Harpsfield's Life of More.

EARLY ENGLISH TEXT SOCIETY

Original Series, No. 186

1932 (for 1931; reprinted 1963)

PRICE 45s.

HOLBEIN'S STUDY OF THE MORE FAMILY GROUP. (BASEL GALLERY.)

The life and death of Sr Thomas Moore, knight, sometymes Lord high Chancellor of England,

written in the tyme of Queene Marie

by

Nicholas Harpsfield, L.D.,

AND NOW EDITED FROM EIGHT MANUSCRIPTS,
WITH COLLATIONS, TEXTUAL NOTES, ETC.,

BY ELSIE VAUGHAN HITCHCOCK

WITH AN INTRODUCTION ON THE CONTINUITY OF ENGLISH PROSE FROM ALFRED TO MORE AND HIS SCHOOL, A LIFE OF HARPSFIELD, AND HISTORICAL NOTES,

BY R. W. CHAMBERS

AND WITH APPENDICES, INCLUDING THE RASTELL FRAGMENTS, CHIEFLY CONCERNING FISHER; THE NEWS LETTER TO PARIS, DESCRIBING THE TRIAL AND DEATH OF MORE; MORE'S INDICTMENT; AND MORE'S EPITAPH.

Published for
THE EARLY ENGLISH TEXT SOCIETY
by the
OXFORD UNIVERSITY PRESS
LONDON NEW YORK TORONTO

OXFORD
UNIVERSITY PRESS

Great Clarendon Street, Oxford OX2 6DP
United Kingdom

Oxford University Press is a department of the University of Oxford.
It furthers the University's objective of excellence in research, scholarship,
and education by publishing worldwide. Oxford is a registered trade mark of
Oxford University Press in the UK and in certain other countries

First Edition published in 1932
Reprinted 1963

Published in the United States of America by Oxford University Press
198 Madison Avenue, New York, NY 10016, United States of America

British Library Cataloguing in Publication Data
Data available

Library of Congress Cataloging in Publication Data
Data available

Original Series, 186

ISBN 978-0-19-722186-0

To

Gertrude Chambers

This Book is Affectionately Dedicated

PREFACE

Three hundred and seventy-four years after it was written, Nicholas Harpsfield's *Life of Sir Thomas More* is now first presented to the public.

In the Introduction to our edition an attempt has been made to show the ancestry and importance of the prose of More and his School—in which School Harpsfield has great significance. That Harpsfield should so far have been generally known only for his *Pretended Divorce* seems without justification in this age of research. That More should have been slighted by so many in the realm of letters is even more astonishing: his importance in history and politics has been allowed to dwarf appreciation of his genius as a writer.

The *Rastell Fragments*, another supremely important product of the More School, have also been curiously neglected, despite Van Ortroy's labours forty years ago.

Our sincere thanks are due to owners who have readily accorded every facility for the study and collation of their manuscripts: especially to the Librarian (Mr. P. W. Wood) and the Governing Body of Emmanuel College, Cambridge; His Grace the Archbishop of Canterbury, and the Lambeth Librarian (Professor Claude Jenkins); the Librarian of the Public Library, Colchester (Mr. G. Rickwood); the owners of the Yelverton Harpsfield; and the Rt. Hon. John Burns.

For permission to reproduce the various illustrations we are most grateful. The Delegates of the Clarendon Press generously gave us leave to use the Emery Walker plates of Quentin Metsys' diptych of Peter Giles and Erasmus, which they had made for Vol. II of Dr. P. S. Allen's *Opus Epist. Des. Erasmi.* The Peter Giles is at Longford Castle in the possession of Earl Radnor, who kindly permits its reproduction here. The Erasmus is now in the Corsini Gallery at Rome; it was earlier in the possession of Count Grégoire Stroganoff, from whom in 1909 Dr. Allen received the negative from which the plate was taken. To Prof. Otto Fischer, Curator of the Basel Gallery, and to the Rector of Chelsea (Archdeacon H. E. J. Bevan), we are much indebted for permitting respectively the reproduction of Holbein's sketch of the More Family Group, and of our photo of the More Tomb in Chelsea Old Church. We also sincerely thank the Governing Body of Emmanuel College, Cambridge, for permission to reproduce a page of the Emmanuel manuscript.

It is a pleasure and honour to acknowledge friendly help from the Rt. Rev. Mgr. P. E. Hallett, Dr. C. T. Onions, and Prof. A. F. Pollard. To the work of Dr. P. S. Allen all interested in the More-Erasmus Circle owe a debt that cannot be estimated. Miss Winifred Jay has supplied us with a valuable summary of references in the City Records to Judge John More and Thomas More (see Historical Note, 19/22–20/2). Others have helped, directly and indirectly; we would mention particularly the encouragement of our Provost, Dr. Allen Mawer; of Prof. A. W. Reed, an ardent toiler in the same field; and of that genial scholar now passed from us—Sir Israel Gollancz. We have also to thank the present Director of the Early English Text Society, Prof. A. W. Pollard; and, for advice on certain difficult points, we are indebted to Dr. Robin Flower of the British Museum.

Our book might have been dedicated to several scholar-friends. We dedicate it, however, to one whose helpfulness in aspects of life other than those of scholarship have made the work possible.

Like John Foxe, we must ask the gentle reader to bear with the "Faultes and ouersightes escaped" (not, we trust, in such numbers as in the *Acts and Monuments*), "imputing the fault rather to the laborious trauayle in the manyfolde matters herein contained, then to any slackenes of our good wyl herein employed."

E. V. H.
R. W. C.

University College, London.
The Utas of St. Peter, 1931.

CONTENTS

	PAGE
PREFACE	vii
INTRODUCTION—	
DESCRIPTION OF THE HARPSFIELD MANUSCRIPTS .	xiii
RELATIONSHIP OF THE HARPSFIELD MANUSCRIPTS .	xxi
THE CONTINUITY OF ENGLISH PROSE FROM ALFRED TO MORE AND HIS SCHOOL	xlv
LIFE AND WORKS OF HARPSFIELD	clxxv
RASTELL'S LIFE OF MORE	ccxv
INDEX TO INTRODUCTION	ccxxi
EDITOR'S SUMMARY OF CONTENTS OF HARPSFIELD'S *Life of More*.	ccxxxi
TEXT	1
APPENDIX I: THE RASTELL FRAGMENTS	219
APPENDIX II: THE PARIS NEWS LETTER	253
APPENDIX III: SIR THOMAS MORE'S INDICTMENT .	267
APPENDIX IV: THE MORE EPITAPH	277
TEXTUAL NOTES	283
NOTE ON MR. THOMAS MOARE, OWNER OF THE EMMANUEL HARPSFIELD	294
HISTORICAL NOTES	297
GLOSSARY	371
GENERAL INDEX	377

LIST OF ILLUSTRATIONS

Holbein's Study of the More Family Group (Basel Gallery) . . . . . . *Frontispiece*

The More Tomb in Chelsea Old Church . *Facing p.* 60

Facsimile of MS. Emmanuel 76, fol. 24ᵃ (reduced) . . . . . . *Facing p.* 87

Diptych of Erasmus and Peter Gilles by Quentin Metsys . . . . *Between pp.* 136 *and* 137

INTRODUCTION

DESCRIPTION OF THE HARPSFIELD MANUSCRIPTS.

I. MS. Emmanuel 76.

MS. 76 in Emmanuel College, Cambridge, is used as the basis of the critical text. Throughout this edition it is referred to as E. **MS. E.**

This manuscript is thus described on p. 69 of the *Catalogue of the Western MSS. in the Library of Emmanuel College*, by M. R. James, 1904 :— **James's description.**

> Paper, $8\frac{1}{8} \times 6\frac{1}{4}$, ff. 57 + 12 + 46 written. Cent. XVI, for the most part in a beautifully neat hand.
>
> Vellum wrapper. Note [1] in the cover by Dr. Farmer attributing the text to Nicholas Harpsfield.
>
> Also this note :
>
> > This booke was founde by Rich: Topclyff in Mr Thomas Moares Studdye emongs other bookes at Greenstreet Mr Wayfarers hovse when Mr Moare was apprehended the xiijth of Aprill 1582.
>
> Contents :
>
> Life of Sir Thomas More.
> Dedication to Will. Roper, signed N.H.L.D. Text ends f. 57 : longe preserue the Realme. Amen.
> Speeches of More on the Act of Supremacy. ff. 12.
> More's Confession of belief. ff. 44.
> Certaine notes of Doctor Hardi[n]s death noted in a sermon made at his monthes minde þe xiiiith of October 1573 in Antwerpe vppon these words *Eamus et nos et moriamur cum eo.* ff. 2.

There can be no reasonable doubt, for the reasons given below (see pp. 294–6) that the "Mr Thomas Moare," who owned the Emmanuel manuscript, was Thomas More of Barnborough, grandson of the Chancellor. **Ownership.**

On "Greenstreet, Mr Wayfarers hovse," see p. 296.

At the beginning of the manuscript is a folding of 4 blank leaves, **Foldings.**

[1] "See Burnett's *Reformation*, Vol. III, App. p. 400. I believe this life was written by Nicholas Harpsfield."

on the verso of the last leaf of which are written the two notes described by James (see above).

The *Life of More*: fols. ii (ii b blank) + 60 (60 b blank) + 2 (blank).

The section of the manuscript comprising the *Life of More* consists of 8 foldings of 8 leaves each. The Epistle Dedicatory begins on the recto of the first leaf of the first folding of 8, and the Epistle is not foliated in the MS.: it is foliated as fols. i^a — ii^a in this edition.[1] Folio ii^b is blank. The *Life* begins on the recto of the third leaf, and this is foliated as fol. 1 in arabic in the MS., and as fol. 1^a in this edition.[2] The arabic foliation of the manuscript is erroneous from fol. 28 onwards. The numbers 27 and 28 are repeated, thus throwing the foliation out by two. After this point the folios are numbered only here and there, and the last folio written is foliated as 57, whereas, even when counting from the folio wrongly marked 28 (which should have been marked 30), the last written folio would count as 58: it is actually fol. 60^a of the *Life*, and fol. 62^a of the whole Harpsfield tract (including the Epistle Dedicatory). The *Life* ends 15 lines from the top of this folio; the remaining two leaves of this eighth folding are blank.

The ink used is now a pale brown.

Hand-writing, Text, etc.

The handwriting of the *Life of More* is uniform throughout, and is an exceptionally fine and carefully executed specimen of the English hand of the earlier Elizabethan period. The MS. is evidently a fair copy, done by an experienced scribe, who was so careful that he made few scribal corrections or slips from beginning to end. There *are* serious errors and omissions in Emmanuel, which can be corrected and supplied from other MSS., but it is certain that most of these already existed in the exemplar which the scribe of Emmanuel had before him.

The text is written continuously, without paragraph breaks. Each page contains about 42 lines and has a catchword. The initial word "IT" of the Epistle Dedicatory is capitalised, and the initial T of "This," beginning the *Life*, is a large capital.

Many titles of books, most proper names, and Latin quotations are written in a fine Italian hand; but no attempt is made, in this edition, to distinguish the names written in Italian script from the others: italics are reserved for Latin words and quotations, and for the expansions of contracted forms—few in number in Emmanuel.

Marginal notes.

The first half of the *Life* has been annotated in a later hand by a Protestant (see facsimile). These comments are trivial and are passed

[1] See pp. 3–6. [2] See p. 9.

over in this edition. They are generally sarcastic or scurrilous, of the following type:—

fol. 1[b]. (*See* p. 11, l. 2.) "A fit exercise for Sunday!" (*Here E reads by error* Sunday *for* soden.)
fol. 2[a]. (*See* p. 13, ll. 23–4.) "Master More a Lay man, to reade in the Church!"
fol. 14[a]. (*See* p. 51, l. 1.) "So doe not I!" (*Concerning Harpsfield's supposition that More was unwilling to become Lord Chancellor.*)
fol. 17[b]. (*See* p. 61, ll. 14–15.) "Antichrists cause and false religion!" (*alongside* Gods cause and religion).
fol. 18[b]. (*See* p. 65, l. 17.) "Whipp on! & smart enough." (*Concerning More's punishment of his body with whips.*)
fol. 25[b]. (*See* p. 95, l. 10.) "Then Sir Tho: Mores wife could sweare too!" (*alongside* By God goe forward).

Authorship. The *Life of More* in Emmanuel 76 has no title. The Epistle Dedicatory is signed "N H L D." The work has been proved to be that of Nicholas Harpsfield, Archdeacon of Canterbury (1519–1575); it was written[1] presumably not later than April, 1557.

Punctuation. The punctuation of Emmanuel is good and regular, and generally near enough to the modern standard to enable the careful reader to appreciate the sense. In order, however, to guard against possible ambiguities, and to make the text as easy reading as possible, the punctuation is modernised in this edition.

An idea of the actual punctuation of the MS. can be gathered from the facsimile.

II. MS. Lambeth 827.

MS. L. MS. 827 in the Lambeth Palace Library[2] is denoted by L in this edition. It is mentioned in Todd's *Catalogue of Manuscripts and Records in Lambeth Palace*, 1812; nothing is known of its earlier history.

[1] See below, p. xxi.

[2] A transcript of MS. Lambeth 827, now in the possession of Dom Bede Camm, was made by the late Mr. Thomas Garner. This was printed in *Manhu* (Vol. II, No. 4. to Vol. VI, No. 58), the monthly magazine of the Chapel of the Adoration Réparatrice, Chelsea. The magazine was discontinued in July, 1914, owing to the war, but the text of Harpsfield was nearly complete—the last words being "yet they dragge all behinde this our worthie captayne" (cf. p. 206, ll. 22–3, below).

Another copy of Lambeth was made by Mr. C. A. Macirone, of the War Office. Extracts from this were made by Mr. Reginald Hine in *The Cream of Curiosity*, 1920.

Pages cropped. The manuscript is a paper quarto in a vellum wrapper. The leaves have been cropped at the outer edge and the bottom, but the words or letters here and there missing are easily supplied from other manuscripts, or, if catchwords, from the top of the next page. Each page had originally a catchword.

Foldings. The Harpsfield *Life* occupies the entire manuscript. The text ends 16 lines from the top of fol. 89ᵇ.[1] It begins on the folio marked 1 : this is really the recto of a second leaf of a folding of 4 leaves, the first leaf being blank. Preceding this folding is a double leaf cut very short.

Hand-writing, Text, etc. Lambeth 827 is in several hands, and sometimes the same hand so varies in slope as to give the impression of a different writer. All the hands except the last are crabbed cursive. The letters are often so crowded that they are somewhat difficult to distinguish, particularly *a* and *u*, *e* and *o*, and the stroke letters *m*, *n*, *u*. All the hands seem to be of the very late sixteenth or early seventeenth century.

The number of lines on a page differs according to the hand: for instance, the first page has 35 lines; the last complete page has 23 lines; fol. 37ᵃ has 41 lines.

The ink is now a pale brown.

The text is written continuously, without paragraph breaks. It is full of slight errors and omissions, corrected usually by the same hands.

III. MS. Rawlinson D. 107.

MS. R². MS. Rawlinson D. 107, in the Bodleian Library, is denoted in this edition by R².

The manuscript is a paper quarto in a vellum wrapper. The leaves measure $7\frac{1}{2} \times 5\frac{1}{2}$ inches.

Foldings. The foldings are irregular. The manuscript contains 135 folios written; at the beginning and end is a blank leaf. The *Life of More* occupies folios 1ᵃ—90ᵇ,[2] ending 6 lines from the top. The Epistle Dedicatory is wanting.

Hand-writing, Text, etc. The handwriting is of the sixteenth century; it is a clear, bold, running hand and the same throughout, though sometimes a much finer pen is used. The ink is now a pale brown, sometimes faded, but the words are always legible.

[1] Fol. 11ᵇ is blank.

[2] For the other contents of this manuscript, see *Cat. Codd. MSS. Bibl. Bodl. Codices Rawlinsoniani D. No.* 107.

The number of lines per page averages about 30.

The text is written continuously, without paragraph breaks. A noteworthy feature is the number of corrected spellings, many letters being inserted above the line, or superimposed, or heavily scored through, or blotted out. These spellings are of considerable interest to the philologist, but would needlessly cumber the collations in this edition.

On the cover of R² are written the following notes:— Notes.

"The counterpart of Mr. Forsters."

"Sealed and deliuered in the presence of vs, William Gough."

IV. MS. Yelverton 72.

MS. Yelverton 72, in the possession of the Calthorpe family, is denoted in this edition by Y. The Harpsfield *Life* is the last of a number of tracts in the volume, one of which is Harpsfield's *Divorce.* These tracts are described in the Appendix to the Second Report of the Royal Commission on Historical Manuscripts (1870), p. 43. MS. Y.

The manuscript is a large paper folio in a vellum wrapper with double tie. The leaves measure approximately 12 × 8 inches.

The *Life of More* occupies folios 319ª—373ª; fol. 350 is blank. The foldings are irregular. Foldings.

The handwriting is of the late sixteenth or early seventeenth century—a firm, neat, running hand. The number of lines per page varies, being approximately 40. A line of writing measures about 6 inches, an inner margin of about 2 inches being left blank. The text runs on continuously, without paragraph breaks. Hand-writing, Text, etc.

V. MS. Colchester (Harsnett) H. b. 35.

MS. Colchester (Harsnett) H. b. 35, in the Public Library, Colchester, is denoted in this edition by C. MS. C.

The manuscript is imperfect, the Epistle Dedicatory and the beginning of the *Life* itself being missing. It commences with the words "hee was sometime somewhat propense and inclyned either to bee Preist" (cf. p. 17, l. 9, below).

C is a paper manuscript, bound in a vellum wrapper. It now contains 166 leaves written, with a blank leaf at beginning and end. The pages measure 5½ × 9 inches.

The foldings are irregular. Foldings.

Hand-writing, Text, etc.

The writing is of the late sixteenth or early seventeenth century, a large, clear, bold hand, and the ink still a good black.

The text is divided into numerous short paragraphs by blank spaces at the end of each. There are no paragraph marks. A line of writing measures 4½ inches, the text being enclosed in margins at the sides, top and bottom. There are 21 lines to a page. Each page has a catchword.

VI. MS. Harleian 6253.

MS. H.

MS. Harleian 6253,[1] in the British Museum, is denoted in this edition by H.

The manuscript is of paper, the leaves measuring 11⅝ × 7½ inches.

Foldings.

MS. H consists of 120 folios, which may be summarily described as follows:—

	Folios.
(1) At the beginning 5 fols., originally blank, but the first (now marked 1*) is now occupied by notes in late hands on some of the MSS. of the More *Lives* in the British Museum.	5
(2) Fol. 6 (now marked 2*) has pasted on the verso an engraving of Sir Thomas More by Elstracke.	1
(3) Fol. 7 (now marked 3*) has on the recto the title: "The life and death of Sir Thomas Moore knight, sometymes Lord high Chancellor of England. Written in the tyme of Queene Marie." (*See title-page of this edition.*)	1
(4) Fols. 8 and 9 (now marked 4* and 5*) contain the abbreviated Epistle Dedicatory, signed "N.H.L.D."	2
(5) Fols. 10—119 (now marked 1—109) are occupied by the *Life of More* and three engravings: on the recto of the folio marked 65, Henry VIII, by Dolaram (verso blank); on the recto of the folio marked 71, Anne Boleyn, by Elstracke (verso blank); on the recto of the folio marked 109, Queen Mary, by Dolaram (verso blank).	109
(6) At the end 2 fols. blank.	2
	120

[1] In the Guildhall Library there is a late nineteenth-century transcript of Harleian 6253, viz. MS. 1225 (M. 1. 6.), one of the MSS. of the Alfred Cock Collection. The spellings and forms are modernised. There are frequent mistakes in transcription—some of these being corrected in another hand.

MS. Harleian 6253 is written in a clear, elegant hand of the early seventeenth century. The text is divided into paragraphs by blank spaces, but there are no paragraph marks. A line of text measures 5 inches, the text being enclosed within blank margins at the sides, top and bottom. There are 26 lines on a page. Hand-writing, Text, etc.

VII. MS. Rawlinson D. 86.

MS. Rawlinson D. 86, in the Bodleian Library, is denoted in this edition by R. It is a paper manuscript in folio, in a vellum wrapper. The leaves measure $11\frac{1}{2} \times 7\frac{1}{2}$ inches. MS. R.

The manuscript is marked as consisting of 94 folios, foliated in a modern hand in pencil. These are apparently counted, and may be summarily described, as follows:— Foldings.

		Folios.
(1) Folding of 1 leaf = 2 folios (1 folio written on the recto).	fol. 1^a occupied by Title: "The Life and Death of Sr Thomas More some tyme Lord Chancellor of England." fol. 1^b (blank). A folio blank on both sides, and not counted in the foliation.	1 (1^a being written).
(2) Folding of 4 leaves = 8 folios.	2^a (*i.e.* the second written, but actually fol. 3^a). 2^b, 3^a (Occupied by abbreviated *Epistle Dedicatorie*). 3^b (blank). 4^a (On this the *Life* begins). 4^b. 5^a–9^b.	8 (written, except for folio counted as 3^b).

(3) Six foldings of 4 leaves (= 48 folios). 48

(4) One folding of 3 leaves (= 6 folios). 6

(5) Four foldings of 4 leaves, of which last is blank and pasted on cover, and not counted in foliation (= 31 folios written). 31

94

The handwriting is a loose, running hand of the seventeenth century, and the same throughout. The ink is now a pale brown. A line of writing measures about $4\frac{3}{4}$ inches. There are margins at Hand-writing, Text, etc.

the sides, top and bottom. The number of lines to a page varies, the average being about 30.

The text is divided into paragraphs by blank spaces, but there are no paragraph marks. Like Harleian 6253, it contains the shortened Epistle Dedicatory; gaps are left in many instances where the exemplar before the scribe seems to have presented difficulty.

VIII. MS. Burns.

MS. B.

This manuscript, now in the Library of the Rt. Hon. John Burns, was sold at Sotheby's Sale, Nov. 15, 1926 (Lot 422 **A**). It is denoted in this edition by B.

MS. B is a paper quarto of 98 leaves (190 mm. by 148 mm.), bound in old calf. It contains, besides the *Life of More*, which comes first in the volume, various religious poems, letters, etc.[1]

The *Life* is imperfect, the Epistle Dedicatory and the beginning of the text (probably 2 folios, about 840 words) being missing.[2] The first leaf preserved has the right-hand top corner torn off.[3]

Hand writing, Text, etc.

The hand is a late sixteenth or early seventeenth century cursive, and the ink a good black. Each page is headed "The lyfe of sir Thomas More knighte," and each has a catchword. The text is continuous, and enclosed in red lines (margins of varying width) at the top, bottom and sides.

Foldings.

The manuscript is foliated in ink. The foldings are irregular.

[1] For description, see Sotheby's Catalogue, Nov. 15–17, 1926.
[2] For commencement of text, see p. 12, l. 11, below.
[3] For words thereby missing, see collations.

RELATIONSHIP OF THE HARPSFIELD MANUSCRIPTS.

The critical edition of Harpsfield's *Life of More*, which follows, is based on the eight manuscripts, *E, L, R², Y, C, H, R, B,* described above (pp. xiii–xx).

The fundamental difference between the transmission of mediæval or Tudor texts in manuscript, and that of the classical authors, is this. In the case of the classical authors there is wont to be a thousand years,[1] more or less, between our earliest extant manuscript and the date when the author lived whose work it records. In the case of mediæval texts the gap is often quite a short one; and in the case of Harpsfield we can reckon some at least of the manuscripts as contemporary. Harpsfield's *Life of More* was written[2] presumably not later than 1557. Harpsfield died 18 December, 1575. The Emmanuel MS. (E), on which our text is based, was confiscated by the authorities only six and a half years[3] after the death of Harpsfield.

Problems of editing from many manu-scripts.

Consequently the textual problems are different. If we can reconstruct the common original from which our extant manuscripts are derived, it will be something much nearer to the author's autograph than in the case of most classical texts. There is therefore less opening for purely conjectural emendation.

But despite these differences, the experience of editors of classical texts is helpful—indeed indispensable.

One of the greatest of Latin scholars who ever lived has written:

> Some ancient authors have descended to modern times in one MS. only, or in a few MSS. derived immediately or with little interval from one. Such are Lucretius, Catullus, Valerius Flaccus, and Statius in his *Siluae*. Others there are whose text, though in the main reposing on a single copy, can be corrected here and there from others, inferior indeed, but still

[1] The New Testament, Virgil, and portions of Livy are exceptions: there the gap is much smaller.

[2] The black-letter edition of More's *English Works*, which appeared in April, 1557, was still occupying Master Sargeant Rastell at the time Harpsfield was writing More's *Life* (see below, p. 100).

[3] See above, p. xiii.

> independent and indispensable. Such are Juvenal, Ovid in his *Heroides*, Seneca in his tragedies, and Statius in his *Thebais* and *Achilleis*. There is a third class whose text comes down from a remote original through separate channels, and is preserved by MSS. of unlike character but like fidelity, each serving in its turn to correct the faults of others. Such are Persius, Lucan, Martial, and Manilius.
>
> If I had no judgment, and knew it, and were nevertheless immutably resolved to edit a classic, I would single out my victim from the first of these three classes: that would be best for the victim and best for me. Authors surviving in a solitary manuscript are by far the easiest to edit, because their editor is relieved from one of the most exacting offices of criticism, from the balancing of evidence and the choice of variants. They are the easiest, and for a fool they are the safest. One field at least for the display of folly is denied him: others are open, and in defending, correcting, and explaining the written text he may yet aspire to make a scarecrow of the author and a byword of himself; but with no variants to afford him scope for choice and judgment he cannot exhibit his impotence to judge and choose.[1]

It is not for an editor of *Beowulf* or the editor of Pecock's *Donet* and *Folewer* to deny that the difficulties of editing a text even from one manuscript may be serious enough for the editor to make a byword of himself. But no one will dispute Professor Housman's dictum that the difficulties of editing a text extant in many manuscripts are altogether greater. These difficulties only begin when the comparatively easy labour of collating all the manuscripts is finished. How decide between the different readings they offer?

Fallacy of following the majority.

The first and most obvious method is to count the manuscripts, and follow the majority. And sometimes, with some texts, the most able editor may find himself, in the last resort, driven to this democratic method of solving his problems. And if every manuscript were copied direct from the author's autograph, it is a method for which there would be something to be said. But manuscripts are mostly copied from each other. Suppose two copies, 'a' and 'b,' made by reliable but not elegant scribes, from the author's autograph. The copy 'a' comes to the scriptorium of a busy monastery, and is often copied, and its copies copied again. These copies are, we may suppose, so numerous, and many so surpass in beauty their common ancestor 'a,' that in the end, worn out in the service of

[1] *M. Manilii Astronomicon liber primus recensuit* A. E. Housman, Londinii, 1903, pp. xxx–xxxi.

the scriptorium, 'a' is thrown on the rubbish heap. Half a dozen copies of 'a' may survive to our day, most of them handsomely done. We will call them A_1, A_2, A_3, A_4, A_5, A_6. Meantime we may suppose that 'b' remains a barren stock, but, by some accident, falls into the hands of Sir Robert Cotton, and is preserved to posterity. Under these circumstances it is clear that the united authority[1] of A_1, A_2, A_3, A_4, A_5, A_6, where these six handsome manuscripts all agree, is no greater than that of the insignificant-looking 'b.'

Yet the genealogical method seldom solves all the problems.

It is interesting to trace how editors gradually came to recognise the importance of the genealogical method of studying manuscripts. Erasmus, when he edited the New Testament, had no conception of it, and indeed, if he had realised it, yet, working as a pioneer in a vast field, he could not have put it into practice in any serious way.[2] The result is the difference between the "Received" Greek text of the New Testament which has come down to us from the sixteenth century, and the critical texts of scholars like Westcott and Hort, which are based on the recognition of the great fact that—

> all textual transmission takes the form of a genealogical tree, diverging into smaller and smaller branches, of which the extant documents are casual and scattered fragments.

Now the recognition of this fact has enabled scholars to dismiss hundreds and thousands of false readings from the texts they have edited. But when we look at modern texts of the New Testament we see that, though in many respects they agree in differing from the old texts, they have not attained certainty or unanimity.

And we have only to return to a study of Harpsfield's manuscripts, with their comparatively simple problems, to see why this is.

If we apply the principle of the genealogical tree to the eight manuscripts of Harpsfield, we shall find that, according to the proved common errors of L R^2 B, of H R, of E H R, of E H R Y, and of L R^2 B H R E Y, and the isolation of C (see below, pp. xxxiii–iv), they group themselves something like this:

[1] In the case of the eight Harpsfield manuscripts, external evidence sometimes proves that the authority of the single manuscript C outweighs the authority of the other seven combined. See below, pp. xxxiii–iv.

[2] "Neither Erasmus nor any other scholar then living could have produced a materially better text without enormous labour, the need of which was not as yet apparent." Westcott and Hort, *Introduction* to their edition of the *New Testament*, 1881, p. 11.

Genealogical tree of the Harpsfield manuscripts.

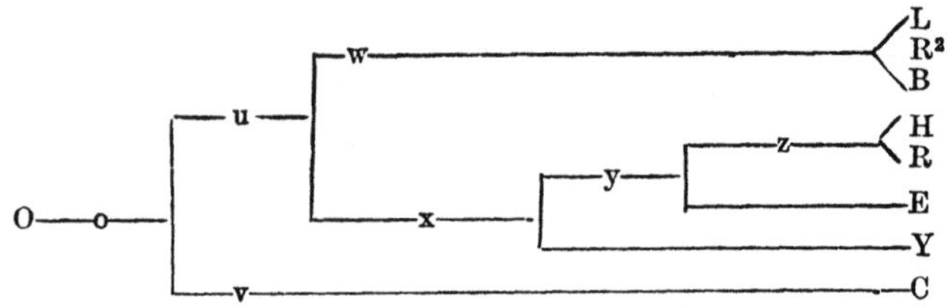

O represents the author's original: the small letters, o, u, v, w, x, y, z, represent parent manuscripts now lost: the capital letters L, R², B, H, R, E, Y, C, represent the extant manuscripts.

But there is also a puzzling connection of common errors between E H R Y and C, E and C, Y and C (see below, pp. xxxv–viii). How can this be expressed in the same tree?

Three stages in the genealogical method of studying manuscripts: (1) Provisional judgment of readings on *a priori* evidence.

A tree like the above can only be taken as giving a rough general impression of the relationship of the manuscripts. For the reasons given below, it is very seldom that we can arrive at a tree which satisfies all the data; and, even so, it can only be arrived at after many imperfect and tentative efforts, which can be classified in three stages:

(1) The only method by which we can arrive at any classification is to begin by examining the individual readings of the manuscripts on their merits, not letting ourselves be influenced by the number of manuscripts which agree or disagree in each case, but judging solely on *intrinsic* probability. For the moment, we neglect all variants unless one is intrinsically more probable than another. The results will, of course, be quite provisional; for subsequently manuscript authority may in some cases be so strong in favour of what at first sight seemed an inferior reading, that we are compelled to believe that, after all, this reading represents the words of the original writer. And in the same way we may be compelled by the weight of manuscript evidence to admit in the end that what we at first thought the better reading is nothing but the felicitous corruption of an isolated scribe. *But we cannot invoke manuscript authority at the beginning: we have still to decide where it lies.*[1]

(2) Estimate, by these readings, of manuscript authority

(2) Having then made lists of the readings which on *a priori* grounds seem inferior or superior, we can judge which are the better and which the worse manuscripts, according as they offer

[1] "To warp our choice in this particular instance by assuming as proved the general conclusions for which we are now collecting materials is, in the full sense of the term, preposterous." Housman, *Juvenal*, xvi.

or do not offer good readings. Further, we can (if we are lucky) classify our manuscripts into groups and sub-groups, united by the common errors which they have inherited from the corruptions of the common ancestors from which they are copied. Obviously, agreement in the correct reading proves no affinity between manuscripts; and even agreement in incorrect readings need imply no affinity if the misreading is one which is likely to have occurred to scribes independently.

and relationship.

(3) We can now begin to speak of manuscript relationship, and of one manuscript as being better than another. But as we decide where the weight of manuscript authority lies, we must look back, and be prepared to alter our original judgment as to readings if "very strong *a posteriori* evidence from the best MSS.," and still more from the best groups of manuscripts, "should seem to overbalance the admittedly inconclusive *a priori* evidence."[1]

(3) Final decision as to readings.

These three stages are repeatedly emphasised by Westcott and Hort: first, provisional judgment of readings on intrinsic, *a priori* evidence; then estimate of manuscript authority and relationship by these readings; then final decision of readings.[2]

And even this "final" decision as to readings obviously leads us back to a reconsideration of the relationship of the manuscripts; for, since only the common possession of incorrect readings proves special relationship, any change in our view as to which is the correct, and which the incorrect reading, alters the evidence for manuscript relationship.

So we go on by a process of gradual approximation to finality, getting our text, and simultaneously our ideas as to the relationships of the manuscripts, gradually more and more into order.

But even this repeated examination and re-examination of the results does not exhaust the complexity of the problem. It is sometimes stated that, when we have got our tree plotted, the determination of the text is comparatively simple. But this is too optimistic a view. Take the very easiest case—where the extant manuscripts can be arranged with fair consistency into three groups. It would seem as if, where two independent groups agree against a third, the two must always be right as against the one. But, in practice, things do not work out so simply. In the case of the

The determination of the text cannot always be settled by a genealogical tree: contradictory affinities in the Harpsfield manuscript groups.

[1] Moore, *Contributions to the Textual Criticism of the Divina Commedia*, p. xxxv.

[2] *Introduction to the New Testament*, 1881, p. 33; *New Testament*, 1885, p. 546.

manuscripts of Harpsfield's *Life of More*, we have three groups of MSS.: L R[2] B form one; E Y H R another; C the third. (For although there is a certain special affinity between the first two,[1] as against the isolated C, nevertheless there is a clear distinction between the group L R[2] B on the one hand as against E Y H R on the other.) Turning then to the collations, we might expect them to organise themselves on this basis: each manuscript would of course have its own individual errors, and there is a little sub-group H R which we should expect to find agreeing in errors peculiar to itself; apart from this we might expect to be confronted with these two family groups, and to find members of each group agreeing together in their ancestral differences as against members of the other group, whilst C, in magnificent isolation, should have no errors except his own and those which he has inherited from his special and distinguished ancestry. A glance at the collations shows that this is not the case. Families break up, and side against each other in a most unfraternal way; and all sorts of unexpected combinations occur.[2] Our notes show no families of "brethren agreeing together in unity," but rather houses constantly divided against themselves: in fact they resemble Parliament on a private members' night, with all the bonds of party discipline relaxed, and Conservatives, Socialists and Liberals voting with or against each other, according as their private conscience may direct.

Three reasons for contradictory affinities among manuscripts: (1) Errors may have occurred independently.

Three reasons, at least, can be given for this:

(1) As stated above, errors which are likely to have occurred independently are obviously no evidence of relationship between manuscripts. The first thing we have to do is very much to enlarge our ideas of the number and scope of errors likely to have occurred independently. Sixteenth-century script may cause two words which look very different in modern print to appear extraordinarily alike; in this way errors may occur independently, without any common ancestry, in a way which at first blush appears impossible. A good example is More's exhortation to his children "to take vertue and learning for their meate, and playe for their sauce."[3] Instead of "sauce" some manuscripts read "fancie," and the division of the manuscripts does not follow exactly according to the families outlined

[1] See errors common to L R[2] B and E H R Y (p. xxxiv below).

[2] See particularly the puzzling connections of apparent error between E (H R) Y and C, E (H R) and C, Y and C (pp. xxxv–viii below); and the errors common to L R[2] B and H R (pp. xliii–iv below).

[3] p. 19. ll. 20–21.

above.[1] But when we consider how easily, in an Elizabethan hand, "sauce" and "fancie" may appear almost identical, there is nothing to prevent the miswriting having been made independently by two or more scribes. The same argument applies to sixteenth-century habits of speech and thought, which may cause one term to be substituted for another, independently, in two or more manuscripts. Many scribes were very unfaithful, and substituted synonyms more or less at random. Consequently two quite unrelated manuscripts will often agree in some wanton alteration, not because they have derived it from a common ancestor, but because, independently, their scribes have chosen to substitute the same synonym.

(2) The corrections of an intelligent scribe may have confused the evidence.

(2) A more complicated and deplorable confusion is caused by the intelligence of certain scribes. The modern editor asks of the scribe first that he be faithful; secondly, that he be stupid: a scribe who uses his intelligence upon the text he is copying is only a source of trouble. Even if the passage be hopelessly corrupt, if the scribe will but transcribe it faithfully, it is likely enough that he will give a clue to the modern editor; for the modern editor has the advantage of comparing many other manuscripts which were not accessible to the scribe. But the scribe who substitutes something which is not in the copy before him, but which he thinks the author *ought* to have written, simply mangles the evidence which he ought to have handed on to the modern editor. If the scribe could rise from his grave, he would of course reply that he had no thought of making things convenient for the modern editor: he was trying to make the text intelligible for the man of his own generation who would have to read it; but the fact remains that *for our purposes* the good scribe, like the good modern printer, is the man who follows his copy even if it flies out of the window.

A good example of this is the unnecessary "of" in the passage about Friar Barnes, "the weake and lame reasons that fryer Barnes brought against her,"[2] where both C and the group E Y H R have an apparently unnecessary "of" inserted before "that." This is hardly likely to have arisen independently: it looks, therefore, like an error common to C and to the group E Y H R, and this, if supported by other evidence, might incline us to attribute a common ancestry to them. But the most likely explanation is that this unnecessary "of" was found in the ancestor of *all* our manuscripts (which need not necessarily have been Harpsfield's autograph), that the manuscript

[1] See below, p. xl. [2] p. 119, ll. 23-24.

which is the ancestor of L R² B made the passage clearer by cancelling this unnecessary "of," and by so doing created what appears to be an agreement in error between C and the E Y H R group.[1] How easily this may have happened is shown by the fact that in MS. E the unnecessary "of" has been struck out. If E had been copied, the copy would obviously have omitted the cancelled word. What we know to have happened in E, can easily have happened in the ancestor of the group L R² B.

It is always possible that a scribe, who improves in this way a corrupt or difficult passage which both his and all the other extant manuscripts have inherited, may create an appearance of agreement in error on the part of all the other manuscripts. In reality the inheritance of error was shared by him with all the other manuscripts, and the fact that he has not chosen to hand down this inheritance conceals, but does not alter, the facts of the affinities of the manuscripts.[2]

(3) Manuscripts may have been compared, and so contaminated.

(3) But when allowance has been made for unexpected agreements due to these two causes, there will remain a large number of difficult cases in which a manuscript contrives to show conflicting affinities, now with one group, now with another, in a way which defies either of the explanations suggested above. The reason is this:

> Comparison of manuscripts, and the transcribing of manuscripts from two sources, one of which was used to supplement deficiencies in the other, were processes constantly going on in the Middle Ages. Thus a monk of St. Martin's, Tournai, tells us that the library had such a reputation that its books were constantly sought by all for the purpose of correcting their copies;[3] and Guigo, prior of the Grande Chartreuse, finding his copy of Hilary on the Psalms corrupt, writes to Peter the Venerable, Abbot of Cluny, asking for the loan of the Cluny

[1] That raises the question whether we ought to read "of" in our critical text. "Of," we have agreed, was probably the reading of the ancestor of all our extant manuscripts. If we believe that ancestor to have been Harpsfield's autograph, then we must give its readings in our text—our business is to reproduce what Harpsfield wrote, not to improve on it. But there may have been a transcript of Harpsfield which, although erroneous, is nevertheless the ancestor of all our extant manuscripts; and we are not bound to respect *its* errors.

[2] Cf. notes on rejected readings in 61/17 and 119/24 below, pp. xxxvi–vii.

[3] Abbot Odo kept as many as twelve young monks at work copying: Unde omnes libros Ieronimi, . . . beati Gregorii, et quoscumque invenire potuit beati Augustini, Ambrosii, Hysidori, Bede, necnon etiam domni Anselmi . . . postea vero Cantuariensis archiepiscopi, tam diligenter fecit describi, ut vix in aliqua vicinarum ecclesiarum similis inveniretur bibliotheca, omnesque pro corrigendis libris suis de nostra ecclesia peterent exemplaria. (Pertz, SS. xiv. 313.)

copy; Peter does not send it because he finds that the Cluny copy has the same corruption of which Guigo had complained. On the other hand, Peter asks for the loan of Augustine's letters; the Cluny copy had been lent to one of the outlying hermitages, and a large portion of the opening correspondence between Augustine and Jerome had been unfortunately devoured by a bear.[1]

This is quoted from an article by one of the editors in the *Review of English Studies*, I, p 8. The bear casually devouring St. Jerome is so dear to us that we cannot abstain from quoting him on all relevant (and some irrelevant) occasions.

This habit of "contamination" or "mixture" has played such havoc with the genealogy of manuscripts that many experienced scholars would discourage the use of any such tree as we have drawn. And all would urge that such trees must only be used with the utmost caution.

Thus Edward Moore writes of the Dante manuscripts, of which he had made a lifelong study, and which are exceptionally complicated and intermixed:

> I have often suspected *either* that a scribe copied different *Canti* or *Cantiche* from different exemplars, *or* that he had two or more exemplars before him. . . . For a few Cantos, two manuscripts sometimes exhibit very striking coincidences, and then the resemblance suddenly disappears, often to be followed by equally remarkable coincidences in some totally different direction, which in their turn cease to guide us long. If such a practice of copying as that just indicated were at all common, all hope of anything like a complete and systematic classification of manuscripts either "genealogically" or even into "families" must clearly be abandoned.[2]

So A. E. Housman tells us of the manuscripts of Juvenal:

> Authors like Juvenal, read and copied and quoted both in antiquity and in the Middle Ages, have no strictly separated families of manuscripts. Lections are bandied to and fro from

[1] Tractatum autem beati Hilarii super Psalmos ideo non misi, quia eamdem in nostro codice quam et in vestro corruptionem inveni. Quod si et talem vultis, remandate, et mittam. Prosperum contra Cassianum, sicut nostis, non habemus, sed pro eo ad sanctum Joannem Angeliacensum in Aquitania misimus, et iterum, si necesse fuerit, mittemus. Mittite et vos nobis, si placet, majus volumen Epistolarum sancti patris Augustini: quod in ipso pene initio continet epistolas ejusdem ad sanctum Hieronymum, et sancti Hieronymi ad ipsum. Nam magnam partem nostrarum, in quadam obedientia, casu comedit ursus. See Migne, *Pat. Lat.*, clxxxvi. 106. Petrus Venerabilis, Cluniacensis abbas nonus, Venerabili Patri Guigoni, Carthusiensi priori (*Epistolarum liber*, i. 24)

[2] *Contributions*, p. xxxiii.

> one copy to another, and all the streams of tradition are united by canals.[1]

And Westcott and Hort agree as to the complexity of the manuscripts of the New Testament:

> Almost every important document combines readings from more than one ancient source.[2]

Liability to contamination in the case of the Harpsfield manuscripts.

We have only to think of the circumstances under which the manuscripts of Harpsfield were multiplied, to see how peculiarly they were liable to this mixture. They were copied by, or for the use of, Roman Catholic gentry: the book was not allowed to be printed, and even the copying of the manuscripts had to be done *sub rosa*. It is quite natural, therefore, that manuscripts like H, though obviously executed with care, are copies of copies, and, in course of transcription, have in many places become unintelligible. Yet Carter, Harpsfield's amanuensis, was travelling about the country, lurking in the houses of Papist gentry, and carrying with him autograph manuscripts of Harpsfield, hoping for an occasion when he might be able to print them. He may well have shown a copy to his host, and his host may well have replied, "I have a copy of that myself, but it is so corrupt that in many places I can't make sense of it." Carter would correct his host's copy from the autograph he carried about with him. He would correct all serious errors, but trifling variants, like *wretched and wicked* instead of *wicked and wretched*, he would not trouble to alter. This corrected copy would, of course, show marks of alteration where it had been corrected. But if yet another copy were made from this corrected copy, all evidence of the correcting hand would disappear. We should then have a copy which had a number of trifling variants in common with the sub-group to which it had originally belonged (these would be the little variants which the corrector had not troubled to alter), but which, in really important matters, was free from the errors common, not only to that sub-group, but to other manuscripts which had not had the advantage of such correction.[3]

For these reasons, manuscripts show traces of the most contradictory affinities. The phenomena considered under (1) and (2) produce an

[1] See *D. Junii Juvenalis Saturæ editorum in usum edidit* A. E. Housman, Londinii, 1905, p. xxiv.
[2] Westcott and Hort, *New Testament*, 1885, p. 544.
[3] Was this the story of the ancestor of the Colchester Harpsfield? MS. C cannot be made to fit satisfactorily into any genealogical tree. See above, pp. xxiii–iv.

appearance of relationship which is quite unreal. That considered under (3) is an actual relationship, superimposed upon another and quite different relationship, and obliterating it to a greater or less degree, according as the correction has been more or less systematically carried out.

Relative value of the Emmanuel, Lambeth and Colchester manuscripts.

Emmanuel is the only manuscript of Harpsfield's *Life of More*, known to be extant, that is complete, with the full Epistle Dedicatory. It is evidently a careful copy of a very good exemplar, and is written out without any improvements or alterations. It has obvious blunders, but these can easily be remedied from other manuscripts, especially from MS. C.

MS. E is in some sense official, in that it belonged to the More family. It was seized by the informer and priest-catcher Topcliff in "Mr. Thomas Moares Studdye" on 13 April, 1582. Thus it was in existence six and a half years after Harpsfield died, and in the possession of one of More's descendants.[1]

Lambeth 827 was the manuscript originally chosen for full transcription for this edition, and a third of it was actually written out. This choice was made entirely on the apparent excellence of its text of the *Life*, as it is clearly a later copy than Emmanuel, and does not contain the Epistle Dedicatory. But as the edition proceeded, the general superiority of Emmanuel over Lambeth became established, and a good deal of the work had to be reconsidered and recast.[2] The agreements of E with manuscripts of the Roper *Life*, the *English Works* of More, and the best readings in the other Harpsfield manuscripts (particularly C) turned out to be commoner than was the case with L; and these superiorities of the E text, combined with its full Epistle Dedicatory, and the early date and interesting history of the manuscript, decided its claim to form the basis of the critical text.

It is, then, partly on account of its more frequent agreement with external authority, that E is superior to L. C, however, is the manuscript most closely reproducing several passages in Roper or More's *English Works* that Harpsfield must have used.

Harpsfield's *Life of More* helps us to estimate the general value of manuscript evidence and the dangers attending attempts at family trees. It contains long passages (filling almost half the book) where the Roper manuscripts or More's *English Works* show what the original words used by Harpsfield himself must have been; and this

[1] See below, pp. 294–6. [2] Cf. above, pp. xxiv–v.

external authority gives us control in forming a critical text of Harpsfield's *Life* of a kind such as we do not often possess in similar critical work.[1] Here we have not only the problem, but often the answer to the problem; and so we are able with more confidence to reconstruct an archetype which we partially possess. External authority proves that MS. C has often preserved readings that all the other seven manuscripts have lost. Without the support of external authority, an editor would hardly dare to follow C against the combined evidence of such manuscripts as E, L and Y. And if such external corroboration did not exist, the correct readings of C alone (see below, pp. xxxiii–iv) would often have been rejected as C's errors. And the corruptions of these readings being then no longer classed as errors common to E H R Y and L R^2 B, the case for their common exemplar ('u'—see above, diagram, p. xxiv) would have fallen to the ground. The errors common to E H R Y and C (see below, pp. xxxv–vii) would then have led to *their* closer grouping, and the plotting of the family tree would have seemed a simpler matter (cf. above, pp. xxiii–iv). But this apparent simplicity would have been fallacious and misleading.

C is rather a late manuscript, and contains some obviously corrupt readings (see below, p. xxxiv); it nevertheless contains, as just stated, a number of readings proved obviously right (see below, pp. xxxiii–iv) by external authority, although these readings are found in no other Harpsfield manuscript, and although sometimes the other seven manuscripts are solidly united against C. It follows that other readings of C must never be dismissed without most careful consideration, especially when, as is not infrequently the case, these readings are supported[2] by E or Y, or E and Y (see collations).

If MS. C had been complete, and of earlier date, it would have been chosen as the basis of the critical text, for its readings when in conflict with those of E (apart from mere scribal slips) have often the superiority.

C, however, usually agrees with E, and in this lies often the superiority of E over L. Where C differs from E (E alone or supported), the text of E, if sense, is not altered on the authority of C alone; but C is followed if supported by sense, by Roper, by More's

[1] In the case of Cavendish's *Life of Wolsey*, we have still more trustworthy means of controlling manuscript evidence. Cavendish's actual autograph exists in the British Museum, and from this the accuracy of the scribes of the extant copies can be exactly estimated.

[2] The possibility of contamination must be taken into account (see above, pp. xxviii–xxx).

English Works, or by other reliable external authority. It *is* supported in these ways so frequently (see below, pp. xxxiii–iv) as to make it highly probable that in a large number of other variants, in passages of Harpsfield's own composition, where there is no Roper or *English Works*, etc., to appeal to, and where the sense is equally good either way, C really does give the right reading against E, and even against the agreement of all or most other manuscripts with E. But as C has many demonstrable errors (see below, p. xxxiv) it is risky to alter E, especially when supported by other good manuscript authority, on the evidence of C alone; for though we might often be restoring Harpsfield's actual words, we might often be unnecessarily corrupting them. In these cases the E reading is therefore retained.

Many variations, such as the differing order of words, or obvious synonyms, are quite unimportant; but it is necessary to take trouble to weigh these unimportant variations, for, especially if they can be checked by external authority, they may throw light on the relative correctness of manuscripts, which relative correctness is of supreme importance when we wish to weigh readings which *do* matter. Even in trifling variations, therefore, the reading of the critical text is made to conform with the reading best supported.

Readings of C differing from those of the other Harpsfield manuscripts, but supported by external authority.

The readings which C *alone* has preserved are often of great importance, and many of them are adopted in the critical text. The following are supported by external authority:

(1) Supported by Roper: *required he answere*, 32/25; *call to minde*, 112/18; *as her husbande had giuen it to him, euen so freely*, 154/4–5; *liuing*, 158/2; *case here then*, 171/18–19; *you were esteemed*, 189/22; *Can it*, 189/27; *for if*, 190/26; *it pleaseth him*, 201/25–6; *and saide to him, My lorde Ambassadour*, 205/19–21.

(2) Supported by More's *English Works*: *and will beginne afreshe*, 94/9; *God, I say, which*, 120/16; *whole Catholike Churche*, 125/8–9; *iest and rayle*, 125/17; *with a coale*, 138/5; *whole corps of christendome to the contrarie in matter touching beleife, as he is by the lawe of the whole corps though there happ*, 177/11–13.

(3) Supported by More's *English Works*, MS. Cleopatra E vi, and Record Office MS. of More's Letter to the King concerning the Parliament Bill: *his dutie toward your grace*, 161/26; *gratious*, 163/6.

(4) Supported by Erasmus' Letter to Ulrich von Hutten: *and sing at the lute and virgenalls*, 94/3–4 (see Textual Notes); *so was he no notable lowe and litle man*, 141/6–7.

If C in these readings had had the support of Roper alone, it might be argued that the text of some ancestor of C had been "improved" from a good Roper manuscript. But it is surely not conceivable that a scribe would also have searched right through More's *English Works* and the Letters of Erasmus to remedy defects in his exemplar. The corresponding passages in the *English Works* take a good deal of finding. It seems much more probable that these readings of C (some of real importance) were inherited from a parent manuscript 'v' (see diagram, p. xxiv), which had not suffered the corruptions of the 'u' group, or which had had errors corrected by some authoritative hand, conceivably that of Carter.[1]

And therefore proof of errors common to L R² B. H R, E and Y.

The readings above being accepted as correct, it follows that their misrepresentations in L R² B, H R, E and Y must be considered errors common to those seven manuscripts, inherited from a common ancestor 'u' (see above, p. xxvi, and diagram, p. xxiv) distinct from 'v,' the ancestor of C. (But there is difficulty in thus isolating C. See above, p. xxiv, and below, pp. xxxv–viii.)

Corrupt readings peculiar to C.

Corruptions peculiar to C consist usually of trifling omissions or careless slips of the scribe, not materially affecting the text: 20/23–4, 33/18, 69/3, 76/30, 81/12, 104/18–19, 104/24, 105/12, 156/9, 165/4, 186/11 (slight, mostly unimportant omissions); 127/18–25, 170/27—171/2, 182/1–4 (omissions due to eye-slip); 35/19 (*so* for *to*), 50/8 (*offence* for *office*), 66/16 (*þis* for *his*), 82/24 (*workes* for *markes*), 83/9 (*whome* for *who*), 103/3 (*Respusius* for *Vespusius*), 108/21 (*others* for *otherwise*), 109/1 (*reforme* for *reformed*), 115/3 (*elders* for *elder*), 121/22 (*living* for *lying*), 126/7 (*woorst* for *woorse*), 128/9 (*alhollandtide* for *Alhalloutide*), 130/6 (*assertions* for *assertion*), 132/1 (*so* for *too*), 144/14 (*at* for *of*), 177/3 (*in no other* for *in other*), 188/16 (*and þat* for *that*), 200/9 (*neuer* for *neyther*), 202/10 (*intend* for *intended*), 202/14 (*This* for *The*), 215/10 (*vnshryved* for *vnshryned*), 215/27 (*not* for *nor*).

(Unnecessary expansions seem to occur in 171/3, 208/8, 208/9, but these are not certainly errors.)

From the collations to the text, similar lists of corrupt readings can easily be constructed for all the other manuscripts. Those of

[1] See above, p. xxx.

C have been collected here in order that the general excellence of the text may be at once appreciated.

Errors common to E(H R) Y C.

The collocation E H R Y C, or E Y C, occurs sufficiently often in the collations, and the combined authority of these manuscripts is sufficiently often rejected, to render some explanation desirable. H and R are such inferior manuscripts that the combination E H R Y C has little more weight than has E Y C, and any argument affecting E Y C may be taken in practice to apply equally to E H R Y C. E, Y and C are all three important manuscripts, and if their common reading is rejected as inferior to that of L R² B, we must be prepared on the one hand to justify this rejection of the evidence of the two traditions of E(H R)Y and C against that of L R² B; and, on the other, to justify the classification of the E(H R)Y group and the C group as from two distinct traditions 'v' and 'x' (see diagram, p. xxiv). From the collations, E (H R)Y C seem to have so many common errors that one might think these necessitated closer grouping of those manuscripts.

Why some readings of L(R² B) are adopted against those of E Y C or E H R Y C.

There is no need to labour the point as to the reason for the occasional adoption of L(R² B) readings. It will be found on examination that where the critical text follows L(R² B), *i.e.* L alone or supported by other members of its group, rather than E(H R)Y C, there is either real superiority of sense in L(R² B), or there is support for L(R² B) from external authority such as Roper or More's *English Works.* And as C and E are followed when thus supported, one must equally follow L(R² B).

The apparent connection between E(H R) Y and C.

With regard to the groupings of MSS. E H R Y C (see diagram, p. xxiv), it must be remembered that external authority often proves that C gives the correct reading where E (H R) and Y go wrong in common, and in common also with L R² B, and this in important cases (see above, pp. xxxiii–iv). From *this evidence* it would seem, therefore, that E(H R) and Y are more closely related to each other, and even to L R² B, than E(H R) to C, or Y to C (see diagram, p. xxiv). Yet E(H R)Y and C *do* err together. These errors are often so trivial and natural that they might be supposed to have occurred independently. But some "common errors" are not so easily dismissed. Do these mean *real* common errors of E(H R)Y C, or merely *apparent* agreement[1] in error, due to the corrections of the intelligent scribe of the ancestor of L R² B? Or must we admit that

[1] See above, pp. xxvii–viii.

E(H R)Y have conflicting affinities,[1] now with L R² B, now with C? The genealogical tree (p. xxiv above) does not here satisfy the data.

Errors (or rejected readings) common to E(H R)Y C.

Take the "errors" (or rejected readings) common to E(H R)Y C:

31/28, E Y C H R *thither* for *hither; thither* is not *certainly* erroneous, though probably so, according to the weight of Roper manuscript authority; it might easily have arisen independently, and proves nothing as to Harpsfield manuscript relationship.

34/15, E Y C R *nowe* for *not;* H here goes with L R² B, reading *not*. *Nowe* is contrary to the sense of the passage; but was it actually in the common exemplar (which was not necessarily Harpsfield's autograph) and corrected independently by the ancestor of L R² B and by H?

44/24, E Y C *his* for *this*. (Most Roper manuscripts[2] support *this*; but note that Dyce has *his*.)

57/5, E Y C *the entrie* for *his entrie*. (Roper supports *his*. H R here represent most faithfully the Roper tradition. See collations.)

61/17, E Y C H R *if it were* for *were*. *Were* (L R² B) is read in the critical text,[3] as the syntax is thereby much improved. But *if it were* may actually be the original reading, though clumsy; it does not necessarily point to any close manuscript relationship: nor is it a certain *error* of a common exemplar of E H R Y C.

65/25, E Y C H R *caused* for *causing;* L has corrected *caused* into *causing*. Probably Harpsfield actually wrote *caused*, which the ancestor of L R² B corrected, thus creating a fictitious apparent agreement in error[4] between E Y C H R.

104/19, 25, E Y C *Zeusis* for *Zeuxis*. (Note that H R here have the correct spelling.) This seems to be an unmistakable error of E Y C. It seems hardly likely that Harpsfield would have written *Zeusis*.

106/14, E Y C *enioyne* for *reioyne*. Here again H R have the correct reading. *Enioyne* is obviously a careless error derived from the *en-* of the preceding *encounter*. It may possibly be Harpsfield's own slip, corrected by some later scribes.

119/24, Y C H R *of that;* before *that* E has *of* crossed through; L R² B *that*. The cancellation in E, very rare in that manuscript, and the occurrence of *of* in such faithful manuscripts as Y C rather point to deliberate omission of a recognised erroneous *of, actually in the exemplar*, by the more sophisticated group L R² B. It seems,

[1] See above, pp. xxv–vi. [2] For Roper manuscripts, see below, p. 283.
[3] Cf. above, p. xxviii, footnote 1. [4] Cf. above, pp. xxvii–viii.

therefore, unsafe to use this passage for evidence of manuscript relationship (see above, pp. xxvii–viii).

125/24, E Y C H R *my* for *any;* L R^2 B *any*, supported by *English Works.* (Mistake probably due to some scribe misreading a carelessly written *any.*)

128/14, E Y C H R *into* for *in* (2). (*in* supported by *English Works.*)

129/15, E Y C *also to;* L R^2 B H R *all to*, supported by *English Works.*

132/24, E Y C omit *though.* (Note that HR, as well as L R^2 B, read *though: though* is necessary for the syntax.)

137/16, E Y C *gett leaue to gett home* for *gett leaue to go home.* (Here again H R have the correct reading.)

145/19, E Y C H R *Zamachus* for *Zimachus.*

145/20, E Y C *Seuilius* for *Seruilius.* (H R agree in the correct reading with L R^2 B.)

164/5, E Y C H R *some* for *soone.*

172/9, E Y C H R omit *his.*

178/1, E Y C H R *say* for *sayde.*

Two interesting errors need special consideration:

125/3, E Y C H R omit *were their writinge neuer so shorte* before *yet were their whole worke.* This is proved a common error by the reading in *English Works:* there is obviously an eye-slip owing to the recurrence of *were.*

141/14–15. See Collations and Textual Notes. There was evidently difficulty in reading the text of the archetype here. L R^2 give the best sense (and are therefore followed in the critical text), but it is doubtful if *betoken* was really in the original. B (of the same family as L R^2) does not read it; the Latin has merely *arguere*, which is adequately represented by *signifie* in all manuscripts. The synonym *betoken* may be the ingenious device of an intelligent scribe. The scribes of Y and C *may* have been independently honest, leaving a gap for what they could not read; the ancestor of E H R makes a bad guess. The evidence is too ambiguous to justify any argument as to manuscript relation.

Errors common to E (H R) and C.

Consider with these "errors" of E(H R) Y C the cases where E(H R) and C have errors in common, but where Y has the correct reading along with L R^2 B:

36/3. E C *requisite;* L R^2 B Y H R *exquisite*, supported by *English Works.*

88/16, E C omit *learned.*

131/23, E C *Lorde;* L R² B Y H R *borde*, supported by *English Works.*

179/7, E C H R *there* for *there three.*[1]

Errors common to Y and C.

There are cases again where Y and C have errors in common, and where E H R have the correct reading along with L R² B:

21/7, Y C *he* for *for that he.* Y and C are not *certainly* wrong here, though *for that he* seems preferable.

23/18, Y C *purposed* for *proposed: purposed* probably erroneously expanded from a contracted form of *proposed.*

48/25, Y C *were* for *was.* (Roper supports *was.*)

60/15, Y C *tendred* for *tendring.*

83/13, Y C *toung* for *tongues.*

108/14, Y C *writhe and wreathe* for *writhe and wrest.*

163/1–2, Y C omit *many.*

198/16, Y C *so soone* for *as soone.*

210/24, Y C *Colledge* for *collegue.* (The same slip occurs in R².)

From these three lists it would appear that C has some connection with the E(H R)Y group, and also with its branches E(H R) and Y individually. Yet the list of certain errors shared by E H R Y and L R² B (see above, p. xxxiv) seems to prove the ancestry of C independent, not only from that of L R² B, but also from that of E(H R)Y. The evidence is so conflicting that a family tree as plotted to cover one set of data cannot cover the other (see above, pp. xxiii–iv).

Errors common to E(H R) and Y.

E (H R) and Y have few common errors apart from those they share with the L R² B group against the correct readings of C (see above, p. xxxiv), or those they share with C against the correct readings of L R² B (see above, pp. xxxv–vii). There is not nearly so close a connection between E (H R) and Y as there is between E and H R (see below, pp. xli–ii). It may be argued, however, that the following common errors justify the representation of Y and the E (H R) group as coming from a common exemplar 'x' (see diagram, p. xxiv) distinct from 'w' and 'v,' the exemplars respectively of the L R² B group and of C:

11/2, E Y *Sunday* for *soden.*

[1] In the two lists of "errors" given above—those of E(H R)Y C and those of E(H R)C—it is to be noted that the inferior MSS. H and R often have the apparently correct readings of L R² B. As stated below, pp. xl, xliii, H R add but little authority to the other manuscripts they support; their varying affinities, generally with E, but often with L R² B, are interesting.

63/14, E Y *that* for *what.*
79/18, E Y omit *fathers.*
104/8, E H R Y *cause* for *caused.*
116/7, E R Y *cast* for *crafte.*
118/14, 118/16, E H R Y *stuffe* for *scuse.*
119/5, E Y omit *vnknowne.*
123/9, E H R Y *aduersaryes* for *aduersary.*
127/3, E H R Y omit *made.*
128/14, E H R Y *into* for *in.*
133/28, E *foreswore,* Y *foresware* for *foresawe.*
135/1, E H R Y omit *vpon.*

Evidence for grouping H R.

H and R have obviously a common exemplar 'z' (see diagram, p. xxiv). Anyone who looks through the collations to the text below, will see very frequently a reading for **H R** not shared by other manuscripts. And although many of these readings are plausible, and might, on purely *a priori* grounds, be correct, there are many more which the sense, or the evidence of the Roper manuscripts or of More's *English Works,* proves to be wrong.

Errors common to H R, but not to E H R.

The following errors peculiar to H R occur in the first fifty pages of the printed text, and may be taken as typical of the relationship of these two manuscripts throughout the work. Their common errors are very frequent, and comprise many careless blunders carried over from their common exemplar, the sense of the passage being thereby often destroyed :

17/26, *puttinge* for *shutting.*
27/13, *to enforme* for *in forme.*
29/17, omit *in matters of great importance.*
31/14, *feared* for *fearing.*
32/26, *most* for *first.*
33/25, H *weare so well,* R *more so well,* for *so well.*
34/24, *soe* for *sore.*
36/20, *was* for *went.*
40/24, omit *spring the.*
41/14, omit *and desired to know of him the very truth.* (Omission not due to eye-slip.)
41/16, *that is said* for *that sort as is saide.*
43/15, omit *and iust iudgement.*
43/23, *euer* for *neuer.*
44/8, *moved* for *offended.*

44/9, *the French kinge* for *the king.*
45/25, *agreeable* for *disagreable.*
49/15, omit *truely.*

There are only very rare cases where the readings of H R, as against those of most or all other manuscripts, seem preferable. The following readings of H R are adopted in the critical text:

(1) 57/5, *his entrie.* (Supported by Roper. L R² B and E Y C vary very slightly.)

(2) 109/15–19, *did . . . lay.* Adopted in the critical text because necessary for good syntax;[1] *did . . . laide* E L R² Y C; B as H R. But *did . . . laide* is quite possibly the reading of 'o,' the common ancestor (which need not necessarily be Harpsfield's autograph), corrected in the sub-group H R, and independently in B.

(3) 132/25–6, *they lacked yet.* The syntax is improved[1] by the addition of *they*, but it must be remembered that pronouns are frequently omitted in the older syntax where considered essential to-day. It should be noted that B also reads *they.* Have the sub-group H R and B again corrected independently?

(4) 214/11, *that it be*; E L R² Y C B *if it be. That* seems necessary. In Tudor script the abbreviation for *that* (*yᵗ*) is not unlike a badly written *yf.* An erroneous *yf* may thus have crept into 'o,' the common ancestor, and been corrected in the sub-group H R.

It should be noted that in reading *sauce*, 19/21, H R agree with C and Roper, where E and the other traditions L R² B and Y go wrong.[2]

H and R are inferior manuscripts and of late date. If they stand in isolation, their evidence is usually of hardly any value. If their readings are in agreement with those of other manuscripts, they add but little authority to the evidence of those manuscripts. The frequent combination E H R (for, as shown below, pp. xli–ii, E H R are obviously closely connected) carries, therefore, practically no more weight than E alone against the authority of other traditions.

[1] One hesitates to "improve" the text on the authority of inferior manuscripts. But see above, p. xxviii, footnote 1.
[2] Cf. above, p. xxvii.

Evidence for grouping E H R.

E H R resemble one another in that they contain—H R, however, only imperfectly—the Epistle Dedicatory, which is entirely omitted in the other five manuscripts.[1] They possess also in common a number of errors not shared by other manuscripts (see below, pp. xli–ii). A remarkable feature of these errors is their uneven distribution.[2] There is a striking absence in the first part of the book, not merely of demonstrable errors common to E H R alone, but even of innocuous variants. On p. 66, ll. 3–4, we have an important omission, due to a slip of the eye from the occurrence of a repeated word. From this point onwards errors common to E H R occur, but the last forty pages are free from any error of importance. The demonstrable common errors of these manuscripts are almost confined to the central portion of the book, pp. 66–180, not much more in bulk than a half of it.

Errors common to E H R.

The errors common to E H R, but not found in other manuscripts, are as follows:

66/3–4, omit *chauncing to espie the same, began to laughe at it. His daughter Margarete.* (Eye-slip, due to recurrence of *Margarete.*)

68/15, omit *all.* (*all* is supported by all Roper manuscripts[3] except J H^2, but note that J H^2 omit.)

78/13, *brothers* for *brother.*

98/8, E R *on the one side,* H *one the one the on side,* for *inside.* (*inside* supported by *English Works.*)

98/12, *in* for *vp* (*vp* supported by *English Works.*)

99/4, *wisely* for *wilily.* (*wisely* is not certainly wrong, but weight of manuscript evidence points to *wilily.*)

102/25, *but* for *full.*

114/19–21, omit *his translation in the dutche tonge hath wonderfully depraued, corrupted and.*

121/19–21, omit *and preachings, and concludeth not more pleasantly then truly, That when a man well considereth those their salutations.* (Eye-slip, due to recurrence of *salutations.*)

122/2, *eyther* for *euer.*

124/21, *with such a* for *with a.* (*with a* supported by *English Works.*)

149/26, omit *then.* (*then* supported by Roper.)

[1] It must be remembered, however, that the beginning of MSS. B and C is lost.
[2] Cf. Moore's note on the Dante manuscripts, p. xxix, above.
[3] For symbols denoting Roper manuscripts, see below, p. 283.

157/24, *that he* for *how he.* (*how he* supported by Roper.)
177/10, omit *his.* (*his* supported by *English Works.*)
180/3, *sure* for *sore.*

Evidence for grouping L R² B.

There are some twenty common errors of importance (see below, pp. xlii–iii) that justify us in grouping together L R² B. The three manuscripts agree (apart from mere scribal slips) very closely, and form a strong combination, their readings needing careful consideration before they are rejected. In the following list of rejected readings, it will be noted that practically every one is either demonstrably against the sense, or is proved to be wrong by external authority:

Errors common to L R² B.

16/30, omit *his.* (Not certainly an error.)

19/4, *yoongest* for *yonger.* (*yoongest* proved error by sense; *yonger* supported by *seconde,* 18/31, and by Roper.)

20/24–5, omit *and by the kinges consent, for great important matters betweene the said merchantes.* (Eye-slip, due to recurrence of *merchauntes and.*)

35/19, omit *lett.* (*lett* supported by sense and by *English Works.*)

35/22, *they* for *we.* (*we* supported by context and by *English Works.*)

37/14, omit *in the while.* (Error proved by *English Works.*)

37/16, *he* for *it.* (Error proved by *English Works.*)

48/17, *the Emperors highnes* for *the Emperour, his highnes.* (Probably *the Emperour his highnes* was taken as possessive.)

53/23, omit *a plaine example of.* (Error proved by Roper.)

55/24, *the same lawe* for *the rigour of the lawe.* (Error proved by Roper.)

58/1, *More* (*more*) for *were.*

69/13–14, *at large composition* for *at a league and composition.*

69/19–20, *you live not to that day* for *some of vs liue not till that day.* (Error proved by Roper.)

88/10, omit *finallye.*

92/8, omit *not in Platoes.* (Eye-slip.)

93/18–20, omit *wisedome in taking that for the best . . . that otherwise could not be holpen; his pietie and godlynes.* (Eye-slip, due to recurrence of *godlynes.*)

94/17, *long* for *large.* (*large* supported by *English Works.*)

103/22–3, omit *it was by most certaine experience found.*

105/3, *opinionable* for *inopinable.*

105/18, *vsed* for *instituted.*

106/12, omit *and manifest.*

106/17, *himselfe with* for *him with.*

109/12, omit *worldly.*

115/10–11, omit *knowledge, penaunce into.* (Eye-slip, due to recurrence of *into.* Error proved by *English Works.*)

130/7, omit *colour of his.*

142/9, omit *to speake.*

145/13, *thinges* for *charges.* (*Charges* supported by Roper.)

147/12, omit *by that meanes.* (Error proved by Roper.)

159/16, omit *consent of.*

160/7, *state* for *Statute.*

163/6, omit *gratious.* (Error proved by *English Works*, etc.)

163/15, omit *yet.* (Error proved by *English Works*, etc.)

175/2, *more* for *now.*

176/15, *to be supreme heade.* (*supreme* omitted in *English Works.*)

176/18, omit *that his grace is head of the Church here.* (Eye-slip, due to recurrence of *here.*)

178/17, *owne* for *newe.*

182/1, omit *seruaunt to the Secretary.* (Error proved by Roper.)

188/14, *it was saide* for *saide.*

188/14, omit *vpon the Inditement.*

189/4, *neede* for *needed.* (Error proved by Roper.)

191/13, omit *first.* (Error proved by Roper.)

207/9–10, omit *as we must of fine force graunt it.* (Eye-slip, due to recurrence of *graunt.*)

Errors common to H R and L R² B.

There are a number of trifling errors common to L R² B and H R (see below, p. xliv)—errors which can often be proved to be such by the authority of Roper or More's *English Works.* In important points the groups L R² B and H R are distinct, and many of the common errors are of the kind that might easily arise independently. But here again we are faced with unexpected combinations, and have to admit the break-up of families.[1]

H R are too inferior to strengthen the authority of L R² B as against that of other manuscripts. The group L R² B H R is of practically no more weight than L R² B alone.

Trivial errors

The following trivial errors are common to L (R² B) and H R:

[1] See above, pp. xxv–vi.

common to L (R² B) and H R.

9/14 (*many* omitted); 10/8 (*he* added); 19/19 (*the* omitted); 25/26 (*shall* for *may*—Roper supports *may*); 32/26 (*excused* for *excusing*); 50/4 (*saide* omitted); 50/18-19 (*many sorrowes and griefs* for *mayne sorowe and griefe*); 52/16 (*also* omitted—Roper supports *also*); 57/22 (*graces* for *gratious*—Roper supports *gratious*); 65/28 (*secrete* omitted); 92/13 (*or* for *and*): 111/15 (*rose* for *did rise*); 122/11 (*such a* for *such*); 143/19 (*sayde* for *same*—Roper supports *same*); 169/7 (*therein* omitted).

Similar trifling errors proved to be so by More's *English Works* are:

123/6 (*the* omitted); 123/8 (*a* inserted); 124/5 (*to* inserted); 163/13 (*againe* omitted).

Comparative values of groups of Harpsfield manuscripts.

It follows from the preceding pages that the manuscripts which really count in estimating the value of any given reading are E, Y, L (R² B) and C. C may sometimes be worth all the rest together, and is certainly so if supported by external evidence (Roper, More's *English Works*, etc.). E C, still more E Y C, are strong combinations. Less strong is the combination E L (R² B). But all three combinations are too strong to be upset unless they make very inferior sense, or unless they are refuted by strong external authority.

THE CONTINUITY OF ENGLISH PROSE FROM ALFRED TO MORE AND HIS SCHOOL.

I. The First English Biographers.

Nicholas Harpsfield, says Lord Acton, was "the most eminent Catholic who, in 1559, neither obeyed the Act of Uniformity nor took shelter from its penalties in flight." This eminent Englishman was the writer of a book which has a claim to be the first scholarly biography extant in English, and the subject of that biography was, in the judgement of Dean Swift, a person "of the greatest virtue this kingdom ever produced."

Dr. Furnivall said long ago that the Lives of the Sinners, if we could get them, would be better worth editing for the Early English Text Society than the Lives of the Saints. Yet, little as we care to read about Saints, it *is* surprising that this is the first edition issued to the world[1] of a book which can claim so important a place in the history of English literature.

We can grant this important place to Harpsfield's *Life*, without any disrespect to Roper or to Cavendish, who were writing simultaneously[2] with him. A full biography is one thing; the memoir, in which a personal adherent records so much of his hero's life as he

[1] The Sisters of the *Adoration réparatrice* printed, in the monthly magazine of their Convent, Thomas Garner's transcript of the Lambeth MS. of Harpsfield's *Life of More.* It ran through 55 numbers, and was not quite completed, as the War, and the consequent paper famine, stopped it. There is no file of this periodical, *Manhu*, in the British Museum.

[2] Harpsfield's *Life* incorporates Roper's notes, and therefore in its finished form must be later. Yet, whilst Harpsfield speaks of Rastell's edition of More's works as in preparation (*we trust shortlye to haue all his englishe workes in print*; see below, p. 100, ll. 15–19, and Note thereto), Roper speaks of the *greate booke of his workes* as if it were already in people's hands. This shows how difficult it is, from such casual references, to decide the priority of works which must have occupied their writers some time. Harpsfield's *Life* was apparently finished for transcription before April, 1557, the date of Rastell's edition of More's *Works.* Cavendish, as Van Ortroy has pointed out, speaks of *themprour Charles the 5 that nowe reygnyth*, and was therefore presumably writing before the news reached England that Charles had made (on 15 Jan., 1556) his final abdication of Spain and Sicily. Yet Cavendish dates the autograph manuscript of his *Life of Wolsey* and his poems, 24 June, 1558 (*compile le xxiiij jour de Junij annis regnorum Philippi Regis & Regine Marie iiij^to & v^to par le auctor G. C.*—MS. Egerton 2402, fol. 149^r).

The first English Biographers.

himself saw, is another. Cavendish followed, with intense sympathy, one portion only of Wolsey's career. Roper is merely supplying, for Harpsfield's use, notes of what he himself knew; and he intentionally leaves to the official biographer not merely gleanings, as Harpsfield modestly remarks, but much of the harvest. From Roper's notes we learn little of More's European eminence; we do not even learn that he wrote *Utopia*. In Cavendish we are told little of the part Wolsey played in English history; Cavendish gives us but one more example of the fall of a great man, to add to the lists compiled by Boccaccio or Chaucer. Still less do we learn of Wolsey's part in European history. Cavendish accompanied Wolsey on his great embassy in 1527; we hear little about Wolsey, except of the pomp of his retinue. What we are told is, how France impressed George Cavendish.

It is obvious that each kind of writing has its own peculiar aims and merits. The writer of the personal memoir, who sets down what he himself has known, can never be out of date. During the four years which most mattered, Cavendish saw all that the Cardinal's gentleman-usher could see; and this stands. But the complete, scholarly biographer suffers under the disadvantage that he may be superseded, by a later and more complete and more scholarly biographer, who will collect an even greater mass of facts, and survey his hero with an even wider range. Where documents have been preserved as carefully, and published as fully, as they have been in the last four centuries of European history, every such biographer has to risk this fate. His is not the luck of Plutarch, who could draw from sources which barbarians in succeeding ages obligingly destroyed; till Plutarch, by the loss of his authorities, becomes himself the authority. Harpsfield had not this great advantage of coming just before an age of darkness:

> O vanagloria dell' umane posse,
> com' poco verde in su la cima dura,
> se non è giunta dall' etati grosse.

Most of the material upon which Harpsfield drew is still extant (though this should not blind us to the very important passages for which he is our sole authority). So he has been unjustly neglected. Father Bridgett's want of appreciation for his great predecessor, who was doing for Tudor days what Bridgett himself was doing for a later age, is one of the few faults that can be found with the excellent Victorian *Life of More.*

The first English Biographers.

The greatest of all biographers are, of course, those who have intimate personal knowledge, and who have also cast their net wide for further information. To this class, which includes Boswell, Lockhart and Trevelyan, Harpsfield of course cannot claim to belong. To judge from the fragments which have survived, the *Life of More* by Judge Rastell *was* of this type. The loss of such an elaborately documented life, written by that one of all More's young associates who had known most of his work, is indeed irreparable. By its combination of elaborate research and intimate personal knowledge, it would seem to have reached a standard to which neither Roper nor Harpsfield attains. And the style was not unworthy of the matter.

But no one can take from Harpsfield the honour of being the first modern to compile, in the English tongue, a complete biography, and thus to present an all-round picture of his hero. It may be replied that this, however great a distinction, hardly entitles the work of a man who died under Elizabeth to a place in the *Early English Texts.* But Harpsfield is emphatically in his place among the *Early English Texts*; he is a link between two ages. Although the first modern biographer, he can also be regarded as almost the last Englishman (of a long succession) to write, on English ground, a treatise upon the life of a saint. What has been said of Stapleton, writing his *Life of More* abroad, in Latin, thirty years later, is also true of Harpsfield: "His primary object was not to write a history, but rather a devotional work for the edification of his readers."[1] We are sometimes reminded of the Old English lives of martyrs, of Oswald or of Edmund. Harpsfield has an ancestry which goes back to Ælfric, and beyond. And for the closest parallel to his *Life of More* of which we have any knowledge in earlier English literature, we have to go back four centuries and a half, to the time when, a generation after the Conquest, Colman wrote in English his Life of St. Wulfstan.[2]

Our age does not love homilies, nor edification; and most English readers will prefer Roper's simple memories to Harpsfield's hagiography. But to those of us who are concerned with the continuity of English literature, this strong devotional tendency in Harpsfield is not without its interest. It associates him intimately with his hero,

[1] Stapleton's *Life of More*, trans. by P. E. Hallett, 1928.

[2] This is, of course, extant only in the Latin translation of William of Malmesbury. An English copy was sent to Rome, to the great Pope, Innocent III, in or about 1202 (*scripturam autenticam de uita ipsius ante centum annos anglicana lingua conscriptam*).

The first English Biographers.

Thomas More. The chief rival to Harpsfield as our earliest biographer is More himself; for the *History of Richard III* might be claimed as biography. Those who so regard *Richard III* can quote More's own words, that *this Dukes demeanoure ministreth in effecte all the whole matter whereof this booke shall entreate.* (Indeed, as biography, *Richard III* belongs to the most modern, denigratory school, which makes the hero so black that the reader desires to whitewash him.) But I doubt if *Richard III* can be called a biography. It is true that More's interest in the character of Richard is what gives unity to the whole book. Still, the book covers only the history of four months, and much of it is not immediately concerned with Richard himself. *Richard III* is rather the first modern treatment of a limited period of English history. With it begins modern English historical writing of distinction.[1]

But the important thing is to note that More, like Harpsfield, is in the devotional tradition. Whilst most competent judges have recognized in his *History of Richard III* the first great piece of modern English history, we must not forget that it is also almost a sermon against ambition. And both as history and as sermon, it has its part to play in the story of the continuity of English prose.

More's *History of Richard III* has a great advantage over Harpsfield's *Life of More*, in that More had access, through Cardinal Morton, to much information of the greatest value which otherwise would have been lost to us. But, though most of Harpsfield's facts are drawn from sources which survived him and are still preserved, it is not so with regard to his standpoint. Coming just before the Elizabethan religious settlement, which was deeply to affect all English life, Harpsfield gives us an outlook which, if we would understand things, we must recapture. I think that it is in this that the value of his biography above all consists. During more than three centuries Harpsfield's work has been neglected; and this is a good example of the fragmentary and puzzled way in which More's memory has been revered by Englishmen; for we have indeed

[1] The so-called "Translator of Livius" can also claim a place in the history of English biography. An Italian humanist, Tito Livio of Forli, had been encouraged by Humphrey, duke of Gloucester, to compile a life of Henry V. An anonymous writer rendered this into English about the same time that More was engaged upon his *Richard III* (1513). The translator added much additional material, and in particular a number of personal anecdotes derived ultimately from James Butler, Earl of Ormonde, so that his translation has some claim to be looked upon as an original work. Shakespeare is indebted, through the "Translator of Livius," to Ormonde.

The first English Biographers.

lost the key to the understanding of his character. To most of his countrymen More has been the typical, and the noblest, example of that very common phenomenon—the man who stiffens in later life, till he forgets what manner of man he was in his youth. Now, that More's character shows growth and development is clear: the temper of the last letter he wrote from prison and the last prayer he wrote in prison could, one supposes, only have come with the lapse of years. It is in striking contrast to the rather "cocky" schoolboy precocity shown in some of his early verse, in his earliest extant letter (to Colet), and in one or two anecdotes of his youth.

But the great importance of Harpsfield's *Life* lies in this, as I shall try, later, to show: it is a complete study of More, written by a man who is so nearly a contemporary, and whose standpoint is so near to More's own, that he can see no inconsistency in the author of *Utopia* and the bosom friend of Erasmus having given his life on behalf of the unity of Christendom. To Harpsfield, More's career seems to be a life of rigid consistency, such as it is not given to many men to live.

II. England and the Memory of More.

"How little," Dr. P. S. Allen writes, "has England done to cherish More's memory! The house that he made at Chelsea is clean gone out of sight; even his tomb in the old church there, with its long plain inscription, is hidden in darkness, almost as though he had died a death of shame. Heroic efforts could not save Crosby Hall from transplantation; and the great Holbein portrait of the Chancellor, immeasurably more beautiful than any reproduction of it, was allowed to go out of the country without a single word of protest. No one has collected More's letters, and there is no critical edition of his English works. It is time that reparation should be made."[1]

Since these words were written, some reparation has been made. Professor Reed has shown how much the origins of Tudor drama have to do with More and his circle. Father Hallett has made and published a translation of the *Life of More* by the exile Thomas Stapleton, a translation which has the honour, after the lapse of more

[1] *The Times Literary Supplement*, 26 Dec., 1918 (p. 654).

England and the Memory of More.

than three centuries, of being the first[1] work of Stapleton's to be published in his native land. And, above all, a beginning has been made towards a complete edition of More's English works, which will be the first issued since 1557; and the collection of More's letters has also been taken in hand.[2]

So far, this revived interest in More has been chiefly, though not entirely, among those who are of his faith. And this is natural, for More will always be remembered, pre-eminently, as a martyr; though all but churls venerate his memory, it must remain peculiarly venerable to those of the faith for which he died.

But we cannot separate More the writer from More the martyr. Other men—the courtier Sebastian Newdigate or the scholar Richard Reynolds—endured, with a courage and patience equal to that of More or Fisher, sufferings which (so far as the human mind can estimate them) were beyond measure more terrible than any which those two martyrs were called upon to bear. Yet More and Fisher filled a larger place in all men's thoughts, both at the time and since. Nor was this due to class feeling:[3] as a matter of fact, Newdigate was of more distinguished birth than More or Fisher. The feeling aroused, at home and abroad, by the death of More and Fisher was a tribute to Fisher's eminence of mind, and More's supreme eminence of mind.

It is curious how often to-day More's eminence of mind is challenged or denied. Yet men of his own day had no doubts about it. Whilst More was still a lad, Morton, the most notable English statesman of the time, predicted it;[4] Colet, the outstanding figure in London during More's early manhood, held him to be "the one genius of Britain";[5] when the news of the death of More and Fisher reached Basle, Erasmus, weary, old and sick, wrote that England, although the parent of good wits, had never seen before, and never would see again, a genius such as that of More. Those who are not satisfied with these testimonials may add Harpsfield's "sure, constant, stable and grounded judgement, that he was and is the oddest and the

[1] I wrote "the only work"; but whilst this book was in the press Stapleton's translation of Bede's *Ecclesiastical History* has also been published (1930).

[2] For a *Calendar of the Correspondence of Sir Thomas More*, by Dr. Elizabeth F. Rogers, see *The English Historical Review*, XXXVII, 546–64 (1922). Dr. Rogers is at work on an edition of the letters.

[3] "The deaths of a few poor monks would soon have been forgiven; the execution of Fisher first really revealed the truth." Froude's *History*, 1856, II, 387.

[4] Cf. below, p. 11.

[5] Cf. below, p. 208 and Note.

England and the Memory of More.

notablest man of all England" . . . "such a one that neither England, as I have said, nor, as I suppose, all Christendom, had the like."[1] The whole drift of Harpsfield's biography is to prove that the little band of martyrs for unity included, in More, a man of such genius that it would be absurd to suggest that they had mistaken the gravity of the issue for which they cheerfully gave their lives.

This belief in More's genius was indeed one of the great fighting assets possessed by his party. It was necessary for the other side to belittle not only More's character but also More's intellect: to prove that he was nothing more than either "a foolish wise man or a wise foolish man."

In these milder days, people of all parties are ready to applaud More's heroism. But, nevertheless, there has been a very marked tendency, especially during the last generation, more and more to decry his intellectual claims: "he was rather fitted to adorn than to extend the domain of letters; and as a statesman he took narrow views and misunderstood the spirit of his time."[2]

And indeed, whilst the nobility of More's character is everywhere admitted, these words represent very fairly the judgement of the last thirty years upon him as a writer of English and a statesman. There is, of course, nothing new in the attribution to him of "narrow views." Protestants of every age, from his day to ours, have been clear about that. "Protestants," says Sir James Mackintosh, "ought to be taught humility and charity, by this instance of the wisest and best of men falling into what they deem the most fatal errors." It is not always with humility and charity that More's "fatal errors" have been reproved, and the reproof has come not only from Protestants. Some of More's severest critics have been those liberal-minded people who have abandoned everything of Protestantism except its prejudices.

But it is a new thing, only characteristic of these past forty years, to belittle More's place in the history of English literature. And it is as a writer of English prose, and as one who influenced other writers, that More particularly concerns us here.

Of the many other ways in which More has been belittled I do not wish to speak now. I have tried elsewhere to vindicate the rigid consistency of More, as a theorist and a practical statesman.[3] We are here concerned with Harpsfield and Rastell, and with Harpsfield's

[1] Cf. below, pp. 11, 211.

[2] Garnett and Gosse, *English Literature, an Illustrated Record*, I, p. 318.

[3] *The Saga and the Myth of Sir Thomas More* (British Academy, Literary History Lecture, 1926).

England and the Memory of More.

sources, the two chief of which are Roper and the autobiographical fragments which Harpsfield collected from More's own works. It is therefore the place of More and his school in English prose that interests us.

III. More and the History of English Prose.

More's supreme position as a writer of English prose had been admitted (as we shall see later) from his own day onwards, and was never more clearly understood than in the early Nineteenth Century. "He is to be considered," says Sir James Mackintosh, "as our earliest prose writer, and as the first Englishman who wrote the history of his country in its present language. . . . The composition [of the *History of Richard III*] has an ease and a rotundity (which gratify the ear without awakening the suspicion of art) of which there was no model in any preceding writer of English prose."[1] And so, through three eloquent and discriminating paragraphs, Mackintosh goes on to mark the merits and the limitations of "the father of English prose," as he calls More. Much the same was the judgement of Henry Hallam, who described the style of *Richard III* as "the first example of good English language: pure and perspicuous, well chosen, without vulgarisms or pedantry."[2]

Such was the verdict of the days before the History of English Literature was a subject of academic study. Nowadays, in schools and colleges, students have been taught to think meanly of More's position in the "pageant of English prose." To speak of More, says Mr. Saintsbury, as "the father of English prose" is "to apply a silly phrase in a fashion monstrously unhistorical."[3] Saintsbury will not allow that More's style compares in "richness, colour and representative effect" with that of Berners, or in "craftsman-like methods" with that of Fisher. That very great scholar, John Earle, in what is still one of the best sketches of the history of English prose, mentions More only to state that he wrote in Latin.[4] Other historians of

[1] Mackintosh, *Miscellaneous Works*, Vol. I, 1846, pp. 412–13.

[2] *Introduction to the Literature of Europe*, 1837, I, pp. 620–21. Hallam describes the account of Jane Shore as "a model of elegant narration."

[3] *Short History of English Literature*, 1905, p. 212. Mr. Saintsbury's position as the master of all who attempt the history or the criticism of English literature, makes it incumbent upon those who differ from him to justify themselves if they can; it is for this reason that I have not felt free to pass in silence over any instance where Mr. Saintsbury's great authority tells against the thesis I am trying to maintain.

[4] *English Prose, its Elements, History, and Usage*, 1890, 1903, p. 435.

More and the history of English Prose.

literature tell us that More "shone," "so long as originality was not required": he was "no creator in literature," only "a most felicitous adapter and translator."[1] So the *Cambridge History of English Literature* bases More's fame on his Latin epigrams and *Utopia*; the best that can be said for his English works is that they "require to be mentioned" and "deserve more consideration than they usually receive."[2] And amongst these English works the *Cambridge History* will not allow us to include the *History of Richard III.* Dr. Lindsay, who treats of More, banishes it from the canon of More's works. Mr. Charles Whibley deals with it, as an anonymous treatise, in a later chapter, together with the work of later historians. To do Mr. Whibley justice, he recognizes the outstanding genius of the *History of Richard III*, though he will not allow us to count that genius to More's credit. Mr. Saintsbury will not even permit so much. Even if we give More the benefit of the doubt, and throw *Richard III* into the scale, still, Mr. Saintsbury tells us, "More's place in the strict History of English literature is very small, and not extraordinarily high."[3]

If he compares these later judgements with those in vogue in the early part of the Nineteenth Century, the student may well ask, with jesting Pilate, "What is truth?"

I trust that one effect of this volume will be to reinforce, as against the modern depreciation of More, the view held a century ago by Mackintosh and Hallam. It will also, I trust, bring out, what has not been recognized before, that More was the originator and master of a school of historical writing. Harpsfield's *Life* is the chief extant memorial of this school.[4]

More was the first Englishman to evolve an effective prose, sufficient for all the purposes of his time: eloquent, dramatic, varied. More

[1] Garnett and Gosse, *English Literature, an Illustrated Record*, 1903, p. 318.

[2] *Cambridge History of English Literature*, III, 1909, pp. 16–17.

[3] Saintsbury, as above, p. 212. Compare also the same writer's *History of English Prose Rhythm*, 1912, pp. 122–23: "More . . . did not do much of real importance in English."

[4] In tracing More's influence, there are three "circles" to be distinguished. There are those who actually lived and worked under More's guidance, in his home in the City, or later at the Great House in Chelsea. Of these, more than a dozen in number, William and Margaret Roper are the principal examples. Of the second group—men who, though they did not live in his house, came under his personal influence—William Rastell, John Heywood and Thomas Lupset are examples. Then we have a third group—those who felt More's influence rather through his writings than through personal contact—of these Harpsfield is the chief. Following the phrase of Erasmus, which Harpsfield records (p. 92), I call the first group More's "Academy," reserving the name "School" for the larger group which includes all three classes.

More and the history of English Prose.

can write a prose which is good equally in argument or in narrative, in carefully constructed passages of sustained eloquence, or in rapid dialogue: at times racy and colloquial, at times elaborate, to the verge of being euphuistic. In some of these kinds, English prose had already attained distinction. The religious writers of the Fourteenth Century—Rolle, Hilton, the author of the *Cloud*—are, in their own particular field, masters of a style fully equal to that of More. In solemn, rhetorical prose Fisher is More's equal; though More, when he tries (which he does not often do) can rival the pulpit eloquence of Fisher. In simple narrative and simple dialogue Malory can reach a height of archaic charm such as More never attempts. But More was the first man who possessed a prose style equal to all the needs of Sixteenth-Century England. And in one thing England was peculiarly lacking. Other writers, Pecock, Fortescue, Fisher, had shown a mastery of a controversial and expository style; what England most needed was a prose style in which contemporary events were recorded in living and dramatic narrative.

England had possessed a prose quite capable of being developed for such a purpose. But the development had been frustrated. Although the first of the great European nations to evolve such a style, England had been passed in the race by her continental rivals, till Sir Thomas More and his disciples gave back to her what she had lost. But that is not all. Many men in England since, if few before, have possessed the power of vivid and dramatic narrative, and thereby have given life to what would otherwise be vast and formless collections of facts. Foxe's *Acts and Monuments* is a striking example. But critics have noticed that More's *Richard III* is "a deliberately designed and carefully finished whole," where "the sense of proportion is never at fault," a praise which no one could possibly bestow upon the *Acts and Monuments*. Though More was never able to complete his book, enough is done to show his sense of structure.

And in this sense of proportion and structure he is followed by Harpsfield.

The depreciation of More is due partly (though only partly) to the weight which modern scholars have chosen to attach to an absurd statement by that incorrigible jester, John Harington. Sixty years after the death of More, and a hundred after that of Cardinal Morton, it pleased Harington to assert that he "had heard" that Morton and not More was the author of *Richard III*. It did not matter that both the Latin and the English versions of *Richard III* contain

More and the history of English Prose.

allusions which point to their having been composed a dozen years or so after Morton's death. Harington was not the man to be worried by considerations like that. It did not matter that More's authorship of both versions is attested by a mass of evidence, from people who knew him well, or were contemporary with those who knew him well.[1] Harington's irresponsible statement was supported, in the year 1856, by some arguments of James Gairdner. Gairdner subsequently came to see that these arguments were mistaken, but he could never catch them up. Historians of literature seem to have taken on trust from the political historians the view that More was not the author of *Richard III*. And, in turn, the political historians seem to have taken it on trust from the literary historians. And the *Dictionary of National Biography* took it from both. It was probably this belief that in *Richard III* More was merely a translator of Morton's work which led to the extraordinary judgement of him as no creator, but a felicitous translator. And, if *Richard III* was dismissed as only translation, we were left with nothing of More's which could be procured without difficulty. It is true that, in the Nineteenth Century, some books of extracts were made, and some devotional works reprinted. But these seem to have had no currency outside Roman Catholic circles, as is shown by the fact that, when Dr. and Mrs. Allen brought out their little book of selections some years ago, it was hailed, even by lovers of More, as being the first collection of extracts from More ever made. That book of selections will do much to reinstate More in his correct place. But it has not yet had time to make people reconsider the judgements of the current histories of literature.

For, to historians of English literature, *Richard III* was disqualified, as not by More, and the reprints, current in Roman Catholic circles, were unknown. There remained, therefore, no source of information save the great black-letter edition of 1557, "the great book of his works." But this is a book easily accessible only to peculiarly fortunate persons, millionaires, or fellows of Colleges rich in Tudor books. And its black-letter is very difficult to read for any length of time.[2]

More owed something of his reputation in the Eighteenth Century

[1] See below, p. 102, and Note thereto.

[2] I think that the very natural irritation which follows upon reading too much of the difficult 1557 volume accounts for Prof. Saintsbury's depreciation of More. "Black letter," he says, "*non legitur* with my eyes." (*History of English Prose Rhythm*, p. 93.)

More and the history of English Prose.

to the fact that then, difficult as this black-letter edition was, it was more easily accessible than the works of most of his contemporaries and successors. Nowadays almost everybody except More has been reprinted, in more or less convenient editions, and the position is reversed.

Above all, since the early Nineteenth Century, Malory's *Morte Darthur* and Berners' *Froissart* have been again easily available. Everyone can now see that it is wrong to speak of More, who is much later than Malory and contemporary with Berners, as "our earliest prose writer," the author of "the first example of good English language." Berners' prose is very good, and Malory's is supremely good, and both write English which, except for an occasional word, is easily intelligible to-day.

All the same, the claim which Mackintosh and Hallam made for More, although incautiously worded, is substantially true. I yield to no one in admiration for Malory, and after two or three years spent with W. P. Ker in editing Berners, I am not likely to underestimate that "great translator." And we may admit that nothing that More wrote interests people to-day for the sake of its subject-matter, in the same way that the battles of Cressy and Poitiers and the love of Lancelot interest them. But that does not alter the fact that the place of More in the history of English prose is a much greater one than that of Malory or of Berners. He inherited a great tradition of English prose; he extended it, in many directions, far beyond the range of Malory or of Berners. And he passed it on to his "school"; it continued to be a tradition; it became part of the inheritance of every educated Englishman.

Nevertheless, to speak of More as "the father of English prose," as was done in the early Nineteenth Century, is wrong. If English prose has any known father, that father is Ælfred Æthelwulfing.

"That great king," wrote Prof. W. P. Ker nearly forty years ago, "has been frequently threatened with ostracism, yet neither the political nor the literary history can do without him, and the literary like the political history of England is continuous."[1]

Yet to-day it is generally denied that there is any continuity in the history of English prose. The two latest pronouncements on the subject which I have read are quite definite:—

> The prose of Alfred and his few contemporaries and successors . . . is in no sense the source from which modern English prose

[1] Craik, *English Prose Selections*, I, p. 16.

More and the history of English Prose.

> has sprung. . . . If English prose must have a father, no one is so worthy of this title of respect as Wiclif . . . Wiclif was the first Englishman clearly to realize the broad principles which underlie prose expression. . . . In a word, Wiclif was the first intelligent writer of English prose, a discoverer in the truest sense of the word. With him begins the long and unbroken line of English writers who have striven to use the English tongue as a means of conveying their message as directly and as forcibly as possible to their hearers and readers. The spirit of Wiclif is the spirit of Sir Thomas More. . . .[1]

Sir Arthur Quiller-Couch is equally certain:—

> From Anglo-Saxon Prose, from Anglo-Saxon Poetry, our living Prose and Poetry have, save linguistically, no derivation.[2]

Again, the student may well ask "What is Truth?" when faced with statements so definite and so contradictory.

W. P. Ker did not attempt to prove his thesis—though he would not have spoken with such certainty unless he had been sure that he could do so.

I will try to show some reasons for believing in this continuity; and I think it will appear that the impress of King Alfred's jewel, appropriate as it is on the cover of every volume issued by the Early English Text Society, is peculiarly appropriate upon the cover of an edition of Harpsfield's *Life of Sir Thomas More.*

IV. The First Emerging of English Prose.

More gave English literature an example of a prose which could be used for many different purposes, and more particularly for lively narrative, depicting the characters and motives of the different actors.

In the Middle Ages, more than one nation of Europe had possessed such a prose: we have only to think of the *Heimskringla* or the *Njals Saga,* or Joinville's *Life of St. Louis.* The absence of such prose from English literature, and more particularly during the great age—the Thirteenth Century—is one of the causes of that depreciation of our mediæval things which is so common in this country, particularly among those who profess special interest in English.

[1] G. P. Krapp, *The Rise of English Literary Prose*, pp. vii–ix.

[2] "On the Lineage of English Literature," in *The Art of Writing* (1923), p. 163. When "Q" goes on to say, "the true line of intellectual descent in prose lies through Bede . . . and not through Ælfric or the Saxon Chronicle" (p. 186), I cannot see why the two things should be regarded as mutually exclusive. I firmly believe in the debt of English literature to both.

The first emerging of English Prose.

This defect in English literature is the more deplorable because, of all the peoples of Modern Europe, the inhabitants of these islands had been the first to win for themselves a scholarly narrative prose.[1] By the Eleventh Century this prose had progressed so far that we may believe that, if fate had been more kind, we should have anticipated by a century or two the achievements of the great mediæval historians of France.

Probably there are few better tests of a people having reached and maintained its place among nations than this power of writing stirring prose in its own tongue. We have had an example in the recent history of Europe; whatever the map might look like, Europe could not cease to believe that there was a Polish nation, so long as novels known to be translated from the Polish were to be found in every circulating library. "Fragments of forgotten peoples" may keep their native ballads or folk-tales; but it is a great achievement to establish a native prose, and to get this prose written down. If this prose is no mere naked chronicle of events or register of edicts, if we can feel character underneath it, then the achievement is great indeed. And this great thing had been done by England before the Conquest, as it had been done by Greece and Rome.

That accomplished scholar whom we have recently lost, J. S. Phillimore, writes:

> Poetry is a wind that bloweth where it listeth: a barbaric people may have great poetry, they cannot have great prose. Prose is an institution, part of the equipment of a civilization, part of its heritable wealth, like its laws, or its system of schooling, or its tradition of skilled craftsmanship.[2]

There is reason for this early development of prose in England.

Greek prose and Latin prose were too firmly established to allow scope to the language of the Teutonic invaders when they broke into the Roman Empire. These Teutonic invaders had their own poetry: it was, as Tacitus has said, the one kind of memorial and annals current among them. But there were strong grounds which prevented them from developing prose. When a Teutonic tribe settled within the Roman Empire, there were Latin or Greek clerks ready to write letters for its chieftains, or to record its laws or its history; so that

[1] The chronology of Old Irish prose, as Dr. Robin Flower has pointed it out to me, agrees remarkably with that of Old English prose in certain respects, whilst differing widely in others.

[2] *Dublin Review*, Vol. CLIII, p. 8 (1913): "Blessed Thomas More and the Arrest of Humanism in England."

the traditions, for example, of the Gothic and Longobardic conquerors were written down, not in their own language, but in Latin. Native prose was choked, before it could spring up, by Latin competition. The exception proves the rule: a Gothic bishop did indeed try to make the Bible intelligible to his people in their own tongue. But the version of Ulfilas was overshadowed by its Greek original; and it led to no general use of Germanic prose among the continental conquerors of Rome.

The first emerging of English Prose.

But, when Gregory the Great sent his missionaries to England, Latin civilization reached a land which was so remote from Rome that Latin could influence the native language without utterly depressing it. It was necessary, as a result of the conversion, to make and record a number of amending clauses in the customary law of Kent, and these were written down, not in the Latin of the missionaries, but in the English of the converts. A tradition was thus started which lasted continuously till the Norman Conquest, and after.

Our information is too scanty for us to trace in detail the earliest development of English prose: we can never know exactly how much King Alfred found to build on: whether, for example, the episode of Cynewulf and Cyneheard in the *Chronicle* is evidence for an early tradition of prose saga. But what Alfred built we do know. As Prof. Ker has said, the voyages of Ohthere and Wulfstan, as recorded by Alfred, are, in one sense, modern literature. "It was a happy inspiration that gave Ohthere and Wulfstan their place in Hakluyt's collection; and indeed many of Hakluyt's men are more old-fashioned in their style, and carry more rhetorical top-hamper than Ohthere."[1]

A comparison of Alfred's words with the Elizabethan translation in Hakluyt's *Navigations* will prove the accuracy of Professor Ker's judgement. *He wolde fandian*, says Alfred of Ohthere, "he wished to search." "He fell into a fantasie and desire to prove and know" is the translation. But besides this fantasie there was also a practical aim: *Swiþost he for ðider, toeacan þæs landes sceawunge, for þæm horshwælum, for ðæm hie habbað swiþe æþele ban on hiora toþum*: "Chiefly he went thither (as well as for the surveying of the land) for the horse-whales [walrus], because they have very fine bones in their teeth." The Elizabethan uses just twice as many words as Alfred:

[1] Craik, *English Prose Selections*, I, pp. 6—7.

The first emerging of English Prose.

> The principal purpose of his travel this way, besides the increase of the knowledge and discovery of those coasts and countries, was for the more commodity of fishing of horse-whales, which have in their teeth bones of great price and excellency.

Sir Arthur Quiller-Couch has expressed his dislike of the "clotted" Elizabethan style when compared with the simple clarity of Malory or Berners.[1] But why go back only to Malory or Berners? Why not do justice to the simple clarity of Hilton in the Fourteenth Century, or of the *Chronicle* in the Eleventh, or of Alfred and the *Chronicle* in the Ninth?

In the two or three pages in which Ohthere's travels are recorded, we get a shrewd idea of the traveller's character: the mixture of curiosity and more practical ends which prompted his exploration; the caution which led him to stop it; a caution which also prevented him dwelling on the many tales which he heard of the lands beyond, "but he knew not the truth of it, for he saw it not himself."

But, besides showing us the character of this exemplary explorer, Alfred has revealed his own in a couple of pages, in his letter on the state of learning in England prefixed to his translation of Gregory's *Pastoral Care*—the letter in which he "enunciates an educational policy of compulsory English in primary schools with optional Latin in secondary education." (How much we have enriched the English language since Alfred's day.)

After the death of Alfred, and of the men whom he had encouraged to share his labours of translating, men like Wærferth, bishop of Worcester, there seems for the moment to have been no succession. Of course, at this early date we are at the mercy of chance, and we should not be justified in calling any period barren, solely on the ground that nothing much has come down from it to our own day. As a proof of how little we know, we might take the sermon on St. Chad,[2] written in the Anglian dialect, apparently quite early—not far removed in date from the time of Alfred, but preserved amid a collection of sermons of Ælfric, transcribed long after the Norman Conquest, in the days of Henry I or Stephen. Such an Anglian sermon can hardly have sprung up in isolation: it seems to be one survival from a great mass of lost prose literature.

But we have some positive evidence that Alfred and his group had few immediate successors in English prose. After the death of Alfred's

[1] "On the Capital Difficulty of Prose" (*The Art of Writing*, p. 120).
[2] Ed. Napier, *Anglia*, X, 131–56 (1888).

son Edward, the *Chronicle* was discontinued for a generation; and when it was at last resumed, the meagre annals were eked out, not with prose, but with verse. One gathers that there was no English historical prose to be found. And Ælfric says that he was led to undertake his work because, for those who did not know Latin, Alfred's were the only reliable translations;[1] yet Ælfric wrote a century after Alfred's death.

The first emerging of English Prose.

Nevertheless, the second and third quarters of the Tenth Century were an exceedingly glorious and prosperous period: the great kings of the house of Alfred were drawing together the scattered provinces of Britain under their rule. An Icelandic poet tells us that "Now is the highest deer-forest subject to valiant Athelstan." On *a priori* grounds, we should expect the glories of Alfred's grandsons and great-grandson to be celebrated in the prose Alfred had fostered. Then later we might expect prose to decay, as the century closed on a darkened world, with the Danes ravaging everywhere, and Antichrist due to arrive any hour. The decadence, during the unhappy reign of Ethelred the Unready,[2] of the prose inherited from Alfred, sounds so plausible that historians, both political and literary, assert it as a dogma. But the evidence points to the exact contrary. During the most successful half-century of Anglo-Saxon history, the period from Athelstan to Edgar,[3] native prose is silent; until, as that period draws to an end, we have the *Blickling Homilies*, which we can date, because they tell us that Doomsday is approaching, that nothing now remains save for Antichrist to come, and that of this last age 971 years have elapsed. It is amid talk of the End of the World and of the Heathen Men that at the very end of the Tenth Century, and in the Eleventh, English prose comes again into its own. Once again the *Chronicle* becomes lively, if highly discontented; we have great masses of homilies; the noble Gospel-translations, with their free and idiomatic rendering; translations of books of popular science; Byrhtferth's *Manual;* even Oriental wonders and romance. It is the variety which is remarkable. We have the cultured prose of Ælfric; the utterly different eloquence of Wulfstan, amazing in its vehemence, which reminds us of an Old Testament prophet; and many competent writers who contributed to the Anglo-Saxon Chronicles. Most outstanding among them are the writers who give us, in the middle of

[1] There are no reliable books, he says, on evangelical doctrine (*þa godspellican lare*) for those who know no Latin, *buton þam bocum þe Ælfred cyning snoterlice awende of Ledene on Englisc, þa sind to hæbenne.* (*Homilies*, ed. Thorpe, I, 3.)

[2] 978–1016. [3] 924–975.

The first emerging of English Prose.

the Eleventh Century, distinct accounts of the quarrel between Earl Godwine and Edward the Confessor. That great philologist, Henry Sweet, has rightly spoken of the story given by the Canterbury chronicler as "one of the noblest pieces of prose in any literature, clear, simple and manly in style, calm and dignified in tone, and yet with a warm undercurrent of patriotic indignation." This Chronicler tells of the insolence of Count Eustace of Boulogne: how, on his return from a visit to his brother-in-law, the Confessor, Eustace and his followers put on their armour before entering Dover, bullied the townsmen, and slew one of them on his own hearth; how a riot was caused, and how Eustace barely escaped alive back to King Edward; how he gave a lying account of all this to his brother-in-law, so that Earl Godwine was commanded to take cruel vengeance on the men of Dover; how Godwine could not agree to destroy his own people, and how he and Harold, though it was hateful to them, had to make a stand against their lord the king; with all the other stages of the sad tale, till we reach the outlawing of Godwine and his sons. The story, like an Icelandic saga, makes us feel the stress of mind of the chief actors. Yet it can be got easily into two octavo pages of modern print.

I am not discussing whether or no this account of Godwine and his sons as good patriots is unbiassed: biassed or no, the Chronicler knew how to write English.

Side by side with this story, told in a way which cannot be bettered, we have an account of the same events told by someone who lived in the territory of the Northern earls, where fighting men were being called up to resist Godwine and his sons. This version makes us feel (as Mr. Spectator would have put it) that there is much to be said on both sides. We see Godwine and his sons truculently demanding that Eustace shall be delivered into their hands to be dealt with as they think fit. Yet, after all, Eustace was the Confessor's guest and kinsman (to say nothing of being destined to be the father of one of the Nine Worthies; though we cannot blame the insurgents for not knowing that a son of Eustace was, half a century later, to rule Jerusalem).

Both stories are convincing; the writers report the case, as it appears to them, without rhetoric. So powerful is the writing that, although for over eight hundred years the actors have been dust, yet modern historians feel the infection, and cannot discuss the story without losing their tempers. To realise the strength of the writing, we need only compare the account of the Southerner—"the stoutest Englishman who ever lived," as Freeman calls him—with Freeman's own paraphrase: the simple vigour of the eleventh-century man contrasts strangely with the dithyrambic diatribes of the nineteenth-century historian. And the Northerner makes as vivid an impression as his Southern contemporary: we feel that the Northern lords could not but rally to the help of their king, hectored by insolent subjects. But the Northerner cares more for England than for either party:

The first emerging of English Prose.

> They [the Northern lords] were so much of one mind with the king, that they would have attacked the army of Godwine if the king had wished it. But some men thought that it would be great folly, were the two sides to come together in battle; *well nigh all that was most gallant in England was in one or other of the hosts.* Such men thought that they would be making an open way to our enemies into the land, and be bringing to pass great destruction among ourselves.

So hostages were given on both sides, matters passed off without a fight, Godwine and his sons went into exile.

Next year they returned, with many armed followers, and a real state of civil strife arose. Under Plantagenet or Lancastrian the civil broils would have become civil war. But as soon as the two hosts came within striking distance, this is what happened (and note that the account is strictly contemporary):

> It was hateful to almost all of them that they should fight against men of their own kin, because there were very few who were worth much in either army who were not Englishmen.

Godwine had Flemings with him, Harold Danes, the Confessor Normans, and neither the Chronicler nor anybody else had the least objection to their slitting each other's throats. But the Midlanders and Northerners in the king's service were not going to fight Godwine's men from the South coast. They reckoned themselves to be of the same kin, and, the Chronicler goes on:

> They did not wish that, by destroying each other, they should put this country at the mercy of foreigners.

Again, a third time, trouble arose, when the Northerners objected to the rule appointed by the Government in the South (as they were destined to do so many times again, till the "inly-working North" raised the banner of the Five Wounds for the last time in 1569). The Northerners expelled Tosti, whom the Confessor had placed over them, and there was talk of coercion from the South. But the con-

The first emerging of English Prose.

temporary Latin life of Edward the Confessor tells us that this was abhorred as civil war (*quasi bellum civile*). I suppose this must be the first time in English history for that phrase to be used of the conflict between North and South.

Now it is an almost universally accepted dogma that Old English prose, the prose of Alfred, had perished in "the shock of the several conquests which brought about a general confusion of English ideals and traditions in the tenth and eleventh centuries,"[1] and further that "there was no English nation in existence in the Eleventh Century,"[2] that "the men of Wessex, of the Severn valley, and of Danelaw knew not one another, and had no common loyalty."[3]

Yet here, a few years before the Norman Conquest, we have a man of Canterbury and a man of the North (for he speaks of "all these Northern parts"), both apparently writing in the standard King's English, and showing few, if any, peculiarities of local dialect; and it is asserted that almost all, Northerners and Southerners alike, felt, as Englishmen, that civil strife was *lað*, hateful.

Surely this needs inquiry.

V. The Alleged Decadence of Anglo-Saxon Prose and Anglo-Saxon Civilization.

Now, to begin with, does not the dogma about the decadence of Anglo-Saxon civilization before the Conquest make the whole history of English literature, and indeed the history of the English mind in the broadest sense, a rather puzzling business? For, if Anglo-Saxondom was perishing of inanition, how comes it that it does not succumb altogether under the vigorous impact of Norman-French conquest, followed as this was by wave after wave of the influence of that French civilization which was the mightiest thing in all the Middle Ages?

And the puzzle becomes all the greater when we turn to the second dogma, distinct but closely related, which, not satisfied with declaring pre-Conquest England decadent and sterile, asserts that England did not exist, save as "a geographical expression"; there was, we are told, only "an aggregation of races, regions, and private

[1] G. P. Krapp, *Rise of English Literary Prose*, p. vii.
[2] Douglas, *The Norman Conquest* (published for the Historical Association), 1928.
[3] G. M. Trevelyan, *History of England*, 1926, p. 111.

jurisdictions."[1] That such an aggregation should have been welded into one nation by the very able and energetic governing class superimposed upon it by the Conquest, and by the large subsequent French immigration, is plausible enough. But, in that case, why was the resultant nation not a Norman-French nation?

Alleged Anglo-Saxon decadence.

Yet it is undeniable that, after a long struggle, what comes at last to the top is not merely the English language, but essentially an English, not a French, civilization; an English mind, not a French.

Few dogmas seem so firmly rooted as this of the decay of Anglo-Saxon civilization. We are told by our latest and most popular (and most deservedly popular) historian that the Norman Conquest did not cause the decline of Anglo-Saxon prose and poetry: it had declined of itself; that this decadence had been all of a piece with the political failure, and that England needed to be hammered into a nation, and that in the Normans she found masters who would do it.[2] And that lamented Italian Saxonist, Prof. Aldo Ricci, who has not left behind him a man more learned in the speech and literature of our oldest England, regarded it as beyond dispute that "the whole of Old English intellectual life came to an almost abrupt end during the reign of Knut."[3]

It is true that there have been protests against such a verdict. It is twenty years since Prof. Oman pointed out that, in some respects, at any rate, the Confessor's reign was not futile; that in some things (its coinage, for example) England had reached a higher level of art in the reign of Edward the Confessor than in the middle of the Twelfth Century; and that if, in other respects, such as building in stone, the Continent had much to teach England, the Confessor's great building at Westminster showed that England was ready to learn. But few seem to have taken any notice of this protest.

Turning to literature, it must be admitted that very little poetry indeed has come down which was written immediately before the Norman Conquest. But Old English poetry was, in the main, not a matter of writing. "For us, poetry means the book-shop. . . . But poetry originally was a public, social thing, and the solitary reader, his lamp and his fire, is not the audience for whom the early poets

[1] G. M. Trevelyan, *History of England* (1926), p. 121.
[2] Trevelyan, as above, pp. 111, 121.
[3] *Review of English Studies*, V, 1–11: "The Anglo-Saxon Eleventh-Century Crisis."

Alleged Anglo-Saxon decadence.

composed."[1] Even when Anglo-Saxon poetry came to be written down, the odds against its survival were enormous. We are apt to forget that the little which we can ever know concerning Old English poetry depends upon the accidental preservation of four great codices, all written a generation or more before the Confessor's time. We have practically no information as to poetry in the Confessor's reign, which is, under the circumstances, a very different thing from saying that we have information that there was practically no poetry.

With reference to both prose and poetry, we must remember that, apart from Homilies and the *Chronicle*, Anglo-Saxon literature is mainly a matter of surprises; it mostly consists of things which, but for the accidental preservation of a single manuscript, we should never have known. Save for the Corpus manuscript of *Apollonius*, who would have expected the Novel in Anglo-Saxon literature? If one single manuscript, *Vitellius A. XV*, had blazed up in the great Cottonian fire, instead of being merely singed, we should have known nothing worth mentioning of *Beowulf* and of other surprising things, which anticipate by centuries the achievements of the other vernaculars of Western Europe. The moral is that we can never argue from negative evidence. The displacement of an English by a Norman ruling class cannot have tended towards the careful preservation of manuscripts in Anglo-Saxon; then for centuries before the Dissolution of the Monasteries they must have been useless curiosities, which a competent monastic librarian would eject; and at the Dissolution whole libraries, like those of Glastonbury or Malmesbury or Crowland, vanished almost utterly. Here, much as in excavating a buried city, we have to conjecture from the little that is left as to the mass which once existed. We dwell on the border-line between partial knowledge and complete ignorance.

But we *can* say that the poem in the *Chronicle* on the Death of the Confessor and the Accession of Harold shows that in 1066 there was still good command of the old technique of alliterative verse. After that, we have only one or two short pieces, like *The Grave* and the poem on Durham; and when, later, the old verse appears in the *Proverbs of Alfred*, the *Brut* of Layamon, or the *Bestiary*, it is in a broken-down and apparently moribund form. Yet the alliterative school of poetry was far from moribund. There must have been some parts of the country where it maintained an energetic life, during Layamon's days and for generations after. For it re-

[1] W. P. Ker, *Form and Style in Poetry*, p. 148.

appears, and this time in full vigour and correctness, in the Fourteenth Century, contemporaneously with many other national triumphs. It must have been very strong on the lips of men when it dived under, or it could never have emerged in this way. For the correct technique of the alliterative line must have been handed on from poet to poet: once lost, it could not have been recovered, although doubtless a different technique might have been formed.[1]

Alleged Anglo-Saxon decadence.

And, with the alliterative verse, emerged in the Fourteenth Century marked peculiarities of the English mind. If we want anticipations of the spirit of Spenser, we shall find them more strongly in *Sir Gawayne and the Green Knight* than in Chaucer. And in *Piers Plowman* we find the English spirit as it still exists. "How much the less man you, if you do not know *Piers Plowman?* For therein is to be found the key to the Englishman of to-day, with the same strength and weakness, the same humour, immutable."[2]

There can be few stranger things in the history of literature than this sudden disappearance and reappearance of a school of poetry. It was kept alive by oral tradition through nine generations, appearing in writing very rarely, and then usually in a corrupt form, till it suddenly came forth, correct, vigorous, and bearing with it a whole tide of national feeling. Two of our three greatest Middle English poets are alliterative poets. And though alliterative verse died out after a century and a half, with the poem on the battle of Flodden, it had nevertheless endured into the Tudor age, and had formed a link between Old England and Modern England.[3]

All which shows how little the absence of documents for some particular type of literature at some particular date justifies us in denying its existence, and asserting a break in continuity. We are therefore not justified in asserting such a break in the continuity of English poetry, and in then extending to prose also, by analogy, this alleged break. On the contrary, the history of alliterative verse

[1] There are, of course, many changes, some of them rendered inevitable by the change in the language; but enough of the old technique remains to demonstrate continuity. See J. P. Oakden, *Alliterative Poetry in Middle English*, 1930, pp. 157, etc. In alliterative poetry (just as in prose) the most serious gap in our records lies, not so much between the Anglo-Saxon and the early Middle English period, as between the earlier and the later Middle English period; between, say. 1240 and 1340. Consequently, as Dr. Oakden shows, even some of the changes help to demonstrate continuity. For we can trace developments in the early Middle English period which are anticipatory of the practice of the alliterative poems of the Fourteenth and Fifteenth Centuries.

[2] Mr. Stanley Baldwin, July 19, 1929.

[3] Compare the lecture by Sir Israel Gollancz on *The Middle Ages in the Lineage of English Poetry*, 1920. (Harrap & Co.).

Alleged Anglo-Saxon decadence.

shows that continuity is demonstrable, despite the paucity of documents for the generations immediately before and after the Norman Conquest. During this period prose differs from alliterative verse in that prose documents are sometimes plentiful, and never entirely wanting.

About the year 1000 they are very plentiful. We have seen that on *a priori* grounds it might seem reasonable to assume that the whole Anglo-Saxon period, from the accession of Ethelred the Unready in 978 to the Norman Conquest, is one of such confusion of ideals and traditions that it cannot have been instrumental in transmitting any prose tradition; and that such is indeed the orthodox view.[1] Yet it was precisely during this period of greatest political and military disaster that Old English prose most obviously flourished. Ælfric is exactly contemporary with the worst period of confusion; but there is no confusion in Ælfric.[2] Ælfric is "the great master of prose in all its forms." "Ælfric works on principles that would have been approved by Dryden; and there is no better evidence of the humanities in those early times than this."[3] And the very documents in which the political and military confusion of the age is most emphasized—Wulfstan's *Address*, the *Chronicle*—show a remarkable power of writing excellent English.

When we come to the period of peace which followed this confusion, under Canute and the Confessor, it is true that we find the body of extant English prose to be very small. But there are laws, letters and charters, and under the Confessor we find evidence of many writers of great ability. Sometimes we have only two or three pages extant of each, sometimes less. But prose cannot have been decadent or moribund when a number of such writers were alive. Many documents have perished. And meantime the copying of the books of Ælfric and other classical English writers went on steadily—a very large number of books of English prose copied in this period have survived. The fact that the literary English, the King's English,

[1] See above, p. lxi.

[2] Saintsbury (*History of English Prose Rhythm*, pp. 41, 42) thinks that the rhythmical passages in Ælfric's *Homilies* are a sign of the decadence of English prose. Such rhythmical passages are found especially in the literature of the pulpit from the time of Ælfric to the Fifteenth Century. But it is noteworthy how entirely free from any rhetoric is the prose of the Chroniclers, especially of those immediately before the Conquest, when they choose to write simply. The insertion into the *Chronicle* of what Plummer calls "quasi-poems" does not interfere with the simplicity of the noble prose passages.

[3] W. P. Ker, *English Literature: Medieval* (1912), p. 55.

is coming to be used all over the country[1] is not consistent with the theory of literary decadence.

Alleged Anglo-Saxon decadence.

"Prose is an institution." It will be helpful to try and find out what was the general state of English civilization during these eighty-eight years of alleged decadence, from the accession of Ethelred the Unready to Harold, to see what is the evidence for the sterility which is alleged to have beset Anglo-Saxon life and literature till the Norman came to give a new impulse to civilization and to art.

We must examine the prose, not in isolation, but as "part of the equipment of a civilization," remembering the truth emphasized by Sir Arthur Quiller-Couch:

> That literature cannot be divorced from life: that (for example) you cannot understand Chaucer aright, unless you have the background . . . that is the *national* side with which all our literature is concerned.[2]

For times so remote as those before the Conquest, it is difficult to get the background. We must use every scrap of information we can find, which may teach us what manner of men the pre-Conquest Englishmen were. We can learn much from the prose; but something also from the drawings in manuscripts—something even from the coinage and stonework.

Nothing is easier than to verify what Prof. Oman has said about the coins.

Let anyone (if possible with a strong "Granny's glass") mount the stairs of the British Museum to the Exhibition of English Coins and Medals, and there look at the coins of the Confessor and of Harold, varying, but all well made. He will find that, for a generation after the Conquest, the coinage continues good. But when the generation dies out which had served its apprenticeship under pre-Conquest kings, he will find coins which, by contrast, impress on him the striking excellence of the Anglo-Saxon work. This relapse cannot be attributed to "the anarchy of the reign of Stephen": the inferior coins begin in the reign of Henry I, and they last through the long reign of Henry II. The contrast can only be attributed to the goodness of the pre-Conquest tradition, and to the damage to this tradition consequent upon the Norman Conquest.

Then let our seeker after Truth come downstairs again and look at the case in which are exhibited some of the wonderful and varied

[1] See below, p. lxxvi.
[2] *On the Art of Reading:* Lecture vi, "On a School of English."

Alleged Anglo-Saxon decadence.

products of the Anglo-Saxon School of illumination, covering exactly a century from the Charter of Edgar to the Conquest (966–1066). The series has a marked character of its own; it is astonishing in its variety and development: the Charter of Canute (*c.* 1020) is utterly unlike Edgar's Charter; and the Arundel Psalter, shortly before the Conquest, shows a new style again, anticipating in a remarkable way the art of later centuries. Our seeker naturally turns to the next case, to see what the Normans could do—he finds that the Museum has no work to exhibit of the two generations after the Norman Conquest.

Further, we may remember that the Norman conquerors were amazed at the wealth of precious things they found in England—a land which in that respect, they said, surpassed Gaul many times over.[1] England reminded them of what they had heard of the riches of Byzantium or the East. A Greek or Saracen would have been astonished, said William of Poitiers, at the artistic treasures of England. For English women, he adds, were accomplished in needlework and embroidery, English artificers in every kind of workmanship.[2]

All this had been fostered by the position of London as a centre of trade.

Long before the Norman Conquest, "English work" had been famous on the Continent. In its greatest days, the Abbey of Monte Cassino, the cradle of the Benedictine order, prided itself upon the possession of a specimen of this English work. How this happened was told by the historian of the Monastery, Leo, about the year 1100. In 1020 some of the monks, visiting Jerusalem, had brought back as a relic a fragment of the towel which our Lord had used when washing the feet of His disciples. What shrine could be found worthy to contain this relic? Fortunately just at that time an English noble had sent into those parts the wonderful reliquary in which, says the historian, the cloth is now enshrined, "most

[1] *Chari metalli abundantia multipliciter Gallias terra illa vincit.* Ut enim Horreum Cereris dicenda videtur frumenti copia, sic Ærarium Arabiæ auri copia. William of Poitiers (*Historiæ Normannorum Scriptores antiqui*, ed. Duchesne, Paris, 1619, p. 210).

[2] Voluptuosum est ea perspectare hospitibus maximis, et qui sæpe nobilium ecclesiarum thesauros viderant. Transiret illac hospes Græcus aut Arabs, voluptate traheretur eadem. Anglicæ nationis feminæ multum acu et auri textura, egregie viri in omni valent artificio. Ad hoc incolere apud eos Germani solebant talium artium scientissimi. Inferunt et negotiatores, qui longinquas regiones nauibus adeunt, doctarum manuum opera. (The same, p. 211.)

cunningly and beautifully worked, with gold and gems, *in the English style.*"[1]

Alleged Anglo-Saxon decadence.

It is in the nature of things that most of this "English work" has left no trace. The very preciousness of the metals in which the Anglo-Saxon craftsman loved to work has naturally led to the melting down of his workmanship. The carved and painted wood, which formed so important a feature of Old English decoration, could not long survive. And so the Saxon hall described in *Beowulf*, and the tapestries with which *Beowulf* describes that hall as hung, have vanished as though they had never been; though the amazing Cuthbert Stole at Durham remains to show what England could do in embroidery at the beginning of the Tenth Century. The main things that remain, as evidence, are naturally the manuscripts, for, terrible as has been the destruction which the Reformation wrought, specimens at any rate have been spared. Old English prose remains, and Old English manuscript illumination, both absolutely national and characteristic. Prose and skilled workmanship are, here again, found together as part of a national heritage.[2] They are an index of the rest which has been lost. "There is no better evidence of the humanities" than the prose, says the literary critic.[3] "Manuscript painting was the basic art of the Middle Ages; it was the principal means of the dissemination of artistic styles," says the critic of Art.[4]

In manuscript illumination England, for a century before the Norman Conquest, is now admitted to have been without parallel in Europe:

> The rich outburst of illumination in England during the Tenth and Eleventh Centuries was not equalled by anything on the Continent during that period. English decorative work produces an effect of informal richness different from anything seen before, and the naïve vigour of the figure representation contrasts strongly with the heavy formality of contemporary Ottonian illumination in Germany.[5]

It is not due to any imperfection in our national collection that from the two generations after the Conquest we find no illuminated

[1] Cumque excogitarent nostri qualiter, vel quanam in parte pignera tanta locarent, contigit dispositione divina, ut eodem ipso die a quodam nobili Anglo transmissus sit in hunc locum loculus ille mirificus, ubi nunc recondita est ipsa lintei sancti particula, argento et auro ac gemmis Anglico opere subtiliter ac pulcherrime decoratus. (*Chron. Mon. Casinensis, auctore Leone*, in Pertz *Monumenta, Scriptorum* VII (1846), p. 649.)

[2] See above, p. lviii. [3] W. P. Ker, as above.

[4] O. E. Saunders, *English Illumination*, p. 1.

[5] The same, p. 31.

Alleged Anglo-Saxon decadence.

MSS. exhibited at the British Museum. For the rest of the Eleventh Century there *is* practically no illuminated work extant, beyond some fine initial letters in the great books at Durham. Between sixty and eighty years after Hastings we begin to get great illuminations again; "massive austerity becomes the prevailing note, in place of the light and winsome freedom of the best Eleventh-Century work." The ugliness of the work, compared with the pre-Conquest style, is undeniable.[1] Sometimes it seems a relapse into barbarism. Compare, with any of the figures of the Evangelists drawn by any illuminator of the Winchester School, the Twelfth-Century Evangelists in the Hereford Cathedral Gospels.[2] The style rapidly improves, but it is not till a century after the Norman Conquest that the old pre-Conquest charm is found once more.

Of course, here again we must allow for the vast amount that has been lost. The two generations after the Norman Conquest can hardly have been as barren in the art of illumination as the paucity of extant documents suggests. Yet our stock of manuscripts, albeit small in proportion to the mass we have lost, is nevertheless large enough to allow us to argue with some safety. When we find that illuminated manuscripts surviving from the despised era, beginning with Ethelred the Unready and ending with the Conquest, outnumber those which we can attribute to the two generations after the Conquest by nearly ten to one, the figures must have significance.

The cultural strength of Old English life during its last stage is in remarkable contrast to the frequent ill-success in war. The history of England during the eighty-eight years from the accession of Ethelred the Unready to the battle of Hastings may at first sight appear to be one long story of national failure and foreign domination. But the disasters under Ethelred, the rule of foreign Danish masters, the alleged "anarchy" and "sterility" of the Confessor's reign, did not interrupt the tradition of English craftsmanship, as subsequently the brutalities of the Norman Conquest indisputably did. Are we not allowing ourselves to be dominated by the traditional "drum and

[1] "The personages in the miniatures have gaunt, long-limbed, ungainly figures, with monotonous and singularly unattractive facial types." *Schools of Illumination*, British Museum, Part II, 1915. Compare the judgement of Dr. A. Haseloff: "La technique légère, libre, sommaire de la période anglo-saxonne, avec son esprit, sa spontanéité, sa liberté d'allures, est remplacée par une lourde peinture à la gouache sur fond de couleur; le contour de toutes les figures dans l'ensemble comme dans le détail est fortement accusé, et au début du moins le style est extrêmement lourd." Michel, *Histoire de l'Art*, II, 309.

[2] MS. Hereford Cath. O. i. viii.

trumpet" view of history, which judges everything by military success or failure? Is it reasonable to ignore the pre-eminence in civilization which enabled the English in the first half of the Eleventh Century to turn the tables on their conquerors? **Alleged Anglo-Saxon decadence.**

Murders like those of Edward the Martyr or Prince Alfred or Beorn, massacres like that of St. Bryce's Day, show that England had a ruling class as brutal as any of that age. And many of the rulers were as incompetent as they were brutal.

All that must be admitted. But the wealth and art of England show that there is another side. And the history of England, for the century before the Norman Conquest, is not merely that of a wealthy and artistic people being plundered by a more noble, if less artistic, race. The essential thing is that the English civilize their conquerors. And even from the fighting point of view the record of Eleventh-Century England is not, as a whole, dishonourable. Maldon was no isolated heroic episode. "Thought shall be the harder, heart the keener, spirit shall be the greater, as our might lessens. Here our good prince lies on the earth hewn to death: that man will repent for ever, who now thinks to turn from this war-play." People who appreciated that formula were not decadent. London repeatedly rolled back, from her walls and from her bridge, the most determined Viking attacks. The most glorious day in the long history of London is 8 September, 994, when the Londoners repulsed both Anlaf and Swegen: that is Olaf Tryggvason, afterwards King of Norway, and Sweyn Forkbeard, King of Denmark. Milton was always a patriotic Londoner, and, looking around for a subject for "a Heroicall poem," he was attracted by this theme.[1] What a pity that, instead, he wrote pamphlets on Divorce. But the absence of John Milton's heroic poem is no reason for ignoring the terse prose of the *Chronicle:*

> 994. In this year came Anlaf and Swegen to London on the Nativity of Saint Mary with four and ninety ships. And they were fighting hard against the town, and sought to set it on fire. But there they suffered more harm and evil than they ever weened that the citizens of any town could have done to them. Yea, the holy Mother of God showed on that day to the citizens the gentleness of her heart, and saved them from their foes.

Was it nothing to have astonished Olaf Tryggvason, the greatest hero of the North? Later in the year Ethelred the Unready made his

[1] Trin. Coll. Camb. MS., fol. 36.

Alleged Anglo-Saxon decadence.

usual peace with the Danes, and sent Bishop Alphege to fetch Olaf, and "received him at the bishop's hands"—that is, stood sponsor to him at confirmation. It must have been an amazing meeting, that of Olaf Tryggvason and Saint Alphege. So Olaf, says the *Chronicle*, "promised (which promise he kept) that he would never again come to England save in peace." For six years Olaf spread vigorously in his realm of Norway the faith he had learnt in England, till the day when, at Svold, he found himself, with eleven ships, facing the united fleets of three Scandinavian powers—Denmark under his quondam ally Sweyn Forkbeard, Sweden under its king Olaf, and the Norsemen who followed Jarl Eirik, Haakon's son. Olaf Tryggvason might have got away without battle, but "My men shall never think of flight," he said, "let God care for my life." So he fell, and England was left to face, on behalf of Christendom, the whole force of the heathen onslaught under Sweyn and Canute. Twelve years after Svold, it was the turn of Saint Alphege, now Archbishop of Canterbury. His town was taken and sacked, and he was a prisoner. Again we have the terse words of the *Chronicle:*

> On the Saturday, the Danes were greatly stirred against the Bishop, because he would offer them no money, and forbade that any ransom should be paid for him. They were likewise very drunken, because wine had been brought from the South. So they took the Bishop, and led him to their hustings. And there they pelted him with bones, and with the heads of oxen. And one of them [1] smote him on the head with an axe, so that he fell to the ground. . . . And next day his body was carried to London, and the bishops Eadnoth and Ælfhun and the citizens received it with all honour, and buried it in St. Paul's. . . .

The end of all the fighting was that Edmund Ironside beat Canute the Great to a standstill, and peace was made, as Alfred had been compelled to make it in his day, on the basis of the partitioning of England. The brief account of Edmund's campaigns in the *Chronicle* is a classic piece of English prose. That Edmund died, worn out, immediately after the peace, does not alter his military achievement. So England was united under the rule of Canute, and under the laws of Edgar, which, says Canute a few years later in his English proclamation, "all men have chosen and sworn to, at Oxford."

Canute's victory enables us to observe again the victory of English civilization. We learn from the *Chronicle* how, not a dozen years

[1] A Christian convert, we learn from other accounts, who did it "with pious impiety" to shorten the agonies of the martyr, mortally wounded.

after the Viking host had done St. Alphege to death, Canute, now a model Christian king, was taking a leading part in the translation of the bones of the martyr from St. Paul's to Canterbury. In the same year Jarl Eirik, who had played the chief part among the heathen sea-kings who destroyed Olaf Tryggvason at Svold, joined with archbishops and abbots in witnessing Canute's grant of Sandwich port to Christ Church, Canterbury.[1] Then Canute made the pilgrimage to Rome and arranged that his subjects should have every facility for a like spiritual experience, all which he graciously explained to them in an open letter. Canute filled Denmark with English bishops,[2] whilst his contemporary and foe, Saint Olaf, was christianizing Norway with English ecclesiastics.[3] And from Norway these English missionaries spread to Sweden.

Alleged Anglo-Saxon decadence.

The story of the share of the English Church in the conversion of Scandinavia has, so far as I know, never been fully told in the English tongue. Norwegians have done justice to it.[4]

Finally, without a blow being struck, the Danish domination in England ended, and the line of Alfred was restored to the throne.

Surely this story of the struggle of two civilizations is really not less remarkable than would have been that of a great military victory, if some English king like Athelstan or Harold had arisen, and destroyed the Scandinavian hosts in battle.

And all this time the King's English of the South was making itself felt in the North of England, in the Eleventh Century, as it did not do again till the Fifteenth. In this standard English prose Canute naturally wrote that charter of liberties which he addressed to all his people, clerical and lay, in England, which Mr. Stevenson has declared to be, in substance and in form, the direct lineal ancestor of Magna Charta.[5] When we find the clergy of York not merely copying this into their Gospel Book for record, but using the same

[1] *Crawford Charters*, ed. Napier and Stevenson, XII. For biography of Eirik, see pp. 142–8 of that edition.

[2] Chnut . . . episcopos ab Anglia multos adduxit in Daniam. De quibus Bernardum posuit in Sconiam, Gerbrandum in Seland, Reginbertum in Fune. (Adam of Bremen, *Gesta Pontificum*, II, 53, in Migne, Vol. 146, 1853.)

[3] Beatissimus rex Olaph . . . habuit secum multos episcopos et presbyteros ab Anglia, quorum monitu et doctrina ipse cor suum Deo præparavit, subjectumque populum illis ad regendum commisit. Quorum clari doctrina et virtutibus erant Sigafrid, Grimkil, Rudolf et Bernard. Hi etiam jussu regis ad Suediam et Gothiam et omnes insulas quæ trans Nortmanniam sunt accesserunt evangelizantes. . . . (The same, II, 55.)

[4] Taranger, A., *Den Angelsaksiske Kirkes Indflydelse paa den Norske.* See especially pp. 142 ff.

[5] *English Historical Review*, XXVII, 4 (1912).

Alleged Anglo-Saxon decadence.

standard Southern English for their Bidding Prayer, for their homilies, and, above all, for their local surveys of property, we have a noteworthy event. Modern historians have made much of the different local legal systems of Anglo-Saxon England as rendering a common nationality impossible. Of course it was an impediment. (Yet it was only in 1926 that the special legal peculiarities of Kentish Law were finally abolished.) But the noteworthy thing is not that the Northumbrian clergy, having their own archbishop, should have also had their own special Code of Regulations, but that these regulations are in the standard English of the South.[1] When, after the Conquest, the authorities in York have to draw up for their new Norman archbishop a statement of his rights, they do it in the standard West Saxon speech.[2] Of course the dialects survived: we have a Northumbrian runic inscription dated in the days of Edward the Confessor and Earl Tosti. But even here, as again in the Fifteenth Century, we find the southern scribal conventions interfering with, and modifying, the proper dialectal forms.[3]

And this King's English, standard over all England, was intelligible over the whole of Northern Europe. "There was one speech only in the North, before William the Bastard won England," says the *Gunnlaugs Saga*,[4] when it tells us of the welcome which a Scandinavian traveller could find in London. For at London the ways crossed: the ancient route which led from Rome to York and the North, and the Viking sea-route which stretched, by the Baltic, through Russia to Byzantium. In the streets of early Eleventh-Century London, a man who had visited Rome might easily have met a man who had visited Micklegarth by the way through *Ryzaland*, who also might have talked with a man who had stepped upon what is now the territory of Canada and the United States.

We have seen that it is the *variety* of Anglo-Saxon prose which is so remarkable. To the translations made in Alfred's day, and to the Laws, Charters and Wills, we have to add Gospel Translations, Monastic Rules, Saints' Lives, Oriental legends both religious and

[1] Liebermann, *Die Gesetze der Angelsachsen*, I, 380.
[2] For the text see Herrig's *Archiv*, CXI, p. 279 (ed. Liebermann).
[3] Text by Max Förster in *Englische Studien*, XXXVI, 446 (1906). For the whole question of Eleventh-Century literary English and its distribution, see Schlemilch, *Beiträge zur Sprache und Orthographie Spätaltengl. Sprachdenkmäler der Übergangszeit (1100–1150)*, Halle, 1914 (Morsbach's *Studien*, XXXIV), esp. pp. 69, etc.; and Flasdieck, *Sprachliche Verhältnisse in altengl. Zeit*, in Paul-Braune, *Beiträge*, XLVIII, esp. 411, etc. (1924).
[4] Cap. 6.

secular, Dialogues, rudimentary Scientific, Medical and Astronomical works, Herbals, Lapidaries, even the Novel, in the story of *Apollonius of Tyre*. The fact that England was placed on the line of so many trade routes must have had something to do with this variety.

Alleged Anglo-Saxon decadence.

In the remarkable development of an official language "England preceded the nations of Western Europe by some centuries."[1] From some points of view it seems as if England was making hay of the European time-table, and Eleventh-Century England was getting into the Fifteenth; as if England was escaping from the Dark Ages without passing through the later Middle Ages at all. I think that it is this which accounts for the real animus which many historians show against the England of the Confessor and of Harold, and the obvious relief with which they hail the figure of William the Conqueror. "This kind of thing won't do," we can hear our orthodox historian saying. "It is quite unprecedented; and thank God, here is William come to put a stop to it."

Whatever the cause, recent historians[2] can see nothing but decadence and futility in Anglo-Saxon history of the Tenth and Eleventh Centuries—and even where they have to admit success, they console themselves by finding it "extremely limited."

Let us just look back upon this record of alleged failure.

"On the day that King Edward was alive and dead," 5 January, 1066, not two centuries had elapsed since Alfred was a fugitive at Athelney, with the whole of England harried and burnt up.

And now England possessed a civilization based upon Alfred's English prose as the national official and literary language. English jewellery, metal-work, tapestry and carving were famed throughout Western Europe. English illumination was unrivalled, and so national that the merest novice can identify the work of the Winchester school. Even in stone-carving, those who are competent to judge speak of the superiority of the native English carver over his Norman supplanter.[3] In building upon a large scale England was behind Normandy. But what little is left to us of Eleventh Century Anglo-Saxon architecture shows an astonishing variety. Its mark is "greater cosmopolitanism, as compared to the more competent, but equally more restricted and traditional architecture of the Normans."[4]

[1] W. H. Stevenson, *English Historical Review*, XXVII, 15 (1912).

[2] With certain notable exceptions, chief among whom must be named Dean Armitage Robinson.

[3] Clapham, *English Romanesque Architecture before the Conquest*, Oxford, 1930, p. 136. [4] The same, p. 152.

Alleged Anglo-Saxon decadence.

This is what we should expect, from the number of the civilizations with which England was brought into contact. The fact that Godwine and Harold had, during the fifteen years preceding the Norman Conquest, successfully resisted the excessive political influence of Edward's Norman favourites, has been misrepresented by modern historians as a provincial obscurantism, a wilful resistance of civilizing influences. That this was not so is shown by the fact that it was just during these years, when Norman political influence was in abeyance, that the great Abbey had been rising at Westminster. Its consecration, eight days before the Confessor's death, shows that the determination of Englishmen to be masters in their own land did not involve a refusal to employ, and to learn from, foreign craftsmen, including Normans.

Since the days of Alfred, the relation of England to the world outside had been that of a bulwark to Western Christendom, standing to receive the first shock of Viking invasion. On the whole, this duty had been performed victoriously, and the most overwhelming victory of all, that of Stamford Bridge, was still to come. Even more important was the leading part which England had played in the civilization and christianization of Scandinavia.

At home, Englishmen had grown to have enough feeling of unity to object to fighting one another. Steadily during the Eleventh Century the names "England," "Englishman," are everywhere superseding the older "West Saxon," "Mercian" or "Northumbrian." More than that, the ideal of a united island of Britain grows in strength. From Edward the Elder to Edward the Confessor we hear of this ideal. The poem on the Confessor's death tells us:

Honoured he ruled · the Welsh and the Scots
And the Britons also · Ethelred's son,
Angles and Saxons · champions strong.
As it lies surrounded · by cold sea waves
That land to Edward · the noble king
Obeyed in loyalty · warriors bold.

With William the Conqueror begins the "unholy game of gambling for French Provinces." Within eight years of Hastings, the *Chronicle* tells how William was leading an *English* army to burn the towns and destroy the vineyards of Maine [1] (which doubtless the English did gleefully, remembering the devastation of their own land by

[1] *Anglo-Saxon Chronicle*, anno 1074.

"Frenchmen" during those eight years). And this "unholy game" "was not to end till the Hundred Years' War was over, after four centuries of wasted effort," and was then to be immediately succeeded by a generation of civil war in England. Freeman has pointed out how Norman and Angevin kings, though not willingly disposed to abate a tittle of the rights of their Saxon predecessors, were distracted by their continental schemes. "The British Empire in which Ethelstan gloried was something which hardly seemed worth keeping in the eyes of Richard I." [1] When English historical prose once again attains eminence, after the mediæval interval, with More's *Richard III*, the very ideal of a united Britain has been forgotten, in the futile pursuit of the crown of France. First comes the lament of Edward IV over civil war, and then we have the claim of Richard to the throne of

Alleged Anglo-Saxon decadence.

> the twoo noble realmes, England and Fraunce, the tone fro this day forward by vs and our heires to rule, gouerne and defend, the tother by goddes grace and youre good helpe to geat again and subdewe.[2]

How thoroughly More recognized the folly of this ideal he showed about the same time in *Utopia* by his story of the Achoriens.

No doubt the England of Richard III or Henry VII was a greater nation than that of Edward the Confessor. The whole of Western Europe had grown mightily; and England, which even in the days of the Confessor was a great trading nation, in touch not only with Normandy and the South, but with Lotharingia, Germany and Scandinavia, had grown with the rest of Europe.

The England of Richard III and Henry VII was a land of glorious buildings, stained glass and goldsmith's work: a land of immense possibilities; but it would be difficult to show anything in which, with the same obvious certainty, "it was *preceding* the nations of Western Europe *by some centuries*," as in this achievement of an official vernacular before and in the days of the Confessor. And this English prose of the Eleventh Century was only a part of a great national movement, which was creating a united England.

How far should we have to travel from Eleventh-Century England in distance and in years, before we find any parallel to the two authors already quoted from the *Chronicle*, writing in places far

[1] Compare Freeman, *Norman Conquest*, I, 142–3 (second edition).
[2] More, *History of Richard III* (*Works*, p. 66).

Alleged Anglo-Saxon decadence.

removed from each other, giving an account of stirring events from different points of view, but in the same standard English speech, a standard speech used by the Northerner and the Southerner alike, although based, of course, upon the King's West Saxon tongue? One of them reports, with approval, that the feeling of England was against war; and he does not say that all the chivalry of Wessex was in one host, and all that of Northumbria in the other, and it was a pity they should destroy one another; but all the chivalry of *England* was in one host or the other, and to fight would have been to help *our* enemies and to destroy *our* selves.

I have always wondered why no one seems to be struck by this English historian of the middle of the Eleventh Century, protesting, in the English tongue, against war between different provinces of England. Dante complains because in his day each Italian city was rent by civic strife within itself:

> Ahi serva Italia . . .
> ed ora in te non stanno senza guerra
> li vivi tuoi, e l'un l'altro si rode
> di quei che un muro ed una fossa serra.

The pre-Conquest Englishman anticipates the constant protests of Sixteenth-Century England against "the wounds of civil war." It is "hateful." Here again John Milton found something in pre-Conquest England which he felt to be heroic. A poem, he thought, might be written on Edward Confessor's "over affection to strangers." The page of Milton's MS. is unfortunately torn, but we can read "wherein Godwin's forbearance of battel [p]rais'd, and the [En]glish moderation [of] both sides [m]agnifid."[1]

Anyway, pre-Conquest English prose reached its highest point in these records which tell how England, under the rule of a monarch whom Maitland calls "holy but imbecile," saved herself from the worst results of civil strife. Twice again England was ruled by ecclesiastically-minded kings of apparently similar character; but neither in the reign of Henry III nor in that of Henry VI did "English moderation" suffice to prevent the waging of pitched battles on English soil.

And it was not till 1603 that the ideal of 1066 of an island-kingdom

> swa ymbclyppaþ cealde brymmas

[1] Trin. Coll. Camb. MS., p. 36.

was realized, in Bacon's magnificent words:

Alleged Anglo-Saxon decadence.

> That this island of Brittany, divided from all the world, should be united in itself, as a full period of all instability and peregrinations.

VI. English Prose under the Norman Kings.

This vigour of English prose and of English life in the first half of the Eleventh Century must be understood if we are to follow the history of English prose at all. Those critics are perfectly right who object that it is absurd to claim continuity by jumping from Alfred to Wiclif. But Ælfric's own words show he looked beyond the period (lacking in reliable translations) which preceded him, back to Alfred;[1] and we shall see that the Sermons of Ælfric were being transcribed throughout the Eleventh and Twelfth Centuries, and were presumably being read even in the early Thirteenth. And by this time other writers of distinction had arisen to carry on Ælfric's work.

The effect of the Conquest upon English prose was slow. It was natural that correct alliterative poetry should cease to be written down, though not to be composed. Old English poetry had its home in the Anglo-Saxon hall, and had to go into the highways when the hall passed into Norman hands. But, unlike English poetry, English prose was not suddenly overthrown: it was too useful. The English charter which the Conqueror issued in 1066 to the Londoners, and which may still be seen at the Guildhall, is typical. But, although the process was slow, it was steady: the effect of the Conquest upon English official prose was that of a gradual stranglehold; upon English historical prose the stranglehold was even slower, but in the end equally effective. Once suppressed, English official prose and historical prose were slower to reappear than English alliterative verse. Official English was hardly known in 1360, when the alliterative revival was already vigorous. But, just at the time when, after a century and a half, that alliterative revival came to an end in England with the poem on Flodden, English historical prose was for the first time reasserting its full power in the *History of Richard III* by Sir Thomas More.

This strangling of English prose was a national disaster, and has much to do with that strange misunderstanding of their own

[1] See above, p. lxi.

English Prose under the Norman Kings.

Middle Ages which obsesses so many good Englishmen. There were many gallant English crusaders, and an English king commanded against Saladin. Yet we have nothing in English prose which we can compare with Joinville's *Life of St. Louis*; nothing in English narrative prose that we can think of together with Westminster Abbey as representative of the England of the Thirteenth Century. The Norman Conquest robbed us of such possibilities. Of course the Conqueror did not land at Pevensey with any deliberate intention of destroying the English nationality and the English language;[1] but it was an inevitable consequence of the Conquest that both were nearly destroyed.

What was taking place is shown very well by the register of the charters of the Norman kings. We have records of at least twenty-six documents issued by the Conqueror in English, and, of course, not a single one in French. But the effect of the Norman-French clerks, allowing nothing but Latin, and entrenched in the monastery schools and the king's court, was bound to be felt as time went on. After the Eleventh Century, such English official documents are of the rarest occurrence till the time when, three centuries later, English begins to be used, very charily, in the latter part of the reign of Richard II.

The English laws were translated into French or Latin, and new English laws recorded in French or Latin, with the curious result that the English people, who for nearly five centuries had been distinguished among the nations of Europe by having their laws written down in their own tongue, began to conduct their legal business, first of all in the French language, and then in no language at all. "Il jecte un graund brickbat que narrowly mist."[2]

Whether the Norman Conquest was a blessing or a disaster we can never know; for although we can make some estimate of what England gained and lost, things being as they were, we cannot even guess what would have been the loss or gain, if one of the single combats between Duke William and an English champion had had a different issue. But we can estimate the loss to our English prose. It seems regrettable that this jargon of "Law French" should have taken the place of the clean English which Alfred and Canute used for their legal business. Yet even here there may be differences of opinion. Sir John Fortescue, the great Fifteenth-Century lawyer

[1] Cf. Freeman, *Norman Conquest*, II, 171; (Third edit., 174).
[2] See P. H. Winfield, *Sources of English Legal History*, Camb., Mass., 1925.

who first used English for discussing Constitutional Law, had a high opinion of Anglo-French. During his exile he had occasion to compare it with the French of France, and regretted that Continental French had been corrupted by barbarisms.[1]

English Prose under the Norman Kings.

It is interesting to note that the substitution of French for English as the language of the law was also not a very sudden change. It is remarkable how many of the manuscripts upon which we depend for our knowledge of Old English law were transcribed after the Norman Conquest: some of them a considerable time after. But, once French had become the language of English law, it was slow to be displaced; it was not altogether displaced till the Eighteenth Century.

The record of English historical prose resembles that of English official prose, except that it is much slower in its decline. Once fallen, it lies prostrate just as long.

In one district in England English was, for some time, protected by circumstances. Bishop Wulfstan of Worcester had been a friend of Harold; but his reputation for piety was so outstanding that, since he submitted to the Conqueror, and was guilty of no disloyalty, he was left undisturbed. He lived till 1095; the great See of Worcester therefore remained, for a generation, under the rule of an Englishman. A considerable number of manuscripts of Anglo-Saxon homilies have come down to us which were apparently transcribed at Worcester under Wulfstan.[2]

It may well be that England owes a great deal to the long life of Wulfstan, which ensured that during the thirty terrible years after the Conquest, one district of England at least remained ecclesiastically under English rule. Winchester culture found refuge in Worcester. It is unwise to generalize on such scanty evidence, yet we cannot but note how many of the documents in which the English spirit reasserts itself belong to the Worcester diocese, or to its immediate neighbourhood.

When Wulfstan died, his biography was written *in English* by

[1] *De Laudibus*, cap. 48: *Lingua, jam in Francia vulgaris, non concordat aut consimilis est Gallico inter legisperitos Angliæ usitato, sed vulgariter quadam ruditate corrupta.*

[2] Keller, W., *Die Litterarischen Bestrebungen von Worcester in Angelsächsischer Zeit*, 1900 (Quellen u. Forschungen), p. 64, etc.; also *Zur Litteratur von Worcester*, 1897, p. 20. A Worcester monk, perhaps somewhere about 1200, glossed, in a tremulous hand, a number of Anglo-Saxon books, for the benefit of those who could not understand them. Several of these have been noted by Keller (p. 20) and others by Dr. Montague Rhodes James, *Catalogue of Manuscripts in Corpus Christi College, Cambridge*, Vol. I, No. 12. See also *Die Hirtenbriefe Ælfrics*, herausg. v. Bernhard Fehr, p. xxi.

English Prose under the Norman Kings.

his chaplain and chancellor Colman,[1] some time between 1095 and 1113. Now there had been lives of the great bishops of the Tenth Century, Dunstan and Æthelwold and Oswald; but these had been in Latin. Such a life of a great statesman and saint, just dead, in the vernacular, was a thing hitherto unknown, not only in England, but in Western Europe. Ari the Wise, who laid the foundations of Icelandic historical writing, is a younger contemporary of Colman. But Colman in England, unlike Ari in Iceland, had no successor as a biographer—his life was to remain without parallel in English till Roper and Harpsfield wrote. This shows how heavily Fate had weighted the scales against English prose. The next great English statesman and saint, after Wulfstan, to have his life written in the vernacular was Thomas à Becket; and this was in French verse, not English prose.

But, at the same time, it is evidence of the vitality of English prose at the Norman Conquest that, a full generation or more after that Conquest, England should have produced so unparalleled a work.

A further proof of this vitality is the way in which the *Chronicles* continued. Of the *Chronicles* which we know were being kept up in the days of Edward the Confessor, all but one were still being added to, a generation after the Conquest,[2] although the fact is often not recognized, owing to accidents of mutilation.[3] The "Worcester" Chronicle[4] breaks off in 1079. This is due to mutilation, but anyway that Chronicle did not apparently carry its record much further. Yet the last writer, to judge by his interest in St. Margaret of Scotland and her genealogy, seems to have written after the union of the West Saxon and the Norman lines by the marriage of Margaret's daughter "good Queen Maud" to Henry I in 1100.[5] And this impression of late date is confirmed by the Chronicler's occasional use of Romance words.[6]

[1] Extant only in the Latin rendering of William of Malmesbury, ed. R. R. Darlington; Camden Society, 1928.

[2] The exception is MS. Cotton Tiberius B. i (C), and it is even possible that this also was being kept up after 1066. It ends, indeed, with the tale of the Northman holding the bridge at the battle of Stamford Bridge. But this is appended to the MS. in much later English: the MS. itself ends, *mutilated*, in the middle of the annal for 1066.

[3] I should like here to echo the plea of Dr. Armitage Robinson for the issue of a facsimile edition of the *Chronicles*. See *The Times of St. Dunstan*, 1923, p. 17.

[4] Cott. Tib. B. iv (D). I use the word "Worcester" as signifying some place in that diocese, not necessarily the city itself. Plummer favours Evesham (II, lxxvi).

[5] See the entry under 1067.

[6] Plummer, II, lxxviii (§§ 75, 76).

English Prose under the Norman Kings.

In the late Eleventh Century the *Anglo-Saxon Chronicle* was being copied, it would seem, at Canterbury, in a bilingual form.[1] This double entry, in English and Latin, shows the transition from the vernacular history of Old England to the Latin history of Norman and Angevin England; nevertheless, the transition was slow.

Nearly half a century after the Conquest we have an odd leaf, with entries for the years 1113, 1114: this testifies to the existence of a lost English Chronicle—how far back, how far forward it went, we do not know.[2] The fragment preserved deals almost exclusively with the king's movements and with promotions in Church and State—especially Church; the noteworthy thing is the correctness, considering the date, of the traditional West Saxon in which the fragment is written.

Further, we know of a Chronicle which was being vigorously maintained in English, somewhere in the South of England, as late as 1121. The home of this Chronicle may have been St. Augustine's, Canterbury.[3] How many different writers contributed to it in the fifty-five years between 1066 and 1121 we do not know. But one of these chroniclers was a great writer. It is he who has left us the sketch of the character of the Conqueror to which all later historians have been indebted; the portrait of William as he appeared to one "who looked on him and of old sojourned in his court." The writer is an English patriot, bitterly distressed at all the evils which have come upon his land: "Who is so hard of heart as not to weep at such misfortune?" Yet he can be just to the Conqueror: "these things we have written concerning him, both good and evil."

Peterborough probably lost its English Chronicle in the fire of 1116; but historical writing in English must have been still vigorous there. For, about 1121, the Peterborough monks appear to have borrowed the English Chronicle, just mentioned, from the South of England, and to have copied it. The borrowed manuscript was then, presumably, returned to its Southern home; how much longer it was kept up, and what happened to it ultimately, we do not know. But the Peterborough copy was continued: the last entry is for the year 1154.[4] With this, the noble record of historical writing in English prose ends, and ends nobly. It does not revive again in a form we

[1] Cott. Dom. A. viii (F). The manuscript ends, mutilated, in 1058, but the hand is agreed to be nearly half a century later.
[2] Cott. Dom. A. ix (H).
[3] Plummer, II, lii–liv.
[4] This is, of course, the Bodleian MS., Laud. Misc. 636 (E).

English Prose under the Norman Kings.

can call great literature till it is nobly re-established by Sir Thomas More. There is a connection, but the descent, as I shall try to show, is collateral, not direct.

VII. Disappearance of English Historical Prose.

The unknown monk of Peterborough who tells us of the miseries of Stephen's reign writes as a man looking back on an era already passed away. All the events of the past twenty-two years, since 1132, are recorded perhaps about the same time, certainly in one handwriting; the writer feels that under the strong young king who has just come to the throne a new age has begun.

Indeed the Angevin line marks a new era in many ways. Our chronicler under Henry II writes an English distinctly more modern than that which his predecessor had used in writing the annals of Henry I. The scribal tradition, if not the language itself, has notably changed. Indeed, if a line must be drawn between Old English and Middle English, it would, I think, have to come between the man who wrote the Peterborough annal for 1131, and the man who wrote (perhaps about 1155) the Peterborough annal for 1132.

It was appropriate that, early in the reign of the young king who was descended, not only from the Conqueror, but also from his Saxon predecessors, steps were taken to canonize Edward the Confessor. We have evidence that, shortly after the Confessor's death, he was believed to have foretold the evil days of foreign dominion which were coming, and to have also foretold that they would never mend "till a branch, cut off and removed three furlongs from its parent stem, should of its own self return, graft itself upon that parent stem, grow green, and bear fruit."[1] How true the prognostication of evil had been, is shown by the *Anglo-Saxon Chronicle*, which, for three generations after Hastings, is one long record of tyranny and disaster. Yet the writers are no mere oppressed peasants: they are educated men, keeping up a literary tradition. The man who wrote the character of the Conqueror, and later of Rufus, speaks like a man of affairs. But, more and more, English was banished from court. Two generations after the Conqueror's landing, William of Malmesbury writes that the Confessor's prophecy is still being fulfilled: "To-day, no Englishman is a duke, or a

[1] *Lives of Edward the Confessor*, Rolls Series, p. 431.

bishop, or an abbot: foreigners devour the wealth of England, and there is no hope of remedy."[1]

Disappearance of English Historical Prose.

But with the accession of Henry II some people at least thought that the evil times were over. Ailred of Rievaulx, a thorough Englishman, brought up in the household of a descendant of the Saxon kings, when he has to deal with the Confessor's prophecy, says that now at last it has been fulfilled. The three furlongs he interprets as the reigns of Harold, William I and William II, kings not of the old line. The branch returns to its stock, voluntarily, when Henry I unites the lines by choosing Queen Maud as his bride. The line grows green with their offspring Matilda; Henry II is the fruit. Now verily, Ailred writes, England has a king of English stock, it has bishops and abbots of that stock, it has knights and chiefs whose race combines both stocks.[2]

Yet, indeed, it is just at this point that English historical prose disappears after a life of some ninety years following the Conquest.

And the reason is obvious. For Henry II ruled the vast Angevin empire, stretching "from the Cheviots to the Pyrenees." When Ailred addressed to Henry, Count of Anjou, and heir to the English throne, but not yet king of England, an account of the Saxon kings who had been his predecessors on the throne which was to be his, that account was naturally in Latin. Ailred's tract is one long panegyric of the Saxon kings, ending with a noble (and certainly true) story of the charity of the "Good Queen Maud," and how she washed the feet of lepers. But English was no longer the language of the court. And so for some of the most noteworthy centuries of English history we have no contemporary record in the English tongue. How much we have lost by that, two examples will show. The historians insist that English literature was dead at the time of the Conquest; yet, so long as there is any *Chronicle* at all, they cannot get on without its telling phrases. "He loved the tall stags as if he were their father"; "When the castles were finished, they filled them with devils and evil men"; "There was not an hide of land in England, but he knew who had it, and what it was worth." Compared with this, rhetorical monastic Latin is poor. Again, let anybody compare the gusto with which Harpsfield tells the story of how William Roper "longed sore to be pulpited,"[3] and

[1] *Gesta Regum*, Rolls Series, I, 278.
[2] Ailred, *Life of Edward the Confessor*, in Migne, CXCV, cols. 773–4.
[3] See below, pp. 84–7.

Disappearance of English Historical Prose.

how More was not able "to call him home," with the same story as told by Stapleton. Stapleton was a great man, but he was using the more hackneyed Latin, and all the virtue of the story is lost. One is reminded of Dante's great defence of his beloved Vulgar—which "is closer to us, in that it is more united to us,"[1] than any learned tongue can be.

But English was not even the second tongue of Henry's Angevin empire. And already the great movement of song had begun in France, which was to set the tune of all modern literature. At the moment when it might have been expected that English would begin to come by its own, fashion came in to reinforce French. By the early Thirteenth Century there had been so much intermarriage that the English as a race were absorbing the Normans. But the prestige of French literature, architecture and civilization was at its height. To realize how great that prestige was, we have only to think of St. Francis of Assisi, "loving to speak French, though he spoke it not well."[2] And there must have been many an Englishman who resembled the Umbrian saint in this, if in no other respect. For the late Thirteenth and most of the Fourteenth Century it is the same. Of the very large number of documents, illustrating citizen life in London in the reigns of Edward I, Edward II and Edward III, which have been published by Mr. Riley, more than two-thirds are in Latin, the remainder either in French or in French with Latin: not one is in English. English prose was cut off from its roots in English life.

And English was further handicapped by phonological changes. The standard English of the days of Edward the Confessor had been well on the way to reach the position of a literary language prevalent over all England. But it was now becoming unintelligible, and in its place the dialects were reasserting themselves. There was no longer an English, though there was a French, current throughout all England.

It is significant that just about the time the *Chronicle* expired at Peterborough, Geoffrey Gaimar was translating the *Chronicle* into French, writing a *History of the English* in rhymed couplets. So history comes again to flourish in the vernacular, but in French

[1] *Convivio*, I, 12.

[2] *Eleemosynam gallice postulabat, quia libenter lingua gallica loquebatur, licet ea recte loqui nesciret.* (*La Leggenda di San Francesco, scritta da tre suoi Compagni*, Roma, 1899, p. 22.)

Disappearance of English Historical Prose.

instead of English, and, it is very important to note, in *verse* and not in prose.

Most significant of all, we find the Anglo-Saxon *Life of St. Edmund* being translated into French verse—not in order that aristocrats as well as the humble may understand it, but, the translator tells us, that *all*, the great, the middle and the lower classes, may now understand it:

> Translaté l'ai desqu'a la fin
> E de l'engleis e del latin
> Q'en franceis le poent entendre
> Li grant, li mien, e li mendre.[1]

This has been duly emphasized by Prof. Vising. And all those who will consult the remarkable evidence collected by him[2] will, I think, feel that, in the century following the cessation of the *Chronicle*, it appeared very possible that French and not English would be the language of England. For a century English prose had survived, but had been steadily losing ground; for a century its fate seemed to hang in the balance; for a century the stranglehold upon English was gradually being relaxed, though the relaxation was not obvious to everyone. It is curious that Higden, towards the end of this third century after the Conquest, should have said so contemptuously of English, *in paucis adhuc agrestibus uix remansit.*[3] For, at the moment Higden spoke of English in this way as almost extinct, the tide was about to turn emphatically. Higden wrote in the middle of the Fourteenth Century. In the third quarter of that century English began to supersede French in the schools, so that Trevisa, making his translation of Higden in 1385, quite faithfully translates his author's words "that English remains scarcely with a few uplandish men," but yet, as we shall see later,[4] has to contradict the statement which had been made, only a generation before, by the author whom he is translating.

Now the question which we have got to answer is this: Was the sudden output of English prose a new thing, or a survival of the old prose of Alfred and Ælfric? It is usual to regard it as a new thing, having its beginning with the Wicliffite translation of the Bible. It is the object of this essay to maintain that this is not so,

[1] Denis Piramus, *Vie Seint Edmund*, 3267–70.
[2] *Anglo-Norman Language and Literature*, 1923.
[3] Ed. Babington, II, 160–61.
[4] See below, p. cx.

Disappearance of English Historical Prose.

but that the old prose of Alfred and Ælfric, despite evil days, had nevertheless lived on, to find a new future opening before it in the Fifteenth Century.

VIII. Survival of Religious Prose. The *Ancren Riwle*.

It may be asked—if there is a break of some three centuries in the continuous use of prose for official records, and a break of as long a time in English historical prose—where does the continuity of English prose come in? Obviously the English *Language* is continuous—it lived from generation to generation on the mouths of men. But can the convention of composing prose in English be proved to be continuous?

The continuity of English prose is to be found in the sermon and in every kind of devotional treatise. When we turn to this religious prose, it is no question of leaping over the centuries, as we have to do in passing from the historical prose of the Peterborough monk about 1155 to the humble beginnings of historical prose in the late Fourteenth and early Fifteenth Centuries. On the contrary, there is a series of links, sometimes working very thin, but never broken.

The foreign prelates and abbots whom William imposed upon the conquered English found in their monasteries a tradition of two things without parallel on the Continent, a splendour of manuscript illumination and a tradition of vernacular composition. We might have expected on *a priori* grounds that they would have encouraged the art and discouraged the language. But, in fact, whilst illumination disappears, manuscripts in the English language continue to be transcribed, not only at Worcester, under Wulfstan, but under Norman rule in many other places. Norman bishops and abbots did not, it would seem, actively persecute the English language. Ind ed, the deliberate outlawry of a language is more characteristic of the Twentieth Century than of the Eleventh.

Of course preaching in the vernacular received a check. For preaching was essentially a bishop's business.[1] And if the bishop knew little or no English—— ? Wulfstan, the solitary Saxon bishop, rivalled his Norman colleagues in the magnificence of his rebuilding; but he is reported to have broken into tears as he saw the old building at Worcester being destroyed: "Our predecessors, it is

[1] Cf. for example William of Malmesbury, *Vita Wulfstani*, ed. Darlington, Camden Society, p. 14.

Survival of Religious Prose.

true," he said, "knew not how to build as we do, but their lives were an example to their flock; we, neglecting the cure of souls, care only to heap up stones."[1] St. Wulfstan himself was an energetic preacher.[2] His Norman colleagues called him "unlearned": his words, uttered more than twenty years after the Conquest, and about a dozen years after the time that Wulfstan had been left the sole remaining Saxon prelate, make a gentle but crushing comment upon them and their magnificent buildings.

An English writer, soon after the Conquest, makes a similar complaint:

> Bede and Ælfric turned books into *English*: Wilfred of Ripon, John of Beverley, Cuthbert of Durham, Oswald of Worcester, Egwin of Evesham, Aldhelm of Malmesbury, Swithun, Æthelwold, Aidan, Birinus of Winchester, Paulinus of Rochester, St. Dunstan, St. Alphege of Canterbury—all these taught our people in *English*; their light was not dark, it beamed fairly; but now those teachings are left, and the people is lost; it is other folk who teach our people; and many of the teachers are lost, and the people with them.

We do not know where these words were composed or who wrote them; apparently written soon after the Conquest, they were apposite enough to be copied perhaps a century later. They are now preserved in the Cathedral library at Worcester.

Nevertheless, despite this complaint, treatises like the *History of the Holy Rood Tree* and *Vices and Virtues* show that the work of teaching our people in English, though checked, was not stopped. Above all, the books of Ælfric and other Old English writers continued to be copied assiduously. A large body of extant manuscripts testifies to this; and we must allow for the very much larger number now lost. An an example we might take the seven surviving manuscripts of the Old English *Heptateuch*. Two are pre-Conquest; one is about the time of the Conquest; and four are post-Conquest, and the latest of these was written perhaps a century after the Conquest. In the latter half of the Twelfth Century we find great collections of Homilies, almost entirely drawn from Ælfric and other pre-Conquest sources.[3] About the end of the century we also find Homilies of

[1] William of Malmesbury, *Gesta Pontificum*, *Rolls Series*, p. 283.

[2] Quandocumque dioceses circumiret, nunquam sine missa, sine sermone populum dimitteret. William of Malmesbury, *Vita Wulfstani*, ed. Darlington, p. 36.

[3] MS. Bodl. 343. Napier (*History of the Rood Tree*; E.E.T.S.) dates this MS. about 1150–75.

Survival of Religious Prose.

which we can trace some, but not most, to Ælfric.[1] We find a homily of Ælfric, in a modernized form, in a collection apparently belonging to some time about the year 1200.[2] We find the West Saxon translation of the Gospels being copied in the middle of the Twelfth Century. Made, perhaps, in the troublous times of Æthelred the Unready, it is being copied, perhaps, in the even more troublous times of Stephen. This copy [3] was again transcribed [4] in the latter half of the Twelfth Century, and some gaps in it were filled up by a new translation by the late Twelfth-Century scribe. He makes but a poor show when we compare his work with the fine idiomatic rendering of the Anglo-Saxon translator; but then he is only a scribe supplying some missing verses: we must not ask literary ability from every copyist.

Alfred's works also continued to be copied. The only complete manuscript of his translation of Boethius which time has left us belongs apparently to the early Twelfth Century, whilst for his translation of St. Augustine's *Soliloquies* we are dependent upon a copy made about the middle of that century.

In the latter half of the Tenth Century, Edgar had taken the monks of England under his care, whilst his wife Ælfthryth was made responsible for all the English convents for women. Together they gave to St. Æthelwold the manor of Sudbourne in Sussex, on condition that he should translate into English the *Rule of St. Benedict.* We know this from the Ely records, for St. Æthelwold in turn gave the manor to the monastery of Ely, which he had re-established. Now all our extant copies of Æthelwold's translation (with one exception) speak of monks, not nuns—yet the survival here and there of a feminine pronoun shows that the original from which these manuscripts were all copied must have been for nuns, not monks. And it seems reasonable to assume that St. Æthelwold would have cast his translation into a feminine form. It would have been a confession of weakness that monks should be supposed unable to study

[1] The "Lambeth" Homilies. These are usually dated *c.* 1175. Mr. Gilson was inclined to place the manuscript between 1185–1225 (Allen, *The Author of the Ancren Riwle*, in *Pub. Mod. Lang. Assoc. Amer.*, xliv, 671). On some likenesses between the *Riwle* and some of the "Lambeth" Homilies, see Miss Allen's article, and also, independently, Prof. Tolkien in *Essays and Studies by Members of the English Association*, xiv, p. 119.

[2] MS. Vespasian A. xxii, fol. 54. It must be remembered that, at this period, the materials for dating vernacular writing are, in the words of Mr. Gilson, "so slight that any opinion must be tentative."

[3] MS. Royal 1. A. xiv (British Museum).

[4] MS. Hatton 38 (Bodleian).

their founder's rules in the original. At any rate, the archetype of our extant copies certainly was for nuns; the subsequent adaptation for men may be paralleled in the textual history of other treatises addressed to women: the *Ancren Riwle* or the *Scale of Perfection*. And here, for the first time, we come across a fact which is the cause of the composition of so much English prose: the fact that women recluses would not be expected to be as familiar as men would be with Latin.[1] It is not fanciful to see, in the Anglo-Saxon version of St. Benedict's *Rule* adapted for nuns, the beginning of a literature which ends with the English works addressed by More and Fisher to Joyeuce Leigh and Elizabeth White.

Survival of Religious Prose.

But my immediate point is that the only copy of St. Æthelwold's translation which has come down to us[2] in the form addressed to nuns, a form which must have been that of the original of all extant copies, was transcribed (apparently for the nunnery of Winteney in Hampshire) about the year 1200.[3]

One further fact has quite recently come to light. A certain anchorite Hugh, some time apparently between 1140 and 1215, asked a certain priest Robert for a Rule. Robert replied *diversas sententias de anglicis libris in latinam linguam transferre studui*. English then, not Latin, was, in early Angevin days, the obvious language in which might be found precepts useful to a recluse.[4] And this was natural, since England was remarkable for the number of its hermits and recluses.[5]

Before the work of Æthelwold and Ælfric was forgotten, a new prose writer arose to carry on their work. The new writer, the author of the *Ancren Riwle*, was, as we shall see, a greater master of prose than even Ælfric, and his popularity was destined to last till the close of the Middle Ages.[6]

This survival and revival of devotional prose is in remarkable contrast to the extinction of historical prose. And the reason for the contrast is obvious. Great bishops and abbots, although they

[1] See J. Armitage Robinson, *Life and Times of Dunstan*, 1923, p. 122.

[2] MS. Cotton Claudius D. iii.

[3] *Die Winteney-Version der Regula S. Benedicti Lateinisch und Englisch*, herausg. v. Arnold Schröer. Halle a. S. (Niemeyer), 1888.

[4] *Regulae tres reclusorum et eremitarum Angliae, saec. XIII–XIV*, by P. Livarius Oliger, O.F.M., in *Antonianum*, III, 151–90, 299–320 (1928). The MS. has *angelicis*, but the word is noted for correction, and the context shows that *anglicis* is meant.

[5] I make this assertion on the authority of P. Livarius Oliger, O.F.M., *Antonianum*, III, 166.

[6] See below, pp. xcvi–c.

Survival of Religious Prose.

might speak Latin among themselves, and French to their secular peers, had to consider the souls of those who could speak neither. So, we are told of Abbot Sampson (1135–1211) that he was eloquent both in French and Latin, could read English books excellently, and was wont to preach to the people at Bury in English, in his native Norfolk dialect; and that for this purpose he had a pulpit set up in the church.[1] The English which Sampson would read would probably be the classical pre-Conquest Old English; what he would preach would presumably be something akin to the speech of the last Peterborough chronicler.

We have then, for the Twelfth and the beginning of the Thirteenth Century, a mass of religious and homiletic literature: some of it a transliteration of translations by Alfred or St. Æthelwold; some of it transliteration of sermons of Ælfric or Wulfstan; some of it apparently derived from pre-Conquest originals now lost. Also, some of it is new. We have, simultaneously, in the Twelfth Century, the rise of Norman-French literature, almost exclusively, at the beginning, in verse; and we find English prose treatises and saints' lives being translated into French verse,[2] just as we find the *Chronicle* being translated into French verse by Gaimar.

But the essential thing is, that side by side with French verse, we have the continuation of the English homily tradition and the tradition of books written for recluses, especially women, in English prose.

One particular group of such English prose writings separates itself out from the rest, first by its literary excellence, and secondly by the quite extraordinary regularity and consistency of the English in which it is written. That English is West Midland. The two most important manuscripts are connected, the one with the Worcestershire, and the other with the Shropshire border of Herefordshire. It may be worth remembering that the Worcestershire district is connected both with the survival of literary English under Wulfstan, and with the revival of English by Layamon.

The language of these treatises is "self-consistent and unadulterated." "It stands out," says Prof. Tolkien, "among Middle

[1] Jocelin of Brakelond, *Cronica*, p. 30; trans. Sir Ernest Clarke, p. 52.
[2] Haxo in *Mod. Philol.*, XII, 345, 559; Gabrielson in Herrigs *Archiv*, CXXVIII, 309.

English texts, not excluding the *Ayenbite* or the *Ormulum*, by reason of the regularity of its phonology and its accidence." It is an English "that has preserved something of its former cultivation." Survival of Religious Prose.

> It is not a language long relegated to the "uplands," struggling once more for expression in apologetic emulation of its betters, or out of compassion for the "lewed," but rather one that has never fallen back into "lewedness," and has contrived, in troublous times, to maintain the air of a gentleman, if a country gentleman. It has traditions, and some acquaintance with books and the pen, but it is also in close touch with a good living speech—a soil somewhere in England.[1]

In this speech have been preserved the lives of the three women saints, St. Katherine, St. Margaret and St. Juliana; the tract on *Holy Maidenhood*; *Soul's Ward*; and, above all, the *Ancren Riwle.*

Something of the literary value of these books can be seen if we compare a few lines of *Soul's Ward* with their original, the *De Anima* of Hugo of St. Victor.

Here is the Latin: it is a description of the joys of the blessed:

> Vivunt vitam sine fine, sine molestia, sine diminutione, sine omni adversitate. Vita eorum visio et cognitio beatae Trinitatis, sicut Dominus ait: Haec est vita aeterna, ut cognoscant te Deum verum et quem misisti Jesum Christum. Sapiunt consilia atque judicia Dei quae sunt abyssus multa.[2]

Here is the English, as closely as it can be expressed in modern speech:

> They live aye in one beauty that is brighter sevenfold, and sheener than the sun; and ever in one strength, to do without any labour all that they will; and ever more in one stay, in all that ever good is, without waning, without anything that may harm or ail, in all that ever is soft or sweet. Their life is the sight of God, and the knowledge of God, as our Lord said: "That is, said he, eternal life, to see and know the sooth God, and Him whom He sent, Jesus Christ our Lord, for our redemption." Therefore they are like Him, in the same beauty that He is, for they see Him as He is, face to face. They are so wise that they know all God's redes, and His runes, and His dooms that derne be, and deeper than any sea-dingle.

Such a free treatment of a Latin original, an original by a famous doctor, is surely not the work of a beginner in the vernacular.

[1] *Ancrene Wisse* and *Hali Meiðhad*, by J. R. R. Tolkien, in *Essays and Studies by Members of the English Association*, xiv (1929), pp. 104, etc. Tolkien suggests Herefordshire as the home of all these treatises.

[2] *De anima*, Bk. IV, §§ 13–15, in Migne, *P.L.* CLXXVII, esp. col. 188.

Survival of Religious Prose.

Translation like this must have literary tradition behind it. It is not struggling " in apologetic emulation of its betters." We see the same thing in the translations of biblical texts in the *Ancren Riwle*, or in passages where the author is following St. Bernard, and where, in comparison with his vivid phrases, Bernard's Latin seems comparatively commonplace. " There is no better evidence of the humanities in those early times than this." It is all in the tradition of Ælfric, and in marked contrast to the later practice of Wiclif and his associates. Wiclif's phrases are often vigorous; the words of so powerful a man must needs be; but if he is overshadowed by the Latin, his English becomes helpless in the presence of that great competitor.

The *Ancren Riwle*.

By far the greatest of the books of this group is the *Ancren Riwle*. The Rule was written for three young maidens of gentle birth who had withdrawn from the world to cells by the wall of a church (*under chirche iancred* [1]) where they lived *niht ond dei upe Godes rode*.[2]

> Much word is there of you, what gentle women ye be; for your goodness and for your nobleness of mind beloved of many; sisters, of one father and of one mother, in the flower of your youth, ye have left all worldly joys, and become anchoresses.[3]

Much of the *Riwle* is the ordinary homiletic instruction; but the author from time to time shows astonishing power. One feels that he might have done almost anything. Nowhere can we find better sinners than in the *Ancren Riwle*. We seem sometimes to be anticipating the character drawing of the Seventeenth Century. There is the flatterer, saying to the knight who robs his poor men, " Ah, Sir, verily thou dost well: for one ought always to pluck and pillage the churl—he is like the withy that sprouteth out the better, the more often it is cropped." [4] And here is the backbiter:

> He casts down his head, and begins to sigh before he says a word; then he talks around the subject for a long time with a sorrowful countenance, to be the better believed: " Alas, well-away, woe is me, that he (or she) has fallen into such repute. Enough did I try, but I could do no good herein. It is long ago that I knew of it; but nevertheless it should never have been

[1] Ed. Morton, p. 142. [2] p. 348.

[3] p. 192. This passage is found in full in one manuscript only, Cotton Nero A. xiv: naturally it was too personal to appear in the other recensions; but there are passing references to the anchoresses being three in number, and of high birth; these are left uncancelled (no doubt by inadvertence) in all manuscripts, and so confirm this fuller reference.

[4] p. 86.

The *Ancren Riwle.*

> betrayed by me; but now that it is so widely known through others, I cannot gainsay it. They say that it is bad; and yet it is worse than they say. Grieved and sorry I am that I must say it; but in truth it is so, and that is a great grief. For many other things he (or she) is greatly to be praised; but not for these, and woe is me therefore. No one can defend them." [1]

However intimately personal it may have been in its original intention, the merits of the *Riwle* led to its widespread use. It became a classic, and, as Miss Hope Emily Allen says, "enjoyed a prodigious popularity in medieval England for at least three hundred years."

The *Ancren Riwle* therefore occupies a vital position in the history of English prose. Its popularity extends over the darkest period of our literature. The researches of Miss Allen are beginning to show us that the cult of the "Rule" is not a fad of the modern grammarian. It is not a conspiracy between those strange yoke-fellows, the philological pedant and the papistical mystic, but a fact of English history with which every serious student must reckon.

Towards the end of the reign of the Conqueror's son Henry, three girls withdrew from the world; they had earlier been maids in waiting to his queen, the good Queen Maud, daughter of St. Margaret of Scotland (the sister of Edgar Ætheling and great-niece of the Confessor). To these maidens, Emma, Gunilda and Christina, the Abbot and Convent of Westminster granted the Hermitage of Kilburn, not later than 1135; the foundation prospered, and about a century later had increased greatly.

The circumstances of the original foundation agree closely with those of the *Riwle*, as does also the fact that the *Riwle* was revised for a larger community, apparently about 1230, under circumstances very similar to those which we know to have obtained at Kilburn at the same time. The parallels are numerous and remarkable enough to lend support to Miss Allen's attempt to identify the two anchorholds. On the other hand, there must have been many groups of friends and sisters who withdrew to the spiritual life amid the turmoil of Norman or Angevin England; and three is a natural number for those who set out on such an adventure of "mighty contests, mystic victories and supreme rewards, won on the frontiers of Paradise": *stella duce, ibant tres.*

The date of the first composition of the *Ancren Riwle* remains a

[1] p. 88.

The *Ancren Riwle.*

matter of dispute, but it must have been about 1230 that the revised version of the *Riwle* (known as the *Ancrene Wisse*) was made, for the use of a very much larger community than the original anchor-hold.[1] But this revised version survives only in one manuscript. All our other manuscripts, and the Latin and French versions, go back to the older stage of the Rule as written for three recluses only.[2] That is to say, the older stage had already, by 1230 or soon after, obtained so wide a currency that the revised version could not supersede it. Compound texts arose, always based upon the original version, but showing here and there sporadic additions resulting from comparison with a copy of the revised version. We might reasonably allow a generation or more, to permit a work, originally written for the private use of three recluses, to have obtained such a currency as that. This would carry the original *Riwle* back to the year 1200 or earlier.

Its language and the allusions found in it seem to me to forbid us carrying the *Riwle* in its present form back to 1135, or earlier.[3] If it was originally written in the reign of Henry I for the three maids of honour of good Queen Maud, then it must have been in a form different from any which has come down to us.[4]

But the *Riwle*, even if we date it *c.* 1200, takes us back to a period when the tradition of pre-Conquest prose was still alive—and its forward links are even more important than its links with the past. It was so authoritative that, about the year 1300, Simon of Ghent, Bishop of Salisbury, seeking for a book of devotion for the use of his sisters, nuns of Tarrent in Dorsetshire, translated the *Riwle* into

[1] This must be the later version, because it contains inconsistent references, sometimes to the original three anchoresses, sometimes to the larger community. It must be after 1224, because of its references to the Friars; on the other hand, Dr. Montague Rhodes James dates the MS. "Thirteenth Century early."

[2] Extant in its simplest form in Cotton MSS. Nero and Titus; extracts in MS. Caius Cambr. The other MSS. (Cotton Cleopatra, Vernon, Pepys) and the French and Latin versions, all show occasional traces of the influence of the revised (*Ancrene Wisse*) version.

[3] Especially the quotations from St. Ailred of Rievaulx. On the other hand, the fact that the dialect of the most authoritative copy (*Ancrene Wisse*, MS. C.C.C.C. 402) is West Midland does not seem to me to tell so seriously against Kilburn. That there might be the same Rule used in London and on the Welsh border is suggested in this version; for there is mention of bringing the anchor-holds of England under one rule: London, Oxford, Shrewsbury and Chester are given as examples.

[4] If we assume a primitive edition of the *Riwle* as early as this, we should not be entitled to treat such a presumed edition as an English document, for we have no evidence that it *was* in English, although we can be sure that the extant Latin and French versions, in their present form, are derived from the extant English version.

The *Ancren Riwle.*

Latin. The *Riwle* was also translated into French; exactly at what date we do not know, but apparently after 1230. For this French version is obviously translated from a composite text, made by inserting some of the additions of the revision (*c.* 1230) into a copy of the older text, and often inserting them in the wrong place.[1] Towards the end of the Fourteenth Century, we find the *Riwle* transcribed into that great collection of religious verse and prose, the Vernon Manuscript; and about the same time it was revised and rewritten in a third recension, which Miss Paues discovered in the Pepysian library some years ago. Long before this time the great prose revival of the Fourteenth Century had begun, a revival which is usually associated with the name of Wiclif, but which should also be associated with other names such as those of Richard Rolle and Walter Hilton. The influence of the *Riwle* is found in the popular religious prose of the time. Miss Allen[2] has pointed to borrowings in the *Chastising of God's Children*, in the *Poor Caitiff*, and in a treatise "the holy book *Gratia Dei*," the structure of which she has done much to elucidate. The popularity persisted well on into the Fifteenth Century. Thus Dr. Owst, in his epoch-making book on *Preaching in Medieval England*, tells us much concerning Dr. William Lichfield, who was Rector of All Hallows the Great in London. He was one of several preachers who were famous *in vita et scientia*, and, when he died in 1448, he left behind him 3083 sermons "written in English with his own hand," besides a collection of material for sermons, "mille exempla." Yet of all this, Dr. Owst has been able to trace in surviving manuscripts only a little tract on the Five Senses, which "reveals a vigorous emotional spirit, with a touch of mysticism." As Dr. Owst points out, this tract is deeply indebted to the *Ancren Riwle*: in fact, Dr. Lichfield—and here I am quoting Miss Allen—in "page after page rifles the rich treasure of imagery in the *Riwle*, sometimes borrowing intact, sometimes altering, or using his borrowings as a point of departure." We have, indeed, "what may almost be called another text of Books II and III of the *Ancren Riwle*."[3]

[1] For other reasons showing the French version to be a translation of the English, see *Essays and Studies by Members of the English Association*, ix, and *The Review of English Studies*, I, 1.

[2] See her most important article, "Some Fourteenth-Century borrowings from *Ancren Riwle*," *Modern Language Review*, XVIII, 1–8 (1923).

[3] Miss Allen, "Further Borrowings from *Ancren Riwle*," in *Modern Language Review*, XXIV, 13 (1929). Miss Allen is not quite certain that Lichfield is the author of the treatise. In any case it seems to be Fifteenth-Century, which is all that is material to the argument above.

The *Ancren Riwle.*

Of the great mass of devotional prose, the overwhelming bulk must have been destroyed: what is left has been studied only by a few indefatigable spirits like Dr. Owst and Miss Allen. When we turn from what Dr. Owst calls (unkindly) "the idle imaginations of professors" to these two monuments of research among forgotten manuscripts, Miss Allen's work on Rolle and Dr. Owst's on Medieval Preaching, we realize how much still remains to be done in the history of English prose and of English thought. Of what has been done already towards demonstrating the continuity of English prose, one example [1] must suffice in this place.

Here is a passage from *The Chastising of God's Children,*[2] as printed by Wynkyn de Worde in 1492:

> Also, whan our lord suffreth vs be tempted in our beginnynge, he playeth wyth vs as the moder wyth the chylde, whiche somtyme fleeth away and hideth her, and suffreth the chylde to wepe and crye, and besely to seke hir wyth sobbyng and wepyng; but thenne cometh the moder sodenly wyth mery chere and laughinge, beclippyng her chylde and kyssyng, and wipeth away the teres. Thus fareth our lorde wyth vs, as for a tyme he wythdraweth his grace and comfort fro vs. In somoche that in his absence we ben al colde and drye, swetnesse have we none, ne sauour in deuocyon. . . .

And here is the original, as it was written by the author of the *Ancren Riwle*:

> Ure Louerd, hwon he iðoleð þet we beoð itented, he plaieð mid us, ase þe moder mid hire ȝunge deorlinge, vlihð from him, and hut hire, and let hit sitten one, and loken ȝeorne abuten, and cleopien, Dame! dame! and weopen one hwule, and þeonne mid ispredde ermes leapeð lauhwinde uorð, and cluppeð and cusseð, and wipeð his eien. Riht so, ure Louerd let us one iwurðen oðer hwules, and wiðdraweð his grace, and his cumfort, and his elne, þet we ne iuindeð swetnesse in none þinge þet we wel doð, ne sauur of heorte. . . . [3]

Whoever the maidens were for whom the *Riwle* was written, they were the cause of great things in English prose. They were the first known to us of a long list of devoted women, for whose consolation so many of the greatest books of Middle English prose were composed.

[1] Pointed out (with others) by Miss Allen in *Modern Language Review,* XVIII, 1 (1923).

[2] *The Chastising* is also extant in several manuscripts, and allusions to it show it to be earlier than the Fifteenth Century. (Miss Allen, as above).

[3] Ed. Morton, p. 230, etc. Morton, of course, edited the *Riwle* from MS. Cotton Nero A. xiv, the spelling and forms of which differ somewhat from those of MS. C.C.C.C. 402 of the *Riwle,* as well as from that of the "Catherine group."

IX. English Prose of the Fourteenth Century: Rolle, Hilton, *The Cloud of Unknowing;* Wiclif and the Wicliffite translations.

But an examination of the remarkable popularity of the *Riwle*, which Miss Allen's careful comparison of our extant documents is only now beginning to reveal to us, takes us too quickly over the centuries. Though the *Riwle* was still read and studied in the Fifteenth Century, it had been surpassed as the most popular work for contemplatives by a group of similar books, written for the most part for (or sometimes by) enclosed nuns or anchoresses. Some of these remained in use, in a modernized form, as manuals of devotion among English Roman Catholic exiles abroad, till the Seventeenth Century. Within the last ten years they have again won a remarkable popularity. And it is no longer possible to ignore their position in the history of English prose.

Whilst the *Ancren Riwle* was at the height of its fame, appeared the second great figure of Middle English prose—Richard Rolle of Hampole, student of Oxford and perhaps also of the Sorbonne, hermit and scholar. He has long had a place in the histories of English literature in virtue of a lengthy verse treatise which he did not write, rather than of the prose tracts which he did. Nevertheless, anyone who reads these tracts must see that, despite their Fourteenth-Century Yorkshire dialect, we have in them modern English prose. The spelling and form of the words, sometimes the actual vocabulary, may be strange; but the arrangement of the words is modern. Yet, when Rolle died, Chaucer was still a boy, and Wiclif a young graduate at an Oxford where Latin and French were the only languages yet recognized.

Rolle's date, his style and his popularity give him a supreme place in the history of English prose. In English or in Latin he was, during the latter half of the Fourteenth Century and the whole of the Fifteenth, probably the most widely read in England of all English writers. Investigation of English wills and of documents bearing on the ownership of books seems to show a dozen owners of manuscripts of Rolle for one or two of the *Canterbury Tales*. Such devotional books were likely to be worn to bits, and not to come down to posterity at all: yet Miss Allen has examined between four and five hundred of them, in Latin or in English, scattered through the libraries of Europe and America.

English Prose of the Fourteenth Century: Rolle.

Although the syntax of Rolle is that of to-day, he is still closely in touch with the older stages of the language:

> On the whole he writes like a modern, but it is his peculiar charm that at times the Anglo-Saxon literary traditions break through, giving his prose cadences and ornaments archaic, but in his case, instinctive. Thus he gives the rare, perhaps unique, example of a style truly belonging to the Middle Age of English prose—something that inherits from the rich national literature before the Conquest. . . . Fortunately Rolle's compositions sometimes expressed the vivacity of his temperament, and they sometimes, therefore, seem to give us the veritable utterances of a medieval Englishman, speaking with the human directness and intelligibility of a modern.[1]

And the matter of Rolle is not less important than his style. Dr. Owst ceases for a moment from his devouring of medieval sermons, to brood on what might have happened if, instead of the Protestant and Industrial revolutions as we have known them, there had been more of Rolle's spirit:

> His gentle contact with those around him, his independent spiritual life, lived in the peace of the open country, with time and taste for reflection, for the quest after beauty and truth, as well as mere "goodness," all these, no doubt, are things far too aristocratic, too slow, too unobtrusive, and too individual for the industrial plutocracies, bureaucracies, democracies of to-day. "Ego dormio, et cor meum vigilat," the hermit's favourite watch-word, rings sadly "out-of-date," like bells of rustic England in summer-time, a dreamy sweetness that is passing, too, for the majority of men.[2]

Here is a pedestrian specimen of Rolle, showing how well he can tell a simple tale:

> Also, umwhile þe fende tempes men and women, þat er solitary by þam ane, on a qwaynt maner and a sotell: He trans-figurs hym in þe lyknes of an awngel of lyght, and apers till þam, and sayes þat he es ane of goddes awngels, comen to comforth þam; and swa he deceyves foles. Bot þai þat er wys, and wil not tyte trow till all spirites, bot askes cownsel of conand men: he may not begyle þam. Als I fynd writen of a reclues, þat was a gude woman; till þe whilk þe ill awngell oft-sythes aperde in þe

[1] *Writings ascribed to Richard Rolle, Hermit of Hampole, and materials for his biography*, by Hope Emily Allen, 1927, p. 8. Whilst this preface is passing through the press, *The English Writings of Richard Rolle* have been published by Miss Allen (Oxford, 1931). The volume will prove invaluable to all students of English prose.

[2] Owst, *Preaching in Medieval England*, 1926, p. 114.

English Prose of the Fourteenth Century: Rolle.

> forme of a gode awngel, and sayd þat he was comen to bryng hir to heven. Wharfore scho was right glad and ioyful. Bot neverþe-latter, scho talde it til hir schryft-fader; and he, als wyse man and war, gaf hir þis counsell: "When he comes, he sayde, byd hym þat he schew þe oure lady saynt Mary. When he has done swa: say *Ave maria.*" Scho dyd sa. Þe fende sayde: "Þou has na nede to se hyr; my presence suffyse to þe." And scho sayde, on all maner scho suld se hyr. He saw þat hym behoved outher do hir wyll, or scho walde despyse hym: Als tyte he broght forth þe fayrest body of woman þat myght be, als to hyr syght, and schewed til hyr. And scho sett hir on hir knees and sayde: *Ave maria.* And als tyte all vanyst away; and for scham never sithen come he at hir. Þis I say not, for I hope þat he sal have leve to tempe þe on þis maner; bot for I will þat þou be war, if any swylk temptacions befall þe, slepand or wakand, þat þou trow not oure-tyte, til þou knaw þe soth.[1]

The spelling is strange, and there are many Northern words and phrases—but, apart from these things, what is there in this passage which is not modern English?

Rolle died in 1349. Wiclif's English sermons and treatises were not written till the end of his life, about 1380; and the first Wicliffite version of the Bible, so often regarded as a landmark in English prose, was not contemplated till 1378, nor completed till 1384. And, whilst Rolle writes modern English, the first Wicliffite version, written thirty-five years after Rolle's death, is almost incredibly crude.

English Prose of the Fourteenth Century: Hilton and The *Cloud*.

More modern than Rolle, because a little later in date, and a little less Northern in speech, is Walter Hilton, canon of the Augustinian house of Thurgarton. Of Hilton's life we know nothing, except that he died on the Vigil of the Annunciation, 24 March, 1396. He is, then, Wiclif's contemporary. I give two quotations from *The Scale of Perfection*, and one from *The Cloud of Unknowing*, sometimes attributed to Hilton, but more often supposed to be the work of some unknown author, writing "during, and probably early in, Hilton's life." Hilton apparently knew the *Cloud*, and quoted from it in the *Scale*.

First, the parable of the pilgrim seeking Jerusalem:

> Þer was a man þat wold gon to Ierusalem. And for he knewe not þe weye, he come to an oþer man þat he hopid knew þe wey þeder, and asked wheþer he miȝte come to þat citee. Þat

[1] *Richard Rolle of Hampole*, ed. Horstmann, 1895, I, pp. 12, 13.

English Prose of the Fourteenth Century: Hilton and The *Cloud*.

oþer man seide to him þat he miȝte not come þeder withoute grete disese and mikil travaile, "for þe wey is longe and periles are grete of þefes and robbours, and many oþer lettynges þer ben þat fallen to a man in þe goyng. And also þer are mony sere weies, as it semiþ ledand þederward. Bot men alday are slayn and dispoiled and mown not comyn to þat place þat þei coveiten. Nerþeles þer is o wey þe whilke who so takiþ hit and holdiþ it," he wolde undirtake þat he schude come to þe Cite of Ierusalem. And he schulde never lese his lif ne be slayn ne dye for defaute. He schulde often be robbed and yvel betyn and suffren mikel disese in þe goynge, bot he schulde ay han his lif safe. Þan saiþ þe pilgrym: "If it be so þat I may have my lif safe, and come to þat place þat I coveite, I charge not what meschef I suffre in þe goynge, and þerfore say me what þu wilt and soþly I bihote for to don aftir þe." Þat oþer man answeres and says þus: "Lo I sette þe in þe riȝt wey: þis is þe wey, and þat þu kepe þe lerynge þat I kenne þe. What so þou heres or sees or felis þat schulde lette þe in þi wey, abide not with it wilfully, tary not for it restfully, behold it not, like it not, drede it not; bot ay go forþ in þi wey and þinke þat þu woldes be at Ierusalem. For þat þu coveites, þat þu desires, and noȝt elles bot þat. And if men robbe þe and dispoile þe, bete þe, scorne þe, and dispise þe, strife not ageyn if þu wilt han þi lif. Bot holde þe with þe harme þat þu has, and go forþ as noȝt were, þat þu take no more harme. And also if men wil tary þe wiþ tales and fede þe with lesynges, for to drawe þe to mirþes and for to lefe þi pilgrimage, make def ere and answer not ageyn; and sey not elles bot at þu wuldes be at Ierusalem. And if men profre þe ȝiftes and wil make þe riche with werdly gode, tente not to hem: þinke ay on Ierusalem."[1]

The second extract is in a lower key. It is practical advice to the recluse, that courtesy may sometimes oblige her to leave meditation in order to comfort and profit her fellow Christians by conversation at her window:

If þou coudist wel lufen þin evencristen, it schulde nouȝt hyndre þe for to speken wiþ þem discretli. Discrecion schalt þou han upon þis manere, as me þinkiþ.

Hooso come to þe, aske hym mekeli what he wile. And if he come for to telle his desese and ben confortid of þi speche, here hym gladli and suffre hym seye what he wyle for ese of his oune herte. And whanne he haþ don, conforte hym if þou kan, goodli and caritabli, and sone brek of. And þanne after þat, if he wile fallen in idel tales or vanites of oþer mennes dedis, answere hym bute litel, ne fede nouȝt his speche. And he schal sone ben irk and sone take his lefe.

[1] MS. Harl. 6579, fol. 84 (Bk. II, cap. 21).

English Prose of the Fourteenth Century: Hilton and The *Cloud*.

If hit be annoþer man þat comiþ for to kenne þe, as a man of holikerke, here hym lowli wiþ reverence for his ordre, and if his speche conforte þe, aske of hym, and make þe nouȝt for to kenne hym; it falliþ nouȝt to þe to kennen a prest, bute in nede. If his speche conforte þe nouȝt, answere litel, and he wile sone taken his leve.

If hit be anoþer man þat comiþ for to ȝieven þe hys almes, ore elles for to here þe speken, ore for to ben kenned of þe, speke goodli and mekli to hem alle. Reprove no man of his defaictes, it falliþ nouȝt to þe, bute if he be þe more homli wiþ þe, þat þou wost wel þat he wile taken it of þe.

And schortli for to seyen, als mikil as þou conceivest þat schulden profiten þin evencristen, namli gostli, maiȝt þou seyen if þou kan, and he wile taken it. And of alle oþer þinges kepe silence as mikil as þou maiȝt, and þou schalt in schort time han bute litel pres þat schal letten þe.

Þus me þinkiþ: do bettur if þou maiȝt.[1]

The third extract, from the *Cloud*, describes the mannerisms of the restless folk, contrasted with the demeanour of the truly devout. Obviously it cannot be written for any of the most strictly secluded men or women:

Many wonderful contenaunces folowen hem þat ben disseyvid in þis fals werk, or in any spice þerof; forby þat doþ hem þat ben goddes trewe disciples, for þei ben evermore ful semely in alle here contenaunces bodily or goostly. Bot it is not so of þees oþer. For who so wolle or miȝt beholde unto hem, þer þei sitte in þis tyme, and it so were þat þeire iȝe liddes were open, he schulde see hem stare as þei were wode, and þer to loke as þei sawe þe devil. Sekirly it is good þei be ware, for trewly þe feende is not fer. Som sette þeire iȝen in þeire hedes as þei were sturdy scheep, betyn in þe heed, and as þei schulde diȝe anone. Som hangen here hedes on syde, as a worme were in þeire eres. Som pipyn when þei schuld speke as þer were no spirit in þeire bodies; and þis is þe propre condicioun of an ypocrite. Som crien and whinen in þeire þrote, so ben þei gredy and hasty to sey þat þei þink; and þis is þe condicioun of heretikes, and of hem þat wiþ presumpcioun and wiþ curiouste of witte wil alweys meynteyn errour. Many unordeynde and unsemely contenaunces folowen on þis errour, whoso miȝte parceyve alle.

Neverþeles som þer ben þat ben so curious þat þei kun refreyne hem in grete partye whan þei comen before men. Bot miȝt þees men be seen in place where þei ben homely, þen I trowe þei schuld not be hidde. And neverþeles ȝit I trowe þat who so wolde streitly ȝeinsey þeire opynion, þat þei schuld sone see hem brest oute in som partye: and ȝit hem þink þat alle

[1] MS. Harl. 6579, fol. 57 (Bk. I, cap. 83).

English Prose of the Fourteenth Century: Hilton and The *Cloud.*

þat ever þei do, it is for þe love of god, and for to meynteyne þe treuþ. Now trewly I hope þat, bot ȝif god schewe his merciful miracle, to make hem sone leve of, þei schul love god so longe on þis maner, þat þei schul go staryng wood to þe devil.

I sey not þat þe devil haþ so parfite a servaunt in þis liif, þat is desceyvid and infecte wiþ all þees fantasies þat I sette here; and neverþeles ȝit it may be þat one, and many one, be infecte wiþ hem alle. Bot I sey þat he haþ no parfite ypocrite ne heretike in erþe, þat he ne is gilty in somme þat I have seide, or peraventure schal sey, ȝif god voucheþ saaf.

For som men aren so kumbred in nice corious contenaunces in bodily beryng þat, whan þei schal ouȝt here, þei wriþen here hedes on side queyntely and up wiþ þe chin, þei gape wiþ þeire mouþes as þei schuld here wiþ hem and not wiþ here eres. Som when þei schulen speke poynten wiþ here fyngres or on þeire fyngres or on þeire owne brestes or on þeires þat þei speke to. Som kan nouþer sit stille, stonde stylle, ne ligge stille, bot ȝif þei be ouþer waggyng wiþ þeire fete or ell sumwhat doyng wiþ þeire handes. Som rowyn wiþ þeire armes in tyme of here spekyng as hem nedid for to swymme over a grete water. Som ben evermore smyling and leiȝing at iche oþer worde þat þei speke, as þei weren gigelotes and nice Japyng Jogelers lackyng kontenaunce. Semeli cher were [full fayr] [1] wiþ sobre and demure beryng of body and mirþe in maner.

I say not þat alle þees unsemely contenaunces ben grete synnes in hem self, ne ȝit alle þoo þat done hem ben grete synners hem self. Bot I sey, if þat þees unsemely and unordeinde contenaunces ben governers of þat man þat doþ hem, in so mochel þat he may not leve hem whan he wile, þan I sey þat þei ben tokenes of pride and coryouste of witte, and of unordeynde schewyng, and covetise of knowyng, and specyaly þei ben verrei tokenes of unstabelnes of herte and unrestfulnes of mynde, and namely of þe lackyng of þe werk of þis book. And þis is only þe skile whi þat I set so many of þees disceytes here in þis writyng forwhi þat a goostly worcher schal prove his werk by hem.[2]

It has been observed [3] that this description is based on a long passage concerning deportment by Hugh of St. Victor. But a comparison of the two only serves to bring out the liveliness and terseness of the English compared with the more rhetorical Latin.

[1] Words supplied from MS. Harl. 959, fol. 96*a*. There is a cross in the margin of MS. Harl. 674 to draw attention to the need for correction.

[2] MS. Harl. 674, fols. 70*b*–72.

[3] By Dom Maurice Noetinger of Solesmes, in *Blackfriars*, March, 1924 (Vol. IV, p. 1460). The relevant passages of Hugh of St. Victor come in his *De institutione Novitiorum*, X, XII, XVII (Migne, *P.L.* CLXXVI, col. 935, 941, 942, 948).

And so, in view of the excellent English prose which was being written in the first half of the Fourteenth Century, and the glorious English prose which we find in the second half, there seems little justification for speaking of Wiclif as "the father of English prose," "the first intelligent writer of English prose," "a discoverer in the truest sense of the word." [1] For, although indignation often supplies him with vigorous phrases, Wiclif cannot be compared as a writer of English prose with Rolle, still less with Hilton. The importance of Wiclif in English history no one would deny; and the 170 manuscripts of the two translations of the Bible which he inspired testify to its importance as an English document. But, so far as the history of English prose goes, the first translation can hardly be called English at all, and the second, though better, is written in an undistinguished style. The contrast with the clarity of Hilton, when *he* has occasion to quote Scripture, is marked. Two examples, taken at random, will suffice. One is from the parable of the Lost Piece of Silver. This runs in the Wicliffite version: Wiclif.

> Ether what womman, havyng ten dragmes, and if sche hath lost o dragme, whethir she liȝteth not a lanterne, and turneth upsodoun the hous, and sekith diligently, til she fynde? And whanne sche hath founden sche clepith togidere frendis and neiȝeboris, seyinge Thanke ȝe me, for I have founden the dragme which I hadde lost.[2]

Contrast with this Hilton's simple and clear phraseology:

> What womman is þat, whilk haþ lost a dragme, þat sche ne wile liȝten a lanterne and kesten here hous up so doun, and seken it, til sche finde it. And whan sche haþ founden it, sche calliþ here frendes to here and seiþ to hem þus: makiþ mirthe wiþ me and melodie, for I have founden þe dragme þat Y hadde lost.[3]

Or again, with the Wicliffite translation:

> And if Y departe alle my goodis into the metis of pore men, and yf Y bitake my bodi, so that Y brenne, and if Y have not charite, it profitith to me no thing,[4]

[1] Krapp, *Rise of English Literary Prose*, p. ix.
[2] Luke xv. 8–9 (First Version).
[3] MS. Harl. 6579, fol. 33 (Charterhouse MS.): *Scale*, Bk. I, cap. 48.
[4] 1 Corinth. xiii. 3 (Second Version).

Wiclif.

contrast Hilton's translation:

> And if I ȝefe al þat I have to pouere men, and mi bodi to þe fier to ben brenned, an I hadde no charite, it profitiþ me riȝt nouȝt.[1]

It is a strange reflection that the Wicliffite translation owes its reputation in some measure to its faults. When Rolle and Hilton and Love and the others had been forgotten, Wiclif alone was remembered. And Wiclif gets credit for being a pioneer, because only on that assumption could the crudity of the Wicliffite translation be explained.

But, just as the Fourteenth-Century religious movement in English prose did not originate with Wiclif, so likewise, as we shall see, the suppression of the Lollards did not mean the suppression of Fifteenth-Century religious prose in England.

Popularity of Fourteenth-Century religious prose in the Fifteenth Century.

The early Protestant reformers assumed that in the Fifteenth Century true devotion was found only among a few persecuted disciples of John Wiclif; and this misrepresentation of the century of the *Imitatio Christi* has persisted, and has obscured the whole history of English prose. The continued popularity of orthodox books of religion throughout the Fifteenth Century has been forgotten—yet it is vital to an understanding of our history. The popularity of Hilton was apparently second only to that of Rolle.[2]

How these books were passed from hand to hand to be studied and pored over, not merely by recluses, but by the pious laity, till they were worn out, is shown by the colophon of MS. Harl. 993, containing Hilton's *Eight Chapters necessary for men that give themselves to perfection*, together with *A devout treatise of discerning of spirits*, supposed to be by the author of the *Cloud*:

> This book was maad of þe goodis of robert holond for a comyn profite. Þt þat persoone þat haþ þis book committid to him of þe persoone þt haþ power to committe it have þe uss þerof þe terme of his lijf preiynge for the soule of þe same Robert. And þt he þat haþ þe forseid uss of commissioun, whanne he occupieþ it not, leene he it for a tyme to sum oþer persoone. Also þat persoone to whom it was committid for þe teerme of lijf undir þe for-seid condiciouns delivere it to anoþer persoone þe teerme of his lijf. And so be it delivered and committid from persoone to persoone, man or womman, as longe as þe book enduriþ.

[1] MS. Harl. 6579, fol. 45b (Charterhouse MS.): *Scale*, Bk. I, cap. 67.

[2] This is Miss Deanesly's verdict, after an examination of wills prior to 1525. See *Mod. Lang. Rev.*, xv, 355.

Popularity of Fourteenth-Century religious prose in the Fifteenth Century.

There is a similar note [1] at the end of MS. Lambeth 472, containing Hilton's *Scale of Perfection* and his *Treatise of Mixed Life*, though in this case the owner is John Killum, and the book after his death is to be delivered to Richard Colop. Both Killum († 1416) and Holland († 1441) were London citizens whose activities can be traced in Hustings Rolls and elsewhere.

The much-abused Fifteenth Century is remembered as a time of sterile quarrels between Lancastrian and Yorkist. But there were also citizens like Killum and Collop and Holland, poring over their books of devotion, and leaving them as legacies to each other, together with money to be distributed in alms, or spent upon the mending of bad roads. There were the craftsmen who built the "perpendicular" churches, and filled their windows with painted glass. It was an age of religious guilds, charitable foundations and libraries; most of which things the Sixteenth Century destroyed.[2]

The criticism which derides the Fifteenth Century is much the same as that which will see nothing in the Anglo-Saxon history of the Eleventh Century save contests between Ethelred and Cnut for the throne of England, or between Leofric and Godwine for influence with the Confessor. These things were. But there were also patient monks in the scriptoria, transcribing homilies of Ælfric and Wulfstan so that the upland men might be taught *in English*: there were the artists and craftsmen upon whose work it is still a joy to look.

The history of England is the history of the English people; and the English people went on, despite the quarrels of their lords:

> Take of English earth as much
> As either hand may rightly clutch.
> In the taking of it breathe
> Prayer for all who lie beneath—
> Not the great nor well bespoke,
> But the mere uncounted folk
> Of whose life and death is none
> Report or lamentation.
> Lay that earth upon thy heart,
> And thy sickness shall depart.[3]

[1] The exact similarity of wording, and almost of spelling, is striking. Such notes are found not infrequently in books of devotion. For further examples, see Miss Allen in *Mod. Lang. Rev.*, xviii, 4 (1923).

[2] See Kingsford, *Prejudice and Promise in the Fifteenth Century*, 1925, pp. 42, 43, 67.

[3] Rudyard Kipling, *A Charm* (*Rewards and Fairies*).

X. The Revival of English Prose.

But the essential thing for us about the so-called "weak," "futile" Fifteenth Century is, that it is the time when English prose recovers from the consequences of the Norman Conquest. The change had begun at the end of the preceding century. We have seen that Higden, writing in the middle of the Fourteenth Century, spoke of English as a mere peasant dialect. This can hardly have been true, for the third quarter of that century saw the momentous change by which English superseded French in the schools.[1] And so, when Trevisa was making his translation of Higden in 1385, he asserted, faithfully following his original, that English remained "scarsliche wiþ fewe uplondisshe men;" but he prefixed the very contradictory statement that now Latin is construed in the grammar schools into English, not into French, so that "children of gramer-scole conneþ na more Frensche þan can hir lift heele."[2]

If this were so, we might reasonably expect great changes when the children of 1385 had become the men of affairs of, say, 1410 or 1420. Which is exactly what we do find. It is interesting to compare the proportions of English to French in legal, civic and official documents by 1375 (when English is practically non-existent),[3] by 1400 (when it is to be found, though it is not common), by 1425 (when it has become common), and by 1450 (when it is winning all along the line). Then (except for its stronghold in Law French) French is driven out of England, just as the English (save for the stronghold of Calais) are driven out of France; the two great consequences of the Norman Conquest vanish together.

The Conquest had injured English prose in two ways. Obviously, because French ousted English; less obviously, because, even where English remained, French fashion had led to the substitution of verse for prose in all writing other than that of the most strictly devotional kind. During the second half of the Twelfth, all the Thirteenth, and most of the Fourteenth Centuries, the rule holds that "to save

[1] See article by W. H. Stevenson in the *Furnivall Miscellany*, 1901, pp. 421–9.

[2] Higden's *Polychronicon*; *Rolls Series*, II, 161.

[3] Latin had been the language for laws and ordinances till, in the proclamation of Henry III (1258), we suddenly find French and English on an equality "for one brief moment." Then French "forces its way to the front" (Pollock and Maitland, *History of English Law*, 1898, I, p. 86), whilst the English proclamation "long remains unique." In 1344 we have an isolated petition in English from Gloucestershire (Record Office, Anc. Pets., File 192, No. 9580). An English Deed of 1376 (South-Western) is printed by Morsbach in the *Furnivall Miscellany*, pp. 347–54. "It is," says Morsbach, "what I take to be the oldest M.E. private legal instrument."

The Revival of English Prose.

someone's soul or to improve someone's morals were seemingly the only motives which could suffice to persuade an Englishman to write his native language except in verse."[1] Chaucer gave his life to verse, but comforted himself, when death drew near, by reflecting on the moral virtue of his prose. Chaucer's prose shows him an "average man of his time."[2] English prose far from the average, English prose of real distinction, was written in Chaucer's day; but, so far as our evidence goes, only by those who had withdrawn from the world in which Chaucer moved.

It was just in the years 1384–90, the years (probably) in which mediæval English poetry reached its summit in the *Canterbury Tales*, that English prose first tentatively began to break away from both of the two restrictions which had confined it so largely to noble but austere works of religious contemplation. It is in these excited years that we find the citizens of London again condescending to use English; at least eleven London-English documents are extant.[3]

Within the same years (1384–90) that the Londoners were making their first hesitating beginnings in English, John of Trevisa, in Gloucestershire, was defying the tradition, which had ruled since Angevin times, that English historical writing should be in verse. In the very interesting dialogue between a Lord and a Clerk, which he prefixed to his translation of the *Polychronicon*, he discusses the propriety of translation; then comes the question—rhyme or prose? The Lord is emphatic: "In prose, for commonly prose is more clear than rhyme, more easy and more plain to know and understand." It is not putting history into English, but putting it into English prose, which is revolutionary. When Layamon had put the *Brut* into English, nearly two centuries before, he had, he tells us, three books before him, and looked lovingly on them. One was "the English book that St. Bede made," that is, Alfred's translation; another was "the book that a French clerk named Wace made, who

[1] A. W. Pollard, *Fifteenth-Century Prose and Verse* (*English Garner*), 1903, p. xix.

[2] W. P. Ker in Craik's *English Prose Selections*, I, 41.

[3] Four of these are connected with the feuds which raged round John of Northampton; six are returns of Guilds. Of the 471 Guild-returns of 1389 enumerated by Canon Westlake, about one-ninth are in English and one-ninth in French—the remaining seven-ninths in Latin. But (apart from the six London Guilds) the English returns are found only in Norfolk. Norfolk seems to have led the way in the civic revival of English. "Norfolk French" means English; "I can no Frenche in feith," says Avarice in *Piers Plowman*, "but of the ferthest ende of Norfolke."

For other Town-records in English (more particularly those of Winchester) see Toulmin Smith, *English Gilds* (E.E.T.S.), 1870.

The Revival of English Prose.

well could write." It is unfortunate that Layamon followed the French fashion and wrote in verse. And this had persisted in England long after the French themselves had learned better, so that when vernacular history was beginning to reassert itself, the wrong mode had been chosen, as in the *Chronicle of Robert of Gloucester*; and so, long after French prose had come into its own with the *Prose Lancelot* or Joinville, English was still lumbering along with rhymed Chronicles. Even a generation after Trevisa, the lesson had not been fully learnt. We have narratives written by several people who accompanied Henry V on his French wars. It is odd to reflect what they might have left us, if these Englishmen of the early Fifteenth Century had possessed that tradition of restrained narrative prose which the Chroniclers had in the days of Edward the Confessor. Instead, the monk Thomas Elmham, who seems to have been at Agincourt as chaplain to the king, writes his story in Latin. John Page tells of the siege of Rouen in doggerel rhyme. John Harding, who had education enough to know that the best verse was an imitation of Chaucer's stanza, gives us this kind of thing:

An hundreth myle to Calais had he then
    At Agyncourt, so homewarde in his way
The nobles ther of Fraunce afore him wen
    Proudly battailed with an hundreth thousand in araye
He sawe he must nedes with them make afraye;
He set on them, and with them faught ful sore,
With nyne thousand, no more with hym thore.

It was as an appendix to the *Chronicle* of John Harding that More's *History of Richard III* was first published, and the contrast is striking.

But, long before More's time, the Fifteenth Century had established English prose as the proper medium, not only for history, but for many other things. From about 1416 we have a steady succession of London documents in English. From 1418 Henry V writes English letters to the City Fathers, just as Alfred or Canute had written English letters to their subjects. In 1422 we find the Brewers of London decreeing that, whereas our gracious lord the king condescends to use the English language when writing of *his* affairs, therefore we, the Brewers of London, in some wise following the same example, will do likewise.[1]

[1] Cum nostra lingua materna, videlicet lingua Anglicana, modernis diebus cepit in honoris incrementum ampliari et decorari, eo quod excellentissimus dominus noster Rex henricus quintus, in literis suis missivis, et diversis negociis

The Revival of English Prose.

English prose before the Conquest had risen to great heights, because it was based upon a vernacular, even if it were a literary form of that vernacular. But the trouble during so much of the Thirteenth and Fourteenth Centuries was, that whilst English nationality had asserted itself, custom still demanded that Latin or French should be used, even by people for whom Latin or French was not the natural means of expression, and who can only use these languages with difficulty, *au meuz ke jeo say*,[1] as Peter of Peckham put it. Prose in England begins to have a great future when, early in the Fifteenth Century, English begins to be used, in place of Latin or French, for the affairs of every day; as in grievances of London citizens. They complain that roads are not kept clean :

> Also that a mud wall in the bailly by the hie strete, bytwene the hous of Shelhard habirdassher and hay Sporyer, fallith doun gobet-mele into the hie strete, and makith the wey foule, in desese of al folk ther passyng and dwellyng.

Another grievance is that the official assayer of oysters has farmed out his office :

> For ofte tyme men han sene þat Cacches han layne with oistres ij dayes or iij, and noght half sold her oistres, and after gon out with þe oistres vnsold, and bryng þe same in ayen with fresshyng of new, þe whiche is a foule deceyt. Wherfore it nedith þe sayere to be trewe in his office. And nought withstondyng þis, John of Ely lateþ this office to ferme to wymmen, þat conne not; ne also is not worship to þe Cite þat wymen shuld haue such thyng in gouernance.

Both complaints are of the same year, 1422 : the year in which the Brewers decided to follow the example of Henry V in "augmenting" the English tongue. To the same year belongs the earliest of the

---

personam suam propriam tangentibus, secreta sue voluntatis libencius voluit declarare, et ob meliorem plebis sue intelligentiam communem, aliis ydiomatibus pretermissis, animo diligenti scripturarum exercicio commendari procuravit; Et quam plures sunt nostre Artis Braciatorum qui in dicto ydiomate anglicano habent scienciam, illud idem scribendi atque legendi in aliis ydiomatibus videlicet latino et Franco ante hec tempora usitatis minime senciunt et intelligunt; Quibus de Causis cum pluribus aliis consideratis in presenti quemadmodum maior pars ducum et Communum fidedignorum facere ceperunt in nostra materna lingua suas materias annotari, Sic et nos in arte nostra, predicta eorum vestigia quodamodo sequentes que nos tangunt necessaria decrevimus memorie infuturum commendare ut patet in sequentibus. (From *The Brewers' First Book.*)

[1] See Vising, *Anglo-Norman Language and Literature*, 1923, p. 17.

The Revival of English Prose.

Paston Letters; and it is about this time that the first Stonor papers written in English are found.

This rising flood of English in everyday use, and the noble devotional prose read and pored over by the serious-minded London citizens—the Killums and the Collops—must both be kept in mind. Attention has been too much concentrated upon a few isolated names, Pecock, Capgrave, Fortescue, Malory, and this has concealed the national character of the movement which was going on. In London, from about 1420, English prose was used for secular purposes almost as freely as for those of religion.

Sometimes we can see a connection between the religious prose inherited from earlier centuries and the use of English for Chronicles. Thus Capgrave, English Provincial of the Augustine Friars, meets us in 1422 as a preacher of a Latin sermon which he later translated into English. Then he translated a Life of St. Augustine for "a noble creatur, a gentill woman," who had "desired of me with ful grete instauns to write on-to hir." Then he was led, at the instance of the master of the Order of Gilbertines, to write a Life of St. Gilbert "for the solitarye women whech unneth can undyrstande Latyn, þat þei may at vacaunt tymes red in þis book þe grete vertues of her maystyr."[1] Now these were things such as a learned ecclesiastic might have done in England any time in the past five centuries. But when Capgrave passes, towards the end of his long life, from writing books of devotion in English for women, to writing a prose Chronicle, we have something which, though natural enough in the Fifteenth Century, had been unknown, so far as our evidence goes, for more than two centuries after the expiration of the *Anglo-Saxon Chronicle.*

But now secular prose is found everywhere. The century had hardly opened when we find the translations of Mandeville, and the beginnings of native history with the English prose *Brut.* The *Master of Game,* the oldest English treatise on hunting, partly translation, partly original, was written by the second Duke of York, and dedicated to Henry V whilst he was still Prince. Prose romance is represented by translations like the *Merlin*, the *Alexander*, the *Troy* and the *Thebes*, the version of the *Gesta Romanorum*, the *Book of the Knight of La Tour Landry.* William Thorpe's account of his long dispute with the archbishop shows sometimes quite surprising

[1] Capgrave's *Lives of St. Augustine and St. Gilbert* (E.E.T.S., O.S. 140, pp. 1, 61).

dramatic force and power of manipulating dialogue. Then we have scientific prose, beginning with Chaucer's *Astrolabe* (1390) and Trevisa's translation of Bartolomæus' *de Proprietatibus rerum.*

The Revival of English Prose.

Never since the Eleventh Century had there been such variety in English prose.

And at this time the possession of a tradition of simple dignified religious prose was invaluable, because with this popularization of English prose there had come a very real danger—a danger to which our prose had not been exposed when it had been out of favour with the great. If in the Thirteenth Century English prose seemed in danger of extinction, in the Fifteenth it was in danger of vulgarization. The danger is shown by the words of the London Brewers about royal patronage and "augmenting the English tongue"—an ill-omened phrase which we shall constantly meet during the next century and a half.

How did the English tongue need "augmenting"?

The best English religious prose about the year 1400 had been as noble in its simple lucidity as any English prose ever written. But English had now to be used, not only for religious treatises, but also for legal and diplomatic documents, for national chronicles, for romances—in fact, for all the purposes for which it had been used in the Eleventh Century, and for others as well. Therefore it certainly needed augmenting. Technical expressions would have to be borrowed. English had lost many words during the centuries of banishment from court; and new ideas had grown up which had naturally been expressed in Latin or French. In this sense the augmenting of the English tongue was no new thing. We can trace its beginnings long before the Norman Conquest, with the borrowing of Latin words. The process is continued with French loan-words in the post-Conquest *Chronicle*, and is in very active progress in the *Ancren Riwle.* Such augmenting was necessary and right.

But there is another sense in which this augmenting of the English tongue was deplorable.

Nothing is more noteworthy about the English of the *Ancrèn Riwle* and its group than a certain tone of self-possession. English does not appear to be aping its betters; it "has continued, in troublous times, to maintain the air of a gentleman, if of a country gentleman." The same is true of the prose of Rolle, or Hilton, or the *Cloud,* or Nicholas Love. But it is by no means so often true of the revived English secular prose. There is an extraordinary clumsiness about

The Revival of English Prose.

the *Petition of the Folk of Mercerie*; English is being used for an unaccustomed purpose. Nor is the *Appeal* of Thomas Usk in easy prose, though it is of great linguistic importance as the first piece of writing by a Londoner which we know to be extant in his own handwriting. Thomas Usk's *Testament of Love* (preserved to us in Thynne's reprint) is a remarkable example of pretentious yet inefficient prose. Usk's excessive apologies are, as so often, only a cover for affectation.

Affectation of another kind we find in the City Fathers, addressing King Henry V. Their English has very much the air of a parvenu pressing into society where he is ill at ease. This is the correspondence which the Brewers had in mind; those who composed the letter to Henry V were indeed doing their best to "augment" the English tongue:

> Of Alle erthely Princes Our most dred sovereigne liege Lord and noblest Kyng, we, youre simple Officers, Mair and Aldermen of youre trewe Citee of London, with exhibicion of alle maner subiectif reverence and servisable lowenesse that may be hadde in dede, or in Mynde conceyved, recommende us unto your most noble and hye Magnificence and excellent Power, bisechyng the hevenly kyng of his noble grace and Pitee that he so wold illumine and extende upon the trone of your kyngly mageste the radyouse bemys of hys bounteuous grace, that the begunnen spede, by hys benigne suffraunce and help yn your Chivaliruse persoune fixed and affermed, mowe so be continued forth, and determined so to his plesaunce, your worship, and alle your reumys proffyt, that we and alle your other lieges to the desired presence of your most noble and graciouse persone, fro which grete distance of place long tyme hath prived us, the sonner myght approche and visuelly perceyve, to singuler confort and special Joye of us alle.

This love of long words, "visually perceive" instead of "see," or, a century later, Elyot's "adminiculation" for "support," was encouraged by French example; with such temptations to magniloquence it was well for English prose that so much of the religious writing was at once so noble and so simple. Of course in claiming so high a place for this religious prose of the Thirteenth, Fourteenth, and Fifteenth Centuries, we must admit some exceptions. *The Ayenbite of Inwit* of Dan Michel is notorious for its incapacity, and a century later Richard Misyn translates Richard Rolle's *Incendium Amoris* in an equally unintelligent way.

Simultaneously with the growth of secular prose, we find, as we might expect, that religious prose becomes more varied—more varied, in fact, than it had been since the Eleventh Century. Chaucer translates Boethius, (as King Alfred had done) and reckons it among his "books of devocioun." About 1400 John Mirk's *Festial* provides a series of sermons which we may compare with Ælfric's *Catholic Homilies*; these sermons became extraordinarily popular, and between 1483 and 1532 some twenty editions at least were printed. As in Anglo-Saxon, so now in Fifteenth-Century prose, we find translations of the *Gospel of Nicodemus* and the *Rule of St. Benedict*; as in Anglo-Saxon times, so now again we find the Bidding Prayer recorded at York. There are many saints' lives—the great translation of the *Legenda Aurea* was made about 1438. We find, in fact, all sorts of religious prose, both orthodox and Wicliffite.

The Revival of English Prose.

Of course, much of this prose is the ordinary mediæval prose of pious instruction. Yet much of it is exceedingly beautiful; for instance the *Revelations of Divine Love* of Dame Juliana of Norwich. A phrase in Hilton's *Scale*, "thus readest thou in every book that teacheth of good living," shows that there must have been many other orthodox books of devotion. Many must have been lost. There was "the book of Margerie Kempe of Lynn." Marjorie Kemp was an anchoress, and some noble fragments of her book have been preserved in a "short treatise" taken from it and printed in 1501. Of this printed extract only one copy survives, in the University Library at Cambridge; the original book has been lost. We must allow for a very large amount of religious literature which has disappeared by mere attrition, "read to destruction."

The first three books of the *Imitatio Christi* were translated into English in the latter half of the Fifteenth Century. Then, at the wish of the Lady Margaret, William Atkinson made his translation; the Lady Margaret herself translated the Fourth Book, from a French version, however, not from the Latin. This was so popular that it ran through half a dozen editions in the first thirty years of the Sixteenth Century, and was then superseded by the equally popular translation of More's friend, Richard Whitford.

The services of printing in general, and of Caxton in particular, in stabilizing English prose, are obvious; but it is unfortunate that Caxton, like the Brewers before him, had got an idea of "augmenting" the language. Strangely enough, modern critics have praised him for his

The Revival of English Prose.

bold adoption of words of foreign origin, which were fitted to enrich the storehouse of English, and to give to our tongue the most valuable quality of facility and variety of expression. It is for this that Caxton deserves the praise due to a weighty contributor to the development of our literary style.[1]

Probably Caxton's long sojourn abroad was bad for his English. His natural love of learned words was fostered by French models. He is following literally a French original when he uses these words to convey the idea that Agamemnon commanded the army besieging Troy:

> The sayd Troye was envyronned in fourme of siege and of excidyon by Agamenon . . . the whiche Agamenon . . . hadde the magystracyon and unyversall governaunce of alle thexcersite and hoost to-fore Troye.

Fortunately Caxton often forgets all about "augmenting" his mother tongue; and then he writes it well. And it must stand to his credit that he printed a vast deal of English prose, much of it far better than his own. But when he altered the older texts, it was often for the worse.

> A comparison of his editions of *The Golden Legend*, *Polychronicon*, and *The Knight of the Tower* with the original English versions leaves the older prose easily first. *Again and again, the modern reader will find the word rejected by Caxton more familiar than its substitute;* again and again, Caxton's curtailments, inversions, or expansions merely spoil a piece of more vigorous narrative.[2]

This passion for "augmenting" English prose, sometimes by an excessive use of synonyms, sometimes by the use of "ink-horn terms," and sometimes by a combination of these embellishments, had begun long before Caxton, and long survived him. It is prevalent throughout the whole of More's lifetime: we find it in the Sermons of Fisher, and in the Chronicles of Fabyan and of Hall. Berners fortunately keeps it out of his translation, but his *Preface* is one of the most glaring examples. Elyot defends himself against those who were offended by his "strange termes," and declares that his style had the approval of King Henry VIII:

> His Highnesse benignely receyuynge my boke, whiche I named *The Governour*, in the redynge therof sone perceyued that I intended to augment our Englyshe tongue. . . . His Grace also

[1] Sir Henry Craik in *English Prose Selections*, I, 97.
[2] Alice D. Greenwood in *The Cambridge History of English Literature*, II, 333.

The Revival of English Prose.

perceyued that throughout the boke there was no terme new made by me of a latine or frenche worde, but it is there declared so playnly by one mene or other to a diligent reder, that no sentence is therby made derke or harde to be understande.

During the bilingual period, a writer of English naturally often coupled his English word with a Romance synonym. When English prose reasserts itself there is therefore an inevitable tendency to tautology. But whilst with the good writers this is held in check, it becomes quite uncontrolled in those who are consciously striving after "sugred eloquence." Two examples from Hall's *Chronicle* will suffice. The first is part of the supposed address of Henry V to his soldiers before Agincourt:

> Welbeloved frendes and countrymen, I exhort you heartely thynke and conceiue in your selues that thys daye shal be to vs all a day of ioy, a day of good luck and a day of victory: For truely if you well note and wisely considre all thynges, almighty God, vnder whose protection we be come hither, hath appointed a place so mete and apt for our purpose as we our selues could neither haue deuised nor wished, whyche as it is apt and conuenient for our smal nombre and litle army, so is it vnprofitable and vnmete for a great multitude to fight or geue battaile in.[1]

Such verbiage is bad enough in passages of rhetoric. But it becomes intolerable when Hall allows it to clog his narrative. In the days of Henry IV certain malicious and cruel persons,

> partly moued with indignacion, partely incensed with furious malencolie, set vpon postes and caste aboute the stretes railyng rimes, malicious meters, and tauntyng verses, agaynst king Henry and his procedynges. He beyng netteled with these uncurteous, ye unuertuous prickes and thornes, serched out the authours, and amongest other were found culpable of this offence and crime, Sir Roger Claryngdon knight and eight gray Friers, whiche accordyng to their merites and desertes were strangeled at Tiborne and there put in execucion.[2]

We are told that Hall was "in the later time of his life not so painful and studious as before he had been," and certainly, in the later portion of his *Chronicle*, Hall takes less pains to "augment" the English tongue. Much of this later portion, dealing with Henry VIII, is written in clean English enough, of which Hall was indeed a master. His danger, like Caxton's, lies in a vulgar desire "to embellish, ornate and make fair our English" by "sugred eloquence."

[1] Hall's *Chronicle, Kyng Henry the fifth*, fol. xvi^{b}.
[2] *Kyng Henry the iiii*, fol. xix^{a}.

The Revival of English Prose.

It is difficult to say whether Harding's versification or Hall's tautology is the worse fault in a chronicler. Anyway, it emphasizes More's services to English prose that, as the first edition of his *Richard III* was incorporated in Harding's *Chronicle*, so was the second in Hall's *Chronicle*.

Ascham's censure of Hall's "Indenture English" and his praise of More's style can be considered side by side :

> If a wise man would take *Halles* Cronicle, where moch good matter is quite marde with Indenture Englishe, and first change strange and inkhorne tearmes into proper and commonlie vsed wordes : next, specially to wede out that that is superfluous and idle, not onelie where wordes be vainlie heaped one vpon an other, but also where many sentences, of one meaning, be so clowted vp together as though *M. Hall* had bene, not writing the storie of England, but varying a sentence in Hitching schole : surelie a wise learned man, by this way of *Epitome*, in cutting away wordes and sentences, and diminishing nothing at all of the matter, shold leaue to mens vse a storie, halfe as moch as it was in quantitie, but twise as good as it was both for pleasure and also commoditie.[1]

Long before, Ascham had enumerated all the qualities which a good historian should have, concluding with the necessity for a style "plain and open," but varied "as matters do rise and fall." He then added : "Sir Thomas More, in that pamphlet of Richard the Third, doth in most part, I believe, of all these points so content all men, as, if the rest of our story of England were so done, we might well compare with France, or Italy, or Germany in that behalf."[2]

It is in the possession of this "plain and open" style, which nevertheless can be varied "as matters do rise and fall," that the excellence of the Fourteenth-Century devotional writers had consisted. In More and his school, following them, we find the same excellence. They avoid the vulgarism and pedantry into which the "augmenters" of English are always falling. More, like Ascham after him, does not eschew alliteration or the duplication of words. But these things are not allowed to become literary mannerisms. They are not used unless "the matters do rise" in such a way as to permit of them.

Those great men, the Translators of the Authorized Version, rightly allowed themselves to vary the phrase when they presented their work to King James I, "whose allowance and acceptance of

[1] *Schoolmaster* (*Works*, ed. Aldis Wright, 1904, p. 260).
[2] Letter to John Astley : *Works*, ed. Giles, IV, 6.

our labours shall more honour and encourage us, than all the calumniations and hard interpretations of other men shall dismay us."

The Revival of English Prose.

And we must allow a similar latitude of phrase to William Rastell presenting to Queen Mary the collected edition of his uncle's works:

> When I considered with my selfe (moost gratious soueraigne) what greate eloquence, excellent learninge, and morall vertues, were and be conteyned in the workes and bookes, that the wyse and godlie man, sir Thomas More knighte, sometyme lorde Chauncellour of England (my dere uncle) wrote in the Englysh tonge, so many, and so well, as no one Englishman (I suppose) ever wrote the like, whereby his workes be worthy to be hadde and redde of everye Englishe man, that is studious or desirous to know and learne, not onelye the eloquence and propertie of the English tonge, but also the trewe doctryne of Christes catholike fayth, the confutacion of detestable heresyes, or the godly morall vertues that appertaine to the framinge and fourminge of mennes maners and consciences, to live a vertuous and devout christen life; and when I further considered, that those workes of his were not yet all imprinted, and those that were imprinted, were in severall volumes and bokes, whereby it were likely, that aswell those bokes of his that were already abrode in print, as those that were yet unprinted, should in time percase perish and utterly vanish away (to the great losse and detriment of many) unlesse they were gathered together and printed in one whole volume; for these causes (my most gracious liege Lady) I dyd diligently collect and gather together, as many of those his workes, bokes, letters, and other writinges, printed and unprinted, in the English tonge, as I could come by, and the same (certain yeres in the evil world past, keping in my handes, very surely and safely) now lately have caused to be imprinted in this one volume, to thintent, not onely that every man that will, now in our dayes, maye have and take commoditie by them, but also that they may be preserved for the profit likewise of our posteritie.

XI. Evidence for the Continuous Influence of Fourteenth-Century devotional Literature, through the Fifteenth, into the Sixteenth Century.

Rastell was right in speaking of More as essentially a religious writer—one concerned with "the godly morall vertues." Yet owing to doctrinal changes, More's devotional books were, as years went on, less and less read by his countrymen. The *Dialogue of Comfort* was reprinted abroad, but at home few except those who

Continuous Influence of Fourteenth-Century Devotional Literature.

possessed the magnificent folio of 1557 could "have and take commoditie" by his religious works. *Richard III*, on the other hand, was constantly reissued in editions of the *Chronicles* of Grafton, Holinshed, and Stow, till it came to be recognized by all as a classic. Even if we dismiss as partisan Harpsfield's judgement that "*all men*" admit the "incomparable excellencie" of that fragment, we still have Ascham's statement that it "doth content *all men*," and nearly half a century later Sir John Harington's dictum that it was "the best written part of al our Chronicles, in *all mens* opinions." Ben Jonson in the early Seventeenth Century quotes it as a classic. So does Samuel Johnson in the Eighteenth, and we have seen how this opinion continues into the first half of the Nineteenth Century.[1]

The contrast between the prose of More's *Richard III* and the pompous tautology of Edward Hall is typical of two prose styles which we can distinguish in the late Fourteenth, Fifteenth, and Sixteenth Centuries. On the one hand, we have an English conscious of its inferiority to the Latin or French which it is seeking to replace, trying to assert its dignity by "augmenting itself," "struggling once more for expression in apologetic emulation of its betters." On the other hand, we have the traditional English of the *Ancren Riwle*—surviving in the works of Rolle or of Hilton, in the *Cloud*, in Nicholas Love or in Thomas More—an English which, while not despising ornament, or eschewing the coupling together of synonyms, never makes that excessive use of tricks which marks those who seek to enrich the English language.

Let the reader turn back to the three extracts given above, from Hilton and from the *Cloud*.[2]

The lofty eloquence of the first passage from Hilton's *Scale*, the straightforward common sense of the second, the humorous observation of the quotation from the *Cloud*—all these remind us of the *Ancren Riwle*. All read like forecasts of the prose of More.

And the links are there, easy to discern. At the time when Rolle and Hilton first set to work to write their books of contemplation addressed to dedicated women, the *Ancren Riwle* was the most popular and widely known book of that type—and we have seen how its influence can still be traced a century later, and even finds its way into books printed by Wynkyn de Worde.

The Vernon Manuscript in the Bodleian is an interesting link in the chain. Here, in a vast volume written towards the end of

[1] See above, p. lii. [2] See above, pp. ciii–vi.

Continuous Influence of Fourteenth-Century Devotional Literature

Chaucer's life, we find the text of the *Ancren Riwle* modernized in language, but in substance the same treatise which had been addressed to the three recluses centuries before.[1] We find a text of Rolle's epistle,[2] "*Thou that list love, hearken and hear of love: in the song of love it is written, 'I sleep and my heart wakes,'*" addressed to a nun of Yedingham; Rolle's *Commandment*,[3] written to a nun of Hampole; Rolle's *Form of Living*,[4] written "to a recluse that was clepet Margarete," that is to say, Hampole's disciple, Margaret Kirkby. Rolle had died a generation before the writing of the Vernon MS. And we find also the earliest version of the *Scale of Perfection*, addressed by Walter Hilton to his "Ghostly Sister in Jesu Christ."[5] We do not know the date of the composition of this, but Hilton was probably still alive when the Vernon MS. was written. It would be interesting to print, as they stand in the Vernon MS., passages addressed to these different recluses so widely separated in date, and to ask those who deny the continuity of English prose to tell us, on internal evidence, when we have the late Fourteenth-Century reviser working over English prose of two centuries before, and when he is transcribing the words of his contemporary, Master Walter.

I am not suggesting that when the young Thomas More wrote his book "Unto his right entierly beloued sister in Christ, Joyeuce Leigh"—a sister of the House of the Poor Clares in London—he had necessarily in mind any single one of the five treatises addressed to cloistered women which I have just mentioned. But he was following a tradition.

Whether there were any books besides law books in the house of More's father in Cripplegate Ward we do not know; but if there were, all that we know from the analogy of books bequeathed in English wills would lead us to expect that they were the works of Rolle or of Hilton. The popularity of the *Scale of Perfection* throughout More's life is proved by the printed editions of *c.* 1494, 1519, 1525 and 1533 (all Wynkyn de Worde) and of 1507 (Julian Notary).

Hilton's *Treatise of Mixed Life*, addressed to "a devout man in temporal estate," is also found in the Vernon MS. and in the contemporary Simeon MS., as a third part, appended to the *Scale*. It

[1] Vernon MS., fols. 371^{v}–92^{v}.
[2] Vernon MS., fols. 338^{r}–39^{r}.
[3] Vernon MS., fol. 334.
[4] Vernon MS., fols. 334^{v}–38^{r}.
[5] Vernon MS., fol. 343^{v}–53^{v}.

Continuous Influence of Fourteenth-Century Devotional Literature.

was printed, together with the *Scale*, in all the editions of Wynkyn de Worde, and in Notary's edition. And it was also printed, apart from the *Scale*, by Pynson (1517) and by Wyer (1531). This makes seven editions, in all, during More's lifetime.

So, when Thomas More determined to be an author, not merely in Latin, but in English also, he had not to make an English prose. He found it ready to hand: not in Chaucer's *Parson's Tale*, not even in Malory, whose book he may perhaps never have opened, but in the living tradition of the English pulpit, and in the large body of devotional vernacular literature dating from the Fourteenth Century and the early Fifteenth.

Now this body of literature dates back to a period earlier than Chaucer or Wiclif: for Rolle, it must be repeatedly emphasized, was dead thirty years [1] before Wiclif began his great movement for the translation of the Bible into the vernacular.

But we have seen [2] that, during the century and a half intervening between the days of Rolle and More's early manhood, this old tradition had been in touch with a yet older tradition—that of the group of writings popular certainly by the early Thirteenth Century, and possibly before, of which the *Ancren Riwle* is the greatest extant survival. Further, the *Ancren Riwle* and its group is an outgrowth of the homiletic tradition of the Twelfth Century, which itself is based upon Ælfric—who, in his turn, deliberately built upon the foundations laid by Alfred.

It is from this homiletic tradition that More sometimes borrows the trick of balanced sentences, many of which can be scanned as rough alliterative lines. It is a tradition which we can trace from Ælfric, through the group of Saints' Lives contemporary with the *Ancren Riwle*, and through Rolle.

Here is More's covetous man, whom you may see,

His hed hanging in his bosom · and his body croked,
Walk pit pat · vpon a paire of patens
Wyth the staffe in the tone hande · and the *pater noster* in the tother hande,
The tone fote almost · in the graue already,
And yet neuer the more hast · to part with anythynge,
Nor to restore · that he hathe euyl gotten,
But as gredy to geat a grote · by the begiling of his neybour
As if he had of certaynty · seuen score yere to liue.[3]

[1] Rolle died in 1349; Wiclif was urging the necessity of an English Bible between 1378 and 1384 (Deanesly, p. 241).

[2] See pp. xcix–c, above. [3] *Works*, pp. 93–4.

Continuous Influence of Fourteenth-Century Devotional Literature.

More had probably caught the rhythm from some preacher.

More was surrounded by the preaching tradition, from which he could hardly have escaped. His earliest extant letter discusses London preaching with Colet. If it had been written in English, one would have called it a rather priggish letter; but much may be allowed to a youngster writing Latin prose. It is an appeal to Colet (then absent in the country) to return to London, where, More assures him, everybody is longing for his pulpit eloquence, with incredibly strong desire and keen expectation.

Erasmus records, and Colet had criticized, the "coldness" with which English preachers read their sermons from manuscript[1]—which at any rate testifies to careful preparation. That Colet's sermons were no mere improvisation follows from what Erasmus tells us: that he had polished his English style by the study of English writers. For, Erasmus adds, just as Italy has Dante and Petrarch, so has England *her* native writers.[2] The modern reader naturally thinks of Chaucer; Chaucer's debt to Dante and Petrarch is a commonplace, and the mere association of ideas sends the mind automatically from one to the other. But Chaucer's debt to Dante—a subject which the schoolboy or girl (caring little about Chaucer and less about Dante) dutifully crams up for his or her school-leaving certificate—was a topic unknown to Erasmus.

What were the books which a preacher, at the beginning of the Sixteenth Century, might reasonably be supposed to have chosen, in order to "polish his style"?

If we would attempt to answer this question, we must begin by ridding ourselves of our literary exclusiveness, which, whilst exalting Chaucer, has banished from the histories of literature the greatest prose-writers of the Fourteenth Century. These prose-writers have been excluded for the very reasons which would have led Colet to seek them: their interest in that contemplative piety which had been handed down from late classical times—a kind of writing which, through translations like *Dionis' hid Divinity*, had deeply influenced the thought of the Fifteenth and early Sixteenth Centuries,

[1] Erasmus tells us that the third of the charges brought against Colet by the Bishop of London was: "Quod cum in concione dixisset quosdam de charta concionari (id quod multi frigide faciunt in Anglia) oblique taxasset Episcopum." (*Opus. Epist. Des. Erasmi*, No. 1211, Tom. IV, p. 524, ed. P. S. Allen, 1922.)

[2] "Habet gens Britannica qui hoc praestiterunt apud suos quod Dantes ac Petrarcha apud Italos. Et horum euoluendis scriptis linguam expoliuit, iam tum se praeparans ad praeconium sermonis Euangelici." (the same, p. 515).

Continuous Influence of Fourteenth-Century Devotional Literature.

and which, so far as our evidence goes, was more commonly studied about the year 1500 than Chaucer's *Canterbury Tales*. Colet may well have known *both* Chaucer *and* Hilton: in view of what Erasmus tells us of Colet's wide reading, he probably did know both. Considering his interest in the "pseudo-Dionysius," it seems difficult to imagine that, when he turned to English authors, he ignored the orthodox devotional writing of the Fourteenth and Fifteenth Centuries. That he did not eschew Wicliffite treatises, if he came across them, we know from Erasmus.[1]

And Colet could hardly have failed to come across the orthodox English books of Hilton and his contemporaries. The religious House with which he was most closely connected was the Charterhouse of Sheen, whither he intended to retire, and where he built himself a home (which not he, but Cardinal Wolsey, was destined to occupy). There is no catalogue extant of the library of this House, but inscriptions in extant books give us some fragmentary information. John Kingslow, the first recluse at Sheen, had given to the Sheen Carthusians *The Chastising of God's Children* as early as 1415.[2] The *Chastising* is a tract which, we have seen, connects the early Thirteenth with the late Fifteenth Century: it contains reminiscences of the *Ancren Riwle*, and its popularity lasted long enough for it to be printed by Wynkyn de Worde. John Dygoun, recluse at Sheen in 1438, possessed a book of Hilton's.[3] He also owned the *Poor Caitiff*,[4] a compilation, apparently, of the late Fourteenth Century, which shows traces of the influence of the *Ancren Riwle*, and, to a greater degree, of Rolle.[5] Benet, Proctor of the Sheen Carthusians, copied out Hilton's *Scale*: the manuscript is still extant,[6] certified, in 1499, by the hand of J. Grenehalgh, a monk of the same House. Grenehalgh also possessed a copy of Wynkyn de Worde's 1494 edition of Hilton's *Scale* and *Mixed Life*. He annotated it copiously. The book had passed,

[1] Nullus erat liber tam haereticus quem ille non attente euolueret . . . (*Opus. Epist. Des. Erasmi*, No. 1211, Tom. IV, p. 523).

[2] MS. Rawl. C. 57. Quoted by Miss Deanesly, *Modern Language Review*, xv, p. 357.

[3] Magd. Coll., Oxford, MS. 93. Dygoun and another scribe copied out the *Imitatio Christi*: he was therefore "one of the earliest English students" of that book. (Miss Deanesly, as above, p. 355.)

[4] Magd. Coll., Oxford, MS. 93. Quoted by Miss Deanesly, p. 356.

[5] Hope Emily Allen, *Writings ascribed to Richard Rolle*, 1927, p. 406; and *Modern Language Review*, xviii, pp. 3–4.

[6] Trin. Coll., Camb., MS. B. 15, 18 (374): No. 354 of Dr. James' Catalogue.

Continuous Influence of Fourteenth-Century Devotional Literature.

by 1500, into the hands of Dame Joan Sewell, sister professed in the adjoining House of Sion, a keen student of Rolle.[1]

Two manuscripts of Rolle can also be traced to the Sheen Charterhouse,[2] but these are in Latin. And this is typical: so far as Miss Allen has been able to trace the origin of the Rolle manuscripts, they come in exceptional numbers from Carthusian houses, at home or abroad; but these manuscripts are all Latin, for the Carthusians were above all things a learned order. It is quite natural, therefore, that we should find a Carthusian translating the *Cloud of Unknowing* from English into Latin.[3] But it is certain that the Fifteenth-Century Carthusians did not confine their interest to Latin works—rather that they felt it their duty, in their life of seclusion, to help the laity outside their walls by composing or transcribing vernacular books. For this purpose one of the Sheen Carthusians compiled a vernacular Life of Christ [4] for a nun. But he feels his work to be rather superfluous: it has already been done by Nicholas Love, Prior of the Charterhouse of Mount Grace in Yorkshire—a House which had peculiarly intimate connection with the Sheen House.

Love's *Mirrour of the Blessed Lyf of Iesu Crist* was founded upon a work wrongly attributed to Bonaventura. But Love treats his original freely, making additions "of much beauty and devotion." [5] He tells us his reasons and his method:

> For þere is no pride, but þat it may be iheled þoruȝ þe mekenes of goddis sone: þere is no covetise bot þat it may be heled þoruȝ his poverte: ne wraþþe but þat it may be heled þoruȝ his pacience: nor malice but þat hit may be heled þoruȝ his charitie. And moreover þere is no synne or wickednesse, but þat he schal want it and be kept fro it, þe whiche byholdeþ inwardely and loveþ and foloweþ þe wordes and the dedes of þat man in whom goddes sone ȝaf hymself to us into ensample of good lyvynge. Wherfore now boþe men and wymmen and every age and every dignyte of þis worlde is stired to hope of everelastyng lyf. And for þis hope and to þis entente, wiþ

[1] See Miss Deanesly's edition of the *Incendium*, and Miss Allen's *Writings ascribed to Richard Rolle*, p. 216.

[2] One must have been taken abroad by a refugee; it came to the English Benedictine College at Douay, and is now in the Public Library there; the other is in Trinity College, Dublin. See Allen, *Writings ascribed to Richard Rolle*, pp. 37, 237.

[3] Pembroke College, Cambridge, MS. 221. Translated by Richard de Methley, Carthusian of Mount Grace.

[4] *Speculum Devotorum*. Camb. Univ., MS. Gg. I. 6: see Deanesly, *Lollard Bible*, p. 325.

[5] Deanesly, *Lollard Bible*, p. 323.

Continuous Influence of Fourteenth-Century Devotional Literature.

> holy writt also ben writen dyverse bookes and tretees of devouȝt men, not onliche to clerkes in Latyn but also in English to lewed men and wommen and hem þat ben of symple understondynge.[1]

The importance of Love's *Mirror* lies in its wide diffusion. "It was probably more popular than any other single book in the Fifteenth Century."[2] This is shown by one of the best forms of evidence—the comparative frequency with which it is referred to in wills.

Whether Prior Nicholas was justified in thinking that his *Mirror* was likely to prove "more speedful and edifying" to simple souls than the Wicliffite translations of the Bible, I dare not discuss. But it is certain that Love's beautiful yet easy and natural prose was more likely to lead to the development of a widely spread good English style than the study either of Hereford's version of the Bible, with its crude and literal painting of English words over a Latin base, or even of Purvey's smoother rendering. And, whilst the large number of manuscripts of both these Wicliffite versions is a fact which we must keep always before us in estimating influences, it must also be remembered that it was only through manuscripts that the influence of these versions could be exercised, for no Wicliffite version was printed till 1731. The numerous[3] manuscript copies of the *Mirror* circulating in the Fifteenth Century were reinforced, before the century ended, by at least four printed editions: those of Caxton (1486, 1490), of Wynkyn de Worde (1494), and of Pynson (1494).[4]

Prior Nicholas recommends to his readers a study of the books of Hilton—the *Scale* and *Mixed Life.* The story of Martha and Mary naturally leads him to this—for Mary is the example of all contemplatives:

> And whoso coveiteþ to knowe þe fruyte of vertuouse silence, ȝif he have affeccioun and wille to trewe contemplatyf lyvynge, wiþouten doute he schal be bettre tauȝte by experience þan by writynge or techynge of man; and neverþeles seynt Bernarde and manye oþere holy fadres and doctoures commenden hiȝely þis vertuous sylence, as it is worþy.
>
> Where of, and oþere vertuouse exercise þat longeþ to contemplatyf lyvynge, and specially to a recluse, and also of

[1] Ed. L. F. Powell, Oxford, 1908, p. 8 (based on the Brasenose College MS., written *c.* 1430).

[2] Deanesly in *Mod. Lang. Rev.*, xv, p. 353 (1920).

[3] Powell mentions twenty-three.

[4] See E. Gordon Duff, *Fifteenth Century Printed Books*, 1917.

> medled lyf (þat is to saye somtyme actyfe and somtyme contemplatyf, as it longeþ to dyverse persones þat in worldely astate haven grace of goostly love) who so wole more pleynely be enformed and tauȝt in Englisshe tonge, lete hym loke þe tretys þat þe worþy clerke and holy lyvere maister Walter Hyltoun the chanoun of Thurgartun wrote in englische, by grace and hiȝe discreccioun; and he schal fynde þere, as I leve, a sufficient scole and a trewe of alle þise. Whose soule reste in evere lastynge blisse and pees—as I hope he be ful hiȝe in blisse, ioyned and knytte wiþ outen departynge to his spouse Jesu, by parfite use of the beste parte, þat he chase here wiþ Marye. Of þe which parte he graunt us felawschippe, Jesu oure lorde God.[1]

Continuous Influence of Fourteenth-Century Devotional Literature.

The London citizens among whom Colet moved, and to whom he preached, included men of the same type as the Killums and the Hollands who, in earlier generations, had caused Hilton's books to be transcribed "for a common profit." When Colet withdrew to the Sheen Charterhouse, he would find the same books being studied. The London printers were making them easier of access than ever: the copy which Grenehalgh, monk of Sheen, was annotating about 1500 was a printed one.

It was therefore hardly possible that Colet could have neglected these books. And a reading of them must have tended to "polish his style" for preaching, as it could never have been polished by a study of the *Canterbury Tales*.

The Carthusians of the House of "Smithfield, near London" shared with their brethren of Sheen this interest in works of devotion in the English tongue, and particularly in books by, or attributed to, Hilton. There is no catalogue of their library known, and we have to depend upon odd notes in manuscripts; but these are of special interest when we remember that More "continued four years and more in great devotion and prayer with the monks of the Charterhouse of London."[2]

One of the many British Museum manuscripts of Hilton's *Scale of Perfection* belonged to the London Charterhouse:[3] it is a copy of the first version; but the care with which it has been corrected from a copy of the later version shows the anxiety of the brethren to have a correct text. The *Cloud of Unknowing* was transcribed by William Tregoose, a brother of the London House: he produced

[1] *The Mirrour*, ed. L. F. Powell, 1908, p. 164.
[2] See below, p. 17. [3] MS. Harl. 6579.

Continuous Influence of Fourteenth-Century Devotional Literature.

about 1500 what is almost a new recension.[1] It must have been somewhat later that William Exmew of the London Charterhouse again transcribed the *Cloud*; his manuscript is now in the possession of the Carthusians of Parkminster.

That the prose of Sir Thomas More is in the direct line of succession from that of these great Fourteenth-Century books has been pointed out by Prof. A. W. Reed:

> No one who has read, for instance, his *Treatise of the Four Last Things*—" Death, Doom, Pain, and Joy "—and is familiar with our earlier prose writers, can fail to observe that More's prose style is like nothing that preceded it so much as the natural, lucid and easy prose of the school of Hilton. Nor is this surprising if we remember that More spent three or four years of his early manhood in the Charterhouse of London, where, and apparently when, Hilton's works were being copied. May we not say with some assurance that he knew, and knew well, the writings of Walter Hilton, and look with interest for the marks of their influence on his own direct and intimate prose? We know that throughout his life he continued to practise the austerities and self-discipline that he had known among the Carthusians. It may seem incongruous to associate More's hair-shirt with his prose style; but both, I believe, derived from his early days of prayer, reading, recollection and discipline beside the monks of the London Charterhouse.[2]

To read these Charterhouse manuscripts is to be brought very near to the most heroic episode in English history. I suppose John Houghton, Prior of the London Charterhouse, must have handled the copy of the *Scale of Perfection* belonging to his House. It was John Houghton and his two fellow Priors whom More watched from his prison when they were being placed on hurdles to be drawn to Tyburn. More, " as one longing in that journey to have accompanied them," said to Margaret, " Lo, dost thou not see, Meg, that these blessed fathers be now as cheerfully going to their deaths as bridegrooms to their marriage." This was on 4 May, 1535. Just three weeks later, three other London Carthusians were arrested—young men of gentle birth who, after the death of Prior Houghton, had by their force of character stepped into the position of leaders. What happened to them is recorded below, in the fragment of Rastell's *Life of More*. " They were brought the 25th day of May

[1] This is now in the Bodleian: MS. Douce 262. Tregoose died in 1514. MS. Bodl. 576 is closely related to MS. Douce 262.

[2] Foreword to *The Minor Works of Walter Hilton*, ed. by Dorothy Jones.

Continuous Influence of Fourteenth-Century Devotional Literature.

to Cromwell to his house at Stebunheyth [Stepney], a mile from London; and refusing constantly to acknowledge the king's supremacy, were imprisoned in the Tower of London, where they remained seventeen days, standing bolt upright, tied with iron collars fast by the necks to the posts of the prison, and great fetters fast rived on their legs with great iron bolts." [1]

One of these three was William Exmew, the transcriber of the *Cloud*; another was Sebastian Newdigate, "who had been a courtier." After these seventeen days of torture they were judged by the same commission before which More himself was to appear three weeks later. It is not recorded whether or no More also watched these three going to execution. The other recalcitrant Carthusians were later put to the same torture: chained up in Newgate so that they could move neither hand nor foot, till they perished in torments, of which starvation must have been the smallest. More's adopted daughter, Margaret Gigs, who had married Dr. Clement, a former member of More's household and then court physician, managed to get access to their prison, and ministered to them in every way she could. When she was shut out, she made pathetic attempts to feed and comfort them through a hole in the roof. Margaret Clement was the most learned lady of her day in medicine and mathematics; Leland has praised her beauty, and at Windsor you can still see Holbein's record of her thoughtful face. You will find an account, in the *Dictionary of National Biography*, of her knowledge of algebra, but nothing as to how she succoured the Carthusians at the grave risk of her life; still less as to how, on the Utas of St. Peter, 1570, thirty-five years to a day after the death of More, Margaret Clement lay dying in exile at Mechlin: "Calling her husband therefore she told him that the time of her departing was now come, for that there were standing about her bed the Reverend monks of the Charterhouse, whom she had relieved in prison in England, and did call upon her to come away with them, and that therefore she could stay no longer, because they did expect her." [2]

Now all this has its place in the history of English prose because (amongst other things) it marks the end of the system by which English prose had been preserved. A whole school of English

[1] See below, pp. 235–6. They were apparently taken first to the Marshalsea and removed to the Tower.

[2] This comes from a Life of Mother Margaret Clement (her daughter) now preserved in the English Convent at Bruges.

Continuous Influence of Fourteenth-Century Devotional Literature.

prose begins—so far as we can trace it—with the three girls of gentle birth who had withdrawn from the world, and had to "bear the arrogance of those who might have been their thralls." It ends, so far as England is concerned, with the death of Exmew and his fellow-martyrs, and then of Fisher and of More. Despite the fact that after the Conquest the English language had been little heard at the Court, that Englishmen, not only of the upper but of the middle classes, had been all trying to write French or Latin, nevertheless English, for centuries never used for purposes of law and government, and rarely used for any great works of literature, had been still written by and for people who were too much in earnest to bother about courtly fashions. These people wrote sometimes in Latin, but also in English, because either to them, or to the enclosed sisters for whom so often they wrote, English was the language of passionate and instinctive utterance. It is strange to reflect how our English prose has been handed down to Tudor times, from the days of King Alfred and Abbot Ælfric, not by clerks working in the royal chancelleries, but through books originally written to be read in lonely anchor-holds or quiet nunneries: retreats like those of the three sisters of the *Riwle*, or the sister to whom *The Wooing of our Lord* was addressed; later, for Margaret Kirkby or for the anonymous nuns of Yedingham or Hampole for whom Rolle wrote; later still, for the sisters addressed by Hilton or by the author of the *Chastising of God's Children*,[1] or by the Sheen Carthusian who wrote the *Speculum Devotorum*.[2] Special mention must be made of the nuns of the Brigittine Monastery of Sion at Isleworth, for whom was written the *Myroure of oure Ladye*,[3] and to one of whom the Carthusian Grenehalgh gave the *Scale of Perfection* which he had annotated.[4] The list might be extended indefinitely, till we come to Joyeuce Leigh, the Poor Clare of the Minories, and finally to Elizabeth White, nun of Dartford, half-sister of John Fisher, for whom, whilst in the Tower, he wrote *A Spiritual Consolation* and *The Ways to Perfect Religion*. But times were changing. The year after Fisher wrote, the dissolution of the monasteries began; in five years they were roofless and their libraries for the most part destroyed. Elizabethan England had little use for this literature. The wonder is that so many copies of its masterpieces were preserved.

[1] Trin. Coll. Camb., MS. B. 14. 19 (483): No. 305 of Dr. James' Catalogue.
[2] Camb. Univ., MS. Gg. 1. 6.
[3] Ed. Blunt, E.E.T.S., 1873.
[4] Lord Aldenham's copy.

Continuous Influence of Fourteenth-Century Devotional Literature.

I have mentioned MS. Harl. 993, made by Robert Holland "for a comyn profite," with a request in return for a prayer for his soul. Underneath this inscription we find:

> James Palmer
>
> James Palmer owneth this Booke, yet without ye least intent to pray for ye Soule of Robert Holland, being a wicked and simple custome of sottishly ignorant Papistes. J. Palmer Junr.

Poor James Palmer, junior: he must have found the *Discerning of Spirits* very hard reading. I wonder what he made of it. Perhaps, after all, he made as much of it as the professor who reads it as a document illustrating the history of English prose, and who therefore has no right to thank God that he is not as James Palmer.

With Exmew, then, ends, for the time, so far as England is concerned, the history of *The Cloud of Unknowing.* But there were other Carthusians than those who appeared to the dying eyes of Margaret Clement. There were men like Maurice Chauncy, who, against their consciences, temporized and took the oath, and who yet repented and withdrew later to the Continent, and formed a community of English Carthusians, first at Bruges and finally at Nieuport. And from them the English Benedictine community abroad derived its love of these books. The Venerable Augustine Baker (1575–1641) writes:

> The copy of the book [*The Cloud of Unknowing*] that we have in this house was written in the year 1582. . . . It is said that the copy from which our said copy was taken was brought over into these parts out of England by the English Carthusians, when they forsook their country upon the schism of King Henry VIII.[1]

So the *Cloud* continued to be studied among these English exiles. Father Baker wrote a long exposition upon it, and its lasting popularity is shown by a transcript (now at Ampleforth) made as late as 1677.

The history of English literature, as it was cherished among the exiles, has still to be written.

In the last few years there has been a very noteworthy revival of interest in these books—not in the main an antiquarian interest, but a real return to the point of view of Rolle or Hilton. The books I have mentioned are almost all accessible to-day, in slightly modernized form, published in the *Orchard Classics*, under the editorship of Dom Roger Hudleston.

[1] *Cloud of Unknowing*, ed. Dom Justin McCann (*Orchard Series*), p. 291.

Continuous Influence of Fourteenth-Century Devotional Literature.

We must all rejoice that the works of Rolle and Hilton and Dame Juliana and Nicholas Love are being printed for the only purpose for which their authors would have wished them to be studied; and it is no wonder that in this age of motor-horns the longing for these quiet books has arisen again. But students of language and literature who refer to these modernized texts naturally assume them to be much more modernized than they actually are, and so overlook their importance in the history of English prose. We find a scribe of Rolle in 1411 stating that *antiqui libri* have been used to correct his text. The Twentieth Century ought not to be less exacting in this matter than the Fifteenth. Miss Allen has now placed a convenient and scholarly edition of the more important of Rolle's English works within the reach of all,[1] but we are still without any critical edition of such noble works as Walter Hilton's *Scale of Perfection*, or *The Cloud of Unknowing*.

And above all it is to be hoped that the Early English Text Society will be able to enlist editors to undertake a working edition of the *Ancren Riwle*—probably the greatest need in the whole field of English literature.

XII. Pecock, Fortescue, Malory; Tyndale and the Bible-translators.

So far, the argument has been that the anonymous author of the *Ancren Riwle*, Richard Rolle, Walter Hilton, and Sir Thomas More are main piers of the bridge which connects Tudor prose with the prose of Ælfric and of Alfred. Each of these writers is the centre of a group: immediately round More we have to place William Roper and William Rastell and Nicholas Harpsfield and Margaret Roper, with her few but memorable letters.

Yet, except the *Ancren Riwle* and its group, and More himself apart from his group, these classics are hardly mentioned in histories of English literature, or represented in anthologies of English prose.[2]

But, it will be asked, what about Pecock, Fortescue and Malory, that queerly assorted trio who appear in every history of English literature, whose names schoolboys during the past half-century have learnt by heart as a sacred formula to put them through examinations? (Although at the same time interest in Pecock has been so small that

[1] Oxford, *Clarendon Press*, 1931.

[2] Rolle is thought of only as the supposed author of *The Prick of Conscience*.

the majority of his extant books have been allowed to remain unpublished till they were edited for the Early English Text Society during the last ten years by the energy of Dr. Hitchcock, seconded by that of Dr. Greet.) And, above all, what of Tyndale and Coverdale, and the wonderful succession of translations of the Bible closed by the Authorized Version of 1611?

The answer is that all these have their place, and a most important place; but a place which can only be properly understood when we see these achievements against the continuous background of English devotional prose. Then, and only then, everything is in its right perspective.

The Authorized Version.

Without this background, the glories of English prose become unintelligible. As evidence of this I would quote the words of Sir Arthur Quiller-Couch describing as a "miracle" the Authorized Version of 1611:

> That a large committee of forty-seven should have gone steadily through the great mass of Holy Writ, seldom interfering with genius, yet, when interfering, seldom missing to improve: that a committee of forty-seven should have captured (or even, let us say, should have retained and improved) a rhythm so personal, so constant, that our Bible has the voice of one author speaking through its many mouths: that, Gentlemen, is a wonder before which I can only stand humble and aghast.[1]

Looked at in isolation, the Authorized Version *is* a miracle. But, in fact, there was such a tradition of English prose behind those who drew up the Authorized Version that even a Committee could not spoil it. All their lives the translators had been repeating or listening to the words of the Prayer Book.[2] All the forty-seven must have known by heart large sections of the Psalter in the already seventy-years-old version of 1540. And if it is retorted that this is only pushing the miracle back from Jacobean to early Tudor days, the answer is that the prose of early Tudor days had in turn been nourished on the Fourteenth-Century English of works like *The Scale of Perfection* or *The Cloud of Unknowing*. What that means, any passage taken at random from the *Cloud* would suffice to show. Here are the closing sentences:

> For not what þou arte, ne what þou hast ben, beholdeþ god wiþ his mercyful iȝe—but þat þou woldest be. And Seinte

[1] *On the Art of Writing*, pp. 122–3 (*On the capital difficulty of prose*).
[2] With the trifling exception that Hadrian Saravia, a refugee from the Continent, was not appointed to the rectory of Tattenhill, Staffordshire, till 1588.

The Authorized Version.

Gregory to witnes, þat alle holy desires growen bi delaies. (And ȝif þei wany bi delaies, þen were þei never holy desires; for he þat feliþ ever les ioye and les, in newe fyndinges and sodeyn presentaciouns of his olde purposid desires, þof al þei mowe be clepid kyndely desires to þe goode, neverþeles holy desires weren þei never.)

Of þis holy desire spekiþ seint Austyne, and seiþ þat al þe liif of a good cristen man is not elles bot holy desire.

Farewel, goostly freende, in goddes blessing and mynne. And I beseche almiȝti god þat trewe pees, hole counseil, and goostly coumforte in god, wiþ habundaunce of grace, evirmore be wiþ þee, and alle goddes lovers in eerþe. Amen.[1]

And, if we wish to go behind that, we may turn to the noble eloquence of many a passage in the *Ancren Riwle*, or of Ælfric, or Wulfstan, or Alfred.

Pecock, Fortescue and Malory are three exceptional writers, whose work, for different reasons, is in rather striking contrast with that great body of English prose which we have been considering.

Pecock.

The style of Pecock is crabbed, though not in the same way that the style of the Wicliffite Bible is crabbed. For, if Pecock's style is not an easy one, there is justification for this want of ease. Pecock's work is a raid into new territory: he strives to conduct in English that kind of philosophical discussion for which Latin had hitherto been regarded as the only proper medium.

In this he has no equal in English till Hooker, "though of course Hooker far transcends Pecock in eloquence and majesty of cadence. . . . But in that ponderousness which is yet never really obscure or inaccurate, both are strikingly alike. They have the same luxuriance of subordinate clauses, though in Pecock it is a luxuriance apt to be wearisome, while in Hooker it is delightful and majestic. We find similiar faults—the superabundance of words, the crowding of facts and inferences in space too small to hold them. And we find similar gifts; above all, the art of expressing complex meanings and subtle doctrines with far-sighted and comprehensive accuracy." [2]

The comparison with Hooker reminds us that Pecock is a hundred and fifty years before his time—herein is his greatness and his weakness. He had to create a vocabulary for his new adventure. In a letter of Edward IV to Sixtus IV we are told (it seems incredible) that after the death of the said Reginald Pecock the writings and treatises

[1] MS. Harl. 674, fol. 91*v*.
[2] Introduction to the *Folewer*, p. lxv.

composed by him multiplied in such wise, that not only the laity, but churchmen and scholastic graduates scarcely studied anything else, "so that the pestiferous virus circulated in many human breasts." If this had been allowed to go on, Pecock's contribution to the English vocabulary would have been vast. As it is, it is not negligible; but if his enemies had met him, as he wished, by argument instead of by force, our language of religious and philosophical controversy would have been based upon Pecock, and eendal and meenal, kunningal and moral virtues would not now be untobethoughtupon. But Pecock and his works were suppressed; faced with the choice of being burnt himself or of handing his beloved works to the hangman to burn, he reluctantly chose the latter alternative. Those few of his books that have survived have in each case survived only in a single copy; the *Repressor* was not printed till 1860, and the rest, as we have seen, have only been printed quite recently. Pecock was a pioneer, and, as so often happens with pioneers, his work was largely lost. In virtue of the originality of his effort he stands out in magnificent isolation from the main body of English homiletic, devotional prose. **Pecock.**

Fortescue's claim to a place in the history of English style is quite unlike that of Pecock. Fortescue writes a lucid, simple prose which contrasts with Pecock's complicated structures. The first sentence of *The Donet* fills 31 lines; the first sentence of *The Folewer*, 40; yet both sentences are quite grammatical and well formed. Now take the opening sentence of Fortescue's *Governance*: **Fortescue.**

> Ther bith ij kyndes off kyngdomes, of the wich that on is a lordship callid in laten *dominium regale,* and that other is callid *dominium politicum et regale.*

Fortescue's beautiful and touching *Dialogue between Understanding and Faith* shows his style at its best; it is the prose which for centuries had been used for such works of edification. Fortescue's outstanding place in the history of English literature is due to the fact that he applied this usual English prose to a quite unusual purpose—to constitutional and political subjects which, till his time, would have been treated in Latin or French. Yet his influence upon the later development of English prose cannot have been much greater than that of Pecock. Fortescue was writing *The Governance of England* just at the time when Caxton was making his first essays in printing. Yet *The Governance* remained unprinted till the Eighteenth Century, whilst Fortescue's Latin *De Laudibus* was printed and reprinted from the middle of the Sixteenth Century, and was popularized in

Fortescue. Mulcaster's translation, so that for centuries it was a powerful book. But Fortescue's English works can have had few readers indeed, and correspondingly little influence, either on English thought or English prose style.

Malory. Malory's influence, on the contrary, must have been great. Yet it cannot have been as great as that of More, for he stands in much greater isolation. As Mr. Saintsbury, Malory's keenest advocate, says of the *Morte Darthur*, "although the greatest book in English between the *Canterbury Tales* and the *Faerie Queene*, it is, from this very finality and retrospective, not prospective, character, out of the general line of progress." [1]

The *Morte Darthur* is indeed "out of the general line of progress." What Malory did (and to some extent Berners after him) was to save for the English tongue something of the mediæval glamour of which William the Conqueror robbed us by bringing it to pass that during that greatest of mediæval centuries, the Thirteenth, there was no English prose, save sermons and exhortations addressed to enclosed sisters.

Even by the days of Chaucer the glamour had gone: in the chivalry of the days of Edward III or Richard II, as recorded by Froissart, we feel an archaism, as if men were trying to recapture the standards of an earlier age. We feel it in Chaucer's three references to the greatest heroes of the Table Round. The knight who came to the court of Cambinskan spoke so well, the Squire says:

> That Gawain, with his oldë curteisye,
> Though he were come ageyn out of Fairye,
> Ne coude him nat amende with a word.[2]

And who could speak of the courteous love-making of that court?

> No man but Launcelot, and he is deed.[3]

As to the tale of Chanticleer, says the Nun's Priest,

> This storie is al-so trewe, I undertake,
> As is the book of Launcelot de Lake,
> That wommen holde in ful gret reverence.[4]

Chaucer is in many ways a modern: when he is mediæval he belongs to those latest Middle Ages which differ greatly from the days when the stories of Arthur were in their first glory.

[1] *A First Book of English Literature*, 1914, p. 60; compare *A History of English Prose Rhythm*, 1912: "Malory . . . is not in the most direct line of rhythmical development."
[2] *Canterbury Tales*, F. 95–7. [3] F. 287. [4] B. 4401–3.

Malory.

So the world to which the *Morte Darthur* belongs had passed away before the book was finished in "the ninth year of the reign of King Edward the Fourth, by Sir Thomas Maleore, knight, as Jesu help him for his great might, as he is the servant of Jesu both day and night." In that same year, Niccolo Machiavelli was christened in the Baptistery of Florence, and Erasmus of Rotterdam was taking such interest in the world as a child of three may do. Launcelot was dead indeed. The world was getting ready to profit by those three great benefactions which Cowley has selected as "things useful to human life": "Printing, Guns, America." [1]

There was little room, it has been said, for Arthurian knighthood in the England of the *Paston Letters*. Yet such is the power of style that Malory, at the eleventh hour, was able to go over the old ground, and make it live once more:

> Thenne they made bothe grete dole, oute of mesure. This wille not avayle, said Sire Percyvale. And thenne he kneled doune, and made his prayer devoutely unto Almyghty Jhesu, for he was one of the best knyghtes of the world that at that tyme was, in whome the veray feythe stode moost in. Ryght soo there came by the holy vessel of the Sancgreal, with alle maner of swetnes and savour.[2]

The *Morte Darthur* reached a third edition in 1529 and a fourth in 1557; Ascham tells us how it was received into the prince's chamber when God's Bible was banished the Court.[3]

Percivale wounded, Galahad in prison, strengthened by the Sangreal, these seem strangely incongruous heroes for the court of Henry VIII and its "upstart aristocracy," growing rich on enclosures and sheep-farming, and casting covetous eyes on the monastic lands, till for ten years there was all over England "a sinister hum, as of the floating of an immense land syndicate, with favourable terms for all sufficiently rich, or influential, or mean, to get in on the ground floor." [4]

But the Tudor aristocracy liked to deck itself in the trappings of that mediæval life, on the plunder of which it was to build its fortunes. We think of Northumberland and Somerset as typical statesmen of that New Age which in a generation turned Mediæval into Modern

[1] *A proposition for the advancement of experimental philosophy.*
[2] Book XI, cap. 14.
[3] This has been interpreted as an allusion to the edition of 1529. It seems more likely to be a reference to the edition of 1557.
[4] R. H. Tawney, *Religion and the Rise of Capitalism*, 1926, p. 143.

Malory.

England; and we think of Thomas Wyatt as playing a hardly less revolutionary part in poetry. It is with some sense of incongruity that we find these three in their youth (together with a dozen other young courtiers) proclaiming that the King had given his Castle of Loyalty to four maidens of his Court, who had given the custody of it to them, and that they would defend it against all comers.[1] The whole story reads like a chapter in Malory, with Henry, like Arthur, entering the lists and tilting against his own knights, though with better success.

"Their marvellous enquests and adventures, the achieving of the Sangreal, and in the end the dolorous death and departing out of this world of them all."

Yet one of the defenders of the Castle of Loyalty came to feel that life at the Court was not consistent with mediæval ideas of knightly duty, and left the service of Henry VIII for a cell in the London Charterhouse. His name was Sebastian Newdigate. We have heard of Sebastian Newdigate already,[2] chained upright by neck and feet for seventeen days together. The tradition in Newdigate's family was that Henry visited him in prison, to break his constancy by an appeal to their old friendship. But, if ever the sweetness and savour of the Sangreal had been felt by the mortal senses of any men, it had been felt by Middlemore, Exmew and Newdigate, when Houghton was celebrating mass in the chapel of the London Charterhouse.[3] And they remained steadfast.

All that the Thirteenth Century imagined of Galahad or Percivale was surpassed by the true history of Sebastian Newdigate. You will search in vain for his name in our *Dictionary of National Biography*, but some fragments of his story will be found within the covers of this book.

And so passed the long summer days of 1535, the great dividing days of English history; during so many of which Sebastian Newdigate stood upright, defending the Castle of Loyalty in somewhat different fashion from that in which he had defended it at Greenwich in the sports of Christmas, 1524. Side by side with him stood William Exmew, who had written out with his own hand that copy of the

[1] Hall's *Henry VIII*, ed. Whibley. II. 21, etc.

[2] See above, p. cxxxi.

[3] These are the words of Chauncy, who must have been present:

"In illa conventuali Missa, sanctissima elevatione peracta, sibilus quidam auræ tenuis, exterius paululum sonans, interius vero multum operans, a pluribus percipitur et auditur auribus corporis, et ab omnibus sentitur et hauritur auribus cordis. Cujus dulci modulatione et sono venerabilis Pater Prior tactus, in tantam est divinæ illustrationis copiam et lacrymarum abundantiam resolutus, quod per longam moram in officio Missæ procedere nequibat. Conventus quoque stabat stupefactus, audiens quidem vocem ac sentiens miram et suavem operationem in corde, nesciens tamen unde veniat aut quo vadat." (Chauncy, *Historia aliquot martyrum anglorum*, ed. 1888, p. 96.)

Fourteenth Century *Cloud of Unknowing* which is now treasured by the Carthusians of Parkminster. And meantime More was writing in the Tower, in the margin of a black-letter Book of Hours,[1] those meditations and prayers which are the crown of the noble body of religious literature to which they belong. It would be sacrilege to quote from them here. Fisher meantime had been writing from the Tower to his sister Elizabeth, a nun of Dartford, *A Spiritual Consolation* and *The Ways to Perfect Religion*. And far away, in his prison at Vilvorde, Tyndale was asking for his Hebrew Bible, grammar and dictionary, that he might continue the translation of the Bible which, he had said long before, was to cause a boy that driveth the plough to know more of the Scripture than his ignorant opponents. "If God spared him life," had been his words. He was to be led out to execution next year, before his task was finished. Yet he had done enough. For, all the time, in some distant printing house, probably that of Froschouer in Zürich, the sheets of Coverdale's Bible were being slowly piled up for transport to England.

"Their marvellous enquests and adventures, the achieving of the Sangreal, and in the end the dolorous death and departing out of this world of them all."

Pecock, Fortescue, Capgrave, Caxton, even Malory, are but tributary to the main stream of continuous English prose, which runs strongest and deepest through the channel of our religious literature. And the Authorized Version of 1611 is the product of this early religious literature, not a miracle to be looked at in isolation.

XIII. Protestant and Catholic.

For although religious changes inevitably meant a change in the kind of books read, and many once popular books came to be studied only by a few recusants and a few refugees, nevertheless, we must be careful not to exaggerate the gulf.

It is possible to represent English prose and English scholarship as checked by Tudor despotism, surviving only among the exiles on the Continent, but handicapped on this side of the Channel, so that humanism only achieves its fulfilment three generations later than it had promised to do when Erasmus visited England. A statement on such lines[2] would have more truth, anyway, than the common misrepresentation which makes English prose begin with Wiclif or

[1] Now in the possession of the Earl of Denbigh.

[2] For a most brilliant account of this side of the case, see *Blessed Thomas More and the Arrest of Humanism in England*, by Prof. J. S. Phillimore, in the *Dublin Review*, Vol. 153 (1913), p. 1.

Protestant and Catholic.

Mandeville, and then vanish (save for a few isolated writers, Pecock, Malory, Fortescue, Caxton) till it reappears with Tyndale, or, as some would have it, with the Authorized Version of 1611.

But we must be cautious how we divide prose into Catholic and Protestant. For the leading reformers were not illiterate artisans, or peasants brought up on nothing but Wiclif's Bible. The important thing to remember is that, whatever side these leading men of the early Sixteenth Century took, they had for the most part received one and the same training. The religious quarrel concealed a continuity which it could not destroy. The dispute as to the expediency of translating the Scriptures into English does not mean that the English language was the peculiar property of the reforming party. Think of Cambridge early in the Sixteenth Century. Of the two great masters of English prose, More and Fisher, the one was High Steward and the other was Chancellor. The great patroness of Cambridge, the Lady Margaret, was a keen student of the works of Hilton,[1] and spent much of her time translating French works of devotion into English;[2] her translation (from a French version) of the Fourth Book of the *Imitatio Christi* was a "best seller" of the early Sixteenth Century. William Exmew, the Carthusian transcriber of the *Cloud*, and two of his fellow-martyrs[3] came, as the Elizabethan life of Fisher takes care to record, from the great foundations which were due to the foresight of Fisher and the munificence of the Lady Margaret. But from these same foundations came Ascham and Cheke, two Protestant champions of the English tongue, and above all of "clean English"; whilst Tyndale studied at Cambridge, Coverdale and Barnes belonged to the Austin Friars of Cambridge, Cranmer was a Fellow of Jesus, Latimer of Clare Hall. The essential thing is that the first generation of Protestants, Cranmer, Latimer, Tyndale, only became Protestants in middle life.

To what extent different enthusiasts for the vernacular may have learnt from each other it is difficult to say. We have a record of Dr.

[1] Wynkyn de Worde states that the Lady Margaret commanded him to print the 1494 edition of Hilton's *Scale*, "her grace for to deserue"; and it was probably his assiduity in printing the devotional books she loved which entitled him later to style himself "Prynter unto the moost excellent pryncesse my lady the kynges moder." See C. H. Cooper, *Memoir of Margaret, Countess of Richmond and Derby*, Cambridge, 1874.

[2] Fisher's Sermon "had at the moneth mynde of the noble prynces Margarete," *Works*, p. 295.

[3] Reynolds and Thomas Green or Greenwood. See also Dom L. Hendriks, *The London Charterhouse* (1889), p. 223, note, and p. 228. Sebastian Newdigate was also a Cambridge man, according to MS. Arundel 152, fol. 277.

Barnes attending a sermon of Fisher's;[1] but as Barnes was there in the character of a penitent, bearing a faggot on his shoulder, his stylistic studies were probably perfunctory. More and Tyndale studied each other's works with attention, and More even gave Tyndale lessons on English style:

Protestant and Catholic.

> And thys thing, lo, though it be no great matter, yet I have thought good to give Tindall warning of, because I would have him write true one way or other, that, though I cannot make him by no meane to write true matter, I would have him yet at the lestwise write true englishe.[2]

Tyndale, on the other hand, held More's writing to be "painted poetry, babbling eloquence."[3] Tyndale's objections are, however, not to More's English, but to his habit of illustrating his argument with digressions which Tyndale thought frivolous.

But, despite differences of style, *they both write the same English.*

More would have thought it a sad misuse of his *Treatise upon the passion of Christ*, that we should turn to it in order to extract the passages of translation, and compare them with Tyndale's "false" translation, to show how small is the difference. Yet let us venture to do so, trusting that (as More wrote in the Tower concerning two other controversialists) "they bee both twayne holye sayntes in heaven."

TYNDALE.	MORE.
And when supper was ended, after that the devyll had put in the hert of Iudas Iscariot Simons sonne, to betraye him:	And whan souper was done, whan the devyll hadde putte in to the hearte of Judas the sonne of Symon of Scaryoth to betraye hym:
Iesus knowinge that the father had geven all thinges into his hondes, and that he was come from God and went to God,	Jesus, knowynge that hys father hadde gyven hym althynges in to hys handes, and that hee was come from godde and goeth to godde,

[1] Bridgett's *Fisher*, p. 51.
[2] *Works*, 1557, p. 448.
[3] "With the confidence of his painted poetry, babbling eloquence, and juggling arguments of subtle sophistry, grounded on his 'unwritten verities' as true and as authentic as his story of Utopia." (*Exposition of Matthew, v, vi, vii*, in Tyndale's *Expositions*, ed. Walter, Parker Society, 1849, p. 100.)

Protestant and Catholic.

Tyndale.	More.
he rose from supper, and layde a syde his upper garmentes, and toke a towell, and gyrd him selfe.	aryseth fro supper, and putteth of hys clothes, and toke a lynnen clothe and dydde gyrde it aboute hym.
After that poured he water into a basyn, and beganne to wash his disciples fete, and to wype them with the towell, wherwith he was gyrde.	Than he dydde putte water in to a basyn, and beganne to weshe the feete of his dyscyples, and wype theym with the lynnen cloth that hee was gyrde wyth all.
Then came he to Simon Peter. And Peter sayde to him: Lorde shalt thou wesshe my fete?	Than commeth hee to Symon Peter, and Peter sayeth unto him: Lorde washest thou my feete?
Iesus answered and sayde unto him: What I do, thou wotest not now, but thou shalt knowe herafter.	Jesus aunswered and sayde unto hym: What I doe, thou knowest not nowe, but thou shalte knowe after.
Peter sayd unto him: Thou shalt not wesshe my fete whill the worlde stondeth. Iesus answered him: Yf I wasshe the not, thou shalt have no part with me.	Peter sayeth unto hym: Thou shalte never washe my feete. Jesus aunswered unto him: If I weshe the not, thou shalte have no parte wyth me.
Simon Peter sayde unto him: Lorde, not my fete only, but also my handes and my heed.	Symon Peter sayde unto hym: Lorde not onely my feete, but my handes and my heade to.
Iesus sayde to him: He that is wesshed, nedeth not save to wesshe his fete, and is clene every whit. And ye are clene: but not all.	Jesus sayeth unto hym: Hee that is wesshed needeth no more but that hee weshe hys feete, but is all cleane. And you be cleane: but not all.
For he knewe his betrayer. Therfore sayde he: Ye are not all clene.	For hee knewe who he was shulde betraye hym. Therefore he sayd: You be not clene all.
After he had wesshed their fete, and receaved his clothes, and was set doune agayne, he sayde unto them: Wot ye what I have done to you?	Than after that he had wesshed theyr feete, he toke his clothes agayne, and whan he was sette downe agayne at the table, he sayd unto them: Wote ye what I have done to you?

Protestant and Catholic.

TYNDALE.	MORE.
Ye call me master and Lorde, and ye saye well, for so am I.	You call me mayster and Lorde, and you saye well, for so I am.
If I then, youre Lorde and master, have wesshed youre fete, ye also ought to wesshe one anothers fete.	Therefore, yf I have wesshed youre feete, beinge youre lorde and youre mayster, you owe also one to weshe an others fete.
For I have geven you an ensample, that ye shuld do as I have done to you.	For I have given you an ensample, that likewise as I have doone to you, soo shoulde you doe to.
Verely, verely, I saye unto you, the servaunt is not greater then his master, nether the messenger greater then he that sent him.	Verely, verely, I saye to you, the bondemanne is not more than his lorde, nor an apostle greatter than hee that hath sente hym.
If ye understonde these thinges, happy are ye yf ye do them.[1]	If you know these thynges, blyssed shall you be if you doe these thynges.[2]

And, in the more rhetorical passages, More can rival the sweep of Coverdale's periods :

COVERDALE.	MORE.
What good hath oure pryde done unto us, or what profit hath the pompe of riches brought us? All those thinges are passed awaye like a shadowe . . . Or like as when an arowe is shott at a marck, it parteth the ayre, which immediatly commeth together agayne, so that a man can not knowe where it wente thorow. Even so we in like maner as soóne as we were borne, beganne	What hath pride profited us, or what good hath the glorye of our riches doone unto us? Passed are all those thinges like a shadowe . . . ; or lyke an arow shot out into the place appoynted : the ayer, that was divided, is by and by returned into the place, and in suche wise closed together again, that the way is not perceved in which the arow went. And in likewise we, as soone as we were borne, be by

[1] John, xiii. 2–17, quoted from Tyndale's edition of 1534, as given in Bagster's *Hexapla*.

[2] John, xiii. 2–17, translated by More, 1534–5, as given in *Works*, 1557, p. 1313.

Protestant and Catholic.

COVERDALE.	MORE.
immediatly to drawe to oure ende, and have shewed no token of vertue, but are consumed in oure owne wickednesse.[1]	and by vanished away, and have left no token of any good vertue behind us, but are consumed and wasted and come to nought in our malygnitie.[2]

Our ears are so accustomed to the cadences of the Authorized Version that we are apt to resent any departure from the wonted phraseology. It is a prejudice which it is very difficult indeed to conquer. Almost everywhere, when we compare the Authorized Version of 1611 with the Great Bible of 1540, the Authorized seems to have the advantage in melody. But in the *Psalter* we feel the exact reverse. Is this not largely because in the *Psalter* it is the phrases of 1540, not those of 1611, which we have by heart? Bishop Westcott finds the phrasing of the Rheims and Douai Bible unrhythmical, whilst admitting the wealth of its language.[3] So excellent a judge as Prof. Phillimore evidently preferred the Douai version, even on the score of prose rhythms.[4]

One value of the comparisons given above lies in the fact that, in these passages, More on the one hand, Tyndale or Coverdale on the other, are writing in absolute independence of each other.

There are differences, but they only serve to accentuate the general likeness. Tyndale gains greatly by observing strictly the old distinction of *ye* as nominative and *you* as accusative, which More, so ready to teach Tyndale the rules of English, strangely neglects. In vocabulary, on the other hand, More often has the advantage. And so, often, has the Douai Bible, which was made on principles which More would have approved.[5] And the revisers of the Authorized Version

[1] Wisdom, v. 8–13: Quid nobis profuit superbia? aut divitiarum jactantia quid contulit nobis? Transierunt omnia illa tanquam umbra . . . aut tanquam sagitta emissa in locum destinatum; divisus aer in se continuo reclusus est, ut ignoretur transitus illius. Sic et nos nati continuo desivimus esse, et virtutis quidem nullum signum valuimus ostendere: in malignitate autem nostra consumpti sumus.

[2] More, *Works*, 1557, p. 1199.

[3] *History of the English Bible*, third edit., 1905, p. 249.

[4] *The Arrest of Humanism in England*, in the *Dublin Review*, Vol. 153 (1913), p. 8.

[5] "And at this point let me suggest a theory of the literary history of English for this epoch: namely, that there was a bifurcation: a main-stream dammed, and a new cut opened; and after the new cut had carried off most of the water, the old stream reopened. Dryden is the meeting-point of the two channels. The true main-stream of English tradition in prose was in the line of Parsons, Campion, Allen and the translators of the Douai and Rheims Bible. These

were not above learning from the Douai version. The result is sometimes curious. Prof. Saintsbury quotes " The Charity passage of the First Epistle to the Corinthians " as one of the best examples known to him of absolutely perfect English prose.[1] But the Charity passage —as anyone can satisfy himself—is in the tradition, not of Coverdale and Tyndale, but of Douai and Thomas More.

Protestant and Catholic.

Yet, details apart, Protestant and Catholic speak the same language.

So that in one sense there is, and in one sense there is not, a Protestant schism in literature. There was no change of speech. But there was a change of outlook. It was impossible that those to whom a translation of the Gospels was accessible should be content to study the Life of Christ in Love's *Mirror*. The whole body of religious literature, so popular till about the time of More's death, ceased to be reprinted. Further, the religious quarrel kept the books of Roper, Cavendish, Harpsfield and Rastell from being printed, and so led to the loss of Rastell's *Life of More*. But, on the other hand, More's *Works* had been printed in one of the best edited and most magnificent volumes which the English press had produced : and though the religious changes prevented any further editions, the great book of 1557 must have had its influence. And we have seen that no religious prejudice prevented a frank acknowledgement of the merits of More's *Richard III*.

It is because they form a link between the two ages, that so much importance attaches to the works of Thomas Lupset, the recent edition of which by an American scholar is a splendid contribution to the history of English prose.[2]

More had befriended Lupset, who nevertheless was too old a man to be a typical member of his " school." Lupset is rather, like More himself, a scholar of Colet, and his works " serve as a means of connecting the humanism of Colet and Fisher with that of Elyot and Ascham."

---

are the inheritors of More. But these admirable writings, proscribed and destroyed by the Government of Elizabeth, have remained (such is the obscurantist force of ancient prejudice) unknown not merely to the blinkered schoolboy but even to many professors and students of literature in our own time. A critical comparison of the prose rhythms in the Catholic and the Government Bible would be a most interesting study.'' (Phillimore in the *Dublin Review*, as above, p. 8, footnote.)

[1] *Elizabethan Literature*, p. 217; *Specimens of English Prose Style*, p. xl.

[2] *The Life and Works of Thomas Lupset*, by John Archer Gee. Yale University Press, 1928.

Protestant and Catholic.

Lupset's themes are those of the ordinary mediæval book of devotion: "A treatise of charitie" addressed to his "good sister" (apparently not a sister by birth; rather, we may guess, an inmate of a religious house) or "A treatise of dieying well." But the treatment shows the influence of humanism, and it can be claimed for the style that, if it does not show the wide range and power of More, it has no trace of the carelessness into which the great Chancellor, writing his long controversial books in hours stolen from sleep, is betrayed by his weariness. Lupset's prose "in its phrasing and sentence structure" has claims to be "a more capable instrument for the idiomatic, lucid and graceful expression of ideas than any English prose of earlier date." [1]

Lupset was *vir in omnibus festinabundus*: he printed More's *Utopia* without permission, and More pleaded Lupset's cause with Erasmus, when the great scholar had to admonish his young admirer for not having been sufficiently careful over the secret of *Julius Exclusus*. We may conjecture that, had he lived into the times of trouble, Lupset, unless the years had brought discretion, might have met an end as violent as that of some of his scholar-friends. But he had done nothing to offend either side when he died in early middle age in 1530. So his books were repeatedly printed in the reign of Henry VIII, and a collected edition appeared early in that of Elizabeth.

Individual books disappear. Much was lost. Much was gained. But the Reformation did not break the continuity of English prose.

XIV. More as the Great Restorer of English Prose.

After this very hurried examination of English prose from the Ninth Century to the Sixteenth, we should, at any rate, be in a position to judge better between the critics of the beginning of the Nineteenth Century, who tell us that More is the father of modern English prose, and those of the beginning of the Twentieth, who will have it that his place in the strict history of English literature is very small.[2]

It was undoubtedly the rediscovery of Malory which led to the depreciation of More; and some of the praise given to More must be admitted to be excessive, as soon as we realize what Malory had done

[1] *Life and Works*, p. xiii. [2] See above, pp. lii–iii.

More the Restorer of English Prose.

before More was born. But in the history of literature we have to consider not merely what writers charm us, but what writers influenced their age, and how.

Few of us nowadays, if any, can read More's *Richard III* with the delight with which we read Malory or Berners. Yet we have seen the place Ascham gives to *Richard III*, whilst he has mere contempt for Malory. Ben Jonson in his *Grammar* never mentions Malory, and quotes Berners once only. But More is the prose writer whom he most frequently quotes: clearly, in Jonson's view, More occupied a special position. Chaucer, Gower, Lydgate and More are to Jonson the four standard English writers of the past age. Whatever Malory may mean to us, neither the style nor the ideals of the *Morte Darthur* gave the men of the Sixteenth Century all they needed.

If it be asked why a man like More, brought up in the traditions of English religious prose, should "content all men," whilst Malory contented some, but annoyed others, a good many answers can be given.

In the first place, although there were doubtless as many frivolous people in the reign of Henry VIII as at any other time of the world's history, nevertheless the people most interested in the writing of English prose were all very much in earnest: Colet and Fisher; Tyndale, Frith and Barnes; Coverdale, Cranmer and Latimer; Elyot and Leland; Roper, Cavendish, Harpsfield and Rastell; Cheke and Ascham—every man of them is too serious to care much for romance. More could give his contemporaries what they wanted; for he had inherited all the seriousness of the religious literature of the Fourteenth and Fifteenth Centuries, but without any imitation of the manners of a former age. More is, in some ways, the antithesis of his fellow-martyr, Sebastian Newdigate. The feats of chivalry of Newdigate the courtier, reminiscent of Arthurian romance, would never have interested More; and, after a long struggle, More had also decided that the Carthusian's life was not for him.

And, whilst here and there a Sebastian Newdigate could be found passing from tournaments with kings to the hermit cell of the Charter-house, no ideals could have been more opposed to those of the Sixteenth Century than the ideals of the *Morte Darthur*. To lead one's life, like Lancelot, as a knight errant, till the time came to end it in a state of perfection with penance and prayers and fastings—such was not the wish of the men who dominated Sixteenth-Century England: "the ideal of going out of the world to seek

More the Restorer of English Prose.

something which cannot be valued in terms of pounds, shillings and pence, is abhorrent to a busy, industrial age."[1] More's contemporaries needed, for the practical purposes of their age, other forms of prose than those by which Malory had put new life into the century-old tales of Lancelot and Galahad, or in which Berners had interpreted Froissart to an English public: Malory's style, "beautiful in itself, was not suited for general purposes—for historical, political, theological, philosophical, scientific and miscellaneous writing."[2] Whatever pleasure it may have given to the lighter-hearted, the humanist was not interested in a decaying chivalry; and the earnest heretic and the earnest orthodox did not care for toys. What really annoys Ascham is the inconsequence of the innumerable episodes: "those be counted the noblest knights that do kill most men without any quarrel." It does not worry *us* if the court of King Arthur sometimes reminds us of *Alice in Wonderland.* Whilst Lancelot is absent, Sir Mador de la Porte, upon no evidence whatever, accuses the unfortunate Guinevere of murder. Whereupon King Arthur, albeit convinced of his wife's innocence, announces that he must be a rightful judge, and therefore Guinevere must be burnt unless some knight will put his body in jeopardy to fight for his queen. We might expect that, in the words of Burke, ten thousand swords must have leaped from their scabbards. But no: the Table Round, one and all, refuse. The queen goes down on her knees to Sir Bors, and, at Arthur's request, he grudgingly consents. Lancelot arrives, and all ends happily. Ascham might have said: "This is good stuff for honest men to take pleasure at." Malory has thrown over it all the glamour of his noble style, so that we feel that his knights, "given the atmosphere, are consistent with themselves and their circumstances." But we must not ask a Sixteenth-Century humanist to accept that atmosphere. Ascham has been held up to scorn for his denunciation of *Morte Darthur*: he has been called a prude and a puritan. But, with his study full of the masterpieces of Greece and Rome, he feels it to be a silly book. He does not think this out-of-date mediævalism dangerous, as dangerous books go; but there is no doubt about his contempt.

Now the Fourteenth-Century religious writers can give us, together with a style not inferior to Malory's, an intensity to which Malory rises only now and again. More's religious writing belongs to the

[1] Pollard, *Henry VIII*, p. 342.
[2] Saintsbury, *First Book of English Literature*, 1914, p. 61.

Sixteenth-Century world, not to the Fourteenth-Century cloister. But in words like the following we feel all the passionate seriousness which we find in Hilton; the preacher is standing aloof from the concerns of men, and marvelling at them:

More the Restorer of English Prose.

> I remember me of a thefe once cast at Newgate, that cut a purse at the barre when he shold be hanged on the morow. And when he was asked why he dyd so, knowing that he shoold dye so shortelye, the desperate wretche sayd, that it didde his heart good, to be lorde of that purse, one nyght yet. And in good faythe me thynketh, as muche as wee wonder at hym, yet se we many that do much like, of whom we nothynge wonder at all. I let passe olde priestes that sewe for vowsons of yonger priestes benefices. I let passe olde men that hove and gape to be executours to some that be yonger than themself: whose goodes if thei wold fal, they recken wold do them good to have in their keping yet one yere ere they dye.[1]

And then More bursts into that alliterative passage, already quoted,[2] which reminds us of the tradition which Richard Rolle had inherited from the times of Ælfric.

And this shows us another reason why the tradition of religious literature meant more to Sixteenth-Century England than Malory's romance could mean: a reason which is to be found in Chaucer's words, "Lancelot is dead." But the Seven Deadly Sins are always very much alive.

A religious writer or speaker must deal with his own age; and he must deal with character. His business is with the ways of the spirit of man. And he will often need to express these ways dramatically. We have seen the intensity with which sinners are depicted in the *Ancren Riwle*. Dr. Johnson said, very unjustly, that there was more knowledge of the human heart in one letter of Richardson than in all *Tom Jones*. In one sense there is more knowledge of the human heart in the one paragraph quoted above from the *Ancren Riwle*[3] (and in many another that might be quoted from the same book or from the later devotional writers) than in all the *Morte Darthur*. The piteous history of the last two books of Malory is grounded on the mortal quarrel which has grown up between those two noble knights and firm friends, Gawayne and Lancelot; yet, earlier, Gawayne and his brethren have been pictured as "the greatest destroyers and murderers of good knights that be now in

[1] More, *Works*, col. 93. [2] See above, p. cxxiv.
[3] See above, pp. xcvi–vii.

More the Restorer of English Prose.

this realm," and secret haters of Lancelot.[1] To us, much of the charm of Malory lies in the variety of the ideals animating the different stories which he has taken over, sometimes only half understanding them. But this variety does not make for elaborate or consistent drawing of character.

Ascham, however, demands of narrative that it show "the inward disposition of the mind," as Thucydides or Homer or Chaucer had done.[2] And he finds that More "contents all men" in his *Richard III*. More had been trained by the religious literature. We may grow weary of the Seven Deadly Sins; but Langland and many another writer show what excellent opportunities they give for the sketching of character. The mischief-maker[3] is sketched by More in words which remind us of the *Ancren Riwle*. Here is the vain man; he is really Cardinal Wolsey, but he comes into a discourse on the sin of Flattery:

> The selfesame prelate that I tolde you my tale of, (I dare be bolde to sweare it, I knowe it so surelye) had on a time made of his own drawyng, a certayne treatice that shoulde serve for a leage betwene that countrey and a greate prynce. In which treatice hymselfe thought that he hadde devised his artycles so wysely and endicted them so well, that all the worlde woulde allowe them. Whereupon longing sore to bee praysed, he called unto him a frend of his, a manne well learned, and of good worshippe, and very wel expert in those matters, as he that hadde bene divers times Embassiator for that countrey, and had made many suche treatices himself. Whan he toke him the treatise, and that he hadde redde it, he asked hym howe he lyked it, and sayde: "But I praye you heartelye tell me the verye trouth." And that he spake so heartelye, that the tother hadde wente he woulde fayne have heard the trouth. And in truste thereof, he tolde hym a faulte therein, at the hearyng whereof, he sware in great anger, "By the masse thou art a verye foole." The tother afterwarde tolde mee, that he would never tell hym trouth agayn.[4]

Malory's world is a narrow one: kings, queens, knights, ladies, and hermits who are knights or archbishops in retreat. But the world of the Sixteenth Century was not exclusively aristocratic, and the religious writers had never been so either. The mother playing with

[1] Book X, caps. 55, 58.
[2] Letter to John Astley. See above, p. cxx.
[3] The passage (in the *Apology*) is summarized by Harpsfield. See p. 130, below.
[4] More, *Works*, 1557, p. 1223.

More the Restorer of English Prose.

her child, we have seen,[1] is one of the most enduring things in English literature, at least as old as the *Ancren Riwle* and found in a tract printed by Wynkyn de Worde. And here is a very similar picture, as Sir Thomas More draws it. More is illustrating the flattery of those spiritual advisers who will not tell great men the truth about their deeds. He is thinking, no doubt, of Henry VIII, "with flattery shamefully abused" by "a weak clergy, lacking grace constantly to stand to their learning." But the picture is drawn from the door of a London house:

> And in such wise deale they wyth him as the mother doth sometyme wyth her chyld; which when the litle boy wyl not ryse in tyme for her, but lye styl a bed and slugge, and when he is up weepeth because he hath lien so long, fearyng to be beaten at scoole for hys late commyng thither, she telleth hym then that it is but earely dayes, and he shal com time inough, and biddeth hym "Go, good sonne, I warrant the, I have sent to thy mayster myself, take thy breade and butter with thee, thou shalt not be beaten at al." And thus, so she may send him mery forth at the dore that he weepe not in her sighte at home, she studieth not much uppon the matter though he be taken tardy and beaten when he cometh to scoole.[2]

Above all, the Sixteenth Century needed oratory rather than romance, for the policy of Henry was to encourage a parliament which he knew how to make into a useful tool. Wolsey had disliked parliaments; but when he was once out of the way, Parliament sat often and long—provided it did, in the end, what was wanted, Henry

[1] See above, p. c.

[2] More, *Works*, 1557, p. 1156. The life-like illustration of commonplaces of the pulpit results sometimes in very close parallels between the *Ancren Riwle* and More. For example—God uses the wicked as his instruments to punish the good; but, nevertheless, he will, in the end, cast the wicked into the fire, as the parent throws into the fire the rod with which he has beaten the child for his good:

Ancren Riwle, (ed. Morton, Camden Soc., p. 184):

> Vor ase þe ueder hwon he haueð inouh ibeaten his child & haueð ituht hit wel, he worpeð þe ȝerd into þe fure, uor heo is nouht nanmore; al so þe ueder of heouene, hwon he haueð ibeaten wel mid one unwreste monne oðer wummon his leoue child uor his gode, he worpeþ þe ȝerd into þe fure of helle: þet is þen unwreste mon.

More, *Apology* (ed. Taft, p. 182; *Works*, p. 922); God suffers the heretics for a time, but they will not be able to prevail against the catholic faith:

> And all the myschyef shall be theyr owne at lengthe, though God for our synne suffer them for a scourge to prevayle in some places here and there for a whyle; whom upon mennes amendement he wyll not fayle to serve at the last, as doth the tender mother, whyche, when she hath beten her chylde for his wantonnes, wypeth hys eyen and kysseth hym, and casteth the rodde in the fyre.

More the Restorer of English Prose.

wished it to talk. Where were patterns of parliamentary eloquence to be found better than in the long tradition of religious rhetoric? And here there was certainly a danger.

The most finished pulpit eloquence of the day is to be found in the sermons of Fisher, whom it has been customary of late to applaud as a writer altogether superior to More. It is urged that More's prose, "as it cannot compare for richness, colour, and representative effect with the style of Berners . . . so it is not to be mentioned with that of Fisher for nice rhetorical artifice and intelligent employment of craftsman-like methods of work." [1]

Now the merit of Fisher's oratory no one will deny. For purposes of comparison with More we will take the extract which Mr. Saintsbury has himself selected:

> That man were put in grete peryll and Ieopardy that sholde hange over a very depe pyt holden up by a weyke and sclender corde or lyne, in whose botome sholde be moost woode and cruell beestes of every kynde, abydynge with grete desyre his fallynge downe, for that entent when he shall fall downe anone to devoure hym, whiche lyne or corde that he hangeth by sholde be holden up and stayed onely by the handes of that man, to whome by his manyfolde ungentylnes he hath ordred and made hymselfe as a very enemy. Lyke wyse dere frendes consyder in yourselfe. If now under me were suche a very depe pytte, wherein myght be lyons, tygres, and beres gapynge with open mouth to destroye and devoure me at my fallynge downe, and that there be noo thynge wherby I myght be holden up and socoured, but a broken boket or payle whiche sholde hange by a small corde, stayed and holden up onely by the handes of hym, to whome I have behaved myselfe as an enemye and adversarye by grete and grevous iniuryes and wronges done unto hym, wolde ye not thynke me in peryllous condycyons? [2]

All this is clear, dignified and eloquent. But when we are asked to admire the "simple but extraordinarily effective plan of coupling a Saxon and a Latin word," [3] we may question if so much coupling in one short paragraph is not rather too generous a use of this figure of speech. Surely duplication, like alliteration, is more effective if not overdone. Are we not getting dangerously near "Indenture English"?

And Berners too, when he tries to be eloquent (which fortunately is not often), falls into this trick of duplication, or even triplication.

[1] Saintsbury, *Short History of English Literature*, 1905, p. 212.
[2] Fisher, *English Works*, ed. Mayor; E.E.T.S., pp. 90–91.
[3] Saintsbury, as above, p. 211.

More the Restorer of English Prose.

Prof. Saintsbury tolerates it as "the novice's practice in a real art": [1]

> What condygne graces and thankes ought men to gyve to the writers of historyes, who with their great labours, have done so moche profyte to the humayne lyfe? They shewe, open, manifest and declare to the reder, by example of olde antyquite, what we shulde enquere, desyre, and folowe; and also, what we shulde eschewe, avoyde, and utterly flye; for whan we (beynge unexpert of chaunces) se, beholde, and rede the auncyent actes, gestes, and dedes, howe and with what labours, daungers, and paryls they were gested and done, they right greatly admonest, ensigne, and teche us howe we maye lede forthe our lyves. And farther, he that hath the perfyte knowledge of others joye, welthe, and highe prosperite, and also trouble, sorowe, and great adversyte, hath thexpert doctryne of all parylles.[2]

As a rhetorical device repetition has its uses. It is in place in the General Confession. But it needs to be used only when it is rhetorically justifiable: sparingly, as More uses it, or as Ascham later uses it. In the very passage [3] in which Ascham censures Hall's "Indenture English," he has himself used, more than once, this trick of coupled synonyms; but with discretion. Or, again, it needs to be used as Pecock uses it, with different shades of meaning in the synonyms—as Hooker uses it to amplify and vary his argument.[4]

But when we are asked to admire Berners' Preface as "the novice's practice in a real art," the answer surely is—What right has Berners to be a novice? If he was not satisfied in his Preface to use the noble, simple style which he uses in translating Froissart, if he needed something more rhetorical, the London printing presses in his day were turning out edition after edition of the most moving and artistic English prose, which might have served as a pattern for his rhetoric.

More brings English eloquence from the cloister where it had taken refuge, and applies it to the needs of Sixteenth-Century England. Thereby he deserves the title which Mackintosh gave him long ago, of restorer of political eloquence. He knows all the tricks. He couples synonyms together when it suits his purpose; but he does not do it with the maddening persistency which Berners, or Elyot, or

[1] *History of English Prose Rhythm*, 1912, p. 95.
[2] Berners' *Froissart*, Translator's Preface.
[3] See above, p. cxx.
[4] Pecock, *Folewer*, ed. E. V. Hitchcock, E.E.T.S., 1924. Introduction, pp. lxii–lxiii.

More the Restorer of English Prose.

Hall, or even Fisher displays: a persistency which had become a real danger to English style. In the same way More uses balanced sentences, and sometimes emphasizes the balance with alliteration, sometimes even with cross-alliteration; the most characteristic cadences of Lyly's *Euphues* are anticipated.[1] But when More has once achieved them, he goes on and tries something else, instead of repeating the trick with the reiterated folly of Lyly.

The way More applies this pulpit eloquence to a political purpose can be seen in a few sentences from the speech which he puts into the mouth of Edward IV on his deathbed. The king is exhorting his Council to unity, for the sake of his young son:

> That we be al men, that we be christen men, this shall I leave for prechers to tel you (and yet I wote nere whither any preachers woordes ought more to move you, then his that is by and by gooyng to the place that thei all preache of). But this shal I desire you to remember, that the one parte of you is of my bloode, the other of myne alies,[2] and eche of yow with other, eyther of kinred or affinitie, whiche spirytuall kynred of affynyty, if the sacramentes of Christes Churche beare that weyghte with us that woulde Godde thei did, shoulde no lesse move us to charitye, then the respecte of fleshlye consanguinitye. Oure Lorde forbydde, that you love together the worse, for the selfe cause that you ought to love the better. And yet that happeneth. And no where fynde wee so deadlye debate, as amonge them, whyche by nature and lawe moste oughte to agree together. Suche a pestilente serpente is ambicion and desyre of vaineglorye and soveraintye, whiche amonge states [3] where he once entreth crepeth foorth so farre, tyll with devision and variaunce hee turneth all to mischiefe. Firste longing to be nexte the best, afterwarde egall with the beste, and at laste chiefe and above the beste. Of which immoderate appetite of woorship, and thereby of debate and dissencion, what losse, what sorowe, what trouble hathe within these fewe yeares growen in this realme, I praye Godde as well forgeate as wee well remember.
>
> Whiche thinges yf I coulde as well have foresene, as I have with my more payne then pleasure proved, by Goddes blessed Ladie (that was ever his othe) I woulde never have won the courtesye of mennes knees, with the losse of soo many heades.

And so the king's dying speech works up to its climax:

[1] . . . rather by pleasaunte advyse too wynne themselfe favour, then by profitable advertisemente to do the children good . . . lest those that have not letted to put them in duresse without colour, wil let as lytle to procure their distruccion without cause. (*Works*, 1557, pp. 38, 49.)

[2] Kindred by marriage.

[3] = "estates" = "men of high rank."

Wherfore in these last wordes that ever I looke to speake with you, I exhort you and require you al, for the love that you have ever borne to me, for the love that I have ever born to you, for the love that our lord beareth to us all, from this time forwarde, all grieves forgotten, eche of you love other. Whiche I verelye truste you will, if ye any thing earthly regard, either godde or your king, affinitie or kinred, this realme, your owne countrey, or your owne surety.[1]

More the Restorer of English Prose.

XV. More and his School: Use of Dialogue: The Chelsea Academy of Dramatic Art.

But the most astonishing thing in More's prose is the dialogue. It sometimes seems as if the great house at Chelsea must have been an academy of dramatic writing and thinking. And this not only in the ways which Prof. A. W. Reed has pointed out. More, as a youth, first drew attention to his ability by the skill with which he could play an impromptu part in an interlude. It is this dramatic temper which gives the *Utopia* its peculiar literary attraction, whilst at the same time it enables More, without committing himself, to put the case for and, more briefly, against Communism; to state the dangers, and, on the other hand, the duty, of serving the king, at the time when he was himself hesitating whether he should enter Henry's service or no.

When he has to combat the heretics, it is on the dialogue that he falls back; and again when, in prison, he has to face the question how far a man may rightly submit to those who would force his conscience.

The dramatic power is so strong in him that sometimes he seems to let the damned Whigs have the best of it. It is this dramatic power which his enemies could not understand. They scoff at him as a "poet,"[2] and they doubt his sincerity.[3] Even in modern times some of his admirers have been led to doubt whether he really felt the seriousness of the situation he had to meet;[4] as his contemporaries disapproved of his acting a humorous part, even on the scaffold.[5]

[1] More, *Works*, 1557, p. 39.
[2] Tyndale, *Expositions*, ed. Walter, Parker Society, 1849, p. 100; Foxe, *Acts and Monuments*, ed. Pratt, IV, 643, 679.
[3] Tyndale, *ibid.*; Bale, *Scriptorum illustrium Catalogus*, 1557, p. 655: "pontificum et Pharisæorum crudelitati ex auaritia subseruiens."
[4] *E.g.* Krapp, *Rise of English Literary Prose*, p. 99.
[5] For example, Hall; see his *Henry VIII*, ed. Charles Whibley, II, pp. 265–6.

More and his School: their use of Dialogue.

I fancy that those who listened to the talk at More's table heard scraps of drama hardly inferior to what might have been heard some eighty years later when a play of Shakespeare's was being acted at the Globe. More's dramatic talent, which had aroused Morton's admiration, could not be suppressed. We know the difficulties under which More wrote his controversial works—in watches of the night, utterly weary; so that later, when in great straits of poverty, he told his friends he would not have done it for any sum of money. Yet, however weary, he could not keep this drama out of his theological discussion.

Many of these dramatic pieces are autobiographical, and Harpsfield made booty of them for his *Life*.[1] Many of them might pass as the work of some writer in Stuart days, who had learnt from Shakespeare. And the range of *dramatis personæ* is hardly inferior. The king is, of course, kept out of it; but the persons rank from Cardinal Wolsey to the humblest yokel. Wolsey we have already heard.[2] Here is the yokel giving evidence before a Commission appointed to inquire into the silting up of Sandwich haven:

> and some laying the fault to Goodwyn sandes, some to the landes inned by dyvers owners in the Isle of Tenate, out of the chanell in which the sea was wont to compasse the Isle and bryng the vessels rounde about it (whose course at the ebbe was wont to scoure the haven, whiche nowe the Sea excluded thence, for lack of such course and scouryng is choked up with sande); as they thus alledged, divers men, divers causes, there starte up one good old father and said, "Ye masters, say every man what he wil, cha marked this matter [as] wel as som other. And, by God, I wote how it waxed nought, well ynough. For I knewe it good, and have marked, so chave, whan it began to waxe worse." "And what hath hurt it, good father?" quod the gentlemen. "By my fayth, maisters," quod he, "yonder same Tenterden steple and nothyng els, that by the masse cholde twere a faire fish pole." "Why hath the steple hurt the haven, good father?" quod they. "Nay by'r Ladye maisters," quod he, "yche cannot tell you well why, but chote well it hath. For, by God, I knew it a good haven till that steple was bylded. And by the Mary masse, cha marked it well, it never throve since."[3]

And here we have some townsmen: the very ancestors of the First, Second and Third Citizens of Shakespeare. It is again an examination before divers great lords, spiritual and temporal, this time to take evidence as to the death of Richard Hunne:

[1] See below, especially pp. 94–5, 95–7.
[2] See above, p. clii.
[3] More, *Works*, 1557, p. 278.

More and his School: their use of Dialogue.

The greatest temporall Lorde there presente, sayde unto a cerayne servaunte of hys owne standynge there beside, "Syr, ye tolde me that one shewed you that he coulde goe take hym by the sleeve that kylled Hunne. Have ye broughte hym hether?" "Syr," quod he, "if it lyke your Lordeshyp, thys manne it was that told me so": poynting to one that he had caused to come thether. Than my Lorde asked that man, "Howe saye ye, syr? can ye dooe as ye sayde ye coulde?" "Forsoothe, my Lorde," quod he, "and it lyke youre Lordeshyppe I sayde not so muche, thys gentleman did sumwhat myssetake me. But in dede I told hym that I hadde a neighbour that told me that he coulde doe it." "Where is that neighbour?" quod my Lorde. "Thys man, syr," quod he, bryng[ing] furth one whiche had also been warned to be there. Than was he asked whether he had sayde that he coulde doe it. "Naye, forsoothe," quod he, "my Lorde, I sayde not that I could doe it my selfe: but I sayde that one told me that he could doe it." "Well," quod my lord, "who tolde you so?" "Forsoth, my lord," quod he, "my neyghbour here." Than was that man asked, "Sir, know you one that can tell who kylled Richarde Hunne?" "Forsoothe," quod he, "and it lyke your Lordeshippe, I sayd not that I knew one surely that could tell who hadde killed hym; but I sayde in dede that I knowe one which I thought verelye could tell who kylled him." "Wel," quod the Lordes, "at the last, yet with muche worke, we come to somwhat. But wherby thinke you that he can tell?" "Nay, forsothe, my Lord," quod he, "it is a womanne: I woulde she were here with youre Lordeshyppes nowe." "Well," quod my Lorde, "woman or man all is one, she shal be hadde wheresoever she be." "By my fayth, my Lordes," quod he, "and she were with you, she woulde tell you wonders. For, by God, I have wyst her to tell manye mervaylous thynges ere nowe." "Why," quod the Lordes, "what have you hearde her tolde?" "Forsothe, my Lordes," quod he, "if a thynge hadde been stolen, she would have tolde who hadde it. And therefore I thynke she could as wel tel who killed Hunne, as who stale an horse." "Surelye," sayde the Lordes, "so thynke all we too, I trowe. But howe coulde she tell it? by the devill?" "Naye, by my trouth, I trowe," quod he, "for I could never see her use anye worse waye than lookinge in ones hande." Therewith the Lordes laughed and asked, "What is she?" "Forsoothe, my Lordes," quod he, "an Egipcian, and she was lodged here at Lambeth, but she is gone over sea now. Howbeit, I trowe she be not in her own countrey yet; for they saye it is a great way hence, and she went over litle more than a moneth agoe." [1]

And here we have the great lady—the "stout master woman"—

[1] More, *Works*, 1557, p. 236.

More and his School: their use of Dialogue.

of the upper or upper-middle class. The man who should dare to pit himself against the many-sided abilities of any of Shakespeare's matrons would deserve the fate of Falstaff. Yet, if we put into one room Volumnia and Lady Capulet, Mistress Ford and Mistress Page, the Countess of Roussillon and Lady Macbeth, Mistress Alice More could hold her own with the best of them, without feeling a moment's embarrassment.

More brings Mistress Alice, under the thinnest veil of anonymity, into the *Confutation of Tyndale's Answer*, where he tells how a husband made an unsuccessful attempt to teach his wife science, explaining how the earth is the centre of all things, and how the centre of the earth is consequently the lowest spot in creation, from which everything ascends in every direction. More makes the husband explain how, if a hole were bored through the earth, and a millstone thrown down it, the millstone would fall to the centre, and there would stop; because if it went beyond the centre it would be falling upwards, " from a lower place to a higher " :

> Now whyle he was tellyng her thys tale, she nothing went about to consider hys wordes; but as she was wont in all other thinges, studyed all the whyle nothing elles but what she myght saye to the contrary. And when he hadde wyth much work and oft interrupting, brought at last his tale to an ende, " Wel," quod she to him as Tindal sayth to me, " I wil argue like and make you a lyke sample. My mayde hath yonder a spynning wheele—or els, bicause al your reason reasteth in the roundnes of the world, come hither, thou gyrle, take out thy spindle and bryng me hither the wharle. Lo sir! ye make ymaginacions, I can not tell you what. But here is a wharle, and it is round as the world is; and we shal not neede to ymagin an hole bored thorow, for it hath an hole bored through in deede. But yet because ye go by imaginacions, I wyl imagin with you. Ymagin me now that thys wharle were ten myle thycke on everye syde, and this hole thorow it stil, and so great that a myl stone might wel go thorowe it: now if the wharle stoode on the tone end, and a mil stone wer throwen in above at the tother end, would it go no further than the myds, trow you? By god, if one threwe in a stone no bigger then an egge, I wene if ye stoode in the nether ende of the hole five myle byneth the myddes, it would give you a patte upon the pate that it would make you claw your head, and yet should ye feele none itche at all." [1]

This is not used by Harpsfield; but several other anecdotes of Lady Alice, some taken from Roper, some from More himself, will be found

[1] More, *Works*, 1557, p. 628.

More and his School: their use of Dialogue.

below.[1] It is obvious that Roper had not spent sixteen years in More's household for nothing, as we can see if we turn to the dialogue which Harpsfield gives from his report.[2]

It is one of the losses of English literature that Roper, who had learnt from Sir Thomas More this power of letting his characters speak, should have written so little. He moved among the great men of four reigns. He saw mediæval England pass into modern England. What he tells us is confined to sixty duodecimo pages.

In Roper we have, at last, a writer whom we can class with the great pre-Conquest writers of the *Anglo-Saxon Chronicle*: a man who can tell his tale, and leave it to work its effect, without any attempt to enforce it. Neither More nor Harpsfield, who are so strongly in the sermon tradition, quite do this.

Precisely as the strength of the Anglo-Saxon narrative is brought out when we compare Freeman's paraphrase, so Roper's power is emphasized by a comparison with modern biographers—albeit some of them are no mean writers. Turn to the narrative of Sir James Mackintosh. Following Roper, Mackintosh tells how More at his trial denied the statement of Sir Richard Rich in a way which deeply wounded Rich's credit. Then, Sir James continues, Rich

> was compelled to call Sir Richard Southwell and Mr. Palmer, who were present at the conversation, to prop his tottering evidence. They made a paltry excuse, by alleging that they were so occupied in removing More's books that they did not listen to the words of this extraordinary conversation.

Of course, the statement of Southwell and Palmer, that they took no heed to the talk, *was* an excuse: Cavendish tells how he made exactly the same excuse when he knew that to speak the truth would ruin him. The conversation *was* so extraordinary that the bystanders must have listened to it; and even if they had been momentarily inattentive, still Rich, if he had gained his object by extracting the words, would certainly have called upon Southwell and Palmer to witness that they had been spoken.

All these things are obvious, and they are emphasized by Mackintosh's adjectives—"paltry excuse," "extraordinary conversation." Yet, if we turn to p. 192 below, we see how much more effective is Roper's simplicity, which leaves the reader to draw his own conclusion.

It is not inappropriate to use the word "miracle" of Roper's refusal

[1] pp. 94–8. [2] See pp. 95–7.

More and his School: their use of Dialogue.

to preach. In his youth, Harpsfield tells us, Roper longed sore to be pulpited, and would have sacrificed much of his very large estate for a chance of preaching at Paul's Cross. This concionatory devil was exorcised, Harpsfield tells us, by the prayers of Sir Thomas More.

The combination, in Roper, of passionate narrative power with quiet self-effacement gives us something which it is hard to parallel in English prose between about 1052 and 1556. And Roper adds all the dramatic skill which characterizes the school of More.

Perhaps the most remarkable proof of this dramatic power of the Chelsea household is in the so-called letter of Margaret Roper to Lady Alington. This is a report of a dialogue in prison between More and Margaret. It is about the length of Plato's *Crito*, to which indeed, in many ways, it forms a striking parallel. Now when, after the death of More and Margaret, this letter was printed, More's own circle could not decide whether the real writer was More or his daughter. And the letter remains a puzzle. The speeches of More are absolute More; and the speeches of Margaret are absolute Margaret. And we have to leave it at that.

And the short letter of Lady Alington, More's step-daughter and a member of his Academy, is hardly less noteworthy. She tells how she has interceded for More with the new Chancellor. The letter is written in haste; but there Lord Audeley stands before us: the poor tool chosen to follow the mighty Chancellors of an earlier age, Morton, Warham, Wolsey, More. He is painted in a few telling strokes: a third-rate time-server, boasting that he has no learning, laughing at his own feeble jokes, callously refusing help. Lady Alington writes well, without any of these adjectives or adverbs which I have used; it is only at the end that her feeling bursts out:

> Now, my good sister, hath not my lord tolde me two prety fables? In good fayth they pleased me nothing, nor I wist not what to say, for I was abashed of this aunswer. And I see no better suite than to Almightie God. For he is the comforter of all sorowes.[1]

William Rastell, More's nephew, has this same power of reproducing a vivid dialogue, as anyone can satisfy himself who will read his report of what passed between Fisher and the Lieutenant of the Tower on the morning of Fisher's execution.[2]

Of the sense of proportion and structure which More shows so markedly in *Richard III*, Roper has nothing. We cannot judge from

[1] More, *Works*, 1557, p. 1434. [2] pp. 242–3, below.

More and his School: their use of Dialogue.

the very fragmentary remains of Rastell's *Life* how far he had this gift. But Harpsfield's *Life of More* has a finished design and a power of marshalling and arranging material which shows that More's example had not been lost on him: with Harpsfield in front of us, we must feel that there was one man at any rate who did not "fail to profit by so fine an example of artistry and restraint"[1] as More's *Richard III*. In addition, Harpsfield owed to More's other works a good many of the anecdotes with which he has enlivened his story. Harpsfield could tell a tale quite well, as he has shown elsewhere; but we do not get many examples of this in his *Life of More*, for he has drawn almost all his narratives from one authentic source or another, and is too faithful to vary the language, or to attempt to recast the tale. Yet that Harpsfield has the knack, as well as Roper or Rastell or More himself, is shown by the gusto with which he tells of Roper's temporary lapse into heresy. Harpsfield is obviously enjoying himself. These four pages say much for the honesty of Harpsfield and the good-nature of Roper.

Use of Dialogue by Cavendish.

Unlike Roper or Rastell or Harpsfield, Cavendish does not seem to have come directly under More's influence. He was married to a relative of More—but there seems no proof of their ever having met, though we know that during a quarter of a century Cavendish was a silent but passionate adherent of the doctrines which were specially associated with the name of his great kinsman.

Cavendish has to the full the gift of dramatization.

The neglect of these Tudor biographies has obscured some things in the history of English literature, and probably also in the history of the English nation. We may take first the history of English literature. For example, all critics have been struck with the suddenness of the development of the Elizabethan drama: "in a space of time almost unparallelled for brevity," we pass from the rhymed doggerel of the old plays to the masterpieces of the Elizabethan dramatists. But if we want to see the dramatic instinct at work in the earlier Tudor period, it is precisely in these biographies that we must look for it. If we ignore biographies and memoirs, if we ignore even theological treatises, we shall often be overlooking the very places where the art of dramatic representation was feeling its way, till it bursts out later on the Elizabethan stage.

Two instances of this may be given.

[1] Whibley in the *Cambridge History of English Literature*, III, 335.

Use of Dialogue by Cavendish.

In that grim masterpiece, *Arden of Feversham*, the way in which the villain, Mosbie, shows his vileness has been praised by John Addington Symonds:

"Fie, no, not for a thousand pound."

"The touch of *not for a thousand pound*," says Symonds, "is rare. Alice never for a moment thought of money. It is the churl who expresses the extreme of scorn by hyperboles of cash."

But the thing had been done thirty or forty years before Mosbie was depicted. Turn to the end of Cavendish's *Life of Wolsey* Cavendish has told how Wolsey had been arrested and handed over to the charge of Master Kingston, Constable of the Tower, who had come north to bring him to London; he has told of Wolsey's dreary journey southward—how he fell ill, how they came to Leicester, how Wolsey went straightway to bed, very sick, and how by Monday he seemed to be drawing fast to his end. Meantime the king had sent a message to Master Kingston about £1500 in ready money that Wolsey was supposed to have had in his possession when he was arrested, and the dying man had to be pestered again and again to tell where the money had gone:

> "For this mony that ye demaund of me, I assure you it is none of myn; for I borowed it of dyvers of my frendes to bury me, and to bestowe among my servauntes, whiche hathe taken great paynnes abought me, lyke trewe and faythfull men. Notwithstandyng if it be his pleasur to take thys mony frome me I must hold me therwith content. . . ."
>
> "But, Sir, I pray you, where is this mony?" "Mr. Kyngeston," quod he, "I will not conceyll it frome the kyng; I woll declare it to you, or I dye, by the grace of God. Take a littill pacience with me, I pray you." "Well, Sir, than I woll troble you no more at this tyme, trustyng that ye wyll shewe me tomorowe." "Yea, that I wyll, Mr. Kyngeston, for the mony is safe anoughe, and in an honest man's kepyng; who wyll not kepe oon penny frome the kyng." And than Mr. Kyngeston went to his [chamber to] soper.[1]

But by eight of the clock the next morning Wolsey was dead, without having told where the £1500 were. After Wolsey had been buried, the journey was continued to Hampton Court, for all concerned to obtain their discharge from the king. Cavendish tells us:

> Uppon the morowe I was sent for by the kyng to come to hys Grace; and beyng in Mr. Kyngeston's chamber in the court, had

[1] MS. Egerton 2402, fols. 87^v, 88^r (Autograph of Cavendish).

knowlege therof, and repayryng to the kyng, I found hyme shotyng at the rowndes in the parke, on the baksyde of the garden. And perceyvyng hyme occupied in shotyng, thought it not my dewtie to troble hym : but leaned to a tree, entendyng to stand there, and to attend hys gracious pleasur. Beyng in a great study, at the last the kyng came sodynly behynd me, where I stode, and clappt his hand uppon my sholder; and whan I perceyved hyme I fyll uppon my knee. To whome he sayd, callyng me by my name, "I woll," quod he, "make an end of my game, and than woll I talke with you;" and so departed to his marke, whereat the game was endyd.

Use of Dialogue by Cavendish.

Than the kyng delyverd hys bowe to the yoman of hys bowes, and went his way inward to the place, whome I folowed; howbeit he called for Sir John Gagge, with whome he talked, untill he came at the garden posterne gate, and there entred; the gate beyng shett after hyme, whiche caused me to goo my wayes.

And beyng goon but a lyttyll distance the gate was opened agayn, and there Sir Harry Norres called me agayn, commaundyng me to come in to the kyng, who stode behynd the dore in a nyght-gown of russett velvett furred with sabelles; byfore whome I kneled down, beyng with hyme there all alon the space of an hower and more, dewryng whiche tyme he examyned me of dyvers waytty matters, concernyng my lord, whysshyng that lever than XX.M. li. he had lyved. Than he asked me for the XV.C. li., whiche Mr. Kyngeston moved to my lord byfore his deathe. "Sir," sayd I, "I thynke that I can tell your Grace partely where it is." "Yea, can [you]?" quod the kyng; "than I pray you tell me, and you shall do us myche pleasur, nor it shall not be onrewardyd." [1]

I am not suggesting that the Elizabethan dramatists owe anything directly to these dialogues, but only that these earlier writers show, half a century before Shakespeare, a quite Shakespearean power of dramatization. We have no reason to think that Shakespeare had ever read a manuscript of Roper, or Harpsfield, or Rastell.

More and Shakespeare's *Richard III.*

Cavendish he certainly had read, in the Chroniclers; and everyone knows the use made of Cavendish in *Henry VIII*; Shakespeare follows his wording, in places, as closely as he follows that of Plutarch in the Roman plays.

But the debt which Shakespeare owes to More's *Richard III* is much greater. For he came under the influence of More early, at the very beginning of his work as a tragic poet. From More Shakespeare takes, not indeed any knack of dialogue, but something of the tragic idea, especially the idea in which Shakespeare's *Richard III* reminds

[1] MS. Egerton 2402, fol. 91.

More and Shakespeare's *Richard III.*

us of Greek drama—the feeling of Nemesis: fate hanging over blind men who can see what is happening to others, but are unconscious of the sword over their own heads. *The vain sureti of man's mind, so nere his deth:* that is the moral of Sir Thomas More's *History of Richard III.* As More says of one of Richard's victims, "When he rekened himself surest, he lost his life, and that within two howres after."

In More's *Richard III*, Hastings is an example of the man quite unaware of the destruction awaiting him: a man who dares to gloat over the disaster which, he knows, is about to fall on others, never dreaming that in an hour or two it is to fall on him as well; ignoring warnings and portents which might have put him on his guard:

> Certain is it also (says More) that in the riding toward the Tower, the same morning in which he was behedded, his hors twise or thrise stumbled with him almost to the falling; which thing albeit eche man wote wel daily happeneth to them to whom no such mischaunce is toward, yet hath it ben, of an olde rite and custome, observed as a token often times notably foregoing some great misfortune.

More goes on to tell how in Tower Street Hastings stopped to speak to a priest. In Hastings' company was a knight who had been sent to fetch him to the Tower, and who was in the secret and knew that Hastings would never leave the Tower alive:

> This knight . . . said merely [= merrily] to him: "What, my lord, I pray you come on, whereto talke you so long with that priest, you have no nede of a prist yet": and therwith he laughed upon him, as though he would say, "Ye shal have sone." But so litle wist the tother what he ment, and so little mistrusted, that he was never merier nor never so full of good hope in his life: which self thing is often sene a signe of chaunge.

More then tells how a friend reminded Hastings of the ill turn which his old enemies, Gray and Rivers, had done him in the past. And these enemies, Hastings knew (though his friend did not) were to be beheaded that day at Pomfret. So Hastings ("nothing ware that the axe hang over his own hed") replied:

> Lo how the world is turned, now stand mine enemies in the daunger (as thou maist hap to here more hereafter) and I never in my life so mery, nor never in so great suerty.[1]

[1] More, *Works*, 1557, p. 55.

Everyone remembers the use which Shakespeare makes of that; how he makes Hastings say:

More and Shake-speare's *Richard III*

> Then was I going prisoner to the Tower,
> By the suggestion of the queen's allies;
> But now, I tell thee—keep it to thyself—
> This day those enemies are put to death,
> And I in better state than e'er I was.

The gibe about the priest is put into the mouth of Buckingham:

> What, talking with a priest, lord Chamberlain?
> Your friends at Pomfret, they do need the priest;
> Your honour hath no shriving work in hand.

And Hastings admits that he is thinking of his enemies, about to be put to death:

> Good faith, and when I met this holy man,
> Those men you talk of came into my mind.

But in the same act we have Hastings' own dying speech:

> Three times to-day my foot-cloth horse did stumble,
> And startled, when he looked upon the Tower,
> As loth to bear me to the slaughter-house.
> O, now I want the priest that spake to me.[1]

XVI. Prejudice.

The masterpieces of Fourteenth-Century English prose were forgotten by generations which despised them as the work of "sottishly ignorant Papists." The modern literary historian would indignantly disclaim such prejudice; but his information has reached him only through prejudiced channels. Earlier generations have entailed ignorance on less wilfully bigoted generations which followed them. So, to many people, Fourteenth-Century English prose came to be represented by the very elementary English into which, about the year 1400, a somewhat unintelligent translator rendered the French text of the *Voyages of Sir John Mandeville.* To others, it came to be represented by the Wicliffite translations. And so "Mandeville" has disputed with Wiclif the title of "father of English prose."

We have taken Middle English prose seriously when it is either most elementary or most frivolous; and we have ignored it when it is most finished and most serious.

[1] *Richard III*, Act III, Scenes ii and iv.

Prejudice.

Secondly, the history of English prose has been stultified by a contempt for the periods immediately preceding the Conquest and the Reformation—a contempt which often amounts to sheer partisanship.

In four years William the Conqueror, in about as long a time Henry VIII, altered the face of England as no other men have ever altered it. We, who watch the overthrow many centuries after, must needs take upon us the mystery of things as if we were God's spies, and demonstrate how thoroughly that which fell deserved to fall. And so the three or four generations which precede 1066 or 1536 are out of favour. The Anglo-Saxon period is held to culminate in Alfred, the Middle Ages in Dante or Chaucer—after that we are weary of them. Into an age which knew nothing of it, we read our own feeling of impending catastrophe. "Disintegration," we say, "Decadence," "Sterility," "Futility." We have lost interest in all things except those which seem to herald the coming change. The pitfall which lies before us all is, as Dr. P. S. Allen has said, that we read history, knowing the event.[1]

One of the many results of that widespread trade and intercourse which the Norman conquerors found already flourishing in England[2] was the way in which books of Oriental adventure like *Apollonius of Tyre* and the *Wonders of the East* had been translated into English prose. These books are recorded in the *Cambridge History of English Literature* as indicating the imminence of "The Coming Change." Yet the *Wonders of the East* and the *Letter of Alexander* can be proved to have been translated into English some two generations before the Norman Conquest, at a date when Normandy was still barbarous.[3]

The Fifteenth Century has suffered as much as the Eleventh. Two of our very greatest historians have stigmatized it as the age of futility: in England and in Europe generally.[4] Yet in that century, such was the skill of the craftsmen of Germany that, when they discovered the art of printing by movable types, they immediately, without any fumbling, produced volumes which compel us to marvel to-day at the technical skill necessary for their making. The rapidity with which the art of printing spread shows also how pressing

[1] "The Point of View" in *The Age of Erasmus*; Oxford, 1914, p. 222.

[2] See above, p. lxx.

[3] See Kenneth Sisam in *Mod. Lang. Rev.* XI (1916), p. 336; and Max Förster, *Berichte der Sächs. Akad. der Wissenschaften*, Bd. 71.

[4] Charles Plummer in his edition of Fortescue's *Governance*, p. 3, quoting and endorsing Stubbs' *Constitutional History*, II, 624.

and urgent was the demand of the age for books. It was a century of exploration. By the end of it America had been rediscovered. It was the century which produced the Maid of Orleans, the *Imitatio Christi*, Leonardo da Vinci, Michael Angelo, Erasmus and Thomas More.

Prejudice.

If we limit our view to England, we find that the secretary of a Venetian ambassador, coming to England about 1500, notes just the same things as William of Poitiers noted in 1066: the well-tilled, fertile soil, the very active trade, and, resulting from these two things, the abundance of precious metals and the skill of English craftsmen in working them. In a single street, leading to St. Paul's, our Venetian found fifty-two goldsmiths' shops, "so rich and full of silver vessels, great and small, that in all the shops in Milan, Rome, Venice and Florence put together, I do not think there would be found so many of the magnificence that are to be seen in London."[1] He was amazed, not only at the number and size of our churches scattered over the land, but at the blaze of treasure inside them. The riches of England he thinks to be greater than those of any other country in Europe:

> But above all are their riches displayed in the church treasures; for there is not a parish church in the kingdom so mean as not to posssess crucifixes, candlesticks, censers, patens and cups of silver. . . . Your Magnificence may therefore imagine what the decorations of those enormously rich Benedictine, Carthusian and Cistercian monasteries must be.[2]

Nowhere in the world had the Venetian seen anything like the interior of Westminster Abbey; and Westminster Abbey was surpassed, he reported, by St. Thomas's shrine at Canterbury.

And all this treasure of carved stone, carved wood, metal-work and painted glass (the poor remains of which we marvel at to-day) was there for all to see, at times of festival and pilgrimage.

Erasmus, visiting England at the same time as the Venetian, is as enthusiastic about the glory of English scholarship as the Venetian is about the glory of English art. There is learning, he says, in Latin and Greek, so recondite and so exact that he has lost little by coming to England instead of going to Italy; it is wonderful how universally and how intensely the classics are being studied in England.[3] But

[1] *Relation of England*; Camden Society, XXXVII, 1847, pp. 42–3.

[2] The same, p. 29.

[3] *Opus Epist. Des. Erasmi*, ed. Allen, No. 118, Tom. I, p. 273 (5 Dec. 1499): tantum autem humanitatis atque eruditionis, non illius protritae ac

Prejudice. nothing, not the beauty of the English ladies,[1] nor the learning of Colet, Grocyn, Linacre and the rest, charmed Erasmus more than the character of Thomas More.

And this character remained a London ideal. A century later, no prejudice prevented the Catholic martyr from being the hero of a London which admired him for having " sealed error with his blood." That is the significance of the play of *Sir Thomas More*, to which, it is lawful to believe, Shakespeare added its three greatest pages.

It may well be, as Mr. Chesterton has said, that More will come to be counted the greatest Englishman, or at least the greatest historical character in English history. And More is a product of Fifteenth-Century London. London trained him, and made him what Erasmus found him when he visited England in 1499.

These things are not the product of an age of futility and decadence.

And, alike in the Eleventh and in the Fifteenth Century, the symbol of our civilization lies in the power of English prose. Books were being multiplied : in the Eleventh Century in the quiet scriptoria of monasteries; in the Fifteenth both by scribes and in the printing houses of Caxton and de Worde. They are there if we choose to look for them, instead of declaring that nothing can be found in so sterile an age. And it is in their English prose that the power of these books lies.

Then the blow fell. The ravaging of England from 1066 to 1070, costly as it was in human life, seems to have done incomparably less damage to the art-treasures of England than did the systematic spoliation which, beginning in the year after More's head fell on the scaffold, contrived, in the course of four or five years, to leave the English people very little of the glory which the Venetian secretary saw, save

" bare ruined choirs."

After the blow has fallen, the attention of the historian—literary and political alike—is concentrated upon the new world, and all that it means. The survival of the old is apt to be disregarded, and the

---

trivialis, sed reconditae, exactae, antiquae, Latinae Graecaeque, ut iam Italiam nisi visendi gratia haud multum desyderem. Coletum meum cum audio, Platonem ipsum mihi videor audire. In Grocino quis illum absolutum disciplinarum orbem non miretur ? Linacri iudicio quid acutius, quid altius, quid emunctius ? Thomae Mori ingenio quid unquam finxit natura vel mollius, vel dulcius, vel felicius ? Iam quid ego reliquum catalogum recenseam ? Mirum est dictu quam hic passim, quam dense veterum literarum seges efflorescat.

[1] The same, No. 103, Tom. I, p. 238 (to Faustus Andrelinus, 1499).

light which it might throw on the continuous life of our nation is obscured. An example of this is the way in which the text of the *Anglo-Saxon Chronicle* is ignored during the reigns of William I, William II and Henry I. Teachers of Anglo-Saxon are apt to take no interest in it, because it is too late; and teachers of Middle English because (till we come to the account of Stephen's reign) it is too early.[1] So a quite artificial gap is created, although, in fact, this survival of Old English prose is vital to any understanding of the history of English literature. In a very similar way the Roman Catholic prose of the Reformation period has been ignored. In some measure this was the inevitable result of the difficulty of printing it in Elizabethan times. But this neglect has continued far too long. **Prejudice.**

The peculiar charm of this prose has been well expressed by an American scholar, who cannot be accused of any prejudice in favour of the Roman Catholic outlook :

> One may wonder if this twofold restraint and propriety was not the result of Cavendish's Catholic training and traditions, and if so, be led to reflect on what was lost to writing in sixteenth-century England through its rejection of Catholic discipline. The only piece of sixteenth-century historical writing which in its simple truth and restraint of feeling merits a place by the side of Cavendish's *Life* is the brief account of Sir Thomas More, by his son-in-law, Roper, and in both cases it was the piety of the writer that gave its peculiar charm to the writing. English style of this period was usually very highly colored and self-assertive. It tended to become either extravagantly popular or extravagantly literary and refined. Both in feeling and in the technic of expression, writers of the time often passed beyond the legitimate bounds of their subject. The excellence of Cavendish's *Life and Death* arises from the fact that the author clearly perceived the limits of his subject and held himself within them.[2]

And, if this is true of Roper and Cavendish, it is also true (as I hope this volume will show) that Rastell and Harpsfield have their part to play in the history of English prose.

Our perspective of English literature and English life and English thought has been impeded by our neglect of these biographers—Roper, Harpsfield, Cavendish, Rastell, and above all of More himself. Ignoring their dramatic narrative, we have had an eye only for the

[1] Mr. A. J. Wyatt in his *Threshold of Anglo-Saxon* is a noteworthy exception, and so is Prof. G. T. Flom, in his *Old English Grammar and Reader*, recently published.

[2] Krapp, *Rise of English Literary Prose* (1915), pp. 420–21.

Prejudice. eccentricities of prose style—the affectations of Lyly's *Euphues*, or Nash, or Greene in his cony-catching tracts—or, later, the magnificence of Sir Thomas Browne or of Milton. We have forgotten how many people in the Sixteenth Century had the power of writing a glorious prose style—straightforward, vivid, simple in the best sense, essentially dramatic. So when, a century and a half later, we come to the noble simple eloquence of Bunyan, to the dramatic narrative of Bunyan or Defoe, to the orderly prose of Dryden, we think we have come to something without example in English literature. But it is not so. We have seen that the lively dialogue of More and his school helps to explain the rapidity with which the Elizabethan drama develops a power of vivid, natural dialogue. Shakespeare's predecessors (and even Shakespeare himself often in his early plays) make their characters converse in doggerel rhyme, in the most wooden way. Suddenly, in the shortest time, we have the development of natural prose dialogue—say, for example, Sir John Falstaff and his associates discoursing at the Boar's Head Tavern in Eastcheap. Shakespeare had only to abandon the rhymed doggerel, to make his characters talk as naturally as More, or Cavendish, or Roper, or William Rastell had made their characters talk. Dame Quickly and Mistress Alice More are sisters under their skins.

I come back finally to the noble lecture in which Sir Arthur Quiller-Couch speaks of the Authorized Version of 1611 as a miracle. There had already been the miraculous outburst of Elizabethan verse, he says,

> And then, as already had happened to our Verse, to our prose too there befel a miracle.
>
> You will not ask me "What miracle?" I mean, of course, the Authorized Version of the Bible.[1]

If we turn from the conceits of Euphuism and the tricks of Nash to the prose of the Authorized Version, it does indeed seem a miracle.

But surely the story is even more wonderful than Sir Arthur Quiller-Couch would allow it to be. We begin with the greatest and noblest of all English kings building up (upon what foundations we do not know) a King's English. We see the civilization of which this English prose was the instrument developing for nearly two centuries; then suffering sudden and catastrophic overthrow; then fighting a losing battle steadily but hopelessly, until, two centuries after the

[1] *On the Art of Writing*, p. 121 (Lecture VI: *On the capital difficulty of prose*).

Conquest, the glories of romance and the niceties of the law had become the province of the French tongue, history and theology of the Latin. Yet, when we might expect to find the English tongue surviving as a mere peasants' speech, and English prose ceasing altogether, we see it consecrated in a series of noble books, written for or by those who had withdrawn to cloister or hermitage in search of a peace which they could not find in feudal England. **Quiet books.**

And those who wrote these quiet books found what they sought.

> They find, iwis, St. Julian's inn, that wayfaring men eagerly seek.[1]
>
> What so thou hearest, or seest, or feelest, that should let thee in thy way, abide not with it wilfully, tarry not for it restfully, behold it not, like it not, dread it not; but aye go forth in thy way, and think that thou wouldest be at Jerusalem. For that thou covetest, that thou desirest, and nought else but that.[2]
>
> Ere thou go to bed, hold a chapter with thy heart, and ask it in what thing it is better than it was.[3]
>
> Let holy reading be ever in thy hands; let sleep fall upon thee as thou lookest thereon, and the holy page meet thy drooping face. Thus earnestly and long must thou read. (Everything one may, though, overdo. Best is ever measure.)[4]
>
> Let no man ween with ease to rise to the stars.[5]
>
> If thou wilt ask, how good is he or she, ask "How much loves he or she?"[6]
>
> For what is a man, but his thoughts and his loves?[7]
>
> But he that so loveth God that he longeth to go to Him, my heart cannot give me but he shall be welcome, all were it so that he should come ere he were well purged. For charity covereth a multitude of sins, and he that trusteth in God cannot be confounded.[8]

[1] *Ancren Riwle*, ed. Morton, p. 350.
[2] Hilton, *Scale*. See above, p. civ.
[3] Rolle, *Daily Work* (ed. Horstman, I, p. 151).
[4] *Ancren Riwle*, p. 286.
[5] *Ancren Riwle*, p. 364: also in the *Ureisun of Oure Louerde*, Morris, *O. E. Homilies* I, 187.
[6] Rolle, *Form of Living*, cap. 10 (ed. Horstman, I, p. 37).
[7] Hilton, *Scale*, I, cap. 88.
[8] More, *Works* (1557), p. 1168.

"The seal set on all."

It may be as impossible for us to recapture the spirit of these books as it would be to illuminate the Benedictional of St. Æthelwold, or build another Westminster or Wells. But we have no right to ignore any of these things.

The last sentence—"Charity covereth a multitude of sins"—anticipates the wording of the Authorized Version.[1] It was written by More, in the Tower, awaiting trial.

And so the cadences of the English tongue were preserved, till at last—the words are those of Sir Arthur Quiller-Couch and not mine—

> The Authorized Version, setting a seal on all, set a seal on our national style, thinking and speaking. Who shall determine its range, whether of thought or of music? You have received it by inheritance: it is yours, freely yours—to direct your words through life as well as your hearts.

[1] Against Tyndale's "Love covereth the multitude of sins."

LIFE AND WORKS OF NICHOLAS HARPSFIELD.

The Harpsfield brothers.

THE life of Nicholas Harpsfield has been briefly told by Anthony Wood,[1] by Lord Acton in a letter to the *Academy*,[2] and by Bishop Creighton in the *Dictionary of National Biography*. From all three Nicholas has received credit which is not strictly his due, by being confused with his elder brother, John. Both were archdeacons, both doctors, John of Divinity, Nicholas of Laws; both were mainstays of the restoration under Mary, and together they suffered long imprisonment under Elizabeth. Apart, it is often difficult to know with which we are dealing; but often the two Dromios appear at one time in one place, and then we can be sure of them.

John was famous in his own day as a preacher and a scholar: such was his eloquence that he was known as "Dr. Sweetlips," a nickname with which, it is needless to add, "bilious Bale" coupled a scandalous interpretation. But the writings of Nicholas have secured him a more permanent fame, which has encroached upon the record of his brother. Acton, in his sympathetic sketch of Nicholas, writes: "At the accession of Elizabeth, when the whole Marian clergy made scarcely an effort to avert the ruin which seemed already irretrievable, Harpsfield struggled almost alone to uphold the failing cause." Acton then goes on to attribute to Nicholas alone the exertions of both brothers, and, since both were active, the combined achievement is distinctly impressive.

Their family.

The Harpsfields of Harpsfield were a Hertfordshire family, holding land from the Abbey of St. Albans, at least since the time of Henry III. They bore arms: *Argent, three harps sable, stringed or.* One of the most famous of the abbots of St. Albans, Thomas de la Mare, whose magnificent brass is still a chief glory of his church, was a member of this family on the spindle side.[3]

[1] *Athenæ Oxonienses* (1691) I. 171. Upon this are based various other biographies, which for the most part merely repeat Wood's facts: those, *e.g.*, in Newcourt's *Repertorium Ecclesiasticum*, Dodd's *Church History*, and Gillow's *Bibliographical Dictionary of the English Catholics*. The little biography, compiled by Charles Eyston of East Hendred from Wood, Pits, and Fuller, about 1707, was not printed till 1878.

[2] IX (1876) pp. 609–10.

[3] J. G. Nichols, *The Herald and Genealogist*, V (1870) p. 129: Article by F. J. Baigent.

The Harpsfield family.

Nicholas Harpsfield, the grandfather of our Nicholas, had at least so much of the learning which was later to distinguish his descendants, that, when he slew a man at Windsor Castle, 21 August, 1471, he could claim benefit of clergy, and get off with a year or so of imprisonment in Wolvesey Castle, in the custody of Wayneflete, bishop of Winchester.[1] Like his grandsons, also, he was a faithful adherent of a falling cause. On 12 February, 1484–5, King Richard III granted him, for his eminent services to Richard, late Duke of York, Edward IV and Richard III, in prosperity and adversity, in England, Ireland, Holland and other places, an annuity of £10 for life.[2] In view of the doubts that have sometimes been thrown on the impartiality of More's *History of Richard III*, it is worth noting that, despite his Yorkist family history, Nicholas the grandson accepts without demur More's charges against Richard III, speaks of the "incomparable excellencie"[3] of More's *History*, and often quotes it in his own *Historia Anglicana Ecclesiastica*. All he can do in defence of Richard is to instance his generosity, and to record his ecclesiastical foundations at York and elsewhere; he moralizes, *nemo tam perdite malus est a quo non aliquid nonnunquam boni proficiscatur*.[4]

Nicholas the Yorkist had at least four sons: John, Nicholas, George and Lewis. Nicholas became a priest; John, George and Lewis members of city companies. Yet John did not abandon his claims to gentility: he is mentioned in a patent roll of 5 Henry VIII as "John Harpesfelde, citizen and draper of London, otherwise called John Harpesfeld of London, gentleman."[5] This John was the father of the John and Nicholas with whose doings and sufferings we are concerned.

Yet the two boys seem to have taken less after their merchant father than after his brother Nicholas. This Nicholas, the son of Nicholas the Yorkist, is liable to be confused with his nephew and namesake, our author. The uncle had been a scholar of Winchester College, scholar and fellow of New College, Oxford, and student of law at Bologna; he became Doctor of Decrees and official of the archdeacon of Winchester,[6] and rector of Wyke. Local piety has

[1] Letter by F. J. Baigent in *The Tablet*, LII (N.S. XX) p. 110 (1878).
[2] Baigent in Nichols, as above, p. 129.
[3] p. 102, below.
[4] *Historia*, p. 603.
[5] 16 June, 1513. See Nichols, as above, p. 129; and Wood's *Athenæ*, under John Harpsfield.
[6] Addit. MS. 12,483 in the British Museum records his ecclesiastical visitation of Hampshire and the Isle of Wight in this capacity, in March and April, 1543.

recovered a good deal of information about him.[1] He died 15 March, 1550, aged 76, and left much of his small estate to the poor of Winchester, and in other charitable bequests. His two nephews, Nicholas and John, were his executors and residuary legatees; Nicholas proved the will, 20 May, 1550, only a short time before he fled the realm to escape from the Protestant rule of Edward VI.

Nicholas Harpsfield at Winchester and Oxford.

This nephew, Nicholas Harpsfield, author of the *Life of More*, was born in 1519, in London, in the parish of St. Mary Magdalen, Old Fish St. Before he was ten he was sent to Winchester to learn the elements, for he tells us that he was present at the funeral of Bishop Fox, in Winchester Cathedral[2] (5 October, 1528). He was admitted a scholar of Winchester College next year, 1529,[3] following

[1] See F. J. Baigent, *The History and Antiquities of the parish church of Wyke, near Winchester*, Winchester (1865), where ten pages (7–17) are devoted to his biography. In virtue of their having been executors to the rector of Wyke, Baigent gives brief biographies of John and Nicholas; and so thorough is the search of archives which he made, that he has recovered several important facts and dates unknown to other biographers. Dr. Nicholas Harpsfield the elder is referred to by Wood at the end of his account of our Nicholas (*Athenæ*, 1691, I. 172), as "bred in *Oxon.*, . . . but what relation the former had to this, I know not."

[2] Quo ego tempore, me admodum puerum exequiis et funeri ejus interfuisse memini, ad prima literarum elementa illic haurienda, a parentibus Wintoniam Londino missum. *Historia Ecclesiastica*, 1622, p. 644.

[3] I am indebted for information to the Archivist of Winchester College, Mr. Herbert Chitty, who writes: "In recording that Nicholas was admitted Scholar in 1529, the Register describes him as being *X A[nnorum] in festo pentecost' preterito*. In 1529 Pentecost fell on 16 May. Therefore, if the Register gives the anniversary of the day of Nicholas' birth, Nicholas was born on 16 May, 1519." Mr. Chitty further points out to me that, since the annual election of scholars had to be held between 7 July and 1 Oct., *festo preterito* in the election of 1529 must refer to Pentecost 1529, not to Pentecost 1528.

John, who had been admitted Scholar in 1528, is described in the Register as *XII A[nnorum] in festo pentecost' preterito*. In 1528 Pentecost fell, as Mr. Chitty points out, on 31 May.

Accordingly, 31 May, 1516, and 16 May, 1519, are given by F. J. Baigent (*History of Wyke*, 1865) as the birth-dates of John and Nicholas Harpsfield respectively. Yet it seems an odd coincidence that both the brothers should have been born on days on which Whitsunday happened to fall in the year of their entering Winchester College. Mr. Chitty further informs me that the frequency with which the great festivals are mentioned in these entries is not compatible with the assumption that the entry signifies in every case that the scholar was actually born on the feast itself. He has very kindly sent me a list of the feast days, mentioned to fix the ages of boys in 1528, 1529; this makes it very clear that "the feast day was not necessarily the boy's birthday, though possibly in some cases it may have been." "It seems to me probable," he adds, "that in many cases the boy's birthday occurred shortly before the feast day mentioned in connexion with his age."

That the brothers were born in the parish of St. Mary Magdalen is recorded, Mr. Chitty tells me, in a small book, probably compiled in the Seventeenth Century, the *Liber Successionis et Dignitatis*, kept at Winchester College, giving particulars of Fellows of New College, Oxford.

in the steps of his brother John, three years his senior, who had been admitted to Winchester in the preceding year. The two brothers were admitted scholars of New College, Oxford (John, 14 Nov., 1532; Nicholas, 11 Jan., 1535) and, after their two years' probation, perpetual Fellows (John, 14 Nov., 1534; Nicholas, 11 Jan., 1537).

Then their paths somewhat diverged. John concentrated on Arts, and later on Theology; Nicholas (like his namesake and uncle) on Civil and Canon Law.[1] He took his degree of B.C.L. on 4 June, 1543. Anthony Wood tells us that, "In 1544, he, being then Bach. of the Civ. Law of about an year standing, was admitted Principal of an ancient hostle (mostly for Civilians) called White hall (on the Site of which Jesus Coll. was afterwards partly built)." [2]

The Regius Professorship of Greek at Oxford.

But I have been unable to verify Wood's further statement that in 1546 he was appointed Regius Professor of Greek.[3] This can only be a mistake. Wood gives no authority, but merely quotes, as evidence of Harpsfield's knowledge of Greek, the words of Leland, who, speaking of the learned men of Oxford, has the lines:

Facundus Curio Minervae alumnus
Harpesfeldius, Atticaeque linguae
Interpres facilis disertus aptus.[4]

But this is surely a reference to John, not to Nicholas. It was John Harpsfield, not Nicholas, who translated into Latin the Commentary of Simplicius on the first book of Aristotle's *Physics*,[5] with a dedicatory letter addressed to Henry VIII; again, it was John who translated the first book of Virgil's *Æneid* into Greek hexameters.[6] Finally, when, after more than twelve years' close imprisonment in the Fleet, the two brothers were seeking permission to go to Bath for

[1] Harpesfelde, John, adm. B.A. 27 Feb. 1536/7; det. 1538, lic. for M.A. 5 Apr. 1541, inc. 3 Aug., disp. Oct., sup. as B.D. for D.D. and disp. 5 Apr. 1554, lic. 20 Apr., D.D. 16 July.

Harpesfelde, Nicolas, adm. B.C.L., 4 June, 1543; disp. July, 1546; lic. for D.C.L., 30 Oct., 1553; D.C.L., 16 July, 1554. *Register of the University of Oxford*, ed. by Rev. C. W. Boase, 1885, I, pp. 187, 205.

[2] *Athenæ Oxonienses* (1691) I, 171–2. Harpsfield only held this office for some two years. For White Hall and its principals, see Wood's *City of Oxford*, ed. A. Clark, Oxford Historical Society (1889) pp. 72, 586.

[3] *Athenæ*, as before; see also Wood, *History and Antiquities of the University of Oxford*, ed. Gutch (1796) ii, 852: the statement "deprived by Q. Mary for being married" is a misprint due to the omission of some words. Harpsfield succeeded Edmund Cranmer, who was so deprived.

[4] *Cygnea cantio autore Joanne Lelando antiquario*, Londini, 1545.

[5] British Museum, MS. Royal 12. F.v. The prefatory dedication to Henry VIII is signed *Joannes Harpysfeldus*.

[6] British Museum, MS. Royal 16. C. viii: *Primus liber Aeneidos Virgilii translatus per Ioannem Harpsfeldum Oxoniensem*. The MS. belonged to Cranmer.

The Regius Professorship of Greek at Oxford.

the restoration of their health, it was John Harpsfield who appealed to the solidarity of humanism by composing letters in Greek to Lord Treasurer Burghley and Sir Thomas Smith, Secretary of State.[1] On the other hand, unless his scribes have done him very great wrong, it does not seem as if Nicholas had any very exhaustive knowledge of Greek.

Thanks to Wood's mistake, however, Nicholas everywhere has the credit of having been Oxford's first Regius Professor of Greek, except in Kirby's roll of *Winchester Scholars*, where the honour is attributed to John. Kirby was probably depending upon one of the MS. books preserved at Winchester College, giving particulars of fellows of New College, Oxford, which, I am informed,[2] speaks of *Johs Harpisfield* as *Græcæ Linguæ Profess. Regius.* The matter is placed beyond doubt by a discovery which has been communicated to me by Mr. H. E. Salter, and Mr. L. Tanner, the Archivist of Westminster Abbey. When Henry VIII endowed the Abbey (5 Aug., 1542) the Dean and Chapter were charged with the payment of £400 per annum for ten Readers or Professors, five in each University: for Divinity, Law, Medicine, Greek and Hebrew—a charge from which immunity was purchased in 1546. The records of the Abbey for periods ending Michaelmas, 1543, and Michaelmas, 1544, are extant, and in both the Reader in Greek at Oxford is John Harpsfield.[3] There is evidence that he had been giving his lectures as early as the autumn of 1541; these Regius professorships were in existence some years earlier than has hitherto been thought.[4] John Harpsfield probably ceased to be Regius Pro-

[1] British Museum, MS. Royal 8. B. xx, fols. 155v, 156v.

[2] By the Archivist, Mr. H. Chitty, to whom, and to the Rev. H. E. Salter I wish to express my thanks for help in trying to solve this problem. They point out to me that the foundation of the Chair is earlier than Wood suggests, for in a Lay Subsidy for Oxford at the Record Office, dated 4 Nov., 1543 (Lay Subsidy: E. 179—162/224), *Thomas* Harpsfyld is returned as "reder of the King's lectour in Greek," with a stipend of £40. The name "Thomas" must be a mistake. No Thomas Harpsfield is known.

[3] The entries which have been communicated to me by Mr. Tanner are as follows:

W.A.M., 37043, fol. 11. d.

Reders in Oxfford.	Et soluit Johanni Harpesfeld pro lectura Grece ibidem pro eodem dimidio anno . . . . xx li.
	(The date of this is July to Michaelmas, 1543).

W.A.M., 37044, fol. 4. d.

Reders in Oxfford.	Johannes Harpesfeld reder of Greke. (Michaelmas to Michaelmas, 1543–44. No amount given).

[4] Mr. Salter writes to me: "John Harpsfield took the degree of M.A. on 3 Aug., 1541, and a few lines lower we read in the Register: *Supplicat mag.*

fessor when "King Henry the Eighth his College" came to an end about 1545. It was reconstituted as Christ Church in 1546, and in the accounts of the expenses for the first year of the College, George Etherige is Regius Professor of Greek.

Here, for the moment, we must leave John Harpsfield. His life, as Archdeacon of London, Dean of Norwich, and popular preacher, is full of interest, but concerns us only in those cases (and they are many) where he has been confused with his brother Nicholas, and has to be distinguished.

Of Nicholas Harpsfield's life during these years of study at Oxford we know nothing more. The only piece of information about himself which he has left us is that he was, by chance, present at the great ceremony when Anne of Cleves was received by the King at Blackheath [1] on 3 Jan., 1540.

Nicholas Harpsfield in exile.

In 1550 Nicholas Harpsfield left England [2] on account of the religious changes under Edward VI, and lived in exile at Louvain with Bonvisi, the Clements and the Rastells,[3] who had left the country about the same time. Returning under Mary, he was admitted archdeacon of Canterbury, 31 March, 1554, in place of Edmund Cranmer, brother of the archbishop, who was deprived for

Preferment under Mary.

Iohannes Harpesfeld, magister artium ultimis comitiis creatus, quatinus gratiose cum eo dispensetur pro sua necessaria regentia. Causa est quod publice prelegit, et decanum Wellensem instituit. The entry is undated, but there can be no doubt that it was before Christmas, 1541; in fact it must be at the very beginning of the autumn term, otherwise John would have been obliged to give the lectures due from a necessary regent. He asks to be excused on the grounds that he gives public lectures, and that he is tutor of the Dean of Wells (Fitz-Williams). He does not definitely say that his lectures were in Greek, but he would not have had the knowledge to lecture in Law, Medicine or Theology."

[1] *Treatise touching the Pretended Divorce*, ed. Pocock, p. 259.

[2] Conscientiæ causa in exilium voluntarium profectus est, anno Domini 1550. Pits, *Relationes historicæ de rebus anglicis* (*De illustribus Angliæ scriptoribus*), Paris (1619) p. 780.

[3] *Antonius Bonvisius* . . . *Thomam Morum* semper et colens et admirans, cum fidei Catholicæ reliquias in Anglia extingui videret, in Lovaniensem Academiam domicilium transtulit, non sane ut ibi mercaturæ terrenæ, sed cælesti vacaret. Erat enim is proximus fidei portus, quo Angli ob fidem eiecti se recipere poterant. Collegit ergo ad se, et fovit eos qui ob fidem exulabant, in primis doctorem artis medicæ *Joannem Clementem* unà cum uxore; *Ioannen Storæum*, et præcipuum totius Angliæ lumen *Nicolaum Harpsfildum*, qui postea regnante *Elizabetha* diuturnos carceres perpessus est. Itemque *Ioannen Boxollum* . . . denique *Gulielmum Rastellum* iurisconsultum unà cum uxore sua, quę Lovanii tunc e vita migravit. Nicholas Sanders, *de origine et progressu schismatis Anglicani*, 1585. fols. 123v, 124. John Storey was executed on 1 June, 1571.

being married.[1] On 27 April, 1554, he was collated to the prebend of Harleston in St. Paul's Cathedral, and two days later to the church of Laindon (with the chapel of Basildon) in Essex.[2] The priest's house at Laindon still retains some of the old oak framework which it must have had in Harpsfield's day. Both prebend and vicarage he received upon the deprivation of John Hodgkyns. The vicarage he resigned in 1558 to make way for his brother John, who was collated to it on 14 May of that year; the prebend he retained until, under Elizabeth, " Joh. Hodgkyns, restitutus," re-entered.

Nicholas' resignation of his Essex cure may have been due to the fact that in the meantime he had been appointed to the rectory of Saltwood, near Hythe.[3]

He took the degree of D.C.L. at Oxford on 16 July, 1554; he had resigned his fellowship of New College in 1553 to work at the Court of Arches, " conferens se ad curiam de Arcubus," where, according to Wood, he had considerable practice.

On 24 March, 1558, Harpsfield was appointed to the living of Bishopsbourne, near Canterbury,[4] which was held forty years later by Hooker. It is odd that the greatest Roman Catholic controversialist of his day should have held the same living as the greatest of Anglican apologists. Harpsfield held it, however, only for a short time.[5]

Harpsfield and Cardinal Pole.

During the whole of Cardinal Pole's tenure of office as Archbishop of Canterbury, Harpsfield was closely associated with him. Before Pole landed in England, he had entrusted Harpsfield with power of absolving all under his jurisdiction who had erred from the unity

[1] *Sede vacante* Registers, N. 60^{v}. See *Calendar of Institutions by the Chapter of Canterbury, Sede Vacante*, ed. C. E. Woodruff and I. J. Churchill (1923), Kent Archæological Society, Records Branch, VIII, p. 24; also Strype, *Memorials of Cranmer* (1812) I. 472. Harpsfield entered into an obligation to pay to William Warham, late archdeacon, during his life, a yearly pension of £40.

[2] Newcourt, *Repertorium Ecclesiasticum* (1708) I, 154–5. (From Bonner's Register.)

[3] Nicolaus Harpsfield admissus 1555, 23 Maii, ad rectoriam Saltwood, cum cap. de Hith, vacantem per deprivationem Roberti Watson, clerici conjugati. Reg. Cant., as quoted in Wood's *Athenæ*, ed. Bliss, I, 493. This is from one of the " *Sede Vacante* Registers," N. 86. See *Calendar of Institutions . . . Sede Vacante*, ed. C. E. Woodruff and I. J. Churchill (1923) p. 110.

[4] Vicesimo quarto die Mensis Martis anno domini predicto [iuxta computationem ecclesie Anglicane 1557] dominus contulit magistro Nicholao Harpesfeld, legum doctori, ecclesiam parrochialem de Busshoppesbourne, Cantuar. dioc. . . . per mortem naturalem domini Ricardi Thorneden. Pole's *Register*, fol. 77 (Lambeth Palace Library).

[5] Thomas Willoughbye was rector on 27 Sept., 1559. See Hasted's *History of Kent*, III, 1790, p. 748.

of the Church, and of communicating a power of absolving to other priests.[1]

We have a very full account of Harpsfield's enthusiastic reception of Pole at Canterbury in November, 1554. Pole arrived about midnight, after a tiring journey, and had to listen to a discourse from the Archdeacon, " which lasted a good space of time," on the providence of God in reconciling the realm to Rome. Harpsfield's oratory moved himself and all who heard him to tears : *Tu es Polus, qui aperis nobis polum regni cœlorum : Aer, flumina, terra, parietes ipsi, omnia denique te desiderant.* This fortunate turn of his discourse, from praise of God to praise of Pole himself, entitled the Cardinal to interrupt the Archdeacon, and with the remark that glory must be given to God alone, to get to his bed in the Archdeacon's house.[2]

Harpsfield's name occurs, together with those of very many magnates, clerical and lay, in the proceedings against Bishop Hooper,[3] against Dr. Rowland Taylor,[4] and against Cranmer.[5]

He is named, with many others, in a commission [6] for the checking of heresy in the diocese of Canterbury in 1556 ; and again, nearly two years later,[7] he is on another commission. On 7 July, 1558, Pole issued an instrument from Lambeth, handing to the secular arm five heretics, of whose heresy his commissioners, Harpsfield, Collins and the rest, had informed him.[8] According to Foxe, the sentence was not carried out till about 10 November, and Foxe makes Harpsfield especially responsible for their death. So Harpsfield has not escaped that calumny which is the peculiar lot of archdeacons (*num archidiaconus salvari potest?*). Foxe assures us :

Harpsfield's treatment of heretics.

> As among all the Bishops, Boner bishop of London, was the greatest boucher against the poore members and saints of Christ ; so of all Archdeacons, Nicholas Harpesfield Archdeacon

[1] Strype, *Ecclesiastical Memorials* (1822) III. 1. 211.

[2] See *Il felicissimo Ritorno del Regno d'Inghilterra alla Catholica Unione,* 1554, a rare tract (Brit. Mus., 862, i. 16) which is reprinted in *Epistolarum Reginaldi Poli* Pars V, Brixiæ (1757), Appendix, p. 307. We read in the letter published at Milan, 24 Dec., 1554 (copy in Grenville Library, 11707), *A Conturberi fu fatta vn' oratione dal' Arcidiano nell' entrare dello allogiamento, nella quale fu chiamato il Cardinale Pater Patriœ et alter Helias.* (*L'entrata del Car. Polo in Inghilterra.*)

[3] Strype, *Ecclesiastical Memorials* (1822) III. 1. 288 (28–9 Jan., 1554/5).

[4] The same, pp. 289–90 (29–30 Jan., 1554/5).

[5] Strype, *Memorials of Cranmer* (1812) II. 1072, 1093, 1094, 1096. See *Processus contra Thomam Cranmer,* quoted in full by Strype.

[6] Strype, *Ecclesiastical Memorials* (1822) III. 1. 476 (April 26, 1556).

[7] The same, III. 2. 120 (28 March, 1558).

[8] The same, III. 2. 123.

of Canterbury (as may by man's sight appeare) was the sorest, and of leste compassion, by whose unmercifull nature and agrest disposition, very many were put to death in that dioces of Canterbury, not only in the blody time of that Quene, but some also in the blessed beginning of our most renowned and most mercyfull Prince and Quene that now is, as by the grace of Christ hereafter shal appere.[1]

Harpsfield's treatment of heretics.

The laste that suffered in Quene Maryes tyme were fyve at Canterburye burned aboute syxe dayes before the death of Queene Mary, whose names folowe here underwrytten: Jhon Cornforth, of Wrotham; Christofer Broune, of Maydstone; Jhon Herst, of Ashford; Alyce Snoth, widowe; Katherin Knight, of Thornham.

These fyve, to close up the finall rage of Quene Maries persecution, for the testimony of that word, for which so many had dyed for before, gave up theyre lyves mekely and paciently, suffering the violent malyce of the Papistes. Which Papistes, althoughe they then might have eyther well spared them, or else differred their death, knowing of the sicknes of Queene Mary; yet such was the implacable despite of that generation, that some there be that saye, the Archdecon of Caunterbury the same time being at London, and understanding the daunger of the Quene, incontinently made all post-hast home, to dispatch these, whom before he had then in his cruell custody.[2]

Later, Foxe gave to Harpsfield only the second place, reserving to Dunning of Norwich the stigma of being the cruellest of all archdeacons.[3] He cancelled one passage about Harpsfield's cruelty, but allowed others to stand.

Both Creighton and Acton refuse to believe Foxe's account. There is no doubt that the Marian persecution was more ferocious in Canterbury than in any other country town. As archdeacon, it was Harpsfield's business to inquire into heresy; whether he was personally responsible for the severity of the persecution at Canterbury, as Foxe asserts, we do not know. Acton says:

Independently of the suspicion that adheres to every unsupported statement of Fox, I hesitate to believe that Harpsfield actually stained his hands with blood. It is true that in his book on the Lollards, and in that part of his Dialogues which

[1] Foxe, *Acts and Monuments.* First Edit. (1563) p. 1546. I cannot trace these alleged severities of Harpsfield under Elizabeth.

[2] The same, p. 1673.

[3] Nicholas Harpesfield . . . was the sorest . . . (onely Dunning of Norwich excepted). Second Edit. (1570) II, p. 2140.

Harpsfield's treatment of heretics.

treats of the English Reformers, he describes their punishment without any sign of compassion or regret. It cannot be said of him, as it can be said of More and Pole, that he was an advocate of toleration; but it cannot be proved against him as it can be proved against them, that he became an advocate of religious persecution. The documents in Fox do not connect him directly with the execution of Protestants. Pole issued a commission to him to examine suspected persons and to hand over those whom he found obdurate to the secular arm. But this commission was not issued until the 28th of March in the last year of Mary's reign. Only five persons were condemned after that, and it was by Pole's own act that they were committed to the stake. (Wilkins, *Concilia*, iv. 174.)

We know the execration in which Bonner and Storey were held after the accession of Elizabeth. There is no evidence that any feeling of the kind was entertained against Nicholas Harpsfield. He was allowed liberty and opportunity to compose works of controversy; and it is stated, not indeed on the best authority,[1] that Archbishop Parker, who must have known all about his conduct, treated him with peculiar favour. One of those who were brought before him left a report of his trial, and the testimony of the prisoner is not altogether unfavourable to the justice and the mercy of the judge: "The Archdeacon intreated me to be ruled by him, and take mercy while it was offered; for, if I were condemned, I must needs be burned. Yet he would not say but my soul might be saved." (Fox, iii. 671).[2]

It is characteristic that Foxe, after first mentioning the charge against Harpsfield as mere hearsay, "Some there be that say," [3] goes on to speak of it as if it were proved,[4] and to contrast Harpsfield unfavourably even with Bonner, because a certain William Living, arrested during Queen Mary's last sickness, was not burnt by Bonner. As if there could be any comparison between the case of Living, arrested a few days before Mary's death, on what was apparently not a serious charge, and that of the unfortunates who, after a long trial,

[1] Acton does not mention the authority. The earliest I have found is Wharton in *Anglia Sacra*, Preface, p. xv (1691).

[2] Acton, *Academy*, IX (1876) p. 610. I quote the words of this great historian, but under protest as regards More. More never advocated either "toleration" as we understand it, nor "persecution" such as that under which both he and the Marian martyrs suffered; and his attitude was consistent.

Acton was evidently quoting from the Ninth Edition of the *Acts and Monuments* (1684). In the more easily accessible editions of Townsend and Cattley, or Pratt, the passage will be found in Vol. VIII, p. 331 (Examination of Matthew Plaise).

[3] VIII, 504.

[4] VIII, 505, 530.

had been handed over by Pole to the secular arm four months before.[1]

As Charles Eyston says, Foxe is "the only historian that gives Dr. Harpsfield an ill word." [2] There must have been some very solid virtues to secure for Harpsfield, despite this bitter attack of Foxe, the high reputation which is allowed him alike by Roman and by Protestant historians.

Harpsfield and the last days of Pole.

Harpsfield was one of those upon whom Pole, overwhelmed with troubles and in failing health, could still rely. On 28 Oct., 1558, Pole issued a commission to Harpsfield to be his official, and another to be Dean of the Court of Arches,[3] that is, judge of the ecclesiastical court of Appeal for the Province of Canterbury, held at the church of St.-Mary-le-Bow. At the same time he was appointed "Dean of the Peculiars," that is to say, of the parishes (of which there were thirteen in London alone) exempt from the authority of their diocesan, and placed directly under that of the Archbishop of Canterbury.[4] Two days later, Pole issued to Harpsfield a third commission, authorizing him to visit All Souls College, which Pole, as Archbishop of Canterbury, had the power of visiting.[5] On 1 Nov. Pole appointed him to a Canonry and Prebend in his Cathedral of Christ Church.[6] It is one of the latest entries in his Register.

Less than three weeks after the issue of these commissions, Mary was dead (17 Nov., 1558), and Pole followed her twelve hours later.

Harpsfield and the Convocation of 1559.

At the meeting of Convocation two months after, Nicholas Harpsfield was presented as Prolocutor for the Clergy by Henry Cole,

[1] Most of the references to "Dr. Harpsfield" in Foxe relate certainly or probably to John: Nicholas is concerned in the post-mortem proceedings against John Tooley, VII, 94–7; the proceedings against Thomas Wats, VII, 122; John Bland, VII, 292–5, 304; Nicholas Sheterden, VII, 306; other cases, VII, 339–41; [VII, 383, 766, where, however, the passage against Nicholas Harpsfield, who is called in the First Edition "a whelpe of Bonner's owne heare," is cancelled in the later editions]; VIII, 253, where Harpsfield is specially attacked; VIII, 300, 321; proceedings against Matthew Plaise, VIII, 329; against Richard Woodman, VIII, 367, 370 (where Roper appears together with Harpsfield) 372; the five last Canterbury martyrs, VIII, 504–6. These references are to Pratt's edition, 1877; but with the exception of the extract from the First Edition (VII, 766) they are applicable to the edition of Townsend and Cattley.

[2] *Pretended Divorce*, ed. Pocock (1878) p. 8.

[3] Strype, *Ecclesiastical Memorials* (1822) III. 2. 121.

[4] Newcourt, *Repertorium Ecclesiasticum* (1708) pp. 440–4.

[5] Strype, as before.

[6] Primo die mensis Novembris anno domini predicto [1558] dominus contulit magistro Nicholao Harpesfeld, legum doctori, canonicatum et prebendam in ecclesia Christi Cantuar., quos magister Ricardus Parkehurst dudum habuit. Pole's *Register*, fol. 81v (Lambeth Palace Library).

dean of St. Paul's, and by his brother John, archdeacon of London.[1]

Fuller's account is as follows:

> In the third Session [of Convocation] on friday *Nicholas Harpsfield*, Doctor of Law, and Archdeacon of *Canterbury* was chosen *Referendary* or *Prolocutor* for the *Clergie*, a place of some Credit, but little pains to discharge, seeing the only remarkable thing which passed in this Convocation, was certain Articles of Religion, which they tendered to the [Bishops that they might present them to the] Parliament [18 Feb.] which here we both Transcribe and Translate, requesting the Reader not to begrutch his pains to peruse them: Considering they are the last in this kinde, that ever were represented in *England*, by a Legall Corporation in defence of the Popish Religion. And though errour doth go out with a *Stink*, yet it is a *perfume* that it does go out: We are so far from denying a grave to bury them, that we will erect the Monument [copied by me out of the original] over this ashes of these dead errours.[2]

The monument is then given by Fuller both in the original Latin and in his translation. It affirms transubstantiation, papal supremacy, and the authority which "ought to belong unto the Pastors of the Church . . . and not unto lay-men . . .":

> This remonstrance exhibited by the lower house of *Convocation* to the *Bishops* was according to their Requests presented . . . to the Lord Keeper of the broad Seal of *England* in the Parliament. . . . We may probably conceive that this Declaration of the Popish Clergy hastened the Disputation appointed on the last of March in the Church of *Westminster*. . . .[3]

The Westminster disputation.

Very naturally, therefore, Fuller, in giving his account of this Westminster disputation, adds, after the name of the "Dr. Harpsfield" who was one of the seven (or eight) disputants on the Roman side, the words "Archdeacon of Canterbury." In this he has been followed by all Harpsfield's biographers, Anthony Wood, Lord Acton and Creighton. It is clear, however, that the disputant was John, not Nicholas. An account of the disputation sent by the Count de

[1] Wilkins, *Concilia*, London (1737) IV. 179. Strype, *Annals of the Reformation* (1824) I. i. 80; "The history of it . . . I take . . . from Archbishop Parker's volume, entitled *Synodalia.*" This is now in Corpus Christi College, Cambridge (MS. 121). See M. R. James, *Catalogue of MSS. in C.C.C.C.*, I, 288.

[2] *The Church History of Britain* (1655) Book IX, p. 54.

[3] The same, p. 56.

Feria to the King of Spain [1] speaks of Dr. Arceu [Harpsfield] *Archdeacon of St. Paul's*, rising four times, with the paper in his hand, and being refused permission to speak each time by the Chairman.

Fuller's account tells us:

> The passages of this Disputation (whereof more Noise then fruit, and wherein more Passion then Reason, Cavils then Arguments) are largely reported by Mr. *Fox*. . . . In this Refusal to begin, *Winchester* and *Lincolne* behaved themselves saucily, and scornfully, the rest stiffly and resolutely; only Feckenham, Abbot of *Westminster* (who it seems the second day was added to the Popish Disputants) carried it with more meeknesse and moderation. Hereupon the Lord Keeper cut off this conference, with this sharp Conclusion, *Seeing my Lords we cannot now hear you, you may perchance shortly hear more of us.*[2]

"For the contempt so notoriously made," the bishops of Winchester and Lincoln were sent to the Tower, and the rest, except Abbot Feckenham, were bound over.[3]

On 4 April, 1559, it is *Johannes* Harpesfelde who, with his fellow disputants, enters into recognizances to appear every day before the Lords of the Council,[4] not to depart from London and Westminster and the suburbs, and to pay such fine as may be assessed on him. "Dr. Harpsfield" accordingly makes twenty-eight appearances before he pays his fine of £40 on 12 May, 1559.

Meantime Nicholas had been getting into trouble at Canterbury. On 9 Feb., 1558/9, we have in the Acts of the Privy Council "A letter Nicholas Harpsfield at Canterbury.

[1] 4 April, 1559, *Calendar of State Papers, Spanish*, 1542–1579. There is a full account of the proceedings in Jewel's letter to Peter Martyr, 6 April, 1559, (*Zurich Archives*; Parker Society); also at the end of Foxe's *Acts and Monuments.*

[2] The same, p. 57. For further details of the conference, see *Calendar of State Papers, Domestic*, 1547–1580: Vol. III, Elizabeth, March 1559:

March	51.	Proposition of the Bishops of Winchester, Lichfield, Chester and Carlisle, and Drs. Cole, Harpsfield, Langdale and Chedsey on the part of the Catholics to conduct the conference at Westminster in writing.
March 31.	52.	Declaration of the Proceedings of a Conference begun at Westminster, concerning certain Articles of Religion; and the breaking up of the said conference by default and contempt of certain Bishops parties of the said conference. Signed by the Privy Council.
March 31.	53.	Draft of the above declaration. Corrected by Cecil.
	54.	Copy of the above proceedings.

[3] See "Declaration of the Proceedings of a Conference begun at Westminster, the last of March, 1559," in Burnet's *History of the Reformation* (1681) Vol. II. See also "Synodalia" (MS. Corpus Christi College, Camb., 121) article 21.

[4] *Acts of the Privy Council*, New Series, VII, 79 (1893).

of apparence to Doctour Harpesfylde, Archedeacon of Cantourburye"; and two days later:

> A letter to Sir Thomas Fynche, knight, and George Maye, one of the Aldermen of Cantorbury, that where the Lordes are informed that Doctor Harpesfeld, Archdeacon of Cantourbury, hath used himself of late very dissorderly in steringe the people as muche as in him lyethe to sedytion, and that it is also reported by some of the servauntes of the Colledge in Christe Church in Cantourbury that Religion could not nor should not be altered, and that one man of that Colledge hath well nere one hundreth harnesses, they are requyred texamyne this matter dylligently, and to call before them all suche whome they shall thinke mete to be examyned herein, or culpable touching the same, and theruppon to cause suche as be faulty to be commytted to warde, and to signifye what they shall fynde out herein hither; and also to serche what armure is in the sayd Colledge, and what hath been delyveryd out, and by whom and for what purpose and to whose handes, and to wryte hyther their knowledge in the same.[1]

Nicholas Harpsfield, together with "all the canons and prebendaries that had any right to vote in the election," was summoned to appear at the Chapter on 1 Aug., 1559, for the election of Parker as archbishop of Canterbury. Harpsfield and six others (the majority) absented themselves; they were for their absence pronounced contumacious by the Chapter, and decreed to incur the pains of contumacy.[2]

The Visitors at St. Paul's.

Eleven days later, Nicholas Harpsfield, as Prebendary of London, was called upon to subscribe "the Book of Religion" and refused, but "in terms of studied moderation":

> Aug. 11, 1559. These three Visitors [Robert Horne, Tho. Huyche and John Salvyn] came into the Church of St. Paul in order to visit. . . . And offering to them, *viz.*, *John Harpsfield*, Archdeacon of London, and *Nic. Harpsfield*, Prebendary, and *John Willerton*, as well the Book of the Queen's *Injunctions*, with Admonition inviolably to observe them, and to take care they were observed by other Ministers of the said Church: as also the Book of Religion received, to subscribe the same. The same *John* and *Nic. Harpsfield* and *J. Willerton* did altogether refuse those *Injunctions*, or to subscribe to the said Religion: Protesting nevertheless that they refused them *Animis non maliciosis aut obstinatis, sed ex ea tantum causa, quod conscientiis non salvis adhuc in ea parte non plene instructis in receptionem*

[1] The same, 54.
[2] Strype, *Life and Acts of Matthew Parker* (1711) p. 52.

Injunctionum aut subscriptionem Religionis, etc. *consentire non potuerunt, i.e.* Not with malicious or obstinate minds, but for this cause only, that they could not consent, their consciences not safe, nor as yet fully instructed for the receiving the injunctions, or for subscribing to the Religion, etc.

The Visitors also enjoyned them, that they should take care, that the Cathedral Church should be purged and freed from all and singular their Images, Idols and Altars: *Et in loco ipsorum Altarium ad providend. Mensam decentem in Ecclesia pro celebratione cœnae Domini ordinaria: i.e.* And in the place of those Altars to provide a decent table in the Church, for the ordinary celebration of the Lord's Supper. And present this notice as soon as possibly might be. The said *Harpsfield, Harpsfield* and *Willerton* refused under the Protestation before mentioned. . . .

Lastly, the Commissaries, by reason of the manifest contumacies of *Harpsfield, Harpsfield* and *Willerton* (refusing to receive the *Injunctions*, and to subscribe to the *Religion*) bound them in penalty of 200 l. to the Queen in their respective Recognizances, as in their Recognizances more fully appears.[1]

These events are recorded in a contemporary diary:

1559. The xj day of August the vesetars satt at Powlles . . . apon master Harpfeld and master Harpfeld and dyvers odur. The xxiij day of October master Harpfeld the archdecon of London was deposyd and dyvers prebendarys and vecurs.[2]

Nicholas was obviously among the prebendaries deposed.

Imprisonment of the two brothers.

There is a gap in the extant Acts of the Privy Council after 12 May, 1559—the day on which we find John Harpsfield paying his fine for the contempt committed by him in the disputation of 31 March. The Acts are available again on and after 28 May, 1562; and on 28 July of that year we find both brothers in the Fleet, to be kept more closely:

xxviij^th of Julye 1562 — This daye the Warden of the Fletes deputye, being called before the Lordes, had commaundment geven him to say to his master from their Lordships that he shuld cause Dr. Scotte, Dr. Cole, the twoo Harpesfieldes, Wood, Somerset and Smyth remaineng prisoners in his warde, to be kept in closse prisonne, so as they may not have conference with anye nor be suffred to have suche resorte unto them as they have been accustomed.

[1] Strype, *Annals of the Reformation*, Second edit. (1725) Vol. I, p. 169. Visitation at St. Paul's. Regist. Grindal.

[2] *Diary of Henry Machyn*, ed. J. G. Nichols (1848) Camden Soc., No. 42.

Their release, 1574.

In the Fleet they remained, it appears, for a further twelve years.[1] On 19 Aug., 1574, we learn from the Acts of the Privy Council of their impending release on bail, to go to Bath for their health :

xix^th^ of Auguste 1574 At Bristowe, the xix^th^ of Auguste. A letter to the Warden of the Fleete . . . that when the two Harpesfildes, John and Nicholas, prisoners under his charge, shalbe sent for by the Archbisshop of Caunterburie, that they may be brought unto him; and when the said Lord Archbishop shall have taken bandes of them, as is appointed, the said Warden is required, having knowledge thereof, to set them at libertie.

A letter to the Archbisshop of Caunterburie, that where sute is made for John and Nicholas Harpesfilde, prisoners in the Flete, that in respect of their infirmities and diseases they might be licensed for the recoverie of their helthes to go and remaine at the Bathes in Somerset shiere till the ende of October next, that his Lordship shall cause them to be sent for before him, and to take sufficient bandes and sureties of them, eche of them for them selfes in ij^c^ li. apece, and ij sureties for eche of them in c li. apece, that they shall not by speche, writing or otherwise induce or intice any person to any opinion or acte to be donne contrarie to the lawes establisshed in this realme for causes of Religion, nor that any persons shall resort to them that do mislike the presente state of Religion, and that they both do make their apparaunce before such of their Lordships as shalbe present at the Sterre Chamber the first day of the sitting in Counsell there after the Feast of All Saintes next coming. . . .

John Harpsfield's Common-place-book.

These extracts from the Acts of the Privy Council are supplemented by a Commonplace-book kept by John Harpsfield between 1572 and 1577. John has written in it copies of defeasance of the bond on which he and his brother were released, and of the letter from the Privy Council to Brian Ansley, Warden of the Fleet, for their discharge[2] (19 Aug., 1574). They had to be back from Bath for the first sitting in Council at the Star Chamber in November. In preparation for this we have in the Commonplace-book drafts of three letters in which John again petitions for leave to go to Bath : one in Greek, dated 8 Nov., 1574, to the Lord Treasurer, Lord Burghley;[3] one in Latin, dated Nov., to the Earl of Sussex, Lord Cham-

[1] On 21 June, 1567, there was a conference on matters of religion between Sir Tho. Cornwaleys, Mr. Provost and Mr. Harpsfield. Gabriel Goodman, dean of Westminster, to Cecil: *Calendar of State Papers, Domestic*, 1547–80, p. 293 (Vol. XLIII, Elizabeth, June–Aug. 1567).

[2] British Museum, MS. Royal 8. B. xx, fols. 189^v^, 190^v^.

[3] fol. 155^v^.

berlain;[1] and one in Greek, dated 1 Nov., to Sir Thomas Smith, Secretary of State.[2] The draft letter to Burghley has a note at the end: 12º *fui cum ipso*. This is a reference to the first meeting, after the Feast of All Saints, "at the Sterre chamber," 12 Nov., 1574, when John and Nicholas made that appearance to which they were pledged.[3] But I know no evidence that the leave to go to Bath was granted: the Harpsfields continue to report "every Starre Chamber daye" with a frequency which must have left little opportunity for distant residence.[4] Meantime John amuses himself by making notes in his Commonplace-book from the historical works of Nicholas, and some of these are dated 1 March, 1575, "apud Munnox," *i.e.* at the house of George Monnox of Walthamstow. But on 29 Nov., 1575, "At the Sterre Chamber," Nicholas makes no appearance:

> This day John Harpesfilde, in the behalf of himself and his brother Nicholas Harpesfilde, being sicke, prayeth that his apparaunce might be recorded, acording to their bandes taken to appere before the Lordes from tyme to tyme, as they shuld sitte in Privey Counsell in the Sterre Chamber, which they have donne all this Terme acordingly.[5]

Sickness of Nicholas Harpsfield.

From December, 1575, to the following May, John entered in his Commonplace-book the metrical abridgement of the *Ecclesiastical History of England* with which he was amusing himself. It begins:

> Dux euangelii fuit Arimatheus Ἰωσήφ

It is varied by a few notes relating to his own affairs; near the beginning we find:[6]

> Moritur frater 18 Deceb̄. 1575, Dominica 4ta Adventus.

Death of Nicholas Harpsfield.

This conclusively proves the inaccuracy of the statement of Pits,[7] that Nicholas Harpsfield lingered in prison till 1583. That date has indeed been discredited since the discovery, more than half a century ago, of a number of entries as to the deaths of prominent Roman Catholics in a Service book at Exeter College.[8] There

[1] fol. 156. [2] fol. 156v.
[3] *Acts of the Privy Council*, ed. Dasent, viii (1894), p. 312.
[4] *The same*, pp. 318, 320, 339, 371, 373.
[5] *The same*, ix, p. 54.
[6] fol. 162b.
[7] Obijt tandem Londini Confessor in carcere post vicesimum captivitatis annum, qui fuit partus virginei plus minus 1583, sub duro Catholicis Elizabethæ regno. (Pits, *Relationes Historicæ de rebus Anglicis*, Paris, 1619, p. 781.)
[8] *Psalterium cum hymnis secundum morem et consuetudinem nigrorum monachorum Abendonensis monasterii*, 1528. See *Academy*, ix (1876) p. 360.

the death of Nicholas is stated as occurring on 18 Dec., 1575, which his brother's entry now finally confirms.

Sickness and death of John Harpsfield.

John survived his brother more than two years, writing notes and accounts in his book, some of which apparently refer to legacies left by Nicholas. He continued to make appearances from time to time at the Star Chamber,[1] and was remitted to the charge of the Bishop of Lincoln, "to remaine with him acording to certen orders sent downe with their Lordships' letters." [2] The object was clearly to give him fewer opportunities than he would have in London of communicating with his co-religionists. But he was a very sick man, and on 5 Nov., 1577, "for that there are not any skillfull phisicions in those partes whose advice he might use for the recovery of his healthe," their Lordships allowed him temporarily "to repaire to the Bishop of London, and there remaine with him till he shall be fully recovered" ; the Bishop is "to se him kept a parte, and admitte suche phisicions and surgeons to resort unto him as he shall knowe not only to be skillfull, but also sounde of Relligion." On 7 June, 1578, he applied again to Burghley for leave to go to Bath :

> "Most honorable, as ever heretofore, so now in extremitie helpe me. A letter is drawen for my repaire to bathe. There lacketh but subscription. Our lord ever have your honorable L. in his blessed tuition. Your honorable L. most bounden oratour John Harpsfeld, overwhelmed with hurttes and maladies." [3]

In August he died, apparently in London; the letters of administration taken out after his death by his niece, Anne Worsopp, describe him as of the parish of St. Sepulchre.[4]

The exact date of his death [5] is recorded in the Calendar prefixed to the Service book which also marks that of his brother :

[1] *Acts of the Privy Council*, N.S., ix, 123, 161.

[2] The same, ix, 388; x, 4.

[3] MS. Lansdowne 27, No. 33, fol. 64.

[4] Wood quotes a book of Administrations (Prerogative Court of Canterbury) beginning 1 Jan., 1571; *Athenæ* (1691), I, 151.

[5] The news of his death reached Douay 23 Oct., 1578. See *Diaries of the English College, Douay*, ed. T. F. Knox (1878): *23 Oct., 1578: accepimus reverendum D. D. Harpsfeldum, propter fidei catholicæ professionem multorum annorum incarcerationes apud hæreticos passum, tum nuper in Anglia obiisse.* This entry has caused considerable confusion because, on the strength of Wood's assertion, it had been supposed that Nicholas alone suffered long imprisonment; the editor therefore naturally took this entry as referring to Nicholas. See correspondence in *The Tablet*, LII (N.S. xx, 1878) pp. 9, 47, 75, 110. But the *Acts of the Privy Council* make it clear that the brothers were imprisoned together, and the difficulty accordingly disappears.

Aug. 19. Obitus Johannis Harpsfilde, 1578.
Dec. 18. Obitus Nicolai Harpsfylde, sacerdotis, 1575.

Portrait of Nicholas Harpsfield.

In the Upper Reading Room of the Bodleian may be seen what purports to be a portrait of Nicholas Harpsfield. It is thus described by Mrs. Poole :[1]

> Bust, three-quarters to l.; head bald, leaning to l., greyish hair; lanky brown beard and long moustache; the face thin and distressed, mouth open; apparently represented as Saint Jerome or some other ascetic saint, beating his breast with a stone held in his r. hand; garment of buff and green fur; dark background; above to r. a shelf with four books with illegible titles on their edges; inscribed NICHOLAUS HARPSFELDUS ARCHIDIACONNS CANTNAIRENSIS. This is possibly not a portrait at all: the inscription has suffered from the restoration of a past generation.
> Panel 18½ × 15½ in. [165].
> Given to the University by R. M. Massey, M.D., in 1730.
> Oxford Exhibition of Historical Portraits, 1904, No. 44.

Bacon records[2] that Sir Thomas More refused to have his hair trimmed on the day of his execution, on the ground that the King and he had a suit for his head, and, till the title were cleared, he would do no cost upon it. Until the title to this head be cleared, as between St. Jerome and Nicholas Harpsfield, it seems unreasonable to ask the Early English Text Society to bear the cost of reproducing it.

Character of Nicholas Harpsfield:

Nicholas Harpsfield, says Fuller, left behind him "the general reputation of a Religious man."[3] Despite the ugly stories which Foxe repeats of his "agrest disposition," Harpsfield's writings, controversial as they are, show a certain moderation which was not pleasing to some of the embittered Roman Catholic recusants of the next generation.

explained by Lord Acton.

Harpsfield's attitude has been explained by Lord Acton :[4]

> To have venerated Sir Thomas More, to have been attached to Cardinal Pole, does not define a man's position amid the religious currents of that age. The distinctive feature in Harpsfield's character is his admiration for Erasmus. He

[1] *Catalogue of Portraits in the possession of the University, Colleges, City and County of Oxford,* compiled by Mrs. Reginald Lane Poole (1912) I, 16.
[2] Apophthegms : *Works,* ed. Spedding (1859) vii, p. 127.
[3] *Church History of Britain* (1655) xvi Cent., ix Book, p. 143.
[4] *Academy,* ix (1876) p. 609.

Character of Nicholas Harpsfield explained by Lord Acton.

remained true to the memory of the great Iconoclast, and continued to defend his reputation long after his influence had become extinct in the Church, when his writings were proscribed, and the last of his friends had passed away. The editor of his ecclesiastical history has struck out a long passage in praise of Erasmus, of which one sentence will sufficiently indicate the tone :

> " Waramus, etsi aegro et invito, ut ipse fatetur, animo ecclesias aliquas pensionibus gravari pateretur, cum tamen raras et singulares Erasmi dotes, summam facundiam atque doctrinam, quibus mirifice universae ecclesiae profuit, et, ut illius verbis utar, tanquam sydus quoddam illustravit, et singularem quandam Erasmi in Angliam et Anglos propensionem, apud quos, relicta Italia, Germania, Gallia, aliisque regionibus, in quibus amplissime illi prospectum fuisset, si in illis commorari voluisset, domicilium sibi constituere potissimum cogitabat, magnumque toti Angliae ex illius praesentia emolumentum manaturum perspiceret, curavit ut viginti librarum annuam, quoad viveret, ex ea ecclesia pensionem decerperet." . . .

He is one of the earliest ecclesiastical writers whose mind fell naturally into an historical attitude, and with whom religious controversy resolves itself into the discussion of fact. In the preface to his *Dialogues* he says :

> " A rebus enim sacris et theologia divelli historia non potest, sine qua infans plane est theologus : ut et hic dici possit, quod olim de navi respondit jureconsultus; si dividas, perdes. Quare nos multo rectius theologo, quam eam olim suo oratori Cicero, attribuemus. Et, si verum dicere velimus, quid aliud fere tota Scriptura est, quam perpetua quaedam historia? ut prudenter quidem nostri fecerint, qui ad controversorum hodie dogmatum explicationem historias quoque adhibuerint."

Nothing is more to his credit than the candour with which he states the case of his opponents. He mentions, as Mr. Pocock has pointed out, the argument of Catharine's advocates, that the dispensation would override even the Divine Law; but he adds that it is not his own opinion. He strives to be just towards Henry VIII, and uses with effect, but with entire fairness, the correspondence of the King and the Cardinal with Rome, which had come into his hands. The assertion that nobody honestly doubted the validity of the dispensation; that its original defects were made good by a second instrument,[1] that Wolsey, finding that the business languished, revived it through

[1] Yet surely Harpsfield *does* state this most explicitly. Compare pp. 46–7, below, and Notes thereon. See, however, *Pretended Divorce*, 193, etc.

the Bishop of Tarbes; that the Bishop of Tarbes made an oration exhorting Henry to put away his brother's wife, and to take in her place the French king's sister (already married to a second husband); that Anne Boleyn was at the bottom of the whole mischief; that she was Henry's mistress; that she was Henry's daughter—all these things, which have been the constant material of controversy, do not figure in Harpsfield's severe and sober pages.

Harpsfield's use of English and Latin.

"Harpsfield died," says Acton, "without having made himself known in literature. The works which occupied the weary years of his captivity could not be published in England." And neglect has persisted.

It is typical of this neglect that an eminent modern scholar should have quoted Harpsfield as an exception to the rule that historians of England of the later Sixteenth Century write in English.[1] Yet Harpsfield's practice does not differ from that of his fellow-countrymen. Like More before him, or Bacon or Milton after him, he writes in English when he is addressing Englishmen; in Latin when he is addressing a wider European audience. *Mutatis mutandis*, his practice is exactly the same as that of John Foxe. During Mary's reign, when publication in English was possible, Harpsfield wrote his historical work in English: meantime Foxe, in exile, naturally published in Latin, at Strassburg in 1554, and, later, at Basel.[2] When the positions were reversed, Foxe published his *Acts and Monuments* in English in 1563. If Harpsfield had written his criticism of Foxe in English, he would hardly have seen it in print;[3] on the other hand, the demand among the learned men of Europe for Harpsfield's Latin polemics was such that a second edition of his *Dialogi sex* was called for within seven years. His *Historia Anglicana Ecclesiastica* was not so fortunate; yet even here the contrast with his English works, unprinted till the nineteenth or twentieth century, is striking. That Harpsfield, when writing Latin, is thinking of a European audience, is shown, for example, by the fact that in the *Historia Wicliffiana* he translates into Latin any English words he

[1] *English Historical Literature in the Fifteenth Century*, by C. L. Kingsford (1913) p. 8.

[2] Mary was dead before the Basel edition was actually published in 1559.

[3] Important books were, of course, printed abroad by, and for, the refugees, in English. This refugee literature has been much neglected, and is now, I am glad to say, being studied by Mr. A. C. Southern. [Meantime, whilst this book has been in the press, a most important work by Miss Helen C. White has appeared, on *English Devotional Literature* (Madison, Wisconsin, 1931), with a chapter on "Recusant Devotional Literature."]

may have occasion to quote, such as " When Adam delved and Eve spanne."

Dialogi sex. The first of Harpsfield's books to be printed was his *Dialogi*, the subject of which is summarized in its title.[1] It was published at Antwerp in 1566. The speakers are Irenæus, an Englishman, and Critobulus, a German. (It is perhaps only an accident that the chief speaker in Spenser's *View of the Present State of Ireland*, the Englishman, recently returned from Ireland, is also called *Irenæus*.) Harpsfield's first Dialogue defends the primacy of the Pope; the second, monasticism; the third, the invocation of saints; the fourth and fifth, images; the sixth attacks John Foxe and his martyrs. Alan Cope, a refugee in the Low Countries, was the editor. For Harpsfield's protection, the book appeared under Cope's name; the true authorship was concealed under letters at the end.[2] It is to be hoped that a copy was smuggled into the Fleet for the author to see. It is a beautiful production of the Plantin press: seldom has a controversialist had his arguments put forward in such lovely type. The most provocative portion was the last Dialogue, dealing with Foxe.[3] Foxe defended himself in the second (1570) edition of his *Acts and Monuments* against these attacks of " Alanus Copus Anglus, a person to me unknowen, and obscure hitherto unto the world . . . (whether he under the armour of other, or other under the title of hys name, I knowe not, nor passe not)."[4]

" Coming now to the matter of the Lorde Cobham," says Foxe, " it shall bee requisite a little by the waye to cope with this Cope," and accordingly he devotes forty-seven of his massive columns to a defence of Lord Cobham against Alanus Copus (pp. 676–699). Foxe admits that he has fallen into some inaccuracies, but complains that his adversary, " if he had knowen any fault nedefull to be corrected, might gentely by letters [have] admonished me therof."

Harpsfield had attacked Foxe on account of errors of names which,

[1] *Dialogi sex, contra summi pontificatus, monasticæ vitæ, Sanctorum, sacrarum imaginum oppugnatores, et pseudomartyres.* The second edition was printed by Plantin at Antwerp in 1573. The first Dialogue was reprinted at Rome in 1698, in the collection of works in defence of the Holy See edited by Archbishop Rocaberti; and a single page (that describing the cross which appeared in the middle of a tree in the parish of St. Donat's, Glamorganshire) was printed in England, privately, at Middle Hill, 1846.

[2] A.H.L.N.H.E.V.E.A.C., which the initiated understood to mean *Auctor hujus libri Nicolaus Harpesfeldus, edidit vero eum Alanus Copus.*

[3] Some account of this controversy will be found in Gairdner, *Lollardy and the Reformation*, I, 358–63.

[4] I, p. 676.

considering the vast mass of his work, were almost inevitable, and which do not in themselves detract from the truth of the *Acts and Monuments* as a whole.[1] Foxe is in the right when he replies : *Dialogi sex.*

> Woulde God, maister Cope, that in all the whole booke of Actes and monumentes, from the beginning to the later end of the same, wer never a true story, but that all were false, all were lyes, and all fables.[2]

Foxe seems to have had a very strong suspicion that his real adversary was not Cope, a young Oxford don who had resigned his preferments and gone into exile, but someone nearer home. Foxe threatens to unmask *and name* this adversary : to " shape you a name accordingly, and in stede of Cope godfather you to bee a perpetuall sycophant . . . and dresse your drousy or rather lowsy dialogues in their right colours." [3] Harpsfield had referred to the " angelic " Houghton.[4] How, retorts Foxe, could Alan Cope, who could have been only nine years old when Houghton was executed in 1535, be of age to judge " of any such angelicall proportion of mans personage " ? " Whiche thyng," says Foxe :

> whiche thyng among many other probabilities, maketh me vehemently to suspect, that these Dialogues, printed in Antwerpe, an. 1566, were brought ouer by M. Cope there to be printed, but were penned and framed by an other Pseudo-copus, what soeuer, or in what fleete so euer he was, vnlesse my markes do greatly fayle me. But as the case is of no great weyght, so I let it passe, returnyng to other matters of more importance.[5]

[1] For example, Foxe had, in his first edition, confused two sufferers, Marbeck, the organist of St. George's Chapel, Windsor, and Filmer. Filmer was burnt, Marbeck pardoned, and long continued his duties at Windsor. Foxe had discovered his mistake before his first edition was issued, and in his " Faultes and oversightes escaped, whiche we desire thee, gentle Reader, gently to beare withal," he had noted : " Finmore, rede Marbeck " ; " Marbecke, reade Finmore." Foxe's apology for errors amid " the laborious travayle in the manyfolde matters herein contained " might melt the severest critic. But " Alan Cope " will not let him off, and makes much of *Marbeci Angli inauditum Martyrium* : A Protestant miracle ! Marbeck must have risen from the dead ! *En tibi enim Ioannem Marbecum psaltem Vindilesoriæ anno Domini* 1543 *&* 28 *Iulij, Martyrium in igne alacri* (*ut Foxi verbis utar*) *constantia subeuntem. At ille adhuc vivit, et Vindelesoriæ eleganter, ut solet, psallit et organa pulsat.* (*Dialogi sex*, pp. 962–3.)

[2] *Acts and Monuments* (1570) I, 691.

[3] ed. 1570, I. p. 691.

[4] *Atqui cum Ioannem illum Houghtonium cogito, non tam hominem, quam Angelum in humana forma intueri mihi videor.* (*Dialogi sex* (1566) p. 994.) This seems to be a recollection of the *Expositio fidelis* (see below, p. 254), where, however, it is not Houghton, but Reynolds, who is described as *vir angelico vultu et angelico spiritu.*

[5] ed. 1570, II. p. 1217.

"In what fleete soeuer" points to Harpsfield; in the next (third) edition [1] the reference is made clearer by giving Fleete a capital F; but the authorship is not revealed.[2] In the fourth edition of the *Acts and Monuments*, when both the Harpsfields were dead, Foxe describes the *Dialogues* as "compiled in latine by *Nich. Harpsfield*, set out by *Alanus Copus*." [3]

There is some ground for believing (and it is a pleasant thing to believe) that, during all this bitter controversy, Foxe knew who his adversary was, but refrained from unmasking his disguise, because of the very serious trouble in which it would have involved the author of that "drowsy" volume which seems to have given Foxe sleepless nights.

***Historia Anglicana Ecclesiastica* and *Historia Wicliffiana*.**

Harpsfield's *Historia Anglicana Ecclesiastica* was not published [4] till nearly half a century after its author's death. It naturally received the enthusiastic praise of Roman Catholic writers, but it is important to note that this praise is also echoed by Fuller, who speaks of it as "no less learnedly then painfully performed, and, abating his partiality to his own interest, well deserving of all posterity." [5] It was not till more than a century after Harpsfield's day that his book was found to fall short of the rising standard of historical accuracy. Henry Wharton, in his *Anglia Sacra*, speaks of it slightingly, though still with respect for its author.[6] Harpsfield was perhaps working under greater difficulties than Wharton realized.[7]

During the half-century which intervened between composition and publication, the book had circulated in manuscript, and the relation of the manuscripts to each other, and to the printed edition, presents some interesting problems. A systematic collation of these manuscripts with the printed edition has never been undertaken. If it should be thought worth doing, it is a labour which falls to a bibliographer of the history of the Church of England; it is assuredly

[1] ed. 1576, p. 1043. [2] See p. 547. [3] ed. 1583, p. 568.

[4] *Historia Anglicana Ecclesiastica, a primis gentis susceptæ fidei incunabulis ad nostra fere tempora deducta*, Douay (1622). The *Historia Wicliffiana* is appended.

[5] *Church History of Britain* (1655) xvi. Cent., ix. Book, p. 143.

[6] *ut . . . tam crassi errores sæpius inveniantur, ut mirum sit hominem, cui neque industria nec ingenium defuit, tam misere labi potuisse.* It is Wharton who asserts that Archbishop Parker helped Harpsfield by giving him the use of the registers of his See: *carcere quidem adeo non constrictus ut Archiepiscopus Cantuariensis, erudito labori favens, omnium Sedis suæ Registrorum usum ipsi indulserit.* (*Anglia Sacra*, 1691, Præfatio, xiv, xv.)

[7] See above, p. clxxxiv.

Historia Anglicana Ecclesiastica and *Historia Wicliffiana.*

not a duty incumbent upon the editor of an Early English Text. I will confine myself to some short notes, which are the result of an examination necessarily very limited.

Anthony Wood writes as if he had compared the printed edition of 1622 with Harpsfield's autograph manuscript. But we shall see that here his memory is deceiving him. As far as I am aware, Harpsfield's original manuscript has not survived. The greater part of a transcript, however, is extant, which has received corrections and additions that can hardly be from any other hand than Harpsfield's. This fair copy is in three distinct fragments, written in beautiful Italian scripts, which contrast sharply with the rugged English hand in which the corrections and additions are made. All three fragments are now preserved in the British Museum. They are:

> i. MS. Arundel 72, which contains the First Book, and 58 leaves of the Second, bringing us to Book II, the middle of cap. 23 (the Seventh Century).[1]
>
> ii. MS. Stowe 105, beginning with fol. 69 (Book II, the middle of cap. 26: the Seventh Century) and ending with the close of the Eleventh Century. This Stowe MS. clearly once formed part of the same volume as MS. Arundel 72; ten leaves have been lost.[2] The Stowe MS. contains not only corrections but some considerable additions, made in what is presumably Harpsfield's hand. The most interesting is one which relates to the exactions of the Danes.[3] This mentions Ethelred's treaty, *Quod extat Saxonice impressum, Lond.* 1568. The reference is to Lambarde's Ἀρχαιονομια, published in that year; this helps us to date the additions. Whilst this addition appears in the printed copy, another long addition does not.[4]

For the Twelfth, Thirteenth and Fourteenth Centuries the British Museum has no MS.

> iii. MS. Arundel 73 contains the Fifteenth Century. It has been corrected in the same way as MS. Arundel 72 and MS. Stowe 105, in what is apparently Harpsfield's hand.

I have quoted already a passage from Lord Acton's account of Harpsfield, in which he mentions Harpsfield's admiration of Erasmus,

[1] Harpsfield's *Historia* is divided into Centuries. Book I covers the first six: after that, each Century has a Book to itself.

[2] *i.e.* corresponding to the passage from p. 84, l. 2, to p. 90, l. 40, of the edition of 1622.

[3] fol. 99 of the MS., as at present paged.

[4] fol. 254 (at end of cap. 6 of the Eleventh Century).

Historia Anglicana Ecclesiastica and *Historia Wicliffiana.*

and instances a passage which Harpsfield had written in praise of "the great Iconoclast," but which his editor had suppressed.[1] Acton does not say from what manuscript he recovered this passage, but the treatment of it in MS. Arundel 73 is noteworthy. It is there written out fair in the Italian hand, with some minute corrections of detail in the hand presumably Harpsfield's.[2] Then the whole passage has been scored through, and, as Lord Acton says, it does not appear in the printed text[3] of 1622.

It seems safe to assume that the scoring through was not the work of Harpsfield. For the minute corrections which he makes prove that, at the time he was revising his *Historia,* he meant the passage to stand. That time, as we have seen, was during the last seven years of his life.[4] The "Erasmus" passage remained for a period, corrected but uncancelled; for the other fair copies have the passage, incorporating Harpsfield's minute alterations.[5] They were therefore presumably transcribed after Harpsfield made his corrections, but before the whole "Erasmus" passage was cancelled. But whilst it is clear that Harpsfield's admiration for Erasmus persisted into the last period of his life, it would be hard to condemn Richard Gibbons,[6] who published the *Historia* half a century later, as "an unfaithful editor." The expunging is not necessarily his. He may have received his copy in a mutilated state.

In view of the length of time which passed before it was printed, there are no doubt many manuscripts of the *Historia* extant in the libraries of Europe. The best I have met belonged to Lord Lumley (1534–1609); it was in four volumes, upon the first page of each of which Lumley has placed his autograph. The first two volumes, now bound together, are in the Lambeth Library;[7] the third is in the British Museum;[8] the fourth, containing the addendum to the History, the *Historia Wicliffiana,* is at Lambeth.[9] Further fragmentary copies are in the Royal Library; these are probably not fragments of one set, for one is in an English hand,[10] the other in a beautiful Italian script.[11] Pits, who wrote his account of Harpsfield

[1] See above, p. cxciv. [2] fols. 96v and 97.
[3] It should come on p. 632, but does not.
[4] Subsequent to Lambarde's Ἀρχαιονομια, 1568.
[5] MS. Arundel 73, fols. 96v, 97, should be compared with MS. Stowe 106, fols. 176–7, and MS. Royal 13. C. xiii, fols. 172–3. For example, *tanti festi* of MS. Arundel is corrected in Harpsfield's hand to *tam festi tamque solennis diei,* and appears in that form in both the Stowe and the Royal MSS.
[6] As does Acton, *Academy,* ix (1876) 609.
[7] Nos. 53, 54. [8] Stowe, 106. [9] No. 140.
[10] 13. C. ix. [11] 13. C. xiii.

whilst the *Historia* was still unprinted, mentions a copy in the English College at Rome; Richard Gibbons, editing the *Historia* in 1622, says that he used two manuscripts, one in his own possession, said to have once been Harpsfield's (*ipsius auctoris fuisse dicitur*), from which, however, some leaves were missing; and a transcript which had been supplied to him from a manuscript in the Vatican.

A difficult problem as to the text of the *Historia Anglicana Ecclesiastica* is raised by the fact that Anthony Wood gives instances of passages which he asserts to have been excised from the section dealing with the Thirteenth Century, expurgations similar in intention to that of which Acton complains in the passage regarding Erasmus. Wood claims to have discovered these excisions by comparing with the printed text MS. Cotton Vitellius C. ix, No. 12, which he states to be Harpsfield's autograph copy of the *Historia Anglicana Ecclesiastica*. But this is not so. MS. Vitellius C. ix, No. 12, certainly is the author's autograph copy. However, it is not Nicholas Harpsfield's *Historia*, but a much briefer metrical *Ecclesiastical History of England*, the work of John Harpsfield, written in his distinctive and crabbed handwriting.[1] It is the same metrical *Ecclesiastical History* upon which we have seen John engaged at the date of his brother's death, and which he entered from time to time in his Commonplace-book, as he composed it. Obviously Wood could not have used it to detect omissions in the printed edition of Nicholas' long prose *Historia*. Wood must be confusing MS. Vitellius C. ix (12) with some manuscript of Nicholas' *Historia* which he had seen. But there is no such manuscript in the Cottonian collection; and the only other manuscript of Nicholas' *Historia* which Wood mentions, that at Lambeth, does not contain the passages which he claims to have found.

Where Wood got them is a problem which I must leave to the bibliographer of English Church History.

Harpsfield's *Life of More*, now for the first time published,[2] is known to be extant in eight manuscripts.[3] *The Life of More.*

[1] The same MS., Vitellius C. ix, also contains (No. 11) a Chronicle from the Flood to 1559, which is likewise in John's handwriting, and is attributed to Nicholas by Wood. If it should be argued that these *are* the work of Nicholas, and that John was merely transcribing his brother's writings, I think that John's Commonplace-book affords a conclusive answer.

[2] Most of it has been privately printed (from a transcript of one manuscript) in the magazine of a Chelsea sisterhood. See above, p. xv, footnote.

[3] See above, pp. xiii–xliv.

The Life of More.

In his *Epistle Dedicatorie* Harpsfield expresses his debt to Roper: "Ye shall receaue, I will not say a pigg of your owne sowe (it were too homely and swinish a terme) but rather a comely and goodly garlande . . . picked and gathered euen out of your owne garden." Still, Harpsfield claims, he has "with poore Ruthe leased some good corne." How very considerable Harpsfield's gleanings are, will be realized by anyone who will examine the authorities which have been placed in the margin of this edition. Harpsfield has certainly "paide some part of the shott."

"Harpsfield," says Acton, "relates nearly everything that is in Roper's *Life of More* without his mistakes." Harpsfield rearranges his matter freely, but the only passages of any moment which he omits are Roper's preface, two passages where Roper enumerates his authorities, and the passage explaining the illegality of the oath tendered to More, and More's comment thereupon: "they that have committed me hither . . . are not by theyr owne lawe able to iustifye my imprisonement." All the omissions save the last are no doubt intentional. It is difficult to find any reason except mere oversight for the last omission.[1] The Statute Book proves that More was not exaggerating the illegality of the treatment he received, and that, as Roper says, a second statute had to be made to remedy that illegality.

But Acton is certainly going too far in saying that Harpsfield repeats Roper "without his mistakes." Roper wrote from memory more than twenty years after, and there are many passages where he may be inaccurate, and some where he certainly is inaccurate. In some of these inaccuracies Harpsfield follows him: the most remarkable instance is where Harpsfield repeats Roper's statement that Catherine's divorce was pronounced at St. Albans, although the *Pretended Divorce* shows that he knew that it was at Dunstable.[2]

Nevertheless, Harpsfield corrects Roper frequently. For example:

(1) Roper had mentioned More's marriage [1505] before his action as burgess of parliament [1504]. Harpsfield rearranges these events in their chronological order.

(2) Roper had spoken of More being made "Treasurer." Harpsfield corrects silently to "Under-Treasurer." [3]

(3) Roper says that the speech of More, excusing himself from

[1] Harpsfield used the passage later in the *Pretended Divorce* (p. 223).

[2] See Note to 148/5–6. For other inaccuracies, see "Historical Notes" to 20/23–21/3; 24/9–10; 46/20–3; 73/6 (perhaps); 200/18–19; 205/16—206/8.

[3] p. 24, l. 10, and Note thereto.

The Life of More.

the office of Speaker, is "not now extant." Harpsfield gives some details of this speech, which can be confirmed from other sources.[1]

(4) Roper asserts that Langland, bishop of Lincoln, put into the King's head the suggestion of the illegality of his marriage with Catherine. Harpsfield qualifies this, "as it is commonly reported," and mentions Dr. Draycott's denial.[2]

(5) Adrian's entry into Rome, barefooted, reported as fact by Roper, is qualified by Harpsfield, "as I haue herde it credibly reported."[3]

(6) Harpsfield names "the French king's sister," which Roper does not.[4]

(7) Roper mentions three occasions on which the King attempted to gain More's consent to the divorce. Harpsfield adds a fourth.[5]

But, above all, the story which Harpsfield gives of Roper's lapse into heresy—an incident about which Roper himself is silent—throws a new light upon the whole of Roper's memoir. It shows us Roper as a man of more independence of judgement than perhaps we should have gathered from his own account; he was not a colourless person whose orthodoxy was due to his never having investigated what could be said on the other side. Roper and Pole were apparently, after Sir Thomas More, the men to whom Harpsfield was most deeply attached, and it is evidence of his honesty that he tells the truth about them both so unsparingly, even in matters which they themselves would perhaps have wished forgotten.[6]

The most remarkable thing about Harpsfield's *Life* is his account of More's trial. Roper was not there himself; he had his information by the "credible report" of Sir Antony St. Leger, Richard Heywood, John Webb, and others who were present. This he wrote down, "so far as his poor wit and memory would serve him," some twenty years later. The account sent within a few days of the trial, to Paris, differs from Roper's account fundamentally. The two versions have, in fact, nothing in common. Harpsfield appears to be following one of the most dangerous of all ways of harmonizing discrepant accounts. He accepts both, *in toto*, merely adding one to the other.

And the *Indictment* proves that, in so doing, Harpsfield is reconstructing the actual event with complete correctness.

[1] p. 26, l. 19, and Note thereto. [2] p. 41, ll. 5–25.
[3] p. 42, ll. 8–15, and Note thereto. [4] p. 43, ll. 8–9, and Note thereto.
[5] pp. 47–8, and Note to p. 44, ll. 17–18.
[6] For the account of Pole's conduct at Paris, see *Pretended Divorce*, p. 205, and *Academy*, ix (1876) 604.

Harpsfield has done his work exceedingly well, using with painstaking accuracy and judicious selection the materials at his command, rearranging, welding out of these matters of diverse style a very readable whole. His is the first serious attempt at a complete *Life* of More, with an account of his literary work. Roper's *Life*—perfect little gem as it is—is, in comparison, a mere sketch.

The Pretended Divorce.

Harpsfield wrote a *Treatise on the Pretended Divorce of King Henry VIII from Queen Catherine of Aragon*. This, as he explains,[1] is an appendix to the *Life of More*—a tail which grows to be bigger than the dog.

A manuscript of the *Pretended Divorce* was found among the papers of William Carter, Harpsfield's amanuensis, when he was arrested by Topcliffe. A copy of this was made, in 1707, by Charles Eyston of East Hendred, and left to his son, "because it lets him see 'tis truly Conscience and not Obstinacy makes him, by still adhering to the ancient Church, stand obnoxious to so many laws." From this copy of Charles Eyston the *Treatise* was edited for the Camden Society,[2] by Nicholas Pocock, in 1878. The spelling of Pocock's edition is modernized, though not consistently. Pocock emended his text by collating three manuscripts, but, as he printed no collations, it is impossible to control his work. These manuscripts are British Museum Additional 33,737 (formerly Grenville xxxi) and two [3] in the library of New College, Oxford.

There are other manuscripts of the *Pretended Divorce*, notably one in the Calthorpe collection.[4]

The *Pretended Divorce* is divided into three books. The first is a translation, much abbreviated, of Bishop Fisher's answer to the book which had been printed in London, both in Latin and English, defending the sentence of those Universities which had given their opinion on the King's side.[5] In the second book Harpsfield gives his own answer to Robert Wakefield and a number of other writers who had defended the King's divorce. He then passes to what is of more

[1] p. 213, below.

[2] New Series, xxi. An edition of part of this treatise, with an extract from the *Life of More*, was published by Lord Acton (Philobiblon Society, 1877).

[3] 311 A. and 311 B. MS. 311 A. is closely related to Mr. Eyston's copy.

[4] Yelverton 72, bound with Cavendish's *Life of Wolsey* and Harpsfield's *More*. See above, p. xvii.

[5] *Gravissimæ atque exactissimæ illustrissimarum totius Italiæ ac Galliæ Academiarum Censuræ*. London, Berthelet, 1530. For Fisher's different writings on the Divorce, see Bridgett's *Fisher*, pp. 163–4.

interest to the modern reader, "an historicall discourse" of the Divorce and of the troubles springing from it. The argument throughout is that Sir Thomas More "upon just and sufficient causes did refuse the oath."

The Life of Jesus Christ.

The Lambeth Palace Library contains a small 4° manuscript of 170 pages (No. 446), "The life of our Lorde Jesus Christe, written in Latin by Nicolas Harpsfield, Doctor of Civill Lawe, faythfully translated." None of the authorities makes any mention of this, but I think there is no doubt that it is a translation of an authentic work of Harpsfield. The manuscript is contemporary, or nearly so. It is written in a very neat hand, very similar indeed to that of the Emmanuel MS. of the *Life of More*, which, as we have seen, is prior to 1582. The MS. was once in the library of Lord Lumley (1534–1609), who seems to have had a special interest in Harpsfield's work; it bears Lumley's autograph. The book is not so much devotional as argumentative and controversial, and the arguments are those which Harpsfield would have used. For example:

> Moreover, with what teares may we sufficiently lament and bewayle the horrible facte of that desperate insolent younge man, who, being felowe of a woorshipfull house in a famous Universitie, steppeth to the aultare, and in the presence of the master, and of the whole company, violently plucketh downe the Sacrament, through it on the pavement, and villanously treadeth it under his cursed feete. The master of the house and company lamenting that abhominable enterprise, but by reason of that wicked time durste not punishe him for it.[1]

Readers of the *Pretended Divorce* will remember the horror with which Harpsfield records this outrage.[2] He would be in residence at Oxford at the time, and it obviously made a deep impression upon him. Again, in the *Life of Christ*, the writer dwells upon two appearances of a cross,[3] one in Kent in 1559, and one the next summer after, within the wood of a tree blown down in Glamorganshire. We know that Harpsfield attached strange importance to these marvels; he dwells upon them in his *Dialogi sex*,[4] and evidently looked upon them

[1] fol. 50.

[2] ed. Pocock, p. 282. The act was committed by Thomas Bickley, then fellow of Magdalen, afterwards Bishop of Chichester. It was recorded, and approved, during the lifetime of Bickley and Harpsfield, by Laurence Humphrey, who, at the time it was done, was a demy, and was subsequently President of Magdalen. See his *Joannis Juelli vita* (London) pp. 72, 73.

[3] fol. 80. [4] ed. 1566, pp. 503–9.

as divine protests against the removal of crosses and ornaments from churches.

Works attributed to Harpsfield: *The Life of Cranmer.*

Le Grand, in his *Histoire du Divorce de Henry VIII* (1688), speaks of a *Life of Cranmer*, in manuscript, by Harpsfield : *il nous a donné la vie de Cranmer qui se trouve dans le même MS. que la lettre de Polus.* This cannot be a mistake based upon allusions to Cranmer in the *Life of More* or the *Pretended Divorce*, for the short passage which Le Grand goes on to translate does not come from either of these works. It may be a mistake; on the other hand, Le Grand was well informed about Harpsfield—he learnt somehow that Harpsfield was released from prison at the end of his life :[1] a fact otherwise unknown, so far as I have observed, to everybody who has ever written about him.

This *Life of Cranmer* is referred to in the second edition of Harpsfield's *Dialogi*, in a chapter interpolated after cap. XL of the Sixth Dialogue.[2] Speaking of Cranmer, the writer says :

> Cetera autem illius facinora prætermittam, quæ ab amantissimo mei, Nicolao Sandero, viro religiosissimo et doctissimo, et præclarissimis ingenii sui monumentis non modo de Anglia nostra, sed de toto etiam orbe Christiano optime merito, commemorantur.

The margin adds :

> in libello de vita Cranmeri nondum edito.

Pits [3] also attributes this book to Sanders :

> Scripsit de vita et moribus Thomæ Cranmeri, hæretici, librum unum.

Yet this evidence is inconclusive. Pits may have drawn from the *Dialogi*, and as to the reference there, we must remember that, if Harpsfield were really the author of the *Life of Cranmer*, it could no more have been safely claimed as his than the *Dialogi* themselves. The attribution to Sanders may be a mere friendly gesture.

Sanders was some eleven years Harpsfield's junior; he was, like him, a scholar of Winchester, scholar and fellow of New College (they were contemporaries as fellows for some time) and Bachelor of Civil Law. Acton has expressed surprise that the comparatively

[1] *Histoire du Divorce*, 1688, Tom. I, p. 253, marginal note : *Quelques-uns tiennent qu'on le fit sortir de prison pendant la maladie dont il mourut peu de jours après.*

[2] ed. 1573, p. 711.

[3] *Relationes historicæ de rebus Anglicis*, p. 775.

moderate Harpsfield should have employed such friendly language about Sanders; but he says:

> Sanders was not yet the noted partisan he soon became. Their ways parted when Pius V., on the strength of a report from Sanders, determined to deprive Elizabeth, and Harpsfield was one of those divines who subscribed a declaration against the bull.[1]

The flattering reference to Sanders just quoted was, however, only published in 1573, three years after Pius excommunicated Elizabeth. Of course Cope, and not Harpsfield, may be the author of this addition. But the fact that Sanders refers to Harpsfield as *præcipuum totius Angliæ lumen* in one of the last books on which he was engaged, and which he left unfinished at his death, seems to show that there was no division between them.

Which of these two friends wrote the *Life of Cranmer* is a problem that I must leave unsolved—also where, if anywhere, that *Life* is now to be found. I am sorry to have no information, for it would probably be exciting reading.

Wood mentions as extant in manuscript Harpsfield's *Impugnatio contra Bullam Honorii papæ primi ad Cantabrigiam*, and Pits mentions his Latin Epigrams and other poems. I have not seen these.

Works attributed to Harpsfield: The *Vita Henrici VIII* or Latin *Chronicle.*

It is necessary to discuss Harpsfield's claim to two other works which have recently been attributed to him.

The Latin so-called *Vita Henrici VIII* is rather a *Chronicle of the Divorce* and the proceedings arising out of it, ending with the death of Catherine. I will call it, for brevity, the Latin *Chronicle*. It has been edited by Ch. Bémont from a manuscript at Paris,[2] and attributed to Nicholas Harpsfield.[3] The editor's eminence naturally lends authority to this attribution, and it is likely to be widely accepted; it is so accepted, for example, by Prof. A. F. Pollard.[4]

Yet the attribution is clearly impossible. Bémont does not seem to have noticed that in 1876 Lord Acton pointed out that, whilst the

[1] *Academy*, ix (1876) p. 609.

[2] Bib. nat., no. 6051 du fonds latin. There is another MS., Arundel 151, fols. 343–389v. Bémont has not used this, but it sometimes gives a better text than the Paris MS. An English version (MS. Sloane 2495) concludes with Catherine's last letter (Latin) to Henry. This is wanting in both Latin MSS. and in Bémont's edition.

[3] *Le premier divorce de Henri VIII, fragment d'une chronique anonyme en Latin*, publié par Ch. Bémont. (*Bib. de l'École des Hautes Études*, fasc. 221; 1917.)

[4] *Wolsey* (1929) pp. 2, 5.

Works attributed to Harpsfield: The *Vita Henrici VIII* or Latin *Chronicle*.

Latin *Chronicle of the Divorce* coincides very remarkably, in a number of passages, with Harpsfield's *Treatise on the Pretended Divorce*, it at the same time differs materially, " in substance and in spirit," from that *Treatise*.[1]

There is no doubt that there *is* a connection. The Paris MS. of the Latin *Chronicle* bears the endorsement :

> *Vita Henrici* 8[ti] *founde in Willm. Carters house* 17 *julii* 1582. . . .

Carter was Harpsfield's amanuensis. And Carter has written on the manuscript :

> This booke was founde in my house amongst doctor Har . . . writinges. Willm Carter.

Bémont is undoubtedly right in his view that the imperfect name *Har*. . . . should be interpreted *Harpsfield's* and not *Harding's*. Further, there are long passages in Harpsfield's *Treatise on the Pretended Divorce* and in the Latin *Chronicle* which run closely together.

And Bémont is no doubt right in his argument that the Latin *Chronicle* was being written about May or June, 1557,[2] and therefore belongs to the same epoch as Harpsfield's *Life of More* [3] and his *Pretended Divorce*. Bémont says that it would have been " un acte de piraterie littéraire " [4] for Harpsfield to have transferred without acknowledgement passages from the anonymous Latin *Chronicle* to his *Treatise on the Pretended Divorce*. But both Harpsfield and the writer of the Latin *Chronicle* are concerned with propaganda rather than with literary vanity : there can surely be no doubt that the one would have taken a fact or anecdote from the other, if he was satisfied as to its truth, without feeling bound to paraphrase the language.

Out of several anecdotes and passages common to the two books, the three most important are these :

> (i) Both tell how Archbishop Warham predicted to his nephew, Sir William Warham, the disasters which a successor named Thomas would bring upon the see of Canterbury. But Harpsfield tells the story at first hand (" This I heard, not long since, of the mouth of the said Sir William, who yet liveth.") [5]

[1] *Academy*, ix, p. 609.
[2] Bémont's edition, p. 11.
[3] See above, footnote to p. xxi.
[4] Bémont's edition, p. 16.
[5] *Pretended Divorce*, p. 178. Harpsfield tells the same story, again with the personal authentication, in his *Historia Anglicana Ecclesiastica : solebat suis, nepoti præsertim suo, Gulielmo Waramo . . . dicere . . . a cuius ego id rursus ore aliquando audivi, etc.* (p. 633).

Works attributed to Harpsfield: The *Vita Henrici VIII* or Latin *Chronicle*.

The writer of the Latin *Chronicle* makes no claim to personal knowledge or first-hand information.

(ii) Both tell how Friar Peto, in a sermon, warned Henry that, as dogs licked the blood of Ahab, so should they lick his blood; how Friar Elstowe repeated the threat; and how it was fulfilled. But it is Harpsfield *only* who adds, " Of this sermon and answer myself have heard the said Father Elstowe report." [1]

(iii) On the other hand, the fulfilment of the gruesome prophecy is given on the evidence of one William Counsell, and here it is the writer of the Latin *Chronicle* who claims personal knowledge: *Gulielmus Consellus ipse mihi narravit.*[2] Harpsfield, on the contrary, here does not claim information at first hand; he merely writes, " This chance one William Consell reported." [3]

All this suggests that the two writers had some kind of connection, but that they were not identical—for, if they were identical, why should the personal touches differ in each of these three stories, told otherwise almost in the same words?

Carter's note, *This booke was founde amongst doctor Har[psfeldes] writinges*, cannot be interpreted as an attribution of the authorship to Harpsfield.

Both Harpsfield and the author of the *Chronicle* go out of their way to pay a compliment to James Bassett,[4] who had recently married Mary, daughter of Margaret Roper; this does not prove their identity, but it suggests that they belonged to the same circle.

The differences absolutely preclude the possibility of common authorship. Harpsfield traces the origin of the divorce to the instigation of Wolsey and Langland; [5] the Latin *Chronicle* makes it begin with the King's love for Anne Boleyn.[6] The Latin *Chronicle* makes Wolsey and Campeggio hold the legate's court on the divorce *apud Fratres Carmelitas* [7] instead of at the Blackfriars—a mistake Harpsfield could never have made.[8]

But the most startling discrepancies come into the story of the condemnation and execution of More and the Carthusians. It is not possible that Harpsfield, who has given us the detailed and accurate account of More's imprisonment and death,[9] based on Roper, on

[1] *Pretended Divorce*, p. 205. [2] Bémont's edition, p. 63.
[3] *Pretended Divorce*, p. 203.
[4] *Chronicle*, p. 68; *Life of More*, p. 83, below.
[5] *Pretended Divorce*, p. 175; *Life of More*, pp. 40–42, below.
[6] p. 46.
[7] p. 49. *Carmelitas* is corrected to *Dominicanos* in MS. Arundel 151, p. 356.
[8] See *Pretended Divorce*, p. 180; *Life of More*, p. 46.
[9] pp. 169–204, below.

Works attributed to Harpsfield: The *Vita Henrici VIII* or Latin *Chronicle*.

More's letters and on the *Paris News Letter*, and filling some thirty-five pages of this edition, could, a few months later, have written the inaccurate account of the Latin *Chronicle*, which omits the most essential things, and confuses even what it does record. Though written about the same time, Harpsfield's *Life of More* is well-documented history, the Latin *Chronicle* is legend. The whole atmosphere is different.

The details of the various attempts to shake More's constancy during his imprisonment, as given by Harpsfield, can be proved accurate from extant documents. The Latin *Chronicle* gives merely an account of an apocryphal interview with Cromwell on 30 June, 1535, interesting only as the earliest known version of a very persistent legend.[1]

Harpsfield tells of the meeting of Margaret with More, on his way back from trial, combining skilfully the accounts of Roper and of the contemporary *Paris News Letter* into a touching and absolutely authentic story. The Latin *Chronicle* gives a short and garbled account, making the meeting take place as More is on his way, not from trial, but to execution, making More's daughter attempt to break down her father's constancy, and making More reply, *Desine, filia mea Eva, patrem tuum tentare,*—a reminiscence of the meeting with Margaret in the Tower many months before, when More had compared her to Mother Eve tempting Adam.[2]

The Latin *Chronicle* makes the execution of Reynolds and the first group of Carthusians follow that of More,[3] though they were actually executed more than two months before. Harpsfield gives the exact date, and tells how More watched Reynolds and his fellow-sufferers going to execution.[4] The Latin *Chronicle* actually represents Reynolds as prior of the Sheen Charterhouse, and seems to confuse him with Houghton; Harpsfield gives a short but quite accurate account of him.[5]

[1] The story that More, pressed to change his mind, said he had changed it—the change relating only to whether or no he would have his beard shaved. See Latin *Chronicle*, p. 72; Stapleton, *Tres Thomæ*, cap. XVI, *sub. fin.*; *Life* by *Ro. Ba.* in Wordsworth's *Ecclesiastical Biography* (1853) II. 106–7; and compare the story in Bacon's Apophthegms, and in the Play of *Sir Thomas More*.

[2] Bémont misses the point, and prints *Ena*, which he suggests may be an abbreviation for Elizabeth. But compare the letter of Margaret Roper: "He smiled upon me and said . . . What howe Mother Eve? Where is your mind nowe? Sit not musing with some serpent in youre brest, upon some new perswasion, to offer father Adam the apple yet once agayne." (More, *English Works*, 1557, p. 1441.)

[3] p. 74. [4] Below, p. 179. [5] Below, p. 179.

Works attributed to Harpsfield: The *Vita Henrici VIII* or Latin *Chronicle.*

There is nothing in favour of the identification of the writer of the Latin *Chronicle* with Harpsfield; there is merely some common material in the *Chronicle* and the *Pretended Divorce*. Yet, upon the attribution to Harpsfield of this inaccurate Latin *Chronicle* rests the assertion that Harpsfield represents Wolsey as a mere victim of Henry VIII,[1] and that he wrote two,[2] or rather three,[3] divergent accounts of Wolsey.

There is no discrepancy between the accounts of Wolsey as given in Harpsfield's *Life of More* [4] and in his *Pretended Divorce*.[5] The one was intended as a supplement to the other. In both, Wolsey is depicted as the originator of the divorce, and the part Langland is supposed to have played at his instigation is mentioned; whilst Langland's denial is reported in the *Life of More*, and is again asserted in the *Pretended Divorce*,[6] with a reference to the fuller account of that denial which had already been given in the *Life of More*. That Wolsey, with the help of Langland, had urged divorce on Henry VIII, had been stated by Polydore Vergil [7] in the edition of his *Historia Anglica* published at Basle in 1555. Harpsfield's account in the *Pretended Divorce* seems based on Polydore Vergil, whose *Historia* probably reached him after he had written his *Life of More*, but before writing his *Pretended Divorce*; his record of Langland's denial is his own.[8]

It is emphatically not the case that Harpsfield sees in Wolsey "a mere victim of Henry VIII." On the contrary, he sees in Wolsey the evil genius of Henry, and indeed of the whole realm of England. "Alas, and woe the time that euer he was borne." [9] It would require overwhelming evidence to make us believe that Harpsfield could have so changed his mind (and that within a few months) as to become the author of the Latin *Chronicle*, who "n'a guère vu en Wolsey que la victime de Henri VIII, et le roi devient d'autant plus

[1] Bémont, p. 9; followed by A. F. Pollard, *Wolsey*, p. 2.
[2] Bémont, pp. 16–17; followed by A. F. Pollard.
[3] Pollard, *Wolsey*, p. 5. [4] pp. 40–3, below.
[5] pp. 175, etc.
[6] *Pretended Divorce*, p. 176: "Thus say some of the Bishop of Lincolne; though himself (*as we have shewed*) denied that he was one of the first movers of this matter." The words "as we have shewed" refer to the account Harpsfield had already given in the *Life of More* (p. 41, below).
[7] p. 685. The passage is quoted in the Historical Notes to 41/2–4, below.
[8] Whilst there is no evidence of a change of mind regarding Wolsey, it is clear that Harpsfield, before completing the *Pretended Divorce*, got access to documents bearing on the Divorce proceedings, which were unknown to him when he wrote his *Life of More*. See, e.g. Note to 46/20–23, below.
[9] See pp. 39–43, below.

odieux, que le cardinal, sa victime, nous paraît plus innocente." And there is not a scrap of evidence in favour of the theory of Harpsfield's authorship.

To sum up: the author of the Latin *Chronicle* moved in the same circle as Harpsfield. They may have known each other well; probably the author of the Latin *Chronicle* knew, and used, Harpsfield's *Pretended Divorce*. Harpsfield, on the other hand, may very well have derived, from the writer of the Latin *Chronicle*, the story of William Counsel, since with regard to that anecdote the Latin *Chronicle* claims first-hand information, whilst Harpsfield does not. What is quite clear is that the author of the Latin *Chronicle* did not know Harpsfield's *Life of More*: had he done so, it would have saved him from the many and gross errors into which he falls regarding More and his fellow-martyrs. The quite unwarranted attribution of the Latin *Chronicle* to Harpsfield is regrettable. It can only lead to confusion by giving the authority of Harpsfield's name to certain inaccurate and confused legends, and must reflect unfavourably upon Harpsfield's reputation as a serious historian.

Works attributed to Harpsfield: *The Life of Fisher.*

It has been further suggested, by Dr. Marie Schütt,[1] that Harpsfield may have been the author of the *Life of Fisher* wrongly attributed to Richard Hall. This, as Dr. Schütt points out, had already been tentatively proposed by Father Bridgett:[2] if Hall be not the author, said Bridgett, "I should have no hesitation in naming Harpsfield." But Bridgett did not pursue this suggestion further, because he was satisfied that Hall was the author.

It has, I think, been conclusively proved by Van Ortroy that Richard Hall cannot have been the author of the *Life of Fisher*, though he no doubt translated it into Latin.[3] The *Life* was written in England,[4] planned—and to some extent even written—under Mary, but continued during the first half of the reign of Elizabeth.[5] The collection of information entailed a good deal of correspondence. The writer, in England, had no doubt excellent reasons for remaining anonymous. Richard Hall (*c.* 1537–1604) became an exile at latest in

[1] *Die englische Biographik der Tudor-Zeit*, Hamburg (1930) p. 80.
[2] *Life of Fisher* (1888) pp. xvii–xviii. But this suggestion does not appear in the second edition (1890) or the third (1902).
[3] *Analecta Bollandiana*, x, 195.
[4] *The same*, p. 197.
[5] *The same*, pp. 186–192.

1562, and never returned to England.[1] He cannot have been the man who, at a much later period than 1562, was concerning himself, in England, with compiling material for, and writing, this *Life*. Much of the correspondence, material and drafts, in various stages, is preserved in MS. Arundel 152. One particular handwriting Van Ortroy found to occur again and again: it is presumably that of the man mainly responsible for the compilation of the *Life of Fisher*: Van Ortroy has christened him "l'anonyme." The translator Richard Hall, however, safe in Belgium, had no motive for remaining anonymous, and it is not surprising that Pits should have associated the *Life* with the name of Richard Hall. Pits has made worse mistakes.[2]

Works attributed to Harpsfield: *The Life of Fisher.*

I do not, however, think that Dr. Schütt is justified in her attempt to identify "l'anonyme" with Harpsfield. The handwriting of the corrector of Harpsfield's *Historia Anglicana Ecclesiastica*, who can hardly be other than Harpsfield himself, is a very distinctive one, and is quite different from that of "l'anonyme." This presents a reason against identifying Harpsfield with the author of the *Life of Fisher* which only the most conclusive evidence could overcome. And there is really no evidence in favour of this identification. Harpsfield, one would have thought, would have found it difficult to conduct, in the Fleet, the very considerable correspondence which the compilation of the *Life of Fisher* entailed. And when he and his brother were released (at a time when the correspondence was still going on) it was under very heavy security that "persons that do mislike the present state of Religion" should not resort to them. So far as we can trace the dates, the correspondence preserved in MS. Arundel 152 comes to an end just about the time of Nicholas Harpsfield's death, and Dr. Schütt finds in this a further argument that Harpsfield is to be identified with the writer of the *Life of Fisher*. The last certain date in the collection is that of a letter, replying to inquiries which had been sent on 8 December, 1575, concerning nine or ten persons who had suffered under Henry VIII. We have seen that on 29 November, 1575, Nicholas Harpsfield was too sick to make his appearance before the lords in the Star Chamber. By 8 December he must have been very ill indeed; he died on 18 December. So far from these dates pointing to Nicholas Harpsfield as the author of the correspondence, they seem to me to point to the reverse. The reply of the Cambridge

[1] *Analecta Bollandiana*, x, p. 196.

[2] The attribution to Hall is based upon Pits. See his *Relationes historicæ de rebus Anglicis (de illustribus Angliæ scriptoribus)*, Paris, 1619, p. 803.

correspondent to the questions sent him is dated 5 J[anuary], that is to say, more than a fortnight after the death of Nicholas Harpsfield. "Yow have apoynted unto me one of Hercules labors," he writes.

It would be pleasant to think that Nicholas Harpsfield was indomitable to the last, that even on his death-bed he was planning the biographies of more martyrs, and setting his friends Herculean tasks in supplying him with information. But I am afraid that both the handwriting of "l'anonyme" and intrinsic probability are against this supposition.

There is no doubt that a careful comparison of the handwritings of MSS. Arundel 151 and 152 with those of known Popish recusants might produce interesting results: but it would be "one of Hercules labors." And it is not "apoynted unto me."

RASTELL'S LIFE OF MORE.

It is unnecessary here to attempt any account of the life of Judge William Rastell. All that can be gathered, from laborious studies at the Record Office and elsewhere, has been collected by Prof. A. W. Reed.[1] Reed's account entitles us to regard Rastell as a man exceptionally conscientious, careful and trustworthy. A. W. Reed on Rastell.

That Rastell had written a *Life* of his uncle was known in Elizabethan days. Sanders, in his *de origine Schismatis*, quotes it as an authority for the scandal which would make Henry the father of Anne Boleyn. It is only fair to Rastell to say that Sanders' marginal note, *Haec narrantur a Gulielmo Rastallo, iudice, in vita Thomae Mori*,[2] leaves us in doubt how far Rastell pledged his credit to this malicious and futile gossip, which had been current on the Continent[3] since about 1536.

Stapleton, writing in Belgium in 1588, mentions having had verbal information about More from Rastell, who was his fellow-exile. Stapleton could not have failed to refer to the *Life* had he known it: it is certainly remarkable that he did not.

We owe the preservation of such fragments as have survived to the efforts to compile a *Life of Fisher*, described above. We have seen that correspondence was carried on, for the collection of information, during the first half of Elizabeth's reign. A reference to Archbishop Parker's bequest of books as having arrived at Cambridge but being yet unpacked, and a reference to "old Mr. Roper"[4] as one of the two surviving people who could give information about Fisher, fix 1576 as about the latest date when we can trace this compilation of material as still going on. MS. Arundel 152.

This correspondence is preserved in MS. Arundel 152, and here are found *Certen breef notes apperteyning to Bushope Fisher collected out of Sir Thomas Moores lyfe writt by Master Justice Restall.*[5] At first they

[1] *Early Tudor Drama* (1926) pp. 73–93; reprinted, with some modifications, from *The Library*, Fourth Series, iv, 25–49 (1924).
[2] *De origine Schismatis* (1585) fol. 15.
[3] See Van Ortroy in *Analecta Bollandiana*, x, 130; xii, 120.
[4] *Analecta Bollandiana*, x, 159, 160.
[5] See below, p. 220, etc.

are mere " brief notes," but then the Extract becomes much fuller. For convenience, we call this Extract A. It is followed by a second Extract (B), and a third (C). References to " the LVIII chapiter of this third Booke " show how great was the bulk of the complete work from which these extracts were taken. That not merely 'A' but 'C' as well is from Rastell's *Life*, is proved by the fact that passages which had been jotted down more shortly among the " brief notes " at the beginning of 'A' recur in fuller form in 'C'.[1] And 'B' is clearly, on internal evidence, an extract from the same work as 'A' and 'C'.

From the materials preserved in MS. Arundel 152 the *Life of Fisher* which goes under the name of Richard Hall was compiled. It is extant in a large number of MSS., one of which has been published by the E.E.T.S.[2] A more authoritative text, together with much of the material on which it is based, has been edited by François Van Ortroy[3] from the Stonyhurst MS. (A. V. 19); from MS. Arundel 152 and a transcript of it in MS. Harl. 7047; and from other sources. Van Ortroy also printed a sixteenth-century Latin translation.[4]

"Hall's" *Life of Fisher.*

There is nothing else in " Hall's " *Life* which can approach in value the information derived from Rastell's *More.* Rastell at the time of Fisher's trial and execution was in London. He was an eye-witness of the execution,[5] and as a law student he would have exceptional motive and opportunity for learning about Fisher's trial, even if he were not present. The very detailed information which he gives (such as the names of the commissioners) agrees exactly with the official records, and must be based either upon very full notes taken at the time, or else upon subsequent consultation of documents, presumably in the reign of Queen Mary.

Other information in " Hall's " *Life* is, however, of interest. One set of stories is derived from an anonymous correspondent who, although he had no personal knowledge of Fisher, had been a student of St. John's:

> Of hys notable actes I have no knowlege, for I was but a young schooler of St. Johns college, when he dyed.

It is from this correspondent that the most generally quoted details

[1] See below, pp. 248–50.
[2] Transcribed from MS. Harleian 6382 by the Rev. Ronald Bayne (Extra Series, cxvii).
[3] *Analecta Bollandiana*, x, xii (1891, 1893).
[4] Barberini Library, cód. xxxiii. 89.
[5] See below, p. 244.

of Fisher's execution are derived.[1] They may be true—but they rest upon the words of one who was not an eye-witness. They are probably the reports that reached Cambridge at the time, and they have nothing like the authority of Rastell's equally pathetic and far more authentic account. They confirm Rastell's account in some details, and are in no respect contradictory to it.

Yet in "Hall's" *Life*, mixed with the first-hand information of Rastell, and the good, if second-hand, information of this Cambridge correspondent, we have some things which can only be called folk-lore.[2] For example, we are told how Queen Anne Boleyn wished to see Fisher's head before it was placed among those of traitors upon London Bridge; how she contemptuously said; "Is this the head that so often exclaymed against me? I trust it shall never do me more harme"; how she struck it upon the mouth with the back of her hand, and how she thereby hurt one of her fingers, which began to pain her.[3] It is a very old story, very much older than Anne Boleyn. Of course the story ought to go on, telling how the wound began to mortify, how all the art of physicians and surgeons proved fruitless, and how the cruel insulter of the dead expired in agonies. But Anne Boleyn could not die of a poisoned finger, because she was reserved for another fate. So the finger heals up, and we are consequently left with a silly and pointless story.

And yet, from amidst much inferior matter, there stands out the account of Fisher's trial and execution, which, as a critic about a century ago remarked, is "written in a style so plain and simple, and with such an air of truth that it seems impossible to doubt it." [4]

This, of course, was subjective criticism. But nearly forty years ago Van Ortroy, working entirely on the manuscript evidence of Arundel 152, showed how just this part, which had been noted as having an "air of truth," could be separated out as the work of the eye-witness, William Rastell.

The parallel of Franciscan studies.

Van Ortroy's work on the biography of Fisher is curiously parallel to work done in the same years on the life of St. Francis. The

[1] MS. Arundel 152, fol. 284, printed by Van Ortroy in *Analecta Bollandiana*, x, 166–7.

[2] There is also a good deal borrowed from known sources, such as the *Life of Wolsey* by Cavendish.

[3] *Life of Fisher*, E.E.T.S. edition, p. 126; *Analecta Bollandiana*, xii, 199. It is to be noted, however, that the most accurate text, that given in MS. Arundel 152, does not contain this story. See *Analecta Bollandiana*, x, 129–30.

[4] *Archæologia*, xxv (1834).

The parallel of Franciscan studies.

great *Speculum Vitae*, printed in the Sixteenth Century, had been regarded as worthless for a serious study of Francis's life, because the late and unhistorical character of much that it contained threw doubt upon all. Then Paul Sabatier showed how three-fourths of the book could be stripped off as accretion, leaving us with a more primitive nucleus, the *Speculum Perfectionis*, which he regarded as the work of Brother Leo, the secretary, friend, confessor and nurse of St. Francis.[1] But even this has been shown by a rigid scrutiny to contain much that is second-hand, till, by the use of the manuscripts at Perugia and in the Irish Franciscan Convent of St. Isidore at Rome, we can resolve even the *Speculum Perfectionis* into its constituent elements. So all the dross is finally separated, and we are left with a small residue of pure gold, the series of tales told by Brother Leo.[2]

In a similar way, Fisher's *Life* was printed in the compilation of Thomas Bailey (1655). This, because of its corruptions, was regarded as worthless; then it was shown to be only a garbled form of an earlier life (wrongly attributed to Richard Hall) which was extant in a dozen manuscripts. Then this in turn was separated out into its constituent elements, a few worthless, others doubtful, some of the highest value.

Between the work of Sabatier and the work of Van Ortroy there are, however, two great distinctions. With the rich material of MS. Arundel 152 before him, Van Ortroy was able to work with a finality to which Sabatier could not attain, and which has only been reached —if it has even now been reached—through the labours of a long succession of Franciscan scholars.[3]

The second contrast is more remarkable. The labours of this long succession of Franciscan scholars are known, by all who take any interest in the subject, all over the world. Van Ortroy's work of forty years ago on Fisher has been, so far as I have been able to judge, utterly ignored. " Richard Hall " is everywhere quoted with the hesitation which historians naturally feel in quoting a man who was

[1] Frère Léon . . . raconte la vie d'un homme dont il a partagé l'existence, dont il fut le secrétaire et l'ami, le confesseur et le garde-malade. (*Speculum Perfectionis*, ed. Sabatier, 1898, p. xviii.)

[2] See *A Study of the Sources of the Life of St. Francis*, by F. C. Burkitt, in Walter Seton's *St. Francis of Assisi, 1226–1926, Essays in Commemoration*; also the same scholar's *St. Francis of Assisi and some of his biographers* (*Second Walter Seton Memorial Lecture*, delivered 20 January, 1931, but not yet published).

[3] Including Van Ortroy, who toiled on behalf of both saints.

not born till after Fisher's death, and who can only retail the traditions of the next generation. No one seems to know that, embedded in "Richard Hall," we have the words of William Rastell, contemporary and eye-witness.

I hope that the printing of the Rastell Fragments, from the actual extracts made abroad and sent to England, will be of value to those concerned both with political and with literary history.

The loss of Rastell's *Life of More* is deplorable. He can tell a story as well as Roper or Cavendish, and his *Life* was evidently documented with scrupulous care. It must have been, as a biography, unrivalled in English till, more than half a century later, we come to the *Henry VII* of Francis Bacon and the *Henry VIII* of Lord Herbert of Cherbury. And it must have had authority as a primary source such as neither of those two works can claim.

INDEX TO INTRODUCTION

Achoriens: More's story of the, an allusion to the Anglo-French wars, lxxix.

Acton, Lord: on Nicholas Harpsfield's character and work, xlv, clxxv, clxxxiii–iv, cxciii–v, ccii, ccvi–vii.

Ælfric: states that Alfred's are the only reliable translations, lxi, lxxxi; appreciations of prose of, lxi, lxviii; his books copied throughout the Eleventh and Twelfth Centuries, lxviii, lxxxi, xci–ii, xciv; presumably read even in the early Thirteenth Century, lxxxi. Also xlvii, lx, xcvi.

Ailred, of Rievaulx. See *St. Ailred, of Rievaulx.*

Alfred, King: "father of English prose," lvi; revelation of character, lx; his reliable translations praised by Ælfric, lxi, lxxxi; his translations of Boethius and Augustine copied in Twelfth Century, xcii.

Alice, Mistress, second wife of Sir Thomas More: anecdotes concerning, clx–clxi.

Alice in Wonderland: cl.

Alington, Lady Alice: dramatic power of her letter, clxii.

Allen, Hope Emily: on the *Ancren Riwle,* xcvii, xcix; on Rolle, c, cii, *n.* 1, cxxvii, cxxxiv. Also ci.

Allen, P. S.: on neglect of More, xlix; his *Sir Thomas More, Selections,* lv; "we read history . . . knowing the event," clxviii.

Alliterative poetry: history of, lxvi–vii, lxxxi.

Alphege, St.: lxxiv.

Ancren Riwle: xcvi–c; versions and influence, xcvii–c; translated into Latin by Simon of Ghent, xcviii–ix; translated into French, xcix; loanwords in, cxv; modernized version in Vernon MS., cxxiii; its sinners, xcvi–vii, cli; parallels between More and, cliii, *n.* 2. Also ci.

Ancrene Wisse, revised version of *Ancren Riwle:* xcviii.

Apollonius of Tyre: lxvi, clxviii.

Architecture, Anglo-Saxon: lxxvii.

Arden of Feversham: clxiv.

Ari, the Wise: lxxxiv.

Arundel 152, MS.: ccxv–xvii.

Ascham, Roger: censures Hall's "Indenture English" and praises More's style, cxx; connected with Cambridge University, cxlii; regards Malory with contempt, cxlix, cl; finds that More "contents all men," clii.

Astrolabe, Treatise on the, Chaucer's: cxv.

Athenæ Oxonienses, Anthony Wood's: clxxv, *n.* 1, clxxvii, *n.* 1, clxxviii, *n.* 2, *n.* 3, clxxxi, *n.* 3, cxcii, *n.* 4, cci, ccvii.

Audeley, Sir Thomas, Lord Chancellor: portrayed in Lady Alington's letter, clxii.

"Augmenting" the English language: cxv, cxvi, cxvii–xix.

Authorized Version: varying the phrase, cxx; described by Quiller-Couch as a "miracle," cxxxv; but based on continuous tradition of English devotional prose, cxxxv–vi; our prejudice with regard to its phraseology, cxlvi; revisers and Douai version, cxlvi–vii; "setting a seal on all," clxxiv.

Ayenbite of Inwit, Dan Michel of Northgate's: cxvi.

Bacon, Francis: describes the island-kingdom of Britain, lxxxi.

Baker, Father Augustine: on the *Cloud of Unknowing*, cxxxiii.

Barnes, Robert: Austin Friar of Cambridge, cxlii; as penitent, cxliii.

Becket, Thomas à: *Life of*, in French verse, lxxxiv.

Bémont, Charles: his opinion on authorship of *Vita Henrici VIII*, ccvii–ccxii.

Beowulf: lxvi.

Berners, John Bourchier, Lord: style, cliv–v. Also lvi, cxlix, cl.

Bestiary: lxvi.

Blickling Homilies: lxi.

Boswell, James: xlvii.

Brewers: "augment" the English tongue, cxv.

Bridgett, Father T. E.: on Harpsfield, xlvi; on Fisher, cxliii, *n.* 1.

Britain: ideal of united island in Anglo-Saxon times, lxxviii–lxxx; ideal of unity described by Bacon, lxxxi.

Brut, English prose: cxiv.

Brut, Layamon's: lxvi, cxi–ii.

Bunyan, John: style, clxxii.

Byrhtferth: *Manual*, lxi.

Cambridge: connection of noted Catholics and Protestants with, cxlii.

Cambridge History of English Literature: on More's work, liii.

Canute: becomes a Christian king, lxxv; his Proclamation the ancestor of Magna Charta, lxxv.

Capgrave, John: his *Lives of St. Augustine and St. Gilbert*, cxiv; his prose *Chronicle*, cxiv.

Carter, William: Harpsfield's amanuensis, xxx, cciv, ccviii.

Carthusians: their torture and execution, cxxx–xxxi.

Cavendish, George: his *Life of Wolsey*, xlv–vi; power of dramatization, clxiii–v; Shakespeare's debt to, clxv; style praised by Krapp, clxxi.

Caxton, William: style, cxvii–xviii; prints Love's *Mirror*, cxxviii.

Charterhouse, of London: copy of Hilton's *Scale* and two copies of the *Cloud* possessed by, cxxix–xxx.

Charterhouse, of Sheen: books of devotion possessed by, cxxvi–vii.

Chastising of God's Children: its borrowings from the *Ancren Riwle*, xcix, c, cxxvi; copy possessed by Charterhouse of Sheen, cxxvi; printed by Wynkyn de Worde, cxxvi. Also cxxxii.

Chaucer, Geoffrey: his prose, cxi; *Treatise on the Astrolabe*, cxv; translates Boethius, cxvii; *Parson's Tale*, cxxiv; on the heroes of the Table Round, cxxxviii.

Chauncy, Maurice: cxxxiii, cxl, *n.* 3.

Cheke, Sir John: connection with Cambridge University, cxlii.

Chesterton, G. K.: praises More, clxx.

Chitty, Herbert: on the Harpsfield brothers at Winchester, clxxvii, *n.* 3; on the Regius Professorship of Greek at Oxford, clxxix, *n.* 2.

Chronicle, Anglo-Saxon: episode of Cynewulf and Cyneheard in, lix; eked out with verse, lxi; lively at end of Tenth Century, lxi; account of the quarrel between Godwine and Edward the Confessor, lxi–iii; poem on death of Edward the Confessor, lxvi; power of its English, lxviii; account of London's repulse of Anlaf and Swegen, lxxiii–iv; and of martyrdom of St. Alphege, lxxiv; and of campaigns of Edmund Ironside, lxxiv; and of Canute's share in translation of bones of St. Alphege to Canterbury, lxxiv–v; late survival of, lxxxiv–v; its annals for reigns of William I, William II and Henry I neglected, clxxi.

Chronicle of Robert of Gloucester: cxii.

Clement, Margaret (= Margaret Gigs): cxxxi.

Cloud of Unknowing: style, liv; extract from, cv–vi; humorous observation, cxxii; translated into Latin, cxxvii; copies by London

Carthusians, cxxix–xxx; studied among English exiles abroad, cxxxiii; closing sentences quoted, cxxxv–vi.
Coins: Anglo-Saxon and post-Conquest, lxix.
Colet, John: his opinion of More, l; begged by More to return to London to preach, cxxv; influence of English writers on his style, cxxv, cxxvi.
Colman: his *Life of St. Wulfstan* in English, xlvii, lxxxiii–iv.
Communism of *Utopia:* clvii.
Confutation of Tyndale's Answer: More's anecdote of Mistress Alice in, clx.
Cotton Vitellius A. xv, MS.: lxvi.
Coverdale, Miles: his Bible, cxli; Austin Friar of Cambridge, cxlii; his style compared with More's, cxlv–vi.
Craik, Sir Henry: on Caxton's style, cxviii.
Cranmer, Thomas: fellow of Jesus College, Cambridge, cxlii.
Creighton, Bishop: on Harpsfield, clxxv.
Cuthbert Stole: lxxi.
Cynewulf and Cyneheard, episode of: lix.

De Anima, of Hugo of St. Victor: its literary value compared with that of *Soul's Ward*, xcv; and with that of *Cloud of Unknowing*, cvi.
De Laudibus, Fortescue's: cxxxvii.
Deanesly, Margaret: cviii, *n.* 2, cxxvii, *nn.* 1, 4, 5, cxxviii, *n.* 2.
Defoe, Daniel: style, clxxii.
Devout Treatise of discerning of Spirits: cviii, cxxxiii.
Dialogue: of More and his School, clvii–clxiii.
Dialogue between Understanding and Faith, Fortescue's: cxxxvii.
Dictionary of National Biography: on authorship of More's *Richard III*, lv.
Dionis' hid Divinity: cxxv.
Donet, Pecock's: cxxxvii.
Douai Bible: cxlvi–vii.
Dover: account in *Chronicle* of quarrel with Eustace of Boulogne, lxii.
Dryden, John: prose style, clxxii.

Earle, John: lii.
Edward the Confessor, King: account in *Chronicle* of his quarrel with Godwine, lxi–lxiii; poem on death of, lxxviii.
Edward IV, King: his death-bed speech as related by More, clvi–vii.
Eight Chapters necessary for . . . perfection, Hilton's: cviii.
Eirik, Jarl: lxxiv, lxxv.
Elmham, Thomas: cxii.
Elyot, Sir Thomas: style, cxviii–cxix.
English Language, Standard: in Anglo-Saxon times, lxiv, lxviii–ix, lxxv–vi, lxxx, lxxxviii.
"English work," in Anglo-Saxon times: lxx–lxxi.
Erasmus: his opinion of More, l, clxx; testifies to Colet's pains to polish his style, cxxvi; praises English scholarship, clxix–clxx.
Euphues, Lyly's: clvi.
Eustace of Boulogne: account in the *Chronicle* of his quarrel with the men of Dover, lxii.
Exmew, William: imprisonment and torture, cxxxi, cxl; transcribes the *Cloud*, cxxxi, cxl–cxli; connection with Cambridge University, cxlii.

Fabyan, Robert: style, cxviii.
Festial, John Mirk's: cxvii.
Fisher, John. See *Rochester, John Fisher, Bishop of.*
Flodden, Battle of, poem: lxvii, lxxxi.
Flower, Robin: on Old Irish prose, lviii, *n.* 1.
Folewer, Pecock's: cxxxvi, *n.* 2, clv.
Fortescue, Sir John: style, liv, cxxxvii–viii; high opinion of Anglo-French, lxxxii–iii; pioneer in using English for constitutional and political subjects, cxxxvii; his English works long neglected, cxxxvii–viii.
Foxe, John: his *Acts and Monuments*, liv; on Harpsfield's treatment of heretics, clxxxii–v; on Harpsfield's *Dialogi sex*, cxcvi–viii.

French: ousts English for historical purposes, lxxxviii–ix.
Froissart, Berners'. See *Berners, John Bourchier, Lord.*
Fuller, Thomas: account of Harpsfield in his *Church History*, clxxxvi–vii, cxciii.
Furnivall, F. J.: xlv.

Gaimar, Geoffrey: his History of the English in French rhymed couplets, lxxxviii.
Gairdner, James: on authorship of More's *Richard III*, lv.
Garnett, Richard: opinion of More's work, liii, *n.* 1.
Gee, John Archer: his *Life and Works of Thomas Lupset*, cxlvii–viii.
Gigs, Margaret. See *Clement, Margaret.*
Godwine, Earl: account in *Chronicle* of his quarrel with Edward the Confessor, lxi–iii.
Gollancz, Sir Israel: lxvii, *n.* 3.
Gospel of Nicodemus: cxvii.
Gospels: translations of the, xcii.
Governance of England, Fortescue's: cxxxvii.
Gratia Dei: borrowings from *Ancren Riwle* in, xcix.
Grave, The: poem, lxvi.
Greenwood, Alice D.: on Caxton's style, cxviii.
Grenehalgh, J., of Sheen: cxxvi, cxxxii.
Gunnlaugs Saga: lxxvi.

Hakluyt, Richard: his *Navigations*, lix.
Hall, Edward: style of his *Chronicle*, cxix–cxx, cxxii; Ascham's censure of his "Indenture English," cxx.
Hall, Richard: the *Life of Fisher* attributed to, ccxvi–vii.
Hallam, Henry: opinion of More's *Richard III*, lii.
Hallett, Mgr. Philip E.: translates Stapleton's *Life of More* (Part III of *Tres Thomae*), xlvii, *n.* 1, xlix.
Harding, John: his rhymed *Chronicle*, cxii.
Harington, John: on authorship of More's *Richard III*, liv–v.
Harold, son of Godwine: account in *Chronicle* of his quarrel with Edward the Confessor, lxi–iii.
Harpsfield, John: age, clxxviii; at Winchester and Oxford, clxxviii; first Regius Professor of Greek at Oxford, clxxviii–clxxx; part in the Westminster disputation, clxxxvi–vii; refuses to receive the *Injunctions* and subscribe the *Book of Religion*, clxxxviii–ix; imprisonment, clxxxix; release, cxc; his Commonplace-book, cxc–cxci; sickness and death, cxcii–iii.
Harpsfield, Nicholas: his opinion of More, l–li; use of dramatic, autobiographical passages relating to More, clviii; sense of proportion and structure, clxiii; vivid description of Roper's temporary lapse into heresy, clxiii; his biographers, clxxv; the Harpsfield family, clxxv–vii; birth, clxxvii; at Winchester and Oxford, clxxvii–viii; in exile during reign of Edward VI, clxxx; preferment under Mary, clxxx–xxxi; association with Cardinal Pole, clxxxi–v; treatment of heretics, clxxxii–v; his part in the Convocation of 1559, clxxxv–vi; in trouble at Canterbury, clxxxvii–viii; refuses to receive the *Injunctions* and subscribe the *Book of Religion*, clxxxviii–ix; imprisonment, clxxxix; release, cxc; sickness and death, cxci–ii; portrait of, cxciii; character explained by Lord Acton, cxciii–v; use of English and Latin, cxcv–vi.
Harpsfield, Nicholas, works of:
Dialogi sex, cxcvi–viii.
Historia Anglicana Ecclesiastica and *Historia Wicliffiana*, cxcviii–cci.
Life of Jesus Christ, ccv–vi.
Life of More, xlv–ix, l–li, lii, cci–iv.
Treatise of the Pretended Divorce, cciv–v.
For works attributed to Harpsfield, see pp. ccvi–xiv.

Heimskringla : lvii.
Henry V, King : letter of City Fathers to, cxvi.
See also *Life of Henry V.*
Henry VIII, King : his Castle of Loyalty, cxxxix–cxl; the tradition of his visit to Newdigate in prison, cxl; "with flattery shamefully abused," cliii; his encouragement of Parliament and Parliamentary eloquence, cliii.
Heptateuch, Old English, xci.
Higden, Ralph : contemptuous statement concerning English in his *Polychronicon*, lxxxix, cx.
Hilton, Walter : quotations from the *Scale*, ciii–v; style (in *Scale*) compared with Wiclif's, cvii–viii; his *Eight chapters necessary for men that give themselves to perfection*, cviii; *Scale* and *Treatise of Mixed Life* recommended by Nicholas Love, cxxviii; studied by the Lady Margaret, cxlii. Also xcix.
History of Richard III. See under *More, Sir Thomas.*
History of the Holy Rood Tree : xci.
Holy Maidenhood : xcv.
Homilies : Ælfric's, xcii; the "Blickling," lxi; the "Lambeth," xcii, *n.* 1.
Hooker, Richard : his style compared with Pecock's, cxxxvi, clv.
Houghton, John : cxl.
Housman, A. E. : on problems of text-editing, xxi–ii.
Hugo of St. Victor : xcv, cvi.
Hunne, Richard : More describes the townsmen's evidence as to death of, clviii–ix.

Illumination, Manuscript : Anglo-Saxon and post-Conquest, lxix–lxx, lxxi–ii; the "basic art" of the Middle Ages, lxxi.
Imitatio Christi : translations of, cxvii.
Incendium Amoris, Richard Rolle's : translated by Richard Misyn, cxvi.

Johnson, Samuel : cli.
Joinville, Jean, Sire de : *Life of St. Louis*, lvii.
Jones, Dorothy : edition of *Minor Works of Walter Hilton*, cxxx, *n.* 2.
Jonson, Ben : draws examples from More's prose, cxlix.
Juliana of Norwich, Dame : her *Revelations of Divine Love*, cxvii.

Kemp, Marjorie, of Lynn : her Book, cxvii.
Kent, laws of : lix.
Ker, William Paton : on Alfred's importance in the history of English prose, lvi; on the *Voyages* of Ohthere and Wulfstan, lix; on poetry, lxv–vi; on Ælfric, lxviii; on prose as evidence of the humanities, lxxi; on Chaucer, cxi.
Kingston, Sir William : pesters Wolsey for the £1,500, clxiv.
Kipling, Rudyard : cix.
Krapp, G. P. : considers Wiclif "the father of English prose," cvii; praises Cavendish and Roper, clxxi.

Lambeth Homilies : xcii, *n.* 1.
Latimer, Hugh : Fellow of Clare Hall, Cambridge, cxlii.
"Law French" : lxxxii.
Layamon : choice of verse for the *Brut*, cxi–ii.
Legenda Aurea : translation of, cxvii.
Leigh, Joyeuce : cxxiii, cxxxii.
Letter of Alexander : clxviii.
Lichfield, William : borrowings from the *Ancren Riwle*, xcix.
Life of Cranmer : attributed to Harpsfield, ccvi–vii.
Life of Fisher, "Hall's" : attributed to Harpsfield by Dr. Schütt, ccxii–xiv; compiled from material collected in MS. Arundel 152, ccxv–xvii.
Life of Henry V. See "*Translator of Livius.*"
Life of Richard III. See under *More, Sir Thomas.*
Life of St. Edmund : translated into French verse, lxxxix.
Life of Wulfstan. See *Colman.*

Lindsay, Thomas M.: on More's *Richard III*, liii.

Lives of Saints: translated into French verse, lxxxix, xciv; *St. Juliana, St. Katherine, St. Margaret*, xcv; *Legenda Aurea*, cxvii.

Livio, Tito, of Forli: author of *Life of Henry V*, xlviii, *n.*

Lockhart, John Gibson: xlvii.

London English: Fifteenth-century documents in, cxi and *n.* 3; cxii–iii.

Love, Nicholas: his *Mirror*, cxxvii–viii, cxlvii; recommends Hilton's *Scale* and *Mixed Life*, cxxviii; his style compared with Wiclif's, cxxviii.

Lupset, Thomas: friend of More and scholar of Colet, cxlvii; style, cxlviii.

Lyly, John: Euphuistic devices anticipated by More, clvi.

Mackintosh, Sir James: on More, li, lii, clv; on More's *Richard III*, lii; his style compared with Roper's, clxi.

Maldon, Battle of: lxxiii.

Malory, Sir Thomas: style, liv, lvi, lx, cxxxix; *Morte Darthur*, "out of the general line of progress," cxxxviii; date, cxxxix; regarded with contempt by Ascham, cxxxix, cxlix–cl; not mentioned by Ben Jonson in his *Grammar*, cxlix; ideals of *Morte Darthur* opposed to those of Sixteenth Century, cxlix–cl; the "atmosphere" of, cl; his characters, cli–ii.

Mandeville, Sir John, *Voyages* of: cxiv, clxvii.

Manhu: Harpsfield's *Life of More* printed in, xv, *n.* 2, xlv, *n.* 1.

Manuscript Illumination. See *Illumination, Manuscript.*

Manuscripts: genealogical method of editing, xxiii–xxx.

Manuscripts of Harpsfield's *Life of More:* description of, xiii–xx; relationship of, xxi–xliv.

Margaret, Lady, Countess of Richmond and Derby: patroness of Cambridge University, student of Hilton, translator (from French version) of Fourth Book of *Imitatio Christi*, cxlii. Also cxvii.

Master of Game: cxiv.

Middlemore, Humphrey: cxl.

Milton, John: considers subject for heroic poem, lxxiii, lxxx.

Mirk, John: his *Festial*, cxvii.

Mirrour of the Blessed Lyf of Iesu Crist, Nicholas Love's: cxxvii–viii, cxlvii.

Misyn, Richard: translates Rolle's *Incendium Amoris*, cxvi.

"Moare, Mr. Thomas": owner of the Emmanuel MS., xiii. See also Note, pp. 294–6.

More, Lady Alice. See *Alice, Mistress, second wife of Sir Thomas More.*

More, Margaret. See *Roper, Margaret.*

More, Sir Thomas: different judgments concerning his genius, character and work, xlviii–ix, l–liii, cxlix, clv; *History of Richard III*, xlviii, lii, liii, liv–v, lxxxi, cxxii, cxlvii, cxlix, clii; debt of Shakespeare to *Richard III*, clxv–vii; *English Works*, xlix, l, cxlvii, cli; importance of his prose, liii–iv; his "Academy" and "School," liii, *n.* 4; Ascham praises his style, "he contents all men," cxx, clii; *Dialogue of Comfort*, cxxi; trick of balanced sentences and alliteration, cxxiv; discusses London preaching with Colet, cxxv; watches Carthusians going to execution, cxxx; his meditations and prayers, cxli; High Steward of Cambridge, cxlii; his opinion of Tindale's English and Tindale's opinion of his work, cxliii; his style compared with Tindale's, cxliii–v; and with Coverdale's, cxlv–vi; and with Fisher's, cliv; the "Restorer of English prose," cxlviii–clvii; contrasted with Newdigate, cxlix; his prose in tradition of earlier devotional writers, cl–clvii; parallels with the *Ancren Riwle*, cliii, *n.*; "restorer of political eloquence," clv–vii; his rhetorical devices, clv–vi; his use of dramatic dialogue, clvii–x; Erasmus's admiration for his character, l, clxx; praised by G. K. Chesterton, clxx.

Morte Darthur. See *Malory, Sir Thomas.*

Morton, John, Cardinal: More's debt to him in *Richard III*, xlviii; opinion of More, l; attribution to him of authorship of More's *Richard III*, liv.

Mosbie: in *Arden of Feversham*, clxiv.

Mother: playing with her child, c; unwilling to see her child weep, cliii.

Myroure of oure Ladye: cxxxii.

New Testament: text of Erasmus compared with that of Westcott and Hort, xxiii.

Newdigate, Sebastian: heroism, l; from Courtier to Carthusian, his imprisonment and torture, cxxxi, cxl; tradition of Henry's visit to him in prison, cxl; a Cambridge man, cxlii; contrasted with More, cxlix.

Njals Saga: lvii.

Notary, Julian: prints Hilton's *Scale* and *Treatise of Mixed Life*, cxxiii, cxxiv.

Oakden, J. P.: *Alliterative Poetry in Middle English*, lxvii, *n.* 1.

Ohthere and Wulfstan, Voyages of: lix–lx.

Oman, Charles: his view of Anglo-Saxon civilization in the reign of Edward the Confessor, lxv, lxix.

Orchard Classics: cxxxiii.

Owst, G. R.: his *Preaching in Mediæval England*, xcix, c.

Oxford: John Harpsfield first Regius Professor of Greek at, clxxviii–clxxx.

Page, John: cxii.

Paston Letters: cxiv.

Pastoral Care, Gregory's: Alfred's Preface to his translation of, lx.

Paues, Anna: xcix.

Pecock, Reginald: works, cxxxv; style, liv, cxxxvi–vii; compared with Hooker, cxxxvi, clv; creation of philosophic vocabulary, cxxxvi–vii.

Peterborough Chronicle: lxxxv.

Petition of the Folk of Mercerie: **cxvi.**

Phillimore, J. S.: his views on English prose in *Blessed Thomas More and the Arrest of Humanism in England*, lviii, cxli, *n.* 2, cxlvi, and *n.* 4, *n.* 5.

Piers Plowman: Stanley Baldwin on, lxvii.

Plutarch: gains by loss of his sources, xlvi.

Pollard, A. F.: cxlix–cl, ccvii, ccxi, *n.* 3.

Pollard, A. W.: cxi.

Poor Caitiff: influenced by the *Ancren Riwle*, cxxvi; copy owned by John Dygoun of Sheen, cxxvi.

Prose, English: unmerited neglect of that of the Eleventh Century, clxviii, clxxi; under the Norman kings, lxxxi–vi; of the Fourteenth Century, ci–cix; of the Fifteenth Century, cx, cxii; its proportion to French prose in legal and official documents of the Fifteenth Century, cx; revival, cx–cxxi; of the Sixteenth Century, clxxi; historical, lxxxi, lxxxiii–xc; official, lxxxi–iii; religious, xc–cix, cxxi–cxxxiv.

Proverbs of Alfred: lxvi.

Psalter: phrases of version of 1540 compared with those of Authorized Version, cxlvi.

Pynson: prints Hilton's *Treatise of Mixed Life*, cxxiv; and Love's *Mirrour*, cxxviii.

Quiller-Couch, Sir Arthur: denies continuity of English prose from Anglo-Saxon times, lvii; on the "clotted" Elizabethan style, lx; on the Authorized Version as a "miracle," cxxxv; and as "setting a seal on all," clxxiv.

Rastell, William: style of his Preface to More's *English Works*, cxxi; view of More as a religious writer, cxxi; *Life of More* (and notes therein concerning Fisher), xlvii, cxlvii, ccxv–xix; power of vivid dialogue, clxii.

Reed, Arthur W.: on influence of More and his circle on Tudor drama, xlix; on influence of Fourteenth-century books of devotion on More's prose, cxxx; research on William Rastell, ccxv.

Repressor, Pecock's: cxxxvii.

Revelations of Divine Love: cxvii.

Reynolds, Richard: l.

Rheims Bible: cxlvi.

Ricci, Aldo: on alleged decadence of Anglo-Saxon prose and civilization, lxv.

Richard III, History of. See under *More, Sir Thomas.*

Rochester, John Fisher, Bishop of: eminence of mind, l; his *Spiritual Consolation* and *Ways to Perfect Religion*, cxli; Chancellor of Cambridge University, cxlii; his style compared with More's, liv, cliv; his style praised by Saintsbury, cliv.

Rogers, Elizabeth F.: collection of More's letters, l, *n.* 2.

Rolle, Richard, of Hampole: ci–iii; style, cii; quotation from, cii–iii; his *Incendium Amoris* translated, cxvi; his treatises in the Vernon MS., cxxiii. Also xcix.

Romances: Fifteenth-century prose, cxiv.

Roper, Margaret: letter to Lady Alington purporting to be from, clxii.

Roper, William: value of his memoir of More, xlv–vi; power of dramatic dialogue, clxi; style compared with that of Mackintosh, clxi; temporary lapse into heresy as described by Harpsfield, clxiii; style praised by Krapp, clxxi.

Rule of St. Benedict: translated into English, xcii; early Thirteenth-century transcript of, xciii; Fifteenth-century prose version of, cxvii.

Sabatier, Paul: his work on St. Francis, ccxvii–xviii.

St. Æthelwold: xcii, xciv.

St. Ailred, of Rievaulx: interprets the Confessor's prophecy, lxxxvii; quotations in the *Ancren Riwle* from, xcviii, *n.* 3.

St. Chad: sermon on, lx.

St. Francis: work of Sabatier on, ccxvii–xviii.

St. Thomas of Canterbury: the wealth of his shrine, clxix.

Saintsbury, George: on More, lii, liii; on Ælfric, lxviii; on the "Charity passage," cxlvii; on Malory, cl; on Fisher, cliv; on Berners, cliv–v.

Salter, H. E.: on the Regius Professorship of Greek at Oxford, clxxix, *n.* 2, *n.* 4.

Sampson, Abbot: preaches in English, xciv.

Sandwich haven: More describes the yokel's evidence concerning, clviii.

Saunders, O. E.: on *English Illumination*, lxxi.

Scale of Perfection, Hilton's: quotations from, ciii–v; earliest version, cxxiii; popularity throughout More's life, cxxiii; copies at Charterhouses of Sheen and London, cxxvi, cxxix; printed by Wynkyn de Worde, cxxiii, cxlii; and by Julian Notary, cxxiii.

Scandinavia: share of England in conversion of, lxxv.

Schütt, Marie: ccxii, ccxiii.

Seven Deadly Sins: as depicted in devotional writers and in More, cli, clii.

Shakespeare, William: debt to "Translator of Livius," xlviii, *n.*; and to Cavendish in *Henry VIII*, clxv; and to More in *Richard III*, clxv–clxvii; contribution to play of *Sir Thomas More*, clxx; doggerel rhyme of his early plays, clxxii.

Simon of Ghent: translates *Ancren Riwle* into Latin, xcviii–ix.

Sir Gawayne and the Green Knight: lxvii.
Sir Thomas More, play of: clxx.
Soul's Ward: xcv.
Speculum Devotorum: cxxxii.
Spiritual Consolation, Fisher's: cxxxii, cxli.
Stapleton, Thomas: his *Life of More* (Part III of *Tres Thomae*) translated by P. E. Hallett, xlvii, xlix; translation of Bede's *Ecclesiastical History,* l, *n.* 1; his Latin style, lxxxviii.
Stevenson, W. H.: on Canute's Proclamation, lxxv; on England's priority in developing a standard official language, lxxvii. Also cx, *n.* 1.
Stonor Papers: cxiv.
Strype, John: his *Ecclesiastical Memorials,* &c., footnotes to pp. clxxxii, clxxxv, clxxxviii–ix.
Svold: last fight of Olaf Tryggvason at, lxxiv.
Sweyn Forkbeard: lxxiii, lxxiv.
Swift, Jonathan: xlv.
Symonds, John Addington: clxiv.
Synonyms: of Fisher, Berners, More, Ascham, Pecock, Hooker, clv.

Tanner, L.: on John Harpsfield as Regius Professor of Greek at Oxford, clxxix, *n.* 3.
Testament of Love, Thomas Usk's: cxvi.
Thorpe, William: cxiv.
Tindale, William: in 1535 in prison at Vilvorde, cxli; at Cambridge University, cxlii; More's opinion of his English, and his opinion of More's work, cxliii, clvii, *n.* 2; his style compared with More's, cxliii–v.
Tolkien, J. R. R.: xcv.
Tom Jones: cli.
Topclyff, Richard: xiii.
Tosti: lxiii–iv.
"Translator of Livius": xlviii, *n.*
Treatise of Mixed Life, Hilton's: cix, cxxiii–iv, cxxviii.
Trevelyan, Sir George: his *Life of Macaulay,* xlvii.
Trevelyan, George Macaulay: on the alleged decadence of Anglo-Saxon prose and civilization, lxiv–v.
Trevisa, John of: translates Higden's *Polychronicon* into English prose, cx, cxi; on use of English and French in England, lxxxix, cx; translates *de Proprietatibus rerum* of Bartolomæus, cxv.
Tryggvason, Olaf: lxxiii–iv.
Tyndale, William. See *Tindale, William.*

Ulfilas: lix.
Usk, Thomas: his *Appeal,* cxvi; and *Testament of Love,* cxvi.
Utopia: the Achoriens in, lxxix; dramatic temper of, clvii.

Van Ortroy, François: work on Fisher, ccxvi, ccxvii, ccxviii.
Vernon MS.: contents of, cxxii–iii. Also xcix.
Vices and Virtues: xci.
Vising, Johan: his *Anglo-Norman Language and Literature,* cxiii, *n.* 1.
Vita Henrici VIII, or Latin *Chronicle:* attributed to Harpsfield, ccvii–xii.
Vitellius A. xv, MS.: lxvi.

Wærferth. See (1) *Worcester, Wærferth, Bishop of.*
Ways to Perfect Religion: Fisher's, cxxxii, cxli.
Westminster Abbey: Venetian Secretary describes its wealth, clxix.
Whibley, Charles: on More's *Richard III,* liii, clxiii. Also clvii, *n.* 5.
White, Elizabeth, half-sister of Fisher: cxxxii, cxli.
White, Helen C.: on *English Devotional Literature,* cxcv, *n.* 3.
Wiclif, John: considered by Krapp "the father of English prose," cvii; his prose compared with Hilton's, cvii–viii; and with Love's, cxxviii.
William the Conqueror: his Charter, lxxxi; his character depicted in *Chronicle,* lxxxv.
William of Malmesbury: xlvii, *n.* 2, lxxxvi, xc, *n.*, xci, *n.* 1.

Wolsey, Thomas, Cardinal: his vanity, clii; his dislike of Parliament, cliii; passages from Cavendish's *Life* of, clxiv–v.

Wonders of the East: clxviii.

Wood, Anthony. See *Athenæ Oxonienses.*

Wooing of our Lord: cxxxii.

(1) Worcester, Wærferth, Bishop of: lx.

(2) Worcester, Wulfstan, Bishop of, (and of York): his *Address to the English*, lxviii.

(3) Worcester, Wulfstan, Bishop of: English MSS. transcribed under, lxxxiii; biography, in English, by Colman, xlvii, lxxxiii–iv; an energetic preacher, xci.

Worcester Chronicle: lxxxiv.

Wulfstan. See (2) and (3) *Worcester, Wulfstan, Bishop of.*

Wyer: prints Hilton's *Treatise of Mixed Life*, cxxiv.

Wynkyn de Worde: prints Hilton's *Scale* and *Treatise of Mixed Life*, cxxiv; and the *Chastising of God's Children*, cxxvi; and Love's *Mirror*, cxxviii; and, at the command of the Lady Margaret, Hilton's *Scale*, cxlii, *n.* 1.

EDITOR'S SUMMARY OF CONTENTS

OF

HARPSFIELD'S *LIFE OF MORE*

		PAGES
Epistle Dedicatory to Master William Roper	.	3–6
Book I.	More's Birthplace, Parentage, Early Life and Marriage . . .	9–19
	His Public Life to his Resignation of the Chancellorship . . .	19–62
Book II.	"His Private, Secrete and Domesticall Life and Trade"	63–99
Book III.	His Books	100–135
Book IV.	His Friends, Fame and Learning .	136–140
	His Appearance and Habits . .	141–142
Book V.	His Life after the Resignation of the Great Seal; his Trial and Martyrdom	143–204
Book VI.	Reflections of Harpsfield upon More's Martyrdom	205–218

The Epistle Dedicatorie to Master William Roper

The Harpsfield manuscripts collated for this edition are referred to by the following symbols:

E = MS Emmanuel 76: the basis of the critical text.
L = MS. Lambeth 827.
R^2 = MS. Rawlinson D. 107.
Y = MS. Yelverton 72.
C = MS. (Colchester) Harsnett H. b. 35. For commencement, see p. 17, l. 9.
H = MS. Harley 6253.
R = MS. Rawlinson D. 86.
B = MS. Burns. (This MS., now in the Library of the Rt. Hon. John Burns, was sold at Sotheby's as Lot 422 A, Nov. 15th, 1926.) For commencement, see p. 12, l. 11.

The readings of other MSS. are to be assumed as being the same as those of MS. Emmanuel, unless otherwise stated. Variations of spelling and inflexion are noted only if of special interest.

Readings adopted from other MSS. into the critical text (based on E) are made to conform in spelling with the probable spelling of E Such readings are placed within square brackets in the text.

In the collations the spelling of variant readings is that of the first MS. cited.

Such common varieties of form as the following, which the scribes seem to have considered interchangeable at their own fancy, are not included in the collations:

accompt, count; afore, before; aforesaid, foresaid; afterwards, afterward; although, though; alwayes, alway; ambassade, embassage; ambassadour, embassadour; amonge, amongst; besides, beside; common weale, common wealth; estate, state; fancy, fantasy; farther, further; moe, more; my, myne; ofte, often; others, other; quitt, acquitt; sithence, sithen(s); thoroughly, throughly; till, vntil; to, vnto; towarde, towardes; truth, troth.

The variation of ye *and* you *and certain verbal forms are noted, as being of special interest.*

In the collations no note is usually taken of a correction in the text of a MS., other than E, where the scribe, seeing he has made an error, crosses the incorrect form through and goes straight on with the correct. If, however, such a correction throws light on the text of the MS. or of other MSS., the correction is recorded.

The notes referred to in the collations are the Textual Notes.

An asterisk in the text calls special attention to the collations below.

Flourished ll and pp of MS. E are transcribed as ll and pp; e.g. Cardinall, Bisshopp.

The paragraphing, punctuation and marginal summary are the Editor's.

The sources of Harpsfield's subject-matter are indicated in the marginal summary—[ROPER], [WORKS], &c. Where no source is given, the matter may generally be assumed to be Harpsfield's own. If necessary, further details are given in the *Historical Notes.*

[MS. Emmanuel 76.]

[fol. 1*a*] To the right woorshipfull M*aste*r William Roper.

Nicholas Harpsfield's Life of Sir Thomas More is a New Year's gift to his patron, William Roper.

IT is, and hath beene, an olde and most auncient custome, not onely among the Christians, but longe also before Christes time, at newyeres tyde euery ma*n*, according to his abilitie, to visite and gratifie with some present his speciall frendes and patrones. Conformable to this custome, I doo at this time (being furnished with no worldly treasure to offer you any riche, pretious gifte) present your woorshipp euen with a paper newyeres gifte; but yet suche as I trust, for the deuotion of my poore heart toward your woorshipp, shal be no lesse acceptable then was the dishe of water presented once by a poore man to one of the kinges of Persia, where the custome was for euery man to welcome and hono*ur* the kinges first co*m*ming into their quarters with some costly gifte. Which waterish gifte the good king, considering the plaine homely dealing and great and gratefull good will of the saide poore man, not onely tooke in good gree, but made more accompt of then of his riche and pretious giftes. Wherefore I trust, and litle doubt, knowing the goodnes of your gentle nature, and considering the matter comprised in this booke, being the life of the woorthy S*ir* Thomas More, knight, but that ye will, of your part, in very good part take and accept this my present. Neyther am I so carefull of the acceptation on yo*ur* behalfe as I am afraide on my owne behalfe, least by my vnskilfull handling some part of the woorthines of this man may seeme to some men to be somewhat impaired, blemished, or defaced. For I doo not so well like of my selfe, or stande so muche in mine owne conceipt, that I take my selfe the meetest man to take such an enterprise in hande. I doo well

Harpsfield laments that he is unworthy to write the Life.

MS. E *only. The* Epistle *is wanting in* L R^2 Y C B. *A shortened* Epistle, *beginning* To enterprise any thing (*see p.* 4, *l.* 24, *below*), *is prefixed to* H R.

remember that the great, famous king Alexander gaue in Co*m*maundement that no man should carue his Image but that renowmed caruer Lysippus, no man paint his Image but the excellent Painter Appelles; thinking that otherwise it would be some disgracing to himselfe and his Image. Howe muche the more ought the liuely Image of this woorthy man (whom not his deade image, being neuer so artificially and exquisitely sett forth, but his notable doinges and sayinges doo to vs most exactly represent) to be by some singuler artificer and workeman | [fol. 1 b] sett forth to the world, and, as I may say, by some other more then my selfe. But yet what soeuer my skill be (which I know well is not correspondent to such an enterprise) I haue somewhat the better contentation for that, if I haue erred, [you also haue erred] in yo*ur* choyse, in that you appointed no meeter person. And I comfort my selfe, and it be in nothing els but that I haue satisfied your request; And am better content to be taken a person vnskilfull then a person slouthfull, vnthankfull and vngratefull, especially in suche a matter as this is, and to such a person as ye are. For as this is a matter very profitable, or rather necessary, to be diuulged, so surely, if I be able in this or any other matter, with any maner of co*m*mendation, to enterprise any thing, or to gratifie any man with my doinges, ye are the onely man liuing in all the earth that by your long and great benefites and charges employed and heaped vppon me, toward the supporting of my liuing and learning, haue most deepely bounde me, or rather bought me, to be at your co*m*maundement during my life. Againe, if there be any matter in the world meete and conuenient to be presented and dedicated to you of any learned man, it is this present Treatise.

But comforts himself that he undertook the *Life* at Roper's request.

He owes more to Roper than to anyone.

And to Roper the *Life* is most fittingly dedicated.

To l. 24, to enterprise, MS. E *only*; *thenceforward to end of* Epistle, MSS. E H R *only.*

15. [*you also haue erred*]] *Omitted in* E. (*Some emendation of the text is necessary, and as the scribe of* MS. E *has several instances of omissions caused by a slip of the eye due to a repeated word, such omission here seems very likely.*) 24. *to enterprise*] *Here begins the shortened* Epistle *in* HR. H *has the heading* Epistle Dedicatorie to M*aster* William Rooper. 29-30. *or rather bought me*] *Omitted in* H.

An account of Roper's lineage.

I am not ignorant that ye come of a woorthye pedegree, both by the Father and mothers side: by the fathers side of auncient gentlemen of longe continuance; and by the mothers side of the Apuldrefeles, one of the chiefest and auncient families in Kent, and one of the three chiefe gentlemen that compelled Will*iam* Conquero*ur* to agree and to confirme the auncient customes of Kent; daughter to the great, wise and right woorshipfull S*ir* John Fineux, chiefe Justice of the Kinges benche; who amonge his woorthy and notable sayinges was wont to say that if ye take away from a Justice the order of his discretion, ye take from him more then halfe his office; whose steppes in vertue, wisedome and learning, as also yo*ur* woorshipfull fathers (who was Attorney to king Henry the eight, and whom ye in the office of the Pregnatorie in the kinges benche haue immediately succeeded, and shall therein by Gods grace longe continue) ye haue, God be thanked, well and gratiously troade after. But yet you and your familie are by no one thing more adorned, illustred and beautified, then by this woorthy man, S*ir* Thomas More, in marying his daughter, the excellent, learned and vertuous matrone, mistris Margarete More. He was your woorthy Father in lawe: what say I? your father in lawe? nay, rather your [fol. ii *a*] verye | father in deede; and though a temporall man, yet your very spirituall father, As one that by his good counsaile and aduise, or rather by his instant and deuout prayers to God, recouered your lost soule, ouerwhelmed and full deepe drowned in the deadly, dreadfull depth of horrible heresies.

By marrying Margaret More, Roper is related to Sir Thomas, who had rescued him from heresy.

MSS. E H R *only.*

1. *come*] came H. 2. *fathers*] father H. 4. *mothers*] Mother H. 6. *William Conquerour*] William the Conquerour H. 7. *to confirme*] confirme H R. 11. *After* discretion, E *has* and learning *crossed through.* 17–21. *well . . . excellent*] well followed the Road after a man whose life is admired illustred and beutified that worthie man Sir Thomas Moore whose daughter you have married the excellent, H; well road after a man whose life you re by no great and adorned illustred and beutified then worthie man Sir Thomas Moore in marrying his daughter the excellent, R, *with gaps left by scribe as indicated.* 22. *woorthy*] *Omitted in* H. 23. *what . . . lawe*] *Interlineated in* R. 25. *As*] *Omitted in* H. 28. *full*] *Interlineated in* R.

For his material for the *Life*, Harpsfield owes much to Roper's notes.

Ye maye therefore especially at my handes vendicate and challenge to you this my Treatise, And that not onely for causes aforesaid but for other also, forasmuch as ye shall receaue, I will not say a pigg of your owne sowe (it were too homely and swinish a terme) but rather a comely and goodly garlande, a pleasaunt, sweete nosegaye of most sweete and odoriferous flowers, picked and gathered euen out of your owne garden; ye shall receaue a garlande decked and adorned with pretious pearles and stones, The moste orient whereof ye haue by your owne trauaile procured and gott together, I meane of the good instructions diligently and truely by your industrie gathered, and whereof many ye knowe well by your owne experience, which ye haue imparted to me, and furnished me withall. Wherefore as all waters and riuers, according to the saying of holy Scripture, flowe out of the ocean Sea, and thither doo reflowe againe, so it is conuenient ye shoulde reape the fruit of your owne lab*our* and industrie, and that it should redounde thither, from whence it originally proceeded; And that we and our posteritie should knowe to whom to impute and ascribe the welspring of this great benefite, and whom we may accordingly thanke for many thinges nowe come to light of this woorthy man, which, perchaunce, otherwise would haue bene buried with perpetuall obliuion. And yet we haue also paide some part of the shott, and haue not beene altogether [negligent]. We haue gleaned, I trust, some good grapes, and haue with poore Ruthe leased some good corne, as by the perusing ye shall vnderstand. And thus I co*m*mitt your Woorshipp to the blessed tuition of the Almightie, who sende you this and many other good and happie newe yeres.

But Harpsfield has added other information.

Yo*ur* Worshipps bounden,

N. H. L. D.

MSS. E H R *only*.

10. *ye*] you H R. 13. *ye*] you H R. 16–17. *of holy . . . conuenient*] of þe Scriptures from whence they come thither they doe reflowe againe, It is convenient H; of the Scriptures
out of and thither doe reflowe
it is convenyent R, *with gaps left by scribe as indicated.* 26. *negligent*] negligent H R; *gap left by scribe in* E. 27. *haue*] hath H. 29. *ye*] you H R. 29. *I*] wee H.

The Life and Death of Sir Thomas More

[I]

[fol. 1 *a*] This excellent and peerlesse man, whose life we haue to endight, besides all other great and beautifull outwarde and perpetuall argumentes that God and nature adorned him withall, was beautified (if such thinges may adde any weight to his co*m*mendation, as they doo in the eyes and consideration of many) as well by the place of his birth, being borne at London, the chiefe and notable principall Citie of this our noble Realme, [as] by the heritage and woorshipfull familie whereof he sprange. His Father, M*aster* John More, was very expert in the lawes of this Realme, and for his woorthines aduaunced to be one of the Justices of the kinges benche, and to the woorshipfull degree of knighthood. Who, besides his learning, was indued with many notable and vertuous qualities and giftes : A man very vertuous, and of a very vpright and sincere conscience, both in geving of counsaile and iudgement; a very mercifull and pitifull man; And, amonge other his good qualities and properties, a companiable, a mery, and pleasantly conceyted man. And therefore, in talking of mens wiues, he would merilye saye that that choice is like as if a blinde man should put his hande into a bagge full of snakes and eles together, seuen snakes for one eele. When he hearde folke blame their wiues, and say that they be so many of them shrewes, he would

Thomas More's birthplace and parentage. Born in London. [7 Feb. 1477, or 6 or 7 Feb. 1478.]

His father, Sir John More, Knight and Justice of the King's Bench, Sir John More's virtue. [MORE'S EPITAPH.

Sir John More's wit and humour. His jokes concerning the fortunes of matrimony. [WORKS, pp. 165, 233.]

MSS. E L R^2 Y H R *only.*

2. *beautifull*] beautifull *underlined, and* bountiful *written above* L. 2. *outwarde*] outwardes H. 3. *argumentes*] ornamentes H R. 4. *beautified*] endued R^2. 5. *commendation*] comendationes L Y. 6. *of many as well by*] of manny with great prerogatiue aboue the vulgar sorte aswell by R^2. 7. *chiefe and notable principall Citie*] cheife and notable place and principall Cittie H. 8. *noble*] *Omitted in* R^2. 8. *as*] L R^2 Y H R; and E. 10. *John*] *Omitted in* R^2. 11. *one of the*] one of his the Y. 14. *indued*] educated H. 14. *many*] *Omitted in* L R^2 H R. 16. *and iudgement*] & in Judgment R^2 Y R. 17. *a*] *Omitted in* Y. 17. *and pitifull*] and a pytifull Y. 18. *good*] goodly R^2. 19. *pleasantly*] pleasant R^2 H. 19. *in*] I *in* Y. 23. *he*] *Interlineated in* R^2. 23. *folke*] men R^2. 24. *that*] *Omitted in* H R. 24. *they be*] their be Y. (*See* Notes.) 24. *of them*] *Interlineated in* R. 24. *shrewes*] shewes H.

merily say that they diffame them falsely, for he would say plainly that there was but one shrewde wife in the world, but he saide in deede that euery man weeneth that he hath her, and that one was his owne wife. But in this kinde of proper pleasant talke his sonne, with whom we nowe be in hande, incomparably did exceede him. This good knight and Justice liued vntill he came to great age, and yet was for the health and vse of his body muche more freshe and actiue then men of his yeres commonly be of. But after he had nowe so longe liued, and especially that he had seene his sonne highe Chauncellour of Inglande, he most gladly and willingly, when God called for it, rendred againe his spirite vnto God, from whom he had receaued it.

Sir John More's long and healthy life. [MORE'S EPITAPH.]

But nowe to returne to his sonne; neyther was he by his parentes, nor by his birth and place, so much adorned and beautified as he did adorne and beautifie them both and the whole Realme beside. In the saide Citie, at St Anto|nies schoole, he learned the principles of the [fol. 1 b] latine tongue, in the knowledge whereof when he had in short space farre surmounted his coequalls, his father, seeing the towardlynes and actiuitie of his sonne, and being carefull for his farther good and vertuous education, procured and obteyned that he shoulde be brought vp in the house of the right reuerende, the wise and learned prelate, Cardinall Morton; who, being a man of quicke witt and deepe iudgement, soone espied the childes excellent disposition and nature: who, among many other

Thomas More sent to St. Anthony's school, where he learns the elements of Latin. [ROPER.]

More in the household of Cardinal Morton. [1490.] [ROPER.]

MSS. E L R^2 Y H R *only.*

1. *diffame*] defamed L R^2 Y H R. (*See* Notes.) 2–4. *but . . . he hath her*] *Omitted in* R^2. 3. *saide*] saithe Y. 7. *Justice liued*] Justice Sir John Moore lyued R^2. 7. *to great age*] to a great age H R. 8. *yet was for*] yet was he for L R^2 H R, yet *being interlineated in* L. 8. *health and vse*] vse & health R^2. 10. *after*] after that H R. 11. *his*] *Interlineated in* R^2. 11. *sonne highe*] sonne þe highe L R^2 H R; son the Right Y. (English Works, Epitaph, *p.* 1421, *reads* sonne lord Chaunceller.) 13. *rendred*] render H. 13. *whom*] whence H; whom, *corrected from* whence, R. 18. *S^t*] S^t, *corrected from* a, R. 19. *of the*] of Y. 20. *when*] *Interlineated in* R. 22. *the*] his Y. 22. *towardlynes*] towardnes L R^2 Y. 23. *farther*] father Y; further *interlineated over a word, apparently* father, *crossed through* R. 23. *education*] educations Y. 25. *wise and learned*] wise & vertuous & Learned R^2. 28. *excellent*] most excellent R^2.

tokens of his quicke and pregnant witt, being very yonge, would yet notwithstanding vpon the [soden] stepp in among the Christmas players, and forthwith, without any other forethinking or premeditation, playe a part with them himselfe, so fitly, so plausibly and so pleasantly, that the Auditours tooke muche admiration, and more comfort and pleasure thereof then of all the players besydes; and especially the Cardinall, vpon whose table he wayted. And often would he tell to the nobles sitting at the table with him: "Whosoeuer liueth to see it, shall see this childe come to an excellent and meruailous proufe." To whose very likely, then, and probable foreiudgement, thende and issue of this mans life hath plainly, openly and truely aunswered. And so farre as we may, as it were for a wonderfull but yet for a true surplusage, adde to his coniecturall foreiudgement our sure, constant, stable and grounded iudgement, that he was and is the oddest and the notablest man of all Inglande, And that he atchieued such an excellent state of woorthines, fame and glory as neuer did (especially laye man) in Inglande before, and muche doubt is there whether anye man shall hereafter. Which my saying I trust I shall iustifie hereafter. In the meane season, good Reader, if thou thinke I passe and exceede iust measure, and wouldest I should shewe by and by what motions I haue that leade me to this

More's impromptu acting. [ROPER.]

Cardinal Morton predicts a great future for young Thomas More. [ROPER.]

And Harpsfield promises to show how More proved himself the greatest man England has ever produced, or probably ever will.

MSS. E L R² Y H R *only*.

1. *his*] his his L. 2. *soden*] suddayne L R² H R (*supported by* Roper's sodeynly); Sunday E; sonnday Y. 3. *Christmas*] christianes Y. 3–4. *without any other*] without any R²; without other H. 4. *premeditation*] premeditateing L. 7. *the players*] þe other players R². 8. *the*] *Interlineated in* R². 9. *often*] after Y. 11. *excellent and*] *Interlineated in* L. 12. *likely*] like L R². 13. *foreiudgement*] foreiudgement, *with* fore *interlineated in* L R; Judgmente R². 13. *this mans*] his L R². 15. *as it were*] & as it were LR². 16. *his*] þis L R². 17. *our sure . . . iudgement*] our sur constantable & grounded H. 18 *the* (2)] *Omitted in* H. 18. *notablest*] latabest L. 19. *And that he*] And yf he R². 19. *atchieued*] attained Y. 21–22. *and muche doubt is there*] and doubt there is H; and much doubt there is R. 22. *hereafter*] heeafter L. 23. *saying*] sainges Y. 23. *Which . . . hereafter*] *Omitted in* L R². 24. *I passe*] a passe Y. 25. *iust*] *Omitted in* R². 25-26. *shewe by and by what motions*] shew by & by shew what mocions H; shew (*interlineated*) by & by shew what mocions R.

censure, I praye thee spare me a litle while, and geue the more vigilant and attentiue eare to the due and deepe consideration of that I shall truely and faythfully sett forth touching this man. And then I hope I shall, if thou be any thing indifferent, satisfie my promise and thy expectation also.

More sent to Oxford. [1492.] [ROPER.]

This Cardinall then that had raysed both to himself and others such an expectation to this childe, being nowe more and more carefull to haue him well trayned vp, that his goodly budd might be a faire flower, and at length bring forth such fruit as he and the others expected and looked | for, thought it best he should be [fol. 2 *a*] sent to the Vniuersite of Oxforde, and so he was; where, for the short time of his abode (being not fully two yeres) and for his age, he wonderfully profited in the knowledge of the latin and greeke tonges; where, if he had setled and fixed himselfe, and hadd runne his full race in the study of the liberall sciences and diuinitie, I trowe he would haue beene the singuler and the onely spectacle of this our time for learning. But his father minded that he should treade after his steppes, and settle his whole minde and studie vpon the lawes of the Realme. And so being plucked from the vniuersities of studies and learning*es*, he was sett to the studies of the lawes onely of this Realme. Which studie he co*m*menced first at Newe Inne, one of the Innes of

His progress in Latin and Greek. [ROPER.]

More removed from Oxford in order to study for the Bar. [ROPER.]

More enters New Inn. [1494.] [ROPER.]

To l. 11, bring, MSS. E L R² Y H R *only*; *thenceforward to p.* 17, *l.* 9, he was, MSS. E L R² Y H R B *only.*

1. *thee*] ye Y. 2. *vigilant and attentiue*] diligent attentive H; dilligent & attentiue R. 6. *thy*] þey L. 7. *then*] *Omitted in* L R². 8. *an expectation to*] an highe expectacioun of Y; L *as* E R² H R, *but with* to *interlineated over* of *crossed through.* 9. *well*] *Omitted in* R². 10. *his*] þis L R². 10. *be a*] be made a L R². 10. *faire*] farr Y. 11. *bring*] *Here commences the text of* B. 11. *and the others*] & others H R; and other[ ] B, *the corner of the page being torn off.* 12. *expected*] [ ] ted B, *the corner of the page being torn off.* 12. *he should*] that he should H R; he s[ ] B, *the corner of the page being torn off.* 13. *of*] of, *corrected to* at, L; at R² B. 13. *Oxforde*] Oxon: R². 13. *and*] an[ ] B, *the corner of the page being torn off.* 14. *fully*] full Y. 17. *setled*] satled Y. 17. *hadd*] *Interlineated in* R. 17. *runne*] runned Y. 19. *the onely*] only R² H. 20. *our*] *Interlineated in* L. 22. *settle*] set Y. 23. *the Realme*] this Realme H R. 24. *learninges*] lerning Y H R. 24. *studies* (2)] studie Y. 25–26. *he commenced first*] he first commenced H.

Admitted to Lincoln's Inn. [1496.] [Roper.]

Made an utter barrister. [Roper, with additions.]

Chauncerie. And when he had welfauouredly profited therein, he was admitted to Lincolnes Inne, and there, with small allowance, so farre forth pursued his studie that he was made, as he was well woorthy, an vtter barrester. Nowe is the lawe of the Realme, and the studie thereof, such as would require a whole man, wholly and entierly thereto addicted, and a whole and entier mans life, to growe to any excellencie therein. Neyther were vtter barresters commonlye made then but after many yeres studie. But this mans speedie and yet substantiall profiting was such that he enioyed some prerogatiue of time; and yet in this notwithstanding did he cutt off from the studie of the lawe muche time, which he employed to his former studies that he vsed in Oxforde; and especially to the reading of St Augustine *de Ciuitate Dei*, which though it be a booke very harde for a well learned man to vnderstande, and cannot be profoundly and exactly vnderstanded, [and] especially cannot be with co*m*mendation openly read, of any man that is not well and substantially furnished as well with diuinite as prophane knowledge; yet did M*aster* More, being so yonge, being so distracted also and occupied in the studie of the co*m*mon lawes, openly reade in the Churche of St Laurence in London the bookes of the saide St Augustine *de Ciuitate Dei*, to his no small co*m*mendation, and to the great admiration of all his audience. His lesson was frequented and honoured with the presence and resort, as well of that well learned and

More's lectures on St. Augustine's *De Civitate Dei* in the Church of St. Lawrence, London. [1501.] [Roper.]

MSS. E L R^2 Y H R B *only*.

1. *And*] *Omitted in* R^2. 2. *Lincolnes*] Licolnes L. 4. *made*] madd Y. (*Note spelling.*) 5. *the Realme*] this Realme Y. 6. *a whole*] an whole R. 7. *a whole*] an whole H R. 7–8. *and entier*] & an entire R. 9. *commonlye*] *The* n *is corrected from* l *in* E. 10. *speedie*] speed Y. 10. *and*] *Omitted in* B. 12–13. *and yet . . . time*] *Interlineated in* R. 15. *Oxforde*] Oxōn R. 17. *a well*] a very well Y. 18. *profoundly and*] *Omitted in* L R^2 B. 18. *vnderstanded*] vnderstode Y. 18. *and* (2)] L R^2 Y H R B; but E. 19. *with*] withoute B. 19. *commendation*] commendacons Y. 19–23. *of . . . openly reade*] *Omitted in* Y. 20. *well . . . as well with*] well an substancially as well with H. 21. *as prophane*] as with profane H R. 28. *and* (1)] *Interlineated over* of *crossed through* Y. 28. *well* (2)] *Omitted in* L R^2 H R B.

Grocyn one of More's audience. [ROPER, with additions.]

great cunning man, M*aster* Grocin (with whom and with M*aster* | Thomas Lupsett he learned the greeke tonge) [fol. 2 *b*] as also w*i*th the chiefe and best learned men of the Citie of London. About the same time the saide Grocin read in the foresaid Citie the bookes of Dionisius Areopagita, but he had not so frequent and so great an Auditorie as had M*aster* More.

More made Reader at Furnivall's Inn. [1501.] [ROPER.]

This intermission and interchaunge of studies was to M*aster* More no lesse comfort and recreation then it was to his auditours good and profitable. So that from this, as it were a spirituall exercise, he returned the lustier and fresher againe to his olde studie of the temporall lawe. And being thought expedient and meete by the whole benche of Lincolnes Inne that he should not keepe and reserue his knowledge to his owne selfe onely, but laye it forth and sowe it abrode to the vse and profite of many others, was made Reader of Furniualls Inne. And in this trade, to the great co*m*moditie of his hearers, he continued three yeres and more.

More burgess of the Parliament about the time of the marriage between James IV of Scotland and Margaret, eldest daughter of Henry VII. [ROPER, with additions.]

About this time he was chosen a Burgesse of the Parliament, in the later dayes of king Henry the seuenth. At which time was there concluded a mariage betweene James, the king of Scott*es*, and Lady Margaret, eldest daughter to the saide king. And because great charges would growe to the king by reason of setting and sending forth the saide Lady, he demaunded of the Parliament about three fifteenes, as it hath beene reported. Nowe considering the continuall custome almost of all times

MSS. E L R^2 Y H R B *only.*

1. *Grocin*] Gorcyn B. 3. *with . . . men*] with the best & cheife learned men H R. 4. *same*] said L H B. 4. *Grocin*] Gorcyn B. 5. *read . . . bookes*] read in the aforesaid Cittye in the bookes of H; R^2 *and* R *as* E L B, *but* aforesaid *for* foresaid; Y *as* E L B, *but* boke *for* bookes. 6. *but he*] but þat he L R^2 Y B. 6. *so frequent and so great*] so great and frequent Y. 6–7. *an Auditorie*] Auditorie H. 8. *interchaunge*] interchanging L. 9. *comfort and recreation*] comfortable B. 11. *a*] as H. 11–12. *and fresher*] and the fresher Y. 12. *his*] þe *interlineated* R^2. 12. *olde*] owne L. 15. *reserue*] conserve B. 17. *Furniualls*] Furnifolds L. 18. *of his*] of all his H R. 22. *was there*] there was HR. 24. *saide*] *Omitted in* H. 25. *to the king*] to the said kinge Y. 25. *setting and sending*] sending and setting Y. 26. *the saide*] of the said R^2. 28. *custome*] customes R^2.

and of all Princes, at least from Henry the first (who gaue his daughter, called commonly Maude the Empresse, in mariage to Henry the Emperour, with no small charges put vpon the commons for the same) and as well the great and present as the longe durable co*m*moditie as it was then likely that should ensue to this Realme by the mariage, it was thought there would be* small reluctation or repining against this Parliament.

More's opposition to the subsidy demanded by Henry VII for this marriage. [1504.] [Roper.]

Howbeit M*aster* More, vpon some apparant grounde, as there is good likelyhood (for he was no rashe, wilfull man, and was easie to be intreated to yeelde to reason) dislyked vpon the saide payment, and shewed openly his minde therein, and with such reasons and argument*es* debated and inforced the matter that the residue of the [fol. 3 *a*] lower house condes|cended to his minde, and thereby was the Bill ouerthrowen. And forthwith M*aster* Tyler, one of the kinges priuie chamber, that was present in the saide house, resorted to the king, declaring vnto him that a beardlesse boye had disappointed and dasshed all his purpose.

The consequent hostility of Henry VII towards More and his father. [Roper, with additions.]

The remembrance of this displeasure sanke deepely into the kinges heart, and bred great and heauy indignation against M*aster* More, readie vpon any small occasion to burst out against him. But yet did the king forbeare, as well least he might seeme thereby to infringe and breake the auncient libertie of the Parliament house for free speaking touching the publique affaires (which would haue beene taken odiously) as also for that M*aster* More had then litle or nothing to leese. But yet was there a

MSS. E L R² Y H R B *only.*

2. *called commonly*] commonly called L R² H R B. 4. *commons*] Comonaltie H R. 5. *longe durable*] long and durable L R² Y B. 6. *the*] *Omitted in* R². 7. *be small*] L R² Y H R B; be no small E. 9. *some apparant*] some good apparaunt Y. 10. *likelyhood*] Likelywoode R². 11. *easie to be intreated*] easely entreated L R² B; easily to be entreated H R. 12. *saide*] same H R. 12. *payment*] parlyament Y. 16. *And*] *Omitted in* B. 16. *Tyler*] Tayler R²; Tailor *crossed through, followed by* Tiler Y; Tyler, *with* y *corrected from* a, R. 18. *saide*] side Y. 18. *declaring*] declareing therein H. 21. *of this*] of of his R². 22. *great*] *The* t *is cropped in* L. 23. *small*] little R². 26. *house*] hou, *with the* se *cropped*, L. 27. *would*] should H R. 29. *then*] *Omitted in* Y. 29. *But yet*] But soone after B. 29. *was there*] their was Y B.

causelesse quarell deuised against his father, whereby he was co*m*mitted to the towre, from whence he could not gett himselfe out vntill the king had gott out of his purse a fine of one hundred poundes.

Dr. Fox, Bishop of Winchester, in order to entrap More, offers to act as mediator for him with the King. [ROPER.]

Neyther yet for all this was M*aster* More altogether forgotten, but pretie priuie wayes were deuised howe to wrappe him in. Amonge other, at a time as he repaired to Doctor Foxe, Bisshopp of Winchester, and one of the kinges priuie Counsaile, and wayted vpon him for a certaine sute, the Bisshopp called him aside, and pretending much fauo*ur*, saide: "If ye will be ruled and ordred by me, I doubt nothing but I shall recouer and winne the king*es* fauo*ur* to you againe;" meaning thereby (as it was coniectured) to wringe out of his owne mouth some confession of his fault and offence against the king, whereby the king might with some better apparant colo*ur* fasten his displeasure vpon him, and openly reuenge the same against him. Returning from the Bisshopp, he fell in co*m*munication with M*aster* Richarde Whitforde, his familier frende, then Chapleine to the Bisshopp, and after one of the Fathers of Sion. To whom after that he had disclosed what the bisshopp saide to him, craving his good and frendly aduise therein: "M*aster* More," sayth he, "Folowe not his counsaile in any wise; for my master, to gratifie the king, and to serue his turne, will not sticke to condescende and agree and it were to the death euen of his owne naturall Father." Whervpon M*aster* More resorted no more to the saide Bisshopp, and | remayning [fol. 3 *b.*] euer after in great feare of the kinges indignation hanging vpon him, and supposing that his longer abode in Inglande

Acting upon the advice of Richard Whitford, the Bishop's chaplain, More returns no more to the Bishop. [ROPER, with addition.]

More's plan to seek safety abroad. [ROPER.]

MSS. E L R^{2} Y H R B *only.*

3. *gott*] gottin Y. 4. *one*] a H; an R. 6. *priuie*] *Omitted in* Y. 6. *wayes*] was H. 11. *ye*] you R^{2} B. 12. *nothing*] not B. 12. *but I*] but that I *in* Y; I *in* H. 13. *to you*] *Omitted in* B. 14. *owne*] *Omitted in* B. 16. *with*] by R^{2}. 21. *of* (2)] *Omitted in* R^{2}. 21. *after that*] after R^{2} H R. 22. *disclosed*] *Final* d *of* disclosed *cropped in* L. 23. *aduise*] ad, *with* uise *cropped*, L. 24. *wise*] case L R^{2} B. 25. *his turne*] his owne turne H. 25. *will not sticke*] will sticke H. 26. *condescende*] condiscent Y. 26. *euen*] *Omitted in* L R^{2} Y; *interlineated in* R. 27. *naturall*] *Omitted in* B. 28–29. *remayning euer after*] euer after remayning L R^{2} B. 30. *him*] *Omitted in* B. 30. *his*] *Omitted in* L R^{2}B.

could not be but to his great daunger, resolued to passe ouer the Seas: which his determination was preuented and cutt off by the death of the king not longe after ensuing. **Exile of More rendered unnecessary owing to death of Henry VII. [1509.] [Roper.]**

And all this while was he vnmaried, and seemed to be in some doubt and deliberation with himselfe what kinde and trade of life he should enter, to folowe and pursue all his longe life after. Surely it seemeth by some apparant coniectures that he was sometime somewhat propense and inclined either to be a priest, or to take some monasticall and solitary life; for he continued after his foresaide reading fowre yeres and more full vertuously and religiously in great deuotion and prayer with the monkes of the Charterhouse of London, without any maner of profession or vowe, eyther to see and proue whether he could frame himselfe to that kinde of life, or at least [for a time] to sequester himselfe from all temporall and worldly exercises. Himselfe saide also afterwarde, when his daughter Margarete Roper (whom of all his children he did most louingly, most entierly and most fatherly tendre*) escaped against all expectation, as we shall hereafter shewe, of a most daungerous sicknes, that if she had dyed, he would neuer haue intermedled with any worldly affaires after. Furthermore, being prisoner in the towre, he tolde his said daughter that his short penning and shutting vp did litle greeue him; for if it had not beene

More had spent four years without vow with the monks of the Charterhouse. [1499-1503.] [Roper.]

More feels drawn to the monastic life. [Roper.]

To l. 9, he was, MSS. E L R² Y H R B *only; thenceforward to end of text* E L R² Y C H R B.

1. *could*] would L. 3. *king*] kinges, *with the* s *partly erased,* Y. 5. *And all*] All H; *in* R all *is preceded by* & *partly obliterated.* 6. *in*] of Y. 7. *and trade of life*] of trade and lyef Y. 8. *all his longe life after*] all his life longe after H. 9. *coniectures*] reason and coniecture Y. 9. *he was*] *Here begins* MS. C. 9. *sometime*] sometimes L; sometyme, *with final* s *cancelled,* B. 10. *propense and*] *Omitted in* B. 10. *to be a priest*] to the preist Y; to bee Preist C. 11. *and*] *Omitted in* B. 11. *after*] *Omitted in* B. 16–17. *for a time*] for a tyme C; *omitted in* E L R² Y H R B. 18. worldly] gostly Y. 20. *most*] *Omitted in* Y. 20. *entierly*] *Interlineated in* L. 21. *tendre*] L R² H R B; tendred E Y; C tendred, *but omits* did *in l.* 20. 23. *haue*] *Interlineated in* L. 23. *haue intermedled*] intermedle B. 24. *affaires*] *This is added in the same hand on the margin, with omission mark in text after* worldly, R². 26. *shutting*] puttinge H R.

for respect of his wife and children, he had voluntarily longe ere that time shutt him selfe in as narrowe or narrower a roome then that was.

But, Harpsfield points out, he was not bound to choose it.

Nowe, if any man will say that, seing the contemplatiue life farre exceedeth the actiue, according as Christe him selfe confesseth : *Optimam partem elegit Maria, quae non auferetur ab ea*, that he meruaileth why *Master* More did not folow, embrace and pursue the saide inclination, To this I answere, that no man is precisely bounde so to doo ; I aunswere farther, that were it so that he had such propension and inclination, God himselfe seemeth to haue chosen and appointed this man to another kinde of life, to serue him therein more acceptably to his diuine hono*ur*, and more profitably for the wealth of the Realme and his owne soule also. Of the | which our iudgement we shall [fol. 4 *a*] render you hereafter suche causes as moue vs so to thinke.

More decides to marry, and lives virtuously in the married state.

In conclusion therefore he fell to mariage, in and vnder the which he did not onely liue free from dishonouring the same with any vnlawfull and filthie company, leaving his owne wife (as many, especially such as be of great wealth and authoritie, the more pitie, often doo) but liued himselfe, his wife, his children and familie, after such a godly and vertuous sort as his house might rather be a mirro*ur* and spectacle, not onely to the residue of the laitie, but euen to many of the Clergie also.

Marries [Jane], eldest daughter of Mr. Colt. [1505.] [ROPER.]

His wife was one *Master* Coltes daughter, a gentleman of Essex, that had ofte inuited him thither, hauing three daughters, whose honest conuersation and vertuous education prouoked him there specially to sett his affection. And albeit his minde moste serued him to the seconde

MSS. E L R² Y C H R B.

1. *for respect*] for the great respect R². 1. *voluntarily*] voluntarie Y. 2–3. *or narrower a roome*] or a narrowar rowme Y ; or narrower roome B. 5. *the actiue*] the actiue lyfe Y. 7. *meruaileth*] maruailed R². 8. *not*] *Omitted in* B. 9. *answere*] aunswered further R². 14. *profitably*] profitable R². 16. *moue*] mooues L. 16. *so*] *Interlineated in* R. 20. *any*] *Omitted in* C. 22. *the more pitie*] þe more þe pittie L B. 23. *his children*] and children R² Y C. 24. *godly and vertuous*] vertuouse & godlie B. 25. *a*] *Interlineated in* R². 30. *his*] *Omitted in* B.

daughter, for that he thought her the fayrest and best fauoured, yet when he considered that it would be both great griefe and some shame also [to] the eldest to see her yonger sister in mariage preferred before her, he then of a certaine pitie framed his fancie toward her, and soone after maried her; neuer the more discontinuing his studie of the lawe at Lincolnes Inne, but applying still the same vntill he was called to the bench, and had read there twise, which is as often as ordinarily any Judge of the lawe doth reade.

Made a bencher of Lincoln's Inn, readin there twice [Roper.]

Before which time he had placed himselfe and his wife in Bucklersbury in London, where he had by her three daughters and one sonne (called John More, to whom Erasmus did dedicate Aristotles workes, printed by Bebelius; and three daughters, Margarete,* maried to M*aster* Will*iam* Roper; Cicelie, maried to M*aster* Giles Heron; and Elizabeth, wife to M*aster* Will*iam* Dancie): which children from their youth he brought vp in vertue, and knowledge both in the latin and the greeke tonges, whom he would often exhort to take vertue and learning for their meate, and playe for their [sauce].

Residence at Bucklersbury. [Roper.]

The family of More: Margaret [b. 1505]; Elizabeth [b. 1506]; Cecily [b. 1507]; John [b.? 1508, 9.] [Roper, with additions.]

As he was borne in London, so was he as well of others as of the saide Citie derely beloued, and inioyed there

MSS. E L R^2 Y C H R B.

1–2. *that . . . yet*] *Omitted in* R^2. 3. *some shame also*] also some shame Y. 3. *to the eldest*] to theldest Y C (*supported by* Roper); the eldest E L R^2 H R B. 4. *her* (1)] þe R^2. 4. *yonger*] yoongest L R^2 B. 5. *of a certaine*] of certaine Y. 6. *discontinuing*] *Corrected from* discontinued R^2; discontinued Y. 6. *his*] þe C. (Roper *supports* his). 7. *applying*] applyed Y. 9. *as often*] *Interlineated in* Y. 9–10. *as ordinarily . . . reade*] as any Judge of the lawe ordinarily doth reade H R. 11. *and his wife*] *Omitted in* Y. 12. *Bucklersbury*] Bucklesbury L R^2. 12–13. *where . . . sonne*] where he had by her one sonn H R. (*See* Notes). 13. *John More, to whom*] John Moore by her to whom Y. 15. *Bebelius*] Bebilius L R^2 B; Bebelinus C. 15. *daughters*] doughtes Y. 15. *Margarete, maried*] L R^2 Y C H R B; Margarete who was maried E. 16. *Giles*] *Omitted in* R^2. 17. *Elizabeth, wife to*] Elyzabethe maried to Y B. 19. *in the*] of the R^2. 19. *the greeke*] greeke L R^2 H R B. 20. *often*] *Omitted in* H. 20. *vertue*] vertues Y. 21. *sauce*] C H R (*supported by* Roper); fancie E L R^2 Y B. 22. *As*] And as C, *with* as *interlineated.* 23. *as of the saide Citie*] and especiallie of þe Citizens of þe said Citye C. 23. *derely*] *Omitted in* H.

More made an Under-sheriff of London. [1510.] [ROPER and ERASMUS.]

His energy, justice and sincerity. [ERASMUS.]

He makes about £400 yearly. [ROPER.]

the first office that he had, being made vnder sheriffe of the | [saide] Citie. The saide office, as it is woorshipfull, [fol. 4 *b*] so is it not verye combersome: for the Judge sitteth vpon Thursday onely, once in the weeke, before noone; no man dispatched in the same office more causes then he did; No man euer vsed himselfe more sincerely and vprightly to the suters, to whom often times he forgaue his owne fee and dutie. In the saide Court it is the order, before they co*m*mence their matter, that the Plaintiffe put* downe three grotes, and the defendant as muche; more it is not lawfull to require of them; by the which office, and his learned counsaile that he gaue his client*es*, he gayned without grudge, griefe or touche of his owne conscience, and without the grudge, griefe or iniurie of any other man, aboue fowre hundred poundes yerely.

More's embassies in the interests of the English merchants. [1515, 1517.] [ROPER.]

Neither was there any matter in controuersie of weight and importance in any of the Princes courtes of the lawes of the Realme that he was not retayned for counsaile of the one or the other partie; yea, he grewe shortly in suche woorthy credite for his witt, learning, wisdome and experience, that before he came to the seruice of king Henry the eight, he was at the sute and instance of the englishe merchauntes, and by the kinges consent, for great important matters betweene the said merchantes and the

MSS. E L R² Y C H R B.

1. *the first*] first R². 1. *that he had*] that euer he had H R. 1–2. *of the saide*] L R² Y C H R B; of the E. 2. *woorshipfull*] very woorshipfull L R² B. 3. *so is it not*] so it is not H R. 3. *it*] *Interlineated in* L. 3. *sitteth*] *Corrected from* sittinge R². 5. *dispatched*] dispatcheth R². 5. *in the same office more causes*] more causes in the same Office H R. 6–7. *euer vsed . . . vprightly*] vsed himselfe euer more sincerely & vprightly L R² B; vsed himself more sincerely and vprightly Y; euer vsed himselfe more sincerely vprightly H. 6. *and*] *Interlineated in* R. 7. *vprightly to the suters*] *On an erasure in* R. 10. *Plaintiffe*] plaintiffes H. 10. *put*] Y C H R; putteth E L R² B. 11. *it is not*] is it not Y. 12. *which*] *Omitted in* B. 12. *that he gaue*] he gaue Y. 14. *and*] or H R. 14. *or*] and L. 18. *and*] or L R² B. 18. *lawes*] Lawe Y. 19. *not*] *Omitted in* R². 19–20. *of . . . partie*] for the one or other partie Y; for the one or of the other H. 22. *came*] come R². 22. *of king*] of þe King L. 23–24. *of the englishe merchauntes*] *Omitted in* C. 24–25. *and by the . . . said merchantes*] *Omitted in* L R² B. 24. *for great*] for the great Y.

merchauntes of the Stilliarde (albeit commonly suche ambassades are committed to Ciuilians) sent twise Ambassadour ouer the Seas. He of his owne selfe and of nature neither desired nor well lyked to be intricated with Princes affaires, and of all other offices he had little minde and fancie to be any ambassadour, And least to this ambassade; for that he lyked not to haue his abode (as he had) and, as it were, to be shutt vp in a Towne nere to the Sea, where neither the grounde nor the ayre was good and wholsome. Againe, whereas in Inglande of very nature he did abhorre from greeuous and contentious alter[c]ations and strifes, though he felt thereby a gaine, suche contentions in a straunge countrey were muche more greeuous and odious to him, and by so muche the more as he felt thereby some damage. For though he were woorshipfully prouided and furnished for the defraying of his charges, yet grewe there some charges [fol. 5 *a*] thereby to him; and he was merily wont to say that | there was betweene a lay man and a priest to be sent in ambassade a very great difference: for the priestes neede not to be troubled or disquieted for the absence of their wiues and children (as hauing none, or suche as they may finde euery where) as the lay man is, and may carie their whole familie with them, as the lay man cannot. He would also farther pleasantly say that albeit he were no yll husbande, no yll father, no yll master, yet could he

More's dislike of such embassies, and his reasons therefor. [MORE to ERASMUS.]

MSS. ELR²YCHRB.

2. *ambassades*] Embassages, *with* ges *corrected from* dors, L. 2. *are*] as Y. 2. *Ciuilians*] the Civillians H. 4. *well lyked*] liked well C. 6. *any*] an H. 7. *for that he*] for he LR²HRB; he YC. 8–10. *nere to . . . good and wholsome*] neare the Sea and wholesome H; R *as* ELR²YCB, *but* neare the Sea *for* nere to the Sea. 12. *altercations*] LB; alterations ER²C; alteracPiouns Y; alterracions HR. 12. *a gaine*] L *has a letter cancelled before* gaine, *and* a *interlineated*; againe YH; gaine R²C. 13. *in a straunge countrey*] in straing countries Y. 14. *greeuous and odious*] Odious & grevous R². 15 *thereby*] *Omitted in* H. 16. *woorshipfully*] worshiplye Y. 17. *there some charges thereby*] there thereby some charges L; thereby some charges R². 18. *was*] *Omitted in* B. 19. *in*] *Omitted in* L. 20. *priestes*] prest Y. 21. *troubled or disquieted*] disquieted or troubled HR. 22. *and*] or H. 24. *cannot*] canot L. 25–26. *no yll husbande, no yll father*] not ill husband nor ill father Y.

More's success in embassy.

not intreate his wife, children or familie, to fast for his pleasure vntill his returne. But yet all this notwithstanding, the office once put vpon him, not desired, expected or looked for on his part, he forslowed nothing for the aduauncing and happie expedition of the same, and so therein demeaned himselfe that after his returne he purchased to himselfe great aduauncement of his estimation, both with the merchantes and with the king himselfe; who, at his returne, offered him for some recompence [of his travaile] an annuall pencion during his life. Which, though it was honorable and fruitfull, yet did he refuse it, least he should be occasioned thereby to relinquishe his former state, condition and office (which he preferred to be muche better) or keepe it with some discontentation of the Citizens of London, who perchaunce might conceaue some sinister suspicion of him, that when any controuersie should afterwarde chaunce (as there did often) betweene the king and the Citie for their priuiledges, he would not beare himselfe vprightly and sincerely, being, as it were, somewhat wrapped in, intangled and affectionated, by reason of this pensition.

More's reason for refusing the pension offered him as a reward. [MORE to ERASMUS.]

The King's desire to get More into the royal service. [ROPER.]

Moreouer the king was in hande with Cardinall Woolsey, then Lorde Chauncellour, to winne him and to procure him to his graces seruice. The Cardinall did not forslowe the matter, but incontinentlye trauelled, and that very earnestly, with him, with many persuasions, which he did amonge other inforce with this, that his seruice must needes be deere to his Maiestie, which could not with his honour with lesse | then he should leese thereby seeme to [fol. 5 b] recompence him. Yet he, being very lothe to shifte and chaunge his state and condition, wrought so with the Cardinall that by the Cardinall the king was satisfied for

More manages for a time to keep out of State affairs. [ROPER.]

MSS. E L R^{2} Y C H R B.

1. *or*] ar Y. 5. *aduauncing*] advancement L R^{2} B. 5. *of*] for B. 6 *his*] hes R^{2}. 10. *of his travaile*] Y C ; *omitted in* E L R^{2} H R B. 19. *vprightly*] vpright Y. 20. *in*] *Omitted in* B. 21. *this*] his R^{2} H. 23. *and to procure*] & procure R^{2} Y B. 26–27. *which . . . inforce*] and which among other he did inforce L R^{2} B. 28. *which*] who L R^{2} B. 29. *leese*] loose H. 30. *Yet*] Yea, *corrected from* Yeat, B. 30. *very*] *Omitted in* H ; *interlineated in* R. 31. *the*] *Interlineated in* R^{2}.

the time, and accepted M*aster* Mores excuse. I say for the time. For this mans woorthy estimation and fame so grewe on euery day more then other, that a while after the king could by no maner of intreatie be induced any longer to forbeare his seruice, and that vpon this occasion.

But the ability he shows in the case of the Pope's ship causes the King to engage him in his service. [ROPER.]

There chaunced a great shipp of his that then was Pope to arriue at Southampton, the which the king claymed as a forfeyture. Wherevpon the popes ambassadour, then resident in the Realme, vpon sute obteyned of the king that he might retaine for his master some Counsailers learned in the lawes of the Realme, and that in his owne presence (him selfe being a singuler Ciuilian) the matter might in some publike place be openly heard, debated and discoursed. Among all the lawyers, no one could be founde so apte and meete as M*aster* More, As one that was able to report to the Ambassadour all the reasons and argumentes on both sides proposed and alleaged. Vpon this the Counsailers of either partie, in the presence of the Lorde Chauncell*our* and other the Judges in the Starre chamber, had audience accordinglye. At what time M*aster* More was not onely a bare reporter to the Ambassadour, but argued himselfe also so learnedly and so substantially that he recouered and wonne to the pope the saide forfaiture, and to himselfe high commendation and renowne.

The King's instructions to More on his entering the Royal service. [WORKS, pp. 1426 (numbered 1427), 1444, 1458; ROPER.]

Being then vpon this occasion retained in the kinges seruice, the king gaue him a notable and woorthye lesson and charge, that in all his doinges and affaires touching the king, he should first respect and regarde God, and

MSS. E L R^2 Y C H R B.

1. *the*] þat L R^2 B. 1–2. *and accepted . . . time*] *Interlineated in* R. 1. *Mores*] More his B. 2. *the*] þat L R^2 B. 2. *For this*] But this L R^2 B. 3. *on euery day more then other*] every day more on then other Y; everie day on more then other C H R; L *as* E R^2 B, *but* other *corrected from* others, *and catchword* others. 4. *intreatie*] meanes or entreaty R^2. 7. *great*] *Omitted in* Y. 7. *his*] him C. (Roper *supports* his.) 7. *that then was*] þat was then C. (Roper MSS. *vary. See* Notes). 7. *Pope*] the Popes H R. 10. *sute obteyned*] suite obteined obteined Y. 11. *Counsailers*] councellour H R. 12. *lawes*] Lawe Y. 18. *proposed*] purposed Y C. 19. *of*] of of R^2. 24. *the pope*] þe Pope, *with* þe *interlineated*, R^2.

afterwarde the king his master. Which lesson and instruction neuer was there, I trowe, any Princes seruaunt that more willingly heard, or more faithfully and effectually executed and accomplished, as ye shall hereafter better vnderstande.

More made Master of Requests and Privy Councillor [1518]; Under Treasurer of the Exchequer [1521]; Chancellor of the Duchy of Lancaster [1525]; and finally Lord Chancellor. [1529.] [ROPER.]

At his first entraunce, being [then] no better rowme voyde, he was made master of the requestes, and within a moneth he was made knight and one of the kinges priuie Councell. After the death of *Master* Weston, he was made vnder Treasourer of Theschequer; and then afterwarde, vpon the death of Sir Richarde Wingefelde, Chauncell*our* of the Douchie of | Lancaster; and at length aduaunced to [fol. 6 *a*] be Lorde Chauncell*our* of Inglande. The which offices, as he obteyned by the kinges goodnes, by his meere voluntary and free disposition, without any sute or solicitation of his owne behalfe, so did he vse him selfe therein with all good dexteritie, wisedome and equitie, sinceritie and incorruption, and in this race of the kinges seruice he ranne painfully, wisely and honorably, twentie yeres and aboue.

More high in favour with King Henry VIII.

Neyther was there any one man that the king vsed more familierly, [nor] with whom he more debated, not onely for publike affaires, but in matters of learning, withall taking a great comfort besides in his merie and pleasantly conceyted witt. And tooke such pleasure in his company that he woulde sometime, upon the sodaine, come to his house at Chelsey to be merye with him.

The King visits More at Chelsea. [ROPER.]

MSS. E L R^2 Y C H R B.

4. *ye*] you L R^2 B. 6. *being then no*] C (*supported by* Roper's having then no); being no E L R^2 Y H R B. 6. *better rowme*] better a roome L R^2 B. 7. *of the*] of B. 7–8. *a moneth*] on munth R^2; one mounthe Y. 8. *he was*] *Omitted in* R^2. 10. *vnder*] *Interlineated in* Y. 10. *afterwarde*] after H B. 11. *vpon*] *Omitted in* B. 11. *Wingefelde*] Winfield L; Winfild R^2; Winkfilde B. 12–13. *to be Lorde*] to the Lord Y. 13. *The which offices*] The which L R^2 B; to the which H. 14. *kinges*] king his B. 17. *and*] *Omitted in* B. 18. *sinceritie*] sincerly R^2. 18. *race*] *Corrected from some other word in* C. 21. *one*] *Omitted in* B. 22. *nor*] L R^2 Y C H R B; or E. 23. *for*] in Y. 23. *publike*] bublique R^2. 23. *but in*] but also in Y. 24. *his*] *Interlineated in* L. 25. *pleasantly*] pleasant H. 25. *And tooke*] And he tooke H R. 25–26. *witt. And tooke . . . sodaine*] wit that he would some tyme taking such pleasure in his companie vpon the sodaine Y. 26. *the sodaine*] a suddeine B.

Whither on a time, vnlooked for, he came to diner to him; and after diner, in a faire garden of his, walked with him by the space of an howre, holding his arme about his necke. Of all the which fauour he made no more accompt then a deepe wise man should doo, And as the nature and disposition of the king (which he deepely and throughlye perceaued) did require, and as in deede he afterwarde in himselfe most of all men experienced. Wherefore euen at this time, when flattering fortune seemed most pleasantly to smile vppon him, and all thinges seemed as faire and beautifull as the lustry of a bright diamonde, he well thought as well vpon the disposition and inclination of the saide Prince as vpon the fraile, instable and brickle state of suche as seeme to be in high fauo*ur* of their Princes.

But More perceives Henry's disposition, and realises the insecurity of kingly favour. [Roper.]

Wherefore, when that after the kinges departure his sonne in lawe, M*aster* Will*iam* Roper, reioycingly came to him, saying these wordes: "S*ir*, howe happy are you whom the king hath* so familierly* interteyned, as I neuer haue seene him to doo anye other except Cardinall Wolsey, whom I sawe his grace walke withall arme in arme"; S*ir* Thomas More aunswered in this sort: "I thanke our Lorde, sonne, I finde his grace my verye good Lorde in deede; And I beleeue he doth as singulerly fauour me as he doth any subiect within this Realme. Howbeit, sonne Roper, I may tell thee I haue no cause to be proude thereof; For if my head

"If my head could win him a castle in France, it should not fail to serve his turn." [Roper.]

MSS. E L R^2 Y C H R B.

1–2. *Whither . . . him*] *Omitted in* B. 1. *vnlooked for*] *Omitted in* L R^2 B. 3. *an*] one L R^2 B. 8. *most*] *Omitted in* H. 8. *men*] other men R^2. 9. *when*] whet Y. 11. *beautifull*] as bewtyfull B. 12. *as well*] *Interlineated in* L. 15. *seeme*] seemed L. 15. *in high fauour*] highe in favour H. 15. *of*] with R^2. 16. *when that*] when R^2. 18. *are*] be R^2. 19. *hath so familierly interteyned*] hath so familiarly entertayned L Y C H B (*order of words supported by* Roper); so familierly hath interteyned E R; hath soe fauourably and famyliarely entertayned R^2. 19–20. *as . . . other*] R *as* E Y C B, *with* neuer *interlineated*; as I neuer have seene to doe any other L; as I neuer haue seene him to doe to any other R^2; as I have neuer sene him doe to any other H. 20. *him*] *Omitted in* B. 21. *sawe*] have seene H. 22. *aunswered*] aunswe *at end of line* B. 24. *beleeue*] doe beleive H. 25. *he doth*] *Omitted in* R^2. 26. *this*] his L. 26. *may*] shall L R^2 H R B. (Roper *supports* may). 27. *thereof*] therat C. (Roper *supports* thereof).

could winne him a castle in Fraunce" (for then was there warre betweene Fraunce and vs) " it should not faile to serue his turne."

The visit to England of Charles the Emperor, and More's oration before him. [Friday, 6 June, 1522.] [HALL'S CHRONICLE.]

After that S*ir* Thomas More had nowe continued about nine yeres in | the kinges seruice, Charles the [fol 6 b] Empero*ur* came into the Realme, and was most honorably and magnificently receaued in the Citie of London. At which time S*ir* Thomas More made a fine and eloquent oration in the presence of the Empero*ur* and the kinge, in their praise and co*m*mendac*i*on, and of the great amitie and loue that the one bare to the other, and the singuler comfort that the subiect*es* of both Realmes receaued thereof.

More is chosen Speaker [18 April, 1523], and pleads his unfitness for that office, likening himself to Phormio before Hannibal. [HALL'S CHRONICLE.]

The saide yere [which was the fourteenth yere of the Kings raigne] a Parliament was summoned, where the Commons chose for their Speaker* S*ir* Thomas More, and presented him the Saturday after in the Parliament chamber, where he disabled himselfe as a man not meete for that office. Among other thinges he brought forth a story of the notable captaine Hanniball, to whom at a certaine time Phormio commenced a solemne declaration touching Chiualrie and the feates of warre, which was well lyked and praysed of many; but Hanniball, being demaunded what he thought thereof, aunswered: "I neuer heard a more proude, arrogant foole, that durst take vpon him to instruct the flowre and master of chiualrie in the feates and affaires of warre." "So," saith S*ir* Thomas, "I may

MSS. E L R^2 Y C H R B.

1–2. *was there warre*] there was warre L R^2 B. 2. *it should*] yt should R^2, *with* yt *interlineated before* yf I *crossed through.* 4. *After that Sir*] After Sir L R^2 B. 5. *about*] *Omitted in* B. 6. *into*] to Y C. 7. *Citie of*] citie of cytie of B. 7. *At*] At At R^2. 9. *the kinge*] kinge R^2. 14–15. *which . . . raigne*] which was the 14th yeere of þe Kings raigne L R^2 Y C H R B (*supported by* Roper); *omitted in* E. 16. *Speaker Sir*] L R^2 Y B; Speaker the saide Sir E C H R. 18. *disabled*] did disable B. 20. *the*] a Y; that H R. 20. *captaine*] papitaine Y. 21. *to whom . . . certaine*] *Interlineated in* R *over the same words crossed through and partly erased.* 21. *at a*] on a R^2; at B. 21. *Phormio*] Phormo R^2; Phoricio Y; Phocinio H R. 22–23. *and the*] and B. 23. *well*] *Interlineated in* L. 25. *thought*] liked Y. 26. *proude, arrogant*] proud & arrogant R^2. 26. *him*] *Interlineated in* R^2. 27–28. *feates and*] *Omitted in* B.

well looke for and feare the like rebuke at the kinges handes, if I should arrogate so muche to my selfe as to speake before a king of such learning, wisdome and experience in publike affaires, [of] the manuring, welding and ordering [of] the same. Wherefore my humble petition is, that the Commons may freely choose some other for their Speaker." But the Cardinall aunswered that the king by good proufe and experience knewe his witt, learning and discretion to be suche as he might well beare and satisfie the office, and that the Commons could not choose a meeter.

In the ende, when the king would not consent to the election of any other, he spake to his grace in forme folowing:—

More's speech before the King when made Speaker, pleading for toleration for himself and freedom of speech for the Commons [ROPER.]

"Sith I perceaue, most redoubted Soueraine, that it standeth not with your high pleasure to reforme this election, and cause it to be chaunged, but haue by the mouth of the most reuerende father in God, the Legate, your highe Chauncell*our*, therevnto geuen your most royall assent, and haue of your benignitie determined, farre aboue that I maye beare, to inhable me and for this office to repute me meete, rather then ye should seeme to impute vnto your Commons that they had vnmeetely [fol. 7 *a*] chosen; I am therefore, and alwaye | shal be, readie obediently to conforme my selfe to thaccomplishment of your high co*m*maundement, in my most humble wise beseeching your moste noble Maiestie that I may, with your graces fauo*ur*, before I farther enter there into,

MSS. E L R² Y C H R B.

1. *and*] *Omitted in* B. 2. *arrogate*] abrogate Y. 3. *before*] to L R² B. 3. *of such*] of so much Y. 4. *in publike*] and publique Y. 4. *of the*] Y C; in the E L R² H R B. 5. *of the same*] L R² Y C; the same E H R B. 5–6. *my humble petition*] my first & humble Peticion H. 6. *freely choose*] choose freely L; freely chose C. 8. *the king . . . knewe*] the kinge knew by good proofe and experience H; R *as* H, *but with a second* knew *interlineated after* experience. 10. *and that*] and H. 11. *choose*] chose C; coose H. 13. *any other*] another L R² B. 13. *in forme*] to enforme H R. 16. *to*] *Interlineated over* who *crossed through* R. 22. *ye*] you L R² H R B. 23. *vnmeetely*] vnhabilly Y. 24. *alwaye shal be*] shallbee allwayes L R² B. 25. *conforme*] confirme Y H. 26. *high*] highnes L R² B. 26. *my*] *Omitted in* R² C H R. (Roper MSS. *vary*. *See* Notes). 27. *moste*] *Omitted in* H R.

make my humble intercession vnto your highnes for two lowly petitions: the one priuately concerning my selfe, the other* the whole assemble of your co*m*mon house.

"For my selfe, gratious Soueraine, that if it mishapp me, in any thing hereafter that is on the behalfe of your Commons in your high presence to be declared, to mistake my message, and in the lacke of good vtterance by my misrehearsall to peruert or impaire their prudent instructions, it may then like your most noble Maiestie, of your aboundant grace, with the eye of your accustomed pitie, to pardon my simplenes, geuing me leaue to repaire againe vnto the co*m*mon house, and there to conferre w*i*th them, and to take their substantiall aduise what thing, and in what wise, I shall on their behalfe vtter and speake before your noble grace, to the intent their prudent deuises and affaires be not by my simplenes and folye hindred or impaired. Which thing, if it should mishappe, as it were well likely to mishapp me, if your gratious benignitie relieued not my ouersight, it could not faile to be, during my life, a perpetuall grudge and heauines to my heart; the helpe and remedie whereof, in maner afore remembred, is, most gratious Soueraine, my first lowly sute and humble petition vnto your moste noble grace.

"Mine other humble request, most excellent Prince, is this: That forasmuche as there be of your Commons, here by your high co*m*maundement assembled, of your Parliament, a great number, which are, after the accustomed

MSS. E L R^2 Y C H R B.

1. *intercession*] intrission H. 1. *two*] *Interlineated in* L. 2. *concerning*] concening H. 3. *other*] *Omitted in* R^2. 3. *the other the*] Y C (*supported by most* Roper MSS.); the other for the E L R^2 H R B. (*See* Notes). 5. *on*] in L R^2 B. 6. *high*] heighnes B. (Roper MSS. *vary. See* Notes). 9. *most*] *Interlineated in* R. (*Some* Roper MSS. *omit. See* Notes). 12. *vnto*] into H R; to B. 14. *on*] in L R^2 Y B. 15. *the intent*] thenten Y; thentent (*corrected from* thentend) the Intent R^2; intent H. 17. *hindred or*] hindered of or H. 18. *were*] *Interlineated in* L. 18. *were well*] well were R^2. 18. *me*] *Interlineated in* L. 19. *relieued*] releaue Y. 19. *could*] would L H R. 20. *to be*] but Y. 21. *remedie*] memory R^2. 23–24. *vnto . . . grace*] *Omitted in* Y. 25. *request*] *Written upon an erasure in* R.

maner, appointed in the co*m*mon house to treate and deuise of the co*m*mon affaires among themselues apart; And albeit, most deere liege Lorde, that according to your moste prudent deuise, by your honorable writt*es* euery where declared, there hath beene as due diligence vsed in sending vp to your highnes Court of Parliament the moste discrete persons out of euery quarter that men could esteeme [meete thervnto], whereby it is not to be doubted but that there is a very substantiall assemble of right wise and politike persons; yet, most victorious Prince, sith among so many wise men neyther is euery [fol. 7 b] man wise alike, nor, among so many men all like well | witted, euery man like well spoken, And it often happeth that likewise as muche follye is vttered with painted, pollished speeche, so many men, boysteous and rude in language, [se] deepe in deede, and geue right * substantiall counsaile; And sith also in matters of great importance the minde is often so occupied in the matter, that a man rather studieth what to say then howe; by reason whereof the wisest man, and the best spoken, in a whole countrey fortuneth amonge, while his minde is feruent in the matter, somewhat to speake in suche wise as he would

MSS. E L R^2 Y C H R B.

2. *common*] commons Y. 2. *among*] of L R^2 B. 2. *themselues*] them self Y. 3. *that*] and R^2. 6. *vsed*] *Omitted in* H R. 6. *highnes*] highe Y H R. 7. *out*] *Omitted in* R^2. 7–8. *that men could esteeme meete thervnto*] C (*supported by most* Roper MSS.); that men could esteeme thereto fitt E L R^2 B; Y R *as* E L R^2 B, *but omitting* fitt; then men could esteeme thereto H. (*See* Notes). 9. *very*] *Omitted in* Y H. 10. *yet*] yt R^2. 12–13. *wise alike . . . well spoken*] wise alike nor amongst so many men all alike well-witted nor euery man like well spoken L R^2; wise in like nor among so many men like well witted every man like well spoken Y; C *as* E, *but omits* all; wise alike nor amonge soe many wise men all like well witted nor euery like well spoken H R; B *as* L R^2, *but* among *for* amongst. (Roper MSS. *vary. See* Notes). 13. *happeth*] happeneth L. 14–15. *painted, pollished*] painted and polished L. 15. *boysteous and rude*] rude and boysterrous H R. 16. [*se*]] so E Y C H R; be soe (soe *being interlineated*) L; bee R^2 B. (*Most* Roper MSS. *read* se; *but see* Notes). 16. *geue*] *Corrected from* geuee E. 16. *right substantiall*] L R^2 Y C H B (*supported by* Roper); right and substantiall E R. 17. *sith*] *Interlineated over* seeke *crossed through* L. 17. *in matters of great importance*] *Omitted in* H R. 20. *the* (2)] *Omitted in* R^2 H R. 21. *amonge*] among other B. 21–22. *in the matter*] *Interlineated in* R. 22. *to speake*] *Interlineated in* R.

afterwarde wishe to haue beene vttered otherwise, and yet no woorse will had when he spake it, then he hath when he would so gladly chaunge it; Therefore, most gratious Soueraine, considering that in your high Court of Parliament is nothing intreated but matter of weight and importance concerning your Realme and your owne royall estate, it could not faile but to lett and putt to silence from the geuing of their aduise and counsaile many of your discrete Commons, to the great hinderance of the common affaires, except that euery of your Commons were vtterly discharged of all doubt and feare howe any thing that it should happen them to speake, should happen of your highnes to be taken. And in this point, though your well knowen and proued benignitie putteth euery man in right good hope, yet suche is the weight of the matter, such is the reuerende dreade that the timerous heartes of your naturall subiectes conceaue toward your high Maiestie, our most redoubted king and vndoubted Soueraine, that they cannot in this point finde themselves satisfied, except your gratious bountie therein declared put away the scruple of their timerous mindes, and animate and encourage them, and put them out of doubt. It may therfore like your most aboundant grace, our most benigne and godly king, to geue to all your Commons here assembled your most gratious licence and pardon, freely, without doubt of your dreadfull displeasure, euery man to discharge his conscience, and boldly in any thing incident among vs to declare his aduise; and whatsoeuer happen any man to say, that it may like your noble Maiestie of your inestimable goodnes to take all in good

MSS. E L R^2 Y C H R B.

1. *wishe*] *A following* d *erased in* L. 1. *to haue*] had R^2. 1–2. *yet no woorse will had*] yet had no woorse meaning L R^2 B. 5. *is nothing*] nothing is L. 5. *matter*] matters R^2. 6. *owne*] *Omitted in* H R. 7. *and putt*] and to put L. 9. *the* (2)] your H R. 10. *common*] commons Y. 10. *euery of*] euery man of H R. (*Most* Roper MSS. *support* euery of. *See* Notes). 12. *it should happen*] sholde happ B. 12. *happen*] *Interlineated in* R^2. 12. *them*] then Y. 15. *right good*] good right Y. 16. *dreade that*] dread of that H R. 17. *heartes*] hart Y. 20. *therein*] therin, *with* r *interlineated*, L. 23. *most*] *Omitted in* H; *interlineated in* R. 24. *king*] prince B. 26. *doubt*] all doubt L R^2 B. 29. *that*] *Omitted in* Y. 29. *noble*] *Omitted in* H.

part, interpreting euery mans wordes, howe vncomely [fol. 8 a] soeuer they be couched, to proceede yet of good | zeale toward the profite of your Realme and hon*our* of your royall person; the prosperous estate and preseruation wherof, most excellent Soueraine, is the thing which we all, [your] moste humble loving subiect*es*, according to the most bounden dutie of our naturall allegiance, most highly desire and praye for."

Wolsey's visit to the Commons. [1523.] [Roper.]

At this Parliament Cardinall Wolsey founde himselfe muche greeued with the Burgesses thereof, for that nothing was so soone done or spoken therein, but that it was immediatlye blowen abroade in euery alehouse. It fortuned at that Parliament a very great subsedie to be demaunded, which the Cardinall fearing would not passe the common house, determined for the furtherance thereof to be there personally himselfe. Before whose co*m*ming, after longe debating there, whether it were better but with a fewe of his Lordes (as the most opinion of the house was) or with his whole traine royally to receaue him there among them: "Masters," quoth S*ir* Thomas More, "forasmuche as my Lorde Cardinall lately, ye wote well, layde to our charge the lightnes of our tonges for thinges vttered out of this house, it shall not in my minde be amisse with all his pompe to receaue him, with his maces, his pillers, his polleaxes, his Crosses, his hatt and the great Seale too, to the intent, if he finde the like fault with vs hereafter, we may be the bolder from our selues to laye the blame vpon those that his grace bringeth [hither] with him." Wherevnto the house wholly agreing, he was receaued accordingly.

MSS. E L R^2 Y C H R B.

2. *be*] *Omitted in* B. 2. *couched*] couched togeather (*with* er *interlineated*) R^2; towched Y. 4. *prosperous*] prosperate R^2. 6. *your*] B (*supported by* Roper); *omitted in* E L R^2 Y C H R. 6. *humble*] *Omitted in* L R^2 B. 6. *loving*] *Interlineated in* R. 7. *most*] *Omitted in* Y. 7. *allegiance*] allegiament Y. 11. *spoken*] sopken H. 11. *but that it*] but it B. 14. *fearing*] feared H R. 18. *his*] the B. 21. *ye*] you L R^2 H R B. 21. *well*] *Omitted in* Y. 22. *our* (1)] your R^2. 22. *our* (2)] your R^2. 22. *charge*] charges Y. 22. *lightnes*] highnes R^2. 23. *out*] *Omitted in* L R^2 B. 24. *his*] all his Y. 26. *too*] *Omitted in* Y. 26. *if*] þat yf R^2. 27. *be*] *Omitted in* R^2. 27. *from*] for B. 28. *those*] them H R. 28. *hither*] L R^2 B (*supported by most* Roper MSS.); thither E Y C H R. (*See* Notes).

Wolsey can get no answer from the Commons or the Speaker. [ROPER.]

Where, after that he had in a solemne oration by many reasons proued howe necessary it was the demaunde there [moued] to be graunted, and farther shewed that lesse would not serue to mainteyne the Princes purpose, he seing the company sitting still silent and therevnto nothing aunswering, and contrary to his expectation shewing in themselues towardes his requestes no towardnes of inclination, sayde vnto them: "Masters, you haue many wise and learned men among you; and sith I am from the kinges owne person sent hither vnto you for the preseruation of your selues and all the Reálme, I thinke it meete you geue me some reasonable aunswere." Whereat euery man holding his peace, then beganne he to speake to one *Master* Marney, afterwarde Lorde Marney; who making him no aunswere neyther, he seuerally asked the same question of diuers other accompted the wisest of the company. To whom, when none of them all | would geue so much as one worde, being before [fol. 8 *b*] agreed (as the custome was) by their Speaker to make aunswere: "Masters," quoth the Cardinall, "vnlesse it be the maner of your house, as of likelyhood it is, by the mouth of your Speaker, whom ye haue chosen for trustie and wise, as in deede he is, in such cases to vtter your mindes, here is, without doubt, a meruailous obstinate silence." And thervpon required [he] answere of *Master* Speaker, who first reuerently vpon his knees excusing the silence of the house, abasshed at the presence of so noble a personage, able to amase the wisest and best learned in a Realme, and after by many and probable argumentes prouing that for them to make aunswere was it neyther

MSS. E L R^2 Y C H R B.

1. *after that he*] after he L R^2 B. 1. *in a*] in H R. 3. *moued*] mooved C (*supported by* Roper); maid moued Y; made E L R^2 H R B. 4. *to mainteyne*] *Omitted in* L R. 5. *company sitting*] company theirunto sitting Y. 5. *still*] *Omitted in* Y. 6 *nothing aunswering*] suing nothing Y. 7. *requestes*] request L Y. 7–8. *towardnes*] towardlynes R^2. 10–12. *for the . . . you*] *Omitted in* B. 15. *him*] *Omitted in* L R^2. 16. *other*] others R^2 Y. 22. *ye*] you L R^2 H R B. 23. *cases*] causes Y. 25. *he*] C (*supported by* Roper); the E L R^2 Y H R B. 26. *first*] most H R. 26. *excusing*] excused L R^2 H R B. (Roper *supports* excusing). 29. *a*] þe L Y. 29. *and* (2)] *Omitted in* C.

expedient nor agreable with the auncient libertie of the house, in conclusion for himselfe shewed, that though they had all with their voices trusted him, yet except euery one of them could put into his [one] head all their seuerall wittes, he alone in so weightie a matter was vnmeete to make his grace aunswere.

Wolsey's consequent anger against More. [Roper.]

Whervpon the Cardinall, displeased with S*ir* Thomas More, that had not in this Parliament in all thinges satisfied his desire, sodenly arose and departed; and after the Parliament ended, in his gallerye at white hall at Westminster, vttered vnto him his griefes, saying: "Would [to] God you had beene at Rome, M*aster* More, when I made you speaker." "Your grace not offended, so would I too, my Lorde," quoth he. And to winde suche quarells out of the Cardinalls head, he begonne to talke of that gallerie, and saide: "I like this gallery of yours, my Lorde, muche better then your gallerie at Hampton Court." Wherewith so wisely he brake off the Cardinalles displeasant talke that the Cardinall, at that present, as it seemed, wist not what more to say to him; but, for reuengement of his displeasure, councelled the king to sende him ambassadour into Spaine, co*m*mending to his highnes his wisedome, learning and meetenes for that voyage; and the difficultie of the cause considered, none was there, he saide, so well able to serue his grace therein. Which when the king had broken to S*ir* Thomas More,

Wolsey's unsuccessful plot to send More to Spain. [Roper.]

MSS. E L R² Y C H R B.

1. *with*] to L R² B. 2. *for himselfe shewed*] for himselfe he shewed L R² B; shewed for himselfe H R. 4. *euery one of them could*] euery one would L R² B; R *as* E Y C H, *but with* of them *interlineated.* 4. *one* (2)] C; owne (= "one") Y; *omitted in* E L R² H R B. (*Most* Roper MSS. *vary between* one *and* owne, *which here* = "one." *See* Notes.) 4. *their*] the Y. 8. *not*] *Interlineated in* R². 10. *at white hall*] at (*crossed through*) in Whitehall L. 11. *vttered*] vtter Y; he vttred L R² H R B. (*Most* Roper MSS. *support* vttered. *See* Notes.) 12. *Would to God*] C (*supported by* Roper); would to good R²; Would God E L Y H R B. 12. *you had beene*] you were R². 15. *talke*] speake Y. 16. *and saide*] *Omitted in* R². 17. *Hampton*] hapton Y. 18. *Wherewith*] *In* R *the* with *is interlineated.* 18. *so wisely he*] he so wisely L R² B; so wisely (*with omission of* he) C. 19. *at that present*] at þat tyme present R². 23. *wisedome, learning*] wisdome bo Learninge R². 25. *he saide, so well*] he said weare soe well H; he said more so well R.

and that he had declared vnto his grace howe vnfitt a iourney it was for him, the nature of the countrey and disposition | of his complexion so disagreing together that [Fol. 9 *a*] he should neuer be likely to doo his grace acceptable seruice there, knowing right well that, if his grace sent him thither, he should sende him into his graue; But shewing himselfe neuerthelesse readie, according to his dutie, all were it with the losse of his life, to fulfill his graces pleasure in that behalfe; The king, allowing well his aunswere, saide vnto him: "It is not our meaning, M*aster* More, to doo you hurt, but to doo you good [would we] be gladd. We will therefore for this purpose deuise vpon some other, and employe your seruice otherwise."

Wolsey fears More. [Erasmus.]

Wolsey's pomp and vanity.

Truely, this Cardinall did [not] heartily loue S*ir* Thomas More, yea, he rather feared him then loued him. And albeit he were adorned w*ith* many goodly graces and qualities, yet was he of so outragious aspiring, ambitious nature, and so fedd with vaineglory and with the hearing of his owne praise, and by the excesse thereof fallen, as it were, into a certaine pleasant phrenesie, that the enormious fault ouerwhelmed, defaced and destroyed the true co*m*mendation of all his good properties. He sore longed and thirsted after the hearing of his owne praise, not onely when he had done some thinges co*m*mendable, but euen when he had sometimes done that that was naught in deede.

MSS. E L R^2 Y C H R B.

2. *for him*] for him to vndertake C. 3. *disposition*] þe disposition R^2 Y. 3. *disagreing*] disagreed Y. 4. *likely*] like B. 5. *there*] therein R^2. 6. *into*] vnto R^2. 7–8. *according . . . were it*] *Interlineated in* L. 8. *all*] although H R. 10–11. *meaning, Master . . . hurt*] meaning to doe yow hurte Master More B. 12. *would we be*] would wee be C (*supported by* Roper); would be Y; we will be E L R^2 H R B. 13. *deuise vpon some*] devise some vpon some Y. 13. *your*] our Y. 15. *this*] the Y. 15. *not*] not L R^2 H B; nowe E Y C R. 15. *heartily*] *Omitted in* L R^2 B. 17. *were*] was B. 18. *so*] such C H R. 20. *the hearing*] heareing H R. 21. *pleasant phrenesie*] p, *crossed through*, frensey R^2. 22. *fault*] faultes B. 23. *commendation*] commendacions R^2. 24. *sore*] soe H R. 26. *when*] whe H. 26–27. *he had sometimes done*] sometymes he had done C; he had done somtimes B. 27. *that that was*] that was H R; that which was B.

Of this vaineglorious, scabbed, itching follye to heare his owne prayse, leaving diuers other that we haue in store, we will shewe you one ensample, and the rather because S*ir* Thomas More doth both tell it, and was also present the same time; Albeit he telleth it vnder dissembled and counterfaite names, as well of the persons as countrey described, wherein I will shifte none of the authours wordes, but as he wrate them, recite them, sauing I will recite them in his owne person, and somewhat abridge them :

Wolsey's Dinner. [Works, pp. 1221-2.]

"So it happed one day that the Cardinall had in great audience made an oration, &c., in a certaine matter, wherein he lyked himselfe so well that at his dinner he sate, he thought, on thornes, till he might heare howe they that sate with him at his borde would co*m*mende it. And when he had sitt musing a while, deuising (as I thought after) vpon some proper pretie way to bring it in withall, At the last, for lacke of a better (least he [fol. 9 b] should haue lett the matter goe to long) | he brought it euen bluntly forth, and asked vs all that sate at his bordes ende (for at his owne messe in the middes there sate but himselfe alone) howe well we lyked his oration that he had made that day.

"When the probleme was once proponed, till it was

MSS. E L R^2 Y C H R B.

2. *other that we*] other we L B; others wee R^2. 3. *one*] an H R. 4. *More*] *Omitted in* L R^2. 4. *both*] *Omitted in* L R^2 B. 4. *was also*] allso was L R^2 B. 5–6. *dissembled*] dissemblinge R^2. 6. *counterfaite*] counterfeited Y. 6. *persons*] parties H R. 7. *countrey*] countries H R B. 8. *wrate*] wroughte L; wrote R^2 C; wrott H. 8. *recite*] receyue Y. 9. *sauing I*] saveing that I, H R. 9. *sauing I will recite them*] *Omitted in* B. 11. *happed*] happened L B. 11. *one day*] that one day Y; one a daie H R. 11–12. *had in great*] had great H R. 12. *&c.*] even B. 13–15. *he sate . . . howe they*] *Omitted in* H. 14. *he thought, on thornes*] as he thought in thornes B. 15. *with him*] within R^2. 16. *he*] *Interlineated in* R^2. 16. *sitt*] satt R^2 B. 18. *for*] for the Y. 19. *lett*] *Omitted in* L R^2 B. 19. *to*] so C. 19. *he*] *Omitted in* B. 20. *euen*] over B. 20. *vs*] *Omitted in* L B. 20. *his*] þe L R^2 H R B. (English Works, *p.* 1221, *support* his.) 22. *we lyked his*] we liked the H R; they liked his L B; they liked þe R^2. 23. *had made*] made L H R B. (English Works, *p.* 1221, *support* had made). 24. *was*] *Omitted in* H. 24. *proponed*] proposed R^2; propounded Y C.

The guests vie with each other in praise of Wolsey's oration. [Works, *as above.*]

full aunswered, no man (I weene) eate one morsell of meate more, euery man was fallen into so deepe a studie for the finding of some [exquisite] praise. For he that should haue brought out but a vulgare and a common co*m*menda*ci*on, would haue thought himselfe shamed for euer. Then sayd we our sentences by rowe as we sate, from the lowest vnto the highest, in good order, as it had beene a great matter of the common weale in a high solemne counsaile. When it came to my part, I will not say for any boaste, me thought, by our Ladye, for my part I quitt my selfe meetely well, and I liked my selfe the better because, me thought, my wordes went with some grace in the englishe tonge, wherein, letting my latine alone, me listed to shewe my cunning. And I hoped to be lyked the better because I sawe that he that sate next me, and should say his sentence after me, was an vnlearned priest, for he could speake no latine at all. But when he came forth with his part with my Lordes co*m*menda*ci*on, the wylie foxe had beene so well accustomed in court with the crafte of flatterie, that he went beyonde me too too farre. And then might I see by him what excellencie a right meane witt may come to in one crafte, that in all his whole life studieth and busieth his witt about no mo but that one. But I made after a solemne vowe vnto my selfe, that if euer he and I were

An unlearned priest outruns More in flattery. [Works, *as above.*]

MSS. E L R² Y C H R B.

1. *one*] a B. 2. *was . . . deepe*] was so fallen in so depe Y C. 3. *exquisite*] L R² Y H R B (*supported by* English Works, *p.* 1221); requisite E C. 4. *should . . . but a*] should but haue brought out a Y. 4. *and a common*] and common L R²; *omitted in* B. 6. *sayd*] *The* y *corrected from another letter* E. 6. *sentences*] sentence Y. 6–7. *sentences . . . order*] sentences from the lowest to þe highest by rowe as we sate in good order R². 7. *from . . . highest*] from the highest to the lowest B. 8. *a* (1)] *Omitted in* H. 8. *a* (2)] an L R² B. 9. *it*] yt, *corrected from* ht, R². 9. *not*] *Omitted in* H. 10. *me*] *Corrected from* my R². 10. *our*] *Interlineated over* my *crossed through* R². 12. *me thought*] I thought L R² B. 14. *latine*] lettere Y. 15. *hoped*] hope Y. 15. *sawe*] saw, *corrected from* sayd, R². 15–16. *that he that sate*] he that satt H R. 16. *should*] woulde B. 18. *with my Lordes*] of my lordes Y B. 20. *in*] at L; to þe B. 20. *with the*] with B. 20. *went*] was H R. 21. *then might I*] then i might I (i *being interlineated*) R²; then I mighte H. 22. *may*] myght R² B. 23. *his* (1)] this B. 23. *busieth*] buslith Y. 24. *after*] afterward B. 25. *he and I*] I and he, Y C. (English Works, *p.* 1222, *support* he and I.)

matched together at that borde againe, when we should fall to our flatterie, I would flatter in latine, that he should not contende with me any more; for though I could be content to be outrunne of an horse, yet would I no more abide it to be [out]runne of an asse.

A Doctor of the Church outflatters the rest by his silent ecstasy. [WORKS, *as above.*]

"But here nowe beganne the game. He that sate highest, and was to speake, was a great beneficed man, and not a doct*our* onely, but also somewhat learned in the lawes of the Churche. A world it was to see howe he marked euery mans worde that spake before him.
[fol. 10 *a*] And it seemed | that euery worde, the more proper it was, the woorse he lyked it, for the cumbraunce that he had to studie out a better to passe it. The man euen so swett with labour, so that he was faine in the while, nowe and then, to wipe his face. Howbeit, in conclusion, when it came to his course, we that had spoken before him had so taken vp all amonge vs before, that we had not lefte him one wise worde to speake after. And yet founde he out suche a shifte, that in his flattering he passed all the many of vs. For when he sawe that he could finde no wordes of praise that would passe all that had beene spoken before* already*, the wylie foxe would speake neuer a worde, but as he that was rauished with the wonder of the wisedome and eloquence that my Lordes grace had vttered in that oration, he fett a longe sigh, with an Oh, from the bottome of his brest, and

MSS. E L R^2 Y C H R B.

1. *that*] þe R^2 B. 4. *outrunne*] ouerrunne R^2 C B. (English Works, *p.* 1222, *support* outrunne.) 4. *an*] a C. 4–5. *would I*] I would H R. 5. *it*] *Omitted in* Y. 5. *outrunne*] L Y H R B (*supported by* English Works, *p.* 1222); ouerrunne E R^2 C. 6. *beganne*] begon B. 7. *and*] *Omitted in* R^2. 8. *also*] *Omitted in* L R^2 B. 12. *that*] *Omitted in* L Y H R. 13. *to studie out a*] *Interlineated in* R. 13. *euen*] *Omitted in* Y. 14. *so that*] that L R^2 H R B. (English Works, *p.* 1222, *have* euen swette . . . so that.) 14. *in the while*] *Omitted in* L R^2 B. 16. *it*] he L R^2 B. 18. *to speake after*] after to speake R^2. 19. *out*] *Interlineated in* L. 20. *that*] *Omitted in* L R^2 B. 22. *before already*] before alredie Y C (*supported by* English Works, *p.* 1222); already before E L R^2 H R B. 23. *that*] *Interlineated in* R^2. 24. *of the*] of H R. 25. *fett*] did fetche R^2; fetcht C. (English Works, *p.* 1222, *support* fett.) 25. *a longe*] along L. 26. *sigh*] sithe C; sith H. (*Note variant forms.*) 26. *brest*] hart Y.

helde vp both his handes, and lifte vp his head, and cast vp his eyen into the welkin, and wepte."

Wolsey no real lover of More.

In this vaineglorious pageant of my Lorde Cardinall, though, as it appereth, S*ir* Thomas More was in a maner forced, contrarye to his sober and well knowen modest nature, to playe a part to acco*m*modate himselfe somewhat to the players in this foolishe, fonde stage playe, yet I doubt nothing, if his answere were certainly knowen, he played no other part then might beseeme his graue, modest person, and kept himselfe within reasonable boundes, and yeelded none other then competent praise. For in very deede the oration was not to be dispraysed or dislyked. But, as we beganne to say, whether it were for that, as it is not vnlikely, that S*ir* Thomas More would not magnifie all the Cardinalls doinges and sayinges aboue the starres (as he many times expected) and crye, *Sanctus, Sanctus, Sanctus,* &c., or that the Cardinall feared him for his excellent qualities, and enuyed him for the singuler fauo*ur* that he well knewe the king bare to him, and thereby doubted least he might stande in his waye to shadowe and obscure some part of his great shining lustre and glorye (which thoughtes that he had nowe and then [among other] it is very probable), or were it for the Parliament sake we spake of, or for some other causes, he neuer entierlye and from the heart loued him. And doubtlesse, if S*ir* | Thomas More had beene of so [fol. 10 *b*] high, immoderate aspiring minde as was the Cardinall, he might haue perchaunce geuen him a fall longe ere he tooke his fall, and haue shifted him from the saddle

MSS. E L R^2 Y C H R B.

4. *appereth*] appeared B. 6. *a part*] aparte L. 7. *this*] the Y. 8. *knowen*] *Interlineated in* R^2. 9–10. *graue, modest*] graue & modest H R. 11. *boundes*] bonds C. 11. *none*] no L R^2. 12. *to*] *Interlineated in* R^2. 13. *beganne*] begon B. 13–14. *were for that*] were that R^2. 17. *Sanctus, Sanctus, Sanctus, &c.*] Sanctus Sanctus &c. L R^2 B. 17. *or that*] or yf R^2. 18. *him* (2)] *Interlineated in* R^2. 19. *to*] *Interlineated in* R^2. 21. *his*] *Omitted in* B. 23. *among other*] L R^2 Y C H R B; *omitted in* E. 23. *it*] yt yt R^2. 24. *Parliament*] Parliaments L. 24. *some*] same R^2. 25. *causes*] cause H R. 25. *and from*] or from Y. 28. *haue perchaunce*] perchance have L R^2 B. 28. *a*] *Interlineated in* L. 29. *fall*] *Omitted in* B. 29. *shifted*] sifted L.

of the Lorde Chauncellourshipp, and might haue sitt therein before he did; whose fall and ruine he neither procured nor desired, as the world well knoweth, and much lesse his great office, wherevnto he woorthily succeeded. Yea, the Cardinall himselfe, when he sawe he should needes forgoe the same, though he neuer bare him, as I haue saide, true hartie affection, yet did he confesse that S*ir* Thomas More was the aptest and fittest man in the Realme for the same: whose great excellent witt and learning, whose singuler qualities, graces and giftes, whose profounde pollitike head in the ciuill affaires, as well inwardly as outwardly, the saide Cardinall by longe time [certainly], and, as I might say, feelingly knewe; As with whom, beside all other experiences of him, he had beene twise ioyned in co*m*mission and sent Ambassadour, once to the Emperour Charles into Flaunders, the other time to the frenche king into Fraunce.

Yet Wolsey recognised More as the fittest person to succeed him as Chancellor. [ERASMUS.]

More and Wolsey joint Ambassadors. [ROPER.]

And thus muche by the way of this Cardinall, whose remembraunce and doinges I would to God I might nowe put away, and here breake off, or that I might haue better matter to write on. But as our former declaration is incident to our matter, so nowe the very consequence and course of our story taken in hande forceth farther to enlarge of his doinges, as alas, and woe the time that euer he was borne. And thrise happie had he beene if he had trode the vertuous steppes that this woorthye man, who followed him in the office of the Lorde Chauncell*our*, treaded. If he had, I say, folowed his modest, softe,

Wolsey compared unfavourably with More.

MSS. E L R^2 Y C H R B.

1. *sitt*] sitten H R. 2. *did*] died Y. 3. *procured*] did procure H. 5. *he sawe*] he sawe þat C. 6. *should*] must B. 6. *though*] thought Y. 10–11. *whose . . . giftes*] *Omitted in* B. 10. *graces*] grace Y. 13. *certainly*] certainely L R^2 Y C H R B; *omitted in* E. 13. *might*] may C. 14. *knewe*] knowe H B. 15. *beene*] but R^2. 16. *Ambassadour, once*] once embassadour Y. 17. *into*] *Corrected from* vnto L. 18. *thus*] this R^2. 18. *muche*] *Interlineated in* R^2. 19–20. *nowe . . . might*] *Omitted in* B. 21. *our*] one L. 22. *our*] the R^2. 22. *very*] *Interlineated in* L. 23. *forceth*] forceth vs B. 24. *his*] *Corrected from* our R. 24. *as*] *Interlineated over* but *crossed through* L. 26. *trode*] tread C B. 26. *that this*] of this H. 26–28. *steppes . . . treaded*] stepps of this worthie man who followed him in the Office of the Lord Chauncellour treaded R. 28. *treaded*] traded L.

Harpsfield blames Wolsey's ambition as the cause of his fall and the subsequent troubles of the Realm.

sober, nothing revenging and nothing ambitious nature, if he had shewed himselfe a true, faythfull, vertuous Counsailer to his Prince, then had he preserued himselfe from the fowle shamefull fall and ruine that he headlong, by his outragious ambition and revengeable nature, cast himselfe in; then had he preserued his Prince from the fowle enormious faultes and cruelties he after fell to; then had he preserued this woorthy man, of whose storye we be in hande, and that noble Prelate, the good Bis|shopp of [fol. 11 *a*] Rochester, and also the blessed, and, as I may say, the liuing Saintes, the monkes of the Charterhouse, with many other, from fowle butcherie slaughter; then finally had he preserued the whole Realme from the heynous and hydeous schismes and heresies wherewith sithens it hath bene lamentably ouerwhelmed. Which thinges, though he neuer intended, or once, I suppose, thought should so chaunce, yet did all these and other many [and mayne] mischiefes rise and springe originally, as it were certaine detestable braunches out of the roote of his cursed and wicked ambition and reuenging nature. A pitifull and lamentable ensample of all posteritie to marke and beholde, and thereby the better to detest and eschewe all such wretched and wicked ambition.

Harpsfield blames Wolsey as the

The beginning and spring, the true though lamentable processe of the which doinges, albeit it be lothsome and ruefull to be remembred, I am nowe driuen, for the

MSS. E L R^2 Y C H R B.

1. *sober, nothing*] sober & nothing L R^2 B. 2. *vertuous*] & vertuous R^2 Y; *omitted in* Y. 6. *his*] the B. 6. *from*] for Y. 9. *the good*] *Omitted in* B. 10. *the*] *Omitted in* R^2. 12. *butcherie slaughter*] butchery & slaughter L R^2 B; butcherly slaughter H. 13. *whole*] *Omitted in* R^2. 13. *had . . . Realme*] had þe whole realme beine preserved C. 14–15. *wherewith . . . bene*] wherewith it hath bene sithence H R. 15. *lamentably*] most lamentably R^2; lamentable H; *omitted in* B. 17. *did all*] did R^2. 17. *other many and mayne*] C; other many and many Y; other many E L R^2; many other H R B. 18. *rise*] arise L. 18. *were certaine*] *Omitted in* R^2. 19. *his*] this R^2. 19. *cursed and*] course and Y. 20. *ambition*] ambitions R^2. 20–23. *and reuenging nature . . . wicked ambition*] *Omitted in* B. 21. *lamentable*] a lamentable C. 23. *wretched and wicked*] wicked and wreched Y C. 24. *The beginning . . . though*] The beginning and true though H R. 25. *albeit*] althoughe B.

better and fuller vnderstanding of our matter * take[n] in hand, a litle at large to open and discouer; I meane of the diuorce betweene king Henry and Queene Katherine, moued and procured by the saide Cardinall: who, for the better atchieuing of his purpose, requested (as it is commonly reported) Langlonde, Bisshopp of Lincolne, and ghostly father to the king, to put a scruple into his graces head that it was not lawfull for him to mary his brothers wife. Howbeit, concerning the saide Bisshopp, though it were so co*m*monly bruted abroade and beleeued, yet haue I heard Docto*ur* Draycott, that was his Chapleine and Chauncello*ur*, say that he once tolde the Bisshopp what rumo*ur* ranne vpon him in that matter, and desired to know of him the very truth. Who aunswered that in verye deede he did not breake the matter after that sort as is saide, but the king brake the matter to him first, and neuer lefte vrging of him untill he had wonne him to geue his consent to others that were the chiefe setters forth of the diuorce betweene the king and Queene Katherine. Of the which his doinges he did sore forethinke himselfe, and repented afterwarde, declaring to the saide docto*ur* that there was neuer any one thing that did so much and so greeuously nipp his [fol. 11 *b*] heart as did that his consent and doing towarde | the saide diuorce.

originator of Henry's divorce of Queen Katherine.

Langland, Bishop of Lincoln, is reported to have suggested the divorce to the King. [ROPER.]

But Harpsfield reports Langland's denial of this rumour.

Yet is it most credible that the saide Cardinall was the

MSS. E L R² Y C H R B.

1. *better and fuller*] fuller and better L R² B. 1. *matter taken*] C; matter to take E L R² Y H R B. (Cf. *p.* 39, *l.* 23, story taken in hande). 2. *a litle*] and a litle L R² B. 2. *large*] *Omitted in* H. 2. *open and*] *Interlineated in* R. 3. *diuorce*] dououce Y. 3. *betweene*] of Y. 4. *who*] wee, *upon a partly erased* wh, R. 5. *atchieuing of*] atcheving H. 9. *Bisshopp*] Byssop of Lyncolne B. 10. *so*] *Omitted in* Y. 14. *and . . . truth*] *Omitted in* H R. 16. *after that sort*] *Omitted in* L R² B; after that H R. 16. *as is saide, but*] as it was sayd L R² B (*being interlineated in* L); is said H R. 16. *brake*] broke L R² B. 17. *vrging of*] vrging H R. 18. *wonne*] wanne L; woun H. 19. *setters*] *Initial* s *corrected from* f, L. 19. *forth*] one (= "on") L; on R² B. 19. *of the diuorce*] of this divorce B. 19–20. *betweene . . . Katherine*] *Omitted in* B. 20. *and Queene*] & the Queene R² H R. 23. *that*] *Omitted in* L R² B. 23–24. *so much. . . heart*] so much grieve & nip his heart L R² B. 24. *saide*] *Interlineated in* R. 26. *yet is it*] yet it is Y H R B; Yt is C.

Cardinal Adrian elected Pope. [1522.] Wolsey's consequent anger with Charles the Emperor. [ROPER.]

first auth*our* and incenser of this diuorce, and that for this cause, as Queene Katherine herselfe layde afterwarde to his charge. The Sea of Rome being at that time voyde, the Cardinall, being a man very ambitious and desirous to aspire to that dignitie, wherein he had good hope and likelyhood, perceauing himselfe frustrate and eluded of this his aspiring expectation by the meanes of the Emperour Charles co*m*mending Cardinall Adrian, sometime his Schoolemaster, to the Cardinalls of Rome, for his great learning, vertue and woorthines, who therevpon was elected Pope (and co*m*ming from Spaine, whereof he had vnder the saide Charles the chiefe gouernment, before his entrie into the Citie of Rome putting off his hose and shoes, and, as I haue hearde * it credibly * reported, barefoote and bare legged passed through the streetes towardes his pallace, with such humblenes as all the people had him in great reuerence)—The Cardinall, [I saie], waxed so wood therewith that he studied to inuent all wayes of reuengement of his griefe against the Empero*ur*: which, as it was the beginning of a lamentable tragedie, so some part of it, not as impertinent to my present purpose, I recken requisite here to put in remembraunce.

Wolsey's revenge against the

This Cardinall therefore, not ignorant of the kinges vnconstant and mutable disposition (soone inclined to

MSS. E L R^2 Y C H R B.

1. *first*] *Omitted in* L R^2 B. 1. *this*] his Y. 2. *layde afterwarde*] afterward layed Y. 3. *being . . . time*] at that tyme being Y. 4. *the Cardinall*] and the cardinall Y. 4. *a man very ambitious*] a man at that tyme ambitious H R. 5. *aspire to*] aspire L R^2. 5. *good hope*] that good hope H R. 5–6. *and likelyhood*] *Omitted in* B. 6. *frustrate*] first rated R^2; frustrated C. 6. *eluded*] deluded H. 7. *this his*] his L; this H R. 12. *the chiefe*] *Omitted in* Y; Chiefe H R B. 13. *the Citie*] the said Cittie Y. 14. *as I . . . reported*] as I haue harde yt credibly reported R^2 Y C H R; as I haue credibly hearde it reported E L B. 14–15. *barefoote*] barefooted L R^2 B. 15. *legged*] legges Y. 15. *streetes*] Streests H. 15. *towardes*] to R^2. 17. *the Cardinall, I saie*] C (*supported by most* Roper MSS.); the Cardinall E L R^2 Y H R B. 18. *therewith*] therat H R. 18. *inuent*] worke & inuente R^2; worke H R. 18–19. *studied . . . the Emperour*] studied all wayes of reuengement to inuente towardes the emperor Y. 18. *all wayes*] alwaies C R. 19. *griefe*] greifes H. 20. *so*] *Omitted in* H. 21. *part . . . impertinent*] part of it was not impertinent Y. 21. *not as*] as not R^2 H R. 22. *requisite*] *Interlineated in* R; exquiset H. 23. *the*] *Interlineated in* B.

withdrawe his deuotion from his owne most noble, vertuous and lawfull wife, Queene Catherine, aunt to the Emperour, vpon euery light occasion, and vpon other, to her in nobilitie, wisedome, vertue, fauour and beautie farre incomparable, to fixe his affection) meaning to make this his so light disposition an instrument to bring about his vngodly intent, deuised to allure the king to cast phantasie [vnto] one of the frenche kinges sisters, the Dutchesse of Alanson, because of the enmitie and warre that was at that time betweene the frenche king and the Emperour, whom for the cause afore remembred he mortally maligned.

Emperor's Aunt, Queen Katherine. [ROPER.]

Wolsey's attempt to bring about the King's marriage with the Duchess of Alençon. [ROPER, with addition.]

And not longe after was he sent Ambassadour to intreate and conclude for the perfiting of the saide mariage. But ô the great prouidence and iust iudgement of God, ô the vnfortunable (but yet condigne) euentes of wretched and mischieuous counsaile! This Cardinall then, [though] neuer Ambassadour, I trowe, before in this Realme set forth himselfe so costly, so pompously and so gorgiously, though he thought by this meane to make himselfe in [fol 12 a] the kinges graces fauour (whom | he already throughly possessed, and altogether ruled) more stedfast, sure and fast, yet was there neuer man that eyther had lesse honour or woorse lucke of his ambassade or of his whole enterprise, as being the very meane and occasion that he was vtterly vndone and ouerthrowen.

Wolsey's embassy to France. [1527.]

MSS. E L R^2 Y C H R B.

1. *withdrawe*] withdray Y. 3. *other*] another R^2, an *being prefixed in margin*; others B. 5. *affection*] fancye C. 7. *deuised*] devising Y. 7–8. *cast phantasie vnto*] cast fancie vnto L R^2 Y R (*supported by* Roper); cast his fantasie vnto H; cast his fancie vnto B; cast phantasie vpon E; caste affection vpon C. 8–9. *the Dutchesse*] and duches Y. 9. *enmitie*] ennitie Y. 13 *after was he*] after he was he L, *the first* he *crossed through, and the second* he *interlineated.* 14. *for*] *Omitted in* H R. 15. *and iust iudgement*] *Omitted in* H R. 16. *vnfortunable*] vnfortunate Y. 16. *but yet*] & yet B. 16. *euentes*] event L R^2 Y B. 17. *though*] Y C; thoughe, *corrected from* thought, B; thought E L R^2 H R. 18. *before*] *Omitted in* H R. 19. *himselfe*] *Omitted in* L R^2 H R B. 20. *though he thought*] thinking L R^2 B; thought C; & thought H R. 20. *meane*] meane *corrected from* meanes R^2; meanes B. 21. *graces*] grace his B. 22–23. *sure and fast*] & sure R^2 B. 23. *neuer*] euer H R. 24. *woorse . . . or*] *Interlineated in* L. 25. *and*] or Y.

The King meanwhile falls in love with Anne Boleyn. [ROPER.]

And forbids Wolsey to treat of the French marriage.

Anne and the King incensed against Wolsey.

For in the meane season had the king (contrary to his minde, nothing lesse looking for) fallen in loue with Lady Anne Bulleine, vpon whom his heart was nowe so throughlye and entierly fixed, that there was a messanger dispatched with letters after the Cardinall, willing him that of other matters he should breake with the frenche king, but in no case of any mariage. The Lady Anne Bulleine was so greeuously offended with the Cardinall for mouing the king touching the saide frenche kinges sister, that she neuer ceassed to presse and vrge the king vtterly to vndoe the Cardinall. Wherevnto the king was otherwise* also* incensed, as we shall hereafter declare, thinking that eyther the Cardinall had chaunged his minde and mislyked the whole mariage, or at least was nothing so forwarde therein, nor conformable to his minde, as he had looked for at his handes.

The King consults More for the first time on the proposed divorce. [ROPER.]

More excuses himself as unmeet to meddle in such matters. [ROPER.

Nowe when this matter was once broched, the king opened it with the first to S*ir* Thomas More, whose councell he required therein, shewing him certaine places of Scripture that somewhat seemed to serue his appetite: which, when he had perused, and therevpon, as one that had neuer professed the studie of diuinitie, himselfe excused to be vnmeete many wayes to meddle with such matters, The king, not satisfied with [this] aunswere, so sore still pressed vpon him therefore, that in conclusion he condiscended to his graces motion. And forasmuch as the case was of suche importance as needed good aduisement and deliberation, he besought his grace of

MSS. E L R[2] Y C H R B.

5. *with*] which L. 5. *after*] after, *corrected from* afters, R[2]. 6–7. *frenche king*] kinge of Fraunce R[2]. 7. *any mariage*] the Marriage H. 8. *offended*] moved H R. 9. *the king*] the French kinge H R. 10. *presse*] pressed R[2]. 11. *vtterly*] *Omitted in* R[2]. 12. *otherwise also*] other wise alsoe L R[2] Y C H R B; also otherwise E. 12. *hereafter*] heeafter L; afterward H. 14. *and*] or Y. 15. *so*] *Omitted in* R[2]. 16. *had*] *Omitted in* C; *interlineated in* R. 18. *opened . . . to*] opened with þe first to L R[2] B; with the first it to H. 19. *places*] praces Y. 22. *had neuer*] neuer had L R[2] B; neuer had Y, *with* neuer *corrected from* neyther. 22–23. *himselfe excused*] excused himselfe R[2]. 24. *this*] L R[2] H R B (*supported by* Roper); his E Y C. 27. *case*] cause R[2] H R. 27. *as* (2)] & B. 28. *aduisement*] advertisement L B.

The King bids More consult with the Bishops of Durham and Bath. [ROPER.]

sufficient respite aduisedlye to consider of it. Wherewith the king, well contented, saide vnto him That Tunstall and Clarke, Bisshopps of Durham and Bathe, with other learned of his priuie Counsaile, should also be doers therein.

More consults the Works of St. Jerome, St. Augustine, &c., and recommends their perusal to the King. [ROPER.]

So S*ir* Thomas More departing, conferred those places of Scripture with the expositions of diuers of the [old] holye Doctours. And at his next co*m*ming to the [fol. 12 *b*] Court, in talking with | his grace of the foresaide matter, he saide: "To be plaine with your grace, neyther my Lorde of Durham, nor my Lorde of Bathe, though I knowe them both to be wise, vertuous, learned and honorable Prelates, nor my selfe, with the rest of your counsaile, being all your graces owne seruaunt*es*, for your manifolde benefites dayly bestowed vpon vs most bounden vnto you, be, in my iudgement, meete Counsailers for your grace herein. But if your grace minde to vnderstande the truth, such Counsailers may you haue deuised as neither for respect of their owne worldly co*m*moditie, nor for feare of your princely authoritie, will be inclined to deceaue you." To whom he named then St. Jerome, St. Augustine, and diuers others olde holy Doctours, both Greekes and Latines; and moreouer shewed him what authorities he had gathered out of them: Which although the king, as disagreable with his desire, did not very well like off, yet were they by S*ir* Thomas More (who in all his co*m*munication with the king in that matter had alwayes most discretely behaued himselfe) so wisely tempred, that he both presently tooke

MSS. E L R² Y C H R B.

3. *of*] *Interlineated in* R. 6. *conferred*] conferred conferred Y; considered H. 7. *of* (1)] *Omitted in* H. 7. *old*] L Y C H R B (*supported by* Roper); *omitted in* E R². 8. *holye*] *Omitted in* B. 9. *foresaide*] sayd L R² B. 13. *with*] with with C. 14. *owne*] *Interlineated in* L. 15. *most*] *Omitted in* B. 17. *minde*] *Interlineated in* L. 18. *truth*] *After* truth, E *has* herein *crossed through*. 18. *such Counsailers*] *Omitted in* R². 19. *for*] in L R² B. 21. *then*] *Interlineated in* R². 22. *St. Jerome, St. Augustine*] St. Augustine, St. Hierome R². 22. *others olde holy*] other holy L R² H. 24. *him*] *Omitted in* H R. 24. *what*] that Y. 25. *disagreable*] agreeable H R. 25–26. *with his desire*] to his desire R².

them in good part, and often times had thereof conference with him againe.

The King appeals to the Pope to pronounce the marriage with Katherine illegal. [ROPER.]

After this were there certaine questions amonge the Counsaile proponed, whether the king needed in this case to haue any scruple at all, and if he had, what way were best to be taken to deliuer him of it. The most part of whom were of the opinion that there was good cause of scruple, and that for discharge of it, sute were meete to be made to the Sea of Rome, where the king hoped by liberalitie to obtaine his purpose; wherein, as it afterwarde appered, he was farre deceaued.

A Commission is appointed. [13 April, 1528.] [ROPER.]

In support of the legality of the King's marriage with Katherine, a dispensation and brief are produced. [ROPER.] Then the King appeals from the Pope to the next

Then was there for the triall and examination of this matrimonie procured from Rome a Co*m*mission, in which Cardinall Campegius and Cardinall Wolsey were ioyned Co*m*missioners, who for the determination thereof sate at the Blacke fryers in London, where a libell was put in for the adnulling of the saide matrimonie, alleaging the mariage betweene the king and the Queene to be vnlawfull. And for proufe of the mariage to be lawfull was there brought in a dispensation, in which, after diuers disputations therevpon holden, there appered an imperfection, which by an instrument or briefe, vpon | [fol. 18 a] searche found in the Treasorie of Spaine, and sent to the Co*m*missioners into Inglande, was supplied; and so should iudgement haue beene geuen by the Pope accordingly, had not the king, vpon intelligence thereof, before the same iudgement, appealed to the next generall

MSS. E L R^2 Y C H R B.

4. *proponed*] propounded Y. 5. *and*] *Omitted in* B. 5–6. *way were*] waye there were C. 6. *be*] *Interlineated in* L. 7. *were*] where R^2. 7. *the*] *Interlineated in* L; *omitted in* R^2 H B. 7. *of the opinion*] of opinion H. 8. *and*] *Omitted in* B. 9. *where the*] where (*upon an erasure*) the the R. 10. *hoped by liberalitie*] by liberality hoped H. 10–11. *as it*] *Interlineated in* R. 11. *afterwarde*] after C. 11. *farre*] *Corrected from* faire R. 12. *the*] a Y; theire B. 13. *in which*] in þe which C. 15–16. *sate at*] satt in H R. 16. *was put*] *Corrected from* put put R. 17. *the*] *Omitted in* R^2. 17. *adnulling*] admitting *underlined in text of* L, *and* adnulling *a correction on the margin;* admitting Y. 18. *and the*] and C H R. 20. *was there*] there was H R B. 24. *was*] *Interlineated in* Y. 24. *supplied*] supposed, *corrected from* pupposed, Y. 24. *so*] *Interlineated in* R^2. 26. *king, vpon intelligence*] king vppon þe intelligence L B.

General Council. [ROPER.]

Counsaile. After whose appellation* [the Cardinall] vpon that matter sate no longer.

The nature of the brief explained.

The supplying we spake of was thus. When that Prince Arthure was deade, to whom Lady Catherine was maryed, there was by the sute of king Henry the seuenth, after long consultation and debating the matter both in Spaine and Rome, a dispensation gotten that Lorde Henry, Prince Arthures brother, might marye her; but yet because some doubted whether that the saide Prince Arthur did euer carnally knowe her or no before his death, whereof might perchaunce in time growe a question against the validitie of the mariage (as in deede afterwarde there did) the two wise kinges of Inglande and Spaine procured another briefe, in the which (for the more aboundant cautell) it was particulerly specified that notwithstanding any carnall copulation, if anye suche happely were betweene the saide Arthure and ladye Catherine, the mariage should be good and auaileable.

More is sent on embassy [to Amiens with Wolsey, July–Sept., 1527].

The King consults More for the second time on the marriage, and desires him to commune with Master Fox. [MORE to CROMWELL; WORKS, p. 1425.]

Before the Cardinall Campegius and Cardinall Woolsey, the popes legates, sate vpon this matter, S*ir* Thomas More was sente beyonde the Sea for certaine of the king*es* affaires. At his returne, when he repaired to the king at Hampton Court, the king brake againe with him of this matter, and shewed him that it was perceaued that his mariage was not onely against the positive lawes of the Churche and the written lawe of God, but also in suche sort against the lawe of nature that it could

MSS. E L R² Y C H R B.

1–2. *appellation the Cardinall . . . longer*] appelations þe Cardinall vpon that matter sate no longer C; appellation vpon that matter they sate no longer E L R² H R B; Y *as* E L R² H R B, *but* the matter. (*See* Notes.) 2. *that*] the R² Y. (Roper MSS. *vary. See* Notes.) 3. *spake*] speake L R² C. (*Note forms.*) 6. *and debating the*] a debating of the Y C. 7. *a dispensation*] and dispensacion Y. 9. *whether that*] whether H. 9. *the saide*] þat sayd R², sayd *being interlineated.* 14. *in the which*] *Omitted in* B. 15. *more*] *Interlineated in* L. 15. *cautell*] *Corrected from* councell R². 17–18. *and ladye*] & þe Lady L R² B; and the said Lady Y. 18. *be good*] *Interlineated in* R². 20. *Cardinall*] Cardinalles H R. 21. *the popes legates*] *Omitted in* B. 21. *this*] þe C. 22. *Sea*] seas B. 24. *againe with him*] with him againe C. 25. *of this*] in this Y; of his C. 26. *his*] this L. 27. *lawe*] lawes H R. 28. *lawe*] lawes H R.

in no wise by the Churche be relieued or dispensed withall; And incontinently layde the Byble open before him, and there read such wordes as moued him and other learned persons so to thinke. But when he had asked S*ir* Thomas More what he thought vpon [these] wordes, and perceaued that S*ir* Thomas Mores minde was not correspondent to his owne minde, willed him to co*m*mon farther with M*aster* Foxe, his Almoigner, and to reade a booke with him that then was in making for the matter.

More and Tunstall are sent ambassadors to Cambrai. [Summer of 1529.] The great benefits More procured for England. [ROPER.]

After which time the sute beganne, and the legates, as we haue shewed, | sett vpon the matter. And while the [fol. 13 *b*] legates were yet sitting, it pleased the king to send S*ir* Thomas Moore with docto*ur* Tunstall, then Bisshopp of London and afterwarde of Durham, in ambassade about the peace, that at their being there was concluded at Cameraye betweene the Emperour, his highnes and the frenche king. In the concluding whereof S*ir* Thomas Moore so woorthily handled himselfe (procuring in our league more benefites into this Realme then at any time by the king and his counsaile was thought possible to be compassed) that for his good seruice in that voyage, the king, when he after made him Lorde Chauncell*our*, caused the duke of Norffolke openly to declare to the people how muche all Inglande was bounde to him.

The King consults More for the third time on the marriage, and prays him to confer

Nowe vpon his co*m*ming home from Cameraye, the king earnestly persuaded S*ir* Thomas More to condiscende to the matter of the mariage, by many wayes prouoking him thereto; for which, it was thought, he the rather soone after made him Lorde Chauncell*our*; eftsones

MSS. E L R^2 Y C H R B.

1. *in*] *Omitted in* B. 1. *by the Churche be*] be by the Church be R, *the second* be *being interlineated*. 3. *read*] *Omitted in* L R^2; shewed B. 5. *these*] L Y C H R B; these, *corrected from* those, R^2; those E. 6. *Mores*] *Omitted in* B. 7. *owne*] *Interlineated in* L. 11. *which*] what R^2 B. 12. *sett*] sate L R^2 B; satt H R. 17. *Emperour his highnes*] Emperors highnes L R^2 B. 19. *handled*] behaued H R. 20. *more benefites into*] more benefittes betwene into R^2, *with* benefittes *interlineated*. 20. *this*] this our R^2. 21. *thought possible*] thought possibly R^2. 22. *voyage*] vioge Y. 24. *Norffolke*] Morffolk H. 25. *was*] were Y C. (Roper *supports* was.) 29. *it was*] as it was Y. 30. *eftsones*] oftesones R^2.

with Bishop Stokesley. [1529.] [ROPER.]

repeting vnto him amonge other motives the new scruple that was founde (as we haue declared) that the former mariage was so directly against the lawe of nature that no dispensation could repaire, reforme and supplye that defecte, as doct*our* Stokesley (whom he had preferred to the Bisshopricke of London, and in that case chiefely credited) was able to instruct him, with whom he prayed him in that point to conferre. But for all [his] conference with him, he sawe nothing of such force as could induce him to chaunge his opinion therein; which notwithstanding, the Bisshopp shewed himselfe in his report of him to the kinges highnes so good and fauourable, that he saide he founde him in his graces cause very towarde, and desirous to finde some matter wherewith he might truely serue his grace to his contentation.

Bishop Stokesley's quarrel with Wolsey. [ROPER.]

This Bisshopp Stokesley, being by the Cardinall not longe before in the Starre chamber openly put to rebuke, and afterwarde sent to the Fleete, thought that forasmuche as the Cardinall, for lacke of such forwardnes in setting forth the king*es* diuorce as his grace looked for, [fol. 14 *a*] was out of his highnes fa|uour, he had nowe a good occasion offred him to revenge his quarell against him, Farther to incense the king*es* displeasure towarde him busily trauelled to inuent some coulourable deuise for the kinges furtherance in that behalfe: which, as before is mentioned, he to his grace reuealed, hoping thereby to bring the king to the better lyking of himselfe and the more mislyking of the Cardinall, whom his highnes therefore soone after of his office displaced, and to S*ir* Thomas More (the rather to moue him to incline to his side) the same in his steede co*m*mitted.

MSS. E L R^2 Y C H R B.

2. *haue*] *Omitted in* C. 4. *that*] the B. 5. *defecte*] defute L. 5. *as*] & H. 6. *and*] *Omitted in* Y H; *interlineated in* R. 6. *case*] cause Y. 8. *his*] B (*supported by most* Roper MSS.); this E L R^2 Y C H R. (*See* Notes.) 9. *as*] that Y. 15. *truely*] *Omitted in* H R. 18. *thought*] *This is the reading of all the* Harpsfield MSS., *but the* Roper MSS. *have* thinking, *which is better syntax.* 23. *incense*] increase L; incease Y. (Roper MSS. *vary. See* Notes.) 23. *towarde*] against L R^2 B. 24. *busily*] he busilie B. 24. *inuent*] finde H. 25. *kinges*] king his B. 29. *therefore*] *Omitted in* R^2. 29. *therefore soone after*] soone after therefore H R.

The fall of Wolsey. [1529.]

The saide Cardinall, a while after, albeit he was taken and receaued and vsed as a legate from the ninth yere of the kinges reigne, as well by the whole Realme as by the king himselfe (and the saide office procured, as it was thought, to him not without the kinges helpe and mediation) yet beside many other great and heynous offences laide to his charge, was by the kinges learned counsaile, for the practising and exercysing of the same office without the kinges speciall licence in wryting, and the whole clergie withall, for acknowledging the saide legantine authoritie, founde fallen in[to] a *Praemunire*. And the prouince of Caunterbury, to recouer the kinges fau*our* and grace (beside like contribution for the rate of the Prouince of Yorke) was faine to defraye to the kinges vse one hundred thousande poundes.

The death of Wolsey. [30 November, 1530.]

The Cardinall, being in his diocesse of Yorke, was arrested, and sent for to make aunswere to such accusations as were layde against him. But the mayne sorowe and griefe that he had conceaued of these his troubles, with farther feare of other greeuous euentes, had so deepely sunke into his heart that it cutt off a great part of his iourney and his life withall. And this ende fell vpon him that was the first and principall instrument of this vnhappy diuorce.

More (against his will) is made Lord Chancellor.

But nowe lett vs returne to S*ir* Thomas More, newly made Lorde Chauncell*our*, which office, I suppose, verilye

MSS. E L R^2 Y C H R B.

1. *a while*] a whle H. 3. *whole*] noble H. 3. *by*] *Omitted in* R^2 B. 4. *saide*] *Omitted in* L R^2 H R B. 5–6. *and mediation*] *Omitted in* R^2. 8. *exercysing*] executing Y. 8. *office*] offence C. 9. *in wryting*] and writing L R^2 B. 10. *the*] of the B. 11. *legantine*] Legantine *or* Legantiue L; Legatiue R^2 Y B; Legantiue C H. 11. *legantine authoritie*] authorytie Legantiue R^2. 11. *into*] L R^2 Y C H R B; in E. (*See* Notes.) 12. *recouer*] recouer R, *with* ouer *corrected from other letters.* 12. *kinges*] king his B. 13. *like*] the like B. 14. *of* (2)] *Interlineated in* R^2. 15. *one*] an Y. 18–19. *the mayne sorowe and griefe*] þe many sorrowes and griefs L R^2 H R B. 19. *these his troubles*] this his troble Y. 20. *euentes*] event L B. 20. *had*] has L. 21. *sunke*] sancte Y; sanke C. 22. *his life*] life L R^2 B. 23. *was . . . instrument*] was the first & principall of L R^2; was first cheife & principall instrument of H; was the first cheife and principall instrument of R (first *being interlineated over* cheife); was the first & principall causer B. 24. *vnhappy*] *Omitted in* C. 25. *But*] *Omitted in* B.

[26 October, 1529.]

he was of himselfe very vnwilling to take vpon him, and [fol. 14 b] would haue earnestly refused the same, but that he | thought it vnmeete and vnseemely to gainsay and contrary the will and pleasure of the king, that so highly and entierly fauored and loued him, and also an euill part to withdrawe and denye his seruice to the whole Realme, that with gladfull and meruailous good mind towarde him wisshed and desired that he of all men might enioye the saide office; who betweene the dukes of Norfolke and Suffolke being brought through Westminster hall to his place in the Chauncerie, the duke of Norffolke, in open audience of all the people there assembled, shewed that he was from the king himselfe straightly charged by speciall Commission, there openly in presence of them all, to make declaration howe much all Inglande was beholding vnto S*ir* Thomas More for his good seruice, and howe woorthy he was to haue the highest roome in the Realme, and howe derely his grace loued and trusted him, for which (saide the duke) he had great cause to reioyce. Wherevnto S*ir* Thomas More, among many other his humble and wise sayinges not nowe in my memorie, aunswered that although he had good cause to take comfort of his highnes singuler fauour towardes him, that he had, farre aboue his desertes, so highly co*m*mended him, to whom therefore he acknowledged himselfe most deepely bounden; Yet neuerthelesse he must for his owne part needes confesse that in all thinges by his grace alleaged he had done no more than was his dutie, and further disallowed himselfe as vnmeete for that roome, Wherein, considering howe wise and honorable a Prelate

The Duke of Norfolk praises More publicly. [ROPER.]

More's modest reply. [ROPER.]

MSS. E L R^2 Y C H R B.

2. *that*] *Omitted in* L R^2. 4. *and pleasure*] *Interlineated in* R. 5. *an euill*] in euill H. 5–6. *to withdrawe and denye*] to deny and withdrawe Y. 7. *and meruailous*] and with mervailous L R^2. 8. *that . . . might*] þat of all men he might R^2, *with* he *interlineated.* 9. *Norfolke*] Morffolk H. 10. *Westminster*] Westmester R^2. 12. *all*] *Interlineated in* R^2. 14. *in presence*] in the presence R^2 H R. 15. *beholding*] behoulden Y. (Roper MSS. *vary. See* Notes.) 17. *in the*] in all the H R. 18. *and howe . . . trusted him*] *Omitted in* H. 18. *derely*] deere B. 19. *he*] ye Y. 22. *good*] *Omitted in* C. 24. *so*] *Omitted in* H. 27. *in*] *Interlineated in* R. 29. *disallowed himselfe*] disabled R^2.

had lately before taken so great a fall, he had, he saide, [therof] no cause to reioyce. And as they had before, on the kinges behalfe, charged him vprightly to minister indifferent Justice to the people, without corruption or affection; so did he likewise charge them againe, that if they sawe him, at any time, in any thing, digresse from any part of his dutie in that honorable office, euen as they would discharge their owne dutie and fidelitie to God and the king, so should they not faile to disclose it to his grace, who otherwise might haue iust occasion to laye his fault whollye to their charge.

More's doors ever open to suitors: his son-in-law's objection thereto. [Roper.]

While he was Lorde Chauncell*our*, being at leasure, as seldome he was, one of his sonnes in lawe on a time saide merily to him: "When Cardinall Wolsey was Lorde Chauncell*our*, not onely diuers of his priuie chamber, but suche also as were but his doorekeepers, gott great gaine." And since he had maried one of his daughters, and | gaue [fol. 15 *a*] still attendance vpon him, he thought he might of reason looke for something; Where he in deede, because he was so readie himselfe to heare euery man, poore and riche, and kept no dores shett from them, could finde none, [it] was to him a great discourage. And whereas els some for frendshipp, some for kinred, and some for profite, would gladly haue had his furtherance in bringing them to his presence, if he should [nowe] take any thing of them, he

MSS. E L R^2 Y C H R B.

1. *before taken*] taken before H. 1. *so great*] *Omitted in* H R. 1. *he saide*] as he said L R^2 B. 2. *therof*] C (*supported by* Roper); therefore E L Y H R B; before R^2. 2–3. *before . . . him*] one (= "on") þe kinges behalfe before charged him R^2; before charged him on the kinges behalfe H R. 3–4. *minister indifferent Justice*] administer indifferent iustice L; administer iustice H R. 6–7. *digresse from any part*] digresse from any parte R, any parte *being on an erasure, and* digresse *interlineated.* 7. *euen*] euer R^2. 8. *and fidelitie*] *Omitted in* Y. 12. *being at leasure*] *Interlineated in* L. 16. *also*] *Omitted in* L R^2 H R B. (Roper *supports* also). 16. *but*] *Omitted in* R^2 B. (Roper MSS. *vary. See* Notes.) 18. *he might of reason*] of reason he might H R. 19. *Where*] when H R. 20. *himselfe*] *Omitted in* Y. 20. *man, poore*] man both poore R^2. 21. *kept*] keepe L. 21. *shett*] shut L H. 21. *could finde none*] could find none *twice over* Y. 21. *it was*] L R^2 H R B; was E Y C. (*Some such pronoun as* it *seems necessary. Most* Roper MSS. *have* which was. *See* Notes.) 23. *frendshipp, some*] frendshipp & some H R. 25. *should nowe take*] should now take Y C (*supported by* Roper); now should take H R; should take L R^2 B; should not take E.

knewe, he saide, he should doo them great wronge, for that they might doo as muche for themselues as he could doo for them; which condic*io*n, though he thought it in S*ir* Thomas More very co*m*mendable, yet to him, saide he, being his sonne, he founde it nothing profitable.

More would see justice done even to the Devil [ROPER.]

When he had tolde him this tale: "You say well, sonne," quoth he; "I doo not mislike that you are of conscience so scrupulous; but many other wayes be there, sonne, that I may both doo your selfe good, and pleasure yo*ur* frende also; for sometime may I by my worde stande your frende in steede, and sometime may I by my letter helpe him; or if he haue a cause depending before me, at your request I may heare him before another; or if his cause be not all the best, yet may I moue the parties to fall to some reasonable ende by arbitriment. Howbeit, this one thing, sonne, I assure thee on my faith, that if the parties will at my handes call for iustice, then, all were it my father stoode on the one side, and the deuill on the other, his cause being good, the deuill shoulde haue right." So offered he his sonne, as he thought, he saide, as muche fauo*ur* as with reason he could require.

More's decree against his own son-in-law, Master Heron. [ROPER.]

And that he would for no respect digresse from Justice, well appered by a plaine example of another of his sonnes called M*aste*r Herone: for when he, having a matter before him in the Chauncerie, and presuming too muche of his fauo*ur*, would by him in no wise be persuaded to agree to any indifferent order, then made he in conclusion a flatt decree against him.

MSS. E L R^2 Y C H R B.

1. *doo*] *Interlineated in* R^2. 2. *doo*] *Omitted in* B. 3. *it*] *Omitted in* L R^2 B. 6. *this*] his L; his *interlineated in* R^2. 6. *You say*] he said Y. 8. *scrupulous*] scripulous H. 8. *wayes*] wise Y. 8. *be there*] there be L. 9. *both doo*] doe both B. 10. *frende*] friendes B. 10. *may . . . worde*] by my word may I *in* H R. 11–12. *may I . . . helpe him*] by my Letter helpe H R. 14. *cause*] case Y. 16. *sonne*] *Interlineated in* R. 16. *on my*] by my R^2. 16. *that if*] and yf Y. 17. *my*] thy H R. 17. *then*] *Omitted in* Y. 17–18. *all were it*] albeit H R. 18. *on the one*] of þe one C. 20. *he thought*] *Interlineated in* Y. 23. *well*] it well B. 23. *a plaine example of*] *Omitted in* L R^2 B. 25. *him*] *Omitted in* B. 25. *too muche*] soe to much R^2, *with* to *interlineated*. 26. *would by him in no wise be persuaded*] would by no meanes by him be persuaded L B; would by noe meanes be perswaded by him R^2. 26. *to* (2)] *Interlineated in* L. 27. *he*] *Omitted in* H R.

More's care with regard to Subpœnas. [ROPER.]

This Lord Chauncell*our* vsed co*m*monly euery afternoone at his house at Chelsey to sitt in his open hall, to the intent that, if any persons had any sute vnto him, they might the more boldly come to his presence, and therevpon bring their complaintes before him; whose maner was also to reade euery bill himselfe, ere he would award any *Subpoena*: which bearing matter sufficient woorthy a *Subpoena*, would* he* sett his hande vnto, or els cancell it.

More's reverence and love for his father. [ROPER.]

Whensoeuer he passed through Westminster hall to his place in the Chauncerie by the Court of the kinges benche, if his Fa|ther [fol. 15 b] (one of the Judges thereof) had bene sett ere he came, he would goe into the same Court, and there reuerently kneeling downe in the sight of them all, dulye aske his fathers blessing. And if it fortuned that his father and he at readinges [in] Lincolnes Inn mett together, as they sometime did, [notwithstanding his high office] he would offer in argument the preheminence to his father, though he, for his office sake, would refuse to take it. And for better declaration of his naturall affection towarde his father, he not only while he laye on his death bedd, according to his dutie, often times with comfortable wordes most kindly came to visite him, but also at his departure out of this world, with teares taking him about the necke, most louingly kissed and embraced him, commending him into the mercifull handes of almightie God, and so departed from him.

And as fewe Iniunctions as he graunted while he was

MSS. E L R^2 Y C H R B.

1. *This*] the Y. 2. *at* (2)] in H. 2. *his* (2)] *Omitted in* H. 3. *had any sute*] had suite H R. 3. *vnto*] vn *of* vnto *interlineated in* E. 3–4. *they might the more boldly*] then might they more boldely L R^2 B. 5. *before*] vnto R^2. 5. *whose*] His B. 8. *would he*] Y C (*supported by* Roper); he would E L R^2 H R B. (*See* Notes.) 13. *would*] should Y. 14. *dulye*] *Omitted in* H R. 16. *at readinges*] at the readinges H R. 16. *in Lincolnes*] Y C (*supported by* Roper); at Lincolnes E L R^2 H R B. 17. *as they sometime did*] as sometymes they did H R. 17–18. *notwithstanding his high office*] L R^2 C H R B (*supported by* Roper); notwithstanding his hight office Y; *omitted in* E. 19. *he*] *Interlineated in* L. 20. *for better*] for þe better L R^2 B. 21. *while*] when H. 22. *death*] deathes R^2. 23. *most kindly*] most *omitted*, kindlie *interlineated, in* R. 26. *into*] vnto B. 26. *mercifull*] *Omitted in* C H R.

More defends his injunctions before the Judges. [ROPER.]

Lord Chauncell*our*, yet were they by some of the Judges of the lawe mislyked: which M*aster* Will*iam* Roper vnderstanding, declared the same vnto S*ir* Thomas More, who aunswered him that they should haue litle cause to finde fault with him therefore; and therevpon caused he one M*aster* Cro[o]ke, chiefe of the sixe Clerkes, to make a dockett conteyning the whole number and causes of all suche Iniunctions as eyther in his time had already passed, or at that present depended in any of the kinges Courtes at Westminster. Which done, he inuited all the Judges to dyne with him in the Councell chamber at Westminster; where after diner, when he had broken with them what complaintes he had heard of his Iniunctions, and moreouer shewed them both the number and causes of euery one of them, in order, so plainly that, vpon full debating of those matters, they were all inforced to confesse that they, in like case, could haue done no otherwise themselves, Then offered he this vnto them: that if the Justices of euerye Court (vnto whom the reformation of the rig*our* of the lawe, by reason of their office, most especially apperteyned) woulde, vpon reasonable considerations, by their owne discretions (as they were, as he thought, in conscience bounden) mittigate and reforme the rig*our* of the lawe themselues, there should from thenceforth by him no more Iniunctions be graunted. Wherevnto, when they refused to condiscende, then saide he vnto them: "Forasmuch as your selues,

MSS. E L R² Y C H R B.

1. *some of the Judges*] some Judges H R. 4. *who aunswered him*] *Interlineated in* R. 6. *one*] *Interlineated in* R. 6. *Crooke*] L B (*supported by* Roper); Crocke E R² Y C H R. 6. *chiefe*] cheife *interlineated over* one *crossed through* R; one cheif Y. 8. *already*] *Interlineated in* R. 9. *or . . . depended*] or that present depended L; or at that present depending H R. 12. *where*] when L. 12. *broken*] broke R². 16. *vpon*] in H R. 16. *of*] *Interlineated over* vpon *crossed through* L. 16. *those*] *Corrected from* these R². 17. *in*] in the H R. 17. *case*] cause R². 18. *offered he*] he offered H R. 20. *the reformation of*] *Omitted in* Y. 20. *the* (3)] *Omitted in* R². 21. *office*] offices Y. 24. *the rigour of the lawe*] the same lawe L R² B. 25. *by him*] from him R². 26. *Wherevnto*] Wherevpon L. 26. *when*] then Y; when *interlineated in* R. 27. *then saide he*] he sayd B.

my Lordes, driue me to that necessitie for awarding out Iniunctions to relieue the peoples iniurye, you cannot hereafter any more iustly blame me." After that he saide secretly to M*aster* Will*iam* Roper: "I perceaue, | [fol. 16 a] sonne, why they like not so to doo, for they see that they may by the verdict of the Jurie cast off all quarells from themselues vpon the Jurie, which they accompt their chiefe defence; And therefore am I compelled to abide the aduenture of all such reportes."

More's charity. [ERASMUS to ULRICH VON HUTTEN.]

All the while he was Lorde Chauncell*our*, yea, and before also, there was nothing in the world that more pleased or comforted him then when he had done some good to other men; of whom some he relieued with his money, some by his authoritie, some by his good worde and commendac*i*on, some with his good counsaile. Neither was there euer any man (woorthy to be relieued) that sought reliefe and helpe at his hande, that went not from him merie and cheerfull. For he was (as a man may say) the publique patrone of all the poore; And thought that he did procure to himselfe a great benefite and treasure as often as he could by his counsaile deliuer and ridd any man in any perplexitie and difficile cause, as often as he could pacifie and reconcile any that were at variance and debate.

The King consults More for

Nowe a litle to speake againe of the kinges great affaires then in hande. The king, shortlye vpon his

MSS. E L R^2 Y C H R B.

1–2. *for . . . relieue*] for according to our releue Y. 4. *saide secretly*] secretly said H R—said *being interlineated in* R. 5. *sonne*] some Y. 5–6. *for they . . . cast*] for they see that by the verdict of the Jury they may cast H. 6. *from*] of H. 11. *that*] *Omitted in* L R^2 B. 12. *or*] and B. 12. *him*] *Omitted in* H. 13. *his*] *Omitted in* H R. 14. *his authoritie*] autoritie B. 14. *some . . . worde*] some with his good wordes Y; some with his good worde C. 15. *some . . . counsaile*] *Inserted after* money *above* (*cf.* l. 14) *in* R^2, *and omitted after* commendacion. 15. *his*] *Omitted in* H. 17. *sought*] sought for H R. 17. *hande*] handes H R B. 18. *from him*] away Y. 18. *cheerfull*] cheirefully C. 19. *all*] *Omitted in* R^2. 20. *thought*] though R^2 Y. 21. *as* (2)] *Interlineated in* R. 21–22. *deliuer and ridd*] rid and delyver Y. 22. *difficile*] difficulte L R^2 B. 23. *pacifie and reconcile*] reconcile & pacify R^2. 23. *at*] in H R. 25. *great*] *Interlineated in* R.

the fourth time on the divorce. More cannot, with his conscience, safely serve his Grace's contentation. [ROPER.]

entrie into the office of the Chauncelloursшipp, moued eftsones S*ir* Thomas More to weigh and consider his great matter; who, falling downe vpon his knees, humbly besought his highnes to stande his gratious Soueraine, as he euer since [his] entrie first into his graces seruice had founde him, saying there was nothing in the worlde had beene so grieuous vnto his heart as to remember that he was not able, as he willingly would with the losse of one of his limmes, for that matter any thing to finde whereby he could with his conscience safely serue his graces contentation; as he that alway bare in minde the most godly wordes that his highnes spake vnto him at his first co*m*ming into his noble seruice, the most vertuous lesson that euer Prince taught his seruaunt, willing him first to looke vnto God, and after God vnto him, as, in good fayth, he saide he did, or els might his grace well accompt him his most vnwoorthy seruaunt. To this the king aunswered, that if he could not therein with his conscience serue him, he was content to accept his seruice otherwise; and vsing the aduise of other of his learned [fol. 16 *b*] | Councell, whose consciences could well ynough agree therewith, would neuerthelesse continue his gratious fauoure towarde him, and neuer with that matter molest his conscience after.

But S*ir* Thomas More, in processe of time, seing the king fully determined to proceede forth in the mariage of Queene Anne, when he with Bisshopps and nobles of

MSS. E L R[2] Y C H R B.

1. *the* (2)] his L R[2] B. 1. *into . . . Chauncelloursшipp*] into his Chancelorship Y. 2. *eftsones*] oftsoones R[2]. 4. *as*] and Y. 5. *his entrie*] his entry H R (*supported by* Roper); his entrance L R[2] B; the entrie E Y C. 5. *first*] *Omitted in* R[2] Y. (Roper MSS. *vary. See* Notes.) 5. *had*] he H R. 6–7. *had beene*] *Interlineated in* R. 7. *that*] *Interlineated in* R[2]. 8. *he willingly*] willinglie he B. 8. *willingly would*] would willingly H. 8. *would*] *Interlineated in* L. 8–9. *one of his*] one his R. 10. *could*] *Interlineated in* L. 11. *as he that*] as that H. 16. *well*] *Interlineated in* L. 18–19. *could not . . . serue him*] could not with his conscience serve him theirin Y. 21. *could*] would R[2]. 21. *could . . . agree*] could well enough agree R, enough *being interlineated.* 22. *gratious*] graces L R[2] H R B. (Roper *supports* gratious.) 26. *forth*] *This is the reading of all the* Harpsfield MSS.; Roper MSS. *vary between* forth *and* further. 27. *and*] *Interlineated over* of *crossed through* Y.

More declares to the Commons the judgment of the Universities with regard to the King's marriage with Anne Boleyn. But is silent as to his own opinion. He pleads to be discharged from the Chancellorship. [15 May, 1532.] [ROPER.]

the higher house of the Parliament were, for the furtherance of that mariage, co*m*maunded by the king to goe downe to the common house, to shewe vnto them both what the vniuersities, as well of other partes beyonde the Seas as of Oxforde and Cambridge, had done in that behalfe, and their Seales also testifying the same—All which matters, at the kinges request, not shewing of what minde himselfe was therein, he opened to the lower house of the Parliament—Neuertheless, doubting least further attemptes should after folowe, which, contrary to his conscience, by reason of his office, he was likely to be put vnto, he made sute to the duke of Norffolke, his singuler deere frend, to be a meane to the king that he might, with his graces fauo*ur*, be discharged of that chargeable roome of the Chauncello*ur*shipp, wherein, for certaine infirmities of his bodie, he pretended himselfe vnable any longer to serue.

More compares the King's office to that of a Shepherd. [Cf. HALL'S CHRONICLE.]

At the commencement of which Parliament, S*ir* Thomas More, standing at the right hande of the king, behinde the barre, made an eloquent oration. The effect thereof was that the office of a Shepherd did most liuely resemble the office and gouernment of a king, whose riches if [ye] respect, he is but a riche man; if his hono*ur*, he is but honorable; and so forth; but the office of a Shepherde, as he well and wittilye declared, acco*m*modating the prosequution thereof to his purpose and the summoning of the present Parliament, comprised

MSS. E L R² Y C H R B.

1. *were*] More, *corrected from* more, L; more R² B. 1–2. *furtherance*] furtheraune R². 2. *mariage*] *Omitted in* L R² B. 5. *Oxforde*] Oxon. R²; Oxenford C. 7. *at*] *Corrected from* as E; as Y. 10. *least*] that L H. 10. *attemptes*] attempt Y. 10. *after folowe*] followe after L R² H R B. 12. *likely*] like H R. 13. *deere*] good L R² B. 15. *of the*] of H R. 19–20. *standing . . . made*] standinge behinde the barre at þe righte hande of þe Kinge made R². 20. *an*] *Omitted in* H. 21. *thereof*] whereof L B. 22. *resemble*] *Interlineated in* L. 22. *and*] and and E. 23. *if ye respect*] L C (*with* he *interlineated in* L *above* ye *and crossed through*); he E R² Y H R; wee B. 23. *he*] *Corrected from* his R². 23. *a riche man*] *In* L a *and* man *are interlineated.* 25. *declared*] *Interlineated over* declareth *crossed through* Y. 26. *prosequution*] persecution B. 26. *thereof*] there R²; *omitted in* H. 27. *the*] to þe C. 27. *the* (2)] this H R. 27. *present*] *Omitted in* B.

in a maner all or the chiefe and principall function of a king.

Nowe, whereas I declared that S*ir* Thomas More, vpon consideration and deepe foresight of thinges hanging vpon the Realme and imminent, was desirous to be exonerated and discharged of that office, pretending infirmities, Truth it is that this was no bare and naked pretence, but that it was so with him in very deede; for he was troubled with a disease in his brest, which continuing with him many monethes, after he consulted with [fol. 17 *a*] the phisitians, who made him aunswere | that longe diseases were daungerous; adding further that his disease could not shortly be holpen, but by a litle and litle, with continuance of longe time, by rest, good diet and phisicke, and yet could not they appoint any certaine time when he should recouer, or be quite ridd and cured. This thing S*ir* Thomas More well weighing with himselfe, and that eyther he must forgoe the office, or forslowe some part of his requisite and dutifull diligence, seing him selfe not able to welde and dispatche the manifolde and weightie affaires of that office, and that with longe continuance in the office he was like to be bereaued of the office and his life withall, determined with himselfe rather to forgoe the one then both.

More's ill-health a true plea for discharge from the Chancellorship. [More to Erasmus.]

And yet his aduersaries and euill willers did spreade and cast rumours abrode to make him the more odious, that with the kinges displeasure he was against his will thrust out of the Chauncellourshipp. And newes

More's enemies declare his discharge from the Chancellorship to be

MSS. E L R^2 Y C H R B.

1. *maner*] matter Y. 1. *function*] functions L. 3. *I declared that*] *Interlineated in* R^2. 4. *consideration and*] *Interlineated in* L. 5. *and imminent*] *Omitted in* B. 5. *to be*] to be to be H. 7. *is*] *Interlineated over* was *crossed through* L. 7. *this*] it L R^2 B. 7. *bare and naked*] naked or bare H R. 10. *after*] *Omitted in* B. 10. *consulted*] had consulted H. 11. *the*] many L R^2 B. 11. *made him aunswere that*] who aunswered that B. 13. *shortly*] *Omitted in* L R^2 B. 13. *holpen*] helped Y. 14. *litle*] a little L C H. 14. *of longe*] and long Y. 16. *or*] & H. 16. *and*] or Y. 18. *the*] that L. 20. *selfe*] *Omitted in* B. 22. *the*] that H. 23. *of the . . . life*] of his life and office H. 24. *with himselfe*] *Omitted in* L R^2 B. 25. *spreade*] speak Y. 27–28. *he . . . thrust*] against his will he was thrust H R.

due to the King's displeasure. [ERASMUS.]

At the appointment of Lord Audley as More's successor, the Duke of Norfolk declares the truth as to More's resignation. [MORE to ERASMUS.]

thereof came with meruailous speede into farre countreys, and that his Success*our* had dimissed out of prison such as he had imprisoned for religion. But a world it is to see the wonderfull malice of these men, who knewe, or might haue soone learned, that at the very same time that his Successour, the Lorde Audley, was first placed in Westminster, the duke of Norffolke, high Treasorer of Inglande, did openly, by the kinges speciall co*m*maundement, declare that S*ir* Thomas More with much adoe, and after his earnest sute and Supplication, was hardly suffred to dimisse the saide office. And surely as the king, in preferring him to that roome, tendred the co*m*mon wealth in choosing S*ir* Thomas More as the meetest man for it (as he was in very deede) so dismissed him vpon his earnest sute, tendring S*ir* Thomas Mores health.

Lord Audley declares the same. [MORE to ERASMUS.]

Nowe the verye same that the duke declared, the saide Lorde Audley, his success*our*, in the kinges owne presence and by his co*m*maundement, did declare and notifie in his oration made the Parliament folowing.

More declares the same in his own Epitaph. [WORKS, pp. 1419-22.]

Which Epitaph his enemies censure as vain-glorious.

Yea, the very same (to represse malitious talke and rumours) S*ir* Thomas More himselfe declared, with the Summarie and effectuall discourse of his life, in a certaine Epitaphe, which he caused to be put vpon his Sepulchre, that he had prouided for himselfe and his wiues at Chelsey. His aduersaries mouthes being at length stopped with so manifest and manifolde apparant matter to the contrarye, lefte that pratling and talking, and beganne, causelesse, to prattle and talke against his

MSS. E L R^2 Y C H R B.

1. *thereof came*] came thereof H R. 2. *and that*] þat L. 2. *Successour*] successours Y. 3. *But . . . is*] But it is a worlde R^2. 3. *is*] was Y. 4–5. *who knewe . . . learned*] who well knew or soone might haue well learned R^2, *the second* well *being interlineated.* 8. *kinges*] King B. 11. *suffred*] *Interlineated over* offered *crossed through* R. 12. *in preferring*] preferringe H. 14–15. *as . . . him*] *Interlineated in* R. 14. *dismissed*] dismissing *with* ing *partly erased, and* ed *substituted* L; he dysmyssed B. 15. *tendring*] tendred Y C. 17. *declared*] declarith Y. 19. *and*] *Interlineated in* L. 20. *made the*] made in the B. 22. *himselfe*] *Omitted in* H R. 26. *wiues*] wife, *corrected from* wive, B. 27. *apparent*] *Interlineated in* L. 28. *lefte*] least R^2 Y. 29. *causelesse*] causelesly C. 29. *prattle and*] *Omitted in* B. 29. *against*] againe Y.

THE MORE TOMB IN CHELSEA OLD CHURCH.

Harpsfield defends More and his Epitaph.

saide Epitaphe as very vaineglorious*. Against whose [fol. 17 *b*] false slaunderous calumnies, the | open tried truth of all his vertuous innocent life doth defende it selfe, And I doubt not Gods owne iudgement agreable thereto, as it did longe before the blessed patient man Job, who*m* his frendes that came in his wofull distresse to visite him, did muche after like maner charge him as these his enemies charged S*ir* Thomas More. For surely he was a man of so excellent and singuler giftes and qualities (into the brest of which kinde of men some spice of vaineglory often times creepeth) so farre from it as lightly a man might be. And in verye truth, in the endighting of this his Epitaphe, he had not so much regarde vnto himselfe, or his owne estimation, as to Gods cause and religion, which he had by open bookes against the Protestant*es* defended; least it might (if such rumours blowen and sowen abrode by them* were taken for truth, that for his fault, or vpon displeasure, he was displaced) somewhat be impaired or hindred. Wherefore true it is, for all their babling, that as he entred into the office with the kinges high and singuler fauo*ur*, with the great good will of the nobilitie, and wonderfull reioycing of the whole people, and vsed the office to the contentation of the king and all sort of good people, and the profite of the whole co*m*mon wealth, So it is true also that he was most fauourably and honorably dimissed, after longe sute, from the saide office. At the which time the king saide to him that in any sute that he should

The King promises More the

MSS. E L R² Y C H R B.

1. *vaineglorious*] C; vaine aud glorious E L R² Y H R B. 2. *slaunderous calumnies*] calumnious (*corrected from* calumnies) slaunders B. 2. *all*] *Omitted in* H R. 3. *vertuous, innocent*] vertues & innocente R². 4. *Gods*] God his B. 9. *so*] such H. 9. *and qualities*] *Omitted in* B. 10. *of*] of the Y. 11. *so farre*] & yet so far B. 11. *lightly*] likely B. 12. *a man*] man C. 13. *had*] maid Y. 17. *them were*] L R² B; them if it were E Y C H R. 19. *be*] *Corrected from* he L. 19. *or*] or or Y. 19. *true*] *Interlineated over* tyme *crossed through* R. 20. *for all*] that for all B. 20. *babling*] brabling Y. 20. *the*] that H R. 21. *great*] *Interlineated in* R. 26. *most*] *Omitted in* R². 26. *honorably*] most honorably R². 27. *At*] *Corrected from* And L. 28. *that* (2)] *Omitted in* L R² H B.

continuance of his favour. [ROPER.]

afterwarde haue to his grace, that eyther should concerne the saide S*ir* Thomas Mores hono*ur* (for that worde it liked his highnes to vse to him) or that should apperteyne to his profite, he should finde his highnes a good and gratious Lorde to him.

MSS. E L R[2] Y C H R B.

1. *afterwarde*] after L R[2] Y B. 1. *haue*] *Omitted in* H. 2. *the saide*] *Interlineated in* L ; *omitted in* B. 3. *to* (2)] *Corrected from* towarde E. 3. *should*] could Y. 4. *his* (2)] *Interlineated in* R[2]. 4–5. *a good and gratious*] a a most gratious R[2]. 4. *and*] *Omitted in* L B.

[II]

More's later life and his death, though also the subject of calumny, were equally blameless, as Harpsfield will show.

True it is also, that notwithstanding the like calumniations and false slaunders of his aduersaries, he liued and dyed also afterwarde (though these men defame him with a newe founde [fond] kinde of treason) most innocently and most honorably. The full declaration of which his life and death doth nowe remaine to be by vs opened and declared.

But Harpsfield will first deal with More's private life and his writings.

But inasmuch as we haue many other thinges touching this man woorthy to be remembred, we will interlace them before. And as we haue hitherto prosequuted his publique doinges in the common affaires of the Realme, himselfe being the highest magistrate, after the king, in the same; and will hereafter also in conuenient place declare [what] accompt he rendred to the Prince and magistrates, being afterwarde a priuate man, of his publique doinges; so will we nowe in the meane while recount vnto you First his priuate, secrete and domesticall life and trade with his wife, children, familie and others; And then, because the world well knew him, and so tooke [fol. 18 a] him, and the | testimonie of learned men and his owne bookes withall bare good and substantiall recorde thereof, for a great excellent learned man, we will not altogether pretermitt his saide bookes, but speake so muche as shall seeme to serue the turne.

First then [will] we laye before you a description and

MSS. E L R^2 Y C H R B.

2. *and false slaunders*] of falce slaunderers Y. 4. *a*] all Y. 4. *fond*] L R^2 Y C H R B; *omitted in* E. 5. *honorably*] horeibly Y. 6. *remaine . . . opened*] remaine by vs to be opened L R^2 Y B. 10. *as*] *Omitted in* L R^2. 11. *the* (1)] *Omitted in* L R^2 Y B. 11. *the* (2)] this H. 13. *and will*] we will H R. 14. *what*] L R^2 C H R B; that E Y. 14. *to*] *Omitted in* C. 15. *afterwarde*] after Y. 16. *so will we nowe*] & now H R. 16. *we*] *Interlineated over* vs *crossed through* L. 16. *the*] *Interlineated in* L. 16. *while*] tyme H R. 17. *priuate*] pivate Y. 17. *domesticall*] modesticall Y. 18. *wife, children*] wife and Children H R. 21. *bookes*] there R^2; boke Y. 22. *learned*] *Omitted in* H. 23. *his saide bookes*] the same bookes L; þe sayd Bookes R^2 H B. 25. *will we laye*] will we lay Y C; we will lay L; we laye E R^2 H R B.

More's practice of confession and attendance at Mass before entering into any matter of importance. [ROPER.]

declaration of some part of his saide private life and doinges. In whom this is principally to be considered, as the roote and head of all his well doinges, that alwayes he had a speciall and singuler regarde and respect to God-warde, and to keepe his conscience whole, sincere and vpright. And this among other was one of his good, vertuous and godlye properties, conditions and customes, that when he entred into any matter or office of importance, as when he was chosen one of the kinges priuie counsaile, when he was sent Ambassadour, appointed Speaker of the Parliament, made Lorde Chauncell*our*, or when he tooke any other weightie matter or affaire vpon him, he would goe to the Churche and be confessed, he woulde heare Masse and be houseled.

More sings in the choir at Chelsea Church. The Duke of Norfolk censures him for acting as a parish clerk. [ROPER, with addition.]

He vsed, yea, being Lorde Chauncell*our*, to sitt and sing in the quire with a surplise on his backe. And when that the duke of Norffolke, co*m*ming at a time to Chelsey to dyne with him, fortuned to finde him in his attire and trade, going homewarde after seruice, arme in arme with him, saide after this fasshion: "God body, God body, my Lorde Chauncell*our*, a parishe clarke, a parishe clarke! you dishon*our* the king and his office"; "Nay," quoth S*ir* Thomas More, smiling vpon the duke, "your grace may not thinke that the king, your master and mine, will with me, for seruing of God his master, be offended, or thereby accompt his office dishonoured." Wherin S*ir* Thomas More did very godly and deuoutly, and spake verye truely and wisely. What would the duke haue saide, if he had seene that mightie and noble

MSS. E L R² Y C H R B.

1. *saide*] *Interlineated in* R. 2. *is*] *Interlineated in* B. 4. *and singuler*] *Omitted in* Y. 7. *vertuous*] virtues L. 7. *properties*] proprieties L. 8. *office*] *Interlineated over* off vs *crossed through* L. 10. *when*] *Interlineated in* L. 12. *matter or affaire*] matters or affaires H ; matter or affaires R; affaire B. 13. *and be*] to be L R² B. 17. *that*] *Interlineated in* L ; *omitted in* H R. 17. *at a*] on a L. 18. *his*] that B. 19. *and trade*] *Omitted in* B. 20. *this*] *Interlineated over* þat *crossed through* L. 21–22. *a parishe clarke, a parishe clarke*] *Once only in* L. 25. *of*] *Omitted in* L R² B. 27. *More*] *Omitted in* C. 28. *spake*] did speake B. 28. *wisely*] visely R². 29. *that*] þe L R² C B.

Emperoure, Charles the great, playing the very same part; or king Dauid, longe before, hopping and dauncing naked before the arke?

More devotes Fridays to godly exercises. [Roper.]

He was sometime for godly purpose desirous to be solitarie, and to sequester him selfe from worldly company. And therefore the better to satisfie and accomplishe this his godly desire, he builded, a good distance from his mansion house at Chelsey, a place called the newe building, wherein there was a chappell, a librarie and a gallerie. In which, as his vse was vpon other dayes to occupye himselfe in* prayer and studie* together, so on the Fryday there vsually continued he from morning till evening, spending his time onely in deuout prayers and spirituall exercises.

More's New Building. [Roper.]

More's Shirt of Hair and other austerities. [Roper, with addition.]

As to the poore for Gods sake he was good and pitifull, so vsed he another rare and singuler kinde of almes of his [fol. 18 b] | owne body, as to punish the same with whippes, the cordes knotted. And albeit by reason he would not be noted of singularitie, he conformed himselfe outwardly to other men in his apparell, according to his state and vocation, yet howe litle he inwardly esteemed such vanities, it well appered by the shirt of heare that he ware secretly next his body; whereof no person was priuie but his daughter onely, mistris Margarete Roper, whom for her secrecie he aboue all other trusted, caus[ing] her, as neede required, to washe the same shirt of heare; sauing that it chaunced once that as he sate at Supper in the sommer, singly in his doublett and hose, wearing vpon the saide secrete shirt

MSS. E L R² Y C H R B.

1. *Emperoure, Charles*] Emperour called Charles C. 4. *purpose*] purposes H R. 5. *to sequester*] sequester H. 11. *in prayer and studie*] L R² Y C H R B (*supported by* Roper); in studie and prayer E. 12. *he*] *Omitted in* H. 13. *till*] to L. 13. *onely*] *Omitted in* H. 15. *for . . . was*] he for Gods sake was B. 17. *the* (2)] and R² Y. 18. *by reason*] *Interlineated in* R. 19. *conformed*] comforted Y. 19. *other*] othe R. 20–21. *yet . . . inwardly*] yet litle inwardly he H. 21. *such*] those H. 21–22. *well appered*] will appeare Y. 22. *the*] *Interlineated in* R². 22. *ware secretly*] secretly ware H R. 23–24. *but . . . onely*] but only his daughter R²; but his daughter B. 25. *other*] *Omitted in* H. 25. *causing*] R² B (*supported by* Roper); causing, *corrected from* caused, L; caused E Y C H R. 26. *same*] sayd R². 26. *shirt*] *Omitted in* H. 26. *it*] he L. 27. *singly*] single R² Y. 28. *secrete*] *Omitted in* L R² H R B.

of heare a plaine linnen shirt without ruffe or coller, that a yonge gentlewoman, mistris Moore, sister to the saide Margarete, [chauncing to espie the same, began to laughe at it. His daughter Margarete], not ignorant of his maner, perceaving the same, priuily tolde him of it. And he, being sory that she sawe it, presently amended it.

More not ambitious of worldly honour or reward. [Cf. ROPER.]

As he was not ambitious and greedie of hon*our* and worldly preferment, and one that in twentie yeres seruice to the king neuer craued* of him any thing* for himselfe; and as he, after that he was by his well deseruing and by the kinges free and meere goodnes aduaunced and promoted, did not looke vp on high, and solemnely sett by himselfe, with the contempt and disdaine of other; so was he nothing greeued, but rather gladd (for, as I haue shewed, he did procure it) when he was ridd of the Chauncelloursshipp. And whereas vpon the holye dayes, during his high office, one of his gentlemen, when seruice at the Churche was done, ordinarily vsed to come to my Lady his wiues pewe, and say vnto her, "Madame, my Lorde is gone"; the next holye day after the surrender of his office and departure of his gentlemen, he came vnto my Lady his wiues pewe himselfe, and making a low cursey, saide [vnto her], "Madame, my Lorde is gone."

More's fun: "Madam, my Lord is gone." [ROPER.]

The burning of More's barns; his fortitude in misfortune;

As prosperitie did nothing lifte him vp with hawtines and pride, so no mischaunce or trouble that very heauily fell vpon him afterwarde, could infringe or breake his

MSS. E L R^2 Y C H R B.

1. *of*] *Omitted in* H. 3–4. *chauncing to espie the same, began to laughe at it. His daughter Margarete*] L Y C B; (*supported by* Roper); R^2 *as* L Y C B, *but omitting* Margarete; *omitted in* E H R. 4. *not ignorant*] being not ignorant L; and not ignorant H. 5. *same, priuily*] sayde priuity R^2. 7–8. *and worldly preferment*] *Omitted in* B. 8. *to*] of H R. 9. *craued of him any thing*] L R^2 Y C B; craued any thing of him E H R. 9–10. *and . . . by* (1)] and as he that was by B. 11. *free and meere*] meere & free H R; meere B. 12. *on high . . . sett*] vpon his high and solemne seate Y. 12. *sett*] satt H; sitt R. 13. *with . . . other*] with contemning other B. 14. *as*] *Omitted in* Y. 15. *when*] when as L R^2 B. 16. *his*] þis C. 17. *at*] of L. 19. *say*] said H R. 19–23. *the next . . . is gone*] *Omitted in* B. 20. *holye*] *Omitted in* H R. 21. *Lady*] Ladies Y. 22. *making*] *Omitted in* H. 22. *a*] *Omitted in* R^2. 23. *vnto her*] vnto hir L R^2 Y C H R; vnter E. 25. *mischaunce*] adversitie B. 25. *or*] and Y; nor B.

great patience and constancie, as we shall declare hereafter more at large. A little before he was made Lorde Chauncell*our*, it chaunced his barnes and all his corne at Chelsey, by retchlesse negligence, to be burnt and consumed with fire, with some of his neighbours houses; whereof he being at the Court and vnderstanding, wrote to his wife a comfortable letter, willing her, their children, and all their familie, to repaire to the Churche and geue [fol. 19 *a*] God thankes, who might take away all the residue | they had besides. And willed diligent searche and inquirie to be made what damage his poore neighbours had taken thereby, which, he saide, should be recompenced and restored (as it was) to the vttermost farthing.

he compensates his poore neighbours who suffered by the fire. [1529.] [WORKS, pp. 1418-19.]

And as in all other thinges he had a grounded and a profounde iudgement, So had he a deepe foresight (when fewe thought litle of it) and, as it proued, a sure ayme of the lamentable world that folowed, and that we haue sithens full heauily felt. And longe before tooke it so in his heart, and suche compassion of it, that he gladly would haue with his owne present destruction * repulsed and redeemed the imminent mischaunces.

More's foresight.

It fortuned he walked on a time with M*aster* Will*iam* Roper, his sonne in lawe, alonge the temmes side at

The three things in

MSS. E L R^2 Y C H R B.

1. *great*] *Omitted in* H. 1. *and*] or H. 1. *declare hereafter*] hereafter declare H R. 4. *retchlesse*] wretchlesse, *corrected from* wretchtches, L. 4–5. *and consumed*] *Omitted in* B. 5. *with some*] & some H R. 5. *houses*] howss H. 7. *her*] *Omitted in* R^2. 8. *geue*] to giue R^2. 9. *who*] which Y. 9. *take*] haue taken H R (haue *being interlineated in* R). 9–10. *they had besides*] besides that they had H R. 10. *And willed*] allso he willed B. 10. *willed*] willing H. 14. *as*] *Interlineated in* E C; *omitted in* Y. 14. *in all . . . had*] he had in all other thinges H R. 14–15. *and a profounde*] & profound H R B. 16. *of it*] one yt R^2. 16. *it proued*] it is prooued L R^2 H R B. 16–17. *a sure ayme*] as sewer any Y. 17. *folowed*] followeth Y. 19. *so in*] *Interlineated in* L *over some word crossed through.* 19. *in his heart*] in harte H; in his harte R, his *being interlineated.* 20–21. *would haue with his own present destruction repulsed*] C; E Y H R *as* C, *but* destruction haue repulsed; would haue repulsed (*omitting* with . . . destruction) L R^2; would repulsed (*omitting* haue *and* with . . . destruction) B. 22. *he walked on a time*] on a tyme he walked H R. 22. *walked*] walking Y. 23. *temmes*] Thames L, *with* Tha *corrected from* tem; Thames R^2 H R; temmes *corrected from* temnes Y.

Christendom that More wished to see. [ROPER.]

Chelsey, and in talking of other thinges, he saide vnto him:

"Nowe would to our Lorde, sonne Roper, vpon condition that three thinges were well stablished in Christendome, I were put in a sacke, and here presently cast into the temmes."

"What great thinges be those, S*ir*," quoth M*aster* Will*iam* Roper, "that should moue you so to wishe?"

"Wouldest thou knowe what they be, sonne Roper?" quoth he.

"Yea, mary, with good will, S*ir*, if it please you," q*uo*th M*aster* W*illiam* Roper.

"In faith, sonne, they be these," [saide] he. "The first is, That where the most part of christen Princes be at mortall warre, they were [all] at an vniuersall peace. The second, that where the Churche of Christe is at this present sore afflicted with many errors and heresies, it were setled in a perfect vniformitie of religion. The thirde, that where the kinges matter of his mariage is nowe come in question, that it were to the glory of God and quietnes of all partes brought to a good conclusion." Whereby, as it was to be gathered, he iudged that otherwise it would be a disturbance to a great part of Christendome.

More foresees the growth of heresy. [ROPER.]

It fortuned also at another time, before the matter of matrimonie was brought in question, When M*aster*

MSS. E L R^2 Y C H R B.

1. *and*] *Omitted in* Y C H. 1. *in*] *Interlineated in* L. 3. *to our Lorde*] to god R^2. 4. *that*] *Omitted in* Y C. 5. *in*] into R^2 H R. 5. *here*] *Omitted in* R^2. 6. *temmes*] (*Spellings as for p.* 67, *l.* 23, *above.*) 7. *be*] are H R. 8. *that . . . wishe*] *Interlineated in* R. 9–12. *Wouldest . . . Roper*] *Omitted in* R. 9. *What . . . Roper*] son Roper what they be L R^2 B. 13. *saide*] said L R^2 Y C H B (*supported by* Roper); quoth E R. 14. *where*] where as R^2, *with* as *interlineated.* 14. *part*] *Omitted in* Y. 15. *warre*] warrs H R. 15. *all at*] L R^2 Y C B (*supported by* Roper); at E H R. 17. *errors and heresies*] errores heresies L, errores *being interlineated.* 18. *in*] with H R. 19. *where*] whereas Y. 19. *his*] *Omitted in* H R. 21. *partes*] parties L R^2 B; persons Y. (*Partes* = "parties." *See* Notes.) 22. *as*] *Omitted in* B. 22–23. *iudged . . . a* (1)] iudged that it would be a L, *with* that *interlineated over* it would *crossed through, and* it would be a *interlineated over* beve *crossed through.* 23. *to*] of Y. 25. *another*] a another R, *with* a *interlineated.*

William Roper, in talke with Sir Thomas More, of a certaine ioye commended vnto him the happy state of this Realme, that had so Catholike a Prince that no heretike durst shew his face, so vertuous and learned a Clergie, so graue and sounde a nobilitie, and so loving,* obedient subiectes all in one fayth agreing together; "Troth it is, in deede, sonne Roper," quoth he, and in commending all degrees and states of the same, went farre beyond Master William Roper; "And yet, sonne [fol. 19 b] Roper, | I praye God," saide he, "that some of vs, as high as we seeme to sitt vpon the mountaines, treading heretikes vnder our feete like antes, liue not the day that we gladly would wishe to be at [a] league and composition with them, to lett them haue their churches quietly to themselues, so that they would be content to lett vs haue ours quietly to our selues."

And when that Master William Roper had tolde him many considerations why he had no cause so to say, "Well," saide he, "I praye God, sonne, some of vs liue not till that day," shewing no reason why he should put any doubt therin.

To whom the saide Master Roper saide: "Sir, it is very desperately spoken." For that worde vsed Master Roper, for the which afterwarde, as he hath tolde his frendes, he cryed God mercy, calling it a vile worde.

Who, by those wordes perceauing Master Roper in a

MSS. E L R^2 Y C H R B.

1–2. *of . . . ioye*] *Interlineated in* L. 3. *had*] *Omitted in* C. 4. *vertuous and*] *Omitted in* L. 5–6. *loving, obedient*] L Y C B (*supported by most* Roper MSS.); loving and obedient E R^2 H R. (*See* Notes.) 7. *in deede*] *Interlineated in* R. 8–9. *the same . . . And yet*] the same yow are to be commended, & yet B. 9. *William*] *Omitted in* R^2. 10–11. *as high*] highe, *corrected from* as, H. 11. *sitt*] set Y. 13. *gladly would wishe*] would gladly wish H R B. 13–14. *at a league and composition*] C (*supported by* Roper); at league and composition E Y H R; at large composition L R^2 B. 14–15. *them . . . quietly to*] *Omitted in* B. 16. *ours*] our church Y; our Churches H R. 16. *to*] *Interlineated over* by *crossed through* L. 17. *when that*] when B. 19–20. *some . . . day*] you live not to that day L R^2 B. 22. *the saide*] *Omitted in* R^2 B. 22. *Master Roper*] Master William Roper L B. 22. *Roper saide*] Roper replied saying B. 23. *very*] *Omitted in* R^2. 25. *calling*] *Corrected from* called R^2. 26. *who . . . perceauing*] Sir Thomas More perceuing B. 26. *those*] these R^2. 26. *Master Roper*] Master William Roper L R^2.

fume, saide merily to him: "Well, well, sonne Roper, it shall not be so, [it shall not be so]."

More foresees and fears the administering of the Oaths. [ROPER.]

Againe, when Cranmer, Archbisshopp of Caunterbury, had determined the matter touching the kinges mariage (to whom a Co*mm*issio*n* was from the king to that intent directed) euen according to the kinges owne minde, and that therevpon the king had sequestred himselfe from the Churche of Rome, pretending that he had no iustice at the Popes handes, S*ir* Thomas More saide to his sonne in lawe, M*aster* W*illia*m Roper: "God geue grace, sonne, that these matters be not within a while confirmed with othes." At the which time the saide M*aster* W*illia*m, seing litle likelyhood thereof, and yet fearing least for his fore speaking it would the sooner come to passe, waxed therefore for this his so saying much offended with him.

More predicts that misfortunes will follow the oppression and casting out of the Clergy. [WORKS, p. 313.]

And whereas in a booke intituled The Supplication of beggers, the autho*ur*, vnder an holy, fonde, pretensed colour of helping the poore and impotent, craftily goeth about to oppresse and cast out the Clergie, bearing men in hande that then, after that the Gospell should be

MSS. E L R^2 Y C H R B.

1. *Well, well*] well R^2. 2. *it shall not be so, it shall not be so*] yt shall not be so, yt shall not be so C; *once only* E L R^2 Y H R B. (Roper MSS. *vary. See* Notes.) 4. *the* (2)] *Omitted in* H. 5. *a Commission was*] was a commission L R^2 B. 5. *from the*] *Cropped in* L. 6. *directed*] derived B. 6–8. *directed . . . from*] derected and therevpon the kinge had requested even accordinge to the kinges owne mynde himselfe from H, *evidently an unintelligent transcript of an insertion like that of* R, *which has* and therevpon the king had sequestered *interlineated between* to that intent directed *and* even according to the kinges owne minde himself from, *with no indication as to where the interlineated words should be inserted.* 6. *kinges*] king his B. 6. *minde*] desire R^2. 7–8. *sequestered . . . the*] sequestered him selfe from þe, selfe from *being interlineated*, R^2. 10. *in lawe*] *Omitted in* B. 10. *William*] *Omitted in* B. 11. *these matters*] this matter Y. 11. *within a while*] a while within R, within *being interlineated.* 12. *At the*] At L R^2 B. 13. *William*] Roper B. 13. *yet*] *Omitted in* H. 15. *waxed*] was, *corrected from* waxed, R^2. 15. *therefore*] *Omitted in* R^2. 15. *this his so saying*] his so saying L B; his sayinge R^2, *with* soe *crossed through after* his; R *as* E Y C H, *but with* this *interlineated.* 16. *much offended*] *Interlineated in* L *over* verie wroth *crossed through.* 18. *of*] of the Y C. 18. *an*] a H. 20. *oppresse and*] *Omitted in* L B. 21. *after that*] after L B.

preached, beggers and bawdes should decrease, ydle folkes and theeves be the fewer, and the Realme increase in riches, and so forth; S*ir* Thomas More sheweth, and truely, as it were an occean Sea of many and great mischieuous euentes that would (as haue in deede) thereof redounde and ouerwhelme the Realme. "Then," saith he, "shall Luthers Gospell come in, then shall Tindalls Testament be taken vp, then shall false heresies be preached, then shall the Sacramentes be sett at naught, then shall fasting and prayer be neglected, then shall holy Saintes be blasphemed, then shall Almightie God be displeased, then shall he withdrawe his grace and lett all runne to ruine, then shall all vertue be had in derision, then shall all vice reigne and runne forth vnbridled, then shall youth leaue labour and all occupation, then shall folke waxe ydle and fall to vnthriftines, then shall whoores and theeues, beggers and bawdes increase, then shall vnthriftes flocke together and swarme [fol. 20 *a*] about, and eche beare him | bolde of other, then shall all lawes be laughed to scorne, then shall the seruauntes set naught by their masters, and vnruly people rebell against their rulers. Then will rise vp rifling and robberie, murther and mischiefe and plaine insurrection, whereof [what] would be the ende, or when you should see it, onely God knoweth." And that Luthers newe Gospell hath taken such effect, not onely in Almaine,

MSS. E L R^2 Y C H R B.

1. *folkes*] folke R^2 B. 2. *in*] with R^2. 3. *riches*] ritche H. 3. *and so forth*] &c L B. 3–4. *sheweth . . . Sea*] shewed truly & as it weare in an Ocean Sea H; R *as* E L R^2 Y C, *but* in an *for* an; B *as* E L R^2 Y C, *but* sheweth trulie *for* sheweth and truely. 4–5. *many . . . mischieuous*] many greate & mischeeuous R^2. 5. *as haue*] *Omitted in* L R^2 B. 6. *ouerwhelme*] overwhelmed Y. 6. *saith*] sayd R^2. 8. *false*] *Crossed through in* R^2. 10. *shall*] shall shall H. 10. *prayer*] praying Y. 13. *then shall all*] *Omitted in* H. 13–14. *vertue . . . derision*] *Interlineated in* R. 14. *then shall all*] *Interlineated in* R. 14. *all*] *Omitted in* C. 15. *youth*] all youth B. 16–17. *then . . . whoores and*] *Omitted in* R^2. 16. *folke*] folkes H; people B. 17. *theeues*] Thewes H. 19. *him*] *Omitted in* R^2. 19–20. *then shall . . . scorne*] *Omitted in* H R. 20. *the seruauntes*] servantes H R. 22. *will*] will *interlineated over* shall R; shall B. 23. *robberie*] robbing Y. 23. *murther and*] *Cropped in* L. 24. *what*] L R^2 Y C H R B; when E. 24–25. *you should see*] you shall see L R^2 Y B; should you see H.

but in other countreys also, in Flaunders and Fraunce, and euen neerer home, the wofull experience doth certainly and feelingly, to the great griefe of all the good, testimonie to the worlde.

And foretells the fall of Anne Boleyn. [ROPER, with addition.]

But that I shall nowe declare, me thinketh may rather hange vppon some priuate and secrete reuelation and diuine information then any worldly and wise coniecture or foresight; by what meanes soeuer he thought it, or for what cause soeuer he spake it, truth it is, that at a certaine time when his daughter Margarete resorted to him to the towre, after that he had firste questioned with her a while of the order of his wife, children and state of his house in his absence, he asked her howe Queen Anne did.

"In fayth, father," quoth she, "neuer better."

"Neuer better, Megge!" quoth he. "Alas! Megge, it pitieth me to remember [into] what miserie, poore soule, she shall shortly come."

Into what miserie she within a while after fell, and ere that yere turned ouer wherein *Sir* Thomas More dyed, all Inglande did well knowe, and was not a litle astonied at so straunge a sight and euent; which neither *Sir* Thomas nor any man els could well by his meere naturalls foresee or foretell.

He was also of so milde, gentle and patient nature, that

MSS. E L R² Y C H R B.

1. *in* (2)] as C. 4. *testimonie*] testify L R² B. 5. *But . . . may*] but þat which now I shall declare me think may L R² B; But that I shall now declare may H. 5. *me thinketh*] *Omitted in* R. 6. *and secrete*] *Omitted in* H R. 6. *reuelation*] *Upon an erasure in* R. 6–7. *and diuine information*] *Omitted in* B. 7. *then*] then then Y. 7. *and*] *Interlineated in* R. 8. *or*] and L R² Y. 8. *or foresight*] *Omitted in* B. 8. *meanes*] meane Y. 8. *thought*] *Interlineated over* spake *crossed through* L. 8. *or* (2)] *Interlineated over & crossed through* L. 9. *cause*] *Interlineated over some word crossed through* L. 10. *when*] when as Y. 11. *to the*] in the R². 12. *with*] *Omitted in* Y. 12. *of the order*] *Omitted in* R². 12. *wife, children*] wife and children L. 15. *In*] *Omitted in* R². 15–16. *neuer better. Neuer better*] *Once only in* L R² B. 17. *into*] L R² Y C R B (*supported by* Roper); vnto E H. 19. *Into*] *Corrected from* vnto L. 20. *turned*] were turned L R² B. 22. *and euent*] *Omitted in* B. 22–23. *Thomas nor*] Thomas Moore nor L R² Y B. 23. *naturalls*] nature H. 24. *or*] and L.

The Water-bailiff jealous for More's reputation. [ROPER.]

of all suche as falsely slaundered him, and wretchedly rayled against him, albeit he knew them, and might easily haue for that punished them, or otherwise waite them a shrewde turne, he would neuer reuenge himselfe. On a time when he was Lorde Chauncell*our* of Inglande, the Waterbayly of London, sometime his seruaunt, hearing where he had beene at dinner certaine merchaunt*es* liberally rayle against his olde master, waxed so discontented therewith that he hastilye came to him and tolde him what he had hearde. "And were I, S*ir*," quoth he, "in such fauo*ur* and authoritie with my Prince as you are, such men surely should not be suffred so villanously and falsely to misreport and slaunder me. Wherefore I woulde wishe you to call them before you, and, to their shame, for their lewde malice to punishe them."

More is tolerant of slander. [ROPER.]

Who, smiling vpon him, saide: "Why, M*aster* Waterbaylye, would you haue me* punish those by whom I receaue more benefite then by all you that be my frendes? Lett them a Gods name speake as lewdly as they list of me, and shoote neuer so many arrowes at me, as longe as [fol. 20 *b*] | they doo not hitt me, what am I the woorse? But if they shoulde once hitt me, then would it in deede not a litle trouble me. I haue more cause, I assure thee, M*aster* Waterbailie, to pitie them the*n* to be angry with them."

And makes the best of everything.

Neyther would he sinisterly or suspiciously take any thing written, spoken, or done by his frendes, peruerting, contorting and wringing it to the woorst (as many doo) but rather make the best of all thinges.

MSS. E L R² Y C H R B.

1. *slaundered*] slandered, *with* ed *interlineated*, L. 1. *wretchedly*] wickedly L R² B. 3. *haue . . . punished*] for þat have punished L R²; haue for that haue punished H; R *as* H, *but with first* haue *interlineated*; have punished B. 3. *waite*] have waighted them L R² B. 5. *of Inglande*] *Omitted in* B. 8. *against*] againe Y. 9. *came*] ran B. 10. *had hearde*] heard H R. 10. *Sir*] *Omitted in* L. 11. *and authoritie*] *Omitted in* B. 15. *to punishe*] punnish C. 17. *punish those*] ponishe those Y C (*supported by* Roper); to punish those E L R² B; punish them H R. 18. *receaue*] haue Y. 19. *a Gods*] in gods C; a God his B. 19–20. *of me*] *Omitted in* L. 20. *longe as*] *Interlineated in* R². 21. *hitt*] hurt Y. 22. *shoulde once hitt*] do once hitt L R² B. 22. *not*] *Omitted in* B. 23. *trouble*] hurt H R. 25. *or*] nor R². 26. *by his*] of his B. 27. *and*] or R² Y. 27. *woorst*] most Y.

More is ready to make friends, and careful to keep them. [ERASMUS to ULRICH VON HUTTEN.]

And lett us nowe a litle consider his demeanure and trade with and towarde his saide frendes, his wife, his children and familie, and otherwise also. As he was not very curious in choosing and pyking out his frendes, and easie to be intreated to enter frendshipp with suche as desired it; so when he was once entred in frendshipp with anye man, to keepe, nourishe and mainteyne the same he was verye vigilant and carefull. And in his owne busines and affaires as he was somewhat negligent, so in folowing and dispatching his frendes matters and affaires there was no* man more painefull and diligent.

More's easy conversation and ready wit. [ERASMUS to ULRICH VON HUTTEN, with additions.]

In conuersation with his saide frendes he was not very scrupulous and ceremonious, though he neuer omitted that that common honestie and ciuilitie required. But he was therein so sweete and pleasaunt that there was no man of so dull and heauie disposition that he did not with his companie quicken, refreshe and exhilerate. For he had a speciall* notable* gifte of eloquence, mery and pleasaunt talke, and yet without any gall or bitternes, hurt or slaunder, in his iesting to any man. This grace

MSS. E L R² Y C H R B.

1. *And*] *Omitted in* B. 1. *lett vs nowe*] now let vs H R B. 1. *a litle consider*] consider a lytle C. 2. *and trade*] *Omitted in* B. 2. *with and towarde*] towardes H; toward R B. 2. *saide*] *Omitted in* B. 2–5. *his wife . . . his frendes*] his wife his children his famylie & otherwise alsoe as he was not very curious in choosinge, in pickinge out of his friendes, *an addition on the margin in* R², *with* * *before* & easy *in text of* R². (*Cf. l.* 5.) 3. *his children*] and children Y. 3. *and familie*] his family H R. 4–5. *in choosing . . . frendes*] in choosing in picking out of his friends L; in picking out of his friends B. 5. *easie*] easily H R. 6. *desired*] desire H R. 7. *in*] into R² Y. 7. *nourishe*] & nourishe R². 9. *And . . . affaires*] And as in his owne busines and affaires C (as *being interlineated*); And as in his owne affaires B. 9. *as*] *Omitted in* L R² C B. 10. *so in*] but in R². 10. *folowing and*] *Omitted in* B. 11. *and affaires*] *Omitted in* B. 11. *no man*] L R² C B; no one man E Y H R. 11. *more*] *Interlineated over* so *crossed through* R. 14. *scrupulous and*] *Omitted in* B. 16. *no*] noe noe R². 17. *After* so, E *has* he *crossed through.* 18. *refreshe*] & refreshe R. 19. *speciall notable*] L Y C; speciall noble R² B; notable speciall E H R. 19–20. *gifte . . . bitternes*] *An addition on margin, with omission of* and yet (*cf. l.* 20) *in* R², *with* * *before* hurte (*cf. l.* 21) *in text of* R². 19. *eloquence*] eloquente B. 20. *and yet*] *Omitted in* L R² B.

is called in greeke [Aἱμυλία], whereof that noble Romane, Paulus Æmilius, was so called; and surely M*aster* More is, if euer there were any, our englishe, though not Paulus, yet Thomas Æmilius.

When he was at home, as his custome was dayly, beside his priuate prayers, with his children to say the seuen psalmes, letanie and suffrages folowing; so was his guise nightly, before he went to bedd, with his wife, children and housholde to goe to his chappell, and there vpon his knees ordinarily to say certaine psalmes and Collect*es* with them.

Family prayer the morning and evening custom of More's household. [ROPER.]

And to prouoke his wife and children to the desire of heauenly thinges, he would sometime vse these wordes folowing vnto them: "It is nowe no mastrie for you children to goe to heauen, for euerye bodye geueth you good counsaile, euery body geueth you good example; you see vertue rewarded and vice punished, so that you are caried vp to heauen euen by the chinnes. But if you shall liue the time when no man will geue you good counsaile, nor no man will geue you good example, when you shall see vertue punished and vice rewarded, if you will then stande faste and firmely sticke to God, vpon paine of my life, though you be but halfe good, God will allowe you for whole good."

More's pious counsel to his family. There is no merit in "being carried up to heaven by the chins." [ROPER.]

[fol. 21 *a*] If his wife or any of his children | had beene diseased or troubled, he would say vnto them: "We may not looke at our pleasures to goe to heauen in Fetherbeddes. It is not the way; for our Lorde himselfe went thither with great paine and by many tribulations, which was the pathe wherein he walked thither, leaving vs example to folowe

Sickness and sorrow are to be met patiently. For people cannot "go to heaven on feather-beds." [ROPER.]

MSS. E L R² Y C H R B.

1. [Aἱμυλία]] *Gap left by scribe after* greeke *in* E R² Y C H R; *omission mark in* L *after* greeke; *gap left by scribe after* called *in* B. *The reading* Aἱμυλία *is the marginal gloss in* E. 3. *any, our*] any of our L R² B. 3. *though*] toung Y. 7. *psalmes*] Phaslmes H; Phalms R. 7. *letanie*] latine Y. 8. *nightly*] mightily H. 10. *certaine*] *Omitted in* H. 15. *to goe*] for to goe H. 17–21. *so that . . . vice rewarded*] *Omitted in* Y. 18. *euen*] *Interlineated in* R. 19. *will*] *Omitted in* R². 22. *my*] *Interlineated in* R². 23. *you* (2)] *Omitted in* L. 29. *by*] *Omitted in* L.

him; for the seruaunt may not looke to be in better case then his master."

They must withstand valiantly the temptations of the devil, who is likened to an ape. [ROPER.]

And as he would in this sort persuade them to take their troubles patiently, so would he in the like sorte teache them to withstande the deuill and his temptations valiantly, saying: "Whosoeuer will marke the deuill and his temptations, shall finde him therein muche like to an ape; for like as an ape, not well looked vnto, will be busie and bolde to doo shrewde turnes, and contrarywise, being spied, will sodenly leape backe and aduenture no farther; so the deuill, finding a man ydle, slothfull, and without resistance ready to receaue his temptations, waxeth so hardie that he will not faile still to continue with him vntill to his purpose he hath throughly brought him. But on the other side, if he see a man with diligence perseuer to preuent and withstande his temptations, he waxeth so wearie that in conclusion he vtterly forsaketh him. For as the deuill of dispositio*n* is a spirite of so high a pride that he cannot abide to be mocked, so is he of nature so enuious that he feareth any more to assault him, least he should thereby not onely catche a fowle fall himselfe, but also minister to the man more matter of merite."

Roper has testified to the equability of More's temper—"never once in a fume." [ROPER.]

This and suche like was the vertuo̅us talke and trade with his saide wife and children. In whom, amonge his other excellent giftes and graces, this was one notable, that ye should neuer see him in any chafe or fretting with his saide wife, children, or familie. M*aster* W*illia*m Roper, his sonne, hath reported that in sixteene yeres and more, being in his house, he could neuer perceaue him as muche as once in any fume.

MSS. E L R² Y C H R B.

1. *may*] *Interlineated over* must *crossed through* L; must H R B. (*See* Notes.) 1. *not*] *Omitted in* H. 3. *in this sort persuade them*] perswade them in this sorte L R² B. 4. *in the like*] in like H. 6. *valiantly*] patiently C. 8. *for . . . ape*] *Interlineated in* R. 8. *looked*] liked Y. 10. *aduenture*] venter B. 16. *perseuer*] presever Y; to persevere B. 18–19. *spirite of*] spirit & of L R² B. 21. *thereby not onely*] not onely thereby H R. 25. *saide*] *Omitted in* B. 25–26. *his other*] other his R². 26. *other*] *Omitted in* H R. 27. *ye*] you L R² B. 30. *his*] *Omitted in* C. 30–31. *as muche*] *Omitted in* H R. 31. *any*] *Interlineated over* a *crossed through* E.

More prepares his family for his suffering and martyrdom. [ROPER.]

In the time somewhat before his trouble he would talke with his wife and children of the ioyes of heauen and the paines of hell, of the liues of the holy martyrs, of their greeuous martyrdomes, of their meruailous patience, of their passion[s] and deathes that they suffred rather then they would offende God; And what an happie and blessed thing it was for the loue of God to suffer losse of goodes, imprisonment, losse of landes and life also. He would farther saye to them that, vpon his faith, if he might perceaue his wife and children would incourage him to dye in a good cause, it should so comfort him that, for verye ioye thereof, it woulde make him merily rúnne to death. He shewed to them [fol. 21 b] before | what trouble might after fall to him; wherewith and the lyke vertuous talke he had so longe before his trouble incouraged them, that when he after fell into the trouble in deede, his trouble to them was a great deale the lesse: *quia spicula praeuisa minus laedunt.* No meruaile nowe, if they hauing suche a patient master and gouernour, his children and familie folowed, as they did in deede, his good aduertisementes and vertuous behauiour.

The learning of More's children. [ERASMUS.]

We haue before shewed howe he trayned vp his sonne and three daughters in vertue and learning and the knowledge of the latine and greeke tonges, In all which they did not (for their age) a litle profite: which was to Sir Thomas More no small comfort and no litle increase of the loue that otherwise (as a most naturall father)

MSS. E L R^2 Y C H R B.

2. *of the*] of B. 2. *ioyes*] ioye H R. 3. *and the*] and B. 3. *paines*] paine, *with final* s *cancelled*, Y. 3. *the holy*] holy L R^2 B. 4. *of their* (2)] & theyr L. 5. *their*] þe R^2. 5. *passions*] L R^2 B (*supported by* Roper); passion E Y C H R. 12. *that, for*] *Interlineated over* for the *crossed through* L. 12. *verye*] every Y B. 13. *runne*] to runne L R^2 B. 14. *before*] *Interlineated in* R. 15. *the lyke*] in like Y. 17. *into the*] into H. 17. *to them was*] was to them was Y; was to them H; R *as* H, *but with erasure of an interlineated* to them *before* was. 18. *the lesse*] lesse Y. 19–20. *suche a patient master*] soe patient a master R^2. 20. *patient*] parent C. 20. *and familie*] *Interlineated in* L. 21. *as they*] and they Y. 23. *howe*] you Y. 25. *of the*] of Y. 26–27. *which . . . comfort*] *Omitted in* H.

he bare to them. Of the which their great towardnes and profiting, not onely *Sir* Thomas More plainely testifieth in his epigrammes, but the renowned Clerke also, Erasmus Roterodamus; who receaued from them sundry letters, written, as he saith, not onely in pure latin, but full also of good, substantiall, wittie matter, which he certainly knewe to haue beene of their owne endighting, though he could hardly persuade the same to other straungers.

Praise of Margaret Roper's learning and virtue.

But of all other mistris Margarete Roper did pricke neerest her father, as well in witt, vertue and learning, as also in merye and pleasaunt talke. She was to her seruauntes a meeke and gentle mistris, to her brother* and sisters a most louing, naturall, amiable sister, To her frendes a very sure, stedfast and comfortable frende; yea, which is a rare thing in a woman, accompted of them to be of such grauitie and prudent counsaile that diuers men of good calling and experience would in their perplexe and difficulte causes consult and deliberate with her; and founde, as they haue reported, as graue and as profitable counsaile at her handes as they doubted to haue founde the lyke at many of their handes that were for their witt, vertue, learning and experience, men of whom there was made very good accompt.

Margaret a perfect mother.

To her children she was a double mother, [as] one not content to bring them forth onely into the world, but instructing them also her selfe in vertue and learning.

MSS. E L R^2 Y C H R B.

1. *he bare*] *Interlineated in* R^2. 1. *great*] *Omitted in* H. 2. *plainely*] *Omitted in* H R. 3. *in his epigrammes*] *Interlineated in* R. 4. *Erasmus*] *Interlineated in* R. 5. *saith*] sayth, *corrected from* sayde, R^2. 6. *full also*] also full Y. 6. *good*] *Omitted in* L R^2 B. 6. *wittie*] writtin Y. 7. *haue*] *Interlineated in* R^2; *interlineated over* to ben *in* R. 12. *as also*] and also Y. 13. *meeke*] meete Y. 13. *brother*] L R^2 Y C B; brothers E H R. 14. *most . . . sister*] most naturall & amyable loveing sister H R. 14. *amiable*] & amiable R^2 Y. 14–15. *a most . . . frendes*] *Omitted in* B. 15. *a*] *Omitted in* R^2. 15. *frende*] *Omitted in* R^2. 18–19. *perplexe*] perplexed L. 20–21. *and as profitable*] and proffitable C. 21. *profitable*] priffittable H. 22. *many*] *Interlineated over* any *crossed through* L. 23. *vertue, learning*] Learninge vertue R^2. 24. *good*] great H. 25. *as*] L R^2 Y H B; and E C R. 27. *her selfe*] hirselfe allsoe R^2.

At what time her husbande was vpon a certaine displeasure taken against him in king Henries dayes sent to the towre, certaine sent from the king to searche her house, vpon a sodaine running vpon her, founde her, not puling and lamenting, but full busily teaching her [fol. 22 *a*] children : whom they, | finding nothing astonied with their message, and finding also, beside this her constancie, such grauitie and wisedome in her talke as they litle looked for, were themselues much astonied, and were in great admiration, neyther could afterward speake [too] muche good of her, as partly my selfe haue heard at the mouth of one of them.

Margaret carries on her ordinary duties when her husband is sent to the Tower.

But aboue all other she was to her father, and to her husbande, such a daughter, suche a wife, as I suppose it was harde to matche her in all Inglande. And albeit this her daughterly behauio*ur* and reuerence was in her notable all her life before, yet neuer so notable as after her [fathers] trouble, affliction and imprisonment; all the which time, as well for her great paines and trauaile she tooke to procure some reliefe and ease to her father, as for her wise and godly talke with him, [as] also for such letters she sent him, and for diuers other considerations, it appereth she was the chiefest and almost the onely worldlye comfort S*ir* Thomas More had. To whom he wrate in that time diuers letters, and amonge

Margaret the chief comfort of her father in his trouble.

As More's Letters witness. [Cf. WORKS, p. 1446.]

MSS. E L R^2 Y C H R B.

1. *what*] which L R^2 B. 2. *against him*] *Omitted in* H R; against B. 3. *certaine sent*] certaine men presently were sent R^2; sent certaine H R. 3. *from*] *Omitted in* R^2. 4. *her* (1)] his H. 4. *vpon a sodaine*] whoe vpon a sudden R^2, sudden *being interlineated over* certayne *crossed through.* 5. *and*] or Y. 5. *busily*] busie Y H. 10. *too*] to L R^2 C H R B; so E Y. 12. *of one*] of þe one C H; R *as* C H, *but with* the *interlineated.* 13. *But . . . she*] but of all other she L R^2 B; But aboue all she H; but aboue all tother she R, all *and* she *being interlineated.* 13. *was . . . father*] was to her father R, was to her *being interlineated.* 13. *and to her*] and L R^2 B; and (*corrected from* was) to her R. 14. *suche*] and such Y H R. 15. *And*] *Omitted in* H R. 16. *daughterly*] daughterlike L. 17. *as after*] *On an erasure in* R^2. 18. *her fathers trouble*] hir fathers trouble L R^2 B; her trouble E Y; his trouble C H; his, *corrected from* her, R. 19. *her*] the H R. 20. *some . . . father*] him releife & ease R^2. 21. *as also*] as allso L R^2 Y C H R B; and also E. 22. *she*] as she H R. 25. *he*] shee H R. 25. *in that*] at þat R^2.

other one aunswering a letter of hers, In [the] which he merily writeth that to declare what pleasure and comfort he tooke of her saide letters, a pecke of coales would not suffise to make him pennes: meaning that he had none other pennes at that time, as he had not in deede.

Margaret a perfect wife, and Roper a perfect husband.

Nowe on the other side, she was so good, so debonaire, and so gentle a wife, that her husbande thought himselfe a moste happy man that euer he happened vpon such a treasure—A treasure, I may well say, for such a wife incomparably exceedeth (as Salomon sayth) all worldly treasure. Who was on his part againe to her so good, so sweete, so sober, so modest, so louing an husbande that, as Erasmus longe agoe writeth, if he had not beene her husbande, he might seeme to haue beene her owne germaine brother. Surely, the saide M*aster* Roper had her in suche estimation, or rather admiration, that he thought, and hath also saide, that she was more woorthy for her excellent qualities to haue bene a Princes wife.

Roper might seem to have been Margaret's own brother. [ERASMUS.]

Erasmus dedicated to Margaret his Commentary on [the Christmas Hymn of] Prudentius. [1523.]

And the saide Erasmus, for her exquisite learning, wisedome and vertue, made such an accompt of her, that he called her the flowre of all the learned matrones in Inglande. To whom, being * as yet * very yonge, but yet adorned with a childe, he dedicated his Commentaries made vpon certaine hymnes of Prudentius. | And [fol. 22 b] to say the truth, she was our Sappho, our Aspasia,

MSS. E L R^2 Y C H R B.

1. *aunswering*] answired Y. 1. *the which*] L R^2 Y C B; which E H R. 4. *not*] *Omitted in* H. 4. *pennes*] pens at that time L R^2 B. 5. *none*] noe L R^2 H R B. 5. *at that time*] then R^2. 7. *so debonaire*] *Omitted in* B. 10. *a treasure—A treasure*] a treasure I a treasure L; a treasure *once only* B. 11. *incomparably*] incomparable Y. 12. *treasure*] treasures L R^2 B. 12. *againe*] *Omitted in* H R. 12. *to her*] *Omitted in* R^2 H R. 13. *an*] a L R^2 Y. 14–15. *not . . . husbande*] *Interlineated in* R; not her husband beene B. 15. *seeme to*] *Omitted in* H R. 17. *suche*] such great H R. 18. *thought*] *Interlineated over* was *crossed through* L; hath thought C. 18. *hath*] *Omitted in* L R^2 B. 19. *her*] *Omitted in* H R. 19. *Princes wife*] princesse R^2. 20. *exquisite learning*] excellent learninge R^2 B, learninge *being upon an erasure in* R^2. 21. *an*] *Omitted in* B. 23. *being as yet*] L R^2 Y C B; as yet being E H R. 25. *made*] *Omitted in* L R^2 B. 26. *our Aspasia*] Aspasia L R^2; our Aspusia H R; Aspacia B.

our Hypathia, our Dam[o], our Cornelia. But what speake I of these, though learned, yet Infidels? Nay, rather, she was our christian Fabiola, our Marcella, our Paula, our Eustochium.

Margaret's emendation of a textual error in St. Cyprian. [Ep. 31.] [Either COSTER or CLEMENT.]

We will nowe, gentle Reader, geue thee a litle taste of her learning and of her readie, pregnant witt. St Ciprians workes had beene in those dayes manye times printed, and yet after so ofte printing there remayned, among other defectes and faultes, one notable amonge all these printes vncorrected and vnreformed. The wordes are these: *Absit enim ab Ecclesia Romana vigorem su[u]m tam prophana facilitate dimittere, et nisi vos seueritatis, euersa fidei maiestate, dissoluere.* Which place when mistris Margarete had read, without any helpe of other sample, or any instruction: "These wordes '*nisi vos*' should be," quoth she, "I trowe" (wherin she saide a very troth) "'*neruos.*'"

Margaret's miraculous recovery from the sweating sickness at the prayer of Sir Thomas More. [ROPER.]

This gentlewoman chaunced amonge other to fall sicke in the time of the great swett; whose recouerie being desperated of her Father, of the phisitians and all others, God seemed to shewe to S*ir* Thomas More a manifest and, as it were, a miraculous token of his speciall fauour. She being then in so great extremitie of that disease

MSS. E L R^2 Y C H R B.

1. *our Hypathia*] or Hipatia R^2. 1. *Dam[o]*] Dama *or* Dania *or* Daina E Y C H R; Samia L R^2; Samiia B. 3. *our christian*] of Christian H. 4. *our Eustochium*] and Estomachin Y; oure Eustochian B. 5. *geue . . . taste*] *Omitted in* B. 6. *readie*] *Omitted in* H R. 7. *had beene*] being L R^2 B. 7. *those*] theis Y. 8. *ofte*] often L; many times R^2. 8. *printing*] printinge, *corrected from* printed, R^2. 9. *other*] *Corrected from* others R^2. 9. *defectes and faultes*] faultes and defects L R^2 B. 10. *these*] those B. 10. *vncorrected*] incorrected L R^2. 11. *enim*] eiim H. 11. *suum*] L R^2 H R; suam E Y C B. 12. *prophana*] prophanae H R. 12. *dimittere*] dimittore H. 12. *et*] *Omitted in* C. 12. *vos*] hos B. 12. *seueritatis*] servitatis H. 13. *fidei*] fedei H. 13. *dissoluere*] disoluere C; disolverre H. 14. *had read*] had heard read L R^2 B. 14–15. *without . . . instruction*] without the helpe of any ensample or any other instruccion H. 14–15. *of other sample*] *Omitted in* B. 15. *or any*] or forther B. 15. *nisi vos*] nisi hos B. 16–17. *a very troth*] very truth L R^2; trulie B. 20. *desperated*] dispaired L R^2 B. 20. *of the phisitians*] of her phisicions L, her *being interlineated over* the, *corrected from* hir *and then crossed through.* 22. *miraculous*] merveylous L R^2 B. 23. *so great*] the greate B.

as by no inuentions or deuises that phisitians in suche case commonly vse (of whom he had diuers, both expert and wise and well learned, then continually attendant vpon her) coulde be kept from sleepe, so that both phisitians and all other there despaired of her recouerie and gaue her ouer; Her Father, as he that most entierly tendred her, being in no small heauines for her, by prayer at Gods hande sought to gett her remedie. Wherevpon going vp after his vsuall maner into his foresaide newe building, there in his Chappell, vpon his knees, with teares most deuoutly besought Almightie God that it would like his goodnes, vnto whom nothing was impossible, if it were his blessed will, at his mediation to vouchsafe gratiously to heare his humble petition; where came incontinent into his minde that a glister should be the onely remedie to helpe her. Which, when he tolde the phisitians, they by and by confessed that if there were any hope of health, that was the very best helpe in deede, much meruailing of themselues that they had not before remembred it. Then was it immediatly ministred vpon her sleeping, which she could by no meanes haue beene brought vnto waking. And albeit after that she was thereby throughly awaked, Gods | markes (an euident vndoubted token of death) [fol. 23 a] plainly appered vpon her, yet she, contrary to all their expectations, was, as it was thought, by her fathers feruent prayer miraculously recouered, and at length againe to perfect health restored. Whom if it had pleased God

MSS. E L R^2 Y C H R B.

2. *case*] cases L. 2. *commonly vse*] do commonly vse L R^2 B. 3. *and wise*] wise C H R. (Roper MSS. *vary*. *See* Notes.) 3. *attendant*] attendinge H R. 4. *coulde*] cold H. 8. *hande*] handes H. 10. *into*] to B. 10. *his*] *Omitted in* H. 13. *impossible*] vnpossible L. 13–14. *at his mediation*] *Interlineated in* R. 14. *mediation*] meditation R^2. 14. *to vouchsafe*] vouchafe R^2. 16. *remedie*] thing C. (Roper MSS. *have* way.) 18. *hope*] helpe Y. 19. *of*] at R^2. 21. *it*] *Omitted in* H R. 21. *her*] *Interlineated in* R^2. 22. *could*] would R^2. 22. *meanes . . . waking*] meanes be brought to wakeing H R B. 23. *awaked*] awake R. 24. *Gods*] God his B. 24. *markes*] workes C. 24. *euident vndoubted*] evident & vndoubted L. 26. *as it was*] *Omitted in* Y. 27. *prayer*] prayers R^2. 27–28. *and at length againe . . . restored*] and againe at lengthe . . . restored L; and againe at length . . . miraculously restored R^2; & restored at length to her former health B. 28. *had pleased*] please R.

at that time to haue taken to his mercie, her father saide that he would neuer haue medled with worldly matters after, as we have before touched.

The family of Margaret Roper.

By this gentlewoman M*aster* Will*ia*m Roper hath yet liuing two yonge gentlemen, his sonnes, being brought vp and learned in the liberall sciences and the lawes of the Realme; and one daughter, late wife to M*aster* Clarke, and nowe wife to M*aster* Bassett, one of our gratious Soueraines Queene Maries priuie chamber, who in the late kinge Edwardes dayes, because he would the better preserue himselfe not to be intangled with the schisme, withdrewe himselfe into Flaunders. This mistris Bassett is very well experted in the latine and greeke tonges; she hath very hansomely and learnedly translated out of the greeke into the englishe all the ecclesiasticall storye of Eusebius, w*i*th Socrates, Theodoretus, Sozomenus and Euagrius, albeit of modestie she suppresseth it, and keepeth it from the print. She hath also very aptly and fitly translated into the saide tonge a certaine booke that S*ir* Thomas,* her grandfather, made vpon the passion, and so elegantly and eloquently penned that a man would thinke it were originally written in the saide englishe tonge.

The learned translations of Margaret's daughter, Mistress Bassett.

Her translation of the *Passionis Expositio*, the Latin portion of More's *Treatise on the Passion*. [WORKS, p. 1350, with addition.]

Here nowe haue I occasion somewhat to interlace of

MSS. E L R² Y C H R B.

1–2. *saide that he*] sayd he L R² B. 2. *would neuer haue*] neuer would haue H R. 2. *with*] *Interlineated in* L. 2. *matters*] matter L R² B. 3. *after*] againe Y. 3. *as . . . touched*] *Omitted in* B. 3. *touched*] *Interlineated in* Y. 4. *William*] *Omitted in* B. 4. *hath*] had B. 4–5. *yet liuing*] *Omitted in* B. 6. *and learned*] *Omitted in* B. 6. *and the lawes*] & Lawes R²; and in the lawes H R. 6. *of the*] of this H R. 7. *late*] *Interlineated in* Y. 7. *wife to*] wife of L. 7. *to Master*] to one master Y. 8. *nowe*] afterwarde B. 9. *Soueraines*] soueraigne H R B. 9. *Queene*] quenes Y. 9. *who*] whome C. 12. *into*] in R². 13. *is*] was B. 13. *experted*] expert B. 13. *tonges*] toung Y C. 14. *translated*] *Omitted in* R². 14–15. *the greeke*] greke Y. 15. *into the englishe*] into English L H B; into the Englishe tonge Y. 15. *ecclesiasticall*] Ecclesiaticall H. 15. *storye*] history L. 16. *Theodoretus*] *Omitted in* H R. 16. *Sozomenus*] Soromenus Y; Zoromenus H R. 17. *Euagrius*] Euagariss H; Euagarus R; Evagoras B. 17–18. *and keepeth it*] *Omitted in* Y. 18. *it from*] it in from B. 20. *Sir Thomas*] L R² Y C H; Sir Thomas More E R B. 21. *and eloquently*] *Omitted in* B. 21. *penned*] penned it B. 22. *saide*] *Omitted in* Y B. 23. *nowe*] *Omitted in* L R² B. 23. *somewhat*] *Omitted in Y.*

Roper's temporary lapse into heresy.

the saide *Master* Will*iam* Roper, but it would require a proper and peculier narration to discourse this man condignelye as his woorthines requireth, but we will, cutting off all other thinges, speake of a point or two onely. The saide *Master* Will*iam* Roper, at what time he maried with mistris Margarete More, was a meruailous zealous Protestant, and so feruent, and withall so well and properly lyked of himselfe and his diuine learning, that he tooke the brydle into the teeth, and ranne forth like a headstronge horse, harde to be plucked backe againe.

Roper's desire to preach heretical doctrines.

Neyther was he content to whisper it in hugger mugger, but thirsted very sore to publishe his newe doctrine and diuulge it, and thought himselfe very able so to doo, and it were euen at Paules Crosse; yea, for the burning zeale he bare to the furtherance and aduauncement of Luthers newe broached religion, and for the pretie lyking he hadd of himselfe, he longed so sore to be pulpited, that to haue satisfied his madd affection and desire, he could haue beene content to haue forgone a good portion of his landes. At which time there were some others of that sect detected for mainteyning of heresies, that catched such an ytche of preaching that, though their heresies lay foystring still in the bottome of

MSS. E L R^2 Y C H R B.

1. *the saide*] *Omitted in* B. 2. *peculier*] a peculiar Y. 3. *condignelye*] his condignitie B. 4. *cutting*] cutt H. 4. *speake*] & speake H R. 4. *two*] *Interlineated in* L. 5. *Roper*] *Omitted in* C. 7. *Protestant*] prodistant Y. 7–8. *and so feruent . . . learning*] & so fervent in divine learning B. 8. *properly*] porperly H. 8. *and his*] as his H R. 9. *the brydle*] his bridle B. 9. *the teeth*] his teeth L. 9. *a*] an R. 11. *content*] contented H R. 11–12. *hugger mugger*] hucker mucker L R^2 B; hokemoker Y; hoker moker C. 12. *thirsted*] thristed Y. 12. *sore to*] soone to to B. 13. *and diuulge it*] *Omitted in* B. 13. *diuulge*] divulgate Y. 13. *it*] *Omitted in* R^2. 13. *able*] well able R^2. 13–14. *able . . . were*] able to do it, if it weare B. 14. *euen*] *Omitted in* B. 15–16. *aduauncement of*] advancement to L, *with* of *crossed through before* to. 16. *broached*] breathed L R^2 B. 17. *he hadd*] *Omitted in* H R. 18. *madd*] madd, *corrected from* mynde, R^2; mynde H. 18–19. *and desire*] *Omitted in* B. 19. *content*] contented H R. 21. *detected*] decected Y. 22. *an*] a Y. 23. *foystring*] foystered L. 23. *still*] *Interlineated in* R. 23. *in*] *Interlineated in* L; *interlineated over* to *crossed through* R^2.

their heartes, at what time with their lippes they professed the contrary, yet, as it is well knowen and themselfe confessed, vpon hope of preaching againe they were content openly to abiure.

This fall into heresie of the same M*aster* Roper, as he [fol 23 b] can coniecture, first did growe of a scruple of | his owne conscience, for lacke of grace and better knowledge, as some doo vpon other occasions. He dayly did vse immoderate fasting and many prayers, which with good discretion well vsed had not beene to be mislyked; but vsing them without order and good consideration, thinking God therewith neuer to be pleased, did werye himselfe euen *vsque ad taedium.* Then did he vnderstand of Luthers workes brought into the Realme, and as Eue of a curious minde desirous to knowe both good and euill, so did he, for the straungenes and delectation of that doctrine, fall into great desire to reade his workes: who, amongst other his bookes, had read a booke of Luthers *de libertate christiana*, and another *de captiuitate Babilonica*, and was with them in affection so bewitched that he then did beleeue euery matter sett forth by Luther to be true. And was with these bookes, by ignorance, pride, false allegations, sophisticall reasons and argumentes, and with his owne corrupt affections deceaued, and fully persuaded

Roper, wearied by immoderate fasting and many prayers, is bewitched by Luther's books and his doctrine that faith alone justifies, and the works of man do nothing profit.

MSS. E L R^2 Y C H R B.

1. *time*] times H R. 1. *professed*] confessed L R^2 B. 2. *as*] *Omitted in* H R. 2–3. *yet, as it is . . . confessed*] yet it is . . . confessed *interlineated in* R. 2–3. *themselfe confessed*] theyr selves confesse it L B; themselues confesse yt R^2; themselves confessed Y. 3. *of*] *Interlineated in* R^2. 4. *abiure*] abiure it L. 5. *heresie . . . Roper*] heresie of þe same Master William Roper L; heresie of Master William Roper R^2 B; heresie Master Roper H R; Y *as* E C, *but with* said *for* same. 8–9. *immoderate*] immoderate, *with* im *interlineated*, R. 11. *good*] *Omitted in* L R^2 B. 12. *therewith*] thereby H R. 12–13. *werye . . . taedium*] weary himselfe vsque ad taedium L; weare himselfe even vsque ad taedium H R. 13. *taedium*] nauseam B. 14. *the*] this H R. 14. *and*] *Omitted in* Y C. 16. *the*] *Omitted in* B. 17. *fall*] fell H. 17. *great*] a great] R^2 B. 18. *other his bookes*] other of his workes R^2; other his workes Y H R. 18–19. *Luthers . . . Babilonica*] Luthers de secundâ captivitate Babilonicâ and another de 1^a libertate Christianâ L, 1^a *being interlineated*; Luthers De captiuitate Babilonica and another de libertate christiana R^2. 20. *with . . . bewitched*] in affection so with them bewitched H R. 20. *then did*] did then H R. 22. *by*] *Omitted in* H R. 24. *fully*] *Omitted in* L R^2 B.

that faith onely did iustifie, that the workes of man did nothing profite, and that, if man could once beleeue that our Sauio*ur* Christe shedd his pretious bloud and dyed on the crosse for our sinnes, the same onely beliefe should be sufficient for our saluation. Then thought he that all the ceremonies and Sacramente*s* in Christes Churche were verye vaine, and was at length so farre waded into heresie and puffed vp w*i*th pride that he wisshed he might be suffred publikely to preache, thinking, as we haue saide, that he should be better able to edifie and profite the people then the best preacher that came [to] Paules crosse, and that he in that doctrine was able to conuince the best docto*ur* in the Realme; and so muche the rather for that he had in open presence (before the world was well acquainted with that doctrine) defaced some that were named doctours of diuinitie, and thought there could be no truth but that which was [come] forth then out of Germanie.

Roper is charged with heresy before Wolsey, but dismissed with a friendly warning.

Who, for his open talke and companying with diuers of his owne sect, of the Stilliarde and other merchauntes, was with them before Cardinall Wolsey conuented of heresie, which merchauntes for their opinions were openly for heresie at Paules Crosse abiured; yet he, for loue borne by the Cardinall to S*ir* Thomas More, his father in lawe, was with a frendly warning discharged; And, albeit he had maried the eldest daughter of S*ir* Thomas More,

MSS. E L R² Y C H R B.

1. *faith onely*] only faith R². 1. *did*] doth Y. 2. *and that*] & H R. 2. *if man*] if a man L. 3. *pretious*] *Omitted in* R². 6. *Christes*] Christ his B. 8. *wisshed he*] wished that he H R. 10. *edifie and profite*] profitt & edify R². 11. *to*] L R² Y C B; at E H R. 12. *he*] *Omitted in* H. 13. *the Realme*] a Realme H R. 13. *the rather*] he rather Y. 14. *well*] *Omitted in* H R. 16. *named*] *Interlineated in* R²; *omitted in* H R. 16. *thought there could*] though their would Y. 17. *which was come forth then out of*] which was come foorth then out of L R²; which was then come forth oute of B; which was set forthe then out of C; which was forth then out of E Y; which was forth then of H R, then *being interlineated in* R. 17. *but that*] but that R, that *being interlineated*; then that B. 19–20. *diuers of*] many of R². 21. *conuented*] convinced B. 24. *by the Cardinall*] *Omitted in* L R² B. 24–25. *his father in lawe*] *Omitted in* B.

24,

and had to him a Lutheran Bille, wherein upon the holye
dayes in steede of his prayers he spent his whole time, thinking
it for him sufficient to gett ones this verie knowledge to be able
among ignorant persons to cable and talke, as he thought, like a
great doctor. And so after continued he in his heresies, but uppon a time Sr Thomas More privately talked in his garden
with his daughter Margarete, and amongst other his sayinges
saide: Megge, I have borne a longe time with thy husbande;
I have reasoned and argued with him in those pointes of religio[n]
and still given to him my poore fatherly counsaile, but I per-
ceave none of all this able to call him home; and therefore,
Megge, I will no longer argue nor dispute with him, but
will cleane geve him over, and gett me another while to God
and praye for him. And soone after, as he verely beleeved, thorough the great mercy of God at the devout prayer of Sr
Thomas More he perceaved his owne ignorance, oversight, malice and follie, and turned him againe to the Catholike faith,
wherein, God be thanked, he hath hitherto continued. And thus
was he induced into these wretched heresies, and none perceav-
eth what deceaved him and many moe, who for the most
part through ignorance do beginne to walke in this waye of heresie, and after in that wicked way do stumble, and finallye
through malice desperately cast them in the ditche of all iniquitie.
And in this notable reclayming and recovering of this gentleman,
God, me thinketh, at the hartie and devout prayers of Sr Thomas
More hath shewed his great tender mercie, as he did longe agoe uppon the great vertuous Clarke St Austen, who after he had
continued nyne yeres a detestable Manichee, and being so nousled
and rooted in their sect that there was no like pleasure to
him in the worlde as to meete in reasoning with some Catholike, whom he, as himselfe thought, was able and did wonderfully confounde, was at length by the fervent devoute
prayers and teares of his good mother Monica reduced to the
true Catholike faith. The said Mr Roper being thus by the
great mercy of God reclaymed from his errours and heresies,
(a goodly fine president for many other of our time, being of
much lesse witt, vertue and learning, to reforme themselves to
the Catholike faith of their mother the holy Catholike Church)
hath beene sithence by the grace of God so stedfastly and so
firmely rooted and fixed in the Catholike faith, and all his
children also, that a man may well say: *Haec mutatio dextrae*
excelsi. And he hath beene sithence the singular helper and patrone
of all Catholikes to relieve and ayde them in their distresse, espe-
ciallye

Roper reclaymed from heresie

O[ratio] the devout praier of Sr Th. More

Manicheus

Haec mutatio dex-
trae diaboli

MS. EMMANUEL 76, FOL. 24a (REDUCED).

whom then of all the world he did, during that time, moste abhorre, though he was a man of most mildnes and notable patience.

Roper, when a heretic, abhors More.

Nowe these easie, short, pleasaunt and licentious lessons did cast him into so sweete a sleepe as he was after loth to wake from it. And [those] lessons he did so well like as he soone after gaue ouer his fasting, praying, [fol. 24 *a*] his primer and all his other prayers, | and gatt to him a Lutheran Bible, wherein vpon the holye dayes, in steede of his prayers, he spent his whole time, thinking it for him sufficient to gett onely thereby knowledge to be able among ignorant persons to bable and talke, as he thought, like a great doct*our*.

Roper considers reading of the Lutheran Bible sufficient to ensure salvation.

And so after continued he in his heresies, vntill vppon a time S*ir* Thomas More priuately talked in his garden with his daughter Margarete, and amongst other his saying*es* saide:

Roper is brought back to the Catholic faith by the earnest prayers of More.

"Megge, I haue borne a longe time with thy husbande; I haue reasoned and argued with him in those pointes of religio*n*, and still geuen to him my poore fatherly counsaile; but I perceaue none of all this able to call him home; and therfore, Megge, I will no longer argue nor dispute with him, but will cleane geue him ouer, and gett me another while to God and praye for him."

MSS. E L R² Y C H R B.

1. *whom*] *Crossed through, and* yet *interlineated* B. 1–2. *world . . . abhorre*] world during that tyme he most abhorred B. 2. *most*] great C. 5. *as he*] that he Y. 6. *after*] afterwarde B. 6. *loth*] both B. 6. *those*] R² Y C B; these E L H R. 7. *as . . . ouer*] that soone after he gave ouer B. 7. *praying*] *Omitted in* R²; prayer H R; & praying B. 8. *his primer . . . prayers*] *Omitted in* B. 8. *gatt to him*] gat him to L; gate to him R²; gott to him H. 9. *the*] *Omitted in* B. 9. *holye*] holly H. 10. *whole*] holy Y. 11. *gett onely thereby*] get thereby onely L R² B. 13. *great*] *Omitted in* C. 14. *after continued he*] after he continued L; still he continued R²; after he contynued B. 14–15. *vppon a time*] vpon a time þat L R² Y H R; *omitted in* B. 15. *talked in his garden*] in his garden talked H R. 16. *his sayinges*] thinges Y. 17. *saide*] he said Y. 18. *a longe*] a long L. 18–19. *a longe . . . husbande*] with thy husbande a long tyme Y. 19. *I haue*] I haue I haue Y. 19. *in*] vpon C. 20. *poore*] best Y. 21. *able*] is able L R² B. 22. *home*] whome L. 23. *nor*] or H. 23. *nor dispute*] *Omitted in* B. 23. *but*] and L. 24. *and gett . . . him*] & praye to god for his conversion B.

And soone after, as he verily beleeued, thorough the great mercy of God, at the deuout prayer of *Sir* Thomas More, he perceaued his owne ignorance, ouersight, malice and folie, and turned him againe to the Catholike fayth, wherein, God be thanked, he hath hitherto continued. And thus was he induced into these wretched heresies, and nowe perceaueth what deceaued him and many moe, who for the moste part through ignorance doo beginne to walke in this waye of heresie, and after in that wicked way doo stande, and finallye through malice do desperately fast sitt in the chaire of all iniquitie.

As St. Augustine was saved by Monica.

And in this notable reclayming and recouering of this gentleman, God, me thinketh, at the hartie and deuout prayers of *Sir* Thomas More, hath shewed his great tender mercie, as he did longe agoe vppon the great, [learned], vertuous Clarke St Austen; who, after he had continued nyne yeres a detestable Maniche, and being so nousled and riped in their sect that there was no like pleasure to him in the world as to matche in reasoning with some Catholike—whom he, as himselfe thought, was able and did wonderfully confounde—was at length, by the feruent deuoute prayers and teares of his good mother Monica, reduced to the true Catholike fayth.

Roper remains ever after a

The said *Master* Roper, being thus by the great mercy of God reclaymed from his errors and heresies (a goodly

MSS. E L R^2 Y C H R B.

1. *And*] *Omitted in* B. 2. *at the deuout*] & devoute B. 2. *prayer*] prayers H R. 6. *into*] vnto H. 7. *perceaueth*] perceaued H; perceaving B. 8. *doo*] *Omitted in* Y. 10. *way*] *An addition on margin in* R^2, *with omission mark before* doe *in text.* 10. *doo*] *Corrected from* to R. 10. *and . . . do*] and doe R^2, *with* through *before* doe *crossed through.* 10 *finallye*] *Omitted in* L R^2 B. 12. *reclayming and recouering*] recoverie and reclaming Y; reclayming & recoverie B. 15–16. *the great, learned, vertuous*] þe great learned virtuous L Y; the great vertuous E C; the great Learned R^2 B; great vertuous learned H R. 17. *and*] *Interlineated in* L. 18. *riped*] ripe L R^2 B. 19. *no like*] not like H. 19–20. *matche in reasoning*] reason B. 20. *whom he*] whom as he B. 21. *able . . . confounde*] able to confounde B. 22. *at length*] at þe length L H B. 22. *deuoute*] & devout L; douout Y. 22. *and teares*] *Omitted in* L. 23. *good*] *Omitted in* L R^2 B. 23. *Monica*] *Omitted in* B. 26. *from*] for Y.

faire president for many other of our time, being of muche lesse witt, vertue and learning, to reforme themselues [and to conforme themselues] to the Catholike faith of their mother, the holy * Church) hath beene [euer] sithens by the goodnes of God so stedfastly and so firmely rooted and fixed in the Catholike fayth, and all his children also, that a man may well say: *Haec mutatio dextrae excelsi.* And he hath beene sithens the singuler helper and patrone of all Catholikes, to relieue and ayde [fol. 24 b] them in their distresse, espe|ciallye such as eyther were imprisoned or otherwise troubled for the Catholike fayth. For which cause in the latter time of king Henry the eight, for relieuing by his almes a notable learned man, M*aster* Beckenshawe, he suffred great trouble and imprisonment in the towre. But his great almes doo not stande within this liste onely, but it reacheth farre further, and so farre that it reacheth to all kinde of poore and needie persons, that, as I trowe, in this kinde no one man of his degree and calling in all Inglande is comparable to him. So that a man may, not without cause, accommodate that place of holy Scripture to him: *Cor viduae consolatus est, oculus fuit caeco, et pes claudo,* and to conclude, *pater erat pauperum.* For the which his great almes sowen vpon the poore so liberallye, I

steadfast Catholic.

Roper very charitable to all Catholics.

For such charity to Master Beckenshawe, Roper suffered imprisonment in the Tower.

MSS. E L R² Y C H R B.

1. *many other of*] many of other of R². 3. *and to conforme themselues*] C; *omitted in* E L R² Y H R B. 4. *the holy Church*] þe holy churche L R² Y C H R; the holy Catholike Church E B. 4–5. *beene euer sithens*] bene euer sithence R² Y C B; beene euen sithence L; beene sithens E H R. 5–6. *stedfastly . . . fixed*] stedfastlie fixed & firmelie rooted B. 8. *excelsi*] excelci H; excelsi, *corrected from* excelci, R; excessit B. 8. *And . . . sithens*] And he hath ben since, *with* since *interlineated* R. 9. *helper and patrone*] patrone & helper R²; helpe & patrone B. 10. *distresse*] distresses R². 10. *such as*] *Omitted in* L R²; such that B. 10. *eyther were*] were eyther L R² B; were H R. 12. *For which*] For the which L R² B; For with H. 12. *time*] end R². 13. *by*] with R². 14. *Beckenshawe*] Beckamshawe L R² B. 14–15. *suffred . . . imprisonment*] suffred long imprisonment B. 15. *doo*] doth Y; did H R. 16. *liste*] *Interlineated in* L; list *interlineated over* lifte R. 16. *reacheth*] reacith Y; reached H R. 17. *and so*] as so H R. 17. *reacheth*] reached H R. 17. *kinde of*] *Omitted in* L R² H B. 18–19. *persons . . . no one*] persons in so much that no one B. 19. *in all Inglande*] in England L R² B. 21 *holy*] *Omitted in* R² B. 22. *et*] es Y. 23. *For the which*] for which H R.

doubt nothing but in the heauenly haruest he shall plentifullye reape mercy and grace and the inestimable rewarde of eternall blisse.

The virtue and learning of Dr. [John] Clement and his wife, [Margaret Gigs]. [MORE to ERASMUS, with additions.]

Lett vs nowe see of some other that were of the familie of this woorthy man, S*ir* Thomas More. Among other doct*our* Clement, also his wife (a woman furnished with muche vertue and wisedome, and with the knowledge of the latine and greeke tonge, yea, and phisicke too, aboue many that seeme good and cunning phisitians) were brought vp in his house. The saide Clement was taken by S*ir* Thomas More from Paules schoole in London, and hath sithens proued a verye excellent good phisitian, and is singulerly seene in the greeke tonge. And yet his vertue surmounteth his learning, and hath aunswered to the expectation of S*ir* Thomas More; who writeth thus of him, being yet a childe, to Erasmus: *Vxor mea te salutat, et item Clemens, qui literis et latinis et graecis ita proficit indies, vt non exiguam de eo spem concipiam, futurum eum aliquando et patriae et literis ornamento.*

Mistress Clement's knowledge of medicine. [WORKS, p. 1173, with addition.]

Nowe to what excellencie [she] grewe in knowledge, and specially of phisicke, in her ripe and latter yeres is eathe to be knowen by that I shall now tell you. It fortuned that S*ir* Thomas More, about a fifteene or sixteene yeres before his death, fell into a tertian ague, and [had] passed three or fowre fitt*es*. But afterwarde

MSS. E L R² Y C H R B.

2. *and grace*] & & grace R². 2. *and* (2)] *Interlineated over to crossed through* R. 2. *the inestimable*] inestimable L R² B. 4. *of*] *Omitted in* B. 6. *also his wife*] also & his wife L R²; & his wife B. 8. *tonge*] tonges L R² H B. 11. *by Sir*] by the said Sir L R². 12. *hath*] *Omitted in* H. 16. *yet*] *Omitted in* H. 16. *yet a*] yet but a R². 17. *qui literis*] qui ita literis Y. 17. *literis*] litteris R². 18. *ita*] *Omitted in* Y. 19. *futurum*] futuram H R. 19. *eum*] enim C. 19. *aliquando*] ali aliquando H R. 20. *literis*] Litteris R². 21. *she*] L Y C H R; he E; his wife R² B. 22. *and specially*] *Omitted in* B. 22. *of phisicke*] in Phisicke H R. 23. *eathe*] eath L, *preceded by* easy *crossed through*; easily R²; easie H R B. 23. *by*] but H. 23. *that*] what Y. 23. *now*] *Interlineated in* R. 24. *about a fifteene*] about xv R² Y H R B. 25. *tertian*] certeine B. 26. *had*] L R² Y C H R B (*supported by* English Works, *p.* 1173); he E.

fell there on him one fitt out of course, so straunge and meruailous that a man would haue thought it impossible; for sodenly he felte himselfe both hott and colde throughout all his body, not in some part the one, and in some part the other, for that had beene, ye wote well, no very straunge thing, to feele the head hott while the handes were colde, but the very selfe same partes he sensibly felt, and right painfully too, all in one instant both hott and colde at once. Vpon this so sodaine and [fol. 25 *a*] rare a chaunce, | he asked a phisitian or twaine that then looked vnto him, howe this should be possible; and they twaine tolde him that it could not be so, but that he was fallen into some slumber, and dreamed that he felt it so. Then mistris Clement, being at that time a yonge girle, whom a kinsman of hers had begonne to teache phisicke, tolde S*ir* Thomas More that there was such a kinde of feuer in deede, and forthwith shewed a worke of Galen, *de differentijs febrium*, where Galen affirmeth the same.

Dr. Clement and his wife voluntary exiles for the Catholic faith.

This godly couple hath, and doth yet continue full blessedly together. Besides all other excellent qualities, this couple is notable for their great constancie in the Catholike fayth; for the which they voluntarily and willingly relinquished their countrey, and banished themselues in the late reigne of king Edwarde the sixt.

John Harris.

There was also in his house a learned and vertuous man called John Harris, that godly and diligently

MSS. E L R² Y C H R B.

1. *on him one fitt*] one fit of him L B; one fitt on him R². 2. *impossible*] vnpossible H R. 4. *not*] now B. 4. *in*] *Omitted in* C. 5. *that*] it B. 5. *had*] *Omitted in* Y. 5. *ye*] you R². 5. *ye wote well*] *Omitted in* B. 6. *to feele*] to felte L. 7. *were*] ar Y H. 8. *sensibly*] very sencibly Y B. 9. *so*] *Omitted in* R². 9–10. *so . . . rare*] so rare & suddaine H R. 10. *a* (1)] *Interlineated in* L. 10. *chaunce*] chaung L; chainge B. 11. *then*] *Corrected from* when Y. 11. *be*] *Interlineated in* R². 12. *they*] the H. 12. *they twaine*] both of them B. 12. *that it*] it L B. 17. *kinde*] *Added on margin in* R². 18. *differentijs*] differencijs L; differentys H. 20. *full*] *Interlineated in* E; most R². 20–21. *full blessedly together*] together full blessedly H R. 25. *late reigne*] latter reigne L R²; last yeare B. 25. *Edwarde*] Eward H. 26. *learned and*] *Omitted in* L R² B.

More's household compared with Plato's Academy. [ERASMUS.]

instructed his youth. Surely, if a man had seene and fully knowen the order, demaine and trade of his children, and of this yonge Clement, and the foresaide maide that was after his wife, and of his other familie, he would haue taken great spirituall and ghostly pleasure thereof, and would haue thought himselfe to haue rather beene in Platoes accademie—nay, what say I, Platoes? not in Platoes, but in some christian well ordred accademie and vniuersitie—rather then in any laye mans house. Euery body there so besett himselfe and his time vpon such good and fruitfull reading and other vertuous exercises. There should you heare of no strife or debate, of no wanton and vnseemely talke, which, with diuers other enormities, were cutt away, because ydlenes, the very pestiferous poysoned bane of youth, was quite excluded, and euery person well and vertuously set aworke.

More's first wife, [Jane], and his education of her described. [ERASMUS to ULRICH VON HUTTEN.]

His first wife he maried a yonge maide, which was verye vertuous and very pliable to all his will and pleasure. By her he had the foresaide three daughters and master John More. And the saide wife dyed very yonge. The said gentlewoman, though she were very yonge and rude, as one brought vp onely in the countrey

MSS. E L R² Y C H R B.

1–2. *and fully knowen*] *Omitted in* B. 2. *demaine*] demeanour L R² H; demeane C R; & demeanour B. 2. *and trade*] *Omitted in* B. 3. *this*] his L R² Y B. 4. *maide that was*] E *has* was *interlineated, and after* maide *an* and *crossed through*; maide, *corrected from* mind, R². 4. *after*] afterwarde B. 5. *haue*] *Interlineated in* R². 6–7. *himselfe . . . beene*] him rather to have beene L B; to be rather R². 7–8. *say I, Platoes*] say I to platos Y. 8. *not in Platoes*] *Omitted in* L R² B. 8. *but*] *Omitted in* B. 9. *and vniuersitie*] *Omitted in* B. 9–10. *then . . . house*] then any landed man his house B. 11. *and his time*] *Omitted in* B. 11. *his*] *Interlineated in* Y. 13. *of no*] or of no H R. 13. *and*] or L R² H R B. 14. *which, with*] with which H R. 14. *other*] other, *corrected from* others, R²; others Y; *omitted in* H R. 15. *poysoned*] & poysened R²; *omitted in* B. 17. *aworke*] on worke H R B. 18. *maried a*] maried was a B. 18–19. *which . . . vertuous*] verie vertuosly bent B. 19. *and very pliable*] & very appliable L R² B; & pliable H R. 19. *all*] *Omitted in* R². 20. *By her*] By *corrected from* Before, *and* her *interlineated* R. 20. *the foresaide*] *Omitted in* B. 22. *gentlewoman*] gentleman Y. 22–23. *The said . . . yonge*] *Interlineated in* R. 22. *were*] was B. 22. *very*] *Omitted in* R². 23. *onely*] *Omitted in* R² B.

vnder her parent*es*, he was the better content to marie that he might the sooner frame her to his owne will, appetite and disposition, as he did in deede; whom he caused to be instructed in learning and all kinde of musicke, And had nowe so fasshioned her according to his owne minde, that he had, and should euer after haue had, a most delectable, sweete, pleasaunt life with her, if God had sent her longer life.

More's children and grand-children live with him.

The saide three daughters, with their husbandes, and his sonne and heire, with eleven nephewes and neeces of his foresaide children, continued in house with him vntill suche time as he was sent to the towre.

More's second wife, [Alice], and his education of her described. [ERASMUS to ULRICH von HUTTEN, with additions.]

After the death of his first wife, he maried a widowe, [fol. 25 b] which continued with him till he suffred; whom | he full entierly loued and most louingly vsed, though he had by her no children, and though she were aged, blunt and rude. And in this he shewed his great wisdome, or rather pietie and godlynes: wisedome in taking that for the best, [or rather making that the best], that otherwise could not be holpen; his pietie and godlynes in cherishing her no lesse louingly and tenderly then if she had beene his firste yonge wife, blessed and adorned with happie and diuers issue of her bodie; whom in very deede he rather maried for the ruling and gouerning of his children, house and familie, then for any bodily pleasure. And yet suche as she was, being also sparefull and geuen to profite,

MSS. E L R² Y C H R B.

1. *vnder*] vnde H. 3. *appetite*] *Omitted in* B. 3. *as*] *Interlineated over* whome *crossed through* L. 4. *kinde*] kindes B. 5. *had*] *Omitted in* L R² B. 7. *sweete*] *Omitted in* L R² B; & swete H R. 7. *life with her*] wife B. 8. *longer*] long L R²; a longer H R B. 10. *and heire*] *Omitted in* B. 10. *eleven*] ane eleuen R². 10. *nephewes and neeces*] Neeces & nephewes R². 11. *foresaide*] *Omitted in* B. 11. *house*] the house B. 14. *him*] *Interlineated in* R². 15. *louingly*] louuingly L, louuing *being on an erasure.* 16. *blunt*] blinde Y. 17. *great*] *Omitted in* H. 18–20. *wisedome in taking that for the best, or rather . . . best, that otherwise . . . godlynes*] wysedome in taking þat for þe beste or rather making þat þe best þat otherwise coulde not be holpen his pyete and godlines C; E Y H R *omit* or rather making þat þe best; L R² B *omit the whole passage*, wisedome . . . godlynes. 23. *and diuers*] *Omitted in* B. 23. *whom*] when B. 23. *very*] *Omitted in* L R² B. 25–26. *yet . . . profite*] yet thoughe she was given to profit B. 26. *being*] and being C.

he so framed and fasshioned her by his dexteritie that he liued a sweete and pleasaunt life with her, and brought her to that case that she learned to playe and sing [at the lute and virgenalls], and euery day at his returning home he tooke a reckoning and accompt of the taske he enioyned her touching the said exercise.

Lady More's banter on her own good resolutions. [WORKS, p. 1184, with additions.]

This wife, on a time after shrifte, bad S*ir* Thomas* be merie. "For I haue," saith she, "this day lefte all my shrewdnes, and* will beginne afreshe." Which merye conceyted talke, though nowe and then it proued true in verye deede, S*ir* Thomas More could well digest and like in her and in his children and other.

More pokes fun at his wife's vanity. [WORKS, p. 1203, with addition.]

Neyther was he in her debt for repaying home againe often time such kinde of talke. Among other thinges, when he diuers times behelde his wife, what paine she tooke in straite binding vp her heare to make her a faire, large forehead, and with straite bracing in her body to make her middle small, both twaine to her great paine, for the pride of a litle foolishe praise, he saide to her: "Forsoothe, Madame, if God geue you not hell, he shall doo you great wronge, for it must needes be your owne of very right, for you buye it very deere, and take very great paine therefore."

This wife, when she saw that S*ir* Thomas More,

MSS. E L R^2 Y C H R B.

1. *and fasshioned*] *Omitted in* B. 1. *her*] *Omitted in* L R^2. 1. *that*] and that Y. 3–4. *and sing at the lute and virgenalls*] and synge at þe lute and virgenalls C; and sing at the Y, *with gap left by scribe sufficient to take in* þe lute and virgenalls *found in* C; and sing E L R^2 H R B. (*See* Notes.) 5. *home*] whome L. 6. *enioyned*] enioyed Y. 6. *the said*] hir said L R^2 H R; hir Y. 7. *Sir Thomas*] L Y C; Sir Thomas Moore E R^2 H R B. 8. *saith*] sayde B. 8. *this day*] *Omitted in* Y. 9. *and will*] C (*supported by* English Works, *p.* 1184); and tomorowe will L R^2 Y B; and to morowe I will E H R. 9. *Which*] with H B. 11. *true*] very true H; not true B. 11. *in verye deede*] indeed R^2 H B. 11–14. *Sir . . . talke*] *Omitted in* B. 11. *digest*] disgest H. 12. *other*] others L R^2. 14. *often times*] oftentyme H; *interlineated in* R. 15. *he*] *Omitted in* R^2. 15. *behelde*] behould Y. 16. *straite*] *Omitted in* B. 16. *her* (1)] his Y. 16. *her* (2)] his Y. 17. *large*] long L R^2 B. 17. *bracing*] lacing B. 19. *pride*] prde H. 19. *foolishe*] *Omitted in* R^2. 19. *he saide to her*] *Interlineated in* L. 20. *you*] *Omitted in* R^2. 22. *for you buye*] seeing you buy B. 24. *that*] *Interlineated in* Y; *omitted in* C.

her husbande, had no list to growe greatly vpward in the world, nor neyther would labour for office of authoritie, and ouer that forsooke a right woorshipfull rowme when it was offered him, she fell in hande with him and all too rated him, and asked him :

More laughs at his wife's love of power, and her indignation at his lack of ambition. Is he content to "make goslings in the ashes"? [WORKS, p. 1224, with addition.]

"What will you doo, that you list not to put foorth your selfe as other folke doo? Will you sitt still by the fire, and make goslinges in the ashes with a sticke as children doo?"

"What would you doo, I praye you?"

"By God, goe forwarde with the first; for as my mother was wont to say, God haue mercy on her soule, it is euer better to rule then to be ruled. And therefore, by God, I would not, I warrant you, be so foolishe to be ruled where I might rule."

"By my troth, wife," quoth her husbande, "in this I dare say you say truth, for I neuer founde you willing to be ruled yet."

When he was prisoner in the towre, and there had continued a good while, his saide wife obteyned licence to [fol. 26 *a*] see him. | Who, at the first co*m*ming, like a simple ignorant woman, and somewhat worldly too, with this maner of salutation bluntly saluted him :

Lady More visits her husband in the Tower; she is not in sympathy with More's opposition to the King's wishes. [ROPER.]

"What the goodyere, M*aster* More," quoth she, "I meruaile that you [that] haue beene alwayes hitherto taken

MSS. E L R² Y C H R B.

1. *her husbande*] *Omitted in* B. 1. *no list*] noe very great list Y; not list B. 1. *to growe . . . vpward*] greatly to gett vpward H. 1. *greatly*] *Omitted in* Y. 2. *nor*] *Interlineated in* L; noe Y. 2. *neyther*] *Omitted in* R² B. 2. *of*] in R²; or Y. 5. *and asked*] asking B. 6. *What . . . not*] what he would doe þat he listed not B. 6. *you* (1)] ye Y H R. 6. *you* (2)] ye H R. 6. *to put*] put Y. 6–7. *your selfe*] himselfe B. 7. *folke*] folkes H. 7. *you*] ye H R. 9–10. *praye you? By God*] pray you goth hee by god said shee R² (o *of* goth *and* said shee *being interlineated*); pray yow quoth he By God B. 11. *euer*] *Omitted in* Y. 12. *then to be*] then be B. 12. *by God*] *Omitted in* B. 13. *would . . . to be*] would not be soe foolish I warrant you to be R². 14. *where I might rule*] when I migh H; Y *as* E L R² C R B, *but* when *for* where. 15. *her husbande*] he R². 17. *yet*] as yet H. 19. *good*] greate B. 21. *too*] *Omitted in* B. 23. *the*] he H. 23. *goodyere*] good ere B. 23–24. *I meruaile*] *Before* meruaile E *has* t ha *crossed through.* 23–24. *I meruaile that you that haue*] C (*supported by most* Roper MSS.); I meruaile that you who haue E Y; I mervaile you that haue H R; I mervaile that you having L R² B. (*See* Notes.)

for so wise a man, will nowe so play the foole to lye here in this close, filthy prison, and be content thus to be shutt vp amonge mise and rattes; when you might be abrode at your libertie, with the fauour and good will both of the king and his counsaile, if you would but doo as all the Bisshopps and best learned of this Realme haue done. And seeing you haue at Chelsey a right faire house, your librarie, your bookes, your gallerie, your garden, your orchyarde and all other necessaries so handsome about you, where you might in the company of me your wife, your children and housholde, be mery, I muse what a Gods name you meane here still thus fondlye to tarye."

More's reply: the Tower is as nigh heaven as is his own house. [ROPER.]

After he had a while quietly heard her, with a cheerefull countenaunce he saide vnto her:

"I praye thee, good mistris Als, tell me one thing."

"What is that?" quoth she.

"Is not this house," quoth he, "as nigh heauen as mine owne?"

To whom she, after her accustomed homely fasshion, not lyking suche talke, aunswered: "Tille valle, Tille valle."

"Howe saye you, mistris Als?" quoth he, "is it not so?"

"*Bone Deus, Bone Deus*, man, will this gere neuer be lefte?" quoth she.

And his house will soon forget its master. [ROPER.]

"Well, then, mistris Alice, if it be so," quoth he, "it is very well. For I see no great cause why I shoulde muche ioye eyther of my gaye house or of any thing

MSS. E L R² Y C H R B.

1. *so wise a man*] a wise man B. 1. *to lye*] & lye H R; as to lye B. 2. *and be*] & to be L. 2. *content thus*] thus content H R. 4. *both*] *Omitted in* B. 5. *all*] *Omitted in* B. 9. *all other*] all other your Y; all your other H. 9. *necessaries*] necessarie Y. 10. *in the*] in H B. 13. *a while . . . her*] quietly heard her a while H. 13–14. *with . . . her*] *Omitted in* H R. 14. *he*] *Omitted in* R². 15. *thee*] yow B. 15. *mistris Als*] wife B. 15. *Als*] Alice L R² Y H R; Alce C. (*So below*, l. 22.) 17. *quoth he*] *Omitted in* H R. 18. *owne*] owne is B. 19. *she*] *Omitted in* H R. 21. *valle*] *Interlineated in* B. 22. *saye*] sayde B. 23. *not*] no H. 24. *Bone* (1) and (2)] Bene Y. 25. *quoth she*] *Omitted in* B. 28. *muche*] so much Y.

belonging therevnto, when, if I should but seuen yeres lye buried vnder the grounde, I should not faile to finde some therein that would bidd me gett me out [of] dores, and tell me it were none of mine. What cause haue I then to like suche a house as would so soone forgett his master?"

So her persuasions moued him but a litle.

More is amused at his wife's fear of his suffocation when locked in by his gaoler. [WORKS, p. 1247, with addition.]

Of some other talke in the towre with his wife, Sir Thomas More telleth a merye, pretie narration, but, as his fasshion is, vnder shadowe of dissembled persons, but in deede meaning of himselfe and this his wife, which you shall nowe heare, speaking himselfe:

"In deede, I wist a woman once that came into a prison to visite of her charitie a poore prisoner there, whom she founde in a chamber (to say the truth) meetely faire, and at the least wise it was stronge ynough; but with mattes of strawe the prisoner had made it so warme, both vnder the foote and rounde about the walles, that in these thinges for the keeping of his health she was on his behalfe gladd and very well comforted. But among many other displeasures that for his sake she was sory for, one she lamented much in her minde, that he should haue the chamber doore vpon him by night made fast by the gayler that shoulde shett him in. 'For by my troth,' quoth she, 'if the doore should

MSS. E L R^2 Y C H R B.

1. *belonging therevnto*] therevnto belonginge H. 1. *when*] where B. 1–2. *but . . . buried*] be but 7 yeeres lye buried L; be but seuen yeres buried R^2; but by seaven yeares buried Y; be but seaven yeares bye buried B. (E C H R *supported by most* Roper MSS. *See* Notes.) 2. *vnder*] in B. 2. *not faile to*] faile but H. 3. *some*] *Omitted in* B. 3. *gett me out*] gett out L R^2 B (Roper MSS. *vary. See* Notes.) 3. *of dores*] of doores R^2 Y C B (*supported by* Roper); of þe doores L H R; adores E. 5. *like*] *Omitted in* B. 5. *a*] an L R^2 B. 5. *as would*] that would Y. 9. *merye*] *Omitted in* L R^2 B. 9. *narration*] talke B. 11. *of*] *Omitted in* H R. 11. *himselfe*] his selfe H. 13. *In deede*] *Omitted in* H R. 13. *wist*] wisht L. 13. *into a*] into L. 14. *charitie*] *The lower half of this word is cropped in* L. 16. *at the least*] at least H R. 17. *mattes*] matters Y. 19. *these*] those Y. 19. *the*] *Omitted in* B. 22. *one*] *Omitted in* B. 22. *he*] shee B. 23. *the*] *Corrected, probably from* hir, L. 23. *vpon*] pon C.

be shett vppon me, I would weene it would stopp vp my breth.'

But dare not show his amusement. [WORKS, *as above.*]

"At that worde | of hers the prisoner laughed in his [fol. 26 *b*] minde, but he durst not laugh alowde, nor say any thing to her, for somewhat in deede he stoode in awe of her, and had his finding there, muche part, of her charitie for almes; but he could not but laugh inwardlye, while he wist well ynough that she vsed on the [inside] to shett euery night full surely her owne chamber to her, both doore and windowes too, and vsed not to open them of all the longe night. [And] what difference then as to the stopping of the breath, whether they were shett [vp] within or without?"

Which narration he doth hansomely applye and accommodate to his purpose.

Lady More has no more effect on her husband's good purposes than had Job's wife on Job's patience.

And thus, loe, though Eve supplanted and ouerthrewe by her pleasant persuasions her husbande, our first father, Adam, in Paradise, yet could not this woman any thing infringe or breake the constant settled good purposes of this woorthy man, her husbande, no, not in his extreme aduersitie; no more then blessed Jobes wife could shake and ouerturne any part of his good patience. And yet surely no stronger nor mightier temptation in all the worlde is there then that proceedeth from the wife. And therefore some thinke and write that though the deuill

MSS. E L R[2] Y C H R B.

1. *me*] her H. 1. *would weene*] weene C. 1. *would stopp*] should stopp B. 1. *vp*] *Omitted in* B. 3. *At*] And at C. 3 *that*] what B. 8. *wist*] wished L. 8. *inside*] L R[2] Y C B (*supported by* English Works, *p.* 1247); on the one side E R; one the one the on side H. 9. *chamber to her*] chamber dore to her H R, dore *being interlineated in* R. 9. *to her, both*] *Omitted in* B. 10. *windowes too*] wyndoes to her B. 10–12. *of all . . . And . . . stopping*] Y C (*supported by* English Works, *p.* 1247); E R *as* Y C, *but omitting* And; all þe long night & what difference as to þe stopping L; all the night longe and what difference as to the stoppinge R[2]; B *as* R[2], *but* is *for* as; all the longe night what difference then as the stoppinge H. 12. *vp*] L R[2] Y C B (*supported by* English Works, *p.* 1247); in E H R. 13. *within*] eather within Y. 14. *Which*] This B. 16. *loe*] *Omitted in* B. 20. *in his* in this C. 20–21. *extreme aduersitie*] extreamity & aduersitye H R. 21. *Jobes*] Job his B. 22. *and*] or L. 22. *and ouerturne*] *Omitted in* B. 25. *and write*] *Omitted in* B.

might haue, by the wordes of his Co*m*mission geuen to him from God, destroyed also Jobes wife as well as he did his children, yet did the wretched, malitious caytiffe full [wilily] spare her, to make her his instrument to the destruction of her husbandes patience.

MSS. E L R[2] Y C H R B.

1. *wordes*] worde B. 1–2. *to him*] him H R. 4. *wilily*] L R[2] Y C B; wisely E H R.

[III]

Of More's books.

It remayneth nowe then, that seing as well the matter it selfe we haue in hande, as our promise, craueth it at our handes, that we speake somewhat of his bookes, whereby he hath consecrate his woorthy name to immortalitie in this transitorie worlde to the worldes ende. And I doubt not, for his great paines and trauell therein, especially for Gods sake, to whom he had his principall respect, he hath receaued his condigne reward in the celestiall worlde that neuer shall haue ende. Whereof some are written in latin onely, [some in English onely], some certaine in both tonges. We will touche summarily of both sortes so muche as may seeme conuenient to our present purpose. And the more willingly this doo we because his bookes be rare, and the print spent vp, and some as well latine as Inglishe neuer yet put to the print. Howbeit, we trust shortlye to haue all his englishe workes, as well those that haue beene sett forth ere this, as some others, in print, wherin M*aster* Sargeant Rastell doth nowe diligently trauell, and imployeth his good and carefull indeuour to the furthering of the saide good purpose.

Rastell is printing More's English Works.

More's Latin *Epigrammata.* [1518.]

Among other his latine bookes are his epigrammes, partly translated out of greeke, partly so wittily and pleasauntly deuised and penned of his owne, as they may

MSS. E L R^2 Y C H R B.

2. *it selfe*] *Omitted in* B. 2. *in hande*] now in hande R^2. 2. *it* (2)] *Corrected from* at L. 3. *speake*] *Corrected, probably from* spake, R. 4. *consecrate*] consecrated B. 5. *worlde to the*] *Omitted in* H. 6. *paines*] *Interlineated over* pointes *crossed through* Y. 7. *his*] a Y. 7. *he hath*] *Interlineated in* R. 9. *haue*] *Omitted in* B. 10. *some in English onely*] L R^2 Y C B; *omitted in* E H R. 10. *certaine*] *Omitted in* C B. 11. *sortes*] poinctes Y. 13. *willingly this*] willing thus L; willing this R^2 Y H B. 13. *doo we*] wee doe B. 13. *bookes*] booke R. 14. *spent*] spirte B. 15. *the*] *Omitted in* Y. 16. *workes*] *Corrected from* bookes R. 17. *that*] as R^2. 17. *haue beene*] haue not beene H R. 17. *others*] other Y. 17–18. *as some others, in print*] as some others not yet in print L R^2 B. 18. *Sargeant*] *Omitted in* Y. 19. *diligently*] most diligently R^2. 19. *imployeth*] implieth B. 20. *to the*] in the H. 20. *purpose*] purposses H. 21. *Among other*] Among all other H R. 21. *his*] of his B. 22. *wittily*] written B.

seeme to be nothing inferiour or to yelde to any of like [fol. 27 *a*] kinde written in our dayes ; And perchaunce | woorthy to be sett and compared with many like wryters of the olde [forerun] dayes. These Epigrammes, as they be learned and pleasaunt, so are they nothing byting or contumelious.

[BEATUS RHENANUS.]

Howbeit certaine merie conceyted Epigrammes that he made of Germanus Brixius, a frenche man, vntruely and falsely setting forth and aduauncing the valiant doinges of the frenche captaine, Herueus, by the Sea against the englishe men, so incensed the saide Brixius, albeit* the thinges that S*ir* Thomas More wrate were true, and yet written in the time of hostilitie and warre, that he wrote a very spitefull booke against the saide S*ir* Thomas More, and so farre forgott himselfe that he went about, as farre as in him laye, to bring him in discredite with king Henry the eight as one that was the kinges enemie. And so when the kinges were at peace, Brixius longe after beganne with M*aster* More his newe and cruell warre. His booke he intituled " Antimorus," which M*aster* More aunswered. And albeit he had a great deale the better hande against Brixius, and that not onely by censure and iudgement of Erasmus, Brixius great frende, but many other learned men Brixius frendes also, yet at the desire of Erasmus, and vpon sight of his letters, he stayed all his bookes,

The anti-Brixius epigrams lead More into controversy.

Brixius's ***Antimorus.*** [1519.]

At the desire of Erasmus, More calls in his ***Epistola ad G. Brixium.*** [1520.]

MSS. E L R^2 Y C H R B.

1. *or to yelde*] *Interlineated in* L; or yeeld H; *omitted in* B. 2. *in our*] in these our R^2. 3–4. *many like wryters of the olde forerun dayes*] many like writers of þe ould forerun daies C; many like wryters of the olde forreine dayes E Y R; many like writers of the old former forrayne dayes L (*final* r *of* former *and* forrayne *interlineated*); many like writers of old former days R^2; many of the old writers in forraigne daies H ; many like authors of the old forraine daies B. 5–6. *byting or contumelious*] biting conuiciously and contumeliously Y; biting contentious or contumelious C. 9. *and aduauncing*] *Omitted in* B. 10. *Herueus*] Hrncus R^2 ; Hercules B. 10. *against*] againe Y; amongst B. 11. *so*] sore B. 11–12. *albeit the thinges that*] R^2 Y C H R; albeit that the thinges that E B; that albeit the things which L. 12. *wrate*] wrought R^2. 13–14. *warre . . . booke*] warre. Wher-vpon Brixius wrote such a spitefull booke B. 14. *the saide*] *Omitted in* B. 15. *about*] *Omitted in* L R^2 B. 15. *farre*] much C. 19. *his*] hes R^2. 19. *His*] This B. 22. *and that*] that B. 22. *by*] by the C. 23. *Brixius great*] his greate B. 23. *but*] & H R. 23. *other*] *Omitted in* L R^2 Y B. 25. *sight*] þe sight C.

newly printed, from further sale, and recouered into his handes some copyes that his frendes had, to suppresse them. So much of Brixius,* which I haue the sooner planted in here because I knowe M*aster* More is herein by some Protestant*es* noted and slaundered.

Life of King Richard the Third (Latin and English). [*c.* 1513.]

He wrote also most elegantly and eloquently the life of kinge Richarde the thirde, not onely in englishe, which booke is abroade in printe, but corrupted and vitiated, but in latine also, not yet printed. He did not perfect and finish the same booke, neyther any sithens durst take vpon him to sett his hande to the penne to finishe it, [either] in the one or other tonge, all men being deterred and driuen from that enterprise by reason of the incomparable excellencie of the saide worke; As all other painters were afraide in the olde time to supplye and perfect the image of Venus painted, but imperfectly, by Apelles, for his excellent workmanshipp therein.

Utopia. [Book II, 1515; Book I, 1516.] An example of a singular good common-wealth.

But the booke that beareth the pricke and price of all his other latine bookes of wittie inuention, for prophane matters, is his Vtopia. He painteth me it forth so liuely and so pleasauntly, as it were an exquisite platforme, paterne and example of a singuler good common wealth, as to the same neyther the Lacedemonians, nor the Athenienses, nor yet, the best of all other, the Romanes common | wealth, is comparable; [full] pretily and probably [fol. 27 *b*] deuising the said co*m*mon wealth to be in one of the

MSS. E L R² Y C H R B.

1. *newly*] new H. 3. *Brixius, which*] L R² Y C B; Brixius the which E H R. 4. *herein*] therein R². 5. *Protestantes*] protestant L. 5. *and slaundered*] & somewhat sclandered L R² Y B. 6. *He . . . elegantly*] he allso wrote elegantly L R² B. 7–8. *which booke is*] which bookes ar Y. 8. *corrupted and vitiated*] vitiated & corrupted R². 10. *same*] sayd R² C H R. 11. *either*] C; neither E L R² Y H R B. 12. *or other*] nor the other H; or the other R. 12. *all*] till all B. 13. *that*] the B. 14. *all*] *Omitted in* B. 15. *in . . . time*] *Interlineated in* L. 15. *supplye and perfect*] perfitt & finish R². 19. *his*] *Interlineated in* L. 19–20. *of wittie . . . matters*] *Omitted in* B. 19. *wittie*] *Corrected from* written L; writtin Y. 19. *inuention*] invecion H. 19–20. *for prophane matters*] *Omitted in* L R². 20. *me it*] it H B; it me R. 21. *an*] in H. 22. *good*] *Omitted in* R². 23. *as to*] and to B. 25. *full*] L R² Y C B; but E H R. 26. *the said common wealth*] the same B. 26. *in one*] one B.

countreys of the newe founde landes declared vnto him at Antwerpe by Hithlodius, a Portingall, and one of the Sea companions of Americus Vespusius, that first sought out and founde these landes; such an excellent and absolute state of *com*mon wealth that, sauing the people were vnchristned, might seeme to passe any state and common wealth, I will not say of the olde nations by me rehearsed, but euen of any other euen in our time.

The common-wealth of Utopia believed by some of More's readers actually to exist.

Many great learned men, as Budaeus and Johannes Paludanus, [seemed to take the same storie as a true storie. And Paludanus] vpon a feruent zeale wisshed that some excellent diuines might be sent thither to preache Christes Gospell; yea, then were here amonge vs at home sundry good men and learned diuines very desirous to take that voyage, to bring that people to Christes fayth, whose maners they did so well like vpon.

A belief not to be wondered at, when we consider the actual discoveries of that time. [WORKS, p. 126, with additions.]

And surely this saide iollye inuention of S*ir* Thomas More seemed to beare a good countenaunce of truth, not onely for the credite M*aster* More was in with the worlde, but euen for that about that time many straunge and vnknowen nations and many conclusions were discouered, such as our forefathers did neither knowe nor beleeue; it was by most certaine experience found, especially by the wonderfull nauigation of *nauis* called Victoria that sayled the world rounde about, that shippes sayle bottome to bottome, and that there be Antipodes, that is to say,

MSS. E L R^2 Y C H R B.

1. *landes*] land B. 2. *Hithlodius*] Hitholdius R^2. 2. *Portingall*] Portugall H R. 3. *Americus*] Almericus L; Amuricus R^2; Americus, *corrected from* Amaricus, B. 3. *Vespusius*] Respusius C. 5. *of*] of a L R^2 Y. 6. *and*] or H. 8. *but euen of*] but of R^2. 8. *euen in*] in H; now in B. 9. *and*] et B. 10. *Paludanus*] Paludamus H. 10–11. *seemed . . . Paludanus*] C; *omitted in* E L R^2 Y H R B. 11. *feruent*] certein B. 13. *Christes*] Christ R^2. 13. *then*] there C. 13. *here*] *Preceding* here, L *has* there *crossed through*; theare H R. 16. *they*] there Y. 16. *well*] *Omitted in* B. 17. *surely*] *Omitted in* L R^2 B. 17. *this*] that H. 18. *to beare*] *Omitted in* B. 19. *credite*] creditte that Y C H. 19. *Master*] Sir Thomas R^2 B. 19. *was in with*] was in L B; was of in R^2. 21. *and many conclusions*] *Omitted in* B. 22. *neither*] neuer L. 22–23. *it was . . . found*] *Omitted in* L R^2 B. 24. *nauis*] navies B. 26. *and that*] & L R^2. 26. *that* (2) . . . *say*] *Omitted in* B.

that walke foote against foote; which thing Lactantius and others doo flatlye denye, laughing them to scorne that did so write. Againe, it is certainly founde that there is vnder the Zodiacke (where Aristotle and others say that for the immoderate and excessiue heate is no habitation) most pleasaunt and temperate dwelling and the most fruitfull countreys of all the world. These and other considerations cause[d] many wise, learned men nothing lesse to mistrust that this had beene nothing but an inuentiue drifte of S*ir* Thomas Mores owne imagination and head, but tooke it for a very sure knowen story.

The tale of Zeuxis and Parrhasius.

Wherein they were deceaued by M*aster* More, as wise and [as] well learned as they were; as Zeu[x]is the Painter was in the olde time, notwithstanding he painted grapes so liuely and exquisitely that the birdes came to picke vpon them as vpon very grapes in deede. But when Parrhasius, another exquisite Painter, had shewed him a certaine table, wherin he had painted a vaile or curtin: "Take away," quoth Zeu[x]is, "this vaile and curtin, that I may see your painting it selfe." Wherat Parrhasius fell vpon a great laughter, saying: "Yester- | day thou didst deceaue the birdes, but this day I haue [fol. 28 *a*] deceaued thee, as cunning a painter as thou art." For in deede it was no curtaine, but a table so artificially painted that it seemed to Zeu[x]is a very curtaine.

MSS. E L R^2 Y C H R B.

1. *that walke*] that they walk L R^2; men that walke C; who walke B. 1. *against*] to Y. 2. *to*] to to R^2. 4–5. *where . . . habitation*] *Omitted in* B. 5. *immoderate*] nordinate H; inordynate R. 7. *countreys of*] Country in L R^2 B; contries in Y. 7. *all*] *Omitted in* Y. 8. *caused*] L R^2 C B; cause E Y H R. 9. *an*] *Interlineated in* R^2. 11. *and head*] *Omitted in* B. 11. *for a*] *Omitted in* H. 13. *and as well*] R^2 Y C H B; and well E L R. 13–14. *as Zeuxis the Painter*] as the painter Zeusis C. 13. *Zeuxis*] R^2 H R B; Zeuxes L; Zeusis E Y C. 14. *in the*] in L R^2 B. 14. *notwithstanding he*] who B. 15. *birdes*] *Interlineated in* R. 18. *a certaine table*] a table (*interlineated*) R^2. 18–19. *a vaile or curtin*] a vaile & a curtaine L; a vaile & curteine R^2 B; *omitted in* C. 19. *quoth*] saith L B. 19. *Zeuxis*] R^2 H R B; Zeuxes L; Zeusis E Y C. 19. *this*] þe R^2; *omitted in* H. 19. *and*] or H. 21. *vpon*] in H R. 21. *Parrhasius . . . saying*] Parrasius laughing greatlie sayde B. 22. *I haue*] haue I, H. 24. *no*] *Omitted* in C. 24. *artificially*] artificiously L. 25. *Zeuxis*] R^2 R B; Zeuxes L; Zuxis H; Zeusis E Y C.

In this booke, among other thinges, he hath a very goodlye processe howe there might be fewer theeues in Inglande, and a meruailous inopinable probleme of sheepe: that whereas men were wont to eate the sheepe, as they doo in other countreys, nowe contrarywise sheepe in Inglande pitifully doo deuoure man, woman and childe, houses, yea, and Townes withall.

Parts of *Utopia* deal with the prevention of theft and turning of English arable land into pasture.

And like a moste thankefull man, he maketh honorable mention of Cardinall Morton, Archbisshopp of Caunterbury and Lorde Chauncell*our* of Inglande, In whose house, as we haue saide, him selfe in his tender youth was brought vp; Albeit it be by the dissembled name of the saide Hithlodius, whom he imagineth to haue bene in Inglande, and to haue beene acquainted with the saide Cardinall.

Cardinal Morton is brought into *Utopia*.

And as this booke in his kinde is singuler and excellent, conteyning and prescribing a common wealth farre passing the common wealthes deuised and instituted by Licurgus, Solon, Numa Pompilius, Plato and diuers other; so wrate he in another kinde and sort a booke against Luther no lesse singuler and excellent. King Henry the eight had written a notable erudite booke against Luthers booke * *de captiuitate Babilonica*, most

More, under the pseudonym of Gulielmus Rosseus, writes the *Responsio ad Lutherum*, a defence of Henry VIII against Luther. [1523.]

MSS. E L R^{2} Y C H R B.

1. *among other*] amonge of other H. 3. *inopinable*] opinionable L R^{2} B. 4. *that . . . sheepe*] *Omitted in* B. 4. *the*] *Omitted in* C. 5. *nowe contrarywise*] so likewise B. 6. *doo*] *Omitted in* H R. 6. *man . . . childe*] men women and children B. 7. *and*] *Omitted in* C. 7. *and Townes*] & the townes H R. 8. *And*] *Omitted in* L R^{2} B. 8. *honorable*] *Omitted in* R^{2}; most honorable Y H R. 11. *as we haue saide*] *Omitted in* B. 11–12. *him selfe . . . vp*] himselfe was in tender youth brought vp L R^{2}; him self was in his tender youth was brought vp Y; C *as* E, *but with* was *omitted*; himself was in his tender youth brought vp H R; he was in his tender youthe broughte vp B. 12. *Albeit it be*] albeit he coloureth it B. 13. *the saide*] *Omitted in* C B. 13. *imagineth*] imgeneth Y; ymagined H R. 16. *in*] is H. 17. *conteyning and*] *Omitted in* B. 17. *prescribing*] describing L. 18. *farre*] *Omitted in* R^{2}. 18. *wealthes*] wealth R^{2} Y. 18. *instituted*] vsed L R^{2} B. 19–20. *Pompilius . . . in*] *Interlineated in* R, *with* others *for* other, *and* wrot *for* wrate. 20. *so*] and so Y. 20. *wrate*] wrought L. 20–21. *wrate . . . against*] wrote he many other kinde of bookes against B. 20–21. *kinde and sort . . . Luther*] sort and kynd against Luther a booke C. 21. *excellent. King*] excellent then kyng C. 22. *a*] in a C. 23. *booke*] R^{2} Y C H R B; bookes E; *cropped in* L. 23. *de*] *Cropped in* L.

Who had scoffed against Henry's *Assertio septem sacramentorum* [1521] in his *Contra Henricum Regem Angliae.* [1522].

euidently and mightily refuting his shamefull, vile heresies against the Catholike faith and Christes holy Sacramentes; which did so greeue and yrke Luther to the very hart, that hauing no good substantiall matter to helpe himselfe withall, he fell to scoffing and sawcie iesting in his aunswere to the kinge*s* booke, vsing almost nothing els throughout his aunswere but the faire figure of rhetorike called sawce mallepert, and playeth the very varlett with the king. To whom S*ir* Thomas More made a Replye, and so doth discipher and open his wretched, vile handlinge of the sacred Scripture, his monstrous opinions, and manifest and manifolde contradictions, that neyther he nor any of his generation durst euer after putt penne to the booke to encounter and [re]ioyne with his Replye. In the which aunswere, beside the deepe and profounde debating of the matter it selfe, he so dresseth him with his owne scoffing and iesting rhethoricke as he woorthelye deserued. But because this kinde of wryting, albeit a meete cover for suche a cupp, and very necessary to represse and beate him w*i*th his owne follye, according to Scripture, *Responde stulto secundum stultitiam eius*, seemed not very agreable and correspondent to his saide grauitie and dignitie, the booke was sett forth vnder the name of one Gulielmus Rosseus onely, suppressing his owne name.

MSS. E L R² Y C H R B.

1. *shamefull, vile*] vile & shamefull L. 4. *good substantiall*] good and substantiall C. 5. *sawcie*] sawce Y. 6. *booke*] bookes Y. 7. *throughout*] through Y. 8. *called*] *Interlineated over an erasure in* R². 8. *sawce*] saucy R² C. 8–9. *and playeth . . . king*] *Omitted in* B. 8. *playeth*] play L; played R²; playinge H R. 9–10. *made a*] made L. 10. *and open*] *Omitted in* B. 11. *Scripture*] Scriptures H R. 12. *and manifest*] *Omitted in* L R² B. 13. *neyther . . . his*] neither he nor his nor any of his H. 14. *booke*] worke H. 14. *and*] *Omitted in* B. 14. *reioyne*] L R² H R; enioyne E Y C; *omitted in* B. 14. *with*] to H R. 15–16. *deepe and profounde*] þe profound & deepe R². 17. *him with*] himselfe with L R² B; him so with H R. 18. *But*] And H R. 19. *albeit a meete*] albeit it be a meet Y. 19. *cupp*] poote Y. 21. *to Scripture*] to the scripture L R² B. 21. *secundum*] secundam H. 21–22. *stultitiam*] stultiam, *corrected from* stultias, H; stultiam R. 23. *saide*] *Interlinated in* R; *omitted in* B. 23. *grauitie and dignitie*] dignity & grauity R². 24. *Gulielmus*] Gulidmus H.

Epistola contra J. Pomeranum. [1525.]

He made also in latine another proper and wittie Treatise printed against a certaine epistle of John Pomerane, one of Luthers standerdbearers in Germanie.

The *Passionis Expositio* [1535] left unfinished by More, and translated into English by Mistress Bassett, More's grand-daughter.

And after he was shutt vp' in the towre, he wrote a [fol. 28 *b*] certaine exposition in latine vpon the | passion of Christe, not yet printed, which was not perfited, and is so plainly and exquisitely translated into Englishe by his foresaide Neece, mistris Bassett, that it may seeme originally to haue beene penned in Englishe by S*ir* Thomas More himselfe.

Translation of the *Life of Pico della Mirandula.* [1510?.]

Some other thinges he wrate also in latin which we praetermitt, and will nowe somewhat talke of his englishe workes; w*hi*ch all, beside the translation of John Picus, erle of Mirandula, and the foresaide life of king Richarde, and some other fewe prophane thinges, concerne matters of religion for the most part.

A Dialogue concernynge heresyes & matters of religion. [1528.]

Tindale's *Answere unto Sir Thomas Mores Dialoge.* [1530.]

The first booke of this sort was his booke[s] of dialogues, made by him when he was Chauncello*ur* of the duchie of Lancaster: which bookes occasioned him afterwarde (as, according to the olde prouerbe, one busines begetteth another) to write diuers other thinges; for whereas he had amongst many other matters touched and reproued Will*iam* Tindalls adulterate and vitiate translation of the newe Testament, Tindall, not able to beare to see his newe religion and his owne doinges withall to haue so fowle an ouerthrowe as S*ir* Thomas More gaue him, after great and longe deliberation and consultation with his evangelicall brethre*n*, tooke in hande to aunswere some

MSS. E L R² Y C H R B.

1. *another*] in other Y. 2. *printed*] *Interlineated in* R². 3. *one . . . Germanie*] one of the standerd bareres of Luthers in Germanie Y C. 6. *yet*] it Y. 7. *and exquisitely*] and is so exquisitlie Y; and so exquisitely C B. 7. *foresaide*] *Omitted in* B. 8–9. *to haue beene*] to be R². 11. *he wrate also*] also he wrott H R. 12. *his*] *Interlineated in* L. 14. *life*] booke B. 15. *fewe*] *Omitted in* L R² B. 17. *his*] his first Y. 17. *bookes*] L R² B (*supported by* bookes, *l.* 19, *below*); booke E Y C H R B. 20. *according to*] concerning B. 21. *other*] *Omitted in* H. 23. *vitiate*] viciall Y. 24. *Testament*] tetament H. 27. *and longe*] *Omitted in* L R² B. 27. *and* (2)] an H. 28. *brethren*] bretherne H. 28. *tooke in*] to in B.

More's *Confutation of Tyndales Answere.* [1532.]

part of his saide dialogues, especially touching his foresaide corrupt translation. But what small woorshipp he wanne thereby, i[t] is eathe for euery man to see, that with indifferent affection will vouchsafe to reade S*ir* Thomas Mores Replye, whereof we shall geue you a small taste.

More's integrity and justice in controversy.

But first we will note vnto you the integritie, the sinceritie and vprightnes, the good and gratious nature and disposition, of the saide S*ir* Thomas More in his wryting, not onely against Tindall, but generally against all other Protestantes. First then it is to be considered in him that he doth not, as many wryters doo against the aduersaries, and all the Protestantes doo against him and other Catholikes, writhe and wrest their wordes to the woorst, and make their reasons more weake and feeble then they are; but rather enforceth them to the vttermoste, and often times farther then the partie himselfe doth, or perchaunce could doo. And was of this minde, that he saide he woulde not lett while he liued, wheresoeuer he perceaued his aduersarye to say well, or himselfe to haue saide otherwise, indifferently for both to say and declare the truth. And therefore himselfe, finding after the printing and the bookes diuulged and commonly read of the debellation of Salem and Bizance (albeit many had read the place, and founde no fault therein) yet he, finding afterwarde that he mistooke certaine wordes of the pacifyer, without any other mans

And his willingness to retract anything wrongly written. [WORKS, after p. 1138.]

MSS. E L R² Y C H R B.

1. *saide*] *Interlineated in* R. 1–2. *his . . . translation*] his former sayd corruption Y. 3. *wanne*] wonne C. 3. *it*] L R² Y C H R B; is E. 3. *eathe*] eth L; easily R²; euident Y; easie C H R B. 7. *first*] *Omitted in* C. 7–8. *the sinceritie*] *Omitted in* H R; sinceritie B. 8. *and* (1)] the R². 8. *the good*] and þe good R². 9. *and disposition*] *Omitted in* B. 9. *the saide*] *Omitted in* B. 10. *generally*] gnerally H. 13. *the*] their R² H R B. 13. *and all*] and as all B. 14. *and other Catholikes*] *Omitted in* B. 14. *wrest*] wreath Y C. 14–15. *wordes to*] *Upon an erasure in* R². 21. *otherwise*] others C. 21–22. *for both . . . truth*] to saye and declare the truth for both Y. 23. *finding*] *Corrected from* findeth Y. 23. *and* (1)] *Interlineated over* of *crossed through* L. 23. *the* (2)] the the R. 23. *diuulged*] deulged Y. 26. *yet*] it Y. 27. *other*] *Omitted in* L R² B.

controlement, of himselfe reformed them. The like he counsailed his learned frendes, especially Erasmus, to doo, and to retracte many thinges that he had written, whose counsaile (wherein he had a notable president so to [fol. 29 *a*] doo in the | woorthy doct*our* St Augustine) if Erasmus had folowed, I trowe his bookes would be better lyked of our posteritie, w*h*ich perchaunce shal be faine either vtterly to abolishe some of his woorkes, or at least to redresse and reforme them.

Erasmus does not compare favourably with More in this respect.

Here is nowe farther to be considered in his wrytinges that he neither hunted after praise and vainglory, nor any vile and filthy gaine or worldly co*m*moditie; yea, so that invenomed and poysoned hereticall bookes might be once suppressed and abolished, he wisshed his owne in a light and faire fire also. Yet did the Evangelicall brethren, after he had abandoned the office of the Lorde Chauncell*our* (as they otherwise spredd and wrate many vaine and false rumours to the aduauncement of their owne newe Gospell and pressing of the Catholikes) [lay] to his charge in their bookes that he was partiall to the Clergie, and had for his bookes receaued a great masse of money of the saide Clergie. And Tindall and diuers other of the good brethren affirmed that they wist well that S*ir* Thomas More was no lesse woorth in money and plate and other moueables then twentie thousand markes. But it was founde farre otherwise when his house was

More did not write for gain or glory; or for partiality to the clergy; or for reward from the clergy; as the heretics asserted.

They affirmed that More was rich. [Works, p. 902.] But after he gave up office,

MSS. E L R^2 Y C H R B.

1. *of . . . them*] reformed them of himselfe R^2. 1. *reformed*] reforme C. 4–5. *wherein . . . Augustine*] *Omitted in* B. fol. 29 *a*. *See* Introduction, Description of MS. E: foliation. 5. *woorthy*] *Omitted in* R^2. 5. *Augustine*] Austin L. 6. *I . . . bookes*] his bookes I trowe H R. 7. *either*] *Interlineated in* R. 10. *Here . . . considered*] Heare it is nowe to be further considered H. 11. *neither*] neuer L. 12. *or*] and B. 12. *worldly*] *Omitted in* L R^2 B. 12. *so that*] that so Y. 12–13. *so that . . . poysoned*] so that the poysoned B. 13–14. *once suppressed and*] *Omitted in* B. 15. *and faire*] *Omitted in* B. 15. *also*] *Omitted in* H B. 15. *Yet*] it Y. 16. *after*] after that L H R. 17. *wrate*] write L B; writt R^2; wrote C H R. 18. *owne*] *Omitted in* C. 19. *and pressing . . . Catholikes*] *Omitted in* B. 19. *lay*] H R B (*necessary for syntax*); laide E L R^2 Y C. 21. *had*] *Omitted in* L R^2 B. 22. *other*] others L R^2 H. 24. *no*] not L. 26. *founde farre otherwise*] farre otherwise founde H. 26. *farre*] *Interlineated in* R.

More was proved to be a poor man; and further search would have revealed no treasure but his wife's gay girdle and her golden beads. [WORKS, p. 1447.]

searched after that he was committed to the towre, where a while he had some competent libertie, but afterwarde vpon a sodaine he was shutt vp verye close. At what time he feared there should be a newe and a more narrower searche in all his houses, because his minde gaue him that some folke thought that he was not so poore as it appered in the searche. But he tolde his daughter, mistris Margarete Roper, that it should make but a game to them that knewe the truth of his pouertie, vnlesse they should finde out his wiues gaye girdle and her golden beades. The like pouertie of any man that so longe continued a Counsailer with the king, and had borne so manye great offices, hath, I trowe, seldome beene founde in anye laye man before, and much lesse sithens his time.

More showed only due reverence to the clergy.

As for partialitie to the Clergie, saving the reuerence due to the saide sacred order of priestes, by whom we are made christen men in Baptisme, and by whom we receaue the other blessed Sacramentes, there was none in him.

And was feared by clerical ill-doers. [WORKS, p. 868.]

And that well felte they that were naught of the saide Clergie, that had so litle fauoure at his handes that there was no man, that any medling hadd with [them], into whose handes they were more lothe to come then into his.

More proved how little of his

As for Fees, Annuities, rewardes, or other commodities that should incline him to be ouer propense and partiall to the Clergie: First touching any fees that he had to his

MSS. E L R^2 Y C H R B.

1. *after that*] after L H. 2. *afterwarde*] after L. 4. *a* (2)] *Omitted in* L R^2 Y H R B. 5. *narrower*] narrowe C B. 6. *that some . . . was*] that folke thought he was L R^2 B. 6–7. *that some . . . poore*] *Interlineated in* R. 6. *folke*] folkes H. 9. *a*] *Interlineated in* L *over a short word cancelled.* 9. *a game*] a gaine Y. 10. *gaye*] gay gold R^2. 12. *Counsailer*] chauncelour L R^2 H B. 13. *borne*] boune R^2. 13. *I trowe*] *Omitted in* B. 13. *beene*] bne Y. 16. *As for*] As for the L. 17. *saide*] *Omitted in* L R^2 C H B. 19. *in*] *Interlineated in* R^2; of H. 20. *naught*] *Interlineated over* not *crossed through* Y. 20. *saide*] *Omitted in* L R^2 C B. 21. *that*] who R^2. 22. *with them*] L, them *being interlineated over* him *crossed through* (them *supported by* Apologye, 1533 ed., *fol.* 79^b, *and* English Works, *p.* 868): him E R^2 Y C H R B. 25. *for Fees*] his Fees H. 25. *or*] & H R. 26. *be*] *Interlineated in* E. 26. *propense and*] *Omitted in* B. 27. *that*] *Omitted in* L R^2 B.

liuing after that he had lefte the saide Chauncellour- [fol. 29 *b*] shipp, | he had not one grote graunted him sith he first wrote or went about to write the dialogues, and that was the first worke that euer he wrate in matters of religion. And as for all the landes and fees that he had, [beside such landes and fees as he had] of the kinges gifte, was not, nor should be, during his mother in lawes life (which liued after he relinquished the office of the Chauncellourshipp) woorthe yerely the summe of one hundred poundes. And thereof had he some by his wife, some lefte by his father, some he purchased, and some fees had he of temporall men. And so may euery man soone gesse that he had no very great part of his liuing by the Clergie to make him very partiall to them.

Income he owed to the Clergy. [WORKS, p. 867.]

Nowe touching rewardes or lucre that did rise to him by his wryting—for the which good father Tindall saide he wrote his bookes, and not for any affection he bare to the Clergie, no more then Judas betrayed Christe for anye fauoure he bare to the Bisshopps, scribes and Pharises—it is a moste open shamefull lye and slaunder. Truth it is, that the Bisshops and the Clergie of Inglande, seing (beside the continuall paines he employed in the affaires of the king and [of] the Realme) the great trauell and lab*our* he tooke in wryting against heretikes,

How More refused reward from the clergy for his controversial writings. [ROPER. Cf. also WORKS, p. 867.]

MSS. ELR²YCHRB.

1. *that*] *Omitted in* R². 1–2. *the saide Chauncellourshipp*] the Chauncelorship L; the said Lord Chauncellourshipp HR. 2. *first*] *Omitted in* H. 3–4. *the dialogues . . . religion*] *Omitted in* B. 4. *first*] *Interlineated in* L. 5. *all*] *Omitted in* H. 5–6. [*beside such landes and fees as he had*]] *Omitted in* ELR²YCHRB. *Supplied from* English Works, *p.* 867. 7. *should be*] should not B. 7. *life*] wife C. 7. *which*] who B. 8–9. *the office . . . Chauncellourshipp*] his Chauncelorship B. 9. *one*] an L. 9. *one hundred*] *It should be noted that* English Works, *p.* 867, *and* 1533 *ed. of* Apologye, *fol.* 75ᵇ, *read* fyftye. 10. *thereof*] therefore L. 10. *he*] *Interlineated in* R. 11. *father, some*] father & some L. 12. *soone*] soundely L. 13. *very*] *Interlineated in* R²R; *omitted in* H. 15. *did rise*] rose LR²HRB; rise Y; should rise C. 15. *to*] *Interlineated in* R. 16. *his wryting*] *Cropped in* L. 18. *betrayed*] bestrayed H. 20. *open*] *Omitted in* LR²B. 21. *and the*] & LR²B. 22. *beside the*] besides his LR²B. 22. *he*] *Omitted in* LR²B. 23. *and of the*] LR²YCHRB; and the E. 24. *heretikes*] heresies LR²B.

for the defence of the Catholike faith and the repressing of damnable heresies, the reformation whereof principallye apperteyned to their pastorall cure, and thinking themselues by his trauells (wherein by their owne confession they were not able with him to make comparison) of their duties in that behalfe discharged, and considering that for all his Princes fauoure he was no riche man, nor in yerely reuennewes aduaunced as his woorthines deserued, therefore at a conuocation among them selues and other of the Clergie, they agreed together and concluded vpon a Summe of fowre or fiue thousande poundes, at the least, to my remembraunce, for his paines to recompence him; to the payment whereof euery Bisshopp, abbott and the rest of the Clergie were after the rate of their abilities liberall contributours, hoping this portion should be to his contentation.

Wherevpon Tunstall, Bisshopp of Durham, Clerke, Bisshop of Bathe, and, as farre as I can [call to minde], Veysey, Bisshop of Exeter, repaired vnto him, declaring howe thankfully for his trauels, to their discharge, in Gods cause bestowed, they reckoned themselues bounden to consider him. And that albeit they could not according to his desertes so woorthely as they gladly would requite him therefore, but must reserue that onely to the goodnes of God, yet for a small part of recompence, in respect of his estate, so vnequall to his woorthines, in the name of their whole conuocation they presented to him that Summe, which they desired him to take in good part.

MSS. E L R^2 Y C H R B.

1–2. *for the . . . heresies*] *Omitted in* B. 1. *and the*] and Y C. 4–5. *confession*] confessions L R^2 B. 7. *his*] the Y. 7. *Princes*] Prince his R. 9–10. *and other . . . Clergie*] *Omitted in* B. 10. *of*] *Interlineated in* C. 12–13. *for his . . . him*] to recompence him for his paynes R^2. 13. *to the*] To the which H R. 14. *of their*] to theire B. 15. *liberall*] liberally L. 15. *contributours*] contributories C. 15. *should*] would H R. 16. *contentation*] good Contentacion H R. 17. *of*] *Interlineated in* R^2. 18. *call to minde*] C (*supported by* Roper); remember E L R^2 Y H R B. 19. *Veysey*] Vosey H R; Vasey B. 20. *howe*] how how R. 20. *trauels*] travell H R. 21. *bounden*] bound L R^2. 22. *that*] *Omitted in* H R. 24. *but must reserue*] but refer B. (*Most* Roper MSS. *support* reserue.) 25. *part*] *Interlineated in* R. 25. *of* (1)] *Omitted in* R. 27. *that*] the B. 28. *him*] *Omitted in* Y.

[fol. 30 a] | Who, forsaking it, saide, That like as it was no small comfort vnto him that so wise and learned men so well accepted his simple doinges, for which he neuer intended to receaue rewarde but at the handes of God onely, to whom alone was the thanke chiefly to be ascribed, so gaue he most humble thankes vnto their honours for all their so bountifull and frendly consideration.

When [they], for all their so importune pressing vpon him that fewe would haue weened he could haue refused it, could by no meanes make him to take it, then besought they him to be content yet that they might bestowe it vpon his wife and children. "Not so, my Lordes," quoth he, "I had leauer see it all * cast * into the temmes, then I or any of mine should haue thereof the woorth of one pennie; for though your offer, my Lordes, be in deede * verye * frendly and honorable, yet sett I so much by my pleasure, and so litle by my profite, that I would not, in good faith, for so muche, and muche more too, haue [loste] the rest of so manye nightes sleepe as was spent vpon the same."

These thinges then being thus premised, let vs nowe see howe substantially Tindall and his felowes haue handled their matters, and lett vs beginne with that that moste

The mis-translations of Tindale and his fellows.

MSS. E L R^2 Y C H R B.

2. *and learned*] & soe learned H. 3. *simple*] *Omitted in* H. 3. *for*] for the L. 5. *the*] *Omitted in* H R. 5. *thanke*] thanks L R^2 H B. (Roper MSS. *vary*. *See* Notes.) 7. *their*] theirs R. 7. *so*] *Omitted in* L R^2 B. (Roper MSS. *vary*. *See* Notes.) 7. *consideration*] consideracions L. 8. *When*] whom B. 8. *they*] C H R (*supported by* Roper); *omitted in* E L R^2 Y B. 8. *their so importune*] their importune R^2; their so importunate H B. (*See* Notes.) 9. *him that fewe*] him in soe much þat few R^2. 9. *weened he*] wende that he Y. 10. *could*] they could B. 11. *be*] *Corrected from* by R^2. 11. *yet*] yt Y. 12. *his wife*] his his wife Y. 12. *Lordes*] Lord H R. 13. *he*] *Interlineated in* R^2. 13. *leauer*] *Interlineated above a word crossed through* L; rather R^2 B. 13. *all cast*] L R^2 C H R B (*supported by most* Roper MSS.): cast all E Y. (*See* Notes.) 13. *temmes*] themes R^2; Thames R. 14. *I or*] *Interlineated in* L. 15. *your . . . Lordes*] my lordes your offer Y. 15–16. *be in deede verye*] be indeede very L R^2 C R B (*supported by* Roper); be in verye deede E; be verie Y H. 17. *would*] could Y. 18. *and muche*] and H R. 19. *loste*] C H (*supported by* Roper); leste Y; lefte E L R^2 R B. 19. *manye*] manie a C. (Roper MSS. *vary*. *See* Notes.) 22. *and his*] & all his R^2. 22. *felowes*] followes B. 23. *that that*] that which R^2 Y B; that H. 23. *moste*] *Omitted in* L.

pinched Tindall to heare of, that is, of his false and corrupt translation of the newe Testament; wherein it is to be considered that, as these good brethren partly denye the verye text it selfe and whole bookes of the sacred Scripture (as the bookes of the Machabees and certaine others, and Luther St James epistle also) and as they adulterate, co*m*maculate and corrupt the whole corps of the same with their wronge and false expositions, farre disagreing from the consent of the holy, auncient fathers and doctours and from the fayth of the whole Catholike Churche; so for the aduauncing and furthering of their saide heresies, they haue of a sett purpose peruerted and mistranslated the saide holy Scripture, and after such shamefull sort that amongst other their mischieuous practises, whereas in the latin Epistle of Saint Paule is read in the olde translation "fornicarij," and in the newe ["scortatores," they haue "sacerdotes,"] that is, "priestes," for the good deuotion they beare to the sacred order of Priesthood. And their Patriarche Luther [with his translation in the dutche tonge hath wonderfully depraued, corrupted and] defiled the saide holy Scripture, as we could by diuers meanes [easily] shewe.

Some of Tindale's mis-translations exposed. [WORKS, pp. 405–444.]

Whom his good scholler Tindall in his englishe translations doth matche, or rather passe; wherein he turneth me this worde "Churche" into "congregation," "Priest" into "seni*our*" and "elder"; which worde "congrega|tion" [fol. 30 *b*]

MSS. E L R^2 Y C H R B.

2. *translation*] traslation R^2. 3. *that*] tha R^2. 4. *of the*] of B. 7. *adulterate, commaculate*] adulterate & commaculate L Y. 9. *holy*] whole Y. 11. *their*] the L. 12. *saide*] *Omitted in* B. 13. *Scripture*] scriptures H R. 14. *other*] all other H R. 14. *their*] *Omitted in* B. 15–16. *whereas . . . translation*] *Omitted in* Y. 16. *and*] *Omitted in* L R^2 B. 17. *scortatores*] C; socrates E R; *omitted in* L R^2 Y H B. 17. *they haue*] L R^2 B; *omitted in* E Y C H R. 17. *sacerdotes*] L R^2 Y H B; *omitted in* E C R. (*See* Notes.) 17–18. *that is, priestes*] *Omitted in* B. 18. *for the*] for their Y C. 18. *they beare*] *Omitted in* L. 19–21. *with . . . corrupted and*] C; B *as* C, *but with* his *omitted*; L R^2 Y *as* C, *but* which translation *for* with his translation; E H R which *for* with, *and following words omitted.* 22. *as*] *Followed by erasure in* R^2. 22. *easily*] easely L R^2 Y C B; *omitted in* E H R. 24. *doth*] *Interlineated in* R. 24. *wherein*] where C. 24. *me*] *Interlineated in* R^2. 25—*l.* 2, *p.* 115. *Priest . . . congregation*] *Omitted in* H R. 26. *and elder*] or elder L.

absolutely of it selfe (as Tindall vseth it) doth no more signifie the congregation of christian men then a faire flocke of vnchristian geese. Neyther * "elder" signifieth any [whit] more "a priest" then* this worde "pr[e]sb[y]teros" * "an elder sticke." Many other partes of his translation are sutable to this, as where, in spite of Christes and his holy Saintes images, he turneth "ydoles" into "images," and for like purpose of setting forth his heresies, "charitie" into "loue," "grace" into "fauo*ur*," "confession" into "knowledge," "penaunce" into "repentaunce," with such like.

For the which—as also for diuers of his false, faithlesse, hereticall assertions as well:
that the Apostles lefte nothing vnwritten that is of necessitie to be beleeued;
that the Churche may erre in matters of fayth;
that the Church is onely of chosen vnknowen electes, touching the maner and order of our election;
touching his wicked and detestable opinion against the free will of man;
touching his fonde, foolishe, and inopinable paradoxes of the elect, though they doo abhominable heynous actes, yet they doo not sinne, and that the elect that once heartily repent, can sinne no more—he doth so substantially and so pleasantlye confute and ouerthrowe Tindall,

More exposes Tindale's false doctrines. [1. WORKS, pp. 459–522.] [2. WORKS, pp. 522–538.] [3. WORKS, pp. 577–608.] [4. WORKS, pp. 719–720.] [5. WORKS, pp. 538–571.]

MSS. E L R^2 Y C H R B.

1. *vseth*] doth vse L R^2 B. 2. *then*] the H. 3. *vnchristian*] vnchristned B. 3. *Neyther elder signifieth*] Neyther this worde praesbiteros for elder signifieth E L R^2 Y B; C *as* E L R^2 Y B, *but* elders *for* elder; H R *as* E L R^2 Y B, *but* Presbiter *for* praesbiteros. (*See* Notes.) 4. *any whit more*] L R^2 Y C R B; not any whitt more H; any more E. 4–5. *then this worde presbyteros an elder sticke*] then an elder sticke E L R^2 Y C H R B. (*See* Notes.) 5. *his*] this Y. 6. *where*] were H. 7. *Christes*] Christ B. 7. *images*] *Omitted in* Y. 7–8. *he turneth . . . images*] *Interlineated in* C; he termeth Idoles & Idoles into Images H. 8. *like*] the like L R^2 B. 10–11. *confession . . . repentaunce with*] confession into repentance & L B; confession into Repentance with R^2. 16. *matters*] matter R. 17. *vnknowen*] *Omitted in* L R^2 B. 21. *inopinable*] inopinionable L, *the first two letters being interlineated*; opinionable R^2; inopiniable H; inopinionable B. 22. *doo*] doe all Y. 22. *heynous*] vicyous H; *written upon* vicyous *in* R. 23. *yet*] yt Y. 23. *they doo*] doe they B. 24–25. *substantially and so pleasantlye*] substantially & pleasantly L R^2 Y B; pleasantly and substancially H R. 25. *confute . . . Tindall*] ouerthrowe Tindall & confute him R^2; confute Tindall B.

that if these men that be envenomed and poysoned with these pestilent heresies would with indifferent minde reade the saide *Sir* Thomas Mores answeres, there were good hope (as it hath, God be thanked, chaunced to manye already) of their good and speedie recouerie. But alacke the while, and woe vpon the subtill [crafte] of the cursed deuill that so blindeth them, and the retchlesse, negligent regarde that these men haue to their soule health, that can be content greedily to glutt in the deadly poyson of their soule by reading and crediting of these mischieuous bookes, and yet will not once vouchsafe to take the wholsome, depulsiue triacle, not to be fetched from Genes, but euen ready at home at their hande in *Sir* Thomas Mores bookes against this deadly, dreadfull infection.

Tindale perverts More's words. More did not assert that the Church existed before the Word, but before the Word was *written*. [WORKS, p. 609.]

But to returne nowe againe to the saide Tindall. Lorde, what open, fowle and shamefull shiftes doth he make for the defence of his wronge and naughtie pestiferous assertions, and with what spitefull, shamefull lyes belyeth he *Sir* Thomas More, and wretchedly depraueth his wrytinges; not be[ing] ashamed (though his plaine manifest wordes lye open to the sight of all men to the contrary) to depraue his aunsweres, and, amonge other, that he should affirme that the Churche of Christe should be before the Gospell was taught or preached: which thing he neyther wryteth, nor once

MSS. E L R^2 Y C H R B.

1. *envenomed and*] *Omitted in* B. 2. *these*] their H. 3. *minde*] mindes R^2. 3. *answeres*] *Interlineated in* R; workes or aunswers R^2. 5. *chaunced to*] chainged so B. 5. *to*] *Omitted in* H. 6. *the while*] *Omitted in* H. 7. *crafte*] L R^2 C H B; cast E Y R. 7. *cursed*] Crused H. 8–9. *and . . . health*] *Omitted in* B. 9. *haue to*] haue of Y. 9. *soule*] soules L C H. 9. *that can*] that they can B. 9. *content*] contented H R. 10. *soule*] soules Y. 11. *of*] *Omitted in* H R. 11. *yet*] it Y. 11. *will*] *Corrected from* would L. 12. *triacle*] triall B. 13. *Genes*] Jenes *underlined, with marginal gloss* Geneva, *in* L; Genna R^2; Jenes Y; Jewes B. 13. *ready*] read H; *interlineated in* R. 13–14. *at their*] in their H R. 15. *deadly, dreadfull*] dreadfull deadly Y. 17. *open*] *Interlineated in* R. 18. *naughtie*] *Omitted in* R^2. 19. *shamefull*] & shamefull R^2. 21. *being*] L R^2 Y C H R B; be E. 22. *lye*] be H R. 24. *he*] *Interlineated in* L. 25. *should be*] *Interlineated over* was *crossed through* R. 25–26. *taught or preached*] preached or taught H R. 26. *thing*] things L R^2.

thought (as a most absurde vntruth), but that it was ([as] it is very true) before the written Gospell. And the saide S*ir* Thomas Moore, seing that by Tindalls owne confession the Churche of God was in the world many hundred yeres before the written lawes of Moyses, doth well thereof ga[fol. 31 *a*]|ther and conclude against Tindall, that there is no cause to be yeelded but that muche more it may be so, and is so in deede, that in the gratious time of our redemption the holy ghoste, that leadeth the Churche from time to time into all truth, being so plentifully effused vpon the same, the Churche of Christe is and hath euer beene in many thinges instructed necessary to be beleeued, that be not in any Scripture comprised.

These and many other stronge reasons to proue the common knowen Catholike Churche, and none other, to be the true Churche of Christe, and that seing we doo not knowe the very bookes of Scripture (which thing Luther himselfe confesseth) but by the knowen Catholike Churche, we must of necessitie take the sounde and true vnderstanding of the saide Scriptures, and of all our fayth, of the saide Churche (which vnderstanding is confirmed in the same Churche from the Apostles time, and by infinite miracles, and with the consent of all the olde fathers and holy martyrs) with other substantiall reasons that S*ir* Thomas More layeth forth, haue so appalled and amased Tindall that he is like a man that were in an inexplicable laberinth and mase, whereof he can by no meanes gett out. And Tindall,

More proves that the Holy Catholic Church is the only true Church of Christ. [WORKS, pp. 614–734; 812–832.]

Tindale, appalled and amazed by More's

MSS. E L R^2 Y C H R B.

1. *thought*] taucht or thought R^2. 1. *as a . . . vntruth*] *Omitted in* B. 1. *as* (2)] L R^2 Y C H R B; and E. 2. *Gospell*] *Interlineated over* truth *crossed through* L. 3. *that*] *Interlineated in* R. 10. *into*] in H. 11. *effused*] infused B. 11. *Churche of*] *Omitted in* H. 12. *and . . . beene*] and euer hath beene L R^2 H R B. 17. *that seing*] seing that B. 20–21. *sounde and true*] true & sound L R^2 C B. 21. *of* (1)] of of R^2. 21. *of the saide*] from the saide B. 24. *and* (1)] *Omitted in* L R^2 B. 25. *all*] *Omitted in* L R^2 B; *interlineated in* R. 25. *the*] *Omitted in* L R^2 B. 26. *that*] yt B. 26. *layeth*] so layeth L R^2 B. 27. *appalled and*] *Omitted in* B. 28. *inexplicable*] explicable Y. 28. *and mase*] *Omitted in* B. 29. *he can*] *Interlineated in* L. 29. *And*] *Omitted in* B.

exposure of him, tries every shift to escape.

Bewildering all with his subtlety. As if "walking all naked in a net." [WORKS, p. 421.]

being thus brought often times to a baye and vtter distresse, he scuddeth in and out like a hare that had twentie brace of greyhoundes after her, and were afearde at euery foote to be snatched vp. And as S*ir* Thomas More also merily, and yet truely, writeth, he windeth him so wilily this way and that way, and so shifteth in and out, and with his subtill shifting he so bleareth our eyen that he maketh vs as blinde as a catt, and so maseth vs in his matters that we can no more see whereabout he walketh then if he went visible before vs all naked in a nett, and in effect playeth the very blinde hobbe about the house.

Sometimes Tindale feebly excuses himself, exhibiting malice, ignorance, error and folly. [WORKS, p. 424.]

Some time when there is none other shifte, Tindall is driuen to [scuse] himselfe and his doinges, as he doth for the worde "praesbiteros," that he translated first "seni*our*" and then "elder": wherein for [scuse] of his fault, at great length he declareth fowre faire vertues in himselfe, malice, ignorance, err*our* and folye. And where he saide he had amended his fault with translating "elder" for "senior," this was a like amending as if he woulde, where a man were blinde of thone eye, amende his sight by putting out * the other.

More confutes the Church

As S*ir* Thomas More aunswered Tindall touching his vnknowen Churche, so did he also fryer Barnes; for in

MSS. E L R^2 Y C H R B.

1. *thus brought often times*] brought thus often times Y; thus oftentymes brought H R. 1. *often*] ofte L. 1. *to a baye*] to be a baie Y. 1. *vtter*] *Omitted in* B. 2. *scuddeth*] studdeth C H R. 3. *afearde*] afreayd Y H R. 5. *More*] *Omitted in* H R. 5. *and*] *Omitted in* L R^2 B. 5. *yet*] it Y. 6. *him*] himselfe R^2. 6. *wilily*] wildly L; willie Y. 6. *this way*] this was B. 8. *eyen*] eyes L R^2 B; eyne Y H. 8. *vs*] *Omitted in* R^2. 9. *maseth*] amazeth L R^2 B; amaseth H R. 10. *visible*] visablie Y. 12. *hobbe*] hobble H; hobb *corrected from* hobble R. 13. *none*] no L R^2 Y H B. 14. [*scuse*]] excuse L R^2 C B; stuffe E Y H R (scuse = *aphetic form of* excuse; *cf. reading of* C B, *l.* 16, *below*). 15. *praesbiteros*] Presbiter H R. 15. *that*] which L. 16. *scuse*] C B; excuse L; ane excuse R^2; stufe Y; stuffe E H R. 17. *at great length*] at length H; at length *interlineated in* R; *omitted in* B. 18. *ignorance, errour*] Error Ignorance H R. 19. *saide*] saieth C. 19. *had amended*] amendeth C; amended B. 19. *with*] in L R^2 B. 21. *where*] yf B. 21. *were*] is H R. 21. *of thone eye*] one the one ey L R^2 Y. 22. *by*] by the Y. 22. *out the*] L R^2 C B (*supported by* English Works, *p.* 424); out of the E Y H R. 23. *More*] *Omitted in* H R.

that point both agreed, and would haue the Churche secrete and hidd in hugger mugger. But in the meane season they handle their matter so handsomely and [so] artificially that their owne reasons plucke downe their owne [vnknowne] Churche. And albeit they would haue vs beleeue the Churche were vnknowen, yet doo [fol. 31 *b*] they geue vs tokens and | markes whereby it should be knowen; and in pervsing their vnknowen Churche, they fall into many absurde, fonde, foolishe paradoxes, that S*ir* Thomas More discouereth. And this vnknowen Churche would they faine reare vp in the ayre, to plucke downe the knowen Catholike Churche in the earth, and so leaue vs no Churche at all. Which Churche to ouerthrowe is their finall and onely scope; for that standing, they well knowe their malignant Churche cannot stande, being by the Catholike Churche both nowe and many hundred yeres before condemned.

of Friar Barnes in *The second parte of the confutacion of Tyndals answere.* [1533.] [WORKS, pp. 735–812.]

These and many other thinges doth S*ir* Thomas More at large full well declare, and setteth the limping and halting goodwife of the bottell at Bottells wharfe in disputations with fryer barnes. In the which the indifferent Reader shall soone see that she did not so muche limpe and halte as did the weake and lame reasons that fryer Barnes brought against her of his vnknowen Church, which she vtterly ouerthroweth.

More's device of confuting Barnes through the Goodwife of the Bottle. [WORKS, pp. 766–770.]

MSS. E L R² Y C H R B.

1. *both*] they bothe B. 2. *hugger mugger*] hucker mocker Y; hoker moker C; hucker mucker B. 3. *handle*] handled R². 3. *handsomely*] hainously C. 3–4. *and so artificially*] L R² Y C H R B; and artificially E. 5. *owne vnknowne*] C; vnknowen L R² H R B; owne E Y. 6. *beleeue the*] beleeue þat þe R². 8. *in*] *Interlineated in* R. 9. *absurde, fonde, foolishe*] fond absurde and foolish R²; absurde foolish B. 10. *this*] the Y. 10. *vnknowen*] vnknowne L, vn *being interlineated.* 12. *in the*] in C. 13. *so*] *Omitted in* H. 14–15. *ouerthrowe*] ouerthowe H. 15. *well*] *On an erasure in* H. 15. *cannot*] canot C. 17. *yeres*] *Interlineated in* H. 17. *before*] agoe B. 18–19. *More at large*] More more at large L R² B. 19. *full well declare*] declare full well Y. 20. *at Bottells*] at the Bottles H. (Second Parte of the Confutacion, 1533 *edition, p.* cccclxxxxiii, *and* English Works, *p.* 766, *have* Botolphs). 21. *disputations*] disputation L R² H R B. 21–22. *In . . . Reader*] Y *as* E L R² C R B, *but omitting* the which; the which Indifferent Reader H. 23. *weake and lame*] lame & weake L R² H R B. 24. *that*] of that Y C H R; *after* reasons E *has* of *crossed through.* 24. *brought*] brough R².

Though the Church that Tindale and Barnes devise is the same, they frequently disagree.

For God has sent among the heretics the spirit of discord and division. [WORKS, pp. 863–4.]

But yet, as they doo, both Tindall and Barnes, agree, as we haue saide, in their secrete, vnknowen Churche, so in other pointes touching their saide Churche, and in many other articles beside, they doo farre square and disagree, and not so muche the one from the other as from their owne selfe; As S*ir* Thomas More sheweth more at large. "For," saith he, "as they that would haue builded vp the Towre of Babilon for themselues against God, had suche a stopp throwen vpon them that sodenly none vnderstoode what another saide; Surely * so * God vpon these heretikes of our time, that goe busily about to heape vp to the skye their fowle, filthy donghill of all olde and newe false, stinking heresies gathered vp together against the true Catholike fayth of Christe that himselfe hath euer hitherto taught his true Catholike Churche—God, I say, [which], when the Apostles went about to preache the true fayth, sent downe his owne holy spirite of vnitie, concorde and truth vnto them, with the gifte of speeche and vnderstanding, so that they vnderstoode euery man and euery man vnderstoode them, hath reared vp and sent among these heretikes the spirite of errou*r* and lying, of discorde and diuision, the damned deuill of hell, which so intangleth their tonges, and so distempereth their braines, that they neyther vnderstande well one of them another, nor any of them well himselfe."

MSS. E L R^2 Y C H R B,

1. *both . . . agree*] both agree Tyndall and barnes Y. 2. *as . . . saide*] *Interlineated in* L; *omitted in* B. 2. *secrete, vnknowen*] secrett and unknowen R^2 Y B. 3–4. *and in*] as in L R^2 Y H R B. 4. *articles*] Article B. 5. *and not*] and yet not C. 5. *the other*] þe the other R. 6. *owne selfe*] owne selues L R^2 B. 7–8. *would haue*] *Omitted in* Y. 8. *of Babilon*] *Omitted in* H R. 8. *themselues*] them selfe Y C. 9. *stopp*] stoope Y. 10. *vnderstoode*] knew L R^2 B. 11. *Surely so*] L R^2 Y C H R B (*supported by* 1533 *edition of* Apologye, *fol.* 65*a*, *and* English Works, *p.* 863); So surely E. 11. *these*] the H R. 11. *heretikes*] herickes R^2. 11. *of*] in H R. 12. *to* (2)] *Omitted in* R. 13. *false*] faultes L. 14. *vp*] *Omitted in* Y. 15. *hitherto*] hereto Y. 16. *which, when*] C (*supported by* English Works, *p.* 863, *and* 1533 *ed. of* Apologye, *fol.* 65*b*); when E L R^2 Y H R B. 17. *true fayth*] true catholike faith L R^2 B. 18. *owne*] *Omitted in* L R^2 B. 18. *vnitie, concorde*] vnity and concord R^2. 22. *sent*] sett H R. 23. *damned*] damnable L R^2 B. 25. *neyther vnderstande*] vnderstand not well R^2. 26. *of them*] *Omitted in* H R.

The bookes of the saide Tindall and Barnes are farced and stuffed more with iesting and rayling then with any good substantiall reason. And notwithstanding a man would thinke that Tindall were in fonde scoffing [fol. 32 *a*] peerelesse, yet, as S*ir* Thomas More | declareth, Fryer Barnes doth farre ouerrunne him, and often times fareth as he were from a fryer waxen a fidler, and would at a tauerne go gett him a penie for a fitt of mirth. And yet sometime will he full demurely and holyly preache and take too vpon him as he were Christes owne deere Apostle; as doo also the residue of brethren that write, and especially Tindall, who beginneth [the] preface [of his booke] w*ith* "the grace of our Lorde, the light of his spirite," and so forth, with such a solemne, glorious, glistering salutation as though it were St Paule himselfe. But S*ir* Thomas More doth accordingly dresse him, and discouer to the worlde fryer Luthers and Tindals and suche other false, fayned, hipocriticall holynes in their so high and solemne salutations [and preachings, and concludeth not more pleasantly then truly, That when a man well considereth those their salutations] and holye preachinges, and considereth their lying and pestiferous heresies in these their holy salutations and preachinges, he may well and truely iudge these their holy counter-

More ridicules the feigned holiness and foolish railing of Tindale and Barnes. Barnes "fareth as he were from a friar waxen a fiddler." [WORKS, p. 735.]

The counterfeit sermons of Tindale and Barnes are worse than Friar Frappe's Christmas mumming. [WORKS, p. 358.]

MSS. E L R² Y C H R B.

1. *are*] are so H R. 1–2. *are farced and stuffed*] are and stuffed C, *with gap left by scribe between* are *and* and. 3. *good*] good and Y. 3–4. *a man*] a man a man Y; some man H; a man R, *preceded by* s *crossed through.* 4. *fonde*] *Omitted in* H R. 6. *fareth*] feareth C; forceth H. 7. *waxen a*] to a H R. 7. *fidler*] sadler C (English Works, *p.* 735, *support* fidler). 8. *him*] *Omitted in* H R. 9. *yet*] yet he H. 9. *and*] *Following* and, E *has* whollye *crossed through.* 10. *too*] so L R² B. 10. *as he*] as if he B. 10. *deere*] deare true Y; *omitted in* B. 11. *of*] of the L R² H R B. 11. *write*] writ Y. 12–13. *the preface of his booke*] L R² Y C H R B; his preface E. 13. *the light*] & the light L. 14. *and so forth*] &c L. 14. *glorious*] gloriouse & R². 16–17. *and discouer*] and dooth discover C. 17. *Luthers*] Luther H R. 17. *and* (1)] *Omitted in* B. 18. *other*] others R² B. 18. *fayned*] fained & L H R. 19. *high*] highlie H. 19–21. *and* (2) . . . *salutations*] L R² Y C B; *omitted in* E H R. 22. *considereth*] considering C. 22. *lying*] living C. 22. *and* (2)] *Omitted in* H R. 23. *heresies*] preachinges H R. 23. *in these* . . . *preachinges*] *Interlineated in* R; *omitted in* B.

feite salutations and sermons to be a great deale woorse then [euer] fryer frappe, who first gapeth and then blesseth, and looketh holyly, and preacheth ribawdry, was euer wont at Christmas to make.

More's answer [*The Supply-cacyon of Soulys*] to Simon Fish's *Supply-cacyon of Beggars.* [1529.] The subsequent repentance of Simon Fish. [WORKS, p. 881.]

And thus will we leaue Tindall and Barnes, and speake of some other of the holye fraternitie. Among who*m* there was one that made the Supplication of beggers, the which S*ir* Thomas More aunswered verye notablye, before he wrate against Tindall and Barnes. This Supplication was made by one Simon Fishe; but God gaue him suche grace afterwarde that he was sorye and repented himselfe, and came into the Churche againe, and forsooke and forsware all the whole hill of those heresies out of the whiche the fountaine of his great zeale, that moued him to write, sprange.

More's *Aunswere to Frithes Letter agaynst the blessed Sacrament of the aulter.* [1532.]

After this S*ir* Thomas More wrate a letter impugning the erroneous wryting of John Frith.

More's *Apologye* for certain things objected to in his writings. [1533.]

And whereas after [that] he had geuen ouer the office of the Lorde Chauncell*our*, the heretikes full fast did write against him, and founde many faultes with him and his wrytinges, He made a goodly and a learned Apologie (of some of his aunsweres in the [saide] Apologie we haue already, vpon occasion, somewhat touched) especially of that they layde to his charge of the slender recitall or misrehearsing of Tindall and Barnes argu-

MSS. E L R^2 Y C H R B.

1. *sermons*] preachinges R^2. 1. *great*] *Omitted in* B. 1. *deale*] *Interlineated in* R^2. 2. *euer*] L R^2 Y C B; eyther E H R. 2. *frappe*] Frappy L R^2 B. 2. *and*] *Interlineated in* L. 3. *ribawdry*] *In* E ri *is interlineated.* 5. *will we*] weele H; will R. 5. *leaue*] leaue of H R. 8. *aunswered*] aunswereth B. 9. *he*] *Omitted in* R. 11. *suche*] such a L R^2 H R B. (Suche *supported by* English Works, *p.* 881). 12. *repented*] *Omitted in* H. 13. *and forsooke and forsware*] and forsware H R; forsaking & forswearing B. 14. *of* (1)] of of H. 16. *impugning*] repugning H. 18. *after that he*] L Y C H R B (*being interlineated in* R); after he E R^2. 19. *Chauncellour*] Chauncellorshipp H R. 19. *the* (2)] *Interlineated in* R. 19. *full fast*] fell full faste Y. 20. *write*] writte Y. 21. *and a*] and L R^2 B. 22. *in the saide*] in þe said C H R; which said L R^2 B; within the sayd Y; in the same E. 23. *vpon occasion*] vpon some occasion L H R. 25. *misrehearsing*] misrehersall L R^2 H B; misrehearsall, *corrected from* misrehearsing, R. 25. *of*] & B.

He contrasts his treatment of Tindale and Barnes and their treatment of him. [WORKS, p. 846.]

mentes, and sheweth that they were calumnious slaunders, and that himselfe vsed Tindall and Barnes after a contrary and better maner then they vsed him: "for he rehearseth" S*ir* Thomas Mores "argumentes in euery place faintlye* and falsely* too, and leaueth out the pithe and the strength and the proufe that moste maketh [fol. 32 *b*] for the purpose; And he fareth | therein as if there were one that hauing day of challenge appointed, in which he should wrestle with his aduersarye*, would finde the meane by crafte to gett his aduersarye before the day into his owne handes, and there keepe him and dyet him with such a thinne dyet, that, at the day, he bringeth him foorth feeble, faint and famished, and almost hunger starven, and so leane that he can scant stande on his legges; and then is it easie, ye wote well, to geue the silly soule a fall. And yet when Tindall" had "done all this, he taketh the fall himselfe." But euery man maye well see that S*ir* Thomas More neuer vseth that way with Tindall, nor with any of those folke, but rehearseth their reason to the best that they can make it themselues, and rather inforceth and strengtheth it (as we haue before declared) of his owne, then taketh any part of theirs therefrom.

MSS. E L R^2 Y C H R B.

1. *that*] *Omitted in* R^2; *interlineated in* R. 2–3. *contrary . . . maner*] contrary manner and better H. 3. *for he*] for Tindall L R^2 B (he *is obviously taken over direct from passage in* Apologye, *fol.* 7 *b*, 1533 *ed.*). 4. *argumentes*] arguement H R. 5. *faintlye and falsely*] faintly & falsely L R^2 Y C B (*supported by* 1533 *ed. of* Apologye, *fol.* 8 *a*, *and* English Works, *p.* 846); falsely and faintlye E H R. 6. *the strength*] strength L R^2 H R B. (The strength *supported by* English Works, *p.* 846, *and* Apologye, 1533 *ed.*, *fol.* 8 *a*.) 6. *and the* (2)] of the H R. 7. *for the purpose*] to the matter Y. 7. *fareth*] feareth Y. 8. *day*] a day L R^2 H R B. (Day *supported by* English Works, *p.* 846, *and* Apologye, 1533 *ed.*, *fol.* 8 *a*.) 9. *aduersarye*] L R^2 C B (*supported by* English Works, *p.* 846, *and* Apologye, 1533 *ed.*, *fol.* 8 *a*); aduersaryes E Y H R. 10. *finde*] fayne R^2. 12. *such a*] such B. 14. *starven*] starued L. 14. *scant*] *Omitted in* L. 15. *on*] *Corrected from* of L. 15. *then*] *Omitted in* R^2. 15. *is it*] it is H R B. 15. *easie*] ethe C. 15. *ye*] you L R^2 H R B. 16. *yet*] *Omitted in* R^2. 17. *had*] *The reading of all the* Harpsfield MSS. *is* had; hath *is read by* English Works, *p.* 846, *and* Apologye, 1533 *ed.*, *fol.* 8 *b*. 19. *vseth*] used B. 19. *any of*] any other of B. 20. *but*] *On an erasure in* H. 20. *reason*] reasons R^2. 20. *that*] *Omitted in* R^2. 21. *themselues*] them self Y C. 22. *as . . . declared*] *Omitted in* B.

And defends the length of his writings. [WORKS, p. 847.]

Whereas nowe farther they founde fault with the length of his bookes, he wryteth, among other thinges, that "it is litle meruaile that it seeme longe and tedious vnto them to reade it ouer within, whom it yrketh to doo so muche as looke it ouer without, and euerye way seemeth longe to him that is wearie [ere] he beginne." "But I finde," saith he, "some men againe to whom the reading is so farre from tedious, that they haue read the whole booke ouer thrise, and some that make tables thereof for their owne remembraunce, and that suche men as haue as muche witt and learning both, as the best of all this blessed brotherhood that euer I heard of."

And ridicules the "compendious eloquence" and "wonderful brevity" of the heretics. [WORKS, p. 848.]

And then for the shortnes of Barnes bookes, that the aduersaries did commende, he writeth that he woteth [nere] well whether he may call them longe or short; "for sometime they be short in deede, because they would be darke and haue their false folyes passe and repasse all vnperceaued. Sometime they can vse such compendious kinde of eloquence that they conuey and cowche vp together with* a wonderfull breuitie fowre folyes and fiue lyes in lesse then as manye lynes. But yet for all this, I see not in effect any men more longe then they; for they preache some time a longe processe

MSS. E L R[2] Y C H R B.

1. *founde*] finde H. 1. *the*] *Corrected from* this R[2]. 2. *wryteth*] writeth that H R. 3. *litle*] *Interlineated over* his great *crossed through* L. 5. *as looke*] as to looke L R[2] H R B. (As looke *supported by* English Works, *p.* 847, *and* 1533 *ed. of* Apologye, *fol.* 10 *b.*) 6. *ere*] H R B; eare R[2] C; or E L; before Y. (English Works, *p.* 847, *and* Apologye, 1533 *ed., fol.* 10 *b, read* ere. Or *is a possible variant of* ere, *but the regular spelling of* E *is* ere.) 7. *saith he*] *Omitted in* L R[2] B. 8. *tedious*] tediousnes B. 9. *the whole booke*] it Y. 10–11. *and that suche men*] & they such men too R[2]. 11. *as haue*] that haue L H R. 12. *blessed*] *Interlineated in* Y. 14. *Barnes*] Tyndalls and Barnes C. 14. *that*] *Omitted in* Y. 16. *nere*] L R[2] Y C H B (*supported by* English Works, *p.* 847, *and* Apologye, 1533 *ed., fol.* 12 *a*); not E R. 19. *can*] *Omitted in* L. 20. *kinde of*] *Omitted in* L R[2] B. 21. *with a*] R[2] Y C B (*supported by* English Works, *p.* 848, *and* Apologye, 1533 *ed., fol.* 12 *b*); with an L; with such a E H R. 23. *for all this*] *Interlineated in* R. 23. *effect*] *Interlineated in* R. 23. *longe*] longer H R. 24. *a longe*] a very longe L; in a long R[2].

to very litle purpose. And sith that of all their whole purpose they proue in conclusion neuer a peece at all, [were their writinge neuer so shorte], yet were their whole worke at last to longe by altogether."

And defends the sharp language he had used against Tindale, Frith and Barnes. [WORKS, pp. 865–6.]

Beside many other thinges, his aduersaries layde to his charge that he handled Tindall, Frith and Barnes vngodly and with vncomely wordes, wherein he thus aunswereth: "Nowe when that against all the [whole] [fol. 33 *a*] Catholike Churche, | both that nowe is, and that euer before hath beene from the Apostles dayes hitherto, both temporall and spirituall, laye men and religious, and against all that good is, Saint*es*, ceremonies, seruice of God, the very Sacramentes and all, and most against the best, that is, to witt, the pretious body and bloud of our Saui*our* himselfe in the holy Sacrament of the aultare, these blasphemous heretikes in their vngratious bookes so villanously [iest] and rayle, Were not a man, weene you, very farre ouerseene, and woorthy to be compted vncourteous, that would in wryting against their heresies presume without great reuerence to rehearse their woorshipfull names? If any of them vse their wordes at their pleasure, as euill and as villanous as they list, against my selfe, I am content to forbeare [any] requiting thereof, and geue them no worse wordes

MSS. E L R^2 Y C H R B.

1. *to very litle*] to a littell L. 1. *that*] *Omitted in* H R. 1. *all*] *Omitted in* L R^2 B. 2. *in conclusion*] *Omitted in* L R^2. 3. *were* (1) . . . *shorte*] were ther writinge never so shorte L R^2 B (*supported by* English Works, *p.* 848, *and* Apologye, 1533 *ed.*, *fol.* 12*b*); *omitted in* E Y C H R. 4. *whole*] *Omitted in* L; *interlineated in* R^2. 4. *at last to longe*] to longe at last L. 7. *vngodly*] *Interlineated in* R *over a misspelling crossed through and partly on erasure.* 7. *and*] *Interlineated in* R. 8. *whole*] C (*supported by* English Works, *p.* 865, *and* 1533 *ed. of* Apologye, *fol.* 71 *a*); *omitted in* E L R^2 Y H R B. 13–15. *and all . . . Sacrament*] *Omitted in* L. 15. *holy*] *Omitted in* R^2. 17. *iest*] C (*supported by* English Works, *p.* 865, *and* Apologye, 1533 *ed.*, *fol.* 71*a*); wrest E L R^2 Y C H R B. 17. *Were*] would Y. 17. *not*] now B. 19. *vncourteous*] verie vncurtuous Y. 20. *presume*] prusume C. 20. *great*] *Omitted in* R^2. 22. *and as villanous*] *Omitted in* R^2. 23. *against*] agayne Y. 23. *my*] *Corrected from* me R^2. 24. *any*] L B (*supported by* English Works, *p.* 865, *and* Apologye, 1533 *ed.*, *fol.* 71*b*); any, *corrected from* and, R^2; my E Y C H R. 24. *wordes*] *Omitted in* R^2.

againe then if they spake me faire; nor vsing themselues towarde all other folke as they doo, fayrer wordes will I not geue them then if they spake me fowle. For all shall be one to me, or rather the woorse the better; For the pleasaunt oyle of heretikes cast vpon mine head can doo my minde no pleasure; but contrarywise, the woorse that folke write of me for hatred that they beare to the Catholike Churche and fayth, the greater pleasure (as for mine owne part) they doo me. But surely their rayling against all other I purpose not to beare so patiently as to forbeare to lett them heare some part of like language as they speake. Howbeit, vtterly to matche them therein, I neyther can though I would, nor will though I could, but am content (as I needes must) to geue them therein the masterie, wherein to matche them were more rebuke then honestie. For in their onely rayling standeth all their revell; with onely rayling is all their roaste meate basted, and all their pott seasoned, and all their pye meate spiced, and all their manchett*es*, and all their wafers, and all their hipocrace made."

The heretics delight in railing. [WORKS, p. 866.]

He addeth farther: "If they" (saith he) "will not (which were the next) be heretikes alone themselues, and holde their tonges and be still, but will needes be babling and corrupt whom they can, lett them yet at the least wise be reasonable heretikes and honest, and write reason, and leaue rayling, and then lett the brethren finde the fault with me, if I vse [them] not after that in

More would treat his opponents gently if they were but "reasonable heretics." [WORKS, p. 866.]

MSS. E L R^2 Y C H R B.

1. *spake*] speake Y C. (*Note variant forms.*) 1. *nor*] but R^2. 1. *themselues*] them self Y. 2. *folke*] folkes H R. 2. *fayrer*] fayere Y. 2–3. *will I*] I will Y. 7. *woorse*] woorst C. 9. *as . . . part*] *Omitted in* B. 11–12. *some part of like*] the like B. 12. *of*] of of R^2. 12. *vtterly*] *Interlineated in* R. 13–14. *though . . . could*] though I oulde L. 14. *I could*] I neither could Y. 14. *but am*] but I am L. 14–15. *as . . . must*] as nedes I must L R^2 B. 16. *then*] the H. 18. *meate*] meates R. 18. *and all*] all H R; *omitted in* B. 21. *hipocrace*] pocrace L; Hipocras R^2; ypocras H R; Ipocrace B. 23. *which were the next*] (*See* Notes). 23. *themselues*] them self Y C. 25–26. *at the least*] at least R^2. 28. *the fault*] *Omitted in* L; fault H R. 28. *them*] L R^2 C H R B (*supported by sense and* English Works, *p.* 866, *and* Apologye, 1533 *ed., fol.* 74*a*); then E Y. 28. *after that*] afterward B.

wordes as faire and as milde as the matter may suffer and beare."

About this time there was one that had [made] a [fol 33 b] booke "of the diui|sion of the spiritualtie and temporaltie," of the which booke the brethren made great store, and blamed S*ir* Thomas More that he had not vsed in his wryting suche a softe and milde maner and such an indifferent fasshion as the saide person did. By occasion whereof S*ir* Thomas More discourseth vpon the saide booke (the authou*r* whereof pretended to make a pacification of the foresaide diuision and discorde), And openeth many faultes and folyes and heynous false slaunders against the Clergie, craftily and smoothly, vnder an holy [collusion] and pretence of pacification, in the saide bookes. To the which S*ir* Thomas Mores discourse there came an aunswere afterwarde in printe vnder the tytle of "Salem and Bizance." To the which S*ir* Thomas More replyed, and so dressed this pretie, politike pacifier that he had no lust, nor any man for him, to incounter afterwardes with the saide S*ir* Thomas.

The pretie, pleasaunt, wittie declaration of the tytle of the saide booke (because it is seldome and rare to be gotten) I will nowe, gentle Reader, set before thine eyes. The said tytle is framed in this sort: "The debellation of Salem and Bizance, sometime two great

(1) In the *Apologye* More exposed the writer [Christopher St. German] of a *Treatise concernynge the Division betwene the Spiritualtie and the Temporaltie.* (2) "The Pacifier" [Christopher St. German] replied in his *Dialogue betwixte two Englishmen whereof one was called Salem and the other Bizance.* [1533.] (3) To which book of "the Pacifier" or "Sir John Somesay," More's answer was *The Debellacyon of Salem*

MSS. E L R^2 Y C H R B.

3. *made*] L R^2 C B; *omitted in* E Y H R. 4. *of the diuision*] *Omitted in* L. 7. *vsed in his wryting*] in writtinge vsed L; in his writinge used R^2 B. 7. *a softe and milde*] a mild & softe R^2. 12. *many*] the many H R. 14. *smoothly*] *Omitted in* H. 14. *an*] and Y. 14. *collusion*] C; conclusion E L R^2 Y H R B. 15. *bookes*] booke B. 15. *To the*] To L B. 15–17. *To the which . . . Bizance*] *An addition on the margin in* R^2 (the title of *being interlineated*) *with asterisk after* bookes (*Cf. l.* 15) *in text.* 17. *of*] *Omitted in* B. 18–25. *To the which . . . Bizance*] *Omitted in* C. 18. *this*] his H R. 19. *pretie, politike*] pretty proper politicke L Y; pretie proper B. 19. *he*] *Omitted in* H. 19. *lust*] list R^2 H R B. 19. *man*] *Omitted in* Y. 20. *to incounter afterwardes*] afterwardes to Encounter L. 20. *the saide*] *Omitted in* B. 20. *Sir Thomas*] Sir Thomas More L R^2 R B. 22. *it is*] the booke is L R^2 Y B. 23. *thine*] thie Y. 24. *said*] *Omitted in* B. 24. *tytle*] *Omitted in* R^2. 24. *in*] after R^2. 25. *sometime*] some times L R^2 Y C B. (Sometime *supported by* English Works, *p.* 929, *and* 1533 *ed. of* Debellacyon, *Title.*)

and Bizance. [1533.]

The full title of More's *Debellacyon of Salem and Bizance.* [WORKS, p. 929.]

townes, which being vnder the great Turke, were betweene Easter and Michelmas last passed, this present yere of our Lorde 1533, with a meruailous metamorphosis enchaunted and turned into two englishe men, by the wonderfull inuentiue witt and witchcrafte of S*ir* John Somesay, the pacifier, and so by him conueyed hither in a dialoge, to defende his diuision against the Apologie of S*ir* Thomas More, knight. But nowe being thus, betweene the saide Michelmas and Alhalloutide next ensuing, in this debellation vanquished, they be fledd hence and vanished, and are become two townes againe, with those olde names chaunged, Salem into Jerusalem, and Bizance into Constantinople, the one [in] Greece and the other [in] Siria, where they may see them that will and winne them that can. And if the pacifier conuey them hither againe, and tenne such other townes with them, embattailed in such dialogues, S*ir* Thomas More hath vndertaken to put himselfe in [the] aduenture alone against them all. But and if he lett them tary still there, he will not vtterly forsweare it, but he is not much minded as yet, age nowe so co*m*ming on, and waxing all vnwildie, to goe thither and | geue [fol. 34 *a*] the assault to such well walled townes, without some such lustie companie as shal be somewhat likely to leape vp a litle more lightly."

MSS. E L R² Y C H R B.

1. *great*] *Omitted in* L B. 1. *were*] was L; where R². 2. *Easter and Michelmas*] Michaelmas & Easter H R. 3. *our Lorde* 1533] our Lord God 1533 L R² Y C. (Our Lorde 1533 *supported by* English Works, *p.* 929, *and* 1533 *ed. of* Debellacyon, *Title.*) 4. *two*] *Omitted in* L. 5. *and witchcrafte*] *Interlineated in* R. 6. *John Somesay*] John (some saie) C; John some saye B. 6. *by him conueyed*] conveyed by him L. 9. *Alhalloutide*] alhollandtide C. 10. *this*] the L. 10. *vanquished*] *Interlineated in* R. 11. *and vanished*] *Omitted in* L; vanished B. 14. *in* (1)] L R² B (*supported by* English Works, *p.* 929, *and by* 1533 *ed. of* Debellacyon, *Title*); into E Y C H R. 14. *in* (2)] L R² C B (*supported by* English Works, *p.* 929, *and by* 1533 *ed. of* Debellacyon, *Title*); into E Y H R. 15. *winne*] Joynn H. 15. *them*] þen C. 17. *other*] *Omitted in* L R² B. 17. *such*] *Omitted in* L. 18–19. *in the aduenture*] C (*supported by* English Works, *p.* 929, *and* 1533 *ed. of* Debellacyon, *Title*); in an aduenture Y; in aduenture E L R² H R B. 19. *alone*] *Omitted in* L R² B. 19. *But and if*] But if H R. 21. *much*] *Omitted in* L R² B. 21–22. *as yet . . . vnwildie*] *Omitted in* B. 24. *somewhat*] *Omitted in* L. 24. *leape*] lipp R. 25. *a litle*] somewhat Y.

This is the tytle of the foresaide booke. And that in very deede the saide S*ir* Thomas More hath most valiantly discomfited the pacifier, and ouerthrowen his two great townes, may easily appere to such as will vouchsafe to reade the saide S*ir* Thomas More his aunswere, The circumstances and particularities whereof to rehearse, would make our present Treatise to growe too bigge.

More discomfits "the Pacifier."

I will onely shewe you a declaration or two of S*ir* Thomas More, whereby you may make some ayme to iudge by the whole doinges of the saide pacifier. "If it were so," sayth S*ir* Thomas More, "that one founde two men standing together, and would come steppe in betweene them, and beare them in hande they were about to fight, and would with that worde put the one pretily backe with his hande, and [all] to buffet the other about the face, and then goe forth and say that he had parted a fraye and pacified the parties, some men would say againe (as I suppose) that he had as leefe his enemie were let alone with him, and therof abide the aduenture, as haue such a frende stepp in betweene to part them."

And ridicules "the Pacifier's" mode of pacifying, who buffets those he professes to defend. [WORKS, p. 872.]

Another of a man that were angry and fallen out with his wife, and happly not without cause. "Nowe,"

And who aggravates a quarrel by

MSS. E L R^{2} Y C H R B.

2–5. *hath . . . More his*] *An addition on the margin in* R^{2}, vouchsafe *being corrected from* wouchsaye, *and with* Moores *for* More his. *Asterisk in text of* R^{2} *after* More. (*Cf. l.* 2.) 3. *discomfited*] discomforted B. 5. *the saide*] *Omitted in* B. 5. *More his*] Moores his Y; his C; Mores B. 6. *particularities*] particulars H R. 8. *onely*] *Omitted in* H R. 8. *a declaration*] one declaration L R^{2} B. 9. *you*] ye Y. 9. *may*] *Interlineated in* R^{2}. 10. *by*] *Corrected from* of R^{2}. 10. *saide*] *Interlineated in* R. 11. *sayth*] sayd R^{2}. 11. *Sir Thomas More*] þe sayde Sir Thomas Moore L Y; Sir Thomas C. 12. *two*] *Omitted in* Y. 14. *about*] *abought* Y. 14. *one*] *Interlineated in* R^{2}. 15. *pretily*] partly L; pertlie Y; partie B. 15. *backe*] from the other bake Y. 15. *all to*] L R^{2} H R B (*supported by* English Works, *p.* 872, *and* Apologye, 1533 *ed., fol.* 93 *b*); also to E Y C. 18. *men*] *Omitted in* H. 18. *would*] will L R^{2} B. 18. *againe*] *Omitted in* L. 19. *leefe*] live C. 19. *therof*] therefore Y. 20. *abide*] to abide R^{2} B. 20. *haue*] to have B. 21. *betweene*] *Omitted in* R^{2}; betwene them H R. 22. *were*] was H R. 22. *and fallen out*] *Omitted in* L. (*The words* and fallen out *are apparently added by* Harpsfield, *as they are not in* English Works, *p.* 872, *or in* Apologye, 1533 *ed., fol.* 94 *a.*)

sly hints and idle gossip. [WORKS, pp. 872–3.]

saith M*aster* More, "if the auth*our* of this booke would take vpon him to reconcile them together, and helpe to make them at one; and therein would vse this way, that when he had them both before him, would tell all the fault*es* of the wife, and sett among them some of his owne imagination and assertion, and then would goe about to auoide his wordes vnder the colour of his faire figure of Somesay (which he co*m*monly vseth in his booke of pacification) eyther by forgetfulnes or by the figure of plaine folye; and then would afterwarde tell her husbande his par[s]verse too, and tell him that he himselfe had not dealt well with her, but haue vsed to make her too homely w*i*th him, and haue suffred her to be too muche ydle, and suffred her to be [too] muche conuersaunt among her gossips, and haue geuen her ouer gaye gere, and sometime geuen her euill wordes, and call her (as I heare say) cursed queane and shrewe, and some say that she behind your backe calleth you knaue and cuckolde"; were not this a proper kinde of | pacification? [fol. 34 *b*

"The Pacifier" has great cause to be ashamed.

And yet is this the liuely paterne and image of M*aster* Pacifiers doinges. Of the which and of his spinning fine lyes with flexe, fetching it out of his owne body as the spyder doth her cobwebbe, fayning and finding fault

MSS. E L R^2 Y C H R B.

1. *Master More*] Sir Thomas Moore L R^2 H B. 6. *imagination*] ymaginations C H. 6. *assertion*] assertions C. 6. *then would*] then they would H. 7. *the*] his H. 7. *colour of his*] *Omitted in* L R^2 B; colour and H. 10. *afterwarde*] after H R. 11. *husbande his*] husbands L R^2 B; R *as* E Y C H, *with* his *interlineated*. 11. *parsverse*] B (*supported by* English Works, *p.* 873, *and* Apologye, 1533 *ed.*, *fol.* 96 *b*); partverse E L R^2 Y C H R; parte worse R^2. 11. *tell him*] say vnto him L R^2 B. 12. *haue vsed*] hath vsed L R^2 H R B. 13. *haue suffred*] hath suffred L H R B; & hath suffered R^2. 14. *too* (1)] *Omitted in* L R^2 Y C H R. (Too *supported by* English Works, *p.* 873, *and* Apologye, 1533 *ed.*, *fol.* 96 *b*). 14. *ydle . . . muche*] *Omitted in* B. 14. *suffred her*] *Omitted in* H R. 14. *too muche*] R (*supported by* English Works, *p.* 873, *and* Apologye, 1533 *ed.*, *fol.* 97 *a*); too H; muche E L R^2 Y C B. 15. *haue*] *Omitted in* R^2; hath H R. 17. *call*] called L H R. (Call *supported by* English Works, *p.* 873, *and* Apologye, 1533 *ed.*, *fol.* 97 *a*). 17. *heare say*] suppose L. 21. *is this*] this is H R. 22–23. *Of the which . . . fine*] with þe which & with þe spinninge of fine L. 23. *fine*] of fine R^2 B. 23. *lyes*] *Omitted in* R^2. 24. *her*] þe L R^2 B.

w*i*th S*ir* Thomas More for these matters and wordes whereof he saith the plaine contrary, he had great cause to be ashamed. Howbeit litle shame could cleaue to his cheekes, but that he would soone shake it away while his name was not at his booke.

We haue nowe one booke [more] written in matter of religion, and of the blessed Sacrament of the aultar by the saide S*ir* Thomas More. We tolde you before of a letter of his wherein he impugned the [wicked] heresie of John Frith. Nowe had the saide Frith, albeit he were prisoner in the towre of London, founde the meanes to make answere to the saide letter, and to conuey it beyonde the Seas, where it was printed. And it was afterwarde brought into this Realme, as S*ir* Thomas More did certainly vnderstande : who minded, when the booke came to his handes, to aunswere it. But nowe in the meane season came there from beyonde the Sea an aunswere to the saide letter, made by some other, and printed without the authours name, intituled "The Supper of our Lorde." "But I beshrewe," quoth S*ir* Thomas More, "such a sewer as so serueth in the Supper that he conueyeth away the best dishe, and bringeth it not * to the [borde], As this man would, if he could, conueye from the blessed Sacrament Christes owne blessed fleshe and bloud, and leaue vs nothing therein but for a memoriall onely bare breade and wine.

More's *Answere to the . . . book which a namelesse heretyke* [Tindale] *hath named the Souper of the Lorde.* [1533(4).]

More "beshrews a sewer" who conveys the best dish from the board. [WORKS, p. 1036.]

MSS. E L R^2 Y C H R B.

2. *the*] the the Y. 4. *would*] *Omitted in* R^2. 6. *one booke more*] L R^2 Y C (booke *being interlineated in* L); one booke E H R. 8. *the saide*] *Omitted in* B. 9. *wherein he impugned*] wherein he *interlineated in* L, *and* impugned *corrected from* impugninge. 9. *wicked heresie*] Y C H R; heresie E L R^2 B. 10. *Nowe . . . Frith*] Now had the said the said Frith R, *with* had the *interlineated.* 10. *Frith* (2)] John Frith B. 11. *were*] was B. 13. *it was* (2)] *Omitted in* B. 14. *afterwarde*] after B. 14. *this*] the Y. 16. *to* (1)] into R^2 Y. 16. *handes*] hande L. 17. *Sea*] seas B. 18. *saide*] same L. 20. *our Lorde*] the Lorde H. 21. *sewer*] shewer Y (cf. *spelling in* 1534 *ed. of More's* Answere, *Preface, fol.* vi *a*); Seinor H. 21. *so serueth*] saveth H. 21. *the Supper*] such a supper H R. 23. *not to*] L R^2 Y C (*supported by* English Works, *p.* 1036, *and* 1534 *ed. of More's* Answere, *Preface, fol.* vi *a*); not in to E H R B. 23. *borde*] boorde L R^2 Y H R B (*supported by* English Works, *p.* 1036, *and* 1534 *ed. of More's* Answere, *Preface, fol.* vi *a*); Lorde E C.

But his handes are too lumpishe, and [this] messe also too great for him to conueye cleane, especially sith the dishe is so deere and so daintie that euery christian man hath his heart bent thereto, and therefore his eye sett thereon to see where it becommeth." This naughtie, namelesse authour *Sir* Thomas More doth not onely by the authoritie of the sacred Scripture and holye auncient fathers, but by his owne reasons and textes that himselfe bringeth forth, plainely and euidentlye conuince.

A Dialoge of Comfort against Tribulacyon; A Treatise to receyue the Blyssed Body of our Lorde sacramentally and virtually bothe; and *A Treatise upon the Passion.* [1534.]

Nowe haue we beside other excellent and fruitfull bookes of his which he made being prisoner in the towre, as his three bookes of comfort against tribulation, a Treatise to receaue the blessed Sacrament | sacramen- [fol. 35 *a*] tally and virtually both, A Treatise vpon the passion, with notable introductions to the same. He wrote also many other godly and deuout instructions and prayers.

Harpsfield considers *A Dialoge of Comfort against Tribulacyon* superior to all other books on the same subject, heathen and Christian.

And surely, of all the bookes that euer he made, I doubt whether I may preferre any of them to the saide three bookes, yea, or any other mans, eyther heathen or christian, that haue written (as many haue) eyther in the greeke or latine of the saide matter. And as for heathen, I doo this woorthie man plaine iniurie, and doo so much abase him in matching and comparing him with them, especially in this point, seing that [though] they were neuer otherwise so incomparable, [they] lacked yet and knewe not the very speciall and principall grounde of comfort and consolation, that is the

MSS. E L R^2 Y C H R B.

1. *But his*] And his H R. 1. *too*] so C. 1. *this*] L (*supported by* English Works, *p.* 1036, *and* 1534 *ed. of More's* Answere, *Preface, fol.* vi *a*); his E R^2 Y C H R B. 2. *for him*] *Interlineated in* L. 2. *conueye cleane*] conuey away cleane R^2. 7. *Scripture*] Scriptures R^2. 8. *and textes*] *Omitted in* B. 9. *forth*] *Omitted in* Y. 12. *as his*] and his H R. 18. *to*] before B. 20. *eyther*] *Omitted in* R^2 Y. 20–21. *in the*] in L R^2 B. 21. *or*] or in R^2. 22. *heathen*] the heathen H R. 22. *woorthie*] *Interlineated in* R. 23. *so*] *Omitted in* L R^2 B. 23. *matching and*] *Omitted in* B. 24. *though*] L R^2 H R B; *omitted in* E Y C. 25. *neuer otherwise*] otherwise neuer H R. 25. *incomparable*] comparable Y. 25–26. *they lacked yet*] B; yet the [= "they"] lacked H R; lacked yet E L R^2 Y C. (H R B *are inferior MSS.; see* Introd., *p.* xl, *on omission of the pronoun.*) 26. *knewe*] kewe L. 27. *of . . . consolation*] of consolation & comforte R^2.

true fayth in Christe, in whom, and for whom, and his glory, and from whom, we must seeke and fetche all our true comfort and consolation. Well, lett them passe, and lett vs then further say, that as the saide *Sir* Thomas More notably passeth many learned christians that haue of the same matter written before, so lett vs adde that it may well be doubted, all circumstaunces well considered and weighed, if any of the residue may seeme muche to passe him, or to be farre preferred afore him. There is in these bookes so wittie, so pithie, and so substantiall matter for the easing and remedying and patiently suffring of all maner of griefes and sorowes that may possibly incumber any man, by anye maner or kinde of tribulation, whether their tribulation proceede of any inwarde temptation of our ghostly enemy the deuill, or by any outwarde tentation of the world threatning to spoyle and bereaue vs of our goodes, landes, honour, of our libertie and freedome, by greeuous and sharpe imprisonment, or finally of our life withall, by any painefull and exquisite cruell death; Against all which he doth so wonderfully, so effectually, and so strongly prepare, defence and arme the Reader, that a man cannot desire or wish any thing of more efficacie or importance thereto to be added. In the which bookes his principall drifte and scope was to stirre and prepare the mindes of englishe men manfully and couragiously to withstande, and not to shrinke at, the imminent and open persecution whiche he fore[sawe], [fol. 35 *b*] and immediatly folowed, against the vnitie | of the

More's principal object therein was to prepare Englishmen for the religious troubles to come.

MSS. E L R² Y C H R B.

1. *in Christe*] of Christe L. 1–2. *and his glory*] *Omitted in* B. 1. *his*] whose L. 5. *passeth*] passed H R. 6. *so*] se H. 12. *and patiently suffring*] *Omitted in* B. 13. *possibly*] possible Y. 14. *kinde*] *Corrected from* kinge R². 14–15. *their tribulation*] it B. 17. *to*] *Interlineated in* R². 17. *bereaue*] breve Y. 18. *of*] *Interlineated over* and R². 18. *freedome*] friends B. 18–19. *greeuous and sharpe*] sharpe & greeueous R². 19. *or*] & H R. 20. *painefull and*] *Interlineated in* L. 20. *and*] or R². 20. *cruell*] *Omitted in* Y. 22. *strongly*] strungly R². 24. *or*] and R². 25. *drifte and scope*] scope & drifte R². 27. *withstande*] with stand R, with *being interlineated.* 28. *foresawe*] L R² C R B; foresworo E; foresware Y; foreshaw H. *In* R fore *is interlineated.*

More's pseudonym "an Hungarian."

Churche and the catholike fayth of the same. Albeit full wittily and wisely, that the bookes might the more safely goe abrode, he doth not expressly meddle with those matters, and couloureth the matter vnder the name of an Hungarian, and of the persecution of the Turke in Hungarie, and of a booke translated out of the Hungarians tonge into the latin, and then into the englishe tonge.

***A Dialoge of Comfort against Tribulacyon* and *A Treatise on the Passion* were written in the Tower "with a coal."**

Of these bookes there is then great accompt to be made, not onely for the excellent matters comprised, and moste wittily and learnedly handled therein, but for that also they were made when he was most straightly inclosed and shutt vp from all company in the towre. In which sort I doubt whether a man should finde any other booke of like woorthines made by any christian. And yet if anye suche be to be founde, and suche as this, much soone should yeeld and geue place to the same; yet surely, there is one thing wherein these bookes of S*ir* Thomas More by an especiall prerogatiue surmounte, or els I am deceaued, all other of this sort, and that is, that they were for the moste part written with none other penne in the worlde then with a coale, as was also his Treatise vpon the passion; w*hi*ch copie, if some [men] had, they might and would more esteeme then other bookes written with golden letters, and woulde make no lesse accompt of it then St Jerome did of certaine bookes of the learned martyr Lucian written

MSS. E L R^2 Y C H R B.

3. *safely*] safer L B. 4. *and*] but B. 4. *couloureth*] couereth L. 6. *a booke*] þe booke L. 7. *Hungarians*] Hungarian H R. 7. *into the*] into L R^2. 9. *there is then*] then there is L R^2 H B; their is then R, then *being interlineated.* 10. *and*] *Omitted in* B. 11. *learnedly handled*] handled most learnedlie B. 13. *inclosed . . . all*] *On an erasure in* R^2. 14. *doubt*] doubdt C. 14. *should*] shall L R^2 B. 16. *be to*] *Omitted in* L R^2 B. 16. *and suche*] *Omitted in* B. 17. *much*] *Omitted in* B. 17. *should yeeld*] should I yeeld L R^2 H R B. 18. *yet*] *Corrected from* & L. 19. *More*] Mores B. 20. *surmounte*] surmounteth B. 20. *or . . . deceaued*] *Omitted in* B. 23. *as was also*] as also was L R^2 B. 23. *his*] a Y. 24. *some men had*] L R^2 Y C B; some had E H R. 26. *make*] *Omitted in* L R^2 B. 26. *Jerome*] Hierome L B. 26. *did*] *Omitted in* Y. 27. *certaine*] som certeine B. 27. *martyr*] Matir H. 27. *Lucian*] St Lucian R^2; Luexan B.

with his owne hande, that perchaunce he happed [vpon], and esteemed them as a pretious iewell.

In these two books More is inspired as was Esaias.

And yet is there one thing that in the valewing and prysing [of] these bookes I esteeme aboue all other, and that is, that in these bookes he is not, as many great clerkes in their bookes sometime are, like to a whetstone, that being blunt and dull it selfe, whetteth and sharpeth other thinges; it was not so with this man; for albeit he wrote these bookes with a deade blacke coale, yet was there another and a most hott burning coale, suche a one, I say, as touched and purified the lippes of the holy prophete Esaias, that directed his hande with the deade coale, and so inflamed and incensed his heart with all to heauenwarde, that the good and wholsome instructions and councell that he gaue to other men in his [fol. 36 *a*] bookes he himselfe shortly after, in moste patient | suffring of the losse of his goodes, landes, of imprisonment, and of death withall, for the defence of Justice and the catholike fayth, experimented and woorthely practised in himselfe, as we shall hereafter in place conuenient more largely shewe and declare.

More suffered his own tribulation with the patience he had preached.

MSS. E L R^2 Y C H R B.

1. *perchaunce*] by chaunce L R^2 B. 1. *vpon*] vppon C; on L R^2 B; *omitted in* E Y H R. 2. *pretious*] most precious B. 3. *that*] *Omitted in* H. 4. *prysing of these*] prising of these Y; prysing these E H R; prayseinge of these L R^2 C B. 4–5. *I esteeme . . . bookes*] *Omitted in* L B. 4. *esteeme*] esteeme them H R. 5–6. *as many . . . are*] *Omitted in* B. 8. *not so*] *Omitted in* R^2. 8. *so with*] so I saye with C. 8. *albeit*] allthough L; albeit that H. 9. *these bookes*] *Interlineated in* R. 9. *bookes*] *On an erasure in* R^2. 11. *a one*] an one L B. 12. *In the margin of* C *is written* cap. 6. 12. *the*] a R^2. 13. *his*] *Corrected from* the R. 16. *shortly*] *Omitted in* L; *interlineated in* R. 16. *after*] afterwarde L. 16. *patient*] *Omitted in* B. 16–17. *suffring of the*] sufferinge þe L. 17. *goodes . . . imprisonment*] goods & landes of his imprisonment L; goods & landes of Imprisonment R^2 B. 20–21. *place . . . largely*] place more conuenient largely L. 21. *shewe and*] *Omitted in* B.

[IV]

More's reputation as a Latin scholar.

And these be in effect the bookes he made eyther in latine or englishe: which his englishe bookes, if they had beene written by him in the latin tonge also, or might be, with the like grace that they nowe haue, translated into the latine speeche, they would surely much augment and increase the estimation and admiration that the world hath already in forreine countreys of his incomparable witt and learning; for the which he was euen while he liued throughout all Christendome meruailouslye accompted vpon and renowned, as appereth by the wrytinges of sundry learned men, with many of which he was well acquainted also by reason of his ambassades into Fraunce and Flaunders, especially with Erasmus and Petrus [Æ]gidius: which two persons, when that one Quintinius, a singuler good Painter, had sett forth and painted in a certaine table, S*ir* Thomas More made thereof certaine verses, declaring that he was sorie that himselfe also was not sett in the same table, who did so intierly loue them both. The saide Erasmus of all men in the world [most] delighted in the companye of S*ir* Thomas More, whose helpe and frendshipp he muche vsed when he had any affaires with king Henrye the eight.

Erasmus and Petrus Ægidius, two friends of More, painted by Quentin Metsys. More's verses about the picture. [More to Petrus Ægidius.]

The love of Erasmus for More.

More's company sought by Henry VIII. [Roper.]

The which king, for the exquisite learning that he well knewe, not onely by his erudite bookes, but by good experience of him otherwise, he was adorned withall, for many yeres vsed vpon the holy dayes, when

MSS. E L R² Y C H R B.

2. *or*] or in H R B. 3. *tonge*] *Omitted in* H. 4. *be*] *Omitted in* B. 5. *translated*] be translated L R² B. 5. *speeche*] tong Y. 6. *augment and increase*] encrease & augment B. 6–8. *estimation . . . that*] estimation which L; admiration and estimation that R². 7. *hath already*] alreadye hath L. 10–11. *appereth*] appeared H R. 12. *well*] *Interlineated in* R. 13. *into*] in B. 14. *Ægidius*] L R² C B; Agidius E Y; Egidius H R. 15. *one*] *Interlineated in* R. 15. *Quintinius*] Quintinus L R² B. 16. *certaine*] *Omitted in* R² B. 18. *sorie*] verie sorrie B. 18. *also was not*] was not also H R. 18. *same*] *Omitted in* B. 19. *who did*] which did Y. 20. *most delighted*] L R² Y C B; delighted E H R. 26. *he was*] that he was L R². 26–27. *he . . . withall*] *Omitted in* B.

Erasmus
aet. 50
From the Diptych painted in May 1517 for presentation to Thomas More
now in the Corsini Gallery at Rome

Peter Gilles
aet. c. 30
From the Diptych painted in May 1517 for presentation to Thomas More
Now at Longford Castle

he had done his deuotions, to sende for him into his trauers, and there to sitt and conferre with him, not onely in matters and affaires of this Realme, but also in astronomie, Geometrie, Diuinitie and other faculties. And otherwhiles would he in the night haue him into his leades, there to consider w*i*th him the diuersities, courses, motions and operations of the starres and planett*es*; with whom he was, as not lightly with any man more, at other times wonderfully familier, as we haue partly touched before, not onely for his learning sake, but because he was of so merye and pleasaunt disposition. And therefore both he and the Queene, after the Counsaile had supte, at the time of their Supper, for their pleasure, would be merye with him. Whom when he [fol. 36 *b*] perceaued so much in his talke to delight that | he could not once in a moneth gett leaue to [go] home to his wife and children, whose company he most desired, and to be absent from the Court two dayes together but that he should be thither sent for againe, he, much mislyking this restraint of his libertie, beganne therevpon somewhat to dissemble his nature, and so litle and litle from his accustomed mirth to disvse himselfe, that he was of them from thenceforth at suche seasons no more so ordinarily sent for as he was wont to be.

Also by Queen Katherine. [ROPER.]

More's liberty thereby much restrained. [ROPER.]

Nowe for his wise, pleasaunt, wittie talke, and for his other qualities, he had beside his learned frendes many other as well in Inglande as otherwhere, but

More's friendship with Antonio Bonvisi.

MSS. E L R^2 Y C H R B.

1. *his* (2)] the B. 2. *trauers*] Traveices H. 3. *and affaires*] *Omitted in* L. 5. *otherwhiles . . . night*] otherwhile in þe night would he L R^2; otherwhiles in the nighte he would B. 5. *in the night*] *Interlineated in* R. 6. *there*] & there B. 7. *motions*] *Interlineated in* R. 7. *motions and operations*] operations & motions R^2. 8. *not*] *Interlineated in* R. 8. *lightly*] likelie B. 9. *wonderfully*] wonderfull Y. 9–10. *as . . . before*] *Omitted in* B. 9. *partly*] *A correction of* presently R^2. 11. *so*] a L R^2 B. 14. *be merye*] be me merry Y. 16. *go home*] L R^2 H R B (*supported by* Roper); gett home E Y C. 19. *thither*] either H R. 19–20. *he . . . restraint*] *Interlineated in* L. 20. *this*] the B. 21. *so*] by H R. 22. *from*] *Corrected from* to L. 23. *of them*] *Omitted in* B. 23. *from*] *Omitted in* H. 25. *pleasaunt, wittie*] wittie pleasaunt L R^2; wittie & pleasant B. 26. *he had . . . frendes*] *Omitted in* H R.

yet none so deere and so entier to him as was the good and gratious right woorshipfull merchaunt M*aster* Antonie Bonuice. To whom he, being prisoner in the towre, a litle before he was arraigned and condemned, wrate a latin letter with a [co]ale; Wherein among other thinges he confesseth himselfe that he had beene almost fortie yeres not a geste, but a continuall nursling, in his house, and the singuler fauo*ur*, helpe and ayde that he had at all times, especially in his aduersities and troubles, felte at his handes; And that fewe did so fawne vpon their fortunate frendes as he did fauo*ur*, loue, foster and hono*ur* him being ouerthrowen, abiected, afflicted and condemned to prison. And S*ir* Thomas More was wont to call him the apple of his eye.

More's Letter to Antonio Bonvisi. [WORKS, pp. 1454–7.]

This woorthy merchaunt would ofte talke of him and also of S*ir* Thomas Cromwell, with whom he was many yeres familierly acquainted, and would reporte many notable and as yet co*m*monly vnknowen thinges, and of their farre squaring, vnlike and disagreable natures, dispositions, sayinges and doinges, whereof there is nowe no place to talke.

Bonvisi contrasts More and Thomas Cromwell.

But because we are in hande with the bookes and learning of the saide S*ir* Thomas More, I will nowe tell you this one thing onely, that I haue heard him report that he would at table and otherwhere wonderfull deepely and clarkely talke with learned men, as well englishe as of other countries; and that he once knewe when a very excellent learned man (as he was taken),

Bonvisi's report of More's victory in argument over a foreign theologian.

MSS. E L R^2 Y C H R B.

1. *and so entier*] and entire Y H R. 1–2. *good and gratious*] gracious & gratious R^2. 2. *merchaunt*] *Omitted in* B. 5. *coale*] C (*supported by* English Works, *p.* 1454); vale E L R^2 Y H R B. 7. *a geste*] guest H. 10. *fewe*] fewe men L R^2 Y B. 12. *loue*] *Omitted in* B. 12. *being*] *Interlineated in* R^2. 16. *also of*] alsoe R^2; of Y. 17. *familierly*] *Omitted in* H R. 18. *as*] *Omitted in* Y. 18. *commonly*] *Omitted in* B. 18. *and* (2)] *Omitted in* B. 20–21. *there is nowe no place*] there is no place now L R^2 Y B; now there is now noe place H; now there is no place now R. 21. *to*] to to R^2. 22. *we are*] we are now H R. 23. *the saide*] the same L; *omitted in* B. 24. *that*] which L. 24. *haue*] *Omitted in* L. 25. *wonderfull*] wonderfully H R. 26. *learned*] other B. 27. *of*] fof H. 28. *when a*] when that a L; that when a B. 28. *as . . . taken*] *Omitted in* B.

a straunger, being in this Realme, chaunced to be at [fol. 37 *a*] the table with S*ir* Thomas More, | whom he knewe not. At which table there was great reasoning betweene the saide straunger and others of many great pointes of learning. At length S*ir* Thomas More sett in a foote, and coped with the saide straunger, and demained himselfe so cunningly and so learnedlye that the saide straunger, which was a religious man, was muche astonied and abashed to heare such profounde reasons at a laye mans hande. And therevpon inquired of suche as were neerest at hande to him what his name was: which when he once vnderstoode, he had no great pleasure afterwarde to encounter any more with him.

More's meekness and courtesy in disputation with learned men. [ROPER.]

And his good blessed disposition and wise behaui*our* in such kinde of disputations is woorth the noting. For among all other his vertues, he was of suche meekenes that, if it fortuned him with any learned man resorting to him from Oxforde, Cambridge, or elswhere (as there did diuers, some for desire of his acquaintance, some for the famous report of his wisedome and learning, and some for sutes of the vniuersities) to haue entred into argumentes (wherein fewe were comparable to him) and so farre to haue discoursed w*ith* [them] therein that he might perceaue they could not without some inconuenience holde out muche farther disputatio*n* against him; then, least he should discomfort them (as he that sought not his owne glory, but rather would seeme conquered then discourage student*es* in their studies, euer shewing himselfe more desirous to learne then to teache) would he by some wittie deuise courteously breake off into some other matter, and geue ouer.

More's employment by the

Of whom for his wisedome and learning had the king suche an opinion that, at suche times as he attended

MSS. E L R² Y C H R B.

5. *length*] lenghe L. 6–8. *and demained . . straunger*] *Interlineated in* R. 7. *cunningly*] cuinglie H. 12. *once*] *Omitted in* Y. 14. *and wise*] & his wise L. 20. *and learning*] *Omitted in* B. 23. *so*] *Omitted in* H. 23. *them*] L R² Y C H R B (*supported by* Roper); *omitted in* E. 27. *glory*] *On an erasure in* H. 30. *would he*] would R²; he woulde B. 32. *had the king*] the kinge had H R. 33. *times*] tyme R².

King for *ex tempore* answers to orations. [ROPER.]

vpon his highnes taking his progresse eyther to Oxforde or Cambridge, where he was receaued with very eloquent orations, his grace would alwayes assigne him, as one that was prompte and ready therein, *ex tempore* to make aunswere therevnto: whose maner was, whensoeuer he had occasion, eyther here or beyonde the Sea, to be in any vniuersitie, not onely to be present at the readinges and disputations there co*m*monly vsed, but also learnedly to dispute among them himselfe.

More's excellent wit and memory a great aid in his literary work.

But nowe it is time to ceasse fro*m* further intreating of his learning and bookes, sauing I thinke good to be by the way marked and noted howe he | could possibly [fol. 37 *b*] write so many and excellent workes; eyther being out of prison, though furnished with bookes, being so continually trauailed in the affaires of the kinges counsaile and of his great offices, but that one great helpe was the excellencie of his witt and memorie, which were both twaine singuler, and one other, that he spared and saued muche time that men co*m*monly mispende in eating and sleeping; or being [in] prison, being, as he was, so vnfurnished of bookes.

More's economy of time. [Cf. MORE to PETER GILES, *Utopia*.]

Harpsfield promises to relate More's actions from the resignation of the Great Seal to his death.

We will nowe pursue the forme and trade of his other actions and doinges, after the time that he had abandoned the foresaide office of the Lorde Chauncell*our* vntill the time that he suffred at Towrehill. But yet it shall not be perchaunce amisse, seing we haue sett

MSS. E L R² Y C H R B.

2–3. *was . . . orations*] was with eloquent Orations receaved H; was with very eloquent Orations receaved R, *with* receyued *crossed through after* was. 6. *had occasion*] had any occasion L. 6. *eyther*] *Corrected from* that R. 6. *the*] *Omitted in* B. 6. *Sea*] Seas L. 9. *among*] with B. 11. *I thinke good*] I thinke it good L H R B; I doe thinke yt good R². 11–12. *to be . . . noted*] by the waye to be noted and marked Y. 15. *affaires . . . counsaile*] kinges affaires B. 16. *and of his*] & his H. 16. *offices*] affaires Y. 17–18. *which . . . twaine*] which both twaine weare H; which bothe were B. 18–20. *and one . . . sleeping*] *Omitted in* B. 18. *one other*] another L R². 19. *men commonly*] comonly men H R. 19. *mispende*] misspend R, mis *being interlineated.* 20. *and*] or L Y. 20. *in*] L R² Y C H R B; *omitted in* E. 21. *so . . . bookes*] vnfurnished of his bookes B. 22. *nowe*] now therfore C; *omitted in* B. 22. *other*] *Omitted in* H. 23. *and doinges*] *Omitted in* B. 23. *that*] *Omitted in* L R² B. 24. *of the*] of H. 25. *yet*] *Omitted in* L. 26. *perchaunce*] *Omitted in* H.

But he will first describe his person.

forth to your sight his excellent learning and some singuler qualities of his blessed soule and minde, somewhat also here to interlace to the contentation of suche as be desyrous thereof, before we goe farther, of his body also, and of other thinges thereto belonging.

More's appearance. [ERASMUS to ULRICH VON HUTTEN.]

Then, as he was no tall man, [so was he no notable lowe and litle man]; all the partes of his body were in as good proportion and congruence as a man would wishe. His skinne was somewhat white, and the col*our* of his face drewe rather to whitenes [then to palenes, farre from rednes], sauing that some litle thinne redde sparkles eueryewhere appered. His heare was blackishe yealowe, or rather yelowe blackishe, his beard thinne, his eyes graye and speckled, which kinde of eyes [do] commonly [betoken] and signifie a very good and sharpe witt. And they say that suche kinde of eyes are least incombred with diseases and faults. His countenaunce was conformable to his nature and disposition, pleasaunt and amiable, somewhat resembling and tending to the fasshion of one that would laugh.

More's voice. [ERASMUS, *as above*.]

His voyce was neyther too boystrous and bigge, neyther too small and shrill. He spake his wordes very distinctly and treatably, without any maner of hastines or stuttering. And albeit he delighted in all kinde of melodie, yet he seemed not of nature to be apte and meete to sing himselfe.

MSS. E L R^2 Y C H R B.

1. *your*] our H R B. 2–3. *somewhat also here*] *Omitted in* L. 3. *also*] *Interlineated in* R. 6–7. *so was he no notable lowe and litle man*] C (*supported by* Erasmus's Letter to Ulrich von Hutten); *omitted in* E L R^2 Y H R B. (*See* Notes.) 7. *all*] so all H R. 8. *would*] could H. 10–11. *then to . . . rednes*] L R^2 Y C H R B (*supported by* Erasmus's Letter to Ulrich von Hutten); *omitted in* E; H *has* plaenes *for* palenes. (*See* Notes.) 11. *sparkles*] spotes B. 12. *His*] *Interlineated in* R^2. 13. *After* rather, E *has* blackishe *crossed through*. 14–15. *eyes do commonly betoken and signifie*] L R^2; eies doe commonly signifie B; eyes be commonly quicke and signifie E H R; Y C *as* E H R, *but with gap left by scribe between* commonly *and* and, *where* E H R *have* quicke. (*See* Notes.) 15. *a*] *Omitted in* Y. 16. *they*] men R^2. 19. *somewhat*] somthing B. 19. *and tending to*] *Omitted in* B. 21. *was*] *Interlineated in* B. 23–24. *hastines or stuttering*] stuttering or hastinesse Y. 25. *melodie*] *Corrected from* memorye L. 25. *of . . . apte*] to be apt of nature B. 25. *to be*] *Omitted in* C. 25–26. *and meete*] *Omitted in* L B; & made R^2. 26. *to*] for to B.

More healthy, though not robust. [ERASMUS, *as above*, with addition.]

He enioyed the health of his body full well; and though he were not very stronge of body, yet was he able to goe throughe with any labour and paine meete and conuenient for him for to dispatche his busines and affaires. He was very litle infested and incombred with sickenes, sauing a litle before he gaue ouer the office of the Lorde Chaun|cell*our*, and especially afterwarde, when he was [fol. 38 *a*] shutt vp in the towre.

More's diet. [ERASMUS, *as above*.]

And nowe somewhat to speake of his dyet. Being a yonge man, he vsed and delighted much in drinking of water. He vsed very small ale, and as for wine, he did but sippe of it onely for companies sake and pledging of his frendes. He more delighted to feede vpon biefe, salte meates and course breade, and that very well leavened, then vpon fine meates and breade. He loued very well milke and fruit and especially egges.

More's interest in animals. [ERASMUS, *as above*.]

It was great pleasure to him to see and beholde the forme and fasshion, the maner and disposition, of diuers beastes. There was not lightly any kinde of birdes that he kept not in his house, as he kept also the ape, the foxe, the wesell, the ferrett, and other beastes that were rare and not co*m*mon. Besydes, if there had beene any thing brought out of straunge countreys, or woorthie to be looked vpon, that was he very desirous to buye, and to adorne and furnishe his house withall, to the contentation and pleasure of suche as came to him: who tooke great pleasure in the beholding of suche thinges, and himselfe also with them.

MSS. E L R^2 Y C H R B.

2. *very*] *Omitted in* L. 4. *for to*] for H R. 5. *litle . . . incombred*] litle encombred & infested L B; litle infected and incombred C. 7. *when*] that H. 8. *in*] into H. 9. *to speake*] *Omitted in* L R^2 B. 12. *onely*] *Omitted in* B. 12. *companies*] company B. 13. *of his*] his B. 13. *more*] moste B. 14–15. *and that . . . breade*] *Interlineated* (*but* very *omitted*) *in* R; *omitted in* B. 14. *very*] *Omitted in* H R. 15. *fine . . . breade*] dainty meates and fine bread R^2. 16. *very*] *Omitted in* L. 17. *to him*] *Omitted in* H. 19. *lightly*] likelie B. 20. *as he*] And he H. 21. *ferrett*] Fynet B. 22. *there*] *Corrected from* they L. 22. *had beene*] weare H; be R.

[V]

Noue then, when he had ridd himselfe of that office, and obteyned that that neyther chaunced to Scipio Aphrican, the great Pompey, Marcus Tullius Cicero, nor to the Emperour Augustus, to be discharged, when they most desyred, of the combersome affaires of the common wealth, nor lightly doth chaunce to men that be intangled therein, and had nowe gotten that which he euer moste desired, that, being discharged of suche offices and troubles, he might [be]sett and bestowe the residue of his life in ghostly and spirituall studyes, meditations and exercises to heauenwarde: This his desire, I say, when God had mercifully and gratiously graunted him, he was the gladdest man thereof in the worlde, and, as partly ye may vnderstande by the premisses, imployed his time accordingly.

More gladly resigns the Great Seal in order to devote his time to pious exercises.

After he had thus geuen ouer the Chauncellourshipp, and placed all his gentlemen and yeomen with Bisshopps and noble men, and his eight watermen with the Lorde Audley, that in the same office next succeeded him, to whom also he gaue his great barge, then calling all his children vnto him, and asking their aduise howe they might nowe in this decaye of his abilitie (by the surrender of his office so impaired that he could not, as he was wont, [fol. 38 *b*] and gladly woulde, | beare out the whole charges of them all himselfe) from thenceforth be able to liue and continue

After his resignation, More discusses economies necessary to prevent the dispersion of his family. [ROPER.]

MSS. E L R² Y C H R B.

1. *then*] *Omitted in* H R. 2. *that that*] þat which R² H R. 2. *neyther*] neuer L; not B. 3. *Pompey, Marcus*] Pompey & Marcus R². 4–6. *when . . . common wealth*] of the combersome affaires of the comon wealthe when they most desired Y. 6. *lightly*] likely R² B. 6. *that be*] being R². 7. *and . . . gotten*] & now had gotten H R. 7. *that which*] that þat L C B; that Y. 7. *euer moste*] euer most R, *with* euer *interlineated.* 8. *offices*] office Y. 9. *besett and*] L Y C; sett and E R² H R; *omitted in* B. 9. *the*] *Omitted in* H. 11. *I say*] *Omitted in* B. 11. *when*] whe H. 12–13. *he was . . . thereof*] he was thereof the gladdest man H R. 13. *ye*] you L R² B; we H R. 14. *premisses*] premisss H. 16. *thus*] this L. 16. *the*] his L. 19. *that*] who L R² B. 19. *same*] sayde L R² H R B. (Roper *supports* same.) 21. *their*] of their H. 22. *nowe*] *Interlineated in* R. 22. *this*] þe L. 24. *charges*] charge H R. 25. *continue*] to continue Y.

together, as he would wishe they should; When he sawe them silent, and in that case not readye to shewe their opinions vnto him, "Then will I," saide he, "shewe my poore minde to you. I haue beene brought vp," quoth he, "at Oxforde, at an Inne of Chauncerie, at Lincolnes Inne, and also in the kinges Court, and so forth from the lowest degree to the highest, and yet haue I in yerely revennewes at this present lefte me litle aboue an hundred poundes by the yere; so that nowe must we hereafter, if we like to liue together, be content to become contributo[rie]s together. But by my counsaile it shall not be best for us to fall to the lowest fare first. We will not therefore descende to Oxforde fare, nor to the fare of Newe Inne, but we will beginne with Lincolnes Inne dyett, where many right woorshipfull and of good yeres doo liue full well. Which if we finde not our selues the first yere able to mainteyne, then will we the next yere goe one stepp downe to Newe Inne fare, wherewith many an honest man is well contented. If that exceede our abilitie too, then will we the next yere after descende to Oxforde fare, where many graue, learned and auncient fathers be continually conuersaunt. Which if our powre stretche not to mainteyne neyther, then may we yet, like poore schollers of Oxforde, goe a begging with our bagges and wallettes, and sing *Salue Regina* at riche mens dores, where for pitie some good folkes will geue vs their mercifull charitie, and so still keepe company, and goe forth and be merie together."

MSS. E L R^2 Y C H R B.

2. *silent*] all silent R^2. 2. *in that case*] *Omitted in* B. 6. *in the*] at the Y B. 6. *forth*] *Omitted in* L. 7. *I*] *Omitted in* B. 8. *aboue*] able H R. 9. *poundes*] pound B. 9. *by the*] by Y. 11. *contributories*] L C; contributours, E R^2 Y H R B. (Roper MSS. *vary. See* Notes.) 11. *my*] *Omitted in* Y. 13. *nor to the*] nor þe L R^2. 14. *of*] of þe L R^2 B; at C. (Roper *supports* of.) 14. *Lincolnes*] *On an erasure in* R^2. 16. *doo*] *Omitted in* H. 16. *full*] *Omitted in* B. 16. *our selues*] *Omitted in* B. 17. *the next*] thext next R; *omitted in* B. 17. *yere*] *Omitted in* B. 18–19. *wherewith . . . contented*] *Omitted in* B. 20. *too*] *Omitted in* B. 20. *after*] *Omitted in* B. 21. *graue*] greate L R^2 B. 22. *our*] *Interlineated in* R. 23. *neyther*] *Omitted in* H B; *on erasure in* R. 23. *yet*] *Omitted in* H R. 24. *begging*] biggine Y. 25–26. *at . . . dores*] at everie riche mans dore B. 26. *folkes*] folke C. 28. *merie*] many B.

And whereas you haue hearde before he was by the king from a very woorshipfull liuing taken into his graces seruice, with whom, in all the great and weightie causes that concerned his highnes or the Realme, he consumed and spent with painfull cares, trauailes and troubles, as well beyonde the Seas as within this Realme, in effect the whole substance of his life; yet with the gaine he gott therby, being neuer wastfull spender thereof, was he not able, after the resignation of his office of the Lorde Chauncell*our*, for the maintenaunce of himselfe and suche as necessarily belonged vnto him, sufficiently to finde [fol. 39 *a*] | meate, drinke, fuell, apparell, and such other necessary charges. But was inforced and compelled, for lacke of other fuell, euery night before he went to bedd, to cause a great burden of ferne to be brought into his owne chamber, and with the blase thereof to warme himselfe, his wife and his children, and so without any other fyres to goe to their beddes.

After his resignation, More had not sufficient means for himself and his dependants. [ROPER.]

Fern had then to be used as fuel in More's household.

Our christian Z[i]machus, Aristides, Epaminondas, Agrippa, Publicola, Se[r]uilius, which are with immortall fame and glorye renowned for their integritie, and for that that, notwithstanding they had the greatest swaie and offices in the co*m*mon|wealth, the first two at Athens, the thirde at Thebes, the residue at Rome, yet dyed they very poore and needie.

This poverty was due to More's integrity during office.

And nowe lett Tindall and his other good brethren say and lye on apace, that he well wist that S*ir* Thomas More, after he gaue ouer the Chauncellourshipp, was no lesse woorth in money, plate and other moueables then

Tindale and the brethren lie concerning More's wealth. [WORKS, p. 902.]

MSS. E L R^2 Y C H R B.

1. *as*] *Omitted in* Y. 1. *you . . . before*] before yow have hearde B. 1. *haue*] *Interlineated in* R. 4–5. *consumed and*] *Omitted in* B. 5. *trauailes*] sorrowes L. 6. *Seas*] sea L R^2 B. 6. *this*] the H R. 7–8. *gaine . . . therby*] gaine of all his paine H. 7. *gott*] gat Y C. 9–10. *office . . . Chauncellour*] Lord Chaunclorship B. 13. *charges*] thinges L R^2 B. 14. *cause*] case R^2. 15. *burden*] bundell Y. 15. *owne*] *Omitted in* B. 17. *his wife*] & his wife R^2. 17. *and his children*] and children Y C. 17. *fyres*] fire L. 18. *to their beddes*] to bed B. 19. *Zimachus*] L R^2 B; Zamachus E Y C H R. 19. *Epaminondas*] Epimanondas H. 20. *Seruilius*] L R^2 H R; Seuilius E Y C; *omitted in* B. 20. *which*] who L R^2 B. 26–27. *say and*] *Interlineated in* R.

twentie thousande markes. The which report the saide S*ir* Thomas hearing, confessed, if he had heaped vp so muche goodes together, he had not gotten the one halfe by right.

More was a poor man. [ROPER.]

As for the landes that he euer purchased, they were not aboue the value of twentie markes by the yere. And after his debtes paide, he had not, his cheyne except, in golde and siluer lefte him the woorth of one hundred poundes.

More arranges for the conveyance of his lands at his death. [ROPER.]

And that he might the more quietly settle himselfe to the seruice of God, then made he a conueyance for the disposition of all his landes, reseruing to himselfe an estate thereof onely for terme of his owne life; and after his deceasse assuring some part of the same to his wife, some to his sonnes wife for a ioynter in consideratio*n* that she was an inheritrice in possession of more then an hundred pounde lande by the yere, and some to M*aster* Will*iam* Roper and his wife in recompence of their mariage money, with diuers remainders ouer.

Which conveyance was set aside, and the lands appropriated by the King, after More's attainder. [ROPER.]

All which conueyance and assuraunce was perfectly finished longe before that matter wherevpon he was attainted was made an offence, and yet after by Statute cleerely auoyded; and so were all his landes that he had to his wife and children by the saide conueyance in suche sort assured, contrary to the order of the lawe, taken away from them, and brought into the kinges handes, sauing that portion that he had appointed to M*aster* Will*iam* Roper and his

But lands immediately conveyed to

MSS. E L R^2 Y C H R B.

1. *report*] *Interlineated in* L. 1. *the saide*] *Omitted in* L B. 2. *Sir Thomas*] Sir Thomas More B. 2. *if*] *Omitted in* H. 3. *goodes*] *Omitted in* B. 3. *not*] *Interlineated in* L. 5. *that*] *Omitted in* L R^2 B. 5. *they*] *Omitted in* L R^2 Y C H R B. (E *is unsupported, but the pronoun seems necessary.*) 6. *twentie*] *After* twentie, E *has* th *crossed through.* 6. *by the*] by Y; a B. 6. *yere*] yeres R^2. 7. *he had not*] *Omitted in* Y. 7. *except*] excepted Y B. 10. *settle*] sett L. 11. *then made he*] he made R^2. 11–12. *the disposition of*] *Omitted in* B. 14. *deceasse*] *On erasure in* R^2. 14. *of the same*] thereof R^2; *omitted in* Y. 16. *an* (1)] *Omitted in* L. 16. *of more*] in more Y. 16. *then*] thn H. 16. *an* (2)] one Y. 17. *lande*] landes L; *omitted in* R^2. 21–22. *was made . . . auoyded*] *Interlineated in* R. 22. *an offence*] and offence Y; over H. 25. *to*] *Interlineated over* of *crossed through* R. 25. *the order of*] *Omitted in* H.

Roper and his wife escaped the King's seizure. [ROPER.]

wife. Which, although he had in the foresaide conueyance reserued, as he did the rest, for terme of life to himselfe, neuerthelesse vpon farther consideration,* two [fol. 39 b] dayes after, by another conueyance, he gaue | the same immediately to M*aster* Will*iam* Roper and his wife in possession. And so because the Statute had vndone onelye the firste conueyance, geuing no more to the king but so muche as passed by that, the second conueyance, whereby it was geuen to the foresaide M*aster* Roper and his wife, being dated two dayes after, was without the compasse of the Statute, and so was that portion to them by that meanes clerely reserued.

More's advice to Secretary Cromwell: ever tell the King what he *ought* to do, but never what he *is able* to do. [ROPER.]

Nowe vpon this resignement of the foresaide office, came M*aster* Thomas Cromwell, then high in the kinges fauo*ur*, to Chelsey to him, with a message from the king. Wherein when they hadd throughly commoned together: "M*aster* Cromwell," quoth he, "you are nowe entred into the seruice of a moste noble, wise and liberall Prince; if you will folowe my poore aduise, you shall, in your counsaile geuing to his grace, euer tell him what he ought to doo, but neuer what he is able to doo; so shall you shewe your selfe a true, faithfull seruaunt and a right woorthy Counsailo*ur*; for if a Lyon knewe his owne strength, harde were it for anye man to rule him."

Which advice Cromwell did not follow.

Which wise and wholsome aduise of S*ir* Thomas More, if the saide Cromwell had folowed accordingly, he had done the part of a good Counsailo*ur*, and perchaunce preserued the king and the Realme from many greeuous enormities they fell in, and himselfe

MSS. E L R^2 Y O H R B.

1. *the*] *Interlineated in* B. 2. *terme*] the terme B. 2. *life*] his lyfe B. 3. *consideration*] L R^2 Y C H B; considerations E R. (Roper MSS. *vary. See* Notes.) 6–7. *had vndone onelye*] onely had vndone B. 9. *the*] *Omitted in* B. 9. *foresaide*] sayde L H R; say R^2; *omitted in* B. 9. *Master Roper*] Master William Roper L R^2 B. 12. *by that meanes*] *Omitted in* L R^2 B. 13. *this*] theis H. 13. *the*] this B. 18. *liberall*] prudent B. 20. *him*] *Omitted in* H. 20. *he ought*] *Omitted in* B. 22. *true*] true and R^2. 22. *faithfull*] *Omitted in* H. 24. *strength*] strenghe L; strenght R^2. 24. *it*] *Omitted in* B. 24. *him*] *Interlineated in* R^2. 25. *aduise*] counsell L. 26. *the saide Cromwell*] Master Cromwell B 29. *in*] into R^2.

from the vtter ruine and destruction he at length fell in.

Thomas Cranmer pronounces the marriage with Queen Katherine void. And the King marries Anne Boleyn. [ROPER.]

A while after this, Thomas, Archbisshopp of Caunterbury, hauing a Commission sent to him to decyde, ende and determine the matter of the kinges [mariage], in open consistorie pronounced at St Albans and gaue sentence diffinitiue against the [mariage] of Queene Catherine, and declared the same voyde, frustrate, and of no maner of validitie or force. Wherevpon the king maried with the Lady Anne Bulleine, to whom longe before, as it is well knowen, he bare* meruailous great loue and affection, and caused her afterwarde solemnelye to be crowned.

More refuses to be present at Anne's coronation; but accepts the Bishops' money for a gown. [ROPER.]

It fortuned that not longe before the kinges comming through the streetes of London from the towre to Westminster to the saide coronation, that Sir Thomas More receaued a letter from the Bisshops of Durham, Bathe, and Winchester, requesting him both to keepe them company from the tower to the coronation, and also to take twentie poundes that by the bearer thereof they had sent him, to buye him a gowne; which he thankfully receaving, and at home still tarying, at their next meeting, saide merily vnto them:

"My Lordes, in the letter which you lately sent me, you required two thinges of me, the one whereof since I was so well content to graunt you, the other therefore I

MSS. E L R² Y C H R B.

1. *from*] for R. 1. *and destruction*] *Omitted in* B. 1–2. *he . . . in*] at length he came vnto R²; he fell in B. 1. *length*] lenghe L. 5. *mariage*] marriage L R² Y C; marying E H R B. (Roper *has* matrymonye.) 6. *open*] vpon H. 6. *St Albans*] St Talbons Y. 7. *sentence diffinitiue*] definitive sentence B. 7. *mariage*] marriage L Y C H R; marying E R² B. 9. *maner of*] *Omitted in* H R. 9. *validitie or*] *Omitted in* B. 10. *with the Lady*] with ladie C H R. 11. *bare*] L R² Y C H R B; bare a E. 12–13. *solemnelye . . . crowned*] to be solemnly crowned R². 15. *streetes*] strete L R². 16–19 *that . . . coronation*] *An addition on the margin in* R, *with omission mark in text before* and also. (*Cf. l.* 19.) 20–21. *by the . . . sent him*] they had sent him by þe bearer (*with omission of* thereof) C. (Roper *supports* thereof.) 20. *bearer*] bearers B. 21. *him* (2)] *Omitted in* B. 24. *letter*] last letter B. 24. *which*] *Omitted in* H. 26. *so*] *Omitted in* B.

thought I might be the bolder to denye you. And like as the one, because I tooke you for no beggers, and my [fol. 40 a] selfe I knew | to be no riche man, I thought I might the rather fulfill, so the other did put me in remembraunce of an Emperour, that had ordeyned a lawe that whosoeuer committed a certaine offence (which I nowe remember not) except it were a virgin, should suffer the paines of death; such reuerence had he to virginitie. Nowe, so happed it that the first committer of that offence was in deede a virgin. Whereof this Emperour, hearing, was in no small perplexitie, as he that by some ensample faine would haue had that lawe to haue bene put in execution. Wherevpon when his counsaile had sitt longe, solemnely debating this case, sodenly rose there vp one of his Counsaile, a good plaine man among them, and sayde: 'Why make ye so muche adoe, my Lordes, about so small a matter? Let her first be deflowred, and then after may she be deuowred.' And so though your Lordshipps haue in the matter of the matrimonie hitherto kept your selues pure virgins, yet take good heede, my Lordes, that you keepe your virginitie still; for some be there that by procuring your Lordshipps first at the coronation to be present, and next to preache for the setting forth of it, and finally to write bookes vnto all the world in defence thereof, are desirous to deflowre you [and when they haue deflowred you, then] will* they* not faile soone after to deuoure you. Nowe, my Lordes," quoth he, "it lyeth not in my powre but that they may deuoure me;

More's parable of the offending virgin. His warning to the Bishops. [Roper.]

More may be devoured, but will

MSS. E L R² Y C H R B.

1. *be . . . you*] the bolder deny you H; be bolder to deny yow R. 6. *I*] *Omitted in* Y. 7. *it were*] *Omitted in* L R². 8–9. *so happed it*] so it happened Y. 9. *of that offence*] *Omitted in* B. 10. *in deede*] *Omitted in* R² B. 12. *to haue bene*] to be R². 13. *sitt*] satt Y C. 14. *solemnely*] *Omitted in* L R² B. 14. *case*] cause L R² B. 14. *rose there*] there rose L R² B. 16. *ye*] you L R² H R. 18. *after*] afterwarde R². 18. *may she*] she may H R. 18. *though*] *Omitted in* B. 21. *be there*] there bee L R² H R B. (Roper MSS. *vary.*) 25–26. *and when they haue deflowred you*] L R² Y C H B (*supported by* Roper); *interlineated in* R; *omitted in* E. 26. *then*] L R² Y C B (*supported by* Roper); *omitted in* E H R. 26. *will they not*] L R² Y C B (*supported by most* Roper MSS.); they will not E H R. (*See* Notes.) 28. *that*] *Omitted in* L R² B.

not be deflowered. [ROPER.]

but God being my good Lorde, I will prouide that they shall neuer deflowre me."

After his resignation, More does not meddle with State affairs, least of all with the King's marriage.

After the saide mariage and coronation so solemnized, *Sir* Thomas More, partlye (as a deepe wise man) foreseing what inconueniences and troubles he might purchase himselfe with intermedling of the princely affaires, and [fore]seing the tempestuous stormie worlde that in deede afterwarde did most terribly insurge, and partly for that he had principally relinquished that office, as well because his health was decayed, as that he would nowe the residue of his life withdrawe and sequester from all maner worldly busines, and wholly besett it vpon godly, spirituall and heauenlye affaires, did not in any wise intermedle and cumber himselfe *with* any worldly matters, and least of all with the kinges great combersome matter of his mariage, or any other of his publike proceedinges. Concerning the which mariage he was not slenderly and [hoverly] informed, but longe, painfully and deepely trauailed, as appereth by that we haue alredie saide, and by his conference with such persons, and at such times, and in such maner, as we haue before declared; but farther also by such conference as he had, as well and aboue all other, with doct*our* Wilson, being both twaine in euery poynt of one opinion (for the which the saide doct*our* was sent to the towre, albeit he did afterwarde

Though he had studied it fully, and conferred thereon with Doctor Wilson, the Archbishops of Canterbury and York, and Friar Nicholas. [MORE to CROMWELL; WORKS, p. 1426.]

MSS. E L R² Y C H R B.

3. *and coronation*] *Omitted in* B. 4. *partlye . . . man*] being a deepe wise man B. 4. *deepe wise*] wise deepe R². 4. *foreseing*] forsawe B. 5. *inconueniences*] inconvenience Y. 6. *with*] with þe C. 7. *foreseing*] foreseeinge L R² C B; seing E Y H R. 8. *afterwarde did*] did afterwarde L R² B. 9. *he had principally*] principally he had B. 11. *withdrawe and*] *Omitted in* B. 11. *sequester from*] sequestre himselfe from R². 11. *all maner*] all manner of L R² H R B; all Y. 12. *besett it*] besett L; sett H R; beset himselfe B. 12. *vpon godly, spirituall*] about spirituall Y; vpon spirituall B. 14. *cumber*] incomber Y H R. 14. *matters*] affayres R². 16. *proceedinges*] *On an erasure in* R². 17. *the which*] this B. 17. *and*] or B. 18. [*hoverly*]] houertly E Y; *couertly* L R² C H R B. (*See* Notes.) 18–19. *deepely trauailed*] depely informed trauailed Y. 19. *as*] as it Y C. 19. *and*] *Omitted in* L R² B. 21. *maner*] manners B. 21. *haue*] *Omitted in* C. 21. *before*] *Interlineated in* R. 22. *as* (1)] which H. 22. *as* (1) . . . *as well*] *On erasure in* R. 22. *as well and*] *Omitted in* B. 25. *to*] to to B. 25. *albeit*] *albet* C.

relent) as with the Archbisshopps of Caunterbury and [fol. 40 *b*] Yorke, | and doctour Nicholas, the Augustine fryer. Howbeit, finding in all this conference no substantiall and sufficient matter to remoue him from his first opinion, with most mildnes and humilitie declared the same to the king, adding that if he might haue beene able to haue done him seruice in that matter, he would haue beene more gladd then of all such worldly commodities as eyther he then had, or euer* should come to| : Whose good minde in that behalfe the king taking in good gree, vsed in persecuting his great matter onely those whose conscience he perceaued well and fully persuaded vpon that point.

He had declared his opinion to the King, who had professed to take it in good part. [WORKS, *as above.*]

After which time S*ir* Thomas More neyther did any thing, nor wrote worde, to the impayring of the kinges part. And though him selfe were fixed and setled, as the euent did shewe, that neither the kinges fawning and flattering of the world vpon him, nor yet any aduersitie or imprisonment, could breake his constancie, yet the matter once passed by lawe, he did keepe his conscience to himselfe, and would not open his opinion in that matter, especially the causes why he refused the othe, eyther to the Bisshopp of Rochester demaunding his iudgement, eyther to doctour Wilson requiring it at his hande, as well before the saide doctour was imprisoned as afterwarde; but did sende them this worde onely, that he had quieted, fixed and settled his conscience, and so he would [they] should doo theirs. And as for the causes of

The matter of the marriage once settled by law, More keeps his opinion to himself. [Cf. PARIS NEWS LETTER. Also MORE to DR. WILSON; WORKS, p. 1445.]

MSS. E L R² Y C H R B.

2. *Nicholas*] Nichoals C. 3. *all*] *Omitted in* H R. 4. *his*] þe L R² B. 9. *he then*] then he H; he then R, *with* he *interlineated.* 9. *euer should*] L R² Y C R B; euer he should E H. 10. *gree*] part Y. 11. *persecuting*] prosecuteing L R² Y C H R B. (English Works, *p.* 1426, *support* persecuting.) 11. *his great matter*] þat matter C. (English Works, *p.* 1426, *support* his great matter.) 15. *wrote worde*] wrote any worde L B; wrot any worde R², wrot *being corrected from* wrought. 17. *fawning*] *Interlineated in* R. 18–19. *aduersitie or imprisonment*] imprisonment or aduersetie Y. 19. *or*] and R². 19. *constancie*] conscience B. 21. *that*] this Y. 22. *the* (2)] that Y. 24. *hande*] handes B. 27. *he*] the H. 28. *they*] L R² Y C H R B; he E. 28. *as*] *Omitted in* B. 28. *causes*] *Omitted in* B.

He will not disclose his reasons for refusing the oath. [MORE to DR. WILSON; WORKS, p. 1445.]

refusing the saide othe, as no man knewe but himselfe, and were kept secrete in his owne conscience, so (as himselfe wryteth to the said doct*our* Wilson) they were perchaunce some other then those that other men would weene, suche as he neuer disclosed to any man, nor neuer intended to doo whiles he liued.

More is innocent of writing against the Articles put forth by the King's Council. [MORE to CROMWELL; WORKS, p. 1422.]

So muche haue I saide, and the sooner, of his moderate and quiet doinges, because it hath beene otherwise reported that he was a busy body, and that there ranne a brute and reporte vpon him that he was about the making and deuising, and meaned to diuulge and publishe in print, an answere to certaine articles put foorth by the king and his counsaile, wherein he was most giltlesse, and purge[d] himselfe thereof by his letters sent to S*ir* Thomas Cromwell.

More accused of bribery and extortion.

The saide mariage being thus passed, and the authoritie of the Pope [thereupon] passing away withall, vpon displeasure that he would not passe, by sentence diffinitiue, against the kinges mariage with Queene Katherine, there rose euery day more and more some quarelling matter against S*ir* Thomas More. And albeit, as well in his other offices as in the high office of the Lorde Chauncell*our*, there were fewe or none that euer were farther from corruption, oppression, extortion and bryberie then this woorthy man, that for his integritie may be well compared with Fabritius and | suche other noble Romanes; yet, as [fol. 41 *a*] the good king of the Lacedemonians, Agis, was called to an accompt for his misruling and misgouernment, whereas

MSS. E L R² Y C H R B.

1. *the saide*] of the said Y; the B. 2–3. *as . . . Wilson*] *Omitted in* B. 5. *neuer* (2)] *Omitted in* R²; ever C. 6. *whiles*] whyle L R²; whilest H R. 10. *vpon*] of L R² B. 11. *meaned*] meaninge R². 11. *diuulge*] divlge Y. 14. *purged*] Y C H R; purge E; did purge L R² B. 17. *thereupon passing away*] thereupon passing awaye Y C; passing away E; passeinge thereupon L; thereupon passinge R² B; thus passing awaie H R. 18. *not*] *Interlineated in* R. 21. *his*] *Omitted in* L. 24. *bryberie*] *The* y *corrected from* b *in* E. 25. *be well*] well be R² H R B. 26. *with*] to Y. 27. *Agis*] *Omitted here in* R². 28. *an*] *Omitted in* R² Y. 28. *accompt for*] account Agis by name for R², name *being corrected from* meene. 28. *misgouernment*] misgouerment Y; misgoverning C; governement H R.

he moste nobly and woorthily gouerned the saide co*m*monwealth, or rather as blessed St Job was falslye and wrongfully noted of Eliphas for suche matters, so was this innocent, good man called to a reckoning before the kinges councell as, forsooth, a great bryber and extortioner.

More is proved innocent of taking a reward from Vaughan. [ROPER.]

He had made, being Lorde Chauncell*our*, a decree against one Parnell, at the sute of one Vaughan, his aduersarye. This Parnell complained moste greeuously to the kinges highnes that, for making of the same decree, he had of the same Vaughan, vnable for the gowte to trauaile abrode himselfe, by the handes of his wife taken a faire gilted cupp for a bribe. Who therevpon, by the kinges appointment, being called before the whole counsaile (where that matter was heynously layde to his charge) forthwith confessed that forasmuch as that cupp was longe after the foresaide decree brought him for a newyeres gifte, he, at her importunate pressing vpon him therefore, of courtesie refused not to receaue it. Then the Lorde of Wilshire, for hatred of his religion preferrer of this sute, with muche reioysing saide vnto the Lordes: "Loe, did not I tell you, my Lordes, that you should finde this matter true?" Wherevpon S*ir* Thomas More desired their Lordshipps that as they had courteously hearde him tell the one part of his tale, so they would vouchsafe of their honours indifferentlye to heare the other. After which obteyned, he farther declared vnto them that, albeit he had in deede with much worke

MSS. E L R^2 Y C H R B.

1. *saide*] same L H R. 2. *or rather*] as rather H. 2. *as*] a R^2. 2. *blessed*] holy H R. 2. *St*] *Interlineated in* R. 2. *In margin of* C *is written* Job 22. 4. *this*] the H R. 5. *forsooth*] *Omitted in* B. 7. *made*] *Omitted in* H R. 9–10. *moste . . . highnes*] to þe kinges highnes most greeuously L R^2 H R B. 10. *making of*] makeinge L R^2 B. 10. *same*] sayd H R. 11. *same Vaughan*] said Vaghan Y. 11–12. *vnable . . . himselfe*] *Omitted in* B. 14. *the whole*] the kings whole H R. 17. *was*] *Omitted in* B. 19. *therefore*] *Omitted in* B. 20. *Wilshire*] Wiltshire L R^2 H R B; Wlsheire Y; Wilsheire C. 20. *for . . . religion*] *Omitted in* R^2 B. 21. *vnto the*] *Corrected from* vntoo L. 22. *did not I*] did I not L R^2 H R B. 25. *him*] them Y. 26. *indifferentlye to heare*] to heare indifferently L. 27. *which*] the which H; R^2 *has* th *crossed through over* which *crossed through.* 28. *worke*] adoe R^2.

receaued that cuppe, yet immediately therevpon he caused his Butler to fill it with wine, and of that cupp dr[a]nke to her; and that when he had so done, and she pledged him, then as freely [as her husbande had geuen it to him, euen so freely] gaue he the same to her againe, to geue vnto her husbande for his newyeres gifte; which, at his instant request, though much against her will, at length yet she was faine to receaue, as her selfe and certaine other there presently before them deposed. Thus was this great mountaine turned scant to a litle molehill.

More is known to have refused money from Mistress Crocker. [ROPER.]

So at another time, vpon a newyeres day, there came vnto him one mistris Crocker, a riche widowe (for whom with no small paine he had made a decree in the Chauncerie against the Lorde of Arundell) to present him with a paire of gloues, and fortie poundes of angels in them for a newyeres gifte. Of whom he thankfully receaving the gloves, but refusing the mo|ney, saide vnto her: [fol. 41 b] "Mistris, since it were against good maner to forsake a gentlewomans newyeres gifte, I am content to take your gloues; but as for your money, I vtterly refuse." So, muche against her minde, inforced he her to take her golde againe.

From Master Gresham More had accepted a cup, but had given him in return one

And one Master Gresham likewise, having at the same time a cause depending in the Chauncerie before him, sent him for a newyeres gifte a faire gilted cupp; the fashion wherof he very well lyking, caused one of his owne, though not in his fantasie of so good a fashion, yet

MSS. E L R[2] Y C H R B.

2. *and of*] & so of R[2]. 3. *dranke*] L R[2] Y C H R B; drunke E. 3. *so*] *Omitted in* L. 4–5. *as her . . . euen so freely*] as hir housband had given yt to him, even so freely C (*supported by Roper*); *omitted in* E L R[2] Y H R B. 6. *his*] a B. 8. *length*] lengh L. 8. *yet*] *Omitted in* H B. 9. *other . . . deposed*] other presently deposed before them H R. 9. *deposed*] were deposed L. 10. *turned scant*] scant turned H R. 12. *at*] *Interlineated in* R[2]. 12. *a*] an other B. 14–15. *in the Chauncerie*] *Interlineated in* R. 16. *fortie poundes of*] x l R[2]; fourtie pounde C. 17. *he*] *Omitted in* L R[2] B. 19. *Mistris*] Mistris Crocker L R[2] B. 19. *were*] was R[2]. 19. *maner*] manners R[2]. 21. *your*] the B. 21. *refuse*] refuse it B. 21. *So*] and so L. 22. *inforced he*] he inforced Y B. 22–23. *her golde*] he gold H. 24. *Gresham*] *After an erasure in* R[2]. 24. *likewise*] alsoe R[2]. 27. *one of*] owne of H.

better in valew, to be brought him out of his chamber, which he willed the messenger in recompence to deliuer to his master; and vnder other condicion would he in no wise receaue it.

of greater value. [Roper.]

Many thinges moe of like effect, for the declaration of his innocencie and cleerenes from all corruption or euill affection, could I here rehearse beside; which for tediousnes omitting, I referre to the Readers, by these fewe fore remembred examples, with their owne iudgementes wisely to weigh and consider the same.

Other examples might be given. [Roper.]

But then was there a more greeuous and daungerous quarell sought against him by reason of a certaine Nonne dwelling in Caunterbury, for her vertue and holynes among the people not a litle esteemed; vnto whom, for that cause, many religious persons, doctours of diuinitie, and diuers other of good woorshipp of the laitie, vsed to resort. Who, affirming that she had reuelations from God to geue the king warning of his wicked life and of the abuse of the sworde and authoritie co*m*mitted to him by God, and vnderstanding my Lorde of Rochester, Bisshopp Fisher, being her ordinarye, to be a man of notable vertuous liuing and learning, repaired to Rochester, and there disclosed to him all her reuelations, desyring his aduise and counsaile therein. Which the Bisshopp perceaving might well stande with the lawes of God and his holy Churche, aduised her (as she before had warning and intended) to goe to the king [her]selfe, and to lett him vnderstande the whole circumstance

The prophecies of the Nun of Canterbury are made a cause of quarrel against More. [Roper.

The Nun discloses her revelations to Fisher, who advises her to go to the King. [Roper.]

MSS. E L R² Y C H R B.

2. *recompence to*] recompence of the other to H. 3. *to his*] his R². 3. *and vnder other*] as on other B. 3. *in*] *Interlineated in* R². 5. *for the declaration*] *Interlineated in* R. 6–7. *or euill affection*] *Omitted in* B. 7. *here*] *Interlineated in* R. 8. *Readers*] reader B. 9. *fore*] foure R². 12. *sought against*] soughte oute against B. 14. *among . . . esteemed*] not a litle estemed among the people B. 16. *other*] others L R² Y H B. 16. *good*] *After an erasure in* R². 19. *abuse . . . committed*] abuse and aucthoritie of the sword committed Y. 19. *and authoritie*] and of the authority R² H R. 19–20. *by God*] from God R². 23. *to him*] *Omitted in* L. 26–27. *as . . . intended*] *Omitted in* B. 27. *herselfe*] L R² Y C H R B (*supported by* Roper); himselfe E. 28. *and to lett*] & let L.

thereof. Whervpon she went to the king, and tolde him all her re[ue]lations, and so returned home againe.

The Nun talks with More, whose conduct in this case is blameless. [1533.] [ROPER.]

And in short space after, she, making a voyage to the Nunnes of Sion, by meanes of one M*aster* Reynoldes, a father of the same house, there fortuned concerning such secretes as had bene reuealed vnto her (some part whereof seemed to touche the matter of the kinges suprema|cie [fol. 42 *a*] and mariage which shortly therevpon folowed) to enter into talke with S*ir* Thomas More; who, notwithstanding he might well at that time, without daunger of any lawe (though after, as himselfe had prognosticated before, those matters were established by statutes and confirmed by othes)* freely and safely haue talked with her therein, Neuerthelesse, in all the co*m*munication betweene [them] (as in processe it appered) had alway so discretely demeaned himselfe, that he deserued not to be blamed, but contrarywise to be commended and praysed.

More asserts his innocence in the matters of the Nun, the Marriage and the Supremacy. [MORE to CROMWELL; WORKS, pp. 1424–28.]

Concerning the saide Nonne, S*ir* Thomas More at large to the foresayd S*ir* Thomas Cromwell discourseth, and plainly sheweth himselfe moste innocent and farre from all blame and sinister suspition, as well in all his doinges with the saide Nonne as in all other his pro ceeding*es*, eyther touching the kinges mariage or his supremacie. Yet all this notwithstanding, at the Parliament folowing was there put into the Lordes house a Bill to attaint the saide Nonne and diuers other religious persons of high treason, and the Bisshopp of Rochester, S*ir* Thomas More, and certaine other

But More and Fisher are attainted of misprision

MSS. E L R² Y C H R B.

2. *reuelations*] L R² Y C H R B (*supported by* Roper); relations E. 3. *space*] time H R. 3. *after*] afterward Y. 3. *voyage*] vioage Y. 4. *meanes*] reason L. 5. *concerning*] *Omitted in* Y. 6. *whereof*] thereof R² B. 7–8. *touche . . . mariage*] touche the supremacie of the kinges maiestie and marriage Y. 9. *into*] *Omitted in* C. 12. *statutes*] statut Y. 13. *freely*] C H R (*supported by* Roper); as freely E L R² Y B. 14. *them*] L R² Y C H R B (*supported by* Roper); *omitted in* E. 15. *as . . . appered*] *Omitted in* B. 15. *had*] he H R. 16. *demeaned*] behaved B. 17. *and praysed*] *Omitted in* B. 18–19. *Sir Thomas More at large*] Sir Thomas more at large H R. 18–19. *More . . . discourseth*] More discourseth at large to Sir Thomas Cromwell B. 21. *all* (2)] *Omitted in* L R² B. 22. *with*] which H. 24. *at the*] the H R. 25. *folowing*] next followinge R².

of misprision of treason; the king presupposing of likelyhood that this Bill would be to S*ir* Thomas More so troublous and terrible that it would force him to relent and condiscende to his request; wherein his grace was muche deceaued. To which Bill S*ir* Thomas More was a suter personally to be receaued in his owne defence to make aunswere; but the king, not lyking that, assigned the Bisshopp of Caunterbury, the Lorde Chauncell*our*, the duke of Norffolke and M*aster* Cromwell, at a day and place appointed, to call S*ir* Thomas More before them. At which time M*aster* Will*iam* Roper, thinking that then he had good oportunitie, earnestly aduised him to labour vnto those Lordes for the helpe of his discharge out of that Parliament bill; who aunswered the said M*aster* Roper he would.

of treason in the case of the Nun, the King hoping by this charge to terrify More into consent to the marriage. [1534.] More summoned to defend himself. Roper begs him to labour for his discharge out of the Parliament Bill. [ROPER.]

And at his co*m*ming before them according to their appointment, they interteyned him very frendly, willing him to sitt downe with them, which in no wise he would. Then beganne the Lorde Chauncell*our* to declare vnto him howe manye wayes the king had shewed his loue and fauour towardes him; howe faine he would haue had him to continue in his office; howe gladd he would haue [fol. 42 *b*] beene to haue heaped more benefites | vpon him; and, finally, [how] he could aske no worldly honour nor profite at his highnes handes that were lykely to be denyed him; hoping, by the declaration of the kinges kindnes and affection towarde him, to prouoke him to recompence his grace with the lyke againe, and vnto those thinges that the Parliament, the Bisshopps and vniuersities had alreadye passed, to adde his consent.

The Lord Chancellor enlarges upon the King's goodness to More, hoping thus to win him over in the matter of the marriage. [ROPER.]

MSS. E L R² Y C H R B.

1. *of* (1)] for Y. 1. *misprision*] suspicion B, *underlined, probably for correction.* 1–2. *of likelyhood*] *Omitted in* R². 14. *the said*] *Omitted in* H R. 14–15. M*aster* *Roper*] Master William Roper L R² B. 15. *he would*] that he would H. 16. *their*] *Interlineated in* R². 18. *sitt*] sett Y. 20–21. *loue and fauour*] fauour & loue L R² B. 21. *towardes*] to B. 22. *to continue*] continue L R² C H R B. (Roper MSS. *vary. See* Notes.) 24. *how he*] L R² Y C B (*supported by* Roper); that he E H R. 24. *could*] would L. 25. *handes*] hande L R² Y C. 26. *kinges*] *Interlineated in* R². 28. *that*] which B. 29. *the Parliament*] Parliament L. 29. *vniuersities*] the vniuersities L R² B. 30. *adde*] yeald Y; add *interlineated over* passe *crossed through* C.

More acknowledges the King's goodness, but remains firm. [ROPER.]

To this S*ir* Thomas More mildlye made aunswere, saying: "No man [liuing] is there, my Lordes, that would with better will doo the thing that should be acceptable to the kinges highnes then I, [which] must needes confesse his manifolde goodnes and bountifull benefites most benignelye bestowed vpon me; howbeit I verily hoped that I should neuer haue heard of this matter more, considering that I haue, from time to time, alway from the beginning, so plainly and truely declared my minde vnto his grace, which his highnes to me euer seemed, like a moste gratious Prince, very well to accept, neuer minding, as he saide, to molest me more therewith. Since which time any further thing that was able to moue me to any chaunge could I neuer finde. And if I could, there is [none] in all the world that would haue beene gladder [of it] then I."

The King's deputies then accuse More of having incited the King to write [1521] the *Assertio septem sacramentorum adversus M. Lutherum,* maintaining the Pope's authority. [ROPER.]

Many thinges more were there of like sort vttred on both sides. But in the ende, when they sawe they could by no maner of persuasion remoue him from his former determination, then beganne they more terribly to touche him, telling him that the kinges highnes had geuen them in co*m*maundement, if they could by no gentlenes winne him, in his name with his great ingratitude to charge him, that neuer was there seruaunt to his soueraine so villanous, nor subiect to his Prince so traiterous as he. For he, by his subtill sinister sleightes

MSS. E L R² Y C H R B.

1. *made*] *On an erasure in* R. 2. *liuing*] C (*supported by* Roper); *omitted in* E L R² Y H R B. 3. *doo the*] doe H. 4. *which*] Y C H R (*supported by* Roper); who E L R² B. 6. *benignelye*] beniglie Y. 7. *that*] *Interlineated in* R. 7. *haue*] *Interlineated in* R. 8. *more*] *Omitted in* H. 10–11. *to me euer seemed*] seemed to mee ever B. 12. *as he*] *Interlineated over* to haue *crossed through* R². 12. *me more*] mee any more L R² B. 15. *none*] C (*supported by* Roper); no man E L R² Y H R B. 15. *that*] *Omitted in* L R² B. 15. *would*] *Interlineated in* B. 16. *gladder of it then*] L Y C B (*supported by* Roper); of that then R²; gladder then E H R. 17. *were . . . vttred*] weare vttered of the like sorte H. 19. *maner*] *Corrected from* meanes *in* R²; meanes or manner B. 20. *terribly*] terrible Y. 22. *by no gentlenes*] by no manner of perswasion or gentlenes B. 23. *his* (2)] this L R² Y C. (Roper *supports* his.) 23. *great*] *Omitted in* B. 26. *subtill*] *Omitted in* L R² B.

most vnnaturally procuring and prouoking him to sett forth a booke of the assertion of the seuen Sacramentes and mainteynance of the Popes authoritie, had caused him, to his dishon*our* throughout all Christendome, to put a sworde into the Popes handes to fight against him selfe.

When they had thus laide forth all the terrours they could imagine against him: "My Lordes," quoth he, "these terrors be argumentes for children, and not for me; but to aunswere that wherewith you doo chiefly burthen me, I beleeue the kinges highnes of his hon*our* will neuer laye that to my charge; for none is there that can in that point saye in mine excuse more then his highnes himselfe, who right well knoweth that I was neuer procurer or counsailer of his Maiestie therevnto; but after it was finished, by his graces appointment and consent of the [fol. 43 *a*] makers of the same, onely a | sorter out and placer of principall matters therein conteyned. Wherein when I founde the Popes authoritie highlye aduaunced, and with [strong] argumentes mightily defended, I saide vnto his grace: 'I must put your highnes in remembraunce of one thing, and that is this. The Pope, as your grace knoweth, is a Prince as you are, and in league with all other christen Princes. It may hereafter so fall out that your grace and he may varye vpon some pointes of the league, wherevpon may growe breache of amitie and warre betweene you both. I thinke it best therefore

More points out that he had remonstrated with the King for having in this book unduly stressed the Pope's authority. [ROPER.]

MSS. E L R² Y C H R B.

1. *procuring . . . sett*] prouokeing & procureinge him to sett L R² B. 1. *him*] *Omitted in* H R. 1–2. *to sett . . . booke*] *Interlineated in* R. 3. *had*] and Y. 4. *his*] *Interlineated in* R. 4. *throughout*] through L. 5. *into*] in L. 9. *these terrors*] *Interlineated in* R. 9. *be*] are Y H; are *interlineated over* be *crossed through* R. 10. *doo*] did B. 11. *kinges . . . will*] kinges highnes will L R² B; kinge of his honorable inclinacion will H. 12. *laye*] *Corrected from* leaue L. 13. *himselfe*] can himselfe B. 15. *but after*] but that after Y. 16. *consent of*] *Omitted in* L R² B. 18. *therein conteyned*] contayned therein L. 18. *therein*] therein *with* in *interlineated* R². 20. *strong*] Y (*supported by* Roper); straunge E C H R; stronge straunge L R² B. 21. *put*] *Interlineated in* R². 21–22. *remembraunce*] mynde L. 22–23. *your grace knoweth*] yow knowe Y. 24. *It*] yet R². 24. *so*] *Omitted in* B. 26. *league*] leauge Y. 26. *amitie*] vnitie L.

that that place be amended, and his authoritie more slenderly towched.'

" 'Nay,' quoth his grace, 'that shall it not. We are so much bounden to the Sea of Rome that we cannot doo to much hono*ur* to it.'

" Then did I further put him in remembraunce of the Statute of Praemunire, whereby a good part of the Popes pastorall cure here was pared away.

But the King had been obstinate. [ROPER.]

" To that aunswered his highnes: 'Whatsoeuer impediment be to the contrary, we will sett foorth [that] authoritie to the vttermoste; for we receaued from that Sea our crowne imperiall'; which, till his grace with his owne mouth tolde it me, I neuer heard of before. So that I trust, when his grace shal be once truely informed of this, and call to his gratious remembraunce my doing in that behalfe, his highnes will neuer speake of it more, but cleere me throughly therein himselfe."

And thus displeasantly departed they.

More rejoices at his resolute stand before the King's Deputies. [ROPER.]

Then tooke S*ir* Thomas More his boate towarde his house at Chelsey, wherein by the way he was verye merye; and for that was M*aster* Will*iam* Roper nothing sorye, hoping that he had gotten himselfe discharged out of the Parliament bill. When he was landed and came home, then walked he and M*aster* Will*iam* Roper alone into the garden together, where the foresaide M*aster* Roper, desirous to knowe howe he had spedd, sayde: " I trust, S*ir*, that all is well because you be so merye."

" It is so, in deede, sonne Roper, I thanke God," quoth he.

MSS. E L R² Y C H R B.

3. *quoth*] sayde L. 3. *shall it not*] it shall not Y. 4. *bounden*] bounde L R² B. 7. *Statute*] state L R² B; Satute H. 7. *Praemunire*] premuniri L; Praemuniri R²; Preemunire H. 10. *that*] C (*supported by* Roper); the E L R² Y H R B. 12. *our*] the L R² B. 13. *it*] *Omitted in* L. 14. *once*] *Omitted in* R². 14. *once truely informed*] once truly throughly R, once truly *being interlineated.* 14. *truely*] truely & throughly H. 15. *gratious*] graces L R² B. 15. *doing*] doeinges R² H B. 16. *highnes*] grace L. 16. *it more*] me more L; it any more H R. 18. *departed*] parted R². 19–20. *towarde . . . Chelsey*] to Chelsey L R² B. 23. *bill*] house B. 23. *came*] come L Y H. 25. *the foresaide*] *Omitted in* B. 25–26. *Master Roper*] Master William Roper L R² B. 27. *be*] are L. 28. *sonne . . . God*] I thanke god sonne Roper L. 28–29. *God, quoth he*] God for it quoth he Y.

"Are you then put out of the Parliament bill?" saide M*aster* Will*iam* Roper.

He had never remembered the Parliament Bill. [ROPER.]

"By my troth, sonne Roper," quoth he, "I neuer remembred it."

"Neuer remembred it, S*ir*?" saide his sonne in lawe. "A case that toucheth your selfe so neere, and vs all for yo*ur* sake. I am very sory to heare it; for I verily trusted, when I sawe you so merye, that all had beene well."

Then saide he, "Wilt thou knowe, sonne Roper, why I was so merye?"

"That would I gladly, S*ir*," saide he.

[fol. 43 *b*] "In good fayth, I reioyced, | sonne," quoth he, "that I had geuen the deuill a fowle fall, and that with those Lordes I had gone so farre as without great shame I could neuer goe backe againe."

At which wordes waxed M*aster* Roper very sadd; for though himselfe lyked it well, yet lyked [it] him but a litle.

More's letter to the King concerning the Parliament Bill. [5 March, 1534.] [WORKS, pp. 1423–4.]

Concerning the saide bill put into the Parliament against him, he wrate a letter to the king. In the which, among other thinges, he wryteth thus: "In this matter of the Nonne of Caunterbury, I haue vnto your trustie Counsailer, M*aster* Thomas Cromwell, by my wryting as plainly declared the truth as I possible can; which my declaration of [his] dutie toward your [grace] and

MSS. E L R^2 Y C H R B.

1. *then*] *Interlineated in* R. 2. *William*] *Omitted in* B. 5. *Sir*] *Interlineated in* R. 6. *case*] *cause* L R^2 B. 8. *that all*] then all H R. 10. *Then saide he*] *Interlineated in* L. 10. *Wilt*] *The* W *corrected from* s *in* E. 10. *knowe*] kowe L. 12. *would I*] I would H. 13. *I reioyced*] I reioyced I reioyced H. 13. *sonne*] some H; *omitted in* B. 13. *quoth he*] *Omitted in* Y. 14. *a fowle*] *Omitted in* Y. 17. *Master Roper*] Master William Rooper C. 18. *himselfe*] Sir Thomas Moore R^2. 18. *yet*] *Omitted in* Y. 18. *lyked it* (2)] L R^2 C H R B (*supported by* Roper); it liked Y; lyked E. 20. *saide*] *Interlineated in* R. 20. *put*] *Omitted in* B. 20. *into*] in R^2 B. 24. *as*] and H. 25. *possible*] possibly L R^2 H. (Possible *supported by* English Works, *p.* 1423; possibly *by* MS. Cleopatra E vi *and* R.O. MS.) 26. *his*] C (*supported by* English Works, *p.* 1423, MS. Cleopatra E vi *and* R.O. MS.); my E L R^2 Y H R B. 26. *grace*] C (*supported by* English Works, *p.* 1423, MS. Cleopatra E vi *and* R.O. MS.); maiestie E H R; highnes L R^2 Y B.

[his] goodnes towardes me he hath, I vnderstande, declared vnto your grace. In any part of all which my dealing, whether any other man may peraduenture put any doubt, or moue any scruple of suspition, that can* I* neyther tell, nor lyeth in my hande to [lett]. But vnto my selfe it is not possible any part of my saide demean*our* to seeme euill, the very cleerenes of my owne conscience knoweth in all the matter my minde and intent so good. Wherefore, most gratious Soueraine, I neuer will, nor [it] can well become me, with yo*ur* highnes to reason or argue the matter; but in my moste humble maner, prostrate at your gratious feete, I onelye beseeche your grace with your owne high prudence and your accustomed goodnes consider and weigh the matter. And [if] that* in* your so doing, your owne vertuous minde shall geue you that, notwithstanding the manifolde and excellent goodnes

MSS. E L R[2] Y C H R B.

1. *his goodnes*] *All the* Harpsfield MSS. *read* your goodness. His goodness *is the reading of* English Works, *p.* 1423, MS. Cleopatra E vi *and* R. O. MS. 2. *all*] *Interlineated in* R. 4. *of suspition*] *Omitted in* L; or suspicion Y. 4. *can I*] L R[2] Y C B (*supported by* English Works, *p.* 1423, MS. Cleopatra E vi *and* R.O. MS.); I can E H R. 5. *lyeth in*] lyeth it in L. 5. *lett*] L R[2] Y C H R B (*supported by* English Works, *p.* 1423, MS. Cleopatra E vi *and* R.O. MS.); tell E. 5. *vnto*] into *corrected to* vnto H. 6. *part*] *Interlineated in* R[2]. 6. *my saide*] *Omitted in* B. 7. *cleerenes*] (*Corrected from* clenenes) L. 8. *knoweth in all the*] knoweth in all that L R[2] B; knoweth all the H. 8. *matter my minde*] matter my minde my mynde Y; matter to be after my mynde H. 9. *most*] my L; my most R[2] B. 9. *neuer will*] will neuer H. 9–10. *nor it can well become me*] Y (*supported by* MS. Cleopatra E vi, *which has* nor well it can bycome me, *and by* R.O. MS., *which has* nor it can bycome me); nor yet can well become me E C R (*supported by* English Works, *p.* 1423); nor can it become mee L; nor yet can yet become me R[2]; nor yet can well become H; nor yet can it become me B. 11. *my*] *Omitted in* H R. 12. *gratious*] graces L R[2] H R; highnesse Y; *omitted in* B. (Gratious *supported by* English Works, *p.* 1423, MS. Cleopatra E vi *and* R.O. MS.) 12. *grace*] *This is the reading of all the* Harpsfield MSS. *and of* English Works, *p.* 1423. MS. Cleopatra E vi *and* R.O. MS. *read* maiestie. 14. *consider*] to consider Y. 14–15. *And if that in your so doing*] And yf þat in your soe doinge R[2] C B (*supported by* English Works, *p.* 1423); And if þat in so doinge L; And in that your so doing E H R; And that if in so doing Y. (MS. Cleopatra E vi *and* R.O. MS. *have* And than if in your so doing.) 15. *shall geue*] shall soe giue H R. 15. *that*] *Omitted in* Y.

that your gratious highnes hath by so many maner* wayes vsed vnto me, I were a wretche of such a monstrous ingratitude as could with any of them all, or any other person liuing, digresse from my bounden dutie of allegiance towarde your good grace, then desire I no farther fauour at your [gratious] [hand] then the losse of all that euer I may leese, goodes, landes, libertie, and finally my life withall, whereof the keeping of any part vnto my selfe could neuer doo me penywoorth of pleasure; but onely should my comfort be, that after my short life and your longe (which with continuall prosperitie to Gods pleasure our Lorde of his mercy sende you) I should once meete with your grace againe in heauen, and there be [fol. 44 *a*] merie with you; where among [mine] other plea|sures this should yet be one, that your grace should surelye see there then, that how soeuer you take me, I am your true beadsman nowe, and euer haue beene, and will be till I dye, howsoeuer your pleasure be to doo [by] me." And he desyreth the king afterwarde that he would neuer suffer by the meanes of such a bill any man to take occasion afterwarde to slaunder him; "which yet," sayth

MSS. E L R^2 Y C H R B.

1. *by*] *Omitted in* L. 1–2. *so many maner wayes*] (*supported by* English Works, *p.* 1424, MS. Cleopatra E vi *and* R.O. MS.); so many maner of wayes E L R^2 R B; so maner waies Y C; so many waies H. 2. *such a monstrous*] such monstrous L B; of soe monstrous R^2, soe *being interlineated.* 4. *of*] of all H. 6. *gratious*] C (*supported by* English Works, *p.* 1424, MS. Cleopatra E vi *and* R.O. MS.); graces E Y H R; *omitted in* L R^2 B. 6. *hand*] Y C (*supported by* English Works, *p.* 1424, MS. Cleopatra E vi *and* R.O. MS.); handes E L R^2 H R B. 6–7. *all . . . leese*] all I can loose L. 8. *of any*] any L; of my B. 8. *vnto*] thereof vnto H R. 10. *life*] *Omitted in* B *here.* 11. *longe*] long lyfe B. 11. *Gods*] god his B. 12. *sende*] to send H. 13. *with*] *Omitted in* L R^2 Y B. 13. *againe*] *Omitted in* L R^2 H R B. (Againe *supported by* English Works, *p.* 1424, MS. Cleopatra E vi *and* R.O. MS.) 14. *mine*] C (*supported by* English Works, *p.* 1424, MS. Cleopatra E vi *and* R.O. MS.); many E L R^2 Y H R B. 15. *yet*] *Omitted in* L R^2 B. 15. *your grace*] you L R^2 B. 15. *surelye*] *Omitted in* L R^2. 16. *then*] than L. 17. *beadsman*] beadman Y. 18. *by me*] Y C (*supported by* English Works, *p.* 1424, MS. Cleopatra E vi *and* R.O. MS.); with me E L R^2 H R B. 19. *desyreth*] desired L R^2 B. 19–20. *neuer . . . meanes*] neuer suffer by meanes L R^2 B; neuer by the meanes H. 21. *afterwarde*] *Omitted in* Y.

he, "should be the perill of their owne soules and doo them [selfe] more hurt then me: which shall, I trust," sayth he, "settle my heart, with yo*ur* gratious fauo*ur*, to depend vpon the comfort of the truth, and not vpon the fallible opinion [or soone] spoken wordes of light and soone chaungeable people."

The Lord Chancellor and the other Deputies persuade the King that it is not possible to press the Bill against More: in the matter of the Nun he is clearly innocent. [ROPER.]

All this notwithstanding, and the report made by the Lorde Chauncello*ur* and the others to the king of all their whole discourse had with S*ir* Thomas More, the king was so highly offended w*ith* him that he plainly told them he was fully determined that the foresaide Parliament Bill should vndoubtedly proceede foorth against him. To whom the Lord Chauncellour and the rest of the Lordes saide that they perceaued the Lordes of the vpper house so precisely bent to heare him, in his owne defence, make aunswere himselfe, that if he were not put out of the bill, it would without faile be vtterly an ouerthrowe [of] all. But for all this, needes would the king haue his owne will therein, or els, he saide, that at the passing thereof he would be personally present himselfe.

Then the Lorde Audley and the rest, seeing him so vehemently sett therevpon, on their knees most humbly besought his grace to forbeare the same, considering that if he should there in his owne presence receaue an ouerthrowe, it would not onely encourage his subiect*es* euer after to contemne him, but also throughout all Christen-

MSS. E L R² Y C H R B.

1. *should be . . . soules and doo*] *All the* Harpsfield MSS. *agree in this reading.* English Works, *p.* 1424, MS. Cleopatra E vi *and* R.O. MS. *have* should by . . . soules doo. 2. *them selfe*] C (*supported by* English Works, *p.* 1424, MS. Cleopatra E vi *and* R.O. MS.); themselves, E L R² Y H R B. 2. *then*] *Corrected from* them L. 5. *or soone*] *All the* Harpsfield MSS. *have erroneously* of *for* or; soone L B (*supported by* English Works, *p.* 1424, MS. Cleopatra E vi *and* R.O. MS.); some E Y C H R; rash R². 6. *soone*] some H R. 8. *the* (1)] *Omitted in* R² C. 8. *of all*] all L R² B. 9. *had*] *Omitted in* L. 10. *them*] him H R. 10–11. *he* (2) . . . *determined*] *Omitted in* B. 11. *Parliament*] *Omitted in* B. 14. *Lordes*] rest of the Lordes B. 15. *make*] to make B. 17. *it . . . of all*] R² C; E H R *as* R² C, *but* to all *for* of all; it were vtterly an ouerthrowe of all L; it wold without faile be an vtter ouerthrowe of all Y B. 19. *that*] *Omitted in* H. 19. *he* (2)] that he H. 21. *and the rest*] *Omitted in* B. 21. *him*] *Interlineated in* L. 23. *to*] *Omitted in* B. 24. *there*] *Omitted in* H R. 26. *throughout*] through L.

dome redounde to his dishonour for euer; adding therevnto that they mistrusted not in time against him to finde some other meete[r] matter to serue his turne better; for in this cause of the Nonne he was accompted, they saide, so innocent and cleere, that for his dealing therein men reckoned him farre woorthier of prayse then reproufe. Wherevpon at length, through their earnest persuasion, he was content to condiscende to their petition.

When More is informed that he is put out of the Bill, he answers: "*quod differtur, non aufertur.*" [ROPER.]

And in the morowe after, M*aster* Cromwell, meeting [fol. 44 b] | with M*aster* Will*iam* Roper in the Parliament house, willed him to tell his father that he was put out of the Parliament bill; but because he had appointed to dyne that day in London, he sent the message by his seruaunt to his wife to Chelsey; whereof when she informed her father, "In fayth, Megge," quoth [he], "*quod differtur, non aufertur.*"

The Duke of Norfolk counsels More: "*Indignatio principis mors est.*" [ROPER.]

After this, as the duke of Norffolke and S*ir* Thomas More chaunced to fall in familier talke together, the duke saide vnto him:

"By the Masse, M*aster* More, it is perillous stryving with Princes, and therefore I would wishe you somewhat to incline to the kinges pleasure, for by God body, M*aster* More, *Indignatio principis mors est.*"

"Is that all, my Lorde?" quoth he; "then in good faith is there no more difference betweene your grace and me but that I shall dye to day, and you tomorowe."

MSS. E L R^2 Y C H R B.

1. *redounde*] to redounde R^2; to redowne B. 3. *some*] *Omitted in* H R. 3. *meeter matter*] C; meeter matters H; meete matter E L R^2 Y R B. (Roper MSS. *vary. See* Notes.) 4. *cause*] case H. 4. *of*] *Interlineated in* L. 4. *the*] *Omitted in* C. 6. *him*] hir B. 6. *then*] then of B. 7. *length*] lenghe L. 8. *content*] contented Y. 9. *petition*] earenest peticion H R. 10. *morowe*] next morneing H; morning R. 11. *William*] *Omitted in* H. 12. *father*] father in lawe B. 13. *but*] & H R. 14. *he*] *Omitted in* L R^2. 15. *to* (2)] at R^2 Y B. (Roper MSS. *vary*; *majority support* to. *See* Notes.) 16. *he*] hee L R^2 Y C H R B (*supported by* Roper *and sense*); *omitted in* E. 16. *differtur*] defertur Y C B. 17. *non*] no Y. 19. *More*] *Omitted in* H R. 19. *chaunced to fall*] were (*corrected from* well) fell L; fell R^2 B. 19. *in*] into H R. 19. *the duke*] the Duke of Norfolke L R^2 B. 23. *God*] Gods L R^2 Y H R B. (Roper MSS. *vary.*) 24. *Indignatio*] Indignato Y. 25. *Is*] I is H R. 26. *is there*] there is H R.

The administering of the Oath of the Succession. More is the only layman summoned to Lambeth. [ROPER.]

So fell it out within a moneth or thereaboutes after the making of the Statute for the othe of the Supremacie and matrimonie, that all the Priestes of London and Westminster, and no moe temporall men but he, were sent for to appere at Lambeth before the Bisshopp of Caunterbury, the Lord Chauncell*our*, and Secretary Cromwell, Co*m*missioners appointed there to tender the othe vnto them.

More's pious exercises before departure. [ROPER.]

His sorrow at leaving his family. [ROPER.]

Then S*ir* Thomas More, as his accustomed maner was (as we haue declared) when he had any matter of weight in hande, went to Churche and was confessed, and heard Masse and was houseled, in the morning early the selfe same day that he was summoned to appere before the Lordes at Lambeth. And whereas he euermore vsed before, at his departure from his wife and children, whom he tenderly loued, to haue them bring him to his boate, and there to kisse them all and bidd them farewell, then would he suffer none of them forth of the gate to folowe him, but pulled the wickett after him, and shett them all from him. And with an heauy heart, as by his countenaunce it appered, w*ith* M*aster* Will*iam* Roper and their fowre seruauntes tooke he his boate there towarde Lambeth. Wherein sitting still sadly a while, at the last he sodenlye rounded M*aster* Will*iam* Roper in the eare, and saide: "Sonne Roper, I thanke our Lorde the field is wonne." What he meant thereby M*aster* Will*iam* Roper then wist | not; yet lothe to seeme ignorant, he [fol. 45 *a*] aunswered: "S*ir*, I am thereof very gladd." But, as he coniectured afterwarde, it was for that the loue [he had to] God wrought in him so effectually that it

His conscience conquers natural affection: "I thank our Lord the field is won." [ROPER.]

MSS. E L R^2 Y C H R B.

1. *within*] *Omitted in* L. 1. *thereaboutes*] two R^2. 2. *othe of the*] *Omitted in* Y H R. 3–4. *London and Westminster*] Westminster & London L R^2 B. 4. *temporall*] *On an erasure in* R^2. 10. *as . . . declared*] *Omitted in* B. 11. *to*] to the R^2 H R. 16. *them*] him L. 16. *him*] them Y. 16. *his*] the Y. 18. *forth of*] throughe H R. 19. *shett*] shut C. 20. *an*] a B. 20–21. *as . . . appered*] *Omitted in* B. 21. *it*] *Omitted in* L R^2. 22. *their*] his H. 23. *Wherein*] Wherein he H R. 23. *sitting still*] still sittinge L. 24. *rounded*] rounned H. 24. *eare*] yeare R^2. (*Note forms.*) 25. *I . . . Lorde*] *Omitted in* Y. 26. *wonne*] wonne I thanke God Y. 26. *William*] *Omitted in* R^2. 29. *it*] that it H. 29–30. *he had to God*] L R^2 Y C H R B (*supported by* Roper); of God E.

conquered all his carnall affections vtterly from his wife and children, whom he moste deerely loued.

The saide Commissioners required him to take the othe lately appointed by the Parliament for the Succession; to whom Sir Thomas More aunswered that his purpose was not to put any fault eyther in the acte [or] any man that made it, or in the othe or any man that sware it, nor to condemne the conscience of any other man. "But as for my selfe," saide he, "my conscience so moueth me in the matter, that though I would not denye to sweare to the Succession, yet vnto [that] othe that there was offered me I cannot sweare without the hazarding of my soule to perpetuall damnation." And farther saide that if they doubted whether he did refuse the othe onely for the grudge of his conscience, or for any other phantasie, he was ready therein to satisfie them by his othe. Which, if they trusted not, what should they be the better to geue him [any] othe? And if they trusted that he would* therein sweare* true, then trusted he that of their goodnes they would not moue him to sweare the othe that they offred him, perceaving that for to sweare it was against his conscience.

More refuses the Oath of the Succession as to him administered. [13 April, 1534.] [MORE to MARGARET; WORKS, pp. 1428–30.]

Vpon this they shewed him a Roll, wherin were the names of* the Lordes and the Commons which at the determination and ending of the saide Parliament had

More is shown the Roll of Lords and Commons

MSS. E L R² Y C H R B.

1. *affections*] affection L R². 2. *deerely*] tenderlie B. 3. *him*] of him B. 6. *eyther*] *Interlineated in* R. 6. *or*] L R² Y C B (*supported by* English Works, *p.* 1428); nor E H R. 7. *or* (2)] nor, *with* n *interlineated*, R². 8. *to condemne*] condemne B. 9–13. *Note mixture of tenses in all the* Harpsfield MSS. *In* English Works, *p.* 1428, *the tense is past throughout the sentence.* 10. *though*] *Omitted in* L R². 11. *that othe*] þat oath C (*supported by* English Works, *p.* 1428); the othe E L R² Y H R B. 12. *that . . . me*] that is offered B. 12. *was*] *Interlineated in* R. 14. *saide*] sayde he B; *omitted in* H. 14–15. *that . . . othe*] whether he as they perchance might thinke did refuse the oath H. 15. *or*] as L. 16. *therein*] *Interlineated in* R. 16. *them*] him L. 18. *any*] L R² Y C (*supported by* English Works, *p.* 1428); an E H R B. 19. *trusted* (1)] truste B. 19. *that*] *Interlineated in* R. 19. *therein sweare*] therein swere C (*supported by* English Works, *p.* 1428); sweare therein E L R² Y H R B. 23. *were*] was B. 24. *of the*] L R² B (*supported by* English Works, *p.* 1429); of all the E Y C H R. 25. *determination*] ending B. 25. *saide*] *Omitted in* B.

who had taken the Oath. [WORKS, *as above.*]

sworne to the saide Succession, and subscrybed their names. Which when they sawe that notwithstanding S*ir* Thomas More still refuse[d] it, they co*m*maunded him to goe downe to the garden.

The Clergy then take the Oath, with the exception of Dr. Wilson and Fisher. [WORKS, *as above.*]

In the meane while were there called in docto*ur* Wilson and all the Clergie of the Citie of London, which all receaued the othe saving the saide docto*ur* Wilson. Wherevpon he was co*m*mitted to the towre; and so was also the good Bisshopp of Rochester, John Fisher, that was called in before them that day, and refused the foresaide othe.

More is accused of obstinacy in refusing the Oath, and in remaining silent as to the cause of his refusal. [WORKS, *as above.*]

When they were gone, then was S*ir* Thomas More called vp againe, and there was declared vnto him what a number had sworne euen since he went aside, gladly, without any sticking. And laide to him obstinacie, that he would neyther take the othe, nor yet tell the cause whye he | refused to sweare: which, he saide, he would [fol. 45 b] doo, sauing he feared that he should exasperate thereby the kinges displeasure the more against him. And yet at length, when they pressed him, he was content to open and disclose the saide causes in wryting vpon the kinges gratious licence, or vpon his co*m*maundement. But it was aunswered that if the king would geue licence, it would not serue against the Statue. Whervpon S*ir* Thomas More by and bye inferred, that seing he could not

MSS. E L R^2 Y C H R B.

1. *saide*] *Omitted in* B. 3. *still refused*] R^2 H R B (*supported by* English Works, *p.* 1429); still refuse L Y C; did still refuse E. 5. *while*] time Y. 5. *were there*] there were B. 5. *in*] *Interlineated in* R^2. 6. *the Citie of*] *Omitted in* R^2. 7. *the saide*] *Omitted in* B. 8–9. *and . . . also*] with B. 9. *also*] *Omitted in* L. 9–11. *that . . . othe*] *Omitted in* B. 10. *called . . . them*] called before them L; called afore them R^2; called in to them before H, to *being interlineated.* 11. *foresaide*] *Omitted in* R^2. 14. *had sworne*] were sworne L, were *being interlineated.* 14–15. *gladly, without*] gladly & without L. 16. *yet*] *Omitted in* R^2. 18. *doo*] *Omitted in* R^2. 18. *sauing . . . thereby*] L C *as* E R^2 Y B, *but omitting* that; saueinge that thereby he should exasperate H; saueing þat thereby he should exasperate thereby R, *the second* thereby *being interlineated.* 20. *length*] lengh L. 20–21. *open and*] *Omitted in* B. 21. *saide*] *Omitted in* L B. 22. *gratious licence*] gracious likeing & licence H. 23. *if*] *Omitted in* B. 23. *geue*] graunte Y. 23. *it*] if it B. 25. *by and bye*] *Interlineated in* R.

declare the causes without perill, then to leaue them vndeclared was no obstinacie in him.

And whereas he saide that he did not condemne the conscience of other men, the Archbisshopp of Caunterbury, taking holde thereon, saide that it seemed by that the matter wherevpon he stoode was not very sure and certaine; And therefore he should therein obey his soueraine Lorde and king, to whom he was certaine he was bounde to obey. S*ir* Thomas More aunswered that he thought that was one of the causes in which he was bounde not to obey his Prince. And if that reason may conclude, then haue we a way to auoide all perplexities; for in whatsoeuer matters the doctours stande in great doubt, the kinges com*m*aundement, geuen vpon whether side he list, soyleth all the doubtes.

More contends that in this matter he is not bound to obey his Prince. [WORKS, *as above.*]

When they could gett none other aunswere of him, he was com*m*itted to the custodie of the abbott of Westminster by the space of fowre dayes; during which time the king consulted with his counsaile what order were meete to be taken with him. And albeit in the beginning they were resolued that with an othe, not to be acknowen whether he had to the Supremacie beene sworne, or what he thought thereof, he should be discharged, yet did Queene Anne by her importunate clamo*ur* so sore exasperate the king against him that, contrary to his former resolution, he caused the saide othe of the Supremacie to be ministred vnto him; who albeit he made a discrete qualified answere, neuerthelesse was forthwith com*m*itted to the towre.

More is imprisoned at Westminster [13–17 April, 1534]; **the King and Council consider the administering of a special oath to More; but Queene Anne exasperates the king against him. More is sent to the Tower.** [17 April, 1534.] [ROPER.

Whom, as he was going thitherwarde, wearing

MSS. E L R² Y C H R B.

1. *the causes*] them R². 3. *saide*] had said C. 3. *that*] *Omitted in* L H R. 3. *condemne*] *Interlineated in* R. 5–6. *seemed . . . matter*] seemed that the matter R². 6. *the*] *Interlineated in* Y. 7. *therein*] *Omitted in* L R² H R B. 8. *to whom*] whom H R. 10–11. *was . . . to*] was not bounde to H R. 11. *his*] the L R² B. 12. *then*] the H. 12. *to*] for to R². 12. *auoide*] *Interlineated over* can avoide *crossed through* L. 13–14. *in great doubt*] in doubte & greate controuersie R². 14. *whether*] what B. 15. *side*] parte L R² B. 16. *none*] no L R² C H. 19. *counsaile*] councellors B. 26. *saide*] *Omitted in* B. 26. *of the*] of B. 27. *albeit*] although L R²

He still wears his chain of gold. [ROPER.]

(as he co*m*monly did) a cheine of golde about his necke, S*ir* [Richard] Cromwell, that had the charge of his conueyance thither, aduised to sende home his cheyne to his wife or to some of his childre*n*. "No, S*ir*," quoth he, "that I will not; for if I were taken in the fielde by mine enemies, I would they should somewhat | fare the better [fol. 46 *a*] by me."

The Porter demands More's upper garment. [ROPER.]

At whose landing M*aster* Lieftenant at the towre gate was ready to receaue him, where the Porter demaunded of him his vpper garment. "M*aster* Porter," saide he, "here it is," and tooke off his cappe, and deliuered it to him, saying: "I am very sory it is no better for you." "Noe, S*ir*," quoth the Porter, "I must haue your gowne."

More's instructions to John a Wood. [ROPER.]

And so was he by M*aster* Lieftenant conueighed to his lodging, where he called vnto him one John A woode, his owne seruaunt, there appointed to attend vpon him, who could neyther wryte nor reade; and sware him before the Lieftenant that if he should heare or see* him at any time speake or write any thing against the king, the Councell, or the state of the Realme, he should open it to the Lieftenant, that the Lieftenant might incontinent reueale it to the Counsaile.

Letters written from the Tower to Margaret.

And not longe after his co*m*ming to the towre, he wrate certaine letters to his daughter, mistris Margarete Roper, whereof one was written with a coale.

And when he had remained in the towre litle more then

MSS. E L R^2 Y C H R B.

1. *as . . . did*] *Omitted in* B. 1–2. *Sir Richard Cromwell*] Sir Richard Cromewell Y C R; Sir Thomas Cromwell E H (Thomas *in* H *being interlineated over* Richard *underlined*); Sir Richard Southwell L R^2 B. (Roper MSS. *vary. See* Notes.) 3. *aduised*] aduised him R^2. 5. *will*] would R^2. 6. *enemies*] enemie B. 6. *somewhat fare*] a little fare R^2; fare somewhat H R. 6. *fare*] *Corrected from* feare L. 7. *by*] for R^2. 8. *whose*] his B. 8–9. *at . . . ready*] was redie at the tower gate B. 10. *vpper*] vppermost L R^2. 11. *to*] *Omitted in* Y. 13. *Noe*] Nay B. 15. *Master*] the L R^2 B. 15. *was he . . . conueighed*] was he conveyed by the Leivtenant B. 17. *owne*] *Omitted in* L R^2 B. 19. *heare or see*] L R^2 B (*supported by* Roper); see or heare E Y C H R. 19–20. *at any time*] *Omitted in* L. 22–23. *might . . . reueale*] incontinently might reveale C. 24. *to*] into H. 27—l. 2, p. 171. *And when . . . to goe to him*] *Omitted in* C. 27. *litle more then*] a litle more than H R; almost B.

Margaret visits her father in the Tower. [ROPER.]

a moneth, mistris Margarete, longing to see her Father, by her earnest sute at length gatt leaue to goe to him. At whose comming, after the seuen psalmes and letanie saide (which whensoeuer she came to him, ere he fell in talke of any worldly matters, he vsed customablye to say with her) among other communication saide vnto her: "I beleeue, Megge, that they that haue putt me here thought to haue done me a high displeasure." And then shewed her, as I haue somewhat shewed you before, that if it had not beene for his wife, for her and his other children, whom he accompted the chiefe part of his charge, he would not haue fayled longe ere that time to haue closed himselfe vp in as straite a roome, and straiter too. "But since I am come hither without my owne desert, I trust," quoth he, "that God of his goodnes will discharge me of my care, and with his gratious helpe supplye my lacke amonge you." And added: "I finde no cause, I thanke God, Megge, to recken my selfe in woorse case [here] then in mine owne house; for me thinketh God maketh me a wanton, and setteth me vpon his lappe, and dandleth me."

More rejoices at the leisure he now has for godly meditation. [ROPER.]

More believes God will provide for his family. As for himself: God maketh him a wanton. [ROPER.]

Neyther did he at any time after his imprisonment once

MSS. E L R^2 Y C H R B.

1. *mistris Margarete*] mistris Roper B. 2. *her earnest sute*] earnest suite L R^2 B; her earnest request H. 2. *length*] last L. 2. *gatt*] gott H R. 3. *comming, after*] coming to him thervpon shortly after and after C, to him . . . and *being interlineated.* 3. *letanie*] latine Y. 4–5. *ere . . . any*] ere he fell in talke with any L Y; ere he fell in talke with her of any R^2; before he fell to any H; before he fell to talke of any R; ere he fell to talke with any B. (Roper *supports* E C.) 5. *vsed customablye*] accustomablie vsed B. 5. *customablye to say*] to say accustomably L; accustomably to say R^2 H R. (Roper MSS. *vary.*) 6. *with her*] togeather allsoe with her R^2. 7. *that they that*] they that H R. 7. *haue putt*] put L. 8. *me a high*] mee highe L; me an high R^2 C. 8. *then*] *Omitted in* H. 9. *as . . . before*] *Omitted in* B. 9. *somewhat shewed you*] shewed you somewhat H R. 11. *chiefe*] chiefest B. 12. *fayled*] fayned L. 12. *that time*] this B. 13. *vp*] *Omitted in* L R^2 B. 16. *of*] oute of B. 16. *care*] cure C. (Roper *supports* care.) 17. *lacke*] wante Y. 18–19. *case here then*] case heere then C (*supported by* Roper); case nowe then B; case then E L R^2 Y H R. 19. *mine*] my Y. 19. *me*] my Y. 20. *and setteth*] setling B. 22. *at any time . . . imprisonment*] after his imprisoment at any time B. 22. *once*] *Omitted in* B.

More never prays God to deliver him from prison or execution. [MORE to MARGARET; WORKS, p. 1448.]

On the contrary, he reckons imprisonment a benefit, and his troubles profitable exercises of patience. [ROPER.]

praye to God to bring him out of the same, or to deliuer him from death, but referr[ed] all thing whollye vnto his onely pleasure, as to him that sawe better what was best for him then himselfe did. Yea, he would say that the king, in taking him from his li|bertie, did him so great [fol. 46 *b*] good by the spirituall profite that he tooke thereby, that among all the great benefites heaped vpon him so thicke, he receaued his imprisonment euen the very chiefe. And thus by [his] gratious demean*our* in tribulation, it well appered that all the troubles that euer chaunced to him, by his patient suffering thereof, were to him no painfull punishmentes, but of patience profitable exercises.

And is content to lose goods, land, and life too, rather than act against his conscience. [WORKS, pp. 1441–2.]

And as he was well content, and not onely patiently but reioycingly also, to beare the losse of his libertie and his close imprisonment; so his heart, being lightned and strengthned by God, and by the vprightnes of his conscience, and the goodnes of the cause for which he was troubled, was in heart content to leese goodes, lande, and life too (as he afterwarde did) rather then to doo any thing against his conscience. And would say that what lawes soeuer they made, he was right assured that his conscience might stande with his saluation; And that they could doo him no hurt by their lawe in the sight of God, howsoeuer it should seeme in the sight of men,

MSS. E L R² Y C H R B.

1. *out of the same*] oute of troble B. 1. *or*] nor B. 1. *to deliuer*] deliuer L R². 2. *referred*] L R² Y C H R B; referring E. 2. *thing*] thinges L Y C H R B; thinges *corrected from* thingy R². (English Works, *p.* 1448, *support* thing). 3. *sawe*] *Corrected from* say R². 3. *better*] *Interlineated in* R. 4. *himselfe did*] he did himself H. 5. *in taking*] takeinge L R² B. 5. *him from*] from him Y C B. 8. *receaued*] reckoned R². 9. *by his gratious*] L R² B (*supported by* Roper); by gratious E Y C H R. 10. *euer*] *Omitted in* Y. 14. *well*] *Omitted in* L. 14. *and* (2)] *Omitted in* L B. 14–15. *but . . . beare*] but alsoe reioycingly to beare R². 15–16. *and . . . imprisonment*] *Omitted in* B. 17. *strengthned*] strenghened L. 18. *the* (2)] his L R. 18. *for which*] for the which Y. 19. *was*] he was B. 19. *in heart*] *Omitted in* L. 19. *content*] contented B. 19. *leese*] loose H R. 19. *goodes*] his goodes H R. 19. *lande*] landes L R² H R. (English Works, *p.* 1442, *support* lande.) 20. *too*] *Omitted in* B. 20. *to doo*] doe Y H. 21–22. *that . . . soeuer*] what lawes soeuer L R² B; that whatsouer lawes H; that whatsoeuer lawes R.

but if they did him wronge; And that his case was like to a riddle, so that he might leese his head and haue no harme.

More's clear conscience leaves him light-hearted and ever ready for merry talk.

And thus being well and quietly settled in conscience, the securitie and vprightnes of the same so eased and minished all the griefes and paines of his imprisonment and all his other aduersitie, that no token or signification of lamenting or sorowe appered in him, but that in his co*m*munication with his daughter, with the Lieftenant and other, he helde on his [olde] merye, pleasaunt talke whensoeuer occasion serued.

More's reply to the Lieutenant's apology for the poor cheer of the Tower. [ROPER.]

The which Lieftenant, on a certaine time co*m*ming to his chamber to visite him, rehearsed the benefites and frendshipp that he had many wayes receaued at his handes, and howe muche bounden he was therefore frendly to interteyne him and make him good cheere. Which, since the case standing as it did he could not doo without the kinges indignation, he trusted, he saide, he would accept his good will and such poor cheere as he had. "M*aster* Lieftenant," quoth he againe, "I verily beleeue, as you may, you are my good frende in deede, and would, as you say, with your best cheere interteyne me, for which I most heartily thanke you. And assure [fol. 47 *a*] your selfe, M*aster* Lieftenant, I doo not | mislyke my cheere, but whensoeuer I so doo, then you maye thrust me out of your dores."

More's imprisonment becomes harder.

After that nowe S*ir* Thomas More had beene a good while in the towre, and not so restrained but that both

MSS. E L R^2 Y C H R B.

1. *but if*] vlesse L; vnlesse R^2 B; but that H R. (English Works, *p.* 1442, *support* but if.) 1. *case*] cause H R. 2. *a*] *Corrected from* so L. 2. *leese*] loese R^2; loose H R B. 6. *and*] or B. 6. *his*] *Interlineated in* R. 8. *appered*] *Omitted in* L. 8. *his*] *Omitted in* L R^2 B. 10–11. *his olde merye . . . talke*] his olde merry pleasaunt talke L C B; his old merry & pleasant talke R^2; his old merry talke Y; olde *omitted in* E H R. 15. *bounden he was*] he was bounden L R^2 B. 17. *since*] *Omitted in* L R^2 B. 17. *standing*] standeth H. 18. *kinges*] king his B. 18. *trusted*] trusted therfore B. 20. *quoth he againe*] quoth Sir Thomas More B. 24. *Master Lieftenant*] *Omitted in* B. 25. *so*] *Omitted in* H. 27. *nowe*] *Omitted in* R^2. 28. *both*] *Omitted in* Y; *interlineated in* R.

his wife and daughter might with licence repaire to see him, he was, as we haue saide before, sodenlye shett vp; where were it by this restraint the sooner to draw him and cause him to incline to the kinges pleasure; or for such very plaine wordes that he vsed to the Commissioners; or that they intended to deale with him and others more sharply and to make sharper lawes, as they

The King may make a farther and a harder law for him, but he will not act against his conscience. [MORE to MARGARET; WORKS, pp. 1447–8.]

did in deede the Parliament next folowing, And as it was saide in deede of some that his obstinate maner, as they called it, in still refusing the othe should peraduenture force and driue the king to make a farther and harder lawe for him. Which thing, when he hearde, albeit he thought that God of his goodnes would not suffer such an vnlawfull lawe to passe, yet was he prest and redye to abide all extremities rather then to doo any thing contrary to his conscience, not slightly and [houerly], but after longe and deepe consideration and studie, enformed, and would him selfe euer say that if he dyed by such a lawe, he should dye in that point innocent before God.

New Laws are made: the Act of Supremacy and the Act of Treason.

In the next Parliament was the foresaide sharpe lawe made that was before feared and talked of, wherein the king was recognised as the supreme head, vnder God, of the Churche of Inglande. And it was ordeyned that whosoeuer should speake against the saide supremacie, he should be taken as a traitour.

Thus More stands in greater peril.

After the making of which Statute, the world beganne to waxe more straite and rough toward Sir Thomas More and suche other as stoode against the kinges newe

MSS. E L R^2 Y C H R B.

1. *and daughter*] & his children R^2. 1. *with licence*] *Omitted in* Y. 2. *sodenlye*] suddenly now R^2. 2. *shett*] shut C. 3. *where*] *Omitted in* C. 5. *that*] which L. 9. *his*] has Y. 10. *called*] termed B. 11. *force and*] *Omitted in* L. 12. *hearde*] heard of B. 12. *albeit*] albeit that H. 13. *that*] *Omitted in* L. 14. *to*] for to B. 14. *prest and*] *Omitted in* B. 15. *abide*] suffer L R^2 B. 15–16. *any . . . to*] any thinge aginst R^2, thinge *being interlineated.* 16. *and*] or H R. 16. [*houerly*]] houertly E Y C H R; ouertly L R^2; covertlie B. (*See note to p.* 150, *l.* 18.) 17. *and studie*] *Interlineated in* L; *omitted in* B. 21–22. *the king was*] was þe kinge C. 23. *And . . . ordeyned*] An edict was stablyshed B. 24. *saide*] same L B. 25. *he*] *Omitted in* C. 25. *as*] for L R^2 B. 26. *After*] And after R^2. 27. *more*] *Interlineated in* R. 28. *other*] others L R^2. 28. *as*] a H. 28. *kinges*] king his B. 28. *newe*] *Omitted in* B.

Supremacie. And as besyde his olde disease of his brest, he was now greeued in the reynes by reason of grauell and stone, and with the crampe that diuers nightes gryped his legges, so dayly more and more there grewe toward him many other great causes of griefe and sorowes; which all he did moderate and temper with patient and spirituall consolation and comfort to heauenwarde.

His health becomes worse. [LETTER to LADY ALINGTON; WORKS, p. 1434.]

First then, after the making of the saide Statute, S*ir* Thomas Cromwell, then Secretary, resorted to him with the kinges Soliciter and certaine other, and demaunded of him what his opinion and minde was touching the saide Acte, and would very fayne haue wronge out [fol. 47 *b*] some|what at his handes, to say precisely the one way or the other, but they could wring nothing from him.

Cromwell and others fail to discover More's opinion on the new Statute. [*Summarised from* MORE to MARGARET; WORKS, pp. 1451–2.]

Not longe after came to him the Lorde Archbisshopp of Caunterbury, the Lorde Chauncell*our*, the duke of Suffolke, the Erle of Wilshire and the Secretary, and beganne afreshe to presse and vrge him to some one certaine, plaine, determinate and peremptorie aunswere touching his opinion of the lawfulnes or vnlawfulnes of the saide Statute. They charged him with obstinacie and malignitie against the king, because he would not directly answer the question. And the Lorde Chauncell*our* and the Secretary saide that the king might by his lawes compell him to make a plaine answere thereto, eyther the one waye or the other. Wherevnto S*ir* Thomas More aunswered that he would not dispute the kinges authoritie, what his highnes might doo in such a case. But he saide that verily, vnder correction, it

On another occasion the Councillors urge that the King may compel More to state his opinion. [*Summarised from* MORE to MARGARET; WORKS, pp. 1452–4.]

MSS. E L R² Y C H R B.

2. *now*] more L R² B. 2. *by reason*] *Omitted in* L. 2. *of grauell*] of the gravell Y B. 5. *griefe*] greefes H R B. 5. *sorowes*] sorrowe L. 6. *which all*] all which L R² B. 6. *and temper*] and temperate R²; *omitted in* B. 6. *patient*] patience H R B. 8. *Sir*] Master B. 9. *then*] the B. 10. *kinges*] king his B. 10. *other*] others B. 10. *and demaunded*] demaunding B. 12. *very*] *Interlineated in* R. 12. *haue*] *Omitted in* H R. 12–13. *out . . . handes*] out of his handes Y. 13. *to say*] & to say L. 14. *or the other*] or other Y. 14. *wring*] not wringe H R. 17. *Wilshire*] Wiltshire L R² H B. 17–18. *and beganne*] who began B. 19. *certaine*] *Omitted in* B. 24–25. *might . . . him*] might compell him by his lawes L; by his lawes might Compell him H R. 27. *dispute*] dispute of L R². 28. *kinges*] king his B. 28–29. *such a case*] such case L; such cases B.

seemed to him somewhat harde: "For if it so were that my conscience" (sayth he) "gaue me against the Statute (wherein howe my conscience geueth me I make no declaration) then I, nothing doing nor nothing saying against the Statute, it were a very harde thing to compell me to saye eyther precisely with it against my conscience to the losse of my soule, or precisely against it to the destruction of my body."

Cromwell urges that, as heretics had been compelled to acknowledge the Pope as supreme Head of the Church, so the King can compel acknowledgment of his Supremacy. [WORKS, *as above.*]

To this M*aster* Secretarye saide that S*ir* Thomas More had ere this, when he was Chauncell*our*, examined heretikes and theeues and other malefactours, and gaue him a great praise in that behalfe. And he saide that S*ir* Thomas More, as he thought, and at [the] least wise Bisshopps, did vse to examine heretikes whether they beleeued the Pope to be head of the Churche, and vsed to compell them to make a precise aunswere thereto. And why should not then the king, sith it is a lawe made here that his grace is head of the Church here, compell men to aunswere precisely to the lawe here, as they did then concerning the Pope?

More points out that the two cases are not parallel: a general law, acknowledged by

S*ir* Thomas More aunswered and saide that he protested that he intended not to defende his part, or stande in contention; but he saide there was a difference betweene those cases, because that at that time as well here as els where through the corps of Christendome, the [Popes]

MSS. E L R[2] Y C H R B.

1. *to him somewhat*] somewhat to him H R; vnto him verie B. 3–5. *wherein . . . Statute*] *Omitted in* B. 4. *nor*] or L. 7. *against it*] against it with my Conscience H R. 8. *destruction*] losse Y. 10. *Chauncellour*] Lord Chauncelour B. 12. *And*] *Before* And *an erasure in* R[2], *apparently of* And. 13. *and*] *Omitted in* H R. 13. *at the least*] C (*supported by* English Works, *p.* 1453); at least E L R[2] Y H R B. 13. *wise*] wise as H R. 14. *did . . . heretikes*] did vse to doe & to examine H. 15. *to be head*] to be supreme heade L R[2] B; to be supreame Y. (Supreme *omitted in* English Works, *p.* 1453.) 17. *why . . . then*] why then should not H. 18. *that . . . here*] *Omitted in* L R[2] B. 18. *here*] *Omitted in* H R. 18. *compell*] to compell R[2]. 19. *to aunswere precisely*] precisely to answer L; to sweare preciselie B. 21–22. *aunswered and . . . intended*] aunswered protesting that he intended B. 23. *he*] *Omitted in* B. 23. *there was*] that there was L R[2] B. 23. *betweene*] *Interlineated over* in *crossed through* R. 24. *because that at*] because at H R B. 24. *at that . . . here*] aswell at þat tyme here R[2]. 24. *here*] *Omitted in* L. 25. *the corps of*] *Omitted in* B. 25. *Popes*] L R[2] Y C H R B (*supported by* English Works, *p.* 1454); *omitted in* E.

power was recognised for an vndoubted thing, which seemeth not like a thing agreed in this Realme and the contrary taken for truth in other Realmes. Whereto M*aster* Secretary aunswered, that they were as well [fol. 48 *a*] burned for the de|nying of that as they be beheaded for the denying of this, And therefore as good reason to compell them to make precise answere to the one as to the other. Wherevnto S*ir* Thomas More answered, that sith in this case a man is not by the lawe of one Realme so bounde in [his] conscience where there is [a] lawe of the whole corps [of christendome to the contrarie in matter touching beleife, as he is by the lawe of the whole corps], though there happ to be made in some place a lawe locall to the contrary, the reasonablenes or the vnreasonablenes in binding a man to precise aunswere standeth not in the respect or difference betweene heading and burning, but, because of the difference in charge of conscience, the difference standeth betweene heading and hell.

all Christendom, differs in weight from a mere local law not acknowledged by the rest of Christendom. [WORKS, *as above.*]

Among other thinges it was saide to him that if he had as liefe be out of the world as be in it, as he had saide, why did he not then speake euen plaine out against the

More is taunted with cowardic if he had as

MSS. E L R^2 Y C H R B.

2. *seemeth*] seemed H R. 2. *like a*] a like H R. 2. *agreed*] agreede vppon R^2; agreed on B. 3. *in other*] in no other C. 5. *burned*] burdened Y. 5. *for the . . . that*] for denienge of that R^2; for denyinge them of that H R. 5. *they be*] *Omitted in* L; they be now H R. 6. *the denying*] denienge R^2 H R. 7. *precise*] a precise L. 9. *in*] in in R. 10. *in his conscience*] L R^2 Y C B (*supported by* English Works, *p.* 1454); his *omitted in* E H R. 10. *where . . . a lawe*] Y C H R (*supported by* English Works, *p.* 1454); E L *as* Y C H R, *but* the lawe *for* a lawe; as where there is a Law R^2 B. 10. *there*] *Corrected from* this L. 10. *is*] *Interlineated in* L. 11–13. *whole corps of christendome to the contrarie in matter touching beleife, as he is by the lawe of the whole corps, though there happ*] C (*supported by* English Works, *p.* 1454); whole corps though there happ E L R^2 Y H R; whole corps B. 13. *to be . . . place*] in some place to be L. 13–14. *to be . . . contrary*] *Omitted in* B. 14–15. *or the vnreasonablenes*] or vnreasonables L; & vnreasonablenes R^2; or vnreasonablenes H R B. 15. *a*] *Interlineated in* R. 15. *to precise*] to a precise L B. 16. *in the respect*] in respect H R. 17. *but*] *Interlineated in* R. 18. *heading*] heaven H R. 20. *that if he*] þat he L. 21. *as be in it*] as be in yt L, be *being interlineated*; as in yt R^2 H R. 22. *he not*] not he B. 22. *then . . . plaine*] speake even then plaine H R.

lief be out of the world as in it, why not speak out against the Statute? But More is not so presumptuous as to hasten his death. [WORKS, *as above.*]

Statute? "It appereth well," [saide] they, "ye are not content to dye, though ye say so." Wherevnto S*ir* Thomas More answered, that he had not beene any man of such holye liuing as he might be bolde to offer himselfe to death, least God for his presumption might suffer him to fall. Howbeit, if God drewe him to it himselfe, then trusted [he] in his great mercy that he should not faile to geue him grace and strength.

More had not done or said anything to justify his imprisonment and execution.

Thus like a meruailous good and profounde wise man S*ir* Thomas More hitherto demayned himselfe, occurring as muche as might be to the slye, craftie driftes of his aduersaryes going about to snare and intrappe him, and to the malignitie of the peruerse time; that as by no rightfull lawe (nor perchaunce by their owne lawe neyther) they could not iustifie his imprisonment at that time as he was sent to the towre, so notwithstanding their newe lawe, woorse then the former, yet was there no matter, I will not say by right and iustice, but not so muche as by their owne vnlawfull and vniust lawe, to be founde in him, that [his] aduersaries might with any outwarde honest apparance haue [that] they sought for, that was his life and bloud; for he had neither spoken nor done any thing to bring himselfe within the least compasse and daunger of the saide lawe.

The martyrdom of the Priors of the Charter-

For the withstanding of the which, about a two monethes before S*ir* Thomas More suffered, the Pri*our* of the Charterhouse of London, the Priors of the Charter-

MSS. E L R^2 Y C H R B.

1. *saide*] sayde L R^2 B; say E Y C H R. 1. *ye*] you L R^2 Y B. 2. *ye*] you L R^2 Y C B. 3–4. *any man of such*] any such man of H R. 3. *man*] *Interlineated in* R^2. 4. *such*] soe, *corrected from* see, R^2. 6. *him to it*] it to him L. 6–7. *himselfe, then trusted he in*] L R^2 Y C B; he then trusted in H R; himselfe then trusted in E. (I *of* English Works, *p.* 1454, *supports* he.) 7. *should*] woulde L R^2 B. 8. *strength*] strengh L. 9. *meruailous . . . profounde*] good and profounde mervelous Y. 15. *neyther*] *Omitted in* B. 15. *not*] *Omitted in* R^2. 16. *as . . . towre*] *Omitted in* B. 17. *newe*] owne L R^2 B. 17–18. *yet . . . matter*] it was no mater Y. 20. *his*] L R^2 B; their E C H R; there Y. 21. *outwarde honest*] honest outwarde R^2; outward B. 21. *honest*] *Interlineated in* Y R. 21. *haue that they*] L R^2 Y C H R B; haue they E. 22–23. *spoken nor done*] done nor spoken L R^2 B; spoken or done C H R. 23. *least*] *Interlineated in* R. 24. *saide*] *Interlineated in* Y. 25. *about a two*] about 2 H R B. 27–*l.* 1, *p.* 179. *Charterhouses*] Charterhouse H R.

houses of Bevalde and Exame, and M*aster* Reynoldes, a singuler learned diuine, well seene in the latine, greeke and hebrue tonge, a vertuous and religious father of Sion, and one M*aster* John Hall, vicar of Thistilworth, were the [fol. 48 *b*] xxixth of Aprill condemned of treason, and | executed the fourth day of Maye. Afterwarde, the [x]viiijth of June, were there [three] other of the saide Charterhouse of London hanged and quartered, and eyght or nyne of the saide house dyed by reason of the closenes and filthines of the prison in Newgate. The xxijth of the saide moneth the good learned Bisshopp of Rochester, doct*our* John Fisher, was beheaded for the same cause at the towrehill.

houses of London, of Bevall and of Axholme of [Richard] Reynolds, a monk of Sion; and of John Hall, vicar of Isleworth; 4 May, 1535. Martyrdom of other Carthusians of London, [19] June, 1535. Execution of Fisher, 22 June, 1535.

The foresaide M*aster* Reynoldes and the three persons of the Charterhouse, S*ir* Thomas More, looking out of his windowe, chaunced to see going towarde their execution; and longing in that iourney to haue accompanied them, saide to his daughter Margarete, then standing there besyde him: "Loe, doest thou not see, Megge, that these blessed fathers be nowe as cheerefully going to their death as bridegromes to their mariage? Wherefore hereby mayest thou see, mine owne good daughter, what a great difference there is betweene suche as haue in effect spent all their dayes in a straite, harde, penitentiall and painfull life religiously, and suche as haue in the worlde, like wordly wretches (as thy poore father hath

More and Margaret watch certain of the martyrs "going to their death as bridegrooms to their marriage." More longs to accompany them. [ROPER.]

MSS. E L R^2 Y C H R B.

1. *Bevalde*] *In* L R^2 *the spelling seems to be* Benald, *in* H R Benold. 1. *Exame*] Spaine H R; Epame B. 1. *and Master*] and one Master C. 3. *tonge*] tonges L R^2 H R B. 3. *a*] *Omitted in* R^2. 3. *and* (1)] *Omitted in* H R. 4. *were the*] were there the B. 6. *day*] *Omitted in* L R^2 B. 6. *xviiijth*] *All the* Harpsfield MSS. *omit* x. (*See* Notes.) 7. *there*] *Omitted in* Y B. 7. *three*] L R^2 Y B; *omitted in* E C H R. 7. *saide*] *Omitted in* R^2 B. 8. *London hanged*] London aforesayd hanged R^2. 8. *and* (2)] *Interlineated in* R^2 *over* þ. 9. *saide*] same L. 12. *John*] *Omitted in* B. 12. *at the*] at R^2. 14–15. *The foresaide . . . Charterhouse*] *In* R^2 *these words are omitted here, but occur after* chaunced to see *below* (*Cf. l.* 16.) 14. *and the three*] and three C. 14. *persons*] Priors B. 15. *Charterhouse*] Charterhowses B. 15. *of his*] at a L R^2 B. 16. *see going*] se them goe Y; see them going C. 16. *towarde*] to L R^2 B. 18–19. *there besyde him*] by him B. 21. *to*] be to L R^2 Y C. (Roper MSS. *vary.*) 21. *their*] the B. 22. *hereby*] thereby R^2; happilie B. 22–23. *what a great*] what greate R^2.

done) consumed all their time in pleasure and ease licentiously. For God, considering their longe continuing vnpleasant life in most [sore] and greeuous penaunce, will no longer suffer them to remaine here in this vale of miserie and iniquitie, but speedily hence taketh them to the fruition of his euerlasting deitie; whereas thy silly father, Megge, that like a moste wicked caytiffe hath passed forth the whole course of his miserable life moste sinfully, God, thinking not woorthy so soone to come to that eternall felicitie, leaueth him here yet still in the world, further to be plunged and turmoyled with misery."

Cromwell's promises of the King's favour and leniency do not deceive More. [ROPER.]

Within a while after, Master Secretary, comming to him into the towre from the king, pretended much frendshipp towarde him, and for his comfort tolde him that the kinges highnes was his good and gratious Lorde, and minded not with any matter wherein he should haue any cause of scruple from thenceforth to trouble his conscience.

As soone as Master Secretarie was gone, to expresse what comfort he conceaued of his wordes, he wrote with a coale (for ynke then had he none) these verses folowing:

More's verses on flattering Fortune. [ROPER; WORKS, p. 1432.]

Ey flattering fortune, looke thou neuer so faire,
Nor neuer so pleasantly beginne to smyle,
|As though thou wouldest my ruine all repaire, [fol. 49 *a*]
During my life thou shalt not me beguile.
Trust shall I God, to enter, in a while,
His hauen of heauen, sure and vniforme;
Euer after this calme looke I for a storme.

MSS. E L R^2 Y C H R B.

2–3. *continuing*] continuall L. 3. *sore*] L R^2 Y C B (*supported by* Roper *and sense*); sure E H R. 4. *them*] him Y. 4. *here*] *Omitted in* L R^2 B. 6. *them to*] *Omitted in* R^2. 6. *deitie*] Dyetie H R B. 7. *that*] *Omitted in* L R^2. 8–9. *his miserable*] his most miserable L R^2; his wicked B. 9. *thinking not*] thinketh not R^2; thinking him not Y. 10. *so soone*] *Omitted in* Y. 10. *leaueth*] but leaueth R^2. 11. *here yet*] yet here L R^2. 12. *turmoyled*] turmoyled *corrected, probably, from* travailed, L; travailed R^2. 14. *into*] in C. (Roper MSS. *vary.*) 16. *kinges*] king his B. 16. *and*] *Omitted in* L. 18. *cause*] kinde L R^2 B. 18. *of*] *Interlineated in* L. 21. *these*] the B. 22. *Ey*] Fie L R^2 Y B. (Roper *and* English Works, *p.* 1432, *support* Ey.) 24. *ruine*] ruines R^2. 26. *to*] *An erasure after* to *in* R^2. 28. *this*] *The reading of all the* Harpsfield MSS., *but most* Roper MSS. *and* English Works, *p.* 1432, *read* thy.

Yea, three yeres before this, he shewed in certaine latine verses that he elegantly made, but not yet printed, in the which he properly and wittily alludeth to his name, that he had litle hope of longe continuance in this transitorie life, and howe he prepared himselfe to the other eternall and euerlasting life :

More's Latin verses: "*Moraris si sit spes*," etc.

Moraris si sit spes hîc tibi longa morandi,
Hoc te vel Morus, More, monere potest.
Desine morari, et caelo meditare morari,
Hoc te vel Morus, More, monere potest.

Nowe albeit, as we haue saide, S*ir* Thomas More had neyther in speaking nor doing transgressed their* newe lawe of the Supremacie (suppressing the open vtterance of his iudgement for such causes as we haue shewed), whether it were a sett matter purposely and for the nonce deuysed by one meanes or other to gett and extort from him a direct and precise answere, or whether the partie of his owne head, to better his state and aduaunce his estimation with the Prince, wilfully sought the destruction of this woorthy man, I cannot certainly tell; but so it chaunced that afterwarde it was layde against him that he had directly spoken wordes to the derogation of the kinges supremacie, and that vpon this pretence. Shortly after that the saide Lorde Chauncell*our* and others had beene with him in the towre, as we haue declared, one M*aster* Riche, afterwarde Lorde Riche, then newly made the kinges Soliciter, S*ir* Richard Southwell, and M*aster*

Rich, Southwell and Palmer are sent to the Tower to take More's books from him. [ROPER, with additions.]

MSS. E L R² Y C H R B.

2. *that . . . made*] *Omitted in* B. 3. *in the which* in whic L. 4. *longe*] his L R² B; his longe H R. 7. *Moraris* Miraris H R. 7. *In margins of* L R² Y C *is written*: in lib. contra epist. J. Pomerani L; in lib. contra epistol. Joh̃is Pomerani R²; In libro contra epistolam Joan Pomerani Y C. 8. *Hoc*] Hec H. 8. *More*] Mori, *corrected from* More, R². 9. *morari* (1)] mirari H R. 9. *caelo*] Celo Y; Ceolo H. 12. *their newe*] L R² Y C B; their owne newe E H R. 13. *of the*] of B. 13. *suppressing*] Supposinge H. 15. *it were*] there was B. 15–16. *and . . . deuysed*] *Omitted in* B. 17. *a direct and precise*] a precise & directe R². 18. *his state*] his owne estate H; his owne state R. 21. *afterwarde*] afterwarde that B. 24. *after that*] after R². 24. *saide*] *Omitted in* B. 25. *as . . . declared*] *Omitted in* B.

Palmer, seruaunt to the Secretary, were sent to S*ir* Thomas More into the towre, to fetche away his bookes from him.

Rich tries to entrap More on the question of the Supremacy. [ROPER.]

And while S*ir* Richarde Southwell and M*aster* Palmer were busie in the trussing vp of his bookes, M*aster* Riche, pretending frendly talke with him, among other thinges of a sett course, as it seemed, saide thus to him :

"Forasmuche as it is well knowe*n*, M*aster* More, that you are a man both wise and well learned, as well in the lawes of this Realme as otherwise, I praye | you therefore, [fol. 49] S*ir*, lett me be so bolde as of good will to put vnto you this case. Admitt there were, S*ir*," quoth he, "an Acte of Parliament that all the Realme should take me for king; would [not] you nowe, M*aster* More," quoth he, "take me for king?"

"Yes, S*ir*," quoth S*ir* Thomas More, "that would I."

"I put case further," quoth M*aster* Riche, "that there were an Act of Parliament that all the Realme should take me for Pope; would you not then, M*aster* More, take me for Pope?"

"For answere, S*ir*," quoth S*ir* Thomas More, "to your first case, the Parliament maye well, M*aster* Riche, meddle with the state of temporall Princes; but to make aunswere to your other case, [I will put you this case]. Suppose the Parliament would make a lawe that God

MSS. E L R^2 Y C H R B.

1. *seruaunt . . . Secretary*] *Omitted in* L R^2 B. 1–4. *seruaunt . . . Master Palmer*] *Omitted in* C. 1–3. *to Sir . . . him*] to þe tower to take away Sir Thomas Mores bookes L R^2; B *as* L R^2, *but* take away all. 4–5. *And . . . bookes*] *Omitted in* B. 5. *the*] *Omitted in* L. 6. *talke*] to talke R^2. 7. *of a sett*] of set C. (Roper *supports* of a sett). 8. *well*] *Interlineated in* L. 11. *you*] *Interlineated in* R. 12. *case*] *Omitted in* L R^2 B. 13. *the Realme*] *Omitted in* L. 14. *would not you*] wold not yow Y C (*supported by* Roper); woulde you not L R^2 B; would you E H R. 14. *nowe*] *Omitted in* B. (*See* Notes.) 14. *Master More*] sir B. 14. *quoth he*] *Omitted in* B. 15. *take*] allow B. 17. *quoth Master Riche*] *Omitted in* B. 19. *you not*] not you L B. (Roper MSS. *vary*.) 19. *Master More*] *Omitted in* Y. 21. *answere*] *Interlineated in* R^2. 21–22. *to . . . case*] *Omitted in* L. 22. *Master Riche*] *Omitted in* R^2 C. 23. *state*] states R^2. 24–25. *I will put you this case. Suppose*] L Y C B (*supported by* Roper); I put you this case suppose R^2; *omitted in* E H R. 25. *the*] that the B. 25. *would*] should L.

should not be God; would you then, M*aster* Riche, say that God were not God?"

"No, S*ir*," quoth he, "that I would not, sith no Parliament may make anye suche lawe."

"No more," saide S*ir* Thomas More (as M*aster* Riche reported of him) "could the Parliament make the king Supreme head of the Church."

Vpon whose onely report was S*ir* Thomas More indyted of treason vpon the statute whereby it was made treason to denye the king to be supreme head of the Churche. Into which Inditement were put these heynous wordes, "malitiouslye, traiterously and diabolically." Many other thinges were conteyned in the saide Inditement, as ye shall hereafter heare.

Upon Rich's report, More is indicted of treason as having spoken *maliciously* against the King's Supremacy. [ROPER.]

S*ir* Thomas More being brought to Westminster hall to his arraignment at the kinges benche before fifteene Commissioners appointed for that purpose, After that his Inditement was read, as well the Lorde Chauncell*our* as the duke of Norffolke saide to him: "S*ir* Thomas More, ye see that ye haue heynously offended the kinges Maiestie; howbeit we are in very good hope (such is his great bountie, benignitie and clemencie) that if you will forethinke and repent your selfe, if you will reuoke and reforme your wilfull, obstinate opinion that you haue so wrongfully mainteyned and so longe dwelt in, that ye shall taste of his gratious pardon."

More is brought to Westminster to answer his indictment. [1 July, 1535.] [ROPER, with addition.]

It is asserted that More may hope for pardon, if he will bend to the King's will. [PARIS NEWS LETTER.]

"My Lordes," quoth S*ir* Thomas More, "I doo most humbly thanke your Honours of your great good will towardes me. Howbeit, I make this my boone and petitio*n* vnto God as heartily as I may, that he will

More prays God to preserve in him his just opinion.

MSS. E L R^2 Y C H R B.

2. *God* (1)] *Omitted in* B. 2. *not*] *Interlineated in* R^2; *omitted in* H. 3–4. *sith . . . may*] sith any parliament cannot H. 4. *anye suche lawe*] such a lawe B. 5. *saide*] *Corrected from* saith, *partly erased*, R^2. 6. *reported*] sayde B. 11. *Inditement*] iudgment B. 11. *heynous*] *Omitted in* L. 13. *saide*] same B. 14. *ye*] you H R B. 17. *that*] þe C. 17. *After that*] after B. 18. *Inditement*] iudgment B. 20. *ye* (1)] you L R^2 B. 20. *ye* (2)] you L R^2 B. 21. *very*] *Omitted in* L; *interlineated in* R. 23. *forethinke*] fore thincke R^2, *with* fore *interlineated*. 25. *ye*] you L R^2 B; yea Y. 28. *will*] willes H R. 29. *boone*] mone Y.

He fears his bodily weakness may prevent his full and effectual answer to the indictment. [PARIS NEWS LETTER.]

vouchsafe | this my good, honest and vpright minde to [fol. 50 *a*] nourishe, mainteyne and vpholde in me euen to the last howre and extreme moment that euer I shall liue. Concerning nowe the matters you charge and challenge me withall, the articles are so prolixe and longe that I feare, what for my longe imprisonment, what for my longe lingring disease, what for my present weaknes and debilitie, that neyther my witt, nor my memorie, nor yet my voice, will serue to make so full, so effectuall and sufficient aunswere as the weight and importance of these matters doth craue."

A chair is brought for him. [PARIS NEWS LETTER, with addition.]

When he had thus spoken, susteyning his weake and feeble body with a staffe he had in his hande, commaundement was geuen to bring him a chaire; wherein being set, he commenced his answere muche after this sort and fasshion:

More's answer to the First Article: **he denies *malicious* opposition to the King's second marriage; he had spoken for discharge of his conscience; for his opinion he had suffered the penalty.** [PARIS NEWS LETTER.]

"Touching the first article, wherein is purposed that I, to vtter and shewe my malice against the king and his late mariage, haue euer repined and resisted the same, I can say nothing but this: that of malice I neuer spake any thing against it, and that whatsoeuer I haue spoken in that matter, I haue none otherwise spoken but according to my very minde, opinion and conscience. In the which, if I had not, for discharging of my conscience to God and my dutie to my Prince, done as I haue done, I might well accompt my selfe a naughtie, vnfaithfull and disloyall subiect. And for this mine errour (if I may call it an errour, or if I haue beene deceaued therein) I haue not gone scot free and vntouched, my goodes and cattels

MSS. E L R^2 Y C H R B.

1. *good*] *Interlineated in* Y. 2. *mainteyne and vpholde*] vpholde & mayntayne L. 2. *in*] *Interlineated in* R. 3. *howre and extreme*] *Interlineated in* L. 3. *euer*] *Omitted in* H. 3. *liue*] *leiue* R^2. 4. *nowe the matters*] now the mater Y; the matters now H R. 5. *and*] *Omitted in* B. 5. *longe*] so longe L R^2; *omitted in* B. 11. *doth*] doe B. 14. *him*] *Omitted in* B. 17. *is*] it is H. 17. *purposed*] proposed L R^2 B. 18. *against*] to B. 20. *spake*] spoake R^2. 21. *I haue spoken*] *Omitted in* B. 22. *spoken*] *An addition on the margin* R^2. 23. *very*] *Omitted in* B. 23. *opinion*] *Omitted in* L; and opynion B. 24. *discharging*] the discharging Y H R B. 24. *of*] *Omitted in* R^2. 27. *mine*] *Omitted in* B. 29. *and* (1)] or R^2 B. 29. *vntouched, my*] vntouched by my L. 29. *cattels*] Chattell H; Cattell R.

being confiscate, and my selfe to perpetuall prison adiudged, where I haue nowe beene shutt vp about a fifteene monethes.

He has never *denied* the King's Supremacy. His *silence* on that matter is no proof against him, since he cannot be charged with scandal or sedition. [PARIS NEWS LETTER.]

"Whereas nowe farther in this article is conteyned that I haue incurred the daunger and penaltie of the last Acte of Parliament, made sithen I was imprisoned, touching the kinges Supremacie, and that I haue as a rebell and trait*our* gone about to robbe and spoyle the king of his due tytle and hon*our*; and namely for that I am challenged for that I would not answere M*aster* Secretarye and others of the kinges priuie counsaile, nor vtter my minde vnto them, being demaunded what I thought vppon the saide Statute, eyther in lyking or [fol. 50 *b*] [dis]lyking, | but this onely, that I was a man deade and mortified toward the world, and to the thinking vpon any other matters then vpon the passion of Christe and passing out of the worlde; Touching, I say, this challenge and accusation, I aunswere that, for this my taciturnitie and silence, neyther your lawe nor any lawe in the world is able iustly and rightly to punishe me, vnlesse you may besydes laye to my charge eyther some worde or some facte in deede."

It is objected that More's silence proves opposition, and that a faithful subject is bound to give his opinion. [PARIS NEWS LETTER.]

To this the kinges Atturney occurring: "Marie," quoth he, "this very silence is a sure token and demonstration of a corrupt and peruerse nature, maligning and repyning against the statute; yea, there is no true and faithfull subiect that being required of his minde and opinion touching the saide Statute, that is not deepelye and vtterly bounde, without any dissimulation, to confesse the Statute to be good, iust and lawfull."

More replies that in the civil law silence

"Truely," quoth S*ir* Thomas More, "if the rule and Maxime of the ciuill lawe be good, allowable and

MSS. E L R² Y C H R B.

1. *confiscate*] confiscated B. 2. *nowe beene*] beene now L R² H R. 2. *vp*] *Omitted in* L. 2–3. *a fifteene*] 15 H R. 10. *would*] will B. 14. *dislyking*] dislikeinge L R² Y C B; mislyking E H R. 15. *vpon*] of Y H R B. 17. *I say*] *Omitted in* L R² B. 19. *and silence*] *Omitted in* B. 19. *your*] the B. 19. *any*] any other H R. 20. *punishe*] puish H. 22. *facte*] Acte H. 22. *in*] and C. 24. *sure*] *Interlineated in* R. 25. *and* (2)] or B. 32. *Maxime*] Maxima L B; Maxim, *with a following letter cancelled*, R²; Maxima *corrected to* Maxime Y.

is taken rather to mean consent; and that a good subject is bound to answer first to his conscience. [PARIS NEWS LETTER.]

sufficient, that *Qui tacet, consentire videtur* (he that holdeth his peace seemeth to consent), this my silence implyeth and importeth rather a ratification and confirmation then any condemnation of your Statute. For as for that you sayde, that euery good subiect is oblieged to answere and confesse, ye must vnderstande that, in thinges touching conscience, euery true and good subiect is more bounde to haue respect to his saide conscience and to his soule then to any other thing in all the world beside; Namelye when his conscience is in such sort as mine is, that is to say, where the person geueth no occasion of slaunder, of tumult and sedition against his Prince, as it is with me; for I assure you that I haue not hither[to] to this howre disclosed and opened my conscience and minde to any person liuing in all the worlde."

More's answer to the Second Article: in his correspondence with Fisher, he had given no information as to his own opinion on the Statute. [PARIS NEWS LETTER.]

The second Article did inforce also the foresaide accusation of transgressing the foresaide last Statute touching the kinges Supremacie; for that S*ir* Thomas More (as it was pretended) wrate diuers letters to the Bisshopp of Rochester, willing him in no wise to agree and condiscende to the said Statute. "Would God," quoth S*ir* Thomas More, "that these letters were nowe produced and openly read; but forasmuche as the saide Bisshopp, as ye saye, hath burned them, I will not | sticke truely to vtter my selfe, as shortly as I may, the [fol. 51 *a*] very tenours of the same. In one of them there was nothing in the world conteyned but certaine familier talke and reco*m*mendac*i*ons, such as was seemely and

MSS. E L R² Y C H R B.

1. *that* (1)] *Omitted in* L. 1–2. *he . . . consent*] *Omitted in* B. 2–3. *silence . . . rather*] silence rather implyeth & importeth L. 3. *implyeth*] employeth H R; imployeth B. 4. *your*] þe L. 5. *as for that*] wheras R². 5. *you*] ye C. 4. *oblieged*] bounde Y. 6. *ye*] you L R² B. 7. *true and good*] good and true C. 8. *saide*] *Omitted in* C. 9. *all*] *Interlineated in* Y. 11. *is* (1)] *Interlineated in* R². 11. *no*] an L R² Y B; *omitted in* C. 13. *that*] *Omitted in* H R. 13–14. *hitherto to*] L R² Y C; hitherto E H R B. 14–15. *my conscience and minde*] my mind & conscience R². 17. *the*] of the H. 17. *foresaide last*] *Omitted in* B. 18. *Supremacie*] suprmacye H. 19. *pretended*] reported B. 20. *of*] *Omitted in* H. 22. *these*] those B. 22. *were*] *Interlineated in* R. 24. *ye*] wee R²; yea Y. 25. *truely*] *Interlineated in* L. 28. *recommendacions*] commendations L R² B.

agreable to our longe and olde acquaintance. In the other was conteyned my aunswere that I made to the saide Bisshopp, demaunding of me what thing I aunswered at my first examination in the towre vpon the saide Statute. Wherevnto I aunswered nothing els but that I had informed and settled my conscience, and that he should informe and settle his. And other aunswere, vpon the charge of my soule, made I none. These are the tenours of my letters, vpon which ye can take no holde or handfast by your lawe to condemne me to death."

More had informed and settled his conscience, and had advised Fisher to inform and settle his. [PARIS NEWS LETTER.]

After this aunswered he to the thirde article, wherein was laide to his charge that, at suche time as he was examined in the towre, he should answere that the Statute was like a two edged sworde, the which if any man would keepe and obserue, he should thereby leese his soule; and in case any man did not obserue it, he should lose his corporall life. "The verye same aunswere," saide they, "the Bisshopp of Rochester made, whereby [it] doth euidently appere that it was a purposed and a sett matter betweene you, by mutuall conference and agrement."

More's answer to the Third Article: the comparison of the Statute to a two-edged sword, made by both Fisher and More, had not been agreed upon between them. [PARIS NEWS LETTER.]

To this Sir Thomas More aunswered that he did not precisely, but conditionally, answere, that in case the Statute were like to be a double edged sworde, he could not tell in the world howe a man should demeane and order himselfe but that he should fall into one of the

MSS. E L R² Y C H R B.

2. *my*] the B. 3. *saide*] *Omitted in* R². 3–4. *demaunding . . . aunswered*] *Interlineated in* R, *but with* thing *omitted.* 3. *thing*] *Omitted in* L R² Y B. 4. *in the*] at þe C. 5. *saide*] *Omitted in* B. 6. *informed and*] *Omitted in* B. 7. *he*] I *in* B. 7. *settle*] sett B. 7. *And*] *Omitted in* B. 9. *my*] the B. 9. *vpon*] of B. 9. *ye*] you L R² Y B. 10. *or*] nor R². 14. *towre*] *An addition on the margin in* R². 15. *was like*] was made like H R. 15–16. *any man*] a man H R. 16. *obserue*] obserue it L R² B. 16. *leese*] loose H R B. 17. *soule*] *Preceded by an erasure in* R². 17. *not*] *Interlineated in* L. 18. *should lose*] should thereby lose H R. 19. *they*] *Interlineated in* R². 20. *it* (1)] L R² Y C H R B; he E. 20. *euidently*] most evidently H R. 20. *it* (2)] is B. 20. *a*] *Interlineated in* R². 21. *purposed and*] *Omitted in* B. 21. *a*] *Omitted in* L R² H R B. 21. *mutuall*] continuall R². 25. *to be*] *Omitted in* Y B. 25. *double*] two Y 27. *himselfe*] his lyfe B. 27. *the*] their Y.

daungers. "Neyther doo I knowe what kinde of answere the Bisshopp made; whose aunswere, if it were agreable and correspondent to mine, that happ happed by reason of the correspondence and conformitie of our wittes, learning and studie, not that any such thing was purposely concluded vpon and accorded betwixt vs. Neyther hath there at any time any worde or deede malitiously scaped or proceeded from me against your statute, albeit it may well be that my wordes might be wrongfully and malitiously reported to the kinges Maiestie."

More therefore pleads not guilty to having actually *denied* the King's Supremacy. [ROPER.]

And thus did S*ir* Thomas More easily cutt and shake off such and like criminations; and among other thinges saide that he would vpon the Inditement haue abiden in lawe, but that thereby he should haue beene driuen to confesse of himselfe the matter in deede, | that was the [fol. 51] denyall of the kinges Supremacie, which he protested was vntrue. Wherefore he thereto pleaded not giltie, and so reserued to himselfe aduauntage to be taken of the body of the matter after verdict to auoyde the Inditement. And moreouer added, that if these only [odious] termes, "malitiously, traiterously and diabolically," were put out of the Inditement, he sawe therein nothing iustly to charge him.

Rich's false oath. More

Wherefore, for the last cast and refuge, to proue that S*ir* Thomas More was giltie of this treason, M*aster* Riche

MSS. E L R² Y C H R B.

1. *kinde of*] *Interlineated in* R. 3. *agreable and*] *Omitted in* B. 3. *happ*] *Omitted in* H R. 3. *happed*] hapned B. 4. *correspondence and*] *Omitted in* R². 5. *wittes*] letters B. 5. *such*] *Omitted in* C B. 6. *vpon*] *Omitted in* B. 6. *betwixt*] betweene R². 7. *there*] *Omitted in* B. 7. *at any time*] *Omitted in* L R² B. 9. *might*] may B. 12. *cutt and*] *Omitted in* B. 13. *such and like*] such like H; these and the like B. 13. *criminations*] *Interlineated over* communications *crossed through* R². 13. *and among*] And wheras among B. 14. *saide*] it was sayde L R² B. 14. *would*] *Corrected from partly erased* should R². 14. *vpon the Inditement*] *Omitted in* L R² B. 14. *abiden*] abyde H. 15. *should*] would H R. 16. *that*] and þat C. 18. *he thereto*] thereto he L. 19. *reserued*] referred B. 21. *only odious termes*] L Y C B; only termes E H R; odiouse termes R². 23. *out*] *Omitted in* B. 23. *the*] the said H R. 23. *therein nothing*] nothinge therin C H R. 25. *that*] *Omitted in* L.

was called for to geue euidence to the Jurye vpon his othe, as he did. Against whom thus sworne, Sir Thomas More beganne in this wise to say: "If I were a man, my Lordes, that did not regarde an othe, I needed not, as it is well knowen, in this place, at this time, nor in this case, to stande here as an accused person. And if this othe of yours, Master Riche, be true, then praye I that I neuer see God in the face, which I would not say, were it otherwise, to winne the whole world." Then recyted he to the Court the discourse of all their communication in the towre, according to the troth, and saide: "In good fayth, Master Riche, I am sorier for your periurie then for mine owne perill. And you shall vnderstande that neyther I, nor any man els to my knowledge, euer tooke you to be a man of suche credite as in any matter of importance I, or any other, would at any time vouchsafe to communicate with you. And I, as you knowe, of no small while haue beene acqueinted with you and your conuersation, who haue knowen you from your youth hitherto; for we longe dwelled [both] in one parishe together, where, as your selfe can well tell (I am sory you compell me so to say) you [were] esteemed very light of your tonge, a common lyer, a great dycer, and of no commendable fame. And so in your house at the Temple, where hath beene your chiefe bringing vp, were you likewise accompted.

exposes Rich's evil character, and laments his perjury. [ROPER.]

More wishes he may "never see God in the face," if Rich's testimony be true. [ROPER.]

"[Can] it therefore seeme* likely to your honorable Lordshipps that I would, in so weightie a case, so vnaduisedly ouershoote my selfe as to trust Master

Is it likely More would disclose to Rich the opinion he

MSS. E L R^2 Y C H R B.

1. *for*] *Interlineated in* R. 4. *needed*] neede L R^2 B. 4. *not*] not be Y. 8. *the*] his B. 10. *the discourse*] the whole discourse L R^2; all the whoale discourse B. 10. *all*] *Omitted in* L. 12. *sorier*] sorrie C H R; more sorry B, more *being interlineated.* 12. *then*] more then C. 15. *suche*] *Interlineated in* Y. 16. *would . . . time vouchsafe*] wold vouchsafe at any time Y. 19. *youth*] youth vp B. 20. *both*] L R^2 Y C H R B (*supported by* Roper); *omitted in* E. 21. *well*] *Omitted in* Y. 21. *sory*] very sorry Y. 22. *were*] C (*supported by* Roper); are E L R^2 Y H R B. 27. *Can*] C (*supported by* Roper); And can L R^2 B; And dothe Y; And maie H R; And E. 27. *seeme likely*] L R^2 Y C H R B (*supported by* Roper); seeme very likely E. 28. *case*] cause B.

has withheld from the King and his noble Lords? [ROPER.]

Riche (a man of me alwayes reputed for one of so litle trust, as your Lordshipps haue hearde) so farre aboue my soueraine Lorde the king or any of his noble Counsailours, that I would vnto him vtter the secretes of my conscience touching the kinges supremacie, the speciall point and onely marke at my handes so longe sought for; a thing which I neuer did, nor neuer | would, [fol. 52 *a*] after the Statute thereof made, reueale eyther to the kinges highnes himselfe or to any of his honorable Counsailours, as it is not vnknowen to your Honours, at sundry seuerall times sent from his graces owne person vnto the towre to me for none other purpose? Can this in your iudgementes, my Lordes, seeme lykely to be true?

Even if More had betrayed his opinion to Rich, he cannot be charged with having *maliciously* denied the King's Supremacy. [ROPER.] The word *maliciously* had been put into the Statute as a precaution against inflicting the death-penalty on insufficient grounds. [ROPER.]

And yet if I had so done indeede, my Lordes, as M*aster* Riche hath sworne, seing it was spoken but in familier secrete talke, nothing affirming, and onely in putting of cases, without other displeasant circumstances, it cannot iustly be taken to be spoken malitiously; for where there is no malice, there can be no malitious offence. And neuer thinke, my Lordes, that so many woorthy Bisshopps, so many honorable personages, and so many other woorshipfull, vertuous, wise and well learned me*n* as at the making of that lawe were in the Parliament assembled, euer meant to haue any man punished by death in whom there could be founde no malice, taking *malitia* for *maleuolentia;* for [if] *malitia* [be] generally taken for sinne, No man is there then that thereof can

MSS. E L R^2 Y C H R B.

1. *a man . . . reputed*] a man alwaies reputed of me B. 1. *so*] *Omitted in* B. 2. *aboue*] aboughte B. 4. *vnto him vtter*] vtter vnto him B. 6. *and*] &, *corrected from* þe, R^2. 6. *at . . . longe*] so long at my handes Y. 7. *sought*] shot Y. 10. *Counsailours*] counsellour L. 10. *as*] *Corrected from* at L. 11. *graces*] gratious R^2. 14. *yet*] *Interlineated in* R^2. 14. *my Lordes*] *Omitted in* R^2. 15–16. *spoken . . . onely*] *Omitted in* B. 15. *but*] *Interlineated in* Y. 16. *in putting*] puttinge H R. 18. *iustly be*] be iustly L R^2 B. 22. *other*] *Omitted in* B. 22. *woorshipfull*] *Omitted in* Y B. 22. *well*] *Omitted in* B. 23. *the* (2)] *Omitted in* Y; þat C. (*Most* Roper MSS. *support* the. *See* Notes.) 24–25. *assembled . . . whom*] *Omitted in* B. 24. *by*] to C (*marked for correction*). 26. *maleuolentia*] Maledicentia H R. 26. *for if*] For yf C (*supported by* Roper); for E L R^2 Y H R B. 26. *malitia* (2)] malice B. 26. *be*] Y C (*supported by* Roper); is E L R^2 H R B. 27. *then*] *A correction of* them R^2; than Y. 27. *thereof can*] can L; can therof B.

excuse himselfe: *Quia si dixerimus quod peccatum non habemus, nosmet ipsos seducimus, et veritas in nobis non est.* And onely this worde 'maliciously' is in this Statute materiall, as this terme 'forcibly' is in the Statute of forcible entrie. By which Statute, if a man enter peaceablye, and put not his aduersary out forciblye, it is no offence; but if he put him out forcibly, then by that Statute it is an offence, and so shall [he] be punished by this terme 'forcibly.'

Malicious denial is the only denial punishable under the Statute. [ROPER.]

"Besides this, the manifolde goodnes of the kinges highnes himselfe, that hath beene so many wayes my singuler good Lorde and gratious Soueraine, that hath so deerelye loued and trusted me (euen at my very first comming vnto his noble seruice with the dignitie of his honorable priuie Counsaile vouchsafing to admitt me) and to offices of great credite and woorshipp most liberally aduaunced me, and finally with that weightie roome of his graces high Chauncellour (the lyke whereof he neuer did to temporall man before) next to his [owne] royall person the highest officer of this noble Realme, so farre aboue my merites or qualities able and meete therefore, of his incomparable benignitie honored and exalted me, by the space of twentie yeres and more shewing his continuall fauour towardes me, and (vntill at mine owne poore humble sute it pleased his highnes,
[fol. 52 b] geuing me licence with his Maiesties | fauour to bestowe

The King's previous favours to More should be sufficient to convince the judges of the folly of attributing to More *malice* against him. [ROPER.]

MSS. E L R^2 Y C H R B.

1. *dixerimus*] dixcerimus Y. 1. *peccatum*] pecatum Y. 2. *seducimus*] seducemus Y. 2. *veritas*] veritus H R. 3. *this* (2)] the L R^2 H R B; þat C. (Roper MSS. *vary. See* Notes.) 4. *terme*] worde C. (Roper *supports* terme.) 6. *out forciblye*] *Interlineated in* R^2. 7. *it . . . forcibly*] *Omitted in* H R. 8. *he*] L Y C B (*supported by* Roper); *omitted in* E R^2 H R. 13. *euen*] ever B. 13. *first*] *Omitted in* L R^2 B. 15. *Counsaile*] Councellour B. 15. *vouchsafing . . . me*] *Omitted in* B. 16. *and to*] to H R; and to B, to *being interlineated.* 16. *offices*] other offices B. 16. *and woorshipp*] *Omitted in* Y. 18. *his*] *Omitted in* Y. 19. *to* (1)] to any C B. (Roper *supports* to.) 19–20. *his owne royall person*] L R^2 Y C B (*supported by* Roper); owne *omitted in* E; his person H R. (*See* Notes.) 20. *this*] his B. 21. *or*] & L B. 24. *me*] *Interlineated in* R^2. 25. *poore*] *Omitted in* L R^2 B. 25. *humble*] *Omitted in* B. 26. *licence*] leaue Y. 26—*l.* 2, *p.* 192. *bestowe . . . God*] bestowe in þe seruice of god þe residue of my life for þe prouision of my soule L R^2 B.

the residue of my life for the prouision of my soule in the seruice of God, of his speciall goodnes therof to discharge and disburden me) most benignely heaping honours continually more and more vpon me—all this his highnes goodnes, I say, so longe thus bountifully extended towardes me, were in my minde, my Lordes, matter sufficient to conuince this slaunderous surmise by this man so wrongfully imagined against me."

Southwell and Palmer are sworn; they profess they paid no heed to the conversation. [ROPER.]

Master Riche, seing himselfe so disproued, and his credite so fowly defaced, caused Sir Richard Southwell and Master Palmer, that at the time of their communication were in the chamber with them, to be sworne what wordes had passed betwixt them. Wherevpon Master Palmer, vpon his deposition, saide that he was so busye about the trussing vp of Sir Thomas Mores bookes in a sacke, that he tooke no heede [to] their talke. Sir Richarde Southwell likewise, vpon his deposition, sayde that because he was appointed onely to looke to the conueyance of his bookes, he gaue no eare vnto them.

In spite of More's proven innocence, the Jury find him guilty. [ROPER.]

More claims the right to take exception

After this were there many other reasons, not nowe in my remembraunce, by Sir Thomas More in his owne defence alleaged, to the discredite of Master Riches forsaide euidence, and proufe of the cleerenes of his owne conscience. All which notwithstanding, the Jurie founde him giltie. And incontinent vpon their verdict the Lorde Chauncellour, for that matter chiefe Commissioner, beginning to proceede in iudgement

MSS. E L R² Y C H R B.

2. *therof*] *Omitted in* B *after* goodnes, *but placed after* me *below* (*Cf. l.* 3). 2. *discharge*] discharge me Y. 3. *heaping*] heaping vp Y. 4. *more and more vpon me*] vppon me more and more B. 4. *all this*] alb this, *corrected from* albeit, R²; All these B. 5. *goodnes*] goodnesses B. 6. *matter*] matters H B. 7–8. *by . . . so*] *Omitted in* B. 9–10. *disproued . . . so*] *Omitted in* B. 10. *fowly*] fowle Y. 11–13. *Master . . . Wherevpon*] *twice over in* E. 11. *that*] *Omitted in* H R. 11. *at the*] at that Y B. 13. *betwixt*] betwene Y. 14. *so*] *Omitted in* B. 15. *Thomas*] Tho, *corrected from* Mo, L. 15. *Mores*] More his B. 16. *to*] L R² Y C H R B (*supported by* Roper); of E. 18. *to looke*] *Omitted in* L. 18. *to the*] vpon the B. 18–19. *conueyance*] conveying B. 19. *his*] this, *with* t *partly erased*, R². 19. *eare*] yeare R². 20. *were there*] there were B. 22. *Riches*] Riche his B. 23–24. *and proufe . . . conscience*] *Omitted in* B. 23. *proufe of the*] *Omitted in* Y. 24. *owne*] *Omitted in* C

against him, S*ir* Thomas More saide vnto him: "My Lorde, when I was towarde the lawe, the maner in suche case* was to aske the prisoner, before iudgement, why iudgement should not be geuen against him." Where-vpon the Lorde Chauncellour, staying his iudgement, wherein he had partly proceeded, demaunded of him what he was able to say to the contrary; who in this sort most humblye made aunswere:

to the judgment following upon this verdict. [Roper.]

"Seing that I see ye are determined to condemne me (God knoweth howe) I will nowe in discharge of my conscience speake my minde plainlye and freely touching my Inditement and your Statute withall.

Seeing he is precondemned, he discharges his conscience. [Paris News Letter.]

"And forasmuch as this Inditement is grounded vpon an Acte of Parliament directly repugnant to the lawes of God and his holye Churche, the supreme Gouer*n*ment of which, or [of] any part whereof, may no temporall Prince presume by any lawe to take vpon him, as rightfully belonging to the Sea of Rome, a spirituall preheminence by the mouth of our Sauio*ur* himselfe, personally present vpon earth, onely to St Peter and his Successours, bisshopps of the same Sea, by speciall [fol. 58 *a*] | prerogatiue graunted; it is therfore in lawe, amongest christen men, insufficient to charge any christian man." And for proufe thereof, like as among diuers other reasons and authorities he declared that this Realme, being but one member and small part of the Churche, might not make a particuler lawe disagreable with the

A Statute rejecting the Pope's Supremacy is repugnant to the laws of God and his Church. [Roper.]

MSS. E L R^2 Y C H R B.

1. *against him, Sir*] against him to whom Sir L. 3. *case*] Y C; cases E L R^2 H R B. (Roper MSS. *vary, but majority support* case. *See* Notes.) 6. *proceeded*] perceaved H R. 8. *most humblye*] must humble Y. 9. *I see*] *Omitted in* Y. 9. *ye*] you R^2 Y H R. 10–11. *in . . . speake*] discharge my Conscience and speake H. 11. *plainlye and freely*] freelie and plainlie B. 14. *an*] *Corrected from* act L. 14. *repugnant*] repugninge L. 15. *holye*] wholy Y. 15. *supreme Gouernment*] supreame head and gouernement H. 16. *or of any*] L R^2 Y C B (*supported by* Roper); or any E H R. 16. *whereof*] thereof R^2 B. 16. *may*] *Corrected, probably from* mee, R^2. 18. *rightfully belonging*] rightly belongeth H R. 20. *earth*] the earthe B. 21. *Sea*] See of Rome B. 22. *in lawe*] a lawe L B. 23. *insufficient*] vnsufficient L; sufficient Y. 26. *and small part*] and a small parte L R^2 B; & smale member H R. 26. *of the Churche*] therof B. 27. *with the*] to the B.

generall lawe of Christes vniuersall Catholike Churche, no more then the Citie of London, being but one poore member in respect of the whole Realme, might make a lawe against an Acte of Parliament to binde the whole Realme; So further shewed he that it was contrary both to the lawes and statutes of our owne lande yet vnrepealed, as they might euidently [perceaue] in Magna Charta (*Quod ecclesia Anglicana libera* sit, et habeat omnia iura sua integra, et libertates suas illaesas*); And also contrary to the sacred othe which the kinges highnes himselfe and euery other christen Prince alwayes with great solemnitie receaued at their coronations; alleaging, moreouer, that no more might this Realme of Inglande refuse obedience to the Sea of Rome then might the childe refuse obedience to his owne naturall father. For, as St Paule saide [of] the Corinthians, "I haue regenerated you, my children in Christe;" so might St Gregorie, Pope of Rome, of whom, by St Augustine his messenger, we first receaued the christian fayth, of vs englishe men truely say: "You are my children, because I haue geuen to you euerlasting saluation, a farre higher and better inheritance then any carnall father can leaue to his children, and by regeneration made you my spirituall children in Christe."

More is accused of stiffly sticking, contrary to the Bishops

Then was it by the Lorde Chauncellour therevnto aunswered, that seing all the Bisshopps, vniuersities and best learned men of the Realme had to this Acte agreed, it was much meruaile that he alone against them all

MSS. E L R^2 Y C H R B.

1. *Christes*] Christ his B. 4. *an*] the B. 5. *further*] *Omitted in* L. 5. *both*] *Omitted in* Y. 6. *statutes*] statute R^2. 6. *owne*] *Omitted in* R^2. 6. *lande*] Realme R^2 B; *omitted in* H R. 7. *perceaue*] R^2 Y C B (*supported by* Roper); see E L H R. 8. *ecclesia*] ecclecia Y. 8. *libera*] L R^2 B (*supported by* Roper); liberata C, ta *being crossed through in ink and underlined in pencil, with cross in margin*; liberata E Y H R. 8. *habeat*] habea H. 9. *libertates*] libertas Y. 9. *suas*] sus Y; sua H. 9. *illaesas*] illesas C H; illasas R. 11. *alwayes*] *Omitted in* H R. 16. *saide*] *Corrected from* saith R^2. 16. *of*] L Y C; to E R^2 H R B. (Roper MSS. *vary*.) 17. *Pope*] *Omitted in* H. 20. *You*] yow ye Y. 20–21. *geuen to you*] given you H. 21. *higher and better*] better and higher H R. 23. *spirituall*] *Omitted in* H R. 27. *of the*] in the B. 28. *meruaile*] mervailed C. (Roper MSS. *vary*.) 28. *against them all*] *Omitted in* B.

would so stiffly sticke thereat, and so vehemently argue thereagainst. The which reason in effect the Bisshopp of Westminster also made against him, whe*n* he appered before the Co*m*missioners at Lambeth.

and learned men of the Realm. [ROPER, with addition. Cf. also PARIS NEWS LETTER.]

To this S*ir* Thomas More replied, saying that these seuen yeres seriously and earnestly he had besett his studies and cogitations vpon this point chiefly, among other, of the Popes authoritie. "Neyther as yet," saide he, "haue I chaunced vpon any auncient wryter or doct*our* that so aduaunceth, as your Statute doth, the supremacie of any seculer and temporall Prince. If there were no moe but my selfe vpon my side, and the [fol. 53 *b*] whole Par|liament vpon the other, I would be sore afraid to leane to mine owne minde onely against so many. But if the number of Bisshopps and vniuersities be so materiall as your Lordshipp seemeth to take it, then see I litle cause, my Lord, why that thing in my conscience should make any chaunge. For I nothing doubt but that, though not in this Realme, yet in Christendome about, of these well learned Bisshopps and vertuous men that are yet aliue, they be not the fewer part that are of my minde therein. But if I should speake of those that are already deade, of whom many be nowe holy Saintes in heauen, I am very sure it is the farre greater part of them that, all the while they liued,

In seven years' study he had found no authority for the supremacy of a secular Prince. [PARIS NEWS LETTER.]

He asserts he is not alone in his view. He claims the support of the Clergy and learned men of the past. [ROPER. Cf. MORE to MARGARET; WORKS, p. 1430.]

MSS. E L R^{2} Y C H R B.

1. *would*] should B. 1. *stiffly*] *Omitted in* H. 1. *vehemently*] vhemently H. 2. *The which reason*] The which reasons L R^{2}; To which reason H R. 3. *Westminster*] Winchester L R^{2} C B. (Westminster *supported by* my Lorde of Westminster, English Works, *p.* 1430.) 3. *also*] *Omitted in* H R. 3. *him*] *Omitted in* H R. 5. *saying that*] saying that he had C, he had *being omitted after* earnestly *below* (*Cf. l.* 6). 5. *these*] *Omitted in* R^{2}. 7. *chiefly*] onely Y. 8. *yet*] *Interlineated in* R. 10. *aduaunceth*] aduaunced L R^{2} B. 10. *your*] our B. 11. *and*] or L B; our R^{2}. 14. *leane to mine*] leaue my H. 14. *onely*] *Omitted in* B. 15. *number*] nmber H. 15. *of*] of the R^{2}. 16. *materiall*] naturall Y. 16. *Lordshipp seemeth*] Lordships seme B. 18–19. *For . . . doubt*] for I nothinge for I nothinge doubt H. 19. *but*] *Omitted in* L. 20. *these*] those L R^{2} C H R B. (Roper MSS. *vary. See* Notes.) 20–21. *learned . . . men*] Learned men & vertuous Bisshopps R^{2}. 21. *fewer*] fower R^{2}. 22. *my*] *Omitted in* R^{2}. 23. *of those*] of all those H R. 23–24. *be nowe*] now be L R^{2} B. 24. *holy*] wholy Y. 24. *very*] *Omitted in* L. 24. *it is*] it it R. 25. *the*] *Omitted in* B. 25. *liued*] lieued R^{2}.

thought in this case that way that I thinke nowe; and therefore am I not bounden, my Lorde, to conforme my conscience to the Councell of one Realme against the generall Councell of Christendome. For of the foresaide holy Bisshopps I haue, for euery Bisshopp of yours, aboue one hundred; And for one Councell or Parliament of yours (God knoweth what maner of one), I haue all the Councels made these thousande yeres. And for this one kingdome, I haue all other christian Realmes."

There is far more support for his view than for that of his opponents. [PARIS NEWS LETTER.]

Then aunswered the duke of Norffolke: "We nowe plainely perceaue that ye are malitiously bent." "Nay, nay," quoth S*ir* Thomas More, "very and pure necessitie, for the discharge of my conscience, enforceth me to speake so muche. Wherein I call and appeale to God, whose onely sight pearceth into the very depth of mans heart, to be my witnes. Howbeit, it is not for this supremacie so muche that ye seeke my bloud, as for that I would not condiscende to the mariage."

He knows why they seek his blood. [PARIS NEWS LETTER.]

When nowe S*ir* Thomas More, for the auoyding of this Inditement, had taken as manye exceptions as he thought meete, and many moe reasons then I can nowe remember alleaged, the Lorde Chauncell*our*, loth to haue the burden of that [Iudgement] wholly to depende vpon himselfe, there openly asked the aduise of the Lorde Fitz James, then Lorde chiefe Justice of the kinges benche, and ioyned in Co*m*mission with him, whether this Inditement were sufficient or not. Who, lyke a wise man, aunswered: "My Lordes all, by St Julian (that was

The Lord Chief Justice admits that "if the Act of Parliament be lawful, then the Indictment is good enough." [ROPER.]

MSS. E L R^2 Y C H R B.

1. *thought . . . way*] thought that in this case that R. 1. *that I*] which I *in* R^2. 1. *thinke*] doe B. 2. *I not*] not I *in* B. 2. *bounden*] bound H R. 2. *Lorde*] Lordes B. 4. *of* (1)] of all Y. (Roper MSS. *vary*; *majority omit* all. *See* Notes.) 5. *holy*] *Omitted in* B. 5–6. *aboue one hundred*] one hundreth H; one hundred R. 6. *one* (1)] an C. 6. *or*] of L; & R^2. 8. *Councels*] Counsailers Y. 8. *these*] this L R^2 Y B. 8. *thousande*] 100 L R^2 B. 9. *other*] othe R. 9. *Realmes*] kingdomes and Countries H R. 11. *perceaue*] perceaved H. 11. *ye*] you L R^2 B. 12. *and*] *Omitted in* H. 17. *ye*] you R^2. 19. *When nowe*] Now when B. 21. *then*] *Omitted in* L. 22. *alleaged*] *Omitted in* B. 23. *that*] the R^2 B. 23. *Iudgement*] *Supported by* Roper. *All* Harpsfield MSS. Indictment. 23. *to depende*] depend H. 24. *himselfe*] himselfe, *with* selfe *on erasure*, R^2. 24. *of the Lorde*] *Omitted in* Y. 25. *of*] in H R.

euer his othe), I must needes confesse that, if the Act of Parliament be lawfull, then the Inditement is good ynough." Wherevpon the Lorde Chauncell*our* saide to the rest of the lordes: "Loe, my Lordes, you heare what my Lorde chiefe Justice saith;" And so immediately gaue [he] iudgement against him.

Sentence is passed against More. [ROPER.]

After which ended, the Co*m*missioners yet further courteouslye offred him, if he had any thing els to [fol. 54 a] alleage for his defence, | to graunt him fauorable audience. Who aunswered: "More haue I not to say, my Lordes, but that like as the blessed Apostle St Paule, as we reade in the Actes of the Apostles, was present and consented to the death of St Steuen, and kept their clothes that stoned him to death, and yet be they nowe both twaine holy Saintes in heauen, and shall continue there frendes together for euer, so I verily trust, and shall therefore right heartily praye, that though your Lordshipps haue nowe here in earth beene Judges to my condemnation, we may yet hereafter in heauen merily all meete together, to our euerlasting saluation. And thus I desire Almightie God to preserue and defende the kinges Maiestie, and to send him good counsaile."

More prays for his judges. [ROPER.]

And for the King. [PARIS NEWS LETTER.]

Thus muche nowe concerning his arraignement. After the which he departed from the barre to the towre againe, ledd by S*ir* Will*iam* Kingeston, a tall, stronge and comely knight, Constable of the Towre, and his very deere frende. Who, when he had brought him from

More returns to the Tower. Sir William Kingston's farewell. [ROPER.]

MSS. E L R^2 Y C H R B.

1. *euer*] allwayes L. 2. *Inditement*] Iudgment R^2. 4. *you*] ye H R. 5. *saith*] *On an erasure in* L. 6. *gaue he*] R^2 Y C B (*supported by most* Roper MSS.); gaue the E L H R. 10–11. *to say, my Lordes*] my Lordes to answere H R. 11. *that*] *Omitted in* R^2 B. 11. *like*] *Omitted in* B. 14. *be they*] they be H R. 15. *twaine*] *Omitted in* L R^2 H B. 16. *together for euer*] for ever together B. 16. *shall*] *Omitted in* H. 18. *haue . . . beene*] have bene now here in earth B. 18. *here in earth*] in earth R^2, in *being interlineated over* one h *crossed through*; here on earthe Y. 18. *to my*] of my B. 19. *yet*] it Y. 19. *all*] *Omitted in* R^2 Y. 19–20. *all meete together*] mete alltogeather H R. 20. *meete*] mette Y. 20. *to . . . saluation*] to the euerlastinge saluation of vs all R^2; to our euerlastinge solace H R. 20–21. *thus I desire*] heare I beseech H R. 23. *his*] the Y. 24. *After the which*] after which L R^2 B. 25. *stronge*] *Omitted in* H R. 27. *deere*] good H R. 27. *him*] *Omitted in* H R.

Westminster to the Olde Swanne towarde the towre, there with an heauy hart, the teares running downe by his cheekes, bad him farewell. S*ir* Thomas More, seing him so sory, comforted him with as good wordes as he could, saying: "Good M*aster* Kingeston, trouble not your selfe, but be of good cheere, for I will praye for you and my good Lady your wife, that we may meete in heauen together, where we shall be merie for euer."

More will pray for Master Kingston and his wife. [ROPER.]

Margaret's farewell to her father. [ROPER.]

When S*ir* Thomas More came fro*m* Westminster to the Towrewarde againe, his daughter, M*aster* Will*iam* Ropers wife, desirous to see her father, who*m* she thought she should neuer see in this worlde after, and also to haue his finall blessing, gaue attendance about the towrewharfe, where she knewe he should passe by, before he should enter into the towre, there tarying for his comming. Whom as soone as she sawe, after his blessing vpon her knees reuerently receaued, she hasting towardes him, and without consideration or care of her selfe pressing in among the middes of the thronge and company of the garde that with holberdes and billes went rounde about him, hastily ranne to him, and there openly in the sight of them all imbraced him, tooke him about the necke, and kissed him moste lovingly. Who well lyking her moste | naturall and deere daughterly affection towarde him, [fol. 54 *b*] gaue her his fatherly blessing and many godly wordes of comfort beside; telling her that whatsoeuer he suffred, though he suffred as an innocent, yet did he not suffer it without Gods holye will and pleasure. "Ye knowe,"

More comforts Margaret. [PARIS NEWS

MSS. E L R² Y C H R B.

2. *an*] a L Y H B. 9–10. *to the Towrewarde*] toward the towre L R² B. 11. *desirous*] desired H R. 12. *see . . . after*] see againe in this worlde Y. 12. *haue*] *Omitted in* H R. 13. *towrewharfe*] Towre whaife H. 14. *knewe*] kewe Y. 14–15. *should enter*] entred B. 16. *as soone*] so soone Y C. (Roper *supports* as soone). 16. *his*] hir L. 17. *hasting*] hastening C; hasted B. (Roper *supports* hasting.) 19. *among*] *Omitted in* H R. 19. *company*] accompanied H R. 21. *hastily ranne*] *Omitted in* Y; ran hastely H R. 21. *to him*] *Omitted in* Y. 23. *her*] his H R. 23. *moste*] most most R; *omitted in* B. 24. *naturall . . . deere*] *Omitted in* B. 24. *daughterly*] daughte by H; daughter by R. 25. *her*] *Omitted in* H R. 25–26. *of comfort beside*] besides of comfort B. 26. *suffred*] did suffer B. 28. *Gods*] God his B. 28. *Ye*] you L R² B.

quoth he, "the very bottome and secretes of my heart; And ye haue rather cause to congratulate and to reioyce for me that God hath aduaunced me to this high honour, and vouchsafed to make me woorthie to spende my life for the defence and vpholding of vertue, iustice and religion, then to be dismaide or to be discomforted."

[LETTER, with additions.]

O noble and woorthy voyce of our noble, newe, christen Socrates! The olde Socrates, the excellent vertuous Philosopher, was also vniustly put to death; whom, when his wife, at that time folowing, outragiously cryed, "Shall such a good man be put to death?" "Peace, good wife," quoth he, "and content thy selfe; it is farre better for me to dye a good and a true man then as a wretched malefact*our* to liue."

Harpsfield compares More and Socrates: both die gladly for conscience' sake.

Well, to come to her againe. This good, louing and tender daughter, the iewell of the englishe matrones of our time, being at length departed from her father, was not for all this satisfied with the former sight of him; and like one that had forgotten her selfe, being all ravished with entier loue of her deere Father, hauing respect neyther to her selfe nor to the preasse of the people and multitude that were there about him, sodenly turned backe againe, ranne to him as before, tooke him about the necke, and diuers times together most louingly kissed him; and at last, with a full heauie hart, was faine to depart from him. The beholding whereof was to many of them that were present thereat so lamentable, that it made them for very sorowe thereof to mourne and weepe.

Margaret again bids her father farewell. [ROPER; PARIS NEWS LETTER.]

MSS. E L R^2 Y C H R B.

1. *secretes*] secreate B. 2. *ye*] you L R^2 B. 2. *to* (2)] *Omitted in* L R^2 B. 4. *to make*] *Omitted in* H. 6. *or to be*] or be R^2; or H R B. 7–8. *O . . . Socrates*] *Omitted in* L. 8. *christen*] *Omitted in* Y. 10. *cryed*] cryenge Y. 11. *good*] iust B. 12. *farre*] *Omitted in* L R^2 B. 13. *a good and a true man*] a good man and a true Y; a true & good man H; a true & a good man R. 13. *as a*] for a H; a R. 16–17. *of our*] after our H R. 17. *length*] lengh L. 20. *deere*] *Omitted in* R^2. 21. *respect neyther*] neither respect H. 21. *preasse*] peace Y. 21. *of the*] of L R^2 C B. (Roper MSS. *vary.*) 22. *and multitude*] *Omitted in* B. 22. *that were*] *Omitted in* H R. 27–28. *that were present thereat*] there present B. 27. *were*] *Omitted in* R. 29. *to mourne*] mourne H.

More's fortitude. [PARIS NEWS LETTER, with additions.]

Yet for all this S*ir* Thomas More, as one quite mortified to the world and all worldly and naturall affections also, and wholly affixed to heauenwarde, albeit he were a most loving, tender, naturall father to his children, and moste deerly and tenderly affectionated aboue all other to this his daughter, hauing nowe moste mightily subdued and conquered euen nature it selfe for Gods sake, with whom he looked and longed euery howre to be and eternally to dwell with, neyther fell to weeping, nor shewed any token of griefe or sorowe, nor once chaunged | his countenance. [fol. 55 *a*]

Sir William Kingston praises More's stout heart. [ROPER.]

Soone after this S*ir* William Kingeston, talking with M*aster* Willi*am* Roper of S*ir* Thomas More, saide: "In good fayth, M*aster* Roper, I was ashamed of my selfe that at my depart[ing] from your father, I founde my heart so feeble and his so stronge, that he was faine to comfort me, [which] should rather haue comforted him."

More sends his hair-shirt and a letter to Margaret. He longs to die on the Eve of St. Thomas. [ROPER.]

So remained S*ir* Thomas More in the towre more then a sevennight after his iudgement; from whence, the day before he suffred, he sent his shirt of heare (not willing to haue it seene) to M*aster* Willi*am* Ropers wife, his deerely beloued daughter, and a letter written with a coale, plainly expressing the feruent desire he had to suffer on the morowe, in these wordes folowing:

MSS. E L R^2 Y C H R B.

1. *Yet . . . this*] *Omitted in* B. 1. *Yet*] yt Y. 1. *Sir*] *Corrected from* as R^2. 2. *and all worldly*] *Omitted in* H R. 2. *also*] *Omitted in* B. 3. *wholly*] holie Y. 3. *albeit*] althoughe L. 5. *deerly and*] *Omitted in* B. 5. *deerly . . . aboue*] dearly affectionated & tendered aboue L, *the* at *of* affectionated *being interlineated.* 5. *affectionated*] affecconed R. 6. *this*] *Omitted in* Y. 9. *neyther*] neuer C. 10. *nor shewed . . . sorowe*] *Omitted in* H R. 10. *shewed*] shewing B. 10. *or*] *Corrected from* & L. 11. *chaunged*] changing B. 12. *William Kingeston*] *On erasure in* R^2. 13–14. *of Sir . . . Roper*] *Omitted in* Y. 14. *of*] at B. 15. *departing*] departeinge L R^2 Y C H R B; departure E. (Roper MSS *vary, but majority support* departing. *See* Notes.) 15. *your*] my R. 16. *faine*] fainte Y. 17. *which*] L R^2 Y C B; who E H R. (Roper MSS. that.) 17. *rather haue*] haue rather Y; have rather have B. 18. *So . . . More*] Sir Thomas More remayned B. 18–19. *in . . . sevennight*] more then a seuennight in the tower R^2. 18. *the*] this Y. 19. *sevennight*] seaventh night H. 19. *the day*] a daye L. 21–22. *to . . . daughter*] to his dawghter Master William Roperes wife B. 23. *the*] his L.

"I cumber you, good Margarete, muche, but I would be sory if it should be any longer then to morowe; for to morowe is St Thomas Even, and the Vtas of St Peter, and therefore to morowe longe I to goe to God; it were a day very meete and conuenient for me. I neuer lyked your maner towarde me better then when you kissed me laste; for I lyke when daughterly loue and deere charitie haue no leasure to looke to worldly courtesie," etc.

Pope brings More word that he is to die that day. [6 July, 1535.] [ROPER.]

And so vpon the next morowe, being Tuesday, St Thomas Even, and the Vtas of St Peter, in the yere of our Lorde 1535 (according as he in his letter the day before had wisshed), early in the morning came to him S*ir* Thomas Pope, his singuler frende, on message from the king and his Counsaile, that he should before nyne of the clocke the same morning suffer death, and that therefore forthwith he should prepare himselfe thereto.

More's gratitude to the King for having given him leisure to prepare for death. [ROPER.]

He is ready and glad to die, and thanks, and will pray for, the King. [ROPER.]

"M*aster* Pope," quoth he, "for your good tydinges I most heartily thanke you. I haue beene alwayes muche bounden to the kinges highnes for the benefites and honours that he hath still from time to time moste bountifully heaped vpon me; and yet more bounden am I to his grace for putting me vnto this place, where I haue had conuenient time and space to haue remembraunce of mine ende. And so helpe me God, most of all, M*aster* Pope, am I bounden to his highnes that it [pleaseth] him so shortly to ridd me out of the miseries of this wretched world, and therefore will I not fayle

MSS. E L R^2 Y C H R B.

1. *cumber you*] can bere now B. 1. *but*] *Omitted in* L R^2 B. 2. *sory*] loath R^2. 2. *any*] *Omitted in* B. 3. *the*] *Omitted in* H R. 3. *Vtas*] Octave B. 5. *very*] *Omitted in* H R. 6. *your . . . better*] yow better for your maners towardes me Y. 8. *leasure*] pleasure B. 8. *to worldly*] to wardly R^2. 9. *Tuesday*] Twesdaie C; Thursdaie H R; wensday B. 9. *St*] & St L R^2 B. 10–13. *and . . . Thomas*] *Omitted in* B. 11. *Lorde* 1535] lord god 1535 R^2 Y. 11–12. *the day before*] that day before L; *omitted in* H R. 13. *singuler*] singuler good R^2 B. 13. *on message*] came on message B. 15. *that*] *Omitted in* R^2. 16–17. *thereto . . . tydinges*] *Omitted in* H R. 18. *beene*] bne Y. 19. *bounden*] bound B. 19. *and*] and the Y. 20. *hath*] hat H. 21. *yet*] it Y. 21. *bounden*] bounde B. 21–22. *am I to*] am I now to L. 24–25. *God . . . Pope*] good Master Pope most of all R^2. 26. *pleaseth*] C (*supported by* Roper); pleased E L R^2 Y H R B. (*See* Notes.) 27. *I*] *Omitted in* B.

earnestlye to praye for his grace, both here, and also in another world."

The King commands him to use few words at his execution. [ROPER.]

"The kinges pleasure is further," quoth M*aster* Pope, "that at your execution you shall not vse many wordes."

"M*aster* Pope," | quoth he, "you doo well to geue me [fol. 55 *b* warning of his graces pleasure, for otherwise I had purposed at that time somewhat to haue spoken, but of no matter wherewith his grace, or any other, should haue had cause to be offended. Neuerthelesse, whatsoeuer I intended, I am ready obedientlye to conforme my selfe to his graces co*m*maundement. And I beseeche you, good M*aster* Pope, to be a meane vnto his highnes that my daughter Margarete may be at my buriall."

More pleads that Margaret may be present at his burial. [ROPER.]

"The king is content already," quoth M*aster* Pope, "that your wife, children and other your frendes shall haue libertie to be present thereat."

"Oh, howe muche beholden then," saide S*ir* Thomas More, "am I to his grace, that vnto my poore buriall vouchsafeth to haue such gratious consideration."

More comforts Pope. [ROPER.]

Wherewithall M*aster* Pope, taking his leaue of him, could not refraine from weeping. Which S*ir* Thomas More perceaving, comforted him in this wise: "Quiet your selfe, good M*aster* Pope, and be not discomforted; for I trust that we shall, once in heauen, see eche other full merilye, where we shall be sure to liue and loue together, in ioyfull blisse eternallye."

Vpon whose departure, S*ir* Thomas More, as one

MSS. E L R^2 Y C H R B.

3. *is further*] is further is forther R^2. 4. *shall*] should H R. 5. *Master . . . well*] Master Pope you doe well quoth he L. 5. *quoth he*] sayth he Y. 6. *warning*] word H R. 7. *at . . . somewhat*] somewhat at that time H R. 9. *haue had*] haue H R. 9–10. *whatsoeuer*] withsoeuer H. 10. *I* (1)] *Corrected from* he R^2. 10. *intended*] intend C. 10. *obedientlye*] *Omitted in* B. 12. *a*] *Omitted in* Y. 13. *may be*] shal be B. 14. *The*] This C. 14. *content*] contented H R B. 14. *quoth*] *Interlineated in* R. 15. *other your frendes*] & other frends L R^2; other of your frendes H R B. 17. *beholden*] beholdinge L R^2 Y B. 17. *then*] *Omitted in* H. 18. *am I*] I ame Y. 20. *Master Pope*] Sir Thomas Pope R^2. 20. *of*] from R^2. 24. *trust . . . other*] trust that once in heauen we shall see each other L; we shall once in heaven H; trust that I shall once in heaven see eche other R, shall *being interlineated.* 27. *one*] *Interlineated in* R^2.

that had beene inuited to some solemne feast, chaunged himselfe into his best apparell. Which M*aster* Lieftenant espying, aduised him to put it off, saying that he that should haue it was but a iavell. "What, M*aster* Lieftenant," quoth he, "should I accompt him a iavell that shall doo me this day so singuler a benefite? Nay, I assure you, were it cloth of golde, I would accompt it well bestowed on him, as St Ciprian did, who gaue to his executioner thirtie peeces of golde." And albeit at length, through M*aster* Lieftenant*es* importune persuasion, he altered his apparell, yet after the example of that holy Martyr Saint Ciprian, did he, of that litle money that was lefte him, sende one angell of golde to his executioner; and so was he by M*aster* Lieftenant brought out of the towre, and from thence led towarde the place of execution.

The Lieutenant prevents More from wearing his best apparel at his execution. [ROPER.]

But More sends gold to his executioner. [ROPER.]

When he was thus passing to his death, a certaine woman called to him at the towre gate, beseeching him to notifie and declare that he had certaine euidences of hers that were deliuered to him when he was in office, saying that after he was once apprehended, she [could] not come by them; And that he would intreate that she might recouer her saide euidences againe, the losse of [fol. 56 *a*] which [would] import her vtter | vndoing. "Good woman," sayth he, "content thy selfe, and take patience a litle while, for the king is so good and gratious to me, that euen within this halfe howre he will disburden me of all worldly busines, and helpe thee himselfe."

More refers the importunate woman to the mercy of the King. [HALL'S CHRONICLE.]

MSS. E L R² Y C H R B.

1. *that had beene*] *Omitted in* H R. 3. *espying*] perceving B. 4. *a*] *Omitted in* R². 4–6. *What . . . Nay*] *Omitted in* B. 6. *shall*] should L. 6. *so singuler a*] such a singuler H R. 7. *I assure you*] I assure yow quoth Sir Thomas More B. 8. *on him*] *Omitted in* B. 10. *length*] lenghe L. 10. *importune*] importunate H R; *omitted in* B. 12. *holy*] wholy Y. 12. *Saint Ciprian*] *Omitted in* B. 12. *that litle*] the little R². 13. *money that was*] money was L R² B. 15. *towarde*] to H R. 19. *and declare*] *Omitted in* B. 21–22. *could not come by them*] L R² Y B (*supported by* Hall); coulde never come by them C; should not come by them E; should not come to them H R. 22. *And that*] & þat L, þat *being an alteration upon* he. 22. *that* (2)] *Omitted in* Y. 24. *would*] L R² Y C B; should E H R. 25. *sayth he*] quoth he L.

More jests on the weakness of the scaffold. [ROPER.]

When he was going vp to the scaffolde, which was so weake that it was redy to fall, he saide merily to M*aster* Lieftenant: "I praye you, M*aster* Lieftenant, see me safe vp, and for my co*m*ming downe lett me shifte for my selfe."

His speech at the scaffold, and the manner of his death. [6 July, 1535.] [ROPER.]

The*n* desired he all the people thereabout to praye for him, and to beare witnes wi*th* him that he should nowe [there] suffer death in and for the fayth of the holy Catholike Churche. Which done, he kneeled downe, and after his prayers sayde, turned to the executioner, and with a cheerefull countenance spake thus vnto him: "Plucke vp thy spirites, man, and be not afraide to doo thine office; my necke is very short; take heede therfore thou stryke not awrye, for saving of thine honestie."

So passed S*ir* Thomas More out of this world to God, vpon the verye same day in which himselfe had moste desired.

MSS. E L R^2 Y C H R B.

1. *vp*] *Interlineated in* R. 3. *I . . . Lieftenant*] *Omitted in* H R. 6. *all*] *Omitted in* L. 7. *with him*] *Omitted in* L. 7–8. *nowe there*] R^2 Y C B (*supported by most* Roper MSS.); nowe E H R; there L. 8. *and*] *Interlineated in* E. 8. *holy*] *Omitted in* R^2 H R. 9. *Catholike Churche*] Churche Catholike, *with mark for transposition*, E. 9. *kneeled*] *Corrected from* knees R^2; kneely H. 11. *thus*] this, *corrected from* thus, L. 13–14. *therfore thou*] therfore that thou Y H R. 14. *stryke*] *After an erasure in* R^2. 14. *honestie*] honestlie H. 16. *vpon*] *Omitted in* L; *interlineated in* Y. 17. *desired*] *After* desired, R^2 *has in later hand and blacker ink* July 6th 1535.

[VI]

Ye nowe perchaunce, gentle Reader, looke that I should satisfie and perfourme my promise, made* you at the beginning of this Treatise, of the incomparable woorthines of this man, and shewe some reasonable cause, as I promised, why that S*ir* Thomas More did not pursue the life contemplatiue at the Charterhouse, or els where, that he had for certaine yeres so gratiously co*mm*enced. Forsooth, this is nowe done already, if [ye] haue geuen a good and vigilant eye [and minde] to all the premisses, which yet, if they will not fully satisfie your expectation in the generalitie, but that ye expect some more and plainer particularities, we will nowe adde somewhat more for a surplusage.

More's incomparable worthiness has been proved, and the reason shown why he did not pursue the contemplative life. But more particulars shall be given.

Who is it then but this woorthy man, for whose woorthines the late noble and newe Charles the mayne, I meane Charles the fift, gaue out such a singuler and exquisite testimonie and praise? For when intelligence came to him of S*ir* Thomas Mores death, he sent for S*ir* Thomas Elliott, our englishe Ambassadour, [and saide to him:

How Charles the Emperor talked with Sir Thomas Elyot of More's death, and paid tribute to his wisdom. [ROPER.]

"My lorde Ambassadour], We vnderstande* that the king, your master, hath put his faithfull seruaunt and graue, wise Counsail*our*, S*ir* Thomas More, to death."

MSS. E L R² Y C H R B.

1. *Ye*] You L B; Yea H. 1. *Ye . . . looke*] Now perchaunce gentle readers you looke R²; Ye now looke perchaunce gentle reader C. 2. *satisfie and*] *Omitted in* B. 2. *made you*] L R² Y C B; made vnto you E H R. 8. *this . . . done*] this is done now L R² B; that is now done H. 8. [*ye*]] we E L R² Y C H R B. 9. *good and*] *Omitted in* B. 9. *and minde*] L R² Y C H R B; *omitted in* E. 10. *premisses*] premisss H. 10. *yet*] *Omitted in* H R. 11. *but that*] but yf R². 11. *ye*] you L R² B; we H. 12. *we . . . adde*] well wee will now adde L Y; we will add H. 14. *Who*] Who Who R. 15. *the* (2)] Le, *corrected from* the, R². 15. *mayne*] Maigne L. 16. *Charles*] *Omitted in* Y. 16. *out*] *Omitted in* Y. 16–17. *and exquisite*] *Omitted in* B. 17. *testimonie and*] *Interlineated in* L. 18. *him of*] *Omitted* in Y. 19–22. *Ambassadour and saide to him: My lorde Ambassadour, We vnderstande that the*] embassadour and saide to him My lorde Embassadour we vnderstand þat þe C (*supported by* Roper); Ambassadour We vnderstande said he that the E R² Y H R B; L *as* E R² Y H R B, *but* sayth *for* saide.

Wherevnto S*ir* Thomas Eliot aunswered that he heard nothing thereof.

"Well," saide the Emperour, "it is too true. And this will we say, that if we had beene master of such a seruaunt, of whose doinges our selfe haue had these manye yeres no small experience, we would rather haue lost the best Citie of our dominions then haue lost suche a worthy Counsailour."

More is adjudged the most learned of laymen, and the most valiant against the enemies of the realm.

Who is it nowe but this woorthy man, that was so exquisitely learned as neuer anye laye man | before [fol. 56 *b*] sithen Englande was Englande? Who is it but this woorthy man, that, of all laie men that euer were in this Realme, hath with his noble, learned bookes, and shall, by Gods grace, doo so muche good as neuer hitherto did any laye man in Englande before? I intende to blemishe and impaire no mans woorthy credite, nor other mens beneficiall actes to the co*m*mon wealth; I knowe full well that comparisons be odious; but yet I trust I may, without any minishing of any mans well deserued praise, saye that albeit there haue beene many noble and valiant subiectes of this Realme and renowned captaines for their chiualrie, yet they dragge all behinde this [our] woorthie captaine. But if ye will nowe meruaile [at] this, and thinke that I doo immoderatelye exceede and passe my boundes, for that it is not knowen that euer he was in any [warlike] expedition, and that, if it were

MSS. E L R^2 Y C H R B.

2. *heard*] had Y. 3. *it*] *Corrected from* is R^2; yet Y. 4. *that*] *Omitted in* C. (Roper *supports* that). 5. *selfe*] selues Y B. 5. *had*] *Omitted in* Y. 6. *manye*] may R^2. 7. *of*] *Corrected from* if R^2. 8. *Counsailour*] Chauncellour H. 9. *woorthy man*] *Before* man, E *has* Counsailour *crossed through.* 10. *exquisitely*] excellently L. 10–11. *before . . . Englande* (2)] *Follows in* H R *after* woorthy man *above* (*cf.* l. 9), *and omitted here after* laye man, *l.* 10. 13. *noble*] *Omitted in* B. 16. *impaire*] *Corrected from* repayre R^2. 16. *other*] any other H R. 17. *I knowe*] And I knowe C. 17. *full*] *Omitted in* C H R. 18. *be*] are H R. 19. *without any minishing*] without diminishinge R^2. 20–21. *noble and valiant*] valiant and noble H R. 22. *this our*] L R^2 Y C B; this E H R. 23. *But . . . meruaile*] If yow marvell B. 23. *ye*] you L R^2 H B. 23. *nowe*] not H. 23. *at*] L R^2 Y C B; of E H R. 24–25. *and passe*] *Omitted in* B. 25. *for that it is*] for as that is Y; forasmuche as yt is C. 25. *knowen*] *Interlineated in* Y. 26. *warlike*] C; worldly E L R^2 Y H R B. (*See* Notes.) 26. *and that*] & if that H.

so, that such notable and singuler exploites and feates as are pretended, it is most certaine, ye will say, he neuer did, yet must I not for all this geue ouer my censure; Sithen it is very true that there was neuer man in Inglande that so couragiously and manlye hath discomfited and triumphed vpon the most greeuous enemies that euer this Realme had. Which my saying cannot seeme to tende eyther to any vntruth or to the defacing of any noble captaines doinges, if we graunt, as we must of fine force graunt it, That the soule is incomparably aboue the price and estimation of the body, and that to debell many soule enemyes is a greater and more glorious conquest then to debell many corporall enemyes; And if we graunt, as we must, that it is a greater benefite to preserue and recouer many soules that eyther were perished [and] brought already in slauerie, or lyke wretchedly to haue perished and to haue beene brought into the deuils thraldome, then to preserue [m]any mens bodies from perill, daunger and captiuitie, or to recouer them from the same. This, if we confesse, and withall that there be no greater enemies in the world to a common wealth then wretched and desperate heretikes (as we must confesse it by the maine force of truth) then I trust no man can denye but that of a laie man S*ir* Thomas More was the moste notable and valiant captaine against these pestilent and poisoned heretikes (and most royally in his noble bookes conquered them)

The enemies of the realm that More conquered were the heretics.

MSS. E L R² Y C H R B.

1. *that . . . singuler*] that such singular & notable L; that noteable H; that notable & singuler R. 2. *ye*] you L R² B. 3. *yet . . . geue*] yet for all this must I not giue H R. 4. *true*] time H R. 5–6. *discomfited and*] *Omitted in* B. 8. *eyther*] *Omitted in* R². 8. *vntruth or*] vntruth as concerninge my selfe or R². 9. *graunt*] graunte it L R² B. 9–10. *as we . . . it*] *Omitted in* L R² B. 10. *fine*] *Omitted in* H R. 12. *soule*] *Corrected from* soules, L; soules R². 14. *as we*] that wee L; as we R², *with* as *interlineated over* yt *crossed through.* 14. *greater*] greate L. 16. *and*] L R² C H R B Y (*being interlineated in* Y); or E. 16–17. *brought . . . perished*] brought alreadie in laverie and wretchedly to haue perished *interlineated in* Y. 16. *in*] *Interlineated in* L. 17. *beene*] *Interlineated in* L. 18. *to preserue*] preserue H. 18. *many*] R² B; any E L Y C H R. (*Cf. l.* 15, many.) 19. *bodies*] body is R². 26. *these*] this Y.

that euer hitherto Inglande bredd, and that the doinges of the notable and woorthy captaines in martiall exploites must yeelde and geue place to his woorthines.

Praise of More's wit.

Who is it then but this woorthy man, of whom Inglande hath had for vertue, learning and integritie of life suche a Counsailour, such a Lorde Chauncell*our*, as of a laie man it had neuer before? Who was it of whose witt John Collett, deane of Powles, a man of very sharpe, deepe iudgement, was wont to his familier frendes to say that all Inglande had but one wit, but of this woorthie | S*ir* Thomas Mores witt? Who was it nowe farther but this woorthy man, that had suche a witt as Inglande neuer had, nor neuer shall haue? Which thinges not onely his bookes and the testimonie of many learned and deepe wise men seeme to confirme, but it is also expresly and plainely so written by the great excellent Clerke, Erasmus Roterodamus, of fine and excellent wittes a meete and conuenient Judge, as one that of all other, I suppose, of our time, after this our woorthy man, had himselfe a most singuler * pregnant witt. The saide Erasmus wordes in latine are these: "*Cuius pectus erat omni niue candidius; ingenium quale Anglia nec habuit vnquam, nec habitura est; alioqui nequaquam infaelicium ingeniorum parens.*"

[Erasmus, to Ulrich von Hutten.]

[fol. 57

[Erasmus' *Ecclesiastes*]

MSS. E L R² Y C H R B.

4. *it*] *Interlineated in* R²; *omitted in* Y C H R. 5. *hath*] *Interlineated in* L. 5. *integritie*] interretie Y; intregritie H. 8. *witt John Collett*] wytt þe greate learned virtuous man John Collett C. 8. *of very*] of a verrie C H R. 9. *wont to his*] wounte in his familiar talke with his C. 9. *to his familier frendes*] *Omitted in* B. 10–11. *but . . . witt*] *Omitted in* B. 11–12. *nowe farther*] *Omitted in* B. 13. *shall haue*] is like to haue R². 15. *and . . . men*] *Omitted in* B. 17–21. *Roterodamus . . . witt*] *Omitted in* L. 17. *In the margin of* C *is written:* In libro de concionatore. *The same gloss* (*cropped*) *occurs alongside the Latin quotation in* L. (*See* Notes.) 17. *Roterodamus*] Rotterdamus H. 18. *meete and*] *Omitted in* B. 20. *woorthy*] *Omitted in* B. 20. *singuler pregnant*] R² Y C B; singuler and pregnant E L H R. 21. *The saide . . . these*] his wordes are these L; The sayd Erasmus his wordes are these R² B. (*See* Notes.) 22. *candidius*] candidus Y. 22–23. *quale Anglia nec*] quale nec Anglia L. 23. *vnquam . . . alioqui*] vnquam est, alioqum H R. 23. *habitura*] habiturus B. 23. *alioqui*] aliquis B. 24. *nequaquam*] nequanquam Y. 24. *infaelicium*] in felicium Y H R.

Ye will perchaunce nowe somewhat incline and bende (as there is good cause) to my iudgement. But yet if all this will not serue for a sufficient proufe of my censure and asseueration of his peerelesse woorthines, we shall adde yet one other thing, but one suche as shall counteruaile not onely any one thing which we haue spoken of his woorthines, but rather counterpaise, yea, and ouerweigh all that euer we haue spoken thereof. And that is, that he was the first of any whatsoeuer laye man in Inglande that dyed a martyr for the defence and preseruation of the vnitie of the Catholike Churche. And that is his speciall peerelesse prerogatiue.

More the first layman in England that died for the unity of the Holy Catholic Church.

And here, I praye thee, good Reader, let vs, being englishe men, consider this inestimable benefite of God effused and powred vpon vs and this Realme, not slightly and [houerly], but attentiuely and deepely, as the greatnes and woorthines thereof doth require of vs. And let vs not be retchlesse, vnmindfull and vnthankfull persons to God. What countrey then was it of all the Prouinces of the Romane Empire that first publiquely and openlye, with their people and their king, receaued and imbraced the christian fayth? Was it not the people of this our Britaine with our blessed king Lucius? And by whom was he christned but by Damianus and Fugatius, sent from Pope Eleutherius purposely, at the sute of the saide Lucius, to christen him and his people?

Harpsfield surveys the history of the Church in England.

Under Lucius, Britain received the Christian faith.

Well, what countrey was it that first forsooke the

MSS. E L R^2 Y C H R B.

1. *Ye*] You L R^2 B. 1. *nowe*] *Omitted in* H. 1. *somewhat*] *Omitted in* B. 2. *if*] if that H. 3. *for a*] of a Y. 4. *we*] you L R^2 B. 5. *adde yet*] yet adde Y. 5. *other thing, but one*] *Omitted in* Y. 5. *suche*] *On erasure in* R^2. 6–7. *not . . . counterpaise*] *Omitted in* B. 10. *defence and*] *Omitted in* H. 11. *of the* (1) . . . *Churche*] of þe Catho vnytie of the Church R^2. 13. *here*] *Omitted in* R^2. 15. *effused*] infused H R. 15. *vpon*] *Omitted in* B. 16. [*houerly*]] houertly E Y C H R; ouertly L R^2; covertlie B. (*See note to p.* 150, *l.*18.) 19. *then was it*] was it then H R. 20. *of the*] in þe L. 21. *people and their*] *Omitted in* H R. 23. *this our*] *Omitted in* B. 23. *Britaine*] Britany R^2; Brytannie B. 23. *with*] *Corrected from* which C. 23. *blessed*] blissid R. 25. *Fugatius*] Eugatius Y. 26. *Lucius*] Lucus Y; king Lucius B. 27. *Well*] *Omitted in* B. 27. *it*] *Omitted in* H R.

There were some who would not tolerate the schism under Henry VIII.

vnitie and fayth of that Sea, and tooke the episcopall myter and the ecclesiasticall supremacie from St Peters owne head, and put it vpon the head of king Henry the eight? Was it | not the people of Inglande? When [fol. 57 b] this fowle Acte was so passed, and that by authoritie of a pretensed Parliament, God of his tender mercy did not so geue vs ouer, but signified his dislyking and high displeasure for this outragiousnes by his meete and apte legates and ambassadours, not of one onely sort, but of all degrees of the Clergie, to adde the greater weight to this ambassade. And loe, those Ambassadours were the Carthusians and the others we spake of. The Carthusians, I say, men [of so singular integritie and vertue, men] of so harde and so penitentiall and of so spirituall and so contemplatiue life, that they might seeme rather angells appering in mens bodies then very men. These persons, though they were all learned, especially the saide M*aster* Reynoldes, who was a profounde, a deepe and exquisite diuine, yet in case there should enter into any man a fonde and foolishe imagination of defect of learning in them, or that they were persons of too base and lowe degree for suche an ambassade, loe, God prouided for all such imaginatiue defect, and sent with them suche a collegue and Bisshopp as a man may doubt whether all Europe had for all respectes any one [other] Bisshopp to matche him; I meane the blessed John

The Carthusians and Reynolds and Hall died for the unity of the Catholic faith.

MSS. E L R^2 Y C H R B.

1. *vnitie and*] vnitie of L R^2 B. 2. *St*] *Omitted in* L. 4. *When*] *Corrected from* was L. 5. *this*] the H R. 5. *authoritie*] the authoritye H. 7. *vs*] *Omitted in* L R^2 B. 8. *outragiousnes*] *Upon an erasure in* H. 11. *this ambassade*] his Ambassage R^2; his Ambassie H. 11. *those*] these L B. 11–12. *the Carthusians*] Carthusians B. 12. *the others*] other L Y. 12. *spake*] speake C; spoke H R. 13–14. *of so singular integritie and vertue, men*] L R^2 C H R B; Y *as* L R^2 C H R B, *but* no *by error for* so; *omitted in* E. 14. *and so penitentiall and of so*] so penytentiall so B. 14–15. *of so* (2) . . . *contemplatiue*] of spirituall contemplative H R. 17–18. *the saide*] *Omitted in* H R. 19. *in case there*] in this case least there B. 20–21. *of learning*] in learnyng B. 22–23. *prouided*] *prouideth* L; prouided *corrected from* prouidet R^2. 24. *collegue*] Colledge R^2 Y C. 24. *Bisshopp*] busshope Y. 25. *Europe*] Erope R. 25. *any one other*] L R^2 Y C H R B; any one E. 26. *him*] *Omitted in* Y.

Fisher, [the good] Bisshopp of Rochester, whose singuler vertue all Inglande well knewe, and whose singuler deepe knowledge in diuinitie all the worlde knewe, as well the Protestant*es* (who neuer durst aunswere to any of his bookes made eyther against the Lutherans or against the Zuinglians) as the king himselfe best of all other, As the person that had before openly confessed that the saide Bisshopp was one of the best diuines in all Christendome.

For the unity of the faith died also Bishop Fisher.

And nowe because this vnitie is to be beleeued and confessed, not of the Clergie onely, but of all the laitie beside, And least, if perchaunce any fonde and peeuishe conceite shall creepe into the head of some light braine that the saide persons might seeme eyther partiall in the matter, as being all of the Clergie, or that they might, if not for lacke of learning, yet by some simplicitie of witt, be in this matter craftily deceaued and circumuented, Beholde the notable supplement made by God of this our woorthy laye man also; suche a one that [fol. 58 *a*] neyther | Inglande, as I haue saide, nor, as I suppose, all Christendome, had the lyke; Euen suche as I haue shewed you alredie, suche that was as meete to be ambassadour for the laitie as was the good Bisshopp of Rochester for the Clergie; suche, I saye, for learning, that there was thereto nothing apperteyning that he [could] not reache too; suche for the excellencie and pregnancie of witt that no craftie, subtill dealing could

These were Clergy. More died as witness for the faith of the Laity.

MSS. E L R² Y C H R B.

1. *Fisher, the good Bisshopp*] R² Y C H R B; Fisher Bisshopp E L. 2–3. *singuler deepe*] singular L; depe H R. 5. *against*] *Omitted in* B. 6. *Zuinglians*] Zwinglians L H R. 6. *In margin of* C *is written* verba regis. 7. *before openly*] openly before H R. 10. *this*] the L R² B. 10–11. *beleeued and confessed*] confessed and beleeved B. 12. *least*] last Y. 14. *saide*] foresaide B. 19. *a one*] an one H R B. 20. *as . . . saide*] *Omitted in* B. 21. *as*] *Interlineated in* R². 21–22. *as . . . suche*] *Omitted in* B. 22. *that*] as R²; that, *corrected from* as, B. 22. *to be*] for to be Y C. 25. *that . . . apperteyning*] that there was nothinge theire to appertayninge Y C; that thereto was nothinge therevnto appertaineing H; R *as* H, *with* to *of* thereto *interlineated.* 26. *could*] coulde C H R B; would E L R² Y. 26. *not*] *Omitted in* H R. 26. *reache*] wreathe Y. 27. *craftie, subtill*] craftie & subtil L R².

intrapp and snare him vnwares, but that he could soone espie and foresee the daunger; such for his vertue besides and deuotion towarde God, and of such integritie of life and in all his doinges, that God would not lightlye of his great mercie suffer him, in so great a point as this, to be deceaued and miscaried out of the right Catholike fayth.

England was the first country to forsake the unity of the Catholic Church and to give the Pope's Supremacy to a temporal king.

So then, as we were the first people that receaued the faith and the popes Supremacie with common and publike agrement, so we were the first that with common consent and publike lawe forsooke the vnitie of the Catholike Churche, and gaue the Popes spirituall supremacie to a temporall king. For albeit the Grecians longe agoe abandoned the Sea of Rome, and of late the Germaines, yet were they neuer so badd or madd as to attribute the saide supremacie to any laye Prince, whiche both the Caluinistes and the Lutherans impugne.

But in England men first died for this unity.

More was the first layman to die for the cause. Later followed Master German Gardiner.

So God prouided that euen in this Realme also should be those that should first of all people in the world confirme and seale the vnitie of the saide Churche with their innocent bloud. Among whom of all laye men (for afterwarde manye other as well of the Clergie as the laitie, especially one excellent learned man, Master Germaine Gardiner, Secretary to my Lorde Gardiner, Bisshopp of Winchester, and should haue beene also for his grauitie, wisedome and learning Secretary to the king himselfe after the Lorde Writhesley, dyed for the sayde vnitie) the very first was our woorthy Sir Thomas

MSS. E L R^2 Y C H R B.

1. *and*] or H R; *omitted in* B. 1. *snare*] *Omitted in* B. 1. *vnwares*] vnawares L R^2 H. 2. *espie and foresee*] foresee and espye R^2. 2. *foresee*] see H. 2. *besides*] *Omitted in* B. 4. *and*] *Omitted in* H R. 4. *in all his*] *Omitted in* B. 8. *as*] *Corrected from* & L. 11. *vnitie of the*] *Omitted in* H. 12. *Catholike*] holy Catho R^2. 12. *spirituall*] *Interlineated in* L. 14–15. *Germaines*] Germaes Y. 15. *or*] nor R^2. 17. *whiche*] *On an erasure in* R^2. 17. *the* (2)] *Omitted in* L R^2 H R B. 19–20. *confirme*] to confirme Y C B. 22. *as well*] both B. 22. *as the*] as of the L R^2; & of the B. 23. *excellent*] *Interlineated in* R. 24. *Germaine*] German L; Germane R^2 B. 24. *Secretary . . . Gardiner*] *Interlineated in* R. 24. *to my*] to the H. 25. *Bisshopp*] busshoppe Y. 25–27. *and should . . . Writhesley*] *Omitted in* B. 27. *Writhesley*] Writheosley H R.

More. Which notable part to playe, and to be therein his messenger for the laitie, it seemeth that God did purposely choose and reserue him, though for the time he were propense and inclined to some lyking towarde a solitarye and religious life.

It seems that God reserved More for this glorious death as our first lay martyr.

[fol. 58 *b*] This man is therefore our blessed | Protomartyr of all the laitie for the preseruation of the vnitie of Christes Churche, As he was before a blessed and true confessour, in suffering imprisonment and the losse of all his goodes and yerely revennewes, for withstanding the kinges newe mariage; for the which matter, if he had suffred death, he had dyed, no doubt, an holy martyr. But yet, because the Protestant*es* thinke it great folye for him that he stoode in the matter, and that scripture could not beare him therein, and many of the Catholikes doubt, for lacke of knowledge of the whole matter, and being somewhat abused with englishe bookes made for the defence of the newe mariage, haue not so good and woorthye estimation of his doinges therein as they haue for his doinges touching the Popes supremacie, wherein they are ryper and more fullye instructed, I thought to haue made in this Treatise some speciall discourse for the iustification of S*ir* Thomas Mores doinges concerning the saide mariage. But forasmuch as this Treatise of it selfe waxeth longe ynough, I will spare and forbeare that discourse here, and adde it afterwarde in a speciall and peculier Treatise all alone by it selfe.

More was imprisoned for conscience, sake with regard to the divorce.

But his right judgment on this matter is not generally understood.

So Harpsfield promises his *Treatise on the Divorce.*

MSS. ELR²YCHRB.

1. *to playe*] to play R, *with* to *interlineated.* 2. *his*] *Omitted in* H. 3–4. *time . . . propense*] time he was propense L R²; time propence H. 4. *were*] was B. 4. *propense and*] *Omitted in* B. 6. *is therefore*] therfore is Y. 6. *blessed*] *Omitted in* R²; *interlineated in* L. 7. *Christes*] Christ his B. 9. *losse*] loose Y. 12. *dyed, no doubt*] no doubte dyed C. 12. *an*] a L. 13. *because*] *Interlineated in* R. 14. *the*] *Corrected from* that Y. 14. *that* (2)] the B. 16. *doubt*] doubted R². 17–18. *for the defence*] for defence L R². 19–21. *doinges . . . instructed*] doinges touchinge the kinges Supremacy which he doth wholy impugne attributinge þe Supremacy in matter ecclesiasticall as of duty right and equity yt doth belonge wholy vnto St Peeters successor Pope of Roome wherein alsoe they are riper & more fully instructed R². 21. *ryper . . . instructed*] more riper and fullye instructed H R. 25. *ynough*] enouge Y. 25. *spare and*] *Omitted in* B 26. *here*] herafter B.

Martyrdom to preserve the unity of the Catholic Church is as glorious as martyrdom for the sake of Christianity.

As Dionysius, Bishop of Alexandria, writes.

To returne therefore againe to S*ir* Thomas Mores death, lett no man be so wicked to thinke this to be no martyrdome in him, or so vnwise to make it more base then the martyrdome of those that suffred because they would not denye and refuse the holye fayth of Christe. For this kinde of martyrdome seemeth to be of no lesse value, but rather of more, then the other, As the noble learned Bisshopp and woorthy Confesso*ur* of God, Dionisius, the Bisshopp of Alexandria, wryteth: "That martyrdome," sayth he, "that a man suffreth to preserue the vnitie of the Churche, [that] it be not broken and rented, is woorthy in my iudgement no lesse co*m*mendation, but rather more, then that martyrdome that a man suffreth because he will not doo sacrifice to Idoles. For in this case a man dyeth to saue his owne soule. In the other he dyeth for the whole Churche."

Sir Thomas More's martyrdom compared with that of St. Thomas of Dover and St. Thomas of Canterbury.

He is therefore a blessed and happie martyr, and, craving leaue of the blessed martyrs St Thomas of Douer and St Thomas of Caunterbury, and speaking it without diminution or derogation of their glori|ous [fol. 59 *a*] death, a martyr in a cause that neerer toucheth religion and the whole fayth then doth the death of the other twaine.

St. Thomas of Dover died to prevent spoliation of his monastery.

The first was slaine of the french me*n* landing at Douer, in his monasterie, all his felowes being fledd, which thing he could not be persuaded to doo. The cause was by reason he would not disclose to the*m*

MSS. E L R^2 Y C H R B.

1. *therefore*] *Omitted in* L R^2 B. 1. *Mores*] Moore his Y. 3. *to*] as to L. 4. *those*] theise Y C. 5. *not*] *Omitted in* R^2. 5. *and refuse*] *Omitted in* B. 5. *holye*] *Omitted in* H. 6. *In the margin of* R^2 C *is written* Euseb: eccliast: hist: lib: 6: ca: 37; *this gloss is inserted in the text of* B *after* writeth *below.* (*Cf. l.* 9.) 7. *of*] *Omitted in* L. 7. *the* (1)] they H. 8. *woorthy*] *Omitted in* L R^2 B. 9. *the*] *Omitted in* R^2. 11. *that it*] H R; if it E L R^2 Y C B. (H R *are inferior* MSS., *but seem here to have the correct reading.*) 12. *no lesse*] of noe lesse H R. 15. *case*] *Omitted in* L R^2 B. 16. *In the other*] In the tother Y. 20. *diminution*] dimminacion H. 20. *or*] *Corrected from* of L. 20. *glorious*] *The* -ous *of* glorious *is on an erasure in* R^2. 21. *death*] deathes R^2. 21. *in a . . . neerer*] that in a Cause it neuer H; Y *as* E L R^2 B, *but* ner *for* neerer; C *and* R *as* E L R^2 B, *but* never *for* neerer. 22. *doth*] *Omitted in* L R^2. 22. *of the other*] of any of the other L R^2 B.

where the iewels and treasure of the monasterye was; for whom after his death God shewed many miracles.

Even King Henry II recognised St. Thomas of Canterbury as a martyr; though of late England has burned his holy bones and proclaimed him traitor.

The seconde is, and was euer, taken of the Churche for a woorthy martyr, and euen of king Henry the seconde also, for whose displeasure (though perchaunce not by his co*m*maundement) he was slaine; Albeit we haue of late (God illuminate our beetle blinde heartes to see and repent our folye and impietie) vnshryned him, and burned his holye bones; and not onely vnshryned and vnsancted him, but haue made him also, after so manye hundred yeres, a traito*ur* to the king that honoured him, as we haue saide, as a blessed martyr, As did also his children and all other kinges that afterwarde succeeded him; Even as they haue taken vp and burned the bones of blessed St Augustine, our Apostle, who brought the fayth of Jesus Christe first into this Realme.

Even as England has burned the bones of St. Augustine.

St. Thomas of Canterbury died because he would not consent to any abridgement of the Pope's authority; More died for the Pope's Supremacy itself.

Yet, as I* saide, there is great oddes in the cause of their martyrdome. For though the king, for displeasure he bare to the Pope for mainteyning and defending St Thomas, did for a litle while abrogate the Popes authoritie, and [went] about before to cutt off and abridge some appeales wont to be made to the Sea of Rome (wherein and for other thinges St Thomas refused to condiscende and agree to his proceedinges) yet neyther did the king take vpon him the supremacie, nor did not in heart, but onely for displeasure, mislyke the Popes supremacie, and shortly restored the Pope

MSS. E L R^2 Y C H R B.

1. *where*] *Corrected from* were L. 1. *was*] laye B. 3. *and was euer*] & euer was H R. 5. *also*] *Omitted in* B. 5. *perchaunce*] *Interlineated in* R. 7. *beetle*] *Omitted in* B. 8. *vnshryned*] vnshreved B. 9–10. *not onely . . . but*] *Omitted in* B. 10. *vnshryned*] vnshryved C. 11. *also*] *Omitted in* R^2. 12. *that*] who L R^2 B. 12. *as . . . saide*] *Omitted in* B. 12. *haue*] *Omitted in* L. 12. *blessed*] *Omitted in* B. 14. *afterwarde*] after H R. 15. *bones*] bookes Y. 18. *as I saide*] L R^2 Y C; as I haue saide E H R; *omitted in* B. 21. *St*] Sir Y. 22. *went*] C; were E R^2 Y H R; was L B. (*Cf. p.* 111, *l.* 3, went about). 23. *and abridge*] *Omitted in* R^2; & abrogate B. 24. *St*] Sir Y. 25. *condiscende*] discend B. 25. *his*] the Y. 27. *nor*] not C. 28. *Popes*] *Interlineated over* kinges *crossed through* L. 28. *shortly*] shortlie after B.

to his former authoritie, and reuoked all his other misdoinges. There is therfore in S*ir* Thomas More a deeper cause of martyrdome then in the other twaine. Howbeit, as St Thomas of Caunterbury and he were of one and the selfesame christen name, and as there was great conformitie in their birthplace at London, and that they both were Chauncellours of the Realme; and in that St Thomas of Caunterburye, | when his [fol. 59 b] troubles beganne, co*m*ming to the king, caried his Crosse himselfe, not suffering his Chappleine or any of the Bisshopps that offred themselues to carye it; And in that S*ir* Thomas More, when his great troubles first grewe on him, caried the crosse in procession himselfe at Chelsey, the Clarke being out of the waye; and that both euer after caryed, though not the materiall Crosse, yet the very true crosse of Christe, by tribulation, to the time, and of all at the time, of their glorious passion; and that there was a conformitie in that S*ir* Thomas More dyed according to his desire on the eve of St Thomas of Caunterbury; so was there great conformitie in the cause of their martyrdome. But some diuersitie otherwise, as well in that we haue shewed, as that St Thomas of Caunterburye, defending the dignitie and priuiledge of the Churche, suffred without any condemnation or iudgement, in his owne cathedrall Churche, his holy consecrate head being there clouen in peeces. S*ir* Thomas More was condemned in Westminster hall, where he and his father before him ministred iustice moste vprightly to all maner of suters, And where a fewe yeres before there was suche a praise, euen

In the cases of St. Thomas of Canterbury and Sir Thomas More, there is some likeness.

But some diversity also: for St. Thomas of Canterbury was murdered at the altar; More was condemned deliberately at Westminster.

MSS. E L R^2 Y C H R B.

1. *reuoked*] revoke H R. 1. *other*] *Omitted in* L. 4–5. *were of one*] were one H. 6. *their*] the Y C. 7. *both were*] were bothe Y. 11. *themselues*] them selfe Y C; *omitted in* B. 16. *yet . . . crosse*] *Interlineated in* R. 16. *very*] *Omitted in* B. 17. *of all*] *Omitted in* B. 17. *glorious*] golrious H. 18. *a*] *Omitted in* L R^2. 19. *on*] in L R^2 B. 22. *otherwise*] other waies H. 23. *St*] Sir Y. 26. *consecrate*] consecrated L R^2 B. 27. *More*] *Omitted in* L. 27. *was*] beinge H. 28. *him*] *Omitted in* B. 29. *iustice*] *Omitted after* ministred *in* H, *but inserted after* suters *below.* (*Cf. l.* 29.) 29. *moste*] *Interlineated in* R; *omitted in* B. 29. *vprightly*] *Omitted in* B.

by the kinges co*m*maundement (as we haue shewed) geuen him, as lightly hath not beene geuen before to any other.

More's head was set upon London Bridge among the heads of traitors.

He was executed at the towre, and his head (for defending the right head of the Churche) by the kinges co*m*maundement (who renting the vnitie of the Churche, and taking away St Peters prerogatiue and of his Successours, had, as I may say, cutt off St Peters head, and put it, an vggly sight to beholde, vpon his owne shoulders) pitifullye cutt off; And the saide head sett vpon London bridge, in the saide Citie where he was borne and brought vp, vpon an high pole, among the heades of traitours: A rufull and a pitifull spectacle for all good Citizens and other good christians, and muche more lamentable to see their christian english* Ciceroes head in such sort, then it was to the Romanes to see the head of Marcus Tullius Cicero sett vp in the [same] Citie and place where he had, by his great eloquent orations, preserued many an innocent from [fol. 60 *a*] imminent daunger and | perill, and had preserued the whole Citie, by his great industrie, from the mischieuous conspiracie of Cateline and his seditious complices.

A more pitiful sight to the citizens of London than the head of Cicero to the Romans.

But yet S*ir* Thomas Mores head had not so high a place vpon the pole as had his blessed soule among the celestiall holy martyrs in heauen. By whose hartie and deuout intercessio*n* and his foresaide co*m*martyrs, and of our Protomartyr St Albon, and other blessed

More and his fellow saints intercede for us in Heaven; and. England, under

MSS. E L R² Y C H R B.

1. *kinges*] king his B. 1. *as . . . shewed*] *Omitted in* B. 2. *lightly*] likelie B. 2. *not . . . before*] not before bene geuen R². 2. *before*] *Interlineated in* R. 5. *the* (1)] of the Y H. 7. *and* (2)] *Interlineated in* B. 8. *as*] *Omitted in* C. 9. *and put it*] *Omitted after* head *here in* R², *but inserted after* beholde *below* (*Cf. l.* 9). 9. *it*] in B. 10. *the saide head*] *Omitted in* B. 11. *in . . . Citie*] *Omitted in* B. 13. *rufull*] ruthfull B. 13. *and a*] & L R² Y B. 14. *for*] to L. 14. *other*] *Omitted in* B. 15. *their*] there our L R² B. 15. *english*] L R² Y C H R B; englishes E. 17. *the* (2)] that B. 18. *same*] C; saide E L R² Y H R; *omitted in* B. 18. *and place*] *Omitted in* B. 19–21. *orations . . . mischieuous*] orations preserved the whole citie & many an innocent from the mischevous B. 20–21. *the whole*] all the whole Y. 22. *Cateline*] Calline Y. 22. *seditious*] *Omitted in* L. 26. *intercession*] Intercessions R². 26. *and* (2)] as L R² B. 27. *Protomartyr*] Protomartirs H R B. 27. *other*] all other H R.

Queen Mary and Cardinal Pole, has returned to the unity of the Catholic faith.

In the which may God long preserve the Realm.

martyrs and Saintes of the Realme, I doubt not but God of late hath the sooner cast his pitifull eye to reduce vs againe by his blessed minister and Queene, Lady Mary, and by the noble, vertuous, excellent Prelate, Cardinall Poole, to the vnitie of the Churche that we had before abandoned. In the which God of his great mercie longe preserue the Realme.

Amen.

MSS. E L R² Y C H R B.

4. *excellent*] and excellent H R B. 6. *his*] *Omitted in* L.

APPENDIX I

THE *RASTELL FRAGMENTS*,

BEING

"CERTEN BREEF NOTES APPERTEYNING TO

BUSHOPE FISHER,

COLLECTED OUT OF SIR THOMAS MOORES LYFE,

WRITT BY

MASTER JUSTICE RESTALL."

NOTE

The *Rastell Fragments* in MS. Arundel 152 were published in *Analecta Bollandiana*, Tom. XII, pp. 248–270, by Franciscus Van Ortroy, an exceedingly careful editor, to whom all students of Fisher are greatly indebted. MS. Arundel 152 is badly damaged by fire at the edges, and often the material binding these damaged edges makes it difficult, or impossible, to read letters still actually existing. It should be noted that in Extracts A and B and the latter part of C, Van Ortroy supplies the missing words or portions of words directly from the transcript of these passages made by the Cambridge antiquarian, Thomas Baker, in MS. Harleian 7047. Now Baker's transcript is modernised to the spelling of his own age (1656–1740), so that it is out of keeping with Rastell's older style. In this edition the passages, words, or letters given within square brackets are based on Baker's transcript of these Extracts, but given in a spelling as near as possible to that of the *Rastell Fragments*. It should also be noted that in the earlier part of Extract C (see below, pp. 231–236, l. 7), which Baker has not transcribed, Van Ortroy rarely attempts to supply the missing portions, so that there his text makes irritatingly little sense. A readable text can generally be made by conjectures having regard to the context and the space available. By the aid of a good lens more of the text can be made out than was read by Van Ortroy, but it is unfortunately at its worst exactly where Baker does not help us, and the reconstructions must not therefore be considered here as equally authoritative.

Sometimes a reading is suggested by the so-called "Hall's" *Life of Fisher*, of which many copies exist. That of MS. Harleian 6382 has been published for the E.E.T.S. by Ronald Bayne, 1921 (Extra Series, No. cxvii).

Though the spelling of the *Rastell Fragments* is carefully preserved in this edition, it has been found better to modernise the punctuation and paragraphing, and to employ initial capitals for proper names.

Extracts A and B are in the same hand; Extract C in a different hand.

With Extract A, cf. Baker's transcript, MS. Harleian 7047, fols. 11ᵃ–13ᵃ.

Preceding Extract A, on the same leaf, are some notes concerning Fisher, which are crossed through by a single oblique line. The same notes are given in fuller form in Extract C: so the notes crossed through before Extract A are here printed for convenience in the footnotes to Extract C, pp. 248–251.

MS. Arundel 152.

[Certen breef notes apperteyning to Bushope Fisher, collected out of Sir Thomas Moores] lyfe writt by Master Justice Restall.

[Extract A], fols. 246ᵃ–247ᵇ.

[fol. 246 *a*] | The kynge, entendinge to forsake *Queen* K*atherin*, sewed to þe Pope to haue a co*m*mission to de[bate þe] validete or Inualidete of his mariage, whiche was denied; *and* then he pretendid þ*at* þe *Queen* [wolde] consent to a devorce, and enter into Religion, *and* thereapon had a co*m*mission.

Henry VIII obtains a Commission from the Pope [Clement VII] to debate the validity of his marriage with Katherine. [1528].

The [commissi]oners were Laurence Campeius, cardinal *and* legat de latere, *and* cardinal Wolsey. [The] kynge gaue Campeius þe B*ushopric* of Salisbury. (Quere if he had yt not before). The Pope, heringe þe kyn[ges] surmisis were vntrewe, reuoked þe co*m*mission, and yet þe cardinals, at þe k*ynges* ymportune [sewte], proceded in debatinge thereof.

The Pope revokes the Commission.

In lent following, viz. 1529 *and* 20. of H*enry* 8, [þe] kynge cawsed W*illiam* Wareham, the archebushop of Cant*erbury*, to send for dyuers lerned m[en of] bothe vniu*er*sites to come unto hym to Lambeth to dispute upon this matter; and þe [kynge], to seame indifferent, willed þe *Queen* to chuse certe*n* of her councel. *And* so she choise [þe sayed] archebushope; *and* Cut*hbert* Tuns*tal*, the B*ushope* of London; Nicolas Weste, B*ushope* of Eley; John [Clarke], B*ushope* of Bathe—al 4 doctors of bothe lawes. *And* wit*h*al she choise J*ohn* Fisher, B*ushope* of R[ochester]; Henry Standishe, B*ushope* of St· Asaphe; Thomas Abel; John Fetherston; Powel; *and* [Ridley]—al 6 doctors of deuiniti, men excelle*n*tly lerned *and* of great vertue. *And*, besides [these, she] had other doctors of deuiniti, *and* others profowndly lerned in þe comon *and* ciuil lawe[s].

The King summons learned men from the Universities to discuss the divorce, and commands the Queen to choose her counsel, 1529.

9–10. *Quere . . . before*] Inserted between *Salisbury* and *The Pope* in same hand, but very cramped, as if an after-thought.

Fisher's book and oration in defence of the marriage of Henry and Queen Katherine.

The B*ushope* of Rochester offered vp to þe legates a boke, whiche he had compiled in def[ense of] þe mariage, *and* made an oracion unto the*m* to take good head of manifolde incon[ueniences] howe þe made any doubte in this mariage where non is.

Henry is angered by More's first refusing the Chancellorship, and by his attitude to the divorce.

After þe death[e of cardinal] Wolsey, þe kynge, not determininge to haue any of þe spiritualty to be lord [chancellor, offer]ed it to S*i*r Thomas Moore, who refusinge it, þe kynge was angri w*ith* [hym, and caused hym to] accepte it; And labored to haue had hym perswaded on his [side in þe matter of his divorce; and] byca[use he could not be perswaded, he hated hym for it.

The packed Parliament and its three Bills against the clergy. [1529].

The | kynge summoned] a Parliament, *and* choise for [fol. 246 *b*] k*nyghtes and* burgases not onlei heretickes, but also [such]e as he and his councel were perswaded to maligne þe cl*a*rgi *and* theire welthe, *and* namely diuers of his owen councellors *and* howsholde seruant*es and* there seruant*es*; *and* so theis, by þe kinges owen drifte, made a complaint to þe kynge, *and* lykewis complayned of þe clargi *and* their abuses in þe perliame*n*t howse, *and* 3 billes were deuised against the*m* for lawes: one for diminishynge of mortuaries; 2. for rebaytinge of þe charges of probates of testame*ntes*; *and* the 3. was inhibitinge þe clergi from occupyinge of farmes, *and* byinge *and* sellinge of cattel, *and* from takinge of pluralite of benefices, *and* non residens.

Fisher withstands these Bills, and is consequently hated by Henry.

The B*ushope* of Rochester spake against thes billes, for þ*at* he sawe thei were maliciusly deuised by heretickes, *and* tended, under coler of reformacion of abuses, to þe utter ruin of þe spiritualty; *and* he affirmed þ*at* this maligninge of þe clergi was for lacke of faythe. Relacion hereof was made to þe kinge, *and* he bearinge dedly grudge againste þe bushope, appoynted one of þe lower howse to mowe þe next day to haue þe B*ushope* punisshed, and so thei complained of þe B*ushope* to þe kynge.

35–36. . . . *Bushope to þe kynge.*] Following this passage is written, in the same hand, in the same line: *See Halles cronacle.* Then follows a note crossed through: *Duringe this perliament a prest was drawen* and *hanged for coyninge money*—again in the same hand.

Henry, urged by More, Fisher and others, makes a proclamation, 1530, for the repression of Tindale's Testament and other heretical books; but later favours the heretics.

The kinge, beinge moued by Sir Thomas Moore, l*ord* chaun[c]elor, and þe B*ushop* of Rochester *and* þe rest of þe bushopes to repres the hereses *and* neue opinions þ*at* began to growe in his realme by þe fauor showed unto heretickes by An*ne* Bulein *and* her confederat[es], made a proclamacion against þe bringinge in, kepinge *and* readinge of Tynd*als* testa[ment] *and* other bokes, *and* he hym selfe in þe Star Chamber, a*nno* 1530, 22. H*enry* 8, comaund[ed] by his awe*n* mowthe þe Justices of peace of euery quarter of his realme to enquire [of] shuche persons, *and* to signify þe k*ynges* prohibicion therein. And þe kinge also promis[ed] þ*at* þe neue testam*ent* shulde shorteli after be trewli translated; but he was disswaded therein for a tyme, *and* afterward*es* faworinge þe heretickes, cawsed a false translacion to be diuulged thorowout al his dominions.

The Pope [Clement VII] rejects the certificate concerning the divorce. This More and Fisher had refused to sign.

The Pope reuo[ked] þe matter of þe mariage to þe Rot at Rome; *and* þe k*ynge* sent thether D*octor* Bonner *and* D*octor* [Kerne], seamynge as thowghe þei cam of the*m* selues onley, *and* not of þe k*ynges* sendinge, *and* thei [to] speake and treat in this matter as of there owen auctorite, *and* so they un[der] suche protestacion certified þe pope þ*at* al þe B*ushops*, clargi *and* noble men in Englan[d] were agreed to haue this diuorce. Þe Pope required a certificat hereof. Þe king labored for this certificat, *and* Sir Tho*mas* M*oore*, B*ushope* Fhisher, *and* þe Q*ueens* councel *and* ot[her] lerned deuines refused to set to there names *and* seales unto it. For whic[h] cawce þe P*ope* reiected þe certificat, whe*n* yt came to Rome.

The King's attempt to persuade Convocation to acknowledge him as Head of the Church. [1531].

The kin[g] moued þe conuocacion by his confederates to acknowledge hym to be hedd [of þe C]hurche, whiche they denied. *And* then þe k*ynges* confederates toke vppon [them to dispu]te ope*n*ly on þe k*ynges* behalfe, *and* by disputac*i*ons they were confounded; [and being but a fewe in] respecte of þe reste, thei p*er*ceuid thei labored in v[ain. Wherefor the kynge sent for diuers of þe Bushopes and þe best of þe conuocacion,

2. *chauncelor*] MS. *chaunelor*. 11. *and*] Interlineated in same hand. 13. *trewli*] Interlineated in same hand.

and exhorted them to agree to his demands, protesting and swering þat he wolde not chalenge therby any neue aucthorite or spiritual iurisdiccion, but onley the uery same þat he and his] | predecessors had alredy of his [fol. 247 *a*] regal power, *and* mynded therby to requ[ire no furder] aucthorite ouer þe spiritualti.

The k*ynges* confederates reported to þe [conuocacion] þe k*ynges* meaning *and* intent, w*ith* his protestacion *and* othe not to make any [neue] clame thereby; *and* thei affirmed þ*at* thei were not good *and* trewe subiects [to þe] k*ynge* þ*at* wolde not gyue there consent unto his demaunde, *and* credit hym in [his] protestacion *and* othe. The conuocacion seamed to be resolued w*ith* those c[rafti] p*er*suasions; but þe good B*ushope* of Rochester denied to graunt it, *and* require[d þe conuoca]cion to consider wel what inconueniencis wold ensue by this graun[t of] supremacey to þe k*ynge* thus absolutely *and* simpliciter, if þe k*ynge* chainged his [mynde] *and* wolde practise þe said supremacey ouer þe B*ushopes and* clargi of his realme.

The [kynges] confederates replied against þe Bushope howe þe k*ynge* had no shuche [meninge] *and* intent as þe B*ushope* feared, alledginge his royal protestacion *and* othe [in] þe worde of a Prince, *and* þ*at* thoughe yt were graunted absolutly [and] sympliciter, according to þe k*ynges* demaunde, yet it shulde *and* muste nedes haue imployed in yt this condicion *and* playne meninge, þ*at* he wolde haue no furder [aucthori]te by it the*n* "Quantu*m* per lege*m* Dei licet": "Whiche is," [q*uoth* thei], "þ*at* he, beinge [a] temporal Prince, cannot by gods lawe entermeddel as supreame hedd w*ith* spirit[ual] iurisdiccion, spiritual lawes, or spiritual matters, to iudge, order, alter [or] chaynge them."

Fisher insists on Convocation qualifying its assent to the King's Supremacy by the words *Quantum per legem dei licet.*

The hole con*uocacion* were by thes crafti p*er*suasions *and* other secr[et] practises *and* allurement*es* emongest the*m* fully p*er*suaded to credit þe k*ynge* herein, *and* to graunt hym his request to be supreame hed of þe churche of Eng[land] absolutly *and* sympliciter. Whiche thinge beinge perceuid by þe B*ushope* of [Rochester], and beinge angri w*ith* there so soden *and* lighte p*er*suasion, *and* w*i*th*a*l veri lothe [þat þe] graunt shuld thus passe absolutly, *and* not beinge able to stai yt otherw[ise, he] counselled þe conuocacion þat, seinge þe k*ynge* had no furder meaninge by his [requeste] the*n* "Quantu*m* per lege*m* dei licet," *and* þat he intendid not to meddel by uertue there[of] w*ith* any spiritual lawes or spiritual iurisdiccion anny further the*n* his predeces[sors] had don before hym, "If you wil neads," q*uoth* he, "graunt hym this his request, yet, for [decla]racion of yo*ur* ful *and* hole meaninge to þe k*ynge and* his successors *and* there posterity, [expresse] these condicional woords in yo*ur* graunte, 'Quantu*m* per legem Dei licet.'"

The k*ynges* con[federates v]rged stil to haue þe graunt passe absolutly *and* sympliciter, *and* to credi[te þe kynges roy]al sollemne othe *and* protestacion made unto the*m* for declaracion [of his meninge therin]. But þe conuocacion aunswered resolutly þat thei wolde [not graunte this title of su]preamacey to be accnowledged to þe k*ynge* w*ith*out t[hese condicional woords, "Quantum per legem Dei licet."

Whereof the k*ynge* by his confederates being made [fol. 247 b] secretly | priuy, and] seinge he coulde not obtayne it otherwise, for al his crafty [pract]isses, to haue it graunted unto hym absolutly, was of force content to [a]ccepte it thus condicionally. But þe k*ynge* toke *and* practised þe supreamacey afterwards absolutely, *and* caused an acte of parliame*n*t to be ennacted, wherein þe supreamacey was gyue*n* hym *and* his successors by his lay perliame*n*t, *and* annexed to þe crowen as a royal title, w*ith*out any maner of condicion, *and* þe crewel pennalty of highe treason to be executed vpon al souche of þe spiritualty *and* temporalty as shulde deny it. And his successors haue practised þe same supreamacey, etc. But al þe B*ushopes*, sauinge þe b*ushope* of Rochester, condescended to þe k*ynge* bothe in this *and* in all his scismatical doinges afterwards.

But the King obtains unqualified acknowledgment of his Supremacy from Parliament, and it is made high treason to deny it. [1534].

27 ff. *an acte of parliament,* &c.] Cf. reference to this passage below, p. 231.

36. . . . *scismatical doinges afterwards.*] Following this passage is a long note in a different hand: *Note that before this tyme, videlicett* anno *22* Henry *8, the kinge having spent a 100,000*[li]

about procuring the Instrumentes of the vniverseties for his devorce, thought to make the bushoppes and clergie to paye it, and therfore signefied that they were in a premunire for acknowledging the power legatine of cardinall Wolsey, and served an action thereof ageinst the bushoppes and *abbottes in the kinges benche. The clergie, by perswasion of the kinges counsell, granted him a 100,000*[li] *; and he theruppon perdoned them all savinge 8 persons. Hall and the heretykes affirm that the convocacion acknowledged the k*[*inge*] *to be supreme head in there supplication of submission vnto him ; but it is fa*[*lse*], *for the kinge refused to pardon them the premunire, vnlesse they wold acknowl*[*edge*] *him in there submission to be there supreme head ; so that his confederattes, and* [*they*] *that had the presenting of it, did put in that tytle in the submyssion with*[*out*] *anie knowledge of the rest of the convocacion. See cardinall Pooles boke,* [*l.*] *1, fo. 19a, where he vseth these wordes vnto the kinge : " Hunc honorem certe p*[*etere*] *non debuisses, hoc dicam petere adhibitis etiam minis non debuisses, ab invitis exprimere* [*non*] *debuisses quemadmodum me quidem presente fecisti, qui certis diplomatis, quibus maxime* [*ab*] *illis tibi concesse pecunie testimonium continebatur, subscribere recusaris, nisi illud esse*[*t*] *ascriptum, tibi eam pecuniam, vt supremo in Anglia ecclesie capiti persolutam esse."*

The book of Cardinal Pole here referred to is *Reginaldi Poli Cardinalis Britanniæ Regem, pro ecclesiasticæ unitatis defensione, libri quatuor.* Rome. 1537.

[Extract B], fols. 307^{a}–308^{a}.

[fol. 307 *a*] | The nune of Canterbury *and* her attaynder, 1533, *and* 25. of H*enry* þe 8. [The] kynge of malice *and* reuenge coulde fynde no other matter as tou[ching] þe nu*n*ne against B*ushope* Fysher but that thei had harde by repo[rte of] others certen woordes þ*at* þe nonne had spoken agaynste þe [kynges] deuorce, *and* had not reueiled them to þe kynge *and* his coun[cel]; and so thei were attented of mysprision of highe treason, [for] conceilment of thos woordes, in þe bill drawen to attaynt þe no[nne. The] k*ynge* sowghte allso to haue attaynted S*ir* Tho*mas* Moore for talkin[g with] her, *and* put in a bill into þe higher howse to attaynt him [of] misprision of highe treason. Sir Tho*mas* Moore wroghte to [Cromwel] for a copy of þe bill, but he wolde not sende it hym; *and* therefore [he] wroghte to þe k*ynge* to purge hym|selfe of it, *and* thereapon þe [kynge d]ischarged Sir Tho*mas* Moore, *and* attaynted ueri wrongefully þe [rest], by parliament makynge þ*at* an offence by acte whiche was [none] before.

In the case of the Nun of Canterbury, Fisher is attainted of misprision of high treason.

The Bill against More has to be withdrawn.

More's letters to Cromwell and the King.

The kynge caused al his bushopes, sauinge þe B*ushope* of [Rochester], to surrender al theire Bulles to hym whereby they were ma[de] bushopes, *and* they toke þe k*ynges* le*tt*res Pattent*es* to be bushopes [al] onley by hym.

All the Bishops, except Fisher, surrender their Bulls to the King and receive in exchange his Letters Patent.

The clargi of London were sworne to þe othe, *and* Sir Tho*mas* Moore, þe B*ushope* of Rochester, *and* Doctor Wi[lson], who had been þe k*ynges* confessor, refused yt, *and* were therefore ymprisoned [in þe] Tower. The B*ushope* of Rochester sayd he wolde not swere to þ*at* othe: [" But," quoth he,] " I woll applie my selfe to þe k*ynges* pleasure so far fourthe as I may w*ith* consc[ience and] lerninge "; offeringe þ*at* he wolde be content to swere unto some [parte of] þ*at* othe, so þ*at* it were qualified, either w*ith* some condicions or excepcion[s, or in some] other manner than it was there set fourthe.

Fisher, More and Dr. Wilson refuse the Oath of Succession (as unlawfully amplified, and as to them administered) and are sent to the Tower. [13th April, 1534].

Note. With Extract B, cf. Baker's transcript in MS. Harleian 7047, fols. 18^{a}–19^{a}. See above, p. 220, Note.

33. *either*] Interlineated in same hand.

But þe comissi[oners, vtterly] myslikinge *with* his condicions *and* accepcions, as repugn[ant to þe kynges] procedinges, *and* he, constantly refusinge to swere t[o þat othe, beinge so] contrari to gods worde, was sent to þe Tower, [wher he was closely] imprisoned and locked [vp in a stronge chamber from all company sauinge one of his seruantes, who, like a false knaue, accused his master to Cromwel afterwards. The (these 3) were wrongefully] | ymprisoned, bycauce þe othe contaigned [fol. 307 *b*] more thinges then were warranted by þe acte of succession. And yet þe k*ynge* kepte the*m* in prison vntil þe next cession of Parliame*n*t, and the*n* made an acte to make there wrongefull ymprisonm*ent* as rightful from the begynninge.

Six corrupt Acts of this Parliament.

Of 6 actes of parlam*ent* made against þe mynds of þe lords and comons, were compassed by sinister *and* corrupte meanes : *

The first acte auctorisinge þe k*ynge* to make B*ushopes* suffragans.

An acte certifyinge þe othe þ*at* eueri of þe k*ynges* subiectes hathe taken, *and* shal hereafter be bounde to take, for due obseruacion of þe acte made for þe swerty of þe succession of þe k*ynge* in þe crowen of England. Note þ*at* before this acte, þe othe was not warranted by þe acte of succession, but wrongefully gyuen, and those foresaid holly men wrongefully ymprisoned for refusinge it.

Thirdly, a particular acte against Sir Tho*mas* Moore, to condemne hym of mysprision, and so to forfait his lands þ*at* þe k*ynge* had gyuen hym, whiche was not paste vnt*il* a yere.

Fowrethely, an acte for þe k*ynge* to be supream[e] hed of þe churche of England, *and* to haue aucthority to reforme *and* redrese dyuers errors, heresies *and* abuses in þe same.

Fyftely, an acte wherby it was mad highe treaso[n] to

16. *were*] Cf., for omission of the relative pronoun, p. 229, l. 21, and p. 250, l. 2, below. 19. *suffragans*] MS. *and suffragans.* 24. *þe othe*] Interlineated in same hand. 36 ff. *Fyftely, an acte,* &c.] Cf. reference to this passage below, p. 231. 36. *wherby it was*] Interlineated in same hand over *to spelle or do* crossed through.

do or speke againste þe k*ynges* supreamacey and other thing[es]. Note dilligently here þat þe bill was earnestly wi*th*stode, *and* coulde not be suffered to passe, vnlese þe rigor of it were qualified wi*th* this worde " [ma]liciusly "; *and* so not eueri spekinge againste þe supreamacey [to be trea]son, but onlei maliciusly spekinge, *and* so, for more p[layne declarac]ion therof, þe word " maliciusly " was twise put into þe [acte, and yet afterwardes], in puttinge þe acte in execucion against [Bushope Fisher, Sir Thomas Moore, the Car]thusians *and* others, þe word " malici[usly," playnely expressed in þe acte, was adiudged] by þe k[ynges commissioners, before whome they were arrayned, to be voyed.]

[fol. 308 *a*] | Syxtly, an acte concerninge þe payem*ent* of first fructes of al digni[tes, benefices] *and* promocions spiritual, *and* also concerninge one annual [pension] of þe x[th] parte of al þe possessions of þe churche spiritual *and* temporal, [etc.].

Note tovchinge þe Carthusians *and* father Reynolds of Syon *and* John Ha[ll, a] seculer preste, vicar of þe pa*r*ishe of Isselworthe, were endited of [highe] treason by 12 men for denyinge *and* not sweringe to þe k*ynges* sup[reamacey], wi*th* one John Feren, a secular prest, who had his pardon for accus[inge] hymselfe *and* þe vicar, 28 Aprilis, 1535. The vicar was accused [for] speakinge wordes ageinst the kinges supremacie; *and* he confessed the*m*, *and* iudgm*ent* was gyue*n* vppon hym acco[rdingly].

The first band of Carthusians [*i.e.* the Priors of the Charter-houses of London, Bevall and Axholme], Father Reynolds of Sion, and John Hall, a secular priest, are condemned to death for denying the King's Supremacy. [Executed 4 May, 1535].

The 4 religius persons were arrayned, *and* þe Car-thusians, [by þe] mowthe of John Howghton, there Prior, confessed that they denied [the kynges] supream-acy, but not maliciusly. The Jury coulde not ag[re] to condemne thes 4 religius persons, by cawse there con-sciences per[swaded] the*m* thei did it not maliciusly. The Judges hereapon resolu[ed] the*m* that whosoeuer denyed þe supremacey, denied it maliciusly; *and* þe

The Judges rule that the word *maliciously* in the Act is void.

19 ff. *Note tovchinge þe Carthusians*, &c.] Note reference to this passage below, p. 232, ll. 13–14.. 21. *were*] Cf for omission of the relative pronoun, p. 228, l. 16, above, and p. 250, l. 2, below. 26. *speakinge* and *ageinst . . . supremacie* are interlineated in a different hand. 31. *that*] Interlineated in same hand.

Cromwell intimidates the Jury.

expressinge of þe worde " maliciusly " in þe acte was a uoyed lim[itacion] and restraint of þe construccion of þe wordes *and* intencion of þe offen[der]. The Jury for al this coulde not agre to condemne the*m*; whereapo[n] Cromwel, in a rage, went vnto þe Jury, *and* thretened the[m], if þei condemned the*m* not. *And* so, beinge ouercome by his thre[tes], thei fownde the*m* giltei, *and* had great thankes; but thei were [after]wards ashamed to showe their faces, *and* some of the*m* toke great [thought] for it.

The writer will send more information if required

If you wold haue this more playnlie *and* largely, w*ith* [þe manner] of there execucion at there deathe, send worde hereafter [into] thes partes, and you shal haue bettor instrucc[ions of them].

[Extract C], fols. 309^{a}–312^{a}.

[The LV chapiter of the third booke].

[fol. 309 *a*] | . . . . [Now shall I shew you somewhat] . . . of the afore remembred vertuous man, Doct*our* John Fysher, bishop of Roch[ester, who al þe] tyme remayned p*ri*son*er* in the Towre of London, by the space of an wholl ye[re] *and* moare; duryng w*hi*che space, many tymes before the last statute made of the [supremacie], The king sent dyu*er*se of his consell *and* of his lerned byshop*es* *and* other his lerned [laymen to the] byshope to consell and p*er*swade hyme to take the Othe, for refusing whereof he wa[s, as ye haue] hard, thus in pryson. But all they labored in vayne, for in no wise wold he co*n*[sente] to take it.

Fisher a prisoner in the Tower more than a year.

Then after the last cession of parlame*n*t, wherein, as ye redde, were [made the] actes of the kyng*es* supremacie *and* of treason for denyeing the same, The king aga[yne sente] dyu*er*se of his consell to this godlie father thus in the towre, both to shewe hyme [þe penaltie] that was in those act*es* co*n*teyned for them that wold not knowledge *and* co*n*fesse the k[ing to be] supreame head of the churche of England; And also to p*er*swade hyme therefore t[o accepte] *and* confesse it for sayving of his life. But he, Forecasting by the reading of those sta[tutes, and by] that þ*at* he had hard, that if he playnelie, by expresse word*es*, shuld saye that [the king] was not, or coulde not be, supreme head of the churche of England, That th[en he] shulde be in dang*er* of death by

Fisher, questioned in prison by the King's councillors, withholds his opinion as to the King's Supremacy.

Knowing that to declare his opinion thereon was dangerous.

Note. The first portion of Extract C, down to *which in no wise they wold eat, being contrarie to ther Rule and profession*, p. 236, l. 7, was not copied by Baker in MS. Harleian 7047. Sometimes it is impossible to restore the missing lines and letters, but one can generally get a rough approximation from the context and estimations of space. Such rough approximations are given within square brackets. From *The king caused*, p. 236, l. 8, onwards, Baker's transcript, fols. 20^{a}–27^{a}, is again of service. See above, p. 220, Note.

14–15. *as ye redde*] Cf. above, pp. 225, 228–9.

reason of thes late made statut*es*; And kn[owing by] his Lernyng that, notw*ith*standing those Lawes so made for the king*es* suprem[acie], neuer the more was the king in dede, nor coulde be, supreme heade ou*er* the Ch[urche of] England; And therevpon he, considering that if he shuld co*n*fesse this matter, [which was] contrarie to his co*n*scyence, he shuld thereby damage his sowle; he therefore to sau[e his bodye] fro death, *and* his sowle vnspotted in this matter, wittely *and* wiselie helde his peace, *and* . . .; And wold not answere any thing to this matter when any of the king*es* consell in[qu]y[ere]d [of him any] thing therein.

When again required by certain of the Council to disclose his opinion on the King's Supremacy, he maintains his silence thereon, but uses the comparison of the Act to a two-edged sword. [June, 1535].

Then Immediatlie after the deathes of the fyve holy me*n*n (which sup[ra] ye redde) the Fourth day of Maie, this byshope was by some of the king*es* consell (sent frome the king to hyme into the Tower of London) requyred on the king*es* p[arte] to tell his Opynyon *and* Learnyng in this matter, And how he lyked thes new La[wes] thereupon. And they sayed vnto hyme that his doyng could be no man*er* daunger [to hyme], because it shuld fullie apeare that he did it not of any malice or Evell will tow[ards the] prynce, but only for the certifeing of the king of his Opynyon, etc. But th[e byshop] right well p*er*ceyued how hereby they went abowt to catche hyme in a snar[e. And] he also, credibly hearing how this word "malicyouselye" in the statute of Treason [was] of none effecte in the Carthusyans co*n*demnaci*o*ns, he therefore wold make no auns[were] to this questyon. But beyng sore pressed vpon, at last he sayed it semyd hyme [that] thes new Lawes were lyke a twoo edged sword: "For if one shuld saye," q*uoth* he, "that [they were] good, they wold kyll his soule. And if he shuld saye they were nought, they w[old kyll] his bodye."

Fisher is entrapped by a messenger from the

The king then, knowing how this bishop so behavyd hymeself [in talke] *and* co*m*munycaci*o*n, that none of his craftie consell*oures* could gett hyme in a tryppe to speake

11. *inquyered*] MS. *indoyd*. 14. *which supra ye redde*] Cf. above, pp. 229–230.

dyrectlie on the one syde or the other in this matter of the supremacie, [he] and his deuelyshe deviso*ures* invented then a Farther Fetche, whiche was this. [He, on] the vij day of Maie, sent one of his suttle consello*urs* to this byshop in the Towre ag[ayne], w*i*th a very secrett message Fro the king, which ye shall heare :

King into stating his secret opinion on the King's Supremacy.

"The king," q*uoth* [this mische]vouse messeng*er* to this blissed byshop, "haith sent me, his trustie consello*ur* and s*er*vant, [to your] good Lordshipe, w*i*th a very secrett message; That is, that I shuld delyu*er* vnto [you] frome his heighnes, on his behalf, that all be it all the byshop*es* of this realme, [except your] self, *and* all the clargie also, except very few, and all the whole p*ar*lam*ent*, as we[ll lords] as comons, haue agreed *and* graunted to his supremacie, Yet his ma*ies*tie, for the [satisfaccion] of his owne co*n*scyence, is marvelouse desyrous to know yo*ur* Lordship*es* opyny[on theron]; because he assuredlie, by great *and* long experyence, haith knowen yo*ur* Lords[hip, and] estymeth yow no lesse than you be inded, that ma*n*n that, as well for yo*ur* p*er*so[n] as for yo*ur* godly vertu *and* pure conscyence, ar one of the cheife Flowers of t[he realme] this day lyving; and so fully knowen, reputed *and* taken, not onely w*i*thin this [realme but] in all owtward p*ar*tes thoroweout all christendome. Wherefore the king f[or this cause] most hartelie *and* most entirelie requyreth yo*ur* good Lordship to certifie hyme, [by me, his sure] and secret messeng*er*, in this behalf, what yo*ur* full opynyon is in this matt[er by your conscience] *and* lernyng. And further," q*uoth* this craftie caytiff, "the king willed [me trulie and] syncerlie to assure you, *and* faythfullie to promise you, on his hono*ur* and [the word of a prynce], that whatsoeu*er* your Lordship shall by me his messeng*er* certifie [to be your opynyon] in this matter, although it be directlie agaynst the lawes [made for the kinges supremacie], shall ther none advauntage thereof be taken against your [Lordship, and that yow

It is pretended that the King has such respect for Fisher's opinion, that his conscience cannot be satisfied without Fisher's consent to the Supremacy.

Fisher is assured, on the word of his Prince, that no harm shall come to him thereby.

13. *very*] Interlineated in same hand. 20. *for*] Interlineated in same hand.

shall not be empec]hed for yo*ur* seid declaraci*o*n of yo*ur* minde; And t[. . .

t]hat whatsoeu*er* aunswer the byshop shuld . . .

| [The byshop did not perceyue that this deuyce] was [fol. 309 *b*] layed to catche hyme in a snare, But thought veryly that the kyng [mente as] trulie *and* as playnely as this message *and* tale told by this messenger imported.

Fisher is glad thus to serve the King.

Wherefore [the by]shop, thinking assuredlie þ*at* no man*er* of hurt nor harme shuld come unto hyme by sending his [opyny]one in this matter by this messeng*er* to the kyng, was willing thereunto, As well for that þ*at* [he] was glade to shewe hymself willing to do to the kyng, his sou*er*aigne lord, all suche pleasure [and] s*er*uice as he possible could, saving his Lif *and* his conscyence, as for that he had some hope [th]at the kyng the rather, by knowing his opynion herein, wold not execute any further rygo*ur* [by] his new Lawes *and* statut*es* agaynst any ma*n*n þ*at* denyed his supremacye onely according to his [con]scyence.

He tells the messenger that the King cannot be Supreme Head in earth of the Church of England.

This byshop therefore for thes causes, *and* trusting vppon the king*es* assured p*ro*mise [th]us made unto hyme by this messenger, and taking also Faythfull p*ro*myse of this messeng*er* that [nether] hurt nor harme shuld come unto hyme for disclosyng his opynyon *and* mynd in this matter, [an]d trusting also vpon this messeng*eres* Othe that none shuld knowe of his Aunswere but onely þe [kyn]g; The byshope, I saye, for thes causes, playnelie *and* Franckelie, in few word*es*, willed [th]is messeng*er* to certifie the king Frome hyme, that he belyved directelie in his co*n*scyence, *and* [kn]ewe by his Lernyng preciselie, that it was very playne by the holy scripture, the [la]wes of the churche, the gen*er*all cou*n*sell, *and* the whole faith *and* generall practise of christ*es* [ca]tholyke churche frome christ*es* Ascension hetherto, That the king was not, nor could be, [by] the Lawe of God supreame head in earthe of the churche of England.

And when the king was by this messenger acerteyned

that this byshop had thus playnely [d]eclared his opynyon agaynst his supremacy, Then was he very gladd thereof, because [h]e had hereby some playne matter to Lay to the byshops charge, to Arayne hyme *and* co*n*demne hyme for speakyng agaynst his supremacie, where before this tyme by no meanes any suche [a]duauntage could be cowght agaynst the byshop; for the kyng Longed very sore to bryng [h]yme to his death, because he wold not agree to the king*es* maryedge w*i*th Anne Boleyn, nor [t]o his supremacye: In so Farrefurth þ*at* where pope Paulus, the third of that name, had elected hyme for a cardynall, *and* mad preparac*i*on to send the cardinal[s] hatt vnto hyme into England, while he was p*r*ison*er* in the Tower, the king hearyng thereof, [and] having spytt *and* indignac*i*on thereof, sayed that the poope myght well send this byshope a cardinal[s h]att: "But I will so p*r*ouyde," q*uoth* the king, "that if he weare it, he shall beare it on his should*eres*, nor any head he shall haue to put it on."

Pope Paul III makes Fisher cardinal. The King vows that he shall bear his Cardinal's hat on his shoulders, "nor any head he shall have to put it on." [May, 1535.]

Anne Bolleyn mad the king a great banckett at Haneworth, twelve myles frome London, *and* allured ther the kyng w*i*th hir dallyance *and* pastyme to graunt unto hir this request, to put the byshope *and* S*i*r Thomas Moore to death.

The King promises Queen Anne that Fisher and More shall be put to death.

Vpon the examinat*i*on of the rest of the Carthusians in London as towching the king*es* supremacye, the cheif of them were imprysoned: vid*elicet* Vmfray Mydlemore, then vicar *and* before the proct*our*; Will*iam* Exmewe, then ther p*roctour* *and* before ther vicar; *and* Sabast*i*an Newegate, who had bene a cowiertier. These were gent*lemen*. They were brought the xxv daye of Maye to Cromwell to his howse at Stebunheyth, a myle frome London; *and* refusing constantlie to acknowledge the kyng*es* supremacie, were imprisoned in the Towre of London; Where they remayned xvij dayes, standing boltt vpp ryght, tyed with Iron collor*es* fast by the neck*es* to the postes of the pryson, *and* great Fetters fast ryved [on] ther legges w*i*th great Iron boltt*es*; so

The second band of Carthusians—Humphrey Middlemore, William Exmew, and Sebastian Newdigate—are condemned for denying the King's Supremacy, and imprisoned, under cruel conditions, in the Tower, 25 May [1535].

straitely tied þ*at* they could nether lye nor sitt, nor otherwise [e]ase themselves, but stand vp ryght, and in all þ*at* space were they neu*er* losed for any naturall necess[itie, nor] voyding of ordure or otherwise. And they could gett no meate but bread alone *and* fleshe, w[hich in] no wise they wold eat, being contrarie to ther Rule *and* pr*o*fession.

[The LVIII chapiter of the third booke].

An indictment of treason is drawn up against these three Carthusians and Fisher.

[The] king caused a speciall comyssion to be made, dated 2° Junij in the 27 yeare of his Raig[ne, dire]cted to the Lord Awdeleye *and* others to enquyer *and* determyne Treasons. And the king*es* [lerned cons]ell drewe an Inditeme*n*t of treason agaynst the byshope of Rochester *and* the three Carth[usians].

Trial of the second band of Carthusians, 11 June [1535].

[Certe]ne of the comissioners satt at the King*es* Benche, 11 of June, being Fryday *and* St. Barnabe[s day, and th]er the Inditeme*n*t was found, and the 3 Carthusians were brought frome the Tower [in þ*er* religy]ous habbytt*es* to the King*es* Bench Barre, *and* ther arraigned, *and* pleaded not giltie. *And* they we[re found] gyltie, *and* Judgeme*n*t of high treason gyven agaynst the*m*. And the xix of June following, [being Satter]day, they were executed in ther religyous habbytt*es*, as the other Carthusians had be[ne].

The second band of Carthusians executed, 19th June [1535].

The king sends physicians to preserve Fisher's life, in order that he may be brought to his public execution.

[The] bushop of Rochest*er* was so sicke *and* feeble þ*at* he kept his bedde in the Tower, *and* in dang*er* of p[resent deathe.] But the king sent phisitions unto hyme to gyve hyme p*re*s*er*uatyves, þ*at* he myght be [able to come to] his publicke arraignement *and* execution. And the charg*es* of the king abowt th[is extraordinary ph]ysicke amownted to 40^{li}.

Fisher's trial, 17 June, 1535.

[When the bys]hope of Rochester, by this phisicke, medicyns *and* dyett, was somewhatt re[couered of his sickeness and we]keness, and somewhat able to be

8. *The king caused*, &c.] From this point onwards, Baker's transcript, MS. Harleian 7047, fols. 20^{a}–27^{a}, enables us to restore the text where damaged. 12. *an Inditement of treason*] It is evident from p. 237, ll. 26–8, below, that a copy of the Indictment against Fisher was contained in the chapter from which this Extract was made. But it was not transcribed for the Extract, for the text here runs on continuously.

brought abroad, he was the seve[ntethe day of June, being] Thursdaye, in the yeare of *our* Lord God 1535, *and* in the seven *and* twenty [yeare of Henry 8], w*i*th a great nombre of bill*es and* glaves *and* halbert*es*, *and* the axe [of the Tower borne before him, the] edge frome hyme, brought frome the Tower [of London, part by horseback, part by water (because he] was yet so lytle recou*er*ed of his fee[blenes and infirmity that he was not able to walke or go any thing) to the court] of the King*es* Benche [in Westminster Hall, before diuers of them that were appointed by þe king commissioners for þ*is* matter, [fol. 310 *a*] as ye redde in] | the LVIIJ chapit*er* of this third Booke. Which commissioners then s[iting there in þe court of the Kinges] Bench, were thes þ*a*t here follow: S*ir* Thomas Awdeley, Lord Chaun[celor; Charles, Duke of] Suffolk; Henry, erle of Cumb*er*land; Thomas, erle of Wilshyer; Thomas Crom[wel; S*ir*] John Fitziams, cheif Justice of the king*es* Bench; S*ir* John Baldewyn, cheif [Justice of the] comon place; S*ir* Will*iam* Pawlett; Sir Richard Lyster, cheif Baron of thexch[equer; *and* S*ir*] John Port, S*ir* John Spelman, *and* S*ir* Walter Luke, Justic*es* of the king*es* Bench; *and* S*ir* An[tony Fitz]-herbard, one of the Justice[s] of the co*m*mon place. Before whome this Byshopp ap[pered w*i*th] a cherefull countenau*n*ce *and* a godlie co*n*stancye.

The names of the King's Commissioners.

And then was he arraigned vpon [the Inditm*en*t] that was fownd agaynst hyme, the copie whereof ye redde in þe LVIIJ chapiter of this [third book]; whereof theffecte was that he malicyouslye *and* treaterously had sayed thes word*es*: "[The king], our sou*er*aigne Lord, is not supreame head in earth of the church of England." Where[vnto the byshope] plaided "not giltie."

Wherevpon a Jurie of xij me*n*n of Freeholders of the shyer of M[idlesex] were empanelled *and* sworne to trye this yssue, whose names here followe: S*ir* Hugh [Vaughan] *and* S*ir* Walter Hungerford, knyght*es*; Thomas Burbage, John Newdigate, Will*iam* [Browne], John Hewes, Jasp*er* Leyke, John Palmer, Richard

The names of the Jury.

23. *Justices of*] MS. *Justice of.*

Harry yong, Henry Lodisma*n*, John [Elrington], *and* George Hennyngha*m*, Esquyers.

The King's messenger deposes that Fisher had denied the King's Supremacy.

And when these xij me*n*n were swor[ne to trye] whether the byshop were gyltie of this treason or not, Then came forth for wyt[tenesse] agaynst hyme onelie he þ*a*t had bene, as ye rede in þe 55 chapit*er* of this iij^{de} booke, the [messenger] fro the kyng to this byshop in the Tower: who ther openlie before the Judg*es* *and* [the jury] *and* the whole presence, where were a great nomber of people gathered to see this [woful] tragedie, deposed vpon a booke that the byshope had by playne *and* expresse wor[des declared] late unto hyme in the Tower, that he knewe by his lear[n]ing *and* belyved in his co*n*s[cience] þ*a*t þe king was not, nor could be, supreme head in earth of the churche of engl[and].

Fisher reports his conversation with the King's messenger, the reason why he had stated his opinion on the Supremacy, and the King's promise that he should receive no harm therefor.

And when this byshop hard this myscheuous man depose this, he sayed unto hy[me: "S*i*r, I] will not denye þ*a*t I so sayed unto yow; but for all my so sayeing I co*m*mytted no treas[on. For] vpon what occac*i*on I so sayed, *and* for what cause, yo*ur* self know right well." And th[ervpon] the byshop declared openlie, not onely the message þ*a*t this ma*n*n came w*i*th to hyme in the [Tower] fro the king, but also all ther co*m*munycac*i*on *and* talke, *and* Further the ernest *and* assu[red promise] that this messeng*er* mad unto hyme on the king*es* behalf, wyth also his owne sole[mn othe] þ*a*t he wold vtter the aunswere to none but to the king, as you haue redde in the 5[5 chapiter] of this third booke. "Nowe, my Lord*es*," q*uoth* the byshop, "what a monstruouse ma[tter is] this: to laye nowe to my charge as treason the thing which I spake not vntill, [besides] this mans Othe, I had as full *and* as sure a p*ro*mise frome the king, by this his trusty [and sure] messeng*er*, as the king could make me by word of mouthe, that I shuld neu*er* be empeched [nor hurt] by myne aunswere that I shuld send unto hyme by this his messeng*er*, whiche I wold ne[uer haue] spoken, had it not bene in trust of my prync*es* p*ro*myse, *and* of my true *and* loving hart tow[ards

3. *when*] Interlineated in same hand. 13. *learning*] MS. *learing*.

hyme], my naturall liege lorde, in satisfyeing hyme *w*ith declarac*i*on of myne opynion *and* con[science] in this matter, as he ernestlie requyred me by this messeng*er* to signifie playnelie [vnto hyme]."

The King's messenger acknowledges that Fisher speaks the truth, but this does not excuse his denial of the King's Supremacy.

Whereunto this shamelesse best, this mischevous messeng*er*, sayed that trew it was þ*at* [he declared] unto hyme that message fro the kyng, *and* by the king*es* co*m*maundem*ent* made hym [that assured] and faythfull p*ro*mise frome the king, *and* sware unto hym also as he had sayed. "But [all this]," q*uoth* this wicked wyttenesse, "do not discharge you any whyte."

Fisher pleads that he had not *malicously* denied the King's Supremacy.

"Oh! my Lord*es*," [q*uoth* the byshop] to his Judg*es*, "how can this onely testymonye burden me, that ought, as the case [standeth], by all eqytie, all Justice, all worldlie honestie, *and* all cyvell humanytie, to be [no whyte] charged here *w*ithall, though in my so doyng I had co*m*mytted treason? And besydes [this, the] very statute that maketh the speakyng agaynst the kyng*es* sup*re*macie treason, is o[nely and] preciselie lymeted where such speche is spoken malicyously. And now all y[e, My lordes]," q*uoth* he, "p*er*ceyve playnelie that in my vttering *and* signifyeing unto the kyng of my[ne opynyon] *and* conscyence, as towchyng this his cleame of supremacie in the churche of Engla[nd, in such] sort as I did, as ye haue hard, There was no man*er* of malice in me at all, [and so I] co*m*mytted no Treason."

The Judges reply that the word *maliciously* in the Statute is of no validity, and that the King's pardon alone can now save Fisher from the penalty of death.

To this was it aunswered to the byshop by some of h[is judges], vtterlie devoyde of worldly shame, and affirmed by some of the resydew, [both that the] word malicyouslie in the statute was of none effecte, for that none could spe[ke agaynst the] king*es* supremacie by any man*er* of meanes but that the spekyng agaynst it [was treason]; and also þ*at* that message or p*ro*mise to hyme frome the king hymeself neyther co[uld, nor did, by] rygor of our law in any wise discharge hyme; but that in so declaring his [mynde and conscience] agaynst the king*es* supremacie, thowgh it were even at the king*es* owne [commandment and] request, he by the statute co*m*mytted treason; *and* nothing myght disc[harge him now of] the crewell penaltie of death, appoynted by the statute for spe[king agaynst the kinges su]premacye, howe so eu*er* the word*es* were spoken, but onelie [the kinges pardon, if it would pl]ease his grace to graunt it hyme.

Fisher is accused of presumption for holding an opinion contrary to that of all the bishops and best learned men of the realm.

Vpon this [point, and onelie by this wyttnesse of the] king*es* owne messeng*er* sent to the byshopp, w[ere the 12 men charged to find the holy lerned] byshopp gyltie of Treas[on. But before the enquest of 12 men went from the Barr to agree vpon þer verdict, there was layd to the byshopes charge, by some of his judges, high pride and great presumption, that he and a few other did dissent and vary in þis matter of the | kinges supremacie] [fol. 310 *b*] from the whole nomber of the byshop*es*, lord*es*, lerned men *and* co*m*mons, gathered together [in the parlia]-ment, with dyu*er*se other thing*es*. Vnto all whiche he aunswered in effect as the holy fathers [Cart]husians *and* Docto*ur* Reynold*es* had done; wherein he shewed hymeself excellentlie *and* p*ro*fowndlie [le]rned, of great co*n*stancie *and* of a m*ar*velouse godlie corage; And declared the whole matter [so] lernedlie, *and* therew*i*th so godlie, þat it made many of them ther present, *and* some of his Judg*es* also, [so] inwardlie to lament, that ther eyes brast owt w*i*th teares to see such a great famouse clarke [and] vertuouse byshopp to be co*n*-demned to so crewell death by such impyouse lawes *and* by such an vnlawfull *and* detestable wyttnesse, co*n*-trarie to all humayne honestye *and* fidelitie *and* the word *and* p*ro*myse of the king hymeself.

The Jury find Fisher guilty.

But pytie, m*er*cye, equytie, nor Justice had ther no place. For the xij men gaue ther verdite þat he was gyltie of the treason, whiche they did by the p*er*swasion *and* threatt*es* of some [o]f his Judg*es* *and* of the kyng*es* lerned consell; neu*er*thelesse the most p*ar*te of the xij me*n*n did this [so]re agaynst ther owne co*n*scyence; And yet durst do no nother for feare of losse of ther owne [l]yves, w*i*th whiche they were sore manased in case they shulde haue discharged this innocent godlie byshope of Treason.

Then Imediatlie vpon this verdite that same Thursdaye, [t]he xvij day of June, was lyke Judgm*en*t of treason gyven agaynst hyme as was agaynst the holy Carthusyans, of drawing, hanging, cutting downe alyue, throwing to the ground, his bowell*es* to be taken out of his belly, *and* be burnt, he being alyve, *and* his head to be cutt of, *and* his body to be deuyded in fowre part*es*, *and* his head *and* qu*arteres* to be putt where the king shuld appoynt.

The Sentence against Fisher.

But this crewell Judgm*en*t thus gyven was not all executed on hyme. For the king p*er*doned hyme all other crewelties saving heading. And so was he onely beheaded, as you shall redde in the next chapiter. And the cause why he was but onely beheaded, was (as me*n* saye) thought not for any pitie or co*m*passion that this crewell king had on this innocent vertuouse byshop, but for þ*at* the king thought that, if he shuld be drawen on [a] hurdell throwe London to the place of execution, as the Carthusyans were, it were lykelie that he, being aged, sycke *and* very weeke, shuld dye by the waye; W*hi*che the king in no wise wold, but that the byshopp shuld suffer death by open *and* publicke execution, to the Terro*ur* of all other byshopp*es* *and* lerned devynes þ*at* shuld grudge *and* repyne at his supremacie.

The Sentence is reduced to beheading, probably because the King knows that Fisher will otherwise die before the execution.

Of the man*er* of the martirdom of this blissid byshoppe.

When this crewell Judgem*en*t was thus gyven agaynst hyme at Westmy*n*ster Hall, he was, parte on horsebacke *and* p*ar*te by Foot, Frome thence co*n*veyed agayne to the Tower of London, w*i*th a great nombre of officers *and* me*n*n bearing halberd*es* and wepons abowt hyme *and* before hyme *and* behynd hyme, w*i*th the axe of the Tower borne all the way before hyme, the edge toward*es* hyme, as the fashyon is in England whe*n*n any co*n*dempned of treason is brought frome Judgme*n*t.

Fisher is conducted back to the Tower.

And when he came to the Tower gate, he turned hyme unto thos that thus had brought hyme fro the Towre to Westm*inster*, *and* frome thence to the Towre agayne, *and* sayed unto the*m*: "I thanke you, Maisters all, for

He thank the guards for their care of him.

13. *not*] Interlineated in same hand. 18. *aged*] Interlineated over *agayne* crossed through.

It is clear that he longs for death in Christ's cause.

the paynes ye haue taken w*i*th me this day in goyng *and* comyng frome hens to Westm*inster* and hyther agayne." And this spake he w*i*th so lustie a corage *and* so amyable a countenaunce, *and* his color so well come to hyme as though he had come frome a great *and* honorable fest. And his gesture *and* his behavyo*ur* shewed such a certayne inward gladnes in his hart, that any [mann] myght easelie see that he ioyouslie longed *and* looked for the blisse *and* Joyes of heaven, and [that he] inwardlie reioyced þ*at* he was so nere unto his death for Christ*es* cause.

On 22 June [1535], the Lieutenant of the Tower brings Fisher word that he is to die that day.

And long was it [not ere] he came unto it. For he thus being brought agayne to the Towre, *and* ther remayn[*ing* fo]wre dayes in his old pryson, very Feeble *and* sycklie of body, but of co*n*stant corage *and* [lusty hear]te, gladde to dye for the truth of Christ*es* catholicke fayth, The xxij day of June n[ext foll]owing, being Twisday *and* the day of Seynt Alben, the first martyr of England, *and* the [day befo]re the even of the Natyuytie of St. John Baptist, abowt fyve a cloke in the m[orning, the] Levetena*n*t of the Towre came to this holy ma*n*n in his chambre, yet in his bedde [asleep, and wa]kyd hyme, *and* shewed hyme þ*at* he was come to hyme w*i*th a message fro*m* the kyng. [And after] some circu*m*staunce vnto hyme vsyd, w*i*th p*er*swac*i*on to reme*m*bre that for age he co[uld not long] lyve, and therefore ought the rayther to be co*n*tent to die, he told hyme that h[is message was to t]ell hyme that the king*es* pleasure was that he shuld suffer in that forno*n*ne.

When Fisher learns the hour of his death, he asks to be allowed to sleep another hour or two

[" Well," quoth the bishop,] " if this be yo*ur* erant hyther, it is no newes unto me; I haue [looked dayly for it]. I pray you, what is it a cloke?"

" It is," q*uoth* the Levetena*n*t, " abowt Fyve."

[" What time," q*uoth* the bishop,] " must be myne howre to goo owt hence?"

" About tenne of the cloke," sayed [the Levetenant.

10. *his*] Interlineated in same hand. 20. *fyve*] Over *fyve* is interlineated *sixe*, but *fyve* is not crossed through. 33. *Fyve*] Over *Fyve* is interlineated *sixe*, but *Fyve* is not crossed through. 36. *tenne*] Over *tenne* is interlineated *nyne*, but *tenne* is not crossed through.

"Well] than," q*uoth* the byshop, "I praye you, lett me slepe an howre or twyne. [For I may say to you, I slept] not much this nyght, not for feare of death, I tell you, but by reas[on of my great sickness and wekeness]."

W*i*th whiche aunswere the levetena*n*t dep*ar*ted frome hyme [till about nine a cloke. At which tyme he] came againe to the byshops chambre, *and* found [him upward, putting on of his clothes; and shewed him that he] was come for hyme.

He insists on wearing his furred tippet to keep him warm till the very hour of execution.

[fol. 311 *a*] "Well," q*uoth* [the byshop, "I will make] | as convenyent hast as my weeke *and* syckely aged body will gyve me leave. *And*, I pray you, reache [me there my] Furryd typpett to put abowt my necke."

"Oh! my Lord," q*uoth* the Leveten*ant* to hyme, "what [nede you be nowe] so carrefull of yo*ur* health? Yo*ur* tyme is very shorte, lytle more than half an howre."

"I think [none other]wise," q*uoth* the bushope; "but, I pray you, yett gyve me leave to put on my Furred typpett, to ke[pe me warme] for the whyle vntill the verie tyme of execution; for I tell you truth, though I haue, I tha[nk our Lord], a very good stomacke *and* willing mynd to dye at this present, *and* I trust in his goodnesse *and* mercy [he will] styll contynewe it *and* encrease it, yet will I not hynd*er* my health in the meane tyme not a m[inute of an] hower, but will p*re*serue it in the meane season with all suche discrete wayes *and* meanes as a[lmighty God] of his gracious goodnes hath p*ro*uyded for me."

Then was he caryed downe out of his ch[amber betwene] twaine in a chayre, *and* so to the Towre gate; where he being delyu*er*ed to the sheriff*es* of Lond[on, he was] w*i*th a great co*m*panye of halberd*es*, bill*es* *and* glavis caryed in a chayre by Fowre of the sher[iffes officers], the sheriff*es* ryding next after hyme, frome thence not farre of to a playne besyd*es* the Tower [of London] comonly called the Towerhill, otherwise called East Smythfeild, where he was brought ne[re to the] scaffold, on whiche he shuld be beheaded. And when he cam to the foott of the scaffold, they [that caryed] hyme wold haue helped hyme vp the stayres of the

He is carried to Tower Hill.

But mounts the scaffold unaided.

scaffold. But then sayed he unto th[em: "Nay, Maisters], now lett me alone, ye shall see me goo vp to my death well ynough myself, wythout help." [And so went] he vpp the scaffold stayres w*i*thout help, to no lytle marveill of them þ*at* knewe his week[ness and] debylitie, by reason of his age *and* infirmytie.

His executioner asks his pardon.

And when he came vp vpon the scaffold, wh[ich was] abowt eleven of the cloke, he that shuld behead hyme cam unto hyme, as the fasion is, *and* [knyled] unto hyme, *and* prayed hyme to foregyve hyme his death. To whome the blissed byshop [aunswered], w*i*th a bold courage *and* a loving chere, that he foregave hyme hartelie, *and* sayed: "I trust [on our Lord] thow shaltt see me dye even lustelie."

It is clear to all how near Fisher is to a natural death.

Then was his gowne taken of Frome hyme [and his typpett]; And he stodde vp there in the sight of the people (where was a wonderous nombre of p[eople gath]erred to see this horrible execution, of whiche myself whas one)—a long, lene slender [body, nothing] in a man*er* but skyne *and* bare bones, so that the most p*ar*te that there sawe hyme m*ar*veyled to see [any man], bearing life, to be so farre co*n*sumed; for he seemed a lene body carcas, the flessh clene wast[ed away], *and* a verie Image of death, *and*, as one myght saye, death in a mans shape, *and* vsing a mans [voice. And] therefore more monstruous was it that the king or any ma*n*n could be so cruell to put such [a man to] death, yea, though he had bene an offend*er*; for very shortelie he must haue dyed by nature. [And surelie], I thinke, if he had bene in the great Turk*es* land, *and* gyltie of a great trespase ther, he w[old neuer for] pytie haue put hyme to death, being all redye so nere the pytt*es* brynke. For it is the [most crewell] thing that can be, to put any to death that is presentlie dyeing. Wherefor in this poynt I think [that this] king Henrie passed all the Turk*es* or Tyrant*es* that eu*er* was redde or hearde of.

He addresses the people,

When this [holy, innocent] byshope, w*i*th his deadly carcas, stod vpp thus on the scaffold, than spake he to

8. *eleven*] Over *eleven* is interlineated *tenne*, but *eleven* is not crossed through. 34. *Wherefor*] *Where* is interlineated.

asking their prayers that his courage may not fail at the last moment.

the people in effecte [as follows]: "Christen people, I am come hyther to die for the fayth of Christ*es* catholyke church. And, I th[anke God], hetherto my stomacke haith seruyd me well thereto, so þ*at* yet hytherto I haue not feared d[eath]. Wherefore I desyer you helpe me, *and* assist me w*ith* yo*ur* prayers, that at the very poynt *and* instant [of my deathes] stroke, *and* in the very moment of my death, I than faynt not in any poynt of the catholike faith [for any] Feare. And I pray God save the king *and* the Realme, *and* hold his holy hand ou*er* it, *and* send the [king a good] counsell."

He prays for King and Realm.

Men marvel at the strength and clearness his voice.

Thes word*es*, or word*es* of like effecte, he than spacke w*ith* a cherefull cou*n*tenau*n*ce [and with such] a stowt *and* constant courage as one no whyt affrayd, but gladd to suffer death. And th[es wordes] spake he so distinctlie *and* perceyveablie, *and* also w*ith* suche a strong *and* very lowde voyce, þ*at* it [made all] the people astoyned; *and* noted it in a man*er* as a myracle to heare so playne, stronge *and* [lowde a voyce] cam owt of so old, weeke *and* syckelie a carcas; for the yongest, strongest *and* healthfulle[st man there] present could not haue spoken stronglyer, lowdyer, playnelyer, nor better to be perce[yued.

He prays, and commends himself to the mercy of God.

Then] after thes fewe word*es*, or the lyke, spoken by hyme, he knyled downe on both his kn[ees, and sayed certene] prayers; *and*, as some reported, he sayed than the psalme or canticle "Te deu*m* laudamus," etc. [to the end, and] "In te d*omi*ne speraui, no*n* confundar in eternu*m*." Then was he blyndfolled w*ith* an ha[ndekerchiefe abowt] his eyes. And than, liftyng vp his hand*es* *and* hart devoutlie toward*es* heaven, he s[ayed a few prayers], w*hi*che were not long, but feruentlie devout. Which done, he layd downe on his [bely, flat on the] floore of the scaffold, *and* layd his lene necke vpon a litle blocke, so that hi[s body was on] the one syde of the blocke, *and* his head on the other syde, so that his necke was i[ust vpon the middes] of the blokke. And than came quickely the execution*er*, *and* wyth a sharpe *and* hev[y axe cut asunder] his nekke, *and* so seu*er*ed the head frome the bodie, his holy soule dep*ar*ting

The death stroke.

[to the bliss of heauen]. And his nekke then bledde so muche that men muche m*ar*veyled to see [so muche blood come out of so ol]d, lene, slender, weeke *and* syckelye a bodie.

Of this bysho[ps blissed bodie and of his head].

Of the manner of his burial.

Then toke the executioner awaye this byshop*es* clothes *and* his [shirt, and left the headless body ly]ing ther nacked vpon the scaffold almost all þ*at* day after. [Yet one at the last for pity and hum]anytie cast a litle strow vpon the dead bodyes pr[iuities. And abowt eight a cloke in the eue]nyng, co*m*maundm*en*t was come to bury the body to [certen men that taried ther abowt the scaffo]ld w*i*th the bodie all þ*at* afternoon with hal-[berdes and billes. Wherevpon one of them toke vp the dead body], without the head, [vpon his halberd, and caried it to a church yard of a parish church there hard by, called Barking; where, on the north side of that church, hard by the church wall, he and his fellows with ther halberds digged a graue (for other graue had he none but this that they digged with ther halberds); and therin without any reuerence they vilely threw this holy innocent bishops dead body, all naked, flat vpon his bely, without any winding sheet or any other accustomed funerall ceremonies; and then] | covered it [fol. 311 *b*] qwycklie w*i*th the yearth; *and* so, following herein the co*m*maundm*en*t of the kyng, [buryed] it verie contemptuouslie.

His head, after boiling, is set upon London Bridge.

His head was the same daye that his bodie thus was buryed, [or els] the next, somewhat p*er*boyled in hott watter, *and* sett vpp on high on London brydge vpon a [poo]le, w*i*th the residewe of the head*es* of the holy Fathers Carthusians, þ*at* suffred death late before hy[me].

And remains fresh and life-like for fourteen days.

Whiche heade of his, so standing vpon London brydge, did not by the space of xiiij [d]ayes any whytt wyther nor wast, but co*n*tynewed styll very Freshe *and* lyvelie, as though it had [be]ne alyve, loking vpon the people comyng into London. Whiche many of the people toke [for] a myracle, þ*at* Almyghtie god, above the course of nature, did extraordynarelie p*re*serve and [cont]ynewe the Freshe and lyvelie colo*ur* of his face *and* head, for the more playne declaraci*o*n and [noti]fieing to the world of this blissed byshop*es* Innocencie *and* holynes. And at the ende of thes xiiij [da]yes, the executione*r* threwe this holie byshopp*es* head into the Ryver of Temys, when he did sett [vp] ther vpon London brydge S*ir* Thomas Moores head, w*hi*ch he did the seventh day of Julie [ne]xt following, as ye shall redde in the 77 Chap*iter* of this third booke.

It is cast into the Thames to make room for the head of Sir Thomas More.

How this holy byshopp foresawe or forknewe his owne death.

This godly byshope long before his deathe, eyther by his great witt *and* p*ro*fownd lernyng (wherebie [he] considered what myseries *and* myschyves shuld come unto England) or els by some specyall [re]velaci*o*n frome God, had foreknowledge þ*at* hymeselff shuld die otherwise than by his naturall [d]eath for the faith of Christes church. For, iij or iiij yeares before his death, when in a Christmas tyme [h]e had caused to be prepared wurshipfull fare *and* honest pastymes for his kynsfolk*es* *and* frend*es* that [t]hen came to visite hyme (as that mane*r* was than moch vsed in England in þe Christmas), he [c]omaunded his officers to entertayne gentylie *and* make hartie good chere unto Frend*es* and [k]ynsfolk*es* so repayryng to hyme, *and* cam also emong them *and* cheryd them very hartelie; And leving [th]em at ther pastymes, went hymeself awaye into his studie to his prayers *and* meditaci*o*ns. Whiche [one] of his cheif Officers *and* trustie s*er*uant*es* p*er*ceyuing, cam unto hyme, *and* sayed:

Fisher leaves his guests to their Christmas feasting and pastimes, in order to meditate on his death, which he foresees will be a violent one.

"My Lord, I pray you, [lev]e of yo*ur* studie for this merye tyme of Christmas, whyle yo*ur* frend*es* be here, *and* come among them, [and] kepe them companye; or els will they thinke themeselves not welcome to you."

"Why," q*uoth* the byshope, "[ha]ue they not all such thing*es* as was prepared for them?"

10. *Chapiter*] MS. *Charp.*

"Yea," q*uoth* his ser*u*ant, "they haue; but what [then]? Yo*ur* lordshipe*s* presence shall more chere yo*ur* frende*s* than all yo*ur* mete *and* ther pastymes."

"Well," [quoth] the byshop, "I pray you be co*n*tent, *and* lett me alone here in my studie. For my frende*s*, I dare saye, [wyl] be content that I followe herein myne owne mynd in myne owne howse. And therefore pray the*m*, [in] my name, to be as mery w*i*thout me as though I were w*i*th them. For as for me, I haue other thinge*s* [to] doo than to chere my geste*s*, or to be present at ther worldly pastymes; for I tell you in secrett, [I] know I shall not die in my bedde. Wherefore it behoweth me to thinke co*n*tyneweallie vpon the [d]readfull howre of my accompt."

Here Followeth some p*ar*te of this bishope*s* lyf, qualities, vertu *and* lernyng, *and* what booke*s* he wrott.

The writer is ignorant of much concerning Fisher, but will describe what he has heard and known.

[N]ow though I, for lacke of knoweledge, can not (as I gladlie wold if I could) declare unto you the whole [tr]ade of the Lif of this byshop blissed (the onely lanterne of lyght to all the byshope*s* of England, of whome not one followed hyme), yet shall I shew you somewhat what I haue hard *and* knowen of his l[e]rnyng, qualities *and* vertu.

Fisher's personal appearance.

He was of stature somewhat passing the height of the meane sort of [men, and to] his lengh slenderly made, *and* went verie vpp ryght. Of co*m*plexion sangwyne, myngled with fl[eme]; And his heare brow*ne* *and* straite; of contenau*n*ce very sadd *and* grave, *and* yet amyable *and* cherefull, without a[ny ligh]tnesse; very wittie was he, *and* frome his youthe wise, discret *and* sobre, w*i*th such a goodlie reuerent [grau]itie þ*at* his behavo*ur* shewed hyme to be a godlie ma*n*n.

24–31. *He was of stature . . . sobre*] Cf. the notes, crossed through, at the beginning of fol. 246[a], MS. Arundel 152: *Of stature he was somewhat passing* [þe] *highe of þe mean sorte of men, slenderli made,* and *went veri vprighte; of complexi*[*on*] *sanguine mixed with* [Here gap within line, sufficient to take in *fleme; And*] *his heire browne* and *strait; of countenance graue, chereful and amiable; veri wittie he was also* and *ueri discreat* and *sober.*

Fisher's early life.

He was borne in Beverley in Yorkeshyere, [of hone]st parent*es*; *and* for a whyle fownd by his father at schole at the vniu*er*sitie of Cambridge; *And* after mad[e fellow]e of St. Johns Hall in Cambridge, *and* ther in co*n*tyneweance of tyme mad first m*aster* of art*es*, then bac[helor of de]uynytie, *and* after doct*our* of that facultie; *and* was chapleyne *and* almost daylie attendaunt of a go[od space to the] Lady Margaret, contesse of Richemont *and* Derbie, mother unto king Henry the seventh (fath[er of the ki]ng Henrie the eight, of whome this story treatyth). Which king Henrye the VII (at the instance [of his mother], the countesse), for the great vertu *and* excellent ler*n*nyng of this holy ma*n*n, doct*our* John Fysher, [about the ye]are of our Lord God m^{le} v^{c} *and* fyve, made hyme byshop of Rochester in the shyer of Kent; So [that he was] byshope of þ*at* sea abowt thirtie yeares.

Consecrated Bishop of Rochester. [November, 1504].

Created Cardinal. [May, 1535].

And duryng the tyme that he was thus in prys[on in the Tower], as ye haue redde, Our holy father, poope Paulus the third, made hyme cardyn[al, so that t]his crewell king kylled in this one ma*n*n a preist, a byshope, *and* a cardinall; who at t[he tyme of his holy] martyrdome was abowe the aige of threscore *and* fowrtene yeares.

His holiness.

[He was in holi]nes, learnyng *and* dylygence in his cure *and* in fulfylling his office of byshope such [that of many hundred yeares] England had not any byshop worthie to be co*m*pared vnto hyme. And if all [contries of Christendome wer]e serched, ther could not lyghtlie

1–23. *He was borne . . . threscore and fowrtene yeares.*] Cf. the notes, crossed through, at the beginning of fol. 246^{a}, MS. Arundel 152: *John Fysher*, Bushope *of Rochester, was borne in Beuerley in Yorkeshere, of honest parentes.* [*He was*] *fellowe of St Johns Colledge in Cambridge, and promoted there in degrees to D.*[*D*]. *He was chaplen and almost daly attendant vpon the lady M*argaret, *countes of R*ichmond *and* [*Darby, mother*] *to k*ynge *H*enry þ*e vij., who at* þ*e instance of his mother, for his great vertu and lerning,* [*made*] *hym B*ushope *of Rochester 1505. So he was bushop of* þat *see about 30 yeres.* [*At* þe] *tyme of his martirdome he was aboute the age of 70 yeares.*

Over *1505* is interlineated *1503*; over *70* is interlineated *74*. In the margin, opposite *John Fysher*, some words of a note can be made out: *this is* [ ] *bare* [ ] *ther more large.*

15. *fyve*] *three* is interlineated over *fyve*, but *fyve* is not crossed through. 19. *as ye haue redde*] Cf. above, p. 235. 23. *fowrtene*] Interlineated over *tenne* crossed through.

emong all other nac*io*ns be found one [that hath been in all things th]e lyke unto hyme, so well vsed *and* fulfilled the office of a byshop as he [did. He was of such high per]fection in holie lif *and* straite *and* austere lyving as fewe were, I suppo[se, in all Christendome in his time, religious or] other.

His charity.

Of his revenewes of his byshopbrycke which pa[ssed not yearly abowe 4 hundred markes, he bestow]ed in ded*es* of charitie as moch thereof as remay[ned after the furnishing of his house and household, which was not somptuous, but rather] meane, *and* yet honest, [according as might well beseem the reuerent honor and degree of a vertuous byshop.

His austerities.

He studied dayly long and some part of the night; he fasted very much and prayed and meditated dayly diuers hours, and much part of the night also. He was very contemplatiue, and many yeares before his death neuer lay he on fether bedde, but on a hard mattrice, nor lay in any linnen sheetes, but only in wollen blanckettes.

He denies himself for the comfort of others.

To scholers he was benign and bountifull, and in his almes to the poor very liberall, as far as his power extended, and did himself visit his poor] | neighbo*ures* [fol. 312 *a*] when they were sicke, *and* brought them both drynke, meate *and* money. And many tym[es to them that lacked] he brought both coue*r*lett*es* *and* blanckett*es* frome his owne bedde, if he could fynd in his ow[ne house none meet] for the sycke pe*r*son.

His care for his flock.

He was of a great, godlie, stowt courage *and* constancye, not deiecte in any [aduersitie, nor] elated w*i*th any prosperitie, as one that vtterlie dis[p]a[r]id in worldlie

2. *so well vsed*] Cf., for omission of the relative pronoun, p. 228, l. 16, and p. 229, l. 21, above. 7–20. *Of his revenewes . . . wollen blanckettes.*] Cf. the notes, crossed through, at the beginning of fol. 246[1], MS. Arundel 152 : *His yerly reuenues of his Bushoprike he bestowed in deades of charity so muche as rema[yned after] þe furnishinge and prouision of his howse, whiche was but mean. His reuenues [were] not paste 400 markes. Many yeres before his deathe he lay not on a [feder bedde], but on a hard mattarice, and not in any lynnen shetes, but onlie in wollen [blankets].*

Over *400* is interlineated *500*, but *400* is not crossed through.

8. *4*] Over *4* is interlineated *5*, but *4* is not crossed through.

31. *disparid*] MS. disgasid. (See Glossary.)

thing*es*. Gentill *and* cour[teous was he to] all menn, *and* very pitifull to them þ*at* were in any myserie or calamytie. He, lyke a good shep*er*d, [wold not go] Frome his Flocke, but contyneweallie fedde them w*ith* preaching of god*es* word *and* example of [good life]. He, lyke a good shep*er*de, did what he could to reforme his flokke both of the spiritualtie *and* [temporaltie], when he p*er*ceyued any of them to range owt of the right waye, ather in maner*es* or doctryne.

To Fisher is due the foundation of two Cambridge Colleges [Christ's and St. John's].

[Very carefull] was he for the bryngyng vp of the youth of England in vertu *and* learnyng: for by his labo[ur and by the] fav*our* þ*at* the countesse of Richemont *and* Derby had hyme in (wyth whome he myght do very moch), [he with his] good counsell *and* perswasion cawsed hir to buylde twoo Famous colleg*es* in the vniu*er*sitie of Cambri[gge, the one] called the , the other called , in which [colleges a] great nombre of studious youthe haue bene brought vpp in vertu *and* good lernyng co*n*tyneweallie, till] hereses ou*er*whelmed all England; so that he myght well be called the father of them þ*at* were [giuen to vertu] and ler*n*nyng.

Fisher made Chancellor of Cambridge University. [1504].

He was also, duryng a great p*ar*te of the tyme þ*at* he was byshop, the protector [of the vniu*er*sitie] of Cambrigge, for the chose hyme to be ther chancell*our*, by w*hi*ch office he had the rule [and care of all] them that were student*es* in that vniuersitie, for whose comoditie *and* p*ro*fitte in lernyng he mad [no less prouision] than he did for his owne shepe.

Fisher's powers as a preacher.

He was also a verie diligent preacher *and* the [notablest in] all this Realme, both in his tyme or before or syns, as well for his excellent lernyng as [also for edifying] audyens, *and* moving the affections of his hearers to cleve to God *and* goodnes, to enbrase ver[tue and to flee] synne. So highlie *and* p*ro*fowndly was he lerned in dyuynytie that he was, *and* is at this da[y, well known],

11–25. *for by his labour . . . Cambrigge*] Cf. the notes, crossed through, at the beginning of fol. 246a, MS. Arundel 152: *The countes by his perswasion builded 2 colledges in Cambridge,* and þe *vn*[*iuersitie*] *chose hym to be there protector.* 17. Gaps within the line in MS. as indicated.

esteymed, reputed *and* allowyd (and no lesse worthie) not onelie for the cheiffeist dyvyne þ*at* was [many yeares] in England, but also for one of the chef flowers of dyuynytie þ*at* lyved in his tyme thoro[weout all] christendome. Whiche haith appered ryght well by his work*es* þ*at* he wrott in his mater[nall speche], but moche more by his lerned *and* famous book*es* wrytten in the Latten tonge.

His English sermons.

In Engl[ish he] wrott dyu*er*se excellent s*er*mons, *and* full of high co*n*templac*io*n *and* morall lessons; whereof [two were] vpon thes word*es* in the v chapit*er* of seynt Paules first epist*le* unto the Thess*alonians*, " Sine intermis[sione orate "]; and vij S*er*mons vpon the vij penytenciall psalmes; *and* an other full of great lernyng for the [supremacie] of the poope *and* the Sea of Rome, etc.

Enquiry should be made as to what books Fisher wrote in English and Latin.

In Latten he wrotte agaynst heresyes thes work*es* fol[lowing]:

Enquyer what book*es* this blissed byshop wrott both in Englyshe *and* Latten.

APPENDIX II

THE PARIS NEWS LETTER

NOTE

The News Letter describing More's trial and death was widely and immediately circulated in Paris. In the Bibliothèque Nationale there are eight copies of it: a list of these is given below. It was also apparently printed at the time in French, but I have not seen any printed copy earlier than 1731, when it was given in an appendix to the new edition of the *Memoirs* of Castelnau (*Les Mémoires de Castelnau, augmentez par J. le Laboureur. Nouv. édit.*, Bruxelles). This reprint was, however, made from a manuscript so corrupt as to be sometimes unintelligible.

The Paris News Letter was immediately translated, and printed n at least two distinct German versions:

> *Beschreybung des urtheyls und todts, weiland des Gross Cantzlers in Engenlandt, Herrn Thomas Morus, Darumb das er desselben Reichs Ratschlag und newen Statuten nit hat wöllen anhangen. Auss einem welschen truck verteutscht.* Sm. 4°. (Brit. Mus. 1202, c. 33(1)).
>
> *Von der Vorurteilung und Tode, ettwan des Grossen Cantzlers von England Hern Thome Mori. Aus dem Welschen ins Deutsch gebracht.* 4°. Dresden, 1536. (Guildhall, Cock Library.)

There are also extant in MS. at least two copies of a translation into Spanish: one (imperfect) in the Archives of Simancas, the other in Madrid. Copies of both these, made in the nineteenth century by, or for, G. Bergenroth, are in the British Museum (Add. MSS. 28587, fols. 336, *etc.*; 340, *etc.*).

But by far the most famous translation was into Latin. This is entitled *Expositio fidelis de morte D. Thomæ Mori & quorundam aliorum insignium virorum in Anglia.* It is in the form of a letter addressed by P. M. to Caspar Agrippa.

This translation must have been made immediately, for it is dated from Paris, July 23rd, seventeen days, therefore, after More's execution. The writer gives, as his authority, what must be the Paris News Letter, and rumours (*Quæ uero sum narraturus partim e schedis Gallice scriptis, quæ hic circumferuntur, desumpsi, partim e rumoribus*). So far as More's trial and death are concerned, the writer of the *Expositio fidelis* has practically nothing to add, except a detail of More's feebleness: *ibat reus baculo innixus tam longam uiam, corpore graui egrotatione in carcere debilitato nihil tamen perturbationis uultu præ se ferens.* He follows the Paris News Letter, occasionally mistranslating, amplifying, or inserting a tag. Then he gives a very brief account of the end of the Carthusians and of Fisher, the source of which is not known: the information available was, as he himself points out, much more scanty than in the case of More.

The *Expositio fidelis* was printed by Froben at Basle in 1535 (Brit. Mus. copy, G. 1576) and at Antwerp in 1536 (B.M. 4823 aaaa. 6). It has been frequently quoted, and is, with Roper, the commonest source for the story of More's trial and death. The Basle edition was, no doubt, printed under the direction of Erasmus, who had moved to Basle from Freiburg-in-Breisgau in the preceding June, and was now staying with Froben. It is perhaps for this reason that the *Expositio fidelis* is frequently attributed to Erasmus. When, as for example by Father

Bridgett, Erasmus is quoted as an authority for More's trial and execution, it is the *Expositio fidelis* which is meant. Yet it is clear that it cannot be by Erasmus. The fact that in it Erasmus is referred to in the third person might be a blind, though it is difficult to see why he should have kept it secret, were he really the author, for it is a peculiarly guarded statement. It is not consistent with the grief and horror which Erasmus elsewhere shows. It is clear that the dating from Paris is no blind, but that it actually was written there whilst Erasmus was at Basle. The tone in which the *Expositio fidelis* is written is even more conclusive. The writer, whilst sympathizing with More, is very moderate in his censure of Henry, merely suggesting that he should have punished More and Fisher more leniently: *pro sua solita clementia cœterisque uirtutibus, per quas nomen ipsius hactenus erat apud omnes nationes gratiosum et amabile.* This contrasts with the vigorous denunciation in the verses attributed to Erasmus:

Extinctum flemus crudeli funere Morum
Et regem immanem ueneremque cruore madentem
Fortunœque uices, et lesœ pellicis iram . . .
Tempus erat mundi cum iam aduentante ruina
Occideret senio iustum, et labefacta deorum
Relligio caderet tot sustentata per annos,
Mortalesque fidem tota de mente fugassent
Et dolus et fastus cumque impietate libido . . .
Ergo aliud meditantur opus dirumque frementes
Pellicis insinuant atrum in precordia uirus
Et stolido regi eripiunt mentemque animumque.
Ille scelus firmare suum majoribus ausis
Enitens sceleri scelus adiicit, et contemptis
Pontificis summi monitis, quibus ille iubebat
Ejiceret Mœcham Talamique in iura uocaret
Legitimam uxorem solitoque ornaret honore
Ipse sibi ius pontificis, nomenque sacratum
Quam late sua regna patent usurpat, et omnem
Sacrilegus ueterem conuellit relligionem
Et grauius peccat ut non peccasse putetur.
Egregia interea pellex, quœ gaudia sentit?
In quorum iugulos miserum non armat amantem? . . .

(*Carmen heroicum in mortem Thomœ Mori*, Excusum Haganau, per V. Kobian, 1536.—B.M. 851.i.10; second, fuller, version, 11408.aaa.30.)

Though the writer of the *Expositio fidelis* speaks of himself as a personal friend of More, his whole attitude is inconsistent with what we have reason to believe Erasmus felt. Further, the writer of the *Expositio fidelis* mentions having been in England in the suite of Cardinal Campeggio: to suppose this inserted with the deliberate purpose of misleading would be hypercritical, and obviously it again excludes Erasmus.

The *Expositio fidelis* has been frequently reprinted, as, *e.g.*, in the edition of More's Latin Works, Basle, 1563, p. 511; and of Erasmus' Works, Leyden, 1703, Vol. III, col. 1763–71. In both these places it is attributed to Gulielmus Courinus Nucerinus, and is supposed to be written to Philippus Montanus. But Courinus Nucerinus (at any rate if he is Gilbert Cousin of Nozeroy, b. 1506, d. 1572) cannot be the writer. Cousin was secretary to Erasmus from 1530 to 1535, first at Freiburg and then at Basle, till he became canon at Nozeroy: he was not in Paris at the time when the news of More's execution came through. (Something is known of Cousin's movements from his letters to Ammerbach in the

Cathedral library at Basle. See Pierre André Pidoux, *Gilbert Cousin, étude sur sa vie : Mémoires de la Société d'Émulation du Jura,* Série 8, Vol. IV, 1910, pp. 35–147, especially 67[51]–69).)

The author of the *Expositio fidelis* is in all probability Philippe Dumont (Philippus Montanus, b. c. 1496, d. 1576) a former pupil of Erasmus, then apparently in Paris. (See *Opus Epist. Des. Erasmi,* ed. Allen, No. 2065, Tom. VII, p. 520; F. Sweert, *Athenæ Belgicæ,* 1628, p. 645.) The letters P. M. in the early editions of the *Expositio fidelis* point to him, and the later reprints, in which the work is attributed to Courinus Nucerinus, nevertheless make Montanus the recipient.

M. Pierre Janelle suggests in a letter to me that the English services of propaganda abroad may have had something to do with the *Expositio fidelis.* "It would be very clever to publish an authentic account of More's trial, professedly by a friend of his, with such half admissions as: after all, he may have been in the wrong, and nobly sacrificed his life for a mistaken sense of right." However this may be, the author of the *Expositio fidelis,* despite his visit to England, knew no English, though he knew something of English life and customs. The curious error "killim" for "guilty" is not a misprint: it must have been accepted by the author of the *Expositio fidelis* from a lost French manuscript of the Paris News Letter, because the same mistake occurs in one of the German translations which was made direct from the French. The *Expositio fidelis* and this German translation were presumably from the same, or from an allied manuscript now lost. MS. fr. 16539 in the Bibliothèque Nationale shows the first stage of this corruption in the form "Gilley" (see footnote, p. 263, l. 6).

With regard to the attribution of the *Expositio fidelis* to Erasmus, the judgment of Stapleton should be noted:

> *Stilus et modus scribendi apertissime clamant authorem illum esse, maxime cum in epistolis eadem fere sed sparsim scripserit* (*Tres Thomæ,* 1588, p. 352; 1612, p. 363).

The most striking parallel between the letters of Erasmus and the *Expositio* which I have noticed is the description of More's piety. Erasmus describes More in his letter to Faber (1532):

> *Sic addictus pietati, ut si in alterutram partem aliquantulum inclinet momentum, superstitioni quam impietati uicinior esse uideatur.*

The phrase is echoed in the *Expositio:*

> *Erat enim mentis tam religiosæ ut propior esset superstitioni quam impietati.*

But the letter to Faber had been printed at Basle in 1534, as an appendix to Erasmus' *Liber de præparatione ad mortem,* pp. 93–100, so that there is no difficulty over its being quoted by a scholar in Paris in July, 1535.

The interest taken in these matters throughout Europe is shown by the fact that there are two other German translations, which, however, were made, not from the original French, but from the *Expositio fidelis.* These are:

> *Glaubwirdiger bericht von dem Todt des Edlen Hochgelerten Herrn Thome Mori . . . durch ein Epistel . . . auss Latein in Teutsch vertholmetschet* [by G. Wickgramm] 4°. (B.M. 697, c. 43.)

> *Ein glaubwirdige anzaygung des tods Herrn Thome Mori.* 1536. (B.M. 699, g. 36.)

For Harpsfield's treatment of these sources, see Historical Note to pp. 183–200.

The Paris News Letter exists in eight manuscripts in the Bibliothèque Nationale. These manuscripts are referred to in the collations to this edition by the following letters:

A = MS. fr. 1701 (ff. 185–90). No title.
B = MS. fr. 2832 (ff. 191–93). No title.
C = MS. fr. 2960 (ff. 64–70). Headed: *Discours sur le procez et execution de Thomas Morus, chancellier d'Angleterre.*
D = MS. fr. 2981 (ff. 44–45). Printed for this edition *in extenso.* No title. The title in square brackets below is that of MS. C.
E = MS. fr. 3969 (ff. 63–67). No title.
F = MS. fr. 12157 (3 feuillets). Headed: *Coppie de la condampnacion de maistre Morus, chancellier d'Angleterre.*
G = MS. fr. 12795 (ff. 29–32). No title; but preceding the text is a note of the copyist Julyot: *J'ay commence a escrire les choses contenus en ce present livre en l'an* 1536. *Julyot.*
H = MS. fr. 16539 (ff. 30–33). Headed: *Memoire touchant le proces de Maistre Thomas Maurus nagueres chancelier d'Angleterre.*

The following diagram represents what appears to be the relation of the eight manuscripts, O indicating the author's original, and x, y, z parent manuscripts now lost:

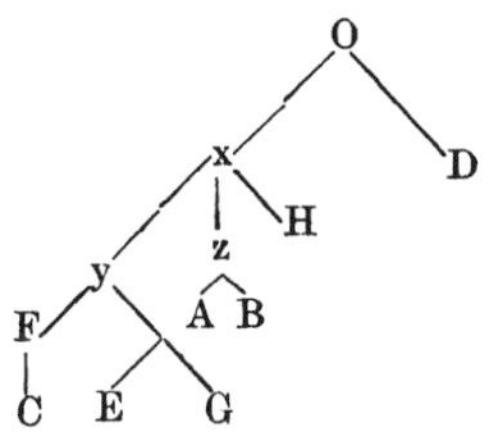

The MSS. derived from 'y' have a note following the text (see below, p. 266), which is wanting in A B H D. MS. C is a late copy of MS. F, which is probably the oldest of the eight, and is dated 4 August, 1535. As may be seen from the collations below, the text of MSS. F and C is very corrupt. MSS. E, G, A, B and D are all of the sixteenth century; MS. H is of the early seventeenth century. MS. D furnishes an excellent text.

The paragraphing, punctuation and marginal summary of this edition are the Editor's. There are no accents in MS. D, and as their absence causes no ambiguities of meaning, they are omitted from this edition.

The readings of other MSS. are to be assumed as being the same as those of MS. D, unless otherwise stated. Variations of spelling are not noted; variations of inflexion are noted if of special interest.

In the collations the spelling of variant readings is that of the first manuscript cited.

Bibliothèque Nationale, MS. fr. 2981.

[Discours sur le procez et execution de Thomas Morus, chancellier d'Angleterre.]

More brought to trial, 1 July, 1535.

Maistre Thomas Morus, nagueres chancellier d'Angleterre, fut mene le premier jour de Juillet, mil V^c trente cinq, devant les juges deleguez par le Roy. Et apres que les charges et informations faictes a l'encontre de luy eurent este en sa presence publiees, les seigneurs chancellier et duc de Norfort s'adresserent vers luy, disant ainsi :

Is promised pardon, if he will bend to the King's will.

" Vous voyez bien, Me Morus, que vous avez grandement erre contre la maieste Royalle. Ce neantmoings, nous esperons tant de sa clemence et benignite que si voulez vous repentir et revocquer de vostre obstinee oppinion en laquelle vous avez si temerairement persiste, que vous obtiendrez grace et pardon."

He prays God to preserve in him his just opinion.

He fears that bodily weakness may prevent his full and effectual

A quoy respondit ledit Morus : " Messeigneurs, je vous remercie tres affectueusement de vostre bonne volunte. Seullement je prie le Dieu tout puissant qu'il lui plaise me maintenir en ceste mienne juste oppinion, en sorte que je y puisse perseverer jusques a la mort. Et quant aux accusations dont l'on me charge, je doubte que ne l'entendement ne la memoire ne la parolle pourront satisfaire a y repondre, eu esgard a la prolixite et grandeur

3. *cinq*] six C. 3. *devant*] devers B. 3. *les juges deleguez*] le juge delegue F C. 4. *que*] *Omitted in* F C E A B H. 5. *luy . . . publiees*] luy et eurent estez en la presence de luy publieez F C. 6. *s'adresserent*] s'adressant A. 6. *vers*] devers H. 8. *Vous* (1)] *Omitted in* C. 8. *bien*] *Omitted in* F C A B. 8. *vous* (2)] *Omitted in* F C A B. 8–9. *grandement*] *Omitted in* B. 11. *et revocquer*] *Omitted in* F C E G. 14. *Messeigneurs*] Messieurs F C. 15. *remercie*] mercie E G B. 15. *tres affectueusement*] tres humblement C. 17. *mienne juste*] juste myenne F C. 18. *y*] *Omitted in* F C E. 19. *dont . . . charge*] dont me charges F C. 19–21. *je doubte . . . y repondre*] B *as* D A, *but* pourroit *for* pourront ; je doubte que l'entendement la memoire ne la parolle puissent satisfaire H ; je croy que mon entendement memoire ne la parolle ne pourroient satisfaire a y repondre F C ; je doubte que n'ay l'entendement ne la memoire ne la parolle pour y satisfaire et repondre E ; G *as* E, *but* la memoire *for* ne la memoire.

des articles, obstant aussi la longue detention de prison, la griefve maladie et debilitation que maintenant je seuffre."

answer to his indictment.

Lors commandement fut faict qu'on luy apportast une chaize pour se seoir. Ce faict, il continua son propos en ceste maniere :

A chair is brought for him.

"En tant que touche, deist-il, le premier article qui contient que pour monstrer ma malice contre le Roy, j'ay en la matiere de son second mariaige tousiours resiste contre sa serenissime maieste, autre chose ne veulx respondre fors que ce que j'en ay dit, c'est selon ma conscience, pour ce que je ne voullois et ne debvois celer verite a mon prince. Et si je ne l'avoys ainsi faict, je luy serois certainement traistre et desloyal. Depuis pour telle erreur, si cela se doibt nommer erreur, j'ay este condampne, mes biens confisquez, a perpetuelle prison, en laquelle j'ay desja este detenu par l'espace de quinze mois. Seullement je respondray au cas principal, sur ce que vous dictes que j'ay encouru la peine du statut

More's answer to the First Article: with regard to the King's second marriage he had spoken only according to his conscience, and for this he had suffered the penalty.

1–2. *prison, la*] prison de la C; prison avec la G. 4. *Lors commandement*] Le commandement C. 4. *Lors commandement fut faict*] Lors fut faict commandement H. 5. *chaize*] chaire C. 5. *se seoir*] soy seoir F; s'asseoir C; se asseoir E G; soy asseoir H; ce soir A. 5. *son propos*] son discours C. 7–11. *En tant . . . respondre*] *Latin here mistranslates:* Quod ad primum attinet articulum, qui conatur ostendere meam in Regem maleuolentiam, in negotio posterioris matrimonii, confiteor ingenue, me semper restitisse illius serenissime Maiestati. Nec est animus super hoc negotio quicquam aliud dicere, *etc. Harpsfield follows the French here; cf. above, p.* 184, *ll.* 17–20. 7–9. *En tant . . . mariaige*] *Omitted in* A. 9. *j'ay*] *Omitted in* F C. 9. *la*] sa G. 9. *matiere*] nature C. 9. *de son second*] du second F C E B H. 10. *serenissime*] *Omitted in* F C E G. 10. *chose ne*] chose je ne F C E H; chose je n'en G. 11. *fors que*] fors ce que E G H. 11. *ay dit, c'est*] ay dit qui est c'est H. 11. *ce que*] *Omitted in* F C A. 11. *c'est*] *Omitted in* F C E; qui est G. 12. *ma*] la F C A E. 12. *ne voullois et ne debvois*] ne vouloye ne deboye F C E G A B H. 13–14. *Et si . . . desloyal*] *Latin amplifies:* Nec hic est ulla proditio quæ intenditur, quin potius ni id fecissem, præsertim in re tanti momenti, unde pendebat mea sententia, et principis honor, et regni tranquillitas, tum uere fuissem quod nunc objicitur, maleuolus, perfidus et proditor. *Harpsfield expands the French here, but does not follow the Latin; cf. above, p.* 184, *ll.* 23–7. 14. *luy*] *Omitted in* F C E H. 14. *certainement*] *Omitted in* E. 15. *pour*] par F C. 15. *si cela . . . este*] si cela doit estre nomme erreur, j'en ay este F E G H. 15. *j'ay este*] je este A. 15–16. *j'ay este . . . prison*] J'ay este condampne a perpetuelle prison et mesbiens confisques H. 17. *en laquelle*] de laquelle F E G; en laquelle prison H. 17. *j'ay desja este*] j'ay este desja F G B; j'ay ja este A H; j'ay este C E.

He had never *denied* the King's Supremacy. He cannot be punished for his silence thereon, since he is not guilty of treasonable word or deed.

faict au dernier parlement depuis que je suis prisonnier, pour autant que par malice, faulcement et traistrement, j'ay oste a la maieste du Roy son nom, son tiltre, son honneur et sa dignite, qui luy ont este octroyez par ledit parlement qui l'a reçeu suppreme chef en terre de l'eglise d'Angleterre soubz Jhesus Crist. Et premierement quant a ce que vous me opposez que je ne voullu respondre autre chose a monseigneur le secretaire du Roy et l'honnorable conseil de sa maieste, quant ilz me interroguerent que je sentois dudit statut, sinon que moy estant mort au monde, je ne pensois point en telles choses, mais seullement en la passion de Jhesus Crist, je vous diz que pour tel mien silence vostre statut ne me peult condamner a mort : car ne vostre statut ne toutes les loix du monde ne punissent personne sinon pour avoir dict ou faict, et non pour ung semblable silence."

It is objected that More's silence proves opposition, and that a faithful subject is bound to state his opinion.

A ce repplicqua le procureur du Roy, disant que tel silence estoit une demonstration et certain jugement d'une maligne pensee contre ledit statut, pour ce que tout subject fidelle et leal a la maieste, estant interrogue sur ledit statut, estoit tenu et oblige de respondre cathegoricquement et sans aucune dissimulation que tel statut estoit bon et sainct.

1. *au dernier*] a votre H. 1. *je*] *Omitted in* E G. 3. *j'ay oste*] j'en oste C; je oste A; j'ai notte E G. 3. *son tiltre*] *Omitted in* B H. 5. *parlement qui*] parlement lequel H. 5–6. *de l'eglise*] d'eglise F C E G. 7. *ce que vous me opposez*] ce que m'avez aposez F C; ce que m'avez opposez E G; ce que vous aposez B; ce que me opposez A; ce que me apposez H. 7. *que je ne voullu*] que je ne vouluz B; n'ay voulu F C E G A H. 8. *a monseigneur*] *Omitted in* F C E G A H, *and in the German. Latin has :* Domino Secretario Regis. *Harpsfield follows the French ; cf. above, p.* 185, *ll.* 10–11. 9. *et l'honnorable*] a l'honnorable F C G; et a l'honnorable E B H. 9. *sa Maieste*] *Omitted in* C. 10. *dudit*] audit F C. 11–12. *en telles choses*] a telles choses F C E G A B H. 12. *en la*] a la F C E G A B H. 13. *diz*] responds H. 13. *tel mien silence*] telle silence E G; telle moyenne sentence F; telle mienne sentence C. 14. *car ne vostre*] Car vostre F E G. 15. *ne punissent*] ne cognoissent G. 16. *ung*] *Omitted in* F E G A. 16. *silence*] *Latin adds :* De occultis enim solus iudicat Deus, *which Harpsfield does not insert.* 18. *et certain*] de certain G. 19. *pour ce que*] Pour ce F G. 20. *tout subject fidelle et leal*] tous subjectz fidelles et loyaulx F C. 21. *estoit tenu et oblige*] estoient tenuz et obligiez F C. 22. *cathegoricquement*] cathericquement F. 23. *bon et sainct*] *So also German :* gut und heylig; *Latin has :* bonum iustum ac sanctum; *Harpsfield here follows the Latin ; cf. above, p.* 185, *l.* 30.

"Certes, s'il est vray," respondit Morus, "ce que dit le droict commun, *Qui tacet consentire videtur*, mon silence a plus confirme vostre statut que contempne. Et en tant que vous dictes que tout fidelle subiect est tenu et oblige de respondre, je dy que, en matiere qui concerne la conscience, le subiect fidelle est plus oblige a sa conscience et a son ame qu'a chose de ce monde, pourveu que telle conscience comme est la mienne ne engendre scandalle ou sedition a son seigneur; vous asseurant que ma conscience ne s'est descouverte a personne vivante.

More replies that in the common law silence is taken rather to mean consent, and that a good subject is bound to answer first to his conscience.

"Quant au second article, ou il est dit que j'ay use et praticque contre ledit statut, escripvant huict paires de lettres a l'evesque de Rochestre, et luy donnant conseil contre vostre statut, je desirerois merveilleusement que telles lettres fussent leues en public. Mais puisque elles ont este bruslees par ledit evesque, ainsi que vous dictes, je veulx voluntairement en dire la substance. Le contenu de aucunes estoit de choses familliers comme requeroit nostre ancienne amytie. Une autre contenoit la responce a une sienne, par laquelle il me demandoit quoy et comment j'avois respondu en la Tour, a ma premiere examination, sur

More's answer to the Second Article: in his correspondence with Fisher he had given no information as to his own opinion on the Supremacy.

1. *Certes*] Et certes C. 1. *respondit*] dit F C E G A B. 2. *le*] *Omitted in* F C E G B. 2. *le droict commun*] *Latin has:* quod habetur in legibus; *German:* in weltlichen Rechten. 2. *commun*] *After this* C *inserts:* use de practique. 2. *mon*] ma F C E G A B. 3. *vostre statut*] le statut F C E G A B. 3. *contempne*] condampne F C. 4–5. *tout fidelle . . . oblige*] tous les fidelles subjectz sont tenus et obligiez F C. 5. *et oblige*] *Omitted in* H. 7. *a sa*] a la F C E G A B. 7. *de ce monde*] du monde F C E G B. 8. *pourveu que*] *Latin has:* maxime si; *Harpsfield follows the Latin:* Namelye when; *cf. above, p.* 186, *l.* 10. 8. *telle conscience*] icelle conscience H. 10. *asseurant*] advissant A. 11. *personne vivante*] personne du monde F C. 13. *paires*] peres A. 14. *et luy*] en luy H. 16. *telles lettres*] icelles lettres H. 16. *en public*] a publicque F H; et publicques C. 17. *bruslees*] boutez A; volees C. 17. *ledit*] *Omitted in* F C E G A B H, *Latin and German.* 18. *voluntairement*] entierement E. 18–19. *la substance. Le contenu*] la substance et le contenu F E G. 19. *estoit de choses*] estoient de choses F C; faisaient mention de choses E; faisoient mention des choses G. 20. *familliers comme requeroit*] familieres aucune requeroit F C E G. 21. *Une autre*] unes autres H; une lettre F C. 21. *la*] *Omitted in* B. 21. *une sienne*] la sienne C. 22. *me*] *Omitted in* F C A B. 23. *en la Tour*] a la Tour F C E G B. 23. *a ma*] a la F C G; en ma E G B.

More had informed his conscience, and had advised Fisher to inform his.

ledit statut, et je luy respondy que j'avois informe ma conscience, et qu'il debvoit informer la sienne. Veritablement, je le prens sur mon ame, ce est le contenu des dites lettres, pour lesquelles je ne puis par vostre statut estre condamne a la mort.

More's answer to the Third Article: the comparison of the Statute to a two-edged sword, used both by More and by Fisher, had not been agreed upon between them.

"Quant au tiers article, qui dit que moy estant examine par le conseil, je respondy que vostre statut estoit comme une espee tranchant des deux coustez, en sorte que celluy qui le vouldroit garder perdroit son ame, et qui y vouldroit contredire perdroit le corps, ce que a pareillement respondu, ainsi que vous dictes, ledit evesque de Rochestre, et que par cela il appert que nous nous estions recordez, je vous responds que je ne respondy que conditionnellement: c'est assavoir que si c'estoit ung tel statut comme une espee tranchant des deux coustez, comment se pourroit gouverner l'homme pour n'encourir l'un des deux perilz? En quelle maniere peult avoir respondu ledit evesque de Rochestre, je ne scay. S'il a respondu comme moy, cela s'est faict pour la conformite de nostre entendement et doctrine, et non pour nous estre recordez. Et me croyez que je ne feiz et ne diz oncques chose malicieusement contre vostre dit statut. Mais bien peult estre que malicieusement l'on a rapporte de moy a la bonne grace du Roy."

Alors furent appelez par ung huissier douze hommes

1. *statut . . . respondy*] statut auquel feiz responce E G. 3. *je le*] et le H. 3. *ame, ce est*] ame que c'est E G B. 3–4. *des dites*] es dites dictes G. 4. *pour lesquelles*] par lesquelles G. 5. *la*] *Omitted in* E G H. 6. *qui dit que*] qui est que H. 7. *je respondy*] je feiz responce H. 9–10. *perdroit . . . contredire*] *Omitted in* C. 10. *qui y vouldroit*] qui le vouldroit F E G B. 10. *contredire*] contemner F. 10. *le corps*] son corps F E G A B. 10–11. *ce que a pareillement*] ce que j'ai pareillement F. 11. *dictes*] dict F. 12–13. *que . . . recordez*] que nous nous aurions recordez F; que nous avions recordez C. 13. *responds*] dis F C E G B H. 13–14. *que je . . . conditionnellement*] je respondis conditionnellement H. 14. *que*] *Omitted in* H. 15. *tel*] *Omitted in* F C E G B. 15. *tranchant*] tranchante F C E G A B. 16. *comment*] comme F C E G A B H. 16. *se*] ce D. 17. *En quelle*] De quelle F C E G. 19. *cela s'est faict*] cela est fait F A B; cela peult estre fait E G. 21. *nous*] *Omitted in* F B. 22. *je ne feiz*] je n'ay faict C. 22. *et*] *Omitted in* F C G H. 23–24. *estre . . . rapporte*] F C A B *as* D H, *but* on a rapporte *for* l'on a rapporte estre qu'on l'a rapporte malicieusement E G.

selon la coustume du pais, et leurs furent bailez lesdits articles affin qu'ilz advisassent et jugeassent si ledit Me Thomas Morus avoit malicieusement contrevenu audit statut ou non. Lesquelz, apres se estre retirez ung quart d'heure, retournerent devant les princes et juges ordinaires, et prononcerent "Gylti," c'est a dire condampne ou digne de mort. Incontinent fut son arrest prononce par monseigneur le chancellier jouxte et selon la teneur de la nouvelle loy.

The Jury find More guilty.

The Lord Chancello pronounces judgment against him.

Cela faict, ledit Morus commença a parler en ceste maniere: "Or, puisque je suis condampne, voire et Dieu scait comment, je veulx librement parler de vostre statut pour descharger ma conscience. Et diz qu'il y a sept ans que j'ay estudie ceste matiere, mais je n'ay leu en aucun docteur approuve de l'Eglise que ung temporel puisse et doibve estre chef de la spiritualite."

Seeing he is pre-condemned, More discharges his conscience concerning the Supremacy. In seven years' study he had found no authority for the supremacy of a secular prince over the spirituality.

A l'heure luy fut son propos interrompu par ledit seigneur chancellier, qui luy dit: "Me Morus, vous voullez estre estime plus saige et de meilleure conscience que tous les evesques, toute la noblesse et universellement tout le Royaulme."

More is accused of setting his opinion above that of all the Bishops and nobility of the Realm.

A quoy respondit Morus: "Millord, pour ung evesque que vous avez de vostre oppinion, j'en ay de sainctz plus de cent de la mienne; et pour ung vostre parlement, Dieu

1. *selon la coustume*] a la coustume F E G; a l'accoustumee C. 1. *leurs furent*] luy furent C. 1–2. *bailez lesdits articles*] les dits articles baillez H. 2. *affin qu'ilz . . . jugeassent*] afin qu'ilz jugeassent et adjurassent F; C *as* F, *but* advisassent *for* adjurassent; qu'ilz jugeassent E G. 2. *Me*] *Omitted in* H. 6. *Gylti*] Gilley H. *Latin and German have:* Killim. 7. *Incontinent*] Et incontinent F C E A B H. 8. *prononce par*] condempne par H. 9. *la teneur de*] la lettre de F C H; *omitted in* E G. 5. *parler*] dire H. 11. *voire et*] *Omitted in* F C E G A B. *Latin:* quo iure Deus nouit; *German:* und Got weis wie. 12. *librement parler*] parler librement F C B. 14. *que j'ay estudie*] que j'estudie F C A. 14. *ceste matiere*] en ceste matiere E G. 14. *mais je*] mais que je A. 14. *leu*] veu F C E G B. 15. *en aucun docteur approuve*] aucuns docteurs approuvez F C G. 15. *l'Eglise*] l'Esglise qui disent F. 15–16. *que ung . . . chef*] que temporels puissent et doibvent estre chiefs F C G. 19. *estime*] *Omitted in* E. 19–20. *plus saige . . . que tous*] le plus sage et le meilleur que tous C. 20–21. *toute . . . tout*] et toute la noblesse unyversellement de tout F C E G H. 22. *Morus*] ledit Morus F C A B. 23. *de sainctz*] des sainctz F C A B H. 24. *ung*] *Omitted in* F C E G.

More asserts that there is far more support for his view than for that of his opponents.

scait quel, j'ay tous les concilles generaulx depuis mille ans; et pour ung royaulme, j'ay la France et tous les autres royaulmes de la chrestiente."

Lors ledit duc de Norfort luy dist: "A ceste heure, Morus, on veoit bien clairement vostre malice."

More calls God to witness that he has spoken only for discharge of his conscience.

The Act of Supremacy, made without the common consent of all Christians, and directed against the union of Christendom, is ill made.

The true reason why they seek More's blood is that he would not give his consent in the matter of the marriage.

Ledit Morus respondit: "Millord, ce que je diz, c'est par necessite, et pour la declaration de ma conscience et satisfaction de mon ame, et de ce faire j'en appelle Dieu a tesmoing, qui est seul scrutateur des cueurs humains. Et diz davantage que vostre ordonnance est mal faicte, car vous avez faict profession et jure de ne faire jamais chose contre l'eglise, laquelle est en toute la chrestiente une seulle et integre, non divisee, et vous seulz n'avez auctorite quelconque, sans le consentement des autres chrestiens, de faire loy ou acte de parlement contre ladite unyon de la chrestiente. Je scay bien pour quelle cause m'avez condampne. Est ce pour ce que je ne voullu jamais par cy davant consentir a la matiere du mariaige du Roy; mais j'espere bien tant en la divine bonte et misericorde que ainsi que sainct Pol, comme il est escript en sa vie, persecuta tousiours sainct Estienne, et que maintenant ilz sont amys en paradis, ainsi nous tous, combien que nous ayons discord en ce monde, en l'autre nous serons ensemble uniz avec parfaicte charite.

More prays for his Judges and the King.

Et sur ce point je prie Dieu qu'il veuille saulver et garder le Roy, et luy donner bon conseil."

1. *quel*] *Omitted in* F C E G A. 1. *les concilles*] les conseilliers A; vos conseillers C. 1. *generaulx*] *Omitted in* F C. 5. *on veoit*] voyt on E G. 5. *bien clairement*] clerement bien F C E G. 5. *vostre*] ta F. 7. *declaration*] descharge E G B H. 8. *faire*] *Omitted in* E. 8. *en*] *Omitted in* F C E G A B. 9. *a tesmoing*] en tesmoing F C E G A B H. 9. *cueurs humains*] erreurs humaines F C. 10. *Et diz davantage que*] et deiz que B; Je dy davantage que E G; Je dis que F C. 11. *profession*] professions F C E G A B H. 15. *de faire loy*] de celle loy B. 16. *unyon de la*] union de F; unyon de la dite E G. 16–17. *Je scay . . . cause*] Je ne scay pour quelle chose ne cause F. 17. *Est ce*] c'est F A B H; Et Ce C. 17–18. *je ne voullu . . . consentir a*] je ne voulus jamais jadis consentir a B; je n'ay consenty jamais par cy devant a F C E G; par cy devant je n'ay voulu consentir a H. 19. *tant*] *Omitted in* F C E G A B. 21. *persecuta*] persecutoit F C. 21. *tousiours*] *Omitted in* F C E G A B. 23. *nous*] aussy nous H. 23. *discord*] discords F C E G A B. 23–24. *en l'autre nous serons*] en l'aultre au plaisir de Dieu nous serons H. 24. *ensemble uniz*] unys ensemble F C E G A B. 25. *point*] *Omitted in* E G.

Ainsi que l'on ramenoit ledit Morus en la grosse Tour, l'une de ses filles, nommee Marguerite, avant qu'il entrast dedans ladite Tour, se gecta au meilleu de la tourbe des archers et satalites, esprise et vaincue d'une extreme doulleur et vexation paternelle, sans avoir aucun respect a l'assistence ne au lieu public, et saillit au col de son dit pere, et par quelque espace de temps le tint estroictement embrasse, sans pouvoir dire aucune parolle. Et apres son trescher pere, par la permission desdits archers, luy dist pour la consoler :

More is led back to the Tower. Margaret bids her father farewell.

"Marguerite, ayez pascience, ne vous tourmentez plus. Ce est la volunte de Dieu. Longtemps a que vous avez congneu le secret de mon cueur."

More comforts Margaret.

Puis elle, estant esloignee de luy comme de dix ou douze pas, de rechef retourna le ravyr au col; a laquelle ledit pere ne dist autre chose, sans espandre larmes et sans mutation de visaige et de parler, sinon qu'elle priast Dieu pour son ame.

Margaret returns to bid her father a second farewell. More asks her to pray for his soul.

P. 264, l. 26–l. 1. *conseil. Ainsi*] conseil. Et ce dit ainsi que H. 1. *ramenoit*] menoit F C E G. 2. *Marguerite*] *Latin expands:* Margareta filiarum Mori natu maxima, mulier præter eximiam formæ uenustatem cum summa dignitate coniunctam, iudicio ingenio moribus & eruditione patris simillima. 3. *entrast dedans*] entra en E. 4. *des archers et satalites*] des archers des satallites F C G; des archers et sagitaires H; des archers E. 4. *esprise*] *Omitted in* F C. 5. *doulleur et*] *Omitted in* E G. 6. *aucun*] aucuns F C E G A B. 6. *ne au lieu public*] ny au peuple B; ne au public H. 6. *et*] *Omitted in* F C E G A B. 7. *dit*] *Omitted in* F C E G A B. 8–9. *aucune parolle*] aucunes parolles F C E G A B. 9. *parolle*] *After this, Latin inserts the tag :* Curæ, inquit Tragicus, leues loquuntur, ingentes stupent. 12. *Longtemps a*] longtemps y a C. 12. *vous*] *Omitted in* F C. 13. *cueur*] *Latin adds :* simulque dedit osculum ex consuetudine gentis, si quem dimittunt. 14. *Puis*] Et puis B; *omitted in* F C. 15. *douze pas*] douze piedz F C E G A B. 15. *le ravyr*] le rembrasser E; l'embrasser G. 15–18. *ravyr au col . . . son ame*] *Latin expands :* inhæsit collo illius, sed elinguis præ doloris magnitudine. Cui pater nihil loquutus est, tantum erumpebant lacrymæ, uultu tamen a constantia nihil dimoto. Nec aliud supremis uerbis mandauit, quam ut Deum pro anima patris deprecaretur. Ad hoc pietatis certamen plurimis e populari turba lacrymæ excidere. Erant et inter satellites, ferum & immite genus hominum, qui lacrymas tenere non potuerunt, etc. *Spanish has :* a la qual el afligido padre corriendo lagrimas de sus ojos sin hazer mouimiento en la habla ni en el rostro no dixo otra cosa sino que rogassen a dios por su anima. 16. *autre chose, sans*] aucune chose sinon sans H. 17. *sans mutation de*] sans muer de H. 17. *visaige et de parler*] visaige ou de parler F; visaige de parler C; visaige et parler B; visaige E G H. 17. *sinon*] *Omitted in* H.

More's speech on the scaffold and the manner of his death.

Le mercredi ensuyvant il fut decapite en la grant place qui est devant ladite Tour, et parla peu avant l'execution. Seullement pria les assistans qu'ilz priassent Dieu pour luy par deça, et que autre part il prieroit pour eulx. Apres les exhorta, et supplia tres instamment qu'ils priassent Dieu pour le Roy, affin qu'il luy voulsist donner bon conseil, protestant qu'il mouroit son bon serviteur et de Dieu premierement.

1. *mercredi*] *So the eight French MSS. of the News Letter; Latin,* die Mercurij sequente; *German,* am volgenden mitwoch; *Spanish,* Miercoles siguiente. *More's execution took place on* 6 *July,* 1535, *and this fell on a Tuesday.* 2. *Tour*] *Latin has:* Mos est illic ut afficiendi supplicio, de ponte plebem alloquantur. 2. *avant l'execution*] a la dite execution E G. 3. *pria*] priant F C E G A B. 4. *qu'ilz priassent*] qui priassent A. 5. *tres instamment*] tristement F C. 8. *premierement*] *Latin adds:* Hæc loquutus prompte constantique uultu flexis genibus ceruicem posuit securim excepturus non sine graui multorum gemitu. Erat enim bonis omnibus charissimus. Quæ hactenus narraui, fere continebantur in scheda apud Parisios iactata . . .

NOTE

Certain manuscripts have a note following the text:

Et voila la fin myserable de Morus qui fut autrefois en grande reputation et bien ayme du Roy son maistre et de tous estime tousjours homme de bien jusques a la mort F C; E G as F C, but *Voila la fin pitoyable* for *Et voila la fin myserable.*

Following this note F has the date: *Fait le iiij*^{eme} *jour du moys d'Aoust l'an mil V*^{c}*xxxv;* C as F, but *jour d'Aoust* for *jour du moys d'Aoust.*

APPENDIX III

SIR THOMAS MORE'S INDICTMENT

NOTE

THE text of this edition follows that of the original indictment (endorsed on back " Billa vera ") of the *Baga de Secretis*, Pouch 7, Bundle 3, m. 7 (referred to below as B). There is a copy of this in the same Bundle, mm. 1^b–3^a (referred to below as B^2), differing only very slightly from it (see Collations below). Two other copies are found in MS. Arundel 152 (British Museum), fols. 288^a–292^b, and fols. 302^b–305^b (referred to below as A and A^2 respectively). A is printed in *Archæologia*, XXVII, pp. 370–4: it is corrupt in several respects, a noteworthy error being that of the English passage, p. 273, below. A^2 is imperfect, owing to the charred edges of the Arundel MS.: its text is nearer that of the original, but owing to an eyeslip, the English passage of p. 273, below, is again corrupt.

In the variant readings below, the spelling is that of the first MS. cited.

[*Baga de Secretis*, Pouch 7, Bundle 3, M. 7.]

Midd'. Jur*atores* present*ant* p*ro* Do*m*ino Rege q*uo*d, Cum p*er* quendam Actu*m* in p*ar*liamento d*omi*ni n*ost*ri Regis nu*n*c apud London' t*er*cio die Mensis Nouembris Anno regni sui vicesimo primo inchoat*o*, *et* abinde eod*em* t*er*cio die Nouembris vsq*ue* ad villam Westm' in Com*itatu* Midd' p*ro*rogat*o*, et postea, p*er* diu*er*sas p*ro*rogacio*n*es, vsq*ue* ad *et* in t*er*ciu*m* diem Nouembris Anno regni sui vicesimo sexto continuat*o*, *et* tunc apud d*ict*am villa*m* Westm' tent*o*, edit*um*, inter cet*er*a, auctoritate eiusdem Parliamenti inactitatu*m* sit, Q*uo*d idem d*omin*us Rex, heredes *et* successores sui, huius Regni Reges accepti, acceptati *et* reputati erunt vnicu*m* sup*re*mu*m* Caput in t*er*ra Anglicane eccl*es*ie, h*ab*ebuntq*ue* *et* gaudebunt, annexum *et* vnitu*m* Imperiali Corone huius Regni, tam titulu*m* *et* stilu*m* inde q*ua*m om*n*ia honores, dignitates, p*re*eminencias, Jurisdicc*io*nes, priuilegia, auctoritates, immunitates, co*m*moda *et* co*m*moditates d*ict*e dignitati supremi Capitis eiusd*em* Eccl*es*ie incu*m*bencia *et* p*er*tinencia, p*ro*ut in eodem Actu, int*er* alia, plenius continet*ur*; Cumq*ue* eciam p*er* quendam alterum actum, in d*ict*o p*ar*liamento d*ict*o anno vicesimo sexto tento, editu*m*, int*er* cetera inactitatum sit, q*uo*d si aliqua p*er*sona, aut alique p*er*sone, post primu*m* diem Februarii tunc p*ro*ximu*m* sequen*tis*, maliciose optau*er*it, volu*er*it, seu desiderau*er*it p*er* v*er*ba vel scripta, aut arte imaginau*er*it,

By the Act of Supremacy of 26 Henry VIII, the King had been accepted as Supreme Head on earth of the Church of England.

By the Act of Treason of the same Parliament, it was made high treason to deprive *maliciously*, in word or writing, the King,

1. *Midd' Juratores presentant pro Domino Rege*] *Instead of this,* B[2] A A[2] *have the following :*
Midd': Inquisicio capta apud villam Westm', in Comitatu predicto, Coram prefatis Johanne FitzJames Milite, Johanne Baldewyn Milite, Ricardo Lyster Milite, Johanne Porte Milite, Johanne Spelman Milite, Waltero Luke Milite, et Antonio Fitzherbert Milite, Justiciariis, &c. dicto die Lune proximo post Festum sancti Johannis Baptiste, per sacramentum Thome Tayllour, Roberti Graunt, Willielmi Russell, Henrici Croke, Roberti Bowden, Eustacii Rypley, Cristoferi Proctour, Henrici Gaffeney, Johannis Grove, Willielmi Grymbylby, Johannis Apswell, Johannis Myller, Johannis Wylkynson, Thome Colte, Willielmi Stevenson, Walteri Phelipps, Juratorum. Qui dicunt super sacramentum suum.

3. *Mensis*] *Omitted in* B[2] A A[2]. 16. *Jurisdicciones*] *Omitted in* A. 19. *alia*] aliam A[2]. 22. *inactitatum*] inactiatum B[2].

Queen, or their heirs, of their dignities and titles.

inventauerit, practicauerit, siue attemptauerit, aliquod dampnum corporale fiendum aut committendum Regalissime persone domini Regis, Regine, aut eorum heredibus apparentibus, vel ad depriuandos eos, aut eorum aliquem, de dignitate, titulo, seu nomine regalium statuum suorum, Quod tunc quelibet talis persona et persone, sic offendentes in aliquo premissorum post dictum primum diem Februarii, atque eorum auxiliatores, consentores, Consiliarii et abettatores, inde legittime convicti existentes, secundum leges et consuetudines huius Regni adiudicabuntur proditores; Et quod quelibet talis offensa in aliquo premissorum que committeretur aut fieret, post dictum primum diem Februarii, reputabitur, acceptabitur, et adiudicabitur alta prodicio; Et offensores in eisdem, ac eorum auxiliatores, consentores, Consiliarii, et abbettatores, legittime convicti existentes de aliqua tali offensa qualis predicitur, habeb[un]t et pacie[n]tur tales penas mortis, et alias penalitates quales limitate sunt et consuete in casibus alte prodicionis, Prout in dicto altero Actu manifeste patet.

The First Article. On 7 May, 27 Henry VIII, in the Tower, before Thomas Cromwell, Thomas Bedell, John Tregonwell, and others, More had *maliciously* refused to give his opinion on the King's Supremacy.

Quidam tamen Thomas More, nuper de Chelchehith, in Comitatu Mydd', Miles, deum pre oculis non habens, set instigacione diabolica seductus, septimo die Maii Anno regni dicti domini Regis vicesimo septimo, statutorum predictorum satis sciolus, false, proditorie, et maliciose, apud Turrim London', in Comitatu predicto, imaginans, inventans, practicans et attemptans, atque volens, et desiderans, contra legiancie sue debitum, prefatum serenissimum dominum nostrum Regem de dignitate, titulo, et nomine status sui Regalis, videlicet, de dignitate, titulo et nomine suis supremi capitis in terra Anglicane ecclesie, depriuare, dicto septimo die Maii, apud dictam Turrim London', in Comitatu predicto, coram Thoma Crumwell Armigero, primario Secretario Domini Regis, Thoma Bedyll Clerico, Johanne Tregonell legum doctore, Consiliariis dicti domini Regis, et coram diuersis aliis

6. *tunc*] *Omitted in* B^2 A A^2. 6. *talis*] titulis A^2. 17. *tali*] tituli A^2. 18. *habebunt et pacientur*] habebit et pacietur B B^2 A A^2. 25. *Regis*] *Omitted in* B^2 A A^2.

personis eiusdem domini Regis veris subditis, per mandatum ipsius domini Regis examinatus et interrogatus, an ipse eundem dominum Regem supremum caput in terra ecclesie Anglicane accipiebat, acceptabat, et reputabat, et eum sic accipere, acceptare, et reputare, vellet, secundum formam et effectum statuti supradicti prius recitati, Idem Thomas adtunc et ibidem maliciose penitus [s]ilebat, responsumque directum ad illud interrogatorium facere recusabat, Et hec verba Anglicana sequencia dictis domini Regis veris subditis adtunc et ibidem edicebat, videlicet, "I wyll not meddyll with any such matters, For I am fully determyned to serue God, and to thynk vppon his passion and my passage out of this worlde;" Posteaque, videlicet duodecimo die dicte mensis Maii, Anno vicesimo septimo supradicto, prefatus Thomas More, sciens quendam Johannem Fyssher Clericum, tunc, et diu antea, in dicta Turre London', pro diuersis grandibus m[i]sprisionibus per ipsum Johannem erga dicti domini nostri Regis regiam maiestatem perpetratis, fore incarceratum et detentum, ac per dictos domini Regis veros subditos, de eius accepcione, acceptacione, et reputacione, eiusdem domini Regis in premissis fuisse examinatum, eundemque Johannem false, proditorie, et maliciose, expresse negasse prefatum dominum Regem sic accipere, acceptare, et reputare supremum caput in terra ecclesie Anglicane fore, Idemque Thomas More, existimans se ipsum et prefatum Johannem Fyssher de premissis alias ex verisimili tunc fore examinandos et interrogandos, diuersas literas dicto duodecimo die Maii, apud dictam Turrim London', in predicto Comitatu Midd', continuando maliciam suam predictam, false, maliciose, et proditorie scripsit, easque prefato Johanni Fyssher in dicta Turre London' tunc existenti porrexit, et, per quendam Georgium Golde, eisdem die, Anno, et loco transmisit et deliberari fecit; Per quas quidem literas predictus Thomas More false,

The Second Article. On 12 May, More (knowing that John Fisher, Bishop of Rochester, then imprisoned in the Tower for various offences against the King, had expressly denied the King's Supremacy) had written to Fisher, *maliciously* upholding his attitude, and acquainting him with his own silence when examined.

6. *supradicti*] predicti B² A A². 7. *adtunc*] tunc A. 8. *silebat*] A; cilebat B B² A². 18. *misprisionibus*] A A²; mesprisionibus B B². 23. *Johannem*] Johannem Fissher B² A A². 35. *transmisit*] transmitti A.

maliciose, et proditorie prefato Johanni Fyssher in dicta eius falsa prodicione consulebat et consenciebat, et, per easdem intimans eidem Johanni dictam [s]ilenciam quam idem Thomas More vt prefertur interrogatus habuisset, responsumque suum negatum, in verbis anglicanis supra scriptis expressis verbis scriptis revelans,

The Third Article. In the said letters to Fisher, More had described the Act of Parliament as "a sword with two edges," &c.

Et, insuper, per easdem literas false, proditorie, et maliciose scribens et asserens hec verba anglicana, videlicet, "The act of parlement" (dictum Actum posterius recitatum innuens) "is lyke a swerde with two edgys, For if a man answere one wey it wyll confounde his soule, and if he answere the other wey it wyll confounde his body;" postmodumque prefatus Thomas More, metuens ne contingeret prefatum Johannem Fyssher in eius responso, supra itterata examinacione ipsius Johannis fiend[a], predicta verba, per ipsum Thomam eidem Johanni Fyssher vt prefertur scripta consiliariis dicti domini regis eloqui,

On 26 May, More had written to Fisher, advising him to formulate his own answer, and not to make use of any words of his, lest they might be suspected of confederacy.

Idem Thomas More, apud Turrim predictam, vicesimo sexto die Maii anno vicesimo septimo supradicto, per eius alias literas scriptas et prefato Johanni Fyssher directas, et apud Turrim predictam deliberatas, eundem Johannem Fyssher false, maliciose et proditorie desiderabat, quatenus Idem Johannes responsum suum secundum eius proprium animum faceret, et cum aliquo tali responso quale idem Thomas prefato Johanni Fyssher antea scripsisset nullatenus intromitteret, Ne forsan dictis Consiliariis domini Regis occasionem putandi preberet quod aliqualis erat inter eosdem Thomam et Johannem confederacio. Attamen, ex dictis literis prefati Thome More prius scriptis, et dicto Johanni Fyssher vt premittitur porrectis et deliberatis, ita insecutum est, videlicet, idem Johannes Fyssher, per dictas literas prefati Thome More false, maliciose, et proditorie doctus et instructus,

1. *prefato Johanni Fissher*] prefatum Johannem Fissher A. 3. *silenciam*] A; cilenciam B B^2 A^2. 10. *innuens*] *Space left for this in* A. 12. *wey*] *Omitted in* A^2. 13. *his body*] the bodye A^2. 13. *postmodumque*] postmodum A. 16. *fienda*] B^2 A A^2; fiendo B. 19. *Turrim predictam*] Turrim London' predictam A A^2. 22. *predictam*] London' B^2 A A^2. 25. *tali*] tituli A^2. 27. *intromitteret*] intromitteretur A A^2. 29. *aliqualis*] equalis A. 30. *confederacio*] consideratio A; consideracio A^2.

et exinde quodammodo animatus, postea, videlicet, tercio die Junii anno vicesimo septimo supradicto, apud Turrim predictam, per Thomam Audeley militem, Cancellarium Anglie, Charolum Ducem Suff', Thomam Comitem Wiltes', dicti Domini Regis nobiles subditos et Consiliarios, et alios eiusdem domini Regis venerabiles subditos et Consiliarios, denuo de premissis examinatus et interrogatus, penitus [s]ilebat, responsumque directum ad id facere nolebat, Sed hec verba anglicana sequencia adtunc et ibidem dictis nobilibus et venerabilibus domini Regis subditis et consiliariis false, proditorie, et maliciose edicebat, videlicet, "I wyll not meddyll with that matter, For the statute is lyke a two edged sworde, And, if I shuld answere one wey, I shulde offende my conscyence; And if I shulde answere the other wey I shulde put my lyfe in ieopardye; wherfore I wyll make no answere to that matter." Prefatusque Thomas More, similiter dicto tercio die Junii, anno vicesimo septimo supradicto, apud Turrim predictam, per dictos domini Regis nobiles et venerabiles subditos et Consiliarios iterum de premissis interrogatus, In dicta eius [s]ilencia false, proditorie et maliciose, adtunc et ibidem perseuerabat, directumque responsum ad premissa facere nolebat, Immo false, proditorie, et maliciose, adtunc et ibidem imaginans, inventans, practicans, et attemptans, atque volens, et desiderans, prefatum dominum nostrum Regem de dignitate, titulo et nomine status sui regalis supradicti depriuare, sedicionemque et malignitatem in cordibus verorum subditorum domini Regis erga eundem dominum Regem inserere et generare, prefatis nobilibus et venerabilibus dicti domini Regis subditis et Consiliariis adtunc

Yet, on 3 June, Fisher, thus *maliciously* instructed and encouraged by More, had refused to give his opinion on the Supremacy, and had compared the Act to a two-edged sword.

And on this same 3 June, More, when examined, had *maliciously* persevered in his silence concerning the Supremacy, and had used the same comparison of the Act to a two-edged sword.

3. *Turrim*] Turrim London' B² A A². 8. *silebat*] A; cilebat B B² A². 9. *verba anglicana*] Anglicana verba A A². 14–17. *I shulde offende . . . that matter*] *This is the reading of both* B *and* B². A (*followed by the transcript of* Archaeologia, XXVII) *runs:* I should put my life in ieoperdye, and answering another way, I put my soule in more ieoperdy, wherefore to this matter I will make no answer at all. A² *omits* offende my conscyence And if I shulde answere the other wey I shulde, *owing to an eyeslip from* shulde *preceding; otherwise its reading is that of* B *and* B². 16. *answere*] aunser B². 17. *similiter*] *Omitted in* A. 21. *dicta*] dicto A; dictam A². 21. *silencia*] cilencia B B²; silentio A; cilenciam A². 21. *false, proditorie et*] false maliciose et proditorie B² A A².

et ibidem subsequencia verba anglicana palam dicebat, videlicet, "The lawe and statute whereby the Kyng is made supreme hed, as is aforesaid, be lyke a swerde with two edges; For, if a man sey that the same lawes be good, then it is daungerous to the soule; And if he say contrary to the seid statute, then it is dethe to the body. Wherfore I wyll make therunto noon other answere because I wyll not be occasion of the shorttyng of my lyfe." Et insuper Juratores predicti dicunt, quod prefati Thomas More et Johannes Fyssher, ad eorum supradictum falsum et nephandissimum proditorium propositum celandum, omnes et omnimodas literas alterutrum scriptas et deliberatas, et eorum unus et alter, immediate post lecturas earundem combussit.

To conceal their treasonable confederacy, More and Fisher had burnt these letters.

The Fourth Article. On 12 June, More, in conversation with Rich, the Solicitor-General, had actually denied the King's Supremacy, *maliciously* depriving him of his title.

Et, post hec omnia et singula premissa vt premittitur peracta et dicta, videlicet, duodecimo die Junii, anno vicesimo septimo supradicto, accessit ad prefatum Thomam More, in predictam Turrim London', Ricardus Ryche, Generalis solicitator dicti domini Regis, habitoque, adtunc et ibidem, inter eosdem Thomam More et Ricardum Ryche colloquio, de diuersis premissa tangentibus, idem Ricardus Ryche caritatiue movebat prefatum Thomam More, quatenus se vellet actibus et legibus suprascriptis conformare; Ad quod idem Thomas, respondendo prefato Ricardo Ryche, dicebat, "Consciencia vestra saluabit vos," Et "consciencia mea saluabit me." Prefatusque Ricardus Ryche, adtunc et ibidem protestans quod tunc non habebat Commissionem, siue mandatum, cum eodem Thoma More de materia illa tractare siue communicare, eundem Thomam More adtunc et ibidem interrogabat, Si inactitatum fuisset auctoritate parliamenti quod idem Ricardus Ryche esset Rex, Et quod si quis id negaret prodicio esset, Qualis esset offensa in prefato Thoma More si idem Thomas diceret quod prefatus Ricardus Ryche erat Rex? Pro certo, vlterius dicebat idem Ricardus, in consciencia eius quod nulla esset offensa,

More had admitted that an Act of Parliament could make Rich King, and that if it were made treason to deny Rich this title, he would be bound to recognise him as such.

5. *it is*] is it A. 6. *it is*] is it A. 7. *noon*] no A. 8. *the*] *Omitted in* A. 10. *prefati*] predicti A A². 19. *Solicitator*] Solicitor A. 19. *adtunc*] tunc A. 25. *Ricardo Ryche*] Riche B². 30. *interrogabat*] interrogabatur A². 32. *esset*] erat A A². 36. *Ricardus*] Ricardus Riche A.

Sed quod idem Thomas More obligatus erat sic dicere, et eundem Ricardum acceptare pro eo quod consensus prefati Thome More per actum parliamenti erat obligatus. Ad quod prefatus Thomas More, adtunc et ibidem respondendo, dicebat, quod ipse offenderet si diceret non, Quia obligatus esset per actum pro eo quod consensum suum ad id prebere potuit, Sed dicebat quod idem casus erit casus levis; Quamobrem idem Thomas adtunc et ibidem prefato Ricardo Ryche dicebat, quod ipse alium casum sublimiorem proponere vellet, sic dicens, "Posito quod per parliamentum inactitatum foret quod deus non esset deus, Et quod si quis impugnare vellet, actum illum foret prodicio, Si interrogaretur questio a vobis, Ricarde Ryche, velitis dicere quod deus non erat deus accordante statuto, Et si sic diceretis, non offenderetis?" Ad quod idem Ricardus, respondens prefato Thome More, adtunc et ibidem dicebat; "Immo, pro certe; Quia impossibile est fiendum quod deus non esset deus. Et quia casus vester adeo sublimis existit, proponam vobis hunc casum mediocrem, videlicet; Nouistis quia dominus noster Rex constitutus est supremum caput in terra ecclesie Anglicane, Et quare non deberetis vos, Magister More, eum sic affirmare et acceptare, tam sic quam in casu premisso quo ego prefectus eram Rex, In quo casu conceditis quod obligaremini sic me affirmare et acceptare Regem?" Ad quod prefatus Thomas More false, proditorie, et maliciose in dictis eius prodicione et malicia perseuerans, predictumque eius proditorium et maliciosum propositum et appetitum preferre et defendere volens, prefato Ricardo Ryche adtunc et ibidem sic respondebat, videlicet, "quod casus illi non erant consimiles, Quia, Rex per parliamentum fieri potest, et per parliamentum depriuari potest, ad quem actum quilibet subditus ad parliamentum existens suum prebeat consensum, Sed, ad primacie casum, Subditus non potest obligari, Quia consensum suum ab eo ad parliamentum prebere non potest; Et, quamquam Rex sic acceptus sit

Rich had admitted that an Act of Parliament could not make it law that God should not be God.

When Rich had proposed that an Act of Parliament could make the King Supreme Head of the Church, More had asserted that no subject could give his consent to the King's Supremacy through Parliament, and therefore could not be bound by the Act; and had asserted that though the King is accepted as Supreme Head in England, such is not the case in many places abroad

4–5. *respondendo*] respondend A. 8. *erit*] erat A. 14. *erat*] esset A. 18. *fiendum*] fieri A. 21. *caput*] capud A[2]. 25. *obligaremini*] obligamini A; obligamini *corrected from* obligarimini A[2]. 25. *sic me*] me sic A.

Thus More had *maliciously* deprived the King of his title.

in Anglia plurime tamen partes extere idem non affirmant." Sicque Juratores predicti dicunt, quod prefatus Thomas More false, proditorie, et maliciose, arte imaginauit, inventauit, practicauit, *et* attemptauit prefatum serenissimum dominum nostrum Regem de dictis dignitate, titulo *et* nomine supradicti status sui Regalis videlicet de dignitate titulo, et nomine suis supremi capitis in terra Anglicane ecclesie penitus depriuare, In ipsius domini Regis contemptum manifestum, *et* Corone sue regie derogacionem, contra formam *et* effectum statutorum predictorum, Et contra pacem eiusdem domini Regis.

APPENDIX IV

THE EPITAPH ON THE MORE TOMB IN CHELSEA OLD CHURCH

NOTE

The description in English below (*Sir Thomas More . . . which epitaphy here foloweth*) is that preceding the copy of the Epitaph in More's *English Works* (1557), pp. 1419–20. The English note (*Under this epitaphy . . . before*) p. 281, between the "epitaphy in prose" and the "epitaphy in versis," is also from *English Works*, p. 1420. Those portions of the marginal summary of the present edition which are given within quotation marks are from the English translation of the Epitaph, *English Works*, pp. 1421–22.

The Latin text below is that of the present Inscription on the Tomb. "It is probable that no part of the original tomb remains other than the inscription slab, the lettering of which has been recut, and even this is doubtful, since Aubrey states in his *Lives of Eminent Men* [Vol. II, p. 463] that More's monument 'being worn by time, about 1644 Sir John Lawrence of Chelsey erected to his memory a handsome inscription of marble.' The whole monument was 'restored,' that is to say, remade, by Mr. J. Faulkner, statuary of Chelsea, in 1833." (See *L.C.C. Survey of London*, Vol. VII, Part III (1921), pp. 24–7.)

Where the present Inscription on the Tomb differs from the Inscription as given by More in his Letter to Erasmus of June 14, 1532 (as printed in *Des. Erasmi Roterodami Epistolarum Opus, Basileæ, ex officina Frobeniana*, 1538), or from the copy in More's *English Works* (1557), the differences (other than mere variations of spelling, *æ*: *e*, &c.) are recorded in the footnotes below, E signifying the Letter to Erasmus, and W signifying More's *English Works*.

Extensions of the abbreviated forms of the Tomb are denoted in this edition by italics. The oblique stroke / indicates the end of a line in the Tomb Inscription.

[An Epitaphy in Latin.]

1532.

Sir Thomas More, being lorde Chaunceller of England, gaue ouer that office (by his great sute and labour) the XVI day of may, in the yere of our lord god a*nno* 1532, and in the xxiiii yere of the raigne of king Henry the eight. And after in that somer, he wrote an epitaphy in latin, and caused it to be written vpo*n* his tombe of stone, which himself (while he was lord Cha*n*celler) had caused to be made in his parishe church of Chelsey (where he dwelled) thre smal Miles fro*m* London. The copye of which epitaphy here foloweth :

More enumerates his public offices.

THOMAS MORVS VRBE LONDINENSI FAMILIA NON CELEBRI SED HONESTA NATVS IN LITERIS VTCVNQ[VE] / VERSATVS ; QVVM ET CAVSAS ALIQVOT ANNOS IVVENIS EGISSET IN FORO ET IN VRBE SVA PRO SHIREVO IVS / DIXISSET : AB INVICTISSIMO REGE HENRICO OCTAVO (CVI VNI REGVM OMNIVM GLORIA PRIVS INAVDITA / CONTIGIT VT FIDEI DEFENSOR QVALEM ET GLADIO SE ET CALAMO VERE PRÆSTITIT, MERITO VOCARETVR) / ADSCITVS IN AVLAM EST DELECTVSQ*VE* IN CONSILIVM ET CREATVS EQVES PROQVÆSTOR PRIMV[M], POST CANCELLARIVS / LANCASTRIÆ, TANDEM ANGLIÆ MIRO PRINCIPIS FAVORE FACTVS EST SED INTERIM IN PVBLICO REGNI / SENATV LECTVS EST ORATOR POPVLI, PRÆTEREA LEGATVS REGIS NONNVNQVA[M] FVIT ALIAS ALIBI, POSTREMO / VERO CAMERACI COMES ET COLLEGA IVNCTVS PRINCIP[I] LEGATIONIS, CVTHBERTO TVNSTALLO TVM / LONDINENSI MOX DVNELMENSI EPISCOPO, QVO VIRO VIX HABET ORBIS HODIE

And his share with Tunstall in the Peace of Cambrai.

13. LITERIS] litteris E W. 13. VTCVNQVE] *So* E W; Tomb *omits colon denoting* V E. 15. SHIREVO] Shyreno E; Shyreuo W. 16. INVICTISSIMO] inuictiss. E; imictissimo W. 17. OMNIVM] ommium W. 18. VERE] vero W. 21. PRIMVM] *So* E W; Tomb *omits contraction mark for* M, *reading* PRIMV. 24–25. NONNVNQVAM] E; nonnuncquam W; Tomb *omits contraction mark for* M, *reading* NONNVNQVA. 26. PRINCIPI] E W; principe Tomb. 27–28. DVNELMENSI] Dunelniensi W. 28. HABET] habes W.

QVICQVAM ERVDITIVS, PRVDENTIVS, / MELIVS. IBI INTER SVMMOS ORBIS CHRISTIANI MONARCHAS RVRSVS REFECTA FŒDERA, REDDITAMQ*VE* MVNDO / DIV DESIDERATAM PACEM ET LÆTISSIMVS VIDIT ET LEGATVS INTERFVIT /

"Which Peace our Lord stablish and make perpetual.'

"QVAM SVPERI PACEM FIRMENT FAXINTQ*VE* PERENNEM." /

He describes himself as having been "grievous to thieves, murderers [and heretics].'

IN HOC OFFICIORVM VEL HONORVM CVRSV, QVVM ITA VERSARETVR VT NEQ*VE* PRINCEPS OPTIMVS OPERAM / EIVS IMPROBARET NEQ*VE* NOBILIBVS ESSET INVISVS, NEC INIVCVNDVS POPVLO, FVRIBVS AVTEM ET / HOMICIDIS MOLESTVS. PATER EIVS TANDEM IOHANNES MORVS EQVÆS ET IN EVM IVDICVM ORDINEM / A PRINCIPE COOPTATVS QVI REGIVS CON[S]ESSVS VOCATVR; HOMO CIVILIS, SVAVIS, INNOCENS, MITIS, MISERICORS, / ÆQVVS ET INTEGER, ANNIS QVIDEM GRAVIS, SED CORPORE PLVSQVAM PRO ÆTATE VIVIDO, POSTQVAM / EO PRODVCTAM SIBI VITAM VIDIT, VT FILIVM VIDERIT ANGLIÆ CANCELLARIVM, SATIS IN TERRA IAM / SE MORATVM RATVS, LIBENS EMIGRAVIT IN CŒLVM. AT FILIVS, DEFVNCTO PATRE, CVI QVAMDIV / SVPERARAT COMPARATVS ET IVVENIS VOCARI CONSVEVERAT, ET IPSE QVOQ*VE* SIBI VIDEBATVR, / AMISSVM IAM PATREM REQVIRENS ET ÆDITOS EX SE LIBEROS QVATVOR AC NEPOTES VNDECIM / RESPICIENS APVD ANIMVM SVVM CÆPIT PERSENESCERE. AVXIT HVNC AFFECTVM ANIMI SVBSECVTA / STATIM VELVT ADPETENTIS SENI SIGNVM, PECTORIS VALITVDO DETERIOR. ITAQ*VE* MORTALIVM / HARVM RERVM SATVR, QVAM REM A PVERO PENE SEMPER OPTAVERAT, VT VLTIMOS ALIQVOT VITÆ / SVÆ ANNOS OBTINERET LIBEROS, QVIBVS HVIVS VITÆ NEGOTIIS PAVLATIM SE SEDVCENS FVTVRÆ POSSIT / IMMORTALITATEM MEDITARI, EAM REM TANDEM (SI CÆPTIS ANNVAT DEVS) INDVLGENTISSIMI PRINCIPIS / INCOMPARABILI

His father, Sir John More, is now dead. And he himself, growing old and feeble, and desiring leisure for godly purposes, has resigned the Chancellorship.

10. ET] *Omitted in* E W. 10–11. HOMICIDIS MOLESTVS] homicidis hæreticisque molestus E W. *In the present Inscription on the Tomb, the state of the marble proves that no writing ever filled the blank space between* HOMICIDIS *and* MOLESTVS. 13. CONSESSVS]E; confessus Tomb, W. 17. VIDERIT] videret W. 20. SVPERARAT] supererat E W. 25. AVXIT] Anxit W. 25. AFFECTVM] adfectum W. 26. SENI] senii E; sonii W. 27. VALITVDO] valetudo E W. 31. SEDVCENS] subducens E W. 31. POSSIT] posset E W. 32. CÆPTIS] cœptis E; chptis W.

BENEFICIO, RESIGNATIS HONORIBVS, IMPETRAVIT : ATQ*VE* HOC SEPVLCHRVM SIBI, QVOD / MORTIS EVM NVNQVAM CESSANTIS ADREPERE QVOTIDIE COMMONEFACERET TRANSLATIS HVC PRIORIS / VXORIS OSSIBVS EXTRVENDVM CVRAVIT. QVOD NE SVPERSTES FRVSTRA SIBI FECERIT, NEVE / INGRVENTEM TREPIDVS MORTEM HORREAT, SED DESIDERIO CHRISTI LIBENS OPPETAT, MORTEMQ*VE* / VT SIBI NON OMNINO MORTEM, SED IANVAM VITÆ FÆLICIORIS INVENIAT PRECIBVS EVM PIIS / LECTOR OPTIME SPIRANTEM PRÆCOR, DEFVNCTVMQ*VE* PROSEQVERE.

He has caused this tomb to be built for himself, and his first wife's bones to be brought hither. "That he may willingly die . . . help him . . . good reader, now with your prayers while he liveth, and when he is dead also."

Under this epitaphy in prose, he caused to be writte*n* on his to*m*be this latte*n* epitaphy in versis folowing, which himself had made XX yeres before :

Chara Thomæ iacet hic Ioanna Vxorcula Mori,
Qui tumulum Aliciæ hunc destino : quiq*ue* mihi.
Vna mihi dedit hoc coniuncta virentibus annis
Me vocet vt puer et trina puella patrem.
Altera priuignis (quæ gloria rara Novercæ est)
Tam pia quam gnatis vix fuit vlla svis,
Altera sic mecum vixit sic altera viuit
Charior in[c]ertum est hæc sit an illa fuit.
O simul, O Iuncti poteramus viuere nos tres
Quam bene si fatum religioq[ue] sinant.
At societ tumulus, societ nos obsecro cœlum
Sic Mors non potuit quod dare vita, dabit.

Here lies Jane, More's first wife. May he and Alice, his second wife, be united with her in the tomb and in Heaven.

2. NUNQVAM] nuncquam W. 6. NEVE] none W. 7. OPPETAT] opetat W. *Following* OPPETAT, Tomb *has a period, but the sense requires a comma.* 8. MORTEM] *Following* MORTEM, Tomb *has a period, but the sense requires a comma.* 9. EVM] cum W. 10. DEFVNCTVMQVE] defunctumcque W. 11–13. See above, p. 278, note. 14. Tomb *omits comma after* Mori; *comma* E W. 15. Tomb *omits period after* mihi; *period* E W. 17. Tomb *omits period after* patrem; *period* E W. 15. *Aliciæ*] Alicie EW; Aliciciæ Tomb. 21. *incertum*] E W; insertum Tomb. 21. *sit*] sic W. 21. *illa fuit*] haec fuerit E W. 23. *fatum*] factum W. 23. *religioque*] *So* E W; Tomb *omits contraction mark for* ue *after* q.

TEXTUAL NOTES

A list of the Harpsfield manuscripts is given above, p. 2; and a detailed description, with a discussion of their relationship, Introduction, pp. xiii–xliv.

In fixing the reading of any particular passage of the Roper matter in Harpsfield, it is obviously important to know the reading of Roper's *Life*, which Harpsfield was following and transcribing. This can only be ascertained by a collation of the extant Roper MSS., which has therefore been done as a preliminary to fixing the text of Harpsfield.

The Roper manuscripts are referred to in the Notes below by the following symbols:

H^1	= MS. Harleian 6166.	British Museum.
H^2	= MS. Harleian 6254.	British Museum.
H^3	= MS. Harleian 6362.	British Museum.
S	= MS. Sloane 1705.	British Museum.
A	= MS. Additional 11388.	British Museum.
A^2	= MS. Additional 4242.	British Museum.
T	= MS. Bodley 966.	Bodleian.
W	= MS. Willis 58.	Bodleian.
M	= MS. Cambridge University Library Mm. IV. 21.	
D	= MS. Dyce 46. Dyce and Forster Collection, S. Kensington.	
J	= MS. Burns. In the possession of the Rt. Hon. John Burns. The MS. used by Hearne.	

M, the Cambridge MS., will be collated itself for the Roper critical text. Though often injured by damp, the words are always legible. For the purpose of these Notes, a transcript of MS. M, in MS. Harleian 7030, has been used. It was made by the antiquarian Thomas Baker (1656–1740) because of the damaged condition of MS. M even at that date.

MS. 544, in the Library of the Société des Bollandistes, Brussels, has also been collated for the Roper critical text.

The Eton Roper (MS. 167) and a manuscript in the possession of Mr. W. Fagg, of 34 Church Road, Crystal Palace, S.E. 19, which are in the third person, and which differ somewhat from the regular Roper tradition, have not been considered for these Notes.

The spelling of the variant readings below is that of the first manuscript cited.

9/23–4. *When he hearde folke blame their wiues, and say that they be so many of them shrewes. A Dialogue concernynge heresyes, English Works*, p. 233, reads: *For whan he heareth folke blame wyues, & say that there bee so manye of them shrewes.* Of all the Harpsfield MSS., Y alone reads *their be*, the rest *they be*. The reading of the archetype of the Harpsfield MSS. seems likely to have been *they be*, and *their be* of Y a corruption from *their wiues* above.

10/1. *diffame.* The weight of Harpsfield MS. authority would seem to prove the preterite *diffamed* the right reading here. But the passage from which the story is taken, in *A Dialogue concernynge heresyes, English Works*, p. 233, reads *dyffame*, the whole passage there being in the present: *he sayeth that they dyffame them falselye. Diffame* is kept therefore in the Harpsfield text as the *durior lectio*, and as supported by *English Works* and by the present *weeneth*, l. 3.

11/2. *soden.* Reading supported by *sodeynly* of Roper MSS. H^3 H^1 H^2 M T W D J A A^2. (S imperfect.)

19/3. *to the eldest.* Reading supported by Roper MSS. H^3 H^1 H^2 M T W D J A A^2. (S imperfect.)

19/6. *his.* Reading supported by Roper MSS. H^3 H^1 H^2 M T W D J A A^2. (S imperfect.)

19/12–15. *where he had by her three daughters . . . and three daughters.* The repetition is awkward and may be erroneous, but is retained as read by the best Harpsfield manuscripts.

19/21. *sauce.* Reading supported by Roper MSS. H^3 H^1 H^2 M T W D J A A^2. (S imperfect.)

23/7. *shipp of his that then was Pope.* Roper MSS. vary: H^3 H^1 A *shippe of his that was then Pope*; T as H^3 H^1 A, but *the Pope* for *then Pope*; H^2 *shipp of his then that was Pope*; M J *shipp of his that then was Pope*; W *shipp of the Pope*; D A^2 *shipp belonging to the Pope.* (S imperfect.)

24/6. *being then no.* Reading supported by *having then no* of Roper MSS. H^3 H^1 H^2 M T W D J A A^2. (S imperfect.)

f 25/19. *hath so familierly interteyned.* Order of words supported by *had soc amilia rlye enterteyned* of Roper MSS. H^3 H^1 H^2 M S T W D J A A^2.

25/26. *may.* Reading supported by Roper MSS. H^3 H^1 H^2 M S T W D J A A^2.

25/27. *thereof.* Reading supported by Roper MSS. H^3 H^1 H^2 M S T W D J A A^2.

26/14–15. *which was the fourteenth yere of the Kings raigne.* Reading supported by Roper MSS. H^3 H^1 H^2 M T W J A *In the xiiij^{the} yere of his graces raygne*; D A^2 *In the 14th yeare of his Maties reighne.* (S imperfect.)

26/16–17. *for their Speaker Sir Thomas More.* The reading of E C H R, *for their Speaker the saide Sir Thomas More*, seems less accurate than the reading of L R^2 Y B, being probably due to the occurrence of *The saide* (l. 14) above.

27/26. *my.* Roper MSS. vary: H^2 M D J A^2 *my*; omitted in H^3 H^1 T W A. (S imperfect.)

28/3. *the other the.* Reading supported by most Roper MSS.: H^3 (on erasure) H^1 M T D J A A^2 *the other the*; H^2 *the other for the* (*for* being interlineated); W *the other concerninge the.* (S imperfect.)

28/6. *high.* Roper MSS. vary: H^1 H^2 M T J A *high*; H^3 W D A^2 *highnes.* (S imperfect.)

28/9. *most.* Roper MSS. vary: H^2 M T W D J A^2 *most*; omitted in H^3 H^1 A. (S imperfect.)

29/7–8. *that men could esteeme meete thervnto.* Reading supported by Roper MSS. H^3 H^1 M S W D J A A^2; H^2 as H^3 H^1 M S W D J A A^2, but omitting *meete*; T as H^3 H^1 M S W D J A A^2, but *woulde* for *could.*

29/11–13. *neyther is euery man wise alike, nor, among so many men all like well witted, euery man like well spoken.* Roper MSS. vary: H^3 H^1 A *neither is any man alike nor amongst soe many like well witted euery man like well spoken*; H^2 S J *neyther is euery man wise alike nor among so many men like well witted euery man like well spoken*; D as H^2 S J, but *alike well witted* for *like well witted;* A^2 as H^2 S J, but *alike* for *like* in both places; M as H^2 S J, but omitting *men like*; T *neither is any man wise alike nor amonge so many like well wittic every man like well spoken*; W *neither is euerie man like nor among so manie men like well witted nor euerie man like well spoken.*

29/16. *se.* The reading of the Harpsfield text is adopted from that of most Roper MSS.: H³ H¹ H² S T D J A A² *see*; M *so*; W paraphrases—*are deepely read.*

29/16. *right substantiall.* Reading supported by Roper MSS. H³ H¹ H² M S T W D J A A².

30/10. *euery of.* Roper MSS. vary: H² M S T W D A² *euery of*; H³ H¹ A *everye one of*; J omits, owing to eye-slip from *Commons* to *Commons.*

31/6. *your.* Reading supported by Roper MSS. H³ H¹ H² M S T W D J A A².

31/28. *hither.* Reading supported by most Roper MSS.: H³ H¹ H² M W D A A² *hether* (*hither*); T *thither*; omitted in S J.

32/3. *moued.* Reading supported by Roper MSS. H³ H¹ H² M S T W D J A; A² *vsed.*

32/25. *he.* Reading supported by Roper MSS. H³ H¹ H² M S T W D A A²; J *the.*

32/26. *excusing.* Reading supported by Roper MSS. H³ H¹ H² M S T W D J A A².

33/4. *one.* Reading supported by most Roper MSS.: H³ H¹ M D J A A² *owne* (=“one”); H² S *one*; omitted in T W. (For the spelling *owne* = “one,” cf. *English Works*, p. 1435: *mine* owne *daughter* . . . *mine* other *daughter.*)

33/11. *vttered.* Reading supported by most Roper MSS.: H³ H¹ H² M T W D J A A² *vttered*; S *he vttered.*

33/12. *to God.* Reading supported by Roper MSS. H³ H¹ H² M S T W D J A A².

34/12. *would we be.* Reading supported by most Roper MSS.: H³ H¹ M S T W A *would wee be*; H² D J A² *we wold be.*'

42/17. *I saie.* Reading supported by Roper MSS. H³ H¹ H² M T W D A A²; omitted in S J.

43/7–8. *cast phantasie vnto.* Reading supported by Roper MSS.: H³ H¹ H² M S T W A *cast fantasye to* (*vnto*); J *cast fanncie to*; D A² *cast his fantacie & affeccion to.*

44/24. *this.* Reading supported by Roper MSS. H³ H¹ H² M S T W J A A²; D *his.*

45/7. *old.* Reading supported by Roper MSS. H³ H¹ H² M S T W D J A A².

47/1–2. *appellation the Cardinall vpon that matter sate no longer.* Roper MSS. vary slightly; most support *the Cardinall*: H³ H² T J A *appealacione the Cardinall vpon that matter sate no longer*; M S *appellation the Cardinall upon the matter sat no longer*; H¹ W D A² *appellation þe Cardinalls vpon that matter sate noe longer.*

48/25. *was.* Reading supported by Roper MSS. H³ H¹ H² M S T W D J A A².

49/8. *his.* Reading supported by most Roper MSS.: H³ H¹ H² M S T D J A A² *his*; W omits.

49/18. *thought.* Roper MSS. H³ H¹ H² M S T W D J A A² *thinkinge.*

49/23. *incense.* Roper MSS. vary: H² M W J *incense*; H³ H¹ S T A *increase* D A² *augment and increase.*

50/11. *into a Praemunire.* The reading of E, *in a Praemunire,* is paralleled, *e.g.* in Harpsfield's *Divorce,* p. 184, *in a premunire.* But *into a premunire* is commoner, and is read here in the Harpsfield text owing to the weight of Harpsfield MS. authority.

51/15. *beholding.* Roper MSS. vary: H² T W D A² *beholdinge*; H³ H¹ M S J A *beholden.*

51/21. *not nowe in my memorie.* Note that the *memorie* is Roper's, not Harpsfield's, the phrase being taken over in the first person direct from Roper.

52/2. *therof.* Reading supported by Roper MSS. H^3 H^1 H^2 M S T W D J A A^2.

52/16. *also.* Reading supported by Roper MSS. H^3 H^1 H^2 M S T W D J A A^2.

52/16. *but.* Roper MSS. vary: H^3 H^1 H^2 M T J A omit; S W D A^2 *but.* In the text *but* has been retained, owing to its support by the best Harpsfield MSS.

52/21. *it was.* Roper MSS. H^3 H^1 H^2 S T W D J A A^2 *which was*; M *was.*

52/25. *nowe.* Supported by Roper MSS. H^3 H^1 H^2 M S T W D J A A^2.

54/8. *would he.* Reading supported by most Roper MSS.: H^3 H^1 H^2 M S T D J A A^2 *would he*; W *he would.*

54/16. *in Lincolnes Inn.* Reading supported by Roper MSS. H^3 H^1 H^2 M S T W D J A; A^2 *at Lincolnes Inne.*

54/17–18. *notwithstanding his high office.* Reading supported by Roper MSS. H^3 H^1 H^2 M S T W D J A A^2.

55/6. *Crooke.* Reading supported by Roper MSS. H^3 H^1 H^2 M S T W D J A A^2.

57/5. *his entrie first into.* Roper MSS.: H^3 H^1 H^2 M T J A *his entrye into*; S W D A^2 *his first entrie into.*

57/22. *gratious.* Reading supported by Roper MSS. H^3 H^1 H^2 S T W D J A A^2; M *graces.*

57/26. *forth.* Roper MSS. vary: H^2 W *further*; H^3 M S T D J A A^2 *forth*; H^1 *for.*

60/11–16. *And surely as the king . . . tendred the common wealth . . . so dismissed him*, &c. The omission of *he* before *dismissed* seems awkward to modern ears, and was perhaps inserted for the same reason by the scribe of MS. B. But in the syntax of the older periods the omission of the personal pronoun, especially that of the third person, is common if easily supplied from the context. See Kellner's *Historical Outlines of English Syntax* §§ 62, 271, 272. See also above, *Rastell Fragments*, 228/16, 229/21, 250/2.

65/11. *in prayer and studie.* Order of words supported by Roper MSS. H^3 H^1 H^2 M S T W D J A A^2.

65/25. *causing.* Reading supported by Roper MSS. H^3 H^1 H^2 M S T W D A A^2; J *caused.*

66/3–4. *chauncing to espie the same, began to laughe at it. His daughter Margarete.* Reading supported by Roper MSS. H^3 H^1 H^2 M S T W D J A A^2.

68/13. *saide.* Reading supported by Roper MSS. H^3 H^1 H^2 M S T W D A A^2; J *quoth.*

68/15. *all at.* Reading supported by Roper MSS. H^3 H^1 M S T W D A A^2; J H^2 omit *all.*

68/21. *partes* = "parties." Supported by Roper MSS.: H^3 H^1 T W D J A A^2 *partyes*; H^2 M S *partes.* (Cf. *English Works*, p. 1450: *as both the* partys *may stand with saluacion . . . I besech our lord bring al* partes *to his blisse.*).

69/5–6. *loving, obedient.* Reading supported by Roper MSS. H^3 H^1 M S T W A A^2; *loving and obedient* H^2 D J.

69/13–14. *at a league and composition.* Reading supported by Roper MSS. H^1 H^2 M S T W D A A^2; H^3 *at a league and compositions*; J *at leagge and composition.*

70/2. *it shall not be so, it shall not be so.* Reading supported by Roper MSS. S W D J A^2; H^3 H^1 H^2 M A repeat three times; T once only.

73/2–4. *albeit he knew them, and might easily haue for that punished them, or otherwise waite them a shrewde turne.* L R^2 B, *have waighted them,* give the modern correct form of the verb, but the *durior lectio, waite,* is more likely to be the true reading. In the older syntax there is frequent failure to employ what we consider the right form of the verb. Cf. below 206/12–14: *That . . . hath with his noble, learned bookes, and shall . . . doo,* where it is not realised that different forms of the principal verb are required after the different auxiliaries.

73/17. *punish.* Reading supported by Roper MSS. H^3 H^1 H^2 M S T W D J A A^2.

76/1. *may.* Reading supported by Roper MSS. H^3 H^1 H^2 M S T W J A A^2; D *must.*

77/5. *passions.* Reading supported by Roper MSS. H^3 H^1 H^2 M S T W D J A A^2.

82/3. *and wise.* Roper MSS. vary: H^3 H^1 W A *and wise*; H^2 M S T D J A^2 *wise.*

82/16. *remedie.* All Roper MSS. here read *way.*

89/22–3. *Cor viduae consolatus est, oculus fuit caeco, et pes claudo . . . pater erat pauperum.* See Job, XXIX, vv. 13–16.

94/3-4. *she learned to playe and sing at the lute and virgenalls,* &c. See Letter to Ulrich von Hutten, *Op. Epist. Des. Erasmi* (ed. Allen), No. 999, Tom. IV, p. 19:

> *Quid enim non impetret, posteaquam effecit vt mulier iam ad senium vergens, ad hoc animi minime mollis, postremo ad rem attentissima, cithara, testudine, monochordo, tibiisque canere disceret, et in hisce rebus cotidie praescriptum operae pensum exigenti marito redderet?*

MS. C seems to have preserved the nearest approach to the passage in Erasmus, where the four instruments are mentioned. The "lute" of C corresponds to *testudine,* "virgenalls" to *monochordo.*

95/24. *that haue.* Reading supported by Roper MSS. H^3 H^1 H^2 M T W D J A A^2; S *who haue.*

97/1–2. *but seuen yeres lye buried.* Reading supported by most Roper MSS.: H^2 M T W J *but seuen yeares lye buried*; S (as H^2 M T W J but with *I should* transposed) *but seaven yeares I should lye buried*; H^3 H^1 A A^2 *but seauen yeres be buried*; D *but one vij yeares be buried.*

97/3. *gett me out.* Roper MSS. vary: H^3 H^1 M S D J A *gett me out*; H^2 T W *get out*; A^2 [damaged] *me out.*

97/3. *of dores.* Reading supported by Roper MSS. H^3 H^1 H^2 M S T W D A A^2; J *of the doores.*

112/18. *call to minde.* Reading supported by Roper MSS. H^3 H^1 H^2 M S T W D J A A^2.

112/24. *reserue.* Reading supported by most Roper MSS.: H^3 H^1 H^2 M S W J A *reserve*; T D A^2 *referr.*

113/5. *thanke.* Roper MSS. vary: H^3 H^1 H^2 M S T A A^2 *thanke*; W D J *thanks.*

113/7. *so.* Roper MSS. vary: H^3 H^1 S W D A A^2 *soe*; H^2 M T J omit.

113/8. *they.* Reading supported by Roper MSS. H^3 H^1 H^2 M S T W D J A A^2.

113/8. *so importune.* All Roper MSS. except S omit *so*: H^3 H^1 H^2 W D J A *importune*; M T *importunate*; S *so importune*; A^2 *import and.* In the Harpsfield text *so* has been retained, as read by the best Harpsfield MSS.

113/13. *it all cast.* Reading supported by most Roper MSS.: H^3 H^1 H^2 M D J A A^2 *it all cast*; S *it cast it all*; T W *it cast.*

113/15–16. *be in deede verye.* Reading supported by Roper MSS. H^3 H^1 H^2 M S T W D J A A^2.

113/19. *loste.* Reading supported by Roper MSS. H^3 H^1 H^2 M S T D J A A^2; W omits.

113/19. *manye.* Roper MSS. vary: H^3 H^2 S T D A^2 *many*; H^1 M W J A *many a.*

114/15–19. *whereas in the latin Epistle of Saint Paule is read in the olde translation* "fornicarij," *and in the newe* "scortatores," &c. By *the olde translation* is meant the Vulgate; by *the newe* Erasmus's Paraphrase. Cf. Vulgate, 1 Cor. VI. 9: *Nolite errare: neque fornicarii, neque idolis servientes, neque adulteri . . . regnum dei possidebunt.* Cf. Erasmus's Paraphrase (Basileæ, 1522), p. 711: *Ne erretis: Neque scortatores, neque cultores simulachrorum neque adulteri . . . regni dei haereditatem accipient.*

All the Harpsfield manuscripts corrupt this passage.

115/3–5. *Neyther "elder" signifieth any whit more "a priest" then this worde "presbyteros" "an elder sticke."* The passage of *The Confutacion of Tyndales Aunswere* (*English Works*, p. 425) from which this is taken, runs:

> *And as very a blockhead wer he that would translate* presbyteros *an elder in stede of a priest, for that this english word elder signifyeth no more a prieste then thys greke woorde* presbyteros *signifyeth an elder sticke.*

The error in the archetype of all the extant Harpsfield manuscripts seems to have arisen through the omission of the words *this worde presbyteros,* and the subsequent insertion of these words in the archetype, either in the margin or between the lines. The words seem then to have been transcribed in the wrong place (*Neyther this worde presbyteros*) and *for* added before *elder* in order to make some apparent sense.

The spelling of *presbyteros* varies in the MSS., that of E being *praesbiteros.*

116/9. *their soule health.* Note survival of old feminine genitive in -*e*. Cf. 207/12, *many soule enemyes.*

122/22–3. *of some of his aunsweres in the saide Apologie we haue already, vpon occasion, somewhat touched.* See above, pp. 109, 110–11, 111, 120, and marginal references. *The Apologye* takes up pp. 845–928 of the *English Works* of 1557.

126/22–3. "*If they*" (*saith he*) "*will not (which were the next) be heretikes alone themselues.*" The passage from which this is derived, *Apologye, English Works*, p. 866, runs as follows:

> *If they wyll not* (*whyche were the beste*) *reuoke theyre false heresyes, nor wyll not* (*whyche were the next*) *be heretykes alone them selfe.*

No doubt Harpsfield meant to quote it so, or did quote it so. There has been at some stage an eye-slip from *will not* to *will not,* possibly by Harpsfield himself, possibly by the writer of the archetype from which all our extant manuscripts are derived.

129/17–21. *some men would say againe . . . that he had as leefe his enemie were let alone with him . . . as haue such a frende stepp in betweene to part them.* Note confusion of number.

130/10–11. *and then would afterwarde tell her husbande his parsverse too.*

I am indebted to Professor A. W. Reed for the following note:

In Heywood's *Proverbes* (*a Dialogue conteyning the number of the effectuall proverbes in the English tounge,* &c., Part II, Cap. 3) the writer is called in to compose a quarrel between the young husband and his elderly wife. She says to him at table:

> *And all fraies by this I trust haue taken end,*
> *For I fully hope my husband will amend.*
> *Well amended (thought I) whan ye both relent,*
> *Not to your owne but eche to others mendment.*
> *Now, if hope fayle, (quoth she) and chaunce bring about*
> *Any suche breache, wherby we fall again out,*
> I pray you tell him his pars vers *now and than,*
> *And wink on me*[1] *also hardly, if ye can*
> *Take me in any tryp.*

This clearly echoes the passage in the *Apologye* (*English Works*, p. 873). The words *pars vers* are, I believe, only our *parse verse*. The idea is taken from a schoolmaster's monotonous, "Smith, parse verse so and so," "Jones, parse verse so and so," "Brown, *ditto*," "Robinson, *ditto*." "Tell him his *pars verse*" means, therefore, "give him his lesson," "let him have it."

The word *parse* is only the Latin *pars*="part of speech," used imperatively. Cf. the verbal use of *parse* in Ascham's *Schoolmaster*, ed. Mayor, p. 3:

> *Let the master read unto hym the Epistles of Cicero gathered togither and chosen out by Sturmius for the capacitie of children. First, let him teach the childe, cherefullie and plainlie, the cause and matter of the letter: then, let him construe it into Englishe, so oft as the childe may easilie carie awaie the understanding of it: Lastlie,* parse *it over perfitlie. This done thus, let the childe, by and by, both construe and* parse *it ouer againe* . . . &c.

Possibly More (for family fun) coined the word *pars verse*. The passage in the *Apologye* in which it occurs shows him coining a similar treasure, *some say*:

> "*I pray you good man* Some say *gete you shortely hence. For my husbande and I shall agree much the sooner if no suche brother* Some say *come within our dore.*"

137/16. *go home.* Reading supported by Roper MSS. H³ H¹ H² M T W D J A A². (S imperfect.)

139/23. *them.* Reading supported by sense and by Roper MSS. H³ H¹ H² M S T W D J A A².

141/6–7. *so was he no notable lowe and litle man.* Cf. Letter to Ulrich von Hutten, *Op. Epist. Des. Erasmi* (ed. Allen), No. 999, Tom. IV, p. 14: *statura modoque corporis est infra proceritatem, supra tamen notabilem humilitatem.*

141/10–11. *then to palenes, farre from rednes.* Cf. Letter to Ulrich von Hutten, *Op. Epist. Des. Erasmi*, No. 999, Tom. IV, p. 14: *quam ad pallorem, quanquam a rubore procul abest.*

141/14–15. *which kinde of eyes do commonly betoken and signifie a very good and sharpe witt.* Cf. Letter to Ulrich von Hutten, *Op. Epist. Des. Erasmi*, No. 999, Tom. IV, p. 14: *quae species ingenium arguere solet felicissimum.* There is nothing in the Latin corresponding to *be quicke*, which is apparently a bad

[1] *i.e.* "tell *him* off, but close your eyes to me."

guess of the archetype of E H R for *betoken* or some other word, which was perhaps blurred, and for which the scribes of Y C leave a gap.

143/19. *same.* Reading supported by Roper MSS. H^3 H^1 H^2 M S T W D J A A^2.

144/11. *contributories.* Most Roper MSS. support *contributories*; H^3 H^1 H^2 M W D A A^2 *contrybutaryes*; T *tributatories*; S *contributours*; J omits, owing to eye-slip from *together* to *together*.

144/14. *of.* Reading supported by Roper MSS. H^3 H^1 H^2 M S T W J A A^2; D *of the.*

147/3. *consideration.* Roper MSS. vary: H^3 H^1 J A *considerations*; M S T W D A^2 *consideracion.* (H^2 imperfect.)

148/5. *mariage.* All Roper MSS. read *matrymonye.*

148/20–21. *by the bearer thereof they had sent.* Reading supported by Roper MSS. H^3 H^1 H^2 M S T W D J A A^2.

149/21. *be there.* Roper MSS. vary: H^3 H^1 S T A *be there*; H^2 M W D J A^2 *there be.*

149/25–6. *and when they haue deflowred you.* Reading supported by Roper MSS. H^3 H^1 H^2 M S T W D J A; A^2 omits, owing to eye-slip from *defloure you* preceding.

149/26. *then.* Reading supported by Roper MSS. H^3 H^1 H^2 M S T W D A A^2; J omits.

149/26. *will they not.* Order of words supported by most Roper MSS.: H^3 H^1 H^2 S T W D A A^2 *will they not*; M *will not they*; J *the will not.*

150/17–18. *not slenderly and hoverly informed.* The sense required is that of *hoverly* = "lightly," "slightly." Cf. Harpsfield's *Divorce*, 170, *hoverly touched* (*N.E.D.*). The reading of E Y, *houertly*, seems a confusion of *overtly* and *hoverly*; *couertly* in L R^2 C H R seems a scribal substitution. Cf. also *A Dialogue concernynge heresyes*, More's *English Works*, 1557 ed., p. 105, *rather nede to be attentely redde and aduised than houerly harde and passid ouer.*

154/4–5. *as her husbande had geuen it to him, euen so freely.* Reading supported by Roper MSS. H^3 H^1 H^2 M T D J A; W as H^3 H^1 H^2 M T D J A, but omitting *it to*; A^2 omits, owing to eye-slip from *him* to *him.* (S imperfect.)

155/27. *herselfe.* Reading supported by Roper MSS. H^3 H^1 H^2 M S T W D J A A^2.

156/2. *reuelations.* Reading supported by Roper MSS. H^3 H^1 H^2 M S T W D J A A^2.

156/13. *freely.* Reading supported by Roper MSS. H^3 H^1 H^2 M S T W D J A A^2.

156/14. *them.* Reading supported by Roper MSS. H^3 H^1 H^2 M S T W D J (interlineated in J) A A^2.

157/22. *to continue.* Roper MSS. vary: H^3 H^1 W A *to continue*; H^2 M T J *contynewe*; D A^2 *continued.* (S imperfect.)

157/24. *how he.* Reading supported by Roper MSS. H^3 H^1 H^2 M T W D J A A^2. (S imperfect.)

158/2. *liuing.* Reading supported by Roper MSS. H^3 H^1 H^2 M T W D J A A^2. (S imperfect.)

158/4. *which.* Reading supported by Roper MSS. H^3 H^1 H^2 M S T W D J A A^2.

158/15. *none.* Reading supported by Roper MSS. H^3 H^1 H^2 M S T W D J A A^2.

158/16. *gladder of it then.* Reading supported by Roper MSS. $H^3 H^1 H^2$ M S T W D J A A^2.

158/23. *his* (2). Reading supported by Roper MSS. $H^3 H^1 H^2$ S T W D J A A^2; M *is.*

159/20. *strong.* Reading supported by Roper MSS. $H^3 H^1 H^2$ M S T W D J A A^2.

160/10. *that.* Reading supported by Roper MSS. $H^3 H^1 H^2$ M S T W D J A A^2.

161/18. *lyked it* (2). Reading supported by Roper MSS. $H^3 H^1 H^2$ M S T W D J A A^2.

161/21. *he wrate a letter to the king.* There are two autograph copies of this letter, MS. Cotton Cleop. E. vi, fol. 176; and the Record Office MS., State Papers, Hen. viii. § 82, p. 254. As will be seen from the collations above, these generally differ very slightly from each other, but considerably from the copy in More's *English Works* (pp. 1423–4), and from the wording of the Harpsfield MSS. For the reading *Nonne of Caunterbury* (l. 23) as against *wykked woman of Canterbery,* see Historical Note to 161/21.

165/3. *meeter matter.* Roper MSS. vary: $H^3 H^2$ W A A^2 *meeter matter*; M T D J *meet matter*; H^1 S *matter.*

165/15. *to* (2). Reading supported by Roper MSS. H^2 M S T W D A; $H^3 H^1$ J A^2 *at.*

165/23. *God.* Reading supported by Roper MSS. $H^3 H^1 H^2$ M S D A; T W J A^2 *Gods.*

166/29–30. *he had to God.* Reading supported by Roper MSS. $H^3 H^1 H^2$ M S T W J A A^2; D *feruor and loue which he had to god.*

167/1–2. *from . . . loued.* All Roper MSS. omit.

170/1–2. *Sir Richard Cromwell.* Reading supported by most Roper MSS.: H^2 M S T W D J A^2 *Sir Richard Cromwell*; H^1 A *Sir Richard Cromwell,* with *Cromwell* underlined and *Southwell* written in margin; H^3 *Sir Richard Southwell.* (Cresacre More, p. 225 (1726 ed.), has *Winkefield.*)

171/4–5. *ere he fell in talke of any.* Reading supported by Roper MSS. $H^3 H^1 H^2$ M S J A; T *or he fell in talke with any*; W *ere she fell in talke of anie*; D *before he would fall in talke of any*; A^2 [damaged] *fell in talke of any.*

171/5. *customablye.* Roper MSS. vary: H^2 M T J A^2 *accustomably*; D *accustomablely*; S *customably*; H^1 A *accustomedly*; W *accustomelie*; H^3 *accordingly.* In the Harpsfield text *customably* is retained as supported by E Y C.

171/16. *care.* Reading supported by Roper MSS. $H^3 H^1 H^2$ M S T W J D A A^2.

171/18–19. *case here then.* Reading supported by Roper MSS. $H^3 H^1 H^2$ M S T W D J A; A^2 *case then.*

172/9. *by his gratious.* Reading supported by Roper MSS. $H^3 H^1 H^2$ M S T W D J A A^2.

179/6–8. *the xviiij*th *of June, were there three other of the saide Charterhouse of London hanged and quartered.* The three Carthusians referred to, viz. William Exmew, Humphrey Middlemore, and Sebastian Newdigate, were brought up for trial at Westminster on 9th June, 1535, and executed on 19th. (See *Letters and Papers,* Vol. VIII, Entries 886, 895.) Either Harpsfield has confused the two dates, or the archetype of the extant Harpsfield manuscripts omitted the *x* by error.

179/21. *to.* Reading supported by Roper MSS. $H^3 H^1 H^2$ M T D J A; S W A^2 *be to.*

180/3. *sore.* Reading supported by Roper MSS. H³ H¹ H² M S T W D J A A².

180/14. *into.* Roper MSS. vary: H³ H¹ M S W D J A A² *into*; H² T *in*.

180/22. *Ey.* Reading supported by Roper MSS. H³ H¹ H² M S D J A; W *Aye*; A² *Ay*; T omits. (Copy of these verses in Brit. Mus. MS. 17 D. XIV has *Ey.*)

180/28. *this.* Roper MSS. H³ H¹ H² S T J A *thy*; M W A² *the*; D *a*. (Note that the sixteenth-century copy of these Verses in MS. 17 D XIV, British Museum, also reads *thy caulme*. In the Harpsfield text *this* has been retained as uniform in the Harpsfield MSS., but its accuracy is doubtful.)

182/7. *of a sett.* Reading supported by Roper MSS. H³ H¹ H² M S T W D J A A².

182/14. *would not you.* Reading supported by Roper MSS. H³ H¹ H² M S T W D J A A².

182/14. *nowe.* All Roper MSS. except S omit; but *nowe* has been retained in the Harpsfield text as supported by all the Harpsfield MSS. except B, which is frequently corrupt.

182/19. *you not.* Roper MSS. vary: H³ H¹ S T W D J A *not you*; H² M *you not*; A² omits, owing to eye-slip from *Pope* to *Pope*.

182/24–5. *I will put you this case.* Reading supported by Roper MSS. H³ H¹ H² M S T W D J A; A² *I will put to you th* [damaged].

189/20. *both.* Reading supported by Roper MSS. H³ H¹ H² M S T W D J A A². (W *in one parrish both together.*)

189/22. *were.* Reading supported by Roper MSS. H³ H¹ H² M S T W D J A A².

189/27. *Can.* Reading supported by Roper MSS. H³ H¹ H² M S T W D J A A².

189/27. *seeme likely.* Reading supported by Roper MSS. H³ H¹ H² M S T W D J A. (A² damaged.)

190/23. *the* (2). Reading supported by Roper MSS. H³ H¹ H² M S T D J A; W *that*. (A² leaf missing.)

190/26. *for if.* Reading supported by Roper MSS. H¹ H² M S T W D J A; H³ *for*. (A² leaf missing.)

190/26. *be.* Reading supported by Roper MSS. H³ H¹ H² M S T W D J A. (A² leaf missing.)

191/1–3. *Quia si dixerimus quod peccatum non habemus*, &c. See 1 John i. 8: *Si dixerimus quoniam peccatum non habemus, ipsi nos seducimus, et veritas in nobis non est.*

191/3. *this* (2). Roper MSS. vary: H³ H¹ H² M T J *the*; S W D *this*; A omits, owing to eye-slip from *is* to *is*. (A² leaf missing.)

191/4. *terme.* Reading supported by Roper MSS. H² M S W D J; H³ H¹ T omit *materiall . . . statute*; A omits, owing to eye-slip from *is* to *is*. (A² leaf missing.)

191/8. *he.* Reading supported by Roper MSS. H³ H¹ H² M S T W D J A, being interlineated in H³. (A² leaf missing.)

191/19(1). *to.* Reading supported by Roper MSS. H³ H¹ H² M S T W D J A. (A² leaf missing.)

191/19. *owne.* Reading supported by Roper MSS. H³ H¹ H² M S T D J A; W omits. (A² leaf missing.)

192/16. *to.* Reading supported by Roper MSS. H³ H¹ H² M S T W D J A. (A² leaf missing.)

193/3. *case.* Roper MSS. vary: $H^3 H^1 H^2$ M T J A A^2 *case*; S W D *cases.*

193/16. *or of any.* Reading supported by Roper MSS. $H^3 H^1 H^2$ M S T W D J A A^2.

194/7. *perceaue.* Reading supported by Roper MSS. $H^3 H^1 H^2$ M S T W D J A; A^2 *apeare.*

194/8. *libera.* Reading supported by Roper MSS. $H^3 H^1 H^2$ M S T W D J A A^2.

194/15–17. *For as St Paule saide of the Corinthians,* &c. See 1 Cor. iv. 15.

194/16. *of.* Roper MSS. vary: H^2 M T D J A^2 *of*; $H^3 H^1$ S W A *to.*

194/28. *meruaile.* Roper MSS. vary: $H^3 H^1$ W A *merueyll*; H^2 M S T D J A^2 *mervayled.*

195/20. *these.* Roper MSS. vary: $H^3 H^1$ M T A *these*; H^2 S W D A^2 *thos(e)*; J omits *of . . . aliue.*

196/4. *of* (1). Reading supported by Roper MSS. H^2 M S T W J A^2; $H^3 H^1$ D A *of all.*

197/6. *gaue he.* Roper MSS. vary: $H^1 H^2$ M S W D A *gaue he*; J T *gaue the*; H^3 *gaue.* (A^2 damaged.)

198/16. *as soone.* Reading supported by Roper MSS. $H^3 H^1 H^2$ M S T W D J A A^2.

198/17. *hasting.* Reading supported by Roper MSS. $H^3 H^1 H^2$ M S T W D J A. (A^2 damaged.)

199/21. *of the.* Reading supported by Roper MSS. $H^3 H^1$ T D J A; H^2 M S W A^2 *of.*

200/15. *departing.* Reading supported by Roper MSS. $H^3 H^1 H^2$ M T W A; D J A^2 *departure.* (S imperfect.)

201/26. *pleaseth.* Reading supported by Roper MSS. $H^3 H^1 H^2$ M S T D A A^2; W J *pleased.*

204/7–8. *nowe there.* Reading supported by Roper MSS. $H^3 H^1$ M S T W D A; A^2 *there nowe*; H^2 J *then.*

205/19–22. *and saide to him: My lorde Ambassadour, We vnderstande that the.* Reading supported by Roper MSS. $H^3 H^1 H^2$ M S T W D J A A^2.

206/4. *that.* Supported by Roper MSS. $H^3 H^1 H^2$ M T W D J A A^2; S omits.

206/12–14. *that . . . hath with his noble, learned bookes, and shall . . . doo.* See above, note to 73/2–4.

206/26. *warlike.* C is unsupported by other Harpsfield MSS., but *warlike* makes better sense than *worldly,* and is borne out by *martiall,* 208/2.

207/12. *soule enemyes.* See above, Note to 116/9.

208/2. *martiall.* See above, Note to 206/26.

NOTE ON MR. THOMAS MOARE, OWNER OF THE EMMANUEL HARPSFIELD.

Mr. Thomas Moare, owner of the Emmanuel Harpsfield.

IN the cover of the Emmanuel College Harpsfield manuscript is written:[1]

> This booke was founde by Rich: Topclyff in Mr. Thomas Moares Studdye emongs other bookes at Greenstreet Mr. Wayfarers hovse when Mr. Moare was apprehended the xiijth of Aprill 1582.

Of the family of the Chancellor, there were three Thomas Mores alive in 1582:

Three Thomas Mores of the family of the Chancellor alive in 1582.

I. Thomas[2] (of Barnborough and Chelsea), b. 1531, d. 1606, eldest son of John More (son of Sir Thomas) and Anne, only child and heir of Edward Cresacre of Barnborough Hall, Yorkshire. Thomas I was born in his grandfather's house at Chelsea; and though after the dispersion of the family and the loss of Sir Thomas More's estates, John More and his family seem to have depended upon the Barnborough inheritance of his wife, which was later conveyed to this eldest son Thomas, Thomas evidently kept up throughout his life some connection with Chelsea, leaving benefactions to the parish in his will.

Thomas I married, in 1553, Mary, daughter of John Scrope of Hambledon, Bucks, and niece of Henry, Lord Scrope of Bolton. They had numerous children (thirteen according to Cresacre More), among them Thomas III (see below), Cresacre (writer of the *Life* of the Chancellor), Mary and Grace (see below, p. 296). The family resided mainly at Barnborough.

II. Thomas junior,[2] fifth son of John More, and brother of Thomas I, b. 1538, and for whom Thomas Cromwell stood Sponsor.[3] He is censured as apostate and "professed minister"[4] (*i.e.* Protestant minister) by Cresacre More, his nephew.

III. Thomas, second son of Thomas I, b. January, 1565. This Thomas never married, and relinquished his inheritance. He entered the English

[1] See above, p. xiii.

[2] The births of Thomas I and Thomas II are recorded at the end of Sir Thomas More's *Book of Hours*, later an heirloom of his son John and his descendants (see *Notes and Queries*, 8th Series, II, 13 August, 1892):

I. Thomas More was borne the viij^th^ day of August in the xxiij^th^ yere of o^r^ souerayne lorde the King Henry the viij^th^ the Date of o^r^ lorde M.VCXXXJ, which day was saynte Seryans day [*i.e.* the Feast of St. Ciriacus] on a twsday at xij of the cloke that day beyng saynt Lawrens yuyns yuyn [*i.e.* the day before the Vigil of St. Lawrence] Godfathers Tho. More K Chancello^r^ of englond, my lord Darcy, M^r^garet daughter of þ^e^ said sr Thomas. Tho. Hungerford at bysshop.

II. Thomas More my v^th^ sone was borne vppon twsday wchich was the seconde day of July bytwene one & ij in the morni'g in the yere of the raygne of Kyng Henry the viij^th^ xxx^th^ The lorde Cromwell erle of essexe / sr Ric' Westo' my lady Knevet / my lorde the bysshoppe of Durham at confyrmacyon.

[3] See above, footnote 2.

[4] See *Life of Sir Thomas More* by Cresacre More, Hunter's ed., p. 291.

College at Rome, 17 November, 1587, and after many years of labour in the Catholic cause, died at Rome, 11 April, 1625.

We cannot, of course, overlook the possibility that the "Mr. Thomas Moare" who owned the Emmanuel manuscript was not of the family of the Chancellor at all. "Thomas More" was a common name.[1] But, considering the status of the owner and the contents of the manuscript, and in the absence of evidence to the contrary, it seems on *a priori* grounds likely that this Mr. Thomas Moare was one of the family, and therefore one of the three Thomases enumerated above.

Thomas More of Barnborough and Chelsea, grandson of the Chancellor, almost certainly the owner of the Emmanuel Harpsfield.

Thomas I (of Barnborough and Chelsea) is almost certainly indicated by the Emmanuel MS. note. He is known to have been an ardent Catholic, and the subject of active persecution in Elizabeth's reign. At the Visitation of Yorkshire in 1584–5, he was in prison for recusancy. In the Heralds' List, drawn up prior to that Visitation, we have an enumeration of "Those reputed to be Gentlemen in each Wapentake, and summoned to appear and enter their pedigree." Among those of

Tyckhull Fee Westrydinge

is noted *Thomas More de Barneburgh, in prisona, recusans.*[2]

There are several references in the *Domestic Papers* to the imprisonment of a Thomas More in the Marshalsea in the years 1582, 1583, 1584, 1585, 1586:

(1) In the list of "Prisonners committed to the Marshalsey before June 82, & yet [23 March, 1583] remayning there": *Dom. Eliz.* Vol. CLIX n. 35.

Tho. More.

(2) In a duplicate list of the prisoners given in (1) above, but containing more details: among the "Recusantes committed to the Marshalsey before June last, and now [23 March, 1583] there remayninge": *Dom. Eliz.* Vol. CLIX, n. 36.

Thomas Moore of Chelsey in Com Midd gent.

(3) Among the "temporall gentlemen Recusantes in the Marshalsey" on 22 March, 1584: *Dom. Eliz.* Vol. CLXIX, n. 26.

Thomas Moore *sent in* *the* 28 *of Aprill*, 1582.

(4) In the Certificate of Alderman Buckle, etc., for search of certain persons and houses, 27 August, 1584, noted in St. Mary Overies Close: *Dom. Eliz.* Vol. CLXXII, n. 104.

In the howse of Elizabeth Bosaunt, widdowe, *Mary More and Grace More, daughters of Thomas More, prisoner*[3] *in the Marshelsie.*

(5) In the Certificate of prisoners in the Marshalsea in July, 1585 (which gives the dates of the several commitments), among the 42 recusants: *Dom. E.* Vol. CLXXX, n. 64.

[1] Another Thomas More of the time can be easily dismissed. On 24th December, 1582, we have information sent by Bishop Whitgift to Walsingham concerning "two massing priests taken in Worcestershire, of some account among recusants," and concerning "other Papists, *Thomas Moore* and Rees Moore, *poor men*, but very dangerous: *the former was Boner's porter in Queen Mary's time.*" (*Dom. Eliz.*, Vol. CLVI, n. 29.) Whitgift was Bishop of Worcester from 24 March, 1576–7, to 14 August, 1583. The Moores here referred to were probably of Worcestershire, and certainly not gentlemen. The Thomas Moore, formerly "Boner's porter," was not likely to have a "studdye" in Mr. Wayfarer's house. Also it is to be remarked that the information against this Thomas Moore is six months later than the apprehension of the Mr. Thomas Moare of the Emmanuel note.

[2] See Foster's *Visitation of Yorkshire made in the years* 1584/5 *by Robert Glover, Somerset Herald*, p. 388.

[3] MS. *prisoners*, certainly an error for *prisoner*, due to *daughters* preceding.

Thomas More *gent* *the* 28 *of Aprill,* 1582.

The chain of evidence connecting the Thomas More who owned the Emmanuel manuscript with Thomas More of Barnborough and Chelsea, grandson of the Chancellor, seems complete. "Mr. Thomas Moare," owner of the manuscript, is apprehended on 13 April, 1582, and is therefore almost certainly identical with the "Thomas More, gent." who is committed [1] to the Marshalsea for recusancy on 28 April, 1582 (see Entries (3) and (5)). "Thomas Moore *of Chelsey,*[2] gent.," recusant prisoner in the Marshalsea, is still there in March, 1583, March, 1584, August, 1584, and July, 1585 (see Entries (1), (2), (3), (4), (5)): he has *two daughters, Mary and Grace.* Thomas More of Barnborough and Chelsea [2] also has daughters Mary and Grace; [3] and he is noted as in prison for recusancy before the Visitation of Yorkshire [4] in 1584-5.

"Greenstreet, Mr. Wayfarer's house."

"Greenstreet, Mr. Wayfarer's house," is probably the famous "Greenstreet" in East Ham, at which Father Parsons in 1580 had been busy establishing a printing-press. This was inevitably a marked house, as Father Parsons' designs had been discovered.

[1] A later commitment, probably of the same Thomas More, who must then have been released for a short spell between July, 1585, and 1 January, 1586, seems to be indicated by the following Entries:

Dom. Eliz. Vol. CXC, nn. 13. i, 22, 23 (three copies).

A. In the Marshalsea list of prisoners in June, 1586, among the "temporall men recusantes":

(*a*) n. 13. i. *Thomas Moore gent comyted by Mr. Justis Yong the First of January 1585* (*i.e.* 1586, new style).

(*b*) n. 22. *Thomas Moore examined by Mr. Justis Yong on newyeres daye last and then by him comyted and sence not examyned.*

(*c*) n. 23. *Thomas Moore comyted on Newyers day last 1585* (*i.e.* 1586, new style).

Dom. Eliz. Vol. CXCV, n. 74.

B. Among the list of "Layemen" in the Marshalsea in (? December) 1586, and noted as "Gentilmenn and meete for Wisbiche":

Mr. More thelder

These Entries, however, do not affect the argument as to the owner of the Emmanuel Harpsfield.

[2] For connection of Thomas of Barnborough with Chelsea, see above, p. 294.

[3] As proved by the inscriptions on the Burford Priory Painting of the More family, Thomas of Barnborough had two daughters, Mary and Grace, who in 1584 would have been respectively 25 and 16 years of age. (See Hunter's ed. of Cresacre More's *Life of Sir Thomas More,* p. 363.)

[4] See above, p. 295.

HISTORICAL NOTES

NOTE.—The difficulty as to the degree of authenticity implied by inverted commas has been discussed by Prof. A. F. Pollard in the Preface to his *Wolsey*. This difficulty is peculiarly troublesome in the Tudor Period, where the *Letters and Papers* usefully provide a vast mass of material in a translated and summarized form. In the following notes, italics are used where a document is quoted in its original language and spelling; quotation marks are used for translations and paraphrases such as those of *L. & P.*, and also for quotations from modern writers.

3/1–5. *IT is, and hath beene, an olde and most auncient custome . . . at newyeres tyde euery man . . . to visite and gratifie with some present his speciall frendes and patrones.* Cf. the opening of More's dedication to Joyeuce Leigh of his translation of the *Life of John Picus, Erle of Myrandula* (*English Works*, p. 1):

> *It is, and of longe time hath bene (my well beloued sister) a custome in the beginnyng of the new yere, frendes to sende betwene presentes or gyftes*, etc.

3/3. *newyeres tyde.* New Year's Day is, of course, January 1, the Feast of the Circumcision, as is explained in the *Ormulum* (l. 4230). So, in *Sir Gawayne and the Grene Knight*, New Year's Day, when Gawayne has to meet his adversary, is January 1. All this despite the legal and ecclesiastical beginning of the year on March 25. Cf. R. L. Poole in *Trans. Brit. Acad.*, X, pp. 113–37, " The Beginning of the year in the Middle Ages."

3/11–12. *the dishe of water presented once . . . to one of the kinges of Persia.* Nicholas has taken this from his brother John's dedication of his translation of Simplicius to Henry VIII: *Nihil veritus quin ut Artaxerses Persarum rex aquam rustici manu oblatam benigne accepit, sic et tua celsitudo, etc.* (MS. Royal 12. F. v.)

4/1–4. *the great, famous king Alexander gaue in Commaundement that no man should . . . paint his Image but the excellent Painter Appelles.* Erasmus also " disables " himself as unfit to portray More adequately, and uses this comparison of Alexander desiring no painter but Apelles. Cf. letter to Ulrich von Hutten, *Opus Epist. Des. Erasmi* (ed. Allen), No. 999, Tom. IV, p. 13 :

> *Caeterum quod a me flagitas, vt tibi totum Morum velut in tabula depingam, vtinam tam absolute praestare queam quam tu vehementer cupis ! Nam mihi quoque non iniucundum fuerit interim in amici multo omnium suauissimi contemplatione versari. Sed primum οὐ παντὸς ἀνδρός ἐστιν omnes Mori dotes perspexisse. Deinde haud scio an ille laturus sit a quolibet artifice depingi sese. Nec enim arbitror leuioris esse operae Morum effingere quam Alexandrum magnum aut Achillem, nec illi quam hic noster immortalitate digniores erant. Tale argumentum prorsus Apellis cuiuspiam manum desyderat ; at vereor ne ipse Fuluii Rutubaeque similior sim quam Apellis.*

5/4. *of the Apuldrefeles.* For this connection, see Hasted, *History of Kent*, 1790, III, 640, under the Manor of Stourmouth, *alias* Northcourt :

> the latter end of K. Henry IV's reign . . . this manor was in the possession of the eminent family of *Apulderfield*, but *sir William de Apulderfield*, a man of much note in the reigns of K. Henry VI and K. Edward IV, leaving an only daughter and heir *Elizabeth*, she carried it in marriage to *sir John Fineux, knt.*, Chief Justice of the King's Bench in the reigns of K. Henry VII and VIII, whose first wife she was. By her he had two daughters, his coheirs, of whom *Jane*, the eldest, carried this manor in marriage to *John Roper*, of *Eltham, esq.* . He was Prothonotary of the King's Bench, and Attorney-general to K. Henry VIII, and resided first at *St. Dunstan's* near *Canterbury*, the seat of his ancestors, but afterwards at *Well-hall* in Eltham, where he died in 1524, leaving by *Jane* his wife, above mentioned, two sons, *William*, who succeeded him at *Eltham ;* and *Christopher*, who became by his will entitled to this manor.

"William" is the William Roper to whom Harpsfield dedicates this *Life*. "Christopher" was the father of John Roper, first baron Teynham, from whom the present (18th) baron is descended.

A letter from Roper's mother to Thomas Cromwell, 16 Nov. [1539], is printed in *Archæologia Cantiana*, iv, 237.

5/8. *Sir John Fineux* (for whom see Fuller's *Worthies*, ed. Nichols, 1811, I, 500) was famous for his maxims, some of which are preserved in MS. Sloane 1523 (fols. 27–8), with those of other famous men. The one quoted by Harpsfield is not, however, found there.

See also Note to 5/4, above.

5/13–14. *your woorshipfull fathers.* In addition to the posts mentioned by Harpsfield, John Roper, William's father (d. 7 April, 1524), held the office of sheriff of Kent in 1521; and, together with his father-in-law, Sir John Fineux (see above, Notes to 5/4, 5/8), was in charge of the Records of Bridewell Palace. Wolsey writes that the king wishes Fineux and Roper to have a convenient house for the Records in their keeping, *L. & P.*, iii. 2, p. 1522 (No. 3678). See also E. G. O'Donoghue, *Bridewell Hospital*, 1923.

John Roper is chiefly memorable as an example of the notorious inability of eminent lawyers to make their own wills. He made a will, 27 January, 1523, which, after leading to trouble between Archbishop Warham and Cardinal Wolsey, had finally to be unravelled by an Act of Parliament in 1529. See *Archæologia Cantiana*, ii, 153–74, where the complete text of the will is given : it is of incredible piety and complexity.

For the Ropers, see E. Hasted, *History of Kent*, 1778–99, *passim*, especially Vol. I, p. 55 (Well Hall) and Vol. III, pp. 589, etc. (St. Dunstan's, Canterbury); and, for a fuller account, the new edition, *Hundred of Blackheath*, ed. H. H. Drake, 1886, p. 189.

5/27. *recouered your lost soule.* See above, pp. 84–90.

9/6. *his birth.* Cresacre More tells us that *Sir Thomas More was borne at London in Milke Streete (where the Judge his father for the most parte dwelt).* This is possible; but it is also possible, for reasons to be given below, that More was born in the parish of St. Giles, Cripplegate, outside the walls, not in Milk Street, which is in the ward of Cripplegate Within, and that the removal of Sir John More to Milk Street took place later.

Cresacre goes on to say that More was born in 1480, in the 20th year of Edward IV. This has caused much trouble, because, if so, More could not have been much more than three, and might have been less, upon the death of Edward IV (9 April, 1483), and could therefore not be expected to have remembered the anecdote recorded in the *Life of Richard III*. The problems arising from this, and affecting More's authorship of *Richard III*, are explained below (Note to 102/6–17).

It was therefore a discovery of great importance when Mr. Aldis Wright found, inscribed upon two blank leaves of a manuscript in Trinity College, Cambridge (MS. O. 2. 21) a series of notes relating to the marriage of John More, and to the birth of six children. (See *Notes and Queries*, 17 Oct., 1868, Ser. IV, Vol. II, pp. 365, etc., 422, etc., 449.)

There can be no doubt as to the identity of this John More. The children include Jane, Thomas, John and Elizabeth; these names we know from Stapleton and Erasmus to have belonged to the only four children of Judge More of whom we have record elsewhere.

The date given for the birth of Thomas More in the Trinity College manuscript —or rather the dates, for, as we shall see, the evidence is ambiguous—fit in with the age marked on the Holbein drawing at Basle, whilst 1480 would be inconsistent with the age on this drawing: the Trinity College manuscript date disposes of the supposed chronological difficulty over More's authorship of *Richard III*. Further, John More is mentioned as having been married in St. Giles, Cripplegate, and it is with this parish of Cripplegate Without that the anecdote in *Richard III* is connected.

The seven entries can therefore be taken as fixing definitely the marriage, and the dates of the birth of the six children, of Judge John More. The entries run as follows:

> *M^d^ quod die dominica in vigilia Sancti Marce Evangeliste Anno Regni Regis Edwardi quarti post conquestum Anglie quartodecimo Johannes More Gent. maritatus fuit Agneti filie Thome Graunger in parochia sancti Egidij extra Crepylgate london.* [24 *April*, 1474.]
>
> *M^ed^ quod die sabbati in vigilia sancti gregorij pape inter horam primam & horam secundam post Meridiem eiusdem diei Anno Regni Regis Edwardi quarti post conquestum Anglic xv^o^ nata fuit Johanna More filia Johannis More Gent.* [11 *March*, 1474–5.]
>
> *M^d^ quod die veneris proximo post Festum purificacionis beate Marie virginis videlicet septimo die Februarij inter horam secundam et horam terciam in Mane natus fuit Thomas More filius Johannis More Gent. Anno Regni Regis Edwardi quarti post conquestum Anglie decimo septimo.* [7 *Feb.*, 1477–8.]
>
> *M^d^ quod die dominica videlicet vltimo die Januarij inter horam septimam et horam octauam ante Meridiem Anno regni Regis Edwardi quarti decimo octauo nata fuit Agatha filia Johannis More Gentilman.* [31 *Jan.*, 1478–9.]
>
> *M^d^ quod die Martis videlicet vj^to^ die Junij inter horam decimam & horam vndecimam ante Meridiem natus fuit Johannes More filius Johannis More Gent. Anno regni Regis Edwardi quarti vicesimo.* [6 *June*, 1480.]
>
> *Me^d^ quod die lune viz. tercio die Septembris inter horam secundam & horam terciam in Mane natus fuit Edwardus Moore filius Johannis More Gent. Anno regni regis Edwardi iiij^ti^ post conquestum xxj^o^.* [3 *Sept.*, 1481.]

> *M^d quod die dominica videlicet xxij° die Septembris anno regni regis Edwardi iiij^ti xxij° inter horam quartam & quintam in Mane nata fuit Elizabeth More filia Johannis More Gent.* [22 *Sept.*, 1482.]

(See *Notes and Queries*, as above, and Seebohm, *Oxford Reformers*, Second edit., 1869, pp. 521–2).

The exact date of the birth of Sir Thomas More is, however, still uncertain: for the 7th of February in the year 1477–8 fell, not on Friday, but on Saturday. John More must therefore have made a slip in his entry, and we are left to choose between three possible dates:

Friday, 7 February, 1476–7.
Friday, 6 February, 1477–8.
Saturday, 7 February, 1477–8.

Mr. Aldis Wright assumed the latest date to be the correct one, and it was not till nearly thirty years later that Mr. Nichols argued for the earliest date (*Proc. Soc. Ant.*, 18 March, 1897, 2nd Ser., XVI, pp. 321–27).

Many of Mr. Nichols' arguments do not seem conclusive, depending as they do upon the ages of More and his children as Erasmus recalls them. In the letter to Ulrich von Hutten (*Opus Epist. Des. Erasmi*, ed. Allen, No. 999, Tom. IV, p. 14, l. 57) Erasmus states that when he first knew More, More was not more than twenty-three. This, as Nichols argues, certainly favours the earlier year, for it is clear that Erasmus first met More in the late summer or autumn of 1499 (Allen, *as above*, I, p. 6; Ep. 104 and Ep. 114, introd.), and, even if born in the earlier year, More would then have been only twenty-two and a half. On the other hand, in the next words, Erasmus says that More has now barely passed his fortieth year (*vix excessit quadragesimum*). The letter to Ulrich von Hutten was written 23 July, 1519; More was then forty-two and a half, or forty-one and a half, according as we take the earlier or the later date: here, then, the inexactitude is less if we take the later. Mr. Nichols gets rid of the inconsistency, and finds a consistent argument for the earlier birth-year, by dating the letter to Ulrich von Hutten two years earlier than the received date. But, as Dr. Allen has shown, the change, for several reasons, is inadmissible. The letter of Erasmus to Ulrich von Hutten is indisputably a reply to an earlier letter from Hutten to Erasmus (*Opus Epist. Des. Erasmi*, ed. Allen, No. 986, Tom. III, p. 613), and this letter, dated 5 June, is proved by a number of allusions to contemporary events to belong beyond possibility of doubt to the year 1519.

So that all we can say is, that these two references of Erasmus to More's age are both of them only approximately correct, and approach to greater exactitude, the first if we adopt the earlier, and the second if we adopt the later date for More's birth. These references therefore cancel out.

From Erasmus' reference to the age of More's son John no argument can be drawn: it is avowedly only approximate.

Neither is there much force in Mr. Nichols' argument that, if we adopt the earlier date for More's birth, Judge More's family are then born at more regular intervals. For, according to Stapleton, there was also a still-born child. Naturally no entry is made of this miscarriage; but it accounts for the hiatus in the chronology of the records.

The only things which seem likely to help us are the drawings and picture by Holbein. The drawing of the More family group (reproduced in this book, Frontispiece) is now at Basle. The ages of the different members of the family there given are obviously authoritative; they are in a hand not unlike that of More's numerous autograph letters, though I would not say that the hand is certainly More's. But clearly the notes were made by his order, or by that of a member of the family; who outside the family would have known the age of More's domestic fool? They are added in ink of a colour different from that of the sketch as a whole, but agreeing in colour with some of the modifications made in the sketch.

The actual painting, for which the drawing is the preliminary sketch, is not now extant, at any rate as Holbein left it. It is represented by the painting at Nostell Priory, which once belonged to the Roper family. This is dated 1530; but at that date Holbein was not in England. Accordingly the art critics are divided between two theories: either the Nostell Priory painting is a copy (made in 1530) of a lost painting by Holbein; or it is Holbein's painting, left incomplete by him when he went back to Basle, and finished by another hand in 1530. For the purpose of fixing the ages of More and his household, these theories are equivalent; the point is that the ages of More's family, as noted on the preliminary sketch, have been copied on the Nostell Priory picture. The ages relate to the period when Holbein was at work on the picture; the date 1530 to the time when it was copied (or completed) by another hand. This wrong dating of the "Nostell Priory" picture was transferred to the "Burford Priory" picture which, as we shall see later, was the origin of the mistaken date which Cresacre More gives for the birth of his great-grandfather, and of many other chronological errors respecting the More circle.

It remains to fix the real date when Holbein was working upon the family group. It was at the end of August, 1526, that Holbein had left Basle with letters of recommendation from Erasmus: "the arts are freezing," says Erasmus, "in this part of the world, and he is on his way to England to pick up some angels there." With such expectations Holbein would perhaps not have delayed his journey down the Rhine and across from Antwerp, and by October he may have been with More in Chelsea, where, according to his early biographer, he was a guest. But all we know for certain is that, on 18 December, 1526, More writes to Erasmus that Holbein is a wonderful artist, and that he will do what he can for him—and he did so by getting him commissions for portraits. If only to give confidence to his friends, More must have set the example by himself giving Holbein a commission: it is reasonable to suppose that Holbein was at work on the family group by December, 1526. No doubt it occupied him for a long period: perhaps he was still engaged on it, and had to leave it unfinished, when he returned to Basle. At Basle we find him in August, 1528, buying a house after his two years' absence. At what date then were the ages of the sitters written in? For we must decide for the earlier or the later date of More's birth according as it seems probable that the inscription which puts him in his fiftieth year refers to a date either before or after 7 February, 1527.

Now here we are helped by another picture of the More family group. This is a very late copy, which was long at Gobions, the seat of the family descended from Sir Thomas More's son John, and Anne Cresacre. It was subsequently at Burford Priory. Into this copy, made in 1593, are painted the figures of Thomas More, the son of John More by Anne Cresacre, of his wife, and of two sons, the younger being that Cresacre More who wrote the *Life* of his great-grandfather about 1615–20. These figures, added to the portraits of Sir Thomas More, his father Judge More, and his son John, as given in the original of

Holbein, make a composite group of five generations of the family. It was clearly from this picture, painted more than twenty years before he wrote his *Life* of More, that Cresacre More got several of his facts and dates. The inscriptions on this picture (so far as they could be deciphered a hundred years ago) are given in the Appendix to Joseph Hunter's edition of Cresacre More's *Life* (1828).

On this picture it is recorded that Anne Cresacre was born in the third year of Henry VIII (*i.e.* between 22 April, 1511, and 22 April, 1512). Such a strictly family record is likely to be accurate on this point. Further, the brass plate, which formerly covered her tomb in the church at Barnborough, agreed with this date, recording that she died on 2 December, 1577, in her sixty-sixth year (Hunter's edition of Cresacre More's *Life of More*, 1828, Preface, p. xliv). She must therefore have been born between 2 December, 1511, and 22 April, 1512.

Now we know from the Basle sketch that it depicts Anne Cresacre in her fifteenth year. Anne Cresacre can only have been in her fifteenth year between 2 December, 1525, and 22 April, 1527.

But here comes in the importance of the further facts pointed out by Mr. Nichols (*Proc. Soc. Ant.*, 31 March, 1898, 2nd Ser., xvii, pp. 133–40). Holbein, it seems almost certain, is to be identified with the Master Hans who was working against time, decorating a Banqueting House at Greenwich for King Henry VIII, and painting, in London, " the plat of Tirwan," a canvas depicting the English camp before Térouenne. On these he was busy for several weeks from 8 February, 1527. It seems probable, therefore, that Holbein's work on the More family group is not merely prior to 22 April, 1527, but also prior to 8 February, 1527, since between that date and 22 April his work for the king in Greenwich and London would have left him little leisure for Chelsea.

Also we can arrange in chronological order the various fragments of his work on the More group: the Basle sketch of the complete group; the studies, now at Windsor Castle, of the different members of the group; and the Nostell Priory painting. There is evidence that the Basle sketch was the first. For in the Basle sketch Lady More is represented as kneeling at a *prie-dieu*, but Holbein has written a note that she is to be seated (*dise soll sitzen*): and in the Nostell Priory painting she *is* seated. In the Basle sketch a musical instrument hangs on the wall; Holbein has made a note that musical instruments are to lie on a shelf (*Klafikordi und ander seytespill uf dem bank*): and in the Nostell Priory painting they *do* lie on the sideboard. Further, in the Nostell Priory painting the positions and attitudes of Elizabeth Daunce and of Margaret Gigs are interchanged as compared with those in the Basle sketch: and the Windsor drawings show them in these changed attitudes.

So it is clear that first came the Basle sketch; then it was decided to make certain changes, and the Windsor drawings and the Nostell Priory painting embody these changes.

This is important, because we know that a sketch of the group was sent to Erasmus—he acknowledges it in a letter to Margaret Roper (quoted below, in Note to 80/20–23) dated 6 September, 1529; this may well be the sketch now at Basle, which Holbein perhaps carried back with him. But whether or no it was conveyed to Erasmus in 1528, it probably belongs, for the reasons given above, to the first period of Holbein's activity in England, the winter of 1526–7, and to a date prior to 8 February, 1527.

Of course, all these arguments are tentative, and only point to probabilities, not certainties. Still, the probability seems to be that the sketch, which is noted as being of More in his fiftieth year, was made *before* 8 February, 1527, and accordingly that More was born in 1477 rather than 1478.

Mr. A. B. Chamberlain, in his splendid monograph on Holbein, accepts Nichols' arguments dating More's birth in 1477, and from this date proceeds to argue the date of the Holbein sketch. I doubt if this can be maintained, since, apart from the sketch, I know of no data enabling us to decide between 1477 and 1478 for More's birth. But the Basle sketch does seem to me to point to 1477 as the more probable year.

9/7–8. *being borne at London, the chiefe and notable principall Citie of this our noble Realme.* The elaboration about London is based upon the letter of Erasmus to Faber: *natus est Londini, in qua ciuitate multo omnium celeberrima natum et educatum esse apud Anglos nonnulla nobilitatis pars habetur.* (*Des. Erasmi Epist. Opus*; Basileæ, 1538, p. 1071.)

9/9. *His Father.* Judge More's *Life* will be found in *The Judges of England*, by Edward Foss, v, 190–203 (1857), and in the same writer's *Biographical Dictionary of the Judges*, 1870, pp. 454–56. Much of this matter had been published by Foss in *Archæologia*, xxxv, pp. 27–33 (1853).

For John More's age, see Note to 10/6–7, below.

9/17, 10/8–10, 12–13. *a very mercifull and pitifull man . . . muche more freshe and actiue then men of his yeres commonly be of . . . most gladly and willingly . . . rendred againe his spirite vnto God.* Harpsfield draws from the description of Judge John More in More's Epitaph (see above, p. 280, ll. 14–19) *homo . . . mitis, misericors . . . corpore plusquam pro ætate vivido . . . libens emigravit in cœlum.* Note how often, in Harpsfield's *Life*, what looks like mere padding has a definite source.

9/19–23. *And therefore, in talking of mens wiues, he would merilye saye that that choice is like as if a blinde man should put his hande into a bagge full of snakes and eles together, seuen snakes for one eele.* Cf. *A Dialogue concernynge heresyes* (*English Works*, p. 165):

> *But nowe if ye were in the case that I haue herde my father meryly say euery man is at the choyce of his wife, that ye shold put your hande in to a blynde bagge full of snakes and eles together, vii snakes for one ele, ye wold, I wene, reken it a perillous choice to take vp one at aduenture, thoughe ye had made your special prayour to spede well.*

The Harpsfield MSS. all read *blinde man* for *blynde bagge*.

Note that in this passage of the *Dialogue*, More is speaking in his own person, and there is therefore no doubt that the reference is to his own father. In many other cases we might have guessed that the stories More tells in his *English Works* (especially in the *Dialogue of Comfort*) referred to his own acquaintances, and especially to members of his own household. But we could not have been certain if Harpsfield had not confirmed the guess. Harpsfield's intimate connection with the Ropers places his identifications beyond doubt. See pp. 90–91, and cf. Note to 10/2.

10/2. *there was but one shrewde wife.* Also from the *Dialogue concernynge heresyes*, p. 233, and also definitely there attributed by More to his father. See above, Note to 9/19–23.

10/6–7. *This good knight and Justice liued vntill he came to great age.* Judge

More died in 1530; his will was proved on 5 December of that year. Sir Thomas was then probably drawing towards the end of his fifty-fourth year (though possibly only of his fifty-third: see above, Note to 9/6). Judge More, as appears from the Holbein sketch at Basle, was twenty-six years older than Sir Thomas: he died, therefore, probably in his eightieth year. Erasmus had an exaggerated idea of his age, making him eighty as early as 1521, but this is obviously a guess: *patrem habet non minorem, arbitror, annis octoginta, mire virenti senectute* (to Budaeus, *Opus Epist. Des. Erasmi*, ed. Allen, No. 1233, Tom. IV, p. 579.) This may have had something to do with the extreme age (ninety) attributed to Judge More by Cresacre More.

Sir John More, then, was probably born in 1451, though the very end of 1450 and the early months of 1452 are not excluded. In the Burford Priory picture it is stated that he died at the age of seventy-seven in 1530; and this is the origin of the birth date, *c.* 1453, given by Foss, the *D. N. B.*, and, in fact, all the authorities. (See above, Note to 9/6.)

10/15. *his sonne.* Harpsfield does not seem to know of any brother, and it is curious that Stapleton asserts that More was an only son (*fratres nullos habuit*). Yet Stapleton was in constant touch with other exiles who must have known the facts. An attempt has been made to account for this by supposing that both John and Edward More died in infancy (Aldis Wright in *Notes and Queries*, Ser. IV, vol. ii, Oct. 1868, pp. 365, 442; quoted in the second edition of Seebohm's *Oxford Reformers*, 1869, p. 524. So too Bridgett's *Life of More*, p. 3). The *D. N. B.* accordingly describes Thomas More as the "only surviving son." But John More is mentioned, as secretary to Thomas More, in letters of Erasmus to Ammonius and of Ammonius to Erasmus (*Opus Epist. Des. Erasmi*, ed. Allen, Nos. 243, 246, Tom. I, pp. 486, 493. See also Nichols, *Epistles of Erasmus*, II, 43, 44, 50, 62). John More seems to have been a scribe, and to have acted as secretary to his brother. There is some reason for thinking that John died about 1512, when he would have been in the early thirties.

10/16. *his parentes.* The document quoted above, under Note to 9/6, proves beyond dispute that More's mother was Agnes, daughter of Thomas Graunger. Thomas Graunger, from whom More presumably derived his Christian name, was elected Sheriff 11 Nov., 1503. According to the *D. N. B.*, he died two days later at the serjeants' feast held on the occasion when John More was made a serjeant. But Stow (who is quoted as the authority in the *D. N. B.*) does not say so. Stow makes him *dine*, not *die*:

> *The xiii of Nouember, was holden within the pallace of the Archbishop of Canterbury, at Lambeth, the Sergeants feast, where dined the King and all his nobles, and vpon the same day, Thomas Granger, newly chosen Sheriffe of London, was presented before the Barons of the Kings Exchequer, there to take his oth, and after went with the Maior vnto the same feast, whiche saued him money in hys pursse, for if that day that feast had not bin kepte, he must haue feasted the Maior, Aldermen, and others Worshipfull of the Citie. This Feast was kept at the charge of tenne learned men, newly admitted to be Sergeants to the Kings law, whose names were . . . Iohn Moore . . .* (*Chronicles of England*, 1580, p. 876.)

The ignorance of More's biographers as to his parentage bears witness to the thoroughness of what Cresacre More calls "King Henry's seizure of all our evidences." Stapleton did not know the name of More's mother (*matris nomen nescitur*), and says that she died while More was still an infant. Cresacre More describes her as a Handcombe of Holiewell in Bedfordshire, and the MS. in the College of Arms (Vincent cxi, p. 370, as quoted in Bridgett) calls her Alice Hancombe of Hancombe, Co. Bedford.

Alice Handcombe may be the name of a subsequent wife; in 1511 there is mention of an Alice, wife of a John More, relict of Will. Huntyngdon of Exeter (*L. & P., Henry VIII*, Vol. I, 1920, sec. edit., 969 (4)); but these may be different persons. And Foss (*The Judges of England*, v, 202) calls Mistress Hancombe of Holywell, on what authority I do not know, Johanna. Then, according to a MS. of Cresacre More's *Life*, used by Hunter for his edition of 1828, John More married a " Mrs. Bowes, widow, before called Barton," but this name is not given in the printed editions of Cresacre More's *Life*. Finally, according to Cresacre, Judge More married Alice, one of the Mores of Surrey; " Alice, daughter of John and sister of Sir Christopher More of Losely, Surrey," is mentioned as John More's *second* wife in the MS. Coll. Arms, xlvii. D. xiv., p. 333 (Bridgett). Foss, again on what authority I do not know, says that she also was a widow (Alice Clarke). Dr. P. S. Allen makes it clear that Judge More, although a dissuader from matrimony, was married, not, as his biographers have stated, three, but four times in all, whatever the names and order of his wives. In the letter to Ulrich von Hutten, as printed in 1519 (*Farrago nova Epistolarum*, p. 333) Erasmus mentions that John More had given Thomas two stepmothers, to both of whom he showed himself a true son. When the letter was reprinted in the *Epistolae ad diuersos* (p. 435) in 1521, Erasmus added *Nuper induxit tertiam* [*sc. nouercam*] : *hac Morus sancte deierat se nihil unquam vidisse melius*. Judge More must then have been nearly seventy when he put his hand into the bag of snakes for the fourth and last time.

More's last stepmother survived him, and died in 1544. She lived at Gobions in North Mimms, and was buried at Northall [Northaw] according to Cresacre. This is the " mother-in-law " [*i.e.* stepmother] to whom More refers in the *Apologye* (*English Works*, p. 867) as still living. Cf. Harpsfield, 111/7.

10/18–19. *St. Antonies schoole.* An account of this school will be found in Stow's *Survey* (ed. Kingsford, Oxford, 1908, I. 75). Stow's description of the discussions in the streets between Antony's "pigs" and Paul's "pigeons" is famous : "and so proceeding to questions in Grammar, they usually fall from words to blows, with their satchels full of books, many times in great heaps, that they troubled the streets and passengers." St. Antony's was a free school attached to the Hospital of St. Antony in Threadneedle Street, and was taught in More's day by Nicholas Holt (cf. Stapleton, 1588, p. 11; 1612, p. 155). Nicholas Holt must be distinguished from John Holt, also a friend of More's, for whom see Wood's *Athenæ*, 1691, I, col. 7–8. John Holt published a grammar called *Lac Puerorum*, dedicated to Cardinal Morton, and prefaced and concluded by epigrams by More in praise of the book : *Thome More diserti adolescentuli in lucubraciunculas Holtiade*. Wood says it was published about 1497, and the dedication to Morton, who died in 1500, confirms this; but the extant editions are later : Wynkyn de Worde [? 1510], Pynson [1520], of both of which there are copies (very rare, if not unique) in the British Museum; fragments of an edition printed at Antwerp are in the Bodleian and the Cambridge University Library. An Accidence and Grammar by Nicholas Holt, " Master to Sir Thomas More," is mentioned in the sale catalogue of the books of Richard Smith; see Smith's *Obituary*, p. xvii (Camden Soc., 1849). But it may be questioned whether this is not an erroneous description of John Holt's *Lac Puerorum.*

More's earliest extant letter was addressed to a John Holt (copy in MS. Arundel 249, fol. 85v.; see *Anglia,* xiv, 1891–2, pp. 498–9).

11/2–3. *would . . . stepp in among the Christmas players.* For an underplot played by boys, in a play belonging to the period of More's youth, and to the household of Cardinal Morton, see *Fulgens and Lucres, a Fifteenth-Century Secular Play, by Henry Medwall,* edited by F. S. Boas and A. W. Reed, Clarendon Press, 1926; and cf. A. W. Reed, *Early Tudor Drama,* pp. 99–100.

12/13. *sent to the Vniuersite of Oxforde.* Cresacre More says that More was "*in Canterbury Colledge,* now called *Christs-Church.*" Anthony a Wood records a different tradition: "Miles Windsore, who came to the University of *Oxon.* in the time of Queen *Mary,* doth tell us more than once that he had his chamber and studied in the Hall of *St. Mary the Virgin,* and constant tradition doth say the like, and 'twas never reported to the contrary before those two authors here cited" [*i.e.* Cresacre More and Hoddesdon] "published their respective books." See *Athenæ Oxonienses,* I, col. 32. Windsor had made notes for a history of Oxford, which passed to Wood; Wood complains that these notes "contained many dotages and fooleries." The statement of Cresacre is supported by the fact that More would naturally go to Canterbury College, since it was the Archbishop of Canterbury who "placed him at Oxford." Canterbury College was a home of Greek studies: it was the college of William Selling and of Linacre (see Allen, *The Age of Erasmus,* 1914, p. 124).

12/15–16. *profited in the . . . latin and greeke tonges.* Harpsfield later (14/1–2) mentions Grocyn and Lupset among those with whom More *learned the greeke tonge* (14/1–2). More himself mentions Linacre: *Quum ipse iam olim idem Aristotelis opus [Meteorologicorum] audirem Græce, eodem mihi perlegente atque interpretante Linacro* (*Epistola ad Dorpium* in *T. Mori Lucubrationes*; Basle, 1563, p. 417). Stapleton (1588, p. 12; 1612, p. 155) assumes that it was at Oxford that More heard Linacre. More may have studied Greek there under Grocyn, who had returned from Italy by 1491, but More's Greek studies were mainly pursued in London. In 1501, about seven years after he had left Oxford, he writes in his letter to John Holt (see above, Note to 10/18–19): "*At in bonis artibus quid proficis?*" *inquis. Egregie scilicet ut nihil supra. Ita enim sepositis latinis litteris grecas sequor.* He goes on to speak of *Grocinus preceptor meus.* Later, in 1504, in his letter to Colet (Stapleton, 1588, p. 23; 1612, p. 165) More speaks of Grocyn as *solus* (*dum tu abes*) *vitæ meæ magister,* and of Linacre as *studiorum præceptor.* Dr. P. S. Allen says that Linacre in 1499 had "just returned from Venice . . . he had been working on Aristotelian commentators, and was soon to lecture on the *Meteorologica*—a course which More, who was working for the Bar in London, attended" (*Age of Erasmus,* p. 129). It was in 1505–6 that More was translating Lucian with Erasmus. Lupset was a much younger man; he was almost certainly born in 1495 (see Gee's *Life of Lupset,* 1928, p. 12). The study with Lupset must be referred to a much later period of More's life.

12/26. *Newe Inne,* when an Inn of Chancery, was connected with the Middle Temple. It was No. 21, Wych St., Drury Lane, and was demolished in the construction of the modern Aldwych. But it had ceased to have much connection with the Inn of Court, and the buildings were long subsequent to More's time. See H. B. Wheatley, *London*, 1891, II. 583; Loftie, *The Inns of Court and Chancery*, where will be found a sketch of New Inn as it stood in the early eighteen-nineties.

13/2–12. *he was admitted to Lincolnes Inne. . . he enioyed some prerogatiue of time.* More's admission is recorded in the *Black Books* (Book II, pt. 1, fol. 34):

> *Thomas More admissus est in Societat. xij die Februar. a°. sup. dicto* [1496] *et pardonat. est quatuor vacaciones ad instanciam Johannis More patris sui.*

At the same time Richard Stafferton was admitted on the same terms, likewise at the instance of John More. Richard Stafferton married More's sister Joan.

From the *Black Books* we learn the different offices which More held: he presented his accounts as "Pensioner" from Easter to Michaelmas, 1507 (Book III, fol. 8); he was elected Butler, Michaelmas term, 1507 (Book III, fol. 12); he lent money towards the New Building (Book III, fol. 18) and was repaid (*ibid.*, fol. 25); in Michaelmas term, 2 Henry VIII, he was elected Autumn Reader [for the following year, 1511] (Book III, fol. 36), and at the Feast of All Saints, 6 Henry VIII, Lent Reader [*i.e.* for Lent Term, 1515] (*ibid.*, fol. 55). Finally, on 24 June, 1520, he is referred to as Mr. Thomas More of the King's Council, when Richard Stafferton, one of the prenotaries of the Sheriff's court of London, son of Master Stafferton, was admitted at his instance, and pardoned four vacations (Book III, fol. 81). The *Records of the Society of Lincoln's Inn* have been printed (Vol. I of the *Black Books* in 1897).

There was a contemporary Thomas More of the Temple, who is liable to be confused with his great namesake. We have evidence of his activity between 1505 and 1517 in the *Middle Temple Records* (ed. C. H. Hopwood, 1904–5). He was Treasurer of the Middle Temple (*Records*, I, 12, 14, 23, 31, 39, 40–9, 51–3) and Lent Reader (I, 18, 37).

13/23–25. *openly reade in the Churche of St. Laurence. . . the bookes of . . . St. Augustine* de Ciuitate Dei. Probably by the invitation of Grocyn, rector of St. Lawrence. The lectures are lost. Stapleton tells us *non quidem eius operis Theologica discutiens, sed Philosophica tantum atque Historica* (*Tres Thomæ*, 1588, p. 17: 1612, p. 160).

14/1–2. *Master Grocin (with whom and with master Thomas Lupsett he learned the greeke tonge).* See above, Note to 12/15–16.

14/4–7. *the saide Grocin . . . had not so frequent and so great an Auditorie as had Master More.* So Stapleton: *vt Grocino relicto, qui antea bonarum literarum palmam tulerat, ad Morum audiendum omnes confluerent* (*Tres Thomæ*, 1612, p. 160).

Yet Grocin's lectures were very fairly attended, according to More's letter to John Holt (copy in MS. Arundel 249, fol. 85v.):

> *Grocinus preceptor meus interpretacionem illius operis diui Dionisii Areopagite quod de celesti hierarchia inscribitur feliciter in ede diui Pauli nuper auspicatus est. Nescias an cum maiore sua laude an audientium fruge. Consessum habet discipulorum, utinam tam doctum quam magnum habet, tum et celebrem numerum eciam ex doctissimis. Nonnulli eciam imperiti confluunt, partim nouitate rei tacti, partim ut aliquid intelligere*

videantur. Plerique rursus ex hijs qui scioli sibi videntur ideo non intersunt ne fateri videantur eu se nescire que nesciunt.

Grocyn's lectures may be dated as about the autumn of 1501 by the description which follows of the entry of Catherine into London as the bride of Prince Arthur (12 Nov., 1501). More gives a satirical account of her Spanish escort, but reports that all admire the princess herself: there is nothing wanting in her which the most beautiful girl should have. More's first extant letter closes with the hope: *ut hoc celeberrimum coniugium Anglie felix faustumque sit;* thirty-three years later he told his judges that it was for his adherence to Catherine that they sought his blood (Harpsfield, p. 196, above; *Paris News Letter*, p. 204). More, as usual, is unchanged amid a changing world.

14/17. *Furniualls Inne.* An Inn of Chancery attached to Lincoln's Inn. About 1640 most of it was rebuilt from designs by Inigo Jones, although the Hall remained till swept away by a second and more complete rebuilding in 1818–20. The old Hall is figured in Wilkinson's *Londina Illustrata.* In the rebuilt Inn Dickens lived and wrote *Pickwick.* Furnivall's Inn was purchased by the Prudential Assurance Co. in 1888, and their offices were later built upon the site. See H. B. Wheatley, *London*, 1891, II. 83; E. Williams, *Early Holborn*, 1927, *passim*, esp. I, 472–92.

14/20–21. *chosen a Burgesse of the Parliament.* The constituency is not known.

15/15–16. *thereby was the Bill ouerthrowen.* All this depends upon Roper. What we learn from the *Rolls of Parliament* is, that forasmuch as the king was entitled to have two reasonable Aids, the one for the making knight of Arthur, late Prince of Wales, deceased, and the other for the marriage of his daughter Margaret, the Commons, considering that this *shuld be to theym doubtefull, uncerteyn and great inquietness for the serche and non knowlege of their severall Tenures, and of their Landes chargeable to the same*, petitioned the king to accept £40,000 in recompense and satisfaction of the said two Aids, and that the king agreed, and, of his more ample grace and pity, remitted £10,000 of this. For this, and details as to the raising of the balance, see *Rot. Parl.*, Vol. VI, pp. 532–42.

Stubbs has cast considerable doubt upon the story told by Roper and Harpsfield:

> The story that Sir Thomas More in a parliament in 1502 prevented the Commons from granting an aid for the marriage of Margaret, although told on good authority, falls to the ground, for the good reason that no parliament was held in 1502, and that in 1504 the grant was actually made. More probably was instrumental in limiting this sum. (*Seventeen lectures on the study of Medieval and Modern History*, 1886, pp. 416–17.)

But it is pressing the words "at which time" unduly, to turn them into an assertion that the parliament was held *exactly* at the same time as the marriage. The words of Harpsfield and Roper are justified by the fact that the parliament of 1504 considered the Aid consequent upon the marriage. According to the *Italian Relation of England* (Camden Society, 37, ed. C. A. Sneyd, 1847, p. 52) a "Fifteenth" was estimated to produce £37,930. It is true that deductions have to be made from this, and that the actual yield of a "Fifteenth" at this date was approximately £29,000. But, even on this reduced estimate, it is clear that if Henry VII had indeed hoped to get three fifteenths as the Aid to which he was entitled for the marriage of his daughter, his purpose would be sufficiently "dashed" by his having to be satisfied with a grant of £40,000 in lieu of the two Aids consequent upon the knighting of his son and the marriage of his daughter. The episode is discussed by F. C. Dietz, *English Government Finance, 1485–1558, University of Illinois Studies in the Social Sciences*, Vol. ix, No. 3, 1920; see especially p. 28. It seems quite clear that the purposes of Henry VII were defeated.

Even the king-lover, Hall, though he seeks to exonerate Henry VII personally, testifies to the discontent aroused by the extortions of Empson and Dudley:

> *And at this vnreasonable and extorte doynge, noble men grudged, meane men kycked, poore men lamented, preachers openly at Paules crosse and other places exclamed, rebuked and detested, but yet they would neuer amende.*
> (*Kyng Henry the VII*, fol. lix, verso.)

See also the Note to 15/21.

15/16. *Master Tyler.* This is presumably Sir William Tyler, knight of the king's body, controller of the king's works, and master of the king's jewels, whose name occurs frequently in the *Rolls of Parliament*, and in Campbell's *Materials for a History of the Reign of Henry VII* (1877, *Rolls Series*). A Master William Tyler of Bath also occurs in the *Rolls of Parliament*, but he is presumably a different person.

15/21 ff. *The remembrance of this displeasure sanke deepely into the kinges heart*, etc. In 1506 More, in the inscription (to Dr. Thomas Ruthall, the king's secretary) of his Latin version of three of the dialogues of Lucian, speaks of Henry VII as "the most prudent of princes." From this, Mr. F. M. Nichols has felt reason to doubt the story of the king's indignation (see *The Epistles of Erasmus*, I, 1901, p. 405):

> The reference in the above letter to the wisdom shown by Henry VII in the selection of his ministers, and the good terms upon which the writer stood with the King's Secretary, may suggest the question, whether there is any sufficient evidence for the commonly received story of Thomas More being himself in disgrace after the parliament of 1504. The description of him in the . . . Epistle [of Erasmus to Richard Whitford] rather suggests that he was already practising with success as a barrister.

Every suggestion of Mr. F. M. Nichols needs to be carefully considered, but I doubt whether the facts throw serious doubt upon the story of Henry VII *conceiving great indignation* towards More, as first told by Roper, and subsequently amplified by Harpsfield. This is rather a different thing from More being "in disgrace." For the essential point of the story is that this indignation was not publicly shown: More was in danger, perhaps, but not in disgrace. The reason for the king's forbearance, *least he might seeme thereby to infringe and breake the auncient libertie of the Parliament house*, is Harpsfield's addition. But Roper's version makes it quite clear that More went on with his Law studies after his marriage [in 1505], *applyinge still the same untill he was called to the Benche*, and having an interview on a matter of business with *Doctor Foxe, Bishoppe of Wynchester, one of the Kinges Pryvie Councell.* It was this interview, which took place not long before the death of Henry VII (1509), which made More suspect that, as Harpsfield puts it, *pretie priuie wayes were deuised howe to wrappe him in.* This is in no way inconsistent with More having earlier, in 1506, dedicated his translation to the king's secretary, and spoken of the king's prudence.

More was no bigoted plain-dealer who could not stoop to a compliment; he speaks of himself as not being *tam superstitiose veracem vt mendaciolum vsquequaque velut parricidium abominer* (*Opus Epist. Des. Erasmi*, ed. Allen, No. 338, Tom. II, p. 193). And to speak of Henry VII as "prudent" was no "flattery," but bare justice. It cannot be held to prove that the speaker did not suspect him of personal ill-will. And even if it could, it would prove nothing: for, on Roper's showing, it was only later that More became aware of these evil designs.

Much more to the point is the very outspoken way in which, when congratulating Henry VIII on his accession, More denounces the abuses of the reign just ended:

Iam delatores uolupe est contemnere, nemo
Deferri, nisi qui detulit ante, timet.
(*Lucubrationes*; Basle, 1563, p. 183.)

There is so much plain speaking that Germain de Brie, later, in his *Antimorus*, publicly censured More for his outspokenness. Considering More's extraordinary equanimity, it is obvious that he had been deeply stirred; and I think it might be reasonably argued that he would not have used the language he does about the *leges nocere coactae* and the tyranny of Henry VII, if he had connived at that tyranny by his silence in parliament. More's poem implies deliverance from a very present fear.

The story of More's resistance in parliament and the revenge plotted by the king and his advisers is confirmed by Stapleton, who adds the detail that Dudley, when going to execution, assured More that, had he acknowledged his fault to the king, it would have cost him his head (*Tres Thomæ*, 1612, p. 181).

In 1508 More paid a short visit to Louvain and Paris; for in the Epistle to Dorpius (1515) he speaks of having seen something of those Universities seven years before, and having made inquiries as to the subjects and methods of teaching (*Lucubrationes*, as above, p. 376). This may well have been preparatory to an intended sojourn abroad.

16/8. *Doctor Foxe, Bisshopp of Winchester*, born about 1448, died 1528, the founder of Corpus Christi College, Oxford.

16/19–21. *Master Richarde Whitforde . . . after one of the Fathers of Sion.* A full account of Richard Whitford and his devotional writings, by Dom Wilfrid Raynal, O.S.B., will be found prefixed to Raynal's edition of Whitford's translation of *The Imitation of Christ* (London, 1872; 1908). There are many traces of his connection with the Bridgettine monastery of Syon at Isleworth, Middlesex, such as his translation into English of the *Martyrology* used in that house, *The Martiloge . . . as it is redde in Syon*, printed by Wynkyn de Worde in 1526, and edited by F. Procter and E. S. Dewick (Henry Bradshaw Society), 1893. The Introduction to that book should be consulted for information about Whitford.

See Aungier (G. J.), *History of Syon Monastery*, 1840, where letters are quoted from Cromwell's visitors as to the stubborn resistance of Whitford. He was, nevertheless, pensioned at the Dissolution, and was protected by the family of Lord Mountjoy. Erasmus dedicated to Whitford his translations from Lucian, with much praise of More, and references to Whitford's friendship to both More and himself.

17/11–15. *for he continued . . . fowre yeres and more . . . with the monkes of the Charterhouse of London, without any maner of profession or vowe*, etc. Prof. A. W. Reed writes to me : " The question of paying-guests in religious houses is interesting," and reminds me that in 1511 Erasmus was discussing whether Ammonius could find rooms for him with the Austin Friars (*Opus Epist. Des. Erasmi*, ed. Allen, No. 243, Tom. I, p. 487). It is evident, however, that Roper and Harpsfield regard More's sojourn with the Carthusians as quite a different thing, and that More was admitted to their inner life.

On the other hand, " there is no proof that he [More] was ever an oblate, for in those days the rule which limits visits or retreats to ten days was not in force " (Dom Lawrence Hendriks, *The London Charterhouse*, 1889, p. 65).

The leading London Carthusians who were later associated with More in resisting the oath—Houghton, Exmewe and Newdigate—had, of course, not as yet entered the London Charterhouse.

See also *Charterhouse in London*, by Gerald S. Davies, Master of Charterhouse, 1922.

18/6. *Optimam partem elegit Maria.* Martha and Mary have always been held to typify the Active and the Contemplative Life. This point as to the superiority of the Contemplative Life has been repeatedly made, by St. Augustine and St. Gregory in their *Sermons*, and others following them. See E. Cuthbert Butler, *Western Mysticism*, 1922, pp. 200–22, 214–15.

18/27–8. *His wife was one Master Coltes daughter*, etc. Some account of the Colts of Netherhall will be given in the forthcoming edition of Roper's *Life* for the Early English Text Society. See the important article on *More and Netherhall*, by Dr. P. S. Allen, in the *Times Literary Supplement*, 26 Dec., 1918.

19/8–9. *called to the bench . . . and had read there twise.* See above, Note to 13/2–12. E. Foss, *The Judges of England*, V, 1857, p. 208, places More's second Readership in the Lent term of 1516, but this seems to be an error due to miscalculating the regnal year.

19/12. *Bucklersbury* "led from the east end of Cheapside to Charlotte Row, the west side of the Mansion House, but has . . . been cut in half and greatly diminished in extent by the formation of Queen Victoria Street." It was " possessed of grocers and apothecaries," whence Falstaff's reference to those who " smell like Bucklersbury in simple time." See H. B. Wheatley, *London*, 1891, I, 297.

19/13–15. *and one sonne called John More, to whom Erasmus did dedicate Aristotles workes, printed by Bebelius.* See *Aristotelis opera quæcunque impressa hactenus extiterunt omnia, excusa per Des. Eras. Roterodamum.* (Basileæ, *apud Io. Beb. mdxxxi.*) The Preface seems to make more of the learning of More's daughters than of that of their brother :

> *Hic ipse* ARISTOTELES *dixisse fertur, sibi turpe esse silere, loquente Xenocrate: longe uero turpius tibi fuerit non philosophari, quum uideas optimas sorores tuas* MARGARETAM, ALOISIAM, CECILIAM, *tam sedulo, tamque feliciter in utriusque lingue̜ scriptoribus uersari. Quanquam omnium acerrimum ad omnem uirtutem calcar esse debet, uir omnibus numeris absolutus pater tuus* THOMAS MORUS . . . *Datum apud Friburgum Brisgoiœ, iii Kal. Martias, mdxxxi.*

19/15–17. *and three daughters. Margarete, maried to Master William Roper; Cicelie, maried to Master Giles Heron; and Elizabeth, wife to Master William*

Dancie. For a fuller account of these daughters and sons-in-law, the reader is referred to the forthcoming edition of Roper's *Life* for the Early English Text Society. In the meantime it may be pointed out:

(1) That Elizabeth was married to William Daunce, not as the *D. N. B.* says, "apparently about 1535," but on 29 Sept., 1525. See letters of A. F. Pollard and A. W. Reed in the *Times Literary Supplement*, 27 March and 3 April, 1930.

(2) In the letter to Ulrich von Hutten, as in the dedication to Aristotle, Erasmus calls Elizabeth *Aloysia*. See Note to 19/13–15, above.

19/22–20/2. *As he was borne in London, so was he as well of others as of the saide Citie derely beloued, and inioyed there the first office that he had, being made vnder sheriffe of the saide Citie.*

I am deeply indebted to Miss Winifred Jay for information as to the references to John and Thomas More in the City Records.

These records are the *Journal or Record of the Courts of Aldermen and Common Council,* till 1495. After 1495 this becomes the *Journal of the Court of Common Council,* a distinct *Repertory or Record of the Court of Aldermen* having been started in that year. The most important entries from the *Journals* [Jor] and *Repertories* [R] were copied into the *Letter Book* [L.B.].

The following is a summary of the extracts with which Miss Jay has supplied me:

Jor. 9. 241, *b.* — 1489. *Isto die concordatur per Maiorem et aldermannos quod Johannes More, legis peritus, pro bono Consilio suo huic Civitati ante hec impenso, habeat annuatim de Camera unam togam.*

R. 2. 98, *b.* — [Oct. 3, 1509. Thomas More, with others, to *see and viewe the comen grounde wheruppon the Master of seint bartholomus hath bilded.*]

Jor. 11. 93. — [Dec. 13, 1509. *Thomas More, mercerus, electus est in isto Communi consilio in unum Burgensem pro Civibus huius Civitatis pro proximo parliamento apud Westm.*

This entry, and perhaps the preceding one, must relate to another Thomas More. Thomas More, Mercer, is referred to as deceased on 20 Oct., 1513 (Jor. 11. 181, *b*).]

Jor. 11. 118, *b.* and L. B. M. 177. — Sept. 3, 1510. *Eodem die Thomas More, gent., electus est in unum subvicecomitem Civitatis london loco Ricardi Broke, gent., qui nuper electus fuit in Recordatorem london.*

This is followed by a number of entries in which More acts as a City official:

R. 2. 97, *b.* — Sept. 19, 1510. With others as arbitrator.

R. 2. 131. — March 2, 1512. With aldermen and bakers *to go to the kynges Counsell to knowe their pleasure for Bysket etc. for the kyng etc.*

R. 2. 141. — Sept. 23, 1512. Business of the Fishmongers.

R. 2. 146. — Nov. 16, 1512. Authority of the Mayor over the Crafts. The wardens of ten companies came before the Recorder and others, *and all this wardeyns before reherced, except the Wardeyns of taillors, have aggreed and consented to the peticion late moved in the parleament house that all Craftes shalbe hereafter be* [sic] *under the Rule of the Maire and aldermen for the tyme beyng; and that all the Wardeyns that have consentea shall go to the parleament to morwe by barge at their cost and appere before the lordes, and to have the comen sergeant and yong Mor to speke and make aunswere for them.*

R. 2. 148. — Dec. 7,1512. Mr. Mor, seriaunt, [*i.e.* More's father], and Mr. Mor, jun. are each appointed on a small Committee, to speak respectively with the Duke of Buckingham and the Bishop of Norwich for the Act concerning Corporations.

Jan. 20, 1513. With others to interview the King's Council for divers causes. R. 2. 151.

Sept. 13, 1513. With others, care of London Bridge. R. 2. 162.

Dec. 11, 1514; Mar. 22, 1515. Forfeiture of some alum *as foreyn bought and sold*: xxs. is given to More *for his grete labour and payn by hym susteyned in that behalff.* R. 2 .206, *b.* R. 3. 15.

May 8, 1515. *Yt ys agreed that Thomas More, Gent., oon of* [the] *undersheryfes of london which shall go on the kinges ambasset in to Flaunders shall occupie his Rowme & office by his sufficient depute un tyll his cummyng home agayn.* R. 3. 22.

Feb. 21, 1516; Aug. 21, 1516. Marriage of the daughter of Mistress Alice Middleton, (More's step-daughter) to Thomas Elryngton, gent. [After his death, she married Giles Alington.] R. 3. 69. R. 3. 156, *b.*

June 10, 1516. Committee to fix price of victuals: *and that Mr. More the yonger shall be assistent to theym.* R. 3. 88, *b.*

Mar. 10, 17, 1517. Office of the gaugership, and tithes. R. 3. 133, *b.*

May 1, 1517, was Evil May Day. On May 12 More was one of a Commission appointed *to go to the kinges grace & to know his plesure when the Mayr & aldremen & diverse of the Substancyall Comeners of this Citie shall sue to beseche his grace to be good and gracious lord un to theym & to accepte theym nowe beying most Sorowfull & hevye for thees late Attemptates doon ageynst their wylles;* and also *to fele my lord Cardynalles mynde concernyng the nombre of persones that shall cume to the kinges grace for the seyd Sute to be made.* R. 3. 143.

July 6, 1517. With the Recorder, to arbitrate between the parishioners of St. Vedast and the Fellowship of Saddlers. R. 3. 149.

July 23, 1518. *Ad istam Curiam Thomas More, Gent., unus Subviccecomes Civitatis in Computatore Pulletr' london, libere et sponte . . . Resignavit Officium predictum in manus Maioris et aldermannorum.* R. 3. 221.

Owing to a mistake in reckoning the regnal year, the date of More's surrender of the office of Under-Sheriff has always been given as 23 July, 1519, which is not consistent with his conviction that he could not properly hold that office and be in the service of the king.

More's official connection with the City was now closed; but More's services to the City, especially in connection with the pacification of the May Day troubles, continued to be a London tradition for a century. His part in this is ignored by Roper, Harpsfield and Stapleton, but Hall (deeply interested in this, as in all City matters) does justice to it in his *Chronicle* (*Henry VIII*, ed. Charles Whibley, 1904, I, 159, etc.). Meantime the exchange of courtesies and good offices continued, the Londoners evidently feeling that in More they had a friend at court:

Feb. 17, 1519. John Melsham, one of More's clerks, was admitted one of the attorneys of the sheriff's court at More's special request and instance. R. 3. 263. R. 5. 103, 104, *b.*

Aug. 18, [? 1519]. Richard Staverton admitted one of the attorneys in the sheriff's court *at the Sute & Request of Mr. John More oon of the kinges Justices & Mr. Thomas More.* R. 4. 18, *b.* R. 5. 142.

Sept. 13, 1520. More begged the Court of Aldermen for the reversion of the Secondaryship for Richard Staverton *which hath maryed the Syster of the seyd Mr. More.* R. 4. 63, *b.*

R. 5. 102, *b*. Feb. 17, 1521. Two of the sheriff's officials had to appear before the King's Council to be censured. The undersheriffs were told to present the serjeants to the Council and specially to Mr. More.

R. 5. 204. July 5, 1521. More present at the Court of Aldermen. It was stated that the king was displeased with the City because divers persons had lamented the death of the Duke of Buckingham, saying he died guiltless.

R. 5. 204, *b*. July 5, 1521. Again present at Court of Aldermen; it was suggested that all the harness of the City should be brought to certain places in the City, so as to pacify and please the king.

Jor. 12, 123. [Aug. 7, 1521. Thomas More, late of London, gentleman, bound himself in a recognizance of £20 to appear before the mayor, and answer to things objected against him. The description, "gentleman," shows that this is *not* Sir Thomas, who had just been knighted (see Note to 24/9–10) and who was still apparently living in London, in Bucklersbury; for in her marriage licence, 2 July, 1521, Margaret More is described as of St. Stephen's, Walbrook: see P. Norman, *Crosby Place*, p. 21].

R. 5. 267, *b*. Feb. 28, 1521 or 1522. Next reversion of clerkship in Mayor's Court promised to William Blakwell, clerk to one of the attorneys of the Sheriff's Court, at the request of *Sir Thomas More, undertresorer of England, a specyall lover and ffrende in the Busynesses and Causes of this Citie.*

R. 4. 118. R. 5. 285. May 9, 1522. More requires the Mayor and Aldermen to search for and imprison Frenchmen, and attach their goods.

R. 4. 134, *b*. Nov. 18, 1522. *Yt ys agreed that Syr Thomas More, undertresorer of ynglande, for his labor and payn that he toke for the Citie in makyng of a preposicion at the Comyng and Receyvyng of Thempperors grace in to this Citie shall have towardes a gown of velvet x li.* (Cf. Note to 26/7–9.)

R. 4. 136. Nov. 20, 1522. More exhibits the king's letter to the Court of Aldermen about the exercising of physic in the City.

R. 4. 170, *b*. Cf. R. 5. 360. R. 6. 71. Nov. 24, 1523. More thanks the Court of Aldermen for promising Staverton the reversion of the Secondaryship of the Counter in Bread St. As Staverton no longer wants it, he asks it for John Wyseman, clerk of the counter, and asks Wyseman's place for an old acquaintance, Reve, a scrivener.

Jor. 12, 285. 1524. Arbitrator in case of *Coke* v. *City* as to the setting up of mills on the Thames.

R. 6. 94, 106, 108. R. 7. 71, *b*. R. 8. 7, *b*. 1525, 1528. Mr. [John] More, Justice of the King's Bench, to have yearly a hogshead of wine from the City.

R. 7. 140. 1526. Mr. More, Justice, to help City make a certificate of Clopton's will.

R. 8. 39. 1529. The Chancellor of the Duchy of Lancaster came in person to recommend, for the post of sword-bearer, his servant, Walter Smith, who had been with him eight or nine years. (Cf. Note to 73/6.)

R. 8. 77. 1529. The Lord Chancellor of England to have a tun of good wine of red and claret. His father to have a hogshead.

R. 8. 86. 1530. More signs the ordinances of the London Parish Clerks.

R. 8. 102. 1530. Bill of Sir Thomas More for £50.

R. 8. 141. 1530. More to have a tun of good wine at Christmas.

20/1. *vnder sheriffe.* The description of the office is derived from Erasmus' letter to Ulrich von Hutten: *Id munus vt minimum habet oneris (nam non sedetur nisi die Iouis vsque ad prandium) ita cum primis honorificum habetur. Nemo plures causas absoluit, nemo se gessit integrius; remissa plerisque pecunia quam ex praescripto debent qui litigant: siquidem ante litis contestationem actor deponit treis drachmas, totidem reus, nec amplius quicquam fas est exigere.* (*Opus Epist. Des. Erasmi*, ed. Allen, No. 999, Tom. IV, p. 20.)

20/23–21/3. *he was at the sute and instance of the englishe merchauntes . . . for great important matters betweene the said merchantes and the merchauntes of the Stilliarde . . . sent twise Ambassadour ouer the Seas.* The Steelyard was the colony of the Hanseatic League in London: it stood on the site of Cannon St. Station, and was "like a small walled German town in the midst of London." Roper and Harpsfield are not correct in making both embassies relate to matters between the English merchants and those of the Steelyard: the second embassy was to Calais, and for the purpose of negotiating, not with the Hanseatic, but with French merchants.

The *First Embassy* is the one made famous by the allusions at the beginning of *Utopia*. The document appointing More and his colleagues ambassadors is given in Rymer's *Foedera*, xiii, 497: 7 May [1515], *De fidelitatibus, industriis, et providis circumspectionibus dilectorum et fidelium nostrorum Cuthberti Tunstall, utriusque juris doctoris, consiliarii nostri, Ricardi Sampson, utriusque juris doctoris, Thomæ Spynell, militis, Thomæ More, armigeri, et Johannis Clifford, gubernatoris Mercatorum nationis Angliæ.*

On 8 May, 1515, the Court of Aldermen permitted More to occupy his office of Under-sheriff by deputy (see Note to 19/22–20/2 above). Much confusion has been caused by the fact that Foss (*The Judges of England*, 1857, V. 209) mentions this leave of absence as having been given on 8 May, 1514, and again in 1515. The earlier date is clearly a duplication, due to miscalculating the regnal year of Henry VIII. There is no such entry for 8 May, 1514—in fact the Court of Aldermen did not meet on that date.

More arrived at Bruges on 17 May. Spinelly writes thence to Henry VIII on the 18th: *I . . . taryed oonly for the comyng of your ambassadours. Doctour Dunstable* [i.e. Tunstall] *and Mr. More aryued in thys towne yis*[*terday*] (MS. Cotton Galba B. iii, 307 (now p. 344); cf. *L. & P.*, ii. 473, p. 135). Meantime matters had been complicated by the addition of Richard Sampson to the embassy. Wolsey had obtained the bishopric of the conquered town of Tournay; but there was also a French claimant, and Sampson, Wolsey's representative in Tournay, had been in a difficult position. Wolsey secured diplomatic immunity for Sampson by adding him to the commission, writing to him some time in May: *ye shall haue assocyat with* [*you*] *yong More.* Sampson being the king's ambassador, his enemies, Wolsey writes, will find it the more difficult to attempt anything against him, and he will be the more able to advance Wolsey's causes: *handyll the mater boldly and foulmynat the censures according* [*to the*] *bryff, not feryng for any excomynycacion of any man* (MS. Cotton Calig. E. iii, 99, Wolsey's autograph, in an execrable hand, and mutilated; cf. *L. & P.*, ii, 534, p. 147). Sampson replied, thanking Wolsey for having added him in the commission *with Mr. Tunstall and yong Moore*, but pointing out the difficulties he would have in promoting Wolsey's interests in Flanders: *I schuld meruelosly prouoke the commons* [*of*] *the countre, which off ther own nature be malicios* [*of the*] *honor or profet off any Inglisman* (MS. Cotton Calig. D. vi, 288^{v}, now 292^{v}.) This forecast was justified, and Tunstall writes to Wolsey an account of their troubles from Bruges, on 9 July (autograph letter in MS. Cotton Galba B. iii, 259, now p. 293^{v}):

As towching master [Sampson] . . . you contynue good lord vnto hym. I assur you he [doth you good] seruice in thes parties and painful also. For in al thes . . . wer not in the kinges commission, he is so persuyd by your ad[uersaries that] he mygth not saffly tary. And now off late notwithstond[ing] he is in commission, he was openly in al the churchys off thys tow[ne] accursyd, whych shewyth the malice off your said aduersar[ies tow]ardes you, and also lytyl good mynd to the kinges grace . . . I besech you to contynue good to hym in helpinge hym [in] thys besines; yff the kinges commission wer not, I assur you they wold [inv]ocare brachium seculare *again hym rygth shortly. And lykwyse I humbly beseche you to contynue good lord vnto Mr. Spinel, which I as[sure] you doth the kinge diligent faithful and trusty seruice as we may perceue. Your grace must help the kinge may continue his gracio[us] fauour towardes hym, for bycause he seruith hys grace, other men doth forsake hym her. Master More at thys tyme as beynge at a low ebbe desyrys by your grace to be set on flote ayen . . .*

By your humble beadman Cuthbert Tunstal.

The same request for more money is made in a letter of Tunstal, Sampson and More to the Council. (In the Record Office; see *L. & P.*, ii. 678, 679, p. 180.)

More later gave an account of this embassy in a letter to Erasmus: *Nostra legatio, quoniam haec tibi curae est, vt mea omnia, satis foeliciter processit* (*Opus Epist. Des. Erasmi*, ed. Allen, No. 388, Tom. II, pp. 195–6. Allen dates this letter, c. 17 Feb., 1516; Nichols in May, 1516). More says that he had expected the embassy to last two months, and that it lasted six; that when the business for which he had been sent was concluded, and further delay seemed likely, he got permission to return, through the mediation of Pace; later he met Pace at Gravelines, outward bound, and in such haste that they had hardly time to greet each other. Pace in his letter to Wolsey, from Antwerp, dated 25 Oct., 1515 (preserved in MS. Cotton Galba B. vi, p. 82, now 100), tells of this hasty meeting; after mentioning some information he had obtained, he adds: *I met wyth Mr. More in the highwaye, and because there was at that tyme no commoditie to wryte vnto your grace, I desirydde hym to make schewe off thys vnto your sayde grace.* (See *L. & P.*, ii. 1067, p. 282: it appears from ii. 1059 that Pace passed through Calais on the 24th.) In this letter to Erasmus, More then goes on to express, humorously, his dislike of these embassies (see Note to 21/19 ff. below) and the pleasure he had derived from the company of Tunstall, Busleiden, and Peter Giles.

In the *Second Embassy* More was associated with Sir Richard Wingfield, deputy of Calais, and Dr. William Knight. A draft commission, dated 26 Aug., 1517, to settle disputes in Calais between French and English merchants, is extant (MS. Cotton Caligula D. vi, 317, now 322–27; cf. *L. & P.*, ii. 3634, p. 1148). A letter of Wingfield and More (in French) to the French commissioners at Boulogne, dated 20 Nov., 1517, is preserved in Cotton Caligula E. i, 130 (now 174, etc.; cf. *L. & P.*, ii. 3803, p. 119).

More was starting for Calais on this second embassy when he wrote to Erasmus, 19 Aug., 1517; he mentions that the plague has been raging in London: *Ego vxorque ac liberi adhuc intacti, reliqua familia tota reualuit. Hoc tibi affirmo, minus periculi in acie quam in vrbe esse. Nunc, vt audio, seuire Caleti incipit, quum nos eo extrudimur legatione functuri; tanquam parum sit in contagione vixisse, nisi sequamur etiam.* More was still by the sea when Erasmus wrote to him, 30 Nov., *O te felicem, qui nunc, vt arbitror, adeo vicinus mari degas.* On

21 Dec., Erasmus, writing to Pace, who was then at Bruges, wonders if More is with him—presumably paying a visit on his way home: *Si Morus est apud te, miror illum tantopere πυθαγορίζειν* [*i.e.* keep silence] . . . *Morum non saluto, quandoquidem ille nihil tale in tuis litteris, ne tam crebris quidem.* (*Opus Epist. Des. Erasmi*, ed. Allen, Nos. 623, 726, 742; Tom. III, pp. 47, 153, 171.)

21/8 ff. *shutt vp in a Towne nere to the Sea.* Strictly, this refers only to the second embassy (1517). Cf. *Opus Epist. Des. Erasmi* (ed. Allen), No. 688, Tom. III, p. 111. More writes to Erasmus from Calais:

> *Nam et relegatus sum in oppidulum maritimum et solo et coelo iniucundum: tum domi qui meapte natura vehementer ab litibus abhorream, etiam quum lucrum adferunt, quantum necesse est hic adferant taedium, quum veniant comitatae damno.*

21/19 ff. *there was betweene a lay man and a priest to be sent in ambassade a very great difference,* etc. From the letter quoted above, *Opus Epist. Des. Erasmi* (ed. Allen), No. 388, Tom. II, p. 196:

> *Mihi nunquam admodum legati munus arrisit. Neque videtur perinde nobis laicis quam sacerdotibus conuenire vobis, qui primum vxores ac liberos aut domi non habetis aut vbique reperitis. Nos sicubi paulo absumus, coniugum protinus ac sobolis desyderio reuocamur . . . a quibus ego, quanquam scis quam clemens maritus, quam indulgens pater, quam mitis dominus, tamen ne tantulum quidem quiui impetrare vt mea causa tantisper quoad domum redirem ieiuni persisterent.*

22/8–21. *the king . . . offered him . . . an annuall pencion,* etc. Cf. *Opus Epist. Des. Erasmi* (ed. Allen), No. 388, Tom. II, p. 196:

> *quanquam mihi reuertenti pensio annua ab Rege decreta est, eaque plane, seu quis honorem spectet seu fructum, neutiquam contemnenda. Quam ego tamen hactenus recusaui, videorque mihi perpetuo recusaturus; quod ea suscepta praesens haec mea in vrbe conditio, quam ego etiam meliori antepono, aut mihi foret relinquenda aut, quod minime vellem, cum aliqua ciuium offensione retinenda.*

The pension was to have been one of £100; it appears as granted to "Thomas More, councillor, for life," on the Record Office lists, 1516 (*L. & P.*, ii. 2736, p. 875).

23/30. *he should first respect and regarde God.* More understood this, not as a mere pious phrase, but as an undertaking that he should have freedom of conscience. He quotes it three times in his Letters—to Thomas Cromwell (*English Works*, p. 1426, numbered 1427); to his fellow-sufferer, Dr. Wilson (*English Works*, p. 1444); and to Margaret Roper (*English Works*, p. 1453).

24/6–7. *being then no better rowme voyde, he was made master of the requestes.* Erasmus, writing to William Nesen from Louvain on 17 April, 1518, says: *Ac Morus ipse totus est aulicus, Regi semper assistens, cui est a secretis.* Writing to More, about the 23rd, Erasmus says: *Quod in aulam pertractus es, vnum hoc me consolatur, quod sub optimo Rege mereberis: nobis certe et litteris ademptus es.* To Tunstall, Erasmus writes on the 24th: *Mori fortunam plane deplorarem, qui sit in aulam pertractus, ni sub tali Rege tamque multis eruditis contubernalibus et collegis non aula sed μουσεῖον videri possit. Sed tamen interea nihil adfertur ἐκ τῆς Οὐτοπίας quod rideamus: et ille sat scio ridere malit quam curuli sublimis vehi.* (*Opus Epist. Des. Erasmi*, ed. Allen, Nos. 816, 829, 832; Tom. III, pp. 286, 295, 303.)

24/9–10. *After the death of Master Weston, he was made vnder Treasourer of Theschequer.* A curious mistake. Weston did not precede, but followed More as Under-Treasurer, and lived for some twenty years after the date at which he is here alleged to have died. He was a prominent figure about the Court, and Roper, from whom the error is derived, must, one would think, have known him well. Roper commits the further error (which Harpsfield corrects) of making Weston Treasurer, not Under-Treasurer.

More actually succeeded Sir John Cutte. Cutte was still Under-Treasurer in July, 1520 (*L. & P.*, iii. 1, 928), and was holding the keys of the Treasury in September, 1520 (*ibid.*, 973). The exact date of More's appointment is not certain : the first known allusion to his preferment is in a letter of Erasmus to Pace, 11 June, 1521 (*Opus Epist. Des. Erasmi*, ed. Allen, No. 1210, Tom. IV, p. 506). Erasmus gives a more detailed account in a letter to Conrad Goclenius (12 Aug., 1521; No. 1223) :

> *Nam quum antea Regi tantum esset a consiliis, nuper nec ambiens nec expetens vltroneo fauore Principis humanissimi et eques auratus factus est, et munus habet apud Britannos cum honorificum imprimis, tum etiam salarii non poenitendi, quod appellatur a thesauris.*

There is a further reference in the letter to Budaeus (*c.* Sept., 1521; No. 1233) :

> *Est enim Principi suo a thesauris. Ea functio apud Britannos vt est splendida cum primis atque honorifica, ita non admodum est obnoxia nec inuidiae nec molestis negociis. Erat competitor, homo sat gratiosus, qui sic ambiebat hoc muneris vt non grauaretur suo victu ciboque gerere. At Rex optimus hic certissimum in Morum fauoris argumentum dedit, qui non ambienti salarium etiam addere maluerit quam gratuitum magistratum admittere.*

In the dedication of his *De arte supputandi* (1522) Cuthbert Tunstall refers to More's labours at the Treasury. Tunstall dedicates his work to More : *cui enim aptiora hæc quam tibi esse possunt : qui totus in supputationibus excutiendis occupatus in regni ærario post præfectum primas tenes.*

24/11. *Sir Richarde Wingefelde.* Died at Toledo, 22 July, 1525. More succeeded him both as High Steward of the University of Cambridge and as Chancellor of the Duchy of Lancaster.

24/21–2. *Neyther was there any one man that the king vsed more familierly.* The importance of More's position at Court about 1526, after he had been made Chancellor of the Duchy of Lancaster, is shown by the *Ordenaunces made for the kinges householde and chambres* (MS. Laud 597; also in MS. Harl. 642; and printed in the *Collection of Ordinances and Regulations* issued by the Society of Antiquaries, London, 1790). These ordinances (made at Eltham in the 17th year of the king) provide (Cap. 74) among other things, for the establishment of a Council of twenty members (" Sir Thomas More, Chaunceler of the Duchie," being one). Since many of these were often absent from the king's Court for " reasonnable impedimentes," ten of the Council, including More, are named for " contynuall attendaunce " :

> *And bycause, percase it may chaunce some of these aforenamed personnes to be absent for some reasonable cause, Be it alwaies prouided and forseen that either the Bishop of Bathe, the Secretarie, Syr Thomas More and the Dean of the chapell or two of them at the lest alwaies be present except the kinges grace gyve licence to any of them to the contrarie, whiche said counsaillours so apointed*

for contynuall attendaunce shall applie themself effectuallie, diligentlie, uprightlie and iustly in the premisses, being euerye day in the forenone by X of the clock at the furthest and at afternone by II of the clock in the kinges dynyng chamber or in suche other place as shall fortune to be appointed for the counsaill chamber, there to be in redines not only in case the kinges pleasure shalbe to comone and conferre with them upon any cause or mater, but also for hering and direction of pore mens compleintes and maters of Justice, whiche direction well obserued the kinges highnes shalbe alwaies furnished of an honourable presence of counsaillours aboutes his grace as to his high honnour doth appertaigne. (MS. Laud 597, fol. 31v; Bodleian Library.)

See also Pollard, "The Council under the Tudors," in the *English Historical Review*, xxxvii, 337–60 (1922), especially p. 359.

24/27–26/3. *his house at Chelsey.* "From June, 1523, to Jan., 1524, More was the owner of Crosby Place in the City of London; but I cannot find any definite evidence to connect him with Chelsea before his purchases of land there in 1524." (Dr. P. S. Allen, *Opus Epist. Des. Erasmi*, No. 999, Tom. IV, p. 17. See also Norman, *Crosby Place*, p. 21.) A truce was made with France on 14 Aug., 1525, so Henry's visit can be dated with some probability in 1524, or the summer of 1525.

26/7–9. *At which time Sir Thomas More made a fine and eloquent oration in the presence of the Emperour and the kinge*, etc. A summary of the oration, in much the same words as those of Harpsfield, will be found in Hall's *Chronicle*, xiiij yere, fol. lxxxxv, verso (p. 250 of Vol. I of the reprint edited by Charles Whibley). Hall adds that More said *how that the Maior and Citezens offered* [to the Emperor] *any pleasure of service that in them laye next their sovereigne lorde.* For the citizens' gratitude to More, see Note to 19/22.

Rymer's *Foedera*, xiii, 768, contains a list of those appointed to meet the Emperor—*Assignati in adventu Imperatoris, ad intendendum regi vicesimo septimo die mensis Maii apud Cantuariam :* More's name occurs in the list of knights. (For examples of More's diplomatic activities, see the same volume, pp. 497, 714, 722.)

26/17. *the Saturday*, i.e. 18 April, 1523, as Prof. A. F. Pollard has pointed out to me, referring to *Rot. Parl.* Suppl., p. lxxvi.

26/19 ff. *Among other thinges he brought forth a story of the notable captaine Hanniball*, etc. Roper speaks of this speech, in which More asked to be discharged from the office of Speaker, as "not now extant," in contrast to the oration pleading for freedom of speech, which he gives verbatim. A summary of the speech "not now extant" had, however, been given in Hall's *Chronicle*, yere xiiij, fol. cvi, verso (p. 279 of Vol. I of the reprint edited by Charles Whibley). Harpsfield's summary is very like Hall's, and is possibly a paraphrase of it; but, if so, his freedom in dealing with Hall's report contrasts with the care with which he follows, verbatim, the speech reported by Roper.

If Harpsfield drew from Hall, he may have refreshed his memory by looking up the story of Phormio and Hannibal in Cicero, *de Oratore*, II, 18 (75), for he gives it more accurately than does Hall.

In the speech written to be delivered in this parliament (it is supposed by Thomas Cromwell), there is confirmation of More having told the story of Phormio: the speaker discusses the policy of invading France, and apologises for expressing his opinion—*In the reasonyng of whiche matter I shall but vtter myne ygnoraunce afore Hanyball, as our ryght wyse spekar rehersid now of late* (*Life and Letters of Thomas Cromwell*, by R. B. Merriman, 1902, I, 37).

27/13–14 ff. *he spake to his grace in forme folowing*, etc. For the historic value of More's speech when made Speaker, see "The Commons' Privilege of Free Speech in Parliament," by Prof. J. E. Neale, in *Tudor Studies presented to A. F. Pollard*, pp. 257 ff.

31/12 ff. *It fortuned at that Parliament a very great subsedie to be demaunded*, etc. It is clear that More (whilst loyally co-operating with Wolsey in persuading the Commons to grant the unpopular subsidy) disliked Wolsey's bullying methods. Hall gives us one side of this very natural attitude; Roper (whom Harpsfield is here following) the other. Hall says:

> *The morow after, sir Thomas More, beyng speker, declared all the Cardinalles oracion again to the commons, and enforced his demaund strongly, saiyng: that of duetie men ought not to deny to paye iiii.s.of the pound. But for all that, it was denied*, etc. (Hall's *Chronicle*, ed. Charles Whibley, I, 285).

If Wolsey realised how much More disliked his arrogance, and *if* there was really the friction between them which Roper and Harpsfield record, Wolsey certainly recovered from his annoyance in a way which does him credit. He wrote a letter, 24 August, 1523, for More to present to Henry after the dissolution of parliament, which is full of kindly feeling:

> *Sir. After my moste humble recommendations. It may like your grace to vnderstande, I have shewed vnto this berer, Sir Thomas More, diuerse Matters to bee by hym, on my behalf, declared vnto your highnes, beseeching the same, that at convenient tyme It may be your pleasure to heare hym make reaport therof accordyngly. And, Sire, wheras it hath been accustomed, that the spekers of the Parliamentes, in consideration of their diligence and paynes taken, have had, though the parliament hath been right soone finisshed, aboue the C li ordynary, a reward of C li, for the better mayntenance of their householde and other charges susteyned in the same, I suppose, Sir, that the faithful diligence of the said Sir Thomas More, in all your causes treated in this your late parliament, as wel for your Subsidy, right honorably passed, as otherwise considered, no man could better deserve the same then he hath done, wherfore your pleasure known therein, I shall cause the same to be auaunced vnto hym accordyngly, Ascertaynyng your grace that I am the rather moved to put your highnes in remembraunce therof, bycause he is not the most redy to speke and solicite his owne cause.*
>
> *At your Mannor of Hampton Court, the 24th day of august by your*
> *most humble Chaplain*
> *T. Car[lis] Ebor.*
>
> *To the kings most noble Grace*
> *Defender of the Faith.*

The original letter was stated in the printed State Papers of 1830 (Vol. I, lxix, p. 124) to have been lost. It was found before 1867 (see *L. & P.*, Vol. iii, Part 2, p. 1355, footnote to No. 3267) and is now numbered as 171 in the Record Office volume, *L. & P.*, Henry VIII (28), III. The manuscript is now in a mutilated and much-damaged condition, and the signature and address are cut off. Fortunately a copy of it had been made (see No. 172 of same volume) by Mr. Raymond, Keeper of the State Papers, with the spelling partly modernised. In the transcript above, the original manuscript has been followed where possible, and Mr. Raymond's copy used where the original cannot be now read or where mutilated.

Two days after this letter to the king, More writes to Wolsey, reporting that the king had ordered that, besides his fee of £100 as speaker, he should receive £100 out of the Exchequer. (MS. Cotton Titus B. 1, fol. 331 [325]; cf. Delcourt, *Essai sur la langue de Sir Thomas More*, pp. 328–9):

> *fferthermore hit may lyke your good grace to vnderstand that at the contemplation of your graces lettres the kinges highnes is graciously content that byside the c. li. for my fe for thoffice of the speker of his parleament, to be taken at the receipte of his eschequer, I shall haue one other hundred poundis owt of his cofres by thandes of the tresorer of his chambre, wherfor in moost humble wise I besech your good grace that as your graciouse favour hath obteigned hit for me, so it may lyke the same to wryte to Mr Wiatt that he may deliver hit to such as I shall send for hit. Wherby I & all myne, as the manyfold goodnes of your grace hath all redy bound vs, shalbe dayly more & more bounden to pray for your grace; whom our Lord longe preserve in honour & helth; at Esthamstede the xxvj*[th] *day of August,*
>
> *Your humble oratour & moost bounden beedman,*
> *Thomas More.*
>
> *To my Lord legates good grace.*

There are many letters of More to Wolsey during the following month. They are official, written by the king's order; but More adds personal passages to compliment Wolsey, and express his indebtedness to him. On 1 Sept. he goes out of his way to express his admiration of Wolsey's letter: *ffor hit is for the quantite one of the best made lettres for wordis, mater, sentence and cowching that ever I redde in my life* (Delcourt, *as above*, p. 329). On 13 Sept. More expresses his gratitude to Wolsey (Delcourt, p. 337), and again more emphatically on 26 Sept. (Delcourt, p. 348):

> *ffinally that hit lyketh your good grace so benygnely to accepte and take in worth my pore service, and so far aboue my merites to commende the same, in that lettre which of myn accustumed maner your grace foreknew the kinges grace shold se (wherby his highnes shold haue occasion to accepte hit in lyke wise: and so lyked your grace in one lettre both geve me your thankes and gete me his) I were, my good lord, very blynde if I perceived not, very vnkinde if ever I forgate, of what graciouse favour it procedeth; which I can never otherwise reanswere than with my pore prayour, which duryng my life shall never faile to pray to god for the preservation of your good grace in honour & helth. At Wodestoke the xxvi*[th] *day of Septembre,*
>
> *Your humble oratour and moost bounden beedman,*
> *Thomas More.*
>
> *To my lord legates good grace.*

If therefore, at this time, there was unfriendliness between Wolsey and More, it must have passed off quickly.

32/14. *Master Marney, afterwarde Lorde Marney.* This must be Sir John Marney. His father, Sir Henry Marney, Lord Privy Seal, had been raised to the peerage on 12 April, 1523, a few days before the meeting of this parliament (see *L. & P.*, iii. 2, App. 41), and died a few weeks later (24 May, 1523). Sir

John is mentioned as "John, Lord Marney," in a Commission of the Peace, Nov. 1523 (*ibid.*).

33/10. *gallerye at white hall*, i.e. York House.

33/19–22. *the Cardinall . . . for reuengement of his displeasure, councelled the king to sende him ambassadour into Spaine.* The comment of Father Bridgett (*Life of More*, p. 195) is to the point: "There was surely nothing in the Spanish climate so deadly as to justify us in attributing to Wolsey the revengeful and murderous motive hinted at by Roper. All seems to be explained, if we suppose that More saw in the Cardinal's proposal a plan to get him away from England, and that More also saw (what the Cardinal did not see) that for him the climate would be perilous."

Sir Thomas Boleyn and Richard Sampson had been sent in the autumn of 1522 (Sampson writes from Laredo on 16 Oct., after an exciting journey: his despatches and those of Tunstall will be found in MS. Cotton Vespasian C. ii and iii). In April, 1523, Sir Thomas Boleyn was recalled, returning home in May. This was about the time of the discussions in Parliament to which Roper refers, and it may well have been proposed to send More to Spain when he was freed from his duties as Speaker. More naturally objected, for it was a well-known trick of Wolsey's to send abroad rivals whose power he feared. Ultimately Tunstall and Sir Richard Wingfield were sent to join Sampson; they left Cowes, 18 April, 1525, and arrived at Toledo, 24 May, 1525. Copies of the instructions to them will be found in MS. Stowe 147, fols. 67v, 86. Wingfield fell ill almost immediately, and died at Toledo, 22 July, 1525, whilst Tunstall and Sampson were both seriously ill. Tunstall reports all this in a letter:

> *To my lorde legates grace: Plese it your grace to vndirstand that it hath pleasid almygthy god to cal Mr. Wingfeld out off thys present lyffe. The maner and fourme off whos deth shal appere vnto you by the kinges lettre which shal come to your knowlege. Wherfor I shal not nede to repete it. He hath written a lettre vnto your grace commendyng vnto the same his wyff and hys chyldern, which gretly ran in his mynd in his seknes . . . Hys seknes had welnygh ouerthrawn me also, for lake off rest and slepe, when he drew nygh to hys end. . . . My compagnion Mr. Sampson, the morow affter hys deth, fel into a fever and ys not yet wel recoueryd. I was not longe befor Mr. Wyngfeld seknes brougth so low by a fluxe that my legges began to fail me. And my stomake and strenght was goon. Yff the feuer had comen, as offte it foloyth that dysese, surly I had not escapyd; but louyd be god, now I am bettyr, and Mr. Sampson past the worste. . . . From Tolledo the Xth day off August* [1525.] *By your graces most humble bedman, Cuthbert London.* (MS. Cotton Vesp. C. iii, fols. 82–4.)

Is it too much to suppose that Roper's suspicions had their origin in a grim jest More may have made when he heard of the ill-health of those who actually did go? "Now I see why my Lord Cardinal wished to send *me*." More's jest could never be distinguished from his earnest: and Roper took everything seriously.

Tyndale refers to Wolsey's habit of sending rivals to Italy or Spain, but does not hint that there was any murderous intent behind it. Compare Note to 49/16–18.

34/15–16. *Truely, this Cardinall did not heartily loue Sir Thomas More, yea, he rather feared him.* From a letter of Erasmus to Faber: *Cardinalis dum uiueret*

Moro parum æquus erat, eumque metuebat uerius quam amabat. (*Des. Erasmi Epist. Opus*, Basileae, 1538, p. 1071.)

39/5–9. *the Cardinall himselfe, when he sawe he should needes forgoe the same, though he neuer bare him, as I haue saide, true hartie affection, yet did he confesse that Sir Thomas More was the aptest and fittest man in the Realme for the same.* Cf. above, Note to 34/15–16. In his letter to Faber, Erasmus records how Wolsey, when he saw that there was no chance of recovering power, had said that in the whole island there was no one capable of taking his place save More alone:

> *Quin ipse Cardinalis Eboracensis, uir, quæcunque fuit hominis fortuna, non stupidus, quum perspiceret nullam superesse spem reditus ad dignitatem pristinam, asseuerauit, in ea Insula nullum esse tanto oneri parem præter unum Morum. Nec hoc erat fauoris aut beneuolentiæ suffragium. Cardinalis dum uiueret, Moro parum æquus erat,* etc. (*Des. Erasmi Epist. Opus*, Basileae, 1538, p. 1071.)

41/2–4. *the diuorce . . . moued and procured by the . . . Cardinall.* Harpsfield tells the story more at length in the *Pretended Divorce*, pp. 175, etc. It is based upon the tale told by Polydore Vergil, Wolsey's bitter enemy, in 1555:

> *Is* [*Volsæus*] *proinde quod cogitarat, cum spe magna id exequi cupiens, cum Ioanne Longland Lincolniensi episcopo de quæstione futura amice communicat, quod is esset, qui regis confessionem audiret. . . . Quo capto consilio, placuit Volsæo prouinciam suscipere, qui suo tempore ad regem adiuit, ac eum specie charitatis & iustitię de eiusmodi iure matrimonii admonet, asseritque id parum uirium uel roboris habere, propter nuptias Catherinæ cum eius fratre coniunctas, uehementerque orat, ne se patiatur diutius in tanto uersari discrimine, cum hic de salute animæ, de posteritate uera regum, de honestate uitæ quammaxime agatur. His auditis, rex primum paulisper stetit tacitus, ut qui plurimum mirabatur coniugium suum damnari, quod initio ueluti iustum æquumque a pontifice Romano, ab optimis ac doctissimis quibusque episcopis probatum de eorumque sententia sancitum fuisset, dein inquit: Bone pater, uide bene quale saxum suo loco iacens mouere coneris, sicut in prouerbio est, habeo equidem uxorem foeminam multo nobilissimam, longe electissimam sanctissimamque, cui nihil objici potest diuortio dignum. Quod uero mulierem nuptam fuisse fratri meo ais, id minime obstat, quoniam ipsa alias sæpe iureiurando testata est, illum propter imbecillitatem tum ætatis tum naturæ nunquam secum corpus commiscuisse. Ita eo die sermo de re ipsa haud longius processit. At triduo post Volsæus incredibili armatus audacia Lincolniensem conuenit eumque ducit ad regem, quem ille sic affatur,* etc. (*Polydori Vergilii Anglicæ Historiæ* libri xxvii; Basileae, 1555, p. 685.)

That Wolsey was the first mover of the divorce was asserted at the time, e.g. by Tyndale in *The Practise of Prelates*, 1530: *he imagined the diuorcement betwene the King and the Queene* (*Workes of Tyndall, Frith and Barnes*, 1572, p. 372).

41/4–42/1. For Harpsfield's view on the origin of the divorce, and his alleged divergent accounts of Wolsey, see above, *Introduction*, pp. ccvii–ccxii.

41/21. *repented afterwarde.* According to Chapuys, this repentance began early: "The bishop of Lincoln, who was at the beginning one of the promotors of the divorce, has said several times since Christmas, that he would rather be the poorest man in the world than ever have been the King's councillor and confessor" (*L. & P.*, vii, p. 8, No. 14, Chapuys to Charles V, 3 Jan. 1534).

42/8–15. *Cardinall Adrian . . . barefoote and bare legged passed through the streetes.* I can find no mention of this act of humility, either in the contemporary account of Adrian's entry into Rome by Gerardus Moringus (*Vita Hadriani Sexti*, pp. 60–1, in C. Burmannus, *Analecta Historica de Hadriano Sexto*, 1727) or in the modern account of Constantin von Höfler, who devotes more than twenty pages to Adrian's arrival at, and entry into Rome (*Papst Adrian VI*, 1880, pp. 187—202). Such an act of humility is not incredible. According to Cavendish, Cardinal Wolsey expressed his intention of making his entry into York, for his installation, "in the vamps of our hosen" (*Life of Wolsey*, ed. Singer, 1827, p. 335).

43/8–9. *one of the frenche kinges sisters, the Dutchesse of Alanson.* A common error, which ultimately finds its way into the Shakespearean *Henry VIII* (III. ii. 85). The Duchess of Alençon is generally known in this country as Margaret of Navarre. A full account of her life and writings has just been written, in two massive volumes, by M. Pierre Jourda (*Marguerite d'Angoulême, Duchesse d'Alençon, Reine de Navarre (1492–1549)*. A marriage between Henry VIII and "the amiable mother of the Renaissance" would have been a remarkable event; but even Wolsey cannot have hoped to bring it to pass. For "Margaret, duchess of Alençon, had already been married to Henry, king of Navarre, in the preceding January. The error comes originally from Polydore Vergil, and has been repeated by later writers. But the princess whom Wolsey had intended his master to marry was Renée, daughter of Louis XII, who was married a year later to Hercules, afterwards Duke of Ferrara" (Gairdner, *English Historical Review*, XI, 681).

44/17–18. *the king opened it with the first to Sir Thomas More.* We have to distinguish four different consultations:

1. Harpsfield, pp. 44–6: Roper (ed. Sampson), pp. 223–4.
2. Harpsfield, pp. 47–8: *not in Roper;* but in More's letter to Cromwell, *English Works*, p. 1425.
3. Harpsfield, pp. 48–9: Roper, pp. 226–7. This seems to be the conference referred to in More's letter to Cromwell (*English Works*, p. 1426), although the details do not altogether agree.
4. Harpsfield, pp. 56–7: Roper, pp. 234–5.

46/12–13. *Then was there . . . procured from Rome a Commission.* For the complicated question of the divorce proceedings, see:

N. Pocock, *Records of the Reformation*, 2 vols., 1870.
P. Friedmann, *Anne Boleyn*, 2 vols., 1884.
S. Ehses, *Römische Dokumente zur Geschichte der Ehescheidung Heinrichs VIII*, 1893.
J. Gairdner, "New Lights on the Divorce of Henry VIII," *English Historical Review*, xi, 673–702, xii, 1–16, 237–53.
Sir John Macdonell, *Historical Trials*, 1927, pp. 149–70.
A. F. Pollard, *Wolsey*, 1929.

See also pp. 221–2, above, and Note thereon.

46/20–23. *a dispensation . . . an instrument or briefe, vpon searche found in the Treasorie of Spaine.* The text of the brief is given in the *Life of Henry VIII*, by Lord Herbert of Cherbury, pp. 266–7 (edit. 1672). The brief was not found in the Treasury of Spain, as Harpsfield says, but among the papers of Ruy Gonzalez de Puebla, who had been ambassador to England 1494–1509, and who was supposed to have brought it back from England, whither it had been originally sent. Neither was the brief sent to England during the divorce proceedings, but only a copy.

See Ehses, *Römische Dokumente zur Geschichte der Ehescheidung Heinrichs VIII*, 1893, pp. xxxi–xliii, and Lord Acton, "Wolsey and the Divorce of Henry VIII", (1877) in *Historical Essays*, 1907, pp. 47–9. Acton doubts the authenticity of the brief.

In this inaccurate account Harpsfield is following Roper word for word. Later, when he wrote *The Pretended Divorce*, he knew that only a copy of the brief was sent to England for the inspection of the Commissioners, and states very fairly the case against its authenticity (*Pretended Divorce*, pp. 193–5).

46/26–47/1. *had not the king . . . appealed to the next generall Counsaile.* Compare More's letter to Cromwell (*English Works*, p. 1427). *And verely sith the kinges highnes hath (as by the boke of his honorable counsaile appereth) appeled to the general counsaile from the Pope . . .*

48/8. *Master Foxe, his Almoigner.* Harpsfield here has slightly misrepresented his source, More's letter to Cromwell of 1533 (*English Works*, p. 1425). More there tells how, after his return from beyond sea (six years before), he had been told to confer with Master Foxe, "nowe hys gracyous [*misprint for* graces] almoygner." Henry's almoners changed frequently, for the post was an avenue to promotion. (See Pollard's *Wolsey*, p. 11, footnote.) The almoner at this date (Sept., 1527) was Dr. Edward Lee, who was absent on an embassy to Spain. He subsequently became Archbishop of York, and was succeeded as almoner by Edward Foxe, who himself later became bishop of Hereford. For Foxe's career, see *D. N. B.*

48/18–19. *Sir Thomas Moore so woorthily handled himselfe.* Note the stress which More himself, in his Epitaph, lays upon the Peace of Cambrai. See above, p. 279, l. 23, to p. 280, l. 6.

49/16–18. *Bisshopp Stokesley, being by the Cardinall . . . sent to the Fleete.* There appears to be no confirmation of this, but it is not incredible, considering Wolsey's high-handed actions (cf. Pollard, *Wolsey*, p. 178). Pollard suggests, however, that Roper may be thinking of Stokesley's later troubles in 1538, when he was accused of infringing statutes 16 Rich. II and 28 Henry VIII, by executing a bull of the Pope. On that occasion he was brought into court in the custody of the marshal, admitted to bail, and subsequently pardoned by the king (3 July, 1538: see *L. & P.* xiii. 1. 1095, p. 399).

There is no doubt that there was some quarrel between Wolsey and Stokesley. It is referred to by Tyndale in his *Practice of Prelates*:

> *And after the same example he furnished the Court with Chaplaines of his owne sworne Disciples. . . . If among those cormorauntes any yet began to be to much in fauour with the kyng, & to be somewhat busie in the Court and to drawe any other way then as my Lord Cardinall had appointed that the plowe should go, anone he was sent to Italy or to Spayne; or some quarel was picked agaynst him, and so was thrust out of the Court, as Stokesly was.* (*Workes of Tyndall, Frith and Barnes*, 1572, p. 368.)

50/25–6. *Sir Thomas More, newly made Lorde Chauncellour.* In Rymer's *Foedera*, xiv, 349 (cf. *L. & P.*, iv. 6025) will be found particulars of the surrender of the Great Seal by Wolsey on 17 Oct., 1529, to the Dukes of Norfolk and Suffolk, of the delivery of the Seal by Henry to More in his privy chamber at East Greenwich on 25 Oct., and of More's taking the oath on the 26th, in the Great Hall at Westminster. On 25 Oct., Chapuys writes to Charles V: "The Chancellor's seal has remained in the hands of the Duke of Norfolk till this morning, when it was transferred to Sir Thomas More. Every one is delighted at his promotion, because he is an upright and learned man, and a good servant of the Queen." (*L. & P.*, iv. 6026, p. 2684.)

50/26–51/1. *which office, I suppose, verilye he was of himself very vnwilling to ake vpon him.* This is emphasized by the fragment of Rastell's lost *Life of More*. See above, p. 222, ll. 6–12.

53/8 ff. *but many other wayes be there*, etc. The comment of Lord Campbell on this shows the change in etiquette between the sixteenth and the nineteenth centuries:

> The first part of the Chancellor's answer can only be accounted for by supposing that he wished not only to mollify, but to mystify his son-in-law; or, that such practices as would now be matter of severe censure or impeachment, were then considered praiseworthy by the most virtuous; he winds up, in a manner to convince us that in no particular, however small, would he have swerved from what he considered right. (*Lives of the Lord Chancellors*, 1856, II, 33–4.)

53/24–28. *Master Herone . . . having a matter before him in the Chauncerie*, etc. The case seems to be that of *Giles Heron* v. *Nicholas Millisante* (Land in Withern wrongfully entered on by defendant during complainant's nonage), *Early Chancery Proceedings*, Bundle 643, No. 32.

For Giles Heron, see the forthcoming edition of Roper's *Life* for the Early English Text Society.

55/6. *Master Crooke, chiefe of the sixe Clerkes.* Among the principal officers of the Court of Chancery were "the Six Clerks in Chancery, or 'Prothonotaries,' whose duty it was to receive and file all bills, answers, replications, and other records in causes on the equity side of the Court of Chancery, and to enter memoranda of them in books, from which they were to certify to the Court, as occasion should require, the state of the proceedings in the various causes." The Six Clerks were abolished in 1842. See M. S. Giuseppi, *Guide to the . . . Record Office*, 1923, pp. 7, 47, 48, 50, 51, 64, 67.

58/18 ff. *At the commencement of which Parliament, Sir Thomas More . . . made an eloquent oration*, etc. This speech of More, comparing King Henry VIII to a Shepherd, was made at the opening of the "Reformation Parliament," 3 November, 1529. Cf. Hall's *Chronicle*, Henry viii, fol. clxxxvii:

> *Sir Thomas More, his Chauncelor, standyng on the righthand of the kyng, behynde the barre, made an eloquent Oracion, declaryng that like as a good shepard whiche not alonely kepeth and attendeth well his shepe, but also forseeth & prouideth for althyng which either may be hurtful or noysome to his floke, or may preserue and defende thesame agaynst all peryles that may chaunce to come, so the kyng, whiche was the sheaperd, ruler, and gouernour of his realme, vigilantly forseyng thinges to come, considered how diuers lawes*

> *before this tyme wer made nowe by long continuance of tyme and mutacion of thinges very insufficient & vnperfight, and also by the frayl condicion of man diuers new enormities were sprong amongest the people, for the which no law was yet made to reforme thesame, which was the very cause why at that tyme the kyng had somoned his high courte of parliament: and he resembled the king to a shepard, or heard man, for this cause, for if a prince be compared to hys riches, he is but a richeman; if a prince be compared to his honour, he is but an honorable man; but compare him to the multitude of his people and the numbre of his flocke, then he is a ruler, a gouernor of might and puissaunce, so that his people maketh him a prince, as of the multitude of shepe commeth the name of a shepherd: and as you se that emongest a great flocke of shepe some be rotten and fauty, which the good sheperd sendeth from the good shepe, so the great wether* [*i.e.* Wolsey] *which is of late fallen, as you all knowe, so craftely, so scabedly, ye, & so vntruly iuggeled with the kyng, that all men must nedes gesse and thinke that he thought in him self that the* [kyng] *had no wit to perceiue his craftie doyng, or els that he presumed that the kyng woulde not se nor know his fraudulent Iuggeling and attemptes: but he was deceiued, for his graces sight was so quike and penetrable that he saw him, ye, and saw through him both within and without, so that all thing to him was open,* etc.

The rest of the speech refers to the "small ponishment" of Wolsey, and directs the Commons to choose a Speaker.

Bridgett (*Life of More*, 3rd edit., pp. 231–2; see also Appendix D, 448) doubts the accuracy of the latter part of the speech, as recorded by Hall, with its bitter reflections on Wolsey. It is hardly the case, however, that this speech "has no confirmation." Some portions of Hall's account are confirmed by the *Rolls of Parliament*, though nothing is said there concerning the attack on Wolsey. The *Rolls* merely record that More described the parliament as called for the remedy of errors and abuses:

> *quæ aut hominum injuria, vel temporum varietate, præter bonum publicum, antehac in hoc regno Angliæ usitat. et errore et præmissa fuerunt, debita nunc correctionis emendatione, sagacique prudentia et circumspectione reformarentur et castigarentur . . . de quibus quidem erroribus et abusibus longa et eleganter disseruit oratione, qua dictorum abusuum et errorum summam, causasque et occasiones eorundem, et quid pro eorum reformatione sit faciendum, singulari quadam eloquentia et facundia declaravit.* (*Rolls of Parliament*, in *Journals of the Lords*, I, cli.)

Nevertheless, there is very little doubt that the passages about Wolsey have been reported by Hall with substantial accuracy. According to Chapuys, More spoke of Wolsey as the "chief defaulter, who having attempted and done many things . . . to the detriment of the crown and kingdom and having besides committed many acts of gross and flagrant injustice, of which they would be hereafter informed, had just been tried and condemned by a Court of Law, as they had no doubt heard." . . . "The Chancellor," says Chapuys, "went on enumerating the misdeeds of the Cardinal." (*Cal. of State Papers, Spanish*, I, 323–4, 8 Nov., 1529.)

59/7–9. *Truth it is that this was no bare and naked pretence . . . for he was troubled with a disease in his brest.* Cf. More's words to Erasmus in the letter of 14 June, 1532, *Des. Erasmi Epist. Opus;* Basileae, 1538, p. 1073 [= Lond., 1642, col. 1507, Lib. xxvii, Ep. 9]:

Sed interim pectus mihi occupauit nescio quid morbi : cuius non tam sensu & dolore crucior, quàm eventus metu, ac timore solicitor. Nam quum aliquot menses eodem tenore semper infestaret, consulti medici responderunt, moram longam in morbis esse periculosam, & curam huius agebant [*aiebant*] *celerem esse non posse, tempore sensim, uictu, pharmacis, quiete medicandum : neque finem medendi præfiniebant, neque salutem satis certam pollicebantur tamen. Hæc ego igitur mecum uersans animo, quum aut depondendum mihi magistratum uiderem, aut operam meam in eo gerendo claudicaturam, quando negotia quę res poscebat obiri per me non possent, nisi mortem ipse obire periclitarer, qua si defungerer, uel sic omnino cum uita simul relinquendum fuit officium, decreui mecum tandem altero potius quam utroque carere.*

59/25–60/3. *And yet his aduersaries and euill willers did spreade and cast rumours abrode to make him the more odious, that with the kinges displeasure he was against his will thrust out of the Chauncellourshipp. And newes thereof came with meruailous speede into farre countreys, and that his Successour had dimissed out of prison such as he had imprisoned for religion.*

From the letter of Erasmus to Faber :

Tantane celeritate istuc usque peruolasse rumorem, clariss. uirum Thomam Morum iure submotum a munere cancellarij, & in huius locum surrogatum alium nobilem, qui protinus liberos dimiserit, quos Morus ob contentiosa dogmata coniecerat in uincula . . . Porrò quod iactant de carceribus an uerum sit nescio. Illud constat, uirum natura mitissimum nulli fuisse molestum, qui monitus uoluerit a sectarum contagio resipiscere. An isti postulant, ut summus tanti regni iudex nullos habeat carceres? Odit ille seditiosa dogmata, quibus nunc misere concutitur orbis. Hoc ille non dissimulat, nec cupit esse clàm, sic addictus pietati, ut si in alterutram partem aliquantulum inclinet momentum, superstitioni quam impietati uicinior esse uideatur. Illud tamen eximiæ cuiusdam clementiæ satis magnum est argumentum quod sub illo cancellario nullus ob improbata dogmata capitis poenam dedit, quum in utraque Germania, Galliaque tam multi sint affecti supplicio. (*Des. Erasmi Epist. Opus ;* Basileae, 1538, pp. 1070, 1072 [= Lond., 1642, col. 1505].)

60/7 ff., 60/18 ff., 60/22 ff. *the duke of Norffolke . . . did openly . . . declare*, etc.; *Lorde Audley . . . did declare*, etc.; *Sir Thomas More himselfe declared . . . in a certaine Epitaphe . . . vpon his Sepulchre . . . at Chelsey.* Cf. *Des. Erasmi Epist. Opus*; Basileae, 1538, p. 1076 [= Lond., 1642, col. 1511]:

Sed de hoc negocio Rex ipse quum aliàs, tum priuatim sæpe, tum bis publice pronunciauit. Nam supra quàm meus pudor pati potest ut recenseam, per os ducis illustrissimi, ducis, inquam, Norfolchiæ, magni thesaurarij Angliæ, quum successor meus homo in primis egregius collocaretur in loco, honorifice iussit de me testatum reddere, quòd ægrè ad preces meas me dimiserit : nec eo singularis erga me bonitas regis contenta, reuocari fecit idem denuo multo post in sua præsentia in solenni conuentu magnatum ac populi, per os successoris mei, in oratione, quam ex more primam habuit in senatu, quem senatum (*ut scis*) *nos perleamentum uocamus. Igitur si tibi ita uidebitur nihil est quod dubites, quo minus edas epistolam. Quod in Epitaphio profiteor hæreticis me fuisse molestum, hoc ambitiosè feci. . . .*

For the text of the epitaph, see above, Appendix IV, pp. 277–81.

64/29–65/1. *that mightie and noble Emperoure, Charles the great, playing the very same part.* Neither Einhard nor the Monk of St. Gall makes any mention of Charles the Great sitting in the choir, although the latter has much to say about his encouragement of ecclesiastical music. It is just possible that Harpsfield is thinking of Fulk the Good, Duke of Anjou, who is said to have sung with his canons in the choir, and to have been ridiculed for doing so by the King of France, Lewis d'Outremer. Much more probably, however, by "Charles the Great" Harpsfield means Charles V, whom, below, he calls "the newe Charles the mayne" (p. 205). Charles V, after his retirement to Yuste, "when well enough . . . always attended the service [mass] in person, occupying his place in the choir. At other times he would sit at his chamber-window, which, as we have seen, opened on the chancel, where the clear, sonorous tones of his voice might be heard, mingling with those of the choristers below." (Prescott, *Life of Charles V after his Abdication*, appended to Robertson's *Charles V*, 1857, p. 366).

65/22–3. *the shirt of heare that he ware secretly next his body.* This was sent to Margaret Roper by More the day before his execution (see above, p. 200). From her it passed to her adopted sister and namesake, Margaret Gigs (Mistress Clement), through whose daughter (Mother Margaret Clement) it passed to the Community of St. Monica's, Louvain, and so to its present guardians, the Canonesses of Newton Abbot, who were founded from the Louvain Community. See C. S. Durrant, *A link between Flemish mystics and English martyrs*, 1925, pp. 183–223.

The shirt of hair returned once again, for a few days, during the exhibition of relics of Sir Thomas More held at 28 Beaufort St., Chelsea, 9–13 July, 1929, to the place where More, one warm summer evening, was noticed to be wearing it (see above, p. 66).

66/2–3. *a yonge gentlewoman, mistris Moore, sister to the saide Margarete*, i.e. Anne Cresacre, wife of More's son John. Information as to Anne Cresacre is available from the inscription on the "Burford Priory" copy of Holbein's painting of the family of Sir Thomas More :

> *Johannes Morus Londinensis armiger Thomæ Mori et Janæ unicus filius ætatis* 19 *duxit uxorem Annam Cresacrem Eboracensem ætatis* 18 *anno* 21 *H.* 8, 1529. *Ille decessit ætatis suæ* 37 *anno primo Edwardi* 6. *Illa obiit ætatis suæ* 66 *anno* 20 *Elizabethæ* 1577.
>
> *Anna Cresacris fuit filia et hæres Edwardi Cresacris ar. hæredis manerii de Baronburgh in libertate Ducatûs Lancastriæ vocati Baronburgh Halle prope Doncastrum in Comitatu Ebor. Edwardus obiit ætatis suæ* 27 *anno* 4 *H.* 8, 1512. *Quæ Anna nata fuit apud Baronburgh Hall anno* 3 *H.* 8, *et mortua est ibidem ætatis suæ* 66 *anno* 20 *Elizabethæ*, 1577.

After the death of John More, Anne married Sir William West (13 June, 1559). She died 2 Dec., 1577; the plate from her tomb, removed to the Hall at Barnborough, is mentioned by Joseph Hunter in his Introduction to Cresacre More's *Life of Sir Thomas More*, London, 1828 (p. xliii). These dates are important, as they help to fix the chronology of all the members of the More family. See above, Note to 9/6.

66/7–9. *As he was not ambitious and greedie of honour*, etc. Cf. Roper's comment, MS. Harleian 6254 [p. 10] :

> *Thus did it by his doings throughe out the whole course of his life appere, that all his travaile and paynes, without respecte of erthly comodities either to*

himself, or any of his, were onely vppon the seruice of god, the prince, and the realme, wholy bestowed and imploied ; whom I herd in his later tyme to say that he neuer asked the kinge for himself the valewe of one penye.

This is one of the very few sentences of Roper which Harpsfield does not use verbally. Compare also Wolsey's letter, quoted above, Note to 31/12, as to More's unwillingness to ask for himself.

72/13–18. *he asked her howe Queen Anne did,* etc. The publication of abstracts of the correspondence of Chapuys shows this forecast to have had less of *secrete reuelation and diuine information* than Harpsfield thought. About the time that More was sent to the Tower, there were rumours of a rival to Anne in Henry's affections (not Jane Seymour, the later rival); by September, 1534, gossip spoke of open quarrels, and in October Anne's influence had waned; the rival was not finally routed till February, 1535. For an account of this and quotations from the correspondence of Chapuys, see Friedmann, *Anne Boleyn,* 1884, II, 35–57.

73/6. *Waterbayly of London.* One of the four gentlemen attendant upon the Lord Mayor. (See A. W. Reed, *Early Tudor Drama,* p. 154.) But the Water Bailiff of this time appears to have come from the Royal Household, not from More's; and as the tale must relate to one who was "sometime seruaunt" of More, Prof. Reed suggests that the anecdote really relates to another of the four gentlemen, the Sword Bearer, Walter Smyth, who was advanced to that office in 1529, after having been some nine years More's servant. See Note to 19/22, above.

73/25–9. *Neyther would he sinisterly or suspiciously take any thing,* etc. So Erasmus, writing to Polydore Vergil (5 Sept., 1525) of some trouble (otherwise unrecorded) between Polydore Vergil and More : *si quid offensus fuit ob nescio quas causas, leuis erit offensio, et ille ne grauium quidem iniuriarum solet meminisse : Opus Epist. Des. Erasmi* (ed. Allen), No. 1606, Tom. VI, p. 159.

74/4–5. *not very curious in choosing . . . his frendes,* etc. See Erasmus to Ulrich von Hutten, *Opus Epist. Des. Erasmi* (ed. Allen), No. 999, Tom. IV, p. 16.

74/21–75/2. *This grace is called in greeke Αἱμυλία, whereof that noble Romane, Paulus Æmilius, was so called.* Harpsfield probably got this from Plutarch. Plutarch, however, does not say that it was the famous Paulus Æmilius who was so named from his eloquence, but the ancestor of the family in the days of Numa, Mamercus, δι' αἱμυλίαν λόγου καὶ χάριν Αἰμίλιος προσαγορευθείς (*Life of Æmilius Paulus,* II : compare *Life of Numa,* VIII.) The old editions of Liddell and Scott used to allow that there might be some connection between the roots of the two words, but this suggestion will not be found in the latest edition.

77/23–78/9. Towards the end of 1521, Erasmus writes to Budaeus of the learning of More's children. See *Opus Epist. Des. Erasmi* (ed. Allen), No. 1233, Tom. IV, p. 577 :

Habet filias treis, quarum maxima natu, Margareta, iam nupta est iuueni, primum beato, deinde moribus integerrimis ac modestissimis, postremo non alieno a nostris studiis. Omnes a teneris annis curauit imbuendas primum castis ac sanctis moribus, deinde politioribus literis. . . . Ante annum visum est Moro mihi specimen aliquod exhibere, quantum in literis profecissent. Iussit vt omnes ad me scriberent, et quidem suo quisque Marte.

Nec argumentum est suppeditatum, nec in sermone quicquam est correctum. Etenim cum illi schedas obtulissent patri castigandas, ille velut offensus incommoda scriptura iussit vt eadem accuratius ac purius describerent. Id vbi factum est, ne syllaba quidem mutata literas obsignatas ad me misit. Crede mihi, Budaee, nihil aeque sum admiratus. In sensibus nihil erat ineptum aut puellare ; sermo talis vt sentires esse quotidie proficientium.

79/1–3. *At what time her husbande* [Roper] *was . . . in king Henries dayes sent to the towre.* The reason for this imprisonment is given later by Harpsfield, p. 89, ll. 12–15 : *for relieuing by his almes a notable learned man, Master Beckenshawe.*

Prof. A. F. Pollard writes to me : " Bekynsaw's story is curious. Besides authorities in *D. N. B.* (iv. 141), there are many letters from him in *L. & P.* for 1539. He was accused in 1543 of conspiring with Pole in Paris, was pardoned (along with John More of Chelsea, *ib.* 1543, i. 610 [62]), became a gentleman-usher to Henry viii (*ib.* 1545, ii. p. 516), and published in 1546 *De supremo et absoluto Regis imperio,* which out-Gardinered Stephen Gardiner's *De vera obedientia,* and is in Goldast. J. W. Allen has a reference to him in his recent *Political Thought in the 16th Century* (p. 163 *n.*). He appears also to have been in the 'plot of the prebendaries' against Cranmer; so does Roper, whose imprisonment in the Tower (in 1543) is mentioned (*L. & P.* 1542, No. 267), and fine of £100. But Roper continued to the end of the reign on commissions of the peace, sewers, etc., and drawing an annuity from monastic lands (*ib.* 1543–6, *passim*)."

80/14–16. *as Erasmus longe agoe writeth, if he* [Roper] *had not beene her husbande, he might seeme to haue beene her owne germaine brother.* See below, Note to 80/23–5.

80/20–23. *And the saide Erasmus . . . called her* [Margaret] *the flowre of all the learned matrones in Inglande.* See *Des. Erasmi Epist. Opus ;* Basileae, 1538, liber xxvi, p. 1048 :

Erasmus Rot. Margaretae Roperae S.D.

Vix ullo sermone consequi queam, Margareta Ropera, Britanniae tuae decus, quantam animo meo persenserim uoluptatem, quum pictor Olpeinus totam familiam istam adeo feliciter expressam mihi repraesentauit, ut si coram adfuissem non multo plus fuerim uisurus . . . Omnes agnoui, sed neminem magis quam te. Videre mihi uidebar per pulcherrimum domicilium relucentem animum multo pulchriorem.

[*Speaks of his wish to see them all, and asks Margaret to persuade her sisters that the letter is addressed to all three.*] *Ornatissimae matronae Aloysiae matri tuae multam ex me salutem dices, eique me commendabis & amanter & diligenter. Effigiem illius quando coram non licuit, libenter sum exosculatus. . . .*

(*Datum apud Friburgum Brisgoiae* postrid. Non. Septemb. MDXXIX.)

80/23–5. *To whom* [Margaret] . . . *he* [Erasmus] *dedicated his Commentaries made vpon certaine hymnes of Prudentius.* See Erasmus' Commentary on the Christmas Hymn of Prudentius, 1523. The first edition in the British Museum is that of 1562, and there the dedication runs as follows :

Erasmus Roterodamus castissimae puellae Margaretae Roperae S.D.

Toties iam prouocor tuis sororumque tuarum literis, optima Margareta, tam sanis, tam argutis, tam modestis, tam candidis, tam amicis, ut etiamsi quis titulos detrahat, Thomae Mori γνήσια τέκνα possim agnoscere. Ne uero semper uideamini cecinisse surdo, studiis quibus obruor, paululum ocii suffuratus, hisce diebus Nataliciis paraui munusculum, quod spero uobis non ingratum futurum. Quod felix faustumque sit. Guilielmus Roperus ea morum integritate, suauitate, modestiaque praeditus, ut ni sponsus esset tuus, germanus uideri posset, dedit tibi auspicatissimas coniugii primitias: aut si mauis, tu illi dedisti, uel ut uerius dicam, uterque dedit alteri παιδίον, quod dissuauietur. En mitto tibi et alterum puerum, multo auspicatissimum, Iesum nascentem Iudaeis, et mox illucescentem gentibus, qui connubii uestri prouentum bene fortunabit, quique studiorum uestrorum uerus erit Apollo, cuius laudes pro fescenninis tuis infantulis lyrae poteris occinere. Solus enim hic dignus est, qui fidibus, qui fistulis, qui uoce, qui musices omni genere sed pręcipue modulatis piae mentis affectibus iugiter celebretur. Non dedignabitur a talibus coniugibus decantari, quorum ea est uitae totius puritas, concordia, tranquillitas simplicitas ut aegre reperias uirginitatis professores qui se ausint comparare. Rarum exemplum hoc praesertim seculo, sed quod uideo breui ad plures permanaturum. Habetis isthic reginam, uelut istius sanctissimi chori Calliopen. Sunt et in Germania familiae non obscurae, quae neutiquam infeliciter meditantur, quod uos hactenus felicissime prętatis. Bene uale, non infimum aeui Britanniaeque tuae decus, et totum istum chorum mihi saluta diligenter.

Basileae ad Christi natalem, Anno mdxxiij. (*Aurelii Prudentii Clementis quae extant poemata omnia . . . in aliquot uero Hymnos D. Erasmi Roterodami . . . Commentaria;* Basileae [1562], pp. 453–4.)

The Commentary follows, on the Christmas hymn.

81/1. *Damo.* The daughter of Pythagoras, to whom he entrusted his writings, with a command not to publish them. She obeyed her father, although she was in great poverty, and was offered much money for them, as is told by Diogenes Laertius in his *Lives of the Philosophers* (ed. Cobet, Paris, 1850, p. 214. Book VIII, Pythagoras, cap. 22).

81/3–4. *our christian Fabiola,* etc. Fabiola (d. 399), Marcella (d. 410), Paula (d. 404), Eustochium (d. 418), all friends of St. Jerome, the last two particularly connected with the convent at Bethlehem. Harpsfield doubtless learnt the virtues of these ascetic ladies from the Works of St. Jerome, where they are abundantly recorded; those unwilling to go to the original source will find them all in Wace and Piercy, *Dictionary of Christian Biography,* 1911.

81/6–17. *St. Ciprians workes . . . "nisi vos" should be . . . "neruos."* See *Vincentii Lirinensis Galli, pro Catholicae fidei antiquitate . . . additum est breue Commentariolum, per Ioannem Costerium . . .* 4°. Lovanii, 1552. The book is not paged, but at the end of section K, Coster refers, in his annotations, to a letter of St. Cyprian, the 7th of the Second Book, beginning *Quanquam benè sibi conscius animus. . . .* He notes a corruption in this letter, not corrected in the Cologne edition of 1544:

> *in qua vir utraque lingua doctissimus, D. Henricus Grauius, multa vulnera persanauit, locum corruptum quidem esse ostendit, interpositis duobus asteriscis, interim tamen nihil adferens, quod eam tabem sanare queat. Sententia uero haec est:* Absit enim ab Ecclesia Romana, vigorem suum tam prophana facilitate dimittere, & nisi vos seueritatis, euersa fidei maiestate, dissoluere, &c. *Igitur quum Clemens, medicinae doctor, natione Anglus, vir ornatissimus,*

> *ac Graecarum literarum peritissimus, mecum subinde pro sua humanitate de literis conferret, atque harum occasione multa de praeclarissimi viri Thomae Mori, quo familiariter dum viueret usus erat, humanitate, pietate, prudentia ac eruditione diceret, meminit quoque subinde Margaretae Mori filiae: cuius ingenium atque doctrinam mirifice praedicabat. Vt autem cognoscas, inquit, vera esse quae dico, adferam tibi ex Cypriano locum deprauatum admodum, quem illa citra exemplaris subsidium sola ingenii sui foelicitate restituit. Erat autem ea sententia, quam supra posui. Nam pro eo quod ibi legimus, nisi vos seueritatis, neruos seueritatis reponendum esse dicebat.*

Coster goes on to explain how the mistake presumably arose; *neruos* written *ñuos*, and misread *nisi uos*.

Compare the Cologne edition of 1569, p. 111, for the same passage.

See also *Opera D. Caecilii Cypriani . . . Adnotationes Iacobi Pamelii . . . .* (Antverpiæ, 1568, fol.), p. 59, Note on Ep. xxxi:

> *& neruos seueritatis*] *Hunc locum feliciter prima sic restituit Margareta Thomae Mori filia, ut testatur Costerius Commentariolo in Vincentium Lirinensem. Antea erat nisi uos, corruptissime.*

81/18–19. *This gentlewoman chaunced . . . to fall sicke in the time of the great swett.* There were, according to Hall, two great attacks of this "sweating sickness," in 1517 and in 1528.

Now on 19 Aug., 1517, More writes to Erasmus about the sickness: "I, with my wife and children, am as yet untouched; the rest of my family [*i.e.* his household, servants, etc.] have recovered." More was then on the point of departing for Calais on a diplomatic mission, and left almost immediately. Allen dates this mission August–December. It seems, then, that Margaret most probably was attacked in the epidemic of 1528.

83/4–9. *By this gentlewoman Master William Roper hath yet liuing two yonge gentlemen . . . and one daughter, late wife to Master Clarke, and nowe wife to Master Bassett, one of our gratious Soueraines Queene Maries priuie chamber.* The *Life* by "Ro. Ba." (printed in Wordsworth's *Ecclesiastical Biography*, II, p. 111, 1853), says more fully: *Margaret . . . had by him* [William Roper] *two sonnes, Thomas and Anthony, and three daughters, Elizabeth, Marie and Margaret.* A letter is extant from Ascham, addressed to Mary, whilst her first husband, Stephen Clarke, was still alive (III. 22, *Dominæ Clarke: Epistolæ*, 1703, pp. 269–71); it contains an interesting reminiscence of Ascham's connection with the Ropers and the Alingtons. Mary's second husband, James Bassett, was the third son of Sir John Bassett of Umberleigh, Devon, and was gentleman of the chamber to Queen Mary. In the Latin *Chronicle of the Divorce* (Bémont) he is styled *incomparabilis ille juvenis, omnibus animi et corporis dotibus cumulatissimus* (p. 68). (According to the same *Chronicle*, Mary Bassett contributed largely to the expenses of printing the great 1557 edition of More's *English Works.*) James Bassett had been for twelve years gentleman-servant to Stephen Gardiner, bishop of Winchester (Foxe, *Acts and Monuments*, ed. Cattley, VI, 231–6). We hear of him often in the *Domestic Papers* (Mary: correspondence with Edw. Courteney, earl of Devonshire; thanking him for the gift of a great horse, etc.); and in the *Venetian Papers* (VI. 3. 1146); he was sent to Philip by Mary *per dar l'avviso certo al serenissimo re del suo esser gravida.* James Basset died 21 Nov., 1557. Mary Bassett long survived him. Her will is printed in *Notes and Queries*, 11th Ser., Vol. VI, 3 Aug., 1912, pp. 87–8. She leaves a bequest "to my goddaughter, Bridget Clement, Dr. Clement's daughter"; and to her son "a ring that was my grandfather More's, and a great hoop of gold that Mr. Bassett gave me for a wedding ring, and a gold ring that King Philip gave me." The legacies to her sons are to be void "if they become heretics." Mary Bassett died 20 March, 1572, and her will was proved 19 April following; William Roper was an executor.

83/12–17. *This mistris Bassett . . . hath . . . translated out of the greeke into the englishe all the ecclesiasticall storye of Eusebius, with Socrates, Theodoretus, Sozomenus and Euagrius.* The British Museum MS., Harleian 1860, contains a Latin version of the First Book of the *Ecclesiastical History* of Eusebius, and an English version of the first five books, translated by "Mary Clarcke," and dedicated, during the reign of Edward VI, to the Lady Mary. This MS. was once bound in purple velvet, and was apparently the presentation copy actually given to the Princess Mary: but it has lost its original binding.

83/18–20. *She* [Mary Bassett] *hath also . . . translated . . . a certaine booke that Sir Thomas, her grandfather, made vpon the passion.* For the Latin text of More's *Passionis Expositio*, see *Opera latina*, fols. 118^a–133^b; for the English translation, see *English Works*, pp. 1350–1404, *An exposicion of a parte of the passion of . . . Iesus Christe, made in latine by syr Thomas More . . . in the tower . . . and translated into englyshe by maystres Marye Basset*, etc.

89/12–15. Roper's imprisonment in the Tower. Cf. above, p. 79, ll. 1–3, and Note thereon.

90/6–7. *doctour Clement, also his wife (a woman furnished with muche vertue and wisedome).* For Clement, see *John Clement and his Books* by A. W. Reed, *The Library*, March, 1926. Clement's *Life* has also been written at length by Wenkerbach (*John Clement: Studien zur Geschichte der Medizin*, XIV, 1925). And much about both Clement and his wife Margaret Gigs will be found in Reed's *Early Tudor Drama.*

The account of both the Clements in the *D.N.B.* is unduly brief, and not altogether accurate. It was Mistress Clement (Margaret Gigs) who succoured the imprisoned Carthusians. The story is told in John Morris's *Troubles of our Catholic Forefathers*, 1872, pp. 27–31, from "the original manuscript *Life*, by Sister Elizabeth Shirley," of Margaret Clement, junior, the daughter of Dr. and Mistress Clement, "the property of the priory of Our Blessed Lady of Nazareth, at Bruges." Much about this will also be found in C. S. Durrant, *A link between Flemish mystics and English martyrs*, 1925. The same story is told by Gairdner (*Lollardy and the Reformation*, ii. 40), but Gairdner confuses Mistress Margaret Clement with her daughter of the same name (born 1540, professed at St. Ursula's, Louvain, 1557; Prioress of St. Ursula's *c.* 1570–*c.* 1607, when she resigned owing to blindness; joined in the foundation of the English daughter-community of St. Monica's; died 1612). The confusion is natural, since some of the most interesting facts we know concerning Mistress Clement are derived from the *Life* of her daughter, Mother Margaret Clement.

90/17–20. *Vxor mea te salutat, et item Clemens,* &c. See *Opus Epist. Des. Erasmi* (ed. Allen), No. 388, Tom. II, p. 198.

90/21–91/19. *Nowe to what excellencie she* [Mistress Clement] *grewe in knowledge, and specially of phisicke,* etc. In *A Dyalogue of Comforte* (*English Works,*

p. 1173) Anthony tells Vyncent this story of " a yonge Gyrle," here identified by Harpsfield as Mistress Clement. See Note to 9/19–23.

91/27. *John Harris* was More's " secretarius intimus." He married Dorothy Colly, Margaret Roper's maid. Stapleton knew them both as refugees in Belgium, and derived from them much of the information, both oral and written, upon which his *Life* of More is based (*Tres Thomæ*, 1612, p. 152). Dorothy was still living at Douai in 1588. A portrait of Harris is introduced into the " Nostell Priory " painting of the More family group; he is standing in the doorway at the back. (Reproduced in Arthur B. Chamberlain's *Hans Holbein the Younger*, 1913, I, 296.) .

92/6–17. *and would haue thought himselfe to haue rather beene in Platoes accademie—nay . . . in some christian well ordred accademie . . . ydlenes . . . was quite excluded, and euery person well and vertuously set aworke.* Cf. Erasmus to Faber, *Des. Erasmi Epist. Opus ;* Basileae, 1538, p. 1073. [= Lond., 1642, col. 1506] :

> *Dicas apud illum esse alteram Platonis academiam : sed contumeliam facio domui illius quum eam Platonis academiae confero, in qua disputabatur de numeris ac figuris geometricis, interdum de virtutibus moralibus : hanc domum rectius dixeris scholam ac gymnasium Christianę religionis. Nullus ac nulla illic est, non vacans liberalibus disciplinis frugiferaeque lectioni, tametsi praecipua primaque pietatis cura est. Nulla illic rixa, nullum petulantius verbum auditur, nemo conspicitur ociosus . . . nec deest sobria hilaritas.*

92/18, etc. *His first wife*, etc. Some account of More's two wives and their family connections will be given in the Notes to the forthcoming edition of Roper's *Life* (E.E.T.S.).

93/13. *he maried a widowe.* Cf. Erasmus to Ulrich von Hutten : *Opus Epist. Des. Erasmi* (ed. Allen), No. 999, Tom. IV, p. 19.

94/3–4. *she learned . . . virgenalls.* See above, Textual Note, p. 287.

100/15–19. *Howbeit, we trust shortlye to haue all his englishe workes . . . in print, wherin Master Sargeant Rastell doth nowe diligently trauell.* A reference to the great edition of More's *English Works*, the dedication of which is dated 30 April, 1557. Harpsfield's *Life* is presumably to be dated, therefore, not later than April, 1557. On the other hand, Roper speaks of " a greate Book of his workes " as if it were already in people's hands; yet Roper's *Life* must be earlier than Harpsfield's.

101/4–6. *These Epigrammes, as they be learned and pleasaunt, so are they nothing byting or contumelious.* Beatus Rhenanus, in an introductory letter addressed *Bilibaldo Pircheimero* (1518), and prefixed to More's epigrams, writes : *Sunt autem huius sales nequaquam mordaces, sed candidi, melliti, blandi, & quiduis potius quam amarulenti.*

101/7–8. *Epigrammes that he made of Germanus Brixius.* On 10 August, 1512, the English ship *Regent* and the French *Cordelière* fought an engagement. The French ship caught fire, and the ships having grappled, the *Cordelière* involved the English vessel in her fate : both captains and most of the two crews perished. The French scholar Germain de Brie (Brixius) wrote a patriotic poem on the occasion, *Chordigeræ Navis conflagratio.* More at the time replied with a number of epigrams, which later he hesitated to print. Writing to

Erasmus, 3 Sept., 1516 (*Opus Epist. Des. Erasmi*, ed. Allen, No. 461, Tom. II, p. 340), More asks Erasmus to consider whether the epigrams on Brixius should be published (*in quibus sunt quaedam amarulentiora, quanquam videri possim ab illo prouocatus conuiciis dictis in patriam*). These epigrams were, however, printed with the rest by Froben, in March, 1518. Brixius had apparently seen them in manuscript, for about August, 1517, Erasmus wrote to dissuade him from replying (ed. Allen, as above, No. 620, Tom. III, p. 42). This letter was appended by Brixius, with his rejoinder, to his *Antimorus* (*Thomæ Mori lapsus inexcusabilis in syllabarum quantitate*) Lutetiæ, 1519. 4°. Erasmus wrote to pacify More and persuade him not to make any retort (ed. Allen, No. 1093, Tom. IV, p. 239). More replied to Erasmus at length (ed. Allen, No. 1096, Tom. IV, p. 251). After hesitation he published his reply to Brixius, *Thomæ Mori Epistola ad Germanum Brixium: qui quum Morus in libellum ejus quo contumeliosis mendaciis incesserat Angliam lusisset aliquot epigrammata . . . ædidit adversus Morum libellum qui suum infamat authorem*, Pynson, 1520. This act Erasmus regrets (to Budaeus, ed. Allen, No. 1184, Tom. IV, p. 442).

101/9–11. *the valiant doinges of the frenche captaine, Herueus, by the Sea against the englishe men.* "Herueus" is Hervé de Portzmoguer, the Breton sailor, who, on 10 August, 1512, commanded *La Cordelière*. In 1845, M. Auguste Jal, marine historiographer of France, wrote a monograph on the episode: *Marie la Cordelière; étude pour une histoire de la marine française.*

102/6–17. *He wrote . . . the life of kinge Richarde the thirde*, etc. The denial of More's authorship of the *Life of Richard III* (or, as it is sometimes called *of Edward V*) is one of the curiosities of literature. More's authorship is contested in the *Cambridge History of English Literature* (III, 17, 334) and in the *D.N.B.* (see *More, Morton*), whilst the most authoritative book on the subject, Kingsford's *English Historical Literature in the Fifteenth Century* (1913, p. 186), entirely suspends judgment.

Yet the evidence is peculiarly plentiful and weighty. As in the case of many other of More's works (the authenticity of which, nevertheless, no one would dispute), the *Life of Richard III* remained unpublished during his lifetime. But three years after More's death, George Croftes, chancellor of Chichester Cathedral, admitted under examination that he had spoken of More's works with Sir Geoffrey Pole, and that Pole "lent me a Chronicle of Mores making, of Richard III" (*L. & P.* xiii. 2, No. 828, pp. 334–5). The same series of examinations shows how undesirable it was even to talk about More; and it is quite natural that when, in 1543, the *Life of Richard III* was published (from a corrupt manuscript) for the first time, in the Continuation of Hardyng's *Chronicle*, More was not distinguished from the other writers whose work was utilized in that Continuation: they were all included in the vague but convenient phrase, "diuerse and sondery autours that haue writen of the affaires of Englande." But there was no hint that the author was unknown, and in the first year in which it was advisable to name the author (1548) the work was republished as More's. In 1550 it was again published as More's; in 1552 Roger Ascham spoke of it as More's, and referred to the high esteem in which it was held; in 1557 Bale enumerated it among More's works; and about the same date we have this reference in Harpsfield. Harpsfield's reference is, so far as I know, the first allusion to the existence of a Latin version. William

Rastell, More's nephew, who had made it his business to collect More's works, printed a more correct text of the English version in 1557, " fro the copie of his own hand." Rastell supplemented gaps in the English text by translating the corresponding passage from the Latin, which, equally with the English, he definitely claimed as More's.

In 1565 the Latin version was printed at Louvain, as More's, in his collected Latin works. William Rastell had withdrawn to Louvain, and it was almost certainly he who was responsible for this edition. The English version was reprinted in 1568 (Grafton), 1569 (Grafton), 1577 (Holinshed), 1580 (Stow), 1587 (Holinshed); and in all these cases it was stated to be by More. In 1588 Stapleton, in the first biography of More to be printed, spoke of his authorship both of the English and of the Latin version.

It is not till 1596, after half a century, during which *Richard III* had been nine times printed, either in English or Latin, as the work of More, with no expression of doubt, that John Harington spoke of *Richard the thirde, written as I have heard by Moorton, but as most suppose by that worthy and incorrupt magistrate, Sir Thomas More.*

The attribution to Morton is intelligible, for More clearly derived much information from him. Sir George Buck (d. 1623) tells us that a book, written in Latin by Morton against Richard III, was used by More in compiling his history, and " was lately in the hands of Mr. Roper, of Eltham, as Sir Edward Hoby, who saw it, told me." More, says Buck, " set forth, amplified, and glozed " the book Morton had given him. But this Latin book written by Morton cannot be identified with the Latin version of *Richard III*. For the Latin version of *Richard III* is not a mere sketch " set forth and amplified " in the English. Both the English and the Latin are elaborate works of art, and correspond closely. And both contain chronological references which forbid our attributing either to Morton. In the opening paragraph of *Richard III* there are allusions, both in the Latin and the English, to Katharine of York as still living, and as having been relieved by King Henry VIII. This marks the date of composition as between 1509 and 1527. There is an allusion, both in the Latin and the English, to Thomas Howard as Earl of Surrey, which dates the passage between 1 Feb., 1513/14, and 21 May, 1524. Both these allusions fit in with the facts stated by Rastell, that the History was written about 1513, and by Sir Thomas More when he was Under-Sheriff (1510–1518). But they rule out Cardinal Morton, who died in 1500. Both the Latin and the English describe the beauty of Shore's wife, *thus say thei that knew her in her youthe*, a sentence natural to More, but out of place in the mouth of Morton, who was her senior by twenty years or more, and must have seen her often enough *in ipso formæ et ætatis flore.* A passage, found in the Latin only, mentions how the author had heard someone mention to his father, shortly after the death of Edward IV, a forecast that the Duke of Gloucester would be king. This is natural if the author be More, who was five or six at the time, but incompatible with Morton being the author, for at that time he was between sixty and seventy. Then there are passages found only in the English which are incompatible with Morton's authorship, such as the mention of the execution of Tyrrel (1502), and the hope of the author *to write the time of the late noble prince King Henry the seuenth.*

Morton is undoubtedly the authority for many of the facts, and there is no reason to disbelieve the statement of Sir George Buck that a Latin book, written by him against Richard III, was More's chief authority, and that the book remained in the Roper family. But the *Life of Richard III*, whether in the Latin or the English, is essentially a product of the Revival of Learning in England. Its attribution to Morton, who was born about 1420, would mean that we must rewrite the history of English scholarship; the attribution of the English version to him would further mean that we must rewrite the history of English style and of the English language. No one ever claimed that Morton was a great scholar or a great writer. It is incredible that he could have been the author of the *Life of Richard III*, and that no one should have known it till Harington in 1596, nearly a century after Morton's death.

The erroneous belief that More was born in 1480 did much to throw doubt on his authorship: for it must have been between April and June, 1483, that the conversation took place, which the author mentions having heard, about the Duke of Gloucester becoming king. But we now know that More was born either in February, 1478, or (more probably) in February, 1477, and so might easily have remembered a conversation of 1483.

For a discussion at greater length, see *More's History of Richard III* by R. W. Chambers in the *Modern Language Review*, XXIII, 405–423, reprinted, with some additions, in Vol. I of the re-issue of the *Workes of Sir Thomas More.*

103/9. *Budaeus.* Guillaume Budé, 1467–1540.

103/9–10. *Johannes Paludanus:* i.e. John Desmarais, Orator of the University of Louvain and a friend of Erasmus. Dorpius, in a letter to Erasmus of Jan., 1517, describes him as the most courteous and, at the same time, the sincerest of men, and in July, 1517, Erasmus writes to More: *Louanii diuersor apud Ioannem Paludanum, huius Achademie Rethorem.* (*Opus Epist. Des. Erasmi*, ed. Allen, No. 597, Tom. III, p. 6. See also prefatory note to No. 180, Tom. I, p. 398.)

103/23–5. *especially by the wonderfull nauigation of* nauis *called Victoria that sayled the world rounde about.* A reference to the ship of Juan Sebastian del Cano, lieutenant of Magellan, and the first circumnavigator, 1519–22.

105/21–3 ff. *King Henry the eight had written a notable erudite booke against Luthers booke,* etc. Henry published the *Assertio* in 1521 (see also pp. 158–60, above). Luther replied in 1522. More's reply appeared under the name of "Gulielmus Rosseus," *Eruditissimi viri G. Rossei opus . . . quo . . . refellit . . . Lutheri calumnias, quibus . . . regem Henricum . . . octavum scurra turpissimus insectatur;* London, 1523. Stapleton asserts that during More's lifetime, *nemo suspicatus aliud fuerit, quam nescio quem Rosseum illius operis authorem fuisse* (*Tres Thomæ*, ed. 1612, p. 218). Yet Tyndale in his *Practise of Prelates* (1530) speaks of More "writing against Martin" in a context which looks as if the reference might be to Rosseus. (*Workes of Tyndall, Frith and Barnes*, 1572, p. 373.) More in his English Works keeps the secret by occasional references to Rosseus (*Works*, pp. 490, 513, 817). Stapleton (ed. 1612, p. 187) asserts that William Ross was the name of a real man who *eodem fere tempore Romam peregrinatus in Italia moritur.* The *Responsio* was printed in the Louvain edition of More's Latin Works (1565–6).

107/2–3. *Treatise . . . against . . . John Pomerane.* Johann Bugenhagen, a Pomeranian, addressed a letter to the English (*Epistola Ioannis Bugenhagii Pomerani ad Anglos*, Wittemberg, 1525). This is also extant in German versions: *Ainn sendprieff Herr Johan Bugenhag Pomeran an dye Christen inn England,* 1525; *Ein sendbrieff an die Christen ynn Engeland, warynnen ein Christlich leben stehet,* Wittemberg, 1525. More's reply was not printed till 1568, at Louvain: "*Doctissima D. Thomae Mori . . . Epistola in qua non minus facete quam pie respondet literis Johannis Pomerani, hominis inter Protestantes nominis non obscuri. Opusculum . . . ex authoris quidem autographo emendato, dum viueret, exemplari desumptum.*" The little volume also contains a portrait of More, several epigrams in his praise, and his own epigram *Moraris.* It was edited and published by John Fowler.

107/4–8. *he wrote a certaine exposition in latine vpon the passion of Christe . . . translated into Englishe by . . . mistris Bassett.* See above, Note to 83/18–20. "Neece," of course, means granddaughter.

107/13–14. *the translation of John Picus, erle of Mirandula.* In the *English Works* of 1557 this book is dated in the Table of Contents as *c.* 1510. Prof. A. W. Reed considers this some five years too late. See *Early Tudor Drama,* p. 73.

108/12–18. *he doth not . . . wrest their wordes . . . but rather enforceth them,* etc. This characteristic of More has been noted by modern critics. G. P. Krapp, of course independently of Harpsfield, uses almost his exact words—More "is a fair disputant, *often stating his opponents' case better than they could do it themselves*" (*Rise of English Literary Prose,* 1915, p. 99). But while Krapp attributes this to More's "self-confidence" and to his "not fully realizing the seriousness of the situation," the evidence of Roper proves that this was not so (cf. above, pp. 68–70). The cause was, as Harpsfield puts it, More's "integritie."

108/26–7. *he, finding afterwarde that he mistooke certaine wordes of the pacifyer.* More made this correction at the end of the errata appended to his *Answer to the first part of the poisoned book which a nameless heretic hath named the Supper of the Lord* (1533). The *Answer* was reprinted in 1557 in the collected *Works,* and this appendix to the *Answer* was at first overlooked, but subsequently printed on a separate sheet and inserted (in some copies) between pp. 1138 and 1139.

The error has nothing to do with the argument. More, to whom the dialogue was an artistic form, to be worked out with regard to character drawing and verisimilitude, had scoffed at the very wooden dialogue of St. German, and had exaggerated one point through a slip of the eye in reading:

> *And therfore albeit that I haue knowen many that haue red it, of whiche I neuer found any that found it, yet sythe it happed me lately to looke theron, and find myne ouersight my self, I wold in no wise leue it, good reder, vnreformed. Nor neuer purpose while I liue, whersoeuer I may parceiue, either mine aduersary to saye well, or my selfe to haue saide otherwyse, to let for vs both indifferently to declare and saye the truth.* (*English Works,* ed. 1557.)

109/1–3. *The like he counsailed his learned frendes, especially Erasmus, to doo, and to retracte many thinges that he had written.* Stapleton says the same, and adds that this letter of More to Erasmus was written by More towards the end of his life, but that Erasmus destroyed it, so that it should not appear among his correspondence (*Tres Thomæ,* ed. 1612, p. 193). More defended Erasmus repeatedly and warmly, but it is quite conceivable that, in view of the encouragement which he found that the heretics received from Erasmus' writings (see, e.g. *Works*, 1557, p. 422), he may have written a private letter, and that neither he nor Erasmus wished it to be printed. Stapleton drew much of his information from John Harris, More's secretary, so that his statements on matters like this carry weight.

112/18. *as farre as I can call to minde.* Harpsfield adopts Roper's expression of doubt in a matter which would not be within his own personal memory.

122/10. *This Supplication was made by one Simon Fishe.* For Simon Fish, of Oxford and Gray's Inn, (d. 1531), see Foxe's *Acts and Monuments*, and the article by Mandell Creighton in the *D.N.B.*

122/21–2. *a learned Apologie.* Edited for the Early English Text Society by A. I. Taft, 1930 (No. 180).

127/3–5. *a booke " of the diuision of the spiritualtie and temporaltie."* Christopher St. German's *Treatise* is printed as an appendix to Taft's edition of the *Apologye*, pp. 203–53 (Early English Text Society).

136/14–19. *Erasmus and Petrus Ægidius : which two persons, when that one Quintinius . . . painted in a certaine table, Sir Thomas More made thereof certaine verses*, etc. On 30 May, 1517, Erasmus wrote to More :

> *Petrus Ægidius et ego pingimur in eadem tabula : eam tibi dono breui mittemus.* See *Opus Epist. Des. Erasmi* (ed. Allen), No. 584, Tom. II, p. 576.

The diptych was sent to More at Calais the following September. Cf. letter of Erasmus to More, 8 September :

> *Mitto tabulas, quo tibi vtcunque adsimus, si qua sors nos ademerit. Dimidium impendit Petrus, dimidium ego . . . vt amborum munus esset commune* (*op. cit.*, No. 654, Tom. III, p. 76).

Later the two pictures became separated. See above, Preface, p. vii.

More's verses on the diptych of Peter Giles and Erasmus are to be found in his letter from Calais to Peter Giles, 7 October, 1517 (*op. cit.*, No. 684, Tom. III, pp. 106–7) :

TABELLA LOQVITVR.

Quanti olim fuerant Pollux et Castor amici,
Erasmum tantos Egidiumque fero.
Morus ab his dolet esse loco, coniunctus amore
Tam prope quam quisquam vix queat esse sibi.
Sic desyderio est consultum absentis, vt horum
Reddat amans animum littera, corpus ego.

IPSE LOQVOR MORVS.

Tu quos aspicis, agnitos opinor
Ex vultu tibi, si prius vel vnquam
Visos ; sin minus, indicabit altrum
Ipsi littera scripta : nomen alter,
Ne sis nescius, ecce scribit ipse ;
Quanquam is qui siet, vt taceret ipse,
Inscripti poterant docere libri
Toto qui celebres leguntur orbe.

Quintine o veteris nouator artis,
Magno non minor artifex Apelle,
Mire composito potens colore
Vitam adfingere mortuis figuris ;
Hei cur effigies labore tanto
Factas tam bene talium virorum,
Quales prisca tulere secla raros,
Quales tempora nostra rariores,
Quales haud scio post futura an vllos,
Te iuuit fragili indidisse ligno,
Dandas materie fideliori,
Quae seruare datas queat perhennes ?
O si sic poteras tuaeque famae et
Votis consuluisse posterorum !
Nam si secula quae sequentur vllum
Seruabunt studium artium bonarum,
Nec Mars horridus obteret Mineruam,
Quanti hanc posteritas emat tabellam ?

138/2–3. *Master Antonie Bonuice.* Antonio Bonvisi, a merchant of Lucca, had settled in England, and had many dealings with the court, both as purveyor of news and banker. His name occurs constantly in the *Calendar* (*L. & P.*) : most of the entries are mere matters of business, but his letters to Wolsey and Cromwell are noteworthy.

For an outline of his life, see *D.N.B.* Since that biography was written, the most interesting addition to our information about him consists in a number of papers concerning Crosby Place, which came into the market in 1907. For these, the account of Bonvisi should be consulted in Philip Norman's *Crosby Place*, 1908, pp. 21–4 (*Comm. for Survey of Memorials of Greater London, Monograph* 9). More sold the lease of Crosby Place to Bonvisi in January, 1524. On 1 April, 1547, Bonvisi made over Crosby Place to William Roper and William Rastell as tenants for 90 years, and on 22 June of that year obtained licence to convey the property to Richard Heywood and John Webb, in trust for himself for life. On 25 Sept., 3rd Edward VI, Antonio Bonvisi *withdrewe himself without, and departed out of England unto the places beyond the sea without lycens of his soverayne lord,* and Crosby Hall was seized by the sheriffs of London. The fee simple of Crosby Place was regranted to Bonvisi 10 May, 1 Queen Mary (1554). We learn (*Inq. post mortem*) that Bonvisi died 7 Dec., 1558.

An inquisition taken at the Guildhall of London, 8 May, 1553, into the goods of *Anthony Bonvyce in a capital messuage called Crosbies Place in Bisshoppesgate strete, London,* gives some indication of how Crosby Hall was furnished in the days of this merchant-prince. See the *Calendar of Patent Rolls of Edward VI*, Vol. V, pp. 24–6.

141/6–7, 10–11, 14–15. See above, Textual Notes, pp. 289–90.

144/13. *Oxforde fare.* Dr. Christopher Wordsworth (*Eccles. Biog.* II. 82) compares the account of the very slender fare of Cambridge, which is given by Thomas Lever in a sermon preached at Paul's Cross in 1550.

145/19. *Zimachus.* Apparently Q. Aurelius Symmachus, the defender of Roman paganism in the latter half of the fourth century, who was certainly "renowned for his integritie." It can hardly be his descendant, Q. Aurelius Memmius Symmachus (father-in-law of Boethius; put to death by Theodoric), for Harpsfield's words seem to imply that here he is dealing with pagan examples. Nor is it clear why Harpsfield should have made the mistake of calling either of these men an Athenian. Is there an error in the text?

145/20. *Seruilius.* Barea Soranus, accused under Nero, and compelled, with his daughter Servilia, to commit suicide. See Juvenal, III, 116; Tacitus, *Annals*, XVI, 30–33; *Hist.*, IV, 10.

146/11–12. *then made he a conueyance for the disposition of all his landes.* In MS. Arundel 152, fols. 305 v.–306 v., may be found the Act of Parliament annulling the deed of feoffement of certain estates made by Sir Thomas More prior to his attainder; also in *Statutes of the Realm*, Vol. III, p. 529. In the same volume of the *Statutes*, p. 528, is the Act repealing the letters patent in favour of Sir Thomas—"An Act concernyng the Attainder of Sir Thomas More." (For contents, see *Archaeologia*, xxvii, p. 362.)

148/5–6. *in open consistorie pronounced at St. Albans.* It is curious that Harpsfield, who is an authority on all that concerns the Divorce, should have copied this error from Roper. The court was actually held at Dunstable Priory: sentence was given on 23 May, 1533. (Three letters of Cranmer to Henry, and one of Bedyll to Cromwell, written from Dunstable, dealing with this matter, are given in *State Papers*, 1830, I, 394–7. The text of Cranmer's sentence will be found in Burnet's *History of the Reformation*, ed. Pocock, 1865, IV, 189, *Collection of Records*, XLVII.) It is also an error to state that the marriage with Anne followed: the king had been secretly married to Anne since about 25 January. Five days after giving sentence at Dunstable, Cranmer, after an inquiry at Lambeth, declared the marriage lawful (see Rymer, *Foedera*, xiv, 470). Harpsfield has "Dunstable" quite correctly in the *Pretended Divorce* (Camden Soc.), p. 198.

150/23—151/1. *doctour Wilson . . . sent to the towre, albeit he did afterwarde relent.* Two letters of More to Dr. Wilson, when his fellow-prisoner, are given in his *English Works*, 1557, pp. 1443-6. For Dr. Wilson, see *D.N.B.*, which gives the date of his committal to the Tower as "10 April, 1534, a week before the arrest of Fisher and More." This is clearly wrong, since More mentions Dr. Wilson being "gentilmanly sent streight vnto the towre" on the day of his own arrest (Monday, 13 April, 1534, according to Rastell: *Works*, 1557, p. 1428). More was delivered as a prisoner to the Abbot of Westminster, and not sent to the Tower till the following Friday (the 17th). Sir Thomas Palmer, writing on the 15th, mentions Dr. Wilson having been "yesterday commanded to the Tower" (*L. & P.* vii, 483). If Rastell is correct, this puts it a day too late.

Wilson ultimately took the oath, and was pardoned, 29 May, 1537 (*L. & P.* xii. 1, p. 607).

151/2. *doctour Nicholas, the Augustine fryer*, i.e. Nicholas de Burgo, an Italian friar, in the pay of the king. Nicholas is mentioned several times in the *Letters and Papers*:

V, p. 304. Reward given by my lord cardinal's command to Fryer Nicholas of Oxford, £5. (Accounts of Treasurer of Chamber, Nov., 1528.)

V, p. 313. Friar Nicholas, one of the king's spiritual learned counsel, 15 July, by way of reward, £6 13*s*. 4*d*. (*The same*, July, 1529.)

V, p. 748. To Friar Nicholas by the king's command, £3 15*s*. (Privy Purse Expenses, Feb. 12, 1530.)

VI, No. 75. Letter to Cromwell, 26 January, 1532/3. Has performed duties of Reader bestowed on him by the king, and for greater advantage has added public lectures, but has received no remuneration, for those who distribute the king's gifts do so arbitrarily.

VI, No. 717. Cromwell's accounts: To Doctor Nicholas de Burgo, £6 13*s*. 4*d*. (1533).

VIII, No. 1054. Stokesley to Cromwell, 17 July, 1535: Much of what I said is in the king's book that Mr. Ampner (Fox), Dr. Nicholas and I made before my going over sea in embassy, and was after translated by my Lord of Canterbury.

Nicholas de Burgo must not be confused with the papal nuncio, Antonio, baron de Burgo.

151/21, etc. *And would not open his opinion in that matter, especially the causes why he refused the othe, eyther to the Bishopp of Rochester . . . eyther to doctour Wilson*, etc. Compare the answer made by More, under examination, regarding his replies to Fisher's inquiries: that he *wrote a letter to Mr. Fissher, wherein he certified hym that this examinat* [i.e. More] *had refused the othe of succession; and never shewed the Counsaill, nor intended ever to shewe any other, the cause wherfor he did so refuse the same*; and again that he had replied to Fisher: "*My Lorde, I am determyned to medle of no thing, but only to geve my mynde uppon Godd, and the summe of my hole studie shal be, to thinke upon the Passion of Christe, and my passage out of this worlde, with the dependences therupon*" (*State Papers*, 1830, I, 433–4). More's letter to Dr. Wilson is given in *Works*, 1443–6: *Finally as touching þe oth, the causes for which I refused it, no man woteth what they be. For they be secret in myne own conscience, some other peraduenture, than those that other menne woulde wene, and suche as I neuer disclosed vnto any man yet, nor neuer entend to dooe whyle I liue.* For the phrase *that he had settled his conscience, and so he would they should doo theirs,* compare pp. 187, 262, above.

153/7–8. *He had made, being Lorde Chauncellour, a decree against one Parnell, at the sute of one Vaughan.* A "John Parnell, gent'" was on the Jury that found More guilty, and is possibly the same man. See below, Note to 192/24–5.

For the following note on the Parnell–Vaughan suit we are indebted to Miss M. C. Dowling:

> The manuscripts relating to the story are in a bad condition, but it is possible to reconstruct the main features of the quarrel.
>
> Geoffrey Vaughan and Richard his son, citizens and mercers of London, had business dealings with John Parnell, citizen and draper, also of London. Parnell agreed to supply kerseys to the Vaughans, who were to pay him partly in money, partly in woad. The Vaughans considered that Parnell had not fulfilled his side of the bargain, and therefore brought against him in the Mayor's court an action of detinue (*i.e.* serving a writ on one who detains goods which ought to be delivered up). Apparently they received no satisfaction, and the matter was transferred to the Court of Chancery. Two suits arose, neither of which bears a date, but they were both addressed to Wolsey, as Chancellor, during the years 1518–29:—

(1) Geoffrey Vaughan *v.* William Paviour, clerk, and John Pernell (P.R.O. Early Chancery Proceedings, C 1/587/15).

(2) Richard Vaughan *v.* John Pernell (C 1/587/41).

Once more the Vaughans gained nothing—no decrees are recorded to these suits—and later, when Sir Thomas More was Chancellor (*i.e.* 1529–32), they united to send in a complaint to him against Parnell (C 1/685/39).

Two indorsements on the Bill add valuable information. The first, written in English, records 9 February, 1529/30, as the date of the examination of the parties by Commissioners. The second indorsement, in Latin, gives the final decree. The case was heard 20 January, 1530/31, and it was decreed that all agreements between the parties were to become void. Further, Parnell was to pay £128 14*s.* to Geoffrey Vaughan, and also £50 to Richard and Geoffrey for their costs. Richard Vaughan was to pay Parnell £20; owing to the bad condition of the document it is impossible to say why this payment was to be made. Apparently, each matter in question was dealt with in turn, and separate payments were ordered. It is possible that Parnell paid even more than the sums already mentioned.

At any rate, Parnell parted company with £158 14*s.*, and if he was the John Parnell of the jury at More's trial, it is evident that he went with few kindly thoughts towards the former Lord Chancellor.

156/4–5. *Nunnes of Sion, by meanes of one Master Reynoldes, a father of the same house.* For the Bridgettine monastery of Sion, near Isleworth, between Kew and Richmond, see G. J. Aungier, *History of Syon Monastery.* For Reynolds, see 179/1–2, above, and Note thereon.

156/26. *a Bill to attaint the saide Nonne.* For the text of this, see *Statutes of the Realm*, Vol. III, pp. 446–51, 25 Henry VIII, c. 12; summary in *L. & P.* vii. 70 (p. 28). Sir Thomas More was put out of the Bill, but the name of John, Bishop of Rochester, remained.

158–60. *a booke of the assertion of the seuen Sacramentes.* See above, p. 105, ll. 21–3, and Note thereon.

161/21. *he wrate a letter to the king.* This letter is given in full by Rastell in *English Works*, pp. 1423–4. Two MSS. of it are extant, both of them in More's own handwriting, one in the Cottonian collection (Cleopatra E. vi, fol. 176, but generally on exhibition among the historical autographs) and one in the Record Office. The differences between More's two autograph copies are not important, but there are serious discrepancies between them and the text as printed by Rastell and used by Harpsfield. The most striking of these is, that where More's autograph MSS. in each case speak of *the wykked woman of Canterbery*, Rastell (227/1) and Harpsfield (161/23) use the non-committal phrase *the nunne of Canterbury*; a passage in which More says that he does not murmur at the king's marriage with this noble woman [Anne Boleyn] but will pray for them both, and their noble issue, is omitted by Rastell: it does not occur in the part of the letter quoted by Harpsfield. These discrepancies were pointed out by John Bruce in 1843 in *Archæologia* (xxx, 149–59). Bruce at the same time defended Rastell from any charge of having deliberately altered the letters; he drew attention to a number of variations of wording, too important to be attributed to the printer, yet showing no motive which should lead us to attribute them to Rastell; above all, he pointed out that Rastell did not know the exact date of this letter to the king, but only that it was written "in February or in March . . . 1533" [*i.e.* 1534, N.S.], whilst both the autograph letters are dated exactly, *at my pore howse in Chelchith the fifeth day of March.* From all this he argued that Rastell had printed from some rough draft of More's, and that the alterations had been made, not by Rastell, but by Sir Thomas himself in the course of revision and transcription.

Bruce did not know of the existence of MS. Royal 17. D. xiv. This is a collection of letters and treatises by More, and is either the source from which Rastell printed, or a transcript of that source. The letter to the king, as given in the Royal MS., shares with Rastell's printed copy those minor verbal discrepancies which rightly led Bruce to regard the printed copy as an earlier draft. Nevertheless the Royal MS. has, not the *nunne of Canterbury* but the *wicked woman of Countorbury* (fol. 383v.). Rastell therefore clearly *had* modified his original here. With regard to More's words about the king's marriage, the matter is not so clear: the substance of the words about Anne Boleyn is found in MS. Royal 17.D.xiv, fol. 390v., but it is added at the bottom of the page. What was the condition of the MS., as used by Rastell, remains therefore uncertain.

The letter to Cromwell, printed by Rastell, is likewise obviously taken from a draft different from that preserved in MS. Cleop. E. vi, and this different draft is preserved in the Royal MS. But Rastell has here also made a change, corresponding to that in the letter to the king. Rastell's text has *In the mater of the nonne*; but the Royal MS. has the *wicked woman* (393), agreeing with MS. Cleop. E. vi.

There is another letter of More to Cromwell, and Burnet accuses Rastell of suppressing this. A late sixteenth-century copy of it is in MS. Arundel 152, fols. 296–9. More in this letter is very hard upon the Nun. He writes:

> *You have done in my mynde to your greate Laude & prayse a verye meritorious deed in bringinge forthe to lighte suche detestable ypocrisie wherbye euerye other wretche maye take warninge and be ferde to sett forthe theire owne devilisshe dissimuled falshed vnder the maner & color of the wonderfull worke of god.*

Burnet first printed this letter (*History of the Reformation*, pt. 2, *Records*, ii, 21, 1680; cf. Pocock's edit. v. 438), and he accused Rastell of "fraud" in deliberately suppressing it, "that one of their martyrs might not lessen the esteem of another." Bruce, on the other hand, argues that Rastell omitted this letter because he was ignorant of it (*Archæologia*, xxx, 151–3). This, however, can hardly be the case, since the letter is found in MS. Royal 17. D. xiv, fols. 376–83.

So Burnet's facts are correct, yet his language is scarcely justified. The Nun of Kent had given her life on behalf of Catherine and Mary, and it would hardly have been possible to publish words reflecting so severely upon her, in a book dedicated to Queen Mary herself. These letters of More to the king and Cromwell are rather painful reading (though they contain nothing discreditable to More), and since Rastell does not claim to be giving a complete collection of More's letters, he would have been guilty of no "fraud" if he had omitted them altogether. To omit one, and make alterations of phrase in two others, was technically a less correct proceeding. But the astonishing thing is, in fact, that Rastell should have printed so much.

165/12–13. *he was put out of the Parliament bill.* Doubt has been thrown upon Roper's statement, and it has been questioned whether More's name ever was in the Bill, because it is not found in the Record Office list of those implicated with Elizabeth Barton (*L. & P.* vii. 70). But there can be no doubt. On Friday, 6 March, 1533/4, there is an entry in the *Journal of the Lords :*

> *Billa in papiro scripta, concernens debitam punitionem* Elizabethe Barton, *Monache et Hippocrite, alias nuncupata* The Holy Maid of Kent, *cum suis adherentibus,* ter *est lecta ; qua quidem Billa, sic lecta, memorati Domini esse consentaneum excogitaverunt, ad cognoscendum an cum Regio animo quadrare potest, ut* Thomas More, *Miles, ceterique in dicta Billa secum nominati, except. Epus.* Rofficien. *egritudine gravis (cujus responsum per suas Literas cognoscitur) coram Dominis in Regio Senatu secus nuncupat.* The Stere Chamber, *accersantur ad audiendum quid pro se ipsis dicere possint.* (Vol. I, p. 72.)

As we know, the king preferred that More's name should be taken out of the Bill; and accordingly we read on Thursday, 12 March :

> *Hodie Billa in pergameno scripta, concernens punitionem* Elizabethe Barton . . . *cum suis adherentibus,* quarta vice *est lecta et per Dominos* consentita.

166/1–3. *So fell it out within a moneth or thereaboutes after the making of the Statute for the othe of the Supremacie and matrimonie,* i.e. the Oath of the Succession. See below, Note to 228/24–27.

169/17. *the abbott of Westminster,* i.e. William Benson, a native of Boston, hence taking the name " Boston." He died in 1549. He is termed " Bisshopp of Westminster," p. 195, ll. 2–3. Westminster became a Bishopric under Henry VIII, 17 Dec., 1540; the bishopric was dissolved by Edward VI, 1 April, 1550. The title " Bisshopp " on p. 195 is therefore erroneous.

170/1–2. *Sir Richard Cromwell.* This is undoubtedly the correct reading. The scribe from whom MSS. L, R[2] and B are derived corrupted *Cromwell* into *Southwell,* and this reading gained such currency that MSS. of Roper were corrected in accordance with it. (See above, *Textual Notes,* p. 291.)

Sir Richard Cromwell was the son of Thomas Cromwell's sister Katherine, and her husband Morgan Williams. He entered his uncle's service, and took his name. He is constantly mentioned in *L. & P.*, and some of his letters are extant; he secured a large share in the plunder resulting from the dissolution of the monasteries. He was the great-grandfather of Oliver Cromwell.

170/16. *John A woode.* Margaret Roper, writing to her father, signs herself *Your owne most loving obedient doughter and bedeswoman, which desireth above all worldly thinges to be in John a woodes stede to do you some service.* For the examination of John a Wood, on 11 June, 1535, see *L. & P.*, viii. 856 (ii, vi, viii), pp. 330–1. His name occurs in some fragmentary accounts relating to prisoners in the Tower : *Wode, servus T. More, militis,* ibid., 1001 (4).

174/20—25. *In the next Parliament was the foresaide sharpe lawe made . . . wherein the king was recognised as the supreme head. . . . And it was ordeyned that whosoeuer should speake against the saide supremacie, he should be taken as a traitour.* These are, of course, two distinct Acts : (1) 26 Henry VIII, cap. 1 : *An Acte concernynge the Kynges Highnes to be supreme heed of the Churche of Englande & to have auctoryte to refourme & redresse all errours, heresyes & abuses yn the same* (*Statutes of the Realm*, III, p. 492); (2) 26 Henry VIII, cap. 13: *An Acte wherby divers offences be made high treason* (*Statutes*, III, p. 508).

178/26–179/1. *the Priour of the Charterhouse of London*: i.e. John Houghton; *the Priors of the Charterhouses of Bevalde and Exame*: i.e. Robert Laurence, Prior of Bevall, and Augustine Webster, Prior of Axholme. For the Carthusians see 229/29–230/14, above, with the Note thereon.

179/1–2. *Master Reynoldes, a singuler learned diuine.* The account of Reynolds and his learning may be from Harpsfield's own knowledge, or it may be taken from Cardinal Pole:

> *Et hic facere non possum quin unum nominatim appellem, quem ego familiariter noram. Ei Reginaldo erat nomen, qui & uitæ sanctitate cum præcipuis illorum erat comparandus, qui exactiorem ad Christi normam uiuendi rationem profitentur; et quod in paucissimis eius generis hominum reperitur, omnium liberalium artium cognitionem non uulgarem habebat, eamque ex ipsis haustam fontibus. Nam tres pręcipuas linguas, quibus omnis liberalis doctrina continetur, probe callebat, & solus ex monachis Anglis callebat. . . . Testimonium sanguine suo . . . dedit tanta quidem animi constantia, ut, quod mihi retulit, qui se ei spectaculo interfuisse, & omnia quæ agerentur attentissime obseruasse diceret, cum in illum feralem laqueum caput insereret, torquem potius regni insigne quam supplicii instrumentum induere uideretur, tanta erat in uultu alacritas.* (Reginald Pole, *Pro ecclesiasticæ unitatis defensione*, [1538], fols. 103v., 104r..)

The author of the *Expositio fidelis* (see pp. 254–6, above) knew Reynolds, and bears witness to his virtues:

> *Cartusianis adiunctus est Reginaldus monachus Brigittensis, uir angelico uultu & angelico spiritu, sanique iudicii: quod ex illius colloquio comperi, quum in comitatu Cardinalis Campegii uersarer in Anglia.*

For Reynolds' appeal to all the rest of Christendom, and all the General Councils, and all the holy doctors of the Church for the last fifteen hundred years, see *L. & P.*, viii., No. 661. Cf. More's claim for the support of his view, pp. 195–6 above.

179/4. *Master John Hall, vicar of Thistilworth.* For John Hall or Hale, vicar of Isleworth, see Gairdner, *Lollardy*, I, 430–2. Hale's crime was not, like that of the Carthusians and Reynolds, merely the assertion that the king was not Supreme Head, but a general indictment of Henry's actions, uttered to one Robert Feron or Fern, of Teddington, clerk. This included what is evidently a reference to the king's treatment of More and Fisher:

> Thus ungoodly he doth handle innocents, and also highly learned and virtuous men, not only robbing them of their living and spoiling them of their goods, but also thrusting them into perpetual prison, so that it is too great pity to hear, and more to be lamented than any good Christian man's ears may abide. (*Baga de Secretis*, vii, 1, as summarized in App. II to the *Third Report of the Deputy Keeper of the Public Records*, p. 237.)

Feron turned king's evidence, and was pardoned. See above, *Rastell Fragments*, p. 229, where the Christian name of Feron is given erroneously as "John."

179/6–8. *the xviiijth of June were there three other of the saide Charterhouse of London hanged and quartered.* This is the second band of Carthusians to be executed. For fuller account see pp. 235–6, and Note thereon.

181/7–10. *Moraris si sit spes*, etc. As is pointed out in the margins of MSS. L R² Y C, the verses appear in the *Epistola contra J. Pomeranum* (Louvain, 1568; for which see Note to 107/2–3). They are on the back of the title-page, and are followed by two other lines invoking a blessing on the reader who shall be mindful of More :

Qui memor es Mori, longae tibi tempora vitae
Sint, et ad aeternum peruia porta mori.

These two additional lines are apparently not claimed as More's, for his poem is described as a quatrain : *D. Thomae Mori Tetrastichon ab ipso conscriptum, triennio antequam mortem oppeteret.*

In the British Museum MS. Royal 17.D.xiv, fol. 453, a copy of these verses is found, also with the two additional lines.

181/27–182/1. *Sir Richard Southwell and Master Palmer.* Sir Richard Southwell (1504–64) is remembered for Holbein's portrait of him in the Uffizi, " one of Holbein's finest portraits of his second English period." It was finished 10 July, 1536. There is a replica in the Louvre, and a crayon study at Windsor. It " displays a very subtle insight into what must have been an unattractive and in many ways despicable nature. . . . Southwell . . . in 1531 . . . was obliged to pay a fine of £1000 before he could obtain pardon for being concerned in a murder, yet three years later he was Sheriff of Norfolk. . . . His treachery helped to bring Sir Thomas More to the scaffold " [this, I think, is stretching the case against Southwell], " and, later on, he played an even more treacherous part at the trial of his early companion, the Earl of Surrey " (Arthur B. Chamberlain, *Hans Holbein*, II, 84). Southwell was still alive when Roper's *Life* and Harpsfield's *Life* were being written and circulated, and the inclusion of his name here is an additional guarantee, if any were needed, of the good faith of Roper's account.

" Master Palmer " is probably Sir John Palmer, who was Sheriff of Surrey and Sussex in 1533, and again in 1543. " He became a noted dicer, and having been constantly in the habit of winning money from Henry VIII at cards, he was hanged, though upon what exact grounds, or at what date, is uncertain." (See *D.N.B.*, under Sir Thomas Palmer, who was brother of Sir John and a distinguished soldier of the garrison at Calais.)

183/8–12. *Sir Thomas More indyted of treason vpon the statute*, etc. See above, Appendix III, More's Indictment, pp. 267–76.

183–200. *More . . . brought to Westminster hall to his arraignment*, etc. For the Paris News Letter and explanatory Note, see above, Appendix II, pp. 253–66. The News Letter must be taken in connection with Roper's account, and the two combined as in Harpsfield, if one is to get the whole story of the Trial. It will be noted that the News Letter entirely omits the Rich episode.

Harpsfield follows the French of the News Letter very closely, but occasionally his wording is nearer that of the Latin of the *Expositio Fidelis*. See above, collations to Paris News Letter, *e.g.* 260/23, 261/8. Note also 261/18, *je veulx voluntairement en dire* : this is not as near Harpsfield's " I will not sticke to utter " (186/24–5) as is the Latin *ipse non gravabor recitare.*

The only actual *fact* which Harpsfield seems to have adopted from the Latin, as against the French, is " susteyning with a staffe " (*baculo innixus*), 184/12–13 (see above, p. 254). Note omission in the French, p. 259, between ll. 3 and 4.

185/31–2. *the rule and Maxime of the ciuill lawe.* See above, 261/1–2, *ce que dit le droict commun.* Prof. Pollard writes: "More undoubtedly said 'the civil law,' but the Frenchman's mistake was natural. Pole, in Starkey's *Dialogue* (E.E.T.S., p. 194), is reported as speaking of *the cyuyle law of the Romaynys, the wych ys now the commyn law almost of al Chrystyan natyonys.*"

190/17–191/4. *it cannot iustly be taken to be spoken malitiously. . . . And onely this worde "maliciously" is in this Statute materiall.* For further discussion of this legal point, see above, 229/2–8, and Note thereupon. This is why Harpsfield stresses the word *malitiouslye*, above, 183/12, 188/22.

191/17–19. *and finally with that weightie roome of his graces high Chauncellour (the lyke whereof he neuer did to temporall man before).* This passage of Harpsfield is taken from Roper. It has often been interpreted to mean that More was the first layman to be made Chancellor, as, for example, by Sampson in his note on this passage in his edition of Roper's *Life*, p. 263. What More says, and says truly, is that he [*Henry VIII*] never gave the Chancellorship to "temporall man before."

Mr. Allen R. Benham has noted the prevalence of this error concerning More in the *Philological Quarterly*, VII, 4 (Oct. 1928), p. 402:

> Dr. J. Rawson Lumby in a note in his edition of More's *Utopia* (*Pitt Press Series*, Cambridge University Press, 1922), remarks, p. 182, "More was the first layman who was Lord Chancellor." Professor F. E. Schelling in *Elizabethan Playwrights* (Harper and Brothers, 1922), p. 26, characterizes Sir Thomas More as "England's first lay chancellor." The facts seem to be otherwise. Lord Campbell in his *Lives of the Chancellors* catalogs at least two lay chancellors in the fifteenth century. Thus (I, p. 275) he names Sir Thomas Beaufort, a layman, as chancellor in 1409 for two years, and *Ibid.*, p. 305, Richard Neville, Earl of Salisbury, Chancellor in 1454. This does not include the case of Sir John Fortescue, who may have been Chancellor toward the close of the reign of Henry VI. Articles in the *Dictionary of National Biography* confirm Lord Campbell's findings in the cases of Beaufort and Salisbury. Professor Kenneth H. Vickers in his *England in the Later Middle Ages* (Methuen & Co., 3rd edition, 1921), p. 336, describes Sir Thomas Beaufort (*anno* 1409) as "the first lay chancellor of the reign" (*i.e.* that of Henry IV). Professor Vickers does not mention Salisbury as chancellor. But at any rate it is clear that Sir Thomas More was not the first Lord Chancellor of England who was a layman.

192/24–5. *the Jurie founde him giltie.*

In Bundle 5, Pouch 7, of the *Baga de Secretis*, the same which contains More's Indictment, is a slip of parchment giving the names of the Jury that found More guilty. The slip contains many names; the following are marked *Jur*:

Thomas Palmer, miles
Thomas Spert, miles
Gregorius Lovell, ar*miger*
Thomas Burbage, ar*miger*
Willielmus Brown, ar*miger*
Jasper Leyke, ar*miger*
Thomas Byllyngton, ar*miger*
Joh*annes* Parnell, gent'

Galfrid*us* Chamber, gent'
Edwardus Stokwod, gent'
Ricardus Bellamy, gent'
Georgius Stokys, gent'

For the possible identification of this "Johannes Parnell, gent." with the Master Parnell against whom More made a decree, see above, Note to 153/7–8.

195/2–3. *the Bisshopp of Westminster.* See above, Note to 169/17.

196/6–7. *for one Councell or Parliament of yours (God knoweth what maner of one).* A parenthesis like this—a mere allusion thrown out as needing no further elaboration—is surely even more convincing than the more definite statements (of which we have many) as to the doubtful character of the "Reformation" Parliament. In this allusive form, it would be strong evidence, even if put into More's mouth by some contemporary narrator of his trial. But it rests upon the Paris News Letter, and there is little doubt that *pour ung vostre parlement, Dieu scait quel,* is a true report of More's words.

Now More had been a burgess of Parliament thirty years before: as Speaker he had defended the privileges of the House, and made the famous petition for freedom of speech in 1523. (See above, pp. 28–31, and Prof. J. E. Neale, on *Free Speech in Parliament,* in *Tudor Studies,* 1924, p. 267.) During the whole of the controversy on the Matrimony and Supremacy he never dropped a hasty word against the agents and ministers of the king; and such words as these, from him, must mean something.

It is expressly stated by Justice Rastell—who was twenty-one in the year that the Parliament was summoned (1529)—that *the kynge . . . choise for knyghtes and burgases* those who would support him against the clergy, and especially *diuers of his owen ccuncellors and howsholde seruantes and there seruantes.* (For the whole passage, see above, p. 222.) This is, of course, the evidence of one who became afterwards, and probably was already at the time, a violent partisan. Yet that the Reformation Parliament consisted mainly of the king's servants is admitted by Edward Hall the Chronicler, an equally violent partisan on the king's side. Hall tells how the king had borrowed money in the fifteenth year of his reign, and how in the twenty-first a Bill was introduced to release him from his debts:

> *This byll was sore argued in the common house, but the moste parte of the commons were the kynges servauntes, and the other were so labored to by other, that the bill was assented to. When this release of the loane was knowen to the commons of the Realme, Lorde, so they grudged, and spake ill of the hole Parliament . . . but ther was no remedy.* (p. 767: ed. Charles Whibley, 1904, II. 169.)

That the Reformation Parliament was carefully packed is also asserted by Richard Hiliard, who claims to have been an eye-witness in one case, and who wrote before the Marian reaction:

> *Ilico regia auctoritate indictum est concilium trium statuum, quod Parliamentum Angli vocant, cuius auctoritate omnia ardua et gravia provinciae negotia stabiliri et definiri solent. Verum in hoc consilio cogendo summa cautio adhibebatur, ut hi soli adessent, qui regio negotio prodesse possent. Et cum illorum, ad quos ex officio interesse parliamento attinet, aliqui electione populi creantur, alii dignitatis aut nobilitatis ratione intersunt, ut eligerentur regis familiares aut sectae Lutheranae homines—nam hi solum in hoc negotio*

se ingerebant—regiis litteris, quibus vel honestissima ratione contradicere summum nefas habebatur, effectum est.

Hiliard goes on to tell how he was at that time in the service of Cuthbert Tunstall, and how, when they were not far from London, they unexpectedly received letters from Cromwell, excusing the bishop from attending Parliament. Tunstall hesitated, but next day received a letter from the king himself, commanding him to return to his diocese :

> *Haec ideo hoc loco recito ut scias qua arte, quo dolo, quibus technis et fraude effectum sit, quod lege, ordine et ratione perfici nequibat. Nec minore fraude, coacto iam concilio, in suffragiis dandis, quam prius in indictione usi sunt.* (MS. Arundel 152, 312 v., printed by Van Ortroy in *Analecta Bollandiana*, xii, 272–3.)

This probably happened in 1533–4, about which time we have the evidence of Chapuys as to the countermanding of members of Parliament, including Tunstall : "the king has taken trouble to have deputies at his will, by countermanding those who, he thought, would oppose him, as the archbishop of York, the bishops of Durham and Rochester, Lord Darcy, and many others" (*L. & P.* vii. No. 121, p. 47; 29 Jan., 1534). Some months later Chapuys mentions that Tunstall has been intimidated by the example of the imprisonment of Fisher and More, and has now been ordered to come to London, "which he was not allowed to do during Parliament, but was even countermanded" (*Ibid.*, No. 690, p. 265, 19 May, 1534).

In the *Life of Fisher* wrongly attributed to Richard Hall is a picturesque statement which has repeatedly been quoted; by Gairdner, for example, H. A. L. Fisher, and Bridgett. But it naturally has not the authority of the contemporary statements quoted above :

> *In this Perlement the common howse was so parcially chosen, that the king had his will almost in all things that himselfe listed. For where in ould time the kinge used to direct his breiffe or writt of Perleament to every cittie, borrowgh and corporate towne within this realme, that they amonge them should make election of two hônest, fitt and skilfull men of their owne number to come to this Perlement, the same order and forme of the writt was now in this Perlement observed. But then with every writt there came also a private lettre from some one or other of the kings counsellors, requiringe them to chuse the persons named in their letters. Who, fearinge their great authoritie, durst commonly chuse none other : so that, where in times past the Common Howse was usually furnished with grave and discreet townes men, apparrelled in comlye and sage furred gownes, now might you have seene in this Perlement few others then roystinge courtyers, servingmen, parasytes and flatterers of all sortes, lightly apparreled in short clokes and swordes, and as lightly furnished ether with learninge or honestie ; so that when any thinge was moved against the spiritualtie or the libertie of the Church, to that they harkned dilligently, gevinge straight their assents in any thinge, that the kinge would require.* (*Analecta Bollandiana*, x, 1, 1891, pp. 335–6. Cf. *Life of Fisher*, MS. Harl. 6382, ed. E.E.T.S., p. 68.)

It is often denied that the Parliament of 1529 *was* packed, although evidence is too conclusive to allow of that denial being made with regard to the Parliaments of 1536 and 1539. But as to the Parliament of 1529, Prof. G. M. Trevelyan assures us with confidence, "The Reformation Parliament was not packed" (*History of England*, p. 304); and Prof. A. F. Pollard says, "There is, in fact, nothing to show that Henry VIII intimidated his Commons at any time, or that he packed the Parliament of 1529. Systematic interference in elections was a later expedient devised by Thomas Cromwell" (*Henry VIII*, 1913, p. 260). The preservation of Cromwell's correspondence supplies us with an "enormous mass of material" for the years 1533–40, unparalleled in the case of any earlier statesman. But it is surely perilous to argue that systematic interference in elections was an expedient devised by Cromwell, or that the Parliament of 1529 "was not packed," because it does not happen that any correspondence has survived relating to 1529 comparable to Cromwell's letter to the Mayor, Sheriffs and Commonalty of Canterbury in 1536. The definite evidence of contemporaries like Rastell, Hiliard and Chapuys, supported by the words of More, "God knoweth what manner of one," seems to show that similar practices were going on in 1529. That none of the private letters requiring the electors to choose the persons recommended should have happened to survive from the earlier year is no evidence that they were not written. It is only by accident that the evidence has survived for Canterbury in 1536.

196/16. Harpsfield here omits a passage which both the Paris News Letter and the *Expositio Fidelis* report—More's censure of the Act of Supremacy in that it was made without the common consent of all Christendom. Cf. above, Paris News Letter, 264/10–16.

196/16–18. *Howbeit, it is not for this supremacie so muche that ye seeke my bloud, as for that I would not condiscende to the mariage.* See Note to 14/4–7, *sub fin.*

199/8–14. *The olde Socrates . . . when his wife . . . cryed,* "*Shall such a good man be put to death?*" etc. This is perhaps an inaccurate recollection of a passage in a letter of Erasmus to Budaeus: "*Moxque mihi venit in mentem Phocyonis, ni fallor, apophthegma, cui bibituro cicutam cum vxor acclamaret, 'Mi vir, innocens morieris': 'Quid,' inquit, 'ais vxor? An me malles nocentem mori?'*" See *Opus Epist. Des. Erasmi* (ed. Allen), No. 1233, Tom. IV, p. 579).

200/18–19; 201/9–10. *more then a sevennight after his iudgement; Tuesday . . . the Vtas of St. Peter.* In making *more then a sevennight* intervene between More's trial and execution, Harpsfield is following Roper; but both are clearly in error. More's trial was indisputably on July 1 (see 258/2, above). St. Peter's day being June 29, the Octave is July 6, and this day, the fifth after his trial, was certainly that of More's execution. (Cf. Hall's *Chronicle*, ed. Whibley, II, 265.) It was, as Harpsfield states, a Tuesday. Two MSS. of Harpsfield, however, have "Thursday," and one "Wednesday"; all MSS. and translations of the Paris News Letter agree upon Wednesday (see 266/1, and collations), although the text printed in Castelnau, 1731, gives the day of the week correctly.

201/13. *Sir Thomas Pope* (? 1507–1559) had been articled to Master Croke, and, as a young official in the Court of Chancery, must have been well known to More. He became a typical member of the new nobility, growing very rich on monastic spoils, whilst at the same time he had no sympathy with "heresy." His foundation of Trinity College, Oxford (in the chapel of which his alabaster effigy may still be seen) has obtained for him a pious memory, and his life has been written at length by Thomas Warton (1772, 1780): for very necessary corrections of Warton, the life in *D.N.B.* should be consulted. A comparison of the incident of More's farewell to Pope, as told by Roper or Harpsfield, and as told by Thomas Warton, is instructive.

203/17–18. *a certaine woman called to him,* etc. See Hall's *Chronicle,* xxvij yere, fol. ccxxvi, verso.

205/16–206/8. *Charles the fift . . . sent for Sir Thomas Eliott . . . and saide . . . the king, your master, hath put . . . Sir Thomas More to death,* etc.

This is the most serious difficulty in Roper and Harpsfield: for Elyot's only known embassy to Charles V had ceased long before More's death. The difficulty has been recently pointed out in a letter by Prof. A. F. Pollard to the *Times Literary Supplement* (xxix, 592, July 17, 1930):

> On the strength of that story Elyot has been credited with an embassy to the Emperor in 1535; and the *D.N.B.*, in an unwonted flight of fancy (xvii. 348, published in 1889, and not corrected in subsequent reissues) tells us how he joined Charles V at Barcelona, accompanied him on his famous expedition to Tunis, returned with him through Italy, and at Naples learnt "from the Emperor himself" the news of More's execution. Yet the publication of vols. viii–x of the "Letters and Papers of Henry VIII" in 1885–7 had failed to reveal any trace of this embassy, had shown that Elyot was in England at the time (1535–6) visiting monasteries and inquiring into the value of other ecclesiastical property, and that the Ambassador who accompanied Charles V was Richard Pate, afterwards Bishop of Worcester.

The *D.N.B.* derived what Prof. Pollard calls its "flight of fancy" from the exhaustive biography of Elyot by H. H. S. Croft, prefixed to his edition of the *Governor* (1883). Croft realized the difficulty of Elyot's known embassy to the Emperor being finished before More's death, but evaded it by identifying Elyot with an anonymous English ambassador whom he found recorded as accompanying Charles to Tunis. As set out by Croft, it all looks very plausible, but in 1885 the publication of *L. & P.* viii showed this explanation to be impossible.

Prof. Pollard continues:

> Elyot however had been Ambassador at the Imperial Court in 1531–2; and this circumstance, coupled with the fact that Henry VIII lost More as a councillor when he resigned the Chancellorship in 1532, and not when he was executed on July 6, 1535, led me to suggest that the story, true in substance, had merely acquired an inaccurate date in recollection or transmission. Further investigation seems to dispose of this explanation. Elyot's mission to Charles V terminated in March, 1532, when Cranmer (soon to be Archbishop) took over his duties at the Emperor's Court at Ratisbon; Elyot left Ratisbon in April, if not in March, and on June 3 was calling on Chapuys in London ("Letters and Papers," V, 869, 910, 1077). More did not resign till May 16 (*ibid.*, 1075), and Elyot, who never saw the Emperor after March or April, 1532, cannot have heard any comment from his lips on either More's resignation or death.

All versions of the story are ultimately derived from Roper. The version given in "Hall's" *Life of Fisher* (E.E.T.S. pp. 128–9) makes Charles praise Fisher as well as More; this seems to be merely an adaptation, fitting the story to its new context. The same version is given by Stapleton (ed. 1612, p. 369). Roper's story must have some foundation in fact. The list of witnesses cited by him proves that he had a very definite scene in his mind: *Which matter was by the same Sir Thomas Eliott to my self, to my wife, to maister Clement and his wife, to master John Haywood and his wife, and vnto diuers other his Freinds accordingly reported* [MS. Harleian 6254, p. 47]. Clement, his wife, and John Heywood were living when Roper wrote, and he would hardly have taken their names in vain.

This confusion of dates in stories which have, nevertheless, some historical foundation, is characteristic of literary sources—witness the Icelandic sagas. As Prof. Pollard remarks, "exact dating is a scientific rather than a literary achievement."

Prof. Pollard suggests that "it is possible that Charles made the remark to Pate, and that Pate repeated it to Roper, or to Harpsfield or to both (they both have the story) during their later exile at Louvain." But I fear that "exact dating" blocks this way out of the difficulty. The matter was reported to Roper *and his wife*: Mistress Roper died in 1544, and was never an exile in Louvain.

On the other hand, I am convinced that Prof. Pollard's original explanation, which he now abandons, is still very defensible. For, though Elyot left the court of Charles V before More's resignation took effect, Charles had known that it was *imminent* for over a year. On 21 February, 1531, Chapuys had written to Charles that More was so distressed at the turn things were taking that he was anxious above all things to resign his office (*L. & P.*, v. 112).

This news must have moved Charles: for More's troubles were closely linked with his championship of the Emperor's aunt (as More hinted at his trial). It is but natural that the Emperor should have burst into an encomium of More, esteeming him above the best city in his dominions.

Elyot on his return to London would find, in mid-May, that the Chancellor's resignation was the topic of conversation. More's relations with Henry were still almost ostentatiously friendly; ill-health was the pretext of his resignation, and he was proclaiming (on the tomb which he was not spared to occupy) how *indulgentissimi principis incomparabili beneficio* he had been released from the cares of office, and allowed to spend the last years of this life in meditating on the next.

That being so, even a wary diplomatist like Elyot may well have allowed himself to repeat the warm praise of Charles, on some occasion when he was in the company of this group of More's young friends.

He would hardly have done so after More's execution; it would not have been loyal for an ex-ambassador to repeat what would have been in effect a censure upon his master. There is no doubt that Elyot at heart sympathized with More. On 29 Jan., 1534, Chapuys, writing to Charles V, mentions Elyot among those who had been in conference with him on behalf of Queen Catherine: "I was moved to write about it by the Queen's order, and the request of several persons, of whom Elyot was not the last, and he was instigated from a good quarter, as he himself told me. Though Elyot ought not to be considered one of the principal, I mention him because you know him" (*L. & P.* vii, p. 47, No. 121). But the imprisonment and execution of More seems to have made Elyot more cautious, and about a year after More's death, we find him writing to Cromwell:

> *I have in as moche detestacion as any man lyving . . . arrogant usurpacions of men callid Spirituall, and masking religious, and all other abusions of Christes holy doctrine and lawes. And as moche I inioy at the kinges godly*

proceding, to the due reformacion of the sayde enormyties, as any his graces poure subiect lyving. I therefor beseche your goode lordship now to lay apart the remembraunce of the amity betwene me and Syr Thomas More, which was but usque ad aras, *as is the proverb, consydering that I was never so moche addict unto hym as I was unto truthe and fidelity toward my soveraigne lorde as godd is my juge.* (Letter of Elyot *To my speciall goode lorde my lord Pryvy Seale*, MS. Cotton Cleop. E iv, fol. 220 [now 260]; cf. *Archæologia*, xxxiii, 353.)

What the authorities about this time thought of discourse with Mistress Clement and Mistress Roper upon the virtues of Sir Thomas More is shown by a question put to Sir Geoffrey Pole in 1538:

> Item, how often within these twelve months or two years you have been in company with Mrs. Roper or Mrs. Clement, and at what places you have met with them? What communication you have had with either of them touching the death of Sir Thomas More? (*L. & P.*, xiii. 2, No. 695, pp. 266–7.)

The Ropers and the Clements were the most devoted of all More's school; but John Heywood the dramatist was hardly less devoted: according to Pits he was most intimate with him (*familiarissimus*), and his championship of the cause for which More died twice brought him near to hanging—the second time at the age of over 80. Heywood's wife was Joan, More's niece, sister of William Rastell. They formed "the little band of the *familiarissimi*" (A. W. Reed, *Tudor Drama*, p. 53). Twenty years later, Roper's mind doubtless went back to many meetings of this little band: one perhaps shortly after More's resignation, another after his death. Roper transfers Elyot's words, by a natural lapse of memory, from an earlier to a later meeting. Thereby he attributes to Elyot an outspoken devotion to More's memory, which in reality Elyot did not show. But Roper had never seen Elyot's exculpatory letter to Cromwell.

208/7–10. *Who was it of whose witt John Collett . . . was wont . . . to say that all Inglande had but one wit, but of this woorthie Sir Thomas Mores witt?* See letter to Ulrich von Hutten, *Opus Epist. Des. Erasmi* (ed. Allen), No. 999, Tom. IV, p. 21:

> *Ioannes Coletus, vir acris exactique iudicii, in familiaribus colloquiis subinde dicere solet Britanniae non nisi vnicum esse ingenium : cum haec insula tot egregiis ingeniis floreat.*

208/21–4. *The saide Erasmus wordes in latine are these:* Cuius pectus, etc. See *Des. Erasmi, Ecclesiastae, sive de ratione concionandi, libri quatuor, opus recens.* (Basileae, 1535), Preface (dated Nonas Augusti), A3r:

> *Quid igitur hac tempestate crudelius, quæ me tot spectatissimis amicis spoliavit. Pridem Guilhelmo Varramo, archiepiscopo Cantuariensi, nuper Guilhelmo Montioio, Episcopo Roffensi & Thoma Moro, qui fuit eius regni supremus iudex, cui pectus erat omni niue candidius, ingenium quale Anglia nec habuit unquam nec habitura est, alioqui nequaquam infelicium ingeniorum parens.*

209/22–25. *Was it not the people of this our Britaine with our blessed king Lucius? And by whom was he christned but by Damianus and Fugatius, sent from Pope Eleutherius. . . .* See Bede, *Hist. Eccles.*, Bk. I, cap. 4, and Plummer's note thereto: "The earliest authority for this story is the recension of the *Liber Pontificalis* known as the 'Catalogus Felicianus,' attributed to the year 530. Thence Bede probably got it. . . . It may safely be pronounced fabulous." See *Dict. Christ. Biog.*, article "Eleutherius."

210/5–6. *authoritie of a pretensed Parliament.* See above, Note to 196/6–7.

212/23–4. *Master Germaine Gardiner.* Secretary to Stephen Gardiner, bishop of Winchester, his kinsman. His case seems to have roused exceptional sympathy, owing to his outstanding ability and his enthusiastic devotion to the cause for which he died. Cresacre More tells us that Germaine Gardiner *auouched at his ende before all the people, that the holie simplicitie of the blessed Carthusians, the wonderfull learning of the Bishopp of* Rochester, *and the singular wisedome of Sir* Thomas More, *had stirred him vp to that courage* (ed. 1726, p. 278). The fullest account of Germaine Gardiner will be found in Gairdner, *Lollardy*, I, 405–13, 416; II, 411–12. There is a brief account by Father Richard Stanton in Dom Bede Camm's *Lives of the English Martyrs*, I, 543–7. (But note that Gardiner was executed 7 March, 1544, not 1545: Stanton's mistake is corrected by Dom Bede Camm in his second volume, p. 655.)

213/12–20. *But yet, because the Protestantes thinke it great folye for him that he stoode in the matter* [i.e. *the kinges newe mariage*, ll. 10–11] . . . *and many of the Catholikes . . . haue not so good and woorthye estimation of his doinges therein as they haue for his doinges touching the Popes supremacie*, etc. This expression of opinion is surprising; it hardly harmonizes with that held by modern historians: that the average Englishman was opposed to the Pope's interference in England, but sympathized with the blameless and injured Catherine. See *e.g.* Trevelyan, *History of England*, 1926, p. 302.

213/25–27. *I will . . . adde it afterwarde in a . . . Treatise*, i.e. *A Treatise on the Pretended Divorce between Henry VIII and Catherine of Aragon.* Ed. by Nicholas Pocock for the Camden Society, 1878.

214/9–16. *Dionisius . . . wryteth*, etc. The passage comes in the Epistle of Dionysius, bishop of Alexandria, addressed to Novatianus:

> *ἔδει μὲν γὰρ καὶ πᾶν ὁτιοῦν παθεῖν, ὑπὲρ τοῦ μὴ διακόψαι τὴν ἐκκλησίαν τοῦ Θεοῦ. καὶ ἦν οὐκ ἀδοξοτέρα τῆς ἕνεκεν τοῦ μὴ εἰδωλολατρεῦσαι γινομένης, ἡ ἕνεκεν τοῦ μὴ σχίσαι μαρτυρία· κατ' ἐμὲ δὲ καὶ μείζων· ἐκεῖ μὲν γὰρ ὑπὲρ μιᾶς τις τῆς ἑαυτοῦ ψυχῆς, ἐνταῦθα δὲ ὑπὲρ ὅλης τῆς ἐκκλησίας μαρτυρεῖ.* S. Dionysii *Quae Supersunt*; Romæ, 1796, pp. 128–9.

214/18–19. *St. Thomas of Douer.* Thomas de la Hale, monk of Dover Priory, killed by the French in their attack on Dover in 1295. *Vita et passio Thomæ de la Hale, auctore Johanne de Tynemouth*, will be found in MS. Bodl. 240, fol. 798, and a translation of this is given in *Dover Priory, a history of the Priory of St. Mary the Virgin and St. Martin of the New Work*, by C. R. Haines, Cambridge, 1930. An account of the raid and a picture of the martyrdom will also be found in the *Chronicon Roffense*, MS. Cotton Nero D. ii, fol. 187r, which is also reproduced in Dr. Haines' book. A short account of the martyrdom of Thomas of Dover is given by Harpsfield in his *Historia Anglicana Ecclesiastica*, Duaci, 1622, p. 453.

215/4–5. *king Henry the seconde.* The comparison between Henry II and Henry VIII may have been suggested by the letter of Paul III to Ferdinand, King of the Romans:

> *Nec tamen hic Henricus* [H. viii] *illius* [H. ii] *impietatem retulit, verum et longe superauit. Ille enim vnum, hic multo plures, ille unius particularis,*

hic Universalis Ecclesiæ iura tuentem, ille Archiepiscopum, hic R. E. Cardinalem neci tradidit. Ille denique . . . poenitentiam sibi a Romano Pontifice impositam humiliter suscepit. (See A. Chacon (Ciaconius), *Vitæ Pontificum*, 1677, Vol. III, col. 575.)

215/9. *burned his holye bones.* For a full discussion of the alleged burning of the bones of St. Thomas, see H. S. Milman, *The Vanished Memorials of St. Thomas of Canterbury*, *Archæologia*, liii, 211–228.

215/10–11. *made him . . . a traitour.* A proclamation (of 16 Nov. 1538, preserved in the Library of the Society of Antiquaries) against *naughtye printed bokes* concludes with fulminations against Becket: *there appereth nothynge in his lyfe and exteriour conuersation wherby he shuld be callyd a sainct, but rather estemed to haue ben a rebell and traytour to his prynce.* (Facsimile, Oxford, 1897; partly reprinted in Burnet's *Reformation*, ed. Pocock, 1865, VI, pp. 221–2; cf. the same, pp. 224–5.)

A full story of the legal proceedings against Becket is given, nearly a century later, in Chrysostomo Henriquez, *Phoenix reviviscens*, Bruxelles, 1626, pp. 199–212, *de Beati Thomæ secundo martyrio.* This story entirely lacks confirmation.

221/9. *Quere if he had yt not before.* Campeggio had held the bishopric of Salisbury since 1524.

221/10–13. *The Pope . . . reuoked þe commission, and yet þe cardinals . . . proceded in debatinge thereof.* Clement VII issued a commission to Wolsey and Campeggio to try the case and pronounce sentence, and Campeggio embarked on 25 July, 1528. Letters were, however, sent after him, which Campeggio understood as forbidding him to begin the trial. Against this he protested. Whilst promising not to proceed to sentence without express commission, he urged that if he did not begin the trial, the English would think he had come to fool them:

> *Ma V.S. advertisca, che se la intende che nè al procedere in causa, nè al sententiare habbia a seguir cosa alcuna senza advertirne etc. io non vedo in caso che 'l Re non si potesse rcmuovere della opinione, come senza scandalizar possa differire, che per virtù della commissione non si habbi a procedere et far el processo, et facilmente gli parrebbe ch'io fussi mandato per uccellarli, et potrebbono sdegnarsi, la qual cosa conosce V.S. quanto possa importare. Ma s'ella intende quelle parole quanto allo atto della sententia, come piu chiaramente si comprende ch'ella ha voluto intendere per la sua de XXVIII, la quale porta il dupplicato della de XXI. la può esser certa, che osservarò quanto la me scrive, et che mai non intenderanno qual sia l'opinion mia, salvo quando sarò sul punto, se pur là si verrà.* (Letter of Campeggio to Salviato, 16 Nov., 1528, in Theiner, *Vetera Monumenta Hibernorum et Scotorum*, Romae, 1864, p. 567.)

Another interpretation of Rastell's words that the Pope "reuoked þe commission" would be to make them refer to the decretal commission for which the English envoys had pressed, the original commission granted to Wolsey and Campeggio being regarded as insufficient. The decretal commission "meant, not a full and open enquiry, but a predetermined verdict" (Fisher, *History of England*, 1485–1547, p. 274). This was given to Campeggio on condition of its being shown only to Wolsey and Henry. In October, 1528, Campeggio wrote

.to the Pope that he could not persuade the Queen to enter a religious house (*di contentarsi con una casta professione di vivere in servitio di Dio et in tranquillità del animo et della conscientia sua*) and that the Pope should determine the question (*che Sua Santità la volesse determinare li*). (Ehses, 1893, pp. 59–60. See also Ehses in *Historisches Jahrbuch*, 1892, p. 476.) On 15 December the Pope sent Francesco Campana, his confidential Secretary, to London to instruct Campeggio to destroy the decretal bull (Fisher, p. 283). The original bull of commission of course remained, and under it the meeting of the Legatine Court was held at the Blackfriars from 31 May, 1529, till it was adjourned on 23 July. Meantime the Pope had called the case to Rome, 15 July, 1529.

It must be remembered that at this point we have only " brief notes collected " out of Rastell's *Life*, and they are necessarily partial. Later the extracts obviously become much fuller.

See also above, 46/12, and Note thereto.

221/19 ff. *willed þe Queen to chuse certen of her councel. And so she choise* . . . This list of Catherine's counsel is also recorded by Sanders (*de origine Schismatis*, 1585, f. 45) in exactly the same order. Sanders no doubt derived it from Rastell's *Life of More*, which he knew. It is the most complete list extant, according to Van Ortroy (*Analecta Bollandiana*, x, 312).

222/1–3. *offered vp to þe legates a boke. . . and made an oracion.* A full account is given by Campeggio. For summary, see *L. & P.* IV. iii, No. 5732.

222/6. *After þe deathe of cardinal Wolsey.* An odd mistake, for More took the oath as Lord Chancellor on 26 Oct., 1529, whilst Wolsey survived till 29 Nov., 1530.

222/13–17. *The kynge . . . choise . . . diuers of his owen councellors and howsholde seruantes and there seruantes.* See above, Note to 196/6–7.

222/21. *3 billes were deuised.* For these see Hall's *Chronicle* (ed. Whibley, II, 166, etc.).

222/27. *The Bushope of Rochester spake against thes billes.* See Hall, as above, II, 167–8.

223/8. *he hym selfe in þe Star Chamber.* See Hall, as above, II, 177, etc.

223/18, ff. *and þe kynge sent thether Doctor Bonner and Doctor Kerne.* This is inaccurate. The document which More and Fisher refused to sign is dated 13 July, 1530. (It is given in Lord Herbert of Cherbury's *Henry VIII*, ed. 1649, p. 303; 1672, p. 331.) But the mission of Carne was in 1531, and Bonner was not sent till 1532.

223/31 ff. *The king moued þe conuocacion . . . to acknowledge hym to be hedd of þe Churche*, etc. Some account of the proceedings of Convocation, and of Fisher's part in the discussion, was written by Richard Hiliard. It will be found in MS. Arundel 152, fols. 312v, 313r, and is printed by Van Ortroy in *Analecta Bollandiana*, xii, 273–5. Hiliard was a contemporary, and wrote before the Marian Restoration.

225/33–4. *his successors haue practised þe same supreamacey.* The use of the plural seems to mark Rastell's *Life* as having been written under Elizabeth.

227/1. *The nune of Canterbury.* See above, Note to 161/21.

227/21. *to surrender all theire Bulles.* Cf. *L. & P.* viii. 121.

228/6–8. *one of his seruantes, who like a false knaue, accused his master to Cromwel afterwards.* This seems a harsh judgment upon Richard Wilson. It is clear from *L. & P.* viii. 856, 858, that Wilson was examined in the hope that he would incriminate Fisher; but Rastell's account below (240/5–6) shows at any rate that they got no evidence out of him which they could use. The *Life* which goes by the name of Richard Hall, closely as it follows Rastell, refuses to follow him here, and excuses Wilson as "a simple fellowe," who, "tirribly threatened to be hanged," confessed to carrying sixteen or seventeen letters between Fisher and More. (See *Life* in E.E.T.S., p. 103.) According to the Latin *Life* in MS. Arundel 152, fol. 208^r, Wilson ultimately became a priest, and took refuge in Belgium: *religionis ergo in Belgica exulavit.* "Hall's" *Life* tells how Wilson could not understand Fisher's scruples about the oath, *for your lordshipp may still thinke as you list* (p. 110); and Van Ortroy (*Analect. Bolland.*, x, 185) comments that this can only have been reported by Wilson himself, who therefore may well be the source of other information given in "Hall's" *Life of Fisher.*

228/15. *Of 6 actes of parlament.* See *Statutes of the Realm,* III (1817), 26º Henry VIII. The six, in the order given by Rastell, are:

Chap. XIV (p. 509).
Chap. II (p. 492).
Chap. XXII (p. 528).
Chap. I (p. 492).
Chap. XIII (pp. 508–9).
Chap. III (p. 493).

228/24–27. *þe othe was not warranted by þe acte of succession, but wrongefully gyuen, and those foresaid holly men wrongefully ymprisoned for refusinge it.* This rather obscure sentence is elucidated by a passage in Roper, which, strangely enough, was not incorporated by Harpsfield, though it is accurate. Roper tells how the Lord Chancellor and Master Secretary put more words into the oath than they were warranted in doing by the Act of Succession: *Which Sir Thomas Moore perceyuinge, said vnto my wife: I may tell thee, Megg, they that haue committed me hither, for refusinge of this oath not agreable with the statute, are not by theyr owne lawe able to iustifye my imprisonement* (MS. Harl. 6254, p. 34). The Chancellor and Secretary, Roper adds, afterwards caused another statute to be made, *for the confirmacion of the oath so amplified with their additions.* The Act of Succession, 25º Hen. VIII, Cap. xxii (*Statutes,* III, pp. 471–4), declared the marriage with Catherine void, that with Anne valid, limited the succession to Anne's children, and ordained that all subjects should swear to keep the Act. The oath administered included an undertaking *to beare faith, truth and obedyence alonely to the Kynges Majestye . . . and not to any . . . foreyn Auctorite or Potentate.* By the Act 26º Hen. VIII, cap. ii, it was enacted that this oath *shalbe interprete, expowned, reputed, acceptyd and adjuged the verie othe . . . mente and entended* (*Statutes,* III, 493). The matter is discussed by John Bruce in *Archæologia,* XXV, 73–4 (1834) and XXVII, 361–2 (1838).

229/2–8. *Note dilligently here þat . . . þe word "maliciusly" was twise put into þe acte.* Richard Wilson in his examination tells how Robert Fisher came to his brother in the Tower, and told him that:

> there was never such a sticking at the passing of any act in the Lower House as was at the passing of the same, said he; and that they stuck at

the last to have one word in the same and that was the word *maliciously*, which when it was put, it was not worth . . . for they would expound the same statute themselves at their pleasure. (Record Office; see *L. & P.* viii. 856, No. 2, p. 326.)

This is confirmed in the interrogation of Fisher himself:

To the first Interrogatorie he saith, That whan thacte by the which wordes are made Treason was a making, Robert Fissher his brother came to hym to the Towre, and said that there was an acte in hande in the Common House by the which speking of certain words against the kyng shulde be made treason; and because it was thought by divers of the said house, that no man lightly coulde beware of the penaltie of the said statute, therefor there was moche sticking at the same in the Comen House; and unlesse there were added in the same that the said wordes sholde be spoken maliciouslie, *he thought the same shulde not passe.* (MS. Cotton Cleopatra E. vi, fol. 165 (169), as printed in *Archæologia* XXV, 95.)

The word " maliciously," as Rastell says, is twice inserted in the Act:

yf any person or personnes after the fyrste daye of February nexte comynge, do malicyously *wyshe will or desyre by wordes or writinge or by crafte ymagen . . . any bodely harme to be donne or commytted to the Kynges moste royall personne, the Quenes, or their heires apparaunt, or to depryve theym or any of theym of the dignite title or name of their royall estates, or sclaunderously and* malyciously *publishe and pronounce, etc.* (*Statutes of the Realm*, I, p. 508, 1817; 26º Henry VIII, cap. xiii.)

229/29–230/14. *Trial of the three Carthusian priors and of Reynolds.* A full account of the trial and execution of the three priors is given by Maurice Chauncy, *Historia aliquot martyrum*; Mainz, 1550.

It is not, however, the source of Rastell's account, for Chauncy entirely misses the legal point, which Rastell so emphatically brings out, that all turned on the word *maliciously.* Chauncy, like Rastell, records Cromwell's intimidation of the jury, but more in detail: the jury would not agree to bring in the accused guilty; late in the day Cromwell sent a messenger, who was informed of this:

Qui renuntians hæc domino suo, in iram concitatus, sine mora remisit ad eos dicens: " Si vos eos culpabiles non inveneritis, vos ipsi mortem transgressorum subibitis." Illi tamen has minas parvipendentes, firmaverunt sermonem suum et tunc temporis noluerunt consentire. Quod ille audiens, mox venit ad eos, et per suas comminationes crudeles compulit eos reddere veredictum, vel potius falsum dictum suum, in condemnationem Patrum nostrorum, reosque eos condemnare læsæ majestatis.

The *Expositio fidelis* (see pp. 254–6, above) gives a very brief account of the death of the Carthusians. Rumour had increased the number to fifteen, which the writer quite correctly believes to be exaggeration: he adds, *aiunt omnium incredibilem fuisse constantiam.*

See also above, 178/26–179/1; and Note thereon.

235/18–19. *nor any head he shall haue to put it on.* The exact phrase varies slightly in different versions. Chapuys, writing to Charles V, says: " As soon as this king heard that the Bishop of Rochester had been created cardinal, he was so angry and indignant at it that he said to many who were present at the time, that he would soon give him another and better hat, for he would send the Bishop's head to Rome for that purpose" (*Cal. State Papers*, Spanish, V, No. 174, p. 492: *L. & P.* viii. 876). The Cambridge correspondent who supplied material for Fisher's *Life* gives the words as Rastell does: *I shall provyde that he shall not have an head to putt it on* (MS. Arundel 152, fol. 284, etc.; *Analecta Bollandiana*, x, 167). So does the anonymous Latin Chronicle edited by Bémont (p. 71): *At ego videro caput cui galerum superinducat ne diu habeat.*

235/20–1. *Anne Bolleyn mad the king a great banckett at Haneworth.* Hanworth Park, some three miles from Hampton Court, was "a small royal seat which Henry VIII took great delight in" (Camden's *Britannia*, ed. Gough, 1789, II, p. 2). In 1532 the park was granted to Anne Boleyn for 99 years, and a little later the house was granted to her for life (*Victoria County History, Middlesex*, II, 393).

Rastell's account is confirmed by Chapuys, who writes on June 16, 1535, to Charles V:

> *Et pour le desennuyer de ces fascheries la dame luy a ces jours faict ung festin en une sienne maison ou elle fit plusieurs braves mommeries . . . la dicte dame a si bien banquete et momme que a ce que ma aujourdhuy envoye dire la princesse, le Roy est plus rasste* [*i.e. rassote*] *delle quil ne fust oncques, quest chose qua augmente grandement la craincte de la princesse.* (Quoted by P. Friedemann, *Anne Boleyn*, 1884, II, 79.)

235 to 236. *Trial and execution of the three Carthusians, Middlemore, Exmew and Newdigate.*

The authorities for this, besides Rastell, are:

(1) The *Baga de Secretis*.
(2) Chauncy's *Historia aliquot martyrum*; Mainz, 1550.
(3) Henry Clifford's *Life of Jane Dormer*, ed. by the Rev. J. Stevenson, 1887. See also *L. & P.*, viii. 846, 895.

A complication has been caused by a strange mistake in Gairdner's *L. & P.*, in which the trials of these Carthusians, and of Fisher, are entered together, under 17 June. This has naturally misled subsequent writers, though Gairdner himself later gave the date correctly (*Lollardy and the Reformation*, I, 486). But H. A. L. Fisher, *History of England*, 1485–1547, writes:

> Fisher was brought to his trial in Westminster on 17 June, together with three Charterhouse monks, Humphrey Middlemore, William Exmew, and Sebastian Newdigate.

It is clear, however, from the *Baga de Secretis*, that Rastell's account is the correct one: that these Carthusians were arrested on 25 May (cf. 235/31, above) and brought to trial on 11 June (cf. 236/15, above). Rastell says that they were fixed to posts for seventeen days. These dates allow portions of two days and sixteen others between the arrest and the trial.

The offices held by these monks and the manner of their torture are also narrated by Chauncy:

> . . . *tres alios venerabiles patres (qui capita remanserant) rapuere, scilicet Patrem Humphridum Middlemore tunc Vicarium existentem, et antea Procuratorem Domus, Patrem Guillelmum Exmew, remotum a Vicariatu Procuratorem factum, et Patrem Sebastianum Newdigate sacerdotem et monachum ejusdem nostrae Domus: hos tres illi immisericordes duxerunt ignominiose ad foetidissimum carcarem, ubi illos per duas integras hebdomadas catenis ferreis circa colla et crura injectis constrinxerunt, et alligaverunt eos*

durissime, cum maxima crudelitate, erectos ad postes et columnas domus, absque ullo relevamine vel solutione pro quacumque necessitate facienda . . . etc. (Chauncy, *Historia aliquot martyrum*; Mainz, 1550; Londini, 1888, pp. 107–8.)

Chauncy's account was probably known to Rastell; but Rastell adds details which are neither in Chauncy nor in Clifford; *e.g.* that the refusal of the Supremacy took place at Stepney (235/32): this is confirmed from the *Baga*.

The story is told at much greater length in Clifford's *Life of Jane Dormer.* Jane Dormer, duchess of Feria, was great-niece of Sebastian Newdigate, and was born not very long after his death. Clifford was her confidential servant: so that although Clifford did not finish his book till 1643, 108 years after the Carthusians suffered, it enshrines family tradition, and has some authority. Clifford says that the three Carthusians were arrested on 25 May, tortured in the Marshalsea for fourteen days (p. 27), then brought before the Lords of the Council, sent to the Tower for eight days, and tried on 18 June. The date of arrest is correct, and the duration of the torture agrees with Chauncy, but the date of the trial is certainly wrong. I know of no confirmation of Clifford's statement that the prisoners were taken in the first instance to the Marshalsea. The *Baga* makes it clear that on 9 June they were in the Tower.

The most interesting thing in Clifford's account is the story of how the king visited Sebastian Newdigate in prison, and made a vain effort to shake his determination. But, of course, it would be perilous to attach importance to so late a tradition.

236/21–2. *And the xix of June following . . . they were executed.* So also Hall's *Chronicle* (ed. Whibley, 1904), ii. 264.

236/26–7. *the king sent phisitions unto hyme to gyve hyme preseruatyves.* Dr. Clement, who was one of the Royal physicians, was probably sent to attend Fisher. For we know that Bonvisi consulted Clement as to the state of Fisher's health, and as to what he should send him. Clement replied that "Fisher's liver was wasted, and that he should take goat's milk" (*L. & P.*, viii. 856, June, 1535). Clement was a fellow-exile with Rastell, and was probably Rastell's informant here.

Van Ortroy has printed a letter by Dr. J. Friar concerning "the Bysshope of Rochester" (*Analect. Bolland.* xii, 166) and he and Father Bridgett both suppose Friar to be the physician concerned; but Gairdner (*Lollardy*, I, 487) has shown conclusively that this letter relates, not to Fisher's sickness but to that of a later Bishop of Rochester (Hilsey) in 1539.

237/6 ff. *part by horseback*, etc. So the *Expositio fidelis*: *partim nauigio, partim equo, ob corpusculi debilitatem.*

237/13–23. *Which commissioners . . . were thes . . . Awdeley . . . Sir William Pawlett . . .* That all these persons were on the Commission for the trial of Fisher can be verified from the *Baga de Secretis* (Pouch vii, Bundle 2). Accounts of all of them (except Sir Walter Luke) will be found in the *D.N.B.* It is interesting to note that Sir William Paulet survived till 1572 (Lord Treasurer, 1550–72).

237/33 ff. *a Jurie . . . Sir Walter Hungerford.* The most outstanding member of the jury is Sir Walter Hungerford, a creature of Cromwell's. Just of this date we have some notes of Cromwell in MS. Cotton Titus B. i, 474: ". . . To remember Sir Walter Hungerford in his well doings. When Master Fisher shall go to execution. . . ." Hungerford was beheaded, together with Cromwell, on 28 July, 1540; his demeanour caused doubts as to his sanity.

240/5–6. *onelie by this wyttnesse of the·kinges owne messenger.* So long as this story of the trick, by which the words necessary for his condemnation were drawn from Fisher, depended upon the not very reliable evidence of Bailey or "Hall," it might legitimately be doubted—although, in fact, it was generally accepted, as, for example, by Lord Campbell.

It was Van Ortroy who demonstrated that it depends upon the word of Judge William Rastell, a contemporary. Yet Van Ortroy doubts the story. He believes that Fisher, when questioned by the Council on 7 May, 1535, really used *to the Council* the fatal words denying that the king was Supreme Head, and that he did this in the confidence that the words could not incriminate him, as they were not uttered *maliciously*. Van Ortroy thinks that, later, Fisher was warned by the letters he had exchanged with More, and became more cautious, but that he was nevertheless condemned on 17 June for the words he had uttered *to the Council* on 7 May. Van Ortroy accordingly dismisses, as fiction, Rastell's statement that these words were uttered, not to the Council, but in confidence to the "mischevouse messenger" (*Analect. Bolland.*, xii, 176–8).

Such doubts must carry weight, for all investigation of Fisher's life really starts from Van Ortroy's researches. Doubt is also expressed by Bridgett (*Life of Fisher*, 3rd edit., 374) and Gairdner (*Lollardy*, I. 487). Other recent writers avoid discussing details.

Yet no evidence whatever has been produced which, on scrutiny, can be held to throw serious doubt on Rastell's story. When the authority was still thought to be "Hall's," and when this story was mixed up with a lot of doubtful matter, it nevertheless was noted as standing out by reason of its intrinsic verisimilitude, its "air of truth." (See above, p. ccxvii.) Rastell, at the date of Fisher's trial, was twenty-seven years old, and was a student of law at Lincoln's Inn. The trial was public. With his uncle's fate hanging in the balance, Rastell must have had the strongest motives, professional and personal, for learning the truth. His account of Fisher's trial and execution is full of the most elaborate detail, and wherever we can verify it (which we generally can) we find it absolutely accurate. What motive can there have been which would lead Rastell to insert such a fiction into his elaborately documented account? He must have expected critical scrutiny, for it was an age of controversy, of embittered polemic about martyrs and pseudo-martyrs. In his *Life of More* Rastell had a story to tell of the most convincing kind, needing no exaggeration. Why should he have thrown doubt on it by introducing fictions about Fisher, which could serve no purpose except to discredit the truth he had to tell about his uncle? *Cui bono?* Who would gain? Rastell was living, alike in England and in Belgium, in close association with the Clements, the Harrises and the Heywoods. They may have been a prejudiced and embittered community, ready to believe scandal. But this was a matter which must have come within the personal knowledge of them all; and they were upright men and women. In England, the matter was also within the personal knowledge of many other people still living. Sir William Paulet, whom Rastell mentions as one of the Commissioners at Fisher's trial, survived till 1572; he was Lord Treasurer from

1550 to his death. Rich survived Rastell, living till 1567. Rastell's later years were largely spent in preparing books for publication, and he must have written his *Life of More* for publication: he could not have foreseen that, owing to his own sudden death, his story of Fisher's trial would remain in manuscript, and its veracity never be discussed till many generations after all eye-witnesses were dead. We have every reason to believe that Judge Rastell was a man of high character. His edition of More's *Works* shows him to have had a very accurate mind. Equally so does his *Collection of Entrees*, a law book upon which he was working about the same time that he was writing his *Life of More*. That he should have invented a fiction, and associated it with some of the most honoured names in the history of English law, such as that of Sir Antony Fitzherbert, is difficult of belief. Judge Rastell had a great reputation to lose, and obviously a great pride in his profession, which led him, even in exile abroad, to toil at his *Collection of Entrees*. Have we any reason to attribute to him an untruth, the folly of which would, if possible, exceed its malice? We can understand the publication, by either side, of scandals which they honestly believed; but not of things which they knew to be untrue, and which they knew the other side could prove to be untrue.

The *Life of Fisher* attributed to Hall speaks of the incident as *openly knowne to the worlde, to the king's great dishonor*; and there are certain additions and corrections in that *Life* which point to the details of the trial being still remembered, *apart from Rastell's account*. The anonymous "messenger" of Rastell is named, in "Hall's" *Life*, as Rich. Rastell says that the "messenger" admitted that Fisher's statement was true, but said that its truth did not discharge him (p. 239, above). "Hall's" *Life*, on the other hand, says that Rich, *nether denying his* [Fisher's] *wordes for false nor confessinge them for trewe, said* "*yf I had said to you in such sort as you haue declared, I would gladly know what discharge this is to you in lawe*" (E.E.T.S. edit., pp. 116, 117).

Apart from Rastell's account, and that of "Hall's" *Life*, which we may thus regard as in some measure at least an independent authority, we have very little evidence as to the actual trial of Fisher, although we have a good deal of information about his conduct both before and after trial. Among the material collected when "Hall's" *Life* was being compiled (and now preserved in MS. Arundel 152) are two brief *Lives* of Fisher, one in English and one in Latin. The English does not help us here. The Latin, for what it is worth, tells against Rastell's account, and would lead us to suppose that Fisher had used the words, not in private to the messenger, but to the Councillors who had previously examined him. Rastell places this examination by the Council, at which, he asserts, Fisher did *not* commit himself, at some date immediately after the execution of the Carthusians, which was on the 4th. It is clear from this Latin life (and from much other evidence) that the examination took place on the 7th—the very day on which, according to Rastell, the interview with the "mischievous messenger" occurred. The Latin *Life* tells us that on 7 May Thomas Cromwell, Thomas Bedell and John Tregonell were sent to examine Fisher:

> *sciscitantur utrum Dominum regem unicum et supremum caput in terra Ecclesiae anglicanae secundum formam statuti in eam sententiam paulo ante editi agnosceret. Ibi Roffensis cardinalis . . . expresse negavit et in foveam quam illi tentatores mortis foderant cecedit et capitalis legis laqueis captus est.* (MS. Arundel 152, fols. 205^{v}, etc.)

We do not know who was the author of the Latin *Life*, or what claim he had to speak with authority. The *Life* was written in Mary's reign, but not finished till 1566 (*Analecta Bollandiana*, x, 134).

Far more important, because contemporary, is the brief account in which Dr. Ortiz, the emperor's ambassador at Rome, reports what Chapuys had written to him two or three days after the trial. This account does not indicate whether Fisher had committed himself to a messenger in private, or to the Council. Van Ortroy thinks that its brevity implies the latter: *Si l'odieux incident* Rich *a réellement eu lieu en plein tribunal, comprend on l'ignorance de Chapuys, ou son laconisme, ou celui d'Ortiz?* (*Analecta Bollandiana*, xii, 177.) I am convinced that we cannot argue in this way. In the exactly parallel case of More, the "odious Rich incident" indisputably took place, yet it is not mentioned in the *Paris News Letter*, full and elaborate as that account is. The fact that Chapuys (or Ortiz) chose to write briefly can give us no indication as to whether Fisher was condemned for having used the words to Rich in private, or more officially to Cromwell, Bedell and Tregonell. The only thing which *is* clear, is that Fisher admitted that he *had* contradicted the statutes: "He replied that he had not contradicted the statutes maliciously, but with truth and holy intention (*con la verdad y santa intencion*), as they were opposed to the Scriptures and to our faith." (Brit. Mus. Add. MS. 28587, fol. 354; *L. &. P.* viii. 1075.)

Our versions agree that Fisher was condemned for having used certain words, which he admitted having used, but denied having used *maliciously*. This is expressly stated by Rastell, "Hall" and Ortiz, and is consistent with the vague words of the Latin *Life*. This makes the essential difference between the case of Fisher and that of More, who denied having used the words for which he was condemned: *if this othe of yours, Master Riche, be true, then praye I that I neuer see God in the face* (see above, p. 189). Only *after* his condemnation did More speak out; Fisher, before his condemnation, had spoken against the Acts. This distinction between the two martyrs is brought out very strongly by Cardinal Pole in a letter *Episcopo Pacensi*. Pole's episcopal correspondent had corrected some misprints in the *Defensio*, and had made an index; but he also submitted some criticisms, thinking that Pole would have done better to have said nothing about More's unwillingness to speak out, which seemed to detract from the heroism of his martyrdom. Pole replies that More, as a layman and a lawyer, was entitled to take advantage of every loophole which the law allowed him; not so Fisher, who was bound, as a Bishop, to speak openly:

> *cujus tempus aperte loquendi et contradicendi tunc fuit statim ut rogatus est, quia hoc conveniebat Personæ, quam gerebat, Episcopi.*

Each, Pole thinks, did what his office dictated:

> *Ego certe, quo magis exitum illius judicii, statum causæ, et personarum quæ in judicium vocabantur . . . considero, eo magis in eam sententiam venio, ut plane existimem, illos duos viros, ut in causa a Deo doctos et confirmatos, sic in modo defensionis divino potius quam humano judicio ductos fuisse.* (*Epistolarum Reginaldi Poli* Pars IV; Brixiae, 1752, p. 80.)

Now Pole's distinction is absolutely sound, if Rastell's story be true, that at Fisher's trial evidence was limited to the outspoken statement which Fisher, as Bishop, had made to the messenger. But, if we dismiss this story of the messenger as false, then Pole's distinction and the account of Ortiz do not agree at all with what we know of the case. We find Fisher conferring with More, and quite as determined as More to avail himself of every advantage which the law allowed him.

The matter, of course, is complicated and difficult. More and Fisher were suffering imprisonment and forfeiture of their goods for refusing to take the oath. The new legislation made it High Treason to *assert* that the king was *not* Supreme Head—a different thing from failing to swear that he was. Obviously, in the course of cross-examination by members of the Council, Fisher might easily have slipped from merely persisting in his refusal to take the oath (which he was free to do) into a denial that the king *was* Supreme Head, which would have been a capital offence. The point is, that as far as we can trace—and we have a good deal of information—Fisher remained convinced that he had *not* uttered the fatal words *to the Council*. Yet at his trial, according to Pole and our other evidence, he admitted to having uttered these very words. And surely he was a man too obstinate and determined to have allowed himself to be browbeaten into admitting to the use of words which he had all along been convinced that he had not used.

Putting the evidence of Rastell and " Hall " aside, all the other evidence leaves us with this insoluble contradiction between what Pole and others tell us of Fisher's admission, and what we should gather from the documents relating to his examination and trial. But if we turn to Rastell and " Hall," everything becomes consistent. Fisher never admitted to having used the words *to the Council*. But he admitted having used them, *privately and in confidence*, to the " mischevouse messenger," when he was asked his opinion, in his character of Bishop, by the king. The documents make this contrast perfectly clear. The most important is the examination of Fisher on 12 June—that is to say, more than a month after the date (7 May) when Fisher had been interviewed by the Council and by the " messenger," and only five days before his trial. Fisher, examined by Bedell and Layton, clerks to the Council, and others, told how his brother Robert Fisher had first brought him news of the Act. (See Note to p. 229/2–8, above.) The only question he remembered having put was, *whether men shulde be bounde to make any answere*; and to this his brother had replied *Nay*. Later, Sir Thomas More had asked him what he had done, and he had replied in a letter to More :

> *that he had made hys answere according to the statute, which condempneth no man but hym that speketh maliciouslie against the king's title, and that the statute did compelle no man to answere to the question that was purposed hym, and that he besought theym that he shulde not be constrayned to make further or other answere than the said statute did binde hym, but wolde suffre hym to enjoye the benefite of the same statute ; which was all theffect of the said lettre as ferre as this deponent* [i.e. Fisher] *doth remembre.* (MS. Cotton Cleopatra E. vi. fol. 165 (169), etc.; as printed in *Archæologia*, xxv, 95, etc.)

The authorities discovered, about the end of May or early in June, 1535, that correspondence was going on between the two prisoners. They cross-questioned Fisher's servant, Richard Wilson, More's servant, John a Wood, and the Lieutenant's servant, George Golde, and their answers are preserved in the Record Office. Now, from the examination of Fisher's servant, it is clear that when Fisher was interrogated *before the Council* on 7 May, far from avowing that the king was not Head of the Church, he, like More, sought to avoid any compromising statement. Fisher was drawn into a discussion by Bedell, and after the Council had gone, he asked his servant Wilson whether he had been too quick with Bedell, to which Wilson replied " No." The danger that, in such a discussion, the fatal denial should slip out, is obvious ; but we have quite definite evidence that Fisher remained convinced that on 7 May he had avoided using the compromising words. (*L. & P.*, viii. 856, n. 19, p. 328.)

The evidence upon which Van Ortroy depends for his belief that Fisher deliberately uttered the words *to the Council* on 7 May, as a matter of fact cuts both ways. We know that, on 6 May, speaking to George Golde, the servant of the Lieutenant, Fisher said that " he saw no so great peril in the statute, unless it were done or spoken maliciously, and he marvelled much that the monks [the three Carthusian priors and Reynolds] were put to execution, saying that they did nothing maliciously nor obstinately " (*L. & P.*, viii. 856, No. 30, p. 329). This, Van Ortroy thinks, shows that Fisher still confided in the word " maliciously," and, relying on it, committed himself to a denial. Of course, there *was* " no great peril " in the statute, unless it had been misinterpreted. We know that when Fisher's brother brought him the news of the statute, he warned him that it would be so misinterpreted : the lawyers " would expound it at their pleasure " (*L. & P.*, viii, 856). Fisher may have " marvelled," but the evidence shows that he knew, before 7 May, that the monks had been hanged, drawn and quartered; this must have tended, one would think, to have made him cautious. We have Rastell's word that it *did* make him cautious (p. 232, above) and that in consequence he would not utter the words *to the Council*, though he did utter them to the " mischevouse messenger."

Fisher's servant, Richard Wilson, admitted many things under interrogation. Clearly he was devoted to Fisher, but terrorized : *tirribly threatened to be hanged : fearing much his life, and beinge but a simple fellowe* (" Hall's " *Life*, E.E.T.S., p. 103). Hence the different views taken of him by Rastell, who calls him a " false knave " (228/7), and in " Hall's " *Life*, which is very sympathetic towards him. Wilson was made to admit that, standing in the Chamber without the partition, he had heard part of the examination on 7 May; that nearly a month later (3 June) he had spoken about it to Fisher, and at first had agreed with Fisher that he could not remember the compromising words having been said : " But a while after he came to his master [Fisher] as he was saying evensong, and said, Yes, that he [Fisher] had answered that he did not think the king might be Supreme Head; but his master denied having said so " (*L. & P.*, 856, No. 19, p. 328).

After his second interrogation on 3 June, Fisher was equally satisfied that he had avoided compromising himself : " he had not made answer," he said, " but the Council was gone even as they came " [*i.e.* without having extracted the necessary denial] (*L. & P.*, 856, as above).

On 14 June, Bedell, Layton and others were still trying to get a denial out of Fisher in the presence of witnesses, and Fisher was still refusing. The final question was :

> *Item, examined wherein, and for what cause, he* [Fisher] *wolde not answere resolutelye to the said interrogatories ?*
>
> *To this interrogatorie he desireth that he maye not be driven to answere, leste he shulde fall therby into the daungers of the Statutes.* (*State Papers*, 1830, I, 432.)

So that, only three days before Fisher's trial, we find the Council still trying to get a denial; which is surely incompatible with the supposition that, more than a month before, on 7 May, in the presence of the same Thomas Bedell, Fisher had deliberately denied the Supremacy. And it is equally incompatible with the supposition that three days later, at his trial, Fisher admitted having used the words *to the Council* on 7 May. The story of the "mischevouse messenger" explains all.

It is quite intelligible that the Council should have been unwilling, except in the last resort, to use a trick which, in the words of "Hall's" *Life*, was "to the king's great dishonor" (p. 110). They naturally tried to make Fisher deny the Supremacy to them, in the presence of witnesses and notaries. They even tried to persuade him, through his servant Wilson, to admit having denied it at some previous date. These things failing, they fell back upon the evidence of the messenger.

All that we know of Rich, and especially his conduct in More's trial, shows him to have been capable of the trick.

But it may finally be objected that in More's indictment the whole of the alleged conversation with Rich is set out in the fullest way. Why, then, in the case of Fisher's indictment, do we have, instead of the name Richard Rich, the vague phrase *diversis dicti domini regis veris subditis*, with no details?

The cases were different. More solemnly denied having used the words, and we are bound to believe him. The turn given to the conversation, as alleged in More's indictment, was then fictitious, and Rich must have been prepared all along for More's denial; he had to depend upon the jury accepting his oath against More's word. In the case of Fisher the words had actually been used. But Rich cannot have had much confidence in the truthfulness of other men: he had got the words out of Fisher, but he had no witness, and he may well have feared that Fisher, in open court, would deny them. The obvious way of getting an admission from Fisher, was to leave him under the impression that he would be accused of uttering the words *to the Council*, and then to spring upon him the betrayal of the private conference. A man in such circumstances would naturally retort, "I used the words under promise of secrecy," thereby admitting the use of the words.

This is exactly what Rastell tells us *did* happen.

241/12–13, ff. *the cause why he was but onely beheaded, was (as men saye) thought* . . . This is derived from the *Expositio fidelis*: "*Cæterum quod mitiore poena affectus est, quam minabatur iudicum sententia, sunt qui in causa fuisse putent, quod metuerint, ne senex & exhausto corpusculo, si per uiam tam longam rheda traheaue tractus fuisset, sponte expiraret.*"

241/33, ff. *And when he came to the Tower gate*, etc. From the *Expositio fidelis*: "*quum satellitibus stipatus reduceretur in arcem, ut ad ostium uentum est, uersus ad satellites hilari placidoque uultu, Plurimam, inquit, optimi uiri, uobis habeo gratiam pro officio, quo me euntem & redeuntem deduxistis. Dixisses hominem ex hilari suauique redire conuiuio, adeo et color erat iucundior . . . ut nemini non esset perspicuum, sanctissimum uirum, ceu iam portui uicinum, toto pectore ad illam beatam tranquillitatem aspirare.*" Dr. Ortiz, writing to the Empress, says that Chapuys had reported on 20 June that, "On his return to the Tower he [Fisher] was followed by a crowd of men and women in great grief, who demanded his blessing when he crossed the water [*i.e.* the Tower-moat] to enter the Tower" (Transcript in B.M. Add. MS. 28587, fol. 354; *L. & P.* viii, No. 1075, p. 422).

242/21–2. *the Levetenant of the Towre came to this holy mann.* The same story is also told in MS. Arundel 152, fols. 284v, 285. This contains the reminiscences of an anonymous Cambridge correspondent, which were utilized in "Hall's" *Life*:

> . . . *Of hys notable actes I have no knowlege, for I was but a yo[ung] schooler of St Johns college, when he dyed. Ye may aske Mr. Langd[ail your] neybour, what he can remembre of hym, and old Mr [Roper]. I know no moo that can say any thyng. I heard say credybly that the mornyng he shuld dye, Mr. W[alsingham] levetenant cam to him into the Bell Towr, hys pryson, very early, [before] fyve of the clock, and sayd to hym that the wryte was com for hys [execution] betwen nyn and ten of the clok. Whom he thanked merely an[d] sayd: Lett me rest a lytle whyle, and then I wyll make me rea[dy]. And after rising, he putt on all hys best apparell very curiously, and caused hys hose to be trussed rownd, and hys head comed, etc. An[d when] hys servant sayd: Syr, I marvell that ye are so curyouse in try[mming] yourself thys day, seyng ye shall putt off all agayn befor noon; he answered agayn; What, man! Doe yow not know that [this is] our maryage day! I must be gay thys day for honor of the mar[yage].* (See *Analect. Bolland.* x, 166–7.)

It is from this same informant that the anecdotes most usually remembered in connection with Fisher's execution are derived: how, whilst tarrying for the sheriffs, he opened the New Testament at adventure, and what he read there; and how the sun shone upon his face as he mounted the scaffold. These touching traditions may well be true; we know from the account of the Bishop of Faenza (see Note to 244/38–245/1, below) that Fisher *had* to wait a long time on the way to execution; but in any case these stories are not like those preserved by Rastell, recorded by an eye-witness. Yet another piece of Cambridge information confirms the story of the request made to the lieutenant:

> *Whether you have heard of any thinge by him spoken at his deathe? Nota: he desyeryd to slepe a lytle whyle, and so he sleptt ij [hours] quietly.* (MS. Arundel 152, fol. 277: *Analect. Bolland.* x, 172.)

244/38–245/1, etc. *than spak he to the people in effecte as follows.* Rastell's account of Fisher's last moments is confirmed by a letter of the Bishop of Faenza, papal nuncio in France, dated 4 July, 1535 (*L. & P.*, viii. No. 985). This letter depends for its story of Fisher's execution partly on the account of Philip Chabot de Bryon, Admiral of France, who had been on a mission to England; but this is corrected by the subsequent account derived from the English Ambassador in France. The Admiral's account told how, on arriving at the Tower Hill (*piazza*), Fisher had to wait for an hour, because the scaffold was not in order. This delay is not mentioned by Rastèll, but it is recorded in "Hall's" *Life* (E.E.T.S. edit., pp. 123–4). (The account there given of Fisher's demeanour during this delay is derived from one who "was but a young schooler of St. John's college, when he dyed." Cf. MS. Arundel 152, fols. 284–5; *Analecta Bollandiana*, x, 166–7.) The Admiral, like Rastell, contrasts the emaciated form of Fisher ("more like a shadow than a man") with the boldness with which he addressed the people. The Admiral's account of Fisher's speech mentions, as does Rastell, Fisher's expression of loyalty to the king, and of willingness to die for the Church. But these are comparatively commonplace features. More striking is the detail which the Bishop mentions, on the report of the English ambassador, that Fisher asked for the prayers of the spectators, fearing that at the last moment his courage and faith might fail:

> *non disse altro, se non ch' essendo di Carne, la quale naturalmente fugge il*

morire, e sapendo che San Pietro rinego tre uolte Christo per timore della morte, et hauendo esso sempre hauto animo di morire se li fusse di bisogno, per amor di Christo, e della Sua Santa Chiesa, e hora mo ch' egli era condotto li, per questo pregaua tutti a voler supplicare sua Diuina Mta. che concedesse tanto di costanza, e fermezza alla sua fragil Carne di poter patire prontamente il supplicio che se li apparecchiaua. Mons. l'Almiraglio mi dice hauer inteso, ch' ei fu misso in quattro parti, secondo la sentenza data, ma l'Amb^re *d' Inghilterra . . afferma la sentenza non esser stata esseguita se non nel tagliar il capo per grandissima grattia ottenuta dal furor infinito in questo di quel Re, e ch' anch' al fine fu per contento ch'il corpo la sera fusse seppellito.* (Brit. Mus. MS. Add. 8715, fol. 85, *Lettere di Ridolfo Pio, Vescouo di Faenza.*)

Fisher's request for prayers lest, even on the scaffold, he should fall from the faith, is, then, recorded by both Rastell and the Bishop of Faenza. Chapuys writes: "They tell me that on the scaffold he was often and often solicited to comply with the king's wishes, grace and pardon being offered to him in the king's name, but that he kept firm to the last, and died most exemplarily." (*Cal. of State Papers, Spanish*, v. p. 504 (1886).) The report of Fisher's dying words confirms the statement of Chapuys, and is confirmed by it.

245/31–2. *he sayed a few prayers.* Although Rastell's account of Fisher's execution is obviously at first hand, the wording here seems to be suggested by the short account in the *Expositio fidelis*: "*Primum regi regnoque bene precatus est. Mox ardenti magis quam prolixa precatione se ipsum Dei misericordiæ commendauit: simulque procumbens in genua, gracili & exhausta ceruice securim excepit.*"

246/6 ff. *Then toke the executioner,* etc. Rastell's account of the insults to Fisher's body is confirmed by Cardinal Pole's *Apologia ad Carolum V, Cæsarem* (cap. xx): "*Nec vero hoc satis, nisi mortui corpus omni contumeliæ objiceret, quod nudum prorsus in loco supplicii ad spectaculum populo relinqui mandaverat, ad quod nemo accedere audebat tyranni metu, præter eos, qui contumeliæ causa accederent, vel qui mortuo indumenta detraxerant.*" (See *Epistolarum Reginaldi Poli* Pars I; Brixiæ, 1744, p. 96.) That permission to bury Fisher's body came in the evening of the same day is confirmed by the account of the Bishop of Faenza, written less than a fortnight later (see Note to 244/38–245/1, above).

As to the final burial-place of Fisher, see Van Ortroy in *Analecta Bollandiana*, xii, 203 (note), and Bridgett's *Life* (3rd edit., 1902), pp. 408, etc.

246/33–6. *Whiche heade of his . . . contynewed . . . as though it had bene alyve.* The author of the *Expositio fidelis*, writing at Paris, just a month after Fisher's execution, mentions having heard of this by letter from the Netherlands: "*Ex amicorum literis cognoui, in Germania inferiore sparsum rumorem, quum Episcopi Roffensis caput esset in ponte Londoniensi de more expositum, non solum non emarcuisse, uerumetiam magis effloruisse, uiuoque factum similius, ut multi crederent fore, ut etiam loqui inciperet. . . .*"

252/9. *he wrott dyuerse excellent sermons.* Rastell, on 28 June, 1532, printed two sermons by Fisher on Matthew v. 20. (A copy is in the possession of Sir R. Leicester Harmsworth.) Prof. A. W. Reed, to whom I owe this note, thinks it strange that Rastell should have forgotten these sermons. I, who have listened to over four thousand sermons, find it not surprising.

GLOSSARY

NOTE.—The Glossary is not a complete concordance, but aims at including all words which differ materially in spelling from that of the present day, or of which the meaning is of interest or of difficulty.

Infinitives which do not occur in the text, if used as headwords, are placed within square brackets.

R.F. = ***Rastell Fragments***, Appendix I.

Abhorre from, *w. v.* shrink with dislike from, 21/11.

Abrogate, *w. v.* abolish, annul, cancel, 215/21.

Accepcions, *sb. pl.* exceptions, *R.F.* 228/2.

Accompt, *sb., obsolete form of* "account," 3/18, &c.

Accompt, *w. v., obsolete form of* "account," 64/26; *p. p.* **accompted,** 32/16, &c.

Acknowen, *p. p.* acknowledged, confessed. **To be acknowen,** to avow, confess, 169/21.

Adulterate, *p. p. adj.* of base origin, corrupt, 107/23.

Aduertisementes, *sb. pl.* admonitions, precepts, 77/21.

Affectionated, *p. p. adj.* unduly inclined, partial, 22/21.

All to + *verbal form,* soundly, completely. **All to buffet,** 129/15. **All too rated him,** 95/4–5.

Almaine, *sb.* Germany, 71/26.

Amonge, *adv.* from time to time, now and then, 29/21.

Angell, *sb.* gold coin of the value of 6*s.* 8*d.* to 10*s.*, 203/13; *pl.* **angels,** 154/16.

Apon, *in* **Thereapon, Hereapon, Whereapon,** &c., *obsolete variant of* "upon," *R.F.* 221/5, 229/35, 230/4, &c.

Argumentes, *sb. pl.* proofs, evidences, tokens, 9/3.

[**Astonie,** *w. v.*] astound, astonish, confound; *p. p.* **astonied,** 72/21, &c.

Awen, *p. p. adj., obsolete variant of* "own," *R.F.* 223/9.

Ayme, *sb.* guess, conjecture of the probability of, 67/17, 129/9.

Beare, *s. v.* (1) *refl.* conduct oneself, deport oneself, 22/19, 71/19; (2) *tr.* (*a*) hold, exercise an office, 27/10; (*b*) support, corroborate, 213/15; (*c*) be fit for, 27/21, &c.; (*d*) endure, 126/11, &c. **Beare in hande,** maintain, assert, 129/13; *pr. p.* **bearing in hande,** 70/20–21.

Beetle blinde, *adj.* mentally blind as a beetle, 215/7.

Behoweth: it behoweth, *impers. vb., obsolete variant of* "it behoveth," *R.F.* 248/12.

Beshrewe, *w. v.* invoke evil upon, curse, greatly blame, 131/20.

Blinde hobbe, 118/11–12. **Blinde,** *adj.* concealed from sight, *and so* misleading, deceitful. **Hobbe,** *sb., a rustic variation of* "Robin," "Robert," *so used for* "Robin Goodfellow," "Puck," *or generally for* hobgoblin, sprite, elf. **Playeth the very blinde hobbe,** "*Some game unknown.*" (*N.E.D.*)

Blyndfolled, *p. p.* blind-folded, *R.F.* 245/29.

Boysteous, *adj., older and obsolete form of* "boisterous," *which is an obscure variant of it,* rough, unpolished, 29/15.

[**Breake with,** *s. v.*] broach a matter; 3 *sg. pret. ind.* **brake . . . with,** 47/24.

Brickle, *adj.* easily broken, 25/14.

Brute, *sb., obsolete form of* "bruit," report noised abroad, 152/10.

[**Brute,** *w. v.*] report, spread abroad; *p. p.* **bruted,** 41/10.

Butcherie, *adj., obsolete form of* "butcherly," 40/12.

Cattels, *sb. pl.* property generally. **Goodes and cattels,** *technical phrase,* "goods and chattels," 184/29.

Cautell, *sb.* precaution, 47/15.

Censure, *sb.* judgement, opinion, 12/1, 209/3, &c.

Ciuilian, *sb.* one learned in civil law, 23/13.

Coale, *sb.* charcoal used for writing or drawing, charcoal pencil, 134/22, &c.; *pl.* 80/3.

[**Commaculate** *w. v.*] defile; 3 *pl. pr. ind.* **commaculate,** 114/7.

Common, *w. v.* commune, have intercourse with, 48/8; *p. p.* **commoned,** 147/16.

Comon Place, *sb. pl.* Common Pleas, *R.F.* 237/19.

Complexion, *sb.* constitution, 34/3. *The* "four complexions" *of man in the physiology of the Middle Ages—the choleric, phlegmatic, sanguine and melancholic—were supposed to depend on the proportion in the body of the* "four humours"—*choler, phlegm, blood and melancholy.*

Condescende, Condiscende, *w. v.* agree, concur, assent, 16/26, 48/27, &c.; 3 *sg. pret. ind.* **condescended,** 15/15; **condiscended,** 44/26.

[**Conferre,** *w. v.*] compare; 3 *sg. pret. ind.* **conferred,** 45/6.

[**Conuent,** *w. v.*] summon on charge of; *p. p.* **conuented,** 86/21.

Cunning, *adj.* learned, skilful, 14/1, &c.

Cunning, *sb.* learning, 36/14.

Curious, *adj.* (1) particular, fastidious, 74/4; (2) inquisitive, 85/15.

Cursey, *sb., obsolete form of* "curtsy," 66/22.

Debell, *w. v.* subdue in fight, vanquish, 207/12, &c.

Debellation, *sb.* conquest, 108/24, 127/25, &c.

Deere, *adj.* (1) high-priced, costly, 22/28; (2) precious in estimation, 132/3.

[**Deface,** *w. v.*] (1) put out of countenance, outface, abash; *p. p.* **defaced,** 86/15. (2) discredit, destroy reputation of; 3 *sg. pret. ind.* **defaced,** 34/22; *p. p.* **defaced,** 3/28, 192/10.

Defacing, *vbl. sb. of* (2) *above,* discredit, destruction of reputation, 207/8.

Defence, *w. v.* defend, 133/22.

Demaine, *sb.* behaviour, demeanour, 92/2.

Demeane, *w. v.* behave, 187/26; 3 *sg. pret. ind.* **demeaned,** 22/6; **demained,** 139/6, &c.; **demayned,** 178/10.

Depulsiue, *adj.* expelling, driving forth, 116/12.

[**Desperate,** *w. v.*] despair of; *p. p.* **desperated,** 81/20.

Difficile, *adj.* troublesome, difficult, 56/22.

Dimisse, *w. v., obsolete form of* "dismiss," 60/11; *p. p.* **dimissed,** 60/2, &c.

[**Disable,** *w. v.*] discredit, belittle; 3 *sg. pret. ind.* **disabled,** 26/18.

Disagreable, *adj.* not agreeing, discordant, 45/25, 138/19, 193/27.

[**Disallow,** *w. v.*] belittle; 3 *sg. pret. ind.* **disallowed,** 51/29.

[**Discouer,** *w. v.*] make known, expose; 3 *sg. pr. ind.* **discouereth,** 119/10.

[**Dislyke vpon,** *w. v.*] disapprove of; 3 *sg. pret. ind.* **dislyked vpon,** 15/12.

[**Dispare in,** *w. v. intr.*] lose hope in; have no hope in; 3 *sg. pret. ind.* **disparid in,** *R.F.* 250/31. *The MS. reads* disgasid, *which seems otherwise unknown. I am indebted for the emendation to Dr. C. T. Onions.*

Doubt, *sb.* fear, dread, 30/11, 30/26, &c.

Eathe, *adj.* easy, 90/23, &c.

[**Effuse,** *w. v.*] pour out; *p. p.* **effused,** 117/11, 209/15.

[**Elude,** *w. v.*] baffle, disappoint; *p. p.* **eluded,** 42/6.

Euentes, *sb. pl.* results, 43/16, &c.

Experted, *p. p. adj.* experienced, 83/13.

[**Fall in hande with,** *s. v.*] set upon a person; 3 *sg. pret. indic.* **fell in hande with him,** 95/4.

[**Farce,** *w. v.*] stuff; *p. p.* **farced,** 121/1.

Farre, *adv.* much, to a great degree, 120/4, 138/19.

[**Fawor,** *w. v.*] *obs. variant of* "favour"; *pr. p.* **faworinge,** *R.F.* 223/14.

[**Fett,** *w. v.*] *synonym of* "fetch"; 3 *sg. pret. ind.* **fett,** 37/25.

Fleme, *sb.* the cold and moist "humour" of the body in the old physiology, *R.F.* 248/27.

[**Foister,** *w. v., from* "Foist"] smell bad or musty; *pr. p.* **foystring,** 84/23.

Fonde, *adj.* foolish, 70/18, &c.

Forethinke, *w. v. refl.* regret, repent, be sorry, 41/21, 183/23.

Forslowe, *w. v.* delay, neglect, 22/24, 59/19; 3 *sg. pret. ind.* **forslowed,** 22/4.

[**Frustrate,** *w. v.*] disappoint, balk; *p. p.* **frustrate,** 42/6.

Germaine, *adj.* akin, having the same parents, "own," (brother, sister, &c.), 80/16.

Geue, *s. v., obsolete form of* "give," 162/15, &c.; 3 *sg. pr. ind.* **geueth,** 176/3, &c.; 3 *pl. pr. ind.* **geue,** 29/16, &c.; 3 *sg. pr. subj.* **geue,** 94/20; 2 *pl. pr. subj.* **geue,** 32/12; 3 *sg. pret. ind.* **gaue,** 176/2, &c.; *p. p.* **geuen,** 27/19, &c.

Geuing, *vbl. sb. of above,* 9/16, &c.

Glister, *sb.* clyster, enema, 82/16.

[**Glister,** *w. v.*] glitter; *pr. p. adj.* **glistering,** brilliant, glittering, "showy," 121/15.

Goodyere: What the goodyere! *a phrase expressing impatience, imprecation,* &c., 95/23.

Goslinges, *sb. pl.* figures of a gosling, 95/8.

Gree, *sb.* part; **in good gree,** in good part, with good will, 3/18, 151/10.

Heading, *vbl. sb.* beheading, 177/16, 18.

Hipocrace, *sb.* hippocras, a cordial made of wine and spices, 126/21.

[**Housel,** *w. v.*] (1) *tr.* to administer the Eucharist to. (2) *pass.* to receive the Eucharist; *p. p.* **houseled,** 64/14.

Hoverly, *adv.* lightly, slightly, 150/18, 174/16, 209/16. (*See Textual Note to* 150/18.)

Hugger-mugger, *sb.* secret, 84/11–12, 119/2.

Impugne, *w. v.* oppose as false or erroneous, challenge, assail (an opinion, document, &c.), 212/17; 3 *sg. pret. ind.* **impugned,** 131/9, &c.; *pr. p.* **impugning,** 122/16, &c.

Incontinent, Incontinentlye, *adv.* immediately, 82/15, 170/22, 22/25, &c.

Indifferent, *adj.* impartial, 12/5, 116/2, &c.

Indifferently(e), *adv.* impartially, 108/21, 153/26.

Inhable, *w. v., obsolete form of* "enable," declare fit, regard as competent, 27/21.

Inopinable, *adj.* not "opinable,"

inconceivable, unexpected, 105/3 115/21.

Instant, *adj.* urgent, insistent, 154/7.

Intreate, *w. v., obsolete form of* "entreat." (1) beg, pray, 22/1; *p. p.* **intreated,** 15/11, &c. (2) handle a matter or subject, 43/13; *p. p.* **intreated,** 30/5.

Intreating, *vbl. sb., obsolete form of* "entreating," handling of a matter or subject, 140/10.

[**Intricate,** *w. v.*] entangle, involve; *p. p.* **intricated,** 21/4.

Javell, *sb.* worthless scoundrel, rascal, rogue, 203/4, 203/5.

Jollye, *adj.* fine, excellent, agreeable, lively, 103/17.

Large, *adj.* wide, spacious, 94/17.

Leades, *sb. pl.* lead roof, 137/6.

[**Lease,** *w. v.*] glean; *p. p.* **leased,** 6/28.

Leese, *s. v.* lose, 15/29, &c.

Legantine, *adj.* pertaining to a legate, 50/11.

Lengh, *sb.* length, height, stature, *R.F.* 248/25.

Lett, *w. v.* hinder, 30/7, &c.

Lewde, *adj.* wrong, villainous, 73/15.

Lewdly, *adv.* maliciously, 73/19.

Libell, *sb.* document of plaintiff, plea, 46/16. (*Not with modern bad sense.*)

Lightly, *adv.* perhaps, probably, 137/8, 142/19, &c.

List, *sb.* desire, 95/1.

[**List,** *w. v. pers. & impers.*] desire; 2 *sg. pr. ind.* **you list,** 95/6; 3 *pl. pr. ind.* **they list,** 73/19; 3 *sg. pret. ind. impers.* **me listed,** 36/14.

Lustry, *sb.* lustre, brilliance, 25/12.

Lyghtlie, *adv.* easily, *R.F.* 249/28.

[**Malign,** *w. v.*] hate; 3 *sg. pret. ind.* **maligned,** 43/12; *pr. p.* **maligning,** 185/26.

Manchettes, *sb. pl.* small loaves or rolls of fine wheaten bread, 126/20.

Maniche, *sb.* "an adherent of a religious system widely accepted from the third to the fifth century, composed of Gnostic Christian, Mazdean and pagan elements," (*N.E.D.*), 88/17.

Manuring, *vbl. sb.* the occupying or cultivation of lánd, 27/4.

Many: the many, *sb.* company, multitude, 37/20.

Markes, *sb. pl.,* 146/1, 6; *R.F.* 250/8. *The* "mark" *was worth* 13*s.* 4*d.*

Mastrie, *sb.* achievement, 75/14.

Mayne, *adj.* mighty, great, 40/17, &c.

Meate, *sb.* food (in general), *R.F.* 236/5.

[**Minish,** *w. v.*] reduce in power; 3 *pl. pret. ind.* **minished,** 173/6.

Minishing, *vbl. sb. of above,* 206/19.

Mo(e), *quasi-sb.* more things, 36/24, &c.; more persons, 195/12, &c.

Mother-in-law, *sb.* step-mother, 111/7.

Motions, *sb. pl.* motives, reasons, grounds of action, 11/26.

Mowe, *w. v. obsolete variant of* "move," *R.F.* 222/34.

Much, *quasi-sb.* a great quantity, many, 134/17.

Naturalls, *sb. pl.* mental endowments, natural powers, 72/23.

Naught, *adj.* naughty, sinful, of bad account, 110/20.

Neece, *sb.* grand-daughter, 107/8; *pl.* **neeces,** 93/10.

Nephewes, *sb. pl.* grand-sons, 93/10.

Nere, *adv., obsolete form of* "never," 124/16, &c.

Nonce : for the nonce, *adv. phrase,* purposely, expressly, 181/16.

Nother : No nother, *pron.* none other, *R.F.* 240/35.

[**Nousle,** *w. v.*] nuzzle, train, educate; *p. p.* **nousled,** 88/18.

[**Occur,** *w. v.*] resist, oppose; *pr. p.* **occurring,** 178/10, &c.

Oddest, *sup. adj.* most renowned, remarkable, famous, 11/18.

Orient, *adj.* precious, excellent, 6/10.

Ouerseene, *p. p. adj.* mistaken, in error, 125/18.

Parsverse, *sb.* lesson, 130/11 (*See Textual Note to* 130/10–11).

Partes, *sb. pl., obsolete form of* "parties," 68/21 (*See Textual Note*).

Pensition, *sb.* pension, 22/21. (*Note spelling.*)

Perplexe, *adj.* complicated, intricate, 78/19.

Persecuting, *vbl. sb.* following up, pursuing, carrying out, going through with, 151/11.

Possible, *adv., variant form of* "possibly," 161/25.

Precisely, *adv.* entirely, absolutely, 164/15.

[**Prefer,** *w. v.*] esteem more, set before others in favour; 3 *sg. pret. ind.* **preferred,** 22/14.

Pregnatorie, *sb.* protonotary, principal notary, chief clerk of a court of law, 5/15.

Prest, *adj.* prepared, ready, 174/14.

Pretensed, *pp. adj.* pretended, false, 210/6.

Pretie, *adj.* (1) artful, crafty, 16/6, 127/19, &c.; (2) attractive, 127/21, &c.

Pretily, *adv.* cleverly, in a cunning manner, 129/15.

Price, *sb.* value, worth. *See below* **Pricke and Price.**

Pricke and Price, *alliterative phrase,* success and the acknowledgment of success, 102/18.

Propense, *adj.* disposed, inclined, 17/10, 110/26, 213/4.

Propension, *sb.* inclination, 18/10.

[**Propone,** *w. v.*], propound, propose; *p. p.* **proponed,** 35/24, &c.

[**Pule,** *w. v.*] whimper, whine; *pr. p.* **puling,** 79/5.

Queane, *sb.* jade, hussy, 130/17.

Reduce, *w. v.* bring back, 218/2; *p. p.* **reduced,** 88/23.

Renowmed, *p. p. adj., obsolete form of* "renowned," famous, 4/3.

[**Repine,** *w. v. tr.*] fret at, murmur at, grudge; *pr. p.* **repyning,** 185/26; *p. p.* **repined,** 184/19.

Retchlesse, *adj., obsolete variant of* "reckless," careless, heedless, 67/4, 116/8, 209/18.

[**Reuoke,** *w. v.*] refer to some authority; 3 *sg. pret. ind.* **reuoked,** *R.F.* 223/17.

[**Ripe,** *w. v. tr.*] make ripe in knowledge; *p. p.* **riped,** 88/18.

Roome, Rowme, *sb.* place, position, 51/17, 51/29, 24/6, &c.

Rot, *sb.* Rota, *R.F.* 223/18.

[**Round,** *w. v.*] whisper; 3 *sg. pret. ind.* **rounded,** 166/24.

Rude, *adj.* uneducated, inexperienced, 92/23, &c.

Ryper, *comp. adj.* more educated, more instructed, 213/21.

Sadd, *adj.* serious, grave, *R.F.* 248/28.

Sangwyne, *adj. and sb.* one of the four "complexions" of the body in the old physiology, being that in which blood predominates over the other three "humours," *R.F.* 248/26.

Scant, *adv.* barely, hardly, 123/14, 154/10.

Scuse, *w. v. and sb., aphetic form of* "excuse," 118/14, 16.

Seene, *p. p. adj.* versed, skilled, 90/13, 179/2.

Seuerall, *adj.* separate, 190/11.

Seuerally, *adv.* separately, individually, 32/15.

Sewer, *sb.* attendant at a meal, server of dishes, &c., 131/21.

Shett, *w. v., obsolete form of* "shut," 97/24, &c.; 3 *sg. pret. ind.* **shett,** 166/19; *p. p.* **shett,** 52/21, &c., **shutt,** 107/4, &c.

Shrewde, *adj.* injurious, harmful, 73/4.

Shuche, Souche, *pron. adj., obs.*

variants of "such," *R.F.* 223/10, &c., 225/32.

Singly, *adv.* simply, 65/27.

Singuler (1) *adj.* special, particular, above the ordinary, 23/13, 26/12, 38/19, &c.
(2) *adv.* particularly, specially, 58/13.

Singulerly, *adv.* particularly, specially, 25/25.

Sith, *conj.* since, 125/1, &c.

[**Soyle,** *w. v.*] assoil, absolve; 3 *sg. pr. ind.* **soyleth,** 169/15.

Sparkles, *sb. pl.* spots, specks, 141/11.

Square, *w. v.* diverge, disagree, 120/4; *pr. p. adj.* **squaring,** discordant, 138/19.

Supplye, *w. v.* complete, 102/15.

Table, *sb.* (1) surface on which picture painted, picture, 104/18, 136/16, &c.; (2) list of contents; *pl.* **tables,** 124/10.

[**Take,** *s. v. refl.*]; 1 *sg. pr. subj.* **take,** reckon, consider, 3/30; *p. p.* **taken,** reputed, esteemed, considered, 4/19, 138/28.

Take . . . vpon, *s. v.* assume airs, 121/10.

Tentation, *sb., obsolete form of* "temptation," 133/16.

Tertian, *adj.* characterised by a paroxysm every third (*i.e.* alternate) day, 90/25.

Testimonie, *w. v.* bear witness, testify, 72/4.

The, *pers. pron.* 3 *pl., unstressed form of* "they," *R.F.* 222/4, 228/8, 251/25.

Tille valle, *exclamation of impatience,* 96/20.

Towardlynes, *sb.* proficiency, aptitude, 10/22.

Towardnes, *sb.* (1) tendency towards, 32/7; (2) proficiency, aptitude, forwardness in learning, 78/1.

Trade, *sb.* course, method, practice, 76/24, 140/22.

Trauers, *sb.* apartment screened off, 137/2.

Treade, *s.v.* 12/21; 3 *sg. pret. ind.* (*weak*) **treaded,** 39/28; *p. p.* **troade,** 5/18, **trode,** 39/26, &c.

Treatably, *adv.* clearly, 141/23.

Triacle, *sb., obsolete form of* "treacle," remedy, balm, 116/12.

Vnderstande, *s. v.* 13/17, &c.; 1 *sg. pr. ind.* **vnderstande,** 162/1, &c.; 3 *pl. pr. subj.* **vnderstande,** 120/25, &c.; 3 *sg. pret. ind.* **vnderstoode,** 120/20, &c.; *p. p.* (*weak*) **vnderstanded,** 13/18.

Vnfortunable, *adj.* unfortunate, 43/16.

[**Vnsanct,** *w. v.*] strike off the calendar of saints; *p. p.* **vnsancted,** 215/10.

Vnthriftes, *sb. pl.* wasters, 71/18.

Vtas, *sb.* octave, 201/3, 10.

Vtter, *adj.* complete, fully qualified, 13/9.

Virtually, *adv.* worthily, virtuously, with due confession and contrition, &c., 132/14.

Waite, *w. v.* be on the watch to inflict, 73/3.

Wanton, *sb.* pet, pampered darling, 171/20.

Weene, *w. v.* think, 152/5; 2 *pl. pr. ind.* **weene,** 125/18, &c.; *p. p.* **weened,** 113/9, &c.

Where . . . or, *correl. conjs.* whether . . . or, 174/3–5.

[**Wit,** *pret. pr. v.*] know; 3 *sg. pr. ind.* **woteth,** 124/15; 2 *pl. pr. ind.* **wote,** 31/21, 123/15; 1 *sg. pret. ind.* **wist,** 97/13; 3 *sg. pret. ind.* **wist,** 33/20, 98/8.

Wood, *adj.* mad, angry, 42/18.

GENERAL INDEX

NOTE.—Unless otherwise stated, the references are to pages of the tex and Appendices, and to the Historical Notes. For references to works of More, see *More, Sir Thomas, works of.*

R. F. = *Rastell Fragments*, APPENDIX I.

Abell, Thomas: one of Queen Katherine's Counsel, *R. F.* 221.

Adam: 98.

Adrian, Cardinal: is made Pope [1522] (to the disappointment of Wolsey), 42; description of his first entrance into Rome, 42 (see Note to 42/8–15).

Ægidius, Petrus [= Pieter Gillis, Peter Gil(l)es]: is painted in diptych with Erasmus, 136 (see Note to 136/14–19).

Æmilius, Paulus: 75 (see Note to 74/21–75/2).

Agis [IV], king of Sparta: called to account by the Lacedemonians, 152.

Agrippa, [Marcus Vipsanius]: 145.

Alban, St.: 217.

Alban, St., Day of: Fisher executed on, *R. F.* 242.

Alençon, Duchess of, sister to the King of France: devised by Wolsey as bride for Henry VIII, 43 (see Note to 43/8–9).

Alexander [III, "The Great," King of Macedonia]: 4 (see Note to 4/1–4).

Alice, Mistress, second wife of Sir Thomas More: is teased by More—"Madam, my Lord is gone," 66; receives letter from More regarding the loss of his barns, 67; a widow, and second wife of More, 93 (see Note to 93/13); More's education of her described, 93–4 (see Note to 94/3–4); her merry banter, 94; her vanity, 94; her indignation at More's lack of ambition, 94–5; visits More in the Tower, 95, 97; is not in sympathy with More's opposition to the King's wishes and his consequent imprisonment, 95–6.

Anne, Queen. See *Boleyn, Anne, Queen of Henry VIII of England.*

Answere to the . . . book which a namelesse heretyke [Tindale] *hath named the Souper of the Lorde.* See *More, Sir Thomas, works of.*

Answere unto Sir T. Mores Dialoge, Tindale's: 107.

Anthony, St., School of: More educated at, 10 (see Note to 10/18–19).

Antimorus, of Germanus Brixius: 101.

Antipodes: 103.

Antwerp: 103.

Apelles: 4 (see Note to 4/1–4), 102.

Apologye. See *More, Sir Thomas, works of.*

Apuldrefeles, family of: 5 (see Note to 5/4).

Aristides: 145.

Aristotle: Erasmus dedicates to young John More his edition of the works of, 19 (see Note to 19/13–15); his belief that there is no habitation under the Zodiac, 104.

Arthur, Prince [of Wales], brother of Henry, later Henry VIII, King of England: first husband of Katherine of Aragon, 47.

Arundel, [William Fitz Alan], Earl of: loses his case against Mistress Crocker, 154.

Aspasia: 80.

Assertion of the seven sacraments [*Assertio septem sacramentorum*]. See under *Henry VIII, King of England.*

Athenians: commonwealth of the, 102.

Athens: 145.

Attorney, Master [*i.e.* Sir Christopher Hales]: asserts that More's silence proves opposition, 185.

Audeley, [Sir Thomas], Lord Chancellor of England [1532–44]: succeeds More as Lord Chancellor, and explains More's resignation, 60 (**see Note to 60/18, etc.**); is given More's eight watermen, 143; one of the King's deputies before whom More is summoned in the case of the Nun of Canterbury, 157; one of those who persuade the King to put More out of the Parliament Bill, 164–5; one of the Commissioners appointed to tender the Oath of the Succession, 166; attempts to discover More's opinion on the Supremacy, 175; one of the Commissioners appointed to try More for treason, and his speeches at the trial, 183 ff.; stays his judgement, 192–3; accuses More of "stiffly sticking," 194–5; appeals for advice to the Lord Chief Justice, 196–7.

See also *R. F.*: the King commissions him to enquire into treasons, 236; one of the Commissioners at Fisher's trial, 237 (**see Note to 237/13–23**).

Augustine, St. [of Canterbury, died *c.* 607]: sent by Gregory to convert the English, 194; his holy bones taken up and burned, 215.

Augustine, St. [of Hippo; Aurelius Augustinus, b. 354, d. 430]: More "reads" in the Church of St. Lawrence the *De Civitate Dei* of, 13 (**see Note to 13/23–5**); More advises the King to consult the works of, 45; converted by his mother, Monica, 88; integrity in controversy of, 109.

Augustus, Emperor [of Rome]: 143.

Aunswere to Frithes Letter agaynst the blessed Sacrament of the aulter. See *More, Sir Thomas, works of.*

Axholme. See *Charterhouse of Axholme, Lincs.*

Baldwin, Sir John, Chief Justice of the Common Pleas: one of the Commissioners at Fisher's trial, *R. F.* 237.

Barking Church [*i.e.* All Hallows-Barking-by-the-Tower]: Fisher's body buried in the churchyard of, *R. F.* 246.

Barnes, Friar [Robert]: More confutes the Church of, 118–19; the Goodwife of the Bottle confutes, 119; disagreement between Tindale and, 120; More ridicules feigned holiness of, 121; in the *Apologye* More defends his conduct towards, 122–3, 125–7; More ridicules the "compendious eloquence" and "wonderful brevity" of the books of, 124–5.

Barns, More's: burnt down, 67.

Barrister: More made an utter, 15.

[Barton, Elizabeth], the Nun of Canterbury. See *Nun of Canterbury* [i.e. *Elizabeth Barton*].

Bassett, Master [James]: one of Queen Mary's Privy Chamber, and the second husband of [Mary], daughter of Margaret Roper, 83 (**see Note to 83/4–9**).

Bassett, Mistress [Mary]: daughter of William and Margaret Roper, married first to Master [Stephen] Clarke, then to Master

[James] Bassett, 83 (**see Note to 83/4–9**); her learned translations, particularly of the *Passionis Expositio* of More, 83 (**see Notes to 83/12–17, 18–20**), 107.

Bath, [John] Clarke, Bishop of [1523–41]: one of the learned men consulted on the divorce, 45; one of the Clergy who request More to accept reward for his controversial writings, 112; one of the Bishops who request More to accompany them to Anne's coronation, 148.

See also *R. F.*: one of Queen Katherine's Counsel, 221.

Beauvale. See *Charterhouse of Bevall, Notts.*

Bebelius: 19 (**see Note to 19/13–15**).

Beckenshawe, Master: a persecuted Roman Catholic relieved by Roper, 89 (**see Note to 79/1–3**).

Bedell, Thomas: Appendix III, Sir Thomas More's Indictment, 270.

Bevalde, Bevall. See *Charterhouse of Bevall, Notts.*

Blackfriars: commission for the trial of the King's marriage at, 46.

Boleyn, Anne, Queen of Henry VIII of England: her hatred of Wolsey, 44; More foretells the death of, 72 (**see Note to 72/13–18**); marries Henry VIII, 148; More refuses to attend the coronation of, 148; Henry VIII is exasperated against More by, 169.

See also *R. F.*: favours heretics, 223; persuades the King to put More and Fisher to death, 235.

Bonner, [Edmund], Dr.: sent by Henry to the Pope to treat with him concerning the divorce, *R. F.* 223 (**see Note to 223/18 ff.**)

Bonvisi, Antonio: More's friendship with, 137–8 (**see Note to 138/2–3**); More's letter to, 138; More and Cromwell are contrasted by, 138; reports More's victory over a foreign theologian, 138–9.

Brixius, Germanus [Germain de Brie]: his literary warfare with More—the anti-Brixius epigrams and *Antimorus*, 101 (**see Notes to 101/4–6, 101/7–8**).

Bucklersbury: More's house at, 19 (**see Note to 19/12**).

Budaeus, [Gulielmus], [Guillaume Budé]: believed the commonwealth of Utopia actually to exist, 103 (**see Note to 103/9**).

Bullen, Anne. See *Boleyn, Anne.*

Calvinists: 212.

Cambrai: More and Tunstall ambassadors at, 48 (**see Note to 48/18–19**).

See also Appendix IV, Epitaph, 279.

Cambridge: More declares to the Commons the judgment of the University of, 58; More's disputations with learned men of, 139; More attends the King on his progresses to, 140.

Campegius, [Laurentius], Cardinal: one of the Commissioners appointed to judge the divorce, 46, 47.

See also *R. F.*: one of the Commissioners appointed to judge the divorce, 221; given the Bishopric of Salisbury, 221 (**see Note to 221/9**).

(1) **Canterbury, William Warham, Archbishop of** [1503–32], **[Lord Chancellor of England,** 1504–15]: summons learned men of both Universities to dispute concerning the divorce, *R. F.* 221; one of Queen Katherine's Counsel, *R. F.* 221.

(2) **Canterbury, Thomas Cranmer, Archbishop of** [1533–56]: determines the matter of the marriage, 70, 148; More's conference on the marriage with, 151; one of the King's Deputies before whom More is summoned in the case of the Nun of Canterbury, 157; one

of the Commissioners appointed to tender the Oath of the Succession, 166; contends that More is bound to obey his Prince, 169; attempts to discover More's opinion on the Supremacy, 175.

See also *Morton, [John], Cardinal*; *Pole, Reginald, Cardinal.*

Canterbury, Nun of. See *Nun of Canterbury.*

Canterbury, Province of: fined by Henry VIII for recognising Wolsey as legate, 50.

[Carne, Edward]. See *Kerne, [Edward], Dr.*

Carthusians: martyrdom of the first two bands of, 179–80 (**see Notes to 229/29–230/14, 235–6**); first to die for the unity of the Catholic faith, 210.

See also *R. F.*: first band of three condemned to death, 229–30 (**see Note to 229/29–230/14**); second band of three brought before Cromwell, and imprisoned under cruel conditions in the Tower, 235–36 (**see Note**); and executed, 236 (**see Note to 236/21–2**); and their heads set upon London Bridge, 246.

Catherine, Queen. See *Katherine, Queen.*

Catiline, conspiracy of: 217.

Chain of Gold, More's: 170.

Chancellor of the Duchy of Lancaster: More made, 24; More writes his *Dialogue concernynge heresyes* when, 107.

Chancellor, Lord, of England. See *Morton, [John], Cardinal*; *Warham, William*; *Wolsey, [Thomas], Cardinal*; *More, Sir Thomas*; *Audeley, [Sir Thomas]*; *Rich, [Sir Richard]*; *Wriothesley, [Sir Thomas].*

Chancery: 53, 54.

Charles the Great, Emperor: 65 (**see Note to 64/29–65/1**).

Charles V, Emperor: More's oration before, 26 (**see Note to 26/7–9**); procures the election to the papacy of Cardinal Adrian [1522], and so incurs the anger of Wolsey, 42; nephew to Queen Katherine, 43; peace concluded between the Kings of England and France and, 48; pays tribute to More's wisdom, 205–6 (**see Note to 205/16–206/8**).

Charterhouse, of Axholme [Lincs]: martyrdom of the Prior [*i.e.* Augustine Webster] of, 179.

Charterhouse, of Bevall [Notts]: martyrdom of the Prior [*i.e.* Robert Laurence] of, 179.

Charterhouse, of London: More spends four years with the monks of the, 17 (**see Note to 17/11–15**); martyrdom of the Prior [*i.e.* John Houghton] and three other of the, 178–9 (**see Notes to 229/29–230/14, 235–6**).

Chelsea: Henry VIII visits More at his house at, 24 (**see Note to 24/27–26/3**); More sits to hear suits every afternoon in open hall at, 54; More's Sepulchre for himself and his wives at, 60; More sings in the Parish Church at, 64; More's New Building near his house at, 65. See also 160, 165.

See also Appendix IV, Epitaph on the More Tomb in Chelsea Old Church.

Christ, Jesus: extols the contemplative life, 18; an example of endurance, 75; betrayed by Judas, 111.

Cicero, [Marcus Tullius]: 143, 217.

Clarke, John. See *Bath, [John] Clarke, Bishop of.*

Clarke, Master [Stephen]: first husband of [Mary], daughter of William and Margaret Roper, 83 (**see Note to 83/4–9**).

Clement, [John], Dr.: marries [Margaret Gigs] the adopted daughter of Sir Thomas More, 90 (**see Note to 90/6–7**); More praises his virtue and learning to Erasmus, 90 (see Note to 90/17-20); he and his wife voluntary exiles for the Catholic faith, 91; his virtuous demeanour, 92.

Clement, Mistress [*i.e.* **Margaret Gigs**]: adopted child of Sir Thomas More, 90; marries Dr. John Clement, 90; her virtue, 90 (see Note to 90/6-7); her knowledge of medicine, 90-1 (see Note to 90/21—91/19); she and her husband voluntary exiles for the Catholic faith, 91; her virtuous demeanour, 92.

Clergy: More foresees the evils that would arise from oppressing the, 70-2; More falsely accused of partiality to the, 109-10; More falsely accused of receiving money from the, 109, 110-13; More feared by evil c., 110; More refuses reward from the, 111-13.

See also *R.F.*: the three Bills against the c., 222 (see Note to 222/27); the c. take the oath, 227.

Clerk, John. See *Bath, [John] Clarke, Bishop of.*

Clerks, the Six: 55 (see Note to 55/6).

Colet, Dr. [John], Dean of St. Paul's: praises More's wit, 208 (see Note to 208/7-10).

Colte, [Jane]: first wife of Sir Thomas More, 18 (see Note to 18/27-8); her children, 19, 92; More's education of, 92-3; early death of, 92.

Colte, Master [John]: gentleman of Essex, and father-in-law of Sir Thomas More, 18 (see Note to 18/27-8).

Commons. See *Parliament.*

Confutation of Tyndals Answere. See *More, Sir Thomas, works of.*

Conveyance of More's lands: 146-7 (see Note to 146/11-12).

Convocation: persuaded to acknowledge Henry's Supremacy only *Quantum per legem dei licet, R. F.* 223-5.

Corinthians: St. Paul's children in Christ, 194.

Cornelia: 81.

Cranmer, Thomas. See *Canterbury, Thomas Cranmer, Archbishop of.*

[Cresacre, Anne]. See *More, Mistress [Anne],* [i.e. *Anne Cresacre*].

Crocker, Mistress: More refuses money from, 154.

Cromwell, Sir [Richard]: conveys More to the Tower, 170 (see Note to 170/1-2).

Cromwell, Thomas, Master Secretary: Bonvisi contrasts More and, 138; More's advice to, 147; More's letters to, 152, 156; one of the King's Deputies before whom More is summoned in the case of the Nun of Canterbury, 157; More writes to the King of his letter concerning the Nun of Canterbury to, 161 (see Note to 161/21); tells Roper that More is put out of the Parliament Bill, 165; one of the Commissioners appointed to tender the Oath of the Succession, 166; attempts to discover More's opinion on the Supremacy, 175, and APPENDIX III (Sir Thomas More's Indictment) 270; threatens More that the King may compel him to state his opinion, 176-7; promises More the King's favour, 180.

See also *R. F.*: More's letter concerning the Nun to, 227; Fisher's servant accuses his master to, 228; intimidates the Jury at the trial of the first band of Carthusians and Reynolds, 230 (see Note to 229/29-230/14); second band of Carthusians brought before, 235 (see Note to 235-6); one of the King's Commissioners at Fisher's trial, 237.

Crooke, Master [John]: prepares

docket of More's injunctions, 55 (**see Note to 55/6**).

Cumberland, Henry [Clifford, first] Earl of: one of the Commissioners at Fisher's trial, *R. F.* **237.**

Cyprian, St. [Bishop of Carthage]: Margaret Roper emends a passage of, 81 (**see Note to 81/6–17**); sends gold to his executioner, 203.

Damianus: 209 (**see Note to 209/22–25**).

Damo: 81 (**see Note to 81/1**).

Dancie, William: marries Elizabeth More, 19 (**see Note to 19/15–17**).

David, King [of Israel]: 65.

Death: More's verses on, 181 (**see Note to 181/7–10**).

Debellacyon of Salem and Bizance. See *More, Sir Thomas, works of.*

De Captivitate Babylonica, Luther's: influence on Roper of, 85; Henry VIII's book against, 105.

De Civitate Dei, St. Augustine's: "read" by More in the Church of St. Lawrence, 13.

De Libertate Christiana, Luther's: influence on Roper of, 85.

Devil: More would see justice done to the, 53; likened by More to an ape, 76; spared Job's wife so that she might destroy her husband's patience, 98–9.

Dialog of Comfort against Tribulacyon. See *More, Sir Thomas, works of.*

Dialogue betwixte two Englishmen whereof one was called Salem and the other Bizance. See *St. German, Christopher.*

Dialogue concernynge heresyes and matters of religion. See *More, Sir Thomas, works of.*

Dinner, Wolsey's: 35–8.

Dionysius, [Bishop of Alexandria]: 214 (**see Note to 214/9–16**).

Dionysius Areopagita: Grocyn lectures on the books [*De Hierarchia Ecclesiastica*] of, 14.

Divorce Question, between Henry VIII and Queen Katherine: 41–9 (**see Notes to 41/2–4, 46/12–13, 46/20–23, 46/26–47/1**), 56–8, 70, 148.

See also *R. F.* 221–2 (**see Note to 221/10–13**), 223.

Divorce, Treatise on the, Harpsfield's: 213 (**see Note to 213/25–27**).

Dover: 214.

Draycott, Dr.: reports that Langland denied the rumour that he first suggested the divorce to the King, 41.

Durham, [Cuthbert] Tunstall, Bishop of [1530–52 and 1553–9]: one of the learned men consulted on the divorce, 45; on embassy with More at Cambrai, 48; one of those who request More to receive reward for his controversial writings, 112; one of those who request More to accompany them to Queen Anne's coronation, 148.

See also (1) *London, [Cuthbert] Tunstall, Bishop of.*

East Smithfield, Tower Hill: Fisher executed at, *R. F.* 243.

Edward VI, King of England: Master Bassett a refugee in the reign of, 83; Dr. Clement and his wife refugees in the reign of, 91.

Eleutherus, Pope: 209 (**see Note to 209/22–25**).

Eliphas: 153.

Ely, Nicholas West, Bishop of [1515–33]: one of Queen Katherine's counsel, *R. F.* 221.

Elyot, Sir Thomas: told of More's martyrdom by Charles the Emperor, 205–6 (**see Note to 205/16–206/8**).

Embassies, More's: for the English merchants, 20–22 (**see Notes to 20/23—21/3, 21/8 ff., 21/19 ff.**); with Wolsey in Flanders

and France, 39; with Tunstall at Cambrai, 48.
Emperor, the. See *Charles V, Emperor.*
Epaminondas: 145.
Epigrammata. See *More, Sir Thomas, works of.*
Epistola ad G. Brixium. See *More, Sir Thomas, works of.*
Epistola contra J. Pomeranum. See *More, Sir Thomas, works of.*
Epitaph, More's: written for his tomb in Chelsea [Old] Church, 60; censured by More's enemies and defended by Harpsfield, 60–1.
See Appendix IV.
Erasmus, [Desiderius]: dedicates to young John More his edition of Aristotle's works, 19 (**see Note to 19/13–15**); praises the Latin letters of More's children, 78 (**see Note to 77/23—78/9**); praises Roper, 80; calls Margaret "flower of all the learned matrons in England," 80 (**see Note to 80/20–23**); dedicates to Margaret Roper his Commentary on [the Christmas Hymn of] Prudentius, 80 (**see Note to 80/23–5**); More praises Dr. Clement to, 90 (**see Note to 90/17–20**); acts as peacemaker in the More–Brixius controversy, 101 (**see Note to 101/7–8**); not so willing as More to retract anything he had wrongly written, 109 (**see Note to 109/1–3**); painted with Ægidius by Quentin Metsys, 136 (**see Note to 136/14–19**); delights in More's company, 136; praises More's wit, 208 (**see Note to 208/21–4**).
Esaias: 135.
Eusebius: Mistress [Mary] Bassett translates the *Ecclesiastical History* of, 83.
Eustochium: 81 (**see Note to 81/3–4**).
Evagrius: his *Ecclesiastical History* translated by Mistress [Mary] Bassett, 83.
Eve: 98.
Exame. See *Charterhouse of Axholme, Lincs.*
Exeter, [John] Vesey, Veysey *or* **Voysey, Bishop of** [1519–51 and 1553–4]: one of those who request More to accept reward for his controversial writings, 112.
Exmew, William, Carthusian: condemned and executed, *R. F.* 235–6 (**see Note**).

Fabiola: 81 (**see Note to 81/3–4**).
Fabritius: 152.
Feron, [Robert]: earns his pardon by accusing John Hall of denying the King's Supremacy, *R. F.* 229 (**see Note to 179/4**).
Fetherston, John: one of Queen Katherine's Counsel, *R. F.* 221.
Fineux, Sir John: 5 (**see Note to 5/8**).
First-fruits: Parliament passes Act concerning, *R. F.* 229.
Fish, Simon: his *Supplycacyon of Beggars*, 122.
Fisher, John. See *Rochester, John Fisher, Bishop of.*
Fitz-Herbert, Sir Anthony, Justice: one of the Commissioners at Fisher's trial, *R. F.* 237.
Fitz-James, Sir John, Lord Chief Justice: appealed to by the Lord Chancellor at More's trial, 196–7.
See also *R. F.*: one of the Commissioners at Fisher's trial, 237.
Flanders: More and Wolsey ambassadors in, 39; evils arising from the spread of Lutheran doctrines in, 71–2; Master Bassett a refugee in, 83.
Fleet: Bishop Stokesley sent by Wolsey to the, 49 (**see Note to 49/16–18**).
Fortune: More's verses on flattering, 180.
Fox, Master [Edward], the King's Almoner, [Provost of King's College, Cambridge, and later Bishop of Hereford]: More is desired to commune with him

on the marriage, 48 (see Note to 48/8).

Fox, Dr. [Richard]. See *Winchester, Dr. [Richard] Fox, Bishop of.*

France: More and Wolsey ambassadors in, 39; evils arising from the spread of Lutheran doctrines in, 71–2.

Frappe, Friar: his Christmas mumming, 122.

French king, the [*i.e.* Francis I]: Wolsey tries to arrange a marriage between Henry VIII and the sister of, 43; concludes a peace with Henry VIII and Charles the Emperor at Cambrai, 48.

Friday: devoted by More to spiritual exercises, 65.

Frith, John: More's *Aunswere* (*Letter*) to, 122, 131; More defends in the *Apologye* his conduct towards, 125–7; his *Answere* to More's *Letter*, 131.

Fugatius: 209 (see Note to 209/22–5).

Furnivall's Inn: More Reader at, 14 (see Note to 14/17).

Furred tippet: on his way to execution, Fisher insists on wearing his, *R. F.* 243.

Galen: Mistress Clement shows More the *De differentiis febrium* of, 91.

Gardiner, German: martyr for the unity of the Holy Catholic Church, 212 (see Note to 212/23–4).

Gardiner, [Stephen]. See *Winchester, [Stephen] Gardiner, Bishop of.*

[Gigs, Margaret]. See *Clement, Mistress.*

[Gil(l)es, Peter]. See *Ægidius, Petrus.*

Goodwife of the Bottle: confutes Friar Barnes, 119.

Gregory [I], St., Pope: sends Augustine to convert the English, 194.

Gresham, Master: More's exchange of cups with, 154.

Grocyn, [William]: one of Sir T. More's audience, 14; "reads" in London the works of Dionysius Areopagita, 14 (see Note to 14/4–7); one of More's teachers in Greek, 14 (see Note to 12/15–16).

Hall, John, vicar of Thistilworth [*i.e.* Iselworth]: execution of, 179 (see Note to 179/4).
See also *R. F.* 229.

Hampton Court: Wolsey's Palace at, 33; the King consults More on the divorce at, 47.

Haneworth: Queen Anne's banquet at, *R. F.* 235 (see Note to 235/20–21).

Hannibal: More's story concerning Phormio and, 26 (see Note to 26/19 ff.).

Harris, John: 91–2 (see Note to 91/27).

Health, More's: 58, 59 (see Note to 59/7–9), 142, 175.

Henry, Emperor: 15.

Henry I, King of England: 15.

Henry II, King of England: recognised St. Thomas of Canterbury as a martyr, 215 (see Note to 215/4–5).

Henry VII, King of England: More incurs the hostility of, 15 (see Notes to 15/15–16, 15/21 ff.); death of, 17.
See also *R. F.*: makes Fisher Bishop of Rochester, 249.

Henry VIII, King of England: his counsel to More on entering the Royal service, 23–4; his love of More, 24, 136–7; visits More at Chelsea, 24–5 (see Note to 24/27—26/3); excuses More from the proposed embassy to Spain, 34 (see Note to 33/19–22); consults More on the divorce, 44–6 (see Note to 44/17–18), 47–8, 48–9, 56–7; peace concluded between the Emperor, the French King and, 48; displaces Wolsey from the Chancellorship, and appoints More, 49; More likens the King to a shepherd, 58 (**see Note to 58/18 ff.**); promises More the continuance of his favour, 61–2; Brixius strives to bring More into discredit with, 101; his Book (i.e. *Assertio septem sacramentorum*) against Luther, 105 (**see Note to 105/21–3 ff.**), 158–60; Erasmus and, 136; employs More to answer orations, 139–40; More's lands seized by, 146–7 (**see Note to 146/11–12**); professes to take in good part More's view of the marriage, 151; Fisher advises the Nun of Canterbury to go to, 155–6; hopes to use More's attainder in the case of the Nun to win his consent to the marriage, 157; his undue stressing of the Pope's authority, 158–60; More's letter concerning the Parliament Bill to, 161–4 (**see Note to 161/21**); highly offended with More, 164; exasperated by Anne against More, 169; recognised by Parliament as Head of the Church, 174 (**see Note to 174/20–25**), and APPENDIX III, 269; More prays for, 197; sends Master Pope to warn More that he is to die that day, and commands More not to use many words at his execution, 201–2; "cuts off St. Peter's head and puts it upon his own shoulders," 217. See also *Divorce Question* and *Wolsey*.

See also *R. F.*: angered by More's refusal of the Chancellorship and his attitude to the marriage, 222; packs the 1529 Parliament, 222 (**see Note to 196/6–7**); angered by Fisher's opposition to the Bills against the Clergy, 222; is moved to repress heresies, but later favours the heretics, 223 (**see Note to 223/8**); attempts to make Convocation acknowledge his Supremacy, 223–5 (**see Note to 223/31, etc.**); obtains from Parliament unqualified consent to his Supremacy, 225; causes Fisher and More to be attainted in the case of the Nun, 227; More's letter concerning the Nun to, 227; causes the Bishops to surrender their Bulls in exchange for his Letters Patent, 227 (**see Note to 227/21**); is authorised to make Bishops suffragan, 228; sends messenger to entrap Fisher into stating his opinion on the Supremacy, 233–4; angered by Fisher's being made Cardinal, 235 (**see Note to 235/18–19**); promises Anne to put More and Fisher to death, 235; sends physicians to Fisher, 236 (**see Note to 236/26–27**); commutes Fisher's sentence to beheading, 241 (**see Note to 241/12–13 ff.**).

Heron, Giles: marries Cicely More, 19 (**see Note to 19/15–17**); More issues a decree against, 53 (**see Note to 53/24–8**).

Herveus [= Hervé de Porzmoguer]: 101 (**see Note to 101/9–11**).

Hithlodius: 103, 105.

[Holy Maid of Kent]. See *Nun of Canterbury* [i.e. *Elizabeth Barton*].

Houghton, John, Prior [of the Charterhouse of London]: condemned and executed, 178–9; speaks on behalf of the first band of Carthusians, *R. F.* 229 (**see Note to 229/29–230/14**).

"Hungarian, an": pseudonym of More, 134.

Hungerford, Sir Walter: one of the Jury at Fisher's trial, *R. F.* 237 (**see Note to 237/33 ff.**).

Hypathia [Hypatia]: 81.

Indictment, Sir Thomas More's: 183. See APPENDIX III.

Injunctions: More defends his, 54–6.

James [IV], King of Scotland: marries Margaret, daughter of Henry VII, King of England, 14.

Jerome, St.: More advises the King to consult the works of, 45; his copy of the learned martyr Lucian, 134–5.

Job: 61, 153.

Job's wife: 98, 99.

John the Baptist, St., Eve of Nativity of: Fisher executed on, *R. F.* 242.

Judas: 111.

Jury: (1) for More's trial, 192 (**see Note to 192**/24–5). (2) for Fisher's trial, *R. F.* 237–8.

Katherine, Queen, daughter of Ferdinand of Spain, and wife, first to Prince Arthur, and after to Prince Henry, sons of Henry VII of England: her delight in More's company, 137. See also *Divorce Question.*

See also *R. F.*: is reported willing to consent to a divorce, 221; her defendants in the Divorce Question, 221 (**see Note to 221**/19, **etc.**).

[Kent, Holy Maid of]. See *Nun of Canterbury* [i.e. *Elizabeth Barton*].

Kerne, [Edward], Dr.: sent by Henry to the Pope to treat with him concerning the divorce, *R. F.* 223 (**see Note to 223**/18 **ff.**).

King's Bench, Court of the: 54.

"King's Book, the" [i.e. *Assertio septem sacramentorum*]: against Luther, stressing the Pope's authority, 105 (**see Note to 105**/21–3), 158–60.

Kingston, Sir William, Constable of the Tower: conveys More back to the Tower after his trial, and sorrows for him, 197–8; praises More's fortitude, 200.

Lacedemonians: commonwealth of the, 102.

Lactantius, [Lucius Caecilius Firmianus]: 104.

Lambeth: More summoned to take the Oath at, 166.

See also *R. F.*: learned men from both Universities summoned to discuss the divorce at, 221.

Langland, [John]. See *Lincoln, [John] Langland, Bishop of.*

Lawrence, St., Church of: More "reads" the *De Civitate Dei* in the, 13–14.

Letters, More's. See *More, Sir Thomas, works of.*

Licurgus: 105.

Life of King Richard the Third. See *More, Sir Thomas, works of.*

Life of Pico della Mirandula. See *More, Sir Thomas, works of.*

Lincoln, [John] Langland, Bishop of [1520–47]: urged by Wolsey to question the lawfulness of Henry VIII's marriage to Queen Katherine, 41 (**see Note to 41**/21).

Lincoln's Inn: More admitted to, 13 (**see Note to 13**/2–12); approves More's readership at Furnivall's Inn, 14; after his marriage, More continues his studies at, 19 (**see Note to 19**/8–9); More and his father meet at readings at, 54; the fare of, 144.

London: More born in, 9 (**see Note to 9**/7–8); More educated at St. Anthony's School in, 10 (**see Note to 10**/18–19); More lectures at the Church of St. Lawrence in, 13; More's lectures attended by the best learned men in, 14; More spends four years with the monks of the Charterhouse of, 17 (**see Note to 17**/11–15); More's home at Bucklersbury in, 19; More's popularity, and office of Under-sheriff in, 19–20 (**see Notes to 19**/22—**20**/2, **20**/1); More will not accept the King's pension for fear of displeasing the citizens of, 22; More's oration before Charles V on his visit to, 26; the Commissioners sit to judge the divorce at Blackfriars in, 46; Stokesley appointed to the Bishopric of, 49; the Water-bailiff of, 73 (see Note to 73/6); Clement taken by More from St. Paul's School in, 90.

(1) **London, [Cuthbert] Tunstall, Bishop of** [1522–30]: ambassador with More at Cambrai, 48 (see Note to 48/18–19).
See also *R. F.*: one of Queen Katherine's Counsel, 221.
See also *Durham, [Cuthbert] Tunstall, Bishop of.*

(2) **London, [John] Stokesley, Bishop of** [1530–39]: his conference on the marriage with More, and his report of More to the King, 49; his revenge against Wolsey, 49 (see Note to 49/16–18).

London Bridge: More's head set upon, 217, *R. F.* 247.
See also *R. F.*: Fisher's head set upon, 246–7.

Longland, [John]. See *Langland, [John].*

Lord, Our. See *Christ, Jesus.*

Lord Chancellor of England. See under *Morton, [John], Cardinal*; *Warham, William*; *Wolsey, [Thomas], Cardinal*; *More, Sir Thomas*; *Audeley, [Sir Thomas]*; *Rich, [Sir Richard]*; *Wriothesley, [Sir Thomas].*

Lucian: the Martyr, 134.

Lucius, King of Britain: said by Harpsfield to have received first the Christian faith in Britain, 209 (see Note to 209/22–5).

Luke, Sir Walter, Justice: one of the Commissioners at Fisher's trial, *R. F.* 237.

Lupset, Thomas: one of More's fellow-students in Greek, 14 (see Note to 12/15–16).

Luther, Martin: More foretells the evils that would follow from the introduction into England of the Testament and doctrines of, 71; Roper is enticed into heresy by the books of, 85; Roper considers that salvation is ensured by reading the Bible of, 87; his controversy with Henry VIII and More, 105–6 (see Note to 105/21–3 ff.), 158–60; John Pomerane one of the disciples of, 107; the mistranslations of, 114; More ridicules the feigned holiness of, 121.

Lutherans: 211, 212.

Lysippus: 4.

Lyster, Sir Richard, Chief Baron of the Exchequer: one of the Commissioners at Fisher's trial, *R. F.* 237.

Maniche: St. Augustine nine years a, 88.

Marcella: 81 (see Note to 81/3–4).

Margaret, Lady, Countess of Richmond and Derby: Fisher chaplain to, *R. F.* 249; endows two Cambridge Colleges at Fisher's persuasion, *R. F.* 251.

Margaret [Tudor]: eldest daughter of Henry VII of England, marries James [IV] of Scotland, 14.

Margaret More (later **Roper**). See *Roper, Margaret.*

Marney, Lord [John]: 32 (see Note to 32/14).

Martyrdom. See under *Carthusians*; *Fisher*; *Hall*; *Reynolds*; *More, Sir Thomas*; *Gardiner, German.*

Mary, Queen of England: Master Bassett one of the Privy Chamber of, 83; England restored to the unity of the Catholic faith under, 218.

Master of Requests: More made, 24 (see Note to 24/6–7).

Maud, the Empress, daughter of Henry I, King of England: marries the Emperor Henry, 15.

Merchants: More's embassies in the interests of the English, 20–22 (see Notes to 20/23–21/3, 21/19 ff.); of the Stillyard, 21 (see

Note to 20/23–21/3), 86; the Water-bailiff of London angered by hearing the railing against Sir T. More of certain, 73; Roper is convented of heresy before Wolsey along with certain, 86.

Middlemore, Humphrey, Carthusian: condemned and executed, *R. F.* 235–6 (see Note).

Middleton, Alice (later **More**). See *Alice, Mistress, second wife of Sir T. More.*

Monica: mother of St. Augustine, 88.

More, Lady Alice. See *Alice, Mistress, second wife of Sir T. More.*

More, Mistress [Anne], [*i.e.* Anne Cresacre, later wife of John More]: laughs at More's shirt of hair, 65–6 (see Note to 66/2–3).

More, Cicely, daughter of Sir T. More: marries Giles Heron, 19 (see Note to 19/15–17).

More, Elizabeth, daughter of Sir T. More: marries William Dancie, 19 (see Note to 19/15–17).

More, Jane. See *Colte* [*Jane*].

More, Sir John, father of Sir T. More: Justice and Knight, 9 (see Note to 9/9); virtues and wit of, 9–10 (see Notes to 9/17 ff., 9/19–23, 10/2); long and healthy life, 10 (see Note to 10/6–7); Sir T. More's courtesy to, and love for, 54; death of, 10, 54.

More, John, son of Sir T. More: birth of, 19; Erasmus dedicates his edition of Aristotle's works to, 19 (see Note to 19/13–15).

More, Margaret. See *Roper, Margaret.*

More, Sir Thomas, Lord Chancellor of England [1529–32]:

I. Early Life, 9–19.

Birth (see Note to 9/6) and birthplace, London, 9 (see Note to 9/7–8); parentage, 9–10 (see Notes to 10/15, 10/16); at St. Anthony's School, 10 (see Note to 10/18–19); in household of Cardinal Morton, 10–11; his impromptu acting, 11 (see Note to 11/2–3); sent to Oxford, 12 (see Notes to 12/13, 15–16); studies for the Bar, 12–13; made an utter barrister, 13; lectures on *De civitate Dei* of St. Augustine, 13–14 (see Note to 13/23–25); Reader at Furnivall's Inn, 14; made burgess of Parliament, 14; incurs hostility of Henry VII by opposing subsidy, 15–17 (see Notes to 15/15–16, 15/21 ff.); four years without vow with the monks of the Charterhouse of London, 17 (see Note to 17/11–15); marries Mistress [Jane] Colte, 18; continues his study of the law, 19 (see Note to 19/8–9); their children, 19 (see Notes to 19/13–15, 19/15–17).

I, contd. Public Life to resignation of Chancellorship, 19–62.

An Under-Sheriff of London, 20 (see Notes to 19/22—20/2, 20/1); his income therefrom, 20; embassies for English merchants, 20–22 (see Notes to 20/23—21/3, 21/8 ff., 21/19 ff.); refuses the King's pension, 22 (see Note to 22/8–21); case of Pope's ship, 23; the King's "notable and woorthye lesson," 23–4 (see Note to 23/30); his public offices, 24 (see Notes); made Lord Chancellor, 24, 49, 50–51 (see Notes to 50/25–6, 50/26—51/1; also Note to 191/17–19); oration before Charles V, 26 (see Note to 26/7–9); chosen Speaker, and his Speech to the King, 26–31 (see Note to 27/13–14 ff.); defends liberties of the Commons against Wolsey, 31–33 (see Note to 31/12 ff.); defeats Wolsey's plot to send him to Spain (see Note to 33/19–22); embassies with Wolsey to Flanders and France, 39; consulted by the King on the divorce question, 44–6 (see Note to 44/17–18), 47–8,

48–9, 56–7; embassy with Wolsey [to Amiens], 47; embassy with Tunstall to Cambrai, 48 (**see Note to 48/18–19**), *R. F.* 279; his incorruptibility and justice, 52–4 (**see Note to 53/8**); reverence and love for his father, 54; defends his injunctions, 54–6; his charity, 56; gives message to the Commons concerning the divorce, 58; pleads to be discharged from the Chancellorship, 58; oration comparing the King to a Shepherd, 58–9 (**see Note to 58/18 ff.**); ill-health, 59 (**see Note to 59/7–9**); More and his Epitaph are slandered by his enemies, though Norfolk and Audeley had explained his resignation (**see Note to 60/7, etc.**); he is also defended by Harpsfield, 59–62 (**see Note to 59/25, etc.**). See also APPENDIX IV, Epitaph.

II. "*Private, secrete and domesticall life and trade,*" 63–99.

Piety and austerity of life, 64–6; shirt of hair, 65–6 (**see Note to 65/22–3**); freedom from worldly ambition, 66 (**see Note to 66/7–9**); fortitude and compassion, 66–7; foresight, 67–72 (**see Note to 72/13–18**); tolerance of slander (*e.g.* as reported by Water-bailiff), 72–3; makes the best of everything, 73 (**see Note to 73/25–9**); friendliness, 74 (**see Note to 74/4–5**); ready wit, 74–5; pious exercises and counsels, 75–7; never in a fume, 76; prepares his family for his suffering and death, 77; the learning and virtue of his children, particularly of Margaret, 77–81 (**see Note to 77/23—78/9**); at his prayer Margaret recovers from the sweating sickness, 81–3; at his prayer Roper is brought back to the Catholic faith, 87–8; education of his first and second wives, 92–4; conversations with Lady More, 94–8.

III. *Books*, 100–135.

Latin works, 100–7; English works, 107–35; integrity and justice in controversy, 108–9 (**see Notes to 108/12–18, 26–7**); disinterestedness in controversial writings, 109–11; refuses reward from the Clergy, 111–13; exposes mistranslations of Tindale, 114–15; exposes Tindale's false doctrines, 115–16; his statements concerning the Church and the written Gospel perverted by Tindale, 116–17; defence of the Holy Catholic Church, 117; routs Tindale, 117–18; confutes Friar Barnes, 118–19; ridicules feigned holiness of Tindale and Barnes, 121–2; answer to Simon Fish, 122; and to John Frith, 122, 131; defence in the *Apologye* of his conduct towards the heretics, 122–7; exposes "the Pacifier," 127–31; controversy with Frith and Tindale, 131–2; prepares Englishmen for the religious troubles to come, 133–4; patience in tribulation, 135.

See also *More, Sir Thomas, works of.*

IV. *Friends, fame and learning; appearance and habits*, 136–42.

Reputation abroad as scholar, 136; verses about diptych of Erasmus and Petrus Ægidius, 136 (**see Note to 136/14–19**); his friendship with Erasmus, Henry VIII, Queen Katherine and Bonvisi, 136–8; contrasted with Cromwell, 138; disputations with learned men, 138–9; *ex tempore* answers to orations, 139–40; wit, memory, economy of time, 140; appearance and habits, 141–2 (**see Textual Notes to 141/6–7, 10–11, 14–15**); interest in animals, 142.

V. *Life after resignation of the Great Seal; trial, and martyrdom*; 143–204.

Gladly resigns the Great Seal,

143; discusses economies with his family, 143–4; poverty after his resignation, 145–6; arranges for the conveyance of his lands at his death, 146–7 (**see Note to 146**/11–12); advice to Cromwell, 147; refuses to be present at Anne's coronation, but accepts the Bishops' money for a gown, 148; by the parable of the offending virgin he warns the Bishops, 149–50; meddles in no wise with the marriage and withholds his opinion thereon, 150–52 (**see Note to 151**/21, **etc.**); innocent of writing against the Articles put forth by the King and his Council, 152; accused of bribery and extortion, 152–5; his attainder for misprision of treason in the matter of the Nun of Canterbury, and his attitude thereat, 156–60; not responsible for "the King's book" against Luther, or the stressing therein of the Pope's authority, 158–60; rejoices at giving the devil a foul fall, 160–1; letter to the King concerning the Parliament Bill, 161–4 (**see Note to 161**/21); put out of the Parliament Bill, 165 (**see Note to 165**/12–13); foretells Norfolk's disgrace, 165; summoned to Lambeth to take the Oath of Succession, 166; his pious exercises before departure, 166; his conscience conquers natural affection, 166; refuses the Oath, 167–8; accused of obstinacy, 168–9; bound to obey his conscience rather than his Prince, 169; in custody at Westminster, 169; sent to the Tower, 169; his chain of gold, 169–70; the Porter's demand, 170; instructions to John a Wood, 170; letters to Margaret, 170; visited by Margaret, 171; rejoices at his leisure for godly meditation, 171–2; trusts his family to God, 171; gladly suffers for conscience sake 172–3; content with the Lieutenant's poor cheer, 173; after the Act of Supremacy and Treason, his imprisonment becomes harder, 173–4; his health becomes worse, 175; when examined in the Tower, he withholds his opinion on the Supremacy, 175–8, Appendix III (Sir Thomas More's Indictment) 270–1, 273–4; threat to compel him to answer, 176; differentiates a law accepted by Christendom from a mere local law, 176–7; taunted with cowardice, 177–8; had not done or said anything to justify his sufferings, 178; envies the martyrs going gladly to execution, 179–80; not deceived by Cromwell's promises, 180; verses on Fortune, 180; and on Death, 181 (**see Note to 181**/7–10); his books are taken from him, 181–2; Rich tries to entrap him, 182–3; indicted of treason, 183; the trial and condemnation, 183–97 (**see Notes to 183–200, 192**/24–5); accused of treasonable correspondence with Fisher, 186–8; prays for his judges and the King, 197; comforts Kingston and Margaret, 197–8; farewell to Margaret, 198–9; is compared with Socrates, 199; his fortitude, 200; sends his hair-shirt and a letter to Margaret (**see Note to 65**/22–3), 200–1; Pope brings word that he is to die that day, 201 (**see Note to 200**/18–19; **201**/9–10); receives the news gladly, 201; is beholden to the King's "gracious consideration," 202; comforts Pope, 202; prevented from wearing his best apparel for his execution, 203; sends gold to his executioner, 203; refers the importunate woman to the mercy of the King, 203 (**see Note to 203**/17–18); jests on the weakness of the scaffold, 204; prayer at the scaffold, 204.

VI. *Reflections of Harpsfield upon More's martyrdom*, 205–18.

Charles the Fifth pays tribute to his wisdom, 205–6 (**see Note to 205/16–206/8**); his valour against the heretics, 206–8; Colet and Erasmus praise his wit, 208 (**see Notes to 208/7–10, and 208/21–4**); first layman in England that died for the unity of the Church, 209, 211, 212–13; justification of his view on the marriage, 213 (**see Note to 213/12–20**); compared with St. Thomas of Dover and St. Thomas of Canterbury, 214–17; his head set upon London Bridge, 217; intercedes for us in Heaven, 217–18.

See also APPENDIX III, Sir Thomas More's Indictment; and APPENDIX II, Paris News Letter, describing More's Trial.

See also *R. F.*: angers Henry by refusing the Chancellorship and by his attitude to the divorce, 222; urges the King to repress heresies, 223; is put out of the Parliament Bill, 227; his letters to Cromwell and the King concerning the Nun, 227; refuses the Oath and is sent to the Tower, 227–8; Act against, 228; the King promises Anne that he shall be put to death, 235; his head set upon London Bridge, 247.

More, Sir Thomas, works of:

Answere to the . . . book which a namelesse heretyke [Tindale] *hath named the Souper of the Lorde:* 131–2.

Apologye: 122–7 (**see Note to 122/21–2**).

Aunswere to Frithes Letter agaynst the blessed Sacrament of the aulter: 122.

Confutation of Tyndals Answere, More's "Replye" to Tindale: 108.
Second Parte: 119.

Debellacyon of Salem and Bizance: 108, 127–8.

Dialog of Comfort against Tribulacyon: 132–4.

Dialogue concernynge heresyes and matters of religion: 107.

Epigrammata: 100–1 (**see Notes to 101/4–6, 101/7–8**).

Epistola ad G. Brixium, More's "Answer" to Brixius's *Antimorus:* 101.

Epistola contra J. Pomeranum: 107 (**see Note to 107/2–3**).

Letters: to Lady Alice concerning the barns, 67; to Antonio Bonvisi, 138; to Cromwell, 152; to the King, 161–4; to Margaret, 170, 200.

Life of King Richard the Third: 102 (**see Note to 102/6–17**).

Life of Pico della Mirandula: 107 (**see Note to 107/13–14**).

Passionis Expositio, More's "exposition in Latin upon the Passion of Christ": 83, 107.

Responsio ad Lutherum, More's "Replye" to Luther's *Contra Henricum Regem Angliae:* 106.

Supplycacyon of Soulys: 122.

Treatise to receyue the Blyssed Body of our Lorde sacramentally and virtually bothe: 132.

Treatise upon the Passion: 132, 134.

Utopia: 102–5.

Verses: on the diptych of Erasmus and Peter Giles, 136 (**see Note to 136/14–19**); on flattering Fortune, 180; on Death, 181 (**see Note to 181/7–10**).

See also APPENDIX IV, Epitaph, for Latin verses on the More tomb.

Morton, [John], Cardinal, [Lord Chancellor of England, 1487–1500], **[Archbishop of Canterbury,** 1486–1500]: More in the household of, 10–11; More's great future predicted by, 11; More sent to Oxford by, 12; comes into *Utopia*, 105.

New Building, More's: used for pious exercises, 65; petition for the recovery of Margaret at, 82.

New Inn: More studies at, 12 (**see Note to 12**/*26*); fare of, 144.

Newdigate, Sebastian, Carthusian: condemned and executed, *R. F.* 235–6 (**see Note**).

Newgate: certain Carthusians die through imprisonment in, 179.

Nicholas, [de Burgo], Dr., the Austin friar: More confers on the King's marriage with, 151 (**see Note to 151**/*2*).

Norfolk, [Thomas Howard, 2nd Earl of Surrey], [3rd] Duke of: praises More when made Chancellor, 48, 51; More makes suit to the Duke for discharge from the Chancellorship, 58; declares the truth as to More's resignation from the Chancellorship, 60 (**see Note to 60**/*7*, **etc.**); censures More for acting as a parish clerk, 64; one of the King's Deputies before whom More is summoned for the matter of the Nun of Canterbury, 157; warns More that *Indignatio principis mors est,* 165; one of the Commissioners appointed to try More for treason, 183 ff.; perceives More is "maliciously bent," 196.

Numa Pompilius: 105.

Nun of Canterbury [*i.e.* Elizabeth Barton]: the matter of the, 155–7 (**see Note to 156**/*26*); More's letter to the King concerning his attainder in the case of the, 161–4 (**see Note to 161**/*21*).

See also *R. F.*: Fisher and More attainted in the case of, 227.

Oath of the Succession, the: More refuses, 166–9; Fisher and Wilson refuse, 168.

See also *R. F.*: the clergy take, 227; More, Fisher, and Wilson refuse, 227; passed by Parliament, 228 (**see Note to 228**/*24–7*).

Old Swan: 198.

Oxford: More sent to, 12 (**see Note to 12**/*13*); More declares to the Commons the judgement of the University concerning the divorce, 58; fare of, 144 (**see Note to 144**/*13*). See also 139, 140.

"Pacifer, the." See *St. German, Christopher.*

Palmer, Master [John]: servant to Cromwell, sent to take away More's books, 182 (**see Note to 181**/*27*—**182**/*1*); professes he paid no heed to the conversation between More and Rich, 192.

Paludanus, Johannes [**John Desmarais**]: believed the Commonwealth of Utopia actually to exist, and wished to convert the inhabitants to Christianity, 103 (**see Note to 103**/*9–10*).

Paradise: 98.

Paris News Letter. See APPENDIX II.

Parliament and **Lower House of the Parliament (Commons):** More burgess of, 14; More opposes the subsidy demanded by Henry VII from, 14–15; More chosen Speaker of, 26; More pleads toleration for himself and freedom of speech for, 27–31; Wolsey's visit to, and More's defence of the liberties of, 31–3 (**see Note to 31**/*12* **ff.**); More declares the judgement of the Universities concerning the divorce to, 58; More's oration before, 58 (**see Note to 58**/*18* **ff.**); recognises the King's Supremacy, 174 (**see Note to 174**/*20–25*); More's reference to the corrupt, 196 (**see Note to 196**/*6–7*).

See also *R. F.*: the King packs the 1529 P., 222; three Bills against the Clergy passed by, 222 (**see Note to 222**/*21*); six unlawful Acts of, 228–9 (**see Note to 228**/*15*).

Parnell, Master [John]: More's decree against, 153 (**see Note to 153/7–8**).
Parrhasius: 104.
Passionis Expositio. See *More, Sir Thomas, works of.*
Paul, St.: mistranslation in the Latin Epistle of, 114; the Corinthians the children in Christ of, 194; More refers at his trial to the presence at the death of St. Stephen of, 197.
Paula: 81 (**see Note to 81/3–4**).
Paulet, Sir William: one of the Commissioners at Fisher's trial, *R. F.* 237 (**see Note to 237/13–23**).
Paul's Cross: Roper eager to preach at, 84; Roper considers himself better able to preach than the best preacher at, 86; merchants abjure at, 86.
Paul's School: Clement taken by More from, 90.
Peter, St.: the spiritual preeminence of, 193; England the first country to deny supremacy to, 210; Henry VIII "cuts off, and (an ugly sight to behold) puts on his own shoulders, the head of," 217.
Peter, St., Utas of: day of More's execution, 201.
Phormio: More's story of Hannibal and, 26 (**see Note to 26/19 ff.**).
Pico della Mirandula, Life of. See *More, Sir Thomas, works of.*
Plato: More's household likened to the Academy of, 92 (**see Note to 92/6–17**); the commonwealth of, 105.
Pole, Reginald, Cardinal, [Archbishop of Canterbury, 1556–8]: England restored to the unity of the Catholic faith under, 218.
Pomerane, John [*i.e.* John Bugenhagen, a Pomeranian]: 107.
Pompey, the Great: 143.
(1) **Pope [Leo X,** 1513–21]: case of the ship of, 23; Henry VIII in his *Assertio septem sacramentorum* unduly stressed the authority of the, 158–60.
(2) **Pope [Adrian VI,** 1522–3]: elected (to the disappointment of Wolsey), 42 (**see Note to 42/8–15**).
(3) **Pope [Clement VII,** 1523–34]. See *Divorce Question.*
(4) **Pope [Paul III,** 1534–49]: Parliament makes Henry VIII Supreme Head of the Church of England, and disowns the Supremacy of the, 174.
See also *R. F.*: creates Fisher Cardinal, 235, 249.
Pope, Sir Thomas: sent by the King to prepare More for death, and his sorrow therefor, 201–2 (**see Note to 201/13**).
Port, Sir John, Justice: one of the Commissioners at Fisher's trial, *R. F.* 237.
Porter of the Tower. See *Tower of London, Porter of the.*
Powell, [Edward]: one of Queen Katherine's Counsel, *R. F.* 221.
Praemunire, Statute of: Wolsey condemned under the Statute of, 50.
Privy Councillor: More made, 24.
Protestants: More's justice in controversy with the, 108; More's attitude to the marriage considered folly by the, 213.
Prudentius: Erasmus dedicates to Margaret Roper his commentary on [the Christmas Hymn of], 80 (**see Note to 80/23–5**).
Psalms, the Seven: See *Seven Psalms, the.*
Publicola: 145.

Quintinius [*i.e.* Quentin Metsys]: his diptych of Erasmus and Ægidius, 136 (**see Note to 136/14–19**).

Rastell, William: preparing for print More's English works, 100 (**see Note to 100/15–19**).
See also Appendix I, *The Rastell Fragments.*

Responsio ad Lutherum. See *More, Sir Thomas, works of.*

Reynolds, Richard, Dr., father of [the Bridgettine Monastery of] Sion: visited by the Nun of Canterbury, 156; accused of treason and executed, 179 (**see Note to 179/1–2**); learning of, 210.

See also *R. F.*: 229–30.

Rich, [Sir Richard, Solicitor-general; afterwards Lord Chancellor, 1547–51]: attempts to entrap More on the question of the Supremacy, 181–3; perjury of, 188–9; More discloses the character of, 189–90.

See also APPENDIX III, Sir Thomas More's Indictment, 274–5.

Richard the Third, Life of King. See *More, Sir Thomas, works of.*

Ridley, [Robert], Dr.: one of Queen Katherine's Counsel, *R. F.* 221.

Rochester, John Fisher, Bishop of [1504–35]: More withholds his opinion on the marriage from, 151 (**see Note to 151/21, etc.**); his interview with the Nun of Canterbury, 155; indicted of misprision of treason in the case of the Nun of Canterbury, 156; refuses the Oath of Succession and committed to the Tower, 168; martyrdom of, 179; More accused of treasonable correspondence with, 186–8; APPENDIX II, Paris News Letter, 261–2; APPENDIX III, Sir Thomas More's Indictment, 271–4.

See also *R. F.*: one of Queen Katherine's Counsel, 221; his book and oration before the legates in defence of the marriage between Henry and Katherine, 222 (**see Note to 222/1–3**); withstands the three Bills against the Clergy, 222 (**see Note to 222/27**); urges the King to repress heresies, 223; persuades Convocation to qualify their consent to the King's Supremacy, 224–5 (**see Note to 223–31, etc.**); attainted of misprision of treason in the case of the Nun of Canterbury, 227; refuses the Oath and is sent to the Tower, 227–8; kept prisoner for over a year, 231; continues to refuse the Oath, 231; withholds his opinion on the King's Supremacy, 231–2; compares the Statute of the Supremacy to a two-edged sword, 232; is entrapped into stating his opinion on the Supremacy, 232–4; created Cardinal, 235 (**see Note to 235/18–19**); Queen Anne persuades the King to put him to death, 235; indicted of treason, 236; ministered to by the King's physicians, 236 (**see Note to 236/26–7**); his Trial, 236–241 (**see Note to 240/56, etc.**); his Sentence, 240–1 (**see Note to 241/12–13 ff.**); thanks his guards, 241–2 (**see Note to 241/33 ff.**); his conversations with the Lieutenant of the Tower on the morning of his execution, 242–3 (**see Note to 242/21–22**); the manner of his death, 243–6 (**see Notes to 244/38—245/1, etc., 245/31–2**); the burial of his body, 246 (**see Note to 246/6, etc.**); his head is set upon London Bridge, 246 (**see Note to 246/33–6**); his head is thrown into the Thames to make room for More's head, 247; foresees his violent death, 247–8; personal appearance, 248; early life, 249; consecrated bishop, 249; virtue and holiness, 249–50; charity, 250; austerity of life, 250; care of his flock, 250–1; causes Lady Margaret to endow two Cambridge Colleges, 251; Chancellor of Cambridge University, 251; power as preacher, 251–2; English sermons, 252 (**see Note to 252/9**).

Romans: commonwealth of the, 102.

Rome: Pope Adrian's first entrance into, 42 (see Note to 42/8–15); Commission to judge the divorce procured from, 46 (see Note to 46/12–13); spiritual pre-eminence of the See of, 193–4.

Roper, Margaret, daughter of Sir Thomas More: marries William Roper, 5, 19 (see Note to 19/15–17); her miraculous recovery from the sweating sickness, 17, 81–3 (see Note to 81/18–19); is trusted with the secret of More's shirt of hair, 65–6; More predicts the fall of Anne Boleyn to, 72; a perfect daughter, wife, and mother, 78–80; praise of the learning and virtue of, 78–81 (see Note to 80/20–23); Erasmus dedicates his Commentary on [the Christmas Hymn of] Prudentius to, 80 (see Note to 80/23–5); is compared with various famous women, 80–1; emends a textual error in St. Cyprian, 81 (see Note to 81/6–17); recovers from the sweating sickness (see Note to 81/18–19); children of, 83 (see Note to 83/4–9); More discusses the heresy of Roper with, 87; More discusses his poverty with, 110; More conveys a portion of his lands to Roper and, 146–7; More is informed by, that he is put out of the Parliament Bill, 165; More's letters from the Tower to, 170, 200; visits her father in the Tower, 171, 179; watches, with her father, the Carthusians and Master Reynolds going to execution, 179; bids her father farewell, 198–9, Appendix II (Paris News Letter), 265; More sends his shirt of hair and a letter to, 200–1 (see Note to 65/22–3); More requests that she may be at his burial, 202.

Roper, William: Harpsfield's Epistle Dedicatorie to, 3–6; lineage of, 5 (see Notes to 5/4, 5/13–14); Harpsfield provided with notes on More's life by, 6; marries Margaret More, 5, 19 (see Note to 19/15–17); congratulates More on possession of the King's favour, 25; More describes to, the three things desirable in Christendom, 67–8; commends the happy state of the Realm to More, 68–70; offended at More's prediction of the administering of Oaths, 70; has never observed More "in a fume," 76; imprisonment in the Tower, 79 (see Note to 79/1–3), 89; a perfect husband, 80; the children of William and Margaret Roper, 83 (see Note to 83/4–9); temporary lapse into heresy of, 84–7; brought back to the Catholic faith by the prayers of More, 87–8; Catholic zeal and consequent imprisonment of, 88–90; More's conveyance of certain lands to, 146–7; urges More to labour for his discharge out of the Parliament Bill, 157; is grieved that More has neglected to do so, 160–1; sends message to his wife that More is put out of the Parliament Bill, 165; accompanies More in the boat to Lambeth, 166; Kingston praises More's fortitude to, 200.

"**Rosseus, Gulielmus,**" *i.e.* Sir Thomas More: More's *Responsio ad Lutherum* written under the pseudonym of, 106 (see Note to 105/21–3 ff.).

Ruth: 6.

St. Albans: 148 (see Note to 148/5–6).

St. Alban's Day. See *Alban, St., Day of.*

St. Anthony's School. See *Anthony, St., School of.*

St. Asaph, Henry Standish, Bishop of [1518–25]: one of Queen Katherine's Counsel, *R. F.* 221.

St. German, Christopher, called

"Sir John Somesay" and "the Pacifier": More, finding that he has mistaken certain words of "the Pacifier," retracts his criticism, 108–9 (see Note to 108/26–7); author of the *Treatise concernynge the Division between the Spiritualtie and the Temporaltie* (see Note to 127/3–5), and of the *Dialogue betwixte two Englishmen whereof one was called Salem and the other Bizance*, 127; More exposes the folly of his so-called pacification, 127–31.

St. John the Baptist, Eve of Nativity of. See *John the Baptist, St., Eve of.*

St. Lawrence, Church of. See *Lawrence, St., Church of.*

Salisbury, Bishopric of: given to Cardinal Campeius, *R. F.* 221 (see Note to 221/9).

Sappho: 80.

Scipio Africanus [Minor]: 143.

Secretary, Master. See *Cromwell, Thomas.*

Servilius: 145 (see Note to 145/20).

Seven Psalms, the [*i.e.* 6th, 31st, 37th, 50th, 101st, 129th, and 141st]: said daily by More and his family, 75; and by Margaret and More on Margaret's visits to the Tower, 171.

Sheep: More deals in *Utopia* with the turning of arable land into pasture for, 105.

Shepherd: More compares the office of a king to that of a, 58 (see Note to 58/18 ff.).

Ship, the Pope's: the case of, 23.

Shirt of hair, More's: Margaret trusted with the secret of, 65–6; a young gentlewoman [Anne More] laughs at, 65–6; sent to Margaret, 200 (see Note to 65/22–23).

Sion: Richard Whitford one of the fathers of, 16 (see Note to 16/19–21); the Nun of Canterbury visits the nuns of, 156 (see Note to 156/4–5); Richard Reynolds a father of, 156, 179 (see Note to 179/1–2).

(1) **Socrates**: More compared with, 199 (see Note to 199/8–14).

(2) **Socrates [Scholasticus]**: his *Ecclesiastical History* translated by Mistress [Mary] Bassett, 83.

Solomon: 80.

Solon: 105.

"Somesay, Sir John." See *St. German, Christopher.*

Souper of the Lorde, Tindale's: 131–2.

Southampton: 23.

Southwell, Sir Richard: sent to the Tower to take away More's books, 181–2 (see Note to 181/27—182/1); professes he paid no heed to the conversation between More and Rich, 192.

Sozomenus: his *Ecclesiastical History* translated by Mistress [Mary] Bassett, 83.

Spain: Wolsey's plot to send More to, 33 (see Note to 33/19–22); Pope Adrian formerly governor in, 42; brief concerning the marriage of Henry and Katherine found in the Treasury of, 46 (see Note to 46/20–23).

Speaker: More made, 26.

Spelman, Sir John, Justice: one of the Commissioners at Fisher's trial, *R. F.* 237.

Standish, Henry. See *St. Asaph, Henry Standish, Bishop of.*

Star Chamber: Stokesley rebuked by Wolsey in the, 49.

Stebunheyth [*i.e.* Stepney]: Cromwell's house at, *R. F.* 235.

Stephen, St.: his martyrdom referred to by More, 197.

Stillyard, merchants of the: 21 (see Note to 20/23—21/3), 86.

Stokesley, [John]. See (2) *London, [John] Stokesley, Bishop of.*

Subpœnas: More's care with regard to, 54.

Suffolk, [Charles Brandon],

Duke of: attends Sir Thomas More to the Chancery on his being made Lord Chancellor, 51; attempts to discover More's opinion on the Supremacy, 175.
See also *R. F.*: one of the Commissioners at Fisher's trial, 237.

Supplycacyon of Beggars, Simon Fish's: 70, 122.

Supplycacyon of Soulys. See *More, Sir Thomas, works of.*

Supremacy, the King's: Parliament recognises, 174 (**see Note to 174**/20–25); the attempts to discover More's opinion on the question of, 175; More accused of denying, 183, 188.
See also *R. F.*: Convocation qualifies its assent to, 224–5; Parliament acknowledges, 225, 228; Parliament passes Act making it treason to deny, 225, 228–9 (**see Note to 229**/2–8); Fisher entrapped into disclosing his opinion on, 232–4.
See also APPENDIX II, Paris News Letter, 259–64; APPENDIX III, Sir Thomas More's Indictment, 269–76.

Sweating sickness: Margaret's recovery from the, 81–3 (**see Note to 81**/18–19).

Sword, two-edged: comparison of the Act of Supremacy to, 187–8.
See also APPENDIX II, Paris News Letter, 262; APPENDIX III, Sir Thomas More's Indictment, 272–4.

Thames, River: 67, 113.
See also *R. F.*: Fisher's head cast into, 247.

Thebes: 145.

Theft: More deals in *Utopia* with the prevention of, 105.

Theodoretus: his *Ecclesiastical History* translated by Mistress [Mary] Bassett, 83.

Thistilworth [*i.e.* Isleworth]: John Hall, Vicar of, 179 (**see Note to 179**/4).

Thomas, St., of Canterbury: More's martyrdom compared with that of, 214–17 (**see Notes to 215**/9, 10–11).

Thomas, St., of Canterbury, Eve of: More executed on, 201.

Thomas, St., of Dover: More's martyrdom compared with that of, 214–15 (**see Note to 214**/18–19).

Tindale, [William]: More foretells the evils that would arise from the introduction into England of the Testament of, 71; More exposes the corrupt translations and false doctrines of, 107, 113–16; his *Answere unto Sir Thomas More's Dialoge*, 107–8; More's justice towards, 108; falsely asserts that More is rich, 109, 145; falsely asserts that More wrote for gain, 111; perverts More's statements as to the relation of the Church and the *written* Word, 116–17; is completely routed by More, 117–18; disagreements with Barnes, 120; More ridicules the feigned holiness of, 121; More defends in the *Apologye* his conduct towards, 122–3, 125–7; More's *Answere* to his *Souper of the Lorde*, 131–2.
See also *R. F.*: Henry's proclamation against Tindale's Testament, 223.

Tower of Babylon: 120.

Tower of London, the: More is not grieved by his imprisonment in, 17–18, 171–2; Roper imprisoned in, 79 (**see Note to 79**/1–3), 89; More's wife visits him in, 95; as near Heaven as is More's own house, 96–7; More's wife fears his suffocation in, 97–8; works of More written in, 107, 134; More's house searched after he was committed to, 110; Dr. Wilson and Fisher committed to, 168; More committed to, 169; Margaret visits her father in, 171, 179; More's examinations in, 175–8, and APPENDIX III (Sir Thomas More's Indictment), 270–1, 273–4. See also 148, 170, 173, 198, 200, 203, 217.

See also *R. F.*: More, Fisher and Wilson sent to, 227, 228; second band of Carthusians imprisoned under cruel conditions in, 235–6 (**see Note**); Fisher brought to his trial from, 237; Fisher brought back from his trial to, 241.

Tower of London, Constable of the. See *Kingston, Sir William.*

Tower of London, Lieutenant of the [*i.e.* Sir Edmund Walsingham]: receives More, 170; apologises for the poor cheer provided, 173; prevents More from wearing his best apparel at his execution, 203; More jokes on the weakness of the scaffold with, 204.

See also *R. F.*: conversations with Fisher on the morning of his execution, 242–3 (**see Note to 242/21–2**).

Tower of London, Porter of the: 170.

Tower Hill: 140, 179.

See also *R. F.*: Fisher executed at, 243.

Treatise concernynge the Division betwene the Spiritualtie and the Temporaltie. See *St. German, Christopher.*

Treason, the Act of: 174.

See also APPENDIX III, Sir Thomas More's Indictment, 269–70.

Treatise on the Divorce, Harpsfield's: promised, 213.

Treatise upon the Passion. See *More, Sir Thomas, works of.*

Tregonwell, John: APPENDIX III, Sir Thomas More's Indictment, 270.

Trial, (1) **Fisher's:** *R. F.* 236–41. (2) **More's:** 183–97.

See also APPENDIX II, Paris News Letter.

Tunstall, [Cuthbert], Dr. See (1) *London,* [*Cuthbert*] *Tunstall, Bishop of;* and *Durham,* [*Cuthbert*] *Tunstall, Bishop of.*

Tyler, Master [William]: reports to Henry VII More's opposition to the subsidy, 15 (**see Note to 15/16**).

Tyndale, [William]. See *Tindale,* [*William*].

Under Sheriff of London: More made an, 20 (**see Notes to 19/22—20/2, 20/1**).

Under Treasurer of the Exchequer: More made, 24 (**see Note to 24/9–10**).

Utas of St. Peter. See *Peter, St., Utas of.*

Utopia. See *More, Sir Thomas, works of.*

Vaughan, Master [Geoffrey or Richard]: More accused of taking reward from, 153–4 (**see Note to 153/7–8**).

Venus: 102.

Vesey, John. See *Exeter,* [*John*] *Vesey, Veysey* or *Voysey, Bishop of.*

Vesputius, Americus: 103.

Veysey, John. See *Exeter,* [*John*] *Vesey, Veysey* or *Voysey, Bishop of.*

Victoria: *nauis* called, 103 (**see Note to 103/23–5**).

Voysey, John. See *Exeter,* [*John*] *Vesey, Veysey* or *Voysey, Bishop of.*

Warham, William. See *Canterbury, William Warham, Archbishop of.*

Water: presented to king of Persia, 3 (**see Note to 3/11–12**).

Water-bailiff of London: jealous for More's reputation, 73 (**see Note to 73/6**).

Westminster, [William Benson *or* **Boston], Abbot of**: 169 (see **Note to 169/17**), 195 ("Bisshopp").

Westminster, city of: 33, 60, 148, 198.

Westminster Hall: 54, 183, 216.
See also *R. F.*: Fisher brought before Court of the King's Bench in, 237.

Weston, [William], Under-Treasurer: death of, 24 (see **Note to 24/9–10**).

Whitehall, 33.

Whitford, Richard, chaplain to Richard Fox, Bishop of Winchester: his warning to More, 16 (see **Note to 16/19–21**).

William the Conqueror: 5.

Wilson, [Nicholas], Dr.: More's conference on the marriage with, 150; refuses the Oath and sent to the Tower, 150 (see **Note to 150/23—151/1**), 168; More withholds his opinion on the marriage from, 151–2 (see **Note to 151/21, etc.**). See also *R. F.*: 227.

[Wilson, Richard]: Fisher's servant, *R. F.* 228 (see **Note to 228/6–8**).

Wiltshire, [Sir Thomas Boleyn], Earl of, [father of Queen Anne]: charges More with bribery and extortion, 153; attempts to discover More's opinion on the Supremacy, 175.
See also *R. F.*: one of the Commissioners at Fisher's trial, 237.

(1) **Winchester, Dr. [Richard] Fox, Bishop of** [1501–28]: tries to entrap More, 16 (see **Note to 16/8**).

(2) **Winchester, [Stephen] Gardiner, Bishop of** [1531–50 and 1553–5]: one of those requesting More to accompany them to Anne's coronation, 148; German Gardiner his secretary, 212.

Wingfield, Sir Richard, Chan- o r of the Duchy of Lancaster before Sir T. More: death of, 24 (see **Note to 24/11**).

Wolsey, [Thomas], Cardinal, Lord Chancellor of England [1515–29], **Archbishop of York** [1514–30]; labours to procure More for the Royal service, 22; case of the Pope's ship tried before, 23; Roper had seen the King walk arm in arm with, 25; praises More when More is chosen Speaker, 27; visit to the Commons, 31–3 (see **Note to 31/12 ff.**); anger against More, and unsuccessful plot to send More to Spain, 33–4 (see **Note to 33/19–22**); no lover of More, yet considered More fittest to be his successor in the Chancellorship, 34, 38–9 (see **Notes to 34/15–16, 39/5–9**); pomp and vanity of, 34; the flatterers at his Dinner, 35–8; twice joined in embassy with More, 39; compared unfavourably with More, 39–40; Harpsfield blames the ambition of, 40; blamed by Harpsfield as the originator of the divorce, 40–1, 41–3 (see **Note to 41/2–4**); his failure to obtain the Papacy, and his consequent revenge against Charles V and Queen Katherine, 42–3; embassy to France to treat of the marriage of Henry VIII and the Duchess of Alençon, 43; one of the Commissioners appointed to decide the divorce, 46, 47; his quarrel with Bishop Stokesley, 49 (see **Note to 49/16–18**); his fall and death, 50; his fall referred to by More when More made Lord Chancellor, 51–2; contrasted with More, 52; Roper and certain merchants convented of heresy before, 86.
See also *R. F.*: 221, 222 (see **Note to 222/6**).

Wood, John a: More's servant, instructions to, 170 (see **Note to 170/16**).

Wriothesley, [Sir Thomas], Lord Chancellor of England [1544–7]: 212.

(1) **York, Archbishop of.** See *Wolsey, [Thomas], Archbishop of York* [1514–30].

(2) **York, [Edward Lee], Archbishop of** [1531–44]: More's conference on the marriage with, 151.

York, Province of: fined by the King for recognising Wolsey as legate, 50.

Zeuxis: 104.

Zimachus: 145 (see Note to 145/19).

Zodiac: 104.

Zwinglians: 211.

Early English Text Society

OFFICERS AND COUNCIL

Honorary Director
PROFESSOR NORMAN DAVIS, M.B.E.
Merton College, Oxford

J. A. W. BENNETT
PROFESSOR BRUCE DICKINS, F.B.A.
A. I. DOYLE
PROFESSOR P. HODGSON
MISS P. M. KEAN
N. R. KER, F.B.A.
C. T. ONIONS, C.B.E., F.B.A.
PROFESSOR J. R. R. TOLKIEN
PROFESSOR D. WHITELOCK, F.B.A.
PROFESSOR R. M. WILSON
PROFESSOR C. L. WRENN

Honorary Secretary
R. W. BURCHFIELD
40 Walton Crescent, Oxford

Bankers
THE NATIONAL PROVINCIAL BANK LTD.
Cornmarket Street, Oxford

THE Subscription to the Society, which constitutes full membership, is £2. 2*s*. a year for the annual publications, from 1921 onwards, due in advance on the 1st of JANUARY, and should be paid by Cheque, Postal Order, or Money Order crossed 'National Provincial Bank Limited', to the Hon. Secretary, R. W. Burchfield, 40 Walton Crescent, Oxford. Individual members of the Society are allowed, after consultation with the Secretary, to select other volumes of the Society's publications instead of those for the current year. The Society's Texts can also be purchased separately from the Publisher, Oxford University Press, through a bookseller, at the prices put after them in the List, or through the Secretary, by members only, for their own use, at a discount of 2*d*. in the shilling.

The Early English Text Society was founded in 1864 by Frederick James Furnivall, with the help of Richard Morris, Walter Skeat, and others, to bring the mass of unprinted Early English literature within the reach of students and provide sound texts from which the New English Dictionary could quote. In 1867 an Extra Series was started of texts already printed but not in satisfactory or readily obtainable editions. At a cost of nearly £35,000, 159 volumes were issued in the Original Series and 126 in the Extra Series before 1921. In that year the title *Extra Series* was dropped, and all the publications of 1921 and subsequent years have since been listed and numbered as part of the Original Series. Since 1921 some ninety volumes have been issued. In this prospectus the Original Series and Extra Series for the years 1867–1920 are amalgamated, so as to show all the publications of the Society in a single list. In 1955 the prices of all volumes issued for the years up to 1936 and still available, were increased by one-fifth.

LIST OF PUBLICATIONS

Original Series, 1864–1962. Extra Series, 1867–1920

(*One guinea per annum for each series separately up to* 1920, *two guineas from* 1921)

O.S. 1. **Early English Alliterative Poems,** ed. R. Morris. 20*s*. 1864
2. **Arthur,** ed. F. J. Furnivall. (*Out of print.*) ,,
3. **Lauder on the Dewtie of Kyngis, &c.,** 1556, ed. F. Hall. (*Out of print.*) ,,
4. **Sir Gawayne and the Green Knight,** ed. R. Morris. (*Out of print, see* O.S. 210.) ,,
5. **Hume's Orthographie and Congruitie of the Britan Tongue,** ed. H. B. Wheatley. 5*s*. 1865
6. **Lancelot of the Laik,** ed. W. W. Skeat. (*Out of print.*) ,,
7. **Genesis & Exodus,** ed. R. Morris. (*Out of print.*) ,,
8. **Morte Arthure,** ed. E. Brock. (*Reprinted* 1961.) 25*s*. ,,
9. **Thynne on Speght's ed. of Chaucer,** A.D. 1599, ed. G. Kingsley and F. J. Furnivall. (*Out of print.*) ,,
10. **Merlin,** Part I, ed. H. B. Wheatley. (*Out of print.*) ,,
11. **Lyndesay's Monarche, &c.,** ed. J. Small. Part I. (*Out of print.*) ,,
12. **The Wright's Chaste Wife,** ed. F. J. Furnivall. (*Out of print.*) ,,
13. **Seinte Marherete,** ed. O. Cockayne. (*Out of print, see* O.S. 193.) 1866
14. **Kyng Horn, Floris and Blancheflour, &c.,** ed. J. R. Lumby, re-ed. G. H. McKnight. (*Out of print.*) ,,
15. **Political, Religious, and Love Poems,** ed. F. J. Furnivall. (*Out of print.*) ,,
16. **The Book of Quinte Essence,** ed. F. J. Furnivall. (*Out of print.*) ,,
17. **Parallel Extracts from 45 MSS. of Piers the Plowman,** ed. W. W. Skeat. (*Out of print.*) ,,
18. **Hali Meidenhad,** ed. O. Cockayne, re-ed. F. J. Furnivall. (*Out of print.*) ,,
19. **Lyndesay's Monarche, &c.,** ed. J. Small. Part II. (*Out of print.*) ,,
20. **Richard Rolle de Hampole, English Prose Treatises of,** ed. G. G. Perry. (*Reprinted* 1920.) 7*s*. ,,
21. **Merlin,** ed. H. B. Wheatley. Part II. (*Out of print.*) ,,
22. **Partenay** or **Lusignen,** ed. W. W. Skeat. 7*s*. 6*d*. ,,
23. **Dan Michel's Ayenbite of Inwyt,** ed. R. Morris. (*Out of print.*) ,,
24. **Hymns to the Virgin and Christ; The Parliament of Devils, &c.,** ed. F. J. Furnivall. (*Out of print.*) 1867
25. **The Stacions of Rome, the Pilgrims' Sea-voyage, with Clene Maydenhod,** ed. F. J. Furnivall. (*Out of print.*) ,,
26. **Religious Pieces in Prose and Verse,** from R. Thornton's MS., ed. G. G. Perry. 6*s*. (*See under* 1913.) ,,
27. **Levins' Manipulus Vocabulorum, a rhyming Dictionary,** ed. H. B. Wheatley. 14*s*. ,,
28. **William's Vision of Piers the Plowman,** ed. W. W. Skeat. A-Text. (*Reprinted* 1956.) 20*s*. ,,
29. **Old English Homilies** (1220–30), ed. R. Morris. Series I, Part I. (*Out of print.*) ,,
30. **Pierce the Ploughmans Crede,** ed. W. W. Skeat. (*Out of print.*) ,,
E.S. 1. **William of Palerne** or **William and the Werwolf,** re-ed. W. W. Skeat. (*Out of print.*) ,,
2. **Early English Pronunciation,** by A. J. Ellis. Part I. (*Out of print.*) ,,
O.S. 31. **Myrc's Duties of a Parish Priest,** in Verse, ed. E. Peacock. (*Out of print.*) 1868
32. **Early English Meals and Manners: the Boke of Norture of John Russell, the Bokes of Keruynge, Curtasye, and Demeanor, the Babees Book, Urbanitatis, &c.,** ed. F. J. Furnivall. (*Out of print.*) ,,
33. **The Book of the Knight of La Tour-Landry,** ed. T. Wright. (*Out of print.*) ,,
34. **Old English Homilies** (before 1300), ed. R. Morris. Series I, Part II. (*Out of print.*) ,,
35. **Lyndesay's Works,** Part III: The Historie and Testament of Squyer Meldrum, ed. F. Hall. 2s. 6*d*. ,,
E.S. 3. **Caxton's Book of Curtesye,** in Three Versions, ed. F. J. Furnivall. (*Out of print.*) ,,
4. **Havelok the Dane,** re-ed. W. W. Skeat. (*Out of print.*) ,,

E.S. 5. **Chaucer's Boethius,** ed. R. Morris. 14*s*. 1868

6. **Chevelere Assigne,** re-ed. Lord Aldenham. 3*s*. 6*d*. „

O.S. 36. **Merlin,** ed. H. B. Wheatley. Part III. On Arthurian Localities, by J. S. Stuart Glennie. 14*s*. 1869

37. **Sir David Lyndesay's Works,** Part IV, Ane Satyre of the thrie Estaits, ed. F. Hall. (*Out of print.*) „

38. **William's Vision of Piers the Plowman,** ed. W. W Skeat. Part II. Text B. (*Reprinted* 1951.) 18*s*. 6*d*. „

39. **The Gest Hystoriale of the Destruction of Troy,** ed. D. Donaldson and G. A. Panton. Part I. (*Out of print.*) „

E.S. 7. **Early English Pronunciation,** by A. J. Ellis. Part II. 12*s*. „

8. **Queene Elizabethes Achademy, &c.,** ed. F. J. Furnivall. Essays on early Italian and German Books of Courtesy, by W. M. Rossetti and E. Oswald. (*Out of print.*) „

9. **Awdeley's Fraternitye of Vacabondes, Harman's Caveat, &c.,** ed. E. Viles and F. J. Furnivall. 9*s*. „

O.S. 40. **English Gilds,** their Statutes and Customs, A.D. 1389, ed. Toulmin Smith and Lucy T. Smith, with an Essay on Gilds and Trades-Unions, by L. Brentano. (*Out of print.*) 1870

41. **William Lauder's Minor Poems,** ed. F. J. Furnivall. (*Out of print.*) „

42. **Bernardus De Cura Rei Famuliaris,** Early Scottish Prophecies, &c., ed. J. R. Lumby. (*Out of print.*) „

43. **Ratis Raving,** and other Moral and Religious Pieces, ed. J. R. Lumby. (*Out of print.*) „

E.S. 10. **Andrew Boorde's Introduction of Knowledge, 1547, Dyetary of Helth, 1542, Barnes in Defence of the Berde, 1542–3,** ed. F. J. Furnivall. (*Out of print.*) „

11. **Barbour's Bruce,** ed. W. W. Skeat. Part I. 14*s*. „

O.S. 44. **The Alliterative Romance of Joseph of Arimathie,** or **The Holy Grail:** from the Vernon MS.; with W. de Worde's and Pynson's Lives of Joseph: ed. W. W. Skeat. (*Out of print.*) 1871

45. **King Alfred's West-Saxon Version of Gregory's Pastoral Care,** ed., with an English translation, by Henry Sweet. Part I. (*Reprinted* 1958.) 30*s*. „

46. **Legends of the Holy Rood, Symbols of the Passion and Cross Poems,** ed. R. Morris. (*Out of print.*) „

47. **Sir David Lyndesay's Works,** ed. J. A. H. Murray. Part V. (*Out of print.*) „

48. **The Times' Whistle,** and other Poems, by R. C., 1616; ed. J. M. Cowper. 7*s*. 6*d*.

E.S. 12. **England in Henry VIII's Time:** a Dialogue between Cardinal Pole and Lupset, by Thom. Starkey Chaplain to Henry VIII, ed. J. M. Cowper. Part II. (*Out of print*, Part I is E.S. 32, 1878.) „

13. **A Supplicacyon of the Beggers,** by Simon Fish, A.D. 1528–9, ed. F. J. Furnivall, with **A Supplication to our Moste Soueraigne Lorde, A Supplication of the Poore Commons,** and **The Decaye of England by the Great Multitude of Sheep,** ed. J. M. Cowper. (*Out of print.*) „

14. **Early English Pronunciation,** by A. J. Ellis. Part III. (*Out of print.*) „

O.S. 49. **An Old English Miscellany,** containing a Bestiary, Kentish Sermons, Proverbs of Alfred, and Religious Poems of the 13th cent., ed. R. Morris. (*Out of print.*) 1872

50. **King Alfred's West-Saxon Version of Gregory's Pastoral Care,** ed. H. Sweet. Part II. (*Reprinted* 1958.) 30*s*. „

51. **Þe Liflade of St. Juliana,** 2 versions, with translations; ed. O. Cockayne and E. Brock. (*Reprinted* 1957.) 25*s*. „

52. **Palladius on Husbondrie,** englisht, ed. Barton Lodge. Part I. 12*s*. „

E.S. 15. **Robert Crowley's Thirty-One Epigrams, Voyce of the Last Trumpet, Way to Wealth, &c.,** ed. J. M. Cowper. (*Out of print.*) „

16. **Chaucer's Treatise on the Astrolabe,** ed. W. W. Skeat. (*Out of print.*)

17. **The Complaynt of Scotlande,** with 4 Tracts, ed. J. A. H. Murray. Part I. (*Out of print.*) „

O.S. 53. **Old-English Homilies,** Series II, and three Hymns to the Virgin and God, 13th-century, with the music to two of them, in old and modern notation, ed. R. Morris. (*Out of print.*) 1873

54. **The Vision of Piers Plowman,** ed. W. W. Skeat. Part III. Text C. (*Reprinted* 1959.) 35*s*. „

55. **Generydes,** a Romance, ed. W. Aldis Wright. Part I. 3*s*. 6*d*. „

E.S. 18. **The Complaynt of Scotlande,** ed. J. A. H. Murray. Part II. (*Out of print.*) „

19. **The Myroure of oure Ladye,** ed. J. H. Blunt. (*Out of print.*) „

O.S. 56. **The Gest Hystoriale of the Destruction of Troy,** in alliterative verse, ed. D. Donaldson and G. A. Panton. Part II. 12*s*. 6*d*. 1874

57. **Cursor Mundi,** in four Texts, ed. R. Morris. Part I, with 2 photolithographic facsimiles. (*Reprinted* 1961.) 25*s*. „

58. **The Blickling Homilies,** ed. R. Morris. Part I. (*Out of print.*) „

E.S. 20. **Lovelich's History of the Holy Grail,** ed. F. J. Furnivall. Part I. (*Out of print.*) „

21. **Barbour's Bruce,** ed. W. W. Skeat. Part II. (*Out of print.*) „

22. **Henry Brinklow's Complaynt of Roderyck Mors** and **The Lamentacyon of a Christen Agaynst the Cytye of London,** made by Roderigo Mors, ed. J. M. Cowper. (*Out of print.*) „

23. **Early English Pronunciation,** by A. J. Ellis. Part IV. (*Out of print.*) „

O.S. 59. **Cursor Mundi,** in four Texts, ed. R. Morris. Part II. 18*s*. 1875

60. **Meditacyuns on the Soper of our Lorde,** by Robert of Brunne, ed. J. M. Cowper. 3*s*. „

61. **The Romance and Prophecies of Thomas of Erceldoune,** ed. J. A. H. Murray. 12*s*. 6*d*. „

E.S. 24. **Lovelich's History of the Holy Grail,** ed. F. J. Furnivall. Part II. (*Out of print.*) „

25. **Guy of Warwick,** 15th century Version, ed. J. Zupitza. Part I. (*Out of print.*) „

O.S. 62. **Cursor Mundi,** in four Texts, ed. R. Morris. Part III. 18*s*. 1876

63. **The Blickling Homilies,** ed. R. Morris. Part II. (*Out of print.*) „

64. **Francis Thynne's Embleames and Epigrams,** ed. F. J. Furnivall. 8*s*. 6*d*. „

65. **Be Domes Dæge** (Bede's *De Die Judicii*), &c., ed. J. R. Lumby. (*Out of print.*) „

E.S. 26. **Guy of Warwick,** 15th-century Version, ed. J. Zupitza. Part II. (*Out of print.*) „

E.S. 27. **The English Works of John Fisher,** ed. J. E. B. Mayor. Part I. *(Out of print.)* 1876
O.S. 66. **Cursor Mundi,** in four Texts, ed. R. Morris. Part IV, with 2 autotypes. 12*s*. 1877
67. **Notes on Piers Plowman,** by W. W. Skeat. Part I. 25*s*. „
E.S. 28. **Lovelich's Holy Grail,** ed. F. J. Furnivall. Part III. *(Out of print.)* „
29. **Barbour's Bruce,** ed. W. W. Skeat. Part III. 25*s*. „
O.S. 68. **Cursor Mundi,** in 4 Texts, ed. R. Morris. Part V. 30*s*. 1878
69. **Adam Davie's 5 Dreams about Edward II, &c.,** ed. F. J. Furnivall. 6*s*. „
70. **Generydes,** a Romance, ed. W. Aldis Wright. Part II. 5*s*. „
E.S. 30. **Lovelich's Holy Grail,** ed. F. J. Furnivall. Part IV. *(Out of print.)* „
31. **The Alliterative Romance of Alexander and Dindimus,** ed. W. W. Skeat. 7*s*. 6*d*. „
32. **Starkey's England in Henry VIII's Time.** Part I. **Starkey's Life and Letters,** ed. S. J. Herrtage. 9*s*. 6*d*. „
O.S. 71. **The Lay Folks Mass-Book,** four texts, ed. T. F. Simmons. *(Out of print.)* 1879
72. **Palladius on Husbondrie,** englisht, ed. S. J. Herrtage. Part II. 6*s*. „
E.S. 33. **Gesta Romanorum,** ed. S. J. Herrtage. *(Out of print.)* „
34. **The Charlemagne Romances: 1. Sir Ferumbras,** from Ashm. MS. 33, ed. S. J. Herrtage. *(Out of print.)* „
O.S. 73. **The Blickling Homilies,** ed. R. Morris. Part III. 12*s*. 1880
74. **English Works of Wyclif,** hitherto unprinted, ed. F. D. Matthew. *(Out of print.)* „
E.S. 35. **Charlemagne Romances: 2. The Sege off Melayne, Sir Otuell, &c.,** ed. S. J. Herrtage. *(Out of print.)* „
36. **Charlemagne Romances: 3. Lyf of Charles the Grete,** ed. S. J. Herrtage. Part I. 19*s*. „
O.S. 75. **Catholicon Anglicum,** an English-Latin Wordbook, from Lord Monson's MS., A.D. 1483, ed., with Introduction and Notes, by S. J. Herrtage and Preface by H. B. Wheatley. 24*s*. 1881
76. **Ælfric's Metrical Lives of Saints,** in MS. Cott. Jul. E VII, ed. W. W. Skeat. Part I. 20*s*. „
E.S. 37. **Charlemagne Romances: 4. Lyf of Charles the Grete,** ed. S. J. Herrtage. Part II *(Out of print.)* „
38. **Charlemagne Romances: 5. The Sowdone of Babylone,** ed. E. Hausknecht. *(Out of print.)* „
O.S. 77. **Beowulf,** the unique MS. autotyped and transliterated, ed. J. Zupitza. *(Re-issued as* No. 245. *See under* 1958.) 1882
78. **The Fifty Earliest English Wills,** in the Court of Probate, 1387–1439, ed. F. J. Furnivall. *(Out of print.)* „
E.S. 39. **Charlemagne Romances: 6. Rauf Coilyear, Roland, Otuel, &c.,** ed. S. J. Herrtage. 18*s*. „
40. **Charlemagne Romances: 7. Huon of Burdeux,** by Lord Berners, ed. S. L. Lee. Part I. *(Out of print.)* „
O.S. 79. **King Alfred's Orosius,** from Lord Tollemache's 9th-century MS., ed. H. Sweet. Part I. *(Reprinted* 1959.) 30*s*. 1883
79 *b*. *Extra Volume.* **Facsimile of the Epinal Glossary,** ed. H. Sweet. *(Out of print.)* „
E.S. 41. **Charlemagne Romances: 8. Huon of Burdeux,** by Lord Berners, ed. S. L. Lee. Part II. *(Out of print.)* „
42. **Guy of Warwick:** 2 texts (Auchinleck MS. and Caius MS.), ed. J. Zupitza. Part I. *(Out of print.)* „
O.S. 80. **The Life of St. Katherine,** B.M. Royal MS. 17 A. xxvii, &c., and its Latin Original, ed. E. Einenkel. *(Out of print.)* 1884
81. **Piers Plowman:** Glossary, &c., ed. W. W. Skeat. Part IV, completing the work *(Out of print.)* „
E.S. 43. **Charlemagne Romances: 9. Huon of Burdeux,** by Lord Berners, ed. S. L. Lee. Part III. *(Out of print.)* „
44. **Charlemagne Romances: 10. The Foure Sonnes of Aymon,** ed. Octavia Richardson. Part I. *(Out of print.)* „
O.S. 82. **Ælfric's Metrical Lives of Saints,** MS. Cott. Jul. E VII, ed. W. W. Skeat. Part II. 20*s*. 1885
83. **The Oldest English Texts, Charters, &c.,** ed. H. Sweet. *(Reprinted* 1957.) 42*s*. „
E.S. 45. **Charlemagne Romances: 11. The Foure Sonnes of Aymon,** ed. O. Richardson. Part II. *(Out of print.)* „
46. **Sir Beves of Hamtoun,** ed. E. Kölbing. Part I. *(Out of print.)* „
O.S. 84. **Additional Analogs to 'The Wright's Chaste Wife',** O.S. 12, by W. A. Clouston. 1*s*. 1886
85. **The Three Kings of Cologne,** ed. C. Horstmann. 20*s*. 6*d*. „
86. **Prose Lives of Women Saints,** ed. C. Horstmann. 14*s*. „
E.S. 47. **The Wars of Alexander,** ed. W. W. Skeat. *(Out of print.)* „
48. **Sir Beves of Hamtoun,** ed. E. Kölbing. Part II. *(Out of print.)* „
O.S. 87. **The Early South-English Legendary,** Laud MS. 108, ed. C. Horstmann. *(Out of print.)* 1887
88. **Hy. Bradshaw's Life of St. Werburghe** (Pynson, 1521), ed. C. Hortsmann. 12*s*. „
E.S. 49. **Guy of Warwick,** 2 texts (Auchinleck and Caius MSS.), ed. J. Zupitza. Part II. *(Out of print.)* „
50. **Charlemagne Romances: 12. Huon of Burdeux,** by Lord Berners, ed. S. L. Lee. Part IV. *(Out of print.)* „
51. **Torrent of Portyngale,** ed. E. Adam. *(Out of print.)* „
O.S. 89. **Vices and Virtues,** ed. F. Holthausen. Part I. *(Out of print.)* 1888
90. **Anglo-Saxon and Latin Rule of St. Benet,** interlinear Glosses, ed. H Logeman. 20*s*. „
91. **Two Fifteenth-Century Cookery-Books,** ed. T. Austin. *(Out of print.)* „
E.S. 52. **Bullein's Dialogue against the Feuer Pestilence, 1578,** ed. M. and A. H. Bullen. 12*s*. „
53. **Vicary's Anatomie of the Body of Man, 1548,** ed. 1577, ed. F. J. and Percy Furnivall. Part I. 18*s*. „
54. **The Curial made by maystere Alain Charretier, translated by William Caxton,** 1484, ed. F. J. Furnivall and P. Meyer. 6*s*. „
O.S. 92. **Eadwine's Canterbury Psalter,** from the Trin. Cambr. MS., ed. F. Harsley, Part II. 14*s*. 1889
93. **Defensor's Liber Scintillarum,** ed. E. Rhodes. 20*s*. „
E.S. 55. **Barbour's Bruce,** ed. W. W. Skeat. Part IV. 6*s*. „
56. **Early English Pronunciation,** by A. J. Ellis. Part V, the present English Dialects. *(Out of print.)* 1889
O.S. 94. **Ælfric's Metrical Lives of Saints,** MS. Cott. Jul. E VII, ed. W. W. Skeat. Part III. 30*s*. 1890
95. **The Old-English Version of Bede's Ecclesiastical History,** re-ed. T. Miller. Part I, 1. *(Reprinted* 1959.) 30*s*. „
E.S. 57. **Caxton's Eneydos,** ed. W. T. Culley and F. J. Furnivall. *(Reprinting.)* 30*s*. „

E.S. 58. **Caxton's Blanchardyn and Eglantine,** c. 1489, ed. L. Kellner. (*Reprinting.*) 42*s.* 1890

O.S. 96. **The Old-English Version of Bede's Ecclesiastical History,** re-ed. T. Miller. Part I, 2. (*Reprinted* 1959.) 30*s.* 1891

97. **The Earliest English Prose Psalter,** ed. K. D. Buelbring. Part I. 18*s.* „

E.S. 59. **Guy of Warwick,** 2 texts (Auchinleck and Caius MSS.), ed. J. Zupitza. Part III. (*Out of print.*) „

60. **Lydgate's Temple of Glas,** re-ed. J. Schick. 18*s.* „

O.S. 98. **Minor Poems of the Vernon MS.,** ed. C. Horstmann. Part I. 24*s.* 1892

99. **Cursor Mundi.** Preface, Notes, and Glossary, Part VI, ed. R. Morris. 12*s.* „

E.S. 61. **Hoccleve's Minor Poems, I,** from the Phillipps and Durham MSS., ed. F. J. Furnivall. 18*s.* „

62. **The Chester Plays,** re-ed. H. Deimling. Part I. (*Reprinted* 1959.) 25*s.* „

O.S. 100. **Capgrave's Life of St. Katharine,** ed. C. Horstmann, with Forewords by F. J. Furnivall. 24*s.* 1893

101. **Cursor Mundi.** Essay on the MSS., their Dialects, &c., by H. Hupe. Part VII. 12*s.* „

E.S. 63. **Thomas à Kempis's De Imitatione Christi,** ed. J. K. Ingram. (*Out of print.*) „

64. **Caxton's Godeffroy of Boloyne, or The Siege and Conqueste of Jerusalem,** 1481, ed. Mary N. Colvin. 18*s.* „

O.S. 102. **Lanfranc's Science of Cirurgie,** ed. R. von Fleischhacker. Part I. 24*s.* 1894

103. **The Legend of the Cross,** &c., ed. A. S. Napier. 15*s.* „

E.S. 65. **Sir Beves of Hamtoun,** ed. E. Kölbing. Part III. (*Out of print.*) „

66. **Lydgate's and Burgh's Secrees of Philisoffres** ('Governance of Kings and Princes'), ed. R. Steele. (*Out of print.*) „

O.S. 104. **The Exeter Book** (Anglo-Saxon Poems), re-ed. I. Gollancz. Part I. (*Reprinted* 1958.) 30*s.* 1895

105. **The Prymer or Lay Folks' Prayer Book,** Camb. Univ. MS., ed. H. Littlehales. Part I. (*Out of print.*) „

E.S. 67. **The Three Kings' Sons,** a Romance, ed. F. J. Furnivall. Part I, the Text. (*Out of print.*) „

68. **Melusine,** the prose Romance, ed. A. K. Donald. Part I, the Text. (*Out of print.*) „

O.S. 106. **R. Misyn's Fire of Love and Mending of Life** (Hampole), ed. R. Harvey. 18*s.* 1896

107. **The English Conquest of Ireland,** A.D. 1166–1185, 2 Texts, ed. F. J. Furnivall. Part I. 18*s.* „

E.S. 69. **Lydgate's Assembly of the Gods,** ed. O. L. Triggs. (*Reprinted* 1957.) 25*s.* „

70. **The Digby Plays,** ed. F. J. Furnivall. (*Out of print.*) „

O.S. 108. **Child-Marriages and -Divorces, Trothplights, &c.** Chester Depositions, 1561–6, ed. F. J. Furnivall. 18*s.* 1897

109. **The Prymer or Lay Folks' Prayer Book,** ed. H. Littlehales. Part II. (*Out of print.*) „

E.S. 71. **The Towneley Plays,** ed. G. England and A. W. Pollard. (*Re-issued* 1952.) 30*s.* „

72. **Hoccleve's Regement of Princes, and 14 Poems,** ed. F. J. Furnivall. (*Out of print.*) „

73. **Hoccleve's Minor Poems, II,** from the Ashburnham MS., ed. I. Gollancz. (*Out of print.*) „

O.S. 110. **The Old-English Version of Bede's Ecclesiastical History,** ed. T. Miller. Part II, 1. 18*s.* 1898

111. **The Old-English Version of Bede's Ecclesiastical History,** ed. T. Miller. Part II, 2. (*Reprinting.*) „

E.S. 74. **Secreta Secretorum,** 3 prose Englishings, one by Jas. Yonge, 1428, ed. R. Steele. Part I. 24*s.* „

75. **Speculum Guidonis de Warwyk,** ed. G. L. Morrill. 12*s.* „

O.S. 112. **Merlin.** Part IV. Outlines of the Legend of Merlin, by W. E. Mead. 18*s.* 1899

113. **Queen Elizabeth's Englishings of Boethius, Plutarch, &c.,** ed. C. Pemberton. (*Out of print.*) „

E.S. 76. **George Ashby's Poems, &c.,** ed. Mary Bateson. (*Out of print.*) „

77. **Lydgate's DeGuilleville's Pilgrimage of the Life of Man,** ed. F. J. Furnivall. Part I. (*Out of print.*)

78. **The Life and Death of Mary Magdalene,** by T. Robinson, *c.* 1620, ed. H. O. Sommer. 6*s.* „

O.S. 114. **Ælfric's Metrical Lives of Saints,** ed. W. W. Skeat. Part IV and last. (*Reprinting.*) 1900

115. **Jacob's Well,** ed. A. Brandeis. Part I. 12*s.* „

116. **An Old-English Martyrology,** re-ed. G. Herzfeld. 20*s.* „

E.S. 79. **Caxton's Dialogues, English and French,** ed. H. Bradley. 12*s.* „

80. **Lydgate's Two Nightingale Poems,** ed. O. Glauning. 6*s.* „

81. **The English Works of John Gower,** ed. G. C. Macaulay. Part I. (*Reprinted* 1957.) 40*s.* „

O.S. 117. **Minor Poems of the Vernon MS.,** ed. F. J. Furnivall. Part II. 18*s.* 1901

118. **The Lay Folks' Catechism,** ed. T. F. Simmons and H. E. Nolloth. 6*s.* „

119. **Robert of Brunne's Handlyng Synne,** and its French original, re-ed. F. J. Furnivall. Part I. (*Out of print.*) „

E.S. 82. **The English Works of John Gower,** ed. G. C. Macaulay. Part II. (*Reprinted* 1957.) 40*s.* „

83. **Lydgate's DeGuilleville's Pilgrimage of the Life of Man,** ed. F. J. Furnivall. Part II. (*Out of print.*) „

84. **Lydgate's Reason and Sensuality,** ed. E. Sieper. Part I. (*Out of print.*) „

O.S. 120. **The Rule of St. Benet** in Northern Prose and Verse, and Caxton's Summary, ed. E. A. Kock. 18*s.* 1902

121. **The Laud MS. Troy-Book,** ed. J. E. Wülfing. Part I. 18*s.* „

E.S. 85. **Alexander Scott's Poems,** 1568, ed. A. K. Donald. (*Out of print.*) „

86. **William of Shoreham's Poems,** re-ed. M. Konrath. Part I. (*Out of print.*) „

87. **Two Coventry Corpus Christi Plays,** re-ed. H. Craig. 15*s.* (*See under* 1952.) „

O.S. 122. **The Laud MS. Troy-Book,** ed. by J. E. Wülfing. Part II. 24*s.* 1903

123. **Robert of Brunne's Handlyng Synne,** and its French original, re-ed. F. J. Furnivall. Part II. (*Out of print.*) „

E.S. 88. **Le Morte Arthur,** re-ed. J. D. Bruce. (*Reprinted* 1959.) 30*s.* „

89. **Lydgate's Reason and Sensuality,** ed. E. Sieper. Part II. (*Out of print.*) „

90. **English Fragments from Latin Medieval Service-Books,** ed. H. Littlehales. (*Out of print.*) „

O.S. 124. **Twenty-six Political and other Poems** from Digby MS. 102, &c., ed. J. Kail. Part I. 12*s.* 1904

O.S. 125. **Medieval Records of a London City Church,** ed. H. Littlehales. Part I. 12*s.* 1904

126. **An Alphabet of Tales,** in Northern English, from the Latin, ed. M. M. Banks. Part I. 12*s.* „

E.S. 91. **The Macro Plays,** ed. F. J. Furnivall and A. W. Pollard. (*Out of print.*) „

92. **Lydgate's DeGuileville's Pilgrimage of the Life of Man,** ed. Katherine B. Locock. Part III. (*Out of print.*) „

93. **Lovelich's Romance of Merlin,** from the unique MS., ed. E. A. Kock. Part I. 12*s.*

O.S. 127. **An Alphabet of Tales,** in Northern English, from the Latin, ed. M. M. Banks. Part II. 12*s.* 1905
128. **Medieval Records of a London City Church,** ed. H. Littlehales. Part II. 12*s.* „
129. **The English Register of Godstow Nunnery,** ed. A. Clark. Part I. 12*s.* „
E.S. 94. **Respublica,** a Play on a Social England, ed. L. A. Magnus. (*Out of print. See under* 1946.) „
95. **Lovelich's History of the Holy Grail.** Part V. **The Legend of the Holy Grail,** ed. Dorothy Kempe. (*Out of print.*) „
96. **Mirk's Festial,** ed. T. Erbe. Part I. 14*s.* „
O.S. 130. **The English Register of Godstow Nunnery,** ed. A. Clark. Part II. 18*s.* 1906
131. **The Brut, or The Chronicle of England,** ed. F. Brie. Part I. (*Reprinted* 1960.) 25*s.* „
132. **John Metham's Works,** ed. H. Craig. 18*s.* „
E.S. 97. **Lydgate's Troy Book,** ed. H. Bergen. Part I, Books I and II. (*Out of print.*) „
98. **Skelton's Magnyfycence,** ed. R. L. Ramsay. (*Reprinted* 1958.) 30*s.* „
99. **The Romance of Emaré,** re-ed. Edith Rickert. (*Reprinted* 1958.) 15*s.* „
O.S. 133. **The English Register of Oseney Abbey, by Oxford,** ed. A. Clark. Part I. 18*s.* 1907
134. **The Coventry Leet Book,** ed. M. Dormer Harris. Part I. 18*s.* „
E.S. 100. **The Harrowing of Hell,** and **The Gospel of Nicodemus,** re-ed. W. H. Hulme. (*Reprinted* 1961.) 30*s.* „
101. **Songs, Carols, &c.,** from Richard Hill's Balliol MS., ed. R. Dyboski. 18*s.* „
O.S. 135. **The Coventry Leet Book,** ed. M. Dormer Harris. Part II. 18*s.* 1908
135 *b. Extra Issue.* Prof. Manly's **Piers Plowman and its Sequence,** urging the fivefold authorship of the *Vision.* (*Out of print.*) „
136. **The Brut, or The Chronicle of England,** ed. F. Brie. Part II. 18*s.* „
E.S. 102. **Promptorium Parvulorum,** the 1st English-Latin Dictionary, ed. A. L. Mayhew. 25*s.* 6*d.* „
103. **Lydgate's Troy Book,** ed. H. Bergen. Part II, Book III. (*Out of print.*) „
O.S. 137. **Twelfth-Century Homilies** in MS. Bodley 343, ed. A. O. Belfour. Part I, the Text. (*Reprinting.*) 25*s.* 1909
138. **The Coventry Leet Book,** ed. M. Dormer Harris. Part III. 18*s.* „
E.S. 104. **The Non-Cycle Mystery Plays,** re-ed. O. Waterhouse. (*Out of print.*) „
105. **The Tale of Beryn, with the Pardoner and Tapster,** ed. F. J. Furnivall and W. G. Stone. (*Out of print.*) „
O.S. 139. **John Arderne's Treatises on Fistula in Ano, &c.,** ed. D'Arcy Power. 18*s.* 1910
139 *b, c, d, e, f, Extra Issue.* **The Piers Plowman Controversy:** *b.* **Dr. Jusserand's 1st Reply to Prof. Manly;** *c.* **Prof. Manly's Answer to Dr. Jusserand;** *d.* **Dr. Jusserand's 2nd Reply to Prof. Manly;** *e.* **Mr. R. W. Chambers's Article;** *f.* **Dr. Henry Bradley's Rejoinder to Mr. R. W. Chambers.** (*Out of print.*) „
140. **Capgrave's Lives of St. Augustine and St. Gilbert of Sempringham,** ed. J. Munro. (*Out of print.*) „
E.S. 106. **Lydgate's Troy Book,** ed. H. Bergen. Part III. (*Out of print.*) „
107. **Lydgate's Minor Poems,** ed. H. N. MacCracken. Part I. **Religious Poems.** (*Reprinted* 1961.) 40*s.* „
O.S. 141. **Earth upon Earth,** all the known texts, ed., with an Introduction, by Hilda Murray. (*Out of print.*) 1911
142. **The English Register of Godstow Nunnery,** ed. A. Clark. Part III. 12*s.* „
143. **The Prose Life of Alexander,** Thornton MS., ed. J. S. Westlake. 12*s.* „
E.S. 108. **Lydgate's Siege of Thebes,** re-ed. A. Erdmann. Part I, the Text. (*Reprinted* 1960.) 24*s.* „
109. **Partonope,** re-ed. A. T. Bödtker. The Texts. (*Out of print.*) „
O.S. 144. **The English Register of Oseney Abbey, by Oxford,** ed. A. Clark. Part II. 12*s.* 1912
145. **The Northern Passion,** ed. F. A. Foster. Part I, the four parallel texts. 18*s.* „
E.S. 110. **Caxton's Mirrour of the World,** with all the woodcuts, ed. O. H. Prior. (*Out of print.*) „
111. **Caxton's History of Jason,** the Text, Part I, ed. J. Munro. 18*s.* „
O.S. 146. **The Coventry Leet Book,** ed. M. Dormer Harris. Introduction, Indexes, &c. Part IV. 12*s.* 1913
147. **The Northern Passion,** ed. F. A. Foster, Introduction, French Text, Variants and Fragments, Glossary. Part II. 18*s.* „
[An enlarged reprint of O.S. 26, **Religious Pieces in Prose and Verse,** from the Thornton MS., ed. G. G. Perry. 6*s.*] „
E.S. 112. **Lovelich's Romance of Merlin,** ed. E. A. Kock. Part II. (*Reprinted* 1961.) 30*s.* „
113. **Poems by Sir John Salusbury, Robert Chester, and others,** from Christ Church MS. 184, &c., ed. Carleton Brown. 18*s.* „
O.S. 148. **A Fifteenth-Century Courtesy Book and Two Franciscan Rules,** ed. R. W. Chambers and W. W. Seton. (*Out of print.*) 1914
149 **Lincoln Diocese Documents, 1450–1544,** ed. Andrew Clark. 18*s.* „
150. **The Old-English Rule of Bp. Chrodegang,** and the **Capitula of Bp. Theodulf,** ed. A. S. Napier. 15*s.* „
E.S. 114. **The Gild of St. Mary, Lichfield,** ed. F. J. Furnivall. 18*s.* „
115. **The Chester Plays,** re-ed. J. Matthews. Part II. (*Reprinted* 1959.) 25*s.* „
O.S. 151. **The Lanterne of Light,** ed. Lilian M. Swinburn. (*Out of print.*) 1915
152. **Early English Homilies,** from Cott. Vesp. D. XIV, ed. Rubie Warner. Part I, Text. (*Out of print.*) „
E.S. 116. **The Pauline Epistles,** ed. M. J. Powell. (*Out of print.*) „
117. **Bp. Fisher's English Works,** ed. R. Bayne. Part II. 18*s.* „
O.S. 153. **Mandeville's Travels,** ed. P. Hamelius. Part I, Text. (*Reprinted* 1960.) 25*s.* 1916
154. **Mandeville's Travels,** ed. P. Hamelius. Part II, Notes and Introduction. (*Reprinted* 1961.) 25*s.* „
E.S. 118. **The Earliest Arithmetics in English,** ed. R. Steele. 18*s.* „
119. **The Owl and Nightingale,** 2 Texts parallel, ed. G. F. H. Sykes and J. H. G. Grattan. (*Reprinted* 1959.) 20*s.* „
O.S. 155. **The Wheatley MS.,** ed. Mabel Day. 36*s.* 1917

E.S. 120. **Ludus Coventriae,** ed. K. S. Block. (*Reprinted* 1961.) 30*s*. 1917
O.S. 156. **Reginald Pecock's Donet,** from Bodl. MS. 916, ed. Elsie V. Hitchcock. 42*s*. 1918
E.S. 121. **Lydgate's Fall of Princes,** ed. H. Bergen. Part I. (*Out of print.*) "
122. **Lydgate's Fall of Princes,** ed. H. Bergen. Part II. (*Out of print.*) "
O.S. 157. **Harmony of the Life of Christ,** from MS. Pepys 2498, ed. Margery Goates. (*Out of print.*) 1919
158. **Meditations on the Life and Passion of Christ,** from MS. Add., 11307, ed. Charlotte D'Evelyn. (*Out of print.*) "
E.S. 123. **Lydgate's Fall of Princes,** ed. H. Bergen. Part III. (*Out of print.*) "
124. **Lydgate's Fall of Princes,** ed. H. Bergen. Part IV. (*Out of print.*) "
O.S. 159. **Vices and Virtues,** ed. F. Holthausen. Part II. 14*s*. 1920
[A re-edition of O.S. 18, **Hali Meidenhad,** ed. O. Cockayne, with a variant MS., Bodl. 34, hitherto unprinted, ed. F. J. Furnivall. (*Out of print.*)] "
E.S. 125. **Lydgate's Siege of Thebes,** ed. A. Erdmann and E. Ekwall. Part II. 24*s*. "
126. **Lydgate's Troy Book,** ed. H. Bergen. Part IV. 18*s*. "

O.S. 160. **The Old English Heptateuch,** MS. Cott. Claud. B. IV, ed. S. J. Crawford. (*Out of print.*) 1921
161. **Three O.E. Prose Texts,** MS. Cott. Vit. A. XV, ed. S. Rypins. (*Out of print.*) "
162. **Facsimile of MS. Cotton Nero A. x (Pearl, Cleanness, Patience and Sir Gawain),** Introduction by I. Gollancz. (*Reprinted* 1955.) 100*s*. 1922
163. **Book of the Foundation of St. Bartholomew's Church in London,** ed. N. Moore. 12*s*. 1923
164. **Pecock's Folewer to the Donet,** ed. Elsie V. Hitchcock. (*Out of print.*) "
165. **Middleton's Chinon of England, with Leland's Assertio Arturii and Robinson's translation,** ed. W. E. Mead. (*Out of print.*) "
166. **Stanzaic Life of Christ,** ed. Frances A. Foster. (*Out of print.*) 1924
167. **Trevisa's Dialogus inter Militem et Clericum, Sermon by FitzRalph, and Bygynnyng of the World,** ed. A. J. Perry. (*Out of print.*) "
168. **Caxton's Ordre of Chyualry,** ed. A. T. P. Byles. (*Out of print.*) 1925
169. **The Southern Passion,** ed. Beatrice Brown. (*Out of print.*) "
170. **Walton's Boethius,** ed. M. Science. (*Out of print.*) "
171. **Pecock's Reule of Cristen Religioun,** ed. W. C. Greet. (*Out of print.*) 1926
172. **The Seege or Batayle of Troye,** ed. M. E. Barnicle. (*Out of print.*) "
173. **Hawes' Pastime of Pleasure,** ed. W. E. Mead. 18*s*. 1927
174. **The Life of St. Anne,** ed. R. E. Parker. (*Out of print.*) "
175. **Barclay's Eclogues,** ed. Beatrice White. (*Reprinted* 1961.) 35*s*. "
176. **Caxton's Prologues and Epilogues,** ed. W. J. B. Crotch. (*Reprinted* 1956.) 30*s*. "
177. **Byrhtferth's Manual,** ed. S. J. Crawford. (*Out of print.*) 1928
178. **The Revelations of St. Birgitta,** ed. W. P. Cumming. 12*s*. "
179. **The Castell of Pleasure,** ed. R. Cornelius. 15*s*. "
180. **The Apologye of Syr Thomas More,** ed. A. I. Taft. (*Out of print.*) 1929
181. **The Dance of Death,** ed. F. Warren. (*Out of print.*) "
182. **Speculum Christiani,** ed. G. Holmstedt. 30*s*. "
183. **The Northern Passion (Supplement),** ed. W. Heuser and Frances Foster. 9*s*. 1930
184. **The Poems of John Audelay,** ed. Ella K. Whiting. 33*s*. 6*d*. "
185. **Lovelich's Merlin,** ed. E. A. Kock. Part III. 30*s*. "
186. **Harpsfield's Life of More,** ed. Elsie V. Hitchcock and R. W. Chambers. (*Reprinting.*) 45*s*. 1931
187. **Whittinton and Stanbridge's Vulgaria,** ed. B. White. 14*s*. "
188. **The Siege of Jerusalem,** ed. E. Kölbing and Mabel Day. 18*s*. "
189. **Caxton's Fayttes of Armes and of Chyualrye,** ed. A. T. Byles. 25*s*. 6*d*. 1932
190. **English Mediæval Lapidaries,** ed. Joan Evans and Mary Serjeantson. (*Reprinted* 1960.) 20*s*. "
191. **The Seven Sages,** ed. K. Brunner. (*Reprinting.*) "
191A. **On the Continuity of English Prose,** by R. W. Chambers. (*Reprinted* 1957.) 14*s*. "
192. **Lydgate's Minor Poems,** ed. H. N. MacCracken. Part II, **Secular Poems.** (*Reprinted* 1961.) 40*s*. 1933
193. **Seinte Marherete,** re-ed. Frances Mack. (*Reprinted* 1958.) 30*s*. "
194. **The Exeter Book,** Part II, ed. W. S. Mackie. (*Reprinted* 1958.) 25*s*. "
195. **The Quatrefoil of Love,** ed. I. Gollancz and M. Weale. 6*s*. 1934
196. **A Short English Metrical Chronicle,** ed. E. Zettl. 24*s*. "
197. **Roper's Life of More,** ed. Elsie V. Hitchcock. (*Reprinted* 1958.) 20*s*. "
198. **Firumbras and Otuel and Roland,** ed. Mary O'Sullivan. (*Out of print.*) "
199. **Mum and the Sothsegger,** ed. Mabel Day and R. Steele. 14*s*. "
200. **Speculum Sacerdotale,** ed. E. H. Weatherly. 20*s*. 1935
201. **Knyghthode and Bataile,** ed. R. Dyboski and Z. M. Arend. 20*s*. "
202. **Palsgrave's Acolastus,** ed. P. L. Carver. 24*s*. "
203. **Amis and Amiloun,** ed. MacEdward Leach. (*Reprinted* 1960.) 30*s*. "
204. **Valentine and Orson,** ed. Arthur Dickson. 24*s*. 1936
205. **Tales from the Decameron,** ed. H. G. Wright. 20*s*. "
206. **Bokenham's Lives of Holy Women (Lives of the Saints),** ed. Mary S. Serjeantson. 21*s*. 6*d*. "
207. **Liber de Diversis Medicinis,** ed. Margaret S. Ogden. 12*s*. "

The Original and Extra Series of the 'Early English Text Society'

208. **The Parker Chronicle and Laws** (facsimile), ed. R. Flower and A. H. Smith. 84*s*. 1937
209. **Middle English Sermons from MS. Roy. 18 B. xxiii,** ed. W. O. Ross. (*Reprinted* 1960.) 42*s*. 1938
210. **Sir Gawain and the Green Knight,** ed. I. Gollancz. With Introductory essays by Mabel Day and M. S. Serjeantson. (*Reprinted* 1957.) 10*s*. ,,
211. **Dictes and Sayings of the Philosophers,** ed. C. F. Bühler. (*Reprinted* 1961.) 45*s*. 1939
212. **The Book of Margery Kempe,** Part I, ed. S. B. Meech and Hope Emily Allen. (*Reprinted* 1961.) 42*s*. ,,
213. **Ælfric's De Temporibus Anni,** ed. H. Henel. 30*s*. 1940
214. **Morley's Translation of Boccaccio's De Claris Mulieribus,** ed. H. G. Wright. 31*s*. 6*d*. ,,
215. **English Poems of Charles of Orleans,** Part I, ed. R. Steele. 31*s*. 6*d*. 1941
216. **The Latin Text of the Ancrene Riwle,** ed. Charlotte D'Evelyn. (*Reprinted* 1957.) 31*s*. 6*d*. ,,
217. **Book of Vices and Virtues,** ed. W. Nelson Francis. 52*s*. 6*d*. 1942
218. **The Cloud of Unknowing and the Book of Privy Counselling,** ed. Phyllis Hodgson. (*Reprinted* 1958.) 40*s*. 1943
219. **The French Text of the Ancrene Riwle,** B.M. Cotton MS. Vitellius. F. VII, ed. J. A. Herbert. 28*s*. ,,
220. **English Poems of Charles of Orleans,** Part II, ed. R. Steele and Mabel Day. 10*s*. 6*d*. 1944
221. **Sir Degrevant,** ed. L. F. Casson. 52*s*. 6*d*. ,,
222. **Ro. Ba.'s Life of Syr Thomas More,** ed. Elsie V. Hitchcock and Mgr. P. E. Hallett. (*Reprinted* 1957.) 35*s*. 1945
223. **Tretyse of Loue,** ed. J. H. Fisher. 28*s*. ,,
224. **Athelston,** ed. A. McI. Trounce. (*Reprinted* 1957.) 15*s*. 1946
225. **The English Text of the Ancrene Riwle,** B.M. Cotton MS. Nero A. XIV, ed. Mabel Day. (*Reprinted* 1957.) 25*s*. ,,
226. **Respublica,** re-ed. W. W. Greg. 18*s*. 6*d*. ,,
227. **Kyng Alisaunder,** ed. G. V. Smithers. Vol. I, Text. (*Reprinted* 1961.) 35*s*. 1947
228. **The Metrical Life of St. Robert of Knaresborough,** ed. J. Bazire. 25*s*. ,,
229. **The English Text of the Ancrene Riwle,** Gonville and Caius College MS. 234/120, ed. R. M. Wilson. With Introduction by N. R. Ker. (*Reprinted* 1957.) 25*s*. 1948
230. **The Life of St. George by Alexander Barclay,** ed. W. Nelson. (*Reprinted* 1960.) 28*s*. ,,
231. **Deonise Hid Diuinite,** and other treatises related to *The Cloud of Unknowing*, ed. Phyllis Hodgson. (*Reprinted* 1958.) 30*s*. 1949
232. **The English Text of the Ancrene Riwle,** B.M. Royal MS. 8 C. 1, ed. A. C. Baugh. (*Reprinted* 1958.) 20*s*. ,,
233. **The Bibliotheca Historica of Diodorus Siculus translated by John Skelton,** ed. F. M. Salter and H. L. R. Edwards. Vol. I, Text. 42*s*. 1950
234. **Caxton: Paris and Vienne,** ed. MacEdward Leach. 30*s*. 1951
235. **The South English Legendary,** Corpus Christi College Cambridge MS. 145 and B.M. M.S. Harley 2277, &c., ed. Charlotte D'Evelyn and Anna J. Mill. Text, Vol. I. 35*s*. ,,
236. **The South English Legendary.** Text, Vol. II. 35*s*. 1952
[E.S. 87. **Two Coventry Corpus Christi Plays,** re-ed. H. Craig. Second Edition. 15*s*.] ,,
237. **Kyng Alisaunder,** ed. G. V. Smithers. Vol. II, Introduction, Commentary, and Glossary. 37*s*. 6*d*. 1953
238. **The Phonetic Writings of Robert Robinson,** ed. E. J. Dobson. 28*s*. ,,
239. **The Bibliotheca Historica of Diodorus Siculus translated by John Skelton,** ed. F. M. Salter and H. L. R. Edwards. Vol. II. Introduction, Notes, and Glossary. 15*s*. 1954
240. **The French Text of the Ancrene Riwle,** Trinity College, Cambridge, MS. R. 14. 7, ed. W. H. Trethewey. 45*s*. ,,
241. **Þe Wohunge of ure Lauerd,** and other pieces, ed. W. Meredith Thompson. 32*s*. 1955
242. **The Salisbury Psalter,** ed. Celia Sisam and Kenneth Sisam. 84*s*. 1955–56
243. **George Cavendish: The Life and Death of Cardinal Wolsey,** ed. Richard S. Sylvester. (*Reprinted* 1961.) 35*s*. 1957
244. **The South English Legendary.** Vol. III, Introduction and Glossary, ed. Charlotte D'Evelyn. 25*s*. ,,
245. **Beowulf** (facsimile). With Transliteration by J. Zupitza, new collotype plates, and Introduction by N. Davis. 70*s*. 1958
246. **The Parlement of the Thre Ages,** ed. M. Y. Offord. 28*s*. 1959
247. **Facsimile of MS. Bodley 34** (Katherine Group). With Introduction by N. R. Ker. 42*s*. ,,
248. **Þe Liflade ant te Passiun of Seinte Iuliene,** ed. S. R. T. O. d'Ardenne. 30*s*. 1960
249. **Ancrene Wisse,** Corpus Christi College, Cambridge, MS. 402, ed. J. R. R. Tolkien. With an Introduction by N. R. Ker. (*At press.*) 30*s*. ,,

The following is a select list of forthcoming volumes. Other texts are under consideration:

Facsimile of the Cotton and Jesus Manuscripts of the Owl and the Nightingale. With Introduction by N. R. Ker. (*At press.*) (*Part of issue for* 1962.)

Ælfric: Catholic Homilies, First Series, ed. P. Clemoes.

The Paston Letters, ed. N. Davis.

The English Text of the Ancrene Riwle, edited from all the extant manuscripts:

Bodleian MS. Vernon, ed. G. V. Smithers.

B.M. Cotton MS. Titus D. XVIII, ed. Frances M. Mack. (*At press.*) (*Part of issue for* 1962.)

B.M. Cotton MS. Cleopatra C. VI, ed. A. H. Smith.

(*It is also hoped to issue a revised edition of Magdalene College, Cambridge, MS. Pepys* 2498.)

Laȝamon's Brut, ed. G. L. Brook and R. F. Leslie. (*Vol. I at press.*) (*Issue for* 1961.)

The Bodley Version of Mandeville's Travels, ed. M. C. Seymour. (*At press.*)

Ywain and Gawain, ed. Albert B. Friedman and Norman T. Harrington.

The York Plays, re-ed. Arthur Brown.

The Macro Plays, re-ed. Mark Eccles.

The Cely Letters, ed. A. H. Hanham.

January 1962

Publisher

LONDON: THE OXFORD UNIVERSITY PRESS, AMEN HOUSE, E.C. 4